OTHER BOOKS BY JOSEPH MCBRIDE

SEARCHING FOR
JOHN FORD

A Life

JOSEPH McBRIDE

FABER AND FABER

First published in the United States in 2001 by St. Martin's Press
175 Fifth Avenue, New York, NY 10010

First published in the United Kingdom in 2003
By Faber and Faber Limited
3 Queen Square London WC1N 3AU

Grateful acknowledgement is made to the following for permission to quote from published or unpublished material: The American Film Institute, for quotations from its documentary film *Directed by John Ford* (1971) and its television special *The American Film Institute's Salute to John Ford* (1973); Peter Bogdanovich, for quotations from his books *John Ford* (Movie Magazine Ltd., London, 1967, and University of California Press, 1968 and 1978 editions) and *Allan Dwan: The Last Pioneer* (Praeger, 1971), reprinted in Bogdanovich's collection *Who the Devil Made It* (Knopf, 1997), and for quotations from his documentary film *Directed by John Ford* (1971), from his articles "The Autumn of John Ford," *Esquire,* April 1964 (reprinted in condensed form in Bogdanovich's collection *Pieces of Time: Peter Bogdanovich on the Movies,* Arbor House/Esquire, 1973), "Th' Respawnsibility of Bein' J...Jimmy Stewart," *Esquire,* July 1966 (reprinted in *Pieces of Time*), and "The Cowboy Hero and the American West...as Directed by John Ford," *Esquire,* December 1983, and from his program notes for "A Tribute to John Ford" (New Yorker Theatre, New York, 1963); President Richard M. Nixon for his essay "Reflections on John Ford," January 6, 1988; Andrew Sarris, for quotations from his books *Interviews with Film Directors* (editor, Bobbs-Merrill, 1967), *The American Cinema: Directors and Directions, 1929–1968* (E. P. Dutton, 1968), and *The John Ford Movie Mystery* (Indiana University Press, 1975); and Anthony Slide, for quotations from Anthony Slide and June Banker, "Interview with Mary Ford" (© Anthony Slide, 1977).

Book Design by Michelle McMillan

Frontispiece by Corbis, Inc.

A CIP record for this book
is available from the British Library

ISBN 0-57-20075-3

2 4 6 8 10 9 7 5 3 1

Contents

You say someone's called me the greatest poet of the Western saga. I am not a poet, and I don't know what a Western saga is. I would say that is horseshit.

JOHN FORD

MY SEARCH FOR JOHN FORD

A man will search his heart and soul,
Go searchin' way out there.
His peace of mind he knows he'll find,
But where, O Lord, Lord, where?

THE THEME SONG FROM
THE SEARCHERS (1956)

THEY CALLED HIM "Bull" Feeney, "the human battering ram." Broad-shouldered and rugged, John Martin Aloysius Feeney stood six feet tall and weighed 175 pounds, but the wary squint in his blue eyes made him always seem to be coming at you from a defensive crouch. His bluff manner had something strangely distant and dreamy about it. There was an unmistakable sensitivity in his melancholic eyes, at odds with his rough, often rowdy conduct on the football field in Portland, Maine. During his senior year, red-headed Jack Feeney was one of the mainstays of the Portland High Bulldogs, a squad that clawed its way to the 1913 state championship in tight, low-scoring games fought out on muddy playing fields. As a fullback and tackle, he was nicknamed "Bull" because of the way he would lower his leather helmet and ram his head into the opposing line, bulling his way toward the goal line or blocking for other ballcarriers with a reckless bravado that compensated for his dismal eyesight.

Off the field, Jack Feeney wore wireless glasses that gave him a solemn, priestlike gravitas. His father thought he would take Holy Orders. But this son of Irish immigrants was an erratic student with an uncertain future. Feeling the sting of being a mick in a Yankee-dominated New England seaport, he may have been taking the path of passive resistance, bred of a sense of not belonging. During classroom discussions he seemed more interested in sketching caricatures of his classmates and teachers, or heroic profiles of cowboys and Indians. The artistic side of his personality also began to emerge in stories he tried unsuccessfully to sell to magazines and in school essays that his admiring principal, William Jack, took home for safekeeping. The boy later remembered Mr. Jack as "the typical Yankee schoolteacher: kindly, commiserative, at times tough; he had great faith in me, he told me I had tremendous potentialities."

When he put his pen or pencil to paper, or listened to Principal Jack lecturing on American history, Jack Feeney awoke from his habitual trancelike classroom state. His discovery that many of the citizen soldiers who fought in the American Revolution were Irish immigrants was a transforming moment, for it roused in him a sense of vital connection to American history and the nation's heroic ideals. That understanding galvanized young Feeney's visual imagination of the American past and served to counterbalance his indignation over the social injustices he experienced as a first-generation Irish-American. It's easy to see that he became "Bull" Feeney partly out of a self-defensive need to create a pugnacious image in a school where ethnic differences often led to fistfights.

Later in life, after he changed his name to John Ford and became Hollywood's most celebrated filmmaker, the duality of his personality grew increasingly pronounced. Mary Astor, who starred for Ford in *The Hurricane,* described him as "Very Irish, a dark personality, [with] a sensitivity which he did everything to conceal." As if deeply ashamed of the vulnerable, probing gaze with which he looked out onto the world, Ford hid his eyes behind dark glasses and, eventually, an eye patch that gave his face a forbidding, piratical appearance.

"Look at the eyes," Ford replied when asked how one should watch a motion picture. He was giving us a clue about how to understand himself: "The secret is people's faces, their eye expression, their movements."

What is it we see in his eyes, through his eyes?

The rich emotionality of such Ford classics as *Young Mr. Lincoln, The Grapes of Wrath, How Green Was My Valley, Wagon Master, The Quiet Man, The Searchers,* and *The Man Who Shot Liberty Valance* is there for all the world to see. But that artistic expression emanated from secret, fiercely guarded places in a man whose personal brusqueness made him unapproachable to all but those in his inner circle. Even those loyal members of his "John Ford Stock Company" were not immune to his bullheadedness. Tales of his rough treatment of actors became as legendary as stories of his withering contempt for producers. "He was a very selfish guy, and he could be a tyrant, yet he got tremendous performances out of people," recalled actor Milburn Stone. "On *Young Mr. Lincoln* I saw him break an old actor's heart, someone who had been a friend. Ford jumped on him all of a sudden and just destroyed the guy." What Ford feared most, perhaps, was being destroyed in the same way himself. "If he had shown his kindly eyes, they would have walked over him on the set," said his daughter, Barbara.

To friends and colleagues, even to family members, Ford always remained somewhat inscrutable. "I've been trying to figure Jack since the day he was born and never could," his older brother Francis admitted. John Ford could be the kindest man in the world, or the meanest. He was capable of the greatest generosity and the most vicious cruelty, both at times directed toward the very same people. Writer Darcy O'Brien, son of Ford regular George O'Brien, summed up Ford's contradictions by calling him "the old sentimental cruel genius bastard son of a bitch, who knew what he was doing, always and for fifty years, and without whom there would be no American cinema as we know it." There was no denying the quality of the results Ford achieved with all his bullying and wheedling, but what was the price of that achievement in human terms? For those who knew him, attempting to understand his character and come to terms with his often perverse behavior became a study of almost Talmudic complexity.

"Jack's courtesy to any individual was always in inverse ratio to his affection," recalled Philip Dunne, the screenwriter of *How Green Was My Valley.* "I knew Jack liked me, because in all the years I knew him intimately he never said a polite word to me, not one."

"He wasn't so tough," insisted actress Olive Carey, a charter member of the Ford Stock Company who met him soon after he arrived in Hollywood in 1914. "He was darling and warm, but he'd put on this big act of being tough. He was an entirely different guy when he was on the set than he was when he was off the set. On the set he was pretty much of a martinet. But off the set he was a pussycat. He really was very sensitive, a pussycat in a lion's costume."

"The real John Ford was very kind, but he was afraid of that," character actor Frank Baker observed. "And the John Ford we know is a legend, a living legend who was created by John Ford himself to protect the other John Ford, the sympathetic, sentimental, soft John Ford."

Ford used filmmaking as his refuge from reality, a way to create a safe, privileged, mythical world that functioned according to his own private rules. It was a world where he could be the unquestioned "Boss," the "Coach," "the Skipper," "the Old Man," the "Pappy" of his large extended family of actors and crew people. The Navajo Indians called him "Natani Nez," which is usually rendered as "Tall Soldier," although the literal translation is "Tall Leader." Ford's devotion to his stock company, casting them in similar roles in film after film from youth to old age, makes them our old friends as well as his and gives his work the haunting resonance of tribal memory. In the words of critic Andrew Sarris, "A Ford set is thus often a community in itself in the process of representing a larger and more lyrical community on the cosmic screen."

There was a stark dissonance between the vision of communal ideals Ford conjured up in his movies—the world as he wanted it to be—and the world he inhabited when he was not working. Baker thought that Ford "was always unhappy. He never had a day's happiness. Will he find peace? Lonely spirit! What was he looking for?" Ford placed the highest value in his work on traditional family life, and mourned its seemingly inevitable destruction in the face of social change. Yet one of the central paradoxes of his life is that this artist who so idealized the family was "not a good family man," his grandson Dan Ford admitted in his 1979 biography *Pappy: The Life of John Ford*. An often absent, sometimes unfaithful husband, Ford was a poor father to his two children, Patrick and Barbara, whose lives were blighted by his domineering, self-absorbed personality. Like the men in his movies, who keep leaving home to "wander forever between the winds," Ford seemed in perpetual flight from family responsibilities. His true family was his movie "family," a more functional group he knew how to control and manipulate because it lived within the realm of his fantasies.

Drink caused a further schism in Ford's already fragmented personality. "He was two different people depending on whether or not he was drinking," said his Irish relative and filmmaking partner, Lord Michael Killanin. Even though Ford usually remained cold sober when working, the rapid and often giddy oscillations of mood in his films from tragedy to comedy reflect the rollercoaster mood swings of an alcoholic personality. Ford romanticized drinking in his films, befitting his legacy as the son of an Irish immigrant saloonkeeper, but alcoholism blighted not only Ford's life but also those of his wife and children. "His family life was like something out of a Eugene O'Neill play," novelist Robert Nathan, husband of Ford regular Anna Lee, told me not long after Ford's death.

But it was telling that Ford was able to stop drinking when he was making films, for those were the only times when he seemed truly happy. "I simply direct pictures," he once said, "and if I had my way, every morning of my life I'd be behind that camera at nine o'clock waiting for the boys to roll 'em, because that's the only thing I really like to do." Between pictures he would go on abysmally self-destructive binges, trying to find oblivion in the bottle while locked in his den, wrapped in a sheet or huddled in a sleeping bag, reading, listening to music, crying, drinking himself sick. Eventually he would emerge from the sleeping bag, sometimes to be hospitalized, and his wife or other caretakers would burn the bag.

What was he trying to escape? Was it the difficulty of maintaining his illusions? The effort involved in keeping up his act? The pain of simply living with all the contradictions that made him an artist?

Ford's melancholia deepened in his later years, when his reputation went into eclipse in his native land. An increasing bitterness toward Hollywood and life itself seemed to overshadow even Ford's own pride in his artistic accomplishments. As the darkness of age and infirmity and disillusionment gathered around him, so too did he begin to question the values expressed in his earlier work, when the promise of America seemed so vibrant.

What Sarris has called "The John Ford Movie Mystery" is not only the mystery of how such moving and complex films emanated from a man with such a rough-hewn exterior. In a deeper sense, it is the mystery of the man himself. Ford was revealing something about himself when he made movies with the titles *The Quiet Man* and *The Secret Man,* for he did everything he could to tantalize, confuse, and confound those who dared to probe the sources of his creativity. Anyone trying to delve into the secrets of his art would be met with monosyllabic replies, curt "I don't know"'s, or cryptic remarks that smacked of calculated indifference or defensive mockery of the hapless questioner. Of course, he wouldn't speak of what he did as "art," describing it as simply "a job of work."

Ford needed to scare off anyone who would try to take away his hard-won artistic independence, a remarkable achievement within the notoriously machinelike Hollywood system, even if that independence was more intermittent than complete. His most powerful smoke screen was the creation and sustenance of his elaborately self-disguising persona.

"Choosing his Western world, and surrounding himself with this sort of Irish defense, as it were—you could never get a sane word out of him because he was a 'mad Irishman'—was the absolutely marvellous decision he made about Hollywood," screenwriter Alexander Jacobs pointed out. "It allowed him to work in complete harmony and peace within his chosen world." (Ford dropped his facade briefly in 1962, confiding to columnist Hedda Hopper, "You know, I don't want this to get out—I pose as an illiterate.")

Something even more fundamental in Ford than career survival instinct forced him to erect such barriers to his inner life. Perhaps it was, at root, the influence of his Irish heritage, with its long tradition of secrecy and obfuscation in the face of foreign occupation. Sly role-playing becomes second nature to an oppressed people, as Ford seemed to be suggesting when he remarked in 1964, "The Irish and the colored people are the most natural actors in the world." Ford himself, as a young man, acted in at least sixteen silent films and serials, mostly his own and his brother Frank's, usually playing a footloose, rough-and-tumble adventurer. He also rode as a Klansman in D. W. Griffith's 1915 epic, *The Birth of a Nation;* played himself in a 1929 talkie, *Big Time,* directed by Kenneth Hawks (Howard's brother); and appeared in *The Battle of Midway* and some of his other documentaries.

"Of course, Jack was one of the great hams of all time," said Olive Carey, laughing heartily as she reminisced about her old friend. "He was a born actor.

A complete, fantastic actor. He was never relaxed, never mellow, never allowed you to relax either. That's why he was such a good director, I guess. He was always playing a part for his own amusement. When he'd walk on the set, he'd have Danny Borzage play 'Bringing in the Sheaves' on his squeezebox. Oh, criminy, what a ham he was!"

Ford was bedeviled by deep-seated insecurities about his masculinity and how his tenderness was perceived by a society that still tends to regard an artistic nature as "feminine." Although he usually was regarded as "a man's director," a label he angrily rejected, Ford's work was dominated by concerns traditionally designated by the society of his time as feminine—family, tradition, the heartfelt expression of emotion. Those concerns are as much "Irish" as "feminine," but in either case they remain somewhat alien to the dominant cultural norms of modern America.

Novelist Thomas Flanagan thinks that some of Ford's contradictions "derive from his double sense of himself as at once American and Irish. . . . Like Eugene O'Neill, he believed that being Irish carried with it a burden of moods, stances, loyalties, quarrels with the world. Working with the most popular of American cultural forms, he was conscious of a majority culture, from which the Irish, despite their bellicose loyalty to it, stood somewhat apart."

As that suggests, Ford's political views were complex and have been inadequately understood. Too often he and his films were roughly equated with the reactionary politics of his favorite actors, John Wayne and Ward Bond, or with some of his own conservative public stands after he returned from service in World War II. His attitude toward the great moral crisis of postwar Hollywood, the anti-Communist witch-hunt, was contradictory. During that era, he switched his political affiliation from Democrat to Republican, and he ended his days supporting Barry Goldwater, Richard Nixon, and the Vietnam War. But simplistically labeling Ford as a flag-waving jingoist ignores much that is disturbing and ambivalent about his view of American history. By refusing to engage in serious discussions of his personal feelings and the themes of his work, and by declining to accept the label of "artist," Ford was protecting his inner self from those who might find his truths threatening or subversive.

When I called Ford from Wisconsin in 1970 to tell him I was writing a critical study of his films with Michael Wilmington, Ford growled, "My God! What for? You certainly picked a dull subject." He attempted to prove as much when he gave me a testy one-hour interview in California that August, published in our 1974 book *John Ford*. "I didn't tell him *anything*," Ford boasted to Henry Fonda.

But Ford's life story was the opposite of dull. It ranged from the early days of silent filmmaking in Hollywood to participating in the Irish rebellion against the British in 1921, filming the D-Day landings on Omaha Beach, serving as a rear admiral in the U.S. Navy, and making a documentary about Vietnam. Ford laid down countless obstacles for biographers, spreading beguiling legends, outrageously false anecdotes and cover stories, and other forms of disinformation around the improbably colorful story of his life, making it into a minefield for the unwary. But what appears most improbable about his story just as often turns out to be true.

When asked once why he didn't write an autobiography, Ford said, "I've led sort of a peculiar life. . . . I've done so many things, been so many places, that I'm afraid an autobiography would be too episodic. And there are certain things in my life that I would like to forget. I didn't murder anybody or rob anybody, but I got mixed up in a couple of revolutions and that sort of thing. . . . [D]uring World War II, for example, I was in the OSS. . . . I remember coming back from a trip once during the war, and I talked before this audience, and I was telling them about some of the strange places I'd visited for the OSS. This very supercilious and sarcastic man came up to me and said, 'Tell me, Commander Ford, when was the last time you were in Tibet?' I said, 'Exactly ten days ago, sir.' He looked so sort of flabbergasted. Then he said, 'I don't believe it.' And I replied, 'Screw you. It happens to be true.' "

When I began working on this biography in 1971, I wrote Ford asking for his cooperation, sending him copies of some essays I had published on his films. He replied that November:

> Dear Joe,
>   I appreciate your interest (especially the up-beat kindly way you treated me) but, honestly, I'm too old and tired to go for a biog—even with a McBride (My McBride of 52 years [Mrs. Ford, the former Mary McBride Smith] is improving, knock wood). However, let me mull it over.
>
> Sincerely, thanks
> John Ford

Uncertain whether it would be wise to press him further, and intimidated by his bluster, I never pursued that tentative opening, his offer to "mull it over." Perhaps it would not have mattered much if I had been able to persuade Ford to talk with me at greater length, because the truth about anyone's life cannot be captured solely in what the person says about it, particularly if that person is a master fabulist like John Ford. The longest interviews with Ford were conducted by Peter Bogdanovich in 1966 for his seminal book *John Ford,* published in 1967, and by family biographer Dan Ford in 1972–73. Those sessions with Ford (preserved on audiotape at the Lilly Library of Indiana University at Bloomington) offer many fascinating insights for subsequent biographers, yet they raise as many questions as they answer.

I've spent substantial parts of these past three decades talking with people who knew and worked with Ford. After paying my respects at the funeral home in West Hollywood where Ford's coffin lay draped in his tattered flag from the Battle of Midway, I spoke with his sister Josephine and his niece Cecil McLean de Prida. Later I visited other Ford relatives in Ireland, Maine, and California; talked with John Wayne about Ford on the set of Wayne's last film, *The Shootist;* went to Henry Fonda's home in Bel Air, where he acted out Ford's socking him during the making of *Mister Roberts,* with me playing Fonda and Fonda playing Ford; heard Harry Carey Jr.'s story about the time that Ford drunkenly kissed him; and was regaled by Pat O'Brien with his uncannily accurate Ford impersonation. I heard the reminiscences of such quintessential Ford actors as Olive Carey, James Stewart, Claire Trevor, Anna Lee, Hank Worden, and Woody Strode; spoke with Navajo Indians who appeared in Ford's Westerns, including the ninety-six-year-old medicine man Billy Yellow; and interviewed the black comedian and character actor Stepin Fetchit in the basement of a strip joint where he was performing in Madison, Wisconsin.

I talked to the actor who played Chief Scar in *The Searchers,* Henry Brandon; the actress who played Ann Rutledge in *Young Mr. Lincoln,* Pauline Moore; and the stuntman who doubled for John Wayne in *Stagecoach,* Yakima Canutt. I heard about the making of *How Green Was My Valley* from its screenwriter, Philip Dunne, and watched *The Searchers* with its cinematographer, Winton C. Hoch. I discussed Ford's work with fellow directors who admired him, including Orson Welles, Jean Renoir, Howard Hawks, Frank Capra, Allan Dwan, Samuel Fuller, François Truffaut, and Claude Chabrol. I visited the Navy Yard in Washington, D.C., to interview the legendary Admiral John D. Bulkeley, winner of the Medal of Honor, Ford's shipmate during the D-Day landings, and the real-life model for Robert Montgomery's PT boat commander in *They Were Expendable.* And I corresponded with former president Richard Nixon about his friendship with Ford and his admiration for Ford's films.

In addition to studying Ford's voluminous collection of correspondence, scripts, and other papers at the Lilly Library, studying other archival accounts, and digging up contemporaneous records from California to Washington, I went to the Library of Congress, the National Archives, and the United States

Information Agency to watch documentary films he made for the U.S. government. And I walked in the footsteps of Ford and his Irish parents while visiting places important to his story, from the ruins of his family home overlooking Ireland's Galway Bay to his birthplace and boyhood homes on the coast of Maine, the sites of his Hollywood homes and studios, and the ruins of the frontier home he burned while making *The Searchers* in Monument Valley ("They left an awful mess down there," my Navajo guide told me, so I picked up and carried away the charred pieces of wood and artificial brick). I visited Tombstone, Arizona, studying the actual topography of the so-called Gunfight at the O.K. Corral, so I could better understand how Ford transformed the sordid real-life story of Wyatt Earp into the grandly romantic Western mythology of *My Darling Clementine*. I ate rattlesnake stew while attending a Navajo squaw dance under the light of the summer moon in Monument Valley and almost fell into the rushing waters of Galway's River Corrib when, visiting the Spanish Arch on a stormy winter night, I tripped over an anchor as I walked backward along the path of a tracking shot Ford made for *The Rising of the Moon*.

In the process of following Ford's trail, I have excavated much of archaeological and psychological significance about his past, but I have learned more about his inner life from seeing and reseeing his films many times over the years. I clearly remember the day that I fell in love with John Ford's movies, because I made a record of it. December 23, 1967. And I remember the exact moment when it happened.

I was on winter break from the University of Wisconsin when Ford's 1948 cavalry Western *Fort Apache* came on television at my home in Milwaukee. Under the credits, magnificently photographed black-and-white vistas of Monument Valley are intercut with scenes of life at Fort Apache, blended together with Richard Hageman's rousing musical score. Ford's directing credit dissolves on and off the screen in his favorite typographical style, the nineteenth-century Playbill typeface—first "Directed by," then "John Ford"— as a stagecoach comes into view, appearing almost magically from a dust cloud under his name. The camera pans along with the tiny coach as it passes one of the valley's majestic rock formations, Gray Whiskers. As we take in that breathtaking sight, the camera tilts up past the coach so the composition can center on the ancient "monument." This visual frisson, Ford's poetic way of conveying the transcendence of the eternal over the temporal, took me into his confidence, inviting me to share his way of seeing the world. From that moment on, I was an ardent Fordian.

Ford's astonishingly prolific career encompassed about 226 films as a director and/or producer between 1917 and 1970. That total includes 137 films he directed (113 features plus 24 short films or television programs) and two feature-length films he only produced. In addition, during his World War II service as chief of the Field Photographic Branch, Office of Strategic Services, Ford supervised the making of at least 87 documentary films of various lengths, some of which he also directed. Not included in the tally of his 226 films are 9 feature films for which Ford directed scenes without credit, 2 films on which he received story credit, and various films and television shows in which he appeared as himself. Many of Ford's silent films are now lost or exist only in part, but various archives have rediscovered some of them in recent years.

I had the opportunity to watch many of Ford's films again, and some for the first time, during the UCLA Film and Television Archive's massive Ford retrospective in 1994. My son John, who was partly named after Ford, was seven years old at the time of the retrospective. John gallantly accompanied me to forty of the movies, from Ford's first feature, *Straight Shooting* (1917), to his last, *7 Women* (1966); John even watched a rare print of the 1918 Western *Hell Bent,* presented with German intertitles. Unfortunately, few people of any age today are able to have that kind of extended and intimate experience with Ford's work. His films are rarely seen as they were intended to be projected, in 35mm on the big screen, rather than on television, which diminishes the stunning beauty of his compositions and the intimacy of his human drama.

The older I am, the more I respect Ford for refusing to explain his work to interviewers. He meant what he told me: "Everybody asks the same questions, all you people, and I'm sick and tired of trying to answer them, because I don't know the answers." Maddening as it once seemed when I was an eager young cinéaste hoping the master would reveal his secrets to me, Ford's intransigence now seems refreshing in an age when every movie comes accompanied with scores of interviews with the director, telling us how to watch it rather than letting us discover it for ourselves. Ford wanted his work to speak for itself. And it is through his work, not through his public or private statements about it, that Ford speaks to us most passionately and clearly.

Why, then, do we need another Ford biography, another attempt to understand the man behind the films?

Ford's public persona has had the unfortunate side effect of confusing many people about what he stands for in his films. In posing as an illiterate, he did the job far too well. Many people have taken him at face value, viewing him condescendingly as an artistic primitive. Although his persona has outlived its function of protecting him from studio meddling, it continues to prevent his being taken as seriously as his work warrants. The disparity between the persona and the work has encouraged a crippling compartmentalization in Ford scholarship. Previous writers on Ford (including myself) have tended to treat his life and his work as separate entities. His films were the true outlet of this secretive man's inner thoughts and feelings, but since those thoughts and feelings were expressed more visually than verbally, they often have been misunderstood— or not seen at all—by critics who think primarily in literary terms. What has been most lacking in previous books about Ford has been a real understanding of how his life and his work are interconnected. Discovering how Ford's great films emerged from his jealously guarded inner life is the object of this biographical search.

Tag Gallagher, author of a kaleidoscopically detailed 1986 study of Ford's films, came to the conclusion that the biographer's task is impossible: "Because John Ford shrouded himself in mystery, his life and personality remain inscrutable. . . . There will probably never be an adequate biography of John Ford, nor even an adequate character sketch, for there were as many of him as there were people who knew him."

Should biographers so willingly admit defeat? Shouldn't we instead take Ford's intransigence as a challenge? There can be no doubt that the absence of an adequate Ford biography has had serious consequences for the director's critical and public reputation. It is partly for that reason that the films themselves are often misunderstood and neglected today in Ford's own country. Their simplicities too often are rejected, their complexities are insufficiently grasped, the man behind them is indistinct. This incomprehension has led to a marginalization of Ford's importance in American culture. It is our loss far more than his.

Sarris described Ford as "America's cinematic poet laureate." Ford is the closest equivalent we have had to a homegrown Shakespeare. He chronicled our national history on-screen with an epic vision that spanned nearly two centuries, from the Revolutionary War to the Victnam War. While Ford's vision of America is intensely patriotic, it does not flinch from confronting the country's tragic failures, the times when we did not live up to our ideals. Whatever the events he depicts, Ford's natural allegiance is always with the spirit of the American common people, as Walt Whitman described them in his 1855 preface to *Leaves of Grass:*

> Their manners speech dress friendships—the freshness and candor
> of their physiognomy—the picturesque looseness of their car-
> riage . . . their deathless attachment to freedom—their aversion to
> anything indecorous or soft or mean—the practical acknowledg-
> ment of the citizens of one state by the citizens of all other

states—the fierceness of their roused resentment—their curiosity and welcome of novelty—their self-esteem and wonderful sympathy—their susceptibility to a slight—the air they have of persons who never knew how it felt to stand in the presence of superiors—the fluency of their speech—their delight in music, the sure symptom of manly tenderness and native elegance of soul . . . their good temper and openhandedness—the terrible significance of their elections—the President's taking off his hat to them not they to him—these too are unrhymed poetry. It awaits the gigantic and generous treatment worthy of it.

That "gigantic and generous treatment" is the work of John Ford. Although his films are not confined to American settings, it is his films about his native country, even more than those he made about his ancestral homeland of Ireland, that have come to define him as an artist. And the images of America that Ford created have helped define our vision of ourselves. Today's most influential American filmmakers—Steven Spielberg, George Lucas, Martin Scorsese, Oliver Stone—revere and emulate Ford. But unfortunately, that doesn't seem to translate to the audiences who go to their movies. Other directors from the past—Orson Welles, Alfred Hitchcock, Frank Capra—seem to speak more directly and urgently to today's younger audiences. Ford movies are shown often enough on television, where they command a loyal following, largely among older viewers. Yet they show up far less often in theaters and schools. I was shocked a couple of years ago when I asked a film teacher at a leading California university what she thought of Ford, and found that she had never seen any of his movies. This was not an isolated instance. I often encountered blank looks when I mentioned Ford's name to people outside the film business, and a story editor for a Hollywood film company asked me, "What are his films?"

Clearly, something is drastically wrong here. A director of Ford's artistic stature, a filmmaker whose canvas of American life is so rich and ambitious, should be central to our culture, a household word. Is the problem solely in ourselves? Or could it also be inherent in his work? Has Ford become marginalized because of his concentration on a pioneer past that seems less and less meaningful to a nation entering a new millennium? And if that is so, what does that say about us?

Ford's films are, among many other things, demonstrations of his obsession with the revelatory clash between legend and truth. The most famous line in any Ford movie is the frontier newspaper editor's declaration in *The Man Who Shot Liberty Valance:* "When the legend becomes fact, print the legend." But the viewer should be wary of taking that opinion as Ford's own, for as Peter Bogdanovich points out, in *Liberty Valance* (as in most of his other films) "Ford prints the fact." Ford would be the last man, however, to deny the enduring potency of legend. It is in the obscure and elusive juncture between legend and fact that the meaning of his life will be found.

"The truth about my life is nobody's damn business but my own," Ford defiantly proclaimed. What was he trying so hard to conceal? What was he hiding behind those dark glasses? Who was this enigmatic man who was, and will remain, as great a national poet as Walt Whitman? As I ride out to "search his heart and soul, / Go searchin' way out there," I hope to find some answers to those questions.

CHAPTER ONE

"'TISN'T THE CASTLE THAT MAKES THE KING"

John Ford was a king: he knighted all those who had the immense luck to work with him.

JEAN RENOIR, 1973

ONE PARISH OVER" from America, as the saying goes, is the barren, windblown west coast of Ireland, the region of Connemara. I journeyed there a few years ago with my Irish wife, Ruth O'Hara, in search of the Feeney family's beginnings. All I knew was that his ancestors came from a village on Galway Bay called Spiddal, a dot on the map eight and a half miles outside the ancient port city of Galway, in the province of Connaught (contemporary spelling Connacht). Ford made *The Quiet Man* an hour or so north and inland from Spiddal, in the County Mayo town of Cong, whose terrain is gentler and more verdant than the rock-scarred, hilly landscape where his parents were raised. With Ruth's mother, Hetty, as our Gaelic-fluent guide, we motored along the coast road from Galway on a brisk, sunny day in January, arriving on the kind of spectacular late afternoon that rewards the pilgrim with endlessly changing panoramas of light and shade, subtly shifting hues, and a magnificent sunset. Near the end of his life, Ford recalled that it was here in Spiddal, while visiting his family's ancestral home as a boy, that he acquired his love of landscape and his eye for composition.

Although I did not know the names of any Feeney relatives when I arrived, it didn't take long to find one. The first place we visited, naturally, was a local pub, An Crúiscín Lán (The Full Jug), a smoky, stiflingly hot place by the sea where I tried unsuccessfully to make small talk with the regulars, who viewed me with instinctive suspicion.

"You're not an *informer*, are you?" one fellow in a tweed cap demanded, fixing me with a forbidding squint.

Naively expecting the kind of lavishly emotional welcome John Wayne's Sean Thornton receives when he ventures into Cohan's Pub in *The Quiet Man,* I found the experience acutely depressing. Most of the townsfolk still spoke Gaelic as their everyday language, and I hadn't reckoned with the deep-seated Irish caution about revealing too much to an English-speaking stranger, even one who came hoping to learn about the town's most celebrated descendant. But eventually my questions elicited the telephone number of Paraic Feeney, a middle-aged civil servant who turned out to be Ford's second cousin, son of his cousin Martin Feeney and the keeper of the local family history. "We're related to very few around here," Paraic told me. "All our relatives went to the States."

I was disappointed to learn that Paraic's father had died in 1984, at the age of eighty-two; I had hoped to hear firsthand from old Martin of Ford's visit to Spiddal in 1921, during the Black and Tan war, when he came to give money and moral support to the cause of Irish independence. Making my heart sink further, Paraic Feeney told me, "My father had a fantastic memory—he could fill three or four volumes." But eventually I would piece together more bits of information about Ford's experiences with Martin Feeney from the director's own papers.

Paraic Feeney's hospitality to strangers arriving in town unannounced was remarkably generous. He invited us into his modern seaside home for a leisurely chat and whiskeys by the fireplace, rewarding my curiosity about his lineage not only by sketching out the family tree but also by announcing that on his nearby land he had preserved the ruins of Ford's father's birthplace. Not that there was much interest in the site, he admitted, but he had a sense of history and hoped that he could share with the occasional interested stranger his pride in his illustrious relative.

"We were living in the old thatched house, the old homestead, when he was making *The Quiet Man,*" Paraic told me. "My sisters, Maura and Brid, were extras in the film. I very distinctly remember John Ford there. And he always made a point to keep up with us. He always wrote us at Christmas. But my father didn't write letters of any consequence, and as the years went by, we kind of lost contact with him. In the end, it just became Christmas."

Spiddal and other towns in Connaught were settled after Oliver Cromwell and his Puritan armies rampaged through Ireland in the middle of the seventeenth century, slaughtering much of the population as they conquered the land. In the aftermath, Cromwell's soldiers and supporters were awarded the best of the Catholic landholdings east of the river Shannon, while, as Robert Kee recounted in his history of Ireland, the dispossessed "were transplanted beyond the Shannon to the more barren province of Connaught. And with this worst humiliation of the Irish Catholic landowners until then—their banishment to a remote corner of their own country in the beautiful sad lands of the west—what came to be known as 'the curse of Cromwell' was complete."

"To hell or to Connaught" was the cry heard in those days, and the words have echoed down the generations. Although a travel book rhapsodized of County Galway in 1841 that its landscape offered a "happy blending of rugged grandeur with gentle beauty," the best farming land was given to the newly created Protestant Irish nobility, while the peasant farmers, including Ford's ancestors, had to make do with what was left. A more realistic account of the civil parish of Moycullen, of which Spiddal is a part, was given in 1844 by *The Parliamentary Gazeteer of Ireland:* "The surface contains some good, or at least tolerable land on the shore of Galway bay, and along the route of the road from Galway to Oughterard; yet even in parts of these districts it is rocky and wild, and all elsewhere it is prevailingly moorish, sterile, and chaotic. . . . Hamlets are very numerous, but in general are both very poor and very small."

Where Ford's ancestors came from before Spiddal is not known for certain. While scouting locations for *The Quiet Man* in 1950 in neighboring County Mayo, Ford wrote his relative and producing partner, Lord Michael Killanin: "My aunt Julia, 93 years of age, who drinks cocktails, smokes and drives her own car . . . tells me that our location in Mayo is near the parish of Dunfeeney from which the Feeneys were driven in days gone by." Perhaps that is why, referring to my own ancestors from Mayo, Ford told me, "[T]he people from Mayo are noted for their shrewdness and smartness. We're a smart, shrewd, poor race. Proud as hell. You don't say 'County Mayo,' say, 'County Mayo, God help us.'" But Paraic Feeney thinks their branch of the family originated to the south, in County Cork or County Waterford, in the sixteenth or seventeenth century.

"Nobody in his right mind would come here," I was told in Spiddal by Barbara Curran, a relative of both the Feeneys and of John Ford's mother, who also was named Barbara Curran. "But today it's the most valuable land in Ireland. They call it now 'the Golden Strip' and 'the Golden Mile.' Before that, it was worth nothing really." The local priest, Father Tom Kyne, admitted that when he was assigned to his parish in Spiddal, "I thought this was the last place on earth."[1]

When you visit this alluring yet forbidding terrain, studded as it is with rocks rising up every few yards out of its rolling hills, you immediately under-

---

1. That phrase appears in Ford's last feature film, 7 *Women* (1966), set in China during the 1930s. "What are you doing here?" one missionary woman asks another. "This is the last place on earth!"

stand why so many people eventually had to depart for more fertile and hospitable lands. As inspiring as the picturesque qualities of the landscape were to
the young John Feeney on his boyhood visits, they didn't put food on his father's table.

Spiddal's Gaelic name, An Spidéal, means "The Hospital." Converted to
Christianity around 520 and established by Saint Ende, the village's patron
saint, Spiddal (sometimes spelled "Spiddle") was so named in medieval times
because it, like other villages near large cities, was designated as an isolation
site for patients suffering from infectious diseases such as cholera and leprosy.
Spiddal is an amalgamation of four smaller villages, the Feeneys coming from
a cluster of about seven houses called Tuar Beeg, a name anglicized as
Tourbeg. Their stone house, Ard Aoibbinn, is located on Cnocán Glas, or
Green Hill.

"Every field has a name," Barbara Curran explained. "If they're not written
down soon, they will be gone forever."

The morning after arriving in Spiddal, we drove the winding road from the
bay up the rolling hillside to the Feeney homestead. We were welcomed by
Barbara's husband, Tim, or as he is known in the Irish, Tadhg O'Curraidhin.
He showed us around what is left of the Feeney home, said to be more than
four hundred years old, and its two adjacent ruined stone buildings.

The most striking aspect of the Feeney homesite is its proximity to the sea.
From its hilly perch, there is a spectacular, unobstructed view of Galway Bay,
only half a mile away, looking out toward the hills of Clare and the three Aran
Islands (known to cinemagoers through Robert Flaherty's 1934 documentary
classic *Man of Aran*). Growing up in such intimacy with the Atlantic Ocean,
the elder John Feeney naturally would have developed a sense of a distant
horizon always awaiting the adventurer, the omnipresent possibility of exile or
escape. Speaking to a crowd gathered in Galway's Eyre Square in June 1963,
John F. Kennedy observed, "If the day was clear enough, and if you went
down to the bay, and you looked west, and your sight was good enough, you
would see Boston, Massachusetts."

What is left of the Feeney home in Spiddal is broken walls, composed of
two large rocks and a myriad of smaller stones pulled from the nearby earth,
melded together with hardened *daib* (clay) around timber joints sturdily plastered with cow dung. The original clay floor has been replaced with concrete,
but the outlines of the stone-slab fireplace that sat in the middle of the large
family room are still visible. There were two side bedrooms, a separate cooking area, and an attached shed for the tools and animals. The thatched roof
made a ceiling eight feet high. The house's unusually small windows were
rimmed with lime and blue coloring.

Dwellings like these were built in a day by clan members and neighbors gathering in the dozens for a communal house-raising, followed by festivities to commemorate the occasion, like the barn-raising ceremonies common in the American West. (Ford re-created such an event in *Drums Along the Mohawk,* set in New York's Mohawk Valley at the time of the American Revolution.) There were several houses scattered nearby for other clan members, including the Feeneys' Thornton cousins, whose name Ford lent to John Wayne's character in *The Quiet Man.*

A modest subsistence was possible in Spiddal for large families except in famine times, although even then, fishing provided a means of survival for many. In addition to the ubiquitous potato, the fields were sown with oats, barley, and rye. For fertilizer, families carried seaweed from the shore on their backs or on donkeys in wicker baskets. They cut turf from the nearby bog for fuel. Besides raising cows and pigs, they kept sheep and made their own clothing from the wool. All they had to purchase in the marketplace was tea and sugar.

But the Feeneys' land was never entirely their own.

They were tenants on the estate of the Morris barony, a sprawling domain then encompassing twenty thousand acres (the manor house and most of the land rights have since been sold by the Morris family). Catholics of Norman origin, the Morrises had lived in Galway since the fourteenth century. The title of Lord Killanin was bestowed upon the head of the clan, a former lord chief justice, in 1900. As landlords the Morrises were beloved by their tenants because they never evicted anyone, even during the worst periods of economic hardship. When one of the Morris women died in a cholera epidemic after giving birth to a boy named George around 1840, the Feeneys took him in to raise as their foster child, an act that created an undying sense of kinship between the Morrises and the Feeneys (George later was knighted).

Less certain were the alleged blood ties between the Morrises and the Feeneys. The Feeneys claimed that the elder John Feeney's paternal grandmother, Barbara Morris, came from the barony's lineage. Eagerly seized upon by John Ford in an effort to link himself more closely with nobility, that possible connection was viewed with some skepticism by his friend and putative cousin Michael Morris, the third Lord Killanin and a grandnephew of Sir George Morris. Ford "always claimed to be a relation of mine," said Killanin, "because I had a great-great-uncle who populated the Spiddal area at a time when the family tree was not very accurate." After meeting Ford in Hollywood in the late 1930s, Killanin became active with him in efforts to help establish a native Irish film industry. Best known for serving as president of the International Olympic Committee from 1972 to 1980, the portly and jovial

Lord Killanin always had an affectionate relationship with Ford, but considered him a bit of a closet snob. Ford exhibited as much of a penchant for putting on airs as Killanin did for modestly playing down his own noble lineage.

The consciousness of the Feeneys' ambivalent heritage, their social duality as poor relations living under the sheltering shadow of the manor house, formed a central part of Ford's vision of his peculiar place in the world. In his Irish-made film *The Rising of the Moon,* produced in partnership with Killanin, a poteen maker (Jack MacGowran) looks ruefully toward a ruined castle dominating the land inhabited by an old tenant farmer (Noel Purcell), saying of him, "From there to a wee thatched cottage . . ." To which another observer (Cyril Cusack) replies, "Well, 'tisn't the castle that makes the king." The paradox of his physical proximity to the upper classes and the social distance he always felt from them would haunt Ford throughout his lifetime.

"We're not all descended from kings, you know," Spencer Tracy's Irish-American Mayor Frank Skeffington wryly admits to his nephew in Ford's 1958 film *The Last Hurrah*. Skeffington is referring to his mother's years in domestic service. Ford's own mother had to work as a domestic after arriving in America. While the Feeneys prospered soon enough in America, the memory of the humble state to which they had been reduced was something he cherished as a source of mingled resentment and pride.

The Feeneys' "wee, humble cottage" in Spiddal (to borrow Barry Fitzgerald's description of Sean Thornton's White o' Mornin' in *The Quiet Man*) was the birthplace of Ford's father, John Feeney. Born on December 3, 1856, he was one of thirteen children of Patrick Feeney and Mary Curran. He would grow into a tall, rawboned man with a jaunty stride, red hair and mustache, the gnarled hands of a farmer and fisherman, and an unashamedly sentimental disposition.

The Gaelic form of the family name, which Paraic Feeney still prefers to use, is variously given as Ó Fiannaidhe, Ó Feinneadha, Ó Feinneida, or Ó Fidhne (the Ó prefix means "grandson of"), or more simply Feinne. The Feeney family line was founded in the year 350 by Brian, son of the Eocha Moy Veagon, king of Ireland. It was a family branch of the Uí Fiachrach at Finghid (now Finned) in County Sligo, part of northern Connaught. The surname comes from the word *fianna,* meaning "militiaman" or "soldier," after the Fianna Eirinn, militiamen who served at the beck and call of ancient kings. It's a root shared with Ireland's revolutionary Fenians, with whom Ford always felt a political allegiance. In his 1950 Western *Rio Grande,* the Sons of the Pioneers, led by Ford's future son-in-law Ken Curtis, sing Peader Kearney's rousing Irish ballad "Down by the Glenside," also known as "The Bold Fenian Men." "I know no better Irish song," declared Ford.

Ford liked to give his own family's name as O'Fienne, pronounced O'Fearna or O'Feeney. Many references list his birth name as Sean Aloysius O'Fienne or O'Feeney, but that's all a load of Fordian blarney. "We never used the 'O' before Feeney," Paraic Feeney told me. "I think he associated that with something more romantic." The town records of Cape Elizabeth, Maine, indicate that Ford was born John Martin Feeney at home on February 1, 1894 (not 1895, as he later claimed). The records of St. Dominic's Church in Portland list him as being baptized under the same name on March 13, 1894. He later chose the confirmation name of Aloysius and used it as his middle name. Although he, like his father, signed his name John A. Feeney, he was not born John Feeney Jr., as Dan Ford's biography of Ford claims, for his father's middle name was Augustine.

John's older brother Francis, who ran away from home to join a circus, changed his last name from Feeney to Ford to avoid disgracing the family, according to Ford's niece Cecelia (Cecil) McLean de Prida. Other accounts, including John Ford's, had Francis taking the name of an indisposed fellow stage performer he was understudying after becoming an actor and stage manager in New York. More prosaically, Francis himself claimed to have taken the name from a passing motorcar.

In 1925, the *Portland Sunday Telegram* belatedly recognized the rise to fame of John Ford, "son of Mr. and Mrs. John Feeney of this City," with an article headlined "Former Portland Boy Now in Forefront of Country's Greatest Movie Directors." The paper explained to its predominantly Yankee readership that John had adopted Francis's "choice of the name of Ford, as short for his family Irish cognomen, difficult to spell."

In any case, as Lindsay Anderson observes in his book on John Ford, the name befits the director's artistic personality with its boldness, strength, and "happy connotations of poetry and industry." The name evokes not only the automobile but also the Elizabethan playwright John Ford, best known for *'Tis Pity She's a Whore.*[2]

Ford's brother Edward, who worked for many years as one of his assistant directors, adopted the name O'Fearna, partly to distinguish himself from his more successful younger brother. Like so many American immigrants, John Ford felt it necessary to change his name to something that didn't make him sound as if he had just stepped off the boat, but his legal name always re-

---

2. Another John Ford left his name in American history long before the filmmaker. Once when Ford was directing a movie with Olive Carey, he teased her about her age, and Ollie cracked to a visiting reporter, "Why don't you ask him who the manager of Ford's Theatre was?" John T. Ford was the owner and manager of Ford's Theatre in Washington, D.C., when President Abraham Lincoln was assassinated there in 1865.

mained Feeney. When he died, it came as a surprise to many observers (including myself) that Feeney was the name he signed to his will and the name that his family inscribed on his coffin.

Ford liked to claim that his mother, Barbara Curran, came to Spiddal from the Aran Islands. That was another bit of romantic embellishment. "Abby," as she was known, was born in the same town as her future husband. John Feeney "lived at one end of this area and my mother at the other," Ford recalled. "They might have seen one another in church, but they met in America." Their failure to meet in Spiddal (if such indeed was the case) seems even odder given that Ford's parents were second cousins. Barbara's grandfather, Nicholas Curran, was also the grandfather of the elder John Feeney through his mother, Mary Curran.

A strikingly attractive girl with a strong jaw, piercing eyes, unusually fine teeth, and a mischievous personality, Barbara also was born in 1856, the daughter of Bridget McLaughlin and Francis "Frank" Curran. It was Bridget's second marriage. She had been infatuated with Curran before a *shaughraun* (matchmaker) set her up with a man named Costello, who died after giving her several children. Bridget had several more children in her second family with Curran, a farmer who suffered from a heart condition. Abby was minded largely by her half sisters, and the forceful manner she developed no doubt had to do with her need to establish her rightful place in this complicated ménage.

Abby's true connection with the Aran Islands was through her grandmother, Margaret O'Flaherty, the wife of Nicholas Curran. Margaret was descended from a fabled clan of rebels known throughout western Ireland as "the Ferocious O'Flahertys." The Normans may have conquered Connaught in the twelfth century, but they never managed to vanquish the O'Flahertys, of whom it was said, "From the ferocious O'Flahertys deliver us." Another of their descendants, and thus a distant cousin of John Ford, was the novelist Liam O'Flaherty. Born in 1896 on Inishmore, the largest of the Aran Islands, O'Flaherty served with the Irish Republican Army in the civil war, and his 1925 novel about that conflict, *The Informer,* became a Ford film ten years later.

By the time Ford's father and mother were born, the worst of the Great Famine had abated. But they grew up hearing stories about its devastation and witnessing its lingering effects.

The Great Famine of 1845–51, also referred to as *an Gorta Mór* ("the Great Hunger"), was one of the defining events of modern Irish history, a tragedy whose impact still is inadequately understood today. As many as one and a half million people died in Ireland from starvation and famine-related disease. Two million others left the country, three-fourths of them emigrating to the United States. The effect of the blight of Ireland's staple crop, the potato, was intensified by mass evictions and by the British government's active indifference to its colony's suffering.

"They are going, they are going, the Irish are going with a vengeance," the London *Times* gloated during that period. "Soon a Celt will be as rare on the banks of the Liffey as a red man on the banks of the Hudson."

As a result of the Famine, "more people left Ireland in just eleven years than during the preceding two and one-half centuries," Kerby A. Miller wrote in *Emigrants and Exiles: Ireland and the Irish Exodus to North America.* "An entire generation virtually disappeared from the land." The Famine was an event of such cataclysmic proportions that those years "burnt themselves deep into the imagination of the people and have haunted their descendants ever since," Irish historian F. S. L. Lyons observed in *Ireland Since the Famine.*

The most acclaimed literary treatment of the subject is Liam O'Flaherty's 1937 novel *Famine,* which the author dedicated to Ford himself. Although Ford never managed to bring *Famine* to the screen, despite showing interest in doing so over a period of fifteen years, the subject had a powerful hold on him from childhood, helping fuel his passion against injustice and his tragic view of human history. But *Famine* clearly influenced his 1940 film of *The Grapes of Wrath,* from the novel by John Steinbeck, whose maternal grandfather was a Famine immigrant. Ford said the story of the Okie migration from the depression-era dust bowl to California "appealed to me—being about simple people—and the story was similar to the Famine in Ireland, when they threw the people off the land and left them wandering on the roads to starve. That may have had something to do with it—part of my Irish tradition—but I liked the idea of this family going out and trying to find their way in the world."

In County Galway, the Famine was felt most strongly during its first few years, before relief measures began to slow its ravenous impact on the population. Ironically, because the area was so poor, it received a greater degree of aid than many other parts of Ireland. Ford attributed his special fondness for Quakers to learning that not only did they come to feed the starving residents of Spiddal, but unlike many other Protestant missionaries, they did so without demanding that Catholics change their religious faith in exchange for a bowl of soup (a much-resented practice known as "souperism"). The Quakers' "humanitarianism during the Famine," in the words of Irish historian Tim Pat Coogan, "shone like a shaft of sunlight on an icy landscape." Ford noted that the Quaker philanthropists in Spiddal also did not engage in the disastrously widespread practice of discouraging poor Irish people from fishing. Such humanitarianism is reflected in *Cheyenne Autumn,* Ford's 1964 film about the flight of starving Cheyenne Indians back to their native home. The heroine is a Quaker schoolteacher (Carroll Baker) who selflessly accompanies the tribe on its journey, which Ford likened to the flight of the Okies in *The Grapes of Wrath*.

Ireland in the post-Famine years was a land of utter despair. The economic decline of rural areas in the face of nineteenth-century industrialization, already under way when the Famine struck, accelerated out of control. The following decades saw what Lyons described as a "headlong exodus from the country which was the instinctive reaction of a panic-stricken people to the spectacle of their traditional way of life breaking into pieces before their very eyes." By 1926, the Irish population was reduced to half what it had been eighty years earlier, declining from its pre-famine level of 8.5 million to less than 4.3 million. Ford's parents were among the 3.5 million Irish men, women, and children who left for North America during that period of social collapse. Many of them never made it but died on the disease-ridden "coffin ships" crossing the Atlantic.

The voyage was so traumatic for Abby Curran that she refused to talk about it in years to come. But her feelings were eloquently expressed in her refusal to return to Ireland, even when she no longer would have had to travel steerage. Like Ma Joad in *The Grapes of Wrath,* if she had to leave her home and "lose everything I had in life," she would not look back.

As if her fate were intersecting with John Feeney's, Abby arrived in America just days before him. She came to Portland, Maine, in May 1872. He stepped off the boat in Boston on the fourth of June. Each was sixteen years old.

John Feeney left Spiddal with something of value. He had the equivalent of a high school education. Catholic schooling for the Irish was outlawed under the British Penal Laws. The Church had to educate its children clandestinely well into the nineteenth century. Students learned their lessons from priests in "hedge schools" or, as in Feeney's case, at night in the basement of a nearby monastery. He became adept in English and mathematics, and his education eventually would enable him to rise from a job as a laborer with the Portland Gas Light Company to become a successful saloonkeeper and political boss.

His future wife, however, never had the advantage of formal schooling. The only job Abby could find in Portland was the one to which most young Irish immigrant women were relegated. She worked as a maid at the Falmouth Hotel. The hotel was owned by J. K. Kilmartin, husband of her half sister Mary, who as a newly arrived teenager had taken a job making pastries at the hotel and stayed on to marry the boss. Not long after coming to America, Abby sent for her eight-year-old sister, Julia, and she later paid for the passage of a teenage brother, Frank.

John Feeney's emigration followed the path of others in his own clan, although details of their dispersal are sketchy. Ford's tales about this period are among his most obviously fanciful, such as his claim that his father went to America to fight in the Civil War. If that was his father's motive, the Irish lad must have been extremely out of touch with current events, because the war had ended seven years earlier. Unpopular though it was with many Irish immigrants, as the 1863 New York draft riots demonstrated, the Civil War did act as a spur to Irish emigration, because it promised a ready job, food, and clothing for any able-bodied man willing to serve as potential cannon fodder. So even people living in the remote wilds of Connemara would have known when the war ended; indeed, Irish emigration slowed considerably in the 1870s, partly for that reason.

Ford claimed that his father "had four brothers in the war—one on the Confederate side who was killed, two on the Union side, and one who was on both sides—he got *two* pensions. But by the time my father arrived, the war was over. I asked him, 'Which side was you going to fight for, Daddo?' He said, 'Oh, it didn't make no difference—either side.'"

Ford's imagination took on Paul Bunyanesque proportions when it came to describing the exploits of his uncle Mike Connolly. Uncle Mike was the prototype for the boastful, larger-than-life Irishmen played by Victor McLaglen in Ford's cavalry movies, a venerable theatrical type whose lineage traces back to Plautus's Miles Gloriosus and Shakespeare's Falstaff. As Ford told the story, incorporating elements of several of his movies from *The Iron Horse* onward, Uncle Mike emigrated in 1858 to Quebec, where he was promptly shanghaied into a chain gang digging a canal. Eventually escaping to live with a friendly tribe of Blackfoot Indians, Uncle Mike wound up in the Union army during the Civil War, accepting money from another man to fight in his place. During the carnage at Fredericksburg, Uncle Mike deserted, migrating west to help build the Union Pacific Railroad. Throughout this epic American saga, Uncle Mike singlehandedly encapsulates much of the pioneer experience, like the George Peppard character in the 1962 Cinerama spectacle *How the West Was Won,* which Ford partially directed. No doubt some of Uncle Mike's story must have been true, but in this case Ford clearly could not resist printing the legend.

Mike Connolly finally settled in Portland, comfortably married to a prosperous widow who owned a boardinghouse. He also had a profitable sideline as a bootlegger. Despite the Yankee majority's pervasive discrimination against the city's growing Irish-American population, Portland had the quality of a "lace-curtain" refuge for many Irish immigrants who found Boston's docks and tenements unbearably crowded. The desolately beautiful southern coast of Maine, with its rocky beaches and fog-shrouded offshore islands, its rolling hills and picturesque lighthouses, was enough like Ireland to make the immigrant feel less homesick.

When Mike returned to Spiddal for a visit in the spring of 1872, flush with success in the New World, one of his admiring listeners was the teenage John Feeney. Mike's assurance of sponsorship was enough to make John decide to leave his native land. While Spiddal offered little hope for bettering one's lot in life, and though America, at least theoretically, held boundless prospects for an industrious newcomer, emigration was far from an easy choice for a young man like John Feeney. It meant saying good-bye, possibly forever, to many of those he loved. It meant cutting himself off from the land and culture that had nourished his soul, and exchanging them for an uncertain, even terrifying future.

With their long tradition of living close to their native hearth, reinforced by the conservative influence of their Catholic religion, most Irishmen took such a radical step with the greatest reluctance, regardless of how compelling their economic motives were for departure. Described by historian Thomas N. Brown as "the most homesick of all immigrants," the Irish always felt a nostalgic longing for the land they had abandoned. That nostalgia was fueled by Irish emigrants' sense of themselves as involuntary exiles, "driven out of Erin" by the endless hardship and sadness they blamed on their English conquerors. The romantic melancholia of newly hyphenated Irish-Americans would be passed on by them to future generations, eventually finding powerful expression in the work of the most prominent Irish-American filmmaker, John Ford.

Though not without its aspects of grimness, Ford's cinematic vision of Ireland is suffused with a deep sense of romanticism, so extravagant in its emotional fervor that it could only have come from a first-generation American. A title in his silent movie *Hangman's House* (1928) tells us that Ireland is "[s]uch a little place to be so greatly loved." And in the opening segment of Ford's *The Rising of the Moon,* set in rural Galway, we hear an Irish tenor singing with mingled longing and regret:

> *The Garden of Eden has vanished, they say,*
> *But I know the lie of it still. . . .*

For Irish-Americans, this sense of themselves as part of a diaspora "reflected a distinctive Irish worldview," Miller observes in *Emigrants and Exiles.* That tragic sense "led Irish emigrants to interpret experience and adapt to American life in ways which were often alienating and sometimes dysfunctional, albeit traditional, expedient, and conducive to the survival of Irish identity." The "exile motif" in Irish-American life has been a current running throughout "the ofttimes tortuous Irish efforts to resolve the tensions between tradition and modernity."

The clash between tradition and modernity is a central theme underlying all of Ford's work, exemplified in his romantic portraits of bygone days, his mournful elegies to their passing, and his obsession with the breakup of families caught in the wake of tumultuous social change. One of his favorite visual motifs is that of leave-taking: the loved one standing silently on a hillside watching someone walk or ride away forever. This endlessly recurring Fordian image had its roots in the primal leave-takings his parents made as they departed Spiddal in 1872.

Irish family farewells, in those days, were a prolonged ritual that caused the most acute anguish to both emigrants and those they left behind. Ford encapsulated that feeling in the scene of the departure of the two oldest sons in *How Green Was My Valley*. These characters are Welsh, but the ceremony of farewell they silently perform with their parents, one son kneeling at their mother's rocking chair and the other gently closing her eyes with his hands as their father reads the Twenty-third Psalm, is very Irish indeed. The departing person often was left with a heightened sense of misery and guilt for making what seemed an unavoidable choice. Following his family leave-takings, John Feeney paid a visit to the town's new church, then under construction, to attend a clandestine mass in the basement and pray for a safe journey. Then he set out on the road to Galway. He was accompanied by Patrick Morris, the Galway tax collector. In Ford's self-consciously mythic telling of the family saga, this member of the gentry looked out for the well-being of his young kinsman, considering him an intelligent young man with a promising future.

John Feeney said the last of his many good-byes in the old Spanish-influenced port city before boarding the boat to Queenstown. From there he embarked on the steamship for America. But it would not be his last day on Irish soil. In time he would return on a sentimental pilgrimage with the son and namesake to whom he passed along his profound attachment to Ireland.

The Irish actor-producer Charles FitzSimons, who appeared in *The Quiet Man* with his sister, Maureen O'Hara, felt that John Ford "had one great emotional tragedy in his life. That was that he hadn't been born in Ireland." Occasionally Ford went so far as to make people believe that he, like his "Daddo," had been born in the thatched cottage overlooking Galway Bay.

Ford's emotional identification with his family's Irish past helps account for his ambivalence toward his hometown of Portland. He always felt like an outsider there, a mick interloper in a hidebound bastion of WASP history and culture. "I love Portland; I don't even know if they like me," he told a friend in later years. Although John "Bull" Feeney had to leave home and change his name to make his mark in the world, Portland also marked him indelibly, helping shape him into the artist he would become.

During his lifetime, Ford was honored throughout the world for his film-making and military exploits. He received four Academy Awards as best direc-tor and became the first recipient of the American Film Institute's Life Achievement Award. He was awarded the Medal of Freedom, the nation's highest civilian honor, and he also received such military honors as the Purple Heart, the Legion of Merit, the Navy Air Medal, and the gold braid of a rear admiral. He was invested with the jewel and cape of a Knight of Malta, the highest honor for a Catholic layman, by Pope Paul VI. And the Navajos of Monument Valley designated part of their landscape as "John Ford Point." But it was not until twenty-five years after his death that his hometown in Maine finally got around to any official recognition of this son of Irish immigrants.

A measure of Portland's long-standing indifference to Ford's artistic stature came when the AFI award was presented shortly before his death in 1973. Al-though professing to be "delighted" by the tribute, the *Portland Press Herald* of-fered remarkably faint praise in an editorial on its native son: "Mr. Ford was not the greatest director ever to set up a scene. His every effort did not become a classic of his art. But he made good motion pictures. . . . We're not quite sure that we would share the President's [Richard Nixon's] classification of him as 'one of the geniuses of his profession,' but he certainly was a man of consis-tent competence."

In July 1998, a Ford statue was erected in front of an Italian restaurant at Gorham's Corner, the hub of the old Irish immigrant district at the intersec-tion of Fore, Center, Pleasant, York, and Danforth Streets. Ford's brother Francis once wrote that Gorham's Corner "could be likened to the hub of a great wheel painted by a crazy artist who, in a spirit of mischief, had added Welch's Alley and Dumphy's Lane to give it that individual touch of two badly broken spokes." Now part of a gentrified district of shops, restaurants, and of-fices overlooking the downtown wharves, the area was settled by famine im-migrants in the 1840s and still retains much of its period flavor, preserving the red brick buildings and cobblestone streets of that rough-and-ready working-class neighborhood.

The impetus for raising the monument to Ford came not from Portland it-self but from a wealthy Louisiana woman named Linda Noe Laine, who be-came friendly with Ford and his wife, Mary, when he made his Civil War movie *The Horse Soldiers* in 1958. After discovering on a visit to Portland that there wasn't even a plaque honoring Ford in his hometown, Laine commis-sioned the statue from New York sculptor George Kelly.

She also sponsored a series of dedication ceremonies bringing together members of Ford's family with representatives of his Hollywood stock company, the Irish government, the Navajo nation, and the navy. Seeing his favorite groups uniting in his honor for Fordian rituals of lavish sentiment and robust patriotic spectacle would have pleased Ford immensely. The festivities at the unveiling included a color guard of sailors from a navy cruiser, the USS *Carney,* the navy band playing military tunes, and a choir singing such favorite Ford songs as "Red River Valley," "My Darling Clementine," "She Wore a Yellow Ribbon," and "Shall We Gather at the River."

But the most deeply moving moment came during a ceremony at city hall. Billy Yellow, a ninety-six-year-old Navajo shaman, or medicine man, who appeared in every film Ford made in Monument Valley, took the stage with three other members of his tribe to chant a prayer in honor of the man they called Natani Nez. Before offering the incantation for everyone to share the film-maker's legacy of "beauty and peace," Yellow told me that he made the long journey to express his gratitude to Ford for offering work to the impoverished tribe over a period of many years and in the process bringing "an interesting life" to the Navajos. "He brought attention to Monument Valley and the People [the Navajos refer to themselves as Diné, meaning "the People"]. 'Natani Nez' literally means 'Tall Leader.' It was just a natural description given to John when he first came to Monument Valley to do *Stagecoach*. We didn't have much contact with white people; he was a leader and he was tall. I respected his sense of humor, and I respected that Ford was a man who was always in charge."

Portland's bronze statue of Ford depicts him seated in a towering director's chair, ringed with castings of rocks from Monument Valley. Holding a pipe and wearing his habitually casual attire of slouch hat, khaki jacket with military shoulder patch, baggy shirt, flannel pants, and work boots, Ford peers intently through his dark glasses in the direction of his father's saloon across the way. But there's only a vacant lot now where Feeney's Saloon once stood at the corner of Fore and Center Streets. Adjacent to that location, fittingly enough, is a pub named for the Irish high king Brian Boru, who defeated the Norsemen at Clontarf in the eleventh century.

Some of Portland's slowness to honor John Ford had little to do with his Irish background, but can be attributed to the general lack of official cultural recognition given to movie directors in America. For all their lionizing in the media, filmmakers still are mostly ignored by civic worthies whose tastes run more to celebrating soldiers and politicians, ballplayers and musicians, poets and painters. Indeed, Laine first offered the statue to the Portland Museum of Art, which was not sufficiently impressed by Ford's credentials. Perhaps the old New England warning "No Irish Need Apply" still holds weight with such institutions.

Although he never quite felt he belonged in Portland, Ford did not turn his

back on the city where he was raised. When he returned home to visit his remaining family members once or twice a year, Ford always made a point of
looking up old friends, including fellow Portland High School football player
Oscar "Ski" Vanier. "He was proud of all the awards on his wall," Vanier recalled, "but he never spoke about his work. Instead he wanted to know about
his old buddies and girlfriends from Portland, and how this year's football team
was doing."

The Portland Observatory stands at the peak of Munjoy Hill, in the heart of
the old Irish-American neighborhood in the city's East End. From the red
wooden tower, 242 feet above sea level, an observer commands a godlike view
of the ships passing through Casco Bay, along the narrow three-mile peninsula
of hometown poet Henry Wadsworth Longfellow's "city by the sea." Through
a telescope one can study details of the islands in Casco Bay, the mountain
peaks beyond, and the Atlantic Ocean four miles to the east. Young John
Feeney spent many hours here in quiet contemplation of the sea, absorbing
the unfolding visual panorama of fishing boats, commercial vessels, and navy
battle cruisers, imagining the human dramas taking place on these distant
ships.

Atop the observatory, flags would be raised to signal ships approaching
Portland harbor. In the immigrant dwellings clustered around the observatory,
local historian Edward H. Elwell wrote in 1876, "[M]any an eye has been
gladdened by the flag thrown out on one of its three flag-staffs, indicating the
approach of some long-absent ship; and many a storm-tossed vessel has been
saved from wreck by the succor sent out through timely intelligence from this
watch-tower." The nineteenth-century homes and apartment buildings that
still dominate Munjoy Hill often have a "widow's walk," a small fenced-in
porch on the rooftop. These platforms are eloquent reminders of the days
when the wives of sailors would wait anxiously behind the railings for their
husbands' return.

Ford's films contain many such scenes of waiting women, wives of fron-
tiersmen and soldiers and seafaring men, posed silently in doorways, on
rooftops and porches, on docks and desert bluffs. "I can't see him—all I can see
is the flags," says a cavalryman's wife in *Fort Apache* as she stands on a rooftop
porch watching her husband's troop ride out at dawn, never to return.

John Feeney's active imagination would have thrilled to echoes of historic
events that occurred on Munjoy Hill in bygone days.

Named after early British settler George Munjoy, who built his home there
in 1661, the hill was the site of battles and peace parlays between white settlers
and Indians during colonial days, of confrontations with the British during the

Revolutionary War and the War of 1812. In the more tranquil years that followed, Munjoy Hill became "the playground of the city; the scene of 'General Musters' and Fourth of July celebrations." After it was stripped of most of its pristine parkland, Munjoy Hill was "degraded in more senses than one," Elwell wrote, when it was "covered with an unsightly huddle of cheap tenement-houses." While true enough to some extent, those coded words unmistakably expressed the Yankee disdain for the Irish and other immigrant laborers who had been pouring into the city since midcentury.

Scorned in less polite speech as "shanty Irish," they came because cheap labor was needed to sustain Portland's economic boom in the second half of the century. Portland became a key shipping center for goods traveling through New England by boat and rail. Boston, Nova Scotia, other parts of Canada, and rural and coastal Maine shipped products via Portland to New York and points south on steamships and sailing vessels. In his boyhood, John Feeney could still see grand five- and six-masted ships sailing with ocean cargo. The ships carried grain and lumber, coal and Maine granite. Maine was also the nation's leading supplier of fish. Goods and people crossed the Atlantic in both directions by steamships making the regular route between Portland and Liverpool.

Many of the Irish emigrated to Portland on those ships from Liverpool, taking up steerage space that later would be filled with Canadian lumber. Others migrated from earlier stopping-off points in Canada and Boston. As in other cities of the eastern United States, the waves of Irish washing ashore during the mid–nineteenth century were mostly relegated to menial jobs in Portland, loading and unloading ships, digging ditches, sweeping streets, stringing electrical wires and laying gas mains, cleaning hotel rooms, and serving as domestics in private households.

On Munjoy Hill the Irish families lived stacked atop other families in three-story wooden apartment buildings, one family to each floor. Many of these "cheap tenement-houses" were (and in some cases remain) comfortable enough dwellings, however modest their appearance. Spacious enough to accommodate the typically large Irish families, these were not the teeming, unsanitary tenements of the larger eastern cities such as New York and Boston. These were the sturdy, well-kept homes of upwardly mobile people who, suffering the scorn of being called "shanty Irish," aspired to the middle-class gentility that eventually would transform them into "lace-curtain" Irish.

Portland's Irish lived in close proximity with members of other minority groups, including Jews, Italians, French-Canadians, and the "colored people" who, Elwell observed, "have always had a proclivity for Munjoy's Hill." There were some frictions between those groups, particularly between the Irish and the French-Canadians, whose expedient political partnership fractured in the early 1900s. Youths from both camps often faced off in street fights. In Ford's memory, however, he and his fellow members of the Portland underclass tended to share a sense of brotherhood. African-Americans "lived with us," he said. "They didn't live in barrios. Our next-door neighbors were black. There was no difference, no racial feeling, no prejudice." Ford also remembered attending Jewish synagogues several times in his boyhood and acting as a Shabbas goy, a gentile hired to perform tasks forbidden to Orthodox Jews on the Sabbath and High Holy Days. From those experiences and his friendships with Jewish families, he picked up a smattering of Yiddish.

Ford's account of the harmony among ethnic groups during his childhood in Portland may have been somewhat exaggerated in retrospect, but there can be no doubt that he was influenced in a positive way by growing up in such a multiethnic environment. The degree of attention he pays in his films to African-Americans and members of other minority groups was highly unusual for a Hollywood director of his day, and even if his portrayals of those groups are still a subject of controversy, they generally were respectful.

Certainly the Irish and other minority groups in Portland had a common bond in recognizing that the worst discrimination they experienced came from members of the Yankee establishment who served as arbiters of the city's social, economic, and geographical boundaries. Edwin O'Connor's 1956 novel *The Last Hurrah* is still the best fictional portrait of the Irish-Americans of New England. In the book, the aging mayor offers a historical narrative of how Boston's Yankee power structure began to change. On a smaller scale, Frank Skeffington's story also describes what happened in Portland: "A hundred years ago the loyal sons and daughters of the first white inhabitants went to bed one lovely evening, and by the time they woke up and rubbed their eyes, their charming old city was swollen to three times its size. The savages had arrived. Not the Indians; far worse. It was the Irish. They had arrived and they wanted in. Even worse than that, they got in."

Because the Horatio Alger myth still carries such potency in America, men who rise to great heights from humble beginnings are prone to exaggerating the extent of their climb. Ford was no exception. Not content with boasting that he came from "a family of peasants" in Ireland (true enough), he frequently described his family background in Maine as impoverished, although he occasionally did so with a winking sense of irony. He once joked that when he was growing up in Maine, "We were so poor we ate lobster three times a day." "Jack lies," his wife, Mary, said. "They were a very respectable family. He was not the poor boy he lets on."

In fact, the Feeneys were quite prosperous by the time of his birth in 1894, twenty-two years after his parents' arrival in America. From his beginnings as a laborer for the Portland gas company, John Feeney branched out by joining his cousin Mike Connolly in the bootlegging racket. Selling whiskey illegally to dockworkers and sailors, John eventually saved enough money to open his first saloon, a speakeasy near the docks in the back room of a building on Center Street. He married Abby Curran in 1875, and they became American citizens in 1878. The first of their eleven children, Mary Agnes (called Maime), was born in 1876, when they were living above the saloon on Center Street. Several of the Connollys lived in the same neighborhood. But Abby was not happy raising a family over a saloon, so the Feeneys soon relocated.

Speaking to his grandson, John Ford observed that his mother was widely considered the most beautiful Irish girl in Portland, and she was smart enough to marry the most successful Irish saloonkeeper in town. Even allowing for some Fordian hyperbole, that observation is closer to the mark than Ford's claims of poverty, although the family had occasional ups and downs caused by the fluctuating strength of the antiliquor movement.

Selling and consuming liquor ostensibly became illegal in Maine in 1851, when Prohibitionists succeeded in passing the "Maine Law," which became a model for other states. But as would happen when the Nineteenth Amendment was the law of the land between 1919 and 1933, dry laws in Maine were honored as much in the breach as in the observance. As the slogan "Rum, Romanism, and Rebellion" indicated, the Prohibition movement always had a strong anti-immigrant, anti-Catholic component, providing a vehicle for nativist fears about the unruliness of the lower classes while also reflecting more altruistic concerns about poor people's health and welfare.

A strongly Republican state from the Civil War onward, Maine, like Massachusetts, tried to use the Prohibition movement as a means of turning back the tide of immigrant political power, concentrated in the rival Democratic Party. Not surprisingly, Irish-American saloonkeepers like John Feeney or his Boston coeval Patrick Joseph Kennedy (grandfather of the first Irish Catholic president of the United States) not only tended to be staunch Democrats, but often wielded political power from their saloons as party ward bosses. If John Feeney had been asked why he became involved in politics, he would have replied as Mayor Skeffington does in O'Connor's *Last Hurrah:* "[T]he main reason I went into politics was because it was the quickest way out of the cellar and up the ladder. . . . it was only when we gained a measure of political control that our people were able to come up for a little fresh air."

Feeney's Saloon operated at several other locations over the years near the downtown wharves, including 517 Fore Street, 196 Federal Street, and 14

India Street. The latter establishment was run by both John Feeney and his eldest son, Patrick, a confirmed teetotaler who eventually took over the family business when his father retired. The senior Feeney was a regular but moderate drinker, confining his alcohol consumption to a couple of sacramental shots of whiskey before dinner. Ford claimed not to remember a single instance of seeing his father intoxicated. Abby Feeney abstained altogether, and like other respectable women of her day, would not have dreamed of entering a saloon. She also forbade her son John to do so. Yet she seems to have accepted her husband's profession without complaint or disapproval, as a practical necessity of life.

Portland's saloons were euphemistically listed in the city directory as "restaurants" or "dining rooms," even though at Feeney's there wasn't much more to eat than a bowl of beans. Liquor could be consumed on the premises or taken home as "package goods." These establishments served as neighborhood gathering houses where the men could unwind after a long day on the docks and share their grievances, hopes, and reminiscences. British sailors from the Liverpool ships were cordially welcomed customers at Feeney's as well, and buckets of beer were carried from the saloon by bellhops to the traveling men and prostitutes who frequented nearby hotels.

The Irish saloonkeeper in those days was an arbiter of neighborhood disputes, an intermediary between political classes, and a dispenser of political patronage. John Feeney would meet newly arriving immigrants at the ships, help them fill out their citizenship papers, and instruct them how to vote. Feeney also presided over party caucuses at the saloon. The natural next stop for a ward boss was to run for office himself, but unlike P. J. Kennedy, who became a Massachusetts state legislator, the amiable, softhearted John Feeney never was interested in that kind of power, preferring to exercise his paternalistic influence behind the scenes.

Feeney's nephew Joseph Connolly, son of his sister Margaret Connolly, helped break new ground for the Irish in the Portland political establishment. Joe taught himself law while working in a law office and, with the support of Feeney and the Democratic machine, rose to become a judge of the municipal court. The governor eventually appointed him to a seat on the Cumberland County Superior Court, such a bold move, considering Connolly's Catholic faith, that it made headlines as far away as Boston. The family took great pride in Joe's appointment, but when he arrived late to a family dinner celebrating the occasion and failed to exhibit suitable contrition, Margaret pointed out in a typically Irish bit of ironic humor that he wasn't the first judge in the family. That honor went to Chief Justice Morris of the Killanin barony.

Ford grew up admiring Judge Connolly, who helped inspire the many affectionate portrayals of folksy judges in his movies. Connolly's influence can
be seen most clearly in Judge Billy Priest, an Irvin S. Cobb character memorably played for Ford by Will Rogers and Charles Winninger. Ford's equally
warm portraits of Abraham Lincoln and other political figures, even such raffish ones as Mayor Skeffington, also owe much to the positive image of politics
he gained from his uncle and father.

Much in Ford's life and work can be traced back to the influence of his father's profession. The darker side, of course, was the director's own chronic alcoholism, interrupted by halfhearted pledges to abstain and frequent hospital
cures following debilitating drunken binges. On the lighter side, jokes about
prodigious consumption of intoxicating spirits are rampant in Ford's movies.
His cinematic world is filled with lovable Irish drunks, typified by the characters played by Victor McLaglen in *Fort Apache* (who reflects after sampling a
barrel of rotgut whiskey, "Well . . . it's better than no whiskey at all, sir") or
Barry Fitzgerald in *The Quiet Man* (who shudders as he offers his curt dismissal:
"America . . . Pro-hi-*bition!*").

Generally a Ford character's drinking is treated with indulgent humor. The
director stages drunken brawls as good-natured, almost balletic rituals of male
bonding and communal celebration. Francis Ford spends most of his time as a
character actor in his brother's movies in a state of inebriation, playing what
Andrew Sarris describes as "a fearsomely fraternal projection of the director's
Irish irascibility amid a drunken devotion to the cause of some almost forgotten campaign." The last word Frank's "Brother Feeney" character utters on
screen, in *The Sun Shines Bright,* is "Refreshments!" There are rare instances in
Ford movies when drinking reveals a character's fatal lack of self-discipline, as
in *The Informer,* when McLaglen's Gypo Nolan informs on his comrade and
then blows the blood money on a drunken spree. But Ford usually goes out of
his way to ridicule Prohibitionists, such as the starchy Ladies' Anti-Liquor
League with their Grand Lemonade and Strawberry Festival in *The Sun Shines
Bright* or Margaret Leighton's hysterically repressed New England Protestant
missionary in *7 Women* ("Take that . . . *bottle* away!").

On a deeper level, Ford's frequent portrayal of his protagonists as noble outlaws, acting for society in ways society itself cannot see, owes much to the romantic tradition of the Irish rebel as political savior and martyr. It also may
owe something to having a father who practiced an illegal profession in America. Feeney's Saloon, like others in Portland, was raided from time to time,
usually with advance warning from law enforcement officers who were on the
take and just keeping up appearances during election season. John Feeney's political influence helped ensure that his and other saloons would remain open.

The farcical nature of such blatant corruption and hypocrisy could not have escaped the eyes of his son.

From Harry Carey's Cheyenne Harry in silent films to John Wayne's Ringo Kid in *Stagecoach,* Henry Fonda's Tom Joad in *The Grapes of Wrath,* and Wayne's Tom Doniphon in *The Man Who Shot Liberty Valance,* Ford expresses his most heartfelt admiration for lawbreakers who selflessly act on society's behalf, despite their ostracism by supposedly "decent" folks. Since Ford always paid tribute to his father's influence and always treated him with the most sincere devotion, he must have grown up believing his father was more of a genuine force for social good than were the puritanical moralists who relegated him to outlaw status. Living under British occupation for hundreds of years caused widespread disrespect among the Irish for the rule of law and made the words "Irish" and "rebel" synonymous. Even though Ford's position in American society was deeply ambiguous, his self-image as an Irish rebel was an integral part of his persona. His friend and colleague Robert Parrish described Ford as "a cop hater by religion, by belief," words that would have brought a warm glow to the heart of his Irish saloonkeeper father.

"If there is any single thing that explains either of us," John Ford once said to Eugene O'Neill, "it's that we're Irish."

A FARAWAY FELLA

For Britain, the Irish are the Indians to the far west, circling the wag-
ons of imperial civilisation. Once in America, of course, the Irish cease
to be the Indians and become the cowboys.

FINTAN O'TOOLE IN
THE LIE OF THE LAND: IRISH IDENTITIES

ASURE SIGN THE Feeneys were climbing up in the world came when they
moved into a spacious farmhouse a few miles down the coast from Portland in the Spurwink district of Cape Elizabeth. Not that they owned it, mind
you. They were only renting the property on the sprawling estate of Charles
E. Jordan, a wealthy member of a prominent Yankee family whose ancestors
helped settle Cape Elizabeth in the seventeenth century. But it was as close to
living on the coast of Spiddal as the Feeneys could come in their new land,
and by Spiddal standards they were living like lords.

John Martin Feency was born in the two-story Cape Cod farmhouse on
Spurwink Road (now Charles E. Jordan Road) in 1894. Abby, who was attended by a doctor named L. B. Thombs, doubtless had serious concerns over
her newborn's survival. Infant mortality was a recurring problem for her
throughout her childbearing years, in an age when small children often fell
prey to disease caused by poor sanitary conditions. Before moving to Cape
Elizabeth, Abby lost three of her infant children, and a fourth died after they
moved to the farm around 1888.

In Portland, Abby had given birth to Maime, Edith, Patrick, Francis, Bridget, and Barbara. Edith (also called Delia or Della) died of measles in 1881 at
about the age of three, when the family was living in a tenement at 53 Center Street inhabited by eleven Irish families, a total of fifty-five people. Such
tenements, informally known as "rookeries" because of flimsy additions
erected in their backyards to squeeze in more immigrants, were breeding
grounds for cholera and typhus. Bridget Feeney died of cholera in 1884,

shortly before her first birthday. Barbara (also called Abby) succumbed as an infant in 1888. Undaunted, Mrs. Feeney gave birth in Cape Elizabeth to Edward in 1889, Josephine in 1891, and Joanna (called Hannah), who died not long after her birth in 1892. John was the tenth child but only the sixth to survive. He was followed by another boy, Daniel, who lived not long past his birth on February 17, 1898.

Parents in those days had to steel themselves against the heartache of losing children, so it's unlikely John grew up with much awareness of the sisters who had died before his birth. But he must have been affected by the loss of a baby brother. A sensitive four-year-old child's feelings of bereavement might mingle with a guilty feeling of satisfaction over the death of a sibling rival. John left no recorded comment on Daniel's death, but it's worth noting that the same name was given in 1944 to the director's second grandson and future biographer.

Ford's sister Josephine, overlooking their short-lived brother Danny, described John to me as her "baby brother." Ford referred to himself as the family's *cudjeen,* the Irish word for baby. Comparing himself to Roddy McDowall's Huw in *How Green Was My Valley,* a film he felt closely echoed his own family life, Ford remembered being "a fresh young kid at the table." Maintaining that privileged position in a large Irish family meant that Johnny Feeney would have been fretted over, indulged, and also, to some degree, ignored by his aging parents. By the time he came along, both were thirty-seven, well into middle age by the standards of the 1890s. Their other surviving children ranged in age from two to eighteen. The eldest child, Maime, assumed much of John's rearing, leaving his father and mother to deal with him more like grandparents than parents.

The simple but elegant house the Feeneys rented in Cape Elizabeth rests on 190 acres of gently rolling farmland, an unexpectedly luxuriant setting for the first several years of Ford's life. Ford never said much about his birthplace for the record, and little has been written about it by his previous biographers, perhaps because his impressions of his boyhood in Cape Elizabeth were largely relegated to the dimness of his subconscious memory. The most striking aspect of the farm is its spectacular view of the ocean. Only half a mile's stroll down a sloping hillside is Higgins Beach, part of a jagged inlet that looks as if it had been torn from the rocky cliffs.

Stones and driftwood are scattered throughout the narrow strip of sand where the future Rear Admiral John Ford, USNR, set out on his first explorations of the sea. "Ever since I was about four years old," he recalled, "I owned a boat. Some old wreck came up, and we caulked it with tar and everything." He acquired another boat as he was growing up.

The stark grandeur of the area around the rocky promontory of Cape Elizabeth has inspired many painters, notably Winslow Homer and Edward Hopper. Hopper's famous painting *Lighthouse at Two Lights* memorializes a landmark still standing only a few miles down the coast at Portland Head. Growing up in such a picturesque setting gave Ford an instinctive appreciation of natural beauty. He claimed to have spent a summer in his boyhood watching Homer (who died in 1910) painting at his studio at nearby Prout's Neck. With their elegant simplicity and balance and their emotional connection with the rugged beauty of the land and sea, Homer's paintings clearly influenced Ford's visual sense. Explaining why, as a young man, he was able to grasp the fundamentals of moviemaking so quickly, Ford said, "[T]he only thing I always had was an eye for composition—I don't know where I got it—and that's all I *did* have. As a kid, I thought I was going to be an artist; I used to sketch and paint a great deal and I think, for a kid, I did pretty good work—at least I received a lot of compliments about it."

During his early boyhood in Cape Elizabeth, he wouldn't have known that his family were only tenants on the land. He would have assumed that they owned the narrow but sprawling three-bedroom farmhouse with its small adjoining barn and its back porch looking out on a field with tranquil groves of birch trees. So it may have come as a harsh letdown when John realized that his family, as they had in Ireland, were living at the sufferance of wealthy landowners. Worse yet, their landlords were blue-blooded Yankees of English descent.

The farm was part of the land taken from the Indians by the Reverend Robert Jordan after he arrived in Cape Elizabeth from England around 1640. Captain John Smith, who mapped New England in 1614, named the settlement after Elizabeth Stuart, granddaughter of Mary, Queen of Scots, the Catholic queen whose martyrdom is the subject of Ford's 1936 movie *Mary of Scotland*, starring Katharine Hepburn. By 1891, when John and Abby Feeney moved there, Cape Elizabeth was regarded as a rustic retreat for wealthy people from Portland, as well as a resort for summer visitors and Portland residents on weekend outings.

John Feeney moved his family to the fresh air of Cape Elizabeth so he could dabble as a farmer and fisherman. He missed the simpler life he had known as a boy. Here he could raise his own garden, using seaweed for fertilizer as he had in the old country, and go rowing in a lobster boat, providing dinner for his family with only a net and his big, rough hands. But he kept the family saloons active in Portland and employed farmworkers to help him raise crops of strawberries and potatoes. He was not abandoning the liquor business for farming but using the farm instead as insurance against the constant ebbs and flows of Maine's Prohibition laws. For the same reason, Feeney established a "package goods" store dispensing liquor at a railroad station just across the state line in Portsmouth, New Hampshire.

There were many other small farmers and fishermen in Cape Elizabeth, which a Portland newspaper described in 1880 as the "garden of Maine." Families grew strawberries, lettuce, peas, carrots, squash, pumpkins, cabbage, and potatoes. Many raised virtually everything they needed to eat in the warmer months while preserving food for the winter. For professional and amateur fishermen alike, the waters close to shore provided ample quantities of lobster, cod, mackerel, haddock, halibut, sardines, and cunners, a popular fish for making chowder.

In so many ways, it would be hard to imagine a more idyllic place for a young boy to grow up in America around the turn of the century. There was as much space for play and adventure as anyone could wish. In the summertime, children had the woods and the ocean to explore, and in the winter months they could go ice-skating on the Great Pond, slide downhill on wooden sleds, or ride in horse-drawn sleighs. For the adults, there were sketching and painting excursions, clambakes, and all-day picnics on the rocky cliffs and in the woods. For indoor entertainment in those more placid days before radio or television, the Cape Elizabethans sang songs and spun stories, held taffy pulls and music festivals in their homes and churches, went to plays and square dances at the Grange Hall, and attended more intimate dances in other halls and hotels.

In his earliest photograph, taken around the time they lived in Cape Elizabeth, little Johnny Feeney sits placidly perched on the arm of a wicker chair, dressed in a sailor suit. His curious gaze is wide and direct, yet his eyes are softly shaped, gentle, and disquietingly sad. There is a look of loneliness about him, a sense of isolation, perhaps attributable in part to the poor eyesight that afflicted him from childhood. He is quite a handsome little boy, but Ford was the first to admit that he did not mature into a particularly handsome man. "I myself am a pretty ugly fellow," he told an interviewer in 1964. "The public wouldn't pay to see me on film."

The only blight in the Feeneys' earthly paradise of Cape Elizabeth was one they knew all too well: the disease of religious and ethnic prejudice. Cape Elizabeth was overwhelmingly Protestant: Episcopalian, Congregationalist, Methodist, and Baptist. A Catholic church had been built there in 1861, but by the time the Feeneys lived in Cape Elizabeth, most of the Catholics in the area attended Holy Cross Church in South Portland. The Feeneys also continued to attend St. Dominic's in Portland while paying Sunday visits to their relatives in the East End. But in the country, where social change lagged behind the times and Irish accents were mostly heard from workers at the resort hotels, the Feeneys, who still spoke mostly Gaelic around the house, were acutely conscious of their outsider status.

Feeney children of an age to attend the one-room country schoolhouse in Cape Elizabeth found themselves the victims of anti-Irish, anti-Catholic hostility. The teacher seemed hostile, and other children mocked them for using Gaelic words, taunting them as papists.

"Kids would run up and see if we had horns," recalled Ford's niece Cecil McLean de Prida, daughter of his sister Maime.

The gains the family had made since coming to America seemed in danger of being reversed. So, largely at Abby's urging, they moved back to Portland in 1898, the year John turned four.

Those first years of his life in Cape Elizabeth were his lost Eden. The modern world already was beginning to intrude into that rustic haven before the family departed. Cape Elizabeth was subdivided in 1895, its northern half becoming suburban South Portland. In 1898, an electric trolley line was run into Cape Elizabeth from Portland. The trolley replaced what was affectionately known as "the Barge," a bus drawn by a team of four horses. Some of the peace and serenity of Cape Elizabeth was lost as city folk swarmed off the trolley cars into the dusty little hamlet and its tree lined country roads. Soon the gasoline engine would be taking the place of the draft horses and oxen that pulled carts and wagons in John's boyhood. Witnessing the old agrarian world changing before his eyes into the clamorous, industrialized twentieth century, John Feeney did not realize that he was finding one of the major themes that would preoccupy him throughout his adulthood.

From his parents, who had seen one old world collapse around them before coming to America, he would have acquired a sense of regret and nostalgia for what is lost whenever a society is transformed. The deep sense of Irish melancholia he would exhibit in his work, mourning the destruction of traditional societies, had its roots both in his parents' exile from rural Ireland and in his own expulsion from his childhood Eden in Cape Elizabeth. He would try to recapture that lost paradise in his life and, more successfully, in his work. Onscreen, the painful sadness of Ford's nostalgia is exquisitely balanced with the consolations of memory.

How Green Was My Valley begins with the grown-up Huw packing his belongings as he prepares to leave his Welsh coal-mining valley forever. The rest of the movie is Huw's reverie of his lost childhood, introduced with these words: "I am leaving behind me my fifty years of memory—Memory. Strange that the mind will forget so much of what only this moment is past and yet hold clear and bright the memory of what happened years ago—of men and women long since dead. For there is no fence nor hedge round time that is gone. You can go back and have what you like of it. So I can close my eyes on my valley as it is today and see it as it was when I was a boy. Green it was, and possessed of the plenty of the earth. . . ."

The departure from Cape Elizabeth was only the first move the peripatetic Feeneys would make over the next several years. The elder John Feeney seemed dissatisfied with the series of houses they occupied in Portland, perhaps because they always had to share them with two or more families. In relatively short order, the family moved from 48 Danforth Street, in the rough neighborhood near Feeney's Saloon and the downtown wharves, to more genteel Munjoy Hill apartments at 65 Monument Street and around the corner at 21–23 Sheridan Street, just a few blocks up the hill from Casco Bay.

Young John's regret over leaving his childhood farm for the crowded, noisy city could only have been compounded by the feeling of rootlessness caused by those moves. He was forced to move three times in the five-year period between 1901 and 1906, when he was between the ages of seven and twelve. The lack of a fixed address in Portland during that critical period in his early life no doubt helped instill in him the intense feelings about home and wandering that animate so much of his work.

Finally all but the paterfamilias became resistant to being uprooted again, refusing to leave the top-floor apartment on Sheridan Street for more than a decade. The Feeneys shared the three-story building for most of those years with the Irish families of Michael H. Myers and Patrick A. Mahoney, who ran the Myers and Mahoney Plumbing Company, for which Ford's brother Eddie went to work. Myers and Mahoney each had five children. Along with the Feeneys' six surviving children—including Maime and Pat, who continued to room with the family as adults—the narrow wooden building on the downward slope of a hill resembled the fairy-tale home of the Old Woman Who Lived in a Shoe. Its oddly shaped nooks and crannies resounded with the shouts of swarming children playing hide-and-seek.

Johnny, who shared a bedroom with Pat, enjoyed living in the apartment on Sheridan Street, with its abundance of playmates and its breathtaking view of the bay. From the three front windows of the apartment, he spent long hours taking in the dramatic sights of ships passing among the myriad islands of the bay, outlined against the hilly horizon. Here, as at the Portland Observatory a few blocks away, he nurtured his growing love of the sea while simultaneously developing what film critic Manny Farber would call his "fascination . . . with lines of action in deep space."

The elder John Feeney eventually managed a part-time return to the soil by purchasing a cottage for the family on Peaks Island in Casco Bay. Easily accessible by steamboat on the three-mile run from the downtown customhouse wharf, the island was a small but thriving vacation resort, as it remains today. In the early 1900s, a visitor could rent a room at one of about twenty hotels and cottages for between four and thirty dollars a week. Some of the hotels were opulent, catering to wealthy and prominent guests who strolled around the island dressed to the nines. Along with swimming, sailing, and year-round indoor ice-skating, the island offered band concerts and two lively summer theaters, the Cape and the Gem, which presented professional touring companies imported from New York. The barnlike Gem Theatre did double duty as a dance hall. After the nickelodeon craze came to Portland in 1908, the Gem added moving pictures to its entertainment repertoire. Patrons could dance to ragtime music while keeping one eye on the screen.

The Feeneys' piece of land on Peaks Island, half a mile from the ocean, was much smaller than the farm they had rented in Cape Elizabeth, but it was a comfortable and tranquil retreat. Best of all, it belonged to no one else. From a high porch atop a flight of wooden stairs, the family could sit in the fresh air and enjoy a dramatic view of waves crashing against the rocky shoreline. The aging John Feeney could get away from his saloons to grow apple and peach trees and raise strawberries, tomatoes, cucumbers, and potatoes. It was all he needed to make him happy.

Whenever Ford reminisced about growing up in Maine, it was the house on Peaks Island he cited as his home. He even left some people with the impression that he was born there. During the summertime he would row his small boat from the island around Casco Bay, studying navy ships up close and exploring the other Calendar Islands, including Great Chebeague Island, whose soil was studded with Indian arrowheads. If he missed the sea during schooldays in Portland, he could look out through his lace curtains over the rooftops of the sloping street and peer directly toward Peaks Island. And from the island's Forest City Landing, he could look back and see the observatory dominating his hill across the bay.

Even after becoming successful in Hollywood, Ford returned each summer to Peaks Island for rest and recuperation, putting the pressures of moviemaking behind him as he puffed his pipe, rowed his boat, and worked in his father's garden. When his father died, the house was left to one of Ford's aunts, who sold it in the late 1940s. But Ford continued to pay visits to friends and relatives on Peaks Island well into his own old age.

Ford always had a warmly affectionate relationship with his father, whom he first addressed as "Daddo" in the Irish style before starting to call him

"Grampy." A highly sentimental and emotionally demonstrative man, Grampy was outgoing, humorous, relatively abstemious, always reliable, and skilled in his profession.

While watching an Independence Day parade with John, Grampy offered him an early lesson in patriotism: "When the flag passes, take off your cap."

"But I don't have a cap on," John protested.

"Then cross yourself, damn it!" his father said.

A dashing figure with his red hair and broad mustache, Grampy Feeney was also a marvelous storyteller who passed on his "touch of the poet" to his sons John and Francis. "Dad used to tell stories about the fairies in Ireland," John recalled, "and he made them so real we actually expected to meet them if we walked down a dark hall." John's older brother Francis, who became an actor, considered his father "the greatest actor who ever lived." Along with his yarns about fairies, elves, and banshees, Grampy told tall tales about his supposed exploits back in Ireland when he carried boulders on his back or swam the length of Galway Bay. John Ford's memory of these yarns was echoed when the Irish characters of his movies would boast about such feats as swimming the English Channel "with an anvil on me chest," as Victor McLaglen puts it in *She Wore a Yellow Ribbon*. Ford attributed his storytelling talent to his father's influence.

Although king of his domain at the saloon, John Feeney knew his place at home. He was content to leave the family finances and most of the parental discipline to the sharp-witted, strong-willed "woman of the house." Abby Curran Feeney was a loving but somewhat stern mother who reminded Ford's wife, Mary, of Britain's Queen Victoria. Abby had the lace-curtain Irish concern with social respectability. She once told Mary, "Don't let anyone see you sweeping the front porch." Her children considered her a master psychologist who understood how to exact absolute obedience with the most economical and intimidating of means. "One word from her and that was it," her daughter Josephine recalled. Sara Allgood's imperious matriarch Beth Morgan in *How Green Was My Valley* "looked like my mother, and I made her act like my mother," Ford pointed out. Ronald L. Davis suggests in his biography of the director that this may account for the ferocious clashes of will that occurred between Ford and Allgood over the most minute details of her characterization, such as how she sliced bread.

"If my father was the head of our house, my mother was its heart," says Huw in *How Green Was My Valley*. That was not true at the Feeneys' house, where the mother dominated and the children's devotion to her was as much enforced as heartfelt. Whenever Abby's boys entered or left the house, they were expected to kiss their mother. If they had done something to cause her disapproval, she would show it simply by turning her cheek. Abby "had complete control over Jack," his niece Cecil attested. "She had control over all of them. Her children never thought of talking back. Barbara was a lovable authoritarian, as was Jack. He was more like her than were any of the others, less like his father."

The mixture of deference and wariness Abby inspired in her son can be seen in a striking photograph taken by a Portland newspaper photographer when Ford came home on Mother's Day 1929, during a break from shooting his navy film *Salute* in Annapolis, Maryland. John is literally kneeling at his mother's feet as she sits in a rocking chair, a long, flowing lace shawl draped around her neck as she adjusts a carnation in his lapel. Ford clutches a pipe in his right hand, looking into her eyes with a peculiarly somber expression. Framed by short white hair, her face seems obdurate with its small eyes and a jutting lower lip issuing from a stony jawline. The gaze passing between them is so intense and intimate that one almost feels embarrassed to regard it; along with deep mutual respect, their gaze makes evident the tenseness of a mutual standoff between two exceptionally strong-willed, unyielding personalities.

Summarizing their relationship with perfect ambivalence, Abby once declared, "All the children are normal, except the youngest, Johnny."

Ford's habit of sentimentalizing mothers in his movies, while ostensibly reflecting his deep love for his own mother, should be a tip-off that beneath that overabundance of feeling, some forbidden emotions may be lurking. Beyond expressing Ford's obvious admiration and respect for his immigrant mother's strength of character, such sentimentality could be a cover for what Davis proposes "may have been a resentment toward his mother he never allowed to surface." Ford may have resented not only Abby's emotional distance but also female authority itself and its linkage with the giving and withholding of love. That such a resentment probably existed in Ford's case, instilling endlessly conflicting feelings of rebellion and guilt, can be seen in his tendency to center his movies around men while avoiding complex portrayals of heterosexual relationships. That reflected his personal preference for male rather than female companionship and his tormented marriage and family life (in which he and his wife addressed each other as "Mama" and "Papa").

The domineering nature of the traditional Irish mother, overcompensating for the social and sexual subordination of Irish women by the Catholic Church, has been seen by many observers as a key factor in the sexual fears and confusion often exhibited by Irish males. Of Ford's adult sexuality a familiar Irish joke could fairly be applied: "He would climb over a dozen naked women to get to a pint of Guinness." Ford's former screenwriter Dudley Nichols commented in 1953 on the way the filmmaker's personal unease with sexuality is reflected in his work: "Ford's weakness, if I may stand in the place of critic for a moment, is that he cannot create in his actors the normal man-woman passions, either of love or the hate that is the dark side of impassioned love. I should guess he does not know it, does not understand it." Putting aside the obvious exception of *The Quiet Man,* which Nichols underrated perhaps because he wasn't asked to write it, those comments are harsh but have a high degree of truth.

Ford was not usually prone to mysticism, but he claimed that he and his mother were so close they often communicated by psychic means, even after he went to Hollywood: "She would send me messages. There were quite a few instances of that." Rather than taking this strange comment at face value, we might see it as the explanation he made to himself for carrying his mother's admonitory voice around inside him during adulthood. Growing up both accepting and resenting their mothers' powerful influence, Irish men often transfer those feelings to women in general, complicating their sexual relationships, which already are marked by the traditionally Catholic separation of the female of the species into the opposing categories of "Madonna" and "whore." Ford's formative experiences and feelings about sexuality in early childhood are lost to his biographers, for he never spoke of them and probably never even recognized what they were. But the influences that formed his sexuality, his attitudes toward women, and his conflicted feelings about his emotional sensitivity and masculinity can be inferred from his movies.

Many great men show little promise in their early lives. Signs of genius, particularly artistic genius, often are more apparent in retrospect, for the conventional measures of achievement frequently fail to recognize a superior mind and imagination in the early stages of development. While erratic performance in school can be a sign of serious cognitive difficulty or emotional disorder, it can also be a sign that a youngster is developing his or her own special way of seeing the world.

The abilities John Feeney possessed were not readily apparent in grammar school, and only a few people seem to have recognized his potential when he was attending high school. Part of his problem was that the field in which he would excel was still in its infancy. He was born only three years after Thomas Edison began experimenting with motion pictures in New Jersey, and he was just under two years old when the French brothers Louis and Auguste Lumière held the first public exhibition of their "Lumière Cinématographe." Predicting John Feeney would find the perfect outlet for his peculiar blend of talents would have been as difficult as predicting that movies, within the space of a single generation, would become the world's most popular art form.

Preserved among Ford's papers is his report card for the 1905–1906 school year. The redheaded and freckled Irish lad was eleven years old when he entered Josephine O'Connor's sixth-grade class at Emerson Grammar School. For the first two months, she graded John "Poor" in spelling and arithmetic, and only "Fair" in reading, language, and geography. His performance in the next three scholastic periods was extremely erratic, such as when he went from "Good" in arithmetic that December to "Poor" in the same subject only two months later.

John exhibited dogged improvement in most other subjects. By the end of the year, he was only "Fair" in arithmetic but had improved to "Good" in reading, spelling, and language, subjects that included "the parts of speech and the kinds of sentences" as well as "poetry and prose to be commited and recited." His best subject was geography. When the class devoted "special attention to capitals, large cities, and places of historic interest" in the United States, it piqued the interest of the future maker of Western movies, bringing him a mark of "Excellent."

History was another of John's favorite subjects in school, although the Portland school curriculum from that period indicates that he would not have taken a history class until eighth grade. That year he studied "United States History through the revolution . . . with reference to the sequence and connection of important events," along with further study of historical geography and maps. He retained a vivid recollection of Lyman's Historical Chart, which displayed color-coded time lines of great world events, and of memorizing and reciting famous orations by Marc Antony and Patrick Henry. Among the books available to his class were Eggleston's *Stories of American Life and Adventure* and *Stories of Great Americans for Little Americans,* Tappan's *Our Country's Story* and *American Heroes Stories,* and Baldwin's *Abraham Lincoln,* as well as similar volumes on world history.

But John's overall school record, by all accounts, was as spotty as his sixth-grade report card. At Portland High School, it would take him three years to complete a course in algebra, although he did well in history and English composition. Since he had no lack of innate intelligence, why was he so resistant to schooling in general, so unmotivated to excel intellectually?

His parents' choice to send him to public rather than parochial schools exposed him to discrimination as an Irish Catholic. Being stigmatized for his ethnic and religious background may have caused him to become somewhat withdrawn in class. His parents' habit of speaking Gaelic at home also may have contributed to his early feeling of being different from other children. Abby Feeney could read Gaelic, but, unlike her husband, she was never able to read or write English. She depended on John and her other children to read her the local newspapers. Even though both of his parents came from Spiddal, they spoke different dialects and frequently bickered over each other's choice of words. John's own way of speaking favored his mother's, which was influenced by the dialect spoken in the more primitive Aran Islands, the homeland of Liam O'Flaherty and the literary turf of the lyrical playwright John Millington Synge, author of *The Playboy of the Western World* and *Riders to the Sea*. Ford felt his Irish heritage gave him a natural aptitude for language and music. He picked up other languages easily, acquiring French from a French-Canadian boy in the neighborhood.

The history of that period in America is replete with examples of children from immigrant families battling their way to success by using their brains instead of their fists. And it's unlikely that discrimination could have been John's major handicap as a sixth grader at Emerson, for his teacher was Irish and so were many, if not most, of his fellow pupils. The red brick schoolhouse was located on Munjoy Hill at 13 Emerson Street, a short walk from his home (the school building is now an apartment house, but its exterior has changed little since Ford was a student).

John's artistic nature probably was one of the principal factors that made him a mediocre student. Dreamily disconnected from his immediate surroundings, he dwelt largely in his own imagination. Much of his time in class was spent drawing sketches of his teachers and classmates. He was able to get by while paying only partial attention to what was happening in class because he could gather his thoughts quickly when called on for a response. Ford was what his friend and fellow Irishman Pat O'Brien called James Cagney—"a faraway fella."

That quality of abstraction may have been part of Ford's personality from early childhood, but it undoubtedly became more pronounced after he suffered a serious illness during his elementary-school years. He caught diphtheria, a debilitating respiratory disease, and was quarantined at his home on Monument Street, missing a year of school. Dan Ford's biography says that Ford was eight years old when he came down with diphtheria, but a report of Ford's physical examination for active duty in the U.S. Navy in October 1941, not publicly released until 1998, states that the illness occurred when he was twelve. That seems more likely, since he was already in sixth grade when he turned twelve in February 1906, making it improbable that he would have missed one of the previous school years. Furthermore, he should have entered high school in the fall of 1908, but did not do so until the fall of 1910. Being absent for seventh grade when he was twelve and thirteen, along with a period he spent attending school in Ireland, could help account for the time gap.

The effects of the isolation and immobilization Ford suffered as a growing boy confined at home during his illness can be gauged from his depiction of Huw's illness in *How Green Was My Valley.* Drawing on his own childhood experience, Ford movingly shows how disrupting such a confinement can be to a child's normal development. Huw's precocious sensitivity and maturity can be traced to those lonely months when his only adventures are the interior journeys provided by the great books lined up in a row alongside his bed: *Treasure Island,* Boswell's *Life of Johnson, The Pickwick Papers, Ivanhoe,* "all the noble books which have lived in my mind ever since." Giving Huw a copy of *Treasure Island,* his pastor, Mr. Gruffyd (Walter Pidgeon), says, "I could almost wish that I were lying there in your place—if it meant reading this book again for the first time."

The widowed Maime took charge of John's nursing because their mother could not abide being around anyone who was seriously ill. While that may have been an understandable reaction in a mother who had already lost five of her children to illness, John must have felt abandoned by his mother during that frightening time in his life. Huw's mother is separated from her son when both fall ill in *How Green Was My Valley.* His nursing is left to his widowed sister-in-law Bronwen (Anna Lee), who lovingly reads him the classics, just as Maime did for John when she read him *Treasure Island,* Grimms' *Fairy Tales,* and Mark Twain's novels *The Adventures of Tom Sawyer, Adventures of Huckleberry Finn,* and *A Connecticut Yankee in King Arthur's Court.* Turning his period of adversity into a profoundly transforming experience, John acquired a strength of character and a contemplative nature that set him apart from other children when he returned to school a year older than his classmates.

Ford's personal experience as a victim of diphtheria and as the brother of a child who died from cholera may help account for his recurring depiction of such epidemics in his films, including a plague in *Arrowsmith,* typhoid in *Doctor Bull,* yellow fever in *The Prisoner of Shark Island,* and cholera in *7 Women,* as well as diseases stemming from malnutrition in *The Grapes of Wrath.* One reason doctors in Ford movies almost always suffer from alcoholism is the fearful physical and emotional toll exacted by their duties.

There was another reason that John seemed withdrawn into his own inner world. "The very vision of the boy was special," Andrew Sinclair poignantly observed in his 1979 biography of Ford. "His eyesight was poor and he could merely see a blur without wearing thick spectacles. When he took them off, his view of the world was changed to blocks of color or the distinctions between light and dark. Only the movement of people or animals or machines would make a whisk of reference in his hazy universe. But the act of putting his thick lenses over his eyes would change the boy's perceptions."

It's a fascinating irony that many important film directors have had poor eyesight. Some even have functioned with only one eye, such as Ford in his later years, Fritz Lang, Raoul Walsh, and Andre de Toth. These men's deficiencies of vision played a crucial part in shaping them into artists, forcing them to compensate by developing an extraordinarily acute visual sense. Ford's urgent need from boyhood to clarify and make sense of what he saw would become his raison d'être. Without being conscious that he went through daily life equipped with the equivalent of a director's viewfinder—the frames of his glasses—he was beginning to create his own style of looking at the world.

Ford's aptitude for art was a trait he shared with his mother, according to his sister Josephine, who thought that John and his brother Francis took after their mother, while Pat and Eddie were more like their father. One of Abby's sisters was an artist, and Abby herself had a strong artistic bent but little means of expressing it other than exhibiting remarkably good taste in fashion. Her sympathy for her son's artistic talents must have been a crucial factor in shaping his personality.

He also was fortunate that drawing received so much emphasis in the Portland school curriculum. Throughout their grammar school and high school years, students received systematic training in drawing plants, buildings, and other objects, as well as in mechanical and geometric drawing. They studied the harmonies of color, which the city's *Annual School Report* for 1906 described as "a comparatively new feature, and not yet very well understood," but one that "warrants its retention as an important part" of every student's art education.

Marada F. Adams, Emerson's principal, was the school's art teacher. Ford took classes from her every year, and was impressed that she made annual trips to Italy to study art, bringing that European influence to her students in Portland. While reminiscing to his grandson near the end of his life, Ford credited Miss Adams with teaching him much of what he learned about the basic principles of art. Her critical importance in his artistic development can be gauged by the fact that she was the only grammar school teacher he ever cited as an influence on his life.

Although his was one of the most robust and painterly visual styles in the history of cinema, Ford liked to claim that his sense of composition was purely intuitive. When I asked how he went about planning his shots, he replied, "Walk on the set, look at the set, look at the locations. You do it by instinct. You tell the cameraman to place the camera here and get in so-and-so and so-and-so, so he does it. That's all there is to it." But through Miss Adams he did become acquainted with artistic fundamentals. Acquired in the premodernist era, when classical principles of harmony still ruled, Ford's training was not advanced or avant-garde in any way, but it put him on solid ground from the beginning of his career, when he went to work in a popular art form that allowed a Hollywood filmmaker to express himself visually just as long as he accepted the doctrine of directorial "invisibility." Ford pushed the boundaries of that doctrine when his growing tastes for expressionism became more overt in the late silent era and the 1930s (as seen in such films as *Four Sons, Hangman's House, The Informer,* and *The Prisoner of Shark Island*), but his greatest work epitomizes the highest qualities of Hollywood classicism.

With its omnipresent backdrop of the sea and the strikingly varied vantage points of its hilly streets, Portland offered the young John Feeney a rich visual panorama to study and absorb, augmenting the lessons he learned from studying the countryside around Cape Elizabeth and watching Winslow Homer at his easel. Nevertheless, Ford told his grandson that the great feeling for scenery that permeates his work as a director was acquired when he visited Ireland as an adolescent. His father made frequent trips back home, and took John along when the boy was about eleven or twelve. Commuting through the Irish countryside for a few weeks while attending a school near his ancestral home, John became fully aware of the pictorial splendor of landscape and its connections with the lives of ordinary people. As Orson Welles once said of him, "John Ford knows what the earth is made of."

John came away with a deep emotional attachment to Ireland. His last memory of that magical childhood trip was of a *céilí* (a traditional group dance) held in their honor the night before he and his father returned to America. The townsfolk danced to an accordion and fiddles while drinking toasts to the health of father and son with potent doses of poteen, the Irish equivalent of moonshine. Here was the genesis of Ford's romantic vision of Ireland that one day would flower in the extravagantly beautiful landscapes of *The Quiet Man*.

Ford's favorite subjects for drawing throughout his lifetime were not landscapes, however, but cowboys and Indians. His boyhood sketches of Western figures tended to be idealized, heroic profiles. Even as an adult, whenever he made casual sketches on the pages of his scripts or correspondence, he usually drew profiles of noble red men wearing picturesque war bonnets. To a lesser extent, he sketched cowboys and military figures crowned with flamboyant hats and helmets. Ford ultimately needed a movie camera to convey his love of landscape, but his overriding concern as an artist with both pencil and camera was always with people's faces and the way their expressions reflect their inner character.

Ford thought it a curious coincidence that he became so fixated on the West before deciding to make his career in the new medium of motion pictures. Before he even saw a movie, he was an avid reader of Western fiction. But there was nothing unusual about an American boy of the early 1900s having a passion for the Old West. Youngsters from every region of the country were devouring pulp Westerns as well as the tales of more respectable authors in the field, such as James Fenimore Cooper, Bret Harte, and Mark Twain.

From the 1880s onward, America was in a headlong rush of nostalgia to recapture its rapidly vanishing frontier. The West was already being extravagantly mythologized in the artwork of Frederic Remington and Charles Russell, dime novels featuring Deadwood Dick and Buffalo Bill, and live "Wild West Shows" featuring the "genuine" Buffalo Bill Cody and his legion of imitators, including many actual cowboys and Indians who made a living recycling their life stories into entertainment. In historical retrospect, the closing of the western frontier and the final defeat of the Native Americans were marked by the same tragic event, the Wounded Knee massacre in 1890. Three years later, the Wisconsin historian Frederick Jackson Turner delivered his famous paper "The Significance of the Frontier in American History" before the American Historical Association in Chicago.

"American social development has been continually beginning over again on the frontier," Turner explained. "This perennial rebirth, this fluidity of American life, this expansion westward with its new opportunities, its continuous touch with the simplicity of primitive society, furnish the forces dominating American character. The true point of view in the history of this nation is not the Atlantic coast, it is the Great West."

At the conclusion of his remarks, offered just a few months before the birth of America's foremost Western mythmaker of the twentieth century, Turner declared that "the frontier has gone, and with its going has closed the first period of American history." The wide and immediate acceptance of his thesis represented the American public's acknowledgment that the nation's formative era could be recaptured only through the artistic imagination.

Immigrants and their children saw better than most people that the true democracy they were seeking in America was represented in the idealism of the westward impulse. That spirit was captured in newspaper editor Horace Greeley's celebrated 1837 declaration "Go West, young man, go forth into the Country," a line modified by Edmond O'Brien's frontier editor in Ford's film *The Man Who Shot Liberty Valance* to "Go West, young man, and grow *young* with the Country." For a boy from an immigrant family whose parents already had been part of a vast westward migration, going west would have seemed both a logical extension of the American Dream and a further act of exile.

Politicians less concerned with egalitarian optimism than with labor agitation and other unrest among the immigrant population passed the Homestead Act in 1862 to stimulate emigration from the industralized East to the under-populated West. But that measure, supported enthusiastically by Greeley, proved largely a failure, for even Americans restless enough to move west generally wanted to settle in cities rather than in rural areas. Still, the myth of the frontier would not die, and an awareness that the Old West was dying only stimulated a greater desire for inhabiting the legendary West of the imagination.

The western pioneers had "plowed the virgin land and put in crops, and the great Interior Valley was transformed into a garden: for the imagination, the Garden of the World," wrote Henry Nash Smith in his 1950 book *Virgin Land: The American West as Symbol and Myth*. ". . . When the new economic and technological forces, especially the power of steam working through river boats and locomotives, had done their work, the garden was no longer a garden. But the image of an agricultural paradise in the West, embodying group memories of an earlier, a simpler and, it was believed, a happier state of society, long survived as a force in American thought and politics. So powerful and vivid was the image that down to the very end of the nineteenth century it continued to seem a representation, in Whitman's words, of the core of the nation, 'the real genuine America.'"

Enter the movies.

The Western was a natural element of the motion picture medium. Even though the first Westerns, such as Edwin S. Porter's landmark film *The Great Train Robbery* (1903), were shot in New Jersey, their vivid images of gunplay and fast-riding men on horseback filled a deep-seated psychological need in an increasingly modernized America. As the medium gradually became more sophisticated, the beauty of the unspoiled wilderness became an ever more popular attraction for moviegoers. So did pictures romanticizing the purity of Indian life before its destruction by the coming of white "civilization."

Most patrons of the early nickelodeons were members of immigrant families yearning to escape the grinding tedium of their lives in squalid urban environments. If the American Dream that brought them across the ocean seemed a bitter illusion to a man digging ditches, a woman or girl toiling in a sweatshop, or a boy selling papers on a city street corner, that was all the more reason Western movies seemed so appealing. Simply by paying a nickel to rest on a rickety chair in a crowded storefront theater, they could take a vicarious journey into wide-open spaces where a person's past meant nothing and individual initiative still counted for everything.

"New England invented the West," Jorge Luis Borges has written. The Argentinian fabulist was not referring simply to the fact that America's western myths were formulated largely by nineteenth-century writers and politicians from the nation's northeastern intellectual hub. Borges also meant that "the ethical preoccupation of North Americans, based on Protestantism, has led them to present in the cowboy the triumph of good over evil." Even such an iconoclastic western writer as Mark Twain, whose energies were largely devoted to ridiculing and rebelling against the strictures of puritanism, could never escape the groundwork laid down by New England moralists.

Ford's portraits of Protestant reformers and Boston Yankees are caustic in the extreme. In *Drums Along the Mohawk,* set at the time of the Revolutionary War, a fanatical Protesant minister (Arthur Shields) offers a prayer for a young female member of the congregation who is "keeping company with a soldier from Fort Dayton. He's a Massachusetts man, O Lord, and Thou knowest no good can come of that." Even Ford was not immune, however, from what his Western classic *Stagecoach* ironically calls "the blessings of civilization." Some of his Westerns, such as *My Darling Clementine,* fit the Borgesian scenario of frontier puritanism, and Ford's attitude toward Indians varies widely from film to film between the extremes of demonization and idealization. Yet Ford generally approaches the Western genre's puritanical and imperialistic foundations with the subversive, or at least deeply ambivalent, attitude of an unreconstructed Irish rebel. Scorning anyone who affects to be socially or morally superior, Ford's Westerns have a deeply ingrained catholicity that usually (though not consistently) embraces social outcasts and minority groups. Like the Jewish immigrant showmen who pioneered the movie business, Ford communicated easily with his audience because he was one of them.

Portland's first nickelodeon opened when John Feeney was fourteen years old. The transformation of the old Portland Theatre on Congress Street into the Nickel Theatre (later the Big Nickel Theatre) was a perfect symbol of the changing nature of American popular entertainment. Long the only legitimate theater in town, the Portland converted to vaudeville in 1901 before succumbing to the nickelodeon craze on New Year's Day, 1908. Soon after that, a second movie house, the Dreamland Theatre, opened on the next block. There already were four or five thousand nickelodeons in America, catering to an annual audience of more than two million people, a third of them children.

"As a kid, I was fascinated by the nickelodeons of that period," Ford recalled. "Any time I got a nickel or a dime I would go to the movies. I loved the glamour of the movies."

He was so enthralled that when the Gem Theatre on Peaks Island started showing movies, he took a job as an usher. Silent-movie theaters changed their programs twice a week, running each film as often as eighteen times a day, so John was able to see an enormous number of one- and two-reel pictures in his first several years as a moviegoer. As can be seen from an advertisement for the Big Nickel Theatre in John's high school magazine, such programs were highly eclectic:

> THE HIGHEST GRADE PHOTO-PLAYS
> *Including*
> Dramas of Shakespeare
> Stories from Dickens, Cooper and other standard authors
> Historical and Educative Features
> Travel at Home and Abroad
> Athletic Sports and the Big Events of the Day
> Western and Indian Pictures with Stirring Scenes and
> a Good Proportion of *Comedy* Subjects.

By sitting through each program repeatedly when he attended nickelodeons, John began to be aware of camera technique and the way editing was used to construct a cinematic sequence. He soon became "hooked on the notion of the movies."

The most exciting and innovative of the early dramatic movies were directed for New York's Biograph Company by a former stage actor named David Wark Griffith. The Kentucky native started with Biograph as an actor in February 1908 and was so uncertain of his future in movies that he almost accepted a job offer that summer in one of the stock companies on Peaks Island. But his wife, actress Linda Arvidsen, told him, "How long is Peaks Island going to last? What's sure about summer stock? What does Peaks Island mean to [theatrical impresarios] David Belasco or Charles Frohman? . . . You don't know what's going to happen down at the Biograph, you might get to direct some day."

Her prediction came true almost immediately, when Griffith was given the chance to direct a stagy melodrama about a child stolen by Gypsies, *The Adventures of Dollie.* Over the next few years, Griffith greatly expanded the vocabulary of the infant medium with such visually dynamic and dramatically expressive short subjects as *The Lonely Villa, Pippa Passes, A Corner in Wheat, An Unseen Enemy, The Musketeers of Pig Alley,* and *The Battle at Elderbush Gulch.* The most important of Griffith's many early forays into the Western genre, 1913's *Elderbush Gulch* was one of the first films we can be sure left a lasting impression on Ford, since he imitated scenes from it in his first feature, *Straight Shooting* (1917), as well as in *Stagecoach.*

Despite the growing popularity of motion pictures and Griffith's artistic advances, most educated people still considered the "legitimate" stage far more

worthwhile than what they disdainfully called the "flickers." A devoted the-
atergoing town, Portland was considered one of the best stops for any road
company in the early decades of the twentieth century. Most of the celebrated
theatrical performers of the era—among them Maude Adams, John and Ethel
Barrymore, George Arliss, George M. Cohan, Nance O'Neill, John Drew,
Carter De Haven, De Wolf Hopper, Lillian Russell, and James O'Neill (father
of playwright Eugene O'Neill)—made regular appearances before appreciative Portland audiences, who were also treated to occasional visits by such legendary names as France's Sarah Bernhardt and Poland's Helena Modjeska.

John Feeney was not only a movie-mad youth, he was stagestruck. In addition to his job as a movie usher at the Gem Theatre, he ushered during his
high school years in the gallery of the elegant Jefferson Theatre at 112 Free
Street, Portland's leading showcase for legitimate drama. He recalled working
six nights a week at the Jefferson, which means that he saw many, if not most,
of the Jefferson's presentations between the fall of 1910 and the spring of
1914. Between escorting gallery patrons to their fifty-cent seats and running
errands for performers, the bespectacled high school student eagerly witnessed
the last great flowering of the American popular theater before it lost much of
its mass audience to movies and radio. John would come home each night to
Munjoy Hill and regale his family with accounts of the plays he saw at the Jefferson. With his prodigious memory, he could spout off so much of the dialogue, with suitably dramatic inflections, that his family felt no need to bother
going to the actual plays.

Not much serious attention has been paid to the influence of theater on
Ford's artistic development. But in his recollections for his grandson's biography, Ford cited both his ushering at the Jefferson Theatre and his frequent
moviegoing as the experiences that fired him with a passion for show business.
(He might have added that serving Mass as an altar boy at St. Dominic's
Catholic Church on State Street helped imbue him with a love of ritual and
ceremony.)

Ford's absorption of such a broad spectrum of theatrical experiences at a
formative age helped him immensely when he became a filmmaker. While his
visual sense was being stimulated by silent movies, his ear for dialogue was
being trained by stage plays. His exposure to so many distinguished performers with their own varied styles of acting taught him to separate theatrical
truth from phoniness, to recognize every variety of performing trick, and to
understand how a skillful actor can move an audience to laughter or tears. John
acquired an instinctive familiarity with the basic elements of blocking,
scenery, costuming, and all the other aspects of stagecraft, as well as a semiprofessional familiarity with actors and backstage personnel and a casual, first-

hand knowledge of how to talk their language. In the process, he acquired a broad acquaintance with the theatrical repertoire of his day, from melodramas to dramas to comedies, as well as a smattering of Shakespeare and other classical theater. He even had the opportunity to hear specialized companies performing plays for ethnic audiences in Yiddish or French, which would help account for his later facility with both languages.

To give just a flavor of the productions Ford may have seen when he was ushering at the Jefferson, the fall season of 1913, at the start of his senior year in high school, offers some shining examples. Douglas Fairbanks Sr., soon to become the silent cinema's greatest swashbuckling hero, came to Portland for three days that October to star in *Dollars and Sense.* Following the Jefferson's resident stock company in Oscar Wilde's *Lady Windermere's Fan,* the exotic Russian-born actress Alla Nazimova swept onto the boards for one night in *Bella Donna.* John Feeney certainly would not have missed a chance to see the celebrated Irish-American musical comedy star George M. Cohan (whose life would be re-created by James Cagney in *Yankee Doodle Dandy*) when Cohan appeared at the Jefferson on October 27 and 28 in his popular vehicle *Broadway Jones.* Cohan's exuberant showmanship was succeeded by a more august form of "theatuh" in early November when the grandiloquent British actor George Arliss appeared in his signature piece, *Disraeli.*

Such a stellar display could hardly be sustained indefinitely. The Jefferson's primacy in Portland entertainment was being challenged during this period by the boom in vaudeville and nickelodeons (two new movie theaters had opened in 1911, and the city's vaudeville houses sometimes played movies as well). For the remainder of the 1913–14 season, the Jefferson's management cobbled together a largely forgettable schedule of productions including *The Warrens of Virginia, Under Southern Skies, Damaged Goods, Graustark, Little Women,* and *Peg o' My Heart.* But sometimes a beginner can learn more from a second-rate production than from a good one. All were grist for John Feeney's theatrical education, like other perennials he may have seen at the theater in previous years, including *Uncle Tom's Cabin, Brewster's Millions, Charley's Aunt, The Trail of the Lonesome Pine,* and *The Girl of the Golden West.* John and his fellow Jefferson playgoers were rewarded for their loyalty when the 1913–14 season ended on May 23 with two performances by Maude Adams in her most acclaimed role, that of the boy who would not grow up in James M. Barrie's *Peter Pan.*

Ford's nostalgic memories of those days and nights around the footlights included some random, accidental encounters with actors and actresses. He remembered fetching buckets of beer from Feeney's Saloon for De Wolf Hopper, famous for his recital of the poem "Casey at the Bat," and for the amiable comedian Maclyn Arbuckle, brother of Roscoe "Fatty" Arbuckle. And he remembered his boyish delight over a cowboy performer named Tex Cooper, a flamboyantly bearded and coiffed Buffalo Bill imitator who rode a real horse onstage in some long-forgotten Western spectacle. Cooper liked to spend part of each evening mingling with the audience, so he took tickets and helped John usher in the balcony. Already a movie actor in two-reel Westerns for the Bison Company, Cooper later became an early member of Ford's acting troupe in Hollywood, his John Ford Stock Company, a phrase he borrowed from his early experience in the theater.

A haunting offstage image of the great actress Ethel Barrymore was seared into Ford's youthful memory. One morning while serving the six o'clock mass at St. Dominic's, he saw a woman "sitting halfway back; she wore a beautiful fur coat; the sun came through a window and touched down on it and made it shine. She had on an Alice blue cloche with a veil." Wearing his altar boy's white surplice as he slowly preceded the priest along the row of kneeling communicants, John Feeney lifted his gold paten under Ethel Barrymore's chin as she bent back her head and lifted the veil. He was surprised to see that "there were tears in her eyes. I recognized her because I'd seen her when ushering in the theater; but I never knew what made her so sad at that time." With his artist's eye for the visual details that evoke emotion, he had produced a little picture in his memory from that unexpected glimpse into another person's soul. It was his first lesson in how to unveil the reality behind an actor's theatrical facade.

At the Jefferson, Ford might have seen productions of plays he later would make into silent films, such as *Cameo Kirby* by Harry Leon Wilson and Booth Tarkington and *Hearts of Oak* by James A. Herne. Ford also may have seen some actors who eventually would star in his movies. Charles Winninger, the rotund comic actor who crowned his long career by playing Judge Priest in Ford's 1953 masterpiece *The Sun Shines Bright,* appeared at the Jefferson in August 1912 with Julia Ring in *The Yankee Girl.* Henrietta Crosman, the majestic leading lady of Ford's 1933 *Pilgrimage,* was a frequent dramatic performer on the Jefferson's stage in such plays as the March 1910 production of *Sham.* *Sham* was followed by a play called *Above the Limit,* starring Charley Grapewin, the comic actor who would give memorable performances in Ford's film *The Grapes of Wrath, Tobacco Road,* and *Pilgrimage.* While Ford may not have seen all these performers onstage, the familiarity he established with the theater in Portland would enable him to shape the actors' flamboyant, larger-than-life personas deftly and lovingly for the screen.

Inevitably, the stagestruck youth had to venture gingerly before the footlights himself. His early absorption in the theater can be seen as another step toward the creation of what Irish journalist Fintan O'Toole calls "this nexus of strange connections between showbusiness, Irishness and the Wild West," as seen most vividly in Ford's filmmaking career. "The meaning of this self-conscious and intricate theatricality is the meaning of exile itself," O'Toole suggests. "Exile is a form of self-dramatization, the assumption of a role, the tailoring of one's personality to an alien audience. Exile makes things that are unconscious—language, gesture, the accoutrements of nationality—conscious. It makes the exile a performer. And that performance involves ambiguity. It involves being who you are and being who you are playing. It involves, for the Irish in America, playing the white man and remembering the Indian that is left behind."

One source claims that Ford made his stage debut in a 1901 play called *King's Carnival,* but if such an event occurred, Ford would have been about seven years old and appearing in some obscure amateur production, for no play of that title is listed in James Moreland's exhaustive manuscript "A History of the Theatre in Portland, 1794–1932." However, Ford Stock Company member Olive Carey, who met him in 1915, remembered his telling her that he did some acting as a youngster with one of the small summer stock companies on Peaks Island. And to his grandson, Ford recollected in vivid detail how serving as a backstage gofer at the Jefferson Theatre eventually brought him the small part of a messenger boy delivering a telegram to Sidney Toler.

The stocky, sardonic actor, best known today for playing the Chinese detective Charlie Chan in a series of twenty-five movies, was one of Portland's favorite actors. Throughout much of Ford's youth, Toler was the star of the resident stock company at B. F. Keith's Theatre on Preble Street. Keith's stage sometimes was occupied by vaudeville performers, and there was a brief period in the spring of 1912 when Toler moved over to the Jefferson with his fellow troupers. The plays they performed there between April 8 and May 11, each for a full week's run, included *The Dawn of Tomorrow, The Deep Purple, Excuse Me, Billy, The Rose of the Rancho,* and *The Third Degree.*

When eighteen-year-old John Feeney ambled out onto the stage clutching his telegram in one of those plays, he secretly was quaking with fear. Toler, the old pro, quickly sensed it and started toying with him mercilessly. Giving John the third degree, he demanded to know what the telegram contained. John said he didn't know, and Toler asked why he did not. John desperately replied that he hadn't read it. Toler demanded to know why a messenger boy wouldn't read a telegram he was delivering.

As a director, Ford became notorious for baiting nervous actors in similar fashion. Perhaps by assuming the role of the tormentor, he was getting his revenge, over and over, for the agony he once underwent from Sidney Toler.

Ford was equally capable of treating actors with great kindness, and in such moments he may have remembered how it felt being a nervous young stage actor. But he nevertheless recalled his humiliating theatrical initiation fondly, for Toler kidded him about it afterward. That bit of one-upmanship, too, would become part of Ford's method of directing actors, a function of his need to gain psychological control over the people around him.

Willis Goldbeck, who worked with Ford as a writer-producer on *Sergeant Rutledge* (1960) and *The Man Who Shot Liberty Valance* (1962), observed that Ford always had a "tremendous insecurity" about his roots as the son of an Irish immigrant saloonkeeper from Maine. Goldbeck thought that insecurity explained Ford's habitual combativeness with his coworkers, his way of maintaining control by diminishing others.

People began to notice the duality in John Feeney's personality when he attended Portland High School. One of him was the budding artist, bespectacled, soft-spoken, and jocular, but so diffident about his ambitions that he barely recognized them himself. Then there was the tough Irish brawler, the man's man and football star. John Feeney needed new names to fit those two personalities. The redheaded youth encouraged his classmates to call him "Jack," a jaunty, regular-guy sort of nickname, and his teammates on the Portland High Bulldogs dubbed him "Bull."

"He couldn't see too well," remembered teammate Oscar "Ski" Vanier. "We'd yell, 'Off tackle,' and he'd put his head down and charge. It didn't matter if there was a stone wall there, he'd drive right for it. That's when we started calling him Bull. . . . He'd fight at the drop of a hat."

The "Bull" persona was a self-protective cover that allowed a sensitive young man to escape probing and ridicule of his tender side during the time of life when one's developing sexual identity is most uncertain. Though his sudden and conspicuous display of aggression during his high school years now appears an obvious attempt at overcompensation, it served its purpose well. Few would have challenged the masculinity of a letterman who played fullback for the Bulldogs in his junior and senior years. Jack Feeney was also a star sprinter on the varsity track team.[1] Most of all, perhaps, he had to convince *himself* that his growing need to express his feelings artistically did not make him "effeminate." Throwing himself into a macho world of male cama-

---

1. When he won the thirty-yard dash in 4.6 seconds against Westbrook Seminary in February 1914, the school magazine, the *Racquet,* reported, "Feeney's form in the getaway and running was perfect and his speed terrific."

raderie is a classic way for an Irish Catholic male to deal with his discomfort around women, a problem Jack increasingly had to face as he approached adulthood. But splitting his personality in this way failed to resolve his deep-seated conflicts over his masculinity, which would bedevil him for the rest of his life, leaving a pervasive imprint on his work.

Playing the role of "Bull" Feeney was also his way of winning social approval at Portland High. By fitting that era's stereotype of the Irishman as a battling lout, he conformed to WASP prejudices and neutralized potential enemies. But there was a price to be paid for such protective coloration. It changed him both inwardly and outwardly. "In my first football game in high school, I had my nose broken in three places, and one ear is still cauliflower-ish," he wrote in 1946. His misshapen face made him look more like a tugboat captain than a poet. He may not have minded that entirely, but seeing himself as "a pretty ugly fellow" added to the social discomfort he already felt as a "mick" in a school that reflected the city's class divisions.

Looking back over his youth in Portland, Ford preferred to minimize the prejudice he encountered. He pointed out that Irish-Americans, by their sheer numbers, were becoming more of a social and political force in Portland during that period. The city nearly doubled its population between 1890 and 1920, largely due to an influx of immigrants, even though Portland's main business, shipping, began to decline after 1900. Ford's diplomatic attitude toward his hometown masked deeper feelings of resentment, however. Those feelings came out in such offhand remarks as his explanation of why he concentrated on football at Portland High, rather than on basketball. He said he wasn't interested in basketball because in those days it was regarded as a sport for WASPs. He also remembered a female high school teacher treating him as a stereotypical rowdy simply because he was Irish and played football. In an even more telling indication of his true feelings about Portland's class divisions, Ford conceded that the reason he left his hometown was that it offered few opportunities for Irish-Americans.

His high school was the city in microcosm. The old school on Commercial Street was a brick-and-granite building dating back to the time of the Civil War. Among its alumni was Admiral Robert E. Peary, who became world-renowned in 1909 by reaching the North Pole (with black fellow explorer Matthew Henson). But the school magazine in 1914 described the building as "a poor specimen of a High School for a city such as Portland." The influx of newcomers to Portland in the early twentieth century caused a crisis of over-crowding during Ford's years at the high school, 1910 to 1914. He was one of about 1,200 students, 560 more than the building's capacity. The spillover had to be accommodated by moving some classes to other downtown facilities, including city hall. A fire at the school in May of Ford's freshman year gutted the structure's interior. That helped galvanize public support for a more modern building, but construction on new wings would not begin until 1916. Tensions between ethnic groups were inevitable during a period of such social volatility, and some of the festering rage manifested itself on the football field.

Football in those days was less a sport than a battle royal. Players wore leather helmets and little padding. Games usually were low-scoring affairs and every point was fiercely contested. The forward pass was just becoming an important offensive play, introducing some finesse to what had been primarily a joust between burly running backs and linemen. The year John Feeney and his fellow Bulldogs won the state championship, 1913, was the year Knute Rockne's Notre Dame team revolutionized football by beating Army with a forward pass. Ford re-created that epochal moment in his 1955 movie about West Point, *The Long Gray Line,* celebrating the Fighting Irish victory by having a nun lead a parochial school band in "The Notre Dame Fight Song."

Brawls were common between teams and spectators alike during Portland High football games. During a contest with the Coburn Classical Institute at Bayside Park in the fall of 1913, slugging matches between players provoked the crowd to swarm onto the field. City police and finally even the mayor had to step in to restore order.

Bull Feeney was rowdy even by the rough-and-tumble standard of the blue-uniformed Bulldogs. Although tall for his day, he was no behemoth and had poor eyesight, but he played football with blinkered guts and blind determination. Bull was the reliable, good-natured brute who would take the ball under his arm, lower his head, and smash his way through the defensive line. He was a key part of what the *Portland Telegram* called the team's "fast and rugged backfield."

In the first game of the championship season, on September 12, 1913, Feeney was sent in during the second quarter and quickly helped run the ball to Deering High's two-yard line. But the opposition linemen beat back Portland's scoring attempt and "the bad feeling between the two schools cropped out," the *Telegram* reported. Deering received a team penalty for rough play and "both John Feeney and [Deering's right guard] Stockford were put out of the game for their rough tactics."

At a school reunion years later, John remembered the referee as "a young lawyer that had just graduated from Bowdoin. He wanted to pick up some easy money officiating football games. . . . I was in the game for only two plays and he threw me out for unnecessary roughness." "That was a simple case of justice," replied one of John's classmates, who was also a lawyer. "[John] had already trampled two men and both of them had to be carried off the field."

In a game against Bangor on October 25, 1913, Portland's captain, Ralph Mahoney, plunged over the goal line from three yards away, but the *Telegram* reported that "the referee saw 'Bull' Feeney pulling his captain along and terming the assistance illegal would not allow the touchdown, and once more set the blue team back 15 yards."

Portland won both games, however, beating Deering 6–0 and Bangor 7–0, and finished the season with eight wins and three losses. Even more impressive was the fact that the Bulldogs held their opponents to only 18 points all season, while scoring 170. Bull Feeney's teammates appreciated his all-out play. He doubled as the team punter, with somewhat erratic results, and even threw an occasional forward pass.

Some of the respect he engendered no doubt was due to his being older than his teammates—nineteen years old in his final season, twenty by the time of graduation—due to missing a year of grammar school. In his junior year, he was chosen as one of the eight members of the executive board of the class of 1914. He already was showing the qualities of leadership and willpower that would enable him to make a quick success in the movie business.

But John's hard-nosed image in high school was reinforced by his habitually lackadaisical attitude toward most of his schoolwork, other than the subjects he liked, English and history, in which he was an honor student. He blamed his general distraction on fatigue caused by his early-morning job driving a delivery wagon for his brother Pat's wholesale fish market at 191 Congress Street. For a dollar a day, John would deliver loads of codfish, haddock, and mackerel to retail markets, a duty that often caused him to arrive late to class— no doubt accompanied by a pungent aroma. He had other part-time jobs during his high school years unloading trucks at the Casco Bay Lines shipping terminal and as a deliveryman and publicist for a local shoe company.

As he had in grammar school, John made it through his classes largely because of his quick memory and his ability to listen, graduating with a so-so four-year average of 84. "He seemed about as unintellectual a person as you could imagine," recalled classmate Robert Albion, who went on to teach oceanography at Harvard. "In one class, he was told he had no imagination." But those whom Jack Feeney allowed to know him better were able to see beneath his rough, devil-may-care facade.

Oscar Vanier recognized that his fellow member of the Bulldogs' backfield not only was fearless on the gridiron but also "had a great mind and a great sense of humor. Someone would tell him a funny story, and the next day Bull would retell it, adding all kinds of new takes to it. Every time you'd see him he'd have a book in his hand, Shakespeare or something." One of the Irish kids raised in the same Sheridan Street apartment house with the Feeneys,

William Mahoney, remembered that John would "do things, like his writing composition, that showed artistry, but at the time you didn't think much about it. They were just things that were funny."

John's budding talents received crucial encouragement from two unusually perceptive men at Portland High. One was his principal, William Blake Jack. A benevolent, prematurely gray-haired Yankee schoolteacher with cool blue eyes and a great passion for history, William Jack was the first graduate of Portland High to become its principal, assuming that post in the fall of 1911 at the age of thirty-three. He had spent the previous nine years teaching history at the school and continued to do so as principal, visiting classrooms periodically to impart his lessons.

Ford would go on to meet such world leaders as Franklin D. Roosevelt, Winston Churchill, Charles de Gaulle, Dwight D. Eisenhower, and John F. Kennedy, but he declared in his old age that William Jack was the greatest man he had ever met, the one who "set the pattern" of his life. Ford said on another occasion that Mr. Jack was "one man whose life would make a great picture. Once when I ran away on a ship from home, he was there on the dock to greet me, asking me how I had enjoyed my trip around the world. I didn't get any farther than Bath [about thirty miles up the coast]."

Mr. Jack's history lessons, which John first experienced as a sophomore, brought the American Revolution alive to the boy's youthful imagination. Speaking in simple but eloquent terms, the teacher told John about the founding fathers and explained the inner workings of the United States Constitution. He even gave this son of Irish immigrants a lifelong fascination with English history. Egalitarian in his principles, Mr. Jack always made a point of stressing to the children of Yankees and immigrants alike the great contributions made by members of every ethnic group throughout American history, from the Revolutionary War onward. To inspire students of French extraction, he would tell his classes about Lafayette; for Poles, he would refer to Kościuszko and Pulaski; and for the Irish, he would cite the large percentage of revolutionary soldiers who were Irish-Americans.[2]

Mr. Jack had the insight to recognize John Feeney's peculiar combination of abilities. He was impressed with the individuality and imagination John brought to the essays and stories he wrote for various classes, as well as by the

---

2. Despite Mr. Jack's lessons, Ford felt the schooling he received in American history was deficient. So when he was an assistant director at Universal a few years later, he took night courses from an associate professor at the University of Southern California. "I went down there two, sometimes three nights a week—down to the American history class," Ford recalled in a 1970 appearance at USC. "So I now know what the Gadsden Purchase is—I never knew before. . . . There were many gaps in my education, and there're still many gaps in it." In exchange for those lessons, Ford gave bit parts to the professor, who was a movie buff.

young man's skill as an artist. Singling him out for long personal talks, Mr. Jack encouraged John to continue developing both of his creative talents. How he would go about combining them was another matter, something neither could have been expected to foresee. The principal did not spare John some flinty-eyed chastisements when he needed them (frequently). But Ford recalled that Mr. Jack's encouragement marked the first time in his life anyone made him realize he had an important contribution to offer the world beyond Portland. The teacher's clear, simple belief in John Feeney's abilities was a vital factor in giving an insecure young man from an immigrant background the courage and confidence to succeed in the mainstream of American life.

At the time, John toyed with the idea of becoming a writer of fiction or, possibly, a screenwriter for silent movies. He tried his hand as a humorist with a parody of "Wearers of the Blue," the corny Portland High athletic fight song written by the school's music director, George T. Goldthwaite. More seriously, John began writing short stories in a class taught by Lucien Libby. Head of the school's English department, "Luke" Libby was one of its most beloved teachers, renowned for regaling his classes with offhand comical remarks. "For instance, class," Libby would say, "if someone tickles me on the ear with a feather and I don't feel it, and he then takes a match and scratches it on my neck—" To which someone in the class would call out, "Gee! He must be a roughneck!" After getting their attention with jokes, Libby made his students appreciate the beauty of words written hundreds of years earlier by Shakespeare and Chaucer. Ford's films are indebted to Luke Libby's easygoing way of intermingling serious lessons with folksy humor. The director worked some of Libby's whimsicality into Henry Fonda's performance as Abraham Lincoln in *Young Mr. Lincoln* (1939) and paid tribute to his teacher's influence by christening one of the ships in *They Were Expendable* (1945) the *Lucien Libby*.

In 1950, after receiving a New Year's message from Ford, Libby wrote him, "Your expression of respect for me moved me deeply. I likewise have great respect for you, John, especially for the lofty standards upheld by you in your cinema productions. I feel that you are accomplishing on a vastly wider scale much the same thing that I have all my life striven, less effectively, to accomplish in the narrow confines of the schoolroom."

John thought enough of several of his high school stories to offer them to magazines. He claimed that one story—naturally enough a Western yarn—was accepted and brought him a check for twenty-five dollars. That stimulated him to keep writing, he said, even though his subsequent stories were rejected. But if a piece of John Feeney juvenilia was published, it has never surfaced. In a 1948 letter to a young man who wanted to be a writer, Ford counseled persistence in the face of rejection, recalling that he had tried unsuccessfully to sell eighteen or twenty stories. If one of those early stories had seen publication, perhaps he might not have turned his entire attention to movies so readily after completing high school.

The gentler side of Bull Feeney also revealed itself in some tentative, courtly dealings with the opposite sex. When a young woman named Edith Koon came to the school as a Greek and Latin teacher during his senior year, John was one of the students in her study hall. "I was in my first year of teaching," she recalled. "I had just gotten out of Wellesley and was quite green. One day I was having particularly bad luck keeping discipline in one of my study periods. He got his gang together and told the class, 'Let's give this young thing a break, because Willie Jack will never let her stay if she can't keep discipline.' He kept order for me the rest of the year." According to Cecil de Prida, John grew infatuated with Miss Koon and they became fast friends. The teacher regarded him as "a very good-looking, dark-haired boy who always had the nicest smile." He earned the slightly older woman's affectionate regard without having to boast about bringing order to her study hall. "I knew nothing of it until he visited my husband and told me about it," she said. That was in 1947, when Edith was the wife of the president of Maine's Bowdoin College, Portland High alumnus Kenneth C. M. Sills, and Ford came to the campus to receive an honorary degree.

Around female students in high school, Jack Feeney was less outgoing. Despite his letter sweater and hail-fellow-well-met personality in masculine company, he felt shy in addressing girls at school and terribly awkward at the closely chaperoned dances. "At the school proms I was a washout," he recalled. "With my two left feet, I could never keep time to 'Dardanella.'" But he still made the effort. Football teammate Ski Vanier remembered that after school, he and Jack would "go up to the pool room by the old Strand Theatre. We would put our money together and the owner would match the amount. Then one of us would play all comers. We were pretty good. We'd take our winnings and head for the dance hall that was on Pitt Street at the time and find some girls."

Jack managed to get affectionate enough with one Irish girl at Portland High, Miriam Ruth Burke, that they became known as a couple. But it was nothing more than a politely chaste romance with Miriam. He was a virgin when he left for California. John also cherished his high school friendship with Alnah James, a classmate from one of Maine's leading families. He was gratified that their difference in social status meant nothing to the patrician young woman, one of the top ten students in their graduating class of eighty-nine girls and seventy-two boys. Alnah, he recalled, would dance with Irish Catholics. At the Portland High commencement ceremonies in June 1914, which featured speeches and a debate on the war in Europe and the peace movement, the kindly Alnah James read a Bible selection on peace. Bull Feeney served as toastmaster at the senior class banquet.

Katherine Cliffton, Ford's longtime research assistant, recalled that he kept in touch with Alnah Johnston (her married name), "whom he admired greatly as a high school boy. He said she was a 'perfect lady, very democratic.' In each of his pictures there was a gracious, perfect lady, democratic and understanding—I thought she was the model. When he was a young man, I gather, he wouldn't aspire to romance, but he said she was one of the nice girls and she took an interest in him. He was a football hero, and in most American towns it wouldn't be hard for a football hero to mingle freely."

One of John's most cherished high school memories was of attending a dance in Boston during his senior year. The Bulldogs were honored guests at a political festivity in the Vendome Hotel after losing 3–0 to Waltham High on November 15, 1913. Boston mayor John F. Fitzgerald, the genial Irishman known as "Honey Fitz," brought his two older daughters, Rose and Mary Agnes, to the dance. Jack Feeney was among the football players delegated to give them a whirl. He didn't remember which Fitzgerald girl he danced with, but it pleased him to think that it might have been Rose, the future mother of the first Irish Catholic president of the United States.

Principal Jack urged John Feeney to leave Portland to seek his destiny and suggested that he forget about going to college. That was unconventional but perceptive advice offered to a young man with such a restless attitude toward schoolwork and such an eagerness to plunge headlong into a practical, real world occupation.[3]

Despite his father's continued hope that he would become a priest, and his own vague dreams of becoming a writer, John finally decided to gratify his lifelong love of the sea by becoming an officer in the U.S. Navy. During his summer vacations, he had spent some time crewing as a deckhand on a tugboat and as a pantry boy or apprentice seaman on various boats operating out of Portland, although his claim that "before I was twenty I had been all over the world" seems unlikely. Near the end of his high school years, John failed the entrance examination for the U.S. Naval Academy at Annapolis. It was a sharp blow that temporarily discouraged, but did not destroy, his ambition to become a seafaring man. He always continued to feel the lure of the sea, as he indicated in his famous remark in 1950 to Lindsay Anderson: "I want to be a tugboat captain."

---

3. Dan Ford's biography says that Mr. Jack encouraged him to go on to college. But on the tape of an interview with his grandson among his papers at the Lilly Library, Ford clearly says the opposite.

"But God made him a poet," Anderson added, "and he must make the best of that."

If it was not providence that intervened at this turning point in John Feeney's life, what happened looks very much like it in hindsight.

While watching a movie in one of the local theaters, one of the Feeney children (some accounts say it was John) saw an astonishing sight on-screen and came hurrying home to alert the rest of the family: Frank Feeney, the prodigal son who had run away to join the circus, was now a movie star. He called himself Francis Ford.

Dapper, sophisticated, and intensely ambitious, Frank had always felt like a misfit in Portland. Twelve years older than his brother Jack, he was a restless and troublesome student, itching to get out and see the world. "My dear old daddy injected a grammar school education into me, and tried to give me a dose of high school, but I preferred the Spanish-American War," Frank wrote in a 1913 autobiographical sketch. He enlisted in 1898, but when the U.S. Army discovered he was only seventeen, he was sent home from training camp.

"I came back and tried everything, from working in a bakery to shoveling snow," he related. He also tended bar in Feeney's Saloon. "But I couldn't make a success of anything. My father told me I didn't have any sense, and that I had better try at being a policeman or get on the stage. The stage looked good to me, as there I wouldn't have to do any work—as I thought at that time—but I've since had a slight awakening."

Frank's account omitted one of the principal reasons he left Portland, his brief marriage at age nineteen to a sixteen-year-old girl he had impregnated, Dell Cole.[4] He also skipped over his sojourn with a circus, the job he was too embarrassed to report to his lace-curtain family. Frank was considered the black sheep of his family; every time he left home on one of his adventures, his parents prayed for his return, but he would always get in trouble and have to leave again. This time, he was determined not to return to Portland until he could come home a success. Determined to go "legit," the handsome young man with a "black Irish" look of brooding, deep-set eyes and dark, wavy hair set about offering his services to New York stage managers. But with his lack of theatrical training, Frank was offered only insignificant roles. He found

---

4. Their son, John Phillips Ford, known professionally as Philip Ford, was a stuntman and double in some of his uncle John's silent movies, as well as an assistant director on his 1928 films *Hangman's House* and *Riley the Cop*. He went on to a career as a journeyman director of B movies and episodic television.

more opportunities as a property man, a job that helped point him toward his eventual directing career by giving him a crash course in stagecraft.

While appearing in a play called *Merely Mary Ann,* Frank met his second wife, actress Elsie Van Name. When Elsie became pregnant, he decided to look for better-paying work. Frank admitted that he "didn't make much of a hit" as a stage actor, "and some said my voice was bad. . . . Did you ever hear of such a direct steer to the movies? I followed the lead of providence while the industry was still young and rather insignificant. But it did not stay insignificant long."

After some bit parts for the Centaur and Edison film companies in New Jersey and the Bronx, Frank joined the G. Méliès Manufacturing Company in Brooklyn as an actor and all-around assistant. Producer Gaston Méliès, who began making Westerns in 1909 in Fort Lee, New Jersey, was the brother of the pioneering French fantasy filmmaker Georges Méliès; the company manager was Gaston's son Paul. Frank and Elsie went along that December when the outfit relocated to a ranch outside San Antonio, Texas, to make Westerns and Civil War pictures under the brand name of the Star Film Company. Besides playing a wide variety of acting roles, Frank took charge of the props and costumes, helped build and paint scenery, chose the locations, and hired the extras. He first tried his hand at scriptwriting with a Western story called *The Noble Outlaw,* but the script was rejected because it contained too many scenes. Undaunted, he soon began directing pictures for Méliès.

Under the Stars and Bars, an October 1910 release about a Confederate soldier captured by Yankees, was his first notable film as both actor and director. Constructed of several long takes filmed with a largely motionless camera, it shows the influence of Frank's theatrical background in effectively treating the borders of the screen as a proscenium arch. The acting, while theatrically stylized, is more natural than in many other two-reel melodramas of the period, and the film's elliptical narrative style enables it to avoid clichés. Frank already employed fairly complex blocking in this early picture, moving his actors around the camera and composing in depth rather than relying on editing. As yet he employed no close-ups, always keeping the actors in full figure. He later explained that since good-quality film was expensive and hard to get in the early days, scenes had to be staged economically, in a single shot and without repeated takes.

But though Frank's sense of composition and montage would grow increasingly sophisticated, there always remained that sense of an invisible proscenium in the films he directed, a visual framework he would pass along to his younger brother and protégé, who used it with greater subtlety. The classical directing style John Ford developed in silent movies and continued to employ for the rest of his career treated the camera as what he called "an information booth. I like to keep it still and have the characters come to it and tell their story."

Frank played the Mexican villain Navarre in *The Immortal Alamo,* the Méliès company's biggest production, filmed in March 1911, with some scenes shot around the actual Alamo in downtown San Antonio. He went to Santa Barbara, California, with the company that April but left it early the following year to work with fledgling producer Thomas H. Ince in the Bison Company. Frank directed and starred in many of Ince's "101 Bison" Westerns, a trademark referring to the company's use of the personnel, animals, and equipment of the Miller Brothers 101 Ranch Wild West Show. Working under the banner of his own unit, the Broncho Motion Picture Company, Frank made two-reelers in Santa Monica Canyon, including the highly successful *Custer's Last Fight* (1912), in which he starred as General George Armstrong Custer.

A wizard with the makeup box, Frank was hailed by Ince in 1919 as "without doubt one of the most finished of all pioneer film performers. It was nothing for him to play an Indian hero in the morning and make up as Abraham Lincoln for the afternoon's work." Frank appeared as Lincoln in several silent films, the most ambitious of which was Universal's 1913 *From Rail-Splitter to President.* "There is nothing I like better than to play Lincoln," Frank said in 1915. "I have a big library devoted to this great man, and I have studied every phase of his remarkable character, and when I am acting the part, I can *feel* the man as I judge him. I have taken the part in six or seven photoplays now, and every one of them has given a different side of his personality. I have shown his youth, his joys and sorrows, his rail-splitting days, his tragic death, his awkward ways, and his capacity for loving." Frank's great ambition was to "show a resumé of [Lincoln's] life in a twelve-part picture," but it never came to pass. John Ford's own fascination with Lincoln—who figures prominently in such films as *The Iron Horse, The Prisoner of Shark Island, Young Mr. Lincoln,* and *Cheyenne Autumn*—was part of his legacy from Frank. But Jack never deigned to cast his brother as Lincoln, even though Frank easily could have played the role in *The Iron Horse* and *Shark Island.*

A surviving episode of one of Frank's 101 Bison serials, *Blazing the Trail,* vividly demonstrates how much John drew from his brother's work as a director. The picaresque story line bears a strong resemblance to that of John's classic *Wagon Master* (1950), in which Frank plays the coonskin-hatted drummer "Brother Feeney." Frank stars in *Blazing the Trail* as an amiable cowboy in a coonskin hat who signs on to guide a small wagon train of settlers heading west, much like Ben Johnson's title character in *Wagon Master.* The serial's first episode contains some beautifully composed long shots, including several that seem precursors of scenes in *Stagecoach* and *The Searchers.* A high-angle shot of Indians on a cliff watching a distant wagon train, a sequence showing the rescue of a captive white woman from an Indian camp, and images of horsemen and wagons silhouetted against the horizon show what John Ford meant when he told Bogdanovich that Frank "was a great cameraman—there's nothing they're doing today—all these things that are supposed to be so new—that he hadn't done."

Some sources claim the film that brought Frank's new profession to his family's attention was one of the early Westerns he made for Méliès, but that was not correct. His 101 Bison Westerns were among the regular attractions at Portland's Big Nickel Theatre; the *Evening Express* noted in 1913 that the 101 Bisons "have proven among the most popular . . . picture subjects of any being shown for the entertainment of Portland motion picture devotees." But according to Frank, the family first spotted him in a railroad movie. Cecil de Prida, a reliable chronicler of Feeney family history, said Frank was already working for Universal when they saw him on-screen, which would mean the sighting probably occurred sometime in 1913. The family asked Judge Joe Connolly, Grampy Feeney's nephew, to find their long-lost son. The judge managed to get a message to Frank through the New York office of Universal. Frank began corresponding with his family, who hadn't seen him for more than seven years.

Frank received an offer from the Universal Film Manufacturing Company in late 1912, a few months after Carl Laemmle's newly organized company, formed from a group of independent producers, began filmmaking operations in Southern California. A German immigrant, Laemmle was a former exhibitor who had turned to production in 1909 in an attempt to gain independence from the Motion Picture Patents Company. Better known as the Trust, the MPPCo had been formed by Thomas A. Edison and Biograph to monopolize the use of Edison's patented cameras and projectors and the films made by their affiliated companies. Independent filmmakers gradually began fleeing from the East Coast to Southern California looking for good weather, more varied terrain, and freedom from the marauding goons of the Trust. In what became known as the "patents wars," the Trust hired gunmen to take shots at cameras operated by crewmen from renegade film companies. Laemmle was at the forefront of independent producers' opposition to the Trust. Befitting its origins, Universal distributed its films mainly to theaters unaffiliated with major chains and located in small towns and the outlying areas of major cities.

Frank Ford, meanwhile, was having friction with Ince (a former Laemmle associate) over Grace Cunard, a young actress Frank had directed for his Broncho Company. Still married to Elsie but separated from her, Frank became Grace's companion and filmmaking partner. Ince wanted Grace in his own unit, but as a 1916 *Photoplay* article about Frank related, "The young lady announced her preference for Director Ford's company and was fired. Whereupon Director Ford, indignant at this rude treatment of a new star, up and jumped to Universal. Her Grace did likewise." When Frank, at Ince's birthday party, announced his intention to leave for Universal, he and the producer had a drunken fistfight. Ince later expressed regret and asked Frank to reconsider, but Frank remained adamant. His association with Universal began in January 1913, when he started making a Western called *The Coward's Atonement*. It was released under the 101 Bison label, which Laemmle appropriated after raiding several other Bison personnel from Ince.

By the time Frank made his miraculous reappearance on the screen of a Portland movie theater, his mother had been anxiously following newspaper accounts of a highwayman who was operating out west in Yellowstone Park, robbing tourist stagecoaches. Since the thief fit Frank's description, Abby was convinced she had located him. But when told a year or so later that he had been spotted in a movie, she at first refused to believe any son of hers could stoop so low as to become an actor. Everyone was impressed with Frank's glamorous new occupation but his hardheaded Irish mother, who declared after watching him act:

"I wish he had held up the stagecoach."[5]

Despite being rejected by the Naval Academy, Bull Feeney had his choice of several football and track scholarships. He accepted an offer from the University of Maine in Orono, about a hundred miles northeast of Portland. Soon after his graduation from Portland High on June 18, 1914, he spent several days checking out the campus.

He enrolled in the school of agriculture, figuring that wouldn't be as hard as studying. But despite his peasant family's ancestral attachment to the soil and his early childhood on a farm, sixteen years of city life had left Jack unprepared for his first assignment, to slop some hogs on the campus farm. He was equally disgusted with the rest of the freshman curriculum. He had already read

---

5. Abby had a hard time grasping the nature of movies. Once when she went to see Frank in a serial, she became alarmed when the episode ended with him hanging from his fingers from a retracting floor over a pit filled with alligators. Abby thought Frank would have to keep hanging there for the following week. She spent the week urging one of her daughters to send a telegram to the studio asking how Frank was doing. Until she saw the next episode, no amount of persuasion would convince Abby that Frank's escape already had been filmed.

Shakespeare and Chaucer in high school, as well as Caesar's *Gallic Wars* in Latin, but found he would have to do it all over again.

The coup de grâce to Jack's halfhearted dalliance with higher education was administered in the university dining hall. As a scholarship student, he would have had to work his way through school by donning a white coat and working as a waiter, serving breakfast and dinner to more prosperous students. Already extremely sensitive to class distinctions, Jack could only have been dismayed to find himself immediately pressed into service in the dining hall, filling such a stereotypical role for an Irish-American from a working-class background. At dinnertime that first day on the job, he was carrying plates of stew on a tray when one of the diners decided to put the young Irishman in his place.

Jack already had seen the wealthy young WASP, a junior, driving around the campus in his own automobile, looking smug and supercilious. The chips on Jack's shoulders bristled to attention when he heard a shout from the dining table:

"Hey, shanty!"

The young man loudly demanded his dinner from the "shanty" waiter.

For a Yankee to call an Irishman "shanty," a shortened form of the derogatory phrase "shanty Irish," was the worst possible insult in that time and place. With its sneering reference to the impoverished tenement life from which the American Irish were only starting to emerge, "shanty" was a far nastier epithet than calling someone a "mick" or a "paddy." Ford offered a mild echo of that experience in *The Long Gray Line* when fresh-off-the-boat Martin Maher (Tyrone Power) takes an entry-level job as a waiter at West Point. Bristling when addressed as "Paddy" by cadets who don't know his name, he continually shouts back, "*Martin's* the name!"

Jack Feeney was always proud of the even fiercer way *he* reacted to the ethnic slur: he threw the plate of stew in his tormentor's face. Called before the dean, he left the campus, never to return . . . until the University of Maine made him an honorary doctor of humanities in 1947. The university made further amends when it later named its school of dramatic arts after John Ford. "Hell, they kicked me out once, I wanta stay kicked out," Ford joked about that, but he accepted the university's honors gratefully, doubtless reflecting on the fact that if he had received a more hospitable welcome in Orono in 1914, he would not have left Maine that summer on his way to Hollywood.

Ski Vanier could not remember Jack ever displaying an interest in movies or a movie career during his high school years: "You'd have never even known that his brother was in the movies. He never mentioned it." Even though Jack harbored a secret desire to become a screenwriter, Frank's way of life must have seemed distant and unreal to his younger brother. That could help explain Jack's vacillation over his career goals during the weeks following his high school graduation. Despite being "hooked on the notion of the movies," he "never realized that later in life I would become a director."

Jack wrote Frank that June asking if there might be a job for him at Universal. Frank was doing so well that he had his own company within the studio, enabling him to put a relative on the payroll without having to persuade the front office. The members of the Feeney clan always followed the concept of familial loyalty common to people from an immigrant background, providing each other with employment whenever they could. Jack was a big, strong kid who could be thrown into almost any job that required manual labor. It's doubtful his hiring would have bothered Universal president Carl Laemmle, for Hollywood was a wide-open town and Laemmle himself had so many relatives working at the studio that Hollywood wags called him "Uncle Carl"; Ogden Nash quipped, "Uncle Carl Laemmle has a very large faemmle." Around the time Jack decided to quit college, a letter fortuitously arrived from Frank inviting him to Hollywood.

So the young man with the cauliflower ear and the poet's soul went forth into the country, went west to find his future. In November 1914, the Portland High School magazine reported:

"John Feeney is closely connected with the Universal Film Company at Hollywood, California."

CHAPTER THREE

"A DOLLAR FOR A
BLOODY NOSE"

For a long time people have said, as they heard the name "Ford" in connection with a picture: "Ford? Any relation to Francis?" Very soon, unless all indications of the present time fail, they will be saying: "Ford? Any relation to Jack?"

THE MOVING PICTURE WEEKLY, JUNE 1917

EVERY GREAT DIRECTOR has a creation myth, a fabulous tale of his beginnings. On inspection, such tales rarely turn out to be true. When asked late in life how he got to Hollywood, Ford replied with epic understatement, "By train." But he was not always so laconic about the cross-country journey he made in July 1914. He could not resist turning that adventure into part of his personal legend.

Ford wanted people to believe that he hopped freights all the way to California, or that he made his way there by working as a cowboy. Once he even told the tall tale that he was punching cows on a ranch during his leisurely progress toward Hollywood when "The boss's daughter, believe it or not, fell in love with me. She was six-foot-two and weighed about 210 pounds, so I stole a horse and rode away . . . and came to California." Young Jack Feeney soon enough would be meeting real-life cowboys whose true stories ran along those very lines, for the Hollywood West of 1914 was a curious mixture of the genuine article and its celluloid counterfeit, a meeting place for the remnants of the passing frontier and the bards of its mythology. Here even a newcomer's name would be subjected to artful revision, along with the more mundane or less savory aspects of his past.

Rewriting the story of his early life as a plot he might have filmed in the days of silent pictures seems to have amused Ford greatly in his later years, as well as lending a more suitably romantic aura to his first cross-country journey, the adventure that would change his life forever. Such Ford movies as *The*

Quiet Man and *The Man Who Shot Liberty Valance* begin with a train pulling into a station, signaling the onset of a transforming experience, but the reality of Ford's train trip in 1914 was far more prosaic and badly in need of mythic embellishment.

Traveling tourist class across the United States in those days was a dusty, jostling experience. But the physical discomfort Jack felt was tempered by the footloose twenty-year-old's exaltation at seeing the nation's cities and small towns, its Great Plains, Rocky Mountains, and the deserts of the Southwest pass before his nearsighted eyes in a grand, ever-moving panorama. The journey must have seemed somewhat unreal, like one of those early picture shows in which patrons sat in a mock train carriage to marvel at a travelogue projected on a screen visible through the window of their compartment. But for a young man with Jack's powers of imagination, this dream come true was like seeing the maps he had studied in geography class become three-dimensional, or watching the fabled places he remembered from William Jack's American history classes come magically to life. His journey was close enough in time to the fast-fading Old West for Jack Feeney to experience something akin to the sense of adventure he would celebrate in his silent epic about the first cross-country railroad, *The Iron Horse.*

Jack boarded a train for Boston on the first leg of the trip, accompanied by a friend from Portland High, an amiable Scot named Joseph A. McDonough, who also wanted to break into the movie business. Carrying a box of sandwiches packed by his mother, Jack was short of cash and had to ration their food carefully. But he and Joe were doing fine until they had to switch trains in Detroit. Ford himself never told the story to the press, but his football teammate Ski Vanier recounted it to a Portland newspaper: "Joe lost a couple of toes when a train ran over his foot. Bull put him in hospital and continued on his way." The unfortunate Joe McDonough eventually made it to Hollywood anyway. Jack found him a job as a property man at Universal, where Joe spent many years as a first assistant director, most notably on four films for director James Whale, but never for his former high school buddy.

The last night on the train, Ford "had to go without dinner because I had no money in my pocket. So I arrived penniless."

Frank Ford and Grace Cunard, his glamorous lover and leading lady, were waiting at the train station when Jack arrived in downtown Los Angeles. Lounging in the back of his brother's luxurious open touring car as they motored through the streets of Hollywood, Jack was less impressed with the city than with the rakish panache Frank displayed in his directorial attire of breeches, jodhpurs, and riding crop, and with the smart and sultry Grace, crisply dressed in a brown business suit. Spinning the wheel deftly as he described the sights to Jack with a cigarette dangling from his mouth, Frank sped through Hollywood and up along the winding, dusty roads of the Cahuenga Pass, near the 230-acre San Fernando Valley ranch the Universal Film Manufacturing Company had purchased the previous year for all-purpose location shooting. Frank stopped the car at the lavish hillside home he was building for himself and Grace with loads of lumber spirited away from the studio when Uncle Carl Laemmle wasn't looking.

When Lillian Gish was asked what Hollywood was like at the time she arrived there in 1912, she replied, "I thought I was in paradise. The air was fragrant. It smelled like lemons." Indeed, much of the land was still covered with lemon and orange groves when the young pioneers of the movie business staked their claim on Hollywood. Today, when the air reeks of sulfur and carbon monoxide, Miss Gish's olfactory image poignantly evokes the unspoiled charm of a vanished era.

Hollywood was not yet a state of mind when Jack Feeney stepped off the train. The Los Angeles suburb was barely even a place three years earlier when its first movie studio, the Nestor Film Company, was opened by David Horsley in a converted tavern at the corner of Sunset Boulevard and Gower Street. The land surrounding Sunset and Hollywood Boulevards was occupied by lemon groves, bean patches, and hay fields. But the film folk were gradually taking over. Hollywood almost doubled its population between 1909 and 1913, growing from 4,000 to 7,500 people. The staid residents of its stately mansions and Victorian homes were ambivalent about the invasion: happy for the new business in their restaurants and stores, but unwilling to socialize with or sell their homes to those raucous nouveaux riches who worked in the disreputable "flickers." Many apartment buildings displayed signs reading "NO DOGS OR ACTORS ALLOWED."

But by 1914, filmmaking was on its way to establishing a major foothold in the Los Angeles area, whether the locals liked it or not. Motion picture studios were scattered throughout the basin, but many had started to cluster around Hollywood because of its central location, surrounded by mountain ranges and valleys suitable for multipurpose filming.

Universal took over the Nestor studio for its Hollywood operations in 1912, the same year that the industry's leading director, D. W. Griffith, moved from New York to Hollywood with the members of his Biograph Company. In 1914, he was making movies at the Majestic Reliance Studios at the juncture of Hollywood and Sunset Boulevards, 4500 Sunset, soon to be renamed the Fine Arts Studio when Griffith formed the Triangle Film Corporation in partnership with Thomas H. Ince and Mack Sennett. In nearby Edendale, Sennett's Keystone Studios was cranking out its highly popular slapstick comedies featuring the Sennett Bathing Beauties and the Keystone Kops.

The first feature-length film made in Hollywood, Cecil B. DeMille's Western melodrama *The Squaw Man,* was filmed in a barn at the corner of Vine Street and Selma Avenue just a few months before Jack Feeney's arrival in Hollywood. And out in the San Fernando Valley, on some of the land owned by Universal, Griffith was busy filming the battle scenes for a Civil War epic called *The Clansman,* whose production cost was soaring to an unprecedented $110,000.

Francis Ford was directing and acting in a less momentous project, *Lucille Love—The Girl of Mystery,* a lurid serial written by its female star, Grace Cunard. Universal boasted of "spending thousands of dollars" to ensure that its first venture into the serial format would be "the greatest moving picture it has ever produced . . . a tense, nerve-gripping, awe-inspiring romance of love and intrigue." An international chase story starring Grace as the flamboyant daughter of a U.S. Army general and Frank as the villain pursuing her, *Lucille Love* was set in such exotic locales as the Philippines, China, the South Sea Islands, and Mexico—all filmed on the Universal ranch.

The ranch maintained standing sets of streets that could be adapted for any use, from a gated Indian city to a Spanish mission. The Los Angeles River flowed through the sprawling grounds of the valley lot, situated below the picturesque Hollywood Hills. Universal kept its own zoo stocked with lions, tigers, leopards, elephants, camels, gorillas, pythons, and boa constrictors. Fifty cowboys and 156 horses were also in residence, the cowboys living in bunkhouses that enhanced the lot's authentic Western feeling. Interior scenes for Universal films usually were filmed five miles away in Hollywood, where the company maintained "the largest stage in the world." The four-hundred-foot-long, sixty-foot-wide platform allowed as many as sixteen films to be shot simultaneously. Retractable diffusers were used overhead to control the natural lighting from the glaring California sun.

Beginning on April 14, 1914, a two-reel chapter of the fifteen-part *Lucille Love* was released every week. *Lucille Love* became a smash hit, launching Frank and Grace on a three-year run of similar serials for Universal. Their fanciful imaginations flourished in the extravagantly melodramatic, visually baroque, partly tongue-in-cheek genre.

R. L. "Lefty" Hough, a property man on *Lucille Love,* remembered that when Jack Feeney came to Universal, the youngster spent his first couple of weeks riding horses at the ranch before Frank put him to work. From the very beginning, Jack impressed Hough as somewhat withdrawn and hard to understand. That impression would remain in force throughout the decades they worked on films together. Jack hung around with stuntmen, extras, and crewmen in his early days at Universal, but though he always felt more comfortable around men than around women, he never seemed entirely "one of the guys." The secretive, eccentric personality he cultivated after becoming a director was not entirely an act, but an outgrowth of the self-protective character traits that even in his youth made him "a faraway fella."

Frank thought his kid brother should start at the very bottom of the movie business, so Jack was handed a shovel and sent to work as a studio ditchdigger, earning the modest salary of twelve dollars a week. That was a bit of a shock to a young man who had given up on college because he couldn't stomach the humiliation of serving as a waiter. Jack's hero worship for Frank was already becoming clouded by the feelings of resentment that would be evident throughout their adult relationship. Frank seemed to be flaunting his superior position in the movie business by giving Jack a menial job that seemed to mock his ambition to be a screenwriter. But Frank had no need of another writer. He and Grace wrote *Lucille Love* themselves, under the pseudonym of "the Master Pen."

Laboring men were more in demand at the studio than writers, for the lavish new Universal City complex, scheduled to open the following March, was under construction at the ranch during the summer of 1914. Under the supervision of William Horsley, David's brother, four hundred men were busy laying roads and building five new stages, production offices, and other support facilities painted white and designed in the California mission style. Actually a functioning city, the new studio had its own police and fire departments, an electrical plant, a water system, a hospital, and an artificial lake, as well as expanded living quarters for about five hundred people, including tepees for seventy-five Indians. Within three years there would be more than six thousand employees at Universal City. There already were some fifteen hundred employees at Universal's Pacific Coast facilities when Jack went to work for the studio in 1914.

Pioneering the factory approach to filmmaking that would soon become the industry norm, Universal "was about to open a producing plant of unprecedented size, capable of generating great amounts of film at limited cost," writes silent-film historian Richard Koszarski. "Special projects like *The Birth of a Nation* had no place in this scheme, and even ordinary feature-length films were not easily accommodated. Laemmle was prepared to leave the high road to the competition, but would his cut-rate policies justify the overhead of this new plant?"

As far as can be verified, Jack Feeney's first actual film experience came near the end of *Lucille Love*'s lengthy production schedule, as an "assistant, handyman, everything" to his older brother, whom he also doubled in some of the action sequences.[1] On the next picture Frank directed, *The Mysterious Rose,* Jack received a promotion to assistant property man. He also took an acting role as a character named Dopey. The two-reel crime melodrama, filmed between August 7 and 15, starred Grace and Frank in their frequent roles as the jewel thief "My Lady Raffles" and her pursuer, a sympathetic Irish-American detective named Phil Kelly (or Kelley, as the character's name sometimes was spelled).

Francis Ford had played a character named John Ford in a 1913 Universal film, *The She-Wolf.* Naturally, everyone who met Frank's brother Jack when he first came to Universal assumed that the young man's last name also was Ford. He was miffed at first, but changed his mind after receiving his first paycheck and realizing the name "Jack Ford" didn't look so bad, especially when accompanied with a dollar sign. He received his first screen credit under his new name when *The Mysterious Rose* was released on November 24. Ironically, Jack played a character named Frank Feeney in a film directed by his brother two months later, *The Doorway of Destruction.* In this two-reeler, an Irish regiment on a suicide mission in India attacks a native citadel, waving an Irish flag made by the mother of Colonel Patrick Feeney (Francis Ford). Other characters in the adventure yarn were named after their brother Eddie and their niece Cecil McLean.

Jack was promoted to an assistant director's position on *The Doorway of Destruction,* although it was not until a few months later, when he worked on Frank's film *The Campbells Are Coming,* that he became what Frank called "a full-fledged assistant." Jack spent two and a half years working for Frank and other directors at Universal, including Allan Dwan, one of the most resourceful and prolific of silent filmmakers. Dwan made the feature-length *Richelieu* and the three-reeler *The Small Town Girl* in 1914 while Jack was a crewman on the lot. "His brother Francis was working for me as an actor," Dwan recalled, "and he asked me to give Jack a job." Jack would also have had the opportunity to watch, if not work with, the pioneer feminist filmmaker Lois Weber, the Irish dramatic director Herbert Brenon, slapstick specialist Al Christie, and

---

1. Some mystifying records at Universal state that Jack directed *Lucile, the Waitress,* a series of four two-reelers filmed in March and April 1914. That information evidently is incorrect, for Jack was in his final year of high school in Portland at the time. I. G. Edmonds's book *Big U: Universal in the Silent Days,* while erroneously listing the year of Jack's high school graduation as 1913, claims that Jack was an extra in a Francis Ford film made that year at Universal, *The Battle of Bull Run,* which could be true only if Jack had made a visit to Frank during school vacation, an event which, if it occurred, has eluded historians. Another indication that Jack might have been working at Universal in some capacity in 1913 was Allan Dwan's comment to Dan Ford that Jack worked on the crew of Dwan films starring J. Warren Kerrigan; two of the three films Dwan made with Kerrigan were fall 1913 releases, and the other was released in July 1914.

actor-director J. Farrell MacDonald, who later would become a regular in Jack's own stock company. Among the other young prop men and assistants working at Universal around the time Ford started were future directors Henry Hathaway and George Marshall.

Since there were no unions in the industry in those days, Jack was able to try his hand at just about every filmmaking job at Universal, from stuntman and actor to property man, camera operator, and assistant director. He was especially proud of his ability as a cameraman. An assistant director in those days often operated the second camera, and in so doing Ford developed his brilliant eye for composition and his knack for capturing action with documentary-style authenticity. Occasionally Frank sent him out to shoot crowd scenes being staged on the lot by other directors, so they could splice the "stolen" shots into their own movies.

Jack's eclectic apprenticeship even included a brief stint in early 1917 as a crewman for the L-Ko Komedy Kompany, a Universal subsidiary run by Laemmle's brothers-in-law Al and Julius Stern. When somebody told Al that L-Ko's comedies were terrible, he snapped, "L-Ko comedies are not to be laughed at!"

Jack Ford's acting roles included wearing a white sheet for D. W. Griffith in *The Clansman,* later retitled *The Birth of a Nation.* During a period in 1914 when Ford was briefly fired (so he said) from Universal, he went to Orange County, south of Los Angeles, to watch Griffith shoot the now-famous sequence of the Gathering of the Klans. Ford was hired to ride as a Ku Klux Klansman, one of a long line of hooded men on horseback: "I was the one with the glasses. I was riding with one hand holding the hood up so I could see because the damn thing kept slipping over my glasses." (A photograph exists of Klansmen riding across a river in the film, with one doing exactly what Ford remembered doing.) While riding under a low-hanging tree branch, Ford was knocked from his saddle, falling to the ground unconscious.

"He came to with no less than Griffith kneeling over him, offering a brandy flask," Griffith biographer Richard Schickel reported after interviewing Ford about the experience. "[Griffith] insisted that he retire from the field for the day, and Ford would remember stretching out comfortably under a tree to watch the rest of the day's shooting on a sequence that he would have cause to duplicate (and surpass) during his great career." (In an alternate version of the story, Ford had Griffith pulling out the flask and pouring a drink for *himself.* That's a stock gag for doctors in Ford movies, and if Griffith wasn't the inspiration for it, history could be rewritten to imply that he was.)

Ford always had the highest reverence for Griffith, telling Peter Bogdanovich, "If it weren't for Griffith, we'd probably still be in the infantile phase of motion pictures. . . . Griffith was the one who made it an art—if you can call it an art—but at least he made it something worthwhile." It was telling that what impressed Ford most about Griffith's films was not so much their spectacle but their intimately human moments. "D. W. was the only one then who took the time for little details," Ford said, citing the famous scene of the homecoming of the Little Colonel (Henry B. Walthall). The returning soldier's sister (Mae Marsh, later a Ford regular) "has put cotton on her dress, pretending it is ermine, and while they talk he picks little pieces off the dress, shyly." The powerfully elliptical way Griffith shows the soldier's mother embracing her son—only her arm visible as it emerges from inside the door of their home—was echoed by Ford when Gold Star mother Hannah Jessop (Henrietta Crosman) reaches her hand out a train window to receive a bouquet of flowers for her son's grave in the 1933 film *Pilgrimage*.

When Bogdanovich asked Ford about his appearances in silent movies, which included two short films in which he starred under his own direction in 1917, Ford feigned astonishment: "I played the lead in a picture? With my looks? Good God!" But Ford was an actor or stuntman in no fewer than sixteen silent films, and that total does not count the many individual installments of the four serials in which he appeared. Jack did double duty as a performer and crewman not only on *Lucille Love* but also on the Francis Ford–Grace Cunard serials *The Broken Coin* (1915), *Peg o' the Ring* (1916), and *The Purple Mask* (1916–17). As Jack's Portland friend Ski Vanier remembered his acting career, "Jack would always be in the barroom brawl scene, that was right up his alley." His split personality as crewman and actor sometimes became confusing. Once Frank was shooting a dance scene and told Jack to put on a tuxedo and start spinning the girls around the floor. It was only when they watched the rushes that they realized Jack played the scene with a hammer protruding from his pocket.

The most prominent role Jack played under Frank's direction was as one of three drifters mistaken for bandits in the comedy Western *Three Bad Men and a Girl,* filmed in December 1914 and released the following February. The characters played by Frank, Jack, and a diminutive actor named Major Paleolagus redeem themselves by rescuing Grace from a band of marauding Mexicans; Frank, naturally, gets the girl. A contemporary reviewer hailed the two-reeler as "an exceedingly clever satire" on the Western genre: "Seventeen cowboys jump to the backs of their horses at one and the same time, revolver shots are exchanged at point blank every three seconds, doors are broken in, and Grace Cunard escapes on a clothesline over a chasm." Appearing in front of a camera, however clumsily, was another valuable part of John Ford's apprenticeship, helping him understand the fears and gratifications experienced by every movie actor.

· · ·

Before officially achieving the rank of assistant director in 1915, Jack continually grumbled to Frank about having to earn his pay as a lowly property man. There were no art directors in those days, and budgets for sets on serials were modest, so the property man had to scrounge up props anywhere he could, sometimes even knocking on doors in the neighborhood to borrow furniture for a few hours. Allan Dwan said of Jack, "The reason he was a hell of a good property man was that if you wanted anything, he would go out and steal it for you." The job involved as much heavy lifting as creativity, but it taught Jack the rudiments of set design as well as how to maximize production resources.

Occasionally he had the opportunity to work on a more opulent scale for Frank and Grace, such as on their action-adventure saga *The Campbells Are Coming*, a more grandiose version of *The Doorway of Destruction*. Both were set during the sepoy mutiny against the British in 1857 India. Universal claimed, no doubt with some hyperbole, that it spent $117,000 to build and destroy a walled Indian city and a besieged British garrison for *The Campbells Are Coming*. The studio's house organ, the *Universal Weekly*, promised exhibitors that the four-reeler contained "enough battle scenes to satisfy the most bloodthirsty junker or war-mad jingo."

The production was troubled; Frank had to fire a cameraman, and he was in such a foul mood that Jack "got his break when Harry Tenbrook, my first assistant, threw the script at me and left me flat."[2] Despite his promotion to first assistant, "My brother John hated pictures and despised Hollywood and wanted to leave what he called a 'hand-shaking industry,'" Frank recalled in an unpublished memoir written in the mid-1930s. "He left me two days after being placed in his new position. Duke Worne [who later played the villain in the first film Jack directed] . . . helped me until we could talk my brother Jack into coming back." Frank wryly noted that Jack, "like a well-known foreign actress of today [Garbo], 'was always going home.'"

Grace directed some scenes for *The Campbells Are Coming* when Frank had to be absent from part of the location shooting in Oxnard, and she usually helped out with the directing when Frank was busy acting. Frank declared that he had "the utmost confidence in her ability to run the whole shebang. . . . Miss Cunard and I are an ideal team. We even work out the story together. Sometimes one of us, sometimes the other has the original idea, and then she usually puts

---

2. Tenbrook was in the cast of the first film in which Frank appeared, Centaur's production *The Girl from Arizona*, made around 1908. Tenbrook later acted in many of the films John Ford directed, usually playing a lovable functionary. His most memorable role is the cook in *They Were Expendable*.

it into scenario form. She can dream scenarios. We play into each other's hands. She is a very competent director herself, you know." Grace also directed a 1914 comedy called *Sheridan's Pride,* a spoof of Universal's 1913 Civil War movie *Sheridan's Ride,* in which Francis Ford played Abraham Lincoln.

Jack's formative experiences as a property man and assistant director influenced his own work as a director in the extraordinary degree of attention he always paid to the visual impact of settings, costumes, and crowd scenes. He later conceded that the training he received from his older brother was invaluable. Asked by Bogdanovich to name his early influences in the movie business, he replied, "Well, my brother Frank. . . . he was really a good artist, a wonderful musician, a hell of a good actor, a good director—Johnny of all trades—and *master* of all; he just couldn't concentrate on one thing too long. But he was the only influence *I* ever had, working in pictures."

One of the lessons Jack learned from Frank was how to keep the entire film in his head throughout the shooting process. As Frank explained, "You need a good memory and the ability to look at things in a large way in undertaking to produce a successful serial. The great thing is to have a good clear picture of what you want at the beginning and never lose sight of the thing as a whole while working on the details. . . . Your audience won't forgive discrepancies in the story. Their memory is uncanny." People who worked with Jack after he became a director marveled at his memory for details and the way he was able to shoot out of sequence while seldom referring to the script.

It was not only Frank's craftsmanship and filmmaking style that influenced Jack but also his seemingly casual but highly authoritative demeanor. In "Brother Feeney," a 1976 article on Frank in *Film Comment,* Tag Gallagher observed, "Descriptions of [Frank] at this date resemble later ones of brother John." Frank was somewhat taciturn on the set, "but running underneath this silence is a stream of humor that may be called distinctively Fordesquian," the *Universal Weekly* noted. Under Frank's "quiet, almost sarcastic manner," Richard Willis wrote in *Motion Picture Magazine,* "there is deep seriousness, and below the veil of indifference there is one of the warmest hearts imaginable." Frank's habit of speaking about the people who worked for him "as though he loved them" was a precursor of Jack's attitude toward his cast and crew, and the habitual reticence Jack adopted toward his work was another trait he shared with Frank. Willis observed that Frank "never boasts; in fact, he is inclined to speak of his work with levity, and he gives a wrong impression to those who do not know him well."

If Jack had been asked at the time to comment on Frank's treatment of him, chances are that his response would not have been so favorable.

Frank's teasing of his younger brother was merciless. His attitude toward

Jack in the early days was indicated in his comments to an interviewer in 1951: "As a prop man he stunk; as an assistant director, he was worse, and as an actor—well, such a ham! When I would tell Jack to put a chair in the corner for a scene, Jack would turn and say, 'Joe, get a chair and put it in the corner'; Joe would turn around and holler, 'Dutch, get a chair and put it in the corner'; Dutch would turn around and holler, 'Jake, get a chair,' etc."

More objective observers, including Lefty Hough and Allan Dwan, regarded Jack as a hardworking, strong-lunged, and imaginative assistant director. Dwan was impressed by Jack's leadership qualities and the blunt, profane way he bossed around the cowboy actors, many of whom were older than he was. In directing crowd scenes for Frank's movies, Dwan recalled, Jack would single out actors and give them bits of business, showing an instinctive directorial ability that won him notice around the studio.

From the very beginning, Frank turned to the former Bull Feeney to perform some of the most dangerous stunts. Frank always had a taste for rough-and-ready action scenes; according to Gallagher, at least one recorded death occurred while he was directing. Contemptuous of anyone who wouldn't risk his life for a rousing scene, Frank joked, "The joint is full of hams and scared cats." He would say to his cast, "Now, boys, remember you are not in a drawing room; don't bow to each other or apologize if you should happen to take a piece of skin away from the man you are fighting. This is to be the real thing—go to it." If they hesitated, he would add the following words, which Jack would adapt for Huw Morgan's boxing scene in *How Green Was My Valley*: "Listen, boys, a dollar for a bloody nose and two for a black eye." If the actors still balked at doing what he wanted, Frank would say in an exasperated voice, "What d'ye mean, it's dangerous? Here, I'll have my kid brother do it!"

Doubling Frank or other actors, Jack risked his life jumping from cliffs on horseback, racing through the Cahuenga Pass in a careening automobile, and leaping seventy-five feet from a moving train rolling over a trestle. In a 1949 *Saturday Evening Post* profile of Ford, his screenwriter Frank S. Nugent reported, "Jack made the leap all right, but carefully blessed himself before jumping—and spoiled the shot."

Some incidents weren't as amusing. According to Lefty Hough, Jack suffered a serious injury not long after becoming Frank's assistant property man. Frank was playing a Confederate general seated at a desk inside a field tent. After fetching a Confederate flag from the Western Costume Company to decorate the set, Jack stepped in to double Francis for a shot in which a cannonball was supposed to blow up the tent. The desk was wired with a dynamite charge, and when it went off, Jack was blown several feet into the air and underwent a lengthy hospitalization.

Nugent claimed that Jack also suffered a broken arm in an automobile chase when the car was catapulted off the road with dynamite. After his arm healed, Nugent related, Jack was running through a battle scene in a Confederate uniform when Frank hurled a powder bomb that "bounced off Jack's head and exploded just beneath his chin. 'That was a close thing,' Frank told him later, when the nurses began admitting visitors. 'Another second and audiences would have realized I was using a double.'"

There seems to be a fair amount of hyperbole in Nugent's colorful account, whose primary source evidently was Jack himself, spinning malicious yarns about Frank thirty-five years after the fact. Nugent may have conflated the powder bomb incident with the explosion inside the field tent; but Hough, who actually witnessed the dynamite charge exploding, said it came close to ending Jack's life. There is no doubt that the abuse Jack took from Frank as a stuntman festered for decades, causing him to devise elaborate ways of taking revenge on his older brother after Frank's career as a director declined.

Jack often hired Frank to act in his pictures, but almost invariably cast him as a besotted old drunk. Frank rarely was allowed to speak any lines when he acted for his brother. There was an obvious element of humiliation in this treatment—"I want to see him *lashed,*" Jack once declared—but Jack's attitude remained somewhat ambivalent. Frank's "Brother Feeney" character is a lovable old coot, and his taciturnity can be seen as a tribute to their mutual beginnings in silent filmmaking. Frank does wonders with the juicy bits of pantomime Jack gives him, such as his repeated punctuation of courtroom rhetoric with tobacco-spitting into a ringing spittoon in *Young Mr. Lincoln.* Still, what Jack boasted about doing to Frank during the shooting of the 1934 Will Rogers movie *Judge Priest* cannot be seen as anything but "pathological," the word Tag Gallagher aptly applied to his attitude toward Frank.

Playing the town bum, Frank lounged in a wheelbarrow in front of a general store. Perhaps suffering from a hangover, he dozed off between takes. Jack quietly instructed an assistant to tie a rope from a carriage to the wheelbarrow. When the director called "Action!" the carriage took off, dragging the semiconscious Frank down the length of the studio street as he swallowed his chaw of tobacco.

"That was for the grenade!" Jack shouted as his older brother came hobbling back to the set.

Following five months of arduous work on his serial *The Broken Coin,* which was so successful that Universal expanded it from sixteen to thirty-two episodes, Francis Ford made a triumphant return to Portland in November 1915. The family's reaction to his first visit home in eight years may have resembled the greeting Ward Bond gives John Wayne in *The Searchers:* "*Well,* the prodigal brother! When did *you* get back?"

Grace Cunard did not accompany her still-married lover—she went instead to visit her mother in Columbus, Ohio—but Jack tagged along as Portland's mayor presented Frank with the key to the city. Frank "was in demand at all the Portland theaters, and many of his nights were occupied in addressing the theater-goers at the motion picture houses," the *Moving Picture Weekly* reported. Frank also made a dramatic visit to a local school for a reunion with his teenage son Phil, who barely remembered him.

The mayor told Frank that if he wanted to make any pictures in Portland, the city would give him any help he wanted, including the services of the police and fire departments. That was all Frank needed to start his creative juices flowing. "I made the long journey across the continent to the old home with the expectation that I would forget all about motion pictures and have a real rest," he said after his return to California. "But after the first few days, I felt the desire to get busy once again and was soon writing two scenarios."

What was intended as a two-week vacation turned into a busy location shoot, stretching their stay to a month. With Jack's assistance, Frank directed and starred in a sea story, *The Yellow Streak,* later retitled *Chicken-Hearted Jim,* and a crime drama, *The Lumber Yard Gang,* released as *The Strong Arm Squad.* All of Frank's work for Universal has been lost, but the disappearance of these two one-reelers is especially regrettable for biographical reasons. Literally "home movies," they featured in their casts not only Frank and Jack but also their mother and father, their brothers Pat and Eddie, their sisters Maime and Josephine, and their niece, Cecil (whose name was used again for the character of the female lead in *The Strong Arm Squad,* played by Elsie Maison).

The Strong Arm Squad was a formulaic detective yarn with Frank's Detective Phil Kelley pursuing a gang of thieves in a chase scene across the roof of the Portland Police Department building. The *Portland Evening Express* reported on November 20 that the band of "desperate thugs" (led by Jack Ford) "were this morning captured on the roof of the headquarters building after a thrilling struggle in which several members of the department took part," including Chief Dandy Bowen. ". . . The local police have been receiving some exceptional training in the ways of the 'movies' during the past week under Mr. [Frank] Ford's expert direction and it looks as though we may lose some of the patrolmen from the force when Mr. Ford concludes his work in his home town and returns to the Pacific coast."

The film's ending, as described by the reviewer for the *Moving Picture Weekly,* took an intriguingly dark and melancholy turn. Jack, the gang leader played by Jack Ford, is the brother of the detective's girlfriend, and "Kelley, torn between love and duty, finally agrees to let the boy go if she will promise to make him leave town." But realizing she has compromised Kelley in the eyes of his department, Cecil handcuffs her wounded brother and summons the detective, who "bends over the boy but finds that death has claimed him." (The script of *The Strong Arm Squad* was credited to Grace Cunard when the film was released in February 1916, so perhaps she and Frank had cooked up the project before he left Hollywood.)

Less is known about *Chicken-Hearted Jim,* which was filmed around Portland and Casco Bay between November 10 and 17. Universal's house organ did not see fit to review the film when it was released in April 1916, and when I asked John Ford about it in 1970, he claimed not to remember it even after making me shout the title at him several times. Perhaps Ford was still thinking of the film as *The Yellow Streak,* the title he once used while reminiscing to an old friend, Portland policeman Pete Flaherty, about shooting at nearby Sebago Lake.[3]

Chicken-Hearted Jim sounds like a veritable Feeney family psychodrama, for Frank played a roguish fugitive who distresses his parents (John and Abby Feeney) with his nightly debauchery. Maime and Josephine played his sisters, and Jack, Pat, and Eddie were crewmen on a schooner to which Frank's "cowardly" Jim escapes. Indulging in some heroic wish-fulfillment, Frank had Jim redeem himself by foiling a mutiny and marrying the captain's daughter, a happy ending echoing Frank's derring-do in Hollywood serials. Indeed, the plot was cribbed from a 1913 Ford-Cunard film, *Captain Billie's Mate,* but the ending may have been Frank's way of expressing gratitude that Portland and the Feeneys welcomed home their black sheep as a hero.

The key part of John Ford's creation myth—how he became a director—was a drastically reshaped version of what actually happened. As directors are prone to do, Ford stressed the elements that made him look most like a wunderkind and minimized the roles other people played in his ascension.

Ford's version, as told in Bogdanovich's 1971 documentary *Directed by John Ford,* revolved around an incident that occurred during the opening ceremonies at Universal City on March 15 and 16, 1915. Thousands of guests, including a trainload of exhibitors and others brought from New York and Chicago by Carl Laemmle, attended a series of events that included a parade by Universal's resident cowboys and Indians, a barbecue, and a grand ball on March 15, as well as a horse race and rodeo on the following day. Various film companies pretended to shoot scenes for the guests' entertainment; the staging of a flood scene by director Henry McRae's 101 Bison Company was planned as the highlight. Not everything went according to the scenario. The

---

3. Further confusion was added by the *Moving Picture Weekly,* whose article "Ten Fords in Francis' Vacation Film" reported that *The Yellow Streak* was the working title of *The Strong Arm Squad.*

flood scene, which was supposed to sweep away a Western set, inundated much of the back lot. One of Frank Ford's assistants, Bennett Moulter, received serious facial burns when a cannon went off prematurely. And the celebration came to a somber conclusion on the second day, when Universal stunt pilot Frank Stites was killed performing a flying exhibition for spectators.

Earlier that day, the director of a Western scheduled to be filmed before the guests failed to show up for work because he was suffering from a hangover. This caused a crisis for studio general manager Isidore Bernstein, because a crowd including Laemmle and a gaggle of beauty pageant contestants was waiting impatiently to see the show. Bernstein turned to Jack Ford, who had spent the previous night working as a bartender at the grand ball, which lasted until four in the morning on the studio's large indoor stage. More conscientious than the director, Ford slept under the bar so he would not be late to work.

"We had a Western street and a bunch of cowboys," Ford recalled, "and Mr. Bernstein came riding up and he says, 'Gee, you're the first assistant. You've got to shoot something while [Laemmle's] here. There's a big bunch of people, over a hundred.' I said, 'What'll I do?' He says, 'Oh, do anything. You have riders, let 'em ride back and forth.' So they rode through the streets shooting at everything for no reason at all, and I said to Mr. Bernstein, 'How was that?' He said, 'Fine.' He talked to Mr. Laemmle and [the studio chief] said, 'Keep on working.'

"I says [to Bernstein], 'What'll I do?' He says, 'Have 'em ride *back* shooting.' So they rode back shooting. Then he says, 'Can't you have a couple of falls in there?' I said, 'Oh, that'll be easy.' But these [beauty pageant] girls are all very pretty and the cowboys are sort of straightening their kerchiefs up, straightening their hats and trying to look as pretty as possible, shining up to these gals. So I says, 'I'll fire a pistol and you, you, and you do a horse fall or fall off your horse.' Well, the cowboys looked at one another, I fired the shot and then every cowboy—I think there were thirty of them—they *all* fell off their horses.

"And I says to Mr. Bernstein, 'That's about it, isn't it?' He said, 'Oh, no, keep on going. What can you do now?' So I put a lot of kerosene and gasoline in the place and burnt the town down, had the cowboys running up and down. . . . They thought it was great. They had a picture coming up with Harry Carey and they had no director. Mr. Laemmle says, 'That Jack Ford, he yells real loud. He'd make a good director.'"

The young Universal actress Olive Fuller Golden, who was playing "sob sister" parts for actor-director Frank Lloyd, later married Harry Carey. She was present when Ford had the set torched during the studio's opening festivities. She told me the incapacitated director Ford relieved of duty was Henry

McRae, who evidently had done too much unwinding at the ball after staging his runaway flood scene. As for the rest of the story about Carl Laemmle spontaneously offering Ford a directing job, she scoffed, "Well, you know Ford, for cryin' out loud. Ford makes up stories—anything to amuse himself. He'd lie like a son of a bitch as long as it amused him."

Even on the face of it, Ford's claim that he received an instant promotion from the studio chief makes little sense. While Laemmle may well have been impressed with the young assistant's bold, imaginative handling of the situation, Jack had been with the company only eight months when Universal City opened, and he did not receive his promotion to director for almost two more years. But Laemmle may have remembered the incident and perhaps commented about Ford's booming voice when other people, including Olive Golden and Francis Ford, recommended Jack as a director.[4] Allan Dwan thought Laemmle also was influenced by reports of Jack's unusual ability to bring crowd scenes to life with bits of individual business.

It was his brother Frank's intercession with Laemmle that brought Jack the opportunity to direct his first picture, *The Tornado,* under the auspices of the 101 Bison Company. His billing then was "Jack Ford." Several years would pass before he became known as the more genteel "John Ford."

Ford remembered being "scared to death" while making his directorial debut. But handing over the direction of a two-reel Western to an assistant was not a major risk for the studio. Universal even made a profit on the deal by insisting that Jack take a pay cut from forty-five to thirty-five dollars a week for the privilege of becoming a director. It does seem somewhat surprising in retrospect that Jack was also allowed to play the lead role in *The Tornado,* which was released on March 3, 1917. But he later described the movie as "just a bunch of stunts," and he came to it with a reputation as a fearless stuntman. Frank said half-jokingly that Jack's directorial debut "wasn't bad except for the acting." Harry Carey also used to poke fun at Jack's acting, referring to him as "Young Lochinvar Rides Out of the West."

The Tornado no longer exists. Most of the films Jack Ford directed at Universal between 1917 and 1921 have been lost to studio fires, chemical decomposition, and other forms of neglect. As a result, reconstructing his early development as a director is difficult. But a handful of his Universal silents have been rediscovered in recent years, including two complete features,

---

4. Cecil de Prida remembered that Jack was given a tryout on a short film codirected with Laemmle's nephew Eddie. No record of this film has been found, but Eddie worked as an assistant on some of the Westerns Ford directed at Universal.

Straight Shooting (1917) and *Hell Bent* (1918), and parts of three others, *The Secret Man* (1917), *The Last Outlaw* (1919), and *A Gun Fightin' Gentleman* (1919). From these surviving films and from scripts and press coverage of the others, it is possible to get some sense of Ford's artistic evolution in that formative period.

The Tornado mostly followed pulp Western formula—bad guys hold up a town, take a girl hostage, and the hero rides to the rescue. But there were a couple of twists that made it seem more personal than the usual cowboy fare. Ford's Jack Dayton (whose name perhaps was a nod to Universal's West Coast story editor, James Dayton) is known as "the No-Gun Man" because he faces the villains unarmed, anticipating the character played by James Stewart in George Marshall's 1939 Western comedy classic *Destry Rides Again*. Dayton is an immigrant who uses the reward money to bring over his mother (Jean Hathaway) from Ireland, a prototypically Fordian situation if ever there was one.

The *Moving Picture Weekly*, which could be accused of a certain bias since it was published by Universal itself as the successor to the *Universal Weekly*, rhapsodized in its review of *The Tornado:* "In his hand-to-hand struggle in the cabin and the jump from the cabin roof to the back of his horse, Jack Ford qualifies as a rough-riding expert. . . . As a climax the hero leaps from his running horse onto a moving train!" But the in-house critic was not alone in his appreciation, for among the papers Ford preserved from this period is a fan letter from Mary Parks of Waco, Texas, who told him she had seen *The Tornado* three times and wanted to see more of him as an actor!

The Tornado was followed by a short Western that Jack probably directed, *The Trail of Hate*. He starred as a U.S. Army lieutenant in the Philippines whose wife and her lover are captured by bandits. After rescuing the couple, the lieutenant holds to a rigid moral stance, refusing to forgive his faithless wife. *Motion Picture News* attributed the film's direction to Frank Ford, perhaps because it somewhat resembled his *Lucille Love* serial, but the *Moving Picture Weekly* more authoritatively listed Jack as the director. *Exhibitors' Trade Review* called *The Trail of Hate* "thrilling . . . teeming with life and color and action."

In another 1917 short Jack directed, *The Scrapper,* he played the title role of a pugnacious cowboy named Buck, who discovers that his girlfriend, Helen (Louise Granville), has become attached to a brothel. Ford's script was a virginal Catholic filmmaker's treatment of sexuality, for it transpires that the girl's involvement with prostitutes is entirely innocent, and one of the scarlet women helps Buck rescue Helen from a fate worse than death. *The Scrapper* found a boisterous reception in Jack's hometown of Portland, according to his sister Josephine, who wrote him a letter reporting their parents' delight in seeing him on-screen. Whenever a movie starring Frank or Jack played in Portland, theater managers would cross out the name "Ford" on the poster and re-place it with "Feeney."

Josephine's letter added that their mother hoped her Johnny would re-member to write home more often. Ford never lost his emotional devotion to his parents, but during this hectic and exciting period in his life he did tend to be a bit neglectful in corresponding with them, as his father also gently re-minded him from time to time. Jack's twelve-hour workdays, six days a week, left little time for letter writing. Nor did he have much time for socializing, al-though he occasionally hung around with cowboy extras and with other assis-tant directors from the studio, including Charlie Dorian, Earl Page, and Bud Bretherton.

From 1916 through early 1917, Jack lived at the Virginia Apartments at 6629½ Hollywood Boulevard, an unprepossessing two-story building that re-sembled a small hotel and catered to movie people. He shared an apartment with an actor considerably older than himself, Mark Fenton, who appeared in movies directed by both Ford brothers. Jack had his parents out to visit from January through March 1917, renting them the adjacent apartment. When Jack pulled a bed from the wall, explaining that it was a Murphy bed, his fa-ther responded, "To hell it is. No Irishman ever built a bed like this."

Jack's directing career was getting started just as his brother's was starting to fade. Theirs was a real-life example of a classic Hollywood situation epito-mized in the various versions of *A Star Is Born*. The tragedy of Francis Ford's career stemmed from a variety of causes, only one of which was bitterness over his younger brother's success.

The major problem was Frank's growing desire for independence from stu-dio control. He first experienced serious problems with Universal during the shooting of the serial *Peg o' the Ring* in 1916. The studio demanded that Frank and Grace cast the German actor Eddie Polo in an important supporting role. Polo, whose primary talent was gymnastics, had quarreled with Frank and Grace over his refusal to wear makeup when he appeared in their earlier serial *The Broken Coin*. After they resisted using Polo again, Universal found an ex-cuse to fire them.

The serial was set in a circus, and every circus movie has to have a fire de-stroying the big top. Universal had rented a tent for the filming. Laemmle or-dered that the tent be handled with great care; the fire was supposed to be faked by carefully setting ablaze a canvas flat erected outside the actual tent. As Frank's assistant director, Jack was supposed to organize a bucket brigade to douse the fire before it got out of control. But on the day of the filming, when Frank signaled the bucket brigade, there was a huge conflagration. The buckets had been filled with gasoline. "Don't stop!" Jack shouted to the camera-men. "Keep cranking!"

In his profile of John Ford for the *Saturday Evening Post,* Nugent claimed it was Jack's own decision to burn down the tent. But Frank, in his memoir, took the responsibility, adding that the tent cost only sixty dollars. According to Nugent, Jack left the set of the circus picture and "went into hiding. He didn't have to be told that he was fired. Two days later, Laemmle hired him back as an assistant director. 'A spectacle like that is worth a circus tent,' he told him. 'But don't do it again.'" Frank also told that part of the story differently, recalling that *he* was fired over the incident, and that the rest of the company left the lot with him in sympathy. In any case, Jack's papers contain a dismissal notice from Universal dated March 28, 1916, when he was working as Frank's assistant for thirty-five dollars a week.

Jacques Jaccard stepped in as director of *Peg o' the Ring* by early April, with Eddie Polo and Ruth Stonehouse cast in the leading roles for the fifth episode. But when Frank went to New York to put his case directly to Carl Laemmle, the studio chief looked at Frank's footage and reinstated him. The serial was completed under the creative control of Frank and Grace; Jack resumed his dual functions as actor and assistant director. But they were exiled for the remainder of the filming to the Hollywood lot of the L-Ko Komedy Kompany, the Universal subsidiary that continued to be Frank's base until 1917.

The clashes with Frank and Grace over *Peg o' the Ring* and its disappointing box-office performance helped sour Universal's attitude toward the rebellious couple. When their next serial, *The Purple Mask* (1916–17), flopped, the studio took the opportunity to suggest that they stop working together. The separation became personal as well. Grace married cowboy actor Joe Moore in 1917, and Frank went back to his wife, Elsie Van Name. Before he left Universal that year to seek greater independence, Frank directed two more films for the studio, the thriller *Who Was That Other Man* and the Indian drama *John Ermine of Yellowstone,* based on the only novel by the great Western painter and sculptor Frederic Remington. Frank continued directing with diminishing success until the close of the silent era in 1928. Grace disappeared from the film business soon after her partnership with Frank ended, living in obscurity until her death at the Motion Picture Country House and Hospital at age seventy-three in 1967. Drink contributed to her downfall, as it did to Frank's in the aftermath of their breakup.

But the rapidly changing nature of the movie business was an even larger factor in their decline. By the late 1910s, silent films were becoming increasingly sophisticated both visually and dramatically. Serials, with their flimsy characterizations, hokey dramaturgy, and slapdash shooting methods, were gradually ceasing to be principal attractions for adults and becoming Saturday-matinee fare for children. The serials made by Frank and Grace were among the better examples of the genre in the silent period, but by the late teens, aggressive serial heroines such as the ones Grace played were out of vogue and Frank seemed to reach a creative impasse. The qualities of boldness and innovation that make someone a successful pioneer are not the qualities needed for more gradual adaptation to changing times. Frank's son Phil later reflected that his father's work did not display the same kind of artistic development as that of other directors in the period, when the Roaring Twenties were sweeping away the old Victorian attitudes that found such vivid expression in early silent melodrama.

Without Frank's support, Jack never would have come to Hollywood in the first place or risen so quickly in his profession. Frank continued helping Jack find work until Frank left Universal in 1917; by that summer, Jack was firmly established and needed no more assistance. Some friction was evident between Jack and Frank earlier in the year, when Grace wrote Jack and his friend from Portland, Joe McDonough, imploring them to return to their jobs with the L-Ko Komedy Kompany. Frank had found the jobs for the two young men, but they seemed to resent the situation. Probably by then Jack was beginning to distance himself from Frank. Grace rather helplessly pointed out in her letter that on a visit to Portland, she had "promised both your mothers that I would do my best for you."

After Jack became a director, Frank must have felt bitter indeed when Universal's *Weekly* insisted on rubbing his nose in his brother's success. Jack had directed only three short films when the magazine presciently but cruelly observed in June 1917 that soon people would no longer be asking, "Ford? Any relation to Francis?" but would be asking, "Ford? Any relation to Jack?" A year later, reviewing Jack's feature *Hell Bent, Motion Picture News* accurately noted that he "must have assimilated all of the older man's tactics and then endeavored to beat him at his own game. But however the two compare, it remains plain that there are few directors who put such sustained punch in their pictures as does this Mr. Ford."

For his part, Jack quietly repaid Frank's mentoring by supporting him financially when times were tough, as they often were in Frank's later years. Jack frequently employed Frank as an actor (however demeaningly) and helped his son Phil along the path to becoming a director. But however steadfast was the Feeney family's loyalty, it could not conceal the deep-seated antagonisms that existed between Jack and his brothers.

Frank's unpublished memoir, "Up and Down the Ladder," written shortly after he acted for Jack in *Judge Priest* (1934), is filled with bitter and sometimes

heartrending complaints about how old-timers who had helped create the industry had been shunted aside by younger men. Frank wrote of Jack, "His
climb up the ladder was rapid and it wasn't long before he passed many then-
famous directors, coming down. He tried to give them a lift, but, well. . . .
That's another story." When the manuscript was written, the tension between
the brothers was such that Frank barely referred to the work of his brother,
"One of the greatest directors that ever lived." Frank claimed that his praise of
The Iron Horse had been "censored by fistic persuasion. My brother Jack (John
to you) has not spoken to me for several months because I refused to correct
this statement. It is the only good thing I have said about him and in it stays . . .
regardless."

When Edward Feeney came out to Hollywood at age twenty-eight in
1917, lugging around his plumbing tools in the trunk of his car, Jack did his
turn in finding work for his older brother at Universal. Ed became an assistant
director and even directed one movie at the studio, the two-reeler *Under Sentence* (1920), a remake of Jack's 1917 feature *A Marked Man*. Ed subsequently
changed his last name to O'Fearna to differentiate himself from his two more
prominent brothers. He worked effectively as Jack's first assistant during much
of the silent period, and became particularly well regarded for his handling of
the logistics of large productions. His vast historical erudition also made him
a great help to Jack with detail work on period films. But Ed, who had a family of seven children, eventually was relegated to second assistant because of
his worsening alcoholism and the unconcealed hostility he and Jack displayed
toward each other. Often they avoided speaking throughout the making of an
entire film except for professional reasons. Sometimes on location their relationship degenerated into physical brawls.

"Each of the brothers is bitterly critical of the others," New York journalist Paul Harrison reported in a 1937 profile of John Ford. "Ed and Francis will
tell you that John is the worst and most conceited director in Hollywood. John
will tell you that Ed is just a blundering assistant director and that Francis is incapable of portraying anything but drunkard roles."

What was at the root of the problem between Jack and Ed? Longtime John
Ford crewman Lefty Hough once asked that question of Jack, but Jack
brushed him off by saying that Ed argued with everybody. Hough later concluded that the feud between the brothers "goes back to the days in Maine
when Eddie and the others ran a saloon and they used to kick [Jack] Ford out
of there and wouldn't let him drink. Ford never got over that. I had to break
up the fights."

Francis Ford's collapse was a devastating case of hubris, caused largely by his
failed attempt to become a mogul. After making an independent film in New

England in 1917, he founded Fordart Films Inc., with his wife, Elsie, joining him as a writer and actress. The company released only one film, a 1918 Phil Kelly wartime yarn called *Berlin via America.* Though it was successful, other Fordart projects failed to materialize, and Frank joined producer Louis Burston to make another serial, *The Silent Mystery.* Encouraged by its popularity, Frank opened his own studio at Sunset Boulevard and Gower Street in Hollywood. According to his son, Frank's work as a director suffered because of the business pressures involved in running the studio. His 1920 serial *The Great Reward,* made with Burston, "was the poorest serial Ford was ever connected with," wrote film historian Kalton Lahue. "His star was on the wane, and before long, he was to fade out of the serial picture, reappearing at intervals only as director."

In 1922, while Frank was getting away from it all in the South Seas, Elsie sold the studio and left him for his business manager. Frank claimed the business manager also had been stealing money from him by not accounting for all the profit the films were making. Frank gamely kept toiling in the low-budget field until talkies arrived and he was forced to reconstitute himself as a grizzled character actor. The inebriated antics that became his specialty unfortunately were reflections of his offscreen life. At one point he opened a tavern in the San Fernando Valley that Jack funded, but when it failed, Frank threw a party for his friends, had the doors locked, and joined them in drinking up all the remaining booze.

Character actor Frank Baker, who worked with both Francis and John Ford for many years, said that Francis "was very much like John, but he and Jack didn't get on very well. That was a funny part of John Ford. Everything that John Ford did, I could see the reflection of Frank. Camera angles and different touches. He'd say, 'How do you like that?' And I'd say, 'I've seen that before,' and he'd go as cold as anything. . . . I am quite assured now that John Ford was perhaps suffering tremendously from a very great inferiority complex, and sitting right at the foundation of that inferiority complex was his brother Francis. He knew that this is where it all came from, and he took it out on Frank for the rest of his life."

In April 1917, just as Jack Ford was beginning his directing career, America entered World War I. Universal's publication the *Moving Picture Weekly* reported a "tremendous outburst of patriotism at the picture capital," including the formation of a volunteer company composed of actors from the studio. Like other young men throughout the country, they were caught up in the patriotic frenzy that descended when the United States belatedly joined the European war, heeding President Woodrow Wilson's call to "Make the World Safe for Democracy."

Despite failing the examination for Annapolis in 1914, Ford had not given up his dream of a military career. But the rejection had made him more cautious, and he was not eager to become mere cannon fodder. His mother shared his concerns, although his family thought he should serve. His sisters Josephine and Maime (who was serving with the Red Cross) wrote him guilt-inducing letters from Portland reporting that a draft call was not necessary in their hometown because so many young men were enlisting. Many of Jack's high school friends were already in uniform. After registering for the draft along with nearly ten million other American men on June 5, 1917, Ford was classified 1A. By then he was twenty-three years old, although he admitted to being only twenty-two.

It's unclear why Ford already was lying about his age at this early stage in his life. The first recorded instance of Ford claiming to have been born in 1895, not 1894, came on an accident insurance policy application he filled out on October 8, 1915, listing his occupation as "Assistant Motion Picture Director—not acrobat or gymnast." On a previous insurance policy taken out in April 1909, when he was a fifteen-year-old student in the seventh grade at Emerson Grammar School, he had listed his age correctly. It's possible Ford shaved a year off his age during high school because of embarrassment over being a year older than his classmates.

Once he reached Hollywood, seeming even younger than he actually was contributed to Ford's precocious sense of his own mystique. A twenty-one-year-old assistant director when he filled out the insurance application in 1915, he claimed he was still twenty. The outbreak of war in Europe the previous November may have influenced his concern about his age at that time. But the falsehood would not have affected his draft classification in 1917, because by then he was well within the period of eligibility, which was between twenty-one and thirty. Ford never bothered to correct the record about his birthdate. The truth finally emerged at his burial in 1973, when his family had his correct year of birth engraved on his coffin. I noticed the date when the flag was removed from his coffin at the cemetery and reported the information in my article on Ford's funeral in *Sight and Sound,* as well as in my 1974 book about his films. The subsequent discovery of Ford's birth record at Cape Elizabeth confirmed that information, but many books and articles still give his date of birth incorrectly, and the Cannes Film Festival held its Ford centenary celebration in 1995, not 1994.

A few days after he registered for the draft, Ford took out a $250 subscription for Liberty Loan bonds, with $5 of that amount to be deducted each week from his $50 salary at Universal. Not wanting to be drafted as an ordinary foot soldier, but preferring something more glamorous and more suitable to his talents, Ford volunteered to be an aerial combat photographer. He was

rejected because of his poor eyesight. His father tried in vain to use his polit-
ical clout to get the decision overruled by the assistant secretary of the navy, a
fellow Portland man. Still hoping to obtain a commission in the Photographic
Section of the U.S. Army Signal Corps to serve as an aerial photographer attached to the Army Air Corps, Jack corresponded in October 1918 with
R. W. Abbott, a colleague from Universal who had gone to work for the War
Department in Washington, D.C. Ford asked Abbott, who was attached to the
Motor Transport Corps, if he could pull strings. Abbott replied on October
31 that he had discussed the request with an officer in the personnel section of
the Signal Corps. Ford was not considered sufficiently qualified to become a
combat cameraman, Abbott reported, but had been put on a list of possible directors. The war ended eleven days later with Jack Ford still a noncombatant.

Evidently feeling ashamed that he had stayed in Hollywood making Westerns while others died in battle, Ford created a phony war record for himself
and maintained the legend of his World War I service for the rest of his life.
He claimed to have been an ordinary navy seaman, a bluejacket, during the
war. He could not bring himself to pretend he had actually been in combat,
simply maintaining that he had been performing routine shipboard duties such
as scraping rust and swabbing decks. But there is nothing in Ford's navy personnel file to indicate that he served in the First World War. Ford was able to
fool many people in Hollywood and elsewhere with his fabricated service
record, but he could not fool himself. A sense of guilt over that youthful deception may have helped account for the conspicuous displays of patriotism
that became increasingly common in his life and work.

Fan letters aside, Ford never harbored much affection for his first three directorial efforts. He regarded them as modest warming-up exercises for the film
he considered his real debut as a director, *The Soul Herder*. Released in August
1917, the three-reeler was the first of twenty-four movies he would make
with Harry Carey over a remarkably fertile four-year period of apprenticeship.
Francis Ford described *The Soul Herder* as "a little gem. Jack was no good until
he was given something to do on his own where he could let himself go—and
he proved himself then."

Jack was introduced to Harry Carey by Olive Golden. Then twenty-one,
she was a vivacious blonde with what the *Moving Picture Weekly* called a "bewitching smile . . . as golden as an Arizona sunset." But only Carey and Jack
Ford ever called her "Goldie." Most people called her "Ollie."

"When I first met Jack in 1914, he was working as a property man for his
brother," Ollie recalled. "It was long before my interest in Carey. I had known
Harry at Biograph [when they acted together briefly in Griffith's 1913 *Sor-*

rowful Shore], but I wasn't in love with him. There was a whole bunch of young guys at the studio. Jack was one of the stag line. We used to sit around the big table in the commissary and have lunch together. We were a bunch of kids interested in having fun and making movies and picking up that check for thirty-five dollars a week."

The ninety-one-year-old Olive Carey's smile turned wistful as she described the youthful Jack Ford, saying softly, "He was a funny boy. He was a nice young guy with imagination and a fantastic sense of humor. He was fey— most directors are. He had the most beautiful walk, a wonderful stride, very graceful, long steps. Duke Wayne told me he imitated Ford's walk. Jack was a sweetheart. I loved him. I loved every bone in his body. Bless his heart. I miss him something awful."

Ollie said she never dated Jack and she never socialized with him after working hours until he began directing Carey. When Ollie was cast as Carey's leading lady in the 1915 Western *A Knight of the Range,* she became romantically involved with the cowboy star. They married in 1917, although the ceremony had to be repeated in 1921 because of questions about its legality.

Henry Dewitt Carey, known as "the Bronx Cowboy," had a most unusual background for a Western star. The son of a wealthy New York judge, he studied law but never took the bar examination. A visit to Pawnee Bill's Western Tent Show when he was sixteen made Harry a Western aficionado and gave him dreams of becoming an actor. While recuperating from pneumonia contracted in a boating accident during his college years, he wrote himself a stage vehicle called *Montana*. The play became a runaway hit, which he modestly attributed to the fact that he rode an actual horse onstage. In 1911, Carey drifted into the movies, playing tough-guy roles in New York for D. W. Griffith's Biograph Company. His most notable Griffith film was *The Musketeers of Pig Alley,* the 1913 two-reeler that laid the groundwork for the gangster genre and helped revolutionize cinematography with its almost three-dimensional deep-focus imagery by Billy Bitzer.

Carey came to California with Griffith but moved to Universal in 1915 to make dramatic films and Westerns. That October, he starred as the saddle tramp and ex–Texas Ranger "Cheyenne Harry" Henderson in *A Knight of the Range*. Based on Carey's own screenplay and directed by Jacques Jaccard, it was heralded by the *Universal Weekly* as "the first of what is to become a series of five-reel Western features." But *A Knight of the Range* failed to make much impact on the audience. Carey's subsequent Westerns for such directors as George Marshall and Fred Kelsey were even more unremarkable. By early 1917, Carey, whose $150-a-week contract was close to expiration, found himself relegated to three-reel programmers. He was not happy with the

string of films he had been making for Kelsey and was looking around for another director.

Ollie Carey remembered what happened next: "Francis Ford said to me, 'I
understand that Fred Kelsey isn't going to be the director anymore. I wonder
if Harry'd give my brother Jack a shot at it.' And I said, 'Well, let's try and find
out.' So I brought Jack over and introduced them, and that was it. They fell in
love and they were together for four years."

"A JOB OF WORK"

I have never thought about what I was doing in terms of art, or "this is great," or "world-shaking," or anything like that. To me, it was always a job of work—which I enjoyed immensely—and that's it.

JOHN FORD, 1966

IN 1948, FORD NOSTALGICALLY dedicated his ravishingly beautiful Technicolor Western *3 Godfathers* to the recently deceased Harry Carey. A remake of the 1919 Ford-Carey Western *Marked Men*, *3 Godfathers* is prefaced with a shot of a lone rider on Carey's horse, pausing on a hill at sunset. As the sound track plays Harry's favorite song, "Goodbye, Old Paint," these words are superimposed: "To the Memory of HARRY CAREY—Bright Star of the early western sky . . ." Breaking the stylized mold of the Western hero typified (at opposite extremes) by the austere William S. Hart and the flamboyant Tom Mix, Harry Carey offered his audience a bracing taste of unglamorized realism. His clothes were dirty and lived-in, his black hat was creased and battered, he wore his pistol tucked casually into the belt of his blue jeans. His face was lined with experience, and he was capable of both venality and heroism. People found it easy to identify with Harry Carey. They simply believed him.

Carey's deep, resonant voice, so impressive in stage roles, was no help to him in silent movies. But in the words of Frank Capra's associate producer Joseph Sistrom, who suggested Carey for his memorable role as the vice president of the United States in *Mr. Smith Goes to Washington,* the actor had "a good American face." His features were pleasantly homely. He was quietly reserved, yet capable of strong emotion. He had the look of a regular guy who, when provoked, could break the law or become a hero, depending on the circumstances. Carey's acting had an unaffected directness refreshingly unlike the florid theatricality audiences were accustomed to seeing on the screen.

A 1919 Universal advertisement featuring a woodcut of Ford directing

Carey in a forest setting described their work as "PLAIN WESTERNS." What that meant, in Ford's words, was that the movies "weren't shoot-'em-ups, they were character stories. Carey was a great actor, and we didn't dress him up like the cowboys you see on TV—all dolled up. There were numerous Western stars around that time . . . and so we decided to kid them a little bit—not kid the Western—but the leading men—and make Carey sort of a bum, a saddle tramp, instead of a great bold gunfighting hero. All this was fifty percent Carey and fifty percent me."

Harry Carey's silent Westerns made an enormous impression on a strapping kid whose name was Marion "Duke" Morrison when he was growing up on a farm in Glendale, California. "Harry Carey projected a quality that we like to think of in men of the West," said John Wayne, adding that Ford "built on his authenticity." Wayne told actor Harry Carey Jr., "I watched your dad since I was a kid. I copied Harry Carey. That's where I learned to talk like I do; that's where I learned many of my mannerisms. Watching your father."

Carey never watched his own movies. "My husband said this was 'a job of work,' and he enjoyed his work," Olive Carey recalled. "He gave everything he had to it. But he never went to see his work. Harry never looked at rushes because he said, 'What's the use of lookin' at 'em?' There was nothing he could do about 'em if he didn't like 'em, so he wasn't going to be bothered." Ford adopted the same attitude toward his craft, habitually referring to moviemaking with the words Harry used, "a job of work." That offhanded-ness was partly a pose on Ford's part, but for Carey it was the real thing.

What Carey enjoyed was not the trappings of stardom or admiring himself on the screen, but the process of actually making the movies. He loved getting away from the back lot and going out into the country to shoot Western scenes with a small group of friends. He loved riding horses, sleeping outside in a bedroll, playing at being a cowboy and making a living at it. The closer the moviemaking process came to reproducing the actual experience of West-ern life, the more Harry liked it.

Ford shared all those inclinations with Carey, but he had to work hard at developing a persona that came so naturally to the actor, that of a genuine westerner, an unpretentious cowboy, a tough guy with a soft heart. Ford's split personality was evident in his means of locomotion. In June 1916, he spent fifty dollars to buy his own horse, a bay saddle gelding named Woodrow. But the car the ambitious young director drove around Hollywood by the late teens was a fashionable 1916 Stutz Bearcat. As Oscar Wilde famously ob-served, "Being natural is such a difficult pose to keep up." However much Ford tried to conceal his true intellectual nature, he could not help construct-ing his own western sensibility far more self-consciously than Carey. Since

Carey was an actor rather than a director, he worked in a more instinctive way, naturally embodying the themes that Ford explored through increasingly complex narratives and imagery.

But Ford shared Carey's deep-seated passion for authenticity. That helped account for the immediate rapport they had on their first meeting, even though Harry was sixteen years older than the twenty-two-year-old director and from a far loftier social background. Carey's English ancestry, his family's wealth, and his father's judgeship were no impediments to his budding friendship with the Irish saloonkeeper's son from Maine, for Carey's attraction to the rugged life of the West bespoke a restless, rebellious spirit that meshed perfectly with Ford's own. Both hated social hypocrisy and reveled in the disreputability of the movie business.

Neither Ford nor Carey was discouraged by the fact that film reviewers who paid serious attention to Hart's moral fables often tended to ignore less obviously "significant" work in the Western genre. By the late 1910s, the Hollywood Western, other than the occasional prestige project, was becoming increasingly marginalized. Falling out of fashion as mainsteam audience tastes gravitated to more "sophisticated" fare, bread-and-butter Westerns came to be regarded largely as undemanding entertainment for children and uneducated adults. Although the Ford–Carey Westerns generally were enthusiastically reviewed in the trade press and elsewhere, intellectual tastemakers mostly ignored them. America's paper of record, the *New York Times,* did not review any of those films. It was not until Ford branched out into other genres in the early 1920s that his work began to be reviewed in the *Times.*

The relative obscurity Ford and Carey labored under in those years was liberating because it allowed them to explore their favorite themes without becoming self-conscious or worrying unduly about how their movies would be received. As long as their Westerns turned a profit for Universal, they were left alone to play and experiment within the confines of the genre. Those confines are far less burdensome than most critics generally assume, for as Jean Renoir once told me, "The marvelous thing about Westerns is that they are all the same movie. That gives a director unlimited freedom."

William S. Hart established the paradoxical figure of the "good bad man" as the archetype around which serious Westerns wove their moral dilemmas, or what were known then as "soul fights." Under Hart's towering influence, Carey and Ford naturally gravitated to the same theme, for which they had their own instinctive affinities. In Fordian terms, the good bad man was the noble outlaw who becomes the savior of a hypocritical society that finds his code of behavior difficult to accept. Their early Westerns usually revolved around the outlaw's spiritual redemption as he revealed his innate nobility. In the process, he often confronted class prejudices and enabled society to behave in a more humane manner. Ford's fascination with noble outlaws would extend far beyond the series of Westerns he made with Carey, showing up throughout his career in such widely divergent films as *Stagecoach, The Grapes of Wrath, The Rising of the Moon,* and *7 Women.*

The first Ford–Carey collaboration, *The Soul Herder,* had the working title *The Sky Pilot.* Both titles were western slang terms for "preacher." Crime and religion were amusingly intertwined in Carey's Cheyenne Harry, an outlaw who masquerades as a man of God. When he rescues a little girl (Elizabeth Janes) from an Indian attack in the desert, she insists he wear the clerical collar and vest of her late father. Playing a preacher brings out the latent decency in Harry's character. Although he forgets himself and gets mixed up in a saloon brawl, his solicitude for the child wins him the heart of her aunt, the attractive young church organist (Fritzi Ridgeway).

Moving Picture World reviewer Arthur W. Courtney enjoyed the "delicious humor" of the scenes in which Harry "rides his horse into the saloon and compels them all to go to church. After the service he tells them that the Lord loves a cheerful giver. . . . He stands at the door with the collection basket in one hand and a gun in the other and forces them all to give up. He uses the money to send the disreputable women back to their families."

The trade reviewer's description of *The Soul Herder* as "an excellent picture for children of all ages" showed how hard it was for Westerns in that era to be appreciated without some overtone of condescension. Yet Courtney also declared that the film "would surely convert those who refuse to admit that Western movies can have a strong moral tone." Even at this early stage in Ford's career, the special qualities he brought to his films were noticed by reviewers who took the time to see them. The ingenious and complementary blending of comedy and drama Ford employed in *The Soul Herder* to reinforce the story's moral themes would become a hallmark of his style. And while it's ironic that Ford, the son of a saloonkeeper, would have his hero behave like a Prohibitionist, one suspects that the director had his tongue at least partially in cheek.

The script of *The Soul Herder* was credited to George Hively, whose name appears as the screenwriter on many of Ford's silent Westerns for Universal; Hively also edited the films. Some are credited to H. Tipton Steck and other writers, and Ford himself received an occasional writing credit in those days. Ford claimed he and Harry Carey were largely responsible for the scripts of all their films, and Ollie Carey remembered the films as being mostly improvised on location by Jack and Harry after they cooked up the story lines in late-night bull sessions. Harry would drink Melwood whiskey and spew out ideas while Jack, who didn't drink at that stage of his life, would make sarcastic remarks, throw in his own suggestions, and take copious notes. "They never would let the studio know what the hell they were doing," Ollie recalled with amusement, "and then Hively would write it after it was all through."

Her account and Ford's probably underestimate the importance of Hively and the other credited writers, who sent scripts out to the location and occasionally were present during the shooting. Furthermore, two of the movies were adapted from well-known literary sources: Hively based *A Woman's Fool* (1918) on Owen Wister's novel *Lin McLean,* and for *The Outcasts of Poker Flat* (1919), Steck ingeniously interwove the title story by Bret Harte with Harte's "The Luck of Roaring Camp." *Marked Men* was adapted by Steck from Peter B. Kyne's oft-filmed novella *The Three Godfathers* (1913). Still, the picaresque nature of the Ford-Carey movies, the director's habitually casual approach to plotting, and the extensive work on location tended to encourage improvisation. And it's not hard to believe that many of their ideas emerged from boozy nocturnal gabfests.

Most of *Wild Women* (1918) consists of Cheyenne Harry's feverish fantasy of being shanghaied to a South Sea island and being pursued by a jealous native queen. Just in the nick of time, he wakes up with a terrible hangover from drinking too many Honolulu cocktails. *Hell Bent,* a 1918 feature recently rediscovered in a print containing German intertitles, is an uproariously tongue-in-cheek comedy with Harry in a drunken state throughout, lurching from one perilous situation to another. That film's "tickling tone of merriment" delighted *Exhibitors' Trade Review,* which described *Hell Bent* as typical of the Ford-Carey cycle, "which means that thrills and excitement are plentifully distributed about, and that speed and more speed is the keynote."

Ford was never a director who cared overly much about exposition or spent much time worrying whether one scene flowed into the next with perfect logic. The stark simplicity of the generic situations in which he placed Cheyenne Harry—gunfights, saloon donnybrooks, holdups, chase sequences—allowed Ford plenty of opportunity to indulge in the kind of nonstop action and comedy that he knew would delight his audience. Western fans already were cognizant enough of genre conventions that they could follow and appreciate his most creative variations and wildest satiric twists.

In the climax of Ford's *Bucking Broadway* (1917), cowboys ride to the rescue of the heroine through the streets of New York (actually downtown Los Angeles). In *Roped* (1919), Cheyenne Harry is a wealthy Arizona cattleman who becomes the mail-order husband of an eastern society woman. *Hell Bent* starts with a writer admiring Frederic Remington's darkly humorous 1897 painting

A Misdeal, which the film then proceeds to imitate; *The Outcasts of Poker Flat* is framed around Carey's Square Shootin' Harry Lanyon reading Harte's title story. The penultimate Ford-Carey silent, *The Wallop* (1921), opens with Carey watching a "Handsome Harry" movie and walking out in disgust. A sly dig at the star by his director? A bit of self-parody in which Harry was complicit? Without the evidence of the actual film it's impossible to tell.

Even at the beginning of his career, Ford enjoyed a remarkable degree of freedom within the studio factory system. Part of this was due to his professionalism as a filmmaker and the cleverness with which he managed to circumvent executive scrutiny. But part of the credit should go to the studio itself. In his book *American Silent Film,* William K. Everson describes Universal as "a bread-and-butter company that rarely aimed at prestige works, [but] was uncommonly successful in avoiding formula. Many of its films, considered little more than programmers in their day, stand the test of time remarkably well, not only because they have such human qualities and so effortlessly reflect the spirit and day-to-day living of their times, but because Universal freed its directors from assembly-line requirements."

One reason Universal didn't bother interfering with Ford was that his films cost so little money. The production cost for the typical Ford-Carey feature probably was no more than $10,000 to $15,000, and the economy began with the director's salary. After taking a pay cut to start directing at $35 a week in early 1917, Ford was offered a one-year contract that September, calling for him to direct *and* act in Universal pictures for $75 a week, with an option for renewal containing escalator clauses rising to $150 a week in the second year. He rejected that offer, signing a marginally better contract as a director and actor guaranteeing him a raise from $75 to $100 a week after the first six months, and escalating in the option year from $125 a week to $150 in the last six months of the contract.

The single major item in the budget of a Ford-Carey Western was the star's salary. While Ford's salary was inching upward, Harry's rocketed from $150 to $1,250 a week by May 1918. Such was the casual nature of the movie business in those days that Harry didn't even know he had become Universal's biggest star until his wife made that discovery while they were visiting the company's New York office.

The line between illusion and reality in the filming of Ford's early Westerns was virtually nonexistent. He and Carey seldom spent much time in the studio during the brief shooting schedules, a few days for a two-reeler, a few weeks for a five- or six-reel feature. They rode on horseback to all-purpose locations around Newhall, about twenty miles north of Universal City, living a rugged life much like that portrayed in their movies. Most of the filming was in the Placerita Canyon, near the Vasquez Rocks. Ford sometimes ventured farther afield, as in three films released in 1919. He used the spectacular San Bernardino Mountains around Big Bear as the setting of *A Fight for Love,* filmed scenes for *The Outcasts of Poker Flat* along Northern California's Sacramento River, and went to Arizona for *The Ace of the Saddle.*

Adopting several members of the Harry Carey Stock Company into his own nascent acting troupe, Ford found great comfort and security in surrounding himself with familiar and reliable players. Molly Malone was the sweet, outdoorsy, somewhat bland ingenue in eight of their films, although Neva Gerber, Gloria Hope, Gertrude Astor, Winifred Westover, and others also served as leading ladies. Olive Carey, who was acting in comedies at Universal for Al Christie and the Stern brothers, never appeared in Ford's early movies with her husband. Asked why not, she replied with disarming candor, "I was getting forty bucks a week. I'm a lousy actress." (She did appear for Ford many years later in *The Searchers, The Wings of Eagles,* and *Two Rode To gether.*)

The colorful cast of supporting characters in the Ford-Carey Westerns included Hoot Gibson, Duke Lee, Vester Pegg, Ted Brooks, Jim Corey, Joe Harris, and Bill Gillis, stuntmen Clarence and Whitey Sovern, and a Western lawman turned actor named Ed "Pardner" Jones. J. Farrell MacDonald, the lovable bald character actor who appeared in more Ford movies than anyone else except Jack Pennick and Harry Tenbrook, began with the director in those early Westerns, as did Tenbrook and future Ford Stock Company members Andy Devine and Chief John Big Tree, a statuesque Seneca Indian who served as one of the models for the buffalo or Indian-head nickel.

Even future director Frank Capra became an extra in the Ford-Carey Westerns. Ollie remembered the twenty-one-year-old Capra as "a nutty young man who came along and said he needed money" during the shooting of *The Outcasts of Poker Flat* on a Sacramento dock in December 1918. Newly discharged from the army and eager to break into the movie business, Capra was paid five dollars for playing a laborer unloading a stern-wheeler riverboat in the film-within-the-film based on "The Outcasts," featuring Carey as Harte's "honest gambler" John Oakhurst. Capra, who became a close friend of Ford's in later years, also worked as an extra for three days on another of his Carey Westerns filmed at Universal City.

While shooting with Carey on location, Ford moved quickly from setup to setup, working with a very small crew, seldom more than a handful of people. Although the heavyset Ben Reynolds photographed *The Soul Herder* and several of their other movies, John W. Brown most often was the cameraman.

Actor Teddy Brooks doubled as the assistant director, and the property man was George McGonigle, better known as "Jerry." There was a camera assistant as well, and occasionally the services of a carpenter or two were required to put up a rudimentary set suggesting the interior of a frontier home. Ford already displayed a penchant for framing characters through doorways, visually underscoring the thematic tension between the wilderness and civilization. If a more elaborate set was needed, such as a saloon, a church, or a prison, Jack and Harry grudgingly returned to the back lot.

Relishing their freedom, they would rush back to Newhall to rough it at the earliest opportunity. Partly for convenience and partly in emulation of Carey's nonchalant attitude, Ford fell into the habit of not bothering to look at rushes during shooting. He would stop by the studio to supervise Hively's editing, but putting together a Ford film in the cutting room was a relatively simple task. Although Hively was "a damn good cutter," Ollie Carey said, "Ford didn't really need a cutter except for the mechanical works of it, because he shot just enough film that would be necessary for the picture. He never overshot. He had an uncanny ability of being able to know exactly how much footage he needed. He had it in his mind all the time. He knew exactly what he was doing." Ford already had conceived one of his cleverest strategies to keep control of his work. Unlike most other directors, he almost never "covered" a scene from various angles he knew he wouldn't need. As he confided to Ollie, part of the reason for his economical shooting was to give the studio precious little leeway to reedit his pictures.

Ford's apprenticeship in serials and low-budget Westerns taught him to employ simple but expressive setups and, whenever possible, to rely on the spontaneity of the first take. When Hoot Gibson's horse slipped and tumbled crossing a river in *Straight Shooting,* Ford kept the camera rolling as Gibson remounted and continued across the river. Such accidents gave a freshness to Ford's pictures that would remain one of his hallmarks throughout his career. "He got some wonderful effects on rainy days" while shooting his silent Westerns, Ollie remembered. "He'd shoot whether it was raining or not. Ford was the first one at every shot. He loved it." Ford quickly developed a reputation for a striking sense of composition. In 1917, *Moving Picture World* found in *The Secret Man* "a generous lot of picturesque scenes, flooded with California sunshine," and declared that in *Bucking Broadway,* "Jack Ford again demonstrates his happy faculty for getting all outdoors into the scenes." A year and a half later, reviewing *The Outcasts of Poker Flat, Photoplay* hailed "director Ford's marvelous river locations and absolutely incomparable photography. This photoplay is an optic symphony."

Ford's pace of production was staggering. He and Harry Carey made seven films together in 1917, five of them feature-length, and they teamed on seven

features the following year. In 1919, Ford directed a phenomenal total of nineteen movies. Those included seven features and two shorts with Carey, five
shorts starring a young cowboy actor named Pete Morrison, and a short starring Pardner Jones, *The Last Outlaw* (remade by director Christy Cabanne at
RKO in 1936 as a Harry Carey talkie). After a hiatus in 1920 when Ford
began branching out into other genres and also directed his first film for another studio, he and Carey made two more features together at Universal in
1921 before ending their splendid partnership.

During that four-year period, Carey and Ford perfectly complemented
each other's abilities. "Harry Carey tutored me in the early years, sort of
brought me along," Ford acknowledged. "I learned a great deal from Harry
Carey. He was a slow-moving actor when he was afoot. You could read his
mind, peer into his eyes and see him think." While Ford encouraged Carey to
explore deeper levels of humanity in his screen characterizations, Carey gave
Ford the confidence to imbue their generic plots with his personal feelings
and his quirky sense of humor. "They adored each other—they were just
complete pals," Ollie remembered. Ford was more fun to know in the early
part of his career, she said, because he "was more active and hadn't gotten so
sadistic. There never was a cross word. The whole company was a working
unit. They were a ball team, y'know? Everybody worked for the fun of it, as
much as for the fact that you were getting paid to do it. There was a camaraderie about the whole thing that made it click."

So much camaraderie that a bunch of them soon began living together.
Ollie found a three-room bungalow in the wilds of Newhall that rented for
seventeen dollars a month. Jack vacated his Hollywood bachelor apartment
and went to stay on the three-acre ranch with the Careys, Brooks, McGonigle,
Pardner Jones, and Jim Corey, who did triple duty as an actor and as a cow-
puncher/handyman. There was only one bedroom, and Jack and Harry preferred to sleep outside in bedrolls, so everyone except McGonigle joined them
in the alfalfa patch. The toilet was in the bathhouse a few hundred yards from
the main house. They all shared a single automobile, a rattletrap dubbed the
"EMF" for "Every-Morning-Fixit." Often they had to hitch up a horse and
have the horse pull the car along until Ollie could get the engine going.

Ollie served as majordomo, buying the food and doing all the cooking on
an old-fashioned woodstove. "Everybody had to chip in when I'd go into the
market once a week, and I used to have trouble collecting," she said. "I'd go to
collect from Jack, and he was always so goddam tight. I'd say, 'This week I need
twenty dollars' or something, and he'd say, 'Why the hell is it always my week
to buy butter?'"

Harry had the unhappy duty of waking his director each morning. Despite
the demands of his profession, Ford was never a morning person by inclina-

tion. The day after he finished shooting a Pete Morrison short called *Gun Law* in March 1919, Ford received a letter of reprimand from Universal for habitually coming to work at the studio at 9:30 or 10 A.M., an hour or so later than the industry norm. Even before he developed a drinking problem in the 1920s and started suffering from morning hangovers, Ford had exceptional difficulty rising in Newhall because of his late-night script sessions with Harry Carey. Harry would rise at dawn and let his dogs out of the garage so they would swarm all over Ford, licking his face until he was forced to crawl from his sleeping bag, bleary-eyed and cursing.

Much of what little free time Ford had in Newhall was spent in discussions with Harry, whether about the next day's shooting or about other topics. Ford eagerly soaked up whatever he could learn from the actor, who was better educated than he was. "There was never a dull moment," Ollie recalled. "There was never any airy persiflage. There was always something interesting going on between him and Harry, always a *subject*. They might be having an argument over something, but they were always expressing their ideas and their views. They had a wonderful association."

When he wasn't talking or sleeping, Ford was reading books. A lifelong autodidact, he enjoyed novels and short stories, but devoured biographies and history books. "He knew a lot about *everything,* even when he was a kid," Ollie marveled. "If a subject came up or he heard about it somewhere and he didn't know a lot about it, he would find out about it that night or the next day. Because he'd go home and he would study up on it. He was avid for knowledge, always."

The authentic western flavor of their primitive living conditions in Newhall was enhanced by the presence of Ed "Pardner" Jones. An imposing figure with a handlebar mustache, Jones claimed to have been a deputy to the legendary marshal Wyatt Earp in Tombstone, Arizona. Renowned for his uncanny accuracy with a rifle, Pardner also was reputed to have slain a notorious outlaw called the Apache Kid. Those claims were dubious, but many in Hollywood believed them. As if such credentials did not make Jones colorful enough, Ford also insisted that Pardner was related to Pat Garrett, the lawman who shot Billy the Kid. "Jack would dream up all these things," said Ollie. "But Ed would never admit it."

Jones acted in Ford silents and was on call whenever the director needed a sharpshooter, taking risks that would not be allowed in filmmaking today. "If we had a gunfight, we'd talk it over with someone who'd been an old lawman—like Pardner Jones—and he'd tell us how it would have happened," Ford recalled. "In those days we didn't have any tricks— If you had to have a glass shot out of somebody's hand, Pardner would actually shoot it out—with a rifle. . . . Pardner couldn't hit the ceiling with a pistol, but then he'd take a rifle and put a *dime* up there twenty-five yards away and hit it. So we tried to do it the real way it had been in the West: none of this so-called quick-draw stuff." In an interview soon after the release of *Marked Men,* Ford unabashedly related how he had put the life of his star, Harry Carey, into the hands of a sharp-shooter (presumably Jones): "I had to find a man who could handle a rifle so well that there could not be a fraction of an inch mistake in his aim, for he shoots at Carey, who is swimming a river, and the bullet is seen to hit just three inches from the star's head."

The 1920 article added that Ford's "continual cry" was: "In everything I want realism."[1] But what does realism mean in the mythic context of the Western? Ford was already beginning to grapple with that question, as Ollie Carey saw in his tendency to weave heroic legends around people like Pardner Jones, who were living in a shadowland between fact and fiction.

The virtual impossibility of sorting out the truth behind the legends of the Old West was brought home most dramatically when Ford became acquainted with the one and only Wyatt Earp. Ford recalled talking with the old lawman in the "very early silent days, a couple of times a year, [when Earp] would come up to visit pals [at Universal], cowboys he knew in Tombstone; a lot of them were in my company. I think I was an assistant prop boy then."

After retiring to a mining town near the Arizona-California border in 1905, Earp lived much of the time in Los Angeles until his death in 1929. He was often seen around movie sets in the silent era, reminiscing with old cronies and hoping to interest moviemakers in telling his story. Earp had not yet achieved the full legendary status he would acquire posthumously, but people who cared about western history were impressed to meet him. Directors Raoul Walsh and Allan Dwan also remembered Earp visiting their sets, although Dwan had the impression that Earp was still "looking for a place in law and order" rather than in the movie business.

Josephine Marcus Earp wrote that her husband's "experience with Holly-wood was like his experience with newspapermen. After he discovered that they paid no attention to what he told them, Wyatt's sly sense of humor was directed toward the movie people. He pulled their legs, telling them the sort

---

1. Ford also boasted about another dangerous stunt in *Marked Men:* "In the second reel I had to find one man who dared risk his life for a thrill, and I found him. His duty was to dash through the railing of a high wooden bridge on a horse and fall sixty feet below in a shallow river. I had six cameramen there to catch the scene from every angle, and I believe that it will stand as one of the most daring feats ever performed before a camera."

of improbable things found in Western fiction stories. To his amazement, they swallowed these tall tales hook, line and sinker, but were always skeptical of the truth. At this point, my husband gave up in disgust, refusing to have anything further to do with those 'damn fool dudes,' as he called them." Both Dwan's version of the Earp saga, *Frontier Marshal* (1939), and Ford's, *My Darling Clementine* (1946), were based on the fanciful 1931 biography by Stuart N. Lake, *Wyatt Earp: Frontier Marshal,* which embroidered the facts with the partial cooperation of Earp himself. In his 1997 biography *Wyatt Earp: The Life Behind the Legend,* Casey Tefertiller wrote of *Clementine,* "Ford did have a few things a little askew, such as killing off Doc Holliday and Old Man Clanton at the O.K. Corral, plus having the fight in the wrong location, but no one quibbles over details when a movie works."

Ford never wanted to admit that he was doing anything less than a semi-documentary re-creation of the October 26, 1881, gunfight at the O.K. Corral, with Wyatt Earp serving from beyond the grave as an uncredited technical adviser. When Earp visited Universal, Ford told Bogdanovich, "I used to give him a chair and a cup of coffee, and he told me about the fight at the O.K. Corral. So in *My Darling Clementine,* we did it exactly the way it had been."

"Jack said that?" Ollie Carey responded. "He's full of crap. *God,* how he romanced!"

Ollie conceded that Ford and Harry Carey probably did meet Wyatt Earp at Universal, but when asked if it was true that Ford heard about the O.K. Corral directly from Earp, she snorted, "Of course not. He made that all up. You know damn well he made it all up."

But who really knows what John Ford and Wyatt Earp had to say to each other? Perhaps it was from Earp that Ford learned what it meant to "print the legend."

Because so many of Ford's silent films are lost, we are left with, at best, a partial understanding of his early artistic development. As Andrew Sarris points out in *The John Ford Movie Mystery,* we "would be ill-advised to speculate about the quality and impact of a Ford film on the screen purely from a printed synopsis or even from a period critique. Something extra-magical seems to happen between the synopsis and the spectacle where Ford is concerned." If we had to choose just one of the Ford-Carey Westerns to survive, it would be a toss-up between *Straight Shooting,* Ford's first feature film, and *Marked Men,* the director's personal favorite among all the movies he made with Carey.

Marked Men was Ford's first version of *The Three Godfathers* but Carey's second. Peter B. Kyne's sentimental religious fable about three outlaws rescuing a baby in the desert originated in 1910 as a *Saturday Evening Post* short story,

"Broncho Billy and the Baby," which served as the basis that same year for G. M. Anderson's *Broncho Billy's Redemption,* the first film featuring his popular "Broncho Billy" screen character. Kyne expanded the story for his novella, which was filmed with Carey by director Edward J. LeSaint at Universal in 1916. "It was done fast, and Harry didn't like it," Ollie recalled. "He and Jack were talking about it, and they decided to make it again." So entranced was Ford to find a story that transposed biblical iconography into a Western setting, he put aside his habitual reticence to tell an interviewer that "as a film subject it stood out as a classic with unlimited possibilities."[2] Unfortunately, *Marked Men* has been lost, but the script (preserved in Ford's papers) and a few stills suggest what a charming and poignant film it must have been. For historical and biographical reasons, however, we are lucky indeed that *Straight Shooting* has survived the vicissitudes of time, serving as an unexpectedly vivid window into Ford's formative period as an artist.

Ford and Carey planned *Straight Shooting* as a five-reel feature, but Universal insisted on its running only two reels. Ford shot the additional footage any way, wangling another four thousand feet of film by telling the studio that some of his exposed footage had been dropped into a river by accident. Some Universal executives were upset when they saw the completed film, and wanted to cut it back to two reels. But Laemmle overruled them, saying, "If I order a suit of clothes and the fellow gives me an extra pair of pants free, what am I going to do—throw them back in his face?" Laemmle's young executive assistant Irving Thalberg also was instrumental in the decision. Released to great popular success on August 27, 1917, *Straight Shooting* revived Carey's career and encouraged Universal to give its new young director a free hand.

Straight Shooting was rediscovered in 1966 in Czechoslovakia's national film archive and given a new premiere at the following year's Montreal Film Festival. A remarkably assured work for a twenty-three-year-old director, *Straight Shooting* displays a sophisticated command of pictorial storytelling. Ford's style is already recognizably his own; some of the themes and visual motifs he would explore in his mature masterpieces, such as *Stagecoach* and *The Searchers,* are present in his feature debut. *Straight Shooting*'s plot about a range war between cattlemen and ranchers may be overly familiar from hundreds of other

---

2. In addition to Ford's two versions and LeSaint's, the six screen adaptations of Kyne's novella include William Wyler's *Hell's Heroes* (1929), Richard Boleslawski's *Three Godfathers* (1936), and a TV movie, *The Godchild* (1974). Ford's silent version had the working titles *The Three Godfathers* and *The Gift of the Desert.* Reminded by Bogdanovich that the title had been changed to *Marked Men,* Ford replied, "They would, the bastards." When Wyler went to see Ford on his deathbed in 1973, Ford told him, "By the way, it's your turn to do *Three Godfathers* again."

Westerns made before and after it, and some of the acting is marred by overde-pendence on melodramatic clichés, but the vigor and sincerity of Ford's ap-proach keep the movie entertaining and emotionally affecting more than eighty years after it was made.

From the opening shot, an iris-out from a man on horseback to reveal a winding herd of cattle and other horsemen in a valley below him, we know we are in the hands of an innate filmmaker with a fresh, painterly sense of composition. In what would become a hallmark of his style, Ford keeps the camera static but uses movement within the frame to create visual variety. As the horseman on the hilltop turns and rides down to meet other horsemen and they all gallop out of frame, three distinct and harmonious compositions succeed each other within a single shot. Ford's debt to his brother Frank is clear throughout *Straight Shooting,* especially in this kind of foreground-background tension deploying figures in the extreme distance, with the cam-era as an "invisible" observer. But Frank's visual sense was less supple than Jack's. Jack had the instinctive knack of creating images whose elegance did not look overly studied, shots in which the movement seemed natural and fluid even though the camera never moved. Frank's images felt cramped and somewhat forced by comparison.

Jack's greater mastery of the medium was evident in his seamless blending of pictorial beauty with documentary-like directness of action. *Straight Shoot-ing* already exemplifies Sarris's eloquent description of Ford's visual style as one that "evolved almost miraculously into a double vision of an event in all its vital immediacy and yet also in its ultimate memory image on the horizon of history." Stemming in part from Ford's quasi-religious habit of seeing everyday life from the perspective of eternity, this duality in the director's vision of the world helps account for the depth he brings to the character of Cheyenne Harry in *Straight Shooting.*

A hired gun for the cattlemen, Harry experiences a change of heart when sent to kill a defiant old farmer, Sweetwater Sims (George Berrell), who has refused to leave his land even after the murder of his only son. Ford's frankness about the venality of Harry's profession keeps *Straight Shooting* from being overly sentimental. Such bracing realism was a regular component of the Cheyenne Harry movies. *Exhibitors' Trade Review* complained that Carey "consistently portrays a rough character" throughout Ford's 1918 film *Three Mounted Men.* "The only wonder of it is that anyone should attempt to hero-ize such a type. There may be such men in the west, but it is best on the screen to show them up as horrible examples of what a man may be." Ford's tolerant understanding of human weakness avoids that kind of black-and-white mor-alizing. He draws some welcome humor from Harry's initial degeneracy in

Straight Shooting, showing him getting drunk with the villainous character (Vester Pegg) he later will vanquish in a street duel. Such likable vulnerability helps make Harry's moral redemption plausible.

The visual device Ford uses to dramatize Harry's moment of decision is strikingly expressionistic, evidence that a tendency so prominent in Ford's later films was present in a latent form well before he was influenced by German expressionist cinema in the 1920s. When Harry approaches the Sims homestead, he sees the old man grieving over the dead boy's grave with his daughter, Joan (Molly Malone), and her boyfriend, Sam (Hoot Gibson). As Harry emerges from the woods in close-up, his eyes are deeply shadowed by the brim of his hat, suggesting how deeply he is disturbed by what he sees. He removes his hat respectfully, and Ford cuts to a shot from Harry's point of view, a blurred, overexposed image of the family tableau. A reaction shot shows the hired killer rubbing his eyes in anguish. On a realistic level, the blurring demonstrates that Harry is viewing the scene through eyes filled with tears. More symbolically, the overexposure seems to connote a holy light streaming from the family gathered around the cross marking the grave, Harry momentarily blinded and emotionally transfigured by what he sees.

Though relatively crude in its conception, the device is noteworthy both for the double meaning Ford is able to draw from it and as one of his earliest attempts to express a character's feelings and thought processes through the manipulation of lighting and iconography. *Straight Shooting* contains many instances of the more naturalistic lighting effects that Ford employed to suggest a character's inner life at times when the director was less in the thrall of what the French critic Philippe Haudiquet describes as his "expressionist temptation." Both before and after Harry's quasi-mystical experience at the grave, Ford films him in close-ups looking toward the family from the bank of a river, tree branches and bushes casting rippling shadows over his face to suggest his inner turmoil. The influence of D. W. Griffith and his great cameraman Billy Bitzer, who pioneered the dramatic "mood" close-up, is strongly felt at moments like these.

Audiences of 1917, just two years after *The Birth of a Nation,* would have been expected to recognize the pervasive influences of that landmark film in *Straight Shooting.* Indeed, the climactic ride to the rescue of the besieged family by Harry and a gang of his outlaw friends could be considered an outright *hommage.* More telling in the context of Ford's overall career was another lesson he learned from Griffith, the importance of carefully inserting revealing details to humanize action and add leavening touches of humor or sentiment. *Straight Shooting* has a number of such memorable moments: Harry reflectively squeezing his horse's tail after the shootout; Joan clasping her dead brother's empty plate to her breast at the dinner table; a sympathetic black or Mexican outlaw sampling and then stealing a jar of jam after helping save the family.

Thematically, *Straight Shooting* inaugurates one of the dominant concerns of Ford's work, the conflict between wandering and stability, or what *The Man Who Shot Liberty Valance* would define in a larger context as the conflict between "wilderness" and the "garden" of civilization. Cheyenne Harry embodies the deep, unresolved ambivalence Ford's protagonists always feel toward the settled home life they idealize but so rarely manage to achieve. Harry's desire to cast his lot with the Sims family and his flirtation with Joan are counterpointed with his melancholic longing as he watches his outlaw pals ride away from the homestead. The film has come down to us with what seem like two contradictory endings—one in which Harry decides to ride away, leaving Joan to Sam's more suitably domestic company, and another ending in which Harry tentatively decides to settle down with Joan. The "happy" ending, which doesn't match the previous scene photographically, may have been grafted onto the film from an earlier part of the story when *Straight Shooting* was reissued in 1925 as a two-reeler titled *Straight Shootin'*. But the film's dual ending seems peculiarly appropriate as an expression of its budding director's divided self.

"Here we are at a time when the Western was still relatively new even though the West was old, and the Old West virtually dead, and yet Ford is already casting a somber spell on the screen, his *mise en scène* already in mourning, his feelings of loss and displacement already fantasized through the genre," Sarris comments. "This elegiac element in his style helps explain why Ford was spotted as a stylist surprisingly early in his career. It is more than a matter of beautiful pictures. The silent screen was saturated with them. It is rather a matter of the dynamic counterpoint between the physical and emotional energy of his players and the reflective overview of his extraordinarily quiet camera."

In a sudden show of independence, Ford once went to Universal City and did not return to Newhall for an entire week. When he came back, Ollie Carey asked, "Where the hell have you been?"

"I've been with Janet Eastman," Ford said.

"Who the hell is Janet Eastman?" she demanded.

"Don't ask me," he replied. "I picked her up in Hollywood."

"That was the first dame he ever slept with," Ollie recalled. "He'd been a virgin up to that point."

No matter what he defensively told Ollie, who seems to have resented his defection from their camp, Ford's first lover was no casual pickup. Judging from four letters he saved from Janet, she was an intelligent and sophisticated young woman with a perceptive appreciation of his sensitivity and wit. Janet was an actress and aspiring screenwriter. Ford may have met her at Universal, for one of her acting credits was as the female lead in *The Raid,* a three-reel Western released by the studio in March 1917. George Marshall directed the film, which starred Neal Hart.

Although Ollie belittled Ford's affair with Janet as "just a passing fancy," Janet's letters indicate that a deeper emotional bond existed. They evidently dated for a few months around late 1918 and early 1919. By then Ford had moved back near the studio, to the Bachelor Lodge at 6511½ Hollywood Boulevard. Even after marrying another man and moving to England, where she continued working in films, "Jan" affectionately addressed Ford as "Sean," "Mon cher Jack," "Honey," and "old dear." In one letter she saucily wrote him, "Je suis quel'enfant ce soir and I wish to be caresse beaucoup; je suis triste pour la presénce de mon amour de ma coeur.[3] Goodnight, sweetheart. Janet loves you."

But they both realized their romance was receding into memory. "I miss your companionship a lot," Janet wrote him in 1920. ". . . Did you ever consider how unusual it is for people having once had a 'crush' to still be sort of 'chums'—well it is—whether you have had opinions on it or not." It's not clear why Ford and Janet stopped dating, but with his Irish reserve and somewhat puritanical attitude toward sexuality, he may have been intimidated by the spirited young woman's forthright approach to romance and by her career ambitions. One of her letters teasingly refers to a woman who "died happy—though spurned by a Feeney."

Ford was restless. He wanted to show the world that he could do more than direct Harry Carey Westerns.

And he wanted to earn more than $150 a week. That was all he was making by the summer of 1919, the most prolific year of his career. Carey, whom Ford had made into a major star, by then was earning fifteen times that amount, $2,250 a week. The gross disparity in salary between director and star helped cause the resentment that eventually drove them apart.

Harry's enormous income enabled him and Ollie to buy a thousand-acre ranch five miles north of Saugus, not far from the Newhall locations of the Ford-Carey Westerns. The Careys turned their "Harry Carey Rancho" into a

---

3. A rough translation of Janet's ungrammatical French: "What a child I am tonight and I wish to be caressed often; I am sad for the presence of the love of my heart."

profitable tourist attraction during the 1920s, complete with a souvenir shop, tourist cabins, and forty live-in Navajos to make rugs and jewelry and parade around during Wild West shows. Ollie often dressed in Navajo clothes, and she and Harry rode around Hollywood in an open Lincoln town car with a Navajo in the backseat.

Ford, never much of a businessman, grew bitter about the Careys' extravagance and his relative poverty. His habit of arriving late to work in the morning, which Universal chided him about in March 1919, may have been his rebellious way of giving himself a raise. His deal with Universal came up for renewal that September, shortly before he reached what he considered the artistic apogee of the Cheyenne Harry series with *Marked Men*. He had passed up Universal's offer in August to direct an eighteen-part serial called *The Strange Case of Cavendish* for $300 a week, but his salary was doubled to that amount anyway.

Before the end of the year, Universal let Ford make his first film set entirely outside the Western genre, *The Prince of Avenue A*. The star was the former heavyweight boxing champion James J. "Gentleman Jim" Corbett, the dapper Irishman whose life story later was romanticized by Raoul Walsh in the 1942 Errol Flynn movie *Gentleman Jim*. Universal had been talking with Corbett for several months about various projects he might make with Ford before they settled on an ethnic yarn by Charles and Frank Dazey.

A precursor to *The Last Hurrah*, *The Prince of Avenue A* (a lost film) dealt with Irish immigrant politics, although in a more lightly entertaining fashion. Corbett played the title role of Barry O'Connor, the son of a ward boss who also operates a family plumbing business. When Barry falls in love with the snobbish daughter of a wealthy politician, his father's political machinations are thrown into turmoil, but all is resolved in a glorious Irish brawl, with Corbett knocking out his adversaries "as lightly as though they were tenpins," wrote reviewer Marion Russell when the film was released in February 1920. Russell appreciated the film's "splendid characterizations" as well as the "cleverness shown by the director in maintaining the atmosphere of the Lower East Side."

No doubt it was Ford's own upbringing as the son of an Irish immigrant ward boss, living in a house full of Irish plumbers, that gave him such effortless command of the urban working-class milieu. Although he thought Corbett had no acting talent, Ford liked his personality, and the director's class sensitivity allowed him to invest genuine emotion in the formulaic story of a brash, upwardly mobile young mick facing social discrimination. *Exhibitors' Trade Review* praised *The Prince of Avenue A* for its "wealth of human interest, good comedy, [and] a bit of pathos. . . . one can always be sure of clever details when Ford has taken a hand at things."

Having proved his versatility, Jack Ford was beginning to consider leaving the limiting confines of Universal. But he made no rash moves and did not make the mistake of his brother Frank in trying to go independent. From Frank's painful experiences, Jack learned the lesson of working within the system to express himself artistically, of using the system for his own purposes rather than challenging it directly. Compared to the impetuous Frank, Jack was a cautious rebel, befitting the more conservative nature of a younger sibling. Frank's one-word characterization of Jack summed up the differences between them. Jack, he said, was "durable."

Jack signed a new eighteen-month contract with Universal in February 1920. After directing a couple of programmers—a comic melodrama, *The Girl in No. 29,* and a *Cameo Kirby* knockoff about the moral reformation of a southern gambler, *Hitchin' Posts*—he was loaned to the Fox Film Corporation later that year. Although a step above Universal in prestige, William Fox's company similarly catered to a relatively unsophisticated clientele with its staple line of sentimental melodramas and bread-and-butter Westerns. Borrowing Ford from Universal was something of a coup for Fox, which was hoping to lure more ambitious filmmakers to its West Coast lot at 1401 N. Western Avenue in Hollywood. The director was attracted by the prospect of higher production budgets, by the somewhat wider range of material Fox offered him, and, not the least of his concerns, by a higher salary (six hundred dollars a week).

The cowboy actor Buck Jones, a likably unpretentious performer who died heroically rescuing fellow patrons from Boston's disastrous Coconut Grove nightclub fire in 1942, was the star of Ford's first two movies for Fox. The first was a delightful bucolic comedy, *Just Pals* (1920), which was rediscovered along with several other Ford silents in the Fox vaults during the early 1970s. Jones's Bim, the town loafer, befriends a ten-year-old drifter (George E. Stone), and they become unlikely heroes in this modestly engaging film that blends Western motifs with small-town nostalgia redolent of such Griffith films as *True Heart Susie* and *A Romance of Happy Valley*. Ford mischievously appropriated some personality traits of his beloved high school English teacher Lucien Libby for the lazy, amiable Bim.

Though such rustic Americana already seemed anachronistic as the country entered the Roaring Twenties, on one level a film such as *Just Pals* offered Fox's target audience emotional reassurance against changing times. But within that reactionary format, Ford was able to be slyly subversive, directing audience sympathy to two social outcasts, a child and a childlike man, in a fable offering a piquant variation on his "noble outlaw" theme. Ford followed *Just Pals* with an offbeat Western from a script by Jules Furthman, *The Big Punch* (1921), in which Jones played a circuit-riding minister. After being framed by a corrupt sheriff and sent to prison, he returns to clean up the godless town. Some audience members may have recognized themselves in Ford's jabs at small-town hypocrisy and prejudice in those two movies, but he was such a skillful entertainer that he managed to make them enjoy swallowing their pill.

On a trip to California in 1919, Ford's father came out to visit him in Newhall. "I never forget his father," Olive Carey told me almost seventy years later. "I met him just that once. Great big hands his father had, from rowing those lobster boats off the coast of Maine. When he said good-bye, he took Jack's hand and put it in Harry's hand. And put Harry's hand over Jack's hand, and said, 'Take care o' me bye. Take care o' me bye.' Very sentimental."

Perhaps the old man sensed something fading between Jack and Harry and was trying to preserve it. But their partnership was nearing its end. Dan Ford blamed his grandfather's jealousy and competitiveness on his struggle with his newfound success in that rough, transitional period. The demands of success, as Hollywood defined it, caused an "identity crisis" as Ford left behind his ethnic roots while seeing himself in mainstream American terms.

In 1921, Ford returned to Universal to make three last Westerns with Harry Carey, *The Freeze Out, The Wallop,* and *Desperate Trails,* and two starring Hoot Gibson, *Action* and *Sure Fire.* By putting aside his long-festering resentments to work again with Carey, Ford may have been trying to demonstrate that he no longer was so insecure about his status in Hollywood after having proved himself at Fox. And perhaps the three Carey films, particularly the unusually dark and somber *Desperate Trails,* constituted a sentimental gesture toward the friend who had launched his career as a director. Ford made sure he had an escape clause: Fox was offering him a long-term contract. But then something happened that poisoned the relationship between Jack and Harry.

"It was trouble over J. Farrell MacDonald and Joe Harris," Ollie Carey told me, her usual ebullience shading into melancholy. "It was Joe Harris, Harry's pal, who made the trouble. That was when Jack and Harry split, in 1921. I didn't see Jack for a long, long time. He had a chance to go to Fox, and Harry told him to take it."

Harris and MacDonald were members of the Ford Stock Company. Harris, who often played the heavy in Ford's silent Westerns, later became the ranch foreman at the Careys' place near Saugus. Harry Carey Jr. (nicknamed "Dobe," as in "adobe," by his father for his brick red hair) considered Harris "part of the family" and described him as "a health nut, a weight lifter who worked out all the time." According to Ollie and Dobe, Harris began spreading malicious stories about Jack Ford, stories that evidently were filled with insinuations about his sexuality. Ford was distressed that Harry found the stories amusing. This may have been the first time, but it would not be the last, that such gossip was inspired by Ford's sensitivity, his diffidence around women, and his admiration for good-looking he-men. But in Ollie's view, Harris and MacDonald "were just old troublemakers, y'know, nothin' better to do than to dig up trouble. Like witches."

"Joe Harris was a good friend of my dad's, and J. Farrell was very close to Jack Ford, but they were like a couple of old ladies," Dobe said. "I mean, they were straight, but they were gossipmongers. And they started carrying rumors back and forth to Ford about my dad and one thing and another. It started a hostility between Pop and Jack and they drifted apart.

"My dad and Joe Harris would sit at the breakfast table and talk about how Ford loved to cast big muscular guys. I could hear them go on like, 'Psychologically, that was Ford's dream, to look like what he was directing. Ford was a frustrated athlete and wanted to be the Irish brawler, a big rough-and-tumble guy. He wanted to be like Victor McLaglen, but he wasn't, so he created it on the screen.' All this stuff. My mother would come in and say, 'Oh, for Christ's sake, you two old farts sit here and talk.' She'd tell 'em to shut up and get on another subject. But Joe Harris kept that resentment alive with my dad.

"My mother never forgave Joe Harris for that. She'd say, 'He's the son of a bitch that split up Jack and Harry.' I said, 'Well, Mom, a director and an actor can't make pictures together forever. They have to go their separate ways sometime, so it probably was destined anyway.' I think that had more to do with it than what my mother says."

Envy of Ford's growing success and resentment over his perceived abandonment of the old cowboy crowd probably had much to do with the nasty teasing and gossip being spread around Newhall. Harry Carey's box-office appeal had begun to wane even before his breakup with Ford. The gaudier new kind of movie cowboy was in ascendance during the Roaring Twenties, led by Tom Mix, Ken Maynard, and Fred Thomson. Carey's contract was dropped by Universal in 1921, the same year Ford left the studio, and he undoubtedly resented his replacement as Ford's leading man by younger, brawnier, and more handsome actors such as Mix, George O'Brien, and John Wayne.

Dobe thought that when his father poked fun at Ford's "infatuation with muscle" and fondness for displaying those actors' physiques, he was not necessarily implying that Ford had homosexual tendencies. Harry appreciated Ford's sensitive qualities because he himself was "a very gentle guy, a totally un-macho type," his son said. "He wasn't like Mix and those guys who had to fight. But I think Joe Harris would imply it [that Ford was homosexual]." Harris disliked Ford because Harris "was totally humorless. So he didn't understand Jack's humor, and all he saw was Jack's sarcasm and his biting wit. Ford used to rib Joe all the time because he knew he was a perfect put-on."

When Dobe was making *Wagon Master* with Ford in 1949, an incident occurred that revealed how defensive Ford still felt over those ancient insinuations about his masculinity. Veteran actor Russell Simpson, at lunch with Dobe and the rest of the company, started reminiscing about the time in the early 1900s when he saw Harry Carey, then an amateur boxer, win an exhibition against a middleweight champion named Battling Nelson. Carey fought Nelson on the stage of a burlesque house across the street from a theater where he was appearing in his Western play *Montana*. Until Dobe heard Simpson's account, he knew about the fight only from Joe Harris, also an eyewitness. "Russell Simpson said, 'You know, young fellow, I saw your father box Battling Nelson.' And Ford went, *'What?'* Russell Simpson said, 'Harry boxed Battling Nelson.' Ford said, 'Where?' He said, 'St. Louis, at such and such a theater. I was there.' Ford said, 'You *saw* it?' Made him mad! Made Ford madder than a bastard, because *he* didn't box Battling Nelson."

Ironically, the gossip about Jack's masculinity was spread only after he finally, and somewhat precipitously, took the plunge into marriage.

In 1920, Ford arrived late at a St. Patrick's Day dance party held by Irish director Rex Ingram at the Hollywood Hotel. It was there that Ford was introduced to a twenty-eight-year-old divorcée named Mary McBryde Smith. A blue-blooded native of Laurinburg, North Carolina, Mary was a Presbyterian of Scottish and Irish descent. With her long black hair, saucer-shaped and divergent eyes, and a prominent nose framed by an oval face, she had the exotic look of a Black Irish Madonna. She also had a salty, sarcastic wit and a taste for bootleg liquor that matched Ford's own growing fondness for booze during those early days of Prohibition.

Mary had been raised in affluence but had grown up yearning for a fixed sense of home. She was the daughter of a stockbroker, C. E. W. Smith, who moved the family to Madison, New Jersey, in her infancy, when he took a seat on the New York Stock Exchange. He later opened a branch office in Paris. One of twelve children, Mary was raised by a nanny and then shunted among various relatives. She was sent to boarding school in Morristown, New Jersey, where her roommate was Dorothy Parker.

Though Mary and Jack Ford came from much different backgrounds, they shared an ancestral sense of displacement. Like the Irish during the Famine, Mary's forebears had been violently uprooted by tragic historical events. She described her family as "a war-fighting family." Her father came from South Carolina, and both sides of her family were prominent in the Confederacy; one of her ancestors was a member of President Jefferson Davis's war cabinet. The Smiths' plantation was burned during the Civil War by Union army troops led by General William Tecumseh Sherman. After her marriage to

Ford, Mary recalled, "He went down with me to visit my folks, and to my horror told all my family what a nice, kindly old gentleman Sherman was, and I had to sit there and take it!" That Civil War incident, and the hackles it raised between Ford and his wife, found their way into his 1950 cavalry movie *Rio Grande*. Colonel Kirby York (John Wayne) and his southern Irish wife (Maureen O'Hara) suffer a long estrangement after he burns her family's home, Bridesdale, during the Civil War.

After the South's defeat, Mary's family reconciled enough with the winning side to become celebrated in United States military circles. She spent nine months of her youth living near the U.S. Naval Academy at Annapolis with an uncle, Victor Blue, an admiral who served as chief of naval operations; another uncle, Rupert Blue, was the army's surgeon general during World War I. An older relative, John Blue, a Confederate veteran who fought with General Joe Johnston's army, became a state senator and railroad builder in North Carolina. (The Blue family name was bestowed by Ford on Ben Johnson's Travis Blue, the title character in *Wagon Master*.)

Mary's mother, the former Fannie Roper, traced her lineage to Meg Roper, daughter of Sir (later Saint) Thomas More, the English Catholic writer and statesman beheaded by Henry VIII in 1535 for opposing the king's marriage to Anne Boleyn.[4] Having a Catholic martyr in the family tree eventually helped Jack's mother accept the fact that he had married a Protestant. "I thought that was very funny!" said Mary. With her mother's roots in America going back to the early seventeenth century, Mary was a lifelong member of both the Daughters of the American Revolution and the United Daughters of the Confederacy. She was so proud of her family background that she could not resist embellishing it. Before meeting Ford, she changed the Scottish "McBride" in her name to the English-seeming "McBryde" because she thought it classier; her Irish husband always preferred the authentic spelling.

Influenced by her uncle Rupert Blue and by her own fascination with the new field of psychology, Mary was trained for a career as a psychiatric nurse. When the United States entered World War I in April 1917, she wrote her uncle volunteering her services to the army. Although commending her patriotic spirit, he told her that since she had no hospital experience, her services would not be useful in the war. But she persisted: "I was particularly interested because I got to thinking about the boys, and what we were going to do with them . . . not while they were away, but when they came home with the jit-

---

4. In Fred Zinnemann's 1966 film of Robert Bolt's play *A Man for All Seasons*, Paul Scofield plays More and Susannah York is Meg.

ters and the nightmares. How are we going to treat them? Because I had two brothers coming home, so that's how I got interested. And I ended up taking a course at Bellevue Hospital in New York." Mary was accepted for reserve training as an army cadet nurse in 1918, a month before the armistice. She married a soldier during the war, but the marriage fell apart when he returned. Following her graduation from the New Jersey State Hospital's nursing school at Morris Plains in June 1919, Mary went to Los Angeles to be with one of her brothers, who was hospitalized with a war injury.

Mary knew little about the movies when she arrived. "I had never heard about Harry Carey," she admitted, "and he was Jack's close friend, and they were living together. And they couldn't understand that I didn't know who Harry Carey was. It was a different life." Friends in Los Angeles warned her about getting involved with those riffraff in Hollywood. Perhaps she was succumbing to her own rebellious streak when she accepted an invitation from her friend Nan Howard, wife of the director William K. Howard, to the St. Patrick's Day dance. Like all dances held at the Hollywood Hotel, it was strictly chaperoned by the hotel's dowager owner, Mira Hershey. "She had an eagle eye, and there was no drinking at those dances," recalled actress Viola Dana. But Nan and Bill thought Mary might enjoy meeting their bachelor friend, the young Irish-American filmmaker.

At the time, Jack was back in residence at the nearby Virginia Apartments. With his roommate, cowboy actor Hoot Gibson, he was living a raucous, even childish, bachelor existence. Ford "was worse Irish than me," Gibson recalled in a 1958 interview. "That time he wanted to play 'My Wild Irish Rose' on the player piano and I wanted to play something else, I forget what, he picked up the piano stool and broke it on my head. And it was my piano!"

"It wasn't 'My Wild Irish Rose,'" Ford responded, "and there was no choice. He had exactly one roll for that piano—'Dardanella.' He'd sit at that thing playing 'Dardanella' morning, noon and night. Even now . . . anytime I have the black luck to hear 'Dardanella,' I notice my fists are clenched and I'm gritting my teeth. One night I had to get some sleep; I had a tough morning ahead. There he sat, him and his 'Dardanella.' Sure I knocked him off the piano stool and smashed it on his head. And then he came at me with a bottle."

Jack arrived sober and wore a necktie the night he met Mary. He seemed stiff and nervous as they were introduced in the hotel's crystal-chandeliered ballroom. But when they began talking, Mary was captivated by his creative, ambitious personality, and most of all by his wry sense of humor.

"To me, he was the greatest man that ever lived in every way," Mary said in a 1977 interview with film historians Anthony Slide and June Banker, almost four years after Ford's death. "I just thought he was great because he had a wonderful sense of humor; he made me laugh. I'd seen a lot of misery, a lot of unhappiness. I don't know, there was something about him. It certainly wasn't his looks. I just fell in love with him. . . . I wouldn't change a day in my life. Each one has been so perfect. Up in my room, I have a large picture of Jack, and people say to me, 'Why do you sit and look at that?' Because every minute of it was a laugh, something worth having."

With his hunger for respectability, Jack was impressed by Mary's blue-blooded background and her connections with the American establishment, from which he still felt excluded. After they met at the dance, they began seeing each other every day. Jauntily arriving in his latest Stutz convertible, a blue 1919 Speedster, he would pick her up in the evening at the Hancock Park home where she was working as a private nurse and take her on the rounds of restaurants and speakeasies.[5] Prohibition went into effect throughout the United States on January 16, 1920, just two months before they met, but it only seemed to stimulate their mutual thirst. Despite their carousing, they did not sleep together before they were married. But the courtship lasted just four months.

During that time, Ford abruptly stopped corresponding with his former girlfriend, Janet. "What in the world is the matter?" she wrote him from England on June 17. "What dire misfortune has misfallen you? Marriage? Illness? A lost fortune? Wrecked Stutz? What? Or is it that I hurt your Irish feelings. . . . If it's a girl that put a stop to the social correspondence, just write a card . . . and I'll understand." There's no indication in Ford's papers whether he ever sent Janet the news about his impending marriage.

Because Mary was a divorced woman, she and Jack could not be married in the Catholic Church. So they exchanged vows in a civil ceremony at the Los Angeles County Courthouse on July 3, 1920, before a small group of witnesses including Universal executive Irving Thalberg and Nan and Bill Howard. Ford's best man was J. Farrell MacDonald. After leaving the courthouse, the newlyweds stopped at a Western Union office and sent a telegram to Jack's parents, announcing that they had been married by a Father Jackson. But the Feeneys eventually saw through the ruse. Mary recalled their "disgust" when they learned that Jack had been married outside the bounds of his faith.

Jack's willingness to marry a non-Catholic was a surprising departure for him, given his traditional Irish background and his continuing, if imperfect, devotion to Catholicism. But it was a measure of his powerful attraction to

---

5. Coincidentally, she was nursing a relative of Sol Wurtzel, the general manager of Fox's West Coast studios. That may have helped lay the groundwork for the long friendship between Ford and Wurtzel.

Mary and all she represented that he was willing to take that rebellious step. It did not come easy, however. Although Mary eventually converted to Catholicism, the fact that they still could not be married in a Catholic ceremony continued to bother him. After her first husband died, the Fords were married in a Washington, D.C., church in 1941. Mary was not especially happy about having to go through with the ritual, as satisfying as it was to Jack.

"Ford really married above himself," Dan Ford observed to me in 1998. Despite the stark differences in their backgrounds and the many tensions that arose in their marriage, Jack and Mary essentially "were a good match, good for each other," their grandson felt. The couple shared a raucous, bibulous, often profane way of coping with life, and a love-hate attitude toward the movie business. Mary was as shrewd as Jack about the way power operated in Hollywood, and though she was something of a spendthrift, she had more appreciation than he did for money and the status it could bring. Status seeking would prove to have mixed effects on his career, but it was a goal they shared in the 1920s.

Dan Ford wrote in his grandfather's biography that Mary was "unimpressed" by Jack's achievements as a filmmaker: "She regarded his movie career as flashy and 'low Irish' and let him know that she felt it lacked substance." Her attitude intensified Ford's insecurities and eventually made him turn to military life for the social validation they both sought. As the daughter of a navy family, Mary may well have been prouder of her husband's navy accomplishments. Ford himself regarded his navy career as comparable in importance to his work as a director, but his need for military status and social acceptance predated their marriage and stemmed largely from his insecurity over his immigrant background. And Mary's somewhat snobbish attitude toward movies—hardly uncommon in that era—did not blind her to Jack's talent and stature as a filmmaker. Her belief that he was "the greatest man that ever lived, in every way" rested partly on that understanding, even if she needed further validation for their life together.

Their joint ambitions, their deep satisfaction in making a home together, and their alcoholic codependency enabled the Fords' often troubled marriage to endure. Humorist Irvin S. Cobb, author of the Judge Priest stories that served as the basis for two Ford films, dubbed Mary "the lion tamer." Mary explained that "you had to be a lion tamer to live with Mr. Ford. . . . When we had a fight, it was a fight, but not very many, because Jack would go upstairs, and he'd do the worst thing a man could do. He just wouldn't speak to me for two weeks. He wouldn't answer my questions. He'd put cotton in his ears, and he just wouldn't hear me. What's the use of trying to talk to anyone like that?" One time she became so aggravated that she announced she was leaving him. He went outside to the car, started the ignition, and leaned on the horn, calling her bluff.

Torn between home and wandering, like the men in his movies, Ford always displayed ambivalence over his decision to settle down. On his honeymoon, he was already expressing regret over the marriage. Two carloads of friends accompanied the newlyweds to Tijuana over the Fourth of July weekend. The wedding date had been chosen because Ford had the following day off, but did he reflect on the irony that his first full day as a married man was Independence Day? Even before they reached Mexico, the Fords were bickering. The highway was clogged with people returning from San Diego because there were no hotel rooms available on the American side of the border, so Mary suggested they turn back to Los Angeles. Jack angrily insisted they go through with the honeymoon and told Mary that if he had known how irritating she was, he never would have agreed to marry her.

Meeting each other's relatives was somewhat traumatic. When Mary telephoned her father and gaily declared that she had married a man named Sean O'Fienne, the worried stockbroker asked whether her new husband spoke English. Jack managed to assuage that anxiety only to offer his faux pas about General Sherman. Nevertheless, Mary recalled, "Everyone liked Jack from the minute they saw him. But his family objected to me." When the couple arrived in Maine for a two-week visit, Grampy Feeney greeted her warmly, but she felt a certain chill emanating from the rest of the clan: "I was an outsider. I was a Protestant. And I had drawn the pick of the stable." Ford's niece Cecil thought Mary had unrealistic expectations of a more effusive welcome. No doubt there was some wariness on both sides of the cultural divide.

His marriage further alienated Ford from his erstwhile friends in Newhall. "There were a lot of sore heads when Jack married me," Mary said. "He had stepped outside the fold; I was the straw that broke the camel's back." Her explanation of his friends' enmity was rather harsh: she thought they considered Jack their meal ticket and an easy touch for a loan. Perhaps that was her way of acknowledging the role she may have played in Ford's decision to abandon his old working group for "classier" colleagues at other studios. His rough-hewn cowboy gang correctly interpreted his marriage as a sign that Jack was putting on airs. Although Olive Carey was loath to admit it, she took a quick dislike to Mary, and the hostility was reciprocated: Mary thought Ollie looked like a cattle rancher. The first time Mary appeared on the set when Jack was working with Harry, Ollie acted territorial, seeming to resent her presence. Mary thought Ollie was used to running the set and didn't want competition.

Many years later, Mary recalled Jack's saying that "he only married me because I didn't want to get in pictures. . . . I never went on the [studio] stages the whole years I was married. Never went near. That was one of the agree-ments we had. I went on one location, and that was *The Iron Horse*.[6]. . . He said, 'If I were a lawyer, you wouldn't sit in my office. If I were a judge, you wouldn't hear my cases.' He said, 'That's where all the trouble starts.' . . . He'd bring [scripts] home, but he'd never ask me to read them. It was very funny, his work was a closed organization as far as the family was concerned."

Ford compartmentalized his dual lives as a filmmaker and a somewhat inat-tentive family man. Mary made the marriage work by accepting its limitations. Asked by Slide and Banker whether she minded being excluded from Jack's working life, Mary replied, "No, I'd had my feelings hurt when I was first married, so I said, 'That's that!' . . . Wives sitting around the set—you're bound to be an outsider in show business. You can't help it. . . . I was very happy to be what I was, with a lovely home and good friends."

Just before their wedding, Jack and Mary leased their first home, a two-bedroom stucco bungalow at 2253 Beechwood Drive in Hollywood, for $150 a month. Movie people still were not welcome as homeowners in most parts of Los Angeles, but the Fords eventually found a charmingly unpretentious brick house in the Majestic Heights section of Hollywood. Sold to them by Mira Hershey of the Hollywood Hotel, the house at 6860 Odin Street was an English-style cottage surrounded by bushes for privacy, with a long winding stone walkway leading up to the front door. The Fords moved in on October 1, 1920, and it would be their home for the next thirty-two years.

Their first child arrived on April 3, 1921, exactly nine months after the wedding. In a nod to his dual Irish and English lineage, the boy was called Patrick, after Jack's oldest brother, and was given two middle names, Michael and Roper. When he became a father, Ford was nearing the end of shooting on his final silent film with Harry Carey, *Christmas Eve at Pilot Butte.* Although the picture would be released as *Desperate Trails,* Ford always remembered it with nostalgia under the working title it carried when his son was born.

The following month, on May 16, a son was born to Harry and Ollie Carey. Redheaded Harry Carey Jr., who in the fullness of time would himself become a beloved mainstay of the Ford Stock Company, often seemed more like a son to Ford than his own son could ever be. Ford encouraged Dobe to call him "Uncle Jack." He was present at the Carey ranch when Dobe was born, along with another friend of Harry's, the legendary New York mayor James J. Walker.

---

6. Mary visited the Nevada location of *The Iron Horse* to celebrate Jack's thirtieth birthday on February 1, 1924, but he seemed uncomfortable with her there and soon sent her home. She also visited him in 1925 on the Victorville, California, location for his Western *3 Bad Men.*

"According to legend, Ford and my dad got plastered together on the day I was born," Dobe related. "Of course, Ford never could drink. Ford used to get drunk on two or three drinks. My father was a John Wayne type of drinker. He either drank a lot or he didn't drink at all; he held it real well. The day I was born they drank a brand of whiskey called Melwood, so Ford nicknamed me 'Melwood.' He and my dad would kid and Ford would point to me and go, 'Mellllood . . . Mellllood,' like saying 'Melwood' drunk, and he always scared the shit out of me."

After their professional breakup, Harry Carey and Ford went on being friends, but things were never the same between them. Ford cast Harry in only one more film, as the stern but humane prison commandant in *The Prisoner of Shark Island* (1936). Dobe thought one of the reasons Ford didn't hire his father more often was that it would have made the director uncomfortable to have Harry on the set watching him. Ford felt much the same toward Carey as he did toward his brother Francis. He was too conscious of the debt he owed Carey not to feel insecure around him.

"About twice a year, he and my dad would get together," Dobe remembered. "But we'd visit Ford on his boat or at his house, because Joe Harris was living at the ranch with us. My father was never in awe of Ford, except possibly on the set, but never off the set. Because Ford was almost, you might say, his protégé at one time. My dad and he would argue with each other, but it was always about stories. My dad would say, 'No, Jack, you didn't write that story, that was mine.' Ford would say, 'You were drunk!' And they'd argue: 'You were off with so-and-so, bullneckin' and drinkin', and I wrote the goddam script and I remember it.' They'd argue about whose idea it was and who thought up the gag in what film, because they made so many together. And then they'd reminisce: 'Remember when so-and-so and . . .'

"I wish I cared then, but I was a kid. I wish I had sat and listened to it, but Ford was so frightening to me that I didn't want to stay around him. I was always afraid of Ford, because even before he had the patch, he always wore dark glasses and I could never tell whether he was looking at me or not. So I gave him a lot of room. I didn't really know him until after we finished *3 Godfathers*" (in which Ford "introduced" Dobe to movie audiences, although he had already made three other films, including *Red River* for Howard Hawks).

The episode involving Joe Harris, which did not reflect well on anyone involved, always remained a sore point in the Carey household. Ollie had the habit of referring to life "before Harry and Jack split up" and life "after Harry and Jack split up." Although Harry seldom expressed his feelings about Jack, he did so once to Dobe near the end of his life. After working for Elia Kazan in *The Sea of Grass* (1947), Harry told his son, "Jesus, that's the best director I've had since Jack."

Surprised, Dobe responded, "Jack Ford?"

"Yeah, well," his father said, "Ford's the best."

The Little Grey House on the Hill, as Ford called his house on Odin Street, became the anchor of his wandering existence.

In 1926, Jack and Mary sent their friends a lovingly produced Christmas card featuring a color engraving of the house, seen from a low angle at the foot of the stairs, with smoke curling from the chimney. Festooned with a red ribbon, the card contained a printed holiday greeting from Mr. and Mrs. John Ford. They now were the parents of two children; a daughter, Barbara, named after Jack's mother, was born on December 16, 1922. But the drawing inside the card was a dramatic glimpse of Ford standing alone, smoking a pipe in a rugged outdoors pose copied from a photograph taken two years earlier on location for *The Iron Horse*. That peculiar Christmas greeting conveyed more about the Fords' life than they perhaps intended. The little grey house on the hill was Jack's idealized refuge, as beautiful and dreamlike in his mind as a scene from one of his movies. A fire was always waiting for him on the hearth, but the woman who tended it and the children she bore him were nowhere to be seen in the Christmas card. The paterfamilias was off in the wilderness doing what he liked best, making a movie. Ford was devoted to his home, at least in the abstract, but for Mary it truly was the center of her life.

Jack's income rose steadily throughout the 1920s, from $27,200 in 1921 ($18,333 from Universal, $8,867 from Fox) to $37,567 the following year, $69,738 in 1925, and $146,302 in 1929. Partly because it was her role, partly because she enjoyed it, Mary was far more concerned than Jack with the outward trappings of success.

Mary always dressed beautifully, in the latest expensive fashions; the kindest thing one could say about Jack's mode of dress was that it was determinedly casual. She liked to go out on the town, to see and be seen; he hated all that. She held luncheons to court the press on his behalf; he professed to disdain such distasteful necessities, even while spending several thousand dollars a year for a publicist and advertisements in the trade press.

Jack enjoyed driving his fancy peacock-blue Stutz, but Mary preferred to be driven by a black chauffeur, a visible difference in Hollywood status. Mary was always complaining that Jack didn't give her anything at Christmas. So for Christmas 1928, he went to the local Rolls-Royce dealership, dressed like a bum as usual. While he was inspecting a new model, the salesman haughtily demanded to know what he wanted. Ford said he would have a certified check for the $20,110 purchase price sent over immediately by his business manager. Before the car was delivered to Mary, Ford tossed a mink coat in the backseat with a note reading, "This ought to shut you up for twenty years." She did not receive another Christmas present from him for twenty years. Mary always forbade Jack to ride in her Rolls, because he refused to stop smoking his pipe in the car.

If their comfortable but unostentatious house on Odin Street seemed as much symbol as substance to Jack, so too did his marriage offer a stability that often seemed more abstract than real. Even when Ford was at home, he often seemed absent, his mind centered on the next day's shooting or lost in some faraway time and place within the pages of a book. Mary also liked to read books, and her brother Wingate Smith commented, "It's a good thing she does. When Jack goes home every night there isn't much talk." Jack was pleased when Mary went to Hollywood premieres and other social events without him, because it made her happy and kept her off his back. As *Photoplay* magazine observed of Ford in the Roaring Twenties, when Hollywood was becoming notorious for wild parties and other scandals, "His idea of a big evening was not the Coconut Grove [nightclub at Los Angeles's Ambassador Hotel]. If somebody couldn't get up a bridge game, he'd rather sit home reading over new short stories and novels that might develop into good movies."

Mary's best friend was Victoria Forde "Vickie" Mix, the wife of cowboy star Tom Mix. Though no relation to the Fords, Vickie had acted as a child with Francis Ford in some of his earliest silent movies. Jack Ford directed Tom Mix in two run-of-the-mill movies at Fox in 1923, *Three Jumps Ahead* and *North of Hudson Bay*, but left the socializing with the flamboyant, quarrelsome couple largely to Mary. Mary liked to shop and carouse with Vickie, who spent her husband's fortune with abandon.

The Fords' largely separate social worlds intersected only when they threw Sunday afternoon parties in their lushly landscaped four acre garden. Most of the guests were people who worked with Jack at Fox, along with Hoot Gibson and other cowboy actor pals. Even some studio executives were invited, such as Sol Wurtzel of Fox and Universal's "boy wonder" Irving Thalberg, who became production head of the newly formed Metro-Goldwyn-Mayer in 1924. Ford was unusually egalitarian in his array of friends, *Photoplay* observed: "The 'grips' could tell you that he was a heck of a good fellow who directed without temperament, sat in on a bridge or poker game whenever the opportunity presented itself, and while the name of his beautiful wife, Mary, was never off the social sheets, his home was 'open house' to everybody in his company from the star to the prop boy." Mary salted the mixture with navy people she knew from her family connections. Whatever their background, their guests had one thing in common, Mary said: "They were all hard drinkers."

A typical Irish Catholic male of his generation, Jack was more likely to take to bed a bottle of booze than a woman. He seemed to regard sex as something that was not supposed to happen often during marriage, an activity incompatible with the sanctity of motherhood and more suited to actresses or whores. Indeed, by the sexist standards of Hollywood, actresses were regarded as little better than whores. It's unclear exactly when Ford started having extramarital dalliances. But Mary admitted that after a while, one reason she stayed away from his sets was to avoid giving his leading ladies an opportunity to gloat (she mentioned the name of Madeleine Carroll, the cool British blonde who starred for Ford in the 1934 Fox film *The World Moves On*). Jack often seemed to view Mary more as a mother figure and nurse than as a wife, yet when he was off on some distant location, their letters to each other expressed mutual longing and devotion, emotions they may have felt more comfortable expressing from a distance.

During the lengthy shooting of Jack's large-scale silent Western *3 Bad Men* at Victorville in 1925, "They built a whole city out there," recalled Priscilla Bonner, who played the ingenue. "We were all living in very comfortable tents with floors. We all ate together; it was very democratic. Mary Ford came up and it was a family feeling. Mrs. Ford was beautiful. Very Madonna-like, with long black hair parted in the middle, combed straight back, with a little knot in back. She was elegant, charming, very simple, very friendly, outgoing, and devoted to him. He didn't chase women. If there were any, I didn't know. I could only tell you his general reputation—he was not a chaser. He was more fatherly, as far as I could see."

There were enough sparks between Mary and Jack to keep the relationship from ever becoming dull. Mary had her own droll ways of coping with Jack's idiosyncrasies. Her method of waking him in the morning was an especially ingenious form of payback for all he did to torment her. Rather than using dogs to rouse him, as Harry Carey had done in Newhall, she used music. After throwing open the windows, she would play "The Battle Hymn of the Republic" at full volume on the gramophone while Jack grumbled and thrashed beneath his sheets. If several verses went by and he still wouldn't get up, she would switch to bugle calls and then to screeching hillbilly music. His throbbing hangover would become so painful he had no choice but to jump out of bed, cursing her sadism.

From the start of his family life, Ford was a distant father, too preoccupied with his own interests and problems to become deeply involved in the daily lives of his two children. Mary was equally impatient with child rearing, so they left the care of Pat and Barbara largely to a nanny, Maude "Steve" Stevenson, whom the children called "Mama Steve." "When we wanted to be with the children," Mary said, "we got away from Hollywood. Our vacations were away, and we had a [summer] cottage in Maine [on Peaks Island]."

Ford's conflicted attitude toward child raising was revealed when he was interviewed in 1925 by a *Los Angeles Examiner* reporter writing an article on spanking. "I have my problems of discipline," Ford admitted. "My wife and I have found that deprivations of privileges, goodies, and the like is much more effective than the application of the hair brush.

"My father was a good old Irish parent and he believed in registering my aberrations very firmly on my mind through the trousers-seat route, but I forgot the lickin's [sic] ten minutes after I was whaled and was in more mischief. We are raising our youngsters on the same system, and hoping it will be for the best. They are a lively pair, always up to something impish and getting into trouble, but we find to be sent to bed early or to be denied an expected pleasure makes them remember to be good longer than I believe any amount of corporal punishment might."

As Pat was growing up, however, Ford disciplined him more cruelly. A sickly child, Pat never seemed to live up to his father's expectations, and Ford took out his frustrations by beating him with a razor strop. Barbara, on the other hand, was allowed to grow up spoiled and undisciplined; whenever she had a problem at school, Mary would take her side and move her to another school. Ford thought Mary coddled both children too much, but in the view of his niece Cecil de Prida, what Ford took for indulgence actually was Mary's self-centered indifference to her children. Their parents' emotional neglect during those formative years blighted the lives of Pat and Barbara, inflicting psychological wounds that never healed.

"All picture kids are neglected," observed Katherine Cliffton, Ford's long-time research assistant. "Pat was quite a bitter fellow, a rather difficult man. I saw him kiss his father's forehead on occasion, but he told me once that his parents weren't home [in his childhood]. They were a strange family. Barbara was a very shy girl. She had her own problems in life." Cliffton felt that Ford "lived his life on the set. His films *are* his life." In light of Ford's aloofness from Pat and Barbara, it was especially ironic that he encouraged his actors and crew people to call him "Pappy," for they seemed more like real family to him than his own children were.

More and more, drink became Ford's preferred method of escape from his family and everything that seemed intolerable about life when he wasn't working. With rare exceptions, he maintained the self-discipline to avoid drinking while he was directing a film. But once shooting was completed, he had a ritual. He would hand Mary two thousand dollars and tell her to call the bootlegger. If the bootlegger couldn't deliver the full order, Mary's navy friends would come to the rescue by supplying some of the alcohol that was used to power torpedoes. The Fords would use it to mix up batches of "torpedo juice" in their bathtub. Her uncle Bunny, who lived in South Pasadena, would provide them with his highly potent homemade wine. During Prohibition, they kept their booze in a secret compartment behind a sliding door in a den next to the dining room.

Until she developed her own serious drinking problem, Mary tended to imbibe most heavily when Jack was around. She served as what psychologists later would call an alcoholic's "enabler," sharing Jack's bottles and making excuses while he embarked on a prolonged bender. Eventually it would be time for him to start shooting a movie again and he would manage to sober up. Sometimes his drying-out process took place in a hospital. That began happening with increasing regularity as the years went by. Going back to work was the only way Ford knew to keep his self-destructive tendencies under some sort of control.

From time to time, prompted by a wretched sense of guilt, he would take a pledge of abstinence. On April 26, 1923, with his Jesuit parish priest as a witness, he wrote on the stationery of Hollywood's Church of the Blessed Sacrament, "This is to certify that on this date I have firmly resolved to abstain from all alcoholic beverages. Jack Ford." Such vows to reform would inevitably be forgotten in a matter of weeks or even days. But despite his often casual approach to religious observance (he jokingly called his parish "Our Lady of the Cadillacs"), Ford could not escape feeling sinful about his weaknesses. He was locked in a terrible cycle of Irish Catholic self-torment from which he never fully escaped.

He used alcohol as his means of finding oblivion and release from the pressures he felt creating works of art in an often chaotic medium that required millions of dollars and hundreds of people to help him realize his visions. As Frank Capra observed, "A megaphone has been to John Ford what the chisel was to Michelangelo: his life, his passion, his cross." But if his artistry was his cross, it was also his only salvation, enabling him to escape periodically into that better world of beauty and nobility he could conjure up with the power of his imagination.

DIRECTED BY JOHN FORD

There was a young fellow named FORD
Who put all his troupers aboard
He took all those green faces
To God's great OPEN SPACES
To make a big feature—OH LORD.

THE IRON HORSE LOCATION NEWSPAPER,
PUBLISHED ON A TRAIN EN ROUTE TO NEVADA,
DECEMBER 31, 1923

FORD SEEMED TO be foundering throughout much of the 1920s. In his personal life, it was a time of emotional confusion, when he seemed beset by conflicting pressures he barely understood. Creatively, that period was among the most uneven of Ford's career, a time of widely divergent subject matter and sometimes bizarre stylistic experimentation. For all its turmoil, however, it was a creative and necessary process. He was an ambitious man in search of his own identity.

With the rediscovery in recent years of several Ford silent films previously thought lost, some unexpected facets of his developing artistic personality have been revealed. But Andrew Sarris's observation in his seminal 1968 survey *The American Cinema* still seems judicious: "If John Ford had died or retired at the end of 1929, he would have deserved at most a footnote in film history. *The Iron Horse* [1924] and *Four Sons* [1928] attracted some attention in their time . . . [and] Ford's technical competence has been established even at this early stage in his career, but up to 1929 he cannot be considered one of the major artists of the medium. His personal vision has not been developed to the level of a Lubitsch or a Lang at this stage of film history."

After his fertile apprenticeship within a narrow generic range at Universal, the early twenties at Fox saw Ford accepting the role of a complaisant journeyman director, directing a wide variety of mostly impersonal projects undertaken to shore up his standing in the industry. With the collapse of his brother Frank's career serving as a sobering warning of what might happen if he tried to buck the system, Jack was at his most pliable and self-effacing from this period into the early thirties. He was able to make a few films that broke new ground and fired his imagination, and he learned how to imbue even the humblest, most hackneyed script with special qualities of craftsmanship, warmth, and humor. But for the most part, he was out to prove that he was reliable and versatile, a man of all genres who could be handed a script the day before shooting and yet make something slick and professional out of it. He succeeded all too well in those limited ambitions, necessary as they might have been to advance his career.

To reward Ford for signing his long-term contract, Fox offered him a trip overseas. What he secretly had in mind was no vacation, but an extraordinary and dangerous adventure. Before departing, he cranked out a pair of melodramas starring Shirley Mason, *Jackie* (about a Russian ballet dancer in London) and *Little Miss Smiles* (about a Jewish family living in a New York tenement). It's hard to imagine Ford could have done much with such uncongenial material as *Jackie,* but he may have been able to work some of his own complex feelings about the American "melting pot" experience into *Little Miss Smiles.* Despite its hackneyed plot, the film offered "pathos and comedy, realistic people and places," noted *Exhibitors' Trade Review.* But Ford was already becoming impatient with artificial stories, slickly detached craftsmanship, and secondhand emotional experiences.

It was time to rediscover who he really was.

In November 1921, Ford left on a trip to Ireland. It was his first pilgrimage since boyhood to the country he considered his true homeland. Ireland had become a battleground in the intervening years. Ford had missed most of the Irish war for independence, but the momentous historical events taking place in the land of his parents' birth had roused his deepest ethnic allegiances.

The rebellion was sparked by the abortive Easter rising in 1916, the proclamation of an Irish republic, and the subsequent executions of fifteen rebel leaders. The night before his execution, Fenian leader Tom Clarke told his wife that "between this moment and freedom, Ireland will go through hell." Since 1919, the Irish Republican Army, led by their daring commandant, Michael Collins, had been conducting a guerrilla war against the British occupying forces. Collins spearheaded the assassination of British spies and Irish informers while organizing "flying columns" of armed volunteers, groups of twenty or thirty armed men who lived on the run, attacking British soldiers. Among the ways the British retaliated was by unleashing ruthless mercenary units called the "Black and Tans," black-and-khaki-uniformed members of the Royal Irish Constabulary whose tactics included random murder, torture, and burning the homes of IRA sympathizers.

By the time Ford arrived in Ireland, a truce had been in place for four months. Negotiations between the British and the revolutionary Sinn Féin party on an Anglo-Irish treaty were nearing their tragic conclusion in London. The atmosphere in Ireland was charged with tension and uncertainty. Flying columns were hiding in the hills, ready to resume the campaign. Sinn Féin leader Éamon de Valera had put Collins in an almost impossible position at the treaty negotiations; many observers felt that Collins was being set up as a scapegoat to take the blame for accepting British demands that Ireland be partitioned into the Irish Free State and the six northern counties still controlled by the Crown.

Ford's regret at missing the most important event of his generation, the world war, must have increased his determination to witness firsthand at least some of the momentous events taking place in Ireland. As an artist who increasingly felt impelled to understand and interpret great historical upheavals, he knew he would benefit greatly from such an experience. Furthermore, he shared his father's strong republican sympathies in the Irish war for independence.

Before leaving, Jack paid a visit to Maine to seek the blessing of the elderly John Feeney. This meeting of minds and hearts between father and son dissolved the spaces that had grown between them, the geographical and generational barriers that Jack now wanted to bridge. The immigrants' son who had changed his name to achieve success in America was going back to touch the ground where his Feeney ancestors had spent hundreds of years as tenant farmers under British rule. Those Feeneys had never lost their pride or their combativeness. At this moment of uncertainty about his own future and his divided identity as a hyphenated American, Ford wanted to draw inspiration from their example.

He also was going to Ireland on a more practical mission. In a 1936 letter to Irish playwright Sean O'Casey, Ford wrote that he had made the 1921 trip to help his family members in Ireland after receiving reports that they were in political and financial trouble. Following the example of his father, a financial supporter of the IRA, Ford was taking cash to his cousin Martin Feeney and his fellow rebels. Perhaps feeling a bit guilty about his newfound prosperity when others were risking their lives for their homeland, Ford would not be the last Hollywood figure to salve his conscience by contributing money to political revolutionaries. But not many Hollywood people would run the risk of traveling to a war-torn land to do so in person. Telling Mary he was going over to fight, he asked her to go with him, but she didn't take the offer seriously. In any case, she didn't feel she could leave her seven-month-old son with his nanny in Hollywood and her ailing father in New York to go off on an adventure she did not understand.

Evidently confusing the War of Independence with the subsequent Irish civil war, Mary claimed that she did not know what side her husband was on. He talked little about the trip in later years, and, as she told her husband's biographer Andrew Sinclair, "I never asked him about it. It was a sore subject, very secret, and I didn't know the difference between the IRA and my ABC."

Sinclair speculates that because of his "Irish penchant for secrecy and clandestine operation," Ford "may have gone to Ireland to report on the war there for American naval intelligence as well as to help in the struggle himself." However, nothing in Ford's U.S. military records or his correspondence files indicates that he was working for the government by that time or had any official involvement with the navy that early in his life, despite his wife's extensive navy connections. Sinclair, who tends to overestimate the extent of Ford's "other career as a secret intelligence agent," further speculates that Ford may have been a member of the Naval Reserve by 1921. But Ford's military records indicate that he did not receive such a commission until 1934.

And despite Sinclair's claim that Ford "disappeared" from his family "for six months in pursuit of Irish freedom," Ford's passport and other evidence indicate that he could not have been in Ireland for more than four days, and probably for even a shorter time than that. He sailed from New York aboard the SS *Baltic* on November 19, 1921, and arrived in Liverpool on November 28. After a layover, he went on to Ireland, departing from Holyhead in Wales on December 2 on the maiden voyage of an Irish mailboat, the *Cambria*. It arrived at the port of Dun Laoghaire, near Dublin, the following day. By December 7, according to a stamp in his passport, Ford was in France, and before that he had stopped off in London, where he saw several friends. Ford spent the last two weeks of his European trip vacationing in Paris, Marseilles, Nice, Monaco, Germany, and Italy before sailing from Southampton for New York via Cherbourg on December 21, traveling on the RMS *Olympic,* sister ship to the lost *Titanic.* While in New York, he celebrated the New Year's holiday and spent a week directing Mary Carr and Lynn Hammond in a prologue to *Silver Wings,* a Fox melodrama directed by Edwin Carewe.

Not all the funds for the overseas trip came from Ford's own pocket. It was through the largesse of the Fox Film Corporation that he was traveling in luxury in a first-class stateroom costing several hundred dollars a day. In a diary he kept for Mary on the liner heading toward Ireland, Ford expressed gratitude to Fox executive Winfield Sheehan not only for arranging the trip but also for encouraging the ship's personnel to treat him with exceptional care and deference.[1] Ford's awestruck descriptions of his opulent surroundings show no sense of irony over the way he set out on his political mission, only the wide-eyed excitement of someone unaccustomed to wealth and the company of

---

1. As a token of thanks for Fox's generosity, Ford returned to Hollywood with a ten-dollar Republic of Ireland bond certificate for Sol Wurtzel. But Ford evidently never presented the gift, which is preserved among his papers at the University of Indiana's Lilly Library.

high society. Rather than hobnobbing with the moneyed elite, he spent most of his leisure time drinking, chatting, and strolling the deck with a Major Wallace of the Indian army. If they talked about politics, Ford did not record it in his diary.

What he did after arriving in Ireland always remained somewhat mysterious. But a letter Jack wrote Mary after his return to New York shows how deeply moved and politically engaged he was by his experiences in Ireland, brief as they were. She was far more concerned with the fact that he had left her critically short on funds. She became increasingly frantic and even had to hide a new car he had just bought so it wouldn't be repossessed. Her anger at her feckless, globe-trotting husband was compounded when he lectured her from New York about the need for greater economy. To prevent such crises in the future, when Jack returned they hired a business manager, Fred Totman, to begin straightening out their finances.

Although often cryptic and filled with lacunae, Ford's contemporaneous account of his visit to Ireland reads like a treatment for a wonderful John Ford movie, as filled with romantic intrigue as *The Scarlet Pimpernel* but grounded in hard and often bitter reality.

Ford traveled to Dublin on the same boat as Michael Collins, who headed the Irish delegation with Arthur Griffith at the treaty negotiations in London. Collins and Griffith, who had left for Ireland earlier on the same day of December 2, were returning with a draft treaty for consideration by their colleagues in de Valera's cabinet. In his book on Ford, British filmmaker Lindsay Anderson finds it hard to swallow the dramatic historical coincidence of Ford and Collins traveling on the same boat, patronizingly calling it "typical Ford— *poetically true, no doubt.*" But Ford documented the Irish delegates' presence on the boat in his letter to Mary. That letter, which also includes a vivid account of a collision between the *Cambria* and another boat, is supported by the historical record, with one exception. Ford incorrectly reported that Griffith was on the boat with them, when in fact Collins was accompanied by the delegation secretary, writer Erskine Childers, and a third delegate, George Gavan Duffy.

The night was windy and the Irish Sea was heavy when the *Cambria* left Holyhead on December 2. Shortly after midnight, it sighted a schooner, the *James Tyrell,* sailing from Liverpool bound for Bridgewater with a cargo of oil cake. The 3,345-ton mailboat, traveling at a speed of twenty-two knots, was later found remiss for having no lookout posted on its forecastle head. It blew its foghorn but could not avoid hitting the schooner about midships, tearing it in half. Three men from the *James Tyrell* were lost. Ford wrote Mary that the impact of the collision caused the big mailboat to shudder for an hour. They picked up four survivors and circled around looking for bodies, but found none.

The survivors were taken below to first-class compartments on the *Cambria*. According to nautical historians Jim Rees and Liam Charlton, while the men were being cared for, "two well-dressed strangers entered the sick bay. The taller of them approached the beds and passed a few words with the occupants. He asked John Hayes [the schooner's eighteen-year-old engineer] how he felt after the ordeal. John replied that he was fine, but could do with a cigarette. The stranger took twenty Players from his pocket, took one out, placed it in John's mouth and then lit it. He left the packet, which was almost full, and went on to the next bed. When the stranger had passed by, the stewardess asked John if he knew who the big man was. When he said he didn't, she told him it was Michael Collins, on his way back to Dublin from Treaty talks in London."

It's not known whether Ford witnessed that encounter, the likes of which would be seen in many a subsequent Ford movie about sailors and soldiers. Evidently Ford never had his own opportunity to talk with "the Big Fellow" before their boat docked belatedly at Dun Laoghaire at 10:15 A.M. That was unfortunate for cinematic history, for such a meeting might have inspired Ford to make a film about the charismatic rebel. "I was particularly interested in Collins," recalled screenwriter Philip Dunne, who wrote Ford's 1941 film *How Green Was My Valley*. "I told Ford, 'You are the guy who should do the life of Mickey Collins. That's a great movie—especially the fact of who killed him.' He was gunned down by the IRA, by the extremists. Ford seemed excited about it—I'd love to have seen him do Collins." But with its raw exposure of divided Irish loyalties, the subject may have been too sensitive for Ford and the commercial marketplace of his time.[2] Ford would have understood the divided soul of a man who knew he was about to sign his own "death warrant," as Collins said after the treaty was concluded back in London on December 6. The resulting bitterness over what many regarded as a betrayal of the cause of Irish nationalism hurled the country into civil war and led to Collins's assassination in 1922.

Ford's cousin Martin Feeney, who lived on their family's ancient homeland in Spiddal, was a member of an IRA flying column, A Corps, First Battalion of the East Connemara Brigade. It was to Martin and his comrades in Con-

---

2. Later attempts by such filmmakers as John Huston and Michael Cimino to make a film about Collins collapsed for political reasons. Irish director Neil Jordan finally brought the Collins story to the big screen in 1996. Although it powerfully depicts the war for independence, *Michael Collins* oddly fails to show the treaty negotiations and oversimplifies the complex events of the civil war.

nemara that Ford journeyed from Dun Laoghaire to offer his funds and moral support. After safely returning to the United States, Ford related part of what happened next in his tantalizingly brief report to Mary:

"At Galway I got a jaunting-car and rode to Spiddal and had a deuce of a time finding Dad's folks. . . . Spiddal is all shot to pieces. Most of the houses have been burned down by the Black and Tans and all of the young men had been hiding in the hills. As it was during the truce that I was there I was unmolested BUT as Cousin Martin Feeney (Dad's nephew) had been hiding in the Connemara Mountains with the Thornton boys, I naturally was followed about and watched by the B&T fraternity. Tell Dad that the Thornton house is entirely burned down."

In his 1936 letter to O'Casey, Ford elaborated on that account. He wrote that upon arriving in Spiddal, he went directly to the thatched cottage of his cousin Michael Thornton, a country schoolteacher and IRA leader. Ford was astonished to find the Thornton home engulfed in flames.[3] Michael's aged parents were standing in the road in silent anger watching truckloads of Black and Tans leaving the scene. Their son was later imprisoned by the British. Following his release, Michael Thornton worked for the Irish Free State before returning to his profession as a schoolteacher. Ford gave the name of his Thornton cousins to John Wayne's character in *The Quiet Man,* Sean Thornton.

Ford left the smoldering ruins of the Thornton home to go searching for Martin Feeney. According to Dan Ford, Martin recalled that Jack found him in the hills, bringing food and money. During his stay in Galway, Jack was accosted frequently by the Black and Tans and once was "roughed up pretty well," Martin said. Finally, the British authorities deported Ford on a boat for England, threatening him with imprisonment if he came back to Ireland.

Without citing a source, Sinclair writes that Ford "became an occasional contributor and collector of IRA funds during its continuing fight against British control of Northern Ireland." There is nothing in Ford's papers to substantiate that claim, although it would not have been out of character for him, and the IRA has always drawn a large part of its support from American sympathizers. The one record that may offer some indication of a Ford contribution to the IRA is his income tax return for 1921. Ford deducted $4,100 for his "business trip" overseas and an additional $2,700 for "entertaining ex-

---

3. This horrific memory image was echoed in Ford's 1956 Western *The Searchers,* when Ethan Edwards (John Wayne) and Martin Pauley (Jeffrey Hunter) discover their family home burning after an Indian attack. Before the action of *Rio Grande* begins, Wayne's Kirby York has burned his wife's home; in *The Man Who Shot Liberty Valance,* Wayne's Tom Doniphon burns his *own* home. Homes are also destroyed by fire in Ford's *Hangman's House* (taking place in Ireland), *Arrowsmith,* and *Drums Along the Mohawk.* In *The Grapes of Wrath,* farmers' homes are destroyed by Caterpillar tractors sent by the banks.

pense" in connection with that trip and his stay in New York. Those figures seem rather high considering that Fox was footing his travel bill, so it's possible that some of Ford's contribution to Martin Feeney's flying column might have been subsidized inadvertently by the U.S. government as a tax write-off.

Ford was not above some mythic embellishment of his exploits in Ireland. When he visited Dublin in 1964 for preproduction on *Young Cassidy,* a fictionalized account of Sean O'Casey's involvement in the Troubles, Ford stayed at the elegant Shelbourne Hotel. That had been the site of some of the assassinations of British officers and spies by Collins's men on the infamous "Bloody Sunday." Talking about those events with his producer Robert Emmett Ginna Jr., Ford pointed out a room in which two British intelligence officers had been shot, saying, "That's where *we* killed them." If Ginna and readers of Sinclair's book, where the account appeared, were led to believe that Ford actually participated in those killings, they were victims of a bit of Fordian mythmaking, for Bloody Sunday occurred on November 21, 1920, a year before Ford went to Ireland.

Still, most of Ford's account of his exploits was grounded in fact, not legend, and Martin Feeney, for one, never ceased being grateful for his American cousin's support. When a government pension was offered to former members of the old IRA in the early 1950s, Martin made an application, but he had some trouble convincing the government of his service record. So he wrote Ford in 1953, hoping his illustrious cousin would help establish his bona fides: "I had four or five years service in the IRA, so'd be very thankful to you if you write a few lines to Dev [de Valera] or to some of the IRA officers such as Ernie O'Malley or any of them crowd."

Ford dutifully wrote O'Malley, a legendary figure who had been one of Collins's leading organizers and a commandant general in the IRA. The author of a classic 1937 memoir of the conflict, *On Another Man's Wound,* O'Malley had become friendly with Ford over the years and helped him in 1951 by directing background extras for some location scenes in *The Quiet Man.* But O'Malley's response to Ford's letter showed no awareness of any direct involvement by Ford in IRA clandestine activities in 1921 or even of Ford witnessing such activities.

O'Malley explained that "you cannot recommend [Martin Feeney], nor de Valera, nor myself, only such people as have known him in action can write about him. . . . I, who had to be responsible for the greater part of three counties, and at the end of the year more, cannot give evidence about a man whom I consider to be a good man unless I was in control of him in action."

But while Ford most likely was only a casual observer of Martin's flying column during a lull in their activities, it cannot be ruled out entirely that he was directly involved in any IRA action. Certainly he saw and experienced enough of the war's horrors to feel entitled to consider himself Martin's comrade.

When a young British TV journalist, Philip Jenkinson, visited Ford at his home in Los Angeles in 1968 to film an interview for the BBC, Ford gave a typically oblique, perversely Irish, yet unmistakable statement of where his sympathies lay on the still-volatile question of Irish independence from British rule. Jenkinson set him off by asking, "Do you see the systematic destruction of the Red Indian as something inevitable or as a blot on American history?"

"That's a political question," Ford responded. "I don't think that has anything to do with pictures. All I could say was 'no comment.' I wasn't alive then. I had nothing to do with it. My sympathy is all with the Indians. Do you consider the invasion of the Black and Tans in Ireland a blot on English history? Being Irish, it's my prerogative to answer a question with a question. Do you consider that a blot on English history?"

"Some historians would," Jenkinson carefully replied, "but some historians would regard the systematic destruction of the Indian as something terrible."

"I'm not talking about the Indians, I'm talking about the Black and Tans," Ford snapped.

"I don't know enough about it."

"It's the same thing," insisted Ford.

Ford's trip to Ireland in 1921 and his renewed awareness of his Irish heritage "helped resolve the identity crisis" caused by the conflicting demands of career and marriage, Dan Ford wrote. In fact, those conflicts in Ford's character would never be fully resolved. But his fierce pride in his background would provide an anchor for his dual careers in Hollywood and, later, in the navy. Ford's romantic sense of himself as an Irish rebel helped define his individuality despite the many accommodations he made, more or less willingly, to the Hollywood and military establishments. Ireland would also become a recurring setting and subject for his films. During the remainder of the silent era, Ford made two films partially set in Ireland, *The Shamrock Handicap* and *Mother Machree,* and one set almost entirely in that country, *Hangman's House.* Irish-Americans figure prominently in such Ford silents as *The Iron Horse, Kentucky Pride, The Fighting Heart, The Blue Eagle,* and *Riley the Cop.* Later he would deal directly with the Irish Troubles in *The Informer, The Plough and the Stars,* and the "1921" segment of *The Rising of the Moon.*

More generally, Ford's growing sense of his ethnic identity enriched his work by heightening his concentration on the themes of forced emigration, assimilation, family, community, history, and tradition. His films of the 1920s are rife with immigrant characters, not only the Irish but also members of other ethnic groups, including Chinese and Italians *(The Iron Horse)*, Frenchmen and French Canadians *(Cameo Kirby* and *North of Hudson Bay)*, and Germans *(Four Sons* and *Riley the Cop)*. If many of those characters are stereotypical, Ford at least was searching for ways to show how immigrants can be integrated into the mainstream of American life, rather than being ignored or forcibly excluded. Ford's sense of commonality with members of other immigrant groups is humorously expressed by an Italian railroad worker in *The Iron Horse* (Colin Chase) who boasts to J. Farrell MacDonald's Corporal Casey, "Me, I Irish now, too—I marry Nora Hogan!" Gradually, Ford learned how to displace his Irish social and cultural values into other contexts with effortless skill, such as when he drew on his feelings about the famine exodus in making *The Grapes of Wrath*. Enabling him to see his characters in a social and historical context larger than themselves, Ford's broadening compass gradually transformed him from a journeyman director into a major artist with his own distinctive vision of the world.

As brief as it was, Ford's trip to Ireland left a lasting imprint that he might have expressed in the words of Victor McLaglen's exiled Citizen Hogan, leaving Ireland to return to the foreign legion at the end of *Hangman's House:* "I'm going back to the brown desert . . . but I'm taking the green place with me in my heart."

From the stories and songs passed down by his uncle Mike about working on the transcontinental railroad, Ford drew his inspiration for his most ambitious silent film, *The Iron Horse*. A celebration of national unity and particularly of the contributions made by immigrants in conquering the West, this was epic filmmaking on the grandest scale. With the release of his fiftieth film in August 1924, the thirty-year-old Ford achieved what he had been working for, to be in the front ranks of American directors. Yet despite the visual magnificence of its best sequences, *The Iron Horse* too often seems dull and clumsy today. The limitations of its dime-novel plot and Ford's inability to integrate the film's stock characters into all the historical pageantry makes *The Iron Horse* far less engaging than his 1926 silent Western *3 Bad Men,* a splendid but less pretentious film that predictably attracted relatively little critical attention.

Ford's growing need to be taken seriously had become evident by 1923, when he made *Cameo Kirby*. This screen adaptation of the Harry Leon Wilson–Booth Tarkington play about a southern riverboat gambler was the first film for which Ford was given an A-picture budget, enabling him to shoot some lavishly picturesque scenes of life in the antebellum South, including a spectacular steamboat race. *Cameo Kirby* marked the first time Ford's screen credit read "Directed by John Ford," rather than the more casual "Jack Ford."

That was Fox's suggestion, and one can hardly regret the director's assumption of such a perfectly apposite *nom de cinéma*. Yet even the usually dashing John Gilbert was weighed down by the glacial stodginess of *Cameo Kirby,* a warning sign of the lace-curtain pretension Ford sometimes mistook for importance during this wildly uneven period in his career.

As Ford's first full-blown treatment of American history, *The Iron Horse* prefigures the masterpieces of his maturity. With documentary-like vividness, the film, photographed by George Schneiderman, seems to magically transport viewers back into a real time and place in the nation's past. During Nevada location shooting in January and February 1924, Ford and the studio lavished great care and resources on re-creating physical details of railroad building, the westward movement of pioneer communities, clashes with Indians, a cattle drive, a buffalo herd, a saloon gun battle, and other seminal elements of Western mythology. The lovingly crafted pièce de résistance is the ending showing the driving of the "Golden Spike" when the Union Pacific and Central Pacific tracks were joined on May 10, 1869, at Promontory Point, Utah. When Ford filmed the scene at the end of his location shooting on February 10, he framed it as a memory image from American history, with the cast gathered around the trains, posing for a photographer recording the ceremony. Although it was only a re-creation of the actual event, for everyone involved the scene "took on a greater significance than is usually felt during the filming of scenes that are inspired by a lesser theme," reported *Fox Folks Junior,* the company newspaper published daily on location.

The effect of such scenes on the audience was equally powerful. When *The Iron Horse* had its East Coast premiere at New York's Lyric Theatre, the *New York Times* reported, "Gray-haired men, whose fathers had constructed railroads in the pioneer days, were much moved by the spectacle in shadows that passed before their eyes. And some of them wept, not so much at the story . . . as at the sight of the men working with sledge hammers on the spike nails, as tie after tie and rail after rail were laid down."

The Iron Horse proclaimed its meta-Western significance with a title card falsely promising to be "Accurate and faithful in every particular of fact and atmosphere" and with a dedication to Abraham Lincoln, who started the race to build the railroad by signing the Pacific Railroad Act in 1862. A hokey prologue set in 1853 in Springfield, Illinois, shows Lincoln as a middle-aged lawyer (played by Reno justice of the peace Charles Edward Bull) giving his blessing to two children who will grow up to be the film's romantic leads. Ford's use of Lincoln iconography underscores this film's theme that the completion of the vast railroad project pulled together a fractionalized nation of immigrants recently torn by civil war. But foregrounding Lincoln so heavy-handedly was the studio's idea, and it seemed largely an opportunity to confer an official imprimatur on an enterprise that rested somewhat shakily on the flimsiest of melodramatic plots.

The vigor and vitality of the film's action set pieces are continually weighed down by the far-fetched, poorly acted story by Charles Kenyon and John Russell about a railroad scout (George O'Brien) slowly discovering that the Indian who killed his father long ago was actually Deroux (Fred Kohler), the white renegade now trying to divert the railroad onto land that he owns. Besides its sneering villain and blandly amiable hero, *The Iron Horse* is burdened with a simpering heroine, played by Madge Bellamy, whose performance was bad enough before the studio decided to build it up with several ill-matching close-ups. "They stuck in about twelve of these close-ups, but of course it ruined the picture for me," claimed Ford, who actually felt a great sense of nostalgia about the experience of making *The Iron Horse,* if not as much for the picture itself.

From today's perspective, and even from the vantage point of anyone in 1924 who knew more than a little about American history, *The Iron Horse* seems naive in its uncritical glorification of western expansion and the myth of industrial progress. Populists and other antimonopolists had been attacking the corrupt railroad interests for decades, but this movie's villain is narrowly focused on his own personal rather than corporate greed. In exalting a government-supported corporate enterprise built on the backs of workingmen who don't expect much reward for their labors, the film conforms to the ideology of 1920s Republicanism. Although *The Iron Horse* appeared the same year the United States placed severe restrictions on immigration, Ford nevertheless places great emotional emphasis on the sweat and camaraderie of Irish, Italian, and Chinese workers. And he satirizes the tendency of one immigrant group to advance in American society by putting down another immigrant group. When the Italians complain about working conditions, their Irish foreman, Corporal Casey, tries to ingratiate himself with *his* superior by proclaiming, "Say, boss, there's no gettin' on with these furriners—I knocked five of thim down—an' even then they wouldn't work." Ford tried his best to undercut the film's solemnity with frequent low-comedy interludes featuring his "three musketeers," the immigrant railroad workers and former Union army comrades played by J. Farrell MacDonald (Casey), Francis Powers (Sergeant Slattery), and James Welch (Private Schultz). Boldly alternating scenes of comedy and drama would become a Ford trademark, a habit much deplored by critics with limited empathy for his Irish irreverence and little understanding of his Shakespearean method of using comedy as a subversively democratic counterpoint to scenes of tragic nobility.

The only principled opposition shown to the railroad in the film comes from the Native American tribes, who naturally view what they dubbed the "iron horse" as a grave threat to their sovereignty and well-being, although those concerns are never explicitly stated. The Indians are more patronized than demonized. Probably believing that he was displaying an enlightened racial attitude by the standards of his time, Ford portrays them as childlike tools of an evil white man, a noble but simple people inevitably swept away by the forces of "progress."

The director recalled that "we had to spend more and more money, and eventually this simple little story came out as a so-called 'epic,' the biggest picture Fox had ever made. Of course, if they had known what was going to happen, they never would've let us make it." He was being somewhat disingenuous, for the primary reason Fox made *The Iron Horse* was to outdo James Cruze's large-scale Western *The Covered Wagon*, an impressively mounted but even more dramatically ponderous film that became a 1923 box-office sensation.

Ford eagerly responded to the challenge of staging both action scenes and intimate vignettes that offered opportunities for visual poetry reminiscent of the paintings of Frederic Remington and Charles M. Russell. From those Western masters, Ford learned the paradoxical method of capturing the grittiness of frontier life and landscapes in moments of intensely romantic, often statuesque beauty. Both Jack and Francis Ford emulated Remington in their Universal Westerns. Russell, who died in 1926, was a frequent guest at Harry Carey's Rancho, where Jack would have had the opportunity to get to know him. "I like outdoor dramas best," Ford said in a 1925 interview. "On the stage, there is the voice to carry a large share of the drama. In pictures there is no opportunity for the tonal gradations that convey such meaning on the stage. The compensatory thrill comes in what the stage lacks—the 'long shots' that bring in a herd of cattle, massive mountain peaks, a chasm of waterfalls, or a huge mob of men and women."

The wintry conditions Ford and his company encountered on the Nevada location—in and around Dodge Flats, three miles north of the old railroad town of Wadsworth on the Pyramid Indian Reservation—were much like the conditions encountered by the men who built the transcontinental railroad in the 1860s.

Fox placed an ad in the *Nevada State Journal* on January 3 announcing that it was "filming a wonderful picture under the direction of John Ford." The company invited 150 citizens of Reno, including entire families, "to come to Wadsworth Sunday, January 6th, and see how the scenes of a big film are made. Trip will be made by special train leaving Reno 9:00 A.M., remaining during the time the scenes are taken and lunch served which will be furnished by the Wm. Fox Company. . . . This is a chance to learn how a great film is taken and to see yourself as a movie actor. . . . The story being filmed is that of the building of the Central Pacific Railroad, and the Wm. Fox Co. will appreciate the wearing of apparel of the 1868 and 1869 period."

The location shoot filled six weeks of arduous but often exhilarating work in a wide variety of terrain (not including a few days in preproduction, shooting the prologue in the towns of Wadsworth and Dodge). Fox executive Sol Wurtzel, who oversaw *The Iron Horse,* deserves a great deal more credit than Ford ever gave him publicly for letting the director keep going in Nevada as long as he did. After making periodic inspection trips to the location, Wurtzel argued the director's case to the New York front office, which at several points was tempted to order Ford back to Hollywood. At one point, studio chief William Fox ran the footage Ford had shot and decided, "Let them finish it." Ford later blamed Wurtzel for forcing Madge Bellamy's close-ups on him, but by and large, Wurtzel remained a close friend and supporter of Ford's throughout his years at Fox, defending the director's personal and artistic idiosyncrasies and enabling him to make his films with relatively little interference. A measure of Ford's true regard for Wurtzel came when Ford made out his last will and testament in 1927, naming Wurtzel as the guardian of his children and executor of his estate.

Heavy snowfalls caused some of the production delays on *The Iron Horse,* but Ford used them to the picture's advantage. Early in the shooting, after being awakened with a report that it had snowed during the night, Ford asked his cameraman, "What'll we do? We only have four weeks to make it." "There must have been snow when they built the railroad," Schneiderman replied, "so why don't we shoot anyway?"

After seeing the footage in Hollywood, Wurtzel sent Ford a telegram:

RECEIVED FIRST DAYS' WORK OF NORTH PLATTE [the set of the Western town]. STREET LOOKS SPLENDID. SNOW MAKES IT DOUBLY REALISTIC AND ATTRACTIVE. BELIEVE AFTER YOU REVIEW SCENES ON SCREEN YOU WILL FEEL THAT ALL TROUBLE OF PRESENT LOCATION WAS WORTHWHILE.

But one day when a rider delivered a Wurtzel telegram urging him to speed up his shooting pace, Ford made a characteristically theatrical show of defiance. Harold Schuster, a future director who was working on the film as an actor and production assistant, remembered: "Ford looked over towards Pardner Jones, who was about a hundred feet away, and yelled, 'Ed, I have a message right here from Wurtzel. I'm going to fold it up and I want you to shoot a hole right through the name.' He walked out and stood there holding the wire with his right hand. Pardner put the rifle to his shoulder and fired. Ford never moved. He unfolded the paper and held it up for all to see. The bullet had gone right through the name. Everyone cheered and we all went back to work."

The first known instance of Ford being called "Pappy" by his cast and crew was on *The Iron Horse*. Often unshaven, smoking an omnipresent pipe, wearing round glasses, and decked out in boots, winding cloth puttees, woolen or leather coat, and a watch cap or Irish tweed hat, Ford resembled a motley cross between a navy skipper on a distant patrol and an eccentric cavalry officer in the Old West. Alternately shouting orders and cajoling his company with a steady stream of wisecracks and caustic humor, he drew on all his physical resources and filmmaking experience to command two hundred people in what amounted to a massive military operation. When the Paiute Indians who appeared in the film (as Cheyenne and Pawnee and even as Chinese) inducted Ford into their tribe, they named him "Chief Goes Ahead" in admiration of his hard-driving leadership.

Most of the company lived on the unheated, flea-ridden circus train that had transported them from Los Angeles on New Year's Eve. Others camped out inside the sets of the town that did double duty on-screen as North Platte and Cheyenne. When the railroad advances in *The Iron Horse*, the hastily built town is shown being dismantled and moved along with it, including its saloon and gambling hall. "Camp Ford," as the film location encampment was known to "the Ford Pioneer Army," was as raucous an outpost as any that actually existed in the Old West. In the 1960s, Ford thought about writing his own account of the making of *The Iron Horse*, commenting, "My wife says it's more pornographic than even current literature."

According to property master Lefty Hough, the company was well supplied with bootleg liquor and with prostitutes from Reno, who would visit the location every Sunday. For five dollars, a nearby brothel offered not only overnight company but also a bath, a haircut, and laundry service.

Two members of the company were married during location shooting, and two people died. While on a booze run, one of the company bootleggers, himself intoxicated, hit a man and killed him. And on January 25, the manager of the circus train's dining car, a young man named Kelly, died of pneumonia in a Reno hospital. The death of Kelly, an Irish-American U.S. Army veteran of the Great War, roused all of Ford's sentimental instincts. In a scene prefiguring similar rituals in classic Ford movies, the director ordered the company to stand in a memorial tribute that morning as a bugler sounded taps for "Comrade Kelly, who bore the name of a fighting race."

The bugler was a British World War I veteran named Herbert "Limey" Plews, who worked as a property man. Ford had Plews play reveille to wake the company each morning. Recognizing that one of his most important tasks was to keep up discipline and morale on the bleak location, Ford created his own makeshift social institutions. Work-related infractions were lightly punished in "trials" conducted by James Marcus, who played the comical judge in the movie. The money collected in fines went to the Children's Orthopedic Hospital of Hollywood ("HELP THE KIDDIES—Jack Ford"). Ford also organized Sunday football games, with himself as coach and quarterback of "the Ford Terriers," and served as impresario for regular musical and comedy entertainments.

In a train car dubbed "Ford's Theatre," cast members and the company musicians performed for the children's charity. Playing the accordion for those festivities was a bit player named Danny Borzage, brother of Fox director Frank Borzage. Danny's squeezebox would be a fixture on Ford's sets for more than forty years, playing such standards as "Bringing in the Sheaves," "Red River Valley," and "My Darling Clementine." On February 10, the director himself appeared at Ford's Theatre as Casey, the conductor, in "An Old-Fashioned Minstrel" entitled *A Southern Pacific R.R. Romance. Fox Folks Junior* joked that Wurtzel and another Fox executive attended the performance "with a view to signing Jack up as a star who will be featured in picture plays glorifying the railroad conductor and other characters of that calling."

Ford showed formidable self-discipline throughout most of the location shoot, generally blowing off steam with what cast member Francis Powers, in a birthday tribute, called "that sense of humorous deviltry which keeps him utterly human and permits him to express his detestation of all pretense, his utter loathing of the unreal. . . . Could anything be more impressive upon the morale of his racially diversified organization than this exquisite touch of buffoonery? And this is done suddenly in the midst of annoying difficulties when the weight of the nervewracking overhead and the neverending responsibility usually drives the humorless director into the gloom of irritating anxieties."

But all the pressure occasionally made "Pappy" misbehave. "The Ford outfit was the roughest, goddamnedest outfit you ever saw, from the director on downward," recalled Hough. "Ford and his brother, Eddie O'Fearna [the first assistant director], were fighting all the time. . . . I had to break up the fights. When we were doing some of the stuff on the tracks, they got in an argument and O'Fearna went after the Old Man with a pickhandle." That fight was caused by a dangerous Ford prank. After giving actor Justin McCluskey a clay pipe to smoke during the filming of an Indian attack on February 6, Ford quietly ordered Pardner Jones to shoot it out of his mouth. When the pipe shattered, McCluskey was frightened out of his wits, and the outraged O'Fearna charged his brother before being wrestled into submission by Hough.

Jack and Eddie also had a battle royal in the train car where the director and his actors were staying. Their nephew Phil intervened, slugging Eddie, which only had the effect of making Eddie remove his glasses so he could fight better. George O'Brien tried to break up the brawl, but Eddie sent the athletic actor reeling with a ferocious punch. Eddie threw an alarm clock at Jack, barely missing J. Farrell MacDonald, who was also trying to stop the fight. MacDonald hurt himself stepping on broken clock parts and had to hobble around the set for the next three days. No one seemed to remember what the fight was about.

Another time, the company went to Truckee, just over the California border from Reno, to shoot scenes of a locomotive being hauled through a snowy mountain pass. During a break, Ford encountered director A. Edward "Eddie" Sutherland, who was there as an assistant to Charlie Chaplin, preparing the filming of snow scenes for *The Gold Rush*. Ford and Sutherland got wildly drunk and removed all the furniture from the room Chaplin was scheduled to occupy at the Summit Hotel, replacing it with empty liquor bottles. According to Hough, it was rare for Ford to drink on location, and though he had a bad hangover that lasted a couple of days, he did not lose any working time. This may have been the occasion O'Brien recounted to his son, Darcy, when Ford "disappeared on location for several days and was finally found lying in a drunken sleep in a boxcar with several of the Irish extras. 'But he made a great picture,' was Dad's attitude. 'That was just Jack. Who knows? He needed it.'"

Ford's toughness and courage earned the respect of his cast and crew. To obtain several spectacular low-angle shots, he put the camera into a pit and had it covered with planks. A small opening was left for the camera to shoot onrushing horses and buffalo, looking up at their hooves passing just inches away. Ford joined his camera crew in the pit for the filming.

When they shot the buffalo stampede, camera operator Arthur Lund recalled, "There was one moment of danger. The buffalo leading the stampeding herd tripped over a loose plank and crashed to [the] ground. His great strength moved a part of the planking and broke some of the boards on the left end of the pit. A few seconds later another buffalo, stumbling on the planks, plunged headlong into our pit; his great bulk crashed to the floor over our heads and sent a small avalanche of dirt upon us. Ford shouted to me to keep cranking, and my assistant scooped dirt away from the slot before the camera. The buffalo struck the ground with such terrific force that he killed himself.

"Director Ford sustained minor injuries about the hands and face from falling planks. A board also struck me on the back of the head knocking me over but I immediately got up and continued cranking my camera."

For another shot showing a hundred galloping horses during the climactic Indian attack, Ford climbed into the pit with George Schneiderman and camera assistant Burnett Guffey. Rubbing his hands nervously with the filthy handkerchief he always carried while filming, Ford gave Eddie final instructions for the scene. Then he yelled up from the pit, "After the scene, if you don't hear any noise from in here, don't bother to look—just fill it up with dirt."

"Several of the spectators fainted after the scene," the location newspaper reported, "but the intrepid trio came up for air blushing modestly thru their makeup of mud and slush. . . . Jack Ford swallowed two handkerchiefs in the excitement."

Ford skipped the film's world premiere in New York on August 28, 1924, ostentatiously preferring to vacation on Peaks Island in Maine. He explained in a letter to friends in New York, "I'd have to wear clothes if I came to see *The Metallic Mustang*. Here, I wear a shirt and pants. And I fish." He did, however, attend a dinner party thrown for the occasion by William Fox at his Long Island estate, Fox Hall. *The Iron Horse* became a runaway hit, playing for months in New York and eventually returning film rentals to Fox of more than $2 million, on a production outlay of $280,000. Justifying Fox's faith in the suddenly hot young director, the film gave the company a newfound prestige within the industry that helped promote its expansion of studio facilities and theater holdings when it went public with an offering of a million shares of stock in 1925.

Fox went all out with the hoopla when *The Iron Horse* finally had its Los Angeles premiere on February 21, 1925, at Grauman's Egyptian Theater on Hollywood Boulevard. Ford enthusiastically participated in ceremonies that served to cement his stature as a leading American filmmaker. Twenty-five Shoshone and Arapaho Indians "with their squaws and papoose[s]" were escorted from Wyoming for the event by Colonel Tim McCoy, a government agent for Indian affairs who subsequently began his own career as a star of Western movies. The Indians paraded through Hollywood in full tribal regalia before appearing in a stage prologue at the premiere, doing war dances and recreating several scenes from the movie along with other performers. The prologue, titled *The Days of 1863–1869*, played with the film throughout its run at the Egyptian. In the theater's forecourt was displayed the *Collis P. Huntington*, one of the old wood-burning locomotives used to help give *The Iron Horse* its intermittent aura of verisimilitude.

But the most authentically Fordian touch in all the opening festivities was supplied by the director's mother. William Fox graciously invited John and Barbara Feeney down from Portland for the New York premiere at the Lyric Theatre. It was the old Irish couple's first visit to the big city, and they were invited with Jack and Mary to the dinner party at Fox Hall. Grampy Feeney astonished the mogul by downing a tall glass of Jameson's Irish whiskey in a single gulp. When the first course was served, Abby patiently explained to the amused butler that she didn't have to eat the fish because it wasn't Friday. The host would not have been amused by her reason for declining to stay at his home. With stubborn immigrant pride, she told Mary she preferred a hotel to Fox's lavish estate because she didn't want to give Jewish people the idea that she could be won over by such deference.

William Fox showed further kindness by escorting the Feeneys to the Lyric Theatre in the absence of their son. The lobby was decked out with blue and gray silk banners and large portraits of Jack and everyone else of importance connected with the movie. Studying the display, Abby made only one comment to Mr. Fox:

"Where's my Eddie?"

John Ford often declared over the years that he was "not a career man." With that cryptic remark, he apparently meant people to think he never placed the prestige of his own career above his practical interest in keeping his studio bosses happy. But as with most of Ford's public utterances, this one could be taken in two or three different ways. If a "career man" means a director who cares only about budget and box-office considerations, then that hardly describes Ford, for his ambitions were never circumscribed by commercial limitations. Perhaps what Ford, with a slyly Irish sense of irony, meant us to read between the lines was that he *was* a career man, but in the more complex sense of being a director who knew that whatever artistic freedom he enjoyed depended on his reliability in turning out films that pleased the general public as well as pleasing him.

Ford's delicately balanced sense of his role within the Hollywood system helps explain why, after making the biggest movie of his young career, he went back to making little pictures, the kind that have tended to be lost or forgotten. In 1924–26, he followed *The Iron Horse* with a drama about an old sea captain (*Hearts of Oak,* starring Hobart Bosworth); a dawdling comedy about a grizzled layabout (*Lightnin'*, with Jay Hunt); an offbeat mixture of sentiment and comedy, *Kentucky Pride,* told from the viewpoint of a racehorse; two George O'Brien vehicles, a boxing picture (*The Fighting Heart*) and a rural romance (*Thank You*); and *The Shamrock Handicap* with Janet Gaynor, a lushly photographed horse-racing yarn that starts in the Irish countryside and moves to America along with the heroine, her prize filly, and its trainer, the ubiquitous J. Farrell MacDonald.

Unlike his brother Frank, whose directing career was nearing its demise in the same period, Jack knew better than to succumb to the lure of escalating budgets and unrealistic, egotistical demands for unlimited freedom. Jack's bread-and-butter line of Fox silent pictures was not calculated to wow the critics, but it solidified his position in the industry as a busy and reliable director who could handle anything that was tossed at him. Sometimes literally: a script would be tossed on his front porch on Monday morning and he would start directing it the same day. Ford also worked anonymously contributing scenes for other directors' pictures, a common practice in the days of the studio assembly-line system. For Fox's 1922 Roman epic *Nero*,[4] Ford imitated Griffith's Gathering of the Klans sequence from *The Birth of a Nation* and directed battle footage. He also directed some World War I footage for two of the studio's most important silents, Raoul Walsh's *What Price Glory* (1926) and the film that won Frank Borzage the first Academy Award as best director, *Seventh Heaven* (1927).

Even in later years, when his position in Hollywood was far more secure, Ford would follow a similar pattern of alternating his big "prestige" pictures with one or more modestly budgeted "program" pictures. As much as he enjoyed flexing his muscles from time to time on a movie of grand proportions, more of his heart could often be found in one of his little movies, such as *Kentucky Pride*. Released by Fox on September 6, 1925, it survives but is seldom revived today.

With unexpected sweetness and charm, *Kentucky Pride* transposes essential Fordian themes—the breakup of family, the tragedy and glory of obedience to duty, pride in tradition—to the animal world. Treated as an ignominious failure when she trips at the finish line and breaks her leg, Virginia's Future, the horse who serves as the film's protagonist and narrator, is sold into servitude with a junk dealer before being rescued by (who else?) J. Farrell MacDonald. Playing an Irish cop named Donovan who was once the horse's groom, he saves Virginia's Future in a balletic donnybrook and joyously parades her to a racetrack so she can see her daughter become a champion, re-

---

4. The rest of *Nero* was directed by J. Gordon Edwards, who had acted with Francis Ford in a play called *The Modern Lady Godiva*. Edwards was the grandfather of future director Blake Edwards, who played a small role in John Ford's 1945 *They Were Expendable*. Ford's uncredited interpolations in *Nero* confused the *New York Times* reviewer, who noted that "though there are some badly botched pieces of composition in the film, there are also many scenes effectively composed."

deeming the honor of the family line. The horses are played by prominent thoroughbreds of the day, and Ford even gives a cameo to the greatest race-horse of the twenties, Man o' War. A story that could have been insufferably corny in the hands of a journeyman director became genuinely moving through Ford's skillful, crowd-pleasing blend of raucous comedy and straight-forward, unashamed sentiment. The deftness of his craftsmanship in *Kentucky Pride*—the kind of art that conceals art—keeps this unknown gem fresh and exuberant today, while *The Iron Horse,* for all its spectacle, plays more like a museum piece.

When Ford was ready to make another big movie in 1925, he returned to the Western genre. Ford learned a great deal about his craft from the impro-visatory, trial-and-error process of making *The Iron Horse,* and the result was *3 Bad Men,* the silent film pointing most clearly to the strengths of his mature masterpieces. Set in 1877 during a Dakota land rush, *3 Bad Men* gracefully blends the epic with the intimate. This seriocomic tale was adapted by John Stone from a novel by Herman Whittaker, *Over the Border.* Although the di-rector's favorite among his silent work was *Marked Men, 3 Bad Men* contains many thematic similarities to that lost Harry Carey Western, as well as casting MacDonald in another leading role as a kindhearted desert rat. Both stories are centered around three outlaws who redeem themselves by protecting pilgrims (a child in the earlier film, a young woman in the latter) who need their help to reach what *3 Bad Men* explicitly calls "the promised land."

Ford again draws ironic parallels with the Bible story of the Three Wise Men, represented here by MacDonald's Mike Costigan and his pals "Bull" Stanley (Tom Santschi) and "Spade" Allen (Frank Campeau). Not only do they serve as matchmakers for Lee Carleton (Olive Borden) and the Irish im-migrant saddle tramp who loves her, Dan O'Malley (George O'Brien), the three outlaws ultimately sacrifice their lives for the couple and are immortal-ized in the name of their child, Stanley Costigan Allen O'Malley. The film's most moving sequence is the series of farewells among the three outlaws as they prepare to meet their deaths. Ford signals the depth of his emotional identification with these noble outlaws by giving his own youthful nickname of "Bull" to Santschi's incongruously gentle character.

The ostensible celebration of the pioneering spirit in *3 Bad Men* is darkened not only by the necessity of the outlaws' deaths but also by the fact that the promised land itself is morally tainted. The ground reserved for new settlers is former Indian homeland, seized by the white government that conquered the Sioux nation in the aftermath of the Custer massacre. Ford leaves that aspect largely implicit, reserving the role of overt villain for the corrupt sheriff of the town of Custer, Layne Hunter (Lou Tellegen). Like Lee Marvin's Liberty

Valance, Hunter rules a gang of murderous thugs and metes out his version of justice with a bullwhip. With his vampirish makeup and dandyish attire, including a large white hat, Tellegen's Hunter is portrayed by Ford in somewhat tongue-in-cheek fashion, as a satirical exaggeration of iconic Western villainy.

Thanks in large part to the magnificent work of cameraman George Schneiderman, *3 Bad Men* contains some of the most complex compositions of any Ford movie and some of his most virtuosic use of chiaroscuro in black-and-white photography. Yet despite its pictorial sophistication, this picaresque adventure saga always unfolds with effortless naturalness, and the images never come across as mannered or overly studied.

Much of the location shooting was done at Jackson Hole, Wyoming, against the spectacular panorama of the Grand Tetons, the setting for sequences of the outlaws and a pioneer wagon train journeying to the Dakota Badlands. Ford filmed the land rush in California's Mojave Desert, basing it on the biggest Oklahoma land rush, the one in 1893: "We used over two hundred vehicles—stages, Conestoga wagons, buggies, broughams, every blasted vehicle there was—and hundreds of men riding horses, all waiting for the signal to cross over riding like hell." The director sprinkles wonderfully comic touches into the midst of the spectacle, such as shots of a straggler driving a wagon at a snail's pace and another wobbling along on a big-wheeled bicycle while being towed by a horse, holding on to its tail.

And in a (literally) running gag about the reckless process of chronicling contemporary history, Ford shows a newspaperman in a moving wagon cranking out extras on his printing press *from within the actual event*. Ford was discovering how to depict historical events not as static pageantry but as re-created documentary, overflowing with irrepressible, unpredictable energy and drama, and yet also seen intermittently from a contemplative distance. Other films have attempted similarly elaborate land rush sequences, but Ford's direction has never been equaled for its scope, verisimilitude, and sheer cinematic excitement.

One regrettable element in *3 Bad Men* is Ford's staging of a sequence in which a crying baby, left behind in the stampede, is about to be trampled by onrushing horses and wagons. At the last moment, with the nearest horsemen no more than ten yards away, a rider reaches down into the shot and lifts the child to safety. As a piece of action direction this is undeniably exciting, but risking an infant's life for the sake of a cinematic thrill is unconscionable. The stunt could have been faked with the use of process photography, but Ford valued realism over safety in this instance, as he too often did in his early years as a director. As if to justify what he had done, Ford later explained, "[S]everal of the people in the company had been in the actual land rush . . . they'd been kids and rode with their parents—so I talked to them about it. For example, the incident of snatching the baby from under the wheels of a wagon actually happened."

The baby in *3 Bad Men* belonged to a stuntman and his wife. She had been driving a wagon in scenes filmed on that location, a dry lake bed near Victorville. Ford paid her to let him use the baby in the picture while she went into town. He later claimed that he told her what he was planning and that she volunteered her husband as the horseman who snatches the child, a trick the man had performed many times for his own amusement. Prop man Lefty Hough, however, remembered these events differently: No one, including the director, told the mother what was going to happen. Ford positioned the left-handed Hough to double the horseman's arm from the running board of an automobile just outside the shot. As the horseman rode by, Hough was to reach into the frame and scoop up the baby, riding off with it. Hough recalled worrying that some of the stunt riders were so concerned with impressing Ford with their speed that they had little thought of anything in their way. The prop man added that if he had dropped the baby, he was prepared to fall on top of it to protect it from being crushed by the horses and wagons. Luckily for all involved, the shot worked smoothly, and no one wound up dead or in jail.

The aftermath of the filming was traumatic for Ford, helping explain why he did not make another Western for thirteen years. The boom in big-scale Westerns initiated by the success of *The Covered Wagon* already was starting to fade by the time *3 Bad Men* was being edited. After a preview audience reacted badly to the film, Fox made heavy cuts. Released on August 28, 1926, *3 Bad Men* received only middling response from reviewers and the public alike, soon fading into obscurity.

"The picture John Ford made wasn't the one that reached the screen," reported Priscilla Bonner, who plays Millie, the sheriff's innocent fiancée. "I was told that Ford got very angry about what was done to the picture and wanted his name taken off it. I went to the first Hollywood screening and I was astonished: Where was I? I worked on it for months, I got rich, but I wasn't in the picture. I don't think I had more than three scenes, just a good-sized bit. There was one scene in which Lou Tellegen beat me with a large bullwhip, a really brutal scene. It wasn't in the picture." Bonner also recalled that during the filming, Ford had clashed with Sol Wurtzel over the scene of Olive Borden taking a bath in a barrel. Ford played the scene largely for laughs, emphasizing the embarrassed reactions of her male protectors, but "Wurtzel told Ford, 'Keep shooting more of Olive in the barrel.' He didn't. He liked Olive very much, he had nothing against her, but he went for action."

Despite what happened to her role in the cutting room, Bonner had only pleasant memories of the director: "John Ford was a joy to work for. He knew exactly what he wanted and he didn't waste time. I worked mostly by myself and with Lou Tellegen, but Ford was friendly and understanding. He was all for [someone's being] a very natural actor and just feeling. He said, 'The camera photographs your innermost thoughts and picks them up. If you concentrate, the camera can look into your innermost feelings.' His personality was quiet. He chewed a handkerchief all the time; he'd pull it and then he'd chew a little bit longer. I always felt at home with him. Some people you were a little bit afraid of—not John Ford."

F. W. Murnau's 1927 masterpiece *Sunrise: A Song of Two Humans* made an enormous impression on everyone in Hollywood. Ford was so enthusiastic that he went public with his reaction while *Sunrise* was still in postproduction. The first film made in America by the great German expressionist director finished shooting at Fox that February. The same month, en route to visit Murnau in Germany, Ford gave an interview to the *Moving Picture World,* which reported: "After seeing rushes of *Sunrise,* Ford declared that he believed it to be the greatest picture that has been produced. Ford said he doubts whether a greater picture will be made in the next ten years."

Sunrise tells a deceptively simple story of a young rural couple (played by two Ford actors, George O'Brien and Janet Gaynor) whose lives are almost destroyed by the husband's infidelity. It is the way Murnau tells the story visually that makes *Sunrise* such a powerful experience: the hypnotic rhythms of the director's sensuously moving camera, the subtly distorted use of both natural and artificial settings, the complex interplay of light and shade, the stylized acting that makes the characters seem like figures in a fable. *Sunrise* was scandalously absent from the American Film Institute's myopic 1998 list of the "hundred greatest American movies," but it remains one of the most beautiful and profoundly influential films ever made in Hollywood.

The influence of German expressionism on Hollywood crystallized but did not begin with *Sunrise*. Such films as Robert Wiene's nightmarish fantasy *The Cabinet of Dr. Caligari* (1919), Murnau's *Nosferatu* (1922) and *Der Letzte Mann/ The Last Laugh* (1924), E. A. Dupont's *Variety* (1925), and Fritz Lang's *Metropolis* (1926) revolutionized world cinema, and their effects were strongly felt by Hollywood directors, cameramen, and art directors throughout that period. There's no record of Ford watching any of those pictures until after he saw *Sunrise,* but it would be surprising if he hadn't seen *The Last Laugh* when it caused a sensation in Hollywood. That was the film that led to Fox's interest in Murnau, one of two directors considered by the studio in 1925 (the other was Ford) for a project set in the Arctic, *Frozen Justice*. The setting inspired

Murnau to conceive of *Frozen Justice* as a poetic fable of simple folk in visually striking surroundings, much as he later would do with *City Girl* and *Tabu*. But Fox was concerned about letting Murnau shoot for months in such a remote location, away from studio control. The project, which resembled Ford's 1923 film *North of Hudson Bay*, was not filmed until 1929 (by Allan Dwan), and instead Murnau came to Hollywood in July 1926 to make *Sunrise*.

Ford's own ingrained tendency toward visual expressionism was already clear in a rudimentary form as early as 1917, when he used a subjectively distorted point-of-view shot in his first feature, *Straight Shooting*. As his films became increasingly sophisticated over the next few years, he could not have helped being influenced at least indirectly by German expressionism and other trends in European cinema, many of whose leading artists were gradually being lured away to Hollywood. As a visual means of externalizing an inner state, German expressionism caught the tortured zeitgeist of the Weimar period, just as cubism and the stylistic experiments of the literary "lost generation" were expressing the inner turmoil of French and American expatriate artists. By the mid-1920s, the silent art form was reaching such a state of perfection that its greatest practitioners in Hollywood, such as Erich von Stroheim, King Vidor, and Ernst Lubitsch, were seeking ever more elaborate means of visual expression.

Ford worked for most of the twenties in genres that tended to be culturally disreputable and critically neglected, such as Westerns and melodramas, but he showed unmistakable signs of growing ambition by the time he made *The Iron Horse* and *3 Bad Men*. Both films allowed him to expand the visual and emotional range of his developing style, although he still had to remain within the rigorous conventions of a mostly outdoor genre patronized largely by unsophisticated moviegoers. Ford's artistry was becoming more conscious and more insistent, however, as seen in his increasingly intricate employment of lighting effects to create dramatic mood and pictorial beauty. It was becoming harder for him to keep maintaining the facade that he was a simple, unschooled craftsman just doing "a job of work." As anxious as it may have made him feel, it was getting harder for him to deny, most of all to himself, that he was an artist.

Emboldened by the startling example of *Sunrise*, Ford temporarily dropped his facade. Like most other directors on the Fox lot, from the ethereally romantic Frank Borzage to the more hard-edged Raoul Walsh and Howard Hawks, Ford immediately began paying the German master the sincerest form of flattery. Ford's overt, even slavish, Murnau imitation, filmed in 1927 and released early the following year with a musical score and synchronized sound effects, was titled *Four Sons*.

Sumptuously photographed by George Schneiderman and Charles G.

Clarke, with frequent use of the moving camera, *Four Sons* made its stylistic homage to Murnau even more explicit by dealing with the travails of a German family decimated by the horrors of the Great War. Ford considered *Four Sons* the "first really good story" he ever filmed. Philip Klein's screenplay was based on "Grandmother Bernle Learns Her Letters," a 1926 *Saturday Evening Post* story by I. A. R. [Ida Alexa Ross] Wylie about a Bavarian mother (Margaret Mann) who comes to America after three of her sons are killed in combat. The fourth, in a bittersweet irony, survives only because, as an American immigrant, he fights on the other side. Klein drew from an uncredited screen treatment of Wylie's story by Herman Bing, the assistant director of *Sunrise,* and Ford reused the spectacular sets from that film (designed by Rochus Gliese) for his Bavarian village, European battlefield, and New York streets.

Just as Murnau veers from the extremes of slapstick comedy to haunting nocturnal imagery in *Sunrise,* Ford goes from a broadly comedic, operetta-like rendition of village life before the war to a nightmarish, extravagantly stylized scene of death on a fog-shrouded battlefield. Along the way there is a stunning tour de force of the boys of the village marching buoyantly off to war, seen from the premonitory perspective of the anguished Mother Bernle. Ford effectively conveys the poignancy of an ordinary woman being buffeted about by world events beyond her control, but the film's visual extravagance sometimes overwhelms the emotional simplicity of the story, its characteristically Fordian situation of an Old World family being torn apart and reconstituted in a new land. In order to allow the American audience to empathize with the enemy—two years before Lewis Milestone's more dramatically complex film of *All Quiet on the Western Front*—Ford melodramatically portrayed the German officer class as villainous misleaders of the common folk. But the humane impulse behind *Four Sons* still carries considerable emotional weight. A rough-hewn American soldier, played by Jack Pennick in the first of his many Ford films, speaks for the audience when he observes, "I guess those fellows have mothers, too."

Before the start of principal photography, Ford made a pilgrimage to the land of his new master, who reciprocated his admiration. He and Mary left for Germany on the SS *Hamburg* in February 1927. Ford's two-month European trip was financed by Fox so he could shoot location scenes for *Four Sons* in the Bavarian Tyrol, although little, if any, of that material wound up in the completed film. During his month in Berlin, Ford gave himself a crash course in German filmmaking techniques. He screened several of the major German expressionist films and spent time with Murnau, who graciously showed him some of the extensive preproduction designs for his pictures and explained his shooting methods. Jack and Mary also visited France, England, and Ireland, where he filmed steeplechase races for another upcoming Fox film, *Hangman's House*. Before departing London for New York on April 13, Ford attended a luncheon in Murnau's honor.

A sign of Ford's growing need to be taken seriously was a thoughtful article he wrote (perhaps with the help of an uncredited ghostwriter) for the June 10, 1928, *New York Times*. His ruminations on the state of his art form were titled, somewhat incongruously, "Veteran Producer Muses." Ford was only thirty-four at the time, but eleven years' experience as a director qualified him as a veteran in the still-nascent movie business. Describing the "amazing invasion" of foreign "pilgrims" that had taken place in Hollywood, Ford expressed delight that the provincial studio town he had known as a beginner was now a cosmopolitan mecca for the world's top filmmaking talent: "In ten years, Hollywood has become the great mental marketplace of the world." But though many people were describing silent film as the "universal language" and decrying the coming of sound for introducing an overly literal sense of realism, Ford questioned that cliché, in terms that obliquely demonstrated his own preoccupations as a director. "The quality of universality in pictures is in itself a pitfall," he wrote, "for the director who strives too hard to represent humanity by rubbing down the rough edges of racial and personal traits is likely to make his work drab and colorless." Ford expressed his belief that a picture with universal appeal must have strongly individualized characters and that it should be "true to its setting—for instance, that Germany should be represented by the sons, since it is essentially a man's country, but that Ireland, being matriarchal, should be visualized as Mother Machree [a reference to his part-sound feature *Mother Machree*, also a 1928 release]."

Although *Four Sons* remained something of an anomaly in Ford's career, the one time he tried to be someone else, his stylistic experimentation was not just a gesture he had to get out of his system, nor was it the only time he went to such extremes. It was a fruitful way of testing his own uncertain artistic inclinations. In this period of transition, as Hollywood was beginning to venture gingerly into sound and Ford himself was jumping from genre to genre in restless attempts at self-definition, his homegrown piece of expressionism was undertaken with an admirable, if somewhat deluded, lack of restraint. Most strikingly, he abandoned his usual practice of keeping the camera a motionless observer and freed it to prowl around the studio with the flamboyant abandon for which Murnau was celebrated.

Not moving his camera was virtually an article of faith for Ford throughout most of his career. Fellow director Fred Zinnemann recalled that Ford once told him, "You know, you could be a pretty good director if you'd stop fooling around with that boom and quit moving the camera so much." When I asked Ford when he thought the camera should be moved, he replied with stubborn simplicity, "When there's a cause for it." But he told me the reason he did *not* like to move the camera: "because it throws the audience off. It says, 'This is a motion picture. This isn't real.' I like to have the audience feel that this is the real thing. I don't like to have the audience interested in the camera. The camera movement disturbs them."

After seeing Ford's 1935 film *The Informer,* the great French director Jean Renoir said, "I learned so much today. I learned how not to move my camera."

Even before making *Four Sons,* Ford had experimented with flamboyantly moving his camera, as in his dynamic, fast-paced tracking shots of Indians on horseback attacking a train in *The Iron Horse* or his slowly moving shots from trains showing crowds of railroad workers and townspeople. But the difference between his tracking shots in *The Iron Horse* and those in *Four Sons* was that there was a "cause" for the camera movements in the Western. The audience knew—could see—that the camera's perspective was simply that of the moving train. There was nothing self-conscious or "arty" about such "invisible" storytelling, the kind that, with rare exceptions, tended to be the preferred mode of visual narrative throughout the history of the Hollywood studio system.

Ford did not feel empowered to challenge that system, to break down that invisible wall, until Murnau received such rapturous acclaim from reviewers for *Sunrise,* which was also a popular success of highly respectable proportions. Fox was then in the midst of an ambitious program of expansion, acquiring hundreds of theaters and upgrading its facilities. Anxious to upgrade its product accordingly, Fox could afford to use its profits from Tom Mix pictures and other programmers not only to become Murnau's patron but also to encourage forays by Ford and other American directors into cinematic high culture. Like the rest of Hollywood, Fox was facing a serious rival in the new medium of radio, as well as preparing halfheartedly for the coming upheavals of talking pictures. Innovation not only was allowed, it was inevitable during this tumultous period, which saw the last poignant efflorescence of an art form on the verge of extinction.

Four Sons was well received by reviewers (*Photoplay* named it the best picture of 1928), and Fox proclaimed it the studio's "Biggest Success in [the] Last Ten Years." Ford's next movie, *Hangman's House* (also a 1928 release), adapted the brooding Murnau manner to an Irish setting, although in a more restrained fashion (fewer tracking shots). This convoluted, lugubrious tale of a fugitive IRA man (Victor McLaglen) returning to kill the blackguard (Earle Foxe) responsible for his sister's death seems more Germanic than Irish in its heavy-handed sense of determinism. But in contrast with the fluffy romanticism of *The Shamrock Handicap* and the fantastic unreality of *Mother Machree,* the fog- and doom-shrouded atmosphere of *Hangman's House* allows Ford to discover greater depth in his mythopoetic view of Ireland. McLaglen's Citizen Hogan is a hopeless outcast in a society torn by the evils of colonialism, the tragedy of civil war, and the pervasive treachery of informing.

In the final shot of the movie, after Hogan has served as matchmaker for a young couple, he watches longingly as they depart, and we realize that he has been secretly in love with the woman, the aristocratic Connaught O'Brien (June Collyer). This moving frisson comes as a complete surprise. It's an open question whether it would have been more or less powerful if Ford had better prepared the viewer for the revelation. The ending of *Hangman's House* nevertheless carries a mystery similar to the famous final shot of *The Searchers,* which has John Wayne unexpectedly, but inevitably, turning away from the family he has reunited.

Hangman's House did not repeat the commercial success of *Four Sons,* but Alfred Rushford Grearson of *Variety* praised it for "some of the most striking touches of composition seen on the screen since those swampland shots in *Sunrise,* which they often resemble." The reviewer added, "For once here is an Irish picture play that should please the Irish. . . . It doesn't on the one hand travesty the Celt, and it doesn't go out of its way to pat him on the back, two attitudes that have done a good deal to justify Irishmen's bitter objections to stage and screen representations of himself [*sic*] and his people."

Hangman's House* is also noteworthy for a sign of greater things to come: the first appearance in a Ford movie of the young man who would become his most important star, John Wayne. A twenty-one-year-old prelaw student and football player at the University of Southern California, Marion "Duke" Morrison had been an extra and bit player in several other movies and was working at Fox as a propman during summer vacations. Unbilled in *Hangman's House,* Morrison is first seen in a fantasy sequence as a man about to be hanged, then shows up again as a spectator at a horse race who becomes so excited that he breaks down a picket fence.

Morrison began working at Fox in the summer before his sophomore year of 1926, lugging around furniture and other props and serving as a general handyman for such directors as Raoul Walsh and Frank Borzage. He soon caught the eye of Ford.

Tall, ruggedly handsome, and incongruously graceful for a football lineman, Morrison struck the kind of effortlessly impressive male figure that the former "Bull" Feeney wished he could have been. Ford found his physical ideal in the Duke, his cinematic equivalent of Michelangelo's David. So, naturally, Ford had to mask his true feelings and all they might have implied by playing the tough guy and cruelly tormenting the young man. An avid fan of USC football and a friend of the team's coach, Howard Jones, Ford encountered Duke working on a set and immediately put him through a macho hazing ritual.

"You one of Howard Jones's bright boys?" the director asked. "Let's see you get down in position."

As Duke assumed a tackle's three-point stance, Ford suddenly kicked his hand, knocking him into the dirt. "And you call yourself a football player," the director sneered. "I'll bet you couldn't even take me out."

Wayne recalled what happened next: "So, not being interested in a motion picture career at that time, I said, 'Let's try it again.'" When Ford assumed his position, Wayne "kicked him and hit him in the chest. He looked up with a little surprise and there was a deadly silence. And right then was the deciding point in my career in motion pictures."

Ford finally said they should get back to work: "That's enough of this bullshit."

The director hired Morrison as a propman on *Mother Machree* and *Four Sons*. Ford later recalled, "I could see that here was a boy who was working for something—not like most of the other guys, just hanging around to pick up a few fast bucks. Duke was really ambitious and willing to work. Inside of a month or six weeks we were fast friends, and I used to advise him and throw him a bit part now and then."

By then Morrison "wanted to be a director, and naturally I studied Ford like a hawk. . . . He kept his distance from everybody—and yet he had a way of talking to you that made you feel he understood you and your problems. He was the first person who ever made me want to be a person—who gave me a vision of a fully rounded human being."

CHAPTER SIX

"WITHOUT A HARBOR, MAN IS LOST"

Q: What do you think of talk in pictures?
A: Oh, it's necessary. I mean, people expect it now.

FORD, INTERVIEWED BY PETER BOGDANOVICH IN
THE 1971 FILM *DIRECTED BY JOHN FORD*

FORD REMEMBERED THE coming of sound as "a time of near panic in Hollywood." But he was not among the many who panicked. Contrary to his
self-perpetuated image as an aesthetic reactionary who made a grudging transition to talkies, Ford actually welcomed the opportunity to combine pictures
with what he called "auditory imagery." While most people in Hollywood
feared they could not cope with the new medium and mourned the imminent
passing of silent pictures, Ford proclaimed in his 1928 *New York Times* article
that "the pictures are just now on the threshold of one of their most important developments, the use of sound as well as of sight images." Although it
would take him a few years to hit his stride in talking pictures, Ford foresaw
with rare prescience that sound would enable him to assert complete mastery
over his medium. Among the "artistic possibilities" he anticipated with the
coming of sound was "the chance to project symphonic qualities for the creation and holding of a mood, so that pictures will no longer be limited to pure
and simple narrative for material."

Ford always considered himself "a man of the silent cinema," but it's important to remember that silent pictures were never truly silent. They always
were shown in conjunction with music from a piano or orchestra. But the
choice and application of music was largely out of the hands of the filmmaker.
When talking pictures arrived, Ford finally was able to control every aspect of
his medium. Rather than allowing the technical restrictions of the early talking pictures to overwhelm him, Ford took them as a challenge. His pictorial
imagery acquired a greater poetic resonance when orchestrated in combina-

tion with all the tools of dialogue, sound effects, and music. Coincidentally or not, this enrichment of his art came at a time when he was more conscious and insistent about his artistry than ever before. His thoughtful piece about the past, present, and future of the medium for the *New York Times* proclaimed his ambitiousness to the world—even if, in later years, he would revert to his old laconic pose of just doing "a job of work."

In *Directed by John Ford,* Ford assured Bogdanovich that talk helps a movie "[a]s long as the dialogue is crisp and cryptic and as long as they're not long soliloquies. Oh, I like talking pictures. They're much easier to make than silent pictures. I mean, silent pictures were hard work. . . . [It was] very difficult to get a point over. You had to move the camera around so much." Liberating his visual storytelling from the interruptions of written title cards allowed Ford's narrative sequences to flow more freely and naturally. And unlike Murnau, whose extremely stylized treatment of reality reached its fullest expression in pantomime, Ford's more supple interplay between reality and stylization benefited from having an auditory sense. That is one reason why, as Welles put it, Ford's films seem to "live and breathe in a real world," even if they seem to be "written by Mother Machree." In fact, the dialogue in Ford's films is one of the most underrated aspects of his work. While it may occasionally be corny and overripe, it's more often rich, colorful, suggestive, musical, and loaded with invention, a by-product of what Lee Lourdeaux calls Ford's "fine Irish ear for the spoken word."

Ford wrote an article for the *Film Daily* in June 1927 about how he planned to use music in his film *Mother Machree,* originally shot as a silent. Unfortunately, only about twenty-five minutes survives of this delightfully stylized 1928 sentimental comedy about an Irish woman, Ellen McHugh (Belle Bennett), who has a series of fairy-tale-like misadventures on her way to being reunited with her son in New York. She encounters such outlandish characters as Terence O'Dowd, the Giant of Kilkenny (Victor McLaglen); Pips, the Dwarf of Munster (William Platt); and the Harper of Wexford (Ted McNamara), of whom O'Dowd says, "'Tis a queer face he has, but music in his soul." Ellen has to display herself in a New York circus and carnival as a "half-woman," a degrading experience symbolizing the schizoid role of the immigrant. Explaining that he came to America because "[t]he bottom dropped out of the giant business in Ireland," O'Dowd picks up a flowerpot in her small furnished room, sniffs some shamrocks, and looks up to heaven, saying wistfully, "The blessed shamrock! There's many a mile of black water 'twixt us and the place where it grew! Sure, the Irish have the pleasantest land in the world and they do be always leaving it." But since his body is covered with tattoos of snakes, he adds, "I never can go back to Ireland now!"

Mother Machree was filmed in late 1926 but not released until January 1928 because of its retooling for sound, which included the addition of a synchronized musical track and sound effects and the on-screen singing of the title song by lyricist Rida Johnson Young and composers Chauncey Olcott and Ernest R. Ball. Demonstrating his already highly sophisticated understanding of how music could work in tandem with pictures, Ford wrote with enthusiasm: "There is a wealth of [musical] material from which to draw. There is the song itself—'Mother Machree.' The earlier sequences are laid in Ireland, along the seacoast. This, alone, presents a veritable mine of Irish folk-songs, heartstirring with their tuneful melodies and their fascinating romance.

"And, as the action shifts to America, with the swiftly-moving activities into which the whole cast is plunged, there is ample opportunity to further enhance the character values in the new environment through what I like to think of as the 'folk-songs' of our country—as well as the unforgettable wartime ballads and marching songs."

What Ford took from his unrestrained forays into expressionism during the late silent period was a heightened form of storytelling that served to expand his stylistic dexterity and allow him a richer range of emotional expression. Tag Gallagher points out that after his exposure to Murnau's influence, Ford discovered new ways of "articulating emotions and moods and states of the soul. . . . Ford found cinema could be completely poeticized."

As Ford's style matured in the 1930s, his "expressionist temptation" became more subtly ingrained in his work. To convey the German mother's heartbreak in *Four Sons* after her sons have left home to be killed in battle or to find a new life in America, Ford dissolves ghostly images of the boys over the empty places at her dinner table. With simpler, more naturalistic means in his 1941 film *How Green Was My Valley*, Ford achieves a more devastating effect by using space, silence, and minimal sound effects and dialogue. After his older brothers leave home in rebellion, Huw (Roddy McDowall) and his grieving father (Donald Crisp) sit wordlessly at opposite ends of a long and otherwise empty dinner table. Huw finally bangs his utensils on the table to draw attention, and his father says softly, "Yes, my son. I know you are there." The comparison between these two scenes demonstrates how much subtler Ford became when he could work with a combination of auditory and pictorial imagery.

Bold and adventurous by nature, and never one to be fazed by the timidity of executives and technicians, Ford nevertheless might not have been quite so sanguine about sound if he had not been working at Fox during that chaotic transitional period. Most Hollywood studios took a cautious, wait-and-see approach to the novelty of sound until Warner Bros. dramatically demonstrated its appeal with the part-talking, part-singing Al Jolson movie *The Jazz Singer* in October 1927. Of all the majors, Fox was closest behind Warners in developing the new medium. William Fox's ambitious expansion plan for his studio, bankrolled by a $6 million stock offering in 1925, not only included larger budgets for feature films, construction of new production facilities in both Hollywood and New York, and a major expansion of its theater chain. Most importantly from the perspective of film history, Fox's expansion plans also included the development of the Movietone sound system.

The Warner Bros. Vitaphone system used a phonograph record to play the sound track, drastically limiting its reliability and quality. The Movietone system, on the other hand, recorded and played sound directly on film. In September 1927, *Sunrise* became the first Fox feature released with a synchronized musical track, as Warners had done the previous year with *Don Juan.* After testing the use of live sound recording in vaudeville shorts and in its popular Fox Movietone newsreels, the studio began incorporating songs and dialogue into its feature films by the beginning of 1928. That May, Fox announced that all its upcoming films would be "Movietoned." Warners, Paramount, and MGM managed to convert to all-talking features before Fox did so in January 1929, but Fox's enthusiastic commitment to sound helped make it flush with profits in 1928–29, vaulting the studio to a financial position in the industry second only to that of Loews, the parent company of MGM.

Fox's financial boom encouraged the artistic experimentation by such directors as Murnau and Ford. Silent-film historian William K. Everson credits the suppleness of Movietone sound with enabling them to move their cameras so freely in the early part-silent, part-sound hybrids. Following his baptism into synchronized sound with *Mother Machree,* Ford continued his exploration of the new medium in *Four Sons,* released the following month, February 1928. *Four Sons* similarly contains a song and a score, while adding the evocative use of a single repeated word of dialogue. Faintly calling out "Mutterchen!" (German for "Little Mother" or "Mama!"), a dying German soldier (George Meeker) is comforted on the foggy European battlefield by his own brother, the immigrant soldier in the American army (James Hall). The devastating emotional effect of that scene was part of the reason *Four Sons* became an enormous hit.

Even after directing his first all-talking picture that September, *Napoleon's Barber,* Ford made two additional "silent" features. *Riley the Cop* (1928) stars J. Farrell MacDonald as a warmhearted Irish-American cop who has never made an arrest in his twenty years on the New York City police force. The opening title gives Riley's philosophy: "YOU CAN TELL A GOOD COP BY THE ARRESTS HE DOESN'T MAKE." Like so many other Irish immigrants, Riley earns respect in his adopted land by wearing a uniform, but he serves as more of a fatherly figure in his multiethnic neighborhood. While tracking a fugitive to Germany, Riley not only manages to clear the young man but also falls in love with a spirited fräulein charmingly played by Louise Fazenda. This delightful, virtually plotless comedy points forward to the relaxed, character-based style of Ford's later work. In a similar vein, *Strong Boy* (1929) cast Victor McLaglen in the title role of a seemingly brutish railway freight handler who reveals his tender side and unexpectedly becomes a hero. Both films have musical accompaniment and synchronized sound effects. It was not until the 1930s that all the nation's theaters were fully converted to sound, an expensive process that put Hollywood more deeply under the control of eastern banks.

The thirty-two-minute featurette *Napoleon's Barber,* a lost film, was based on a play by Arthur Caesar about an anarchistic French barber (Frank Reicher) who gives a shave to Napoleon (Otto Matiesen) on his way to Waterloo. Pontificating in verse about what he would do to Napoleon if he had him in his chair, the barber only belatedly realizes the identity of his customer, who stalks out saying he can stand a bad barber and a revolutionist but cannot tolerate bad poetry. This divertissement premiered in November 1928 at Fox's New York showcase, the Roxy Theater, on a program of all-talking shorts and was commended by *Variety* reviewer Sidne Silverman for its "splendid" production values. Ford later boasted about how he successfully battled sound technicians to let him take cameras and microphones outdoors to film two sequences of Napoleon conversing with his officers and with the barber's young son (Philippe de Lacy). The director was particularly proud of the sound effect of Josephine's coach clattering across a bridge. The *New York Times* thought *Napoleon's Barber* "may win converts for this new type of entertainment."

Ford's first all-talking feature was more problematical. *The Black Watch* (1929), an adaptation of Talbot Mundy's novel *King of the Khyber Rifles,* stars Victor McLaglen as a British army officer undertaking a secret mission in India in the early days of World War I. Ford's virtuosic direction of the battle sequences, featuring elaborate use of backlighting by the master cinematographer Joseph H. August and a complex orchestration of montage and music, harked back to the derring-do heroics of Francis Ford's 1915 silent feature *The Campbells Are Coming.* Jack made *The Black Watch* as a part-talkie, but after he finished his work on it, Fox general manager Winfield Sheehan hired British cast member Lumsden Hare to direct some additional talking sequences. They included unintentionally comical love scenes with McLaglen and Myrna Loy as Princess Yasmani. Ford thought Hare's scenes were "really horrible—long, talky things, had nothing to do with the story—and completely screwed it up. I wanted to vomit when I saw them."

Hare received a "staged by" credit for his interpolations on *The Black Watch*. Some reviewers didn't know where to lay the blame, thinking Ford was another silent-movie director who had trouble handling dialogue scenes. The same credit was given to Ford's codirector Andrew Bennison on the 1930 gangster film *Born Reckless,* whose dialogue scenes are so wooden and tedious they make the entire film seem comatose. *Born Reckless* is perhaps the least competently directed film to bear Ford's name; it's hard to spot much in it that looks like his style. Two or three more turkeys like these and his career would have been in grave trouble.

The best way to break free of studio control was to go as far away from Hollywood as possible. Making a talkie on a distant location was still considered avant-garde when Ford filmed *Salute* in the spring of 1929 on location at the U.S. Naval Academy in Annapolis, Maryland.

The story was a forgettable bit of piffle about interservice football and romantic rivalry, adapted for the screen by James Kevin McGuinness, a professional Irishman who had helped write *Strong Boy* and *The Black Watch*. With their shared interests in booze and Irish Catholicism, Ford and McGuinness became close friends; they called each other "Sean" and "Seamus." What made *Salute* such a refreshing departure was not its formulaic story but its authentic, spacious look in an era when most films were burdened with cramped artificiality. Ford liberated Joe August's camera for an abundance of atmospheric outdoor scenes on the academy grounds and a vigorously filmed Army-Navy football game.

For football doubles and bit players, Ford took along twenty-five members of the USC Trojans, who had crowned an undefeated season by winning the Rose Bowl. They were recruited by ex-teammate Duke Morrison, who had dropped out of the university in 1927 to work full-time for Ford as a propman. Among the Trojans was a brash, thick-faced lug named Wardell "Ward" Bond, who bulled his way onto the train leaving Los Angeles for the location shoot. With his outrageous crudity, Bond quickly earned his place in Ford's heart as his favorite all-purpose character actor and whipping boy.

"Who's that great big ugly guy?" Ford asked when he first spotted Bond. The director later sketched Bond as a lascivious gorilla in a droll series of caricatures (published in Dan Ford's *Pappy*). Ford noted that Bond was "very unsophisticated, but he wanted to be a man of the world."

Ford was more amused than indignant over Bond's insensitive behavior during the making of *Salute,* such as the time he barged into the director's hotel room and appropriated twenty dollars from his dresser for drinking money. Bond never seemed to mind Ford's incessant jibes, practical jokes, and assorted humiliations, because he relished all the attention the director lavished on him. "Let's face it, Bond is a shit," Ford would say. "But he's my favorite shit!"

According to John Wayne's biographers Randy Roberts and James S. Olson, "Soon after the cast and crew arrived in Annapolis, Ford took up with a local, redheaded groupie who wanted to become an actress. . . . Oblivious to the fact that Ford was sleeping with the woman, Bond made one of his trademark passes—sneaking up behind her, sticking his tongue into her ear, and then, with the formalities over, introducing himself. She pirouetted quickly, French-kissed him on the spot, and jumped from Ford's bed to Bond's. In a lusty mood that night, Ford unsuccessfully tried to locate her, asking Wayne and several other crew members if they had seen the young woman. The next morning, when Duke saw her stumble out of Bond's hotel room, he burst in and confronted a smiling Bond: 'Jesus Christ, Ward,' Duke boomed. 'Don't you know she's Ford's girl? The old man's gonna fire you.' Bond did not give Ford a chance. Scared and chagrined, he packed his bags, hitchhiked into Baltimore, and boarded a westbound B & O train. A few hours later, when Ford learned why Bond had missed his scene, He told Wayne: 'Get over to Western Union and wire that dumb, ugly son of a bitch to get his big ass back here.' Bond got the wire in Pittsburgh. The next morning, he was back on the set—smiling."

When Fox contract player Stepin Fetchit arrived on location for his role in the movie, Ford made a pointed gesture of kinship that forever endeared him to the black comedian, who considered Ford "one of the greatest men who ever lived. . . . [H]e was staying in the commandant's house during that picture, and he had me stay in the guest house. At *Annapolis!*" Ford assigned Duke Morrison to serve as Stepin Fetchit's dresser.

Ford's typically sly and convoluted satire of racial stereotyping shaped the comedian's character in the film, a servant named Smoke Screen, who decks himself out in the admiral's dress uniform and tells his young master, the midshipman Paul (William Janney), "I'se your Mammy!" For nearly a quarter of a century, Ford employed Stepin Fetchit (the stage name of Lincoln Perry) to ridicule and subvert the conventions of American racism. For this both men have been maligned by humorless critics who fail to understand what the African-American film historian Albert Johnson observed in 1971, that "cooler second sight must admit that Stepin Fetchit was an artist, and that his art consisted precisely in mocking and caricaturing the white man's vision of the black: his sly contortions, his surly and exaggerated subservience, can now be seen as a secret weapon in the long racial struggle."

Ford always had warm memories of filming at Annapolis, not only because it gave him time to forge lasting friendships with Duke, Ward, and Stepin Fetchit, but also because it drew him more deeply into the world of the navy. In California, Jack and Mary often socialized with her navy friends, but while living at Annapolis for several weeks he cultivated friendships with the navy brass and had a taste of what it would be like to be one of them. Marching around in a crisp white-and-blue uniform, saluting and receiving salutes, attending fancy-dress balls, hearing endless renditions of "Anchors Aweigh": the life Ford portrayed on-screen was one he yearned for himself, a vocation that combined male camaraderie with patriotic fervor and the acceptance he craved from the American establishment—and from his wife.

That June, taking a break from shooting studio interiors for *Salute,* Ford briefly returned to acting, playing himself in *Big Time,* a seriocomic Fox film about a family of vaudevillians who find employment in talking pictures. Starring Lee Tracy, Mae Clarke, and Stepin Fetchit, *Big Time* was the first complete film directed by Kenneth Hawks, younger brother of Ford's friend and colleague Howard Hawks and husband of actress Mary Astor, whom Ford later directed in *The Hurricane.* Ken Hawks was a promising talent who, his brother recalled, "seemed to be developing into a fellow who was much warmer than I was—a little bit more like Frank Borzage." But Ken died while directing his next picture, *Such Men Are Dangerous.* He was one of ten men killed on January 2, 1930, when two camera planes collided over Santa Monica Bay. Ford contributed five hundred dollars to the "Air Relief Fund" raised among Fox employees to benefit the families of the victims.

Ford's growing passion for the navy led in short order to two more movies, *Men Without Women* (1930), a peacetime drama about crewmen trapped on a doomed submarine, and *Seas Beneath* (1931), a seriocomic World War I naval combat yarn. Released in both talking and silent versions (only the latter survives), *Men Without Women* took its title from Ernest Hemingway's 1929 book of short stories, for which Fox paid the author five hundred dollars. But otherwise Ford's film had nothing to do with Hemingway, and women were featured prominently in the first part of the story, plying their trade at a prolonged sailors' revel centered around "the world's longest bar" in Shanghai.

Written by Dudley Nichols from a story by James Kevin McGuinness, *Men Without Women* was critically acclaimed for the taut moral drama of its second half, revolving around a disgraced sailor who redeems himself by sacrificing his life to save his fellow crewmen. Praising Ford's "inborn sense of dramatic values," the *Film Spectator* observed that "there is a strong human streak in him, because at heart he is a sentimentalist with a tender, poetical, and whimsical outlook on life. *Men Without Women* is a truly great motion picture. It shatters all our highly respected screen traditions." Writing forty-five years later, Andrew Sarris found the film's "mood of romantic despair" still impressive, while noting that "never before had a Ford film been endowed so elegantly with life-and-death suspense."

In retrospect, the most noteworthy aspect of *Men Without Women* is that it inaugurated Ford's long and fruitful partnership with Dudley Nichols, who would become his most important screenwriter throughout the 1930s. A former New York newspaperman who had become known for his coverage of the Sacco and Vanzetti trial, Nichols was an outspoken liberal whose strongly held beliefs deeply influenced Ford during the depression era. He also was a navy veteran of World War I and had some Irish ancestry, two factors that encouraged their quick rapport. Nichols's superb craftsmanship, his allusive dialogue, his penchant for symbolically charged gestures and imagery, and his solid grasp of dramatic structure contributed greatly to several of Ford's major films and left a lasting imprint on his artistic personality.

But in a 1953 letter to Lindsay Anderson, Nichols revealed that he had always felt insecure in his relationship with Ford. He had the sense that Ford "was always trying to displace" him by looking around for a more compatible screenwriter. (In fact, Frank S. Nugent filled that role for Ford after World War II, eclipsing Nichols.) Nichols thought his willingness to argue with Ford, usually without much success, worked to his disadvantage, since "I may not be capable of giving the kind of blind loyalty he desires."

For Nichols, who became an activist in the Screen Writers Guild's fight for recognition during the thirties, insisting on an equal voice for the writer with the director was a fighting principle. Throughout his Hollywood career, the elegantly attired, wavy-haired, somewhat withdrawn writer was perpetually talking about escaping to do some serious writing back east. But when he finally did so, he found the experience intensely frustrating, because he realized with painful bitterness that his talent resided in Hollywood, where writers are not truly respected. Nichols displayed the kind of restless, self-aggrandizing intellectual persona that Ford disdained, preferring to mask his intellect with the complacent facade of a rude workman, an untutored and instinctual genius. Nichols was sharp enough to see through Ford's act, which probably accounted for the director's fascination with Nichols's mind and his ambivalence toward the challenge it presented.

At the beginning, however, Ford and Nichols seemed to thrive on their mutually fertilizing differences, enabling each other to grow as artists by exploring and developing new aspects of their crafts. Nichols admittedly "knew nothing about film" when he began working with Ford, other than having fond memories of *The Iron Horse*. But he had been a drama critic, and Ford suggested he approach the script as if it were a play in several dozen scenes. That made it easy for Nichols. When the film went into production, Nichols began learning how to visualize scenes by watching what Ford did with his script. Gradually the process became more natural for the screenwriter, whose best work exhibits a finely polished sense of cinematic structure.

As far-reaching as Nichols's influence on Ford was, it has been somewhat overrated. While he helped give Ford's work greater moral weight and intellectual depth in such films as *Pilgrimage* (1933), *The Informer* (1935), *Stagecoach* (1939), and *The Long Voyage Home* (1940), Nichols also helped push Ford down the path of self-consciousness and occasional pretension. Becoming more aware of his themes and the social attitudes underlying them was beneficial to Ford, helping crystallize his developing artistic personality and emboldening him to express himself more forcefully. Ford's growing need to be taken seriously and to be granted more stature by both Hollywood and the critics was enhanced by his association with Nichols. Eventually, though, Ford would reject Nichols's penchant for preaching and what the writer called "stylized symbolism" for a more natural, less overtly "artistic," subtler and richer style of filmmaking.

Some critics credit Nichols with introducing Ford to serious moral issues and to certain archetypal situations, such as that of the small group of men whose values are tested under duress in an isolated setting. But Ford was dealing with similar moral issues of sacrifice, loyalty, and duty from the time of his earliest Harry Carey Westerns. The beleaguered male group existed less formally in several of Ford's 1920s features, such as *3 Bad Men* and the navy melodrama *The Blue Eagle,* before Nichols increased the tension by circumscribing the Fordian group in such films as *Men Without Women* and *The Lost Patrol* (1934). Nichols's greatest contribution to Ford's work was to make him more aware of what he wanted to say and to enable him to say it more clearly. Nichols was a phase Ford had to go through to reach full artistic maturity.

Ford made a film in 1930 whose style was more in keeping with the relaxed, spontaneous mode of filmmaking that characterizes the best of his later work. Seldom revived today, *Up the River* is an utterly delightful, disarmingly offbeat lampoon of the prison movie genre.

Fox originally commissioned a serious study of prison life from screenwriter Maurine Watkins, then dropped the project in early 1930 when MGM released its successful prison drama *The Big House*. Ford managed to revive the studio's interest in *Up the River* by turning it into an absurdist comedy about a midwestern penitentiary where life is so convivial that two escapees break back in for the big baseball game against a rival prison. The director did an uncredited rewrite with William Collier Sr., the veteran actor who plays Pop, the prison's salty but wise old lifer. Collier received another of those vague "staged by" credits, in this case perhaps a backhanded acknowledgment of his role as a script doctor and gag writer.

Although the jocular *Up the River* in many ways represents the antithesis of the Dudley Nichols approach to filmmaking, it has thematic and structural affinities with Ford's dramatic films about men testing their character in isolated fortresses. But it does so in a breezy, offhand, often ironic manner, brimming over with what Ford liked to call "grace notes." By that he meant directorial touches, often nonverbal, that reveal character or capture emotion. Such frissons are the cinematic equivalent of the compressed, allusive phrasing of lyric poetry. In his best work, Ford values these seeming digressions above the sometimes laborious necessities of narrative.

Up the River was Spencer Tracy's first feature film and Humphrey Bogart's second. Ford discovered Tracy on Broadway playing a killer in prison in the 1930 play *The Last Mile.* The two Irish Catholics, who shared similar guilt feelings over their heavy drinking and womanizing, proved a good creative match. Tracy's screen persona is already fully formed as the brash, cynical, charismatic St. Louis, lionized by his fellow inmates for his pitching prowess and his indifference to prison rules (laxly enforced by the kindly Irish warden, Robert Emmett O'Connor). Bogart, in his early "Anyone for tennis?" phase, is excessively callow as Steve, a young rich kid gone wrong. Ford's comic imagination is most stimulated by Warren Hymer, who gives an unexpectedly touching comic performance as St. Louis's moronic sidekick, Dannemora Dan. A favorite Ford type, the lovable village idiot, Dan never loses his blinkered sense of dignity while constantly being mistreated by the slickly opportunistic St. Louis.

One of the most uproarious scenes begins with Dan marching in a religious revival procession as part of the "Brotherhood of Hope," carrying a drum being beaten to the tune of "Brighten the Corner Where You Are." As the supposedly reformed ex-con exhorts a street-corner crowd, "And remember, brothers, crime don't pay," Ford cuts to St. Louis cockily pulling up in a fancy convertible with two flashy dames. He and Dan get into a slugging match and are returned to their idyllic, interracial penitentiary, which resembles a college campus, complete with coeds, amateur theatricals, a brass band, a fight song, and even an athletic mascot (a zebra). The occasional undercurrents of suffering and despair in *Up the River* only strengthen Ford's joyous, ironic affirmation of community in this subversive film portraying prison life as preferable to the hypocrisy and emotional isolation of the outside world.

Unlike most Americans, Ford was insulated at first from the devastating effects of the Great Depression. While the bottom was falling out of the national economy, his income was rising to lordly levels, from $146,302 in 1929 to $160,943 in 1930.

Thanks largely to the popularity of talkies, film industry profits were booming, leading people to consider Hollywood "depression-proof." But by 1931, theater attendance was beginning to drop significantly as the novelty of talkies wore off and the nation's unemployment worsened. Studios found it increasingly difficult to keep up with their financial obligations, including the high costs of financing the transition to sound. The economic chaos at Fox eventually disrupted Ford's comfortable haven at the studio, forcing him to start freelancing. By 1933 his income had fallen to almost half what it had been three years earlier.

In March 1929, William Fox, flush with the success of his studio and theater-chain expansion program, made the fatal mistake of overreaching his financial means. He and his family spent close to $50 million to buy a controlling interest in Loews Inc., which owned a giant theater chain as well as the industry's leading studio, MGM. "The new Fox-Loews merger created the largest motion picture complex in the world," notes film historian Douglas Gomery. "Its assets totaled more than $100 million and an annual earning potential existed of $20 million. Fox assumed a substantial short-term debt obligation in the process, but during the bull market of the late Twenties he could simply float more stock and bonds to meet his needs."

Fox's troubles began when he was seriously injured in an auto accident in the summer of 1929. That October, while he was still recuperating, the market crashed. He found it impossible to float the additional stock he needed to retire $30 million in loans he had used to help finance his expansion program. In addition, the Federal Trade Commission brought an antitrust suit against Fox that November because of his Loews acquisition. Unable to meet his short-term debts, Fox fell into acrimonious disputes with his bankers, and a suit was filed seeking to place his producing and theater corporations into receivership. Meanwhile, the Fox Film Corporation, after showing a profit of $9 million in 1929, lost $3 million in 1930. The following year, William Fox decided to retire from the motion picture industry and sell his stock for $18 million to Chicago businessman Harley L. Clarke, president of the General Theaters Equipment Company, who succeeded him as president of the Fox operations.

In the midst of all this chaos, there was a drastic slowdown at Fox. Ford was still being paid on his contract, which ran through October 1932, but he and Mary were accustomed to living comfortably, and they seemed slow to realize how tight things were becoming in Hollywood. With nothing happening at the studio, Jack took a three-month trip in 1931 to the Far East with George

O'Brien and returned in April to find himself with only $5,000 in the bank. He was forced to hire an agent, Harry Wurtzel, who conveniently enough was the brother of his good friend, Fox executive Sol Wurtzel. Ford never became as close to Harry as he was to Sol, and he eventually became disenchanted with his agent's efforts in his behalf. But in 1931, Harry succeeded in persuading Sol to renegotiate Ford's contract with Fox to make it nonexclusive, allowing him to work elsewhere between assignments at his home studio. The move was only partly successful economically and artistically. Ford had to accelerate his workload while accepting projects that he might otherwise have disdained. In 1931–32, he directed one routine picture at Fox and three of varying quality at Goldwyn, Universal, and MGM, while his total income slipped from $139,859 in 1931 to $103,315 in 1932. When he returned to Fox for two pictures in 1933, the worst year of the Great Depression, his income fell to $88,545.

Ford also suffered some losses in the stock market, although they were not crippling because he was always a relatively conservative, if unskilled, investor. He began playing the market in 1924–25 by purchasing $3,000 in Richardson Music Company stock, which he wrote off as a loss after the company filed for bankruptcy in 1933. In 1925–26, he invested $12,000 in the Western Costume Company, but dropped it all when that firm went bankrupt in 1931. Despite the market crash, Ford still reported $5,074 in stock profits on his 1929 income tax return. Eight days after the crash, he bought one thousand shares of stock in Fox Theatres for $19,300, but unloaded them on December 5, 1930, at a loss of $14,303. He wrote off another $3,238 investment in that shaky company in 1933. Ford's biggest stock loss, however, came on investments outside show business. He sold shares of AT&T and Ford Ltd. (the British division of the Ford Motor Company) at a loss of $32,067 in 1932. But he made up for 60 percent of his total stock market losses of $79,608 between 1930 and 1933 by earning $48,463 in stock dividends.

The cautionary example of his brother Francis, whose directorial career had ended with the coming of sound, made Jack all the more determined to show his versatility and reliability during the depression years. To Harry Wurtzel, Ford insisted that he was "a journeyman director, a traffic cop in front of the camera, but the best traffic cop in Hollywood." He was being a bit disingenuous—his artistic ambitions were never less than temporarily dormant—but "traffic cop" is a fair description of his role on *The Brat* (1931), the most unlikely project he tackled in that period.

The Fox romantic comedy stars Sally O'Neil as a footloose gamine who becomes the protégée of an unscrupulous writer (Alan Dinehart). It was the sort of brittle, stage-bound material that was better suited to the talents of George Cukor or Gregory La Cava. Most unusually for Ford, the script often borders on lewdness in its teasing innuendos about an impoverished woman's sexual and economic exploitation by a high-society cad. Ford was handicapped further by his undistinguished cast, yet he still managed to direct *The Brat* with engaging professionalism and a fair amount of gusto.

Beneath Ford's professionalism, however, could be seen a certain amount of self-disgust over his occasional backsliding into hackwork. Perhaps that was one reason he often wallowed in such heavy drinking binges during this period. He could not help feeling despondent over making something like *The World Moves On* (1934). A Fox historical saga following the fortunes of a Louisiana dynasty over a period of a hundred years, *The World Moves On* is one of the dullest and most pointless films he ever made. "I did the best I could, but I hated the damn thing," he admitted. ". . . You were getting paid big money and there was very little income tax, so you swallowed your pride and went out there and did it." This may have been the film on which Ford remembered the studio ordering him to shoot the script exactly as written. To spite the front office, he followed that order with perverse literalness, turning in a laboriously paced, seemingly endless director's cut that had to be shortened drastically before it could be released.

The real trick to being a self-respecting filmmaker, Ford confided to French critic Jean Mitry in 1955, was "to turn out films which please the public, but which also reveal the personality of the director." During the early sound era, when Ford was struggling to consolidate his position within the studio system at a time of dizzying technological and economic change, he was simultaneously searching for his artistic identity. He often had to resort to subterranean cunning to maintain his individuality and insinuate his personality into genre films. One way was through his sly, pointed, deeply Irish sense of humor. Explaining why he inserted a comedy baseball interlude into the World War I sequences of *Born Reckless,* Ford said, "In those days, when the scripts were dull, the best you could do was to try and get some comedy into it." Visual stylization was an even more pervasive method of self-expression for Ford, as he explained to *Photoplay* in 1936: "Lighting, as a matter of fact, is my strong point. I can take a thoroughly mediocre bit of acting, and build points of shadow around a ray of strong light centered on the principals, and finish with something plausible—anyway, that's my one boast."

Ford increasingly recognized how useful it was to have his favorite character actors—his John Ford Stock Company—constantly on the set to help him create a particular emotional or comic mood at a moment's notice. Knowing these people's attributes so well enabled Ford to use them as a form of cinematic shorthand. "After all, you've got to tell your story through the people who portray it," he told *Photoplay.* "You can have a weak, utterly bad script—and a good cast will turn it into a good picture. I've thwarted more than one handicap of that kind with the aid of two or three really fine actors. With the exception of the stars who are signed for parts by the studio in advance, I insist on choosing names for myself. And I spent more time on that task than on any other."

Once he had cast the parts, Ford seemed to direct actors mostly by indirection or osmosis. Jean Arthur, who made her feature film debut for Ford in the 1923 silent *Cameo Kirby,* was delightful as the leading lady of his 1935 gangster comedy-drama *The Whole Town's Talking,* which also stars Edward G. Robinson. "Ford always had a handkerchief or a pipe hangin' out of his mouth," she recalled. "He chewed on it and you never knew what he said. And Robinson had a pipe that *he'd* chew. They'd stand there, these two guys, and never give you any directions at all or *anything* much. I'd say, 'How do I know what I'm gonna do if you don't *talk?*' And they said, 'Well, we talk with our brains. We don't need to verbalize things.'" But when I asked if she found it difficult acting for Ford, Arthur replied, "Oh, no. You know what he's thinking anyway. He's just—it's all over him. A darling, darling man. I don't think he gave much direction, but everybody seemed to understand what they were supposed to do." The reason Ford always chewed on his handkerchief or pipe, she thought, was "so he wouldn't have to talk." Ford's fellow director George Stevens told me, "I think Jack found in motion pictures the only medium in which he could express himself, from the muted films of his early period to the more vocal films of his later period."

Gloria Stuart, the beautiful and exceptionally intelligent young actress who was Ford's leading lady in both *Air Mail* (1932) and *The Prisoner of Shark Island* (1935), is best known today for her Oscar-nominated role as Old Rose in James Cameron's *Titanic* (1997). Although she liked Ford personally and enjoyed his droll sense of humor, Stuart found his taciturn way of working somewhat frustrating: "In both Ford pictures I don't remember what I call directing. He was very good with the camera. I don't remember much dialogue between John and actors." When they made *Air Mail,* she observed, Ford "was not a great big famous director. He was one hired independently at Universal. And I think the Yiddish word is *potchkeh* [time-wasting]—it was really a *potchkeh* picture, low-budget and everything." But she added that Ford "always had top scripts and top actors. It's very hard to go wrong that way."

Marking Ford's first return to Universal in eleven years (for a salary of thirty-six thousand dollars), *Air Mail* is a routine but well-told aviation adventure yarn written by Dale Van Every and Lieutenant Commander Frank "Spig" Wead and starring Ralph Bellamy as the beleaguered chief of pilots at a desert airport, coping with a reckless subordinate (Pat O'Brien). Wead was a retired navy flier who had turned to screenwriting after breaking his neck falling down the stairs of his home in 1927; John Wayne plays Wead in Ford's 1957 biographical film *The Wings of Eagles.* Wead and Ford became good friends, habitually exchanging a stream of sexual banter that seemed Ford's way of kindly emphasizing Wead's virility despite his crippling injury ("He loved women, and I think that finished women for him, so his heroes were always womanizers," Howard Hawks observed). The desperate gallantry of Wead's heroes stems from their ability to carry on in circumstances ordinary people would find utterly demoralizing. Ford, who sublimated his own frustrations into creating a better world on-screen, viscerally responded to Wead's sense of selfless duty.

Ford and Karl Freund, the cinematographer of Murnau's *Der Letzte Mann* and Lang's *Metropolis,* filmed *Air Mail* with intricate, extremely dark compositions, emphasizing the harrowing toll exacted from the pioneering mail pilots in the performance of their daily routine. Ford's pacing is meditative in contrast with Hawks's more dynamic and absurdist handling of a similar Wead story in the 1936 *Ceiling Zero.* The sobriety of Ford's approach, depicting a small outpost surrounded by constant physical and moral danger, invests *Air Mail* with a German expressionist feeling of oppressive doom that helps redeem it from the clichés of the genre. Though hewing closely to his narrative line, Ford finds room for an occasional poetic touch (a downed flier dying in the snow as "Silent Night" plays softly on the sound track) or a bit of comedic commentary (watching Pat O'Brien performing daredevil stunts, one Indian mutters to another, "Aviator—drunk").

Another genre film Ford made in 1932 holds up less well today. Hollywood's biggest studio, MGM, hired him for thirty-five thousand dollars to direct *Flesh,* an odd programmer starring one of the studio's most popular actors, Wallace Beery. For most of its running time, *Flesh* is a broad but amiable comedy about a kindhearted German wrestler named Polakai who naïvely falls in love with a hardboiled American dame, Lora (Karen Morley). But Beery and Morley almost seem to be acting in different movies. Her astringent, sympathetic performance as a despondent ex-con torn between Polakai and her criminal boyfriend (Ricardo Cortez) steals the show as *Flesh* gradually becomes the tragic story of a man's spiritual degradation, in the Germanic vein of *The Blue Angel* or *The Last Laugh.* The strange dissonances in the screenplay can be attributed to its truly bizarre pedigree: the writers included such names as Edmund Goulding, Moss Hart, and (uncredited) William Faulkner. Ford makes Beery's beer-garden comedy entertaining, if overly buffoonish, but if the director thought he could twist *Flesh* into an exercise in pseudo–German expressionism, he miscalculated. Arthur Edeson's lighting style never quite matches the story's downbeat mood, remaining mostly in the brightly escapist MGM house style.

What's truly expressionistic about *Flesh* is the reflection Ford finds of himself in Polakai: Bull Feeney's empathy with the ugly man's helpless feelings of love and selfless devotion for a beautiful but sadly untrustworthy woman. "I'm such a funny-looking fellow and rough," confesses Polakai, "and I couldn't expect Lora to love me." Even though the couple is finally reunited, it is only through the screen of a jailhouse barrier, a remarkably gloomy "happy ending" for this most unromantic love story.

The decade of the 1930s was a tumultuous period for Ford personally as well as professionally. Tag Gallagher observes that in the depression era, Ford's "personal depression was not financial but moral." A pattern began to emerge in which the discipline he maintained while making a movie was utterly abandoned between movies. Serious episodes of drinking, sometimes dangerous enough to require hospitalization, became more common in his life. Sexual infidelities also occurred more frequently, although the full extent of his philandering is impossible to document. When Ford had a medical checkup in September 1934 after complaining of feeling nervous and fatigued, his doctor found he had an enlarged heart, a swollen abdomen, a greatly enlarged liver, and an infected prostate gland. Vainly advising him to stop drinking, the doctor prescribed prostate massages as well as a brief course of the sedatives phenobarbital and Nembutal to help him sleep.

Ford's anxiety and depression were reflected in his troubled relationship with his children. He and Mary were only sporadically involved in the lives of Pat and Barbara, who were entering their critical adolescent years in the early thirties. Pat was cruelly rejected by his father, who seemed infuriated by Pat's boyish imperfections and was far too self-centered to respond to his emotional needs. Once, at the family dinner table, Ford was leaning back in his chair, striking a characteristic pose and chewing on his napkin, when he realized that Pat was imitating him. Rather than being amused or flattered by this expression of filial devotion, Ford lashed out at his son for presuming to be like him. Pat was punished by being ordered to bed. Not surprisingly, Pat became moody and embittered and was sent to a nearby military school,[1] transported back and forth by the family chauffeur in Mary's Rolls-Royce.

---

1. The Black-Foxe Academy in Hollywood, run by Earle Foxe, who starred for Ford as an arrogant stage star in the now-lost silent film *Upstream* and played villains in *Four Sons* and *Hangman's House.*

Pat recalled his relationship with his father in a 1979 interview: "My conversations with him, as his only son—that I know of—[were] 'Yessir,' until one day I said, 'No sir,' and then I was no longer around. . . . In fact, our family life was pretty much like that of a shipmaster and his crew, or a wagon master and his people. He gave the orders, and we carried them out."

Barbara was quick-witted and vivacious, if emotionally erratic, and her father openly favored her over Pat. But she also suffered from his neglect. When Jack was traveling in 1926, Mary wrote him, "The first thing Bobby says every morning is 'I miss my Daddy so much.' We all do!" As a form of overcompensation, Barbara was so indulged by both parents that she had trouble concentrating and following school discipline. Rather than deal with her underlying problems, they continually jumped Barbara from school to school. After the kidnapping of the Lindbergh baby in 1932, Jack and Mary found the excuse they needed to justify shipping their two children far away from home, to attend a private school in Honolulu. Pat and Barbara found happier lives in Hawaii, in part perhaps because their parents came to visit only when Jack was between films.

Ford's mounting dissatisfaction with his home life was manifest in his increasing tendency to escape to faraway lands. Because of a spat over some forgotten issue, he left Mary behind while he took a trip to the Far East from January 16 through April 11, 1931.

The story goes that the day before his departure, Ford asked George O'Brien, who had recently starred for him in *Seas Beneath,* to come along. There are two versions of what happened when they left on the Norwegian tramp steamer *Tai Yang.* Ford's recollection was that when Mary arrived with the children at the dock in San Pedro, she began to cry, and O'Brien commented on how touching it was to see her reaction.

"You'd cry too, if you were her," said Ford.

"Why?" O'Brien asked.

"Because you've got her ticket."

The way O'Brien recalled it, however, was that Mary came to the dock alone and alarmed him by suddenly bursting into tears.

"Why are you crying, Mary?" O'Brien called down to her. "We'll be back by spring!"

"You'd cry, too. You've got my ticket," she said in this account.

Contrary to legend, however, Ford's decision to take O'Brien with him was not made at the last minute. On January 8, eight days before the *Tai Yang* departed, the *Los Angeles Examiner* reported that Ford and O'Brien would be making the trip together.

But Mary's anger at being bypassed for O'Brien was real and needed no embellishment. She took a measure of revenge by heading off to vacation by herself at Waikiki Beach. While writing from the boat to warn her teasingly about not getting involved with Hawaiian beach boys, Ford felt it necessary to joke about his preference for male companionship. He told her that the trip was so invigorating, "Even O'Brien looks at me admiringly. (However, it will do him no good!)"

If Ford took O'Brien along because he thought another man would be more tolerant of his unbridled behavior away from home, he was severely disappointed. Neither man ever discussed publicly the rift that developed between them on the trip. O'Brien, who thought Ford was fleeing the pressures of success, would say only that after spending four months with Ford, "I knew less about him than ever before. He was the most private man I ever met."

In a 1996 article about his father's relationship with Ford, novelist Darcy O'Brien wrote that he often asked his father what had happened. "Eventually, worn down by my inquiries, he revealed that Ford got so drunk in Manila that he lay for days drinking in bed, refusing to listen to George's entreaties to sober up enough to go on with the trip.

"'Poor Jack,' George told me, 'had a case of booze with him in the hotel room and just wouldn't stop. I remember one time, I begged him to quit, we had a dinner to go to, or something, but he just told me to go to hell, you know. It was kind of pathetic, son. He got mad at me, and I remember him kicking under the bedclothes, and empty bottles rolled out onto the floor.'

"Now, in telling this story, my Dad expressed neither anger nor, in the deep sense, judgment about Ford's self-indulgence. A true conservative, George O'Brien accepted the defects in human nature, whether general or particular. In Ford's case, one of these defects was a tendency to go on benders. . . . What my father perhaps did not understand, however, at the time in Manila, and may never have understood, was that however much John Ford enjoyed or required periods of absolute alcoholic oblivion, he remained the slyest of foxes, and the most manipulative; and used his indulgence as a test of the loyalty of friends, employees and, of course, his wife. If I may say so, and I don't see why not, it is a very Irish trait, to test the limits of friendship or love by doing something so awful, so despicable, so hard to bear, so, in a word, foul, as to provide proof, or the lack of it, of someone's loyalty."

Abandoning the sodden Ford in his Manila hotel room, George O'Brien continued alone on his Asian journey for about ten days. Then, his son related, O'Brien returned to "a sobered-up Ford to continue their journey eastwards toward China, and could have had no idea of the price he would pay for this unassuming show of independence.

"He did not work for John Ford again for seventeen years, and never had the lead again in a Ford picture."

Ford also abandoned his more recent protégé, John Wayne, although for a somewhat shorter period of penance.

Perversely, Ford turned his back on Duke not long after he won the director's lasting respect by volunteering to perform some unusually dangerous stunt work on *Men Without Women*. In November 1929, they were shooting off Catalina Island when several professional skin divers balked at entering choppy seas to double for sailors being rescued from the disabled submarine. Duke, working props, impulsively volunteered to take the place of all the professional divers, an act of daring and courage that Ford always recalled as the moment when Duke began to stand out in his eyes. "There was something special about Duke even then," Ford said later. "Sure—he was callow and untutored, but he had something that jumped right off the screen at me. I guess you could call it star power."

When he played his first starring role in the spring of 1930, Duke Morrison was rechristened John Wayne. Ironically, it was not Ford who gave Duke his first big break but another Fox director, Raoul Walsh, in the Western *The Big Trail*. Ford claimed that he suggested Duke to Walsh, but Walsh insisted that he spotted Duke moving furniture on the lot. Peter Bogdanovich, who interviewed both Ford and Walsh, reported that Walsh "liked the way [Duke] walked—a kind of slower, more deliberate version of Ford's own rolling sailor's walk—and convinced the studio that the kid could carry the expensive epic Western."

Even though Ford admired Walsh—in 1964, he listed Walsh's silent feature *The Honor System*[2] as his favorite film after *The Birth of a Nation*—Ford evidently thought Walsh was intruding on his turf by elevating his prop boy to stardom. He and Walsh even staked out competing claims of helping devise Duke's new name. Fox executive Winfield Sheehan started the naming process by decreeing that Marion Morrison was an unacceptable name for a cowboy star. According to Dan Ford's account, John Ford suggested that Duke name himself after a figure he admired in American history, and Duke mentioned the Revolutionary War general Mad Anthony Wayne. Ford supposedly re-

---

2. *The Honor System* (1917), a lost film, starred Milton Sills as a furloughed convict who is kidnapped while trying to get back to an Arizona prison to uphold its honor system. Ford's whimsically eclectic list of his ten favorite films, published in *Cinema* magazine, also included his own *3 Godfathers* (1948), *Ninotchka* (Ernst Lubitsch, 1939), *The High and the Mighty* (William Wellman, 1954), *Tol'able David* (Henry King, 1921), *The Song of Bernadette* (King, 1943), *Lady for a Day* (Frank Capra, 1933), *Going My Way* (Leo McCarey, 1944), and *The Alamo* (John Wayne, 1960).

jected "Tony" Wayne as "too Italian," proposing his own first name instead. Walsh, on the other hand, told Wayne's biographer Maurice Zolotow that it was *he* who mentioned Mad Anthony Wayne and that Sheehan rejected "Tony" as "too Italian." In the Walsh version, Duke was not even consulted when his new name was being devised. All that's certain in this matter is that for Ford and Walsh, those two master bullshit artists, naming the Duke was a cherished example of "When the legend becomes fact, print the legend."

What should have been Wayne's ticket to major stardom instead turned out to be a fiasco that set his career back by a decade. A wide-screen production that attempted to capture the scope of *The Iron Horse* and *The Covered Wagon* in talking pictures, *The Big Trail* was filmed in a 70mm, wide-screen process called "Grandeur Pictures." It is a remarkably beautiful film, and Wayne makes a strong and handsome lead, though rough around the edges. Unfortunately, *The Big Trail* was rudely rejected by audiences and reviewers when it premiered in October 1930. Few theaters could play its oversize image, and the picture looked far less impressive in 35mm prints. The $2 million epic was a colossal bomb, sending Wayne back into B movies and helping make large-scale Westerns out of fashion throughout most of the thirties.

After Duke returned from four months of location shooting on *The Big Trail,* Ford mysteriously froze him out of his life. He snubbed Duke when the actor said "Hi, Coach" on the studio lot. After three such frustrating incidents, Wayne gave up. He and Ford did not speak again for more than three years. Duke's banishment ended just as abruptly as it had begun. In the summer of 1934, Wayne was visiting Catalina Island at the same time as Ford. Ford sent his ten-year-old daughter Barbara to deliver a message to Duke: "Daddy wants to see you." Duke may have been back in Ford's circle of friends, but that did not mean he was offered any roles in Ford movies or that Ford ceased his habitual teasing and belittlement. By then Wayne had left Fox and was trapped in a long, demoralizing run of B Westerns that would keep him on the lower level of the industry until Ford finally chose him to star in *Stagecoach* (1939). The most charitable explanation for Ford's treatment of Wayne throughout most of that decade is that Ford felt Wayne still needed a great deal of seasoning and maturing before he was ready to star in another A picture. But that rationalization leaves out as much as it explains, and Wayne was terribly hurt and baffled by Ford's behavior.

"To this goddam day I don't know why he didn't speak to me for years," Wayne told Dan Ford in 1976. Wayne biographers Randy Roberts and James S. Olson observed, "It was in Ford's nature not to say and Duke's not to ask. Such matters, sensitive, fragile, perhaps even touching on the deep sadness that seemed so much a part of Ford's personality, were not discussed. Perhaps Ford, who viewed himself as a mentor and even surrogate father, resented Duke's decision to make *The Big Trail* with Raoul Walsh. Perhaps the old man was punishing Duke. Or it could simply have been Ford's legendary, unpredictable mean streak."

Ford's most prestigious film of the early thirties was *Arrowsmith* (1931), an adaptation by playwright Sidney Howard of Sinclair Lewis's Pulitzer Prize–winning 1925 novel. Made on loan-out to independent producer Samuel Goldwyn and released through United Artists, *Arrowsmith* was acclaimed for what now seem all the wrong reasons.

Its choppy, overly elliptical narrative pays respects to the novel's themes without treating any in sufficient depth; the dialogue is rife with speechifying (including a scene in which the title character prays that he might avoid "pretense"); and Ronald Colman's British accent and declamatory acting style make his midwestern doctor even more of a pompous fool than Lewis intended. Some of these flaws stem from the novel, in which, as E. L. Doctorow observes, every character "speaks in overly self-indicating paragraphs. Both characters and events are delivered in hasty catalogues and events seem to be sketched on the pages." What's most interesting today about Ford's version of *Arrowsmith* is not how closely it reflects the novel but how this wildly uneven, sometimes downright weird movie obliquely reflects some of the personal conflicts tormenting Ford at a critical juncture of his life.

The story of Martin Arrowsmith, whose egomaniacal ambition destroys both his family and his sense of personal integrity, must have struck Ford as a cautionary tale. Impatient with the mundane life of a small-town doctor, Arrowsmith yearns for medical "glory," which he achieves by leaving his practice for a well-heeled New York laboratory and concocting a serum for bubonic plague. But in the process, his infant son dies because he is out in the field testing a blackleg serum on cattle; his wife (Helen Hayes) dies because she is infected with plague in the West Indies when he is off testing his cure on natives; and the natives are subjected to morally repugnant experimentation in the name of science. Ford's critical perspective on Arrowsmith's destructive hubris is sharp and clearly expressed, although it is expressed more visually than verbally. Tag Gallagher oddly complains that the director is "too subtle" in condemning the racist attitudes of Arrowsmith and his fellow scientists, including a dignified black doctor (Clarence Brooks) who offers his people as guinea pigs. But Ford's horrified condemnation is unmistakable for anyone who has eyes to see.

Arrowsmith's opening title somewhat misleadingly calls it "The story of a man who dedicated his life to service and his heart to the love of one woman." While devoted to his wife in theory, Arrowsmith finds it difficult to deal with her actual needs. His perpetually restless wandering is exasperating to Leora, a former nurse who abandoned her career for marriage. When she expresses frustration over her traditional role as the wife who's left behind, his smug response is simply, "Ah, stand by, old girl." She tells him, with perhaps purposely ambiguous grammar, "Oh, can't you see, I haven't got any life beside you." These conflicts were familiar to Ford after eleven years of increasingly unsatisfying and argumentative married life. His neglect of his wife and children for work, booze, his male friends, and fruitless affairs with other women gave Ford an edginess and desperation that he instilled in Colman's characterization of Arrowsmith. Arrowsmith never actually cheats on his wife, but he is painfully tempted when a wealthy seductress (Myrna Loy) makes herself available in the West Indies. The scenes of Arrowsmith alone in his room impotently longing to be with her are intercut with Loy undressing in her room; both are filmed in deep shadows that almost seem to dissolve the spatial and emotional barriers between them. Ford further intercuts these scenes with the loyal, self-abnegating Leora dying of plague back home. The intercutting makes it seem as if a man's desire equals consummation equals guilt—a very Catholic equation, making lust of the heart as serious a sin as actual adultery.

Unable to resolve Arrowsmith's conflicts in any truly coherent dramatic way because he was too confused about them in his own life, Ford once again sought self-expression in quirky directorial touches inserted here and there in cracks of the narrative. When Arrowsmith proposes to Leora in a restaurant and she murmurs, "I want soft music," he puts some money in a jukebox and out blares the *William Tell* Overture, comically warning her of the frenetic partnership that lies ahead. A subtler omen of incompatibility comes when they go to the county clerk's office to exchange marriage vows. Entering behind them is a very odd couple: a bearded old codger in a Union army uniform with an extremely young bride. Ford's personality also insinuates itself in his characteristic use of an expressionistic lighting mode for scenes of high emotion. That style dominates the later parts of the film: the plague sequences accompanied by mournful black choruses, the burning of a native village to destroy the disease, the horror-film lighting as Arrowsmith finds his elderly mentor Professor Gottlieb (A. E. Anson) having a stroke or suffering from senile dementia.

At Sam Goldwyn's request, Ford made a written pledge not to drink during the shooting of *Arrowsmith*. It was a telling sign of Ford's malaise in this period that the studio chief had to enforce a discipline Ford normally was able to impose on himself. Ford's unhappiness and distraction while making *Arrowsmith* was reflected in its extreme stylistic unevenness, its highly episodic nature, and its schizoid variations in mood.

Ford's inner turmoil was also evident in his complicated relationship with Helen Hayes, the stage star and wife of playwright Charles MacArthur, who gives a feisty and touching performance as the ill-fated Leora. She was equally outspoken on the set, which both irritated and intrigued the director. Ford was an "Irish bully, but a loving one," recalled Hayes, who was Irish-American herself. She found those traits stimulating and considered Ford a "fine director." But Ford wanted to go beyond a working relationship. "He got stuck on me a little, to use an old-fashioned phrase, and took to calling me all the time."

Ford's dissatisfaction with *Arrowsmith* eventually came to a head in a rift with Goldwyn that led him to walk off the picture in disgust; perhaps he was simply tired of working on it and needed an excuse to quit. Assistant director H. Bruce Humberstone had filled a set with extras, and Ford insisted on having it empty to create the mood he wanted. Goldwyn made the mistake of coming on the set and expressing his disagreement with Ford. "If you're going to direct this picture, go ahead and do it," Ford snapped. "If you decide to let me finish directing this picture, call me up at home." Ford stalked off the set and drove home. When he reached Odin Street, he found five telephone messages from Sam Goldwyn imploring him to return to the studio.

Instead Ford went on a bender. The Goldwyn Company finally located him boozing it up on Catalina Island. He straggled into the studio on October 9 in an incoherent state. After two more instances of such behavior while he was supposed to be shooting retakes and supervising the editing, Ford was removed from the picture by Goldwyn. Ford's home studio, Fox, was informed of his behavior, which was verified by four signed statements from eyewitnesses. Goldwyn insisted that Fox return $4,100 of the fee he had paid to borrow Ford. As a result, Fox notified Ford on October 22, 1931, that his contract was being terminated "because of your willful failure, neglect and refusal to render the services contracted to be rendered by you." The studio issued a cover story that the high-salaried director was being let go for reasons of economy. Ford's career had hit its lowest ebb. Ironically enough, his work on *Arrowsmith* would be hailed by critics who knew nothing about his ignominious discharge from the picture.

After freelancing for Universal on *Air Mail* and MGM on *Flesh,* Ford was accepted back at Fox in May 1932. In his new two-picture contract, his salary was cut to $40,000 per film, $10,000 less than he had been making at Fox before the *Arrowsmith* incident, and he had to agree to waive story approval. But in 1933 Ford nevertheless managed to make under that contract two films he would have no reason to regret, *Pilgrimage* and *Doctor Bull.*

Ford impulsively decided to take another trip to Hawaii and the Philippines, this time with Mary in tow. Later, writing off the vacation on his taxes, he told the IRS it was undertaken to prepare a picture called *Shanghai Interlude* (no such picture was ever made, although the whimsical title may have been an allusion to the opening sequences of *Men Without Women*). The Fords' dilatory excursion began on October 31, 1931, and ended when they returned to California on March 8. It was supposed to be Jack's way of making up to Mary for taking George O'Brien along on his previous trip to the Philippines. But rather than healing the growing emotional distance between them, the trip ended by making that distance a permanent condition. They quarreled in Honolulu over Jack's disapproval of Mary's expensive needs for clothing and a retinue of servants. Jack mentally escaped the situation by becoming maudlin and incoherent with drink in his bed at the Royal Hawaiian Hotel. Finally he became so ill that she had to have him hospitalized to be dried out.

When Ford recovered, he and Mary traveled to Manila with Pat, Barbara, and the children's nurse, Maude Stevenson. Mary had summoned them to Hawaii while he was in the hospital. But Jack became restless in Manila and took off for the Dutch East Indies with Larry de Prida, Fox's representative in the Philippines. De Prida, who had become friendly with Ford when the director visited Manila with George O'Brien, later married Ford's niece Cecil McLean. Jack and Larry were accompanied to the East Indies by an artist, Malvina Hoffman, whom they met aboard ship. Hoffman was heading to Bali to sketch native dancers, and they tagged along. It's not hard to imagine Mary's bitter disappointment and loneliness as Jack was roistering his way through Bali, Java, and Sumatra.

On January 2, 1932, while the Fords were still overseas, Mary's thirty-five-year-old brother John Willis Smith committed suicide at their home on Odin Street. The father of two young children, Smith was a former car salesman and had been living in Los Angeles for a year. He drove into the Fords' garage on Odin Street at eleven that morning and killed himself by carbon monoxide poisoning. In early afternoon, the gas-filled garage exploded in flames, hurling the doors of the garage against the house across the street. The Fords' next-door neighbor ran over to find the car in flames. Smith's burned body was in the backseat, clasping a suicide note. Police said he was distraught over being estranged from his wife, who lived in New York.[3]

After returning to Odin Street from her dismal vacation two months after

3. Mary was one of four surviving siblings in the Smith family, including a sister, Margaret, and two brothers, J. T. R. "Bunny" and Wingate. Wingate, who was seriously injured while serving in the U.S. Army during World War I, made his living as a golf pro before coming to Hollywood in 1928. He worked regularly with Ford as an assistant director from the 1930s until the end of Ford's career, outliving his brother-in-law by less than a year.

her brother's suicide, Mary somehow managed to make her peace with her marriage. She accepted Jack as he was, concentrating on his positive qualities and realizing that his more deplorable habits would never change. He found sustenance in his home life despite its profound imperfections.

Ford seemed to be offering his own philosophy of marriage in an exchange from his 1933 Will Rogers film *Doctor Bull*. Rogers's small-town doctor ruminates to his friend, the widow Janet Cardmaker (Vera Allen), "You know, some old early settler had the thing about right when he said that most of life is a storm and without a harbor, man is lost."

"And a woman?" Janet asks.

"Oh," he replies, "a woman don't need refuge like a man."

"I wonder," she muses.

On September 29, 1933, exactly one week after the release of *Doctor Bull*, Mary Ford was injured in what Los Angeles newspapers tactfully called an "odd" or "unusual" automobile accident. Jack, who was driving, was heading home with Mary and an unidentified friend early that morning when the car rounded a corner at Melrose and Martel Avenues in Hollywood. "Narrowly escaping death," Mary reportedly "had been thrown against the door, which was opened by the force of the impact, and had fallen to the pavement, striking her head on the curb." Unconscious, she was taken to the hospital with what was first thought to be a skull fracture. X rays showed that she had only cuts and bruises, and she was discharged the following day.

Mary's philosophy of married life could have been summed up in the words spoken by Leora Arrowsmith to her errant spouse: "You're a rotten husband. I'd rather have you than all the decent ones in the world."

Ford's frustrations over his limited power as a director working within the Hollywood studio system eventually boiled over into public protest. His previously apolitical stance and growing identification with the conservative ethos of the U.S. Navy in the early thirties had led some liberals in Hollywood to view him with suspicion. But as he became involved in the Hollywood labor battles of the depression era, Ford was driven to a newfound political activism, reawakening his Irish heritage of Democratic, prolabor, antiauthoritarian politics. Although Ford was not a "joiner" by nature, his friend and screenwriter Philip Dunne recalled, he was a supporter of FDR and "a rebel in every direction."

In a 1936 interview with Emanuel Eisenberg of *New Theatre*, Ford complained that a director faced "a constant battle to do something fresh. First they want you to repeat your last picture. You talk 'em down. Then they want you to continue whatever vein you succeeded in with the last picture. You're a comedy director or a spectacle director or a melodrama director. You show 'em you've been each of these in turn, and effectively, too. So they grant you range. Another time they want you to knock out something *another* studio's gone and cleaned up with. Like a market. Got to fight it every time. Never any point where you can really say you have full freedom for your own ideas to go ahead with."

Ford's unhappiness over the Hollywood system in the early thirties was largely attributable to the factorylike methods the studios increasingly used to organize production. With the coming of sound and the massive outlays of capital required to refurbish theaters and production facilities, studios and the banks controlling them relied on assembly-line techniques that tended to minimize the importance of the director. The average director was handed a script a day or two before the start of shooting and was excluded from the cutting room. The director's authority was further eroded by the increasingly common "unit" system of assigning more than one director to a picture, and by the growing role of the associate producer as a buffer between the director and the studio head. Ford had much more clout and job security than most Hollywood directors, particularly after signing a ten-picture nonexclusive contract with Fox in September 1934. But not even directors of Ford's stature were immune from studio supervision and interference, and those without such stature had little recourse because there was no minimum contract establishing wages and working conditions for directors.

Ford was one of twelve directors who met in King Vidor's living room on December 23, 1935, and contributed one hundred dollars each to form the Screen Directors Guild over fierce opposition from the Hollywood studios.[4] As Ford recalled, he and the other directors gathered "to talk about our mutual problems. Now directors, because of the nature of their profession (some might say the cussedness of their natures, too), are among the greatest individualists in the world. But all of us in that room realized the need to band together to protect the integrity of motion picture direction." Vidor, the guild's first president, recalled that the impetus for its founding was the studios' decision to institute industrywide pay cuts in March 1933. On March 3, the day before the inauguration of President Franklin D. Roosevelt, the national economic crisis came to a head with panicked investors making runs on banks throughout the country. Roosevelt proclaimed a four-day national bank holiday beginning on March 5 while emergency reforms were begun in the eco-

---

4. The other founders were Frank Borzage, Lloyd Corrigan, William K. Howard, Gregory La Cava, Rowland V. Lee, Lewis Milestone, A. Edward Sutherland, Frank Tuttle, Richard Wallace, and William Wellman.

nomic system as part of FDR's New Deal. The Hollywood studios had been trying without success to impose salary cuts for several years, but the bank holiday, combined with plunging theater attendance and the drying up of Wall Street investment capital, finally gave them the excuse they needed.

The Academy of Motion Picture Arts and Sciences, which had been established in 1927 as a company union to counteract the growing Hollywood labor movement, was pressed into service by the studio bosses to institute the pay cuts. At an emergency meeting with the Association of Motion Picture Producers on March 7, the Academy board decided on "immediate and radical steps": a cut of 50 percent for any studio employee earning more than fifty dollars a week and 25 percent for those earning less than that amount. The cuts were said to be only temporary, but many in Hollywood feared they would become permanent.

Frank Capra, then a member of the Academy board, remembered a bizarre encounter with Ford in the midst of the pay-cut negotiations. At 5:54 P.M. on March 10, Capra was having his hair cut in the basement of the Hollywood Athletic Club when the building was shaken by a major earthquake centered in nearby Long Beach. He ran out of the building, but returned after the shaking subsided, and decided to calm his nerves with a steam bath. He found Ford in the steam room, calmly reading a newspaper: "Then I recognized him—my idol! The fabulous John Ford. To start a conversation, I remarked, 'Some earthquake, huh, Mr. Ford?' 'What earthquake?' he muttered sourly without looking up from his paper. To ease into introducing myself, I said, 'You've heard about the big pay-cut meeting the Academy's holding with the—' Still reading, he cut me short: 'That's all a lot of horseshit.' On that neat appraisal I sneaked out."

On March 13, after the International Alliance of Theatrical Stage Employees refused to go along with the Academy pay cuts, every studio had to stop production, a situation unprecedented in Hollywood history (Ford was then in the midst of directing *Pilgrimage* at Fox). An unsatisfactory compromise was worked out exempting some workers from cuts and lessening the impact on others, enabling production to resume on March 14 and 15. By mid-April, with the national crisis somewhat abated, full salaries were restored at most of the studios. But only independent producer Samuel Goldwyn retroactively paid his employees their lost wages.

"We finally realized how the producers were using the Academy and us," Vidor recalled. "What a lot of people didn't know was the fact that many producers and executives were subtracting the cuts from their employees' checks but not from their own. . . . The realization was very strong that we [directors] must have an organization to speak for us, and not the individual alone."

Ford first played a leadership role among Hollywood directors when he became president of the Motion Picture Directors Association in 1927. Primarily a fraternal organization, the MPDA had been founded in 1915 by, among others, Francis Ford and J. Farrell MacDonald. The Screen Directors Guild (predecessor of today's Directors Guild of America) was a more militant organization, although it lagged behind the formation in 1933 of the Screen Actors Guild and the Screen Writers Guild. The SDG was incorporated in January 1936 with seventy-five members, but as board member Rouben Mamoulian recalled, "It was tough to get important directors in because they had a lot to lose, big salaries to lose—the bigger the directors, the more reluctant they were." Many people in Hollywood charged the SDG with being "Communist-inspired," Vidor recalled, and there were "certain directors who were being such rugged individualists that they were holding out, key directors."

Though Ford was the SDG's first treasurer and often served on the board of the guild over the years to come, he always turned down overtures to run for the presidency, generally preferring to exert his influence behind the scenes. But he was prominently involved throughout the thirties in helping lead the guild's drive for recognition, and he eventually served as a member of the committee negotiating with the producers. Several years of bitterly fought negotiations were required before the directors' and the writers' guilds finally achieved recognition from the studios.

In a speech to SDG members during the salary-cut crisis, Ford put his principles into a broader context than simply the complaints of directors desiring more creative autonomy. Showing as much solidarity with the lowest-paid workers in Hollywood as with his fellow directors, Ford's speech marked the beginning of his period of dramatically increased political awareness and activity. Influenced by the New Deal and by Popular Front agitation for progressive change in the years leading up to World War II, Ford would become so militant that by 1937 he would declare himself "a definite socialistic democrat—*always* left."

Ford's speech to the SDG in 1933 offered what he called "a few dry gloomy facts" about the present financial crisis. He began by forcefully arguing that the squeeze on Hollywood labor and the temporary suspension of production was not justified by the financial condition of the film industry, but was instead an expedient scare tactic.

"Look, gentlemen," he said, "I don't think that we are stupid enough to deny that the picture racket is controlled from Wall Street. . . . [T]he banking industry is going on a sitdown strike. Why? To bring about a financial crisis. So that wages and wage earners can be pushed back to where they were in 1910."

Calling for a unified front with the rest of the Hollywood labor movement,

he told his fellow guild members, "I firmly believe that that kind of cooperation is plainly our duty unless we are satisfied to remain an insignificant and
exclusive club. Let's try to get back to the old days—when the people on the
set looked to the director for leadership. Let's pitch in with our coworkers and
try to find a way out of this mess. Let's work in the industry, with the industry, and for the industry. Let's not be high-hat. Let's help the others. I grant you
that the producers haven't recognized us, but for Christ's sake, and I say that
with reverence, let's not get into a position where the workers of the industry
don't recognize us."

Ford boiled down his arguments to basic human terms, declaring that Wall
Street greed was "the real reason why the favorite grip or gaffer is not working. Why so many familiar faces are missing from the studio. Why some of
those nice old ladies that used to get a few days a week are begging piecework
from wardrobe departments and asking for charity. Let's not kid ourselves. The
unemployment situation in the business right now is appalling. I, for one,
would like to cooperate with the other people in the game and find out what's
at the bottom of this."

Ford found it much harder to express compassion to people face-to-face.
Character actor Frank Baker, who appeared in many Ford movies, told Tag
Gallagher a revealing story about Ford's perverse approach to personal charity.
An old actor Ford had known at Universal came to his office during the depression era begging for money so his wife could have an operation. Ford
physically attacked the man, throwing him to the floor and demanding, "How
dare you come here like this? Who do you think you are to talk to me this
way?" When the man hobbled away, Ford sent his business manager after him
with a thousand-dollar check. Ford arranged for the operation, bought the
couple a house, and helped support them for the rest of their lives.

At the time of the Hollywood studio shutdown in March 1933, Ford was directing his first great film.

I first heard about *Pilgrimage* in the late 1960s from David Shepard, the distinguished film historian then working with the American Film Institute to
rescue lost and forgotten American films from decades of neglect by the studios that produced them. Based on an *American Magazine* story by I. A. R.
Wylie, the woman who also provided the source material for *Four Sons, Pilgrimage* deals with a possessive mother, Arkansas farmer Hannah Jessop (Henrietta Crosman), who sends her son (Norman Foster) to his death in World
War I rather than lose him to the girl he loves. Although stark and corrosive
in its lack of sentimentality, *Pilgrimage* has such tremendous emotional power
that it became a commercial success and even received some good reviews

when released in the summer of 1933. But as a "women's picture" and four-handkerchief weepie, this is the kind of movie that is never taken seriously by intellectuals who automatically sneer at those genres, and it had all but vanished from the landscape of film history, remaining unseen for decades. So it was startling when Shepard declared *Pilgrimage* to be Ford's masterpiece.

Although I would hesitate to make such a categorical statement about any one film from Ford's rich and varied body of work, *Pilgrimage* belongs without question on a short list of the director's greatest films. What's so fascinating about *Pilgrimage* from a biographical point of view is the way it departs from Ford's usual tendency to idealize motherhood. From the first film he directed, *The Tornado,* in which he played a cowboy who brings his mother over from Ireland, Ford habitually treated mothers with iconic reverence. The many lovingly bounteous mothers in his movies include Margaret Mann in *Four Sons,* Alice Brady in *Young Mr. Lincoln,* Jane Darwell in *The Grapes of Wrath,* Sara Allgood in *How Green Was My Valley,* Irene Rich in *Fort Apache,* Mildred Natwick in *3 Godfathers,* Olive Carey in *The Searchers,* and the invisible Irish mother whose spectral voice croons solace to John Wayne's character in *The Quiet Man.* When an interviewer once asked Ford why "the theme of the family" is so important in his work, he replied simply, "You have a mother, don't you?"

But while Ford celebrates the bedrock values of traditional family life, his films also mourn the inevitable dwindling and loss of such values. The theme of the destruction of family was present even in his first feature, *Straight Shooting,* but it became an increasing preoccupation after Ford reached middle age and had to face up to the many imperfections of his own family life. The departure for Ford in *Pilgrimage* is that it locates the source of destruction within the family itself, in a mother whose excessive devotion and pathological jealousy literally cause her son's death. There are some less-than-admirable mothers in a few other Ford films, including *Stagecoach, 7 Women,* and his lost silent Westerns *A Woman's Fool* and *Roped;* in *Rio Grande,* the prideful southern woman played by Maureen O'Hara has grave, if understandable, conflicts with her son and estranged husband. But *Pilgrimage* is unique among surviving Ford films for making a deeply flawed mother its central focus.

In a striking coincidence, Ford's mother died shortly after he finished shooting *Pilgrimage.* Barbara Curran Feeney succumbed to a long illness at the age of seventy-seven on March 26, 1933, at her home in Portland. Ford never commented publicly on his mother's death, but it can readily be imagined that he took it very hard indeed. His awareness of his mother's impending mortality may help explain why he invested such profound emotion in *Pilgrimage.* Ford may never have felt as much resentment toward his mother as Norman

Foster's Jim Jessop does toward his mother in *Pilgrimage,* but given the nature of Irish matriarchy and Abby Feeney's domineering personality, Ford probably did feel somewhat stifled by his mother's obdurate strength and the fierce demands of her love. The usual sentimentality toward motherhood in Ford's movies may have stemmed in part from his own feelings of inadequacy as a son—his inability to measure up to his mother's demanding standards of perfection—and from his guilt over his "desertion" of his parents to pursue a career at the opposite end of the country. Ford's ability to empathize with Hannah Jessop probably also owes much to guilt feelings over his hard-hearted mistreatment of his own son.

Pilgrimage is one of the most extreme examples of Ford's tendency, as a romantic pessimist, to explore the dark side of his ideals, their failure to transform mundane reality into something nobler and more enduring. The most important of his ideals—home, family, tradition, sacrifice—are embodied by women. So it is not surprising that Ford dwells with particular obsessiveness on female suffering and loss.

Especially by the standards of a popular melodrama made in 1933, the rigorous lack of sentimentality Ford maintains throughout *Pilgrimage* is astonishing. Hannah Jessop is a flinty, hard-hearted old woman proud of her descent from Indian-killing pioneers. When her son falls in love and declares his independence, Hannah is confronted with the dilemma faced by all Ford women, the tendency of the male to wander from the home. But Hannah's solution is chilling: she enlists him in the army, after earlier refusing to let him go. The town barber, who doubles as an army recruiter, is taken aback by the bluntness of her declaration, "I want the army to take him away." After prolonged hesitations, she puts pen to paper, signing what she clearly knows is her son's death warrant. To the girl Jim loves, Mary Saunders (Marian Nixon), Hannah admits, "I'd rather see him dead than married to you."

There is only one war scene in *Pilgrimage,* and it is shocking in its brevity: a mere ninety-six seconds elapses on a French battlefield before Jim is dead, buried alive in a collapsing trench. When Hannah is notified of his death by the town mayor (Francis Ford), her grief is palpable from her acute physical pain, but her stoical nature can allow it no verbal expression. Ford instead conveys her deepest inner feelings in one of his most heartrending moments of visual poetry: her hands are seen reassembling the pieces of a ripped-up photograph of her smiling son. The fact that we never saw Hannah tear up the picture makes her silent gesture an even more powerful metaphor for her belated attempt to undo the tragic mistakes of the past.

Ford's blend of filmmaking styles in *Pilgrimage* is masterful and daring. Jim's literal suffocation in the Argonne Forest is metaphorically foreshadowed by the early sequences at the family farm in Three Cedars, Arkansas. Strongly echoing Murnau, as they did in the World War I movie *Four Sons,* Ford and his longtime cinematographer George Schneiderman use a painted sky and studio sets of misty, soft-focus fields and marshes to give Jim's life with his mother a feeling of stifling confinement. Then, when Hannah is coaxed into joining a boatload of other Gold Star Mothers to make a pilgrimage to their sons' graves in France, the film opens up like a flower. The visual expansiveness of the film's second half contrasts sharply with the claustrophobic nature of the scenes in Arkansas. Much as Mark Twain does with his boatload of pilgrims in *Innocents Abroad,* Ford finds rich humor in sheltered American ladies encountering a more sophisticated world. These sequences owe much to the heartfelt simplicity and wit of Dudley Nichols's dialogue (Philip Klein and Barry Connors are also credited for their prior work on the screenplay). Although Nichols barely mentioned the film in his long letter to Lindsay Anderson in 1953 about working with Ford, it is among his finest work as a screenwriter. He seems to dismiss it for being about motherhood, like *Four Sons;* perhaps its daring pirouette from tragedy to comedy also made *Pilgrimage* seem less significant to Nichols than his more critically "respectable" works.

The healing power of the Fordian comic spirit is embodied in the raucous Carolina hillbilly Tilly Hatfield, who befriends Hannah on the boat to France. Magnificently played by Lucille La Verne, best known as the villainess in Griffith's *Orphans of the Storm,* the earthy, pipe-smoking Tilly, whose spirit has weathered the loss of three sons in war, has an indomitable strength that points forward to Jane Darwell's Ma Joad in *The Grapes of Wrath.* The comic relief Tilly provides during the film's somewhat grotesque mass ritual of formalized grief is akin to the humor shouted in the face of death at an Irish wake. But Ford never mocks the women's suffering. One of the most moving scenes is Hannah's outburst on the boat in front of the other mothers, confessing that she doesn't deserve to be in their company because they truly loved their sons and she sent hers to his death. When Hannah is helped to her cabin, Tilly solemnly intones, more to herself than to anyone else, "She sure musta loved that boy a heap." Her compassion and forgiveness are visually reinforced by Ford's lap dissolve to a somber tracking shot of Hannah walking slowly across a Parisian bridge, a lonely figure in the rain, perhaps even contemplating suicide.

Like George Bailey in Frank Capra's *It's a Wonderful Life,* Hannah is rescued from her own despair by coming to the aid of someone else about to commit suicide. She atones for her son's death by adopting the distraught American boy Gary Worth (Maurice Murphy) as a surrogate son. Fox was concerned about centering *Pilgrimage* around a largely unsympathetic old woman and pressured Ford to devote a considerable amount of screen time to Gary and his cute but insipid girlfriend, Suzanne (Heather Angel). An English actress with a finishing-school accent, Angel is hopelessly inappropriate as a French commoner snubbed by Gary's haughty mother (played by Hedda Hopper before she became a gossip columnist). But this casting lapse remains a minor flaw in the film, because Crosman's change of heart is so emotionally convincing. After reuniting Gary and his mother, she tells them, "I'm going to find my own boy now. He's out there in the Argonne—somewhere." Following a Murnau-like tracking shot as she walks through a fog-shrouded cemetery, Hannah asks Jim to forgive her and collapses on his grave. The critical importance the Catholic director places on Hannah's willingness to confess and make amends for her sin ("*I* killed him") is what makes her spiritual redemption possible, bearing out the religious overtones of the film's title. Hannah reunites her own family by apologizing to Jim's girlfriend, Mary, and embracing their illegitimate son, Jimmy (Jay Ward). Since this is the first time his grandmother has ever acknowledged his presence, Jimmy understandably reacts in fear. The film ends on a shot of Hannah clasping the inert little boy in her arms, hugging and kissing him fiercely and possessively. Even in her moment of redemption, Ford shows that there is something terrifying and oppressive about the power of Hannah's love.

Crosman was not Ford's first choice for Hannah Jessop. When *Pilgrimage* was first mentioned in the press as a possible Ford project in November 1932, it was reported that the director wanted Mae Marsh for the part. Marsh played leading roles in such D. W. Griffith films as *The Birth of a Nation, Intolerance,* and *The White Rose,* and *Pilgrimage* is as strongly influenced by Griffith as it is by Murnau. The sequence of Hannah waking during a storm with a psychic realization that Jim has died is reminiscent of a similar sequence in Griffith's 1919 film *The Greatest Question;* Hannah's arm reaching out from a train window to accept Mary's bouquet of flowers for Jim's grave echoes the homecoming scene in *The Birth of a Nation* with the mother's arm reaching out from a doorway to embrace her son as he returns from the Civil War. Casting Mae Marsh would have made the film's Griffith *hommage* complete. But her stardom had not survived the demise of silent pictures, so Ford was overruled by Fox. He always remained a loyal friend to Marsh, casting her in small but memorable parts into the early 1960s.

Henrietta Crosman's only important screen role before *Pilgrimage* was a comic one, as the matriarch in George Cukor's 1929 film *The Royal Family of Broadway*, adapted from the Edna Ferber–George S. Kaufman send-up of the Barrymore clan. But Ford may have remembered her from seeing one of her regular appearances in Portland when he was an usher at the Jefferson Theatre. The great performance Ford drew from Crosman in *Pilgrimage,* with its echoes of Greek tragedy in a rustic American setting, probably owes something to his understanding of her stature as a major actress of the American theater. Crosman lived until 1944 and appeared in a few more movies, but she never found another role to equal *Pilgrimage.* When she appeared onstage for the film's opening at New York's Gaiety Theater, she told the audience, "My hair is growing white. If you like Hannah Jessop, you will make me the happiest woman in New York."

The actor who plays her son, Norman Foster, had a brief run as a leading man in thirties films before going on to a long career as a journeyman director, making such movies as *Journey into Fear, Rachel and the Stranger,* and *Davy Crockett, King of the Wild Frontier.* When I innocently asked Foster in 1971 if the visual style of *Davy Crockett* was something of an homage to Ford, he surprised me by shouting angrily, "It has *nothing* to do with Ford! It's *my* visual style!" Foster, I discovered, bitterly disliked Ford, who bullied and ridiculed him throughout the shooting of *Pilgrimage.* Perhaps Ford did so because he found Foster an overly callow actor, and perhaps he also thought such treatment would put Foster in the right mood to play a morose, mother-dominated young man.

Ford employed an unusual method in shooting close-ups for several scenes in *Pilgrimage.* He filmed Foster and other actors looking directly into the camera, rather than from the slightly oblique angle customary in "invisible" Hollywood storytelling. Foster was convinced that Ford did so maliciously, in order to make him look ridiculous. But Ford used the same technique with Marian Nixon and the child actor Jay Ward; the director pointedly did *not* do so with Crosman, who never looks the camera in the eye. Breaking down the "third wall" between the audience and the characters most affected by Hannah's cruelty seems Ford's way of making a disturbing story even more uncomfortable to watch by having the actors stare at the audience accusingly.

What rankled Foster most about the way Ford treated him, however, was that throughout the shooting, the director mockingly called him "Jasper." Foster had no idea what that nickname signified. Finally, at the end of the shooting, he asked Ford why he called him "Jasper." Ford pointed to the black janitor who had been quietly sweeping the floor of the soundstage every day.

"See him?" the director said. "His name is Jasper."

Without a harbor, man is lost" could have been Ford's credo during those tempestuous years. Paradoxically enough, he found his own harbor by going to sea.

In 1934, two events occurred that would have a profound effect on the remainder of his life. That June, he bought the 106-foot ketch *Faith,* which he renamed the *Araner.* On September 21, he was commissioned as a lieutenant commander in the U.S. Naval Reserve. By reinventing himself as a seafaring man, Ford found a measure of peace and tranquillity.

In a sentimental gesture in memory of his late mother, Ford named the *Araner* after the Aran Islands off the west coast of Ireland, from which her people had come. Owning the *Araner* put Ford back in touch with his rapidly receding Irish roots and with the elemental life he had known as a boy growing up by the sea in Portland. Darcy O'Brien, George's son, observed that the *Araner* was "a classic example of the Irish American's not wanting to lose touch with the old country, but announcing a new prosperity at the same time."

Purchased for the fire-sale price of $16,500 from a financially strapped Pasadena businessman, Ford's yacht had been built eight years earlier in Massachusetts. Designed by John Hanna, the *Araner* was refurbished and personalized by Ford, who had it repainted a jaunty green and white. The luxurious interior included two fireplaces, red carpets, a master suite with a four-poster bed, four guest cabins, and quarters for six crewmen. Ford lovingly cared for the *Araner* and continued to pour great sums of money into it over the years. "It was terribly expensive," said Mary, "but it was our life . . . and Jack had his relaxation." Ford also used the boat for business purposes, entertaining important guests from Hollywood and the navy and holding script conferences with writers. On his 1934 tax return, Ford deducted one thousand dollars for *Araner* expenses, claiming that having Columbia Pictures president Harry Cohn as a guest on the yacht "resulted in his securing an assignment to direct a picture" (*The Whole Town's Talking,* released in 1935). But the IRS allowed only half of that deduction. For decades, Ford battled with the IRS over his deductions for the *Araner,* many of which were disallowed.

The *Araner* resolved some of the tensions Ford, like the heroes of his movies, always felt between the desire for a home and the need to wander. With the *Araner* he had a home that could remain anchored or sail from place to place, depending on his moods. The *Araner* was not exactly an all-male clubhouse—Mary and the children frequently went with him—but if Ford wanted to forget about family responsibilities, the *Araner* was the perfect vehicle. Even more than the Little Grey House on the Hill, it became his real home.

If the yacht often served as the site for a floating party, the boozy balancing act it represented brought a measure of stability to Ford's life. The *Araner* was his escape valve from the pressures of life in Hollywood, a party house for drinking and playing cards with his pals, and a quiet haven where he could read, think, and rest his mind and body between pictures. Ford explained to an interviewer in 1936 how he prepared his pictures: "Usually I take the story and get every line of printed material I can find on the subject. And then I take the boat and simply cruise until I've read it all. I eat, sleep, and drink whatever picture I'm working on—read nothing else, think of nothing else; which is probably the reason the continuity and mood of my products stay at an exact level."

Ford usually kept the *Araner* moored at the harbor in San Pedro, where it was cared for by its master, George Goldrainer, and his successor, Rip Yeager. During the summer Ford would sail the *Araner* to Catalina Island for stays of two or three weeks. Ford spent most of his time in the deckhouse, which was dominated by a large oak poker table. With pals such as Wayne, Bond, Henry Fonda, Dudley Nichols, Wingate Smith, actor Grant Withers, and producer Gene Markey, Ford played poker or bridge. When he had a writer aboard, such as Nichols or, later, James Warner Bellah or Frank Nugent, Ford spent part of his time in story conferences, kicking around ideas for a new picture. The writer periodically would disappear into his cabin to work on the script, occasionally emerging to show his pages to Ford. Ford was not always in the mood for work. Once Nichols approached Ford at the poker table and presented him with a completed script, cautioning him that it was the only copy. Ford tossed it out a porthole into the sea.

Each winter Ford sailed to Mexico on the *Araner* for sport fishing and carousing in fishing villages. He and his regulars were particular devotees of nightlife in Mazatlán, where they would prowl through bars slugging down tequila, accompanied by a hired mariachi band playing the director's favorite sentimental Mexican tunes. The musicians would follow the drunken Americans when they staggered back onto the boat to get even more plastered until they passed out cold.

The flavor of life on those bibulous Mexican excursions is captured by some of the wry entries by the master of the *Araner*, Goldrainer, in the ship's log, such as these for New Year's Eve 1934:

> 1:18 P.M. Went ashore—got the owner, Fonda, Wayne, and Bond out of jail. Put up a bond for their behavior.
>
> 9:30 P.M. Got the owner, Fonda, Wayne, and Bond out of jail again. Invited by Mexican officials to leave town.

The following day:

> Owner went to Mass—brought priest to *Araner*—purpose to sign pledge [to quit drinking]: pledge signed—celebrated signing of pledge with champagne, later augmented with brandy. . . .

Mr. Bond started telling Mr. Ford, owner, how to fish from the
Araner.

Mr. Ford coins new expression. Told Mr. Bond to go fuck himself.

Drink was the only means that Ford had to "relax and shut off his mind,"
Wayne explained. Ford's mind was so active during the making of a film that
people who worked with him testified he was constantly directing the film in
his head, day and night. The effort would become so exhausting and stressful
that he sought mental oblivion between pictures.

"Ford was an excellent drinking companion," reported screenwriter Philip
Dunne, an occasional guest on the boat during the 1930s. The son of the
celebrated Irish-American humorist Finley Peter Dunne, creator of "Mr.
Dooley," Philip Dunne met Ford shortly after coming to Hollywood and
beginning work as a reader at Fox in 1930. Their shared fondness for Mr.
Dooley's dialect humor and their mutual love of Irish history led to a casual
friendship long before they began working together when Ford filmed
Dunne's screenplay of *How Green Was My Valley* in 1941. A prominent liberal
and activist in the Screen Writers Guild, Dunne was an ally of Ford's in the
Hollywood labor movement. Ford was one of a handful of people given the
honor of meeting Finley Peter Dunne when the humorist visited his son in
California in 1935.

"I probably made four trips over to the *Araner* [while it was] anchored over
there at Catalina," Philip Dunne recalled. "I never saw it go anywhere. We'd
either fly over or go over on a boat. We'd drink and then we'd talk about the
Phoenix Park murders.[5] We'd get more and more 'mick' as the evening went
on. Neither of us was really entitled to it. It's a game; Ford used to play that
game. Gene Markey would be with us a lot, because Gene was Irish too. But
Gene used to laugh at us. He'd say, 'Nobody could understand a word you're
saying.'"

Sometimes Dunne would see the darker side of Ford's drinking habit:
"When he was drunk he'd get incoherent. He was not fighting drunk, he
would be sort of distant. I don't think Ford was really a man who had friends
in the usual sense, because he was a dominant figure. He was a leader, and I
don't think leaders have friends. That's why any of us who worked with Ford,

---

5. In May 1882, during bitter conflict in Ireland over the issues of land reform and home rule, the newly
arrived British chief secretary, Lord Frederick Cavendish, and his undersecretary, Thomas Burke, were
stabbed to death in Dublin's Phoenix Park by a band of assassins belonging to a secret society, the Invinci-
bles.

liked Ford, and knew him socially but were not followers would not get very intimate with him, and why he had stooges and followers who were [his intimates]. Wayne and Bond were not friends, they were more stooges. Ford loved to insult people. He actually used to reduce Wayne to tears, have him all blubbery and humiliate him in front of the company. I think Ford, having been an actor himself, had very little respect for the craft of acting."

Ford's dual personality was epitomized in his bifurcated life as a man of the sea. His boozy behavior on the *Araner* was counterpointed by the reverence he displayed for military tradition and his fascination with spit-and-polish discipline as an officer in the U.S. Naval Reserve. He bought an array of navy uniforms and wore them spotlessly, in revealing contrast to the determinedly sloppy attire he wore on board the *Araner* or on the sets of his movies. But Ford honored military discipline as much in the breach as in the observance. Dunne thought Ford always remained "extremely ambivalent" toward the navy side of his existence: "Is there such a word as 'tri-valent'? He could be in *all* three directions. And he was a rebel in every direction."

Dunne somewhat cynically disparaged the navy's acceptance of Ford by claiming, "Anybody with a private boat could get a Naval Reserve commission. That's one of the things that went with the boat, went with the territory." But Ford's ambition to be a navy man traced back to his frustrated attempts to enter Annapolis and serve in World War I. He carefully cultivated his navy connections for several years before receiving his commission. The friendships he developed with officers through Mary's social contacts and through making his films about the navy were as critical to Ford's commission as, if not more so than, owning a boat.

Ford applied for the commission on July 10, 1934. He claimed twenty years of yachting experience and four years as a dockhand on seagoing vessels, but came closer to the truth when he admitted, "Outside of a few years spent before the mast, the whole of my training has been in the motion picture industry." Indeed, his stature in the industry was one of his most attractive assets in the eyes of the navy brass. In one of Ford's letters of recommendation, Rear Admiral Frank H. Schofield wrote the secretary of the navy that Ford's qualifications included "experience in the handling of men, interest in the Navy, [and being] alert, resourceful, and related by marriage to the Navy as he married the niece of Rear Admiral Victor Blue." Recognizing Ford's potential for enhancing the image of the navy through his work as a filmmaker, Captain Herbert A. Jones, director of naval reserves for the Eleventh Naval District headquarters in San Diego, added his praise of Ford's "general Navy-mindedness" and "influential 'contacts' throughout the United States."

Ford's commission was approved despite a navy medical report that he was not physically qualified for appointment. The major problem was the director's weak eyesight: 8/20 in the right eye (corrected to 15/20) and 4/20 in the left eye (corrected to 10/20). He also suffered from "slight" nephritis (a chronic inflammation of the kidneys) and "[p]oor dental condition." To convince the navy that he remained, like Jack Benny, only thirty-nine years old, Ford had his brother Frank submit a false statement that he was born in 1895, rather than in 1894. Jack's desire to serve his country, to prove that he truly belonged in its inner circles, was so important to him that he managed to prevail over the medical examiners. Strings were pulled, and his disqualification was waived. Ford officially entered the U. S. Naval Reserve as a lieutenant commander on October 3, 1934.

In his 1979 Ford biography, Andrew Sinclair not only claims that Ford may have been spying for the United States government during his trip to Ireland in 1921 (extremely unlikely in light of Ford's Irish allegiances and aversion toward informers), but he also states that Ford's two trips to Asia in 1931–32 were disguised spying missions for U.S. military intelligence. Without specifically documenting all his information, Sinclair writes that Ford was recruited for Naval Intelligence by Rear Admiral William S. Sims and Captain Ellis Zacharias, a Japanese-speaking intelligence expert who ran his own semiofficial unit of naval reserve officers gathering information on Japanese and German activities in Mexico and Asia. Sinclair claims that while Ford was directing *Salute* at Annapolis in 1929, he "met the leaders of naval intelligence and was given a mission in the Pacific . . . secretly to report on harbor access and defenses."

George O'Brien, however, said that if Ford was doing any spying during their raucous adventures in Asia in 1931, he didn't realize it. "The preposterousness of this notion is pretty obvious, given that their every move was recorded in the press," wrote O'Brien's son Darcy. "But the glamour of it doubtless pleased and amused both of them. I recall my father's laughing about it and assuring me it was nonsense, as much as he, like Ford, loved the Navy and fancied himself 'on duty' in or out of uniform throughout his life." Ford's extensive military records, released in 1998, contain no indications that Ford was working for Naval Intelligence in any official capacity in 1931–32. Ford's tax returns for those years include no payments of any kind from the U.S. government. The only mentions of his Asian trips on his tax returns are as write-offs for business expenses, ostensibly related to preproduction activities on film projects.

Nevertheless, the possibility of Ford's having had some informal, unsalaried, clandestine role in military intelligence during that period cannot be ruled out. His early involvement may well have been an "off-the-books" relationship. What his military records do indicate is that he performed reconnaissance missions in Mexico for the navy between 1935 and 1939, turning in secret reports and receiving citations for spying on the Japanese military presence in Baja California. In contrast with Sinclair's portrait of Ford leading a "boyish" double life inspired by a "playful sense of conspiracy," Ford in fact was deadly serious about his spying. He fully recognized the grave implications of the rise of fascism in Germany and Japan during the 1930s and was prescient in his understanding that war was becoming inevitable. His inside knowledge no doubt stemmed in part from his closeness to superior officers, with whom he took pains to ingratiate himself, both for the sake of his own career interests and out of a genuine desire to be of vital service in military reconnaissance during an impending national emergency.

Among Ford's military records is a document revealing that there was indeed a hidden purpose behind his obtaining a navy commission. In a 1941 autobiographical sheet prepared for the navy, Ford wrote, "In 1931 I was asked by Admiral Frank H. Schofield, Captain Herbert Jones, and Lieutenant Commander Gail Morgan to prepare a course in naval photography; its uses, tactical, historical, and propaganda. In 1934 I was commissioned as a Lieutenant Commander in the Naval Reserve to forward this work, upon the recommendation of Admiral Schofield." In a report during World War II on the formation in 1940 of his combat photography unit, the Field Photographic Branch of the U.S. Navy, Ford added further details, writing that he had been ordered by Captain Jones in 1934 to plan a course in "Naval and Combat Photography." He explained that the navy wanted him to use his positions in the Naval Reserve and the film industry, as well as his experience as a yachtsman, "in studying infra-red and other supersensitive films and complementary filters as to their efficacy on sea and in the air, particularly in tropical waters."

Ford had much more in mind for his future seafaring ambitions than simply playing the role of gentleman sailor.

But just as Ford movies often mock the very institutions and traditions they idealize, so too did Ford satirize his new career as a navy man. He formed his own private yacht club, a strictly tongue-in-cheek organization that encouraged the wearing of uniforms, the more ridiculously ornate the better, and whose stated purpose was to promote boozing.

The Emerald Bay Yacht Club, founded in 1938, was a permutation of an equally jocular organization Ford had started earlier in the decade as the Young Men's Purity, Total Abstinence, and Snooker Pool Association (the last three words eventually were replaced by "Yachting Association"). That group was composed of fellow members of the Hollywood Athletic Club, where Ford liked to hang out in the afternoon, taking steam baths and sweating off his hangovers. The president of the Young Men's Purity (etc.) Association was the African-American steam-room attendant at the athletic club, John "Buck" Buchanan.

Ford renamed his club after an Irish-sounding bay on Catalina and gave himself the title of "commodore," with Gene Markey serving as the "vice-commodore." The members included *Araner* cronies such as Wayne, Bond, Nichols, and Dunne; Irish novelist and Ford cousin Liam O'Flaherty; the director's agent, Harry Wurtzel; fellow directors Frank Borzage, Tay Garnett, and Emmett Flynn; actors Preston Foster, Frank Morgan, and Johnny Weissmuller; and producer Merian C. Cooper. Some members occasionally held ad hoc meetings at the Hollywood Athletic Club or on the *Araner*, but the Emerald Bay Yacht Club "wasn't really a club—it didn't exist," Philip Dunne explained. "It was something that met once a year." As part of the initiation ceremony, a new member had to stand motionless, looking upward, as a cold beer was poured into his white dress pants.

When the members came together at their annual St. Patrick's Day party at the House of Murphy restaurant in Hollywood, all they did, Dunne admitted, was "just got drunk." The first such party had been held at the Ambassador Hotel's Coconut Grove and ended in a food fight that caused Ford's group to be banished from the fashionable nightclub. Although his yacht club was conceived in irreverence as a raspberry blown in the face of social snobbery, in practice it catered to Ford's most adolescent instincts, much like the forced, tediously macho humor that mars most of his military films. The embarrassingly childish food fight in Ford's 1957 navy movie *The Wings of Eagles* is reminiscent of the Coconut Grove debacle.

Ford's mocking attitude toward social prejudice has led to a serious misunderstanding about the club. Because Hollywood Jews were excluded from the established golf and yacht clubs in Southern California, they had to form their own private clubs. Sinclair's biography claimed that Ford therefore gave his Emerald Bay organization an anti-Semitic slogan in a "gesture of defiance" against Jewish clubs in Los Angeles: "Its infamous slogan was 'No Jews and no dues'—Ford's riposte as a film technician and a Gentile, and thus excluded from some of the smart yacht clubs of the mainland. Yet he himself was to resign from one of his clubs because of the blackballing of a Jewish army officer."

Dan Ford reports in his biography, however, that the slogan of the Emerald Bay Yacht Club was actually "Jews but no dues." That version was confirmed by club member Philip Dunne, who said that he never heard of the alleged anti-Semitic slogan: "Obviously I wouldn't have gone in for anything like that. I don't think that watchword ['Jews but no dues'] was anti-Semitic. I think they were making a point [about] the fact that there were clubs that wouldn't *have* Jews. So they'd say, 'Well, *we* do.'" Also known as "The Yacht Club for People Who Don't Like Yacht Clubs," Ford's familial group had several Jewish members, including Harry Wurtzel, whom Dudley Nichols affectionately referred to as their "Rabbi."

One of Ford's most important creative partnerships was forged with the actor who declared, "I never met a man I didn't like."

Between 1933 and 1935, Will Rogers made three highly popular movies for Ford at Fox: *Doctor Bull,* based on James Gould Cozzens's novel *The Last Adam; Judge Priest,* from the Judge Priest stories by southern humorist Irvin S. Cobb; and *Steamboat Round the Bend,* based on the novel by Ben Lucian Burman. The hallmarks of Ford's mature style are present in these amiable and unpretentious pictures: the interweaving of comedy and drama, the loving focus on Americana, the way a dreamlike past tends to crowd out the present, the loose and colorful approach to dialogue and performance, the delight in treating seemingly irrelevant asides with greater importance than the narrative. And above all, Ford found in Rogers a protagonist whose moral sense harmonized with his own.

Wise, tolerant, humorous, but also a lonely and melancholy figure, the Rogers character in Ford's films is successively a healer, a judge, and a showman—and all of those at once. Whether he's called Dr. George Bull, Judge William Pittman Priest, or Dr. John Pearly, he's a modest and diffident man roused to fight against social injustice. Simultaneously nostalgic and progressive in his outlook, Rogers mediates between warring factions in American life, providing a human link between past and present. He manages the seemingly impossible feat of keeping tradition alive while recognizing the necessity for social change. These three movies hold up remarkably well today, and Rogers's inspired collaboration with Ford left a lasting imprint on the director's approach to filmmaking.

The most beloved American of his time, so popular he was seriously discussed as a candidate for president in 1932, Will Rogers offered both soothing and astringent medicine for a country whose institutions were in a state of crisis. With his folksy, deceptively illiterate brand of satire—as he says in *Judge Priest,* "The first thing I learned in politics was when to say ain't"—Rogers punctured the fat-cat complacency that had brought such illness to the body politic. As a cure he offered common sense. In addition to his huge success as a radio personality and political columnist, Rogers became the movies' biggest box-office attraction by 1934, partly due to his work with Ford. At the time of his death in an August 1935 plane crash, Rogers ranked second at the box office only to the phenomenally popular Fox child star Shirley Temple.

Ford and Rogers were such a perfect match that they might have gone on to a long series of films together, as Ford did with Harry Carey in the early years and with Henry Fonda and John Wayne in years to come. Rogers bore striking similarities to Carey, physically and spiritually and in his casual, seemingly artless acting style. During the filming of *Judge Priest* in 1934, Rogers reminded the readers of his syndicated newspaper column that Ford "used to direct Westerns, and made some great ones with Harry Carey, the most human and natural of the Western actors." Rogers wrote that "one of the likable things about Jack is that he remembers. . . . Well, the other day on a big set, a jury and courtroom trial, Jack had all his old cowpuncher pals, I had known most of them for many years, too, and it sure was good to see 'em again." Marveling at the history lessons he was picking up from listening to Irvin S. Cobb, Rogers added, "This old boy Ford is no cluck on history, either, you get a lot from him; but his stories are mostly about Irish wars. He can lick the English for you as entertainingly as Cobb can the Yankees. Funny part—Ford is a Yankee from Maine."

It was Fox executive Sol Wurtzel who recognized Ford's kinship with Rogers and brought them together. As early as 1929, it was announced that Fox planned to have Ford direct Rogers in a film version of Mark Twain's comic novel about time travel, *A Connecticut Yankee in King Arthur's Court.* Ford had read and loved the book during the months when he was bedridden with diphtheria as a child in Portland and needed a magic carpet for his imagination. But the film, released in 1931 as *A Connecticut Yankee,* was directed instead by David Butler, who had acted for Ford in *The Village Blacksmith, Hoodman Blind, The Blue Eagle,* and *Salute.*

The first role Rogers played for Ford, the title character in *Doctor Bull,* is a Connecticut Yankee, an old-fashioned small-town physician combating epidemics of both typhus and puritanical narrow-mindedness. But in real life Rogers was the farthest remove from a Yankee; he liked to joke that his ancestors *met* the *Mayflower.* "My father was one-eighth Cherokee and my mother was quarter-blood Cherokee," he wrote. "I never got far enough in arithmetic to figure out just how much 'Injun' that makes me, but there's nothing of which I am more proud than my Cherokee blood." As a mixture of red and white, Rogers transcended ethnic classification, for his was a quintessentially American personality, believable in almost any kind of setting the country had to offer. For Ford, Rogers plays an insider who is also an outsider, a leader who acts for society in ways it cannot see, a mediator who eventually helps a recalcitrant populace to a better understanding of its basic values.

Ford's affinity for such conciliatory figures stemmed back to the benign political paternalism embodied by his father, the Democratic ward boss, and his uncle, Judge Joseph Connolly of the Cumberland County (Maine) Superior Court. While loyal to somewhat antiquated and clannish codes of behavior, such men devoted themselves to creating a new social harmony by healing divisive wounds between warring social and ethnic groups. Using somewhat unorthodox means unavailable to the old-line establishment, they manipulated the tools of government so it would behave more humanely and follow what Lincoln called "the better angels of our nature."

Early in their collaboration, Will Rogers gave Ford an elaborate explanation of how a certain scene should be directed. Telling Rogers to direct the scene himself, Ford walked off the set. Rogers went to Fox production chief Winfield Sheehan and embarrassedly confessed that Ford had wandered away and that he had no idea what to do without him. After that, Ford had no trouble with Will Rogers. But Ford wisely indulged his friend "Bill"'s penchant for improvisation, allowing him to do elaborate riffs on the script.

"I don't think he ever read a script at home," Ford recalled. On the set, Rogers would look at his lines and ask the director, "What does that mean?" Ford would say, "Well, that's rather a tough question. I don't know what it means exactly." "Then," recalled Ford, "we would finally figure out what it meant, and I'd say to him, 'Say it in your own words!' And he'd go away, muttering to himself, getting his lines read, and when he came back, he'd make the speech in typical Rogers fashion, which was better than any writer could write for him."

Adapting to Rogers's easygoing acting style was natural to Ford, who liked dialogue to sound as if the actor had just thought it up, even if it had to be written that way (the exceptionally colorful dialogue for *Judge Priest* and *Steamboat Round the Bend* was credited to two first-rate screenwriters, Dudley Nichols and Lamar Trotti). Rogers's dilatory habits when beginning his workday also suited Ford just fine, because it always took the director a while to get up to speed in the morning. Rogers took breaks during the day to bang out his immensely popular daily newspaper column on a portable typewriter, often while sitting on the running board of a car. Ford indulged Rogers's preference for a leisurely shooting pace, knowing that his efficient shooting methods and Rogers's ability to do a scene in a single take would make up the time and keep them on track.

Harry Carey Jr., whose 1994 book *Company of Heroes: My Life as an Actor in the John Ford Stock Company* is the best account of Ford's working methods, recalled that in the 1950s, "I used to sit up in his bedroom on Copa de Oro [Road, in Bel Air], at the side of his bed. He was always lyin' around in bed, even before he was sick. And I got to where I could just ask him [things], talk to him like I would talk to my own father. I had no idea about doing a book or anything, I just was interested. I said to him one time, 'What was it like directing Will Rogers?' And he really surprised me, because he was such a *strong* bastard. He said, 'Oh, you didn't direct Will.' I couldn't believe it, I said, 'Really? You didn't give him any direction?' He said, 'No. Nobody directed Will. You let Will do what he wanted. That's the only way you could handle Will.'"

Rogers and Stepin Fetchit shared a remarkable harmony of acting styles. In a newspaper interview in February 1935, three months before they began work on *Steamboat Round the Bend,* Stepin Fetchit was quoted as saying of Rogers, "Paht of the time he suhprises me. Paht of the time I suhprise him. But mos' of the time we suhprises each other." (Actually, Lincoln Perry, aka Stepin Fetchit, spoke more conventional English off-camera, but his self-conscious crafting of his image was evident in his instruction to the reporter: "If you put anything I say in the papah, it might be wise to kind of transpose it into my dialeck.")

Ford enthusiastically encouraged the affectionate interchanges between the two actors and even included a delightful parody by Rogers of his screen partner in *Judge Priest.* The film also has Rogers singing two songs with the great Hattie McDaniel, "My Old Kentucky Home" and an improvisatory duet.[6] In his personal and professional isolation, Judge Priest finds that he has more in common with blacks than whites. This casual, understated theme of brotherhood between the races is extended into an actual business partnership between Doctor John and Jonah in *Steamboat Round the Bend.* Doctor John also hails a black man he passes on the river as his "brother."

What a radical departure the Stepin Fetchit–Will Rogers screen relationship represented is eloquently explained by V. S. Naipaul in his 1989 book *A Turn in the South:* "Stepin Fetchit was adored in my childhood by the blacks of Trinidad. He was adored not only because he was funny and did wonderful things with his seemingly disjointed body and had a wonderful walk and a wonderful voice, and was given extravagant words to speak; he was adored by Trinidad black people because he appeared in films, at a time when Hollywood stood for an almost impossible glamour; and he was also adored—most importantly—because, at a time when the various races of Trinidad were socially separate and the world seemed fixed forever that way . . . Stepin Fetchit was seen on the screen in the company of white people. And to Trinidad blacks—who looked down at that time on Africans, and laughed and shouted

---

6. In an instance of thoughtless Hollywood racism, her last name is misspelled in the credits as "McDaniels." In many of her early film appearances, McDaniel did not even receive screen credit. She later became the first black actor to win an Academy Award, for her supporting role as Mammy in *Gone with the Wind*.

and hooted in the cinema whenever Africans were shown dancing or with spears—the sight of Stepin Fetchit with white people was like a dream of a happier world."

Healing America's intolerance is one of the major themes of Ford's Rogers trilogy. The communities in these films are torn by prejudice and injustice. As his character name indicates in *Judge Priest*, Rogers plays a figure who combines the conciliatory and ameliorative functions of both jurist and clergyman. He is a celibate because the love of his life exists only in his memory: like Hannah addressing her dead son in *Pilgrimage*, the judge communes with his dead wife by talking to her in a graveyard. His humanity is shown in what he calls "a hankerin' for the spirit of the law and not the letter." To borrow Chesterton's description of a judge in one of his Father Brown stories, Judge Priest is "one of those who are jeered at as humorous judges, but who are generally much more serious than the serious judges, for their levity comes from a living impatience of professional solemnity, while the serious judge is really filled with frivolity, because he is filled with vanity."

Like its remake, *The Sun Shines Bright*, *Judge Priest* centers on a series of incidents in which the judge shames the community into an awareness of its intolerance—he defies class barriers by helping his nephew woo a girl from a disgraced family, pointedly involves his black factotum in his legal activities, and exonerates the girl's father from a trumped-up assault charge by revealing his Civil War heroism. That stirring flashback, showing the rescue of a Union officer by a Confederate, is narrated by none other than Henry B. Walthall, the Little Colonel from *The Birth of a Nation*. Melodramatically accompanied by an African-American band outside the courthouse playing "Dixie," this spectacle is stage-managed by Judge Priest, serving as the director's on-screen surrogate. Combining a celebration of brotherhood under fire with a shameless manipulation of the jury's Confederate sympathies is the judge's way of bringing the community together while acknowledging and subtly mocking the enduring strength of their prejudices.

According to Stepin Fetchit, who repeats his role as the judge's companion Jeff Poindexter in *The Sun Shines Bright*, the reason Ford remade *Judge Priest* was that Fox cut a scene from the film in which the judge rescues Jeff from a lynching: "They cut it out because we were ahead of the time. . . . [In *The Sun Shines Bright*,] the Negro that gets saved was played by a young boy—I was older then. But they kept it in." Ford described Rogers's speech against lynching in *Judge Priest* as "one of the most scorching things you ever heard." All that survives in the film is an ironic allusion to the missing scene: when Jeff, in a Lincolnesque conciliatory spirit, announces that he's going to play both

"Dixie" and "Marching Through Georgia" (the hated anthem of Sherman's Yankee marauders) at the courthouse, the judge dryly comments, "I got you out of *one* lynchin'. Catch you playin' 'Marching Through Georgia,' I'll *join* the lynchin'."

In *Steamboat Round the Bend,* set along the Mississippi River in the Deep South of the 1890s, there's a terrifying and altogether unfunny reaction shot of Stepin Fetchit running from an armed mob of angry whites. Even more remarkably, it is followed by a scene of the black man joining forces with a white preacher to confront the mob together, concocting an ingenious ploy that manages to make the mob seem both venal and ridiculous. This film goes so far in its satirical take on racial and historical themes that it sometimes verges on surrealism.

Stepin Fetchit makes his first appearance emerging from the mouth of a dummy whale in the wax museum of a bankrupt carnival sideshow. Christened David Begat Solomon but generally known by the all-American moniker of George Lincoln Washington, he is dubbed "Jonah" by Rogers's John. The doctor recognizes Jonah as the director's beloved figure of the holy fool. While they run their sideshow on the steamboat, the doctor and Jonah freely transform the wax figures for their own purposes, changing King George III into George Washington, Ulysses S. Grant into Robert E. Lee, and two of Jesus' apostles into the outlaws Frank and Jesse James. This evolving gallery of famous men serves as a metaphor for the mutability of American history and the fluidity of the country's social divisions. By improvising more popular new personalities for their pantheon figures, Doctor John and Jonah farcically mock the schisms in the national character and demonstrate the resilience of a heterogeneous country whose motto is "E Pluribus Unum."

"*Steamboat Round the Bend* should have been a great picture," Ford recalled, "but at that time they had a change of studio and a new manager came in who wanted to show off, so he recut the picture, and took all the comedy out." That's hardly the case, but the film has a highly episodic structure and spends too much time on its melodramatic plot about Doctor John rescuing his dim-witted nephew Duke (John McGuire) from being hanged for committing a justifiable homicide.

The "new manager" Ford blamed for the recutting was the production chief of the newly created Twentieth Century–Fox studio, Darryl F. Zanuck. Zanuck's and Joseph Schenck's Twentieth Century Pictures absorbed the faltering Fox Film Corporation in August 1935, shortly before *Steamboat Round the Bend* was scheduled to be released. The contretemps between Ford and Zanuck—the first but not the last time they would clash over Ford's preference for poetic imagery over narrative—marked an inauspicious start to what would be a long, fruitful, but sometimes argumentative relationship.

. . .

When shooting was completed on *Steamboat Round the Bend* six weeks before Rogers's death, Ford invited Rogers to accompany him to Hawaii on the *Araner*. But Rogers, who loved wilderness adventures, had planned a trip to Alaska with the renowned aviator Wiley Post. "Jack begged him to come along, but you know Will," Mary recalled. "He was just as enthusiastic about aviation as Jack is about yachting. He had supreme confidence in Wiley Post."

Rogers told Ford, "You keep your duck and go on the water. I'll take my eagle and fly." The plane carrying Rogers and Post crashed in fog near Point Barrow, Alaska, on August 15, 1935, killing both men instantly. Rogers was only fifty-five. "We had a terrible time with Jack," Mary said. "He went all to pieces. He was superstitious, and those last words of Will's kept going through his ears."

When Ford recovered his bearings, he held a memorial mass for Rogers at a church in Honolulu. He gathered with him other Fox personnel who happened to be on the island: Shirley Temple, Janet Gaynor, director Henry King, and executive Sol Wurtzel. They later adjourned to a nearby hotel for a Hawaiian version of an Irish wake.

Every Hollywood studio ceased production during Rogers's funeral services at Forest Lawn in Glendale on August 22. Fifty thousand people filed past the coffin, and that night the Hollywood Bowl was filled for a public tribute. Flags flew at half-staff throughout the country; twelve thousand movie screens went dark for two minutes of silent remembrance.

Worried about how movie audiences would react to seeing him again so soon after his death, Twentieth Century–Fox cut a shot of Rogers waving good-bye to the young couple at the end of *Steamboat Round the Bend* before the film was released on September 6. The studio thought viewers would interpret the wave as Rogers saying good-bye to the world and that it would send them out of the comedy feeling depressed. As a consequence, the ending of *Steamboard Round the Bend* is rather abrupt, rather than the lingering farewell that might have seemed more appropriate. But the film was a hit, and so was Fox's subsequent release of another previously unseen Rogers picture, *In Old Kentucky*. The public could not get enough of its beloved Will Rogers.

CHAPTER SEVEN

SEAN AND KATE

Q: *Then you do believe, as a director, in including your point of view*
in a picture about things that bother you?
A: *What the hell else does a man live for?*

FORD, INTERVIEWED BY EMANUEL EISENBERG
IN *NEW THEATRE*, 1936

THE INCREASINGLY PERSONAL nature of Ford's work in the mid-1930s
was manifested in his growing preoccupation with Irish subject matter. As
he looked more deeply within his soul and became more confident in his ability to express his feelings on screen, Ford gravitated to stories that reflected his
ambivalence toward his ethnic identity, his Irish Catholicism, his guilt-ridden
conflicts over money and marital fidelity, and his attempts to reconcile the demands of commercial success with artistic and political integrity. He tested his
growing power within the film industry by trying to persuade reluctant studio
executives to let him film three Irish projects close to his heart: his cousin
Liam O'Flaherty's 1925 novel *The Informer*, Sean O'Casey's 1926 play *The
Plough and the Stars*, and Maurice Walsh's 1933 short story "The Quiet Man."
All three projects eventually reached the screen, but each presented enormous
difficulties, and Ford was unable to find backing for his film of "The Quiet
Man" until the early 1950s.

Ford first became acquainted with O'Flaherty when the novelist came to
Hollywood to work as a screenwriter in 1932. They soon became drinking
buddies. While knocking back enormous quantities of Guinness stout and
Irish whiskey, Ford and the left-wing writer from the Aran Islands had many
enlightening political discussions, often while sailing on the *Araner*. O'Flaherty
reinforced Dudley Nichols's influence on the leftward development of Ford's
political thinking during that period of worldwide political and economic
crisis. Ford took an option on *The Informer* in 1933 and began pitching it
to the studios. The book had been filmed in England by German-American

director Arthur Robison in 1929, but that version did not find an American distributor. Hollywood saw little box-office potential in O'Flaherty's unrelentingly grim story of a renegade Irish Communist named Gypo Nolan who turns in a comrade for a reward of twenty pounds during the civil war of 1921–23.

Ever since his brief visit to strife-torn Ireland in 1921 to observe and support his cousin Martin Feeney's IRA activities, Ford had felt a powerful allegiance to the cause of Irish nationhood. But despite his closeness to O'Flaherty, Ford was less interested in *The Informer* as a vehicle for his or the novelist's political views than as a morality play about the eternal conflict between idealism and human weakness. Such a conflict was raging within Ford's dark personality during the depths of the depression, when his social conscience and growing artistic ambition were making him increasingly discontented with the strictures of the studio system. In Gypo, Ford also could see a cautionary image of his own tendency toward self-destructive and guilt-ridden behavior; the casting of Victor McLaglen, a larger and coarser simulacrum of Bull Feeney, reinforced the connection. O'Flaherty depicted Gypo as a furtive, isolated, and brutish figure waging an unsuccessful attempt to avoid succumbing to the dark side of human nature. The book describes him as being "like some primeval monster just risen from the slime in which all things had their origin."

Before Ford finally received a green light from RKO in October 1934, *The Informer* was rejected by Fox, Columbia, MGM, Paramount, and Warner Bros. because of its downbeat nature and politically sensitive subject matter. But Ford claimed that the reason he had such trouble convincing a studio to let him film *The Informer* was that he could not find an executive who would take the time to read the book. He said he eventually succeeded only because of the intercession of an "old friend" who had read the book, Joseph P. Kennedy. The father of future president John F. Kennedy had formed RKO in 1928 with RCA president David Sarnoff to make talking pictures with the RCA Photophone sound process. According to Ford, Kennedy told RKO's staff producers that "he wanted them to get me to direct a picture. They informed Joe I didn't want to do a Western but a picture about 'a rebellion in Ireland.' Joe asked how much it would cost. When one of the producers said around $200,000, Joe said, 'Let him make it. It won't lose any more than some of those you've made.'" However, Kennedy had sold out his remaining interests in the film business in 1930. Three months before RKO agreed to make *The Informer,* Kennedy became the chairman of the Securities and Exchange Commission. So if he had anything to do with pushing the project, it could only have been on an informal basis.

Furthermore, Ford already had directed a successful film for RKO, *The Lost Patrol* (1934), a desert adventure yarn about a British army patrol cut down, one by one, by unseen Arab snipers. Today *The Lost Patrol* seems stilted and floridly overacted by some of its cast members (particularly Boris Karloff as a wild-eyed religious fanatic), but in its time it was regarded as an unusually serious adventure film, setting a new standard by focusing more on character revelation than on action. The executive who brought Ford to RKO to make *The Lost Patrol* was Merian C. Cooper.

RKO during the thirties "ranked as a major studio only because of its nationwide theater chain," notes film historian Douglas Gomery. "RKO produced the best and worst feature films because its owners and managers were always under the gun to find a way to make money. Rarely was a management team in place for more than a few years when it was let go and replaced by studio bosses with different ideas. Production executives came and went with regularity."

Merian Cooper lasted only sixteen months as RKO's head of production in 1933–34, but he was one of the most fabulous characters who ever worked in the movie business. After failing to complete his studies at Annapolis, Cooper joined the U.S. Army and participated in General "Black Jack" Pershing's Mexican border expeditions against Pancho Villa. He flew in World War I and was captured by the Germans when his plane was shot down over the Argonne Forest. Following the war, Cooper worked in Poland with the European food relief program headed by Herbert Hoover. Kevin Brownlow's study *The War, the West, and the Wilderness* relates the next part of Cooper's colorful and improbable saga: "The Allied intervention was at its height when, with Major Cedric Faunt-le-Roy, he formed the Kościuszko Squadron to fight the Bolsheviks. Again he was shot down, this time by Budënny's cavalry, and he became a prisoner of the Red Army. Sentenced to death, he made an epic escape and returned to the United States. Cooper had been impressed by Theodore Roosevelt's *Through the Brazilian Wilderness,* and by its message: 'If you want to be an explorer, make sure you do it while you're young.'"

Joining forces with a former combat cameraman he had known in Europe, Ernest B. Schoedsack, Cooper made an acclaimed pair of ethnographic documentaries in Turkey and Siam, *Grass* (1925) and *Chang* (1927). Cooper served as executive assistant to RKO production chief David O. Selznick in 1931–33 before ascending to that post when Selznick moved to MGM. With Schoedsack, Cooper produced and directed RKO's classic 1933 monster movie *King Kong,* which satirizes their own filmmaking adventures. At the time Ford met Cooper, Ford was essentially an armchair adventurer whose stirring film images were created more from imagination than experience. "Coop"'s real-life exploits and military background earned his immediate respect and admiration. Bold to the point of recklessness, but personally reserved, the amiable, pipe-smoking southerner resembled the larger-than-life but unassuming adventurers whom Ford romanticized in his films.

Cooper, for his part, not only appreciated Ford's superior filmmaking talent but was unfazed by Ford's eccentricities or drinking habits. He was one of the few executives and producers who ever managed to work comfortably with Ford, allowing the director to feel creatively unfettered while still keeping tight rein on production details. Working with Cooper, Ford felt relaxed and confident enough that he did not need to assert his autonomy by acting rebellious or, as he sometimes did, by sabotaging his own work as a form of passive resistance. Ford's drinking problem, which threatened to disrupt his career in the early thirties, became more manageable after he began working with Cooper. Their association would continue for many years. Cooper eventually became Ford's producing partner in Argosy Pictures, which made some of the director's greatest films, including the Cavalry Trilogy, *The Quiet Man*, and *The Sun Shines Bright*.

If Cooper was the exception that proves the rule in Ford's dealings with producers, Cliff Reid, associate producer on *The Informer*, was the archetypal butt of Ford's producer jokes. Being associate producer on a John Ford film was a thankless job at best, and Ford delighted in telling sadistic stories at Reid's expense. His favorite was about the shooting of *The Lost Patrol* in the desert outside Yuma, Arizona. Work went slowly because of the effect of the intense heat on the cast and crew. Reid pestered Ford with telegrams from Hollywood demanding that he shoot faster. Ford ignored the demands. Finally Reid himself showed up on location, debarking from an airplane in a tropical outfit topped with a pith helmet. Within twenty minutes, Ford claimed, "the producer had disappeared. They'd taken him to the hospital. Yep. Heat prostration."

Such treatment made Reid "terrified" of Ford, according to writer-producer Nunnally Johnson. Reid had little authority on the set of Ford movies, as is evident from the credit appearing above the title of *The Informer*: "A John Ford Production." On the first day of shooting, Ford assembled the company and announced, "This is an associate producer." Taking Reid's chin in his hand and turning it slowly into profile, Ford continued, "Take a good look at him, because you will not see him again on the set until the picture is finished shooting." Then Ford shook Reid's hand and added, "Thank you, Cliff. I'll see you at the rushes."

Katharine Hepburn recalled that Reid "usually did Ford's pictures because Ford liked someone who did not talk back to him"; but Dudley Nichols described Reid more favorably as a producer with "unshakable confidence in

Ford." Ford took every possible advantage of that confidence. Toward the end of shooting on *The Informer,* Reid appeared on the set and timidly approached Ford to congratulate him for being ahead of schedule. Robert Parrish, who worked on the film as an actor and apprentice film editor, recalled that when Reid came to visit, Ford was sitting in his director's chair chewing his hand-kerchief. That meant he wanted to be left alone with his thoughts. Usually Ford's coworkers realized they should stay away from him at such moments. Ford acted as if he did not notice Reid's arrival. But then the associate pro-ducer blurted out, "The stuff looks great, Jack. . . . I just saw the rushes. You're going to love them."

"Eddie!" Ford called to his brother and second assistant Eddie O'Fearna. "Have we finished shooting yet?"

"Not yet, Jack. We still have half a day to go."

"Then what's this front-office son of a bitch doing on the set?"

Reid's face turned color and there was a long, tense silence. Ford turned to cameraman Joseph H. August:

"Joe, the front office likes the rushes, so there must be something wrong. We'll have to keep shooting until we find out what it is. We won't finish tonight after all."

Ford then demanded of Reid, "What rushes did you see, Cliff?"

"The Donald Meek interrogation scene," Reid answered, "and believe me, Jack, he's sensational. When Preston Foster asks him . . ."

Ford told his brother, "Call Donald in. We'll reshoot his interrogation scene this afternoon."

Ford not only redid that scene, but shot for two additional days, redoing an-other scene with Wallace Ford and Una O'Connor as well as adding close-ups and background shots for the main titles. The new material cost the studio twenty-five thousand dollars. One suspects this maneuver was Ford's devious means of bullying Reid into letting him shoot retakes he had always intended to film at the end of principal photography.

When Ford was preparing *They Were Expendable* at MGM in 1944, he told studio chief Louis B. Mayer that he wanted to hire Reid as the film's associate producer. Mayer asked why he wanted Reid, whose career had been in the doldrums.

"Because he's the best goddam associate producer in the business," Ford replied. "Did a hell of a job on *The Informer.*"

Today, I fear that the art of telling stories by motion pictures is becoming lost," Ford wrote in 1937. ". . . I'll venture the prophecy that if somebody today made a picture completely without dialogue, told the story only with the camera, and then 'dubbed' in sound effects and music after the filming was completed, the production would be a smash hit." *The Informer* comes as close to fitting that description as any film Ford made after the advent of talking pictures. Following the same expressionistic path Ford took in the late silent period with *Four Sons* and *Hangman's House*, *The Informer* is a tour de force of visual storytelling, presented with what John Wayne admiringly described as "a sparsity of words."

O'Flaherty's Dostoyevskian novel, which expresses Gypo Nolan's tortured psychological state through a relentless accumulation of vividly detailed imagery, was ideally suited for such an experiment. The author conceived of *The Informer* as "a sort of high-brow detective story" whose style would be "based on the technique of the cinema. It should have all the appearance of a realistic novel and yet the material should have hardly any connexion with real life."

In his 1943 essay "The Writer and the Film," Dudley Nichols explained how he approached his adaptation of *The Informer*: "In 1935 this was in a certain sense an experimental film; some new method had to be found by which to make the psychological action photographic. At that time I had not yet clarified and formulated for myself the principles of screenwriting, and many of my ideas were arrived at instinctively. I had an able mentor as well as collaborator in the person of John Ford and I had begun to catch his instinctive feeling about film. I can see now that I sought and found a series of symbols to make visual the tragic psychology of the informer, in this case a primitive man of powerful hungers. The whole action was to be played out in one foggy night, for the fog was symbolic of the groping primitive mind; it is really a mental fog in which he moves and dies. A poster offering a reward for information concerning Gypo's friend [Frankie McPhillip, played by Wallace Ford] became the symbol of the evil idea of betrayal, and it blows along the street, following Gypo; it will not leave him alone. It catches on his leg and he kicks it off. But still it follows him and he sees it like a phantom in the air when he unexpectedly comes upon his fugitive friend."

Ford and his masterful cinematographer Joseph August flooded the picture with shadows, fog, and backlighting. That technique was not simply a means of externalizing Gypo's moral conflicts; it was also a matter of necessity. Ford had to make *The Informer* for a production cost of only $242,756, which meant that he had to make do virtually without sets.[1] All *The Informer* had to offer in the way of so-called production values were a few canvas flats repre-

---

1. Ford and Nichols agreed to cut their usual salaries and take a percentage of the profits. Ford was paid only $15,750 for directing *The Informer,* but he had 12.5 percent of the net profits and continued to receive modest profit participation checks for the rest of his life. He had a similar arrangement with RKO on *The Lost Patrol,* which cost $253,787; he earned $15,000 plus 12 percent of the net. In 1936 alone, those two films brought profits to Ford of $35,218, mostly from *The Informer.*

senting the streets of Dublin and some nondescript interiors. In a further sign
of the studio's lack of faith, only eighteen days were allowed for shooting, and
midway through the schedule, RKO moved the production from its main lot
on Melrose Avenue down the street to a dusty rental facility, the California
Studio (now Raleigh Studios). "Which was good," Ford recalled, "because
[studio executives] no longer came in each day to tell me how depressing the
story was and what a failure the picture was going to be."

Ford did not regard the meager production values as a handicap. He said he
could have made the movie for half the budget. He was excited by the artistic
challenge of creating a state of mind by orchestrating the interplay of light and
shadow; inadvertently, RKO had allowed him to make an art movie. Sometimes his expressionistic approach works brilliantly. In the opening sequence,
Gypo emerges from the fog into a shadowy Dublin street scene. After ponder-
ing the wanted poster and a superimposed memory image of the fugitive
Frankie McPhillip, the clumsy giant angrily tears down the poster and wanders aimlessly toward a pub, comically banging his head on a hanging sign-
board. He stops to listen to a street singer (Denis O'Dea) singing "The Rose
of Tralee," a ballad of romantic longing that seems to awaken a distant flicker
of tenderness in Gypo's thick, dimly comprehending features. At the sudden
approach of a squad of Black and Tans, Gypo backs anxiously off into the fog.
The commanding officer frisks the street singer, who continues his tune in-
souciantly while turning slowly for inspection. In the same motion he catches
a coin flipped by the officer and casually snaps a salute, lending an unexpected
touch of humanity to an encounter between political enemies. All this is accomplished without a bit of spoken dialogue.

The Dublin atmosphere is hardly realistic, although some reviewers mistook its stylization for realism, and the overtly political aspects of the story are
so deemphasized that the reviewer for Britain's *Picturegoer* was deluded into
writing, "Controversial matter concerning the Black and Tans and the revolutionary forces is carefully avoided, and there is nothing in the picture to hurt
the susceptibilities of either side." While Ford's emphasis is more psychological than political, his shrewd evocation of the atmosphere of betrayal expresses
a deeper, more poetic truth about Irish society. He conjures up the awful, self-
destructive temptation of an impoverished people to turn against themselves
for the sake of monetary rewards offered by their colonial rulers.

Perhaps the most memorable scene in *The Informer* is the death of Frankie
McPhillip. Frankie is trapped by the Black and Tans while trying to escape
from his house by climbing through a second-floor window. He is machine-
gunned while hanging by one hand, as if in a crucifixion. In the foreground
of the frame, we see the dying man's hand slowly slipping from the win-

dowsill. In the eerie silence after the burst of machine-gun fire, the sound of Frankie's fingernails scratching on the wood is harrowing. Ford borrowed that aural detail from one of the extras in the film who remembered seeing and hearing a similar occurrence. "That particular sequence almost caused me a lot of trouble," Ford recalled. "There was a convention of producers being held at the time, so the rushes were sent up for them to see one afternoon; I asked them what they thought of the scene—and they told me it was all right, not to worry because the sound department could cut out the unfortunate sound of the scratching nails! I'm really afraid I insulted them a little during the next five minutes."

When the news of McPhillip's death is telephoned to the headquarters of the Royal Irish Constabulary, a senior officer takes the blood money and drops it on the table in front of Gypo. "Twenty pounds. You'd better count it. Show him out the back way," says one of the Black and Tans, pushing the money toward Gypo with a riding crop. Demonstrating that even the enemy regards Gypo's act of informing with utter contempt, the gesture with the riding crop conveys far more powerfully than words that the informer, like his blood money, has become untouchable.

In Bogdanovich's *Directed by John Ford,* John Wayne uses this scene to illustrate Ford's ability to express complex emotions with the utmost economy of dialogue and gesture. Ford "has such an analytical mind," Wayne comments. "He knows the difference between the trivia and the meat of a scene. . . . He would have Dudley Nichols rewrite scene after scene after scene—this is before the picture started—and then just reach down and take a line out of this one, a line out of this one, and then three lines out of all this wonderful writing but flowery language of Dudley Nichols. . . . I know that they had a long, highly dramatic scene when the British officer paid off Vic McLaglen as the informer. And when [Ford] finished with the scene, it was a silent scene." Ford may have crossed out some of Nichols's "flowery language" when they worked on the script together on the *Araner* during a cruise to Mexico with Wayne, Fonda, and Bond that began on December 19, 1934, and lasted into the following month. However, Nichols told Lindsay Anderson that *The Informer* was the only script he ever wrote that did not require a second draft, and the scene in the shooting script of Gypo receiving the reward money is virtually identical with the scene as it appears on-screen.

Unfortunately, not all of the film's devices are as organic as the use of the riding crop. Much of *The Informer*'s symbolism, such as the ubiquitous wanted poster pursuing Gypo through the streets of Dublin and the use of a blind man to symbolize Gypo's conscience, now seems overly obvious. Despite the visual virtuosity of Ford and August, the film's general lack of subtlety makes it appear both corny and pretentious, a deadly combination. Ford admitted in 1966 that *The Informer* was not one of his favorite pictures because it "lacks humor—which is my forte."[2]

But the 1935 audience, several years removed from the end of the silent era, was unaccustomed to seeing such self-consciously "artistic" stylization in an American movie. Darryl F. Zanuck, one of Hollywood's savviest production executives, considered *The Informer* "a visual masterpiece almost unparalleled in cinema history," an opinion he never changed. "John Ford has directed it with a fine eye for picture effect, both atmospherically and dramatically," observed the *National Board of Review Magazine*. ". . . [S]ubtle and powerfully suggestive is the way [Ford] has paralleled the blind twistings of Gypo's inner nature with an exterior presentment of dark foggy streets peopled with dim figures and dimmer shadows." *New York Times* reviewer Andre Sennwald called *The Informer* "an astonishing screen drama" but seemed to lack the critical vocabulary to describe it clearly: "Having no patience with the childlike rigmarole of routine film manufacture, [Ford] recites Mr. O'Flaherty's realistic drama of the Dublin slums with bold and smashing skill. In his hands *The Informer* becomes at the same time a striking psychological study of a gutter Judas and a rawly impressive picture of the Dublin underworld during the Black and Tan terror."

Not everyone gave *The Informer* such rave reviews. Incorrectly predicting that it would be "a spotty grosser" despite being "forcefully and intelligently written, directed, and acted," *Variety*'s Tom Landry, like Sennwald, misleadingly characterized *The Informer* as a work of ashcan realism: "Story is melodramatic enough to have a good deal of action, along with grim close-ups of poverty and squalor." The more perceptive Otis Ferguson of the *New Republic* wrote that while *The Informer* "opens a lot of new possibilities for Hollywood . . . its persistent inadequacies make it more disappointing than many pictures with less to recommend them." Ferguson objected to Ford's "constant reliance on symbolic fade-ins and ghostly voices, on an elaborately cued and infirm musical score [by Max Steiner]," and to the director's tendency to "drive every nail down three inches below the surface."

---

2. The other Ford film released in 1935, *The Whole Town's Talking* from Columbia, deals with much the same theme, the struggle between good and evil within human nature, although in a largely humorous manner. (The screenplay, based on a novel by W. R. Burnett, was written by Robert Riskin and Jo Swerling, best known for their work with Frank Capra.) Edward G. Robinson plays the dual role of a timid office worker and a notorious gangster named "Killer" Mannion. This dark comedy of mistaken identity is as expressionistic as a German silent film in its stylized depiction of man's duality, but no one seemed to notice because *The Whole Town's Talking* presents itself as lighthearted escapism.

The Informer is marred by its grossly bathetic ending of Gypo falling dead at the foot of a cross as he spreads his arms in a Christlike pose and bellows, "Frankie! Your mother forgives me!" Presenting Gypo's repentance in such operatic fashion only underscores its implausibility. But otherwise McLaglen's performance is a near-miraculous feat of direction. Although the British actor had played leading roles for Ford as gallant military men in such films as *Hangman's House* and *The Lost Patrol,* his range was limited. Most of his work for Ford in talking pictures is as an Irish buffoon, broadly but delightfully played; he tended to employ a stage-Irish accent in such roles. *The Informer* is a different story altogether.

His Gypo is a moving portrait of a man of limited intelligence groping for truth and understanding while allowing his better instincts to be submerged into his animalistic nature. If the film's attempt at Christian redemption for Gypo is unconvincing, it's no fault of McLaglen, who reveals enough humanity in this venal lug to lift him into the realm of tragedy. A walking embodiment of guilt and original sin, McLaglen's Gypo is like a huge errant child who wanders the streets of Dublin bleeding money as he tries to rid himself of the evidence of his crime. The tragic pity we feel for Gypo is partly a tribute to McLaglen's intense absorption in the character, and partly a result of the director's empathetic response to Gypo's human failings. The conflicted needs that tempt this Irishman to betray his friend and political comrade—money, drink, sex, and an American identity—were among the motivating forces Ford found so troublesome in his own life.

Ford had to fight RKO to cast McLaglen. "The studio spent weeks trying to foist better-known heavies on me," said Ford, "but I knew Vic could do the job, and I knew I could handle him exactly as I wanted to. I won in the end—and you saw the performance he gave." Ford directed McLaglen with cunning calculation, bullying and tricking him into giving a great performance. Since he wanted McLaglen to grope for his lines to convey Gypo's slow-witted, half-drunken condition, Ford continually changed the schedule to keep McLaglen unfamiliar with his scenes and surreptitiously filmed what the actor thought were rehearsals. He would send McLaglen off to run his lines with cast member J. M. Kerrigan at the nearby Melrose Grotto bar, and then would abruptly call a tipsy McLaglen back to the set to shoot his scenes.

The most celebrated story about Ford's (mis)treatment of an actor is about the trick he played to get McLaglen into the right mood for his big scene in the picture. Knowing McLaglen was terribly nervous about playing the scene in which the anguished Gypo defends himself to his IRA brethren, Ford told him it was no longer scheduled for the following morning. Suggesting McLaglen take the opportunity to let his hair down, Ford sent him to a party in the com-

pany of Kin and Rosina Wai, Hawaiian friends of the director who were visiting Hollywood. Just as Ford expected, McLaglen drank himself into oblivion,
only to be awakened by an early-morning call to report to the set: the trial
scene was back on the schedule. Abjectly hungover, woozy, dry-mouthed and
stammering, McLaglen fumbled his way through the scene in desperation, in-
coherently reaching for words and gesturing clumsily as he tried vainly to save
his skin. (In later years, Ford insisted it was "absolutely untrue" that he had
pulled such a trick on McLaglen, or hedged by saying, "Victor was just mulled
enough to be confused in the scene, which is exactly what Gypo Nolan was.")

For his pains, McLaglen won the Academy Award for best actor. Ford became a bit testy about all the praise McLaglen received, telling an interviewer
in 1936, "You don't think *The Informer* went over because of McLaglen, do
you? Personally, I doubt it. It was because it was *about* something. I'm no
McLaglen fan, you know."

Belying his frequent protestations that he was no artist, Ford approached *The
Informer* with such seriousness that when the film was poorly received at an industry preview and he heard RKO executives saying they regretted making it,
he went outside and vomited. When he recovered, he headed off to get drunk
with Dudley Nichols. They came upon Irish actor Dudley Digges slumped on
the running board of a car, weeping. Digges tearfully embraced them, extravagantly praising their work. That rescued the writer and director from alcoholic despair and helped ease Ford's feeling that Hollywood was treating him
"like a leper" for making such an arty film.

The Informer opened weakly at the box office on May 1, 1935, but eventually caught on with the public thanks to its critical prestige. On January 2,
1936, the New York Film Critics honored it as best picture and chose Ford as
best director. *The Informer* also was named the best film of the year by the *New
York Times* and the best American film by the National Board of Review. At
the Academy Awards ceremony on March 5, Ford, Nichols, and composer
Max Steiner won Oscars along with McLaglen. *The Informer* placed second to
MGM's *Mutiny on the Bounty* in the balloting for best picture. After the Oscars,
RKO mounted a belated advertising push for *The Informer,* finally enabling the
film to turn a profit.

That year's Oscar ceremony at the Biltmore Hotel in downtown Los Angeles was something of a shambles. Because of ongoing bitterness over the role
of the Academy in the 1933 pay-cut controversy and in its attempts to stem
the rise of the Hollywood labor movement, the Hollywood guilds—the
Screen Actors Guild, the Screen Writers Guild, and the newly formed Screen
Directors Guild—called their second annual boycott of the Oscars. "No one
can respect an organization with the high-sounding title of the Academy of

Motion Picture Arts and Sciences which has failed in every single function it has assumed," the SDG wrote its members. "The sooner it is destroyed and forgotten, the better for the industry."

The studio bosses sent telegrams ordering their stars to attend, but the tactic backfired by causing more to support the boycott. After liberally papering the house with studio employees, Academy president Frank Capra managed to attract a sprinkling of celebrities by inviting pioneer director D. W. Griffith to receive an honorary Oscar. Languishing in alcoholic obscurity, unable to find work in the industry he had almost singlehandedly created, Griffith came from his home in Kentucky to make an emotional acceptance speech. He also presented the awards for best director, actor, and actress (Bette Davis for *Dangerous*). McLaglen and Davis showed up to receive their Oscars, but Ford and Nichols stayed away.

Capra sent a statuette to Nichols, but the writer promptly returned it with a letter he released to the press on March 9:

> My awareness of the honor given the screenplay of *The Informer* and my gratitude to those individuals who voted the award only make this letter the more difficult. But as one of the founders of the Screen Writers Guild—which was conceived in revolt against the Academy and born out of disappointment with the way it functioned against employed talent in any emergency—I deeply regret that I am unable to accept the award.
>
> To accept it would be to turn my back on nearly a thousand members of the Writers Guild, to desert those fellow writers who ventured everything in the long-drawn-out fight for a genuine writers' organization, to go back on convictions honestly arrived at, and to invalidate three years' work in the guild, which I should like to look back upon with self-respect. My only regret now is that I did not withdraw my name from nomination and avoid this more embarrassing situation.

After it was reported that Ford, who was treasurer of the SDG, would refuse his award as well, the director issued a denial on March 8: "I am proud to have received the honor. If I had planned to refuse it, I would not have allowed my name to go in nomination." He privately accepted his Oscar a week after the ceremony. Ford's decision caused some unhappiness among his fellow members of the SDG, which was still struggling for recognition in negotiations with the producers and would not achieve it until 1939. Dan Ford writes in his biography that because Ford accepted his Oscar in 1936, the guild voted him out of office and he remained inactive in the guild for the rest of his life.

But in fact, Ford kept his post as treasurer until May 1938, when he was re-elected to the SDG board of directors, and he never ceased being a major figure in the guild.

After the producers agreed in July 1937 to hold contract talks with the SDG, Ford became a member of the guild's first negotiating committee. Howard Hawks was chairman of the committee, which opened talks with the producers on August 4; in addition to Ford, the other members included Eddie Sutherland, Herbert Biberman, and Rouben Mamoulian. At the time, King Vidor still was president of the guild, but Capra, who had joined the SDG that July, succeeded Vidor the following May. Capra was juggling a dual allegiance, simultaneously serving as president of the Academy, which he helped ease out of the labor controversy but still found a valuable power base in the SDG's battle for recognition. Capra eventually took charge of the laborious negotiations along with the guild's counsel, Mabel Walker Willebrandt. Later claiming all the credit for the SDG's first minimum basic agreement, Capra disparaged the guild's original negotiating committee, contending that they failed to win a contract "because they had no balls. Because they got scared off. Because they thought they were too big to go begging. They talked to each other big but they didn't talk to the producers big. Those guys didn't want to work."

Capra's contemptuous statement unfairly maligned Ford and others who risked their careers to advance the fledgling organization when Capra, by his own admission, was still "stooging for producers" as Academy president. But for all the courage displayed by Ford and the other founders of the guild, there is no doubt that the SDG was the least militant of the three major guilds, "a company of gentlemen adventuring in unionism," in the felicitous phrase of screenwriter Philip Dunne. It finally took the street-fighting ability of Capra and Willebrandt to win recognition and achieve a minimum basic agreement for the SDG in 1939. Still, the groundwork for that agreement had been laid by Vidor, Ford, Hawks, Mamoulian, and the other early members. Ford summarized their goals in a 1937 statement to the press that reflected his own difficult relationships with the studios in that period:

> Changes are due in the motion picture industry from the director's standpoint. With the coming of sound, the "committee method," so-called, came into being. Previously, the method of making pictures had been the "combination method"—the producer, the writer, and the director. And the director started on the idea with the writer and followed through until it was completed on the screen.

My complaint toward the "committee method" is that no one man's idea is carried through in entirety. The picture, by necessity, becomes a composite work. If books were written under the "committee method," I'll venture to say that they would not maintain their clear flow of story. Through the Directors Guild, we hope to eliminate the "committee method." We feel that the Guild fills a very great need. The producers have associations; every other division of the industry is organized; why not us? . . .

We feel that, through the Guild, we can work in closer harmony with the producers. Thus, by direct conference, we hope we can eliminate many of the petty annoyances and difficulties that arise through the "committee method" of picture-making.

We also hope to maintain our position and prestige as directors through the Guild. In this respect, the Guild will be primarily helpful to the newer and younger directors. As a matter of fact, the only thing we are asking is the protection of the younger directors. The young fellows who have been coming up have been "whipped around" a bit. If this tendency continues, the newer generation of directors will be relegated to something of the position of stage manager with a road show. And we don't want this to happen. . . .

Ford became seriously interested in filming "The Quiet Man" in 1935, the same year he made *The Informer.* He took an option on the film rights to Maurice Walsh's seriocomic story on February 25 of the following year.[3] Originally published in the *Saturday Evening Post* in 1933, it is the tale of an Irish-American boxer named Shawn Kelvin, "slightly under middle height," who returns to his native Kerry after killing a man in the ring. Shawn does his patriotic duty as a member of an IRA flying column during the War of Independence, but yearns for lasting peace in "a quiet place on a hillside."

To win the hand of a fiery-tempered local woman named Ellen O'Grady, he finds to his chagrin that he must fight her bullying brother. When Walsh published an expanded version of the story in his 1935 collection *Green Rushes,* he changed the central characters' names to Paddy Bawn Enright and Ellen Roe Danaher. Ford's 1952 film version calls them Sean Thornton (John

---

3. Ford paid Walsh a nominal $10 for the story rights, but an additional $2,500 as an advance on the sale of the rights to a film company; Walsh eventually received another $3,500 when Republic Pictures purchased the rights for the 1952 film version. One of Ford's biggest box-office hits, it brought in domestic rentals of $3.8 million.

Wayne) and Mary Kate Danaher (Maureen O'Hara). Though essentially a fairy tale, Walsh's story is less lighthearted and romantic than the film Ford eventually made from it. Paddy Bawn is a fiercer, more introverted figure than Wayne's troubled but essentially good-natured Sean Thornton, and the story's more recent background of political troubles casts a deeper shadow over the community. So while in retrospect it may seem odd that Hollywood took so long to warm up to "The Quiet Man," those elements probably accounted for some of the hesitancy.

"If you're thinking of a general run of social pictures, or even just plain honest ones, it's almost hopeless," Ford said in 1936. "The whole financial setup is against it. What you'll get is an isolated courageous effort here and there. . . . Look at Nichols and me. We did *The Informer*. Does that make it any easier to go ahead with [Sean] O'Casey's *The Plough and the Stars*, which we want to do after *Mary of Scotland*? Not for a second. They *may* let us do it as a reward for being good boys. Meanwhile we're fighting to have the Abbey Players imported intact and we're fighting the censors and fighting the so-called financial wizards at every point."

It has been said that you can tell when a director is in love with an actress by the way he photographs her on-screen. The tip-off is that dreamy glow a woman's face assumes in her director's rapturously adoring close-ups. Ford's obsessive fascination with Katharine Hepburn during the making of RKO's *Mary of Scotland* (1936) is evident in every frame of her performance as Mary, Queen of Scots. In an interview at the time, Ford made no effort to disguise his intimate feelings for Hepburn:

"When they gave me *Mary of Scotland* to do, my first thought was of Hepburn. She was already set for the role, and it wasn't as if she were just any talented pretty young actress who could be dressed in anything and photographed casually. . . . I asked the studio for a print of every picture Katharine had ever made—*Bill of Divorcement, Morning Glory, Little Women, Alice Adams,* all of them—and then I called in the wardrobe department and set men and the story adaptors; together we looked up portraits and old woodcuts of the period costumes Mary, Queen of Scots wore, and photographs of the rooms in her castle. We sketched gowns and ruffs, we planned backgrounds and settings in rough outline.

"When we had some sort of working basis for departure, we locked ourselves in a projection room and, one each night so long as they lasted, ran the Hepburn pictures. We studied every angle of her strange, sharp face—the chiseled nose, the mouth, the long neck—and then adjusted the sketches to fit her personality. We planned photographic effects, decided how best to light her features and what makeup to use in order to achieve for her a genuine majesty."

Mary of Scotland is less noteworthy as a movie than as visual evidence of the grandest romantic passion Ford ever pursued. Nichols's high-toned adaptation of what Andrew Sarris aptly calls Maxwell Anderson's "blank-minded verse" play is only intermittently worthy of the mercurial young actress and the director's display of overwhelming devotion. Prompting rhetorical excesses like those that would drain all the energy out of his film of *The Plough and the Stars,* *Mary of Scotland* feeds into Ford's worst artistic impulses. Ponderously paced, turgid in diction, virtually humorless, suffocated by the claustrophobic elegance of sixteenth-century settings and costumes, and sentimentally biased toward the lost cause of the martyred Catholic queen, the film comes alive only when Ford moves his camera in as close as possible to Hepburn's glowing face, allowing her to fill the screen with a tremulous religious fervor that strongly resembles sexual ecstasy.

Ford's frequent use of close-ups, while aesthetically justifiable as a way of conveying Mary Stuart's tragic isolation from her people, represents such a departure from the director's usual practice that it demonstrates his interest in Hepburn to the exclusion of all other elements in the story. Similarly, Mary's melancholy romantic scenes with her lugubrious lover, the earl of Bothwell (Fredric March), seem pro forma in contrast with the romantic scenes she plays to the man sitting just offscreen, staring quietly at her through his darkly tinted glasses. Hepburn remembered that Ford "really lost interest in [*Mary of Scotland*] when he found out it was a weak story." But his interest in the leading lady only intensified throughout the course of the shooting.

Hepburn undertook *Mary of Scotland* with reluctance. "I never cared for Mary," she later admitted. "I thought she was a bit of an ass. . . . The script was not very interesting. I never quite understood why Jack Ford was willing to direct it."

She would have preferred that the film be directed by George Cukor, who was responsible for her screen debut in *A Bill of Divorcement,* as well as her sparkling Jo in the 1933 *Little Women.* But the Cukor-Hepburn combination was anathema to RKO production chief Pandro S. Berman in early 1936. The studio had just released *Sylvia Scarlett,* Cukor's fey, gender-bending comedy with Hepburn masquerading as a boy. Although highly regarded by modern audiences more attuned to the gay director's intricately comedic take on sexual ambiguity, *Sylvia Scarlett* in its day was a notorious flop.

Berman, who served as the producer of *Mary of Scotland,* assigned the project to Ford, probably thinking Hepburn would benefit from having a robustly "masculine" director known for his no-nonsense approach with women. Berman had no personal fondness for Ford, considering him "about the meanest man I ever met. He was nice to me because I was running the studio. But, God! he could be a mean man when he wanted to."

Ford jumped at the chance to direct Hepburn. They had met in 1932, when he directed her first screen test. Fox was considering a film version of *The Warrior's Husband,* a farce Hepburn had been doing onstage in New York before she signed her contract with RKO. The scene she chose was not from *The Warrior's Husband,* however, but from a play Philip Barry had written for her, *The Animal Kingdom.* In the test, which still exists at the UCLA Film and Television Archive, Hepburn plays Daisy Sage, an unconventional young woman boldly proposing to the man she loves, who stuns her with the news that he plans to marry another woman. As it turned out, neither Ford nor Hepburn was involved in the film version of *The Animal Kingdom,* which starred Ann Harding and was directed by Edward H. Griffith. But the screen test, in retrospect, carries a premonition of the intense but ultimately futile romantic relationship that later developed between Ford and Hepburn.

From the start of shooting on *Mary of Scotland,* Hepburn adopted a teasing attitude toward Ford, testing his masculine authority. "I found him fascinating but impossible," she recalled. "He was definitely the skipper of his own life and you had better not disagree with him too often. Actually, his 'gang,' so to speak, was all male—but some of the time he would tolerate me."

When Ford arrived on the set to begin shooting on February 25, 1936, he found Hepburn sitting in his director's chair. Her feet propped up on a table, she was smoking an Irish clay pipe. The four other actresses who played characters named Mary also were smoking pipes. Ford clearly was not amused at this parody of his directorial persona. But he played it cool, offering no verbal response even when one of the actresses became ill and Hepburn continued puffing provocatively all day long.

A stickler for cleanliness, Hepburn harped on Ford's aversion to bathing and his habitually sloppy attire. When she realized he wore the same shirt to the set day after day, she crept up behind him with a blue pencil and surreptitiously marked a cross on the sleeve. Toward the end of filming, she asked him why he never changed his shirt. When Ford denied that was the case, she infuriated him by revealing her gag with the pencil mark.

Another time when she mocked his unkemptness, he snapped, "Listen, Katharine, I'll play you a round of golf."

"For a hundred dollars a hole!" she responded.

"And if you lose," Ford went on, "you'll agree to come to this studio at least one day dressed like a woman."

"And if I win, will you agree to come to the studio at least one day dressed like a gentleman?"

Turning to screenwriter Dudley Nichols, Ford said, "Listen, Dudley, let's put that unhappy ending back on this picture. Let's behead the dame after all."

Ford's tolerance of such jousting with an actress was highly unusual. People were banished forever from his kingdom for lesser offenses to his dignity. But he was so captivated by Kate's insouciant personality that he forsook his usual lunchtime naps in his dressing room to flirt with her at a crowded table in the studio commissary. His most remarkable concession came on April 10, when he was rehearsing a scene in the castle tower between Hepburn and Fredric March. It was the kind of long, wordy love scene he always tended to avoid.

"This is a goddamn lousy scene!" he exploded.

"It's the best scene in the picture!" she retorted.

"Well, if you like it so much, why don't you shoot it?"

He told an assistant to hand Hepburn the script and a megaphone, then stalked off the set and let her direct the scene. Ford's gesture was ambiguous. Did it signify indifference to the script, generous confidence in her judgment, sexual tension over directing another man to romance her, or all three? Whatever the case, Hepburn was grateful for the opportunity. Ever after that, Ford encouraged her to become a director, but she never tried it again.

Hepburn's free-spirited nature affected Ford like an aphrodisiac. The independent way she lived her life seemed liberating to a man burdened by a guilt ridden sense of family duty and addicted to work as a substitute for sensual pleasure. But the twenty-nine-year-old actress's lack of inhibition also frightened him, threatening his fragile sense of self-control.

Ford felt similarly ambivalent toward Hepburn's WASPish background. She discerned a common bond of secretiveness stemming from their shared New England heritage, but Ford could not help seeing her as a Connecticut patrician who, in her words, "sort of came over on the *Mayflower*." Ford was attracted to women from that class, but could never forget his origins when he was around them or their families. Kate's formidable mother, Katharine Houghton Hepburn, was a prominent suffragist and a leader in the birth control movement. Like her husband, the Hartford surgeon and urologist Dr. Thomas Hepburn, she was a firm believer in eugenics, a pseudoscientific movement that promoted mandatory sterilization and other means for "the protection of our race stock against hereditary deterioration."[4]

Mrs. Hepburn raised an eyebrow when she met Ford and learned that he

---

4. Quoted from proceedings of the Connecticut Society of Social Hygiene, prepared by Dr. Hepburn.

came from an Irish family of "thirteen" children (there actually were eleven Feeney children). Although Ford was inclined to believe (correctly) that people like Mrs. Hepburn harbored a thinly disguised anti-immigrant agenda, he good-naturedly parried her alarm by pointing out that she herself had borne six children. Kate shared her mother's attitudes about immigrant breeding habits—she expressed similar shock to Ford about his large family even during their final visit together in 1973—but she always assuaged Ford's Irish pride by lovingly addressing him as "Sean." She had a romantic fascination with his Irish background, and they talked about traveling together to Galway and the Aran Islands.

In her disappointingly cryptic 1991 autobiography, *Me: Stories of My Life,* Hepburn disclosed little about her relationship with Ford: "Obviously, he was an extremely interesting man. We became friends, and from time to time during his life we met. I would go sailing on his boat." During breaks from shooting *Mary of Scotland,* they also played contentious rounds of golf at the California Country Club and spent quiet evenings together at Hepburn's Laurel Canyon estate. George Cukor served as a beard for one of their weekend cruises on the *Araner.* Before becoming involved with Ford, Hepburn had an affair with her agent, Leland Hayward, and when Cukor signed the logbook of the *Araner* on April 12, he puckishly wrote, "Poor Leland!" That Sunday Kate posed for an intimate photograph as she sat bare-legged on the deck, beaming at the camera as she casually massaged Jack's foot.

Their relationship became so intense by the time filming was completed on April 23 that Ford traveled with her to New York City and Fenwick, her family estate on Long Island Sound. For Ford, this romantic vacation was a refreshing change from his usual practice of drinking himself into a nearly comatose state between pictures. Kate's father, though not a heavy drinker, shared other traits in common with Ford. Both were tyrannical and possessively devoted to Kate. According to Hepburn biographer Anne Edwards, "Dr. Hepburn had not been too keen on the young Irish Catholic boy Kate had been enamored of as a young girl. Ford impressed him little better. As far as Dr. Hepburn was concerned, Ford was a philandering married man using Kate poorly."

While Kate somewhat grudgingly admired Ford's forceful personality and rough masculine authority, she appreciated the emotional sensitivity and poetic nature that lay beneath his macho facade. She was exhilarated by his creative independence and his disdain for what other people thought of his work. She was frustrated by his perversely Irish sense of humor, but fascinated by the mysteries of his stubbornly clandestine personality. His rich contradictions— she described him as "enormously rough, terribly arrogant, enormously tender . . . never smug, never phony, and enormously, truly sensitive"—intrigued and perplexed her. At the end of his life, she confessed to Ford that she had never managed to figure him out, but called him the most fascinatingly complex man she had ever known. "I'm not sure you even understand yourself entirely," she told him. She thought he had a dual personality, as reflected in his Hollywood and navy careers. Ford retorted that they *both* had split personalities. He described Hepburn as "half pagan, half Puritan," a phrase that he admitted could be applied to himself as well.

As Hepburn's subsequent romantic relationship with Spencer Tracy also demonstrated, she was attracted to troubled, moody Irishmen who drank heavily because they were conflicted over their masculinity and their artistic natures. Such torment was fostered by their inability to resolve those roles in a male-dominated society that tended to regard artistic talent as evidence of effeminacy. With these dark souls, whom she described as similar in "being able to be devastated by the world," she could be more than a lover. She could act as missionary and nurse, trying to save them from their own self-destruction.

Hepburn had displayed a terror of intimacy ever since she was thirteen and her beloved older brother Tom hanged himself just hours after telling her, "You're my girl, aren't you? You're my favorite girl in the whole world." Hepburn's young romantic life, which included a brief marriage to a wealthy but ineffectual socialite, seemed clouded by emotional skittishness and persistent rumors of bisexuality. She had rebuffed Leland Hayward's offer of marriage, driving him into the arms of actress Margaret Sullavan. Whether or not Kate was conscious of her own psychological dynamic, the relationships with Ford and Tracy were safer ones for her to pursue. These men were already married and, however much they loved her, could never leave their wives.

The Ford-Hepburn romance was first revealed to the public by Dan Ford in his 1979 biography *Pappy*. While making *Mary of Scotland,* he wrote, "[T]hey fell in love. . . . [Jack] was obsessed by Kate and found with her a degree of happiness and a peace of mind that he had never known before." That straightforward picture became somewhat muddied, however, when Dan Ford challenged Barbara Leaming's lengthy account of the romance in her gushy 1995 biography *Katharine Hepburn.*

"Many evenings, Kate spoke to Sean through the setting sun," Leaming writes of a time in 1937 when Hepburn was touring in a play. "On her dressing table at the theater, she kept his photograph propped against a toy elephant. As she studied the face in the picture, she imagined that Sean laughed at her. When she went on stage, in her mind's eye she saw him float in midair just beneath the balcony. . . . For Ford, everything had happened quickly. He was not a man who had expected to find happiness outside work. . . . Kate was life-affirming; he had never experienced that in a woman. . . . her loving presence in Ford's life had thrown him into turmoil unlike any he had known."

Writing in the letters column of the *New York Times Book Review,* Ford's grandson denounced Leaming's book as "a cheap, exploitative work of fiction, a Gothic novel that pretends to be a biography. . . . I believe that she has greatly exaggerated the degree and the intensity of the Ford-Hepburn relationship." He went on to claim that the letters between Ford and Hepburn in the John Ford collection at Indiana University's Lilly Library—materials the library obtained from Dan Ford after he had used them as the basis for his own book—"do not substantiate [Leaming's] claim that Katharine Hepburn and John Ford had an intense affair in the mid-1930's."

On the face of it, that statement seems inconsistent with Dan Ford's own book, whose disclosure of the romance was itself considered indiscreet or exaggerated by some intimates of the director. Perhaps by 1995 the grandson had second thoughts about the wisdom of having made such a revelation. However, judging from the correspondence and other information in the Ford collection, there can be no doubt that Ford and Hepburn had, at the very least, a serious affair of the heart, which may or may not have been physically consummated. The affair, which lasted for several months in 1936–37, left them with lifelong feelings of mutual devotion. That is abundantly clear from several hours of deeply moving audiotapes of Ford talking with Hepburn from his deathbed in 1973 (material recorded partly at Hepburn's behest, to help draw out Ford's reminiscences for *Pappy*).

Stripped of rhetorical attacks, the debate between Dan Ford and Barbara Leaming revolves around his charge that she "greatly exaggerated the degree and the intensity" of the relationship. Neither of those two biographies tells a finely nuanced story of that complex relationship as Ford experienced it, nor does either admit that the full truth remains somewhat elusive in nature. Leaming's book attempts to fill the many gaps in the record with liberal dollops of conjecture, invariably interpreting Ford's motives and behavior to fit her overheated thesis that he was tragically helpless to escape the torment of his marriage to Mary, whom the book grossly caricatures as a "monstrous" harpy.

Leaming portrays Mary habitually scorning her husband as "shanty Irish" while belittling his work and even trying to destroy him as a creative artist. She seems to have taken this notion from Dan Ford's comment that Mary regarded Jack's movie career as "flashy and 'low Irish' and let him know that she felt it lacked substance." But rather than damaging Ford as a creative artist, Mary's belief that his movie career "lacked substance" probably helped goad him to do more important work. Mary's view of Jack's filmmaking, while not entirely worshipful, showed sound critical judgment: she said in 1977 that her favorite Ford film was *Young Mr. Lincoln* and her least favorite was *Tobacco Road*. Would he have made better films if he had left Mary for Kate? Not even Leaming makes that claim. Indeed, she argues the opposite: that Ford had a rush of creative energy after giving up on his relationship with Hepburn. Ford recognized that even the somewhat illusory stability of his home life with Mary was essential to his functioning as a creative artist. And it seems extremely unlikely that a proudly Irish man who left college after throwing a plate of stew at a WASP who called him "shanty" Irish would put up with a WASP wife who habitually used the same epithet.

Although it plays down his grandmother's alcoholism and goes into little detail about the rougher edges of the marriage, Dan Ford's portrait of Mary is far more accurate and nuanced than Leaming's. In his letter to the *Times,* he describes Mary as "both an elegant woman and a stabilizing factor in John Ford's life. She was instrumental in making him the man he was."

Claire Trevor, who starred in Ford's 1939 *Stagecoach,* was friendly with both Jack and Mary and often spent weekends with them on the *Araner,* along with her husband, agent and producer Milton Bren. Mary, recalled Trevor, "was always so dignified. She must have had a sense of humor to live with him. He couldn't have been easy. He was such a strange man, with so many foibles. Tough father. Tough husband. He sat in the same chair for twenty years. He dug a hole in it with an arm [by habitually twisting the index finger of his right hand]. His wife wanted to re-cover it. He refused, he wouldn't give it up. Finally she said she would cover it with the same fabric, and he agreed. He was the boss in his home."

Because Leaming harbors such a simplistic view of Mary, her highly romanticized Hepburn biography seems dumbfounded and uncomprehending at the very real, if often tormented, bond that existed between Ford and his wife. Their marriage, for all its flaws, lasted fifty-three years. When the Fords celebrated their golden wedding anniversary in 1970, they were asked the secret of staying married in Hollywood. Jack said, "Keeping your mouth shut." Mary advised, "Don't believe anything you hear and don't believe anything you see." To a female friend, she was even more precise about her coping strategy: "I've been married fifty years. Do you want to know how I did that? For the first third of my marriage, I didn't believe what I heard. For the next third, I didn't believe what was written. And for the last third, I didn't believe what I saw." Mary offered further advice to Hollywood wives in her 1977 interview with film historians Anthony Slide and June Banker: "[T]he first week you're married, you start getting anonymous telephone calls if you want to listen to them. I've begged many and many of them to put cotton in their ears, and stay with their husbands, but they won't do it. They insist on answering that phone."

And yet, despite her studiously practiced habit of denial, Mary could not help learning more than she wanted to know about Jack's closeness with Katharine Hepburn. Dan Ford observes in *Pappy* that the relationship "had blown the lid off any pretense of monogamy, and after it was over, Mary seemed to have given John a free rein to indulge in extramarital affairs—her only stipulations being, first, that she wasn't to know about them, and second, that they were not to become public knowledge." Although Ford subsequently had "several minor affairs . . . his real vice was alcohol, not women."

In contrast to the implications of the Ford family's own biography, Leaming flatly states that Ford "did not sleep with" Hepburn. "From the first, he made clear that he was not interested in an affair," Leaming writes. "He wanted marriage and a life together. To show Kate that he considered this relationship different, Ford talked about various women with whom he had had affairs in the past. Still, she sensed that he wasn't being entirely truthful. Kate could not believe he had ever really been unfaithful to Mary."

Again, no source is cited for these sweeping assertions. It appears that Leaming based this passage upon a single, rather mysterious letter she found among Ford's papers.

Addressed simply to "My Darling," the December 1938 letter is from someone who identifies herself only as "Mimi" and "Miss D." Written in the form of a play, it contains an account of her supposed conversation with "Miss Katie Hepburn" and a "Miss M." "I've been putting this off until I got the proper Noël Coward mood," writes "Mimi."

Set in "Hepburn"'s sitting room, the letter has "Katie" saying to "Miss D.": "I got the most divine letter from Jack. He sends his love to you and tells me to be very sweet to you. . . . How was he when you saw him last? Does he seem well and happy? Is Mary here? Where are the children? . . . Of course I think Mary is a remarkable woman.[5] I think she is insensitive and crude, but still she hasn't had an easy time of it. I think Jack is wonderful but he must be a very difficult man to live with. He probably is better off married to that type of woman than to some fascinating creature with whom [he] would have been very happy. Had he been happy, he never would have been the artist that he is today. What do you think?"

---

5. Ford later used the phrase "a remarkable woman" to describe Hepburn in one of their 1973 conversations, and Anne Edwards adopted it as the title of her Hepburn biography.

"Miss D." replies, *"Shit."*

"Did you know Mary?" continues "Hepburn." "Did you like her? Mary used to be very fond of me until she found out about Jack and me. She thought I double-crossed her. I know she doesn't like me anymore because many people have told me all the things she has said about me. But I can't blame her for that. . . . Of course Jack is really wonderful. We were so close. He was so beautifully relaxed with me. I think I'm one woman who could make Jack very happy. I think I could be very good for him—we could have a wonderful life together. I think Jack loved me. Don't misunderstand—he never made a pass at me, but that proves it—doesn't it.

"I thought a great deal about marriage with him or living with him. But decided against it. I don't think Jack should ever divorce. I think I could of [sic] forced the issue—but then I don't know really. Every time we talked of it he would just smile. But this you can be sure of—if he wouldn't divorce for me, he would do it for no one. Jack has bragged to me about all the women that he has had affairs with, but I don't believe him. I think he just talks big. I believe that Jack has been absolutely faithful. . . . I think if anyone could have made Jack happy, I am that person. Jack really loved me—don't you think so?"

To which "Miss D." retorts, "I *doubt* it."

"That's about everything that was said—what an evening," the letter writer comments. "I can't understand her behavior . . . oh well—you figure it out." She concludes with loving comments to the unidentified recipient, who may or may not have been Ford.

This letter clearly is at least somewhat fanciful. The writer admits as much by casting it in the form of a play, interrupting "Hepburn"'s remarks with skeptical comebacks by "Miss D.," and prefacing the entire dialogue with the suggestive phrase, "If it is what it should be . . ." Furthermore, it seems to be a poison-pen letter by someone hostile to Hepburn and jealous of her relationship with Ford; its tone often seems to mock Hepburn's haughty manner of speaking. But without citing the letter or offering the reader any way to assess its accuracy, Leaming uncritically adopts its assertions as central themes of her book.

It certainly is conceivable that Ford was too inhibited by his Catholicism and marriage vows to sleep with Hepburn. "I never believed he had a romance with Katharine Hepburn," said Claire Trevor. "I read that, but he was too moral. She was too New England. He was not a womanizer, because of his religion and his background; he was devoted to his family. He was not a woman's man. He was not charming in the ordinary way, but he probably revered women more than most men, with his whole being."

Perhaps Ford was giving us a self-portrait in *Mary of Scotland* in the person of David Rizzio (John Carradine), the devoted but sexless and somewhat effete secretary and confidant to Hepburn's Mary Stuart.[6] But in the absence of a smoking-gun piece of correspondence, and with Ford long gone and the aged Hepburn now too infirm to be interviewed on the subject, we will never know exactly what transpired behind closed doors in their relationship. However, according to Ford's niece Cecil de Prida, a generally reliable chronicler of family history, the relationship became so serious that Ford "wanted out" of his marriage.

Mary naturally enough was jealous of the younger woman's glamour and vigor. She took a stand against Hepburn, whom she felt had betrayed her trust. According to Cecil, Mary was willing to let Jack have custody of Pat, but "threatened to take Barbara, the apple of [Jack's] eye." Hepburn countered by offering Mary $150,000 if she would divorce Jack and let him have Barbara. Mary refused, and Jack, said Cecil, "stayed because of the kids, particularly Barb." Cecil also reported Mary's telling John Wayne's first wife, Josephine, that "Jack is very religious, he'll never divorce me. He'll never have any grounds to divorce me on. I'm going to be Mrs. John Ford until I die."

If Hepburn did make such a monetary offer (there is no other documentation), Mary's justifiable outrage can only be imagined. And no matter how little fatherly affection Jack showed toward Pat, Jack almost certainly would have been repulsed by having his family offered such an appalling choice, amounting to the sale of one of his own children. Leaming mentions the alleged offer but seems oblivious of the role it might have played in ending the Ford-Hepburn relationship. Dan Ford's book, for whatever reason, does not mention such an offer, even though Cecil reported it to him in an interview for *Pappy*.

There are only a few letters and telegrams between Ford and Hepburn at the Lilly Library from the period of their affair. Though that correspondence is inconclusive on the issues of sex and marriage, it offers abundant and unmistakable evidence of love, passion, and deep mutual admiration, as indeed can be found in the tapes of Ford and Hepburn conversing in 1973. However, while Hepburn's expressions of affection in her correspondence are unabashed, Ford's are more oblique and guarded; his letters indicate mixed feelings about how far he should pursue their romance.

---

6. Ford always resented Carradine, who had an ego to rival his own, but Ford's nastiness to him on this film may have been a projection of the director's own self-loathing. Carradine recalled, "I was getting ready to do a scene in *Mary of Scotland,* and Ford was sitting behind me. Suddenly I heard, 'You stupid, lanky, Irish sonofabitch.' I just about turned around and cold-cocked him. Donald Crisp grabbed me and pulled me away and said, 'Don't you know what he's up to? . . . He's trying to get you mad 'cause he thinks you'll get more drive into the scene.'"

Visiting the Hepburns in Fenwick may have given Ford some second thoughts, but a far worse experience was awaiting him. Before heading home to Hollywood, Ford paid a visit to his aging father in Portland. Shortly after Jack returned to California, John Feeney died on June 22, 1936, at the age of eighty-two. Grampy Feeney's death hit Jack hard; he now was parentless. He reached out to Hepburn in Fenwick, but she was not home when he telephoned. She didn't know how to find him to return the call; she knew she could not contact him at home. Finally addressing a letter of condolence five days later to Ford's office at Twentieth Century–Fox, where he was preparing the Shirley Temple film *Wee Willie Winkie,* Hepburn stressed how fortunate he was to have had such a happy visit with his father just before the old man's death. She closed her endearments to Ford by regretting how difficult it was for them to express their feelings toward each other in words.

In order to paint this unhappy episode as the turning point of the Ford-Hepburn relationship, Leaming makes a series of wild conjectures: "The news [of his father's death] threw Ford into feverish uncertainty. Deeply superstitious, he seemed to take it as God's comment on the decision he had just made [supposedly, to leave his wife]. . . . Ford did not receive [Kate's letter] until after he returned from burying his father. By that time, he seems also to have buried any clear sense that he deserved a chance at life with Kate. His Catholic conscience—primitive and unshakable—took over. Had Kate been at Fenwick to receive his call on the 22nd, perhaps she might have been able to work her magic on him. . . . As it was, he had only Mary, who seized the opportunity to turn old John Feeney's death to her advantage."

This key element of Leaming's overheated romantic narrative is obvious nonsense. Ford's relationship with Hepburn did not end until April 1937, more than nine months after his father's death.

Anyone familiar with Ford's roughhousing approach to romance in his movies would understand the way he expressed his affection in a letter to Kate on January 16, 1937, declaring that he wanted to give her a big kick in the ass. This was in line with a comment he reportedly made to her while directing *Mary of Scotland:* "You'll give your best performance or I'll break you across my knee."

Hepburn was on the road when he wrote her, performing the title role in a touring production of *Jane Eyre.* She used her relationship with Ford as a model for Jane's forthright, unintimidated behavior toward her gruff employer, Mr. Rochester (Denis Hoey). Ford heartily congratulated Kate on news of her continuing success in the play, shipped her a pair of cotton long johns to keep her warm in the midwestern winter, and said he was eager to come see her performance before the tour ended in April.

But Kate was then being subjected to cross-country, in-person wooing by the wealthy, eccentric aviator and sometime film producer Howard Hughes. Stories appeared in the Los Angeles papers on January 22 claiming that Hepburn and Hughes were planning to marry. That apparently triggered an odd, extremely oblique response from Ford three days later. Writing Hepburn's British secretary, Emily "Em" Perkins, whom he had met on *Mary of Scotland,* Ford pretends to be a sailor in love with Miss Perkins and hoping to make a home with her. Complaining that she has betrayed him with a British musician on the *Queen Mary,* the "sailor" threatens to slug the musician or sue him for alienation of affections unless Em agrees to reimburse the sailor for his presents of fancy underwear.

What Hepburn made of this convoluted jape is unknown. But Ford never did see her in *Jane Eyre.* The proximate cause seems to have been an incident that occurred later in January when Hepburn was staying at the Park Plaza Hotel in St. Louis. Ford had Cliff Reid call to arrange a telephone conversation with Hepburn that night after the play. But Ford failed to call her at the appointed time. After waiting forty-five minutes, Hepburn had to leave for a meeting with the board of the Theater Guild, an appointment she had delayed in anticipation of talking with Ford. Rather than feeling responsible for causing her such inconvenience, Ford irrationally chose to take umbrage. Consciously or not, he may have provoked or aggravated the situation to give himself an excuse for pulling away from her and leaving the field clear for Howard Hughes.

By the time Hepburn played Indianapolis on March 1, the end of her romance with Ford was in sight. Writing "Sean" at the Hollywood Athletic Club, Hepburn admitted, "I can only say that I am facing (& have been for a time) the first crisis in my life. . . . You have given me strength and understanding, and I count you my dearest friend. . . . I would give a lot to talk to you and know what you think of me and . . . a lot of things."

After the tour ended in Baltimore, Hepburn made her decision. She agreed to join Hughes on his yacht for a cruise to Nassau and Jamaica. En route by train to Florida on April 10, she wrote Ford that she was disappointed he had never come to see her play and had chosen to go to Hawaii instead. She told him she had reached the conclusion that in human relations, particularly romantic ones, people "must say yes or no—but not maybe. Maybe is a feeble way of saying no. . . . Clarity is a necessity as everyone gets so mixed up, they don't know what is important to them. I used to be a great exponent of clarity, & I shall try to be again."

But she added with great poignancy, "Oh, Sean—it will be heavenly to see you again—if I may, and if I may not, I can drive by Odin Street in an open Ford & think a thousand things. In my mind and heart your place is everlasting."

It was over. Ford evidently never told her so directly, but he had opted to stay with his wife and children. His Irish Catholicism and overwhelming need for stability were important factors in determining his ultimate preference for Mary, who was content to be a homebody. Kate may have been a more exciting and adventurous companion, but she was no one's idea of conventional marriage material. Ford was not kidding when he told her, "You're a hell of a fine girl. If you'd just learn to shut up and knuckle under you'd probably make somebody a nice wife."

Ford had enough sense to recognize that their relationship would not have much of a future, or perhaps too volatile a future for a man who needed to regard his home as his port in the storm. As imperfect and often miserable as his marriage was, he was not about to throw away his home and children for an unpredictable life with a mercurial, independent woman with a demonstrable aversion to marriage. Nor was prolonged sexual passion, marital or extramarital, ever high on Ford's agenda; working and drinking were his true escape devices from the strictures of family responsibility and the leaden weight of mundane reality.

In a 1983 essay on Ford in *Esquire,* Peter Bogdanovich commented that Ford and Hepburn seemed "a match made in heaven. But, on the other hand, they both knew how badly their relationship might damage their individual careers and their ability to do what they had evidently been born at precisely the right time to do. They both knew how good they were and how much they still had to accomplish.

"When he and Hepburn decided they could never work together again, they both would have known the degree of happiness they were giving up. The decision, a kind of glorious and idealistic sacrifice, is echoed in most of Ford's subsequent pictures: the burden of duty, tradition, honor, and family is among his central themes. . . . In *The Quiet Man,* Ford's single most passionately romantic picture, made in Ireland [when he was] fifty-seven, the Maureen O'Hara character combined the best qualities of the two women who, apart from his mother, Ford most loved: her name in the film was Mary Kate."

Ford's relationship with Hepburn had already begun to cool by July 1936, when he began making his film version of Sean O'Casey's play *The Plough and the Stars.* The emotional turmoil in his private life may help explain why Ford so badly botched a dream project. O'Casey's play about the Easter rebellion of 1916 is one of the landmarks of Irish drama, but Ford's film version turned out to be among the worst debacles of his career.

The Plough and the Stars provoked a legendary riot on February 11, 1926, the fourth night of its initial production at Dublin's Abbey Theatre. Irish nationalists disrupted the play, objecting to its tragicomic depiction of the failed uprising. During the melee at the Abbey, police had to be called out to restore order, but not before cast member Barry Fitzgerald slugged one of the protestors, sending him flying into the stalls. The Abbey's cofounder, poet William Butler Yeats, proclaimed from the stage that "the fame of O'Casey is born here tonight," but O'Casey's anger over the play's reception provoked him to leave Ireland. The event was dramatized in *Young Cassidy,* a 1965 film based on O'Casey's early years and directed by Ford and Jack Cardiff. Ford's admiration for O'Casey led him to ask the playwright to write the screen adaptation of *The Informer,* but O'Casey declined.

Much to Ford's unhappiness, RKO did not let him import the Abbey Players intact for his film version of *The Plough and the Stars.* The studio insisted on the Brooklyn-born Irish-American Barbara Stanwyck as the female lead, Nora Clitheroe. Ford did get Fitzgerald to make his Hollywood debut reprising his celebrated role as Fluther Good. Others from the original production who appeared in the screen version included Arthur Shields (Fitzgerald's brother), F. J. McCormick, and Denis O'Dea; Eileen Crowe, who withdrew from the play during rehearsals, was cast in the film despite O'Casey's strong disapproval. Some other Irish players sought by Ford decided not to sign Hollywood contracts.

The casting turned out to be a mishmash, with the weakest links being Stanwyck and Preston Foster as her husband, Jack Clitheroe (a role originated by McCormick). Foster was a native of Ireland and had appeared in *The Informer* as IRA commandant Dan Gallagher, but there was little resonance of his ethnic background in his bland personality. Ford had offered the part of Jack to Spencer Tracy. Although Tracy had remained friendly with Ford after they worked together on *Up the River,* Tracy found the director overbearing and always resisted being part of his stock company. When Tracy rejected *The Plough and the Stars,* Ford felt betrayed, and they did not work together again until Hepburn brought about their reunion for *The Last Hurrah* in 1958.

Ford tried his best to populate *The Plough and the Stars* with authentic faces in minor roles. He told an interviewer on the Dublin set, "For these pictures that deal with the Irish uprising I've looked up former Black-and-Tan soldiers, former rebels, former onlookers, and given them parts; it adds to the sincerity because in the mass demonstration scenes they remember their own experiences and have real tears in their eyes—and every now and then some extra will offer a suggestion that lends to the authenticity of the production. Some of them—Arthur Shields for instance—were really in the Dublin Post Office when it fell. They were in this pub we've reproduced when the call came to mobilize."

According to Ford, RKO's new production chief, Sam Briskin, did not understand the point of O'Casey's play. Briskin demanded to know why the Irish were fighting the British in the midst of World War I. Ford replied that the Irish wanted the same thing George Washington sought for his people in the American Revolution: liberty. Briskin said he thought the Irish already *had* liberty. When Ford finished shooting, Briskin was still dissatisfied. "Why make a picture where a man and woman are married?" he asked. "The main thing about pictures is love or sex. Here you've got a man and woman married at the start—who's interested in that?" Briskin ordered Ford to shoot new romantic scenes of Nora and Jack as an unmarried couple.

Faced with an uncontrollable threat to his work, Ford responded by going on an alcoholic binge. Mary and the children were away, and his condition became perilous. Katharine Hepburn recalled, "One day Cliff Reid came to me and said that they had to have Ford do some work on one of his pictures and that Ford was on a bender at his house in the Hollywood Hills and wouldn't cooperate. Could I help? . . . So I went over to Ford's house, and somehow I got him into my car and I drove him to the RKO lot where I had a nice big dressing room. And I got him into my room. And somehow I persuaded him to drink a lethal dose of whiskey and castor oil.

"I have never seen anyone so sick. It was terrifying. I thought he was going to die. And he thought he was going to die. Then he fell asleep and I thought he was dead.

"Finally, after about two hours he woke up. I took him to the Hollywood Athletic Club and they pulled him together. . . . Wow! I'll never forget it. I really nearly killed him."

Hepburn was under the mistaken impression that Ford "fixed the picture" before his Hawaiian cruise aboard the *Araner*. In fact, he refused to make the changes RKO demanded. The studio assigned an assistant director, George Nicholls Jr., to shoot the new scenes with Stanwyck and Foster. Ford tried unsuccessfully to have his name removed from the picture. "Completely ruined the damn thing—destroyed the whole story," he fumed (he also said that *Mary of Scotland* had been "cut badly after I left"). This kind of butchery, to which Ford would never be fully immune despite his stature in the industry, caused him to leave RKO for a long-term contract with Twentieth Century–Fox and further spurred his militancy on behalf of the Screen Directors Guild.

Although Ford said his cut of *The Plough and the Stars* was released in Ireland and England, the version released in the United States in December 1936 is a mess. The continuity is choppy, and documentary footage is awkwardly juxtaposed with scenes shot in the studio (RKO used footage of the 1919–21 War of Independence, *not* the 1916 rising). The mixture of comedy and drama, usually managed by Ford with aplomb, is clumsy in the extreme. The interpolated love scenes are dreadfully dull, and Stanwyck gives a performance of unmodulated whining and hysteria. The result is a stagy historical pageant that alternately displays the cynicism of working-class Dublin toward the rebellion and sentimentally celebrates the heroes of a gallant "lost cause." Only a few stirring scenes of rebellion, marching, and street anarchy, lit by Joseph August with a suitably dank melancholia, surmount the ruination of a once promising project.

CHAPTER EIGHT

"NO PLACE FOR AN AUTEUR"

Critics of the Thirties always joked about the fact that the Hollywood system compelled Ford to make three Wee Willie Winkies *for every* Informer. *The joke, then as now, was on the critics.*

ANDREW SARRIS IN
THE AMERICAN CINEMA (1968)

DARRYL'S A GENIUS, and I don't use the word lightly," Ford told a Zanuck biographer in the late 1960s. "Of course in this industry every idiot nephew of some executive producer is a genius, but he actually was. He was head and shoulders above all other producers." Ford added, with some exaggeration, "We had an ideal relationship."

In late 1935, between the making of *The Informer* and *Mary of Scotland* at RKO, Ford returned to Twentieth Century–Fox to direct his first of twelve films for the new production chief, *The Prisoner of Shark Island*. Nunnally Johnson, a Southerner who served as that film's associate producer, wrote the provocative screenplay about Dr. Samuel A. Mudd, the Maryland country doctor who set John Wilkes Booth's broken leg and found himself imprisoned as a conspirator in the assassination of Abraham Lincoln. *Shark Island* finished shooting on January 17, 1936, and was released less than a month later, on Lincoln's birthday.

Once Ford had discharged his remaining obligations to RKO with *The Plough and the Stars* in the fall of 1936, he went back to Fox to make the Shirley Temple film *Wee Willie Winkie*. Although Ford had a nonexclusive contract with the studio during the Darryl F. Zanuck era, Fox remained his principal place of work until the coming of World War II. His first postwar film was made for Zanuck, and they continued working together intermittently until 1952.[1]

---

[1]. Ford's other films for Zanuck were *Four Men and a Prayer, Submarine Patrol, Young Mr. Lincoln, Drums Along the Mohawk, The Grapes of Wrath, Tobacco Road, How Green Was My Valley, My Darling Clementine, When Willie Comes Marching Home,* and *What Price Glory.* Fox also released Ford's 1942 navy documentary *The Battle of Midway.*

Ford initially was somewhat wary about working with Zanuck because of his unhappiness over the cuts Zanuck made in *Steamboat Round the Bend* shortly after taking the production reins at the newly amalgamated studio. The short, feisty executive, who liked to swing a sawed-off polo mallet while striding around his office during story conferences, was as headstrong as the director. Ford thought Zanuck had a "Napoleon complex." Their creative relationship, never without tension, flourished only after an early test of wills.

When Ford began shooting *The Prisoner of Shark Island,* Nunnally Johnson became concerned about the overly broad southern accent Warner Baxter was using in the role of Dr. Mudd. "Can't you tell Warner to speak normally?" the writer asked Ford. "Southerners don't know they've got an accent to begin with until they hear somebody mocking it, and then they get their backs up." Ford said he had mentioned the problem to Baxter, but the actor, in Johnson's words, "had an ego about equal to Ford's and he kept on using the accent." Later, at rushes, Johnson asked Zanuck how *he* thought the accent sounded. Zanuck pronounced it "godawful." Infuriated to learn about Baxter's defiance, Zanuck, who rarely appeared on the sets of films during production, marched onto the soundstage and took Ford aside.

"What about this accent that Baxter's using?" Zanuck demanded.

"Well, what about it?" asked Ford.

"I think it's giving a bad effect," said Zanuck. "Have you spoken to him about it?"

"Yes."

"Well, can't you do anything with him about it?"

"If you're not satisfied with the way I'm directing this," Ford snapped, "you can get somebody else!"

"Are you threatening me?" Zanuck shouted. "Are you threatening me you'll walk off this set? Don't ever threaten me. I throw fellas off this set. They don't quit on me."

"I was embarrassed," recalled Johnson. "I thought Zanuck was going to punch him in the nose. Ford had him outweighed by forty or fifty pounds. I was glad to get away from there. I just didn't want to witness this sort of thing. . . . [A] few months later I got on John's boat, and around the boat were [Fox associate producer] Gene Markey and two or three other fellows. Markey said, 'How'd you get along with Darryl?'

"Ford didn't realize that the only person who was a witness happened to be sitting there. He said to Gene, 'Oh, well, we had a little meeting. We had a little discussion. There's been no trouble since.' Then he looked up and saw I was listening and said, 'You were there, Nunnally.'

"I said, 'I remember,' but I didn't make a point of it."

The ruins of the Feeney family home in Spiddal, County Galway, Ireland, where John Ford's father, John Augustine Feeney, was born and raised before emigrating to America in 1872 JOSEPH MCBRIDE

The author (1986) inside the ruins of the Feeney family home RUTH O'HARA

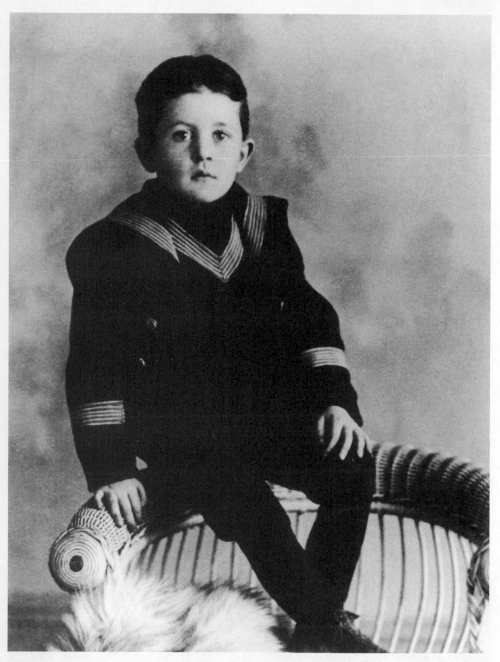

The future rear admiral John Ford as a sailor-suited boy in Maine, when his name was still John Feeney *PROJECTIONS* 4/FABER AND FABER

CERTIFICATION OF VITAL RECORD

STATE OF MAINE

CERTIFIED ABSTRACT OF A CERTIFICATE OF LIVE BIRTH
DEPARTMENT OF HUMAN SERVICES

CHILD	FULL NAME OF CHILD John Martin Feeney	DATE OF BIRTH February 1, 1894	
	SEX Male	BIRTHPLACE Spurwink	
ATTENDANT	NAME AND TITLE OF ATTENDANT L. B. Thombs, M.D.	ADDRESS —	
MOTHER	MAIDEN NAME OF MOTHER Barbara Curran	RESIDENCE OF MOTHER Cape Elizabeth	
FATHER	FATHER'S NAME John A. Feeney		

NAME OF CLERK RECORDING THIS BIRTH	CITY OR TOWN	DATE OF FILING
Noah B. Knight	Cape Elizabeth, ME	1894

I HEREBY CERTIFY THAT THE FOREGOING IS A TRUE ABSTRACT OF A CERTIFICATE OR RECORD WHICH IS IN MY OFFICIAL CUSTODY.

ATTEST: *Linda C. Cohen*   STATE REGISTRAR/MUNICIPAL CLERK
Linda C. Cohen
DATE ISSUED: TOWN OF:
FEB 1 6 1993   South Portland
This copy not valid unless prepared on engraved border disclosing seal and signature of Registrar.
VS-10 R186

ANY ALTERATION OR ERASURE VOIDS THIS CERTIFICATE

The birth records of John Martin Feeney (later known as John Ford) show that he was born in 1894, a year earlier than he claimed, and that his birth name was not Sean Aloysius O'Fearna or another of his fanciful variants. "Spurwink" refers to the district of Cape Elizabeth in which the Feeneys lived; their home was on Spurwink Road, now Charles E. Jordan Road.

STATE OF MAINE
DEPARTMENT OF
HUMAN SERVICES

3

RECORD OF BIRTHS.

Date of Birth	Place of Birth	Name of child (if any)	Sex and Condition			Name of Father
Feb. 1ˢᵗ 1894	Spurwink	John Martin	M	10ᵗʰ Living	W	John A. Feeney
" 1ˢᵗ "	Knightville	Ernest Parsons	M	3ᵈ Living	W	Edwin H. Marshall
" 2ⁿᵈ "	So. Portland	Fridiaca Marie	F	1ˢᵗ Living	W	Fred. G. Orr
" 9ᵗʰ "	Knightville	Warren Henry	M	3ᵈ Living	W	B.A. Squires

Handwritten birth record

TOWN OF CAPE ELIZABETH, MAINE.

TOWN OF
CAPE
ELIZABETH,
MAINE

Maiden name of Mother	Color of Mother	Residence of Parents	Occupation of Father	Birthplace of Father	Birthplace of Mother
Barbara Curran	W	Cape Elizabeth	Farmer	Ireland	Ireland
Eva C. Pearson	W	Knightville	Clerk	No. Yarmouth Me	Cape Elizabeth
Annie L. Violette	W	So. Portland	Machinist	London Eng	" "
Sarah E. Goodwin	W	Cape Elizabeth	Stenographer	Oswego N.Y.	Plattsburg N

Recorded by Noah B. Knight

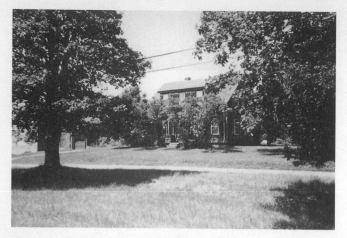

Ford was born in this comfortable farmhouse at Cape Elizabeth, Maine (1998 photo).
JOSEPH McBRIDE

From his earliest childhood, Ford lived close to the sea. This is the view of the ocean from the field behind his birthplace (1998 photo).
JOSEPH McBRIDE

"Ever since I was about four years old, I owned a boat": Higgins Beach, half a mile down the hill from Ford's boyhood home at Cape Elizabeth, where he sailed his first boat (1998 photo)
JOSEPH McBRIDE

As a twelve-year-old child, Ford missed a year of school while quarantined in bed with diphtheria. It was then that he acquired his lifelong love of books, like the bedridden Huw Morgan (Roddy McDowall) in his 1941 film of Richard Llewellyn's novel *How Green Was My Valley*, which won Academy Awards for best picture and best director.

From the vantage point of his family's top-floor apartment in Portland, Maine, young John Feeney spent many hours in his youth watching the boats in nearby Casco Bay. The Feeneys shared this building at 21–23 Sheridan Street with two other Irish families (1998 photo). JOSEPH MCBRIDE

Covering his sensitivity with a roughneck facade, "Bull" Feeney, "the human battering ram" (*back row, far right*), was a star fullback on Portland High School's 1913 state champion football team during his senior year. Among others pictured are his pal Oscar "Ski" Vanier (*front row, far left*) and coach Edmund K. Arnold (*second row, far right*). PETER E. GRIBBIN/PORTLAND HIGH SCHOOL

The old Portland High School on Commercial Street, where Ford completed his formal education in 1914. Although generally lackadaisical in his classes, he was an honor student in his two favorite subjects, English and history. PETER E. GRIBBIN/PORTLAND HIGH SCHOOL

The Ford statue by George M. Kelly at Gorham's Corner in Portland across from the former site of Feeney's Saloon. This photograph was taken on the day of the statue's dedication in July 1998, when Ford was belatedly honored by his hometown. JOSEPH MCBRIDE

The ride of the Klansmen in D. W. Griffith's epic film *The Birth of a Nation* (1915): the Klansman at right holding the hood over his eyes is probably Ford, who recalled, "I was riding with one hand holding the hood up so I could see because the damn thing kept slipping over my glasses." Epoch/Photofest

Ford's most important influence as a filmmaker was his brother Francis, with whom he had a love-hate relationship. Frank had a successful career as an actor and director in the early days of silent films, but in talkies he was relegated to character roles, such as this one in *The Quiet Man* (1952), his penultimate film under his younger brother's direction. Republic Pictures

"Bright Star of the early western sky . . .": Harry Carey, the star of Ford's first silent Westerns for Universal, in their 1919 film *The Outcasts of Poker Flat*, based on two stories by Bret Harte UNIVERSAL

A scene shot along the Sacramento River for *The Outcasts of Poker Flat*. *Photoplay* hailed "director Ford's marvelous river locations and absolutely incomparable photography. This photoplay is an optic symphony." UNIVERSAL/MUSEUM OF MODERN ART/FILM STILLS ARCHIVE

The figure of Abraham Lincoln always had a great symbolic resonance for Ford, seen here directing Nevada judge Charles Edward Bull as Lincoln in *The Iron Horse* (1924). This epic Western about the building of the first transcontinental railroad established Ford as a major American filmmaker. FOX FILM CORP./PHOTOFEST

Easily the finest of Ford's extant silent films, *3 Bad Men* (1926) is a relaxed, picaresque Western set in 1877 during a Dakota land rush. FOX FILM CORP.

Portrait of John Ford in the
1930s Fox Film Corp.

Portrait of John Ford in 1936,
at the time he directed his film
version of Sean O'Casey's play
The Plough and the Stars RKO

Ford's first great film was *Pilgrimage* (1933), the story of a domineering mother who causes her own son's death in World War I. Norman Foster plays the Arkansas farm boy, with the veteran stage star Henrietta Crosman giving a powerful performance as his mother, Hannah Jessop. FOX FILM CORP.

One of Ford's three delightful films with Will Rogers (*leaning out of window*), *Judge Priest* (1934) satirized America's racial divide and provided an example of healing in the friendly relationship between the Kentucky judge and his factotum Jeff Poindexter, played by Stepin Fetchit (*wearing coonskin coat*). FOX FILM CORP. / ACADEMY OF MOTION PICTURE ARTS AND SCIENCES

Ford won his first Academy Award as best director for *The Informer*, his highly expressionistic 1935 film version of Liam O'Flaherty's novel. Victor McLaglen also won an Oscar in the title role of the befuddled Irish traitor Gypo Nolan. RKO/ NOSTALGIA MERCHANT

Ford (*far left*) was a leading figure in the formative years of the Screen Directors Guild. In the late 1930s, he watched as SDG president Frank Capra (*third from right*) presented honorary life memberships in the guild to pioneering director D. W. Griffith and guild counsel Mabel Walker Willebrandt. Also pictured are (*from left*) Frank Strayer, Rouben Mamoulian, J. P. McGowan, W. S. Van Dyke II, William Wyler, Leo McCarey, and George Marshall. UCLA THEATER ARTS LIBRARY/WILLIAM WYLER COLLECTION

Pauline Moore as the ill-fated Ann Rutledge, with Henry Fonda in the title role of *Young Mr. Lincoln* (1939), one of Ford's most haunting and luminous treatments of American history TWENTIETH CENTURY–FOX

An icon is born: John Wayne's entrance scene in his first starring role for Ford, as the Ringo Kid in *Stagecoach* (1939), with Andy Devine and George Bancroft (*pointing gun*) UNITED ARTISTS/WISCONSIN CENTER FOR FILM AND THEATRE RESEARCH

During the filming of the classic chase sequence in *Stagecoach* on Lucerne Dry Lake in the Mojave Desert near Victorville, California, Ford can be seen leaning out the back window of the stagecoach, directing from amid the action. UNITED ARTISTS/WISCONSIN CENTER FOR FILM AND THEATRE RESEARCH

The screenwriter who most influenced Ford's artistic development, Dudley
Nichols, confers with him in 1940 about their adaptation of Eugene
O'Neill's sea tetralogy *The Long Voyage Home*. UNITED ARTISTS/WISCONSIN
CENTER FOR FILM AND THEATRE RESEARCH

Ford surrounded by memorabilia in
the study of "the Little Grey House
on the Hill," his unpretentious
home on Odin Street in Hollywood
(1941) TWENTIETH CENTURY–FOX/
ACADEMY OF MOTION PICTURE ARTS
AND SCIENCES

Embodying the uncommon American common man, Henry Fonda was Ford's favorite protagonist during the director's Popular Front period of the late 1930s. Fonda is seen here as Gil Martin, the farmer-turned–Revolutionary War soldier in *Drums Along the Mohawk* (1939). Twentieth Century–Fox/ Wisconsin Center for Film and Theatre Research

Henry Fonda as the radicalized dust bowl refugee Tom Joad in *The Grapes of Wrath* (1940). Ford was attracted to John Steinbeck's proletarian novel because it reminded him of the hardships of his Irish ancestors during the Great Famine of the nineteenth century. Twentieth Century–Fox

Ford's need to maintain his authoritative image required that he behave as if he had prevailed in the showdown. But Ford had little choice but to capitulate. Playing with only a hint of a southern drawl, Baxter was effective, if uninspired, in the role of Dr. Mudd. Ford's necessary acquiescence to Zanuck's authority demonstrated the limit of even a great director's power in the heyday of the studio system.

Darryl Zanuck's Twentieth Century–Fox was no place for an Auteur," Philip Dunne contended. "Movies were made on what amounted to an assembly line: writers wrote, directors directed, actors acted, cutters cut, and Zanuck himself supervised every detail of each stage of production. At Twentieth, the script was the star. . . . Zanuck's big hits depended primarily on the scripts which were written under his supervision."

Dunne, who worked with Zanuck for many years as a screenwriter and eventually also as a director, regarded him as "the executive par excellence: intelligent, decisive, totally in support of his subordinates as he was totally in charge of their work. Above all, he had the real executive's essential knack of knowing how to handle people. He knew when to coddle, when to bully, and when to exhort."

In most cases, a director was assigned to a project by Zanuck only when the script was ready to shoot. And the director was expected to follow the script religiously. "You did not write scripts *for* directors, not in Zanuck's studio," Dunne explained. "You wrote them for Zanuck. He was the boss. He said to me once, 'If I could start with a bestseller, something that's already a proved hit, and assign one of you guys'—he named three of us, Nunnally Johnson, Lamar Trotti, and me—'I wouldn't care who directed it.' The director was the necessary evil. Nunnally Johnson said that if a director changed a word in the script, it was as if you had insulted American womanhood and trampled on the flag. When I changed a line in my own script as a director, I got a rocket from Zanuck right away. It said, 'God damn it, for twenty years I've been protecting you from other directors. Now you've forced me to protect you from yourself.' And he was right. All I had to do was pick up the phone and let him know I made a change. You had to have one hell of a good editor in charge."

Zanuck's strict supervisory policy over scripts naturally caused tensions with such an independent-minded director as Ford. "When he worked for Zanuck, they had a few clashes," Dunne said, "because Ford, after all, was a very temperamental, feisty character, he'd flare up over any kind of criticism. That happened with Darryl, but he didn't win any arguments with Zanuck. There was no question who was the boss. I do think it's true that there were two director Fords. There was the individual, independent Jack Ford, and then

there was the one who worked for Zanuck. Zanuck was such an overpower-
ing personality that he was stronger than Ford. Of course, he also had the *position* to be stronger."

Ford and Zanuck did not always agree on projects or how to make them,
but even the sparks that flew in their arguments generated creative energy in
the director. Not only did Zanuck help Ford rediscover his commercial bearings, but in the process Zanuck made story choices that tapped into Ford's
strengths as a popular artist. Zanuck started as a writer, and his true brilliance
lay in his shrewd story sense and his gutsiness in being able to make even controversial material play with great effectiveness for a mass audience.

When he took over Fox, Zanuck inherited a studio that had long specialized in pastoral subjects and period films. A native of Wahoo, Nebraska,
Zanuck had his own strong bias toward such subject matter, leading Hollywood wags to refer to his studio as "Nineteenth Century–Fox." In his biography of Zanuck, George F. Custen notes that while the executive concentrated
on period films partly to avoid controversy from pressure groups, "the archi-
tect of Fox's rural nostalgia policy was not merely being regressive. Nostalgia
was a move in a game in which Zanuck distracted audiences with the past, so
he could deal selectively in films like *The Grapes of Wrath* with serious present-
day issues."

Under Zanuck's aegis, Ford began turning out films that, in contrast to
those he had made at RKO, were more emotionally direct and less interested
in style for its own sake. Ford's films for Zanuck in 1935–41, though highly
uneven in quality, included such artistic triumphs as *Young Mr. Lincoln, The
Grapes of Wrath,* and *How Green Was My Valley.* The deepening of Ford's artistic sensibility during that period stemmed in large part from his decision to
concentrate more intensely on American history and stories with strong sociopolitical themes, an artistic and emotional urge that owed much to the
stimulating influence of Zanuck's fondness for such subjects.

Perhaps the principal reason Zanuck was able to draw such good work from
Ford, despite their differences, was that Zanuck admired the director so
strongly. "I have finally come to the conclusion that John Ford is the best director in the history of motion pictures," Zanuck declared in 1968. ". . . Ford
could get more drama into an ordinary interior or exterior long shot than any
director and . . . his placement of the camera almost had the effect of making
even good dialogue unnecessary or secondary. . . . I think he made more outstanding hits than any other director—on all subjects. He was an artist. He
painted a picture—in movement, in action, in still shots. He would never
move a camera setup—move in or zoom in. You would look at the set and
think maybe you need a close-up, but you didn't. He was a great, great pictorial artist."

. . .

Ford accepted that he had to make occasional trade-offs with Zanuck to win more important victories. He learned to choose his battles with great care, avoiding direct confrontation whenever possible. Ford was "a man who made an art of the oblique approach," wrote Dunne. ". . . Jack was as Irish as any native American born in Maine could hope to be. He was not a devious man in the sense that he lied or cheated; he merely preferred the labyrinthine approach to the head-on assault."

Such strategies were part of the habitual secretiveness of Ford's Irish personality, a habit he developed, like the native Irish, largely out of self-protection, as a means of prevailing in an often hostile environment. "None of us can figure out what is in John Ford's mind," declared the exasperated David O. Selznick. Ford liked it that way. Working for such a brilliant Hollywood game player as Zanuck enabled Ford to refine his deviousness to a high art.

Ford's carefully cultivated eccentricities helped him get his own way creatively to the maximum extent possible while still appearing to be deferential to the conventional guidelines of the studio factory system. This necessary duality was the primary reason he posed as someone who didn't consider himself an "artist." By claiming that he regarded moviemaking as "just a job of work," Ford gave Zanuck and other executives the illusion that they were more in control of his films than they actually were. Ford was shrewd enough to save direct confrontation for times when only such a potentially risky approach could solve a problem. And even then he usually devised unexpected methods of confrontation.

On one film at Fox during the 1930s, Ford requested eighty-five extras for a courtroom sequence. The studio sent down only fifty. So Ford told his assistant director, Wingate Smith, to set up folding chairs outside the soundstage and had the extras sit there while he shot the sequence with the courtroom seats empty of spectators. While shooting the mine disaster sequence for *How Green Was My Valley* at Fox in 1941, Ford was criticized by the front office for using too many extras. So he reshot the scene with only the principal actors emoting on an otherwise empty set.

Perhaps the most famous of all John Ford stories is the one about an incident that occurred during the making of *Wee Willie Winkie*. Cinematographer Arthur C. Miller left an account of the incident in his memoirs "to eliminate any doubt that it actually happened." He recalled, "One of the would-be executives from the production office appeared where we were working on the back lot. Such appearances were so unusual, unless they were summoned, that Ford's attention was attracted and he beckoned the executive to him. Ford was sitting in his chair with the script on his lap. As the executive approached, Ford

asked what was on his mind. The man explained that they had just held a production meeting and had reached the conclusion that the picture was four days
behind schedule. Without changing his expression, Ford looked at him for a
few seconds, and then casually opened the script, tore out four pages, handed
them to the astounded man, and said, 'We're on schedule. Now beat it.'"

Ford never did shoot those four pages; perhaps he didn't want to anyway.
He may have been saving the gag for just such an occasion. This kind of outrageous power play was part of the barrier he erected between himself and
studio executives to make them afraid to approach him in the future. Another
part of Ford's legendary pose of indifference was his frequent claim that he
never looked at rushes (the daily screening of unedited footage). "You see, I'm
not very proud of my own work," he told Zanuck biographer Mel Gussow
with a "deadpan expression." When Ford did not turn up to watch rushes during the first days of shooting on *The Prisoner of Shark Island,* Zanuck ordered
him to begin doing so immediately. Ford had the strips of film delivered to the
soundstage and ostentatiously sat in his director's chair studying them frame by
frame through a magnifying glass. Zanuck was not amused. According to
Robert Parrish, who worked as an editor on several Ford films at Fox, the director's supposed lack of interest in rushes was a pose, part of his carefully cultivated persona as a rough-hewn craftsman whose artistry was largely
subconscious. Ford would watch the rushes by himself or with his editors. No
one else was allowed in the screening room. Later the director would act as if
he hadn't seen the rushes.

When holding a private screening of one of his films, even one of his great
classics, Ford liked to say beforehand, "I've been wanting to see this picture
myself. I never saw it after it was all put together." As Parrish noted, "When
the screenings were over, he would shamelessly wipe away a tear and say, to
whoever happened to be present, 'I'm glad I waited until I could see it with
you.' Experienced Ford watchers would look at their feet in embarrassment,
but first-timers were quite often taken in." In a humorous variation, sometimes used with more savvy people who were clued in to his shtick, Ford
might say when mentioning one of his films that he particularly liked, "I *saw*
that." Then he would break into a mischievous grin.

What made such corny routines seem plausible was Ford's well-known
habit of ceding control of the final editing to Zanuck. "He knew I hated to
go into the projection room," said Ford, "so I had this tacit agreement that he
would cut the picture. If it was up to me I'd cut everything out. He'd say,
'What do you think of it?' and I'd say, 'It's just another picture.' He was a great
cutter, a great film editor." Ford went on to give Zanuck even more credit for
his postproduction expertise: "One of his greatest assets was to supply the
proper music—and sound effects. He held music down to a minimum. . . . In

Grapes Darryl used a single, lightly played accordion—not a big orchestra—and it was very American, and very right for the picture." (The theme music for the film, "Red River Valley," was played on the accordion by Danny Borzage, who provided music on Ford's sets from *The Iron Horse* onward.)

"Ford avoided one huge point of controversy [with Zanuck] because he always left the day shooting was over," Dunne noted. "He paid no attention to the postproduction chores. He wanted to go off on the *Araner.* When he did something like *The Informer* or *The Quiet Man* or *The Long Voyage Home,* which were really Fordian epics, he was really in charge. But when he worked for Zanuck he was doing it more as a hired hand."

Indeed, it was standard operating procedure at Fox for Zanuck to have final say over the editing, mixing, and scoring of all the films his studio produced. During postproduction, said Dunne, "No director was sacred. Actually, Ford got much better treatment than most directors." Still, Ford's willingness to absent himself from the studio during most or all of the postproduction process—a practice that today would be considered bizarre for a major director—seems hard to reconcile with his artistic stature. Taken at face value, it seems particularly irresponsible coming from a director who was a militant leader of the Screen Directors Guild, whose platform stressed the crucial importance of directors achieving more control over editing and other aspects of postproduction. But in fact, Ford's ostensibly hands-off posture toward such matters was an even more sophisticated move on the Hollywood political chessboard.

He was able to take such an approach only because he took the precaution of "cutting in the camera." That meant he shot as little nonessential footage as possible, avoiding repeated takes or "covering" the scene from many angles as most directors did in that era. "All a cutter had to do with Ford's takes," explained Parrish, "was to cut off the slate number and put them together, in sequence. This was Ford's own guarantee against possible butchery by front-office executives or wandering meddlers. Ford left them no extra footage to fool around with." This ploy enabled Ford to avoid some, though not all, of the pitched battles that so often occur between filmmakers and studios during postproduction.

The wedding of Angharad (Maureen O'Hara) in *How Green Was My Valley* offers a revealing example of Ford's strategy. "Ford concentrated on the entire picture at all times—never on a single day's work," cinematographer Arthur C. Miller remembered. "There was not a dolly or a boom shot in the entire picture. Occasionally, for the sake of composition or to accommodate the action, the camera would make a slight pan or tilt, but the mechanics of a moving camera never became noticeable. . . . The bride and groom came down the stone steps from the church, built on a small rise, and they moved through the gathering of well-wishers and got into a waiting carriage. The carriage, drawn by two horses, promptly pulled out of the scene. The camera panned slightly to the left in a hardly noticeable manner to show the minister [Walter Pidgeon] who had performed the wedding ceremony and who had consequently lost forever the girl he loved. The minister was standing near the entrance to the church framed by a large oak tree, just a tiny figure in the distance. This was one of those rare occasions when Ford did his thinking out loud. Looking at the minister in the distance for a few seconds, he mumbled, 'If I make a close-up, somebody will want to use it.' Dismissing the thought, we moved to another location in the village."

In addition to exercising such discipline over his shooting methods, Ford devised some deviously clever tricks to safeguard his editorial control even further. One was his habit of sitting in his director's chair immediately under the lens of the camera. At the same time he called "Cut," he would put his fist in front of the lens. That way, if the cameraman was inclined to keep the camera running a bit longer than Ford wanted, the extra footage at the end of the scene would be rendered unusable.

A subtler trick was his habit of violating the rules of "screen direction"—the convention of classical Hollywood moviemaking style dictating that action in successive shots should follow the same direction on the screen in order to give the appearance of seamless motion. Ford deliberately flouted that rule throughout much of his work, especially in his later movies. Some critics have assumed that he was being sloppy or that he just didn't care about smooth continuity; it's clear from the films themselves that carefully matching shots was never one of his highest priorities. Ford's standard explanation for violating screen direction was that he always wanted the flexibility of shooting in whatever direction was best suited for pictorial effect. In the case of the famous sequence of the Indian chase in *Stagecoach,* which disregards the rules with breathtaking abandon, Ford's excuse was that the budget was too low to allow the luxury of frequently shifting the camera to film the action from various directions. But Ford had a more covert reason behind this habitual stylistic anomaly.

Cinematographer Winton C. Hoch, who photographed such Ford classics as *The Quiet Man* and *The Searchers,* told me that the principal reason Ford made a practice of violating the rules of screen direction was to prevent editors from making cuts on movement. If a character enters or exits the frame from the "wrong" direction, as he or she often does in a Ford movie, the editor is forced to begin the shot before the character enters the frame and hold it until after he clears the frame, rather than cutting into the middle of the shot to speed up the action. By doing it his way, Ford was able to control the tempo and duration of each scene without having to participate in the actual editing process. Hoch only once (on *The Quiet Man*) dared to challenge Ford on screen direction, meeting a predictably icy response: Ford set up an entirely different composition just to show him who was boss.

Naturally, such sly subterfuge mightily frustrated executives who jealously guarded their prerogative to meddle with the finished product. Zanuck often clashed with Ford over his fondness for a deliberate, even dawdling storytelling pace. Zanuck's filmmaking credo was "They don't call them *moving* pictures because they *stand still*—they *move!*" As Dunne recalled, "Directors—and writers too—often were distressed by what we called Zanuck's 'nervous scissors,' his tendency to cut too deeply in his constant obsession with a faster pace." Ford's files contain numerous memos from Zanuck lecturing him on that subject.

A typical Zanuck memo praised the early rushes of Ford's 1939 film *Young Mr. Lincoln* as "honest and real," but asked, "Do you feel that at times the tempo is apt to be a trifle slow? I don't mean that we should speed up [Henry] Fonda [as Lincoln], as it is the slowness and deliberate character that you have given him that make his performance swell, but I have had a feeling that at times we seem to be a little draggy as far as mood is concerned." Suggesting that Ford pick up the tempo with secondary characters "so that we don't take the chance of having all of it done in one key," Zanuck added, "I may be wrong about this, but I wish you would give it some thought." Despite whatever influence Zanuck had on the shooting and editing of *Young Mr. Lincoln*,[2] the film keeps a leisurely tempo perfectly appropriate to the subject matter, so it appears that Ford essentially prevailed in that instance. When Zanuck nagged Ford about the same issue during the making of his next film, *Drums Along the Mohawk*, Ford responded from location, "Your letters and wires about tempo frighten me. Both the script and the story call for a placid, pastoral, simple movement, which suddenly breaks into quick, heavy, dramatic overtones. All this requires care."

Zanuck was almost as impatient over Ford's penchant for inventing small, offbeat touches not strictly necessary to the narrative. When Elia Kazan and John Steinbeck were preparing *Viva Zapata!* at Fox in 1950, Zanuck jocularly warned them against anything that might make it seem "as if we are trying to make an art or 'mood' picture. The kind of thing John Ford does when he is

---

2. Ford told Bogdanovich he regretted Fox's decision to drop a "lovely scene" showing Lincoln having a nonverbal encounter outside a Springfield theater with the young actor John Wilkes Booth. Based on Ford's description of the scene, however, it does seem as if Zanuck showed sound judgment in eliminating such a heavy-handed bit of foreshadowing.

stuck and has run out of plot. In these cases, somebody always sings and you cut to an extreme long shot with slanting shadows." While Ford sometimes indulged himself by embroidering such moments in movies whose narrative elements bored him, in his best work such "grace notes" (as he called them) are the conduit he reserves for his deepest feelings. Ford was always less interested in narrative per se than in the lyrical poetry he could draw from and around the narrative line. He would film his long shots in the early morning or late afternoon, when the shadows were deepest, and save the closer shots for the middle of the day.

After Ford screened his cut of *Grapes* for Zanuck, the studio chief congratulated him profusely and Ford replied, "Thanks—and try not to spoil it, will you, sonny?" He was not entirely kidding. Ford's occasional displeasure over Zanuck's reediting of his work eventually turned to bitterness after Zanuck made substantial changes in the director's 1946 Western *My Darling Clementine*.

Ford, who never forgot a slight, also harbored undying resentment against Zanuck for passing on *Stagecoach* (1939) and not allowing him to make other offbeat, seemingly noncommercial projects. Wrong as he was about *Stagecoach*, Zanuck showed wisdom in discouraging Ford from his ill-conceived notion in March 1938 to do a Hollywood remake of Jean Renoir's classic antiwar film set in World War I, *La Grande Illusion*. Ford wanted to change the French prisoners to Englishmen; his casting ideas included Victor McLaglen (in the Jean Gabin role), George Sanders (in the Erich von Stroheim role), J. Edward Bromberg (in the Marcel Dalio role), and David Niven or Cesar Romero (in the Pierre Fresnay role). Calling *La Grande Illusion* "one of the most magnificent pictures of its type that I have ever seen," Zanuck told Ford, "I think that it would be a criminal injustice to attempt to remake the picture in English. The most wonderful thing about the picture is the fine background, the authentic atmosphere, and the foreign characters, who actually speak in the language of their nationality. Once you take this away, I believe you have lost 50% of the value of the picture." (When Renoir came to work at Fox in 1941, he was "particularly pleased by the friendliness of John Ford, being an enthusiastic admirer of his work. He took me aside in the studios and said to me in French: 'Dear Jean, don't ever forget what I'm going to tell you. Actors are crap.' Of course he only meant bad actors.")

Ford charged in later years that Zanuck lacked "artistic integrity" and was interested only in making "safe commercial pictures." But Zanuck's courageous decision to make *The Grapes of Wrath,* even if he softened some aspects of its controversial source material, certainly belied Ford's argument. Still, Ford could not help feeling that his more personal tastes and instincts as a filmmaker were being somewhat stifled under Zanuck's control. Dan Ford's biography seems uncomfortable with some of his grandfather's tastes and instincts, suggesting that Zanuck was right in cutting the "broad sight gags" Ford enjoyed. Despite Ford's complaint that Zanuck was "ruining" his films, his grandson felt that Zanuck actually was "steering him toward his best work." Zanuck may indeed have been steering Ford toward his best work, but most of it was done somewhere else. Andrew Sarris derides the Zanuck-centered "rationale for Ford's rising career. . . . It was as if John Ford's directorial soul were the arena for a titanic struggle between the romantic artifices of Dudley Nichols and the realist humanism of the Fox contingent. What was actually happening was that Ford's art was becoming richer and more complex as he played off one aesthetic against another. He was not yet fully in command of his career, but he was discovering his true talents and affinities through productive experience."

Some of the elements Zanuck disliked about Ford's style are among those that made his work most truly personal. If Ford sometimes goes overboard with his comic relief—never more so, in fact, than with the excruciating antics of William Tracy's Dude Lester in *Tobacco Road* (1941), a Zanuck production—it's also true that Ford's interweaving of tragedy and comedy is, like his tendency toward narrative digression, one of the key components of his artistic personality. The great films Ford made away from Zanuck abound with visual and dramatic poetry and with the subversive sense of humor that gives his worldview a Shakespearean balance and perspective.

Inevitably, the quirks of style and demeanor Ford developed to outwit Zanuck and other studio executives became an integral part of his artistic vision. His sparing use of the close-up, for example, gives that highly emphatic tool far greater impact than if it were diluted by overuse. By withholding close-ups, Ford places greater emphasis on people's social roles than on their isolated, subjective viewpoints. Conversely, Ford's disruption of the classical rules of screen direction works on the audience as a subtle alienation effect. As Hoch pointed out, a close-up of the superannuated Colonel Nathan Brittles (John Wayne) looking toward his fellow soldiers in *She Wore a Yellow Ribbon* from the "wrong" direction achieved "the effect Ford wanted—which was Duke being rejected by the group." That blend of estrangement and yearning for social integration helps account for the complex emotional tone of Ford's way of seeing the world.

In his book on Ford, the French critic Philippe Haudiquet observes that the director had "an obsession with justice." *The Prisoner of Shark Island* (1936), Ford's first film for Zanuck, burns white-hot with outrage over what it portrays as one of the most egregious cases of injustice in American history. Georgia native Nunnally Johnson's screenplay about Dr. Samuel Alexander Mudd trenchantly criticizes the vengeful mentality of the North in the aftermath of the Civil War and the assassination of Abraham Lincoln. The film presents Mudd (Warner Baxter) as an innocent victim of social hysteria who is charged with being an assassination conspirator simply for ministering to an injured man he does not recognize as the fugitive John Wilkes Booth (Francis McDonald). However, the film's unambiguous stance on the still unresolved question of Mudd's culpability makes *The Prisoner of Shark Island* problematical in terms of historical representation.

The Maryland country doctor whose disgrace inspired the saying "His name is Mudd" received a pardon from President Andrew Johnson in 1869 but has never been fully exonerated, despite the continuing efforts of his descendants. Fox bought the film rights to *The Life of Dr. Mudd* by his daughter, Nettie Mudd Monroe, although the book was not credited as a basis for Johnson's screenplay. In the 1997 book *His Name Is* Still *Mudd: The Case Against Dr. Samuel Alexander Mudd,* Edward Steers Jr. argues that Mudd, as part of an underground of Confederate sympathizers in Maryland, was guilty of being an accomplice with Booth in a failed plot to abduct Lincoln and exchange him for Confederate prisoners of war, and of knowingly aiding Booth's escape in the hours following the assassination. Frederick Stone, the lawyer who represented Mudd at his conspiracy trial, said later, "The court very nearly hanged Dr. Mudd. His prevarications were painful. . . . He denied knowing Booth when he knew him well. He was undoubtedly accessory to the abduction plot, though he may have supposed it would never come to anything."

Since the Lincoln assassination was never properly investigated, many questions and doubts persist today about various people's involvement with Booth. The gross injustices perpetrated by the federal government in prosecuting Mudd have helped keep open the question of his possible innocence. The doctor's role in putting down a yellow-fever epidemic during his imprisonment at Fort Jefferson on the island of Dry Tortugas also has contributed to the rehabilitation of his image by those who believe that in treating Booth's broken leg he was simply following his Hippocratic oath.

The heroic depiction of Dr. Mudd in *The Prisoner of Shark Island* may be an example of the tendency toward historical amnesia later criticized by the director in *The Man Who Shot Liberty Valance.* But as audiences have been accustomed to do with the Western genre, *Shark Island* perhaps should be approached more for its mythic qualities than for its claims of historical accuracy. If taken with that large grain of salt, which admittedly involves a certain amount of wish fulfillment in dealing with the ambiguities of American history, *Shark Island* can be taken on its own terms, as an allegory about the need to "bind up the nation's wounds."

The healing that might have occurred between North and South had Lincoln lived is suggested in the opening scene of the bone-weary president

(Frank McGlynn Sr.)[3] addressing a crowd of celebrants on the night of the South's surrender: "You have a band with you. There's one piece of music I've always liked. Heretofore it hasn't seemed the proper thing to use it in the North. But now, by virtue of my prerogative as president and commander in chief of the army and navy, I declare it contraband of war and our lawful prize. I ask the band to play 'Dixie.'" The assassination sequence that immediately follows on-screen ends with a close-up of Lincoln's inert face as a lace curtain is dropped between him and the camera. The camera slowly pulls focus to give Lincoln's image the softly crosshatched contours of a tapestry, Ford's visual equivalent of saying, "Now he belongs to the ages."

Employing a visual style fully as virtuosic as that of *The Informer,* Ford and cameraman Bert Glennon depict Dr. Mudd's nightmarish ordeal in military court and prison with starkly expressionistic camera angles, subtly distorting wide-angle lenses, and heavily shadowed compositions. But this film's Goya-esque vision of torture and suffering is conveyed with greater emotional urgency and less abstraction than was displayed in Ford's more-lauded exercise in expressionism. *Shark Island* does not dwell on pictorial effects for their own sake, but maintains the relentless narrative drive so characteristic of Zanuck's filmmaking philosophy.

The most fascinating aspect of *The Prisoner of Shark Island* is its complex depiction of the shifting relationships between whites and blacks in the Reconstruction era. Whatever his role in the events surrounding Lincoln's assassination, it is indisputable that Dr. Mudd was a slave owner and Confederate sympathizer. Nor do Ford and Johnson elide those aspects of Mudd's character in order to make him a more sympathetic figure.

Despite the film's general tone of sympathy toward the South (the theme song is the haunting, dirgelike "Maryland, My Maryland") and its occasional lapses into racial caricature, Ford movingly depicts the growing bond of brotherhood between Dr. Mudd and his former slave, Buckingham Montmorency "Buck" Milford (Ernest Whitman). Buck is so devoted to Dr. Mudd that he enlists in the Union army and has himself posted to Dry Tortugas to help his ex-master escape. There is great dignity nonetheless in Whitman's portrayal of a man whose loyalty and charity transcend all manner of injustice; the turning point in Buck's relationship with Dr. Mudd comes when they are left to die together in solitary confinement and Mudd ministers to his stricken friend. Yet Mudd is still capable of threatening the fort's rebellious black sol-

---

3. McGlynn was well known for playing Lincoln; he played the title role in the John Drinkwater stage play *Abraham Lincoln.* He was also the director of one of Francis Ford's earliest films, *Pardners,* made in New York for the Edison Company.

diers, whom he calls "boys" or "nigras," when he needs their help in caring for yellow-fever victims. One of the soldiers responds, "That ain't no Yankee talkin' just to hear hisself talk—that's a Southern man and he mean it. Yes sir!"

At the end of the film, when Mudd and Buck return home to the accompaniment of "Dixie," Buck is still riding in the back of the carriage. That the old racial system largely remains in place is made even more emphatically clear when Buck, who has risked his life for his master, thanks *him* for the privilege. Then, in one of the sweetest "grace notes" in all of his work, Ford shows where his deepest emotional allegiance lies in this grim chapter of American history. He reserves the film's final shot not for Dr. Mudd's reunion with his family but for Buck's joyous reunion with his wife, Rosabelle (Etta Mc-Daniel), and their twelve children, who gather around their quietly heroic father in the slanting late-afternoon light.

Tag Gallagher makes the intriguing suggestion that the role of Dr. Mudd would have had far more resonance if it had been played by Ford's longtime leading man in silent movies, Harry Carey. Working with Ford for the first time since 1921, Carey leaves a strong impression of honor and integrity in his secondary part as the stern but sympathetic commandant of the military prison. One of the film's most memorable moments comes when the commandant visits the prison hospital to thank Mudd for risking his life to stop the outbreak of yellow fever. Ford cuts to a close-up of the commandant telling Mudd he will request a presidential pardon for the doctor "because I do love the flag I serve and because I'm jealous of its honor."

The same year they made *The Prisoner of Shark Island,* Ford and Carey were involved in an RKO remake of their 1919 two-reel Western *The Last Outlaw.* With an updated story credited to Ford and Evelyne Murray Campbell, the 1936 talkie version is an amiable B movie directed by silent-film veteran Christy Cabanne. Carey is moving and funny in the title role of an aging outlaw released from prison into the modern world, a Rip Van Winkle figure forced to adjust to such changes as automobile traffic and singing cowboys in the movies. Carey bought the story rights from RKO in 1942, and the following year he and Ford began discussing remaking it again, this time as an A picture. Ford's Argosy Pictures signed a contract in January 1945 to make *The Last Outlaw* for United Artists, but Ford was still in military service at the time and the project did not reach fruition before Carey's death in 1947.

One day," recalled Ford, "Darryl said, 'I'm going to give you something to scream about. I'm going to put you together with Shirley Temple.' He thought that combination would make me and everybody howl. I said, 'Great,' and we just went out and made the picture [*Wee Willie Winkie,* 1937]. . . . The picture made a lot of money—and she adored me." Ford was being somewhat forget-ful, or perhaps disingenuous. He may not actually have screamed at the news, but even though Temple was the greatest box-office attraction in movies, he was far from happy when he received the assignment.

"How do you do, Miss Temple?" Ford said when they met in the studio's wardrobe department. "I am the man you are going to direct in *Wee Willie Winkie.*"

Temple's autobiography, *Child Star,* reports that Ford initially "made no bones about his indifference toward me, saying, 'Working with a child star is a most horrible thing.' . . . Previous directors had lifted me onto their laps and peppered me with conversation, as friendly as Ford was distant. When not is-suing me explicit instructions, Ford usually passed me by, sucking and chew-ing on his handkerchief, his eyes invisible behind deeply tinted glasses and a Donegal tweed cap with downturned brim pulled low over his forehead. With everyone else his instructions were sweeping and general, leaving it to the ac-tors to work out the details. With me he was deliberate, as if he knew not what to expect and dared not leave me alone to interpret my role.

"Confronted with Ford's elusive personality, I seized every chance to in-volve him in casual conversation. Borrowing an extra stopwatch from the con-tinuity girl, I went around timing everything I could and eventually interrupted Ford.

"'Ford V-8,' I said, 'did you know you took two minutes and thirty-five seconds to light your pipe that time? The last time you took two minutes and twelve seconds.'

"Shooting me an annoyed glance, he turned away with grumpy noises and sucked noisily on his pipe."

Confronted with the second leading lady in a row who campaigned for cre-ative equality by teasing her director, Ford gradually warmed up toward his eight-year-old star. He began calling her "Temple Temple" and she recipro-cated with "Mr. Ford Ford." He sometimes needled Shirley by sarcastically using her mother's nickname for her, "Presh" (for "Precious"), which she hated. But when he realized that Shirley owed much of her popularity to her precocious intelligence, Ford began to relax and treat her with more adult humor, a sure sign of his growing affection and respect for her professionalism. He was delighted when she would turn her back and whisper cues to British actors who were slow at remembering their lines. And when she would not stop teasing him about his practice of taking a tea break with the largely British cast every day at four o'clock, Ford retaliated by marching back and forth in front of her dressing room, chanting, "Shirley Temple is unfair to di-rectors! Shirley Temple is unfair to directors!"

Temple finally understood the secret John Ford tried so hard to hide from those who knew him: "Outwardly, he is a rugged person, but inside he's kindly and even sentimental."

Set in 1897 at a British army cantonment in "Raj Pore," India, *Wee Willie Winkie* is loosely based on the whimsical Rudyard Kipling story about a six-year-old British boy named Percival William Williams, who wins acceptance as a fellow Scottish Highlander by performing a heroic rescue. Percival is nick-named "Wee Willie Winkie" after the Scottish nursery rhyme. Changing the boy to an American girl named Priscilla Williams, the screenplay by Ernest Pascal and Julian Josephson has her matchmaking for her young widowed mother (June Lang) and making peace between the Black Watch and the re-bellious Pathan leader Khoda Khan (Cesar Romero). In story developments echoing Temple's off-camera relationships with Ford and her costar Victor McLaglen, Priscilla also softens the heart of her grandfather, Colonel Williams (Sir C. Aubrey Smith), and forms a poignant friendship with McLaglen's Sergeant Donald MacDuff, who teaches her the soldier's manual of arms.

Zanuck provided the key to the unusual emotional depth of this Shirley Temple vehicle. At a story conference on July 25, 1936, he said, "My idea about doing this picture is to forget that it is a Shirley Temple picture. That is, not to forget that she is the star, but to write the story as if it were a *Little Women* or a *David Copperfield*. . . . All the hokum must be thrown out. The characters must be made real, human, believable. . . . And it must be told from the child's viewpoint, through her eyes."

That creative decision, and Ford's assignment as director, demonstrated Zanuck's shrewdness and originality. As Andrew Sarris notes in *The American Cinema,* "Despite the monstrous mythology of Shirley Temple, *Wee Willie Winkie* contains extraordinary camera prose passages from the wide-eyed point of view of a child."

"Passages of visual poetry" would be even more fitting. *Wee Willie Winkie* provides a case study of how Ford approached what could have been a pot-boiler and infused it with his own artistic sensibility. If there were any real jus-tice in Hollywood, Ford would have won an Oscar for a film such as this one, whose truly superior craftsmanship is all the more impressive for seeming so effortless. With larger-than-life romanticism, Ford deftly creates a child's sto-rybook vision of the world, then introduces unexpectedly touching moments as reality impinges on the consciousness of the innocent protagonist. This styl-ized feeling was heightened in the film's original release by tinting the daytime scenes sepia and the nighttime scenes blue, reviving a practice from the silent cinema. In one shot of breathtaking beauty, Priscilla, left behind in a moun-tain tent, watches through a translucent veil as the rebel horsemen ride off to battle; it is as if the child is seeing the events of her life projected on her own inner movie screen.

The luxury of a sizable ($1 million) budget for *Wee Willie Winkie* provided Ford with a handsome re-creation of a British army outpost and a spectacular rebel stronghold, both constructed in the hills near Chatsworth in the San Fernando Valley. The director also had ample time to create scenes that were not mentioned in the script.

Ford's cameraman, Arthur C. Miller, found it difficult to formulate a theory of Ford's working method "because when John Ford made a picture, he could not be compared even to himself from one day to the next. He was one hundred percent unpredictable and had no special method or formula for proceeding. Only one thing is certain and that is that Ford made the pictures himself without any interference." Miller also came to understand that "the script he works from is no more than an idea. He concentrates on making a completed picture, and to do so, he is continually prepared to deviate from the script whenever an idea strikes him. For this reason, the entire cast was required to be present each day, whether or not they worked, so that he could change or improve or add someone to a sequence without having to wait for the actor or to abandon the idea."

Ford's instinctive, improvisational method of working with actors was rewarded on *Wee Willie Winkie* in the magnificent performance he drew from McLaglen as the taciturn but lovable Sergeant MacDuff. The character was thinly developed in the script, so Ford kept adding scenes and bits of business for McLaglen.

One robust, wintry day in Chatsworth, recalled Miller, "Dark storm clouds had begun gathering in the sky. . . . No one expected to do any work until the weather cleared, and that looked as though it might take a long time. Mr. Ford and I stood on the porch of the building, each holding a cup of coffee. As we watched the fast-moving dark clouds and the swaying trees, Ford turned to me and asked if I didn't think this would be a good time to do the burial sequence. After a moment's thought, I said I couldn't remember any burial sequence in the script. With a mischievous grin, he asked me the color of the cover of the revised script I had read. I told him it was blue. 'That wasn't the final script,' Ford said."

Ford turned to the rest of the company and announced, "We've got everybody here—let's bury Victor!"

In the words of the cameraman, "A casket draped with a British Union Jack, resting on the flatbed of an army vehicle, drawn by four black horses and with an honor guard marching in slow step, and the wind whipping back and forth as though in protest against the menacing black clouds in the sky was one of the most dramatic and effective sequences in the picture."

This seemingly off-the-cuff flourish of genius added greatly to Ford's legend, but it evidently was something of a ruse. Ford later admitted that the decision to add the scene had been made in advance, back at the studio: "D. Z. said, 'Victor McLaglen is so good in this, and we kill him off halfway through,' and I said, 'I'd like to keep him.' We had all those bagpipes, and D. Z. said, 'Can you give him an impressive military funeral?'"

Even more memorable is the scene immediately preceding the funeral. Ford shows exquisite delicacy in directing Temple as she softly sings "Auld Lang Syne" at the deathbed of Sergeant MacDuff while he clutches a bouquet of flowers she has stolen from a neighbor's garden. The child's uncomprehending reactions to the hushed, shadowy atmosphere of death and MacDuff's gentle, halting words of farewell make the scene extraordinarily moving. As her song ends, the camera begins a slow and graceful movement past MacDuff toward Priscilla. The sergeant's hand falls still at the bottom of the frame and she backs uncertainly away from the deathbed, a mature awareness of death beginning to impinge just slightly on her wide-eyed innocence.

"Death scenes in movies are notorious booby traps," Temple observed. "One plucked heartstring too many and everything turns into discord and audience indifference. In this case Ford's direction was unfaltering and supremely sensitive, memorable for both critics and audiences. McLaglen's last gasp did not drag on, and my song was phrased and paced to support the action, not dominate it. With his brawny hero counterposed with an innocent child under the encompassing shadow of death, every nuance of movement and sound coalesced in a scene of power and purity. . . .

"When the cameras had stopped, McLaglen raised on his elbow and placed one massive hand over mine: 'If I wasn't already dead,' he said, 'I'd be crying too.'

"Ford came over and put his arm around my shoulder, as he would have a boy. My grief had come across with perfect restraint, he said, holding me firmly and punctuating his compliments with gentle hand pressures.

"That we could be friends I had never doubted. But now we were colleagues."

Wee Willie Winkie remains the star's favorite among all her films: "I marched, drilled, did the manual of arms, and had a wooden rifle. It was wonderful."

A bizarre epilogue to *Wee Willie Winkie* occurred when a review by novelist Graham Greene in the London magazine *Night and Day* provoked a successful libel suit by Twentieth Century–Fox on behalf of Shirley Temple. "I kept on my bathroom wall, until a bomb removed the wall, the statement of claim— that I had accused Twentieth Century–Fox of 'procuring' Miss Temple for 'immoral purposes,'" Greene bitterly recalled in his 1958 essay "Memories of a Film Critic." He was forced to pay a settlement of five hundred pounds and apologize to, as he called her, "that bitch Shirley Temple." The magazine, which agreed to pay three thousand pounds, went out of business.

The studio's lawsuit alleged that the words of Greene's October 28, 1937, review "meant and intended and were understood to mean that the infant Plaintiff [Temple] was a depraved and degraded child, that the said film was of a lewd and unhealthy type designed to appeal to the baser instincts; that the American Company [Twentieth Century–Fox Film Corporation] had exploited the childhood of the infant Plaintiff for its own gain and had trained her in habits of sexual suggestiveness; that the American Company had caused and procured the infant Plaintiff to play the leading part in the said film for which she had accordingly become well fitted by virtue of her sexual precocity; that the said film was one which should be shunned and avoided by all decent-minded people but that the English Company [Twentieth Century–Fox Film Company, Ltd.] had nevertheless caused it to be exhibited and had thereby deliberately exploited its disgusting character."

Incredibly enough, these lurid accusations do not entirely misrepresent the content of Greene's review of *Wee Willie Winkie,* although they miss its semi-humorous intent. Already well established in his reputation as an acidulous critic of American films, particularly some of those turned out by Fox, he fired a warning shot across the studio's bow when he reviewed Temple's 1936 film *Captain January.* Greene wrote in the *Spectator* that she "acts and dances with immense vigour and assurance, but some of her popularity seems to rest on a coquetry quite as mature as Miss [Claudette] Colbert's and on an oddly precocious body as voluptuous in grey flannel trousers as Miss [Marlene] Dietrich's."

His review of *Wee Willie Winkie* pursued that vein of criticism with unusual vehemence, claiming that "infancy is her disguise, her appeal is more secret and more adult. Already two years ago she was a fancy little piece (real childhood, I think, went out after *The Littlest Rebel*). . . . Now in *Wee Willie Winkie,* wearing short kilts, she is completely totsy. Watch her swaggering stride across the Indian barrack-square: hear the gasp of excited expectation from her antique audience when the sergeant's palm is raised: watch the way she measures a man with agile studio eyes, with dimpled depravity. . . .

"Her admirers—middle-aged men and clergymen—respond to her dubious coquetry, to the sight of her well-shaped and desirable little body, packed with enormous vitality, only because the safety curtain of story and dialogue drops between their intelligence and their desire. . . ."

Such a review reveals more about Greene's dark sense of satire than it does about the actual film in question, but Fox had some reason not to shrug off his provocation. According to Greene biographer Norman Sherry, "Greene's review did not appear in America, but stories printed suggested that Greene believed Shirley Temple was a midget with a seven-year-old child of her own. Perhaps this is one reason why Twentieth Century–Fox decided on a libel action." Furthermore, Greene was neither the first nor the last to point out the sexual implications of Shirley's precocity, only the most outrageously direct about calling attention to those undercurrents.

As Jeanine Basinger wrote in her 1975 book on Temple, "Beneath the surface of her screen image lurked hidden, disturbing messages. That she was an out-and-out baby sexpot was pointed out even in her own day, as her constantly kissing little mouth unquestionably held an adult's promise. . . . Her little body was roundly formed, with a pair of smooth thighs always visible beneath the short, short dresses which barely grazed the bottoms of her ruffled underpants. . . . She had an adult's control over her body and a definition to her gestures that were beyond her age. For nearly six years she managed to make time stand still, as she miraculously maintained a balance between adorable child and vamping coquette."

No doubt these complexities can be found beneath the surface of *Wee Willie Winkie,* revolving as it does around the child's innocently loving relationships with four adult men. Ford's awareness on some level of such undertones to the Temple mystique could help account for the fierceness of his initial resistance to working with her. But rather than exploiting her innocence in *Wee Willie Winkie,* Ford both celebrates it and mourns the beginning of its inevitable passing as the already fatherless Priscilla, losing her surrogate father in battle, is confronted with the adult realities of death.

Ford made no public statement about Greene's review, and his personal reaction, if any, has not been recorded. He certainly seemed to hold no grudge against Greene when he bought the film rights to the novel Greene was researching in Mexico at the time of the libel settlement, *The Power and the Glory.* Published in 1940, and retitled *The Labyrinthine Ways* for the American market, it was filmed by Ford in 1947 as *The Fugitive.* Perhaps in his own dark unconscious, Ford was taking revenge for the *Wee Willie Winkie* review by making such an utter travesty of the author's greatest novel. *The Fugitive* is arguably the worst film Ford ever directed; Greene was never able to bring himself to see it because "everything I heard about it was so awful."

The first (and last) film Ford made for Samuel Goldwyn after being fired from *Arrowsmith, The Hurricane* (1937) is a slick, expensive, commercially successful "job of work" that seems to have been approached by the director with only the most superficial level of personal involvement. This is the kind of film Ford had in mind when he responded to a question from a French interviewer who asked what he thought he would achieve when he decided to make a career in motion pictures. Spacing out his words so the listener could not fail to understand his meaning, Ford said, "I thought . . . I would achieve . . . *a check*."

Adapted by Nichols from a 1936 romantic adventure novel by Charles Nordhoff and James Norman Hall, the authors of *Mutiny on the Bounty, The Hurricane* uses a devastating storm in the South Sea islands as a metaphor for nature's revenge on the hubris of colonialism. The hurricane sequence, staged by second-unit director James Basevi and filmed by Ford with the help of associate director Stuart Heisler, is a tour de force of special effects. But Ford's Murnau-like idealization of the island paradise of Manukura is hampered by the overuse of phony studio settings, and the film's shallow, glibly schematic characterizations keep it planted squarely in the realm of melodrama. The warped sense of justice displayed by the evil French colonial governor (Raymond Massey) is matched in Manichean terms by the guileless sweetness of the unjustly imprisoned native he sadistically torments (Jon Hall). In the end, these two combatants are among a handful of people who survive the wrath of a seemingly godless nature, a force that indiscriminately wastes the rest of the island's population.

Ford's interest in *The Hurricane* waned after Goldwyn reneged on a promise to let him film it largely in the South Seas. For atmosphere the director had to make do with a few second-unit location shots taken in Samoa, some seafaring scenes he filmed aboard the *Araner* off Catalina Island, and wind machines blowing sand and water on the Goldwyn back lot in Hollywood. The studio-bound look was not mitigated by the sleek, overly glamorized actors playing Polynesians, including Hall, male model handsome and vacuous, and Dorothy Lamour, decked out in sultry makeup and her famous sarong. Ford "didn't give a damn about the picture," felt screenwriter Ben Hecht, who screened the footage at Goldwyn's request and announced, "I think it stinks." "So do I," said Goldwyn. "I want you to rewrite it and you've only got seventy-two hours to do it." For a fee of twenty-five thousand dollars, Hecht whipped up new dialogue scenes that Ford shot "without reading them," the writer averred.

The attitude of passive resistance Ford adopted toward working with Goldwyn indicated that he knew he had made a mistake and this time was determined to get through it without unduly damaging his career. *The Hurricane* bolstered Ford's tenuous standing at the box office, and his one-hundred-thousand-dollar salary and 12 percent of the net profits helped assuage his sour feelings toward Goldwyn. To borrow a tongue-in-cheek remark Ford made to needle me about my admiration for *The Searchers, The Hurricane* "made a lot of money, and that's the ultimate end." Before returning to Fox, Ford performed another commercial chore for Goldwyn when he directed some action scenes for Archie Mayo's 1938 film *The Adventures of Marco Polo.*

If Ford needed to be reminded why he should prefer Zanuck's more benevolent tyranny to the heavy-handed meddling of other Hollywood moguls, Goldwyn provided the perfect lesson. But part of the price Ford paid for working under contract to Fox was occasionally being assigned to turn out an unabashed potboiler. He directed two such pictures for Zanuck in 1938, *Four Men and a Prayer* and *Submarine Patrol.* Ford's directorial touch is visible only fitfully in these efficient but largely impersonal adventure yarns.

Some of Ford's feeling for the seafaring life shines through even the phoniness of the studio-bound visuals of *Submarine Patrol,* a comedy-drama about a ragtag civilian crew manning a wooden submarine chaser during World War I.[4] The director was operating under an additional handicap, for Zanuck demanded that, to appease the female audience, "We must be as clever as we can in keeping the war out of the picture." When the film was press-screened, the Fox publicity department angered Ford by suggesting that reviewers refrain from judging ingenue Nancy Kelly until they saw her performance in Henry King's *Jesse James.* Ford wrote a blistering letter to Fox about this "adverse criticism from my own studio of my direction. I presume I am no longer wanted at Twentieth Century–Fox to direct pictures, especially pictures with women." Adding that the insult "caused me much humiliation," Ford retaliated by boycotting a party in his honor at Zanuck's home. He claimed he had been unable to return from sea because the *Araner* had engine trouble.

There are some salvageable scenes in *Submarine Patrol* nonetheless, including one that ranks among the finest examples in Ford's work of the camaraderie displayed by adversaries in combat. When the American ship's lieutenant orders the tolling of eight bells in farewell salute to a dead German officer, Quincannon (Ford stalwart J. Farrell MacDonald) murmurs, "God have mercy on their souls." One of the swabbies, confused by the gesture, asks an older sailor, "Hey, Guns, don't—don't we cheer or nothin'?" To which

---

4. William Faulkner, who had done some uncredited writing on *Flesh,* worked on the screenplay of *Submarine Patrol,* which was adapted from a novel by John Milholland, *The Splinter Fleet.* According to associate producer Gene Markey, Faulkner's version contained "good Faulknerian dialogue, but it had nothing whatever to do with our story." Faulkner complained that Markey "told me to follow the storyline, but I can't find the storyline." Faulkner also spent twelve weeks working without credit on Ford's 1939 Fox film *Drums Along the Mohawk.*

Guns (another Ford regular, Jack Pennick) disgustedly replies, *"No."* Chastened, the swabbie joins him in saluting.

There was little opportunity for such heartfelt emotion in *Four Men and a Prayer,* a formulaic story about four sons avenging the murder of their father, a British army officer, by an international munitions cartel. "I just didn't like the story, or anything else about it, so it was a job of work," Ford recalled. "I kidded them slightly." Sometimes, he admitted, a director "must hypnotize himself to be sympathetic toward the subject matter. Sometimes we are not. Being under contract you make pictures that you don't want to make, but you try to steel yourself, to get enthused over them. You get on the set, and you forget everything else. You say these actors are doing the best they can. They also have to make a living. As a director I must help them as much as I can."

The only sequences that do seem to engage Ford's feelings in *Four Men and a Prayer* are those of the sons' reunion with their elderly father and their discovery of his sudden, mysterious death. The homecoming of Colonel Loring Leigh's four sons from around the world after the old man's unjust dismissal from military service has the feeling of a premature Irish wake, mourning and celebrating the importance of their long-distant father as a motivating force in their lives. The actor who plays the father is C. Aubrey Smith. As Ford's sister Josephine Feeney pointed out, the crusty old trouper with a white walrus mustache bore a strong resemblance to Ford's own father. It's easy to see that Ford was able to express his feelings of grief and loss over Grampy Feeney's recent death in these touching scenes of undying filial devotion (Ford visually echoed some of the shots in an even more personal film, *How Green Was My Valley*). Ford pays tribute to his earlier deceased mother as well, by having the men of the Leigh family lift their glasses to their mother's portrait (a device Ford adapted for Mayor Skeffington's daily ritual of placing a flower before the portrait of his dead wife in *The Last Hurrah*).

But as was most often the case with Ford when a film subject failed to capture his imagination, he distracted himself by finding excuses for prankish humor. His victim on *Four Men and a Prayer* was the debonair young British actor David Niven, who was cast as the playboy aviator of the family. In his delightful autobiography *The Moon's a Balloon,* Niven recounts Ford's elaborate practical joke, which the actor evidently did not realize was a parodistic replay of Ford's mistreatment of Victor McLaglen on *The Informer.*

On Niven's twenty-eighth birthday, March 1, 1938, the company was having cake on the set when Ford sauntered over and casually told him, "David, tomorrow you have very little to do—you'll just be background—so tonight go on out and enjoy yourself—really tie one on."

"I hate getting drunk," Niven recalled, "but I felt that I had more or less been ordered to do so and I did my best to oblige." He reported to the studio in the morning "very drunk indeed and thinking how pleased John Ford would be. We were rehearsing the first scene. All I had to do was bind up the arm of George Sanders, who had been shot."

Ford suddenly said, "Hold it. What's the matter with you, Niven? Why don't you stand still?"

"Sorry, Mr. Ford."

"Just a minute. Are you drunk or something?"

"Well, I did have a few, Mr. Ford . . . I thought you said . . ."

"Cut the lights," Ford announced. "Send for Mr. Zanuck. Tell him I have a drunken actor on my set—ask him to come down right away."

While Niven quickly began sobering up, the glowering studio chief arrived on the set.

"What's the problem, Jack?" asked Zanuck.

"Goddamned limeys," muttered Ford, "they're all alike . . . give 'em an inch . . . this actor reported for work drunk."

"Let me see a take," Zanuck ordered, looking askance at Niven.

"Put a white coat on him," Ford instructed the crew, "and give him the first-aid box . . . all right, now try to pull yourself together, for Christ's sake . . . on your cue pull the stethoscope out of your pocket, then open the box and take out a dressing. OK, let's go."

Fumbling with the newly added props, Niven played the scene with Sanders and Richard Greene as best he could, while the studio chief watched him with a fixed stare.

"I tried to concentrate on my cue," Niven remembered, "and when it came, I put my hand in the pocket for the stethoscope and pulled out a large snake. Trying manfully to continue the scene, I dropped it on the floor and opened the first-aid box. When I saw it was full of little green turtles, I let out a yell and flung it in the air."

Ford yelled, "Print it," while the rest of the company, including Zanuck, who had been a party to the gag, cracked up. The scene "was run constantly in private projection rooms thereafter," Niven reported.

NATANI NEZ

*There is no fence nor hedge around time that is gone. You can go
back and have what you like of it, if you can remember.*

THE NARRATOR (IRVING PICHEL) IN
HOW GREEN WAS MY VALLEY (1941)

FORD's *ANNUS MIRABILIS* of 1939 saw the release of *Stagecoach, Young Mr.
Lincoln,* and *Drums Along the Mohawk,* the director's informal "Americana
trilogy." By immersing himself in the American past and bringing it so stir-
ringly alive in those three films, Ford reached his full-blown maturity as an
artist, triumphantly finding the themes and motifs that would involve him for
the remainder of his career.

At a time when the world stood at the brink of war and America's role as a
world power was being challenged by the demands of isolationists and inter-
ventionists alike, Ford used his 1939 excursions into the American past as a
means of urgently reexamining national values. Focusing on the formative
years of the republic and its western expansion, he acknowledged some of the
darker elements of the early American story while glossing over others that he
preferred, at this point, not to examine too closely. If the patriotic messages
sent forth from these films were somewhat ambivalent, since they were
couched in terms of nostalgia for a brighter and now vanished past, Ford's
look back into American history at this turning point in his career nevertheless was suffused with optimism about the future of his country and its democratic way of life.

It's only a slight exaggeration to say that 1939 was the year John Ford discovered America.

Not coincidentally, the end of the thirties also marked the high point of
Ford's Popular Front period. Hollywood liberals and leftists joined forces in
those years, concerned about the rise of fascism in Europe and Japan, as well

as about the continuing economic problems of the Great Depression. At a time when isolationism was still rampant and served to inhibit President Roosevelt's foreign policy, Ford was well ahead of most other Americans in his concern about the probability of war between the democracies and the fascist powers. That concern was reflected not only in his filmmaking but also in his service in the navy reserve and his involvement in Hollywood political organizations.

American leftists during the Popular Front period emphasized patriotic rhetoric as a way of finding common ground with liberals in defense of basic democratic principles. That urgent patriotic groundswell no doubt influenced Ford's cinematic focus in his 1939 trilogy about western pioneers, Abraham Lincoln, and the Revolutionary War, as well as his decision to film John Steinbeck's controversial 1939 protest novel about the mistreatment of migrant workers, *The Grapes of Wrath.*

Ford's heartfelt patriotism was expressed in symbolic, almost pop-art terms in *Drums Along the Mohawk,* whose ending offers one of the director's most joyously optimistic, if somewhat naïve, affirmations of American national unity. At the end of the Revolutionary War, when the first American flag arrives at a fort in New York's Mohawk Valley, Ward Bond runs it up the flagpole in a burst of patriotic frenzy to the tune of "My Country, 'Tis of Thee." The pioneer couple Gil and Lana Martin, played by Henry Fonda (in a tricornered hat) and Claudette Colbert (wearing a red bonnet and a blue-and-white dress), pridefully watch the flag-raising along with a beaming black servant (Beulah Hall Jones) and a Christian Indian who salutes the flag (Chief Big Tree). All are symbolically gathered in multiracial harmony to celebrate the birth of the nation. For Ford, the fact that the new nation was "conceived in liberty" is enough for the African-American and the Native American to celebrate, even though their own personal liberty has yet to be won. Perhaps this flaw in the fabric of American democracy is obliquely acknowledged in the film's final lines when Gil says, "Well, I reckon we better be gettin' back to work. It's gonna be a heap to do from now on."

Ford's militancy on behalf of the Screen Directors Guild helped ease him into publicly supporting more controversial political causes that reached beyond Hollywood in the late thirties. Although he was a Catholic and the Church supported the Fascist revolt of General Francisco Franco against the Spanish Republican government, Ford became an active backer of the Loyalist cause in the Spanish civil war, serving as one of the founders of the Motion Picture Artists Committee to Aid Republican Spain, along with Dudley Nichols, Dashiell Hammett, Donald Ogden Stewart, Lester Cole, Melvyn Douglas, Fredric March, John Garfield, and others. The MPAC, which eventually grew to a membership of fifteen thousand, held rallies and benefits to raise support for Loyalist soldiers and Spanish refugees. In July 1937, novelist Ernest Hemingway came to Hollywood to seek funds for the Loyalists. Hemingway was guest of honor at a party held at the home of March and his wife, Florence Eldridge, both of whom had acted in *Mary of Scotland*. They invited Ford to their gathering, at which Hemingway screened a documentary film, *The Spanish Earth*, that he had helped Dutch filmmaker Joris Ivens make on the battlefront. Ford was not particularly a fan of Hemingway's work, but after spending some time talking with the writer about the fighting in Spain, he wound up donating an ambulance to the Spanish government.

Bob Ford, one of the sons of Francis Ford, was a member of the International Brigade in Spain. From Albacete on September 30, 1937, Bob wrote his uncle Jack a thank-you letter for the ambulance. Confessing surprise that Ford was interested in their cause, Bob expressed pleasure that American liberals like his uncle were supporting the Loyalist forces. Assuring Ford that, contrary to Fascist propaganda, the brigade was not entirely made up of Communists, Bob added that Ford would be intrigued to learn that there were many former IRA men in the British battalion.

Ford must have felt chastened to be responding to Bob's letter from a ranch on the Hudson River in upstate New York, near West Point, where he had gone to dry out from another alcoholic binge. "I am glad you [have] the good part of the O'Feeney blood," Ford wrote his nephew. "Some of it is *very* God-damned awful—we are liars, *weaklings* & selfish drunkards, but there has *always* been a stout rebel quality in the family and a peculiar passion for justice. I am glad you inherited the good strain. *Politically,* I am a definite socialistic democrat—*always* left." But Ford added that, having paid close attention to the development of the Soviet Union, he was convinced that Communism was not the answer to the world's problems because it ran the risk of bringing about despotism.

Suggesting that Bob keep a combat diary with an eye to writing a book, Ford advised him to be on the alert for details of both comedy and drama. He cautioned his nephew to be as careful as possible in battle against the Fascists. In an anti-Semitic "joke" that seemed particularly at odds with the cause for which Bob was fighting, Ford added that he hoped a Jew wouldn't be feeding Bob ammunition.

In early 1938, Ford became a vice president, along with Philip Dunne and Miriam Hopkins, of the newly formed Motion Picture Democratic Committee, whose president was novelist Dashiell Hammett. Dunne, who became acting president when Hammett was taken ill, worked closely in the organization with actor Melvyn Douglas and his wife, Helen Gahagan Douglas, the actress

and future congresswoman. Dudley Nichols was the MPDC's financial director. The organization was prominent among the Hollywood Popular Front
groups "whose primary *raison d'être* was the advancement of the causes of lib-
eralism, anti-fascism, and anti-racism at the local, state, and national levels,"
Larry Ceplair and Steven Englund write in *The Inquisition in Hollywood: Politics
in the Film Community 1930–1960.* "Their work involved lobbying for civil
rights and civil liberties legislation and campaigning for progressive and liberal
candidates for electoral office."

Dunne recalled that Ford "never attended a meeting [of the MPDC], but
remained a loyal contributor until the organization was wrecked by the schism
of 1939 [the shattering of the Popular Front in the wake of the Nazi-Soviet
Non-Aggression Pact]. Those who remember Rear Admiral Ford as a conservative in his later years, perhaps finding him guilty by association with his
rightist friends, John Wayne and Ward Bond, forget that in the 1930s he sailed
with his political helm aport."

Ford was more actively involved with the Hollywood Anti-Nazi League,
another broadly based coalition of leftists and liberals united by their opposition to fascism. The first organization in Hollywood to raise funds on behalf
of the Spanish Loyalists, the league also sponsored a campaign to "Lift the Em-
bargo" imposed by the U.S. Congress on supplying arms to the combatants.
Along with actor Eddie Cantor, screenwriter Dorothy Parker, and others,
Ford addressed a public rally held by the group at the Shrine Auditorium on
January 30, 1938, the fifth anniversary of Adolf Hitler's rise to power. The
rally's theme was "The Nazi Menace in America."

That spring Ford became involved in a labor issue that seemed relatively innocuous at the time but would have unexpected ramifications years later for
his friend and colleague Frank Capra. The film community, and particularly
the guilds, mobilized an outpouring of support for the Los Angeles Newspaper Guild's strike of the *Hollywood Citizen-News,* which began on May 17,
1938. The *Citizen-News* "had been more liberal than the *Los Angeles Times,* but
anything was more liberal than the *Times,*" recalled Dunne, then a board
member of the Screen Writers Guild. "It wasn't much of a paper. But this was
a union time, and these were our fellow writers." The strike was caused by
publisher Harlan G. Palmer's firing of five staff members in retaliation for the
Newspaper Guild's attempt to unionize his paper. The SDG *Bulletin* invited
members to join the picket line outside the *Citizen-News* building on North
Wilcox Avenue, near Hollywood Boulevard, and on May 23 the board of the
Directors Guild voted to support the strike.

Ford joined the picket line on the first day of the strike, along with fellow
SDG board members Capra and Herbert Biberman. Dunne and Robert

Montgomery, the president of the Screen Actors Guild, also were there representing their guilds. "We spent about five minutes walking up and down the picket lines and had our pictures taken," Dunne recalled. A photo of Ford, Capra, and Biberman standing in front of the newspaper building "as they joined the picket line" appeared in the *Hollywood Citizen-News Striker* (an ad hoc publication by the striking employees) on June 1 under the heading "Film Directors Give Aid." There was a mild backlash within the Directors Guild. At a board meeting on June 6, the conservative director Howard Hawks criticized the publication of the picketing invitation in the *Bulletin,* and the board reserved the right to approve such action in the future.

The House Committee on Un-American Activities was created on May 26, just nine days after Ford appeared with his colleagues on the picket line. HUAC was already turning its sights on Hollywood as part of its mandate to investigate "the extent, character, and objects of un-American propaganda activities in the United States."[1] Referring to a report in the West Coast Communist Party newspaper *People's World,* HUAC placed an item in a file on Capra indicating that: "The 30 May 1938 issue of the *People's World* described CAPRA as a member of the picket line in the Hollywood Citizen's [sic] News Strike which was Communist inspired." That citation, among similar charges, would cause problems for Capra during the postwar Hollywood blacklist era, forcing him to call on Ford for help.

During the same period of the late thirties when Ford considered himself "a definite socialistic democrat—*always* left," he served in a semiofficial capacity as a spy for U.S. Naval Intelligence. Ford's spying missions to Mexico are amply documented in his U.S. Navy personnel file and his personal papers, but Dan Ford's biography, written before John Ford's official navy file was released, mocks his grandfather's accounts of these missions. The book's account of a mission to Baja California in 1939 suggests that Ford was "fantasizing" and that his objective was not gathering genuine intelligence but "advancing himself in the Navy."

Pappy does not quote the letter of commendation Ford received from the navy in January 1940 for the seven-page report he filed on possible Japanese military activity in Mexico. The navy praised his "initiative in securing the

---

1. HUAC became a laughingstock to many that year when it was revealed that one of the members of the film colony who had come under its scrutiny was Shirley Temple. She and other stars had sent greetings to a French newspaper which the committee alleged was owned by the Communist Party. *Variety* acidly observed that "about everybody in Hollywood except Mickey Mouse, Charlie McCarthy and Snow White has been signed up" as a Communist dupe.

valuable information contained in your very interesting Intelligence Report of 30 December 1939 on Lower California and the Gulf of California. Your efforts to obtain this information, voluntarily and at your own expense, are considered very commendable."

Japanese infiltration south of the Mexican border was of particular concern to the man who supervised Ford's missions, Captain Ellis M. Zacharias, chief intelligence officer of the Eleventh Naval District at San Diego, the district in which Ford served as a naval reserve officer. Zacharias worried that Japanese fishing trawlers might be surveying Mexican waters for the Imperial Navy and stockpiling supplies and equipment for possible later use by submarines. Ford's cover as a yachtsman, sport fisherman, and carouser gave him the perfect opportunity to sail from port to port observing Japanese activity. While some of the fishermen and other Japanese whom Ford observed on such trips may well have been innocent of any military purpose, it's too easy in hindsight to discount the genuine fears the United States had about the vulnerability of Mexico, Central America, and South America to such infiltration in the years prior to the onset of war with Germany and Japan. There is no doubt that such fears were exaggerated. Public hysteria over a possible Japanese invasion led to one of the worst episodes of injustice in American history, the interning of Japanese-Americans in concentration camps for the duration of the war. But during the early days of America's involvement in the war, the Japanese military did make some attempts to attack the western states with submarines, miniature airplanes, and balloon bombs.

General William J. "Wild Bill" Donovan, director of the Office of Strategic Services (OSS), reported in 1943 that Ford had "devoted himself to the study of intelligence matters" during much of his time in the Naval Reserve before World War II. On September 15, 1941, four days after being called to Washington for active duty in the navy, Ford wrote in a navy document that he had performed "several Naval Intelligence assignments" as a lieutenant commander in the Naval Reserve. "I have made numerous voyages [on the *Araner*] to Hawaii, Panama, the Mexican Coast, and various places on the Pacific," he elaborated in a 1941 navy biographical sheet. "Trips to the Mexican Coast have been mainly at the suggestion of Captain Zacharias, USN." This kind of activity began soon after Ford received his commission in September 1934, and continued at least until February–March 1941, when he undertook a three-week mission to Mazatlán and La Paz.

In his October 1935 annual fitness report for the navy, Ford wrote, "Under Instructions from Director Naval Reserve 11th Naval District [Capt. Herbert A. Jones] have made research covering camera photography and camouflage problems. As Master of my 108-foot Ketch *Araner* have cruised Coast of Mexico to Acapulco visiting en route La Paz, Mazatlán—Tres Marías [Islands]—

Cleopha—Manzanillo—Have just completed a round trip to Hawaii on *Araner* visiting all the Islands. Visited the Sub Base V-4 . . ." Jones described Ford in the same report as an "Excellent officer, enthusiastic, loyal, intelligent, influential in his community. Has been working intensely in an effort to collect photographic and camouflage information likely to be of value to the Navy."

Ford's intelligence activities eventually led to his formation of the Field Photographic Branch of the OSS to document military activity in World War II and provide mapping and other photographic reconnaissance information. Ford began organizing Field Photo, as it was called, on an unofficial basis as a Naval Reserve unit in 1939, but it was not fully operational until September 1941. Ironically, the navy declined to accept Ford's unit for wartime service, forcing him to turn for backing to Donovan's newly formed overseas intelligence agency. However, Ford's prewar activities in concert with Naval Intelligence and the conditions of his recruitment into the Naval Reserve clearly indicate the navy's awareness that he would be a valuable asset in any future combat situation.

As part of his preparation during the 1930s, Ford studied how to make training films and conducted a study of aerial and sea photography. He exaggerated somewhat when he claimed to have "pioneered combat and sea photography" for the navy. But it was true that he "visualized the great importance of photography in times of peace and war," as his commanding officer, W. W. Waddell, wrote in February 1941. In addition to providing data for the Office of Naval Intelligence, Ford's reconnaissance and mapping of Mexican waters gave him valuable practice in the art of photographic documentation.

Ford's reports were "of considerable *importance*," he was told in a 1936 letter of commendation from navy lieutenant commander A. A. Hopkins. "For your own personal information, [I] will state that of the six yachts who [*sic*] have been requested to make observations during the past two years, the *Araner*, its owner and commander are the only ones who have made entrance to the area you explored and who have brought back the data wanted." The ONI noted in July 1936 that Ford had contributed "valuable and most interesting data on Scammon Lagoon" in Baja California. For that report, Ford spent two days with *Araner* captain George Goldrainer and crew members photographing and charting the area from launches. Ford wrote that while he had seen no indication of a Japanese presence, the isolated lagoon was "close enough to shipping lanes to serve as an ideal place to either stockpile supplies or to serve as a rendezvous point for submarines and sub tenders."

On his 1939 trip to Baja California and the Gulf of California, Ford was accompanied by Mary; his longtime cinematographer George Schneiderman;

Schneiderman's wife, Rita; John Wayne; Ward Bond; Preston Foster; and
Wingate Smith. Mary and the Schneidermans provided assistance in Ford's espionage activities, but the others were just along for the carousing. The entire
group spent a fair amount of time in Mexican bars while cruising the route
from Magdalena Bay to Cabo San Lucas and Mazatlán. Ford and Schneiderman amused themselves on the *Araner* at one point by making a 16mm movie
composed of "artistic" studies of beer bottles.[2]

Upon his return to Los Angeles, Ford prepared his seven-page report for
Zacharias, the most detailed such document available in his files. Most of the
report concerns his reconnaissance of Muertos Bay at Guaymas, where he
spent three days fishing. Schneiderman used a still camera with a telephoto
lens to take photographs of Japanese trawlers. Ford also included observations
of a fellow passenger on a train trip in Mexico, "a large Japanese, [an] obvious
Army type" carrying an expensive Leica camera with a telescopic lens. This
man gave orders to groups of other Japanese he met at various stops along the
way, and Ford thought he was a spy: "Takes pictures only of bridges and oil
tanks. He was sublimely indifferent to the scenery and the picturesque Mexican hills we passed through."

Ford's report on Muertos Bay contains many details about ships and naval
uniforms, but what is most remarkable is the way it reflects his keen eye for details of human behavior. This power of observation, when translated into cinematic terms, helps account for his visual and dramatic authority as a director.
He wrote in his report:

> When entering Guaymas harbor, I thought for a moment I was in
> Moji Straits. The Japanese shrimp fleet was lying at anchor. Four-
> teen steam trawlers two to two hundred and fifty tons . . . two
> mother ships five to six hundred tons. . . . I believe the Company
> that owns them is Nippon Kaisha. . . . the majority of the stock is
> owned by the Imperial Family, the remainder by Matsui.
>
> The most striking point concerning this fleet is its personnel.
> This has me completely baffled. The crews come ashore for lib-
> erty in well-tailored flannels, worsted and tweed suits . . . black
> service shoes smartly polished. . . . The men are above average
> height . . . young . . . good-looking and very alert. All carrying

---

2. Dan Ford's jaundiced assessment of this trip may have been influenced by a misleading description Henry
Fonda gave him of Ford's behavior. Fonda claimed that by the time they arrived in Guaymas, Ford was too
drunk to do anything except go to the hospital to dry out. But in light of Ford's detailed descriptions of Guaymas harbor, it's likely that Fonda confused this 1939 trip with another visit he made to Mexico with Ford.

themselves with military carriage. . . . None of these young men spoke English. Some had a smattering of Spanish. I cannot compare them to any ratings in our service . . . unless possibly to the University Naval Reserve Units such as the one at the University of California. . . .

Aboard each trawler three or four young officers were stationed, who never went ashore unless in uniform. The uniform, with the exception of the cap, badge and stripe was the regulation braid-bound Imperial Navy uniform, smartly cut and well pressed. The cap badge while not regulation had the Rising Sun motif.

The Ensign stripe was black, tilted. These young men were tall, straight as ramrods, high cheek-boned, with aquiline features, definitely aristocratic. For want of a better word I would call them the Samurai or military caste. (During three trips to Japan I have studied this type very closely. I'm positive they are Naval men.) . . .

I beg to submit the following opinion. It is my belief that the crews and officers of this shrimp fleet belong to the Imperial Navy or Reserve. The crews are not the same class of fishermen that I have seen so many times in Japan. It is my opinion that these young men are brought here from time to time to make themselves absolutely familiar with Mexican waters and particularly the Gulf of California. . . . It is plausible to assume that these men know every Bay, Cove and Inlet in the Gulf of California, a Bay which is so full of islands, and so close to our Arizona borderline.

They constitute a real menace. Although I am not a trained Intelligence Officer, still my profession is to observe and make distinctions. I have observed well in Japan. I will stake my professional reputation that these young men are not professional fishermen.

In a 1943 report, Commander W. H. Vanderbilt, USNR, head of strategic services for the ONI, described Ford as "fully qualified as an intelligence officer. I doubt if he has the technical experience for certain official duties, but he is a man of broad knowledge, wide experience, and sound judgment."

Throughout most of the 1930s, there was little market for "prestige" Westerns. Diehard fans of cowboy movies had to draw their satisfaction mostly from crudely made and often childish B Westerns, many featuring such singing cowboys as Gene Autry, Tex Ritter, and Dick Foran. Even John

Wayne took an embarrassed turn as "Singin' Sandy" in Monogram's *Riders of Destiny* (1933), complaining later that warbling with someone else's singing voice made him feel like "a goddam pansy." When I asked Ford why he waited until nearly the end of that decade to make his first sound Western, he replied, "Westerns were a sort of—people said they were a drug on the market. No-body was making Westerns.[3] . . . I'm considered a Western director, but I haven't directed so many Westerns as all that, you know." While Ford's point was to make me remember that his body of work contains many different types of films, it is also a fact that he directed *fifty-four* Westerns during the course of his long career.

In April 1937, sixteen-year-old Pat Ford told his father he had read a short story in *Collier's* magazine that he thought might make a good movie. "Stage to Lordsburg" by Ernest Haycox is a terse and exciting character study of a small group of pilgrims and outcasts making a perilous crossing by stagecoach through Indian country. The story reminded John Ford of "Boule de Suif" ("Ball of Fat"), Guy de Maupassant's corrosive tale about a prostitute who sleeps with a Prussian officer to ensure the safety of her ungrateful fellow pas-sengers at a stagecoach station during the Franco-Prussian War. Ford recog-nized that "Stage to Lordsburg" could serve as the framework for a comparable morality play about American bourgeois hypocrisy, an unusually sophisticated and thought-provoking Western that might enable him to return in style to the genre he had always loved best. That August, working closely with Ford, Dudley Nichols adapted the story into his finest screenplay, as terse and economical as it is rich in psychological depth.

But Ford had not made a Western since *3 Bad Men* in 1926. His extensive track record in silent Westerns meant little to Hollywood executives a decade later, when silent movies were literally regarded as relics from another era. Ford's recollection that "Nobody was making Westerns" in the thirties was somewhat misleading. Production of Westerns actually was on the increase in the mid-1930s. From the decade's low point of 65 Westerns in 1933, produc-tion rose to a peak of 145 in 1935, 28 percent of Hollywood's total output of movies. But the overwhelming majority of the Westerns being made were B's; in 1937, only three A Westerns were released, and in 1938, just four. That helps explain why Ford spent a frustrating year and a half shopping "Stage to

---

3. In April 1935, when Darryl F. Zanuck was still running Twentieth Century Pictures, Ford approached him with a project about General George Armstrong Custer titled *Glory Hunter*. Zanuck read a synopsis and found the treatment of Custer so unsympathetic that he wondered why Ford would want to make such a picture. Undaunted, Ford eventually made what was, in effect, his Custer picture with *Fort Apache* (RKO, 1948), starring Henry Fonda as a glory-seeking martinet who leads his cavalrymen into a massacre.

Lordsburg" around Hollywood in 1937–38 as a big-budget Technicolor Western with his former RKO comrade, Merian C. Cooper, before producer Walter Wanger finally agreed to make it as a modestly budgeted black-and-white picture for release through United Artists.[4]

Cooper, a major investor in the Technicolor Corporation, had formed a production company called Pioneer Pictures with the wealthy financier John Hay "Jock" Whitney in 1936, to make films in the new three-strip Technicolor process. Pioneer merged later that year with Selznick International Pictures, established in 1935 by independent producer David O. Selznick to make films for release through UA. Whitney was board chairman of Selznick International and one of the company's main financial backers, along with his sister, Mrs. Charles Payson, and their cousin Cornelius Vanderbilt "Sonny" Whitney (who produced Ford's 1956 Western classic *The Searchers* with Cooper). When Pioneer merged with Selznick's company, Cooper came aboard as a vice president and executive producer. Cooper's deal with Selznick International allowed him complete control of his productions, although Selznick retained veto power over any project he deemed uncommercial.

These interlocking relationships eventually brought Ford into a collision course with Selznick. While Ford was still at RKO, he had signed a contract with Cooper, who considered him "the very best director alive," to make two Technicolor films for Pioneer at a salary of $85,000 apiece. Ford's contract with Pioneer was assumed by Selznick International as part of the merger. Cooper recalled that the Ford deal "aroused the ire of every studio head in Hollywood, including David, as Ford's last picture, *Mary of Scotland,* only paid him $45,000, and I was told that I was ruining the price of the directors as no other director was getting that kind of money."

(That was a typical bit of Hollywood hyperbole, reflecting the tensions then existing between studios and directors over the SDG's demand for recognition. Ford's deal with Pioneer was eclipsed by Frank Capra's $100,000 per picture, plus 25 percent of the net profits, under the terms of his 1935 five-picture contract with Columbia. Ford himself received $100,000 and 12 percent of the profits from Samuel Goldwyn for directing *The Hurricane* in 1937. He was paid a salary of $75,000 per film from Fox in the late 1930s, but earned only $50,000 from Wanger on *Stagecoach.*)

Ford bought the film rights to Haycox's "Stage to Lordsburg" for $7,500.

---

4. Twentieth Century–Fox production chief Darryl Zanuck angered Ford by refusing to read the script. Columbia's Harry Cohn was willing to let Ford make *Stagecoach,* but the deal evidently was contingent upon Ford also directing the film version of Clifford Odets's play *Golden Boy* (Rouben Mamoulian directed that 1939 film). Other studios that passed on *Stagecoach* included MGM, Warner Bros., and Paramount.

Before approaching Selznick with the project, Ford and Cooper agreed on the casting of the two lead actors, Claire Trevor and John Wayne, and obtained verbal commitments from both. A reliable, believably unglamorous young actress cast mostly as a brassy gal with a heart of gold, Trevor had been working in Hollywood since 1932. Suddenly hot in 1937 with her part as the streetwalker in William Wyler's Goldwyn Company film version of Sidney Kingsley's play *Dead End,* she was perfectly cast in Ford's Western. Her character, Dallas, is a kindly but emotionally battered prostitute who desperately hopes for a better life with Wayne's escaped outlaw, the Ringo Kid (in Haycox's story, the characters are called Henriette and Malpais Bill).[5]

"Ford was always sort of interested in me as an actress," Trevor recalled. "I was very flattered by it, but I wasn't in the same awe of him I later had. He had not made much before *Stagecoach* that people thought was important. He was known, but they weren't absolutely on their knees about him. He had a weird personality—he was a character. He seemed like a sloppy person, he dressed in comfortable clothes, loose pants. He was always chewing on a handkerchief or pipe. He looked like some straggler off the set."

Before offering her *Stagecoach,* Ford wanted Trevor to star in *Salome, Where She Danced,* about a Mata Hari–like exotic dancer and spy. That film was directed instead by Charles Lamont for Walter Wanger in 1945, starring Yvonne De Carlo. When Ford called Trevor to his set at Fox to discuss *Stagecoach,* she recalled, "I had cold sores, fever blisters all around my mouth. I came down and held a handkerchief over my face. Ford said, 'Let me see—oh, Lord.' He asked me if I would do him a favor and make a test with a young man. He said, 'The backers don't want him, the producer doesn't want him. *I* want him'— John Wayne."

Wayne had been in the career doldrums ever since the commercial failure of *The Big Trail.* He had spent most of the thirties toiling ignominiously for such quickie studios as Monogram and Republic. Ford would needle him by saying, "Christ, if you learned to act you'd get better parts." But if movies like *The Star Packer* and *Westward Ho* won little respect for Wayne in Hollywood, he was developing a loyal following among young moviegoers and a solid, relaxed professionalism. "When is it my turn?" Wayne sometimes demanded of Ford, half-jokingly, when they sailed on the *Araner.* "Just wait," Ford would say, "I'll let you know when I get the right script." Ford had been keeping his eye on Wayne's development and still thought "Duke wasn't ready" for a major role.

---

5. In what may have been his humorous homage to *Dead End* as well as a pun on her character's name in *Stagecoach,* Ford addressed Trevor as "Dull-Ass" when they worked together.

"He had to develop his skills as an actor. . . . I wanted some pain written on his face to offset the innocence." Finally, by the summer of 1937, Ford decided that Duke was ready.[6] But he made him sweat about it.

On a weekend cruise to Catalina on the *Araner,* Ford tossed Wayne a copy of Nichols's script. "Read this for me," he said. "I'm having a hell of a time deciding whom to cast as the Ringo Kid. You know a lot of young actors, Duke. See what you think." Wayne knew Wanger wanted Gary Cooper for the part, but that Ford wanted someone younger, fresher, and less expensive. So, after reading the script, Duke suggested Lloyd Nolan. Ford scoffed at the idea. It wasn't until the following night, when they docked at San Pedro, that Ford growled, "You idiot, couldn't you play it?" Wayne later gave varying accounts of his reaction: usually he recalled being astonished by the offer, but he told Dan Ford that he realized Ford wanted him for the part and had simply been toying with him; Wayne claimed that his suggestion of Lloyd Nolan was a joke. Whatever the case, Wayne now had his second chance at stardom.

But when Ford and Merian Cooper pitched the "Stage to Lordsburg" package over dinner with Selznick, "To my surprise," Cooper recalled, "David was not impressed. First he said we had no big-name stars, and secondly 'it was just another Western.' He said we'd do a lot better if we did a classic. . . . Ford and I both jumped David hard on this. Jack Ford can state a case as well as anybody who ever lived when he wants to take the time to do it; I'm not too bad myself, and over coffee, we argued that this was a *classic* Western with *classic* characters and we finally convinced him and got the go-ahead. But the very next morning, David called and asked us to come in and see him and the very first thing he says was that he had given our 'Western' 'deep thought' and it was his studied conclusion that the picture would not 'get its print costs back' unless we put stars into the two leads. . . .

"He thought we would be highly pleased when he told us that he could get Gary Cooper and Marlene Dietrich instead of Wayne and Trevor. I was dumbfounded. . . . Besides the fact that they were bad casting, they were both too old, and I had given my word to both Wayne and Claire Trevor through Ford that we would use them. . . . We argued all morning, but I couldn't shake him and he couldn't move me, so right then and there I resigned. . . . I threw the cash and the long-term contracts overboard on what was to me a point of honor. After I left, Jack told David that he'd made a contract with me personally to make *Stagecoach* regardless of what company made the picture, so he left

---

6. Not the summer of 1938, as most accounts have it. The earlier date is established by Selznick's correspondence regarding his dealings with Ford about *Stagecoach*.

too." (Cooper continued to help Ford with the production of *Stagecoach*, although his involvement was unofficial once Walter Wanger arranged the production funding.)

Selznick was furious over the situation with Ford, writing Whitney and the company's treasurer, John Wharton, on June 29, 1937: "We must select the story and sell it to John Ford, instead of having Ford select some uncommercial pet of his that we would be making only because of Ford's enthusiasm. . . . I see no justification for making any story just because it is liked by a man who, I am willing to concede, is one of the greatest directors in the world, but whose record commercially is far from good." Selznick cited *The Informer* as Ford's "one really great picture" but listed *Mary of Scotland* and *The Plough and the Stars* as examples of his "outstanding failures."

Selznick vainly tried to interest Ford in projects other than "Stage to Lordsburg." They included a biographical film about the early American traitor Benedict Arnold; a story about World War I aviators to be produced by Cooper, *Lafayette Escadrille;* and *The Little Shepherd of Kingdom Come,* based on the novel by John Fox about a farm boy who fights for the Union in the Civil War (previously filmed in 1928). Selznick even talked about Ford as a possible director for the company's upcoming film version of Margaret Mitchell's Civil War novel *Gone with the Wind*.

Selznick admitted feeling "somewhat wounded" by his dealings with Ford, "as this is the first time in my career that someone has said that he did not want to work for me." In retrospect, it seems inevitable that Ford and Selznick would be unable to collaborate. As obstinate as Ford, Selznick was well known for his domineering tactics toward directors and his need to be the primary creative force in his productions. Furthermore, Selznick was a powerful antagonist of Ford and his fellow SDG members in their battle for creative and economic parity with producers.

In a letter to his lawyer, Dan O'Shea, on July 16, Selznick blamed Ford's refusal to work for the company on the director's being so "annoyed" that he could not make "Stage to Lordsburg": "Coop tells us that Ford feels he is free of any commitment to us. . . . [but] I don't think we should be chumps about this, and if Ford actually has a commitment with us I see no reason for releasing him." Admitting, however, that he was of two minds on the subject of Ford, Selznick added, "He is an excellent man, but there is no point in treating him as a god, and if he doesn't want to be here I'd just as soon have some other good director."

Despite his blunder in passing up the chance to make *Stagecoach,* Selznick did have something of a point about Ford's fondness for "uncommercial pet" projects. That was one of Ford's many perversities: Katharine Hepburn observed that he "loved his hits—adored his failures." While some of his pets,

Stagecoach among them, proved successful artistically and commercially, Ford was taking a calculated risk by making them. As he explained to Peter Bogdanovich, "I knew they weren't going to be smash hits—I did them for my own amusement. And it didn't hurt anybody—they didn't *make* any money, but they always got their initial cost back. . . . What I used to do was try and make a big picture, a smash, and then I could palm off a little one on them. You can't do it anymore."

But too many "outstanding failures" would have limited Ford's ability to keep working steadily in Hollywood and his freedom to palm off an occasional "little one."

We're all set to revolutionize the industry again," Dudley Nichols declared a few weeks before the opening of *Stagecoach* in 1939. Nichols and Ford, sounding like an impish vaudeville team as they discussed the film with a New York journalist, exulted over the subversive nature of their achievement.

"We're particularly attached to this one," said Nichols, "because it violates all the censorial canons."

"There's not a single respectable character in the cast," declared Ford. "The leading man has killed three guys."

"The leading woman is a prostitute," Nichols added.

"There's a banker in it who robs his own bank," Ford noted.

"And don't forget the pregnant woman who faints," Nichols went on.

"Or the fellow who gets violently ill," said Ford, referring to the drunken doctor.

Stagecoach literally was a political vehicle for Ford and Nichols, a way of looking at America's past and present. This meta-Western can be read as a justification of American Manifest Destiny on the eve of World War II, a scathing critique of capitalist corruption and Republican hypocrisy, and a celebration of the egalitarian values of the New Deal. The self-consciousness of the filmmakers' mission in crafting a morality play loosely modeled on Maupassant's "Boule de Suif" was made more accessible to a mass audience by their ritualistic incorporation of many of the most familiar motifs of the Western genre. In his 1950 essay "The Evolution of the Western," the French critic André Bazin called *Stagecoach* "the ideal example of the maturity of a style brought to classic perfection. John Ford struck the ideal balance among social myth, historical reconstruction, psychological truth, and the traditional theme of the Western *mise en scène*. None of these elements dominated any other. *Stagecoach* is like a wheel, so perfectly made that it remains in equilibrium on its axis in any position." *Stagecoach* established Ford once and for all as the Western filmmaker par excellence. Despite the deepening and enrichment of his subsequent work in the genre, no other Ford Western, not even *The*

Searchers, has achieved anything like the same stature in the popular consciousness.

"Stage to Lordsburg," the Haycox story upon which *Stagecoach* officially is based, provides rough sketches for some of the characters, but the film's sharp social criticism is more deeply influenced by Maupassant. As Garry Wills notes in his 1997 book *John Wayne's America: The Politics of Celebrity,* Ford and Nichols found it commercially expedient to conceal their "arty" source from Hollywood by "present[ing] their biting comedy of social manners as a modern Western."[7] Once the film was completed and nearly ready for release, however, the *Stagecoach* creative team felt safer trying to alert the New York press to their true intentions. Ford may even have been trying to send a humorous signal by releasing publicity photographs showing himself directing scenes in Monument Valley incongruously wearing a beret, as if to say, "Yes, after all, I *am* an artist."

Westerns typically received little respect from American reviewers in those days; most publications, including the Hollywood trade papers, did not even bother to review every bread-and-butter Western. As Leslie A. Fiedler observed in his 1968 book *The Return of the Vanishing American,* "[H]ow certain we used to be, in that irrecoverable recent past, that the distinction between high literature and popular culture was final and beyond appeal: quite like that between White men and Indians, us and them." But even before *Stagecoach* was released on March 2, 1939, it was immediately recognized by most reviewers as a classic of the genre. In advance reviews, the *Motion Picture Herald* called it "the *Covered Wagon* of today's screen"; *Daily Variety* pronounced it "a splendid Western melodrama which is able to match the best in Western literature"; and the *Hollywood Reporter* described *Stagecoach* as "One swellegant Western that even the carriage trade will go for."

Frank S. Nugent of the *New York Times,* a future Ford screenwriter, declared in his March 3 review, "In one superbly expansive gesture . . . John Ford has swept aside ten years of artifice and talkie compromise and has made a motion picture that sings a song of camera. It moves, and how beautifully it moves, across the plains of Arizona, skirting the sky-reaching mesas of Monument

---

7. Late in life, Ford credited some of the story elements in *Stagecoach* to Ben Hecht. Dissatisfied with Nichols's first attempt at adapting Haycox's story, Ford invited Hecht for a weekend cruise to Catalina on the *Araner,* hoping the writer would find the script lying around and offer some free advice. "It's a good story fundamentally," Hecht said, "but it lacks color." According to Ford, Hecht came up with the idea of making Ringo (in the story, Malpais Bill) not simply a rancher out for vengeance but also "a kid just out of prison." Ford erred, however, in remembering that Hecht suggested making Dallas a prostitute, for the equivalent character in the story (Henriette) is also a prostitute.

Valley, beneath the piled-up cloud banks which every photographer dreams about." The audience's familiarity with the story material "doesn't cheat Mr. Ford of his thrills," Nugent noted. "His attitude, if it spoke its mind, would be: 'All right, you know what's coming, but have you ever seen it done like this?' And once you've swallowed your heart again, you'll have to say: 'No, sir! Not like this!'"

Claire Trevor recalled that when she attended the triumphant press preview on February 2, 1939, at the Fox Westwood Theatre in Westwood Village near the UCLA campus, she was "overcome" by her first viewing of the film: "I forgot I was in it, it was so riveting. As I walked up the aisle, [Hollywood columnist] Jimmy Starr said, 'It's a very good Western.' I almost hit him in the face. It was a *classic*. It was a great movie!" (*Daily Variety* reported that at the time of the preview, Ford "sat at a telephone in Portland, Me., awaiting the verdict from a stooge.")

Stagecoach proved popular with the general public, grossing $956,928 in its first ten months of release in the United States. Ford was honored with his second New York Film Critics Award and his second Oscar nomination as best director.[8] While the film has often been credited with spurring a new wave of interest in Westerns among general audiences, it's more accurate to describe *Stagecoach* as the most important example of Hollywood's 1939–40 Western renaissance. Other major Westerns made during that period, some of which were in the works at the same time as *Stagecoach,* included *Union Pacific, Northwest Passage, Jesse James, Dodge City, The Oklahoma Kid, Frontier Marshal, Destry Rides Again, The Return of Frank James, The Westerner, Arizona, The Dark Command, Santa Fe Trail*, and *Virginia City,* as well as Ford's own *Drums Along the Mohawk,* a lavish Technicolor Western set during the Revolutionary War and released by Fox in November 1939. Of all these films, however, *Stagecoach* has been the most revived, revered, and imitated.

"*Stagecoach* is for most people the archetypal Western; yet in many ways it runs exactly counter to the expectations of the genre, most evidently in the presentation of its women," Janey Place contends in her book on Ford's Westerns. It's true that *Stagecoach* operates by paradoxical inversion, snubbing its nose against "respectable" American bourgeois values while exalting raffish egalitarianism. The film counterposes the good whore against the snobbish eastern woman, the noble outlaw against the corrupt banker, the drunken but

---

8. *Stagecoach* received seven Oscar nominations, including one for best picture (the winner was *Gone with the Wind*). Ford's film won in two categories: Thomas Mitchell for best supporting actor and Richard Hageman, Franke Harling, John Leipold, and Leo Shuken for best musical score.

tolerant Irish doctor against the gallant but narrow-minded southern gentleman, etc. But such schematic inversions create their own clichés; and not only have such figures as the whore with a heart of gold become commonplace in subsequent Westerns, there also were many precedents in previous Westerns, Ford's included.

John Wayne's bighearted outlaw "the Ringo Kid" is, of course, a lineal descendant of the "good bad men" played by William S. Hart and by Harry Carey in Ford's silents. Naive but instinctively courtly, Ringo doesn't even realize Dallas is a whore throughout most of the movie and thinks people are snubbing her at the dinner table because she's seated with him. When she finally makes him see the truth, that doesn't change his opinion of her; just as he doesn't define himself as a criminal, he can see beyond someone else's unjustly imposed social role. As Doc Boone (Thomas Mitchell) puts it when he and Dallas are run out of town at the beginning of the film by the puritanical Ladies' Law and Order League, "We're the victims of a foul disease called social prejudice."

Like Wayne, Trevor brings an emotional honesty to a familiar character that lifts it above the cliché. In *Stagecoach,* Ford paradoxically shows the whore becoming a Madonna. Dallas helps Doc Boone deliver the baby of Lucy Mallory (Louise Platt), the cavalry officer's wife from back east (in Haycox's story, there is no doctor and the cavalryman's wife is not pregnant). As Dallas holds the child for the others to see, she says joyously, "It's a little girl," and Ford transforms Dallas with radiant lighting, revealing her inner goodness. "That scene was so beautifully lighted, with her eyes sparkling, and she did it so beautifully," Platt commented. "You know she's going to be a warm, wonderful mother and wife and any man would be lucky to get her—and it's just that one line. To me, that's magic."

Some of the characters in *Stagecoach,* however, including the savage Indian warriors and the comical or duplicitous Mexican servants, are unmodulated caricatures dating back to the earliest days of the genre. John Carradine's Hatfield, the fatalistic southern gentleman turned cardsharp, is a figure straight out of Bret Harte (whose story "The Outcasts of Poker Flat" Ford had filmed in 1919) or the stage melodramas Ford watched as a youthful theater usher in Portland (he filmed one of them, Booth Tarkington's *Cameo Kirby*). And while it's amusing to hear the banker, Gatewood (Berton Churchill), spout Herbert Hooverish Republican blather ("I have a slogan which should be blazoned on every newspaper in the country: 'America for Americans. The government must not interfere with business . . .'"), Gatewood is so unredeemably rotten he lacks only a mustache to play the kind of villain who would foreclose on a widow's mortgage.

What redeems *Stagecoach* from predictability is the three-dimensional am-

bivalence and depth Ford and his cast bring to at least some of these characters as they journey through a dream landscape of the American past. Much
of what struck 1939 viewers as groundbreaking about *Stagecoach* was its unusually sophisticated depiction of bedrock American class conflicts, revealed
through the intricately orchestrated clash of representative personalities under
pressure in a perilous situation. Like all period films that capture the public
imagination, *Stagecoach* was as much about the time when it was made as it was
about the past. While showing that some of the social conflicts of the depression era were little changed from those of the 1870s, *Stagecoach* proposed solutions to those conflicts in the vigor, generosity, and freedom from hypocrisy
exemplified by such figures as the Ringo Kid, Dallas, and Doc Boone.

The film's metaphorical reflection of the American immigrant experience
calls forth Ford's most complex and compelling emotional and artistic responses. As an Irish-American from New England, Ford could feel in his
bones the sting of the condescension with which Ringo and Dallas are treated
by their "respectable" fellow passengers. As Ringo puts it, "I guess you can't
break out of jail and into society the same week." One of the ironies of *Stagecoach* is that even its "respectable" characters would hardly qualify for respectability back east; whether they like to admit it or not, they are all exiles
and immigrants in their western journey. Perhaps the real meaning for Ford of
this moral fable is the immigrant's struggle for respect in a snobbish and hostile WASP society that has difficulty surviving without his help, surrounded as
it is by barely controllable threats from racial subgroups. Ford's egalitarianism
is qualified, however, by the film's casual indulgence in racist caricatures of Indians and Mexicans, whose lack of "civilization" is not seen as a virtue, even
though Dallas says of the Ladies' Law and Order League, "There are worse
things than Apaches."

Ringo is the wild, untamed natural man of American legend, the Natty
Bumppo character (described by Fiedler as "that first not-quite-White man of
our literature") lighting out for the territory at the end, the new frontier, leaving the country for Mexico to reenact yet again the immigrant experience.
Ringo's ethnic background is not specified, but he has symbolic affinities with
both the Irishman and the Indian. With him goes Dallas, the sexually unbridled woman, who turned to her "outlaw" state as a result of being orphaned
when her parents were massacred by Indians.

Ringo and Dallas are sent on their way by Doc Boone and the sympathetic
marshal (George Bancroft). Doc is Ford's surrogate figure, a liberal-minded,
fatalistic, priestlike drunk who even bears a strong physical resemblance to the
director. Doc's line in the closing scene, "Well, they're saved from the blessings
of civilization," perhaps was a conscious echo by Nichols of the ending of
Mark Twain's *Adventures of Huckleberry Finn:* "But I reckon I got to light out

for the territory ahead of the rest, because Aunt Sally she's going to adopt me and sivilize me, and I can't stand it. I been there before."

The moral drama of *Stagecoach* required a suitably grandiose visual setting. Ford found it in the spectacular mesas and buttes of Monument Valley, the isolated area of the Navajo Indian reservation where Utah meets the northeastern corner of Arizona. In *Stagecoach,* as in six later Ford films,[9] Monument Valley would serve as the director's dream landscape of the American past. "I think you can say that the real star of my Westerns has always been the land," Ford said in a 1964 interview. ". . . My favorite location is Monument Valley. . . . It has rivers, mountains, plains, desert, everything the land can offer. I feel at peace there. I have been all over the world, but I consider this the most complete, beautiful, and peaceful place on earth."

When Ford journeyed there to begin filming *Stagecoach* in October 1938, Monument Valley was little known and seldom visited by tourists. It was then the farthest point in the continental United States from a railroad (the nearest line was 180 miles away). There were few roads, and the only communication with the outside world was by means of a single telephone line and an emergency radio phone. The Navajos were still living much as they had in 1885, when the story of *Stagecoach* takes place.

The first film partly shot in Monument Valley was the 1925 silent version of Zane Grey's novel *The Vanishing American,* directed by George B. Seitz. Even before that, cartoonist George Herriman had used Monument Valley as the surreal setting for his Krazy Kat comics, as it later would be for Chuck Jones's Roadrunner cartoons. There are several conflicting accounts of how Ford came to shoot parts of *Stagecoach* in Monument Valley. Ford later claimed, without further elaboration, that he knew about the place from having driven through it on the way to Santa Fe, New Mexico. It's sometimes said that Olive and Harry Carey, or George O'Brien, or even John Wayne alerted him to this spectacular location. The commonly accepted version credits Ford's enlightenment about the valley to Harry Goulding, who for many years ran a trading post and lodge there with his wife, Leone ("Mike"). In this account, Goulding was seeking a new source of revenue for his business and for the impoverished Navajo tribe, which had been hit especially hard by depression-era

---

9. *My Darling Clementine, Fort Apache, She Wore a Yellow Ribbon, The Searchers, Sergeant Rutledge,* and *Cheyenne Autumn.* Two Ford films sometimes thought to have been filmed in Monument Valley, *Wagon Master* and *Rio Grande,* actually were filmed 120 miles north of there, around Moab, Utah. In his beautifully illustrated 1994 book *Il West di John Ford,* Carlo Gaberscek carefully documents Ford's use of Monument Valley and other western locations.

cutbacks in government subsidies. "Those poor old Indians couldn't even get coffee, and they're coffee-drinkin' gee-whizzes," Goulding recalled. So he went to Hollywood with a set of photographs of Monument Valley, arriving unannounced at the offices of producer Walter Wanger. Goulding talked his way into seeing the film's location manager, Danny Keith, who summoned Ford to look at the photographs. Ford was so excited that he chartered a plane and flew to Monument Valley the next day to see the site. "[W]e left $200,000 down there and the Indians ended up fat and sassy," Ford related.

This may be one of those instances in which, as Robert Frost put it, "History is just gossip." The *Stagecoach* company spent about $60,000 on the location shoot in Monument Valley, not $200,000, which would have been nearly 10 percent of the film's entire production cost of $531,374 (it was budgeted at $546,200). Records indicate that twenty-six members of the company stayed at the Gouldings' trading post. Another twenty-two were housed in a barracks that had been built by the Civilian Conservation Corps. But Ford and thirteen other key personnel stayed, like most prominent visitors in those days, at the inn and trading post run by John Wetherill and his wife at Kayenta, twenty-five miles south of Monument Valley. As Garry Wills points out, "In the John Ford mythology, the Gouldings have completely displaced the Wetherills, who were there before them and first brought film companies to the area." Citing Wanger documents, Wills reports that the Gouldings approached the film company through the Wetherills. The Gouldings' trading post had the advantage of being more convenient to the valley location sites. Obliterating the memory of the Wetherills' inn and the CCC barracks, Ford and Goulding concocted the story that Goulding built a barracks to house the entire company.

But in the final analysis, the question of who brought Ford to Monument Valley seems relatively insignificant beside the fact that Ford brought Monument Valley to the moviegoing public and appreciated its potential to bring mythic grandeur to his vision of the West. In *Stagecoach,* Ford's intercutting between the petty squabbles inside the coach and the magnificence of the landscape outside comments metaphorically on the existence of a greater system of moral and spiritual values, recognized more by the audience than by the characters themselves. Monument Valley not only was virtually unspoiled land for Westerns when Ford first went there to shoot, enabling him to make the landscape seem his own, but it largely remained so during Ford's lifetime; with occasional exceptions, other filmmakers tended to avoid the place out of deference to the master. Today, however, Monument Valley has been reduced to a cliché by overexposure in print advertisements and television commercials.

There is a strange irony involved in Ford's visual metaphors for rural Ireland, the land of his ancestors, and for the American West, the land of his dreams. The rocky, starved soil so many people fled is seen as a lush, green, endlessly fertile valley, and the American Dream to which they escaped is a desert valley slashed intermittently by rivers that serve only to emphasize its essential aridity. Yet the America of Ford's stories is presumably a land of fertility and opportunity, or why did the immigrants leave home in the first place?

Henry Nash Smith, analyzing the mythic West in his book *Virgin Land,* speaks of the "static, dreamlike" quality of the symbols employed by Western novelists. The seductiveness, and the terror, of a dream lies in its feeling of stasis, its sense of illusory possibilities. D. H. Lawrence could have been describing Monument Valley when he wrote, "White men have probably never felt so bitter anywhere, as here in America, where the very landscape, in its very beauty, seems a bit devilish and grinning, opposed to us." Yet Ford considered Monument Valley the most peaceful place on earth, a sign of how deeply at home he felt in this externalization of his own psychic landscape.

Compared with Ford's later Western classics shot in Monument Valley, *Stagecoach* contains a relatively small number of scenes actually shot there and none featuring John Wayne or the other principals. The film's modest production cost allowed for an efficient forty-seven days of shooting, from October 31 to December 23, 1938. Only the first seven days of that schedule were spent in Monument Valley—involving a troop of cavalrymen, a band of Indian warriors, and doubles for the coach passengers—before the company moved to Lucerne Dry Lake in the Mojave Desert near Victorville, California, to shoot the famous set piece of Indians chasing the stagecoach.

Here Yakima Canutt performed two of the most memorable stunts in movie history. Doubling for Wayne, he jumped from the coach to a team of running horses; playing an Indian in the same sequence, Canutt leapt from a running horse to the lead horse of the coach team, then was shot and dragged beneath the coach. Ford seemed shaken by the latter stunt, Canutt recalled: "I believe that he thought I was going to fall to the outside of the horses instead of in between them. My bit of acting at the end of the stunt [trying to get up and then falling to the ground] may also have fooled him. He probably thought I had really hurt myself." After the stunt was completed, Canutt saw Ford "leaning against the camera car looking at the ground. One of the camera operators said that he didn't think he got it, a second didn't know for sure, and the third cameraman said he was pretty sure he had it but couldn't be positive." Canutt offered to repeat the stunt, but Ford shook his head, saying, "I'll never shoot that again. They better have it."

The company returned to Goldwyn Studios to shoot interiors, including scenes with the actors riding a mock-up of the stagecoach as it bounced in front of process screens. That footage looks hokey in a way Ford films seldom do; the process backgrounds jiggle distractingly through the windows of the coach. Such artificiality plays a large part in making *Stagecoach* less alluring to the eye than most later Ford Westerns.[10]

But many of the long shots of the stagecoach wending its way through Monument Valley are truly stunning; it can only be surmised how much greater their effect was on contemporary audiences encountering those spectacular vistas for the first time. Ford's artistic instincts were sharpened and stimulated by the overwhelming reality of the landscape. One morning the director was awakened by his assistant, Wingate Smith, with a report that snow had fallen during the night. Because there was no mention of snow in the script, the company was expecting to spend the day resting indoors. But Ford took them out and filmed a long shot of the stagecoach entering a snowy landscape, one of the most beautifully atmospheric sights in the picture. Back in Hollywood, Ford covered the contingency by ad-libbing a couple of lines for the stagecoach driver (Andy Devine), explaining why he chose that route: "I'm using my head. Those breech-clout Apaches don't like snow."

They say I took pleasure in killing Indians in the movies," Ford said toward the end of his career. "But while today film people shed tears over the fate of the Indians, write humanitarian pamphlets and make declarations of intention without ever, *ever* putting their hands in their pockets, more humbly I gave them work. . . . More than having received Oscars, what counts for me is having been made a blood brother of various Indian nations. Perhaps it's my Irish atavism, my sense of reality, of the beauty of clans, in contrast to the modern world, the masses, the collective irresponsibility. Who better than an Irishman could understand the Indians, while still being stirred by the tales of the U.S. Cavalry? We were on both sides of the epic."

No real sympathy for the Indian point of view is evident in *Stagecoach,* however. The most Ford does is to romanticize the "noble savage" in the fashion of Frederic Remington's paintings and sculptures, portraying the Indians as a beautiful but warlike and doomed race giving way to the inexorable advance of white society. The sympathy Ford felt for Indians became more pronounced as time went on, reaching its finest expression in *Fort Apache* (1948) and receiving its fullest, if most problematical, treatment in *Cheyenne Autumn* (1964). But while his portrayal of Indians was seldom again as one-

---

10. The final shoot-out also was filmed at Goldwyn, although the opening scenes in the town of Tonto were filmed on the Western street at Republic Studios. Other location scenes were shot on the Kern River near Kernville and at Chatsworth, Calabasas, and Newhall. Ford filmed at the same picturesque Newhall location, Beale's Cut, that figures prominently in *Straight Shooting* and *The Iron Horse.*

dimensional as it was in *The Iron Horse* or *Stagecoach,* Ford's attitude toward the subject always contained fascinatingly unresolved contradictions. He was always "on both sides of the epic."

The Apaches in *Stagecoach* are seen as a simple force of nature, noble in appearance but destructive in action. Ford even indulges the racist notion of the "fate worse than death" (i.e., interracial rape) in two scenes involving the Southern gambler, the first as he removes his cloak to cover the half-naked body of a blond woman violated by Indians and the second when he prepares to kill the praying cavalry officer's wife to prevent her falling into the hands of marauding Indians, a shot Ford copied directly from D. W. Griffith's 1913 Western *The Battle at Elderbush Gulch.* The relatively uninteresting portrayal of Indians in *Stagecoach* is one reason it seems less artistically resonant than most of Ford's later Westerns. For as Fiedler points out, "The heart of the Western is not the confrontation with the alien landscape . . . but the encounter with the Indian, that utter stranger for whom our New World is an Old Home."

Despite their own reservations about Ford's portrayal of Indians, the Navajos of Monument Valley, whom Ford affectionately called the "Navvies," always had the greatest respect for him as a person. It was on *Stagecoach* that they gave him the name of "Natani Nez," meaning "Tall Leader." "Everybody was all in love with him," Harry Goulding recalled. ". . . They took him in as a Navajo. There was a great, beautiful ceremony. They gave him a sheepskin that they would give a Navajo, say a Navajo doctor that had just been one of the greatest, somebody'd really done somethin'. You could see 'em when they looked at him, just spelled all over 'em, that he was like them. That damn man, sometimes I wonder if he didn't come from a Navajo squaw."

The late Lee Bradley, a Navajo who had worked as an interpreter on *The Vanishing American,* served in that capacity on *Stagecoach* and the other Ford Westerns made in Monument Valley, as well as playing occasional parts himself (his brother Frank sometimes helped with the interpreting). Whenever Ford was planning to do location work on the reservation, Lee Bradley and Goulding would recruit Navajos as horsemen, bit players, extras, and laborers. Lee's daughter, Lillian Bradley Smith, recalled, "My father used to say John Ford was a close friend of his, almost like a brother, partly because they both had an Irish background. My grandpa was half Irish, and my great-grandfather Arthur Bradley was Irish. He was in the U.S. Cavalry."

Ford was superstitious by nature, but he scoffed when Goulding told him during the making of *Stagecoach* that there was a Navajo shaman, or medicine man, who could produce whatever kind of weather the director desired for scenic effect in Monument Valley. The medicine man was named Hosteen Tso, which translates as "Mr. Big" or "Mr. Fat"; Ford called him "Fat." The director facetiously placed an order with Fat, asking for thunderstorms the next day and then a day with a clear sky and only a few snowball clouds, followed by a dust storm. When Fat seemingly conjured up the weather he requested, Ford became a believer. This routine went on for years. "Mr. Ford made a lotta pictures out here, and ole Hosteen Tso was always the first man on the payroll," Goulding said. But one day, the story goes, Fat promised to deliver a certain kind of weather and it didn't happen. When asked what went wrong, he said that his radio was broken.

That droll brand of humor, pulling the leg of the unsuspecting white man, is one of the Navajos' least known attributes, usually kept among themselves as a form of covert amusement. Most of the Indians in Ford's films take their business seriously, although some of their humor occasionally shines through, such as when the Navajos in *Wagon Master* say the Mormons are their brothers because "they're not big thieves like most white men, just little thieves."

A prime example of Navajo humor appears in Tony Hillerman's 1994 novel *Sacred Clowns,* one of the author's popular series about Navajo tribal policeman Jim Chee. Hillerman has Chee and other Navajos attending a drive-in theater screening of Ford's *Cheyenne Autumn,* which one character describes as "'that old movie that used Navajos as extras, and they were supposed to be Cheyennes but they were talking Navajo, and saying all the wrong things? The one that they always bring back to that drive-in movie at Gallup? Sort of a campy deal, like *The Rocky Horror Picture Show?*'" The novel relates that "talking about the movie during the movie—celebrating the small victory of The People over the white man that this John Ford classic represented—was the reason Navajos still came to see it, and the reason the owner of the Gallup Drive-In still brought it back. . . . Scenes came in which somber-looking Cheyenne leaders responded to serious questions in somber-sounding Navajo. When converted back into English by the translator the answers made somber sense. But they produced more happy bedlam among the audience. . . . What he really said tended to have something to do with the size of the colonel's penis, or some other earthy and humorous irrelevancy." (Navajos I interviewed confirmed that members of their tribe did indeed ad-lib mocking dialogue in some Westerns filmed in Monument Valley. Ella Begay reported, "In one, I don't know if it was a John Ford movie, they ask the Indians to surrender and the Indians say, 'Yes, you crawl around like snakes on your bellies.'")

One of the standing jokes about Ford Westerns among the Navajos was how unrealistic the battle scenes between whites and Indians always were. Lillian Bradley Smith, who watched the filming of most of those movies, recalled with amusement, "In Ford movies they would fire a gun and seven Indians would fall off their horses. They got paid for horse falls. The joke is that only one was supposed to fall off." Mrs. Smith's daughter, Barbara White, added, "We would watch the movies at the Chapter House, the community meeting place in Kayenta. If people saw someone they knew [on-screen], everyone got a chance to applaud. We always had a laugh about why only one of the white men would get killed and the rest of the white men would survive. Not enough of them got shot. If that happened, people would laugh. They were happy when the Indians beat the whites."

"There was always a part that did not fit in right" in Ford Westerns, Mrs. Smith said, "and there were other parts that fit in. They would bring down costumes from Hollywood that were not really authentic but served their purposes. I'm pretty sure Ford tried to make the films true to life. It all depends who the scriptwriter was; whoever wrote the script was important. We see American movies and sometimes we don't understand what is happening, what they're about."

One of the most inauthentic aspects of Ford's Westerns is that the Indians are often played by members of the wrong tribes. With a few exceptions, the Apaches of *Stagecoach* are played by Navajos. In other Ford films Navajos appear as Sioux, Cheyenne, Arapaho, and so on. The Apache scout in the opening scene of *Stagecoach* is played by a Seneca, Chief John Big Tree (born Isaac Johnny John), whose career in movies began in 1915. A statuesque man who served as one of the models for the Indian head on the old buffalo nickel, Chief Big Tree first acted for Ford in the 1919 silent Western *A Fight for Love*. He also appears in *The Iron Horse, Drums Along the Mohawk,* and as Pony That Walks, Ford's most memorable Indian character, in *She Wore a Yellow Ribbon*. Ironically, during the making of *Stagecoach,* the Navajos objected to having some of the Apaches played by actual Apaches. As the film company reported in its publicity notes: "Director Ford employed both Navajos and Apaches. The Navajos protested because the two tribes have been enemies for years. However, Ford had to have a few Apache types for closeups to show the features of actual Apaches, some of whom actually descended from Geronimo's followers—three of whom were with Geronimo in their youth." Ford later claimed that the actor playing Geronimo was a half-Apache, half-Navajo grandson of the great warrior.

The Navajo medicine man Billy Yellow was one of the Indian horsemen on all the films Ford made in Monument Valley. Yellow said it didn't matter to Navajos that they sometimes were asked to play members of other tribes as well as their own, because "at the time Hollywood was so new to us." When I asked what he thought of the treatment of Indians in Ford's Westerns, Yellow surprised me by replying that he had never seen any of Ford's Westerns. In fact, he had never seen a motion picture in his ninety-six years, although when we talked that summer evening in 1998, he was going to see clips from some Ford movies at the tribute to his old friend in the city hall of Portland, Maine. Yellow still lived the traditional Navajo life in a Monument Valley hogan, without electricity or running water. His existence resembled that of a man from the nineteenth century, a character from a John Ford movie.

Yellow was most grateful to Ford for his financial support of the Navajos: "Back then for the Navajos the economy was low and he brought jobs for the Navajos to be in the movies." Asked how the Navajos felt when Ford cast them as villains, Yellow said, "It was a job and we just didn't concern ourselves about that. Ford was a very generous man. He fed all the Navajos there. The pay was good. Sometimes you couldn't get it until the end of shooting, but he always paid."

Each Navajo who worked on *Stagecoach* earned $3 a day. That was much less than Hollywood extras and stuntmen were paid, so the company can be accused of taking unfair advantage of Indian labor. But it's also true, as Yellow's comment indicates, that $3 in cash was a boon for a Navajo in those days. The annual per capita income for members of the tribe was measured in 1940 at $82, compared with $579 for the United States as a whole.[11] One time when Ford arrived on location in Monument Valley, he found the Navajos serenading him (in their own language) with Franklin D. Roosevelt's campaign theme song, "Happy Days Are Here Again." Ford joked that whenever he visited Monument Valley, he had to kiss more babies than a politician.

The pay scale on Ford Westerns rose incrementally over the years, and as Barbara White pointed out, "After Ford would make a movie, usually in the summer because it was good weather, people would have money and would run to the store and buy what they needed. They would stock up on pots and pans and staples for the winter at least." Ford did not forget his friends when they were between movies. In December 1948, shortly after he finished filming *She Wore a Yellow Ribbon* in Monument Valley, a blizzard struck, threatening both people and animals with starvation. Yellow remembered, "In 1948, Ford airlifted food in. A lot of families got food with aircraft. What I remember most is the bales of hay dropped from aircraft for the livestock. And Ford would send money by check when people needed it between films, any families that needed money."

There was one quality about Ford's direction that Yellow especially ad-

---

11. That calculation of the Navajos' per capita income did not include government benefits. There were about 50,000 Navajos in 1940, of whom an estimated 9,000 to 13,000 lived off the reservation, which covers approximately twenty-five thousand square miles in the Four Corners area of Arizona, New Mexico, Utah, and Colorado. At the time of the 1990 U.S. Census, there were 148,983 Indians living on the Navajo reservation. They had a per capita income of $4,106, compared with $14,420 for the United States in general.

mired: "I liked John Ford's decisiveness. What I liked about John is that when it was time for action and it was a good shot, the older folks did not have to do it over and over again. The horses didn't have to do it again. But I was young and I wished I did a lot more takes, because I enjoyed it.

"John was very patient even though he didn't speak the language. He was respectful. He had a sense of humor. He always worked—I remember him always sitting at a table doing paperwork, figuring out what he was going to shoot. Sitting in a chair under a tree, under a rock, under a shade house built for the picture. He didn't seem to mind the heat at all."

"Ford would sit around and chat after making the day's work," Lillian Bradley Smith remembered. "Sometimes we would gather round and he would be saying how he got out here—he was in military service and got into Monument Valley [sic]. He said when he started making movies, 'At first I didn't do a good job, but later I was better.'" She added that John Wayne "always was real nice to us, to Navajos. We all got along with him right well."

"John Wayne and John Ford were similar," Yellow observed. "John Wayne also had a sense of humor. Wayne was a good guy. We loved him." Because of the camaraderie they shared with Wayne, many Navajos were shocked in 1971 by what the actor said when *Playboy* interviewer Richard Warren Lewis asked if he had any empathy with American Indians. "I don't feel we did wrong in taking this great country away from them, if that's what you're asking," Wayne responded. "Our so-called stealing of this country from them was just a matter of survival. There were great numbers of people who needed new land, and the Indians were selfishly trying to keep it for themselves. . . . This may come as a surprise to you, but I wasn't alive when the reservations were created. . . . what happened 100 years ago in our country can't be blamed on us today. . . . What happened between their forefathers and our forefathers is so far back— right, wrong, or indifferent—that I don't see why we owe them anything." Until that interview appeared, the Navajos had no idea Wayne personally harbored such brutal sentiments. "If he did say that, I don't know why he would do so," Smith responded, "because he was out there with the People."

When I visited Monument Valley in July 1973, a month before Ford's death, I spoke with a young Navajo who was wearing a fatigue jacket and told me he had recently returned from military service in Vietnam. I asked what he thought of Ford, and he replied, "Is he the old guy with the eye patch? He's OK." But this young man was so infuriated by Wayne's comments in *Playboy* that he told me if Wayne ever came back to make another movie in Monument Valley, "He'd better watch out, because I'll be sitting up there in those rocks with my M1 rifle and I'll pick him off." Wayne never did go back to Monument Valley.

. . .

Wayne's first appearance in *Stagecoach* is one of the great star entrances in film history. As the stagecoach comes to a sudden halt at the sound of his offscreen voice, Ford cuts to a stylized tracking shot of Ringo with a saddle in one hand and a rifle in the other, his face dusty and sweat-stained, his brow furrowed under his cowboy hat. Twirling the rifle, he shouts "Hold it!" as the camera rushes in to a close-up of his face so abruptly that the camera operator briefly loses focus. Although the shot was done against a studio backdrop and could easily have been redone, Ford chose to keep the imperfection, perhaps because it makes Wayne's introduction seem even more breathless and unexpected.

Ford's loving depiction of Wayne on-screen contrasted starkly with the director's harsh treatment of the actor during the filming of *Stagecoach*. "Ford put him through agonies on that picture," Claire Trevor remembered. "He would stop in the middle of a rehearsal, take Duke's chin in his hand, and say, 'What are you doing? Don't act with your chin. It's *here* [gesturing to the eyes]—*here's* where you think. Not with your chin, for Chrissake. Up here.' Like you would a child. Most actors would walk off the set. But he took it, took it, *took* it. Duke was his whipping boy. He knew why, so he stood for it. Ford was only cruel when he had to be. He was trying to take away Duke's bad habits. You can't help having bad habits if you make B movies. I felt embarrassed for him, it was very upsetting, but he was improving every day all through the picture. Ford gave him a style which he kept."

"Jack Ford was a hypnotist and could do anything with actors, if he liked them," fellow director Allan Dwan observed. "Jack gave Wayne character."

Ford seldom let up on Wayne. He would say, "Stop slurring your dialogue and show some expression." He would call Wayne "a big oaf" and a "dumb bastard." Early in the shooting, Wayne had a scene that required him to wash and dry his face. Ford made him do it over and over again until Wayne's face was almost raw. "Can't you wash your fucking face?" Ford demanded. "For Chrissakes, *wash* your face! Don't you ever wash at home? You're dabbing your face, you're *daubing* it!"

"I was so fucking mad I wanted to kill him," Wayne admitted. " . . . He would turn me inside out. I would want to murder him. But Ford knew what he was doing. . . . He knew I was ashamed of being a B-Western cowboy in the company of these big stars. . . . I had a great deal of time in the picture when other people were talking, and all my stuff was just reactions. They became very important throughout the picture; they built my part. . . . Ford treated me with great care."

Sometimes Ford would vary his approach by taking Wayne aside and having him quietly read his lines for an upcoming scene. Ford would murmur, "Jesus, that was nice." (Wayne also ran his lines in the evenings with Yakima Canutt and worked on movement with the veteran Western actor Paul Fix.) Wayne realized that by hounding him in front of the company the way he did, Ford neutralized any possible jealousy and resentment the more experienced actors might have felt. Even though Wayne received only $3,700 for acting in *Stagecoach,* less than any of the other principals (Trevor received the most, $15,000), everyone knew that Wayne had the star-making role. Ford's bullying ensured that Wayne had "the whole cast on my side." The topper came when one of the youngest members of the cast, Tim Holt, finally told Ford, "Stop picking on Duke!"

Thomas Mitchell, with his extensive stage and screen experience, could not be intimidated by the director. One time when Ford tried to bully him, Mitchell came up with the perfect riposte: "That's all right, I saw *Mary of Scotland.*" Speechless, Ford left the set for fifteen minutes. When he came back, nothing more was said about the incident. Mitchell later described Ford as "the meanest s.o.b. on location I ever saw. He chews up actors and spits them out. He brutalizes the crew. He's a tyrant. And I'd crawl over those damned rocks at high noon to work with him again."

By any standard, some of Ford's barbs against Wayne crossed the line between necessity and gratuitous cruelty, such as when he taunted Wayne by saying, "I really should get Gary Cooper for this part. Can't you walk, for Chrissake, instead of skipping like a goddam fairy?" That remark carried an unintended irony, for as Olive Carey recalled, Wayne told her he imitated Ford's walk. Ollie described Ford's walk in terms that could be construed as feminine: she called it "beautiful" and "graceful." And she described Ford's personality as "fey." By mocking Wayne's masculinity with his absurd and homophobic remark, Ford was exposing his anxiety over his own masculinity and trying to ensure that no one would think *he* walked "like a goddam fairy." Wayne parried the remark deftly. When Ford showed him some of the early rushes and asked what he thought of his performance, Wayne responded, "Well, hell, I'm playing you, so—*you* know what that is."

"Ford was a tender, loving man, and he was a delicate, artistic man," Harry Carey Jr. observed. "You could see that his hands and eyes were so gentle. Yet he was intrigued with machoism. He wanted to be a two-fisted, brawling, heavy-drinking Irishman. He wanted to do what John Wayne did on screen and clean up a barroom all by himself, which Ford couldn't do. . . . So he created that on the screen."

Yet Wayne's characters for Ford are tender as often as they are macho. The combination of gentleness and authority Wayne brought to the role of Ringo represented Ford's idealized version of himself, an image the director artfully created on-screen but had trouble incarnating in reality. When Wayne's screen image is heroic, as it is throughout *Stagecoach,* he reconciles the contradictions warring in Ford's nature; but when Wayne plays an antihero, such as Ethan Edwards in *The Searchers,* he rawly exposes those contradictions. But even after *Stagecoach,* it would take years for Ford to recognize Wayne's full potential.

Aside from causing her distress with his treatment of Wayne, Ford "was absolutely wonderful to me," Claire Trevor said. "He was much rougher with men. He never was social on the set; I don't think he had any social graces. Ford was not gentle or polished—he would get right to the core. He was sarcastic. The atmosphere between him and me was perfect. I felt creative and I felt he was creative. John Ford was an artist, so exciting to work for. I would have done anything for him. If he had said, 'Claire, there's a cliff there, jump off it,' I would have.

"There was a chemistry between us. I knew exactly what he wanted; I knew what he was talking about before he finished a sentence. Ford never gave anyone line readings. [He gave direction with] his entire personality—his facial expressions, bending his eye. He didn't verbalize. He wasn't articulate, he couldn't really finish a sentence. He'd start to say something—'Now you go down there, you know, you're not happy . . .'—he might give you that understanding. And I'd say, 'I know what you mean.' He gave you a clue, just an opening. If you didn't produce what he wanted, he would pick you apart.

"There was a nice intimate scene between Ringo and me. We came to the spot where we were supposed to do it. Ford was reading the script—'What *is* this?' It was me saying good-bye to Ringo and Ringo riding off two pages. He read it and he tore up the pages: 'It's too mushy.' It broke my heart. Don't you love that? That was typical of him. He was right. There was not an extra word in that script. It was absolute perfection. And every scene moved the story forward. It was a *moving picture.*"[12]

When Kenneth Tynan asked Orson Welles in 1967 which directors he most admired, Welles gave an oft-quoted response: "The old masters. By which I mean John Ford, John Ford, and John Ford." In other interviews, Welles elab-

---

12. Most television copies of *Stagecoach* today give only a weak approximation of the original's rich photographic texture, so crucial to its orchestration of emotion. The camera negative no longer exists. After being chopped up by a distributor to make trailers, it was lost entirely to nitrate decomposition. In the late 1960s, American Film Institute archivist David Shepard approached John Wayne for a loan of his personal 35mm nitrate print so it could be copied for preservation. Wayne donated the print to the AFI collection at the Library of Congress as a preservation master. An excellent 35mm copy can be viewed at the library in Washington, D.C.

orated: "John Ford was my teacher. My own style has nothing to do with his, but *Stagecoach* was my movie textbook. I ran it over forty times. . . . I wanted to learn how to make movies, and that's such a classically perfect one. . . . Every night for more than a month [while preparing *Citizen Kane* in 1940], I would screen [*Stagecoach*] with a different technician from RKO and ask him questions all through the movie."

Some techniques in *Kane* that have been described as Welles's innovations, such as the use of ceilings on sets to facilitate the use of low-angle setups and wide-angle lenses, had been used by Ford and his cinematographer, Bert Glennon, in *Stagecoach*. Welles's cinematographer on *Kane*, Gregg Toland, was fresh from working with Ford on their two brilliantly photographed 1940 films, *The Grapes of Wrath* and *The Long Voyage Home*. Welles learned much from Ford about how to bring off the subtle orchestration of complex movement within a confined space, and how to use chiaroscuro for maximum cinematic effect. Welles recalled being "constantly encouraged by Toland, who said, under the influence of Ford, 'carry everything in one shot—don't do anything else.' In other words, play scenes through without cutting, and don't do alternate versions."

Many in Hollywood ridiculed and attacked Welles when he first came to town in 1939, seeing him as a threat to their standard method of operations and resenting his contract with RKO, which guaranteed him a virtually unprecedented degree of creative freedom. Ford, however, was one of several veteran directors who went out of their way to welcome him. Welles told Peter Bogdanovich that Ford "came on the set while we were shooting *Kane*— to wish me luck, you know—and there was a first assistant (let's call him Eddie)[13] who we later learned was an informer for the anti-*me* faction in the front office. Ford's greeting to him was the first hint we had of his real status. 'Well, well,' he said, 'how's old snake-in-the-grass Eddie?' That was the tipoff." For the wrap party on the final day of shooting, October 23, 1940, at the RKO-Pathé studio in Culver City, Welles had a soundstage converted into a Wild West saloon. At the climax of the party, a stagecoach appeared on the set in tribute to Welles's cinematic master.

In the 1941 Oscar competition, both Welles and Ford were nominated for best director. Perhaps fittingly, given Welles's high esteem for Ford, Ford won

---

13. Edward Donahue, who had worked as Ford's first assistant, but actually the company's man, on the RKO films *The Informer* and *Mary of Scotland*. One reason Ford so often used his brother-in-law Wingate Smith and his brother Edward O'Fearna as assistants was that their family connections guaranteed that they were loyal to him rather than to the studio.

the award for *How Green Was My Valley,* which also won the Oscar for best picture. As Andrew Sarris remarks, Ford was forty-seven when he made *How Green Was My Valley* and Welles was twenty-five when he made *Kane,* "but both films are the works of old men, the beginnings of a cinema of memory."

Welles's next film, *The Magnificent Ambersons,* began shooting on the day *How Green Was My Valley* was released, October 28, 1941. With its emphasis on the evanescence of memory and its mournful depiction of a family and society in decline, *Ambersons* shows the Ford influence more directly than *Kane.* These affinities did not go unrecognized by Ford.

"Once, after I'd made a couple of pictures of my own, I got a sort of diploma from him—you might call it a citation," Welles recalled. "This had been put together in a bar in some sleazy fishing village in Baja California, and it was written, none too soberly, on the back of an old piece of cardboard. Many ornate and official-looking stamps were pasted all over this document, including several Mexican beer labels. Well, of course I had it framed. For many years, until somebody pinched it, it was the only award I ever used for decoration in my office. The text was brief. There was just this simple statement: 'Orson Welles has been elected.' The name of the institution doing me this honor wasn't given, but Duke Wayne had scrawled his signature as vice-president of something illegible across the Great Seal of Cresta Blanca. And there were those other names . . . all those hairy good companions of Ford's famous clan. . . . I was so pleased and complimented to receive that document from John Ford and his merry crew."

Bogdanovich observed that when Ford, in his old age, spoke of Abraham Lincoln, there was "such an extraordinary sense of intimacy in his tone (and as much affection as there was in a reference to John Wayne as 'this big oaf"), that somehow it was no longer a director speaking of a great President, but a man talking about a friend."

Thanks in part to the influence of his brother Frank, who often played Lincoln in his own films, Lincoln became a familiar figure in John Ford's work long before *Young Mr. Lincoln.* He is a key character in *The Iron Horse* and *The Prisoner of Shark Island* (whose French title is *Je n'ai pas tué Lincoln,* or *I Did Not Kill Lincoln*), and he even makes a cameo appearance in one of Ford's films about Ireland. In *Mother Machree* (1928), the central character, Brian McHugh, is seen as a boy in 1899, dreaming about America as he reclines in a straw pile outside his house in the fishing village of Ballymoney. "The Battle Hymn of the Republic" plays on the sound track as Ford shows Brian (Philippe de Lacy) reading a book about Lincoln and looking at an illustration titled *"Lincoln reading by the firelight."* Near the end of Ford's career, Lincoln is seen briefly in *The*

Civil War, Ford's segment of *How the West Was Won,* and the Great Emancipator's memory is evoked in *Sergeant Rutledge, The Man Who Shot Liberty Valance,* and *Cheyenne Autumn.* For Ford, Lincoln is the archetypal figure of justice, a man who dispenses legal wisdom with a priestlike humor, charity, and tolerance. He is the forefather of the Fordian lineage of folksy, humane judges and politicians that also includes Judge Priest and Mayor Skeffington.

A heartfelt yet not unambiguous expression of Ford's faith in the fundamental decency of American values, *Young Mr. Lincoln* concentrates those values in one uncommon common man, played by Henry Fonda with an uncanny combination of awkwardness and grace. This magical film draws its strength and charm from what the great Russian director Sergei Eisenstein described as its "stylized daguerreotype manner that is in unison with the moral character of Lincoln's sentences" and from its genesis in a "womb of national and popular spirit." Eisenstein added that the "informal plot, almost plotless or anecdotal, looks on closer inspection like a thoroughly composed image synthesizing all those qualities that shone in the historical-political role played by this American giant."

When Fox first offered Fonda the role, he declined "because I didn't think I could play Lincoln. Lincoln to me was a god." The studio persuaded him to do a test wearing a false nose and wart. "The next day I went in to see it, and I'm sitting in the projection room. . . . I see this guy and I thought, 'Well, I'm a son of a bitch! It looks like Lincoln!' Then he started to talk, and *my* voice came out, and it destroyed it for me. I said, 'I'm sorry, fellows, it won't work.' " Later, when Ford was assigned to the picture, he called Fonda in for a meeting. "I remember going into his office the way a recruit would go in to the admiral. . . . He looked up at me from under the hat he had on . . . and either the handkerchief in his mouth or the pipe or whatever he was chewing on, and said, 'What the fuck is all this shit about you not wanting to play this part?' He can only talk by using all the bad words! What he was doing was shaming me. He said, 'You think you'd be playing the goddam Great Emancipator, huh? He's a goddam fucking jake-legged lawyer in Springfield, for Christ's sake!' "

At this point in his career, Ford was somewhat torn between Wayne and Fonda as his ideal screen hero. Fonda was in the ascendancy during Ford's Popular Front period, perhaps because he seemed a more liberal, less authoritarian type than Wayne. And yet there are some overlapping areas between the two actors: Wayne always displays a likable hesitancy and vulnerability in his roles for Ford, and Fonda always has a tendency toward self-righteousness and rigidity. Even Fonda's Lincoln, for all his egalitarianism, is somewhat authoritarian, self-righteous, and condescending. Ford lovingly satirizes Lincoln's awkwardness and rigidity by showing him dancing like a mechanical figure to the tune of "Oh, Dem Golden Slippers" with his future wife, Mary Todd (Marjorie Weaver); the director later used the same tune for the classic scene of Fonda's Wyatt Earp dancing at the church dedication in *My Darling Clementine*.

The impressionistic scenes showing Lincoln's maturation in New Salem and Springfield, Illinois, give not only a précis of his early life but also, in the pageantry of the Independence Day parade, a brief history of the United States from 1776 to the Age of Lincoln. Elderly veterans of the Revolutionary War and the War of 1812 (including Francis Ford in his "Brother Feeney" guise) have the places of honor in the parade, along with a backwoods girl casually playing the part of Miss Liberty. The portrait of Lincoln that emerges is carefully and subtly constructed as a series of metaphors for his ultimate role in American history as the president who waged civil war to preserve the Union and, as a secondary issue, bring an end to the institution of slavery.

The central metaphor, expressed both dramatically and visually, is that of Lincoln as a symbolic reconciler of opposing forces in American life. All his actions as a young man are supercharged with our common knowledge of his destiny. We see it in the way Lincoln awkwardly shifts his hands and legs while making his maiden political speech in New Salem, cheats in a tug-of-war at an Independence Day celebration in Springfield, delicately balances a pie in either hand and takes interminable samples while judging a baking contest, and plays "Dixie" on his Jew's harp while riding his donkey along a country road ("What's that tune you're playin'?" "Don't know—catchy, though"). "[T]he idea of the picture," said Ford, "was to give the feeling that even as a young man you could sense there was going to be something great about this man."

Young Mr. Lincoln perfectly exemplifies Sarris's description of Ford's style as "a double vision of an event in all its vital immediacy and yet also in its ultimate memory image on the horizon of history." The cherishing of a momentary image, immutable in its delicacy and precision of framing, begins to assume obsessive proportions as shot after shot rolls inexorably away. It is as if the very perfection of the image is the cause of its transience. The populist optimism that suffuses Ford's pioneer films of 1939 begins to be weighed down by a haunting regret for the loss of possibilities, the loss of primitive simplicity, and, in particular, the loss of family.

Nowhere is this mingled sense of destiny and loss more poignantly encapsulated than in the Ann Rutledge scene of *Young Mr. Lincoln*. The tracking shot that follows Lincoln and Ann (Pauline Moore) on their casual stroll along a riverbank has a rhapsodic languor that becomes, in retrospect, hypnotic and oppressive, like the dark tree trunks and split-rail fence that pass between them and the moving camera. As Ann prods the hesitant Lincoln to go to college and make something of himself, he concentrates on her with a fixed stare, as if to burn her image into his memory. "You're awfully pretty, Ann," he tells her finally. Looking down shyly, she responds, "Some folks I know—don't like red hair." In a strange reverie, underscored with Alfred Newman's haunting "Ann Rutledge Theme," Lincoln murmurs, "I love red hair." At the end of this scene, the last time we see Ann in the film, she briefly passes into a deep shadow at the left edge of the frame before exiting the shot, a subtle foreshadowing of her premature death. (Although Bert Glennon shot the rest of the film, this scene, filmed on location alongside the Sacramento River, was photographed with particular beauty by Arthur C. Miller.)

Lincoln casually tosses a stone into the river, and the ripples emanating in its wake are transformed, in a slow dissolve, into churning cakes of ice. Then, in an image Ford and screenwriter Lamar Trotti borrowed from Judge Priest's conversation with his dead wife, Lincoln is seen talking to Ann at her gravestone, as if she were still present, still alive, still guiding his destiny. Unsure whether he should stay in New Salem or pursue a career in the law, he plays a little game with her, pretending to let a falling stick decide. When it falls toward the gravestone, he says, "Well, Ann, you win—it's the law." We hear a faint foreshadowing of "The Battle Hymn of the Republic," and Abe adds with a conspiratorial smile, "Wonder if I coulda tipped it your way just a little." *Young Mr. Lincoln* seamlessly and paradoxically melds the romantic "great man" theory of history with a Tolstoyan sense of historical determinism. While Lincoln's actions seem predetermined, they always stem from the uniqueness of his character. Ford remains true to his Catholic beliefs in insisting that Lincoln has a free will in choosing his destiny.

The buxom, brown-haired Fox contract player Pauline Moore, who plays Ann Rutledge with such a touching combination of country naïveté and almost mystical foresight, described the role as "one of the few things I ever did that I felt like a real person. I had no interest in being a glamour girl." But she remembered the filming as a disappointingly "casual" experience: "I respected John Ford, so I looked forward to growing up under his guidance. But it didn't happen. We were up on the Sacramento River. It was late in the afternoon before they got to my part. I had been sitting there sewing little dresses for my two daughters. Ford said to me, 'Do you know your part?' I said, 'Yes.' He said, 'Take off your lipstick.' I said, 'Fine.' The makeup man *did* make a mask of me. Then I saw Ford take a pencil and put a big X on a couple of pages. I thought, 'Oh, no, that's my part!' [Ford cut six lines and a few other words from the three-page scene, which Moore had done earlier in a screen test.] He didn't waste any time; he called me and we did it. He never said a word. I had to ask them, 'Was it all right?' and they said, 'Yes.' I felt that John was just a gentle-man doing his job. He knew what he wanted."

The film's climactic trial sequence presents Lincoln as a wily politician, a manipulator of popular emotion who stage-manages events to achieve what he considers a higher state of truth and justice. He engages in folksy, humor-ously pointed antics to influence the judge, jury, and spectators on behalf of his clients and at the same time for his own political advancement. As his po-litical rival Stephen A. Douglas (Milburn Stone) observes, "Mr. Lincoln's a great storyteller. Like all such actors, he revels in boisterous applause."

Lamar Trotti, whom Zanuck described as "practically an authority on Lin-coln," based the trial on one he witnessed as a crime reporter in Georgia. Trotti's script added a famous detail from the Duff Armstrong trial of 1857, when Lincoln dramatically demonstrated his client's innocence by consulting an almanac. The studio-censored antilynching scene Trotti wrote for *Judge Priest* is transmuted here into a scene of Lincoln standing down a mob who storm the Springfield jailhouse to lynch his clients, two innocent brothers, Matt and Adam Clay (Richard Cromwell and Eddie Quillan).

The boys' mother (Alice Brady), whom Lincoln admiringly calls "a simple country woman," steadfastly refuses to testify against either son. Like the pie-judging contest Lincoln can't seem to decide because of his equal fondness for both pies, but raised in this case to the level of a life-or-death issue, the trial's pitting of brother against brother metaphorically evokes the dilemma Lincoln will have to face with the fratricidal bloodshed of the Civil War. The young lawyer shames his fellow townsfolk into backing down from lynching by em-ploying a masterful combination of threatened physical violence, ingratiating wit, moral homily, and scriptural quotation ("Blessed are the merciful"). Elo-quent as the scene is, it was allowed to reach the screen only because the po-tential victims were white, making it seem less threatening to American moviegoers in a decade when lynchings still claimed the lives of thousands of southern blacks. And as Fritz Lang observed of his own 1936 antilynching film *Fury,* the idea of showing that it would be equally wrong to lynch someone who was guilty also would have been out of the question.

Early in the film, Lincoln is seen leaning against a tree reading *Blackstone's Commentaries.* His own commentary on the law is at once simple and pro-found—"By jing, that's all there is to it—right 'n' wrong." We are meant to think of the way he came to apply his basic principles to the great moral issue of slavery, even though slavery was barely a concern for him in his youth and so is only briefly alluded to in the film. In the final sequence, as Lincoln sym-bolically walks to the top of a hill amidst thunder and lightning, Ford abstracts the man into his legendary image by dissolving to the statue in the Lincoln

Memorial. When rain began falling on the Fox back lot as Fonda was walking up the hill in long shot—one of those happy accidents for which Ford was famous—Ford mused aloud, "The tears of the multitudes."[14]

The least of Ford's three 1939 films, *Drums Along the Mohawk,* based on the historical novel by Walter D. Edmonds, represents something of a regression with its storybook presentation of American history. Compared with the sophisticated development of the main characters in *Stagecoach* and the mythic simplicity of *Young Mr. Lincoln, Drums* takes a cartoonish approach to character and grossly oversimplifies the history of the Revolutionary War period.

The first Ford film made in color—not counting the use of color tinting in such films as *The Iron Horse, Mother Machree,* and *Wee Willie Winkie—Drums* is a gorgeous piece of Technicolor cinematography by Bert Glennon and Ray Rennahan. Ford's romantic imagery takes full advantage of the spectacular locations in Utah's Wasatch Mountains, standing in for upper New York State's Mohawk Valley. But the color is so lush, so pop-artish in its boldness and intensity, that the costumes and decor count for as much as the people. Ford's dissatisfaction with the script by Lamar Trotti and Sonya Levien, difficult location conditions and weather that played havoc with the shooting schedule, and the director's physical exhaustion after making *Stagecoach* and *Lincoln* also contributed to making *Drums* seem sluggish and only intermittently involving.

It's telling that Ford avoided making a color feature for almost another decade after *Drums Along the Mohawk.* Color, he told Bogdanovich, is "much easier than black and white for the cameraman; it's a cinch to work in, if you've any eye at all for color or composition. But black and white is pretty tough—you've got to know your job and be very careful to lay your shadows properly and get the perspective right. In color—there it is; but it can go awfully wrong and throw a picture off. There are certain pictures, like *The Quiet Man,* that call for color—not a blatant kind—but a soft, misty color. For a good dramatic story, though, I much prefer to work in black and white; you'll probably say I'm old-fashioned, but black and white is real photography."

The other major reason for the air of unreality in *Drums* is the casting of Claudette Colbert as Lana, the upper-crust wife of the yeoman farmer Gil Martin (Henry Fonda). Usually seen in sophisticated comedies, Colbert had a

---

14. The scene was shot on what is now Avenue of the Stars in Century City. When Ford revisited the location in 1970 for the filming of the TV documentary *The American West of John Ford,* Henry Fonda asked him, "Do you remember where you are? Do you recognize this?" Ford replied, "No, I don't. This is the damnedest place. . . . I have no idea where the hell we are." The former Fox back lot was sold in 1961 and became the posh business and residential development Century City.

glamorous image that clashed with the pioneer setting, and Ford seemed to resent her presence in the film. Temperamentally averse to Ford's bullying tactics, Colbert refused to give in when she thought he was wrong. "They pay me to direct, honey, what do they pay you to do?" Ford snapped at one point. When I asked her if Ford considered her difficult, Colbert replied haughtily, and perhaps with just the slightest trace of irony, *"Me?* Difficult?" But she admitted she was not used to roughing it the way Ford liked his actors to do on location; she found it particularly distasteful to have to use a wooden outhouse. Partly as a result of his lack of rapport with Colbert, Ford seemed to invest far more sympathy in the character of the hard-boiled old widow Sarah McKlennar, magnificently played by Edna May Oliver, who received an Oscar nomination.

Colbert has one unforgettable scene in the movie, but it's mostly a director's scene, that of Lana watching Gil marching off to war; the climactic long shot of Lana collapsing on a hilltop, with the line of men seen in the distance below her, is one of Ford's finest pictorial images. *Drums Along the Mohawk* is a film that can be appreciated only for such isolated set pieces. The long, brilliantly paced montage of Fonda running silently through the forest, pursued by three Indians, is another such sequence. Then there was the big battle scene that Ford *didn't* film; instead he had the battle-shocked Gil, returning home to his wife, describe it to her in halting tones, letting us imagine the horrors he experienced.

On the other hand, *Drums* gives the bizarre impression that one nasty Englishman with a piratical eye patch (John Carradine) is responsible for stirring up virtually all the trouble between the settlers and the Indians. Crudely depicted as murderous savages, the Indians are seen as disrupting the Edenic tranquillity of the Mohawk Valley and the life of the idealized white pioneer couple. The fact that it was the white settlers who first disrupted the lives of the Native Americans hardly seemed to register in Ford's consciousness at this stage of his career.

Ford does make halfhearted attempts at showing sympathy for the Indians. His portrait of the militant preacher Reverend Rosenkrantz (played by the Irish actor Arthur Shields) satirizes the bloodthirsty attitude the film otherwise portrays as necessary to the survival of white civilization. The preacher calls the Indians "sons of Belial" and offers a blasphemous prayer for victory to "Lord Jehovah, O God of battles," but later collapses in anguish after he personally sheds blood. There's also a Native American Uncle Tom figure named Blue Back, played by Chief Big Tree. A friend of Gil's, Blue Back is a comical figure who is supposed to be sympathetic because of his nonthreatening nature. But he comes off as a pathetic traitor to his own people, accepted by the whites as a sort of domesticated pet. Depicting Indians as noble savages, as Ford does in *Stagecoach,* at least allows them more dignity than this kind of condescension. Asked why Ford's view of Indians became more sympathetic in the years following *Drums Along the Mohawk,* his longtime research assistant Katherine Cliffton said simply, "He came to know them."

Robin Wood observes that *Drums* was "perfectly conceived for (or a perfectly logical product of) its contemporary historical moment—America just emerging from the depression; the world on the brink of a war to defend Democracy against Fascism. The film shows the American people (in microcosm) struggling against hardship and disaster, overcoming them and preparing for new effort." But Wood notes that the film qualifies that ostensibly optimistic vision at every turn: "Ford's allegiance to the past, his rootedness in a tradition that by 1939 was already obsolete, are expressed above all in his compositional sense, perhaps the last distinguished manifestation of the Romantic vision of a possible harmony between nature and humanity . . . [and yet] the sense of harmony and wholeness is everywhere counterpointed with a sense of transience. . . . In fact, the central Fordian paradox is already implicit in *Drums Along the Mohawk:* his dedication to the development of a civilization that will inevitably render obsolete the very values he celebrates."

In his essay "The Irish in John Ford's Films," the novelist and historian Thomas Flanagan writes, "Someone has suggested that Ford's most Irish film is *The Grapes of Wrath.*" That may seem paradoxical in light of Ford's many cinematic treatments of Ireland itself, but the spirit and themes of *The Grapes of Wrath* are very much in keeping with what the director called "my Irish tradition." For as Flanagan notes, *Grapes* is "about poverty and exodus." When Ford read John Steinbeck's novel around the time of its publication in the spring of 1939, he was struck by the similarity between the book's dispossessed Okies, "wandering on the roads to starve," and the Irish evicted by their landlords in the Great Famine, the subject of Ford's cousin Liam O'Flaherty's 1937 novel *Famine.*[15]

Ford's powerful emotional response to the book stemmed from his atavistic memory of how his ancestors struggled to keep from starvation during "the Great Hunger" before leaving their homeland as part of the vast Irish emigration to America. The westward journey of the Joad family from their former home in Oklahoma to an uncertain future in California, where they are treated as little better than animals, powerfully echoes the experience of Famine immigrants in coming to America. Ford's 1940 film version softens

15. Asked about Steinbeck's novel in an interview with George Bluestone for *Novels into Film* (1957), Ford claimed, "I never read the book." That leg-pulling remark was made "with just the slightest trace of whimsy and bravado," Bluestone reported.

some of the more radical socioeconomic themes of Steinbeck's Pulitzer Prize–winning novel, but it is suffused with a fine sense of outrage over the treatment received by these poor, proud, and industrious newcomers.

The return of Tom Joad (Henry Fonda) from prison at the beginning of the film only to find that his family farm, like so many others, is deserted "bears an uncanny resemblance to folk memories of the abandoned Famine villages of Connaught and Munster," Flanagan points out. "Tom is like the Irish rebel son of such memories, sweet-natured but quick-tempered and capable of murderous rage. And, as the Joad family splinters, the patriarch senile and the father helpless, it is the mother, massive and nurturing, who becomes the source of strength. The Joads, descendants of Ford's cowpunching plainsmen, are the ethnic opposites of the Irish, but the myths echo against each other." The family's overloaded truck, creaking its way to California with them and all their possessions, "resonates against memories of the Irish coffin ships headed across the Atlantic. . . . In this film, Ford's thematic material, Ireland and the West, touch each other."

The Grapes of Wrath represents the climax of Ford's Popular Front period. Showing the director at his most engaged, it is the only nondocumentary film he ever made that directly confronts a major contemporary social issue. Ford's films had begun turning increasingly to the past, to historical issues with more distant resonance for his audience. Ford's cinema was a theater of memory and meditation rather than a meeting hall for calls to social action. But the plight of the migrant farmworkers touched him deeply, as it did many Hollywood liberals and leftists during the late thirties. "I was sympathetic to people like the Joads, and contributed a lot of money to them," Ford recalled in 1964. Although he insisted with the hindsight of his more conservative old age that he "was not interested in *Grapes* as a social study . . . I was only interested in the Joad family as *characters*," he admitted, "I bucked to do that picture, and put everything I had into it."

The Grapes of Wrath was such a controversial project for a Hollywood studio to undertake that when second-unit director Otto Brower went on the road to shoot semidocumentary footage of the Joads' trip to California, Fox used a dummy title for the production, *Highway 66*. The book was banned and even burned in some places for its scathing depiction of the social injustices suffered by the migrants at the hands of the California agricultural interests and law enforcement agencies. Zanuck's courageous decision to make the film, bolstered by the book's status as a runaway best-seller, was opposed by the California Chamber of Commerce and the Agricultural Council of California, which called for a boycott of all Fox pictures.

Partly because of that opposition, and partly because of the film's relatively low budget of $750,000, most of the principal photography for *The Grapes of*

Wrath was done on Fox soundstages, the studio back lot, and nearby locations. Some scenes were shot at the federal Resettlement Administration's Arvin Sanitary Camp for migrant workers in Kern County, as well as in the surrounding countryside (the camp, known to its residents as "Weedpatch," was renamed the Farmworkers' Wheat Patch Camp on-screen). Ford rapidly completed principal photography in forty-three days of shooting between October 4 and November 16, 1939, and *The Grapes of Wrath* was ready for release only two months later.

The dust bowl migration brought about a million impoverished people to California between 1935 and 1939; the migration and labor unrest peaked in 1937. These newcomers were collectively known as Okies although some came from Texas, Arkansas, and western Missouri as well as from Oklahoma. They temporarily displaced many of the migratory workers of foreign descent, mostly Mexicans and Asians, who until then had made up the majority of California farmworkers and whose working conditions attracted even less sympathy. The Okie exodus was caused by drought, soil erosion, and dust storms and by the large landowners' widespread evictions of tenant farmers and sharecroppers. Ironically, government programs intended to help farmers by removing land from production only exacerbated the problem, forcing displaced farmers to turn to picking fruit in California.

Steinbeck's exhaustively detailed, semidocumentary approach to this socioeconomic crisis in *The Grapes of Wrath* reflected the novel's origins in investigative journalism. He first traveled around California migrant camps in 1936 to research an impassioned seven-part series for the *San Francisco News,* "The Harvest Gypsies." Steinbeck charged that the large growers in the Imperial Valley were exploiting their workers by paying starvation wages and keeping them in line with "a system of terrorism that would be unusual in the Fascist nations of the world." When Zanuck purchased the film rights to *The Grapes of Wrath,*[16] Steinbeck was skeptical of Hollywood's ability to deal honestly with such material. He asked Zanuck if he believed what the book was saying about the exploitation of migrant workers. Zanuck told Steinbeck that he had hired a detective firm to investigate the charges levied by the novel and found that "the conditions are much worse than you reported." Screenwriter Nun-

16. The title was drawn from Julia Ward Howe's Civil War anthem "The Battle Hymn of the Republic," which in turn borrowed the image from the Book of Revelation. Steinbeck's wife, Carol, suggested calling the novel *The Grapes of Wrath*. The author commented that he liked the title "because it is a march and this book is a kind of march—because it is in our own revolutionary tradition and because in reference to this book it has a large meaning."

nally Johnson had the impression that Zanuck's own visits to migrant camps had a liberalizing effect on his political beliefs.

"When I purchased *The Grapes of Wrath,* this company was controlled by the Chase National Bank, which was the biggest stockholder," Zanuck recalled. "I was told that the chairman of the board of the Chase National Bank, Winthrop Aldrich, . . . would probably raise hell with me because I was attempting a controversial subject that did not hold capital in too high a light. . . . When Steinbeck came out here for the first story conference he was highly suspicious and finally told me that he had been told and warned that the whole scheme was for the purpose of taking the social significance out of the story and he would never have sold the book to me if he had realized this company was actually controlled by big banking interests."

The Fox production chief assured Steinbeck that he was "willing to take any legitimate or justified gamble" with the material. Zanuck subsequently went to New York and "saw Mr. Aldrich on business matters. Out of the blue he said, 'I hear you have purchased a book titled *The Grapes of Wrath.*' I expected the ax to fall but instead he said, 'My wife Winnie is crazy about it and I started reading it last night and it was so fascinating I couldn't put it down. It should make a wonderful movie.'" That anecdote illustrates the remarkable resilience of the American capitalist system even in the midst of economic chaos. In a 1940 article for the *Nation,* "Slumming with Zanuck," Michel Mok noted the irony of the film's New York premiere, which was attended by stars in jewels and furs and by executives of the banks and land companies that had evicted people like the Joads. Despite his assurances to Steinbeck, Zanuck worked closely with Johnson to make the book's political viewpoint less radical and less threatening to corporate interests.

They toned down the earthiness of the novel for censorship reasons, eliminated most of Steinbeck's ruminations on the need for an organized revolt of the underclass, and somewhat softened the author's generally despairing view of the American socioeconomic system. In the most significant structural change, Zanuck and Johnson reversed the order of the sections showing the Joads first living happily in a clean, well-run government camp but then working under severely regimented conditions for meager wages at a peach ranch. Putting the government camp section second, closer to the end of the film, made the story seem far more optimistic, suggesting that President Roosevelt's New Deal might be able to solve the migrant-worker problem by government intervention. Considering that Zanuck was a Republican and temperamentally inclined to side more with capital than labor, that was a major concession on his part. When Grant Mitchell was cast as the camp superintendent and made up to look remarkably similar to FDR, it underscored the film's liberal political message that the American economic system is capable of reforming itself.

When a sympathetic employer in the novel named Mr. Thomas tells Tom Joad that farmworker unrest is being blamed on "red agitators," Tom asks a fellow worker, "What the hell is these reds anyways?" The worker replies by sardonically quoting another employer: "A red is any son-of-a-bitch that wants thirty cents an hour when we're payin' twenty-five!" A similar line was included in the script but was not used in the film. Tom asks in the film, "Listen, what is these reds, anyway? Every time you turn around somebody callin' somebody else a red. What is these *reds* anyway?" To which Mr. Thomas (Roger Imhof) responds, "Oh, I ain't talkin' about that one way or the other." That reply could be taken as an expression of the filmmakers' own equivocation on the subject, but as Ford directs the scene, the tone in Tom's voice clearly mocks red-baiting as a response to social problems. For all his criticisms of the adaptation, George Bluestone in *Novels into Film* concedes that *Grapes* "came as close as any film in Hollywood's prolific turnout to exposing the contradictions and inequities at the heart of American life."

Nowhere is this more memorably conveyed than in the grimly powerful flashback of the hapless Muley (John Qualen) telling how his family home was literally pushed off the land by Caterpillar tractors. Muley's son points a shotgun at a bank representative who explains, impatiently but not without empathy, that the blame for their eviction lies in executive offices far removed. In a rage of frustration, Muley asks the well-dressed man in his fancy car, "Then who *do* we shoot?" The scene's emotional epiphany is Muley's tearful, despairing apostrophe to the land as he grasps a handful of dirt: "And that's what makes it ourn—bein' born on it—and, and workin' on it—and dyin'—*dying* on it. And not no piece o' paper with writin' on it!" The camera looks down compassionately on Muley's squatting figure, his face hidden from view by the brim of his hat; Muley's defeatism throws into relief the Joads' stoical refusal to be crushed by similar circumstances.

Tom's defiance is encapsulated in his parting words to his mother: "I'll be all aroun' in the dark. . . . Wherever there's a fight so hungry people can eat, I'll be there. Wherever there's a cop beatin' up a guy, I'll be there." After that overwhelmingly moving scene, Ford planned to end the film with the long shot of Tom, in silhouette, silently walking up a hill at sunrise. Ford recalled that he wanted to end "on a down note, and the way Zanuck changed it, it came out on an upbeat." However, Ford's ending would have been ambiguous rather than simply downbeat. Although Tom was forced to leave his family, he was heading off to a new life as a political activist. "[A]s long as I'm an outlaw anyways," he tells his mother, "maybe I can do sump'n." Ford's ending would have given a subversive yet still heroic twist to the iconography of Fonda's Abe Lincoln walking up the hill to face his destiny in *Young Mr. Lincoln*. Zanuck and

Johnson both took the responsibility for the decision to end the film instead with Ma Joad's uplifting speech, lifted from a spot two-thirds into the book: "[W]e keep a-comin'. We're the people that live. They can't wipe us out. They can't lick us. We'll go on forever, Pa, 'cause we're the people."

Delivered with fierce confidence by Jane Darwell, the speech is undeniably moving. But the writing and placement of this self-conscious thematic summary by a character not usually given to such grand remarks skirts the edge of sentimental cliché. Upon reflection, the viewer may feel he or she is being sent out of the theater with an unduly optimistic view of a tragic situation, a Hollywood happy ending pasted over a national disgrace. This scene appeared in the shooting script as an addendum dated November 1, 1939, when Ford was still involved in principal photography. But the story goes that when Zanuck asked Ford what he thought about the new ending, Ford said it sounded fine and told Zanuck to direct it himself. It's evident that Ford was less than entirely enthusiastic about the idea but accepted it anyway; his decision not to shoot the ending himself was a clear sign of distancing himself from the decision. Ford told Bogdanovich that while Tom leaving was the "logical end" of the story, "the mother had a little soliloquy which was all right."

Ford's preferred ending with Tom heading off to his uncertain future would have put the emphasis, as in some of his later films, on the loner status of the protagonist rather than on the community he represents. But perhaps Zanuck was right after all. This urgent work of populist filmmaking needed to send audiences out on a note of defiant, indomitable courage. Dust bowl balladeer Woody Guthrie had a similar credo: "Don't ever let nothin' get you plumb down."[17]

While *The Grapes of Wrath* can be appraised in terms of how much has been lost from Steinbeck's book, it also can be looked at in terms of how much the filmmakers have retained from the novel. What remains is powerful enough to make the film Hollywood's strongest indictment of depression era socioeconomic conditions. Other Hollywood films had dealt with the national

17. At the request of Victor Records, Guthrie wrote a song version of the movie in seventeen verses, "Tom Joad." Set to the tune of the outlaw ballad "John Hardy," "Tom Joad" became a classic in its own right. After the lyrics were published in the *Daily Worker,* the song was included in Guthrie's 1940 two-album set *Dust Bowl Ballads.* Guthrie reviewed the film in "Woody Sez," his column for the Communist Party newspaper: "Seen the pitcher last night, *Grapes of Wrath,* best cussed pitcher I ever seen. . . . Shows the damn bankers, men that broke us and the dust that choked us, and comes right out in plain old English, and says what to do about it. . . . Go to see *Grapes of Wrath* pardner, go to see it and don't miss. You was the star in that picture."

calamity—including William Wellman's *Wild Boys of the Road* (1933), King Vidor's *Our Daily Bread* (1934), and Frank Capra's *Mr. Deeds Goes to Town* (1936)—but none matched the feeling of raw authenticity Ford achieved. Johnson's script also has some advantages over the novel, presenting a simpler, leaner narrative line in place of Steinbeck's often repetitious structure and keeping the biblical simplicity of his dialogue while jettisoning his preachy rhetorical interludes. And what Zanuck and Johnson muted in the screenplay, Ford and cinematographer Gregg Toland compensate for with searingly eloquent imagery.

After seeing the film in December 1939, Steinbeck expressed relief to his agent: "Zanuck has more than kept his word. He has a hard, straight picture in which the actors are submerged so completely that it looks and feels like a documentary film and certainly it has a hard, truthful ring. No punches are pulled—in fact, with descriptive matter removed, it is a harsher thing than the book, by far. It seems unbelievable but it is true." Steinbeck's opinion remained constant over the years. He told Henry Fonda in 1958 that he had watched a 16mm print of the film that "[director Elia] Kazan had stolen from Twentieth Century–Fox. It's a wonderful picture, just as good as it ever was. It doesn't look dated."

The Grapes of Wrath was Ford's first collaboration with Toland, Hollywood's greatest cinematographer of that period; they subsequently worked together on *The Long Voyage Home* and the World War II documentary *December 7th*. Toland photographed *Grapes* on loan-out from the Samuel Goldwyn Studios, where his most important films had included William Wyler's *Dead End, Wuthering Heights,* and *The Westerner.* The cinematographer's creative personality was so strong that he left his stylistic mark on every director he worked with, including Ford and Welles. Ford and Toland studied and imitated the work of such depression-era still photographers as Dorothea Lange, Walker Evans, Margaret Bourke-White, and Ben Shahn, as well as Pare Lorentz's U.S. government documentary films *The Plow That Broke the Plains* (1936) and *The River* (1937), whose imagery had previously influenced Steinbeck. The filmmakers benefited greatly from the participation of Tom Collins, the Weedpatch camp manager who had helped Steinbeck with the research for his novel and served as the film's technical consultant.

Toland's celebrated use of the "deep focus" technique, allowing objects far from the camera to remain as sharp as those in the foreground, gives a feeling of three-dimensional reality to the images in *The Grapes of Wrath*. The virtuosity of Toland's work is subtle and naturalistic, rarely employing the extreme, show-offy deep-focus effects he would display in Ford's subsequent film, *The Long Voyage Home*. Ford marveled that Toland "did a great job of photography [in *Grapes*]—absolutely nothing but nothing to photograph, not *one* beautiful thing in there—just sheer good photography." The film abounds with unforgettable images such as those of the Joads' arrival at the Hooverville camp, tracking shots that let us see the camp through their eyes as they drive slowly through the rows of tents and makeshift shacks, passing hungry people with questioning, accusatory faces. Toland's use of low-key lighting in *Grapes* is audacious but never arty, always employed for emotional and poetic effect, as in the haunting nocturnal scenes of Tom's return to his deserted home, Ma's burning of her keepsakes before their departure for California, and the impromptu roadside funeral of Grandpa Joad (Charley Grapewin).

The same spare eloquence resonates through most of the performances. Fonda had to agree to an onerous seven-year contract with Fox to play Tom Joad, and he paid for the opportunity with a string of mostly forgettable projects. But his Tom Joad, coiled with feral rage yet still capable of the most selfless generosity, is the performance of a lifetime. The one weak link in the cast is character actress Jane Darwell, who often lapses into bathos as Ma Joad. Philip Dunne felt that Darwell's "corny" performance "ruined the picture"; Dunne would have preferred the formidable Louise Dresser, who was seriously considered for the role. Ford wanted the gaunt, rustic-looking Beulah Bondi, whose ability to navigate a wide emotional range between kindliness and an almost fanatical intensity would have brought more nuances to the character.

Welles disliked *The Grapes of Wrath* because Ford "made that into a story about mother love. Sentiment is Jack's vice. When he escapes it, you get a perfect kind of innocence." Such innocence can be found, however, in the poignant scene of Tom dancing with his mother as he serenades her with "Red River Valley" (the traditional song used so effectively as the movie's theme music, played by Danny Borzage on his accordion). The theme of mother love is, of course, a very Irish, very Fordian preoccupation. And there is something very truthful about the inevitable clash between Tom's radicalization and his mother's conservative influence in trying to hold the family together. In that archetypal conflict between the Fordian "noble outlaw" and his idealized mother figure can be found much of the director's heart and soul.

Confounding the so-called industry experts, *The Grapes of Wrath* was a success at the box office (grossing $1.1 million, the best performance of any Fox film that year). It also received rapturous critical acclaim. In his oft-quoted *New York Times* review, Frank S. Nugent wrote, "In the vast library where the celluloid literature of the screen is stored there is one small, uncrowded shelf devoted to the cinema's masterworks, to those films which by dignity of theme and excellence of treatment seem to be of enduring artistry. . . . To that shelf of screen classics, Twentieth Century–Fox yesterday added its version of John

Steinbeck's *The Grapes of Wrath*. . . . Direction, when it is as brilliant as Mr. Ford's has been, is easy to recognize, but impossible to describe. . . . *The Grapes of Wrath* is just about as good as any picture has a right to be."[18]

Ford won his second Academy Award for directing the film, which was nominated for six other Oscars, including best picture. Its only other winner was Jane Darwell in the supporting actress category. Henry Fonda was nominated for best actor but was bypassed by the Academy in favor of his close friend James Stewart, who was honored with a consolation Oscar for *The Philadelphia Story* after being bypassed by the Academy for *his* part of a lifetime in 1939's *Mr. Smith Goes to Washington*. *Grapes* won the best picture award from the New York Film Critics Circle, which also recognized Ford for directing both it and *The Long Voyage Home* in 1940.

The reputation of *The Grapes of Wrath* has suffered somewhat as socially conscious filmmaking has become less fashionable. Auteurist critics have tended to downgrade *Grapes* in the Ford canon because it is based on such an important literary work and because Zanuck exerted such influence over the production. But those factors should not prevent people from recognizing the enduring quality of *The Grapes of Wrath*.

Ford revisited—and parodied—the themes and milieu of *The Grapes of Wrath* a year later in *Tobacco Road,* Fox's film version of Erskine Caldwell's 1932 novel and the long-running stage adaptation by Jack Kirkland. Unlike Steinbeck's novel, Caldwell's revels in the comedy and pathos of proletarian defeatism. Ford evidently welcomed the opportunity to unwind from the liberal gravitas of *The Grapes of Wrath* with this bizarre divertissement about a decadent white-trash family in rural Georgia. Starring Charley Grapewin as the shiftless and raucous old farmer Jeeter Lester, *Tobacco Road* looks like something Ford would have made on a drunken bender, interrupted by crying jags and bouts of hymn singing ("Brighten the Corner Where You Are"). Schizoid in the extreme, it alternates between the crudest, most grating low-comedy scenes Ford ever directed and some deftly sketched moments of sentiment as moving as any he ever put on the screen.

Andrew Sarris writes that Ford transformed Jeeter "from a greedy barnyard

---

18. Shortly after writing that review, Nugent was hired by Fox as a screenwriter. This has been seen as a cynical move by Zanuck to get rid of a critic who frequently panned the studio's films (Fox had cut back on its advertising in the *Times* in 1939 to protest Nugent's reviews, particularly his slams at Tyrone Power). Nugent spent his four years at Fox critiquing scripts before production and not being allowed to write screenplays. His break as a screenwriter did not come until he wrote Ford's *Fort Apache* (1948).

animal to a seedy but serious mainstay of tradition." True enough, for Grapewin's wonderful performance enriches and ennobles a character that could have been merely a caricature. The elegiac montage of Jeeter and his wife, Ada (Elizabeth Patterson), leaving the land to make their way to the poorhouse is heartbreakingly beautiful, the melancholy stillness of Ford's compositions lit with late-afternoon chiaroscuro by the masterful Arthur C. Miller. But for the director of *The Grapes of Wrath* to stoop to ridiculing impoverished sharecroppers as lazy and stupid, as Ford does throughout much of *Tobacco Road,* is inexcusable. William Tracy's hideous screeching as the moronic Dude Lester and the embarrassing spectacle of Ward Bond and Gene Tierney writhing toward each other in the dirt to convey sexual passion are among the lowest points in Ford's oeuvre.

It's almost as if *Tobacco Road* were directed by Ford's evil twin, the dark-hearted mess he became whenever he crawled into his sleeping bag between pictures to drink himself incoherent. Nunnally Johnson, who wrote the screenplay for *Tobacco Road,* correctly described it as a "fiasco."

On the studio set of a London pub during the making of *The Long Voyage Home* (1940), Ford posed for a revealing publicity photograph. He leaned on the end of the bar smiling sheepishly and hoisting a beer in the company of some of his actors and several of the most prominent American painters of the day—Thomas Hart Benton, Grant Wood, Luis Quintanilla, Georges Schreiber, and Ernest Fiene. Ford said it was producer Walter Wanger's idea to pay those and four other painters to observe the filming "and paint anything they wanted on the set. I didn't like the idea at first, but the artists proved to be a grand bunch of guys." By posing for the picture, Ford was sending a not-so-subtle signal that he wanted to be regarded as their peer, a filmmaker whose work stood comparison with the finest art his country could produce.

Not even *The Informer* does as much visual preening for attention as *The Long Voyage Home.* That's not to say that the work of Ford and cinematographer Gregg Toland was anything less than stunning. An almost abstract exercise in the creation of a doom-laden mood with deep pools of light and shadow, filmed largely on cramped studio sets, this adaptation of sea plays by Eugene O'Neill is one of the most avant-garde films ever made in Hollywood. Ford had an unusual degree of artistic freedom because he made the film as a coproduction between Wanger and Argosy Pictures, the director's newly formed partnership with Merian C. Cooper (Ford was chairman of the board and Cooper was president). Filmed in thirty-seven days, *The Long Voyage Home* was made for a modest $682,495 (only $6,000 over budget), largely at the Goldwyn Studios, but with a few exteriors at Wilmington Harbor.

Ford and Toland broke all the rules of conventional Hollywood cinematography by shooting directly into floodlights, showing water cascading into the lens during a storm sequence, and setting up shots with the extreme foreground-background tension made possible by Toland's deep-focus technique. From the opening tour de force of silent storytelling—native women coming onto a British ship bearing fruit and rum on a sultry night in the West Indies—to the ending shot of shadows descending on the deck, leaving the solitary Donkeyman (Arthur Shields) in silhouette as he grieves for a lost shipmate, *The Long Voyage Home* is masterfully filmed yet extravagantly overwrought. Ford's high regard for Toland's work was evident in the fact that the great cinematographer receives credit on the same title card as the director, a gesture Welles would repeat on Toland's subsequent film, *Citizen Kane.*

After screening *The Long Voyage Home* at the University of Chicago in 1968, Ford recalled the genesis of the project: "I was talking with Eugene O'Neill (he was a very dear friend of mine) about it, and he said, 'Jack, you must have seen my trilogy *The Long Voyage Home*' [actually a tetralogy of one-act plays written between 1913 and 1917: *Bound East for Cardiff, In the Zone, The Long Voyage Home,* and *The Moon of the Caribbees*]. And I said I had. So he suggested combining them into a picture, and I said, 'That's a wonderful idea.' So we knocked it out. And after it was finished, United Artists set aside a projection room once a month [in San Francisco] and Gene would come and watch *The Long Voyage Home.* He loved it. And that's probably the greatest professional compliment I've ever had." After first seeing the film in July 1940, O'Neill told Ford in a telegram: "MY CONGRATULATIONS ON A GRAND DEEPLY MOVING AND BEAUTIFUL PIECE OF WORK. IT IS A GREAT PICTURE AND I HOPE YOU ARE AS PROUD OF IT AS I AM."

Dudley Nichols's brilliant adaptation honors O'Neill by not following the plays slavishly but instead offering appropriate verbal and visual equivalents to the playwright's rough-hewn prose poetry. Updated to World War II, the film is largely set aboard the British merchant marine ship SS *Glencairn,* transporting a load of TNT through the war zone en route to England. As the title indicates, the dramatic focus is explicitly on the archetypal Fordian male conflict between the urge to wander and the yearning for home. The men of the *Glencairn* envy people who have homes on land, but they dread the constraints of such a life and prefer the rootless company of their fellow sailors. The irony of their "freedom" at sea is how trapped they are in their claustrophobic quarters and their perilous profession. Conveying an omnipresent atmosphere of fear and resignation, stifled sensuality and profound loneliness, *The Long Voyage Home* benefits greatly from Ford's bleak, unromantic understanding of the fate of seamen.

The most memorable performance in *The Long Voyage Home* is offered by John Wayne as the good-natured and boyish Swedish sailor Ole Olsen. Wayne managed a creditable and endearing Swedish accent, thanks to lessons from Danish actress Osa Massen. The night before reporting to work on *The Long Voyage Home,* Wayne had been filming "until probably midnight on a picture that we'd made in six days for Republic [*Three Faces West*]. . . . I wanna tell you, [playing Ole] was quite a switch from the night before, [when I was] knocking people around and jumping on a horse." Ole yearns to see his mother on their farm outside Stockholm ("Just like a little boy I feel home-sick"), but he keeps missing the boat home whenever he drinks anything stronger than "yinyer beer." In the first of her four roles for Ford, Mildred Natwick is funny and touching as the forlorn, tipsy prostitute Freda, guilt-ridden over her complicity in helping a crimp (J. M. Kerrigan) slip Ole a Mickey Finn.

Despite his fine work in this film as the only sailor with a hopeful future, Wayne still was not taken entirely seriously by Ford as an actor. Continuing to try him out for size as a heroic figure, Ford was enamored of Duke's person-ality but as yet did not think him capable of playing complex characters. When editor Robert Parrish, who hoped to become a director, asked Ford how he drew such powerful performances from Wayne in *Stagecoach* and *The Long Voy-age Home,* Ford told him, "Count the times Wayne talks. That's the answer. Don't let him talk unless you have something that needs to be said."

Not surprisingly, the bleak and arty *Long Voyage Home* was a succès d'estime but not a popular favorite. It was nominated for best picture and five other Academy Awards, including screenplay and cinematography, but won none—that year Ford received his Oscar for directing *The Grapes of Wrath.*

With war coming ever closer to America in 1940, the need for modern, so-phisticated combat photography units was becoming more urgent. Ford had foreseen that need when he joined the Naval Reserve in 1934 and began plan-ning for possible American involvement in war with Germany and Japan. His reconnaissance missions to Mexico and elsewhere on behalf of the navy, which continued until February 1941, were part of those preparations. But despite the outbreak of war in Europe in September 1939, the United States remained largely isolationist, and its military bureaucracy was slow to mod-ernize photographic operations. Impatient with the situation and unaccus-tomed to going through official channels, Lieutenant Commander John Ford, USNR, took it upon himself in 1939 to begin organizing what originally was called the Naval Volunteer Photographic Unit, devoted to "carrying out the original plan" for which he had been commissioned.

"John Ford's Navy," as it was known in Hollywood, recruited and trained experienced technicians from the studios' camera, sound, laboratory, and crafts departments. Ford received valuable organizational assistance from Gregg Toland, who trained the unit's cinematographers; sound engineer Edmund H. Hansen, a lieutenant commander in the Naval Reserve, who ran the sound division; and the dapper, diplomatic Lieutenant Commander Alfred J. "Jack" Bolton, USN (Ret.), who served as a liaison between Hollywood and the navy.

Ford submitted a written proposal to the navy in 1940 for acceptance of his volunteers as a Naval Photographic Organization to document naval combat activities for operational, intelligence, historical, and propaganda purposes. The proposal also was signed by Bolton; Hansen; Ford's *Air Mail* screenwriter Frank W. "Spig" Wead, a retired lieutenant commander in the navy; and Ford's producing partner in Argosy Pictures, Merian C. Cooper, then a captain in the U.S. Army Air Corps Reserve. They explained that a more modern photographic organization was needed because the current war already had seen an unprecedented use of photography in naval and other military operations, particularly by the Germans. Pointing out that the use of film reconnaissance and documentation of combat could change the course of battle, they set forth some far-reaching proposals. Predicting the use of radio and television to transmit films of operations and intelligence, they noted that "the development of television for such purposes is an urgent naval photographic research problem, not beyond early realization."

Most of the proposal, however, was spent discussing the morale and propaganda value of motion pictures to obtain "the complete support of the nation" for naval operations: "To our own people, radio, newspapers, [and] motion pictures blast contrary ideas back and forth. Some say our Navy is old-fashioned. . . . The average man has no conception of our Navy's weight, prowess, power, high morale, and striking force. A series of films which show factually the power of the American Navy is bound to give a psychological lift to the whole nation. Let them see the rigors of training; the skill of execution in maneuvers; how money is spent for sea power. . . .

"The German nation in seven years was changed from an indifferent, apathetic, despondent people into a mighty military machine, by the use of radio, printed words and motion pictures, until they were prepared to follow one man and fight the world.

"Our use would be different. Our morale purpose is to show that a Democracy can and must create a greater fighting machine, in spirit and being, than a dictator power."

In April 1940, through Bolton's intercession, Ford's navy acquired official status as the Naval Reserve Photographic Section of the San Diego–based Eleventh Naval District. Ford was appointed recruiting officer to enlist photographic personnel and instructors to study the use of photography in "tactics, ballistics and training and historical films." Believing strongly in the cause of the upcoming fight against fascism, Ford threw himself with enthusiasm into the practical tasks at hand, serving without pay. But his emotions were especially stirred by the ceremonial aspects of military command, the drilling, training, and parading with the full panoply of flags, uniforms, and weaponry. Seeing World War II service as an exciting adventure that would make up for his failure to win acceptance to Annapolis and his lack of service in World War I, Ford approached the upcoming fray with something of a Walter Mittyish perspective. In a 1941 navy biographical sheet, Ford boyishly noted that though he had won two Academy Awards and three awards from the New York Film Critics Circle ("supposedly the greatest honor in the industry"), as well as honors for his films from Italy and Belgium, "I state with pardonable pride that I am the proud possessor of the Small Arms Expert's medal."

Ford's Photographic Section started regular weekly training with 38 officers and 122 enlisted men. By May 1941, it had signed up such men as Cooper; cameramen Joseph H. August, Sid Hickox, John Fulton, Alfred Gilks, and Harold Rosson; editors Otho Lovering and Robert Parrish; and special effects technician E. R. "Ray" Kellogg. At its full strength, the section included about 300 men, many of whom joined after the draft was reinstated in September 1940 and American involvement in the war seemed increasingly inevitable. Before Pearl Harbor, about a third of Ford's men volunteered for active service in the U.S. Navy.

Every Tuesday night from eight to midnight, his ragtag band of volunteers drilled and received instruction on Twentieth Century Fox soundstages, thanks to Zanuck, who had military ambitions of his own. The men used weapons from the Fox prop department and uniforms borrowed from the Western Costume Company. They took supplemental classes on Monday and Wednesday evenings at other locations, including the Los Angeles Naval Reserve Armory, learning how to use various types of camera and sound equipment under wartime conditions and how to develop and print their own motion pictures and stills in the field or on board ship. The training sessions included Toland's "Ten-Minute Talk on Elementary Photography" and a course in "Military Indoctrination" taught by Ford, Bolton, Jack Pennick, and Ben Grotsky. Pennick, a pug-faced ex-marine, was Ford's loyal drillmaster, and Grotsky, a colorful character from Brooklyn, came out of retirement as a chief petty officer in the navy to join the unit.

Ford's attempts to have his Photographic Section accepted as part of regular navy operations were frustrated. His unorthodox approach to documentary filmmaking was threatening to military bureaucrats used to following safe, established procedures. Partly to show the brass what the unit could do, and partly for their own training, Ford's enlisted men made a film of the mobilization and induction ceremonies of the newly formed California State Guard, held at the Santa Anita racetrack. Shot in 1940 as a shakedown assignment without help from their commissioned officers, the completed film was shown throughout California to encourage enlistment in the guard. But the navy stalled when Ford volunteered his men. Undaunted, sure they would be needed, they continued training in the expectation that America soon would enter the war.

As chairman of the Research Council of the Academy of Motion Picture Arts and Sciences, Darryl Zanuck began coordinating Hollywood's production of military training films in 1940 under contract from the government. Zanuck was commissioned a reserve lieutenant colonel in the Army Signal Corps in January 1941. Actively campaigning for America's entry into the war alongside embattled Britain, he not only produced training films at Fox but also turned the studio's resources to making entertainment features with war-related themes, such as *A Yank in the RAF* (1941) with Tyrone Power and Betty Grable. Over the objection of the Signal Corps, which was jealous of its longtime role in supervising the making of army training films, Zanuck was delegated in July 1941 by chief of staff General George C. Marshall to undertake a tour of training camps and service schools to study the use of training films. He returned with a recommendation that their production and distribution be modernized and centralized under a Hollywood executive commissioned into service for that purpose.

When the Selective Service Act became law in 1940, authorizing the drafting of 630,000 men, there was an urgent need for four basic training films to be shown at all army reception centers: *Sex Hygiene, Personal Hygiene, The Articles of War,* and *Military Courtesy and Customs of the Service.* Without waiting for all the financial arrangements to be made with the government for production of those films, Zanuck authorized Fox to go ahead with the first two pictures as soon as the scripts were approved by the War Department. Ford was assigned the direction of *Sex Hygiene,* a half-hour film for the Signal Corps to educate inductees about the dangers of venereal disease.

Shot quickly at Fox and ready for use by March 1941, the black-and-white *Sex Hygiene* is suitably horrifying but also seems somewhat tongue-in-cheek. Coming directly from making *Tobacco Road,* Ford was in a bawdy mood when he filmed the scenes of soldiers (including George Reeves, later famous as

TV's Superman) playing pool in an army canteen before one young man makes the mistake of slipping off to a brothel. The results of his and others' sexual follies are displayed in a graphic illustrated lecture by a medical officer, intoned in stentorian fashion by Charles Trowbridge, who later was promoted by Ford to admiral and/or general in *They Were Expendable, When Willie Comes Marching Home,* and *The Wings of Eagles.* Perhaps it is fitting that the one Ford film dealing explicitly with sexual themes makes the subject seem so thoroughly revolting.

"Ford just loved it!" recalled the film's editor, Gene Fowler Jr. ". . . I think he took a perverse pleasure in showing this shocking stuff." Zanuck once dropped into Ford's office when the director was interviewing a syphilis victim covered with sores. "He don't scare me," growled Zanuck. "Send him down to makeup." Another time Ford sent wheelchair-bound syphilitics to an adjacent soundstage so they could watch scantily clad dancing girls filming a musical number.

The film's preachiness, urging total abstinence as the best safeguard against VD, seems laughably unrealistic even by 1941 standards, but *Sex Hygiene* reportedly did its job well in scaring the bejesus out of millions of GIs. When Bogdanovich asked Ford what his own reaction was to the film, Ford replied, "I looked at it and threw up."

It's ironic that Ford considered *How Green Was My Valley* his most autobiographical film, because he came to the project so late in its development. Richard Llewellyn, an Englishman of Welsh descent, wrote the best-selling 1939 novel about the decline of a turn-of-the-century mining village in south Wales. Ford was not the first director assigned to the film by Zanuck. William Wyler spent three months preparing the picture. He cast many of the parts, oversaw the construction of the sets designed by Richard Day and Nathan Juran, and spent ten weeks working on the script with Philip Dunne. In Dunne's view, Ford made little contribution to the script beyond adding some bits of business and lines of dialogue, the most memorable of which is Barry Fitzgerald's reply to a half-blind man who asks him to help search for miners trapped in a cave-in: "'Tis a coward I am—but I will hold your coat." But while others were primarily responsible for shaping the adaptation of the novel before Ford was assigned to the project, Dunne nevertheless acknowledged to me that Ford "did what any good director does—he made it his picture while he was shooting it."

Jealous of the blockbuster success of David O. Selznick's *Gone with the Wind,* Zanuck initially envisioned *How Green Was My Valley* as his answer to Selznick on a similarly grandiose scale. It was to be a four-hour Technicolor epic shot on location in Wales, starring Tyrone Power as the grown-up Huw Morgan, Laurence Olivier as the preacher Mr. Gruffydd, Katharine Hepburn as Angharad, and Greer Garson as Bronwen (none of these actors appeared in Ford's film). Zanuck rejected scripts by Liam O'Flaherty and Screen Writers Guild president Ernest Pascal because he thought they put too much emphasis on the struggle over the unionization of the coal mine in the village of Cwm Rhondda. The fact that Zanuck was making the film at all was remarkable, because he was a dedicated foe of organized labor, a leader of the Hollywood hierarchy in its battle against the formation of the directors' and writers' guilds. In a story conference on May 22, 1940, Zanuck said:

"I was very disappointed in the [Pascal] script, mainly because it has turned into a labor story and a sociological problem story instead of a great, human, warm story about real living people. . . . I got the impression that we are trying to do an English *Grapes of Wrath* and prove that the mineowners were very mean and that the laborers finally won out over them. All this might be fine if it were happening today, like *Grapes of Wrath,* but this is years ago and who gives a damn? The smart thing to do is to try to keep all of the rest in the background and focus mainly on the human story as seen through Huw's eyes."

Like the screenwriter who preceded him, Philip Dunne was a leading figure in the SWG, which was still fighting for recognition from the producers when he drafted the shooting script in the summer of 1940. Dunne managed to satisfy Zanuck's concerns by using the political conflict as a backdrop to the drama of the Morgan family. Even so, Zanuck grumbled that Dunne had talked him into "making a goddam pro-labor picture," a comment the writer called "absolute nonsense" since "nobody ever talked Darryl Zanuck into making anything he didn't want to make." They compromised on the qualified endorsement of the union by the liberal-minded preacher: "First, have your union. You need it. Alone you are weak. Together you're strong. But remember that with strength goes responsibility—to others and yourselves. For you cannot conquer injustice with more injustice—only with justice and the help of God."

"Innocuous as it may sound today, in 1941, when the picture was released, it was a daring and even radical statement," Dunne wrote. "At that time, the very right of labor to organize was a hot political issue. . . ." However, the screenplay and to an even greater extent the film portray the coming of the union to the valley not as an unalloyed triumph but as a tragic necessity.

Ford brought to the film's depiction of labor strife his experience of several years taking a stand amidst bitter tension between the SDG and the studios. His conflicting liberal and conservative instincts are reflected in the schism in the Morgan family between the older sons' belief in unionism and their father's stubborn defense of patriarchal capitalism while attacking unions as "socialist nonsense." Ford understands the emotional arguments on both sides, but his allegiances are staunchly pro-union. He depicts the coal mine as a malevolent force blighting the valley and its people, looming over the homes of the miners and periodically belching out hellish black smoke and flames, spreading its slag and smog over the once verdant valley. And yet we feel Ford's ambivalence toward social change when the young Huw Morgan (Roddy McDowall) asks Gruffydd (Walter Pidgeon) what it means that the men have gone out on strike. The minister somberly replies, "It means that something has gone out of this valley that may never be replaced."

Even after the political issues of the screenplay were settled, Zanuck and Dunne still had to solve the problem of running time. The Fox front office in New York was becoming uneasy with the costly project, so Zanuck decided that the script should be cut in half to a conventional two-hour length and that the film should be made in black-and-white. Because of the outbreak of war in Europe, location shooting was out of the question, so the spectacular set of the winding street of homes leading up to the mine was constructed on the Fox ranch in the Malibu hills. Ford was busy making *Tobacco Road,* so Wyler was borrowed from Goldwyn to direct *How Green Was My Valley,* with Gregg Toland to serve as cinematographer. Wyler and Dunne spent several weeks fine-tuning the adaptation, which skillfully interweaves drama and comedy as a way of keeping this tragic story bearable to watch. But they were finding it hard to tell the sprawling story of Huw Morgan from boyhood to manhood, when a child actor was to be succeeded on-screen by Tyrone Power.

I always felt that Roddy is the real auteur of the picture," Dunne told me with a wry smile.

Roderick McDowall, thirteen years old when he played Huw, was the son of a British merchant marine officer who had evacuated his wife and two children to New York during the London blitz in 1940. A movie actor since the age of five, Roddy made his American film debut in Fritz Lang's 1941 Fox film *Man Hunt.* He was one of six young Britons tested in New York for the role of Huw.

"The other five were perfect little Freddie Bartholomews, with Eton accents and everything," recalled Dunne, who watched the screen tests with Wyler in California. "And then there was this sort of gangly-looking, strange-looking kid. Somebody—I'm told it was Lew Schreiber, the casting director—said, 'Oh, you don't want to see this. The kid's wall-eyed, not very pretty.' But Willy and I got a glimpse of the test and we both said, 'No! Let's see it!' When the lights came up, the first thing I said was, 'Willy, that solves our length problem.' I put it that way because we had this whole big problem of another movie starting with Ty Power. I said, 'This solves our length problem, because they'll *never* forgive us if we let that boy grow up'—he was so good in the test. Willy said, 'Absolutely, you're right.' Later, when I went on the set with Ford, he was rehearsing the scene where the cruel teacher [Morton Lowery] tells Huw to sit on the dunce's chair. Ford said, 'Watch him feel for the chair with his ass. He knows how to act, this kid.'"

Only the hands of the grown-up Huw are shown on-screen as he packs his belongings in his mother's shawl and prepares to leave his valley in the film's opening shot. While the camera moves past Huw toward an open window, the narrator (Irving Pichel) marvels that the mind will "hold clear and bright the memory of what happened years ago." The scene gradually changes, as if by Huw's magical desire, to show his lost Eden, his alluring memory images of "so much that was good that is gone." The decision to use this kind of distancing, reflective, often contrapuntal narration, then considered an almost avant-garde technique in Hollywood, came not from Ford (as *Time*'s reviewer thought) but from Zanuck, who said in his first script meeting with Dunne, "We should do much of the picture with [Huw] as an offstage commentator, with many of the scenes running silent with nothing but his voiceover."

But after Dunne rewrote the script to focus on Huw's boyhood, the project was abruptly canceled. Not only was the New York office worried about "Willy's reputation as an extravagant director," Dunne reported, "they just thought it was a bad script, a bad story. They said, 'No stars. Who cares about it? It's a tragedy. Who cares about a lot of Welsh miners whose family breaks up?' Zanuck endeared himself to me forever by writing a letter to the New York office saying, 'This is the finest script I've ever had, and I'm going to make this picture. If I can't make it now, I'll make it later. And if necessary I'll take it to another studio.' Which was a big threat."

New York acquiesced.

Zanuck sent for me," wrote Dunne, "and there in his office sat Jack Ford, chewing on his handkerchief and greeting me with insulting remarks about the script. Ford had agreed to bring in the picture for a million dollars, and on that basis New York had told Zanuck he could go ahead."

Ford accepted some, but not all, of the casting choices of Wyler and Zanuck. As Dunne noted, "the one really phony actor" in the picture is Walter Pidgeon, who gives a stiff and insipid performance as Gruffydd. But Pidgeon's was the marquee name that helped sell the picture. Roddy McDowall, on the other hand, gives perhaps the finest performance by a juvenile actor in movie history. When I offered that opinion to McDowall in 1997, he showed his innate modesty and film scholarship by gently correcting me: "Oh, no— Jackie Coogan in *The Kid*."

Ford, who had done such a sensitive job directing Shirley Temple in *Wee Willie Winkie,* felt a symbiotic affinity with the emotions of the wide-eyed, intelligent, unusually somber young Huw, who grows up in the same time period as the director's boyhood. McDowall later said he was never conscious of Ford's direction: "He was so terrific to me, which was very wise, 'cause if he hadn't been, I would have tightened up like a drum. So I think he was a very shrewd psychologist."

Three other cast members went on to become key members of the John Ford Stock Company. The veteran Scottish actor Donald Crisp won an Academy Award for his sturdy and quietly moving supporting performance as the family patriarch, Gwilym Morgan. Wyler's choice for Bronwen, Huw's beloved sister-in-law, was a native Irishwoman, Greer Garson, but Ford preferred the British actress Anna Lee, a lovely, ladylike blonde. Born Joanna Boniface Winnifrith in England and always called "Boniface" by the director, Lee continued acting for her beloved "Pappy" Ford until the end of his career in Hollywood, usually in roles similar to the one she played in *How Green Was My Valley,* that of a grieving widow. Ford became the godfather to her sons John and Tim Stafford, both of whom acted in his 1963 film *Donovan's Reef,* and he gave away Lee in her 1970 marriage to novelist Robert Nathan.

For Huw's emotionally stifled sister, Angharad, Ford bypassed Wyler's preference, Katharine Hepburn; Ford no doubt would have found it difficult to work with Hepburn in the aftermath of their failed romance, particularly on a film that would have required her to enact a failed romance. He turned instead to a fresh Irish face, the ravishing twenty-one-year-old redhead Maureen O'Hara. Discovered by Charles Laughton in the Abbey Theatre company, O'Hara starred with Laughton in Alfred Hitchcock's *Jamaica Inn* (1939) as well as in her first American film the same year, *The Hunchback of Notre Dame.* "I went over to Twentieth Century–Fox to see John Ford," she recalled, "and we discussed his family in Ireland, his parents in Maine, how he grew up. I apparently said something about one of his aunts—'Oh, was she a shawlie?' That means a lady who wears a shawl. And he never forgot it. He always said that the first time he sat and talked movies with me, I insulted his family and called his aunt a shawlie. He just loved to say that. And without a test or anything, I was hired."

Chosen by Ford over Zanuck's preferred actress, Fox contract player Gene Tierney, O'Hara brought an understated passion to Angharad, the role that established her as the director's archetypal leading lady. They went on to make four more features together: *Rio Grande, The Quiet Man, The Long Gray Line,* and *The Wings of Eagles.* Ford's immediate and powerful affinity with O'Hara is evident in her luminous close-ups in *How Green,* filmed with an emotional intensity not seen in his work since his direction of Hepburn in *Mary of Scotland.* Asked by McDowall in a 1991 interview to describe Ford, O'Hara called him "[v]ery sentimental and a terrible prevaricator" who would use any emotional ploy to elicit a performance from an actor. But she added, "The wonderful thing was that he was the boss on the set, and nobody dared step out of line. Which gave the performers such a feeling of security. All you had to worry about was your performance."

Filming *How Green* was a happy and memorable experience for all concerned, with the exception of the distinguished Irish actress Sara Allgood, best known for creating the role of Juno Boyle in the Abbey's 1924 production of Sean O'Casey's *Juno and the Paycock*. Ford argued with Allgood throughout the shooting, even though (because?) as Beth Morgan she was playing a character he modeled after his own mother. But as Anna Lee told me before McDowall's death in 1998, an unusually strong "family" feeling always existed among the film's surviving cast members, a bond encouraged by the director: "Roddy is my love. And Maureen called her daughter Bronwyn after me, after my character. Every year Pappy would give a party for 'The Ladies of the Green Valley,' and we'd all get together, all the women characters from the picture, from Maureen O'Hara to Mae Marsh and Ruth Clifford.

"Pappy liked any actor whom he thought was a professional, but he could not abide an actor who either wanted more or wanted to show off a little or wanted to be known as a star. I remember him saying to somebody, I think it was Walter Pidgeon, 'No stars in my pictures.' Which was true—*he* was the star. A lot of people have said to me, 'You never became a big star in Hollywood. It was because you did all those pictures for John Ford.' And I said I would rather have been a member of John Ford's Stock Company than have won two Oscars as a star."

Ford's long-standing anti-British animus underwent a dramatic transformation in *The Long Voyage Home,* which includes the burial at sea of a British sailor with "Rule, Britannia" playing on the sound track. *How Green Was My Valley* goes further, offering a prayer for the monarch (Queen Victoria) and the Welsh Singers' rendition of "God Save the Queen." Zanuck influenced the film's deference to Great Britain, decreeing, "In view of what is happening today, we certainly don't want to attack the English manner of things, right or wrong." Ford "certainly changed his mind during the war," Lee confirmed. "He'd often tell me that England in World War II was one of the bravest countries he'd ever seen."

Lee nevertheless took the precaution of making up a fictitious Irish great-grandfather named Thomas Michael O'Connell to ensure that Ford would cast her in the film. She also decided not to tell the director that she was pregnant. In the scene of Bronwen learning of the death of her husband, Ivor Morgan (Patric Knowles), Lee had to collapse in a doorway. She suffered a miscarriage, losing one of the twins she was carrying. She told herself afterward that it probably was for the best because the one surviving twin "was all I could handle." Ford visited her in the hospital and always felt guilty about the incident. On every subsequent picture they did together, he was fiercely over-protective. Before she started work, he would line up the cast and crew and demand to know if she was pregnant.

Ford pulled a similar stunt when Philip Dunne made one of his rare appearances on the set of *How Green Was My Valley.* Dunne found the cast and crew lined up serenading him to the tune of "The Farmer in the Dell":

> *We haven't changed a line,*
> *We haven't changed a line.*
> *It's just the way you wro-ote it,*
> *We haven't changed a line.*

Another time Ford summoned Dunne to the set because Sara Allgood objected to the comical scene of Huw's parents discussing his schooling with Gruffydd. Ford "said that the actress decided the scene wouldn't play," Dunne recalled. "So he showed me the scene. I tore it out of the script. I said, 'Now it plays.' You know, that's his old gag. That's what he wanted. He turned to her and said, 'You see, the son-of-a-bitching writer won't help.'" The scene was played virtually as written.

Ford did change some other lines in the screenplay and did his usual creative tightening to substitute visual for verbal storytelling. But his contribution to telling the story goes well beyond the tinkering of a mere *metteur en scène.* The director made *How Green Was My Valley* "live and breathe in a real world."

By the time shooting began on *How Green* in June 1941, Gregg Toland was busy shooting Wyler's film *The Little Foxes,* so Ford hired his frequent Fox collaborator Arthur C. Miller as cinematographer. He and Miller brought an extraordinarily three-dimensional feeling to the village of Cwm Rhondda with an unusual depth of field and their use of split lighting of interior and exterior sets to convey a sense of harmony between man and nature. Ford's characteristic fondness for full group shots and his sparing use of close-ups underscore the cohesive power of social rituals and paradoxically hold this Welsh community together visually even while showing it in the process of forced dissolution. Ford creates an acute feeling of nostalgia to counterpoint the sense of loss that gradually consumes the characters and their village. With its prescient metaphor of the green valley turning black from the waste slag of the coal pits, the film shares a central thematic concern with Welles's 1942 film of Booth Tarkington's novel *The Magnificent Ambersons,* the story of an American city destroyed by the polluting force of the automobile.

The almost tangible physical texture of the village and the mine in *How Green Was My Valley* lends conviction to the subtly dreamlike quality of Ford's staging. Particularly in the early sequences depicting Huw's memories of a happier time, Ford's extensive use of silent footage, balletically stylized, over-laid with narration and Alfred Newman's exquisite musical score, gives the film a larger-than-life, almost fairy-tale feeling. Huw's first encounter with Bronwen as she comes from the next valley to meet her new in-laws is like a scene out of a child's storybook. When Bronwen shyly enters the Morgan home, Huw's mother greets her with "There's lovely you are," and the camera gracefully swings over to a big close-up of Huw. He regards her with dewy-eyed wonderment as the narrator says, "I think I fell in love with Bronwen then. Perhaps it is foolish to think a child could fall in love, but I am the child that was—nobody knows how I felt, except only me." The scene concludes with Bronwen's introduction to her future husband and his four adult broth-ers, lined up and bowing with touching, comical awkwardness.

Ford brought to *How Green Was My Valley* his own reverie of growing up as the "fresh young kid at the table" in a big Irish family. Indeed, the director has been criticized for treating the Welshmen of Cwm Rhondda as if they were his fellow Irishmen, an accurate observation but scarcely a flaw in this Fordian film of memory that deals so feelingly with universal situations of family and communal life. Dunne, watching the rushes, was "horrified" to hear Donald Crisp tipsily singing an Irish drinking song at the wedding celebration—a memorable scene that no doubt greatly helped Crisp win his Oscar. The writer charged onto the set to challenge Ford about the discrepancy. "Ah, go on!" replied Ford. "The Welsh are just another lot of micks and biddies, only Protestants."

Ford could not help thinking of these people as Irishmen, because he saw them not in rational terms but through the intensely emotional prism of his lifelong concern about the destruction of traditional communal ways of life, a theme reflected, as it so often is in his work, in the breakup of a family. Ford's poetic vision of Cwm Rhondda is based less on Llewellyn's book or Dunne's script than on his own boyhood feelings of loss and remembrance. Perhaps the most poignant scene Ford ever directed about family separation occurs when Huw draws lines across a map of the world showing where his older brothers and sister have gone, telling his mother, "And you are the star shining on them from this house, all the way across the continents and the oceans."

The moral decay of Ford's lost paradise, a narrow-minded community flawed by intolerance and Victorian puritanism, is vividly portrayed in the tragic love story of Angharad and Gruffydd. More than any other couple in Ford's work, these two carry melancholy echoes of his love affair with Katharine Hepburn.

Dunne disliked Ford's direction of "the scene where Angharad goes to Gruffydd's quarters at night to try to plead with him so she doesn't have to marry the other guy [the mine owner's son, Iestyn Evans, played by Marten Lamont]. It seemed to me that there was only one way to play the scene physically and that was to have her advancing and him retreating. In other words, she is trying to throw herself at him and say, 'Why?' And his key line to her was, 'I have a duty towards you, let me do it.' Ford played it with Gruffydd coming to her and taking her hand and all kinds of things.

"Ford was always known as a director who couldn't do love scenes. He liked love stories between men. I'm not suggesting that there's a homosexual component, but as you'll recall there are two strong men who love and hate each other, and that's the Ford formula, a friendly rivalry or whatever you want to call it—men without women. Ford was always strongest at that. That's what I thought, and I was scared stiff. I knew what Willy [Wyler] would get out of those scenes, and I do think the love scene was wrong in that conception of having him chasing her around the set, not [wrong in] the way she played it."

However, it could be argued that even if Ford usually is uncomfortable directing love scenes, he excels in evoking the emotion that dominates this scene: unrequited passion. When Gruffydd, who failed to stop his congregation from excommunicating an unmarried mother (Eve March), invokes duty in rejecting Angharad's fervent romantic overtures, the minister's rationale seems the cowardly cover of Victorianism he uses to explain his emotional impotence. Perhaps, too, Ford's Catholicism made him think of Gruffydd not as a minister but as a priest, a man duty-bound to remain celibate. Gruffydd is a man like Ford himself, who seeks in his work the fulfillment that he cannot find in his personal life. But Gruffydd's rejection of Angharad is a tragic choice that, by blocking her natural fecundity and thereby stifling the future, is as symbolically responsible as the coal mine for blighting the life of their community. If Ford had not shown Gruffydd making fumbling attempts at expressing his feelings physically, the scene would have been simply one of a woman offering herself to a passive and unresponsive man, rather than this heartbreaking depiction of a passionate woman trying desperately to break through a conflicted man's emotional repression.

Dunne, like Miller, thought that one of Ford's best directorial decisions in *How Green Was My Valley* was not cutting to a close-up of Gruffydd as he watches Angharad and her wealthy new husband depart their wedding ceremony. Instead, Gruffydd remains a tiny figure in long shot in the church graveyard as the image darkens around him. "That was Ford," Dunne acknowledged. "I didn't write it that way. I wrote it that you saw him carefully packing up the paraphernalia of the wedding. He had married them, and now he's methodically putting everything away. I wanted to say, 'See, he is the preacher, he's going through his job and his heart is breaking,' without ever having to say so. The fact that he's putting this stuff away [means] he's putting his own life away. That was my way of doing it. But he did it pictorially, which is a better way."

Dunne thought Ford had "one of the greatest strokes of luck a director ever had" when the wedding veil suddenly caught a gust of wind and billowed behind Maureen O'Hara as she walked down the steps from the church. O'Hara recalled, "Everybody said, 'Oh, that Ford luck! How wonderful that was! What an effect it had!' *Rubbish!* It wasn't 'Ford luck.' It was three wind machines placed by John Ford, and I had to walk up and down those steps many times while he worked out that the wind machine would do *exactly* that." As she climbs into the carriage, the actor playing her husband, Marten Lamont, reaches out to catch her veil. Dunne thought, "The man shouldn't have *touched* it when the veil spiraled up. My God, what a shot! Luckily, Joe LaShelle, who was the operator, just gave it a little tilt with the camera." I told Dunne I thought the gesture of restraining the veil (probably planned by Ford, like the rest of this meticulously composed shot) is an eloquent metaphor for the repressiveness of Angharad's loveless marriage. "Well, I guess so," the screenwriter responded. "I didn't think beyond that. I said, 'My God, you get a break like that, you leave it alone.'"

In his 1973 eulogy for Ford, François Truffaut described the director as "rugged but inwardly tender" and admitted, "For a long time when I was a journalist, I criticized his conceptions of women—I thought they were too nineteenth century—but when I became a director, I realized that because of him a splendid actress like Maureen O'Hara had been able to play some of the best female roles in American cinema between 1941 and 1957."

O'Hara "was never better than she was in *How Green*," Anna Lee felt. The same can be said of Lee herself, who explained Ford's unusual way of directing women: "Pappy was notorious for not being a woman's director, but I think that was because he really preferred working with men. At first I was a little confused, because I'd been used to directors who actually directed. You see, the strange thing with Ford is you never felt he was actually directing you. If you had a big scene, he'd go off in a corner with you and he'd talk about something usually completely different. And I never knew quite what he was up to, but I supposed it was a form of hypnotism, because you came back and then he'd say, 'Start working.' He never gave you a line reading, which I think is the worst thing a director can do. Somehow or other you gathered what he wanted. And you'd do the scene and you'd find yourself doing things which I'm sure must have come from him, although he never told you to do it. It was really very, very weird.

"Then he always had that trick with his handkerchief. If it was a scene that he thought you were going to be good in, he always stuck his handkerchief into your costume. I remember he did that in my apron in that scene where I come down the hill after Ivor is dead. He just puts in the handkerchief before the scene starts and you think, 'Oh, that's a good-luck talisman or something.' His handkerchiefs, all of them, were shredded at the end [from his chewing on them]. For a long time, I kept one of his handkerchiefs. I'm afraid that it probably went out because somebody thought it was a throwaway, it was chewed so much.

"He was wonderful to work with. I was never so happy in my life than when he told someone that there were only three actresses he cared to work with in Hollywood—Katharine Hepburn, Maureen O'Hara, and Anna Lee."

The single most disturbing aspect of *How Green Was My Valley* is Huw's tragic choice to "go down the colliery with you, sir" (he tells his father) rather than leaving the valley for college to become a doctor or lawyer. Tag Gallagher describes Huw's decision as characteristic of his "wasted, psychotic life. . . . once again in Ford it is a question of duty and tradition gone astray."

It might be added that the boy's decision is a highly complex compound of several elements, including his disenchantment with schooling because of the discrimination he has found outside the valley; his desire to stay close to the woman he chastely loves, his widowed sister-in-law Bronwen; his sense of solidarity with his father, his departed brothers, and their fellow members of the working class; and most of all, his survivor guilt and sense of duty to his aging parents. Blindly putting duty above self is Huw's misguided legacy from his tutor, Mr. Gruffydd, a failed moral leader from whom he learns self-destructive denial and a self-deceptive habit of dreamlike idealism. As Gallagher notes, Ford does not intend us to endorse Huw's decision to ruin his life, which we judge from within the film's framing device of Huw as a chastened man in his fifties finally leaving his boyhood home.

In that light, it is ironic that *How Green Was My Valley* remains one of Ford's most beloved movies. Like Frank Capra's 1946 *It's a Wonderful Life,* Ford's 1941 classic retains a deep hold on the public's emotions despite (and perhaps because of) the fact that it tells an essentially bleak story of the futility of an ordinary man's existence. Both films show the destruction of a once idyllic way of life through the eyes of a well-meaning but masochistic hero who, because of his romantic illusions, fails to leave his hometown until it is too late. And like *Wonderful Life, How Green Was My Valley* has a fantasy happy ending that, at least for critical viewers, serves to underscore the tragedy. In what Ford intended as a cinematic equivalent of a curtain call, he shows Huw, his parents, and his siblings reunited in memory images that even more pointedly resemble a vision of life after death.

When *How Green* opened on October 28, 1941, the United States was on the eve of entering World War II. Ford's bittersweet vision of a lost Eden proved hugely appealing to an audience contemplating a dark and uncertain future. Among the five Academy Awards the film received were Zanuck's first for best picture at Twentieth Century–Fox and Ford's third Oscar as best director. *How Green* was also honored for Crisp's performance, Miller's cinematography, and the interior decoration by Day, Juran, and Thomas Little; it was nominated but did not win for its screenplay, score, film editing, sound recording, and Sara Allgood's supporting performance.

By the time the Oscars were announced on February 26, 1942, the ceremony seemed even more insignificant than usual to Ford. He was in the uniform of the U.S. Navy, filming a war being fought for the survival of civilization. If Ford had never returned from his wartime service, *How Green Was My Valley* would have made a fitting valedictory. He may even have designed it that way, as a summation of the themes of his prewar work and an emotional recapitulation of his own nearly "fifty years of memory."

CHAPTER TEN

"YES—THIS REALLY HAPPENED"

He was the only one of the Hollywood directors that fought who did not forget his men.

CAPTAIN MARK ARMISTEAD, USN (RET.),
ONE OF FORD'S NAVAL AIDES IN WORLD WAR II

As JAPANESE DIVE-bombers and fighter planes swooped over the Midway Atoll in the central Pacific on the morning of June 4, 1942, America's greatest filmmaker was there filming the attack for history. Standing atop the powerhouse on the narrow, triangular sliver of land called Eastern Island, John Ford aimed his 16mm handheld camera directly at the oncoming planes, "yelling at the attacking Zeroes to swing left or right—and cursing them out when they disobeyed directions," Ford screenwriter Frank Nugent reported in his *Saturday Evening Post* profile of the director. One Japanese plane circled in close to where Ford was standing. Just a few yards from Ford's camera, the pilot broke into an enigmatic smile before swerving away from the powerhouse. Ford always remembered that as the most frightening and yet also most exhilarating moment he ever experienced.

Accompanied by a twenty-four-year-old Hollywood assistant cameraman, U.S. Navy Photographer's Mate First Class Jack MacKenzie Jr., Ford started filming the attack shortly after it began at 6:30 A.M. "An obvious and clear target, the power house was repeatedly strafed," wrote William J. Donovan, director of the Office of Strategic Services (OSS), which included Ford's Field Photographic Branch. "Struck by a piece of flying concrete, Commander Ford was rendered unconscious, recovered, carried on, and was subsequently wounded by shrapnel. Despite the extraordinary dangers to which he was subjected voluntarily and the wound which he received, he remained to finish the task assigned to him."

The bomb that knocked Ford unconscious missed the powerhouse by only twenty feet. MacKenzie, who was reloading his camera at the time, recalled being "bounced flat on my face by the terrific explosion of a bomb." Ford reported that he was knocked "goofy for a bit," but not before capturing the sight of that "one big chunk" of concrete hurtling toward the camera in a shower of debris. "We almost lost Commander Ford," MacKenzie said. "He got a piece of metal in his arm from the bomb that exploded when it missed the power house. The Commander was photographing action with a little magazine 16mm camera at the time. He didn't miss any shots either up to the time he got hurt."

The plane that almost killed Ford and MacKenzie was shot down. They scrambled down to ground level before the powerhouse was knocked out by the Japanese. Together the veteran filmmaker and his young cameraman filmed spectacular color footage of a burning hangar, antiaircraft guns defending the island, and sailors and marines dashing around in the midst of raging black smoke and flames, trying to dodge the strafing.

In *The Battle of Midway,* the poetic documentary Ford assembled to commemorate the historic three-day battle, we see young marines raising the American flag in the midst of the thirteen-minute attack on Eastern Island. Ford filmed the stirring scene from the marines' ground-level point of view. He recalled that it was "time for the colors to go up, and despite the bombs and everything, these kids ran up and raised the flag." Just as the flag reaches the top of the pole, it is hit by a gust of wind and billows proudly from the pole, spotlighted by sunlight breaking through the waves of black smoke and flames. Henry Fonda aptly described this as "one of the all-time great shots." Ford lowers the sound of "The Star-Spangled Banner" slightly during the raising of the flag so the narrator can tell us in awestruck tones:

"Yes—this really happened."

Ford's transition from re-creating history to recording actual history marked a momentous turning point in his life and work. Transforming some of his values and deepening others, World War II gave a greater sense of authority to his artistic vision. In *The Battle of Midway* and his other wartime work, Ford advanced the task he had begun in earnest with his Americana trilogy of 1939: chronicling the saga of the United States in the most popular medium of his time, motion pictures. Even while maintaining the legend that he was nothing more than a "hard-nosed, hard-working" director, Ford consciously set out during the war to become America's national poet.

Ford reported for active duty on September 11, 1941, to the chief of naval operations in Washington, D.C. He took his physical examination at the U.S. Naval Dispensary (a waiver had already been obtained on his eyesight to permit him to serve on active duty). Although officially a member of the navy, Ford was assigned immediately to the "additional duty" that would become his principal mission during the war. Donovan asked Secretary of the Navy Frank Knox to let him incorporate Ford's photographic unit of naval reservists and other Hollywood volunteers into what was then called the Office of the Coordinator of Information (COI). Recognizing the potential of film for wartime training, reconnaissance, propaganda, and documentation of combat missions, Donovan was not fazed, as the navy brass had been, by Ford's reputation as a maverick but welcomed his unorthodox imagination and boundless initiative. With Donovan, in the words of historian R. Harris Smith, "[s]tandard operating procedures were almost taboo. Effective action was the sole objective."

Ford was so accustomed to getting his own way on the set in Hollywood, subject only to the benign dictatorship of Darryl Zanuck, that he often had trouble submerging his rebellious streak and becoming a team player during the war. His peculiar blend of authoritarianism and anarchism made him perfectly suited to Donovan's outfit but sometimes caused him difficulties with military brass. "He'd taunt them—he loved to do that—and he got away with it," Rear Admiral John D. Bulkeley, the World War II hero whose story Ford filmed in *They Were Expendable,* told me in a 1987 interview. "John Ford was a born leader, instinctively a leader, and *used* it. Men followed him willingly."[1]

Philip Dunne related the following Ford story: "I don't know if the story is apocryphal or even where it came from, but it was a widely spread story that during the war, Ford got so fed up with the navy protocol and all the tradeschool bullshit that was going on that he was supposed to have said to a bunch of fellow officers, when somebody was asking what they did in the movies when they finished a movie. 'Oh, when we finish the picture and wrap it up, we all get on a bus and go down to San Diego and fuck navy wives.'"

Dunne tended to believe the story because "it's the kind of thing he'd say to a bunch of navy officers. I think somebody had made some disparaging remark about the movie business."

Ford's strengths and weaknesses as an officer from the navy's point of view were set forth in his annual fitness report on September 15, 1941, by Captain I. C. Johnson, director of the Naval Reserve in the Eleventh Naval District at San Diego. Ford received the highest possible marks for initiative ("far beyond

---

1. Bulkeley was promoted to the rank of vice admiral shortly before his retirement from active duty in 1988, after fifty-five years of service. At the time of our interview, he was president of the navy's Board of Inspection and Survey.

the requirements of his commission"), intelligence, leadership, loyalty, attention to duty, presence of mind, endurance, industry, and aptitude for success. He was given an only slightly lower rating for judgment. But he received lesser marks for tact, cooperation, military bearing, and neatness of person and dress. Those were not regarded as minor failings in the navy. Indeed, Ford's style of military dress was so idiosyncratic it made news in Washington. A local columnist told his readers on January 26, 1942, "Ford was observed the other day wearing tropical khaki Army shirt and trousers, a tan Hollywood pullover sweater, and the insignia of an Army lieutenant colonel hung from one collar point. He was tieless and hatless. His friends attributed his attire to the Hollywood influence!"

Ford's Field Photographic Branch became part of the COI's Photographic Presentation Branch, contained within the agency's Intelligence Division. When Ford arrived in Washington, his Hollywood producing partner Merian C. Cooper was already working in the Photographic Presentation Branch, although Cooper would soon be back on active duty as a colonel with the U.S. Army Air Forces.[2] Cooper used his influence with Donovan to smooth Ford's way into the COI, suggesting on September 9 that "in order to have the prestige necessary to do the job we want him to do, he should be promoted to a Commander." Notoriously easy about passing out promotions, Donovan made Ford a commander, out of line, on October 7. In June 1942, Donovan's year-old clandestine intelligence service was transformed into the OSS, the predecessor of the postwar Central Intelligence Agency. Donovan was stripped of his propaganda division, which became part of the new Office of War Information, but Ford and Field Photo remained with the OSS.

Ford's wartime patron was one of the most remarkable American figures of his time. Affectionately known as "Wild Bill," a nickname acquired during his heroic U.S. Army service in World War I, Donovan was a Republican lawyer and former assistant attorney general who had amassed wealth, prestige, and an unusually wide circle of contacts both inside and outside of government. Eleven years older than Ford, Donovan was that rare combination, an intellectual man of action. Tall and movie-star handsome with silvery white hair, a former football star at Columbia University, Donovan was cool, hard-

---

2. Before the war, Ford and Cooper took an option on C. S. Forester's adventure novel *The African Queen* but let it go after entering government service (John Huston made the film in 1952). After serving as an assistant executive and intelligence officer in the Pacific early in the war, Cooper became chief of staff to General Claire Chennault with the "Flying Tigers" in China and later was deputy chief of staff for all U.S. Army Air Forces units in the Pacific under General Douglas MacArthur.

driving, and often ruthless, and he inspired the utmost loyalty from those who served him. If Ford recognized a kindred spirit in Donovan's brilliance as an organizer and a leader of men, he could only admire Donovan's diplomacy, physical fearlessness, and lifelong abstemiousness.

A second-generation Irish-American from Buffalo, New York, the grandson of Famine emigrants, Donovan also inspired intense admiration and respect from Ford as an Irish Catholic who had made it into the deepest inner reaches of American society without betraying his ethnic or religious allegiances. Donovan's paternal grandfather was associated in America with the underground Fenian movement on behalf of Irish independence. The grandfather's home "was visited by Irish intellectuals and Irish independence leaders long after the Fenians had been drawn into the Sinn Fein ('We, Ourselves') movement, a forerunner of the Irish Republican Army," British biographer Anthony Cave Brown wrote in *The Last Hero: Wild Bill Donovan.* "That, too, was undoubtedly important in the shaping of [Wild Bill's] political attitudes, for in his dealings with the British during World War II he was to display, occasionally, a Fenian stubbornness and, more frequently, dislike of some of the institutions of the British Empire."

During World War I, as commander of the First Battalion of the Sixty-ninth Infantry Regiment of the New York National Guard, known as the "Fighting Irish" or "Fighting 69th," Donovan became the most decorated American officer of the war, winning the Medal of Honor, Distinguished Service Medal, Distinguished Service Cross, Purple Heart, and the French Légion d'Honneur and Croix de Guerre. After a triumphant homecoming parade in April 1919, Donovan's "Micks" (as he liked to call them) marched off to civilian life to the strains of "Garry Owen," the Irish tune often heard in Ford's Westerns as the marching song of the U.S. Cavalry.

Parading with his men through the streets of New York City was a matter of ethnic pride to Donovan, his biographer observed: "The American Irish Catholic had long been considered inferior, and here was an opportunity not only to show that the Irish people and Catholic faith were as vital as any other. Also here was an occasion to offer to the electorate a crop of warriors that had proved their human worth on that hardest of all places—the battlefield." Ford shared Donovan's sense that Irish Catholics still had to prove themselves full partners in American society. In January 1942, Ford wrote his agent, Harry Wurtzel, that Catholics and Jews, as groups outside the social mainstream, had a special stake in ensuring the defeat of the Axis powers. Ford added that though the coming year would be arduous, he was certain of victory, an optimism few in Washington shared in the early days of America's entry into the war.

Radio Berlin announced that "America's secret service is under a renegade Irishman named Wild Bill," but Donovan, like Ford, put his Irish sympathies to one side to become a staunch ally of Britain throughout World War II. Donovan was a leading advocate to Roosevelt of American aid to Britain in 1940–41, and he received crucial early backing and training from British intelligence and its chief in the United States, William Stephenson. As a militant but pragmatic Catholic, Donovan was also a fierce anti–Communist and had such a transforming influence on the thinking of the American intelligence and foreign-policy establishments during those years that he came to be regarded as one of the leading architects of the cold war.

Unlike many other nations, the United States approached its entry into World War II without a formal overseas spy organization. Recognizing the urgent need for such a service, Roosevelt created the COI in June 1941 as his own personal reporting agency, with off-the-shelf financing from the President's Emergency Fund. His executive order granted COI the "authority to collect and analyze all information and data, which may bear upon national security; to correlate such information and data, and to make such information and data available to the President and to such departments and officials of the Government as the President may determine." More vaguely, the COI was also allowed "to carry out, when requested by the President, such supplementary activities as may facilitate the securing of information important for national security not now available to the Government." What Roosevelt and Donovan understood by that broad directive was, in the words of OSS historian R. Harris Smith, "espionage, sabotage, 'black' propaganda, guerrilla warfare, and other 'un-American' subversive practices."

Other governmental intelligence services were ordered to cooperate in furnishing information to the COI, a provision that was not always followed willingly and sometimes was ignored completely. Staffed largely with businessmen, lawyers, and academics, the COI was regarded as a rival by Army Intelligence, the Office of Naval Intelligence, the FBI, and other government intelligence services. David K. E. Bruce, the future diplomat who served as OSS chief in London, wrote that agencies opposed to the COI "forgot their internecine animosities and joined in an attempt to strangle this unwanted newcomer at birth." The problem was only partly alleviated when its successor, the OSS, was put under the control of the Joint Chiefs of Staff.

There were so many Ivy Leaguers and other blue bloods in Donovan's group that Washington wags quipped that OSS stood for not only "Oh So Secret" but also "Oh So Social." And because of the many left-wingers who joined the OSS ("I'd put Stalin on the OSS payroll if I thought it would help us defeat Hitler," Donovan said), some called the agency "Oh So Socialist." As Edward Hymoff wrote in *The OSS in World War II,* "There was a cross-section of first-generation Americans and *Mayflower* Americans, Republicans and Democrats, Socialists and Communists, mechanics and artists, second-story men and ex-cops, and many who had little or no aversion to danger and adventure."

Among the men Donovan recruited were playwright Robert E. Sherwood, as chief of propaganda and information, with a staff that included writers Thornton Wilder and Stephen Vincent Benét; Archibald MacLeish, the poet and librarian of Congress, who recruited academics for the Research and Analysis Branch; U.S. Marine Corps Captain James Roosevelt (the president's eldest son), Donovan's military aide and liaison to other government agencies; Allen Dulles, a prominent New York lawyer and future head of the Central Intelligence Agency, who served as the OSS intelligence chief in Switzerland; the former Republican governor of Rhode Island, William Vanderbilt, executive officer of the OSS's Special Operations Branch; future Supreme Court Justice and United Nations ambassador Arthur Goldberg, the first chief of the OSS Labor Branch; historian Arthur Schlesinger Jr., a political intelligence analyst; future blacklisted screenwriter and director Abraham Polonsky, a writer for a "black radio" station based in London and beamed to Germany; actor Sterling Hayden, who served with Tito's guerrillas in Yugoslavia; and the erudite baseball player Moe Berg, who performed dangerous top-secret spying missions.

"[O]ne of Donovan's gifts," noted Anthony Cave Brown, "was that he was able to attract into government service, to keep, and to win the complete loyalty and devotion of the most brilliant yet motley group of peacocks ever assembled in a Washington agency—a factor that was to cause much trouble with the military."

Ford naturally approached the war with worries about his own survival and, beyond that, about how a prolonged absence from feature filmmaking would affect his future in the movie business. But in addition to his strong sense of patriotic duty, he was one of those OSS men who relished "sensation, intrigue, the idea of being a mysterious man with secret knowledge," as Donovan's psychological chief, Harvard's Dr. Henry Murray, described the attraction of clandestine service.

Forty-seven years old and in relatively good health when he entered active duty, Ford thrived physically and psychologically during the war. In an exuberant letter from Hawaii in April 1942, he told Mary that it had been years since he felt or looked so good. Although he promised her that he wouldn't take a drink for the duration, he still went on occasional alcoholic binges, but they were briefer by necessity, and his frequent travels around the world kept him shipshape.

By the end of 1942, 5,177 Hollywood people had joined the military services, including such stars as James Stewart, Clark Gable, Henry Fonda, Tyrone Power, Robert Montgomery, David Niven, George O'Brien, Douglas Fairbanks Jr., Melvyn Douglas, Ronald Reagan, George Brent, and Gene Autry. Donald Crisp, at age sixty-two, was active in military intelligence, as he had been in the First World War. Even Francis Ford enlisted in April 1943, but he was discharged during basic training when the army learned his real age (sixty-five). Many others in Hollywood, on the other hand—most prominently John Wayne—preferred to stay at home, furthering their careers and reaping the benefits of the box-office boom in wartime entertainment.

Few major directors were willing to give up their careers for active service. Others among them included Frank Capra, John Huston, William Wyler, George Stevens, George Cukor, and W. S. Van Dyke. When the army chief of staff, General George C. Marshall, was looking for a Hollywood director to make morale films for the Army Special Services Division, Ford recommended Capra.[3]

Serving in what was essentially a desk job—making the *Why We Fight* series and other films as well as distantly supervising army combat photography units in the latter years of the war—Capra became frustrated that he was never able to film actual combat, unlike some of his colleagues. Huston made the most celebrated of all World War II documentaries, the army's *San Pietro* (1945), a grimly realistic portrait of the Italian campaign; Wyler filmed *The Memphis Belle (A Story of a Flying Fortress)* (1944) for the Eighth Air Force and the Army Air Forces First Motion Picture Unit; and Stevens, serving in the Signal Corps' Army Pictorial Service (APS) under Capra's distant supervision, had his own unit filming combat in Europe and North Africa.

Philip Dunne wanted to join Field Photo but had misgivings. He told Ford, "I don't know that I'm going to like very much being a lieutenant (jg) when Ford is the commander. You know that's not a good relationship. But on the other hand, you promised me that I would be sent way off somewhere with a camera crew to film combat."

Ford replied, "You won't be a wafflebottom."

"You mean I won't have to sit there with you?" asked Dunne.

"That's it—you go!" said Ford.

According to Dunne, Ford put his name in for a commission, but the navy rejected him on security grounds. In a foreshadowing of McCarthyism, Dunne was considered suspect by the Office of Naval Intelligence because of

---

3. At least that is what Capra told me. There is no documentation in his, Ford's, or Marshall's papers about what must have been an informal recommendation. But when I asked Marshall's wartime secretary, Frank McCarthy, if Ford had recommended Capra, McCarthy replied, "That's very possible. General Marshall knew Ford."

his liberal political activities before the war, including membership in various Popular Front organizations. Dunne eventually received a full security clearance as a division chief in the Motion Picture Bureau of the Office of War Information, working under Robert Riskin, the screenwriter whose credits had included Ford's film *The Whole Town's Talking*.

Whatever respect Ford may have had for his old pals John Wayne and Ward Bond faded when neither man showed much interest in serving his country. Disqualified from service because of epilepsy, Bond acted as an air-raid warden, prompting Ford to write Wayne sarcastically in the month after Pearl Harbor, "How does Uncle Ward look with a tin hat and a pair of binoculars?" In a letter to Mary that March, Ford made an acerbic comment about Bond and Wayne sitting on a California mountaintop listening for a possible Japanese attack: "Ah well—such heroism shall not go unrewarded—it will live in the annals of time."

Wayne was an unlikely candidate for the draft because he was thirty-four and the father of four small children when the United States entered the war. But he wrote Ford in May 1942, "Have you any suggestions on how I should get in? Can I get assigned to your outfit, and if I could, would you want me? . . . No, I'm not drunk. I just hate to ask favors, but for Christ sake you can suggest, can't you?" Wayne later claimed that his wife, Josie, hid a letter from Donovan telling him that he could join Field Photo. However, as Wayne biographers Randy Roberts and James S. Olson point out, "There is no such letter in Donovan's public and private papers. Did [Wayne] believe that he was such an American institution by 1942 that he could not enlist as a private? This statement is difficult to take at face value, when one considers that Gable, Power, Fonda, and Stewart—far more important stars than Wayne—were willing to share a foxhole or a cockpit or a ship deck with teenage American soldiers or sailors."

Nevertheless, in the spring of 1943, Wayne again wrote to ask if there was an opening in Field Photo. Ford's executive officer, Lieutenant Frederick A. "Freddie" Spencer, told Wayne he could enlist as part of the unit's army allotment. But Wayne temporized by saying that he first had to make one more movie, an excuse he repeated that August, when he told Ford he needed one last "fling before going off to battle." Dunne learned that "Wayne was offered a job with Ford and turned him down. According to Bob Parrish, Ford remained furious at [Wayne] for years."

Wayne's career as a star of A pictures had just begun to take off when the war broke out, and after a decade toiling in cheap Westerns he was reluctant to sacrifice his newfound momentum. Accordingly, Republic Pictures continually filed deferment requests on his behalf, which were granted because the government considered the film industry "an activity essential in certain instances to the national health, safety, and interest, and in other instances to war production."

Wayne's personal life was in serious disarray during the war years. In May 1943, he separated from his wife, Josephine, to be with Esperanza "Chata" Baur, a young Mexican actress he had met two years earlier; Chata married Wayne two years after his divorce was granted in 1944. Mary Ford, like many Hollywood wives, sided with Josie Wayne. "Can't you write and try to beat something into Duke's head," Mary urged Jack in June 1943. "It's a damn shame that with a war going on he has to think about his lousy stinking tail. I only think of those gorgeous kids. It's really tragic." Although reluctant to intervene and hardly qualified to give a lecture on marital fidelity, Jack wrote Wayne an oblique, largely jocular, letter chiding him for being a poor correspondent: "If you can take enough time from playing with those Mexican jumping beans, I would be very much interested in knowing what's cooking, good looking!" Without going into particulars, Ford ended by bluntly telling Wayne that he was a "damn fool."

"I could never help John Wayne," Mary said in 1977. "I tried and tried and tried. Not a happy man." She was almost as disgusted during the war by the behavior of Wayne's partner in carousing, Ward Bond, who left *his* wife, Doris, in 1943. In one notorious episode, when Bond was lying in Ford's bed half asleep and refusing to go drinking, Wayne poured vodka on Bond's chest and set him on fire. Mary complained to Jack, "Bond is drunk three-fourths of the time and as Pat says, 'When the cat's away how the mice will play.' Guess without you they're bound for destruction." Mary was so fed up with her experience with Wayne that she decided not to intervene in Bond's marital breakup.

Since Wayne was developing a gung ho screen image that eventually would make him seem the quintessential American fighting man, he felt somewhat guilty about being so self-indulgent when millions of other American men were in actual service. In the words of his third wife, Pilar Pallete, "He would become a 'superpatriot,' for the rest of his life trying to atone for staying at home" (Bond similarly became a superpatriot and militant anti-Communist in the postwar years). Wayne partially assuaged his conscience by going on a USO tour in late 1943 and early 1944 to entertain troops in the South Pacific and Australia. But even that had an ulterior motive. "I better go do some touring—I feel the draft breathing down my neck," Wayne said. At Ford's suggestion, Wayne did some poking around on the tour to gather information on U.S. Army General Douglas MacArthur, who had a frosty relationship with the OSS. Upon his return, Wayne filed a report with Donovan and was rewarded with a certificate for serving in the OSS. Wayne never even bothered to pick up the certificate from Ford, and today it remains among Ford's papers at Indiana University's Lilly Library.

After the war, as Gary Wills reports in *John Wayne's America: The Politics of Celebrity,* Wayne sometimes was made to feel uncomfortable on the *Araner* because Ford liked to communicate in navy lingo aboard his yacht. Ford once needled his star in front of screenwriter James Warner Bellah by pointing out that Wayne wore a navy uniform only in movies.

The *Araner* itself served in World War II. At the navy's January 1942 request, Ford granted a charter for the boat to become the flagship of a fleet running antisubmarine patrols off the California coast. Ford was glad to be freed of the financial responsibility for maintaining the *Araner,* since his income dropped dramatically during the war. After earning $186,022 in 1941 ($1,132 of that from the navy), he made only $31,251 in 1942, $21,169 in 1943, and $30,773 in 1944. He earned between $3,630 and $3,883 a year from government service in 1942–44. To pay his 1941 income tax, Ford had to borrow money from Fox, and he dipped into his savings to support his family during his four years of active duty. He never received the compensation of one dollar that was due for the use of the *Araner.*

Ford's only request in exchange for granting the charter was permission to fly the Naval Reserve flag on the *Araner* after the war. The flag of the Pearl Harbor Yacht Club was retired for the duration. To keep an eye on the boat and its expensive furnishings until it was returned by the navy in July 1944, Ford quietly arranged for stuntman Frank McGrath to be included on the navy crew as his personal watchdog. McGrath was rewarded for his loyal service with work on many postwar Ford films.

Field Photo's Washington headquarters was in the South Agriculture Build ing at Fourteenth Street and Independence Avenue. It started with 28 officers and 123 enlisted photographic specialists, broken down into fifteen film crews. Eventually there were about six hundred people on the roster. Most were navy men, but some came from the army, marines, and Coast Guard. Field Photo made up 1 percent of all the people included under the umbrella of the wartime OSS. It has been reported incorrectly that Ford's budget for the first full year of the war was $5 million. The actual figure was $1 million, $115,000 less than Donovan had requested but still a sizable amount, 7 percent of the total COI budget for 1942 of $14.1 million.[4]

---

4. All the units making wartime films for the War Department spent a total of about $50 million. The entire series of seven *Why We Fight* films cost only about $400,000.

Like any good leader, Ford knew how to delegate authority. Daily organizational details were handled by Chief Boatswain Ben Grotsky and by Freddie Spencer before his transfer to England in 1943 to run the unit's London office. But to whip Field Photo into a semblance of military order, Ford relied most heavily on Chief Warrant Officer Ronald J. "Jack" Pennick, the ex-marine drillmaster he affectionately called "the big six-foot-four-and-a-half mick." The selfless, indefatigably loyal Pennick, whose rugged exterior concealed a gentle nature and an aristocratic family background in Virginia, served as Ford's aide-de-camp throughout the war. Donovan once said of Pennick, *"There* is the most perfect soldier I have ever met."

Next to Pennick, Ford's key aide during the war was Lieutenant (jg) Marcus E. "Mark" Armistead, an industrious young man who had been working in a Hollywood equipment rental house when Ford approached him for the loan of cameras and other hardware. Armistead not only filled those needs but signed up as a member of Ford's Naval Reserve unit. He replaced Spencer at the London post in 1944 and personally took charge of Field Photo's extensive aerial reconnaissance photography of Europe in preparation for the Allied invasion. Using 35mm Mitchell cameras mounted in B-25 bombers, the Intelligence Documentary Photographic Project was known informally as "Ippy Dippy Intelligence."

Ford's personal bivouac in Washington during the early months of the war was a tiny room (number 501) in the Carlton Hotel. From time to time he bunked on a yacht at anchor in the Potomac, the *Saramia.* Armistead purchased the yacht as a floating hotel, renting cabins to fellow officers. Ford commandeered the master bedroom. Never changing the bedsheets in his disheveled quarters, Ford held court in his pajamas, scattering cigar ashes and candy bar wrappers and treating Armistead like a manservant. Often dispatched on nocturnal personal errands for his "Skipper," Armistead wearily recalled that Ford was a night owl during the war years, surviving on daytime naps.

"A strange movie director is Mr. Ford," Frank Farrell wrote in a November 1941 profile for the *New York World Telegram.* "In Hollywood he is not of Hollywood. In the Navy he chooses to talk of Ireland. In Washington the thing he wanted most to do was visit an art gallery." Farrell noted that Ford was living out of an open wardrobe trunk in the center of his hotel room. His uniform was hanging neatly in a closet, but when he dressed for an evening out, he rummaged in the trunk to find a casual jacket and a shapeless pair of pants. Ford carried no money in his pockets, only a handkerchief, a pocketknife, and a rabbit's foot. "There wasn't a trace of Hollywood anywhere in his modest apartments," wrote Farrell. "On the bureau were some letters from home, a couple of pipes, cigars, and several books. That trunk, the whole atmosphere, was one of temporary quarters of a man who might set out to sea with an hour's notice. That is what John Ford may have to do. And everybody wants to know why." But when asked why he quit Hollywood for military service, Ford made no grand statements, simply saying that in the current world situation, "I just think it's the thing to do." Farrell admiringly concluded that "there is not a better man in the world for the job."

Ford paid a ceremonial farewell to his Hollywood self when he and some of the cast of *How Green Was My Valley* attended the film's premiere in New York on October 28. The Rivoli Theater event was a benefit for the Navy Relief Society. The following evening, Ford dined at the White House with Franklin and Eleanor Roosevelt.

Like the women in Ford movies who are left behind when their men go wandering around the world, Mary saw Jack rarely during his four years at war. When he left for Washington in September 1941, he carried only a briefcase and told her he would be gone for a couple of days on a business trip. Mary later claimed that she saw him for only twenty-four hours between then and his demobilization in 1945. That was an exaggeration, but not by much. As the war went on, Jack wrote Mary many seemingly heartfelt expressions of tenderness and longing, but his initial indifference toward her loneliness verged on the pathological.

"Honey, it was swell hearing from you last night," he wrote from Washington on October 2, 1941, "but, Ma, you can't call up long distance just when you're blue and lonesome. It's just too damned expensive. We've really got to adjust—not financially necessarily, but mentally." Since she was discouraged from calling, Mary instead traveled to Washington to talk with him in person. The recent death of her first husband finally made it possible for the Fords to be married in the Catholic Church, and the ceremony was held that December in the National Cathedral.

On the early afternoon of December 7, 1941, Jack, Mary, and Barbara, with Merian Cooper and three other guests, were lunching at the Alexandria, Virginia, home of Rear Admiral Andrew C. Pickens and his wife, Harriette. Ford could hardly have chosen a more appropriate setting for that momentous day, for the Pickens home, dating from America's colonial days, seemed to encapsulate the nation's history.

The gathering was interrupted by a maid calling the admiral to the phone. Upon his return, Pickens solemnly announced that the Japanese had bombed Pearl Harbor, and the United States was at war. Harriette Pickens also rose, pointing out a carefully preserved hole in the wall made by a musket ball during the Revolutionary War. "It's no use getting excited," she said. "This is the seventh war that's been announced in this dining room."

All over America that Sunday, citizens listened in shock to radio reports about the coming of war in a place whose name many did not even recognize. But for Ford, the bombing of Pearl Harbor seemed almost anticlimactic. He had known for months, years, that the war was coming; the only question was where and when something would happen to bring America into combat. Still, the scale of the catastrophic events at Pearl Harbor was devastating.

The United States lost 2,403 military personnel, including about 1,200 men on the battleship *Arizona;* another 1,178 were wounded. Much of the Pacific Fleet lay in ruins. Slow to rearm itself all through the isolationist thirties, even while the Axis powers were building up their mighty arsenals, the United States now struggled desperately to make up for lost time and opportunities. The months following Pearl Harbor would bring a string of terrible losses in the Pacific. Ford had no illusions about how difficult it would be to win back control of the sea after such a debacle. The need for better military preparedness became a recurring theme in his work. After the attack on the Philippines in Ford's 1945 film *They Were Expendable,* an admiral (Charles Trowbridge) admits, "Pearl Harbor was a disaster, like the Spanish Armada. . . . We know all about those destroyers out of commission tied up around San Diego. We could use them here. But they're not around. They won't be."

"The attack on Pearl Harbor startled us like some gigantic dissonant firebell in the night of our false security," OSS veteran David Bruce wrote in a postwar analysis of intelligence operations. "We felt betrayed and indeed we were. We were betrayed by the complete failure of our intelligence agencies. Any intelligence service worthy of the name should have foretold this event."

Ford's own feelings of betrayal about Pearl Harbor and his enthusiasm for the unconventional approach of OSS would bring him into conflict with military brass, including those in the navy who had rejected his unit and driven him into Donovan's service.

Not much of the film footage shot by Ford's unit was seen by the public during the war. Two Field Photo documentaries—*The Battle of Midway* and *December 7th* (1943)—received Academy Awards, but Ford and his men concentrated largely on secret photographic missions for the OSS, functioning with a good deal of autonomy under Donovan's benevolent auspices. "Our job was to photograph both for the records and for our intelligence assessment, the work of guerrillas, saboteurs, Resistance outfits," Ford said in a 1962 newspaper interview, one of his first public statements about his secret activities during the war. "Besides this, there were special assignments."

Officially a navy project with Field Photo serving as silent partner, *The Battle of Midway* received a wide theatrical release by Twentieth Century–Fox in

September 1942. *December 7th,* made for the navy and the War Department, was shown to workers in war-related industries after a much longer version was shelved because of its controversial viewpoint on the disaster at Pearl Harbor. Another Field Photo film screened for war workers, *War Department Report*—a forty-six-minute compilation of battle footage, analysis of Axis military and industrial strength, and pep talks about America's superior resources—received an Oscar nomination for best documentary feature of 1943. Along with other government combat photography units, Field Photo also contributed footage to newsreels and to Capra's *Why We Fight* series, which was shown to the public around the world. Some of Ford's own color-film coverage of the Allied invasion of North Africa in November–December 1942 was incorporated in a forty-one-minute documentary produced by Darryl F. Zanuck for the Army Signal Corps and released to theaters by Warner Bros. in 1943 as *At the Front in North Africa.*

Most of Field Photo's work was never intended for public consumption. The unit made training films for OSS personnel (some include appearances by Ford);[5] undertook extensive aerial reconnaissance filming and still photography; and produced reports on areas of vital interest to military planners. Field Photo documented more than fifty combat missions, including the Doolittle Raid on Japan and the Normandy Invasion, but only a fraction of that footage was seen in newsreels. Frank Nugent later described Ford's unit as "the official eye of the American high command." Its secret films were shown to a select audience, including President Roosevelt, the Joint Chiefs of Staff and other military brass, and military intelligence officers. Many once-classified Field Photo films have since been made public, but few of the dozens of films made by the unit have been widely distributed, and some still remain hidden in government vaults.

Ford personally handled some of the directing and photographing chores, but because of the scope and range of Field Photo's activities, he mostly functioned like a studio chief or executive producer, assigning and training photographic crews and supervising their projects, some more closely than others. Much of what they shot was strictly utilitarian documentary footage, with little or no attempt at aesthetic shaping. Unlike propaganda films aimed at least in part at civilian audiences, such as the *Why We Fight* series and Ford's own *The Battle of Midway,* most Field Photo films tended to be less emotional than

---

5. Admiral Bulkeley recalled seeing one Field Photo training film in which Ford "portrayed himself as a typical OSS [agent] who set himself up as a dummy importer-exporter in some phony business. He went through the whole monkey business. They still do that, of course. That's only a cover for the real whatever-they're-doing. He played that guy—he loved to do that."

analytical, offering hard-boiled presentations for professionals who did not need preaching or soft-soaping. Some of the films were not even edited but were simply reels of raw footage from the field.

Nuts-and-bolts training films made by Ford's unit included *OSS Basic Military Training, Blind Bombing, Ground to Air Transfer, The 8-Man Fol-Boat, The E 2-Man Fol-Boat, Nylon Rubber Boat, Suspended Runway, A Report on Airborne Rockets Prepared by the Joint Committee on New Weapons and Equipment of the Joint Chiefs of Staff, Joan and Eleanor* (code names for the two halves of a high-frequency communication system), and *Personnel Inspection of Field Photographic Branch* (with Jack Pennick and Ray Kellogg demonstrating drills and inspections). Among the more ambitious films were *Undercover,* an eighty-minute cinematic training course for secret agents infiltrating enemy territory; and reports on the Axis powers, such as *Meet the Enemy (Germany), German Air Power, German Manpower, This Is Japan, Japanese Behavior,* and *Natural Resources of Japan.*

Other Field Photo "special assignments" included *Crete,* a frank analysis of how the Germans conquered the British-occupied Mediterranean island in twelve days with superior air power; *Inside Tibet,* a thirty-nine-minute color travelogue following the journey of a U.S. military and diplomatic mission; *Burma Butterflies, Chinese Commandos, Preview of Assam,* and other reports on OSS activities in the China-Burma-India Theater of Operations; *Seabees,* a forty-four-minute documentary on the activities of Navy Construction Battalions (CB's) throughout the world; *Project Gunn,* a report on a mission to rescue Allied war prisoners in Romania; *Cayuga Mission,* detailing OSS assistance to partisans in Italy; *We Sail at Midnight,* a lackluster documentary for the Maritime Commission about "victory ships" leaving New York Harbor for Great Britain; *Mission to Giessen,* the clumsily dramatized story of an OSS agent parachuted into Germany to obtain tactical intelligence during the final months of the war in Europe; and *Manuel Quezon: In Memoriam,* Ford's stately and elegiac coverage of the exiled Philippine president's 1944 funeral services at St. Matthew's Cathedral in Washington, D.C., and burial at Arlington National Cemetery. The eighteen-minute color film on Quezon contains little footage on the life of its ostensible subject but features many shots of American military brass, as well as a shot of Ford in uniform and dark glasses among the mourners at the cathedral, flanked by two U.S. sailors as he ostentatiously recites his rosary.

A Field Photo unit led by Ray Kellogg assembled photographic evidence to aid in the Allied prosecution of Nazi war criminals at the Nuremberg trials in 1945–46. *Nazi Concentration Camps,* a fifty-nine-minute compilation of atrocity footage filmed largely by U.S. Army Lieutenant Colonel George Stevens, is preceded by sworn affidavits by Stevens and Kellogg attesting to its authenticity. Kellogg's statement was sworn before Ford, whose signature appears on-screen. Although Ford helped set up the unit's operations at Nuremberg, he had little to do with production of the *Nazi Concentration Camps* film or four others made in conjunction with the trials: *That Justice Be Done,* a ten-minute documentary contrasting the principles of the Allied tribunal with the injustices of the Third Reich; *The Nazi Plan,* a compilation of captured German newsreel and propaganda footage assembled by George Stevens and Budd Schulberg; *Nazi Supreme Court Trial of the Anti-Hitler Plot, Sept. 1944–Jan. 1945,* a forty-four-minute condensation of German footage of the court proceedings; and *Nuremberg,* a seventy-six-minute record of the trials and German atrocities filmed and assembled by Kellogg, Pare Lorentz, and Stuart Schulberg.

A few Field Photo projects were never completed or shown even secretly. In his memoir *Growing Up in Hollywood,* Robert Parrish humorously describes his involvement in filming a report on the defenses of the State Department Building, adjacent to the White House (it is now the Old Executive Office Building). Incensed at a government edict forbidding OSS operations within the United States, Ford mischievously decided to expose the inadequacy of the building's security. Predictably, the surreptitious filming by two sailors from a nearby rooftop, using a 35mm camera with a telephoto lens mounted on a rifle stock,[6] caused the building's marine guards to react in panic. Petty Officer Second Class Parrish and Petty Officer First Class Bill Faralla were arrested and detained for two days; Ford managed to extricate them from more serious trouble by insisting on presiding over their court-martial proceedings in the tongue-in-cheek manner of Judge Priest. This escapade brought about no change in government policy toward the OSS but undoubtedly contributed to the suspicion among career intelligence officers that Ford was a dangerously loose cannon.

Perhaps the most unusual Field Photo project was a film on the National Gallery of Art. Directed by Parrish and photographed in both color and black and white by Navy Lieutenant (jg) Arthur E. Arling (the principal camera operator on *Gone with the Wind*), this twenty-minute 1942 documentary showcased the gallery's fabulous collection of French impressionist paintings, many of which had been sent to America for safekeeping. A pet project of David Bruce, the film, in Donovan's words, was made to "show the French peasants that Americans are cultured." But it ran afoul of Free French general Charles de Gaulle and one of his deputies, writer André Malraux. They managed to

---

6. Called the Cunningham Combat Camera after its inventor, RKO technician Ray Cunningham, it was developed for Field Photo but proved dangerous for combat photography because of its weaponlike appearance.

kill the film by warning that French peasants would throw rocks at the screen and shout, "Barbarian Americans have stolen French masterpieces."

Three days after Pearl Harbor, Ford reported to New York for transport to the U.S. Naval Air Station at Reykjavík, Iceland. It was his first overseas assignment on active duty. At President Roosevelt's personal request, he was sent to make a quick cinematic report on the docks, airport, military buildings, and roads at Reykjavík, a key transit point for Allied convoys traveling through North Atlantic waters infested by German U-boats.

Ford gave Ray Kellogg primary responsibility for directing and photographing *Iceland*. The eleven-minute, black-and-white film analyzes such problems as gale-force winds damaging ships and aircraft, logistical difficulties unloading supplies on the docks, and midocean refueling operations in a convoy en route to Halifax. Screened by FDR and other high government officials, *Iceland* "proved to be of enormous value later in connection with the activities of the United States in establishing bases in the region," Donovan recalled. "The manner in which Captain Ford handled the organization and planning of this expedition was singularly outstanding, and was a forerunner of further important, highly technical, and difficult missions which were later organized to all parts of the world."

On December 23, Ford left Washington to make a film on the security of the Panama Canal Zone. Ordered two days before Pearl Harbor by U.S. Navy Secretary Frank Knox, *Canal Report* now was of even greater urgency. Considered a possible target of the Germans or the Japanese, the canal (in the words of the film) was "one of the world's most strategic points" and carried "the life blood between the two [American] fleets." Incensed over the navy's lack of preparedness at Pearl Harbor, Ford was determined to tell the president the unvarnished truth about what he found in Panama. Robert Parrish recalled that the top brass felt Ford and his OSS unit were best suited for the job because regular army or navy filmmakers might be inclined to cover up security problems at the canal. Taking along two cameramen, Lieutenants Allen G. Siegler and Alfred L. Gilks,[7] Ford shot *Canal Report* quickly, trying to avoid attracting attention. What he turned in was a cinematic equivalent of his prewar intelligence reports warning about the danger of Japanese infiltration south of the border.

The narration Ford wrote and personally delivered for *Canal Report* offered precise visual and verbal evaluations for Roosevelt of various points of concern: "The most vulnerable link is the Madden Dam, which stores water for

---

7. Gilks later did the second-unit cinematography on *The Searchers.*

the [canal's] lock levels . . . notice how white it is and what a moonlight target it could be . . . it would need a heavy concentration of anti-aircraft guns to protect it [ellipses in the original script]." Panama City was a "moonlight target of tortuous streets where a few well-placed bombs might knock out a power supply or tie up military traffic. . . . [T]here are about sixty thousand souls here where Balboa once stared in wild surmise."

Ford's characteristic ambivalence about the human cost of war was evident in a scene showing an internment camp for people of German and Japanese descent. Turning his camera on a Japanese child, he said she "was born in the camp . . . and after her birth certificate could be written 'A.P.H.' . . . 'After Pearl Harbor.' But to an Army nurse there is always one injunction . . . 'Suffer little children' . . . the child isn't bad either." However, as he had done after his trips to Mexico, Ford raised an alarm about spies among the civilian population. Showing U.S. warships lying at anchor at the Pacific entrance to the canal, he noted that the names of the ships were exposed, a glaring security risk. And he called attention to the presence of visitors, "Friends and wives and ladies of leisure and perhaps a secret agent or two," adding that "it seems as though [one woman] might be memorizing something." The United States eventually manned the Canal Zone with several thousand troops. Partially as a result of that vigilance, which owed something to the early alarm raised by Ford, the canal remained undisturbed throughout the war.

Donovan and Ford could hardly have picked a more incendiary subject for their next major film project, which bore the working title *The Story of Pearl Harbor: An Epic in American History.* Controversy over the lack of preparedness by army and navy forces in Hawaii began almost immediately after the attack. The January 25, 1942, report of a special investigating body, the Roberts Commission, led to the retirement of Admiral Husband E. Kimmel, commander in chief of the Pacific Fleet, and Lieutenant General Walter C. Short, the army's Hawaiian Department commander. Further investigations and finger-pointing continued until 1946, producing many volumes of testimony yet never entirely resolving the question of why abundant warnings of Japanese belligerence went largely unheeded. Even today there are those who believe that President Roosevelt provoked the attack and deliberately let it occur in order to draw the reluctant nation into the war.

Donovan biographer Anthony Cave Brown asserts that "the root cause of the intelligence failure that produced the Pearl Harbor disaster" was that "the Army and the Navy had ignored the presidential order that Donovan was to see all intelligence having a bearing on national security." Since the United States had broken the top-secret Japanese code in 1940, a steady flow of deciphered Japanese Foreign Office cable traffic, known as the MAGIC intercepts, was provided to a select group of high-ranking officials. But because the army and the navy "did not trust the security disciplines of a new civilian organization such as Donovan's, vital intelligence was withheld from [COI's Board of Analysts] before, during, and after the attack."

Secretary of the Navy Knox, a fellow Republican and close friend of Donovan's who had personally conducted the first preliminary investigation of Pearl Harbor just days after the bombing, approved Donovan's proposal to make what Knox called "a complete motion picture factual presentation of the attack on Pearl Harbor on 7 December 1941. As you well know, the President has stressed the highly historic importance of this date and I believe that it should be handled by the best talent available." *December 7th* went well beyond Knox's expectations, however, becoming the most controversial film made by Ford's unit during the war. The original eighty-three-minute version of the film argues not only that the military was caught off guard during the attack but also that it was blind to spying by much of the Japanese-American population of Hawaii. That version ran afoul of the military brass and was ordered shelved. It was not until 1943 that Ford received approval for the release of a severely truncated and far milder version.

December 7th can be seen in part as Donovan's vehicle to strike back at military intelligence for failing to keep him in the loop. Ford's willingness to publicly criticize his own branch of the service may have stemmed in part from his lingering resentment against the navy brass for refusing to accept his reserve unit. There is no doubt, however, that Ford passionately believed in the need for greater military preparedness, a theme that is spotlighted not only in *December 7th* but also in some of his later features, such as *They Were Expendable* and *The Wings of Eagles*. In Ford's cavalry Westerns, the resentment felt by officers over their inadequate support from the distant government in Washington owes much to the director's emotional identification with the men who fought and died in such garrisons as Pearl Harbor and Midway.

In return for agreeing to teach cinematography to the men of Ford's Navy Reserve unit, Gregg Toland had been promised a film to direct. Accordingly, Ford assigned Toland to *December 7th* as director and cinematographer, with Lieutenant Samuel G. Engel serving as writer-producer (a screenwriter and producer for Fox before the war, Engel later worked with Ford on *My Darling Clementine*).

Ford expected *December 7th* to be a quick, "newsreel-like operation," Parrish recalled. "When no film arrived from Pearl Harbor after six weeks, Ford flew out to Honolulu," departing from San Francisco on January 24, 1942. Ford discovered that Toland and Engel had concocted an ambitious but bizarrely misguided scheme to turn *December 7th* into a feature-length hodge-podge of documentary and dramatization. They planned to combine the small amount of actual footage of the attack that had been filmed by navy person-nel[8] with extensive re-creations using sailors at Pearl Harbor and soldiers at the adjacent Hickam Field, miniatures of American ships and Japanese planes filmed by Ray Kellogg, staged scenes of prewar life on the island of Oahu, and dramatized scenes with actors philosophizing about America's reluctance to enter the war.

Those lengthy exchanges between Walter Huston as "U.S." (Uncle Sam) and Harry Davenport as "Mr. C." (Uncle Sam's conscience) were to be shot later at Fox, and a fantasy sequence with Dana Andrews playing a dead American sailor was to be filmed near the studio at the National Cemetery in Westwood. Par-rish reported that Ford was "apprehensive about the idea of presenting a feature-length film with Hollywood actors and Toland's political philosophy to Donovan when what was wanted was a brief, factual report about what had happened at Pearl Harbor and who was to blame. He learned that Toland had little regard for military protocol and was stepping on a lot of toes in the sensi-tive post–December 7 era, and that some of the veteran regular Navy officers (as opposed to wartime reserves) were anxious to scuttle the Toland operation."

While quietly mulling how to handle the situation, Ford shot footage of the rebuilding of damaged ships at Pearl Harbor, one of which was still ablaze when he arrived on the scene. *December 7th* describes that operation as "a twenty-four-hour-a-day, around-the-clock job of salvage and repair that will stand forever as one of the great achievements in maritime history."[9] Ford also spent a day directing some of the reenactments of the attack, pressing friends on Oahu into service as actors.

An admiral and three other officers showed up to watch Ford at work. After Ford directed a scene to his own satisfaction, the admiral suggested a piece of business to improve it. As Parrish related, Commander Ford "looked at him for a few seconds, then he looked at his two stars, and then he said, 'Yes, sir. Let's do it again.'" Ford redid the scene as the admiral wished and began preparing another setup. This time Ford "listened while the admiral explained an intricate camera move that he felt sure would give the next shot more 'punch.' Ford was noted for making some of the best films ever made and sel-

---

8. C. P. Daugherty, Plc, Fleet Camera Party, USS *Argonne,* shot 200 feet of 16mm black-and-white film, and Lieutenant Commander Edward Young, USS *Mugford,* shot 250 feet of 8mm Kodachrome.

9. Some of the footage was edited into a secret four-minute film, *U.S.S. Kearny,* also known as *Damage Repair of the WWII Destroyer.*

dom moving the camera. When the admiral finished, Ford stared out at the harbor and what was left of the U.S. Pacific Fleet. He then slowly lit his pipe and turned to the admiral.

"'Sir,' he said, 'do you ever direct complete movies, or do you just kibitz when you have nothing better to do?' He turned his back on the admiral and walked over to Jack MacKenzie, his cameraman. 'Put the camera on a tripod and set it up here,' he said. 'Let's stop wasting time. We've got a lot of work to do today.'

"The next day Ford was given urgent orders from the admiral's office to leave Pearl Harbor. Before he left, he warned Toland and Engel to be careful, to 'be inky,' and not to let anyone know what they were doing, but when he saw them exchange glances, he suspected that his warnings were falling on deaf ears. And when Engel winked at Toland and rolled his eyes, Ford was convinced of his suspicions. He saluted and said to his two lieutenants, 'You're doing a fine job, lads. Keep up the good work.'"

On April 8, Ford left Pearl Harbor on a top-secret mission aboard the cruiser USS *Salt Lake City,* under the command of his old Naval Intelligence comrade, Captain Ellis M. Zacharias. One of seven ships protecting the carrier *Enterprise,* the flagship of Vice Admiral William F. "Bull" Halsey, the *Salt Lake City* was headed for a rendezvous at sea with the remainder of Task Force Sixteen, including the carrier *Hornet.* Secured by cables to the flight deck of the *Hornet* were sixteen U.S. Army Air Corps bombers whose crews were led by Lieutenant Colonel James H. Doolittle.

On the morning of April 18, Ford was aboard the *Hornet* documenting the historic sixty minutes when the Doolittle Raiders took off for their daring attack on Japan. Their B-25 bombers had to be launched from the carrier in rough seas beginning at 8:20 A.M., eight hours ahead of schedule and 824 miles from Tokyo, after the task force was spotted by Japanese patrol boats.

The Doolittle Raid inflicted only modest physical damage on Japan, but it succeeded in what Doolittle explained were its "three real purposes. One purpose was to give the folks at home the first good news that we'd had in World War II. It caused the Japanese to question their warlords. And from a tactical point of view, it caused the retention of aircraft in Japan for the defense of the home islands when we had no intention of hitting them again, seriously, in the near future. Those airplanes would have been much more effective in the South Pacific where the war was going on." By dispelling Japanese illusions that the homeland could not be bombed, the raid also panicked the Imperial high command into speeding up plans for an attack on the U.S. Naval Air Station at Midway, which proved to be the decisive battle of the war in the Pacific.

When I asked General Doolittle about Ford in a 1987 interview, he said he did not remember Ford's presence when the raid was launched. Perhaps the general simply had forgotten about Ford being there, and no doubt he had too much on his mind forty-five years earlier to take cognizance of the filmmaker. Unlike the Army Air Forces cameraman traveling on the mission, Ford shot no preliminary footage of Doolittle and his fellow Raiders posing with the skipper of the *Hornet*, Captain Marc A. Mitscher. Ford reserved his supply of film for the action—the ships of the task force heading toward their rendezvous with the Raiders, the B-25s landing on the *Hornet*, the heavily loaded planes rising slowly from the carrier into an overcast sky—and for shots of the faces of the ordinary seamen supporting the heroic mission. Cutting in the camera, Ford alternated views of planes taking off with shots of cheering, waving, and saluting sailors and marines. He incorporated three close-ups of the task force commander, Admiral Halsey, watching from the bridge of the *Hornet*. But Ford characteristically reserved one of his "grace notes" for a shot of African-American sailors waving farewell to the ascending planes. Some of Ford's edited-in-the-camera footage has been used in newsreels and documentaries over the years.

When the press asked President Roosevelt in April 1942 where the bombers had been based, he cryptically replied, "I think they came from a new secret base at Shangri-La" (an allusion to the almost inaccessible Tibetan monastery in James Hilton's novel *Lost Horizon*, filmed in 1937 by Frank Capra). Ford chafed at the continued secrecy surrounding the raid, writing Captain Zacharias in 1943: "Zach, will you please send my orders regarding the *Salt Lake* cruise so that I might have my papers in order? I know it is still secret according to you, but there have been so many magazine articles about it, I thought by this time the Japs might have caught on." Combining Ford's footage with miniatures, MGM commemorated the Doolittle Raid in *Thirty Seconds over Tokyo*, a 1944 film directed by Mervyn LeRoy and starring Spencer Tracy as Doolittle. But even then the *Hornet* could not be identified as the launching site.

After Pearl Harbor, the Japanese "continued to expand, threatening every unprotected island in the Central, South, and Southwest Pacific," wrote historian Forrest C. Pogue. "For nearly six months victories mounted steadily on the enemy side of the ledger until some despairing persons in the States began to think the unthinkable, 'What if we lose this war?' At last, in early May in the Battle of the Coral Sea and in early June at Midway, the orgy of Japanese conquest was brought to a halt."

Ford's presence at the historic Battle of Midway of June 3–6, 1942, was not, as Henry Fonda (one of the film's narrators) believed, just another case of the director's vaunted "luck of the Irish." In early April, Commander Joseph Rochefort of the Navy Combat Intelligence Office outstation on Hawaii informed Admiral Chester W. Nimitz, commander-in-chief of the U.S. Pacific Fleet, that a large Japanese operation was being planned against Midway. The heavily fortified atoll eleven hundred miles west of the Hawaiian Islands was the United States's outermost bastion of defense in the central Pacific. The intelligence about the pending attack came from MAGIC intercepts. Dan Ford's biography claims Donovan tipped off his grandfather in Washington that the Japanese code had been broken and an attack on Midway was impending. If Donovan did have advance information of the attack, he must have gleaned it from a source other than the actual MAGIC intercepts, for as Brown's Donovan biography reports, the National Security Agency "declared in 1981 that Donovan's name was never on any Top [Secret] List."

Ford told his grandson that he did not learn the whole story when Nimitz asked him on May 25 to arrange Field Photo coverage at Midway. Donovan later wrote for the record that Nimitz asked Ford for photographic documentation of "a dangerous mission. Ford volunteered to proceed himself, taking one enlisted man with him, arriving at Midway on May 28." The enlisted man Ford requested was his young navy photographer on *December 7th*, Jack MacKenzie Jr., who had worked at RKO before the war (MacKenzie's father was also an RKO cameraman).

At Midway, Ford was informed by a navy friend, Commander F. M. "Massie" Hughes, that the Japanese code had been broken and the attack was imminent. On June 3, Ford flew reconnaissance over the ocean with Hughes, the leader of a patrol squadron. Hughes piloted one of twenty-three PBY-5 Catalina flying boats patrolling a seven-hundred-mile arc in search of the enemy fleet. Describing Ford's "temporary additional duty in connection with Photographic Flight Intelligence," Hughes wrote that "while on an extended patrol flight in plane number 23-P-1, in position 320 miles north of Midway, this flight was in contact with two unidentified enemy planes, apparently Japanese seaplane fighters." Aiming his 16mm camera, Ford asked Hughes to reduce speed so he could get a better shot of the fighter planes. Cursing as he demanded to know if Ford wanted to return alive, Hughes took evasive action, revving his engine to eighty miles an hour. Diving into the clouds, Hughes reported the position of the enemy cruiser ships that launched the pursuit planes. It was one of the key pieces of intelligence provided that day by PBY pilots tracking the Japanese fleet. As Nimitz wrote in his June 28 report on the battle, "Had we lacked early information of the Japanese movement, and had we been caught with Carrier Task Forces dispersed, possibly as far away as the Coral Sea, the Battle of Midway would have ended far differ-ently."

Back at Midway that evening, Captain Cyril T. Simard, commandant of the U.S. Naval Air Station, "asked Ford to act as an observer and attempt to obtain a photographic record of the impending attack," Donovan recalled (Ford's record listed him on temporary duty at Midway as a "Photographic and Intel-ligence Officer"). Simard suggested that Ford station himself atop the Eastern Island powerhouse "with two phones for the purpose of reporting the progress of the attack to the officers concerned." Ford agreed, saying it would be "a good place to take pictures."

"Well, forget the pictures as much as you can," said Simard, "but I want a good accurate account of the bombing. We expect to be attacked tomorrow."

Awakened shortly after dawn by the news of approaching Japanese planes, Ford threw on his clothes and scrambled to his perch with his camera and two hundred feet of 16mm Kodachrome film. His 1946 navy citation for the Le-gion of Merit stated that Ford "courageously took station on top of the Mid-way Island power plant, where he remained a clear target as the enemy waged a savage, unexpected [sic] and continuous air attack." During the attack, Ford spotted and reported 76 enemy planes. They were among 108 planes in the first wave of an invasion of the two Midway Islands, Sand and Eastern.

Ford trained his camera on the aircraft hangar on the narrow, triangular sliver of land of which Eastern Island was composed, figuring that it would be a prime Japanese target. The battle had been under way for only two minutes when a bomber pilot scored what Ford called "a very lucky hit, he must have hit some explosives in it, the whole thing went up." Flying in low, Japanese level bombers sought to neutralize antiaircraft fire while dive-bombers and Zeroes strafed ground targets defended by marines. "Those Marines are great boys," Ford told a reporter after returning to the States. "Outnumbered by their attackers, they fought viciously, blasted more than a score of Jap planes out of the sky and met each new assault with renewed determination."[10]

Even after being wounded by shrapnel from the bomb that exploded near the powerhouse, Ford kept filming and also "succeeded in delivering by tele-phone a running, verbal report of the battle, thereby aiding the Commanding Officer in the disposition and use of the defending American forces through-out the action."

"I just kept reporting," Ford recalled. "I'd say, 'There's a plane up there, one

---

10. The total number of Japanese planes destroyed in the battle was 332, of which about 10 were shot down over Eastern Island.

of our planes shot down, man in a parachute, Japs have shot the parachute, the man landed and the PT boat went out. . . .' I just reported those things and took the picture. I was getting paid for it. That's what I was in the Navy for."

After their close call, Ford and MacKenzie prudently climbed down from the powerhouse, which was badly damaged when hit by a Japanese dive-bomber eight minutes into the battle. Giving MacKenzie one succinct piece of advice—concentrate on filming *faces*—Ford followed his own precept as he took dramatic shots of marines firing antiaircraft guns and raising the flag in the midst of the attack. "I shot film and continued to change the film magazines and to stuff them in my pockets," Ford recalled. "The image jumps a lot because the grenades were exploding right next to me. Since then, they do that on purpose, shaking the camera when filming war scenes. For me it was authentic because the shells were exploding at my feet."

To BBC TV interviewer Philip Jenkinson in 1968, Ford claimed, "I am really a coward. I know I am, so that's why I did foolish things. I was decorated eight or nine times, trying to prove that I was not a coward, but after it was all over I still knew, know, that I was a coward. . . . Oh, we'd go ahead and do a thing, but after it was over, your knees would start shaking." Nevertheless, for his actions under fire at Midway he was awarded a Purple Heart along with a citation for distinguished service stating, "Your courage and devotion to duty were in keeping with the highest traditions of the naval service." If Ford saw cowardice within himself, that was only because he truly understood the meaning of courage. As Mark Twain put it, "Courage is resistance to fear, mastery of fear—not absence of fear. Except a creature be part coward it is not a compliment to say it is brave."

During the three days of the Battle of Midway, the Empire of Japan met its first major defeat after nearly seven months of war with American forces. Extending over three hundred sea miles, the battle was decided on June 4 when American planes destroyed all four of the Japanese battleships taking part in the invasion. Most of the footage of air and sea combat in Ford's documentary was shot by U.S. Navy Lieutenant Kenneth M. Pier, who flew on planes off the *Hornet* "with a little 16mm camera you could carry in your coat pocket— and did he do a swell job!" said MacKenzie. "His film had a lot to do with the success of the picture that was released to the public." (When Bogdanovich asked Ford how much of *The Battle of Midway* he photographed himself, Ford replied, "I did all of it—we only had one camera.")

Twenty Americans were killed during the bombing of Sand and Eastern Islands. They were among a total of 362 Americans and 3,057 Japanese who died in the battle. Ford later claimed he was "wounded pretty badly" at Midway and that he had to be treated without medicine because (as the film shows) the naval station's hospital was destroyed in the bombing. In fact, Ford's wound was relatively minor and received proper treatment by a marine medic, Lieutenant Commander Frederick S. Foote. That day Foote described Ford's injuries with precision in a handwritten medical report: "Wound, gunshot, upper left forearm. Result of action from enemy fire this date. A 3″ surface wound treated with [M]erthiolate and sulfanilamide powder. Arm is slightly bruised from elbow to wrist. Tetanus antitoxin given. Not incapacitated for duty." (The words *gunshot* and *shrapnel* are used interchangeably in navy documents about Ford's wound; while reminiscing with his grandson, Ford said he was wounded by shrapnel.)

Two days after the battle ended, Ford cabled Mary from Midway:

"OK. LOVE. JOHN FORD."

Pointedly distinguishing itself from the fakery of *December 7th*, *The Battle of Midway* begins with the title, "This is the actual photographic report of the Battle of Midway." The fact that "this really happened" gives *The Battle of Midway* much of its emotional power. And yet, paradoxically, this first-person, handheld account of history in the making is Ford's most purely poetic film. It gives us the very essence of the man, offering an unmediated, unashamed look into his heart and soul. Tag Gallagher notes that Ford "did not again stand so far off from his material after *The Battle of Midway* as he did before it."

Documentary film historian William T. Murphy has described *The Battle of Midway* as "crude propaganda" that "substitutes moral and emotional feelings for information," offering "no broad perspective of the battle." But Ford's purpose in making the eighteen-minute film was not to elucidate military strategy or provide a comprehensive historical record. Instead he used poetic imagery to convey the feeling of the battle as it was experienced by the men who fought it, thereby enabling the American public to understand the sacrifices necessary to preserve their way of life. Ford brought to the documentary genre his orientation as a fictional filmmaker accustomed to giving emotional inflections to reality with lighting, composition, acting, and music. Andrew Sarris wrote that *The Battle of Midway* is only "ostensibly a documentary. . . . [Ford] focuses here on the ordinary scale by which the most gallant heroes are measured. It is not the battle itself that intrigues Ford, but the weary faces of rescued fliers plucked out of the Pacific after days of privation."

"Men and women of America—here come your neighbors' sons. . . ." Pilots are seen emerging from their planes, some being helped or carried out and placed in ambulances, as the sound track plays "Onward, Christian Soldiers." Ford's personal emotional investment in this elegiac sequence was so great that he literally put himself into it. A brief shot of the director turning toward the cam-

era—wearing a khaki dress uniform, smoking his pipe, and smiling—is inter-cut with two shots of his friend Massie Hughes being lifted from an airplane onto a stretcher. Over the shot of Ford we hear the narrator saying, as if speak-ing for Ford himself, "Well done, Massie Hughes."

Ford left Midway on June 14, stopping briefly in Honolulu and Los Angeles en route to Washington. Haggard and unshaven, his wounded arm bandaged, Ford met Parrish in Honolulu, handing him a 16mm copy of the Midway footage (in eight cans) for editing. Ford told Parrish that he wanted him to cut the film in Hollywood rather than Hawaii: "As soon as it's discovered in Hon-olulu that I've smuggled the film past the Navy censors they'll come snooping around with enough brass to take it away from us." Concerned that the Mid-way footage would get tied up in military bureaucracy and never be released, Ford told Parrish, "Go to your mother's house and hide until you hear from me." By the time the military brass got wind of what they were doing, Ford said, the film would be completed. "Besides, I'll tell them that it's not my fault if an enlisted man steals eight cans of top-secret film and runs home to his mother."

Parrish asked Ford whether he should edit the footage into a straight doc-umentary or a propaganda film.

"What's a 'propaganda' film?" Ford said with distaste.

"Well, I mean is it for the public or for the OSS?"

"It's for the mothers of America. It's to let them know that we're in a war, and that we've been getting the shit kicked out of us for five months, and now we're starting to hit back."

Ford finagled Dudley Nichols and MGM producer-writer James Kevin McGuinness into writing narration for the film, working separately without each other's knowledge. While supervising Parrish's editing of the picture and Alfred Newman's scoring at Fox (including Danny Borzage's "Red River Val-ley" accordion music from *The Grapes of Wrath*), Ford combined the writers' material into a choral commentary read by Fox actors Henry Fonda, Jane Dar-well, Donald Crisp, and Irving Pichel (the film director whose reverent voice also narrates *How Green Was My Valley*). In a recording session that lasted only about twenty minutes, Ford had both Crisp and Pichel read the line "Yes—this really happened," which the director had first dictated in a screening room, before deciding to use Pichel's rendition.

The script indicates that the narration after the opening battle footage should undergo "A COMPLETE CHANGE OF TONE, TO A HOMEY QUAL-ITY: ALMOST GOSSIPY." This led to a dispute between Ford and Parrish, who particularly objected to the emotional voice of the typical American mother represented by Darwell. As B-17s take off, we hear her cry out, "Good luck! God bless you, son!" Later, over shots of the rescued fliers and a bombed-out hospital, she intones in a measured, hymnlike rhythm, "Get those boys to the hospital, please do! Quickly! Get them to clean cots and cool sheets. Give them doctors and medicine, a nurse's soft hands. . . ." Parrish thought those lines were too corny, but Ford told him to consider how his mother would react if he were one of the exhausted fliers.

Two other versions of *The Battle of Midway,* one revised for air force personnel and the other for showing to war workers, exist at the National Archives. Using a more conventionally belligerent narration by a hard-edged male voice, the version for war workers demonstrates how much of the film's power is lost without the original narration that Parrish found objectionable. Ford's orchestration of emotional surrogates from those beloved family sagas *The Grapes of Wrath* and *How Green Was My Valley* has the effect of putting the average American or Briton into the film, which describes Midway as "our outpost—your front yard."

When the film was virtually completed, Ford told Parrish that each of the armed services was "claiming credit for the victory" and that they all would attempt to prevent the American public from seeing *The Battle of Midway* "if they're not equally represented." He instructed Parrish to measure the footage allocated to each service. Parrish already had given equal time in the funeral sequence to shots of Captain Simard of the navy and Colonel Harold D. Shannon, commander of the Sixth Marine Defense Battalion at Midway. But on the August day when the film was to be screened at the White House, Ford reached into his pocket and pulled out a five-foot close-up he had filmed at Midway of his OSS colleague James Roosevelt saluting. Parrish objected that if the shot was inserted in the sequence, there would be a gap in the sound track with the music briefly going silent as the narrator says, "Major Roosevelt."

"Good," said Ford. "It'll give the audience time to think."

The question of whether *The Battle of Midway* would be released to the public hung in the balance when Ford and Donovan showed the film to President Roosevelt. The White House audience also included Eleanor Roosevelt; members of the Joint Chiefs of Staff; presidential press aide Stephen Early; and FDR's chief of staff, Admiral William Leahy, a vigorous opponent of Donovan and the OSS.

"The president talked throughout the screening," Parrish recalled, until the shot of his son came on-screen. The room fell silent and remained so until the end. "When the lights came up, Mrs. Roosevelt was crying. The president turned to Admiral Leahy and said, 'I want every mother in America to see this picture.'"

Technicolor made five hundred 35mm prints of *The Battle of Midway,* which theater owners eagerly booked. Ford assigned Parrish to monitor public reaction that September at New York's Radio City Music Hall. Parrish was astonished when people screamed and wept and had to be helped out of the theater by ushers. The reaction to the film was even more surprising because it came over Fordian touches that Parrish had thought too corny, such as Jane Darwell's plea, "Get those boys to the hospital, please do! Quickly!"

Although *The Battle of Midway* no longer has quite that visceral impact on audiences, it remains an extraordinarily vivid and eloquent meditation on war, one of the rare pieces of propaganda that is also a timeless work of art.

The task of mourning the battle's heroic dead was not confined to a single film. Ford made a separate film commemorating VT-8, a squadron of torpedo planes aboard the *Hornet*. Twenty-nine of the squadron's thirty fliers and all fifteen of its planes were lost within a matter of minutes on the morning of June 4. The catastrophe occurred when the *Hornet* and another carrier, the USS *Enterprise,* caught the four Japanese aircraft carriers as they were recovering planes from the first strike and preparing for a second wave of attacks.

"By mischance the American torpedo bombers came in without fighter protection, and Zeroes knocked them down in a terrible slaughter; not a single torpedo reached the enemy flattops," wrote historian James MacGregor Burns. "But the intrepid torpedo bombers drew so much attention that American dive bombers were able to make their long plunges and rain their missiles on cluttered flight decks. In a few minutes three Japanese carriers were infernos of explosions and fire. Dive bombers got the fourth carrier later in the day."

The only survivor of Torpedo Squadron Eight was Ensign George Gay, who watched the destruction of the three carriers while clinging helplessly to a floating seat cushion from his downed airplane. When it was learned that a cameraman on the *Hornet* had taken 16mm color footage of the ill-fated squadron before they took off on their suicidal mission, Donovan suggested editing the footage into a short film for private distribution to their families. Simple and understated in its eloquence, similar in tone to the sequence in *The Battle of Midway* of sailors quietly watching the sunset the evening before the battle, *Torpedo Squadron 8* has great poignancy as a last record of these men's lives before their heroic sacrifice. Ford had Joe August and other personal emissaries hand-carry 8mm copies of the elegiac eight-minute film to the families.

Torpedo Squadron 8 rarely has been screened in public. The decisions to keep the film private and not to incorporate the footage into *The Battle of Midway* probably stemmed from fear of a negative effect on the morale of the American public. Twentieth Century–Fox developed a feature film project called *Torpedo Squadron 8,* centered around Ensign Gay, but despite early support from the navy, that project was dropped, according to the *New York Times,* when "a certain high government official" protested that such a film "would carry a defeatist implication."

Not knowing about Ford's film on VT-8, Philip Dunne had an uncomfortable encounter with him at the time: "When I had to go to Washington, I'd drop in on him. He ran the *Midway* short for me. And I said, 'Gee, it's wonderful, it's the greatest thing. And I wish to hell that somebody had managed to get cameras on those planes when they got the four Japanese carriers. *That* was the story of Midway.' He said, 'All right, you want to do that, *you* go get yourself a camera!' He'd flare up over any kind of criticism."

Fox transformed its *Torpedo Squadron 8* project into *Wing and a Prayer* (1944), a more upbeat story about a fictional torpedo bomber squadron in the period between the bombing of Pearl Harbor and the Battle of Midway. Directed by Henry Hathaway, the film incorporates footage of the actual battle. *Times* reviewer Thomas M. Pryor observed that it "misses out on the epic sweep of the actual Midway campaign. The Navy's own documentary, *Battle of Midway,* remains the classic screen account of that historic engagement."

Some of Ford's Midway footage, reformatted for the wide screen, was interwoven with staged scenes in Universal's bombastic 1976 feature *Midway,* which *Times* reviewer Vincent Canby described as "a kamikaze attack against one of the greatest sea battles of modern times. The battle—history—survives while the movie blows up harmlessly."

Ford was fully aware of the potential public relations benefits of being wounded under fire. With his future Purple Heart clearly in mind,[11] he wrote on July 3 to a chief pharmacist's mate at Midway, "Leaving the Midway Islands in such a hurry and so early in the morning, I neglected to get a discharge from you at the Field Hospital. Could you have Doctor Fleet or yourself endorse my orders for the benefit of my Naval record: Lacerations, abrasions, concussions, and whatnot. My arm is in good shape although it gives me much pain and I still have to report for treatment. Therefore, the aforementioned is necessary."

Upon his return to Los Angeles, Ford made sure that his exploits received wide media coverage. "FORD FILMED BATTLE OF MIDWAY" read the ban-

---

11. After the war, Ford proudly served as commander of the Hollywood chapter of the Military Order of the Purple Heart.

ner headline in the *Hollywood Reporter* of June 18. The following day's War Extra of the *Los Angeles Examiner* proclaimed, "Director Ford Wounded." His wound was such big news that it was headlined above the main story, "CHURCHILL IN U.S. FOR 2ND FRONT PARLEY." Ford's old friend Hedda Hopper trumpeted his actions to her nationwide radio audience on June 20, and Hearst syndicated gossip columnist Louella Parsons hailed Ford as "Hollywood's own personal hero. John got back from Midway Island with a shrapnel wound in his arm, which was swollen to twice its natural size. After he had it treated by a local doctor, he flew to Washington to edit the pictures he filmed of the Battle of Midway, where he received his wound. He didn't even have the shrapnel removed. He will attend to that little matter later."

Despite Ford's pose of indifference toward Academy Awards, he went out of his way to set up a screening of *The Battle of Midway* in Washington for Walter Wanger, the producer of *Stagecoach* and *The Long Voyage Home,* who was then serving as president of the Academy of Motion Picture Arts and Sciences. When Wanger called *The Battle of Midway* "magnificent . . . definitely award material," Ford snapped, "Oh, for Christ's sakes, Walter, I'm not interested in awards. I just want to remind you Hollywood guys that somebody's out there fighting a war." Parrish, who was present at the screening, recalled that Wanger "winced slightly, but he kept his dignity." Wanger told Ford the Academy would have a hard time picking one war film for the documentary Oscar.

"Why can't you have more than one award?" Ford asked.

As a result, the Academy gave four Oscars for documentaries that year. The others went to the U.S. Army's *Prelude to War* (the first of Capra's *Why We Fight* series), Russia's *Moscow Strikes Back,* and Australia's *Kokoda Front Line.*

When the news broke about Ford's Midway exploits, Louella Parsons reported an encounter with Mary, who looked almost unrecognizably thin. "Mary is a wise Navy wife who never talks," wrote Parsons. "All I could get her to say about John's bravery in filming the Battle of Midway, with an arm rendered almost useless from wounds, was: 'I hope we can all see the pictures.' . . . But you won't get her to say that she fought the Battle of Midway from her chair, or that she burns the midnight oil thinking of her husband filming movies right where the shelling and bombing are the thickest. Mary will tell you she wouldn't have John do anything else."

Mary was just putting on a brave public face. Jack Bolton, their friend in the navy's Los Angeles public relations office, told Ford that she was "pretty miserable just sitting on the hilltop worrying about you and waiting for you to come home."

On his way back from Midway, Ford made a brief stopover to see her in San

Francisco. He sent her a coded message saying that he was going to visit a certain man whom she knew was the manager of the Mark Hopkins Hotel. At the appointed time, Mary met Jack at the hotel. "I only saw him for about ten minutes," she recalled, "but he wanted to tell me he was all right." She had learned to appreciate the need for secrecy after being told of the impending Doolittle Raid by an admiral's wife at a luncheon in Pasadena. Mary mentioned the information to Joe August, who became alarmed and warned her not to talk about it.

Ford became increasingly homesick as the war dragged on. In a particularly tender letter from sea in June 1943, he told Mary, "I pray to God it will soon be over so we can live our life together with our children and grandchildren and our *Araner*—Catalina would look good now. God bless and love you Mary darling—I'm tough to live with—heaven knows & Hollywood didn't help—Irish & genius don't mix well but you know you're the only woman I've ever loved." She replied that she offered daily prayers of gratitude for their marriage, and went on to express regret for having done nothing important enough to make him proud of her. Imagining their twenty-fifth wedding anniversary in 1945, Mary hoped they would get drunk on brandy and take a celebratory cruise on the *Araner* with a group of equally intoxicated friends.

Toward the end of the war, Jack's messages from abroad were becoming so ardent that Mary wryly told Ray Kellogg, "I wonder if Jack's all right. It sounds like he's falling in love with me."[12]

Upon returning home from Washington after Pearl Harbor and settling in for the duration, Mary realized she needed to do something to keep herself busy in Jack's absence. Before the war she had done some volunteer work for Navy Relief and for the Assistance League, an organization helping needy Hollywood workers during the Great Depression. At the suggestion of Doris Stein, wife of MCA talent agency chief Jules Stein, Mary became vice president of the Hollywood Canteen, which opened its doors on October 17, 1942.

Located in an abandoned nightclub at 1415 Cahuenga Boulevard in the heart of the Hollywood business district, the Canteen was founded by John Garfield and Bette Davis along with Carroll Hollister and J. K. "Spike" Wallace as a safe but lively entertainment hangout for servicemen passing through

---

12. Ford's niece Cecil and her husband Lorenzo "Larry" de Prida, who were living in Manila when the war started, were captured and interned there by the Japanese. The U.S. State Department and Congressman Robert Hale (R-Maine) tried to secure their release, but they were not freed until 1945, along with their daughter Patricia Ann, born in the internment camp in 1943.

Southern California to and from the Pacific theater of operations. Davis served as president, and Jules Stein was the Canteen's business manager. Forty-two Hollywood unions lent their help free of charge. Each night two big bands, performing in two shifts, entertained as many as sixteen hundred servicemen. Virtually every Hollywood star came to entertain or serve the troops, who were served coffee, soft drinks, cocoa, cakes, ice cream, and sandwiches. No liquor was allowed.

Bob Hope was chairman of the entertainment committee, and bandleader Kay Kyser was in charge of musical entertainment. Regular bandleaders included Tommy Dorsey, Harry James, and Freddie Martin, with classical conductors such as Arthur Rubinstein and Leopold Stokowski directing the Sunday afternoon concerts. Hope and Bing Crosby did a radio show from the Canteen, and in 1943 Davis and Garfield were among the all-star cast of the Warner Bros. movie *Hollywood Canteen,* a flag-waving musical revue directed by Delmer Daves.

The main attraction at the Canteen, however, was not the music but the dazzling lineup of female stars and starlets dancing with the boys in uniform, waiting on tables, and serving behind the snack counter. A serviceman could take a whirl around the dance floor with the likes of Davis, Marlene Dietrich, Olivia de Havilland, Hedy Lamarr, Joan Crawford, Gene Tierney, and Betty Grable. Hostesses were officially discouraged from dating servicemen in this surreal romantic fantasyland, but illicit flings inevitably resulted. Operating in a state that still outlawed miscegenation, the Canteen practiced only partial racial integration: African-American servicemen were restricted to dancing with black hostesses recruited by the wife of actor Clarence Muse (Muse later appeared in Ford's film *The Sun Shines Bright*).

Mary Ford took a job at the Canteen no one else wanted. From four in the afternoon to midnight seven days a week, she ran the kitchen and snack bar. She recruited Dietrich, Spencer Tracy, Basil Rathbone, Reginald Gardner, Cesar Romero, Red Skelton, and Danny Kaye as dishwashers and busboys. Ronald Colman and Walter Pidgeon were among the waiters. Mary's recruiting was made easier by her husband's friend and admirer Hedda Hopper, who had a brief tryout for the Ford Stock Company in *Pilgrimage.* Hopper would call Mary every Monday morning to find out which stars had been working in the kitchen and vent her wrath against those who shirked the duty.

When people thanked Mary for all she did for the Hollywood Canteen, she would reply, "Are you kidding? Look what the Canteen's done for me." Nevertheless, she suffered greatly from loneliness during the years Jack was in the service.

Barbara, eighteen when the war started, remained at home with her mother. She wanted to make a career in the film industry and even aspired to become a director. Harry Wurtzel arranged for her to be interviewed by director Henry King in December 1942 for the lead role in Fox's religious tale *The Song of Bernadette*. But when King chose Jennifer Jones instead, Barbara found a job as an assistant cutter at the studio, hoping to work for her father in that capacity after the war.

Twenty-year-old Pat, a burly 6'4" and 220 pounds, was attending the University of Maine at the time of Pearl Harbor. After his graduation in August 1942, he married a Maine girl named Jane Mulvany. Rejected for a navy commission because of his poor eyesight, Pat enlisted as an apprentice seaman. His father tried unsuccessfully to obtain him an assignment to serve aboard the *Araner*. Instead, Jack Bolton wangled him a position as a navy public information officer in Los Angeles.

While serving in that post, Pat presented his parents with their first two grandchildren, Timothy John (born on February 3, 1944), and the director's future biographer Daniel Sargent (born on February 13, 1945). After Timothy arrived, Ford wrote Spig Wead that the baby was "absolutely beautiful. He looks exactly like me." "Pappy is now a Grandpappy," Ford's OSS secretary, Evangeline "Vangie" Ostrander, told Wead. "He walks around with a silly grin on his big Irish puss and hasn't pinched me for ten days. Am I slipping or is he slipping?"

Unhappy with his desk job, Pat considered his navy career a failure. He thought about becoming a war correspondent and begged his father to find him a position on the staff of Gene Markey, Ford's Hollywood producer friend who was running a Naval Intelligence unit attached to the Joint Anglo-American Southeast Asian Command in New Delhi. Ford at first tried to discourage that notion, but then he agreed to pull strings with the Office of Naval Intelligence in March 1944. The effort was unsuccessful because of Pat's eyesight, his youth, and the likelihood that the war would be nearing its end by the time he could be trained for intelligence work.

That January, Pat wrote his father complaining about having to serve in the public relations department, which he characterized as dominated by Jews (Pat used an anti-Semitic slur for young male Jews) and sons of wealthy families. He felt the department was largely ineffectual and lamented that he was contributing nothing to the war effort.

Pat's scapegoating of Jews for his career frustrations evidently was an attitude shared by his uncle Wingate Smith, Ford's assistant director. "Unc" had rejoined the army and was serving at "Fort Fox," where some army training films were made, on Western Avenue in Hollywood. Pat told his father that as a professional military man, Wingate was unhappy about having to answer to Jewish officers. Continuing to express such bigotry after he left the service and entered the film industry, Pat may have been taking out on other people the resentment he felt toward his cold and tyrannical father but did not dare express.

It's dismayingly evident from Ford's correspondence with both his wife and son that a certain amount of anti-Semitism was considered acceptable among them, even if they were too discreet to express such sentiments in public. While it seems ironic that these resentments reached their most intense expression in the midst of a war against Nazism, anti-Semitism in the United States began to diminish after the war, as the lessons of the Holocaust and the increased social mobility of Jewish veterans helped break down some of the old barriers. But a sign of prejudice that persisted into the era of the postwar Red Scare was a tendency among right-wing anti-Semites to use the words *Jew* and *Communist* as if they were synonymous.

Mary Ford became incensed during the war about what she perceived as a Communist-Jewish cabal attempting to take over the board of directors of the Hollywood Canteen in order to use the club as an outlet for leftist propaganda. In a letter to Jack on December 8, 1943, she complained that the Canteen was now dominated by Jews and that Jews had discriminated against one of the Fords' Irish friends. She bluntly expressed pleasure in thinking that anti-Semites in the Canteen would reassert control from the Jews, whom she felt were trying to influence the programs and policies of the Canteen. One such conflict arose when some of those Mary considered leftists wanted to have the navy's shore patrol and army MPs removed from keeping order at the Canteen. Pat admiringly told his father that Mary was handling that battle in the manner of a Prussian aristocrat.

Mary recalled that some Canteen board members, such as Bette Davis, Jules Stein, Bob Hope, and Kay Kyser, held secret meetings at her house on Odin Street to make decisions without involving leftists. Evidently Mary's scornful attitude toward Jews did not extend to those who, like Stein, were aligned with her conservative faction. Nor did she object in 1943 when Eddie Cantor gave Christmas presents to the Canteen for more than ten thousand servicemen.

One Hollywood leftist Mary particularly resented was John Garfield, who had founded the Canteen with Davis. In a January 1944 letter to Jack, Mary complained about problems she was having with the Screen Actors Guild and Garfield. Describing Garfield as a Communist, she referred to him by his birth name, Garfinkle. Such venom foreshadowed the political conflicts that would tear Hollywood apart in the postwar era, when the House Committee on Un-American Activities investigated alleged Communist influence in Hollywood, prompting the studios to initiate the blacklist in 1947. Screenwriter Dalton Trumbo, one of the blacklisted Hollywood Ten, was among the people Mary identified as a leader of the attempt to radicalize the Hollywood Canteen. Garfield, a former member of the left-wing Group Theatre and a prominent Hollywood progressive, also refused to cooperate with HUAC and was blacklisted shortly before his death from a heart attack in 1952 at the age of thirty-nine.

John Ford's growing conservatism during the war years was greatly influenced by the company he kept in the military and the OSS, beginning with Donovan himself. While the outcome of the war still hung in the balance, Donovan's pragmatism allowed him to enter into expedient alliances with Communists in various parts of the globe. One of the films made by Field Photo, *Farish Report,* documents the OSS alliances with both the Yugoslav partisans under their Communist leader, Marshal Tito, and the anti-Communist, pro-Serbian Chetniks supported by King Peter, the young monarch in exile, and led by Draza Mihailovic. The film's narrator describes those fighting the Nazis in Yugoslavia as "barefoot, cold, and hungry people, people whose courage and endurance must be observed to be understood. To us they were not Communists or reactionaries, Partisans or Chetniks, but merely brave people who looked to us for aid with the confidence that it would be forthcoming."

But the experience of the radical writer Abraham Polonsky working with the OSS and the Free French demonstrates how anti-Communist Donovan's agency became in the latter part of the war. Polonsky recalled, "As the war came to a close [the OSS] wouldn't let us bring any arms in for those partisan groups who were Communists. [The OSS] did not want them to be armed after the war was over. During the last year of the war there was already in motion, within Army Intelligence, anti-Communist programs for the postwar future."

Despite Ford's prewar activism on behalf of the Spanish Republic, the Hollywood Anti-Nazi League, and the Screen Directors Guild, and his 1937 claim to be "a definite socialistic democrat—*always* left," he increasingly adopted the U.S. government's hardening anti-Communist line during the postwar years. Ford's attitude toward the postwar Hollywood blacklist would prove complex and sometimes contradictory. But initially he aligned himself with Hollywood's most militantly anti-Communist elements, becoming one of the founding members of the Motion Picture Alliance for the Preservation of American Ideals in February 1944. Among the deductions on Ford's 1944 income tax return was a forty-dollar contribution to the Alliance.

Perhaps because he was on active duty in the navy and had to avoid overt political activity, and also in part because he was taking something of a wait-and-see attitude toward the Hollywood political climate, Ford was not among the first officers of the MPA, but he would become one during the Red Scare. Not the last breathtaking turn Ford would take in response to changing political currents, his decision to align himself with what Ceplair and Englund describe as "a prominent group of Hollywood anti-Rooseveltians" demonstrated how much Ford's political beliefs were based on knee-jerk emotionalism and an anxious, self-defensive expediency. Ford's Irish Catholicism was a strong factor in predisposing him toward the anti-Communist cause, as it was for *Going My Way* director Leo McCarey, another MPA founder, and Ford's friend and screenwriter James Kevin McGuinness, chairman of the MPA's first executive committee and later its executive director. The group's formative meetings were held in McGuinness's home. In the words of John Wayne biographer Maurice Zolotow, "John Ford, himself an Irish rebel to the core, was nevertheless anxious about the anti-religious and anti-American quality of some of the Marxian sounds he heard, and he had discussed it with Duke."

Wayne was a founding member of the MPA and became its president in 1949, declaring, "We don't want a political party here that any bully boy in a foreign country can make dance to his tune." The group's first president was director Sam Wood, who was such a rabid anti-Communist that his will specified that his own daughters could not receive inheritances unless they filed affidavits swearing that they "are not now, nor have they ever been, Communists." Walt Disney, a bitter foe of organized labor, was founding vice-president. Other MPA founders included directors King Vidor, Victor Fleming, Clarence Brown, and Norman Taurog; actors Clark Gable, Adolphe Menjou, Gary Cooper, Robert Taylor, Ginger Rogers, Barbara Stanwyck, Irene Dunne, Pat O'Brien, and Donald Crisp; screenwriters John Lee Mahin, Howard Emmett Rogers, Rupert Hughes, Borden Chase, and Morrie Ryskind; art director Cedric Gibbons; antilabor leader Roy Brewer; and stuntman and second-unit director Cliff Lyons (who frequently worked with Ford in later years).

John T. McManus of the liberal New York newspaper *PM* recognized the danger the MPA posed to freedom of expression in Hollywood, describing it in March 1944 as "a group formed in Hollywood by a handful of noted reactionaries headed by Sam Wood, the director who pulled the anti-fascist punch of the film *For Whom the Bell Tolls* [Paramount's 1943 adaptation of Ernest Hemingway's novel about the Spanish civil war]." The MPA had the "stated purpose of running a witch-hunt," McManus noted, and though the group was dominated by "the Know-Nothing bloc among Metro-Goldwyn-Mayer producers, led by James K. McGuinness, a protégé of the notorious [Fox executive and former New York City police commissioner] Winfield Sheehan, the MPA's board of directors managed to attract a few men of unblemished background among Hollywood craftsmen."

"We believe in, and like, the American way of life," the MPA declared in its "Statement of Principles." ". . . In our special field of motion pictures, we resent the growing impression that this industry is made up of, and dominated by, Communists, radicals, and crackpots. . . . We pledge ourselves to fight, with every means at our organized command, any effort of any group or individual to divert the loyalty of the screen from the free America that gave it birth."

Wood went a step beyond that in his inaugural address, advancing the kind of jingoistic, nativistic agenda that would later make Ford, the son of immigrants, acutely uncomfortable: "The American motion picture industry is, and will continue to be, held by Americans for the American people, in the interests of America, and dedicated to the preservation and continuance of the American scene and the American way of life." The 1947 HUAC hearings, which Ford opposed even while remaining active in the MPA, relied heavily on allegations provided by Wood and other members of the MPA, as did the subsequent Hollywood blacklist.

Throughout his lifetime, Ford prided himself, publicly at least, on what he considered his record of tolerance toward Jews and other members of minority groups. After all, as a second-generation Irish-American he was a member of a minority group that had known oppression. As evidence of his enlightened attitude during World War II and the Nazi Holocaust, Ford pointed with pride to his role in helping the OSS repatriate some Jewish refugees from Budapest by bus and plane at the end of the war. In addition, Ford's tax returns show that he made donations to Jewish charities ranging from a $1,000 donation to Temple Israel in 1929 to a $2,313 gift to the National Jewish Hospital in 1966. On a visit to Spain in 1962, he bought an antique menorah (for under $30) and donated it to Temple Israel of Hollywood through Columbia Pictures production manager Jack Fier. Director Samuel Fuller, who was Jewish, said, "Ford was terrific! He wore a chain around his neck, under his shirt. If he was talking to a Catholic, he pulled out his cross. If he was talking to a Jew, he would pull out his Star of David. . . . He had the full panoply."

Others have questioned Ford's sincerity in such ostentatious professions of brotherhood and his sophistication in dealing with issues of discrimination. One of Ford's business managers, Bea Benjamin, who was Jewish, told Dan Ford that she considered his grandfather anti-Semitic. Asked what made her think so, Benjamin replied that Ford liked to say that some of his best friends were Jews, a familiar gentile mantra that she considered tellingly defensive on his part. Ford's prominent role in the Motion Picture Alliance also contributed to such suspicions. From its inception, the MPA often was "accused of being anti-Semitic," as McGuinness himself put it in April 1944, calling the group "the victim of a smear campaign." McGuinness and fellow executive committee member Howard Emmett Rogers replied to that charge by pointing to several prominent American Jews who were leading anti-Communists. But the movement to purge liberals and radicals from Hollywood became increasingly tinged with anti-Semitic overtones, particularly during the HUAC hearings.

The virulent anti-Semitism expressed by Mary and Pat in their letters to John Ford seems to have been offered without any concern that the paterfamilias might have a negative reaction. Indeed, the Ford collection at the Lilly Library contains no letters from Ford responding favorably or unfavorably to those remarks by his wife and son. Furthermore, in some of his other correspondence, Ford used stereotypical and derogatory language about Jews.

A January 1942 letter to his agent, Harry Wurtzel, contains Ford's suggestion that Wurtzel hire a Jewish lawyer to make a subtle legal threat against a journalist planning an article that Ford thought would be unsympathetic. In a somewhat paranoid fashion, Ford linked the journalist with Fifth Columnists, isolationists, and others undermining the war effort. When Wurtzel intervened, the journalist assured him of his goodwill toward Ford, and after the war he was hired to do publicity work for Ford's Argosy Pictures. In a July 1943 letter to Wurtzel, Ford similarly instructed him to hire a "hebe lawyer" to handle a difficult negotiation.

Ford's ethnic badinage with Wurtzel could be construed as a symptom of that era's less sensitive attitude toward language that today would be considered offensive. Ford clearly did not expect Wurtzel to be offended by his repeated advice to hire a Jewish lawyer; Ford's comment about the need for Catholic-Jewish solidarity against the Axis powers came in one of those same letters. If Wurtzel felt offended by Ford's ethnic stereotyping, he evidently did not say so to Ford.

However, in an October 1943 letter to Mary while traveling on a Navy ship, Ford referred to a Jewish doctor on board as "The Yid." Ford's casual use of this derogatory word refers to someone with whom he presumably did not have the kind of teasing friendship he shared with Wurtzel. Ford included another slur against Jews in a letter he wrote the following October to Major General Albert C. Wedemeyer, a right-wing army man of German descent and anti-Semitic views who had studied as an exchange student at the German War College (Kriegsakademie) in Berlin in 1936–38. Ford's comments to Wedemeyer, whom he presumably considered a receptive audience, indicate a general animus against Jews in Hollywood: "My militaristic ego has been somewhat deflated. I have been ordered to Hollywood to do a commercial picture called *They Were Expendable,* and I am leaving tonight. While I will at least get a chance to spend Christmas with the folks and play with my grandsons' electric train, still I'm a bit ashamed that a great warrior like me should be in mockie-land while the good people are fighting."

Mockie, sometimes spelled "mockey" or "mocky," is a derogatory term for "Jew," probably deriving from the Yiddish word *makeh,* meaning a boil, a sore, or a plague.[13]

All this evidence indicates that Ford quietly shared his wife's bias against Jews and helped raise their son to be an anti-Semite. Ford's largely unblemished public record in his dealings with Jews simply meant that he was smart enough to keep his prejudice close to his vest, particularly in an industry in which he dealt frequently with Jewish colleagues, leading him to think of Hollywood as "mockie-land."

When Ford arrived in Algiers on November 12, 1942, he was greeted by a familiar face. Darryl F. Zanuck was there on behalf of the U.S. Army Signal Corps organizing the film coverage of the Allied invasion of North Africa, which had begun four days earlier. "Can't I *ever* get away from you?" Ford demanded. "I'll bet a dollar to a doughnut that if I ever go to Heaven, you'll be waiting at the door for me under a sign reading 'Produced by Darryl F. Zanuck.'"

The navy ordered Ford to the British Isles "on a mission the nature of which cannot be divulged for reasons of security." Sailing aboard the USS *Samuel Chase,* he arrived in London on August 31, taking a room at Claridge's and setting up shop at OSS headquarters, 72 Grosvenor Street. From there he organized crews and secured equipment to film the impending invasion of French Morocco and Algeria, code-named Operation Torch. The complicated logistics of the photographic operation included plans for the exposed 16mm color film footage and black-and-white stills to be sent back daily by courier from North Africa to the London office of the APS. Ford and Jack Pennick departed on October 28 for Scotland, the starting point of their sixteen-day sea journey to Algiers.

Following the October 23–November 4 British victory in Egypt over German general Erwin Rommel's Afrika Korps at El Alamein, Operation Torch was launched on November 8. It ultimately proved successful in preventing

---

13. When quoting from this letter in his biography of his grandfather, Dan Ford recorded "mockie-land" as "'movie land.'" Scott Eyman's 1999 authorized biography *Print the Legend: The Life and Times of John Ford* quotes the word "mockie-land" correctly, but Eyman seems not to understand its meaning. He writes, "As for Jews, [Ford] would occasionally address Harry Wurtzel with anti-Semitic jibes ('Dear Christ-Killer') of the sort that only good friends can get away with. . . . Except for the letters to Harry Wurtzel, Ford's private correspondence is completely free of racial or religious slurs." Eyman also fails to acknowledge Ford's use of the anti-Semitic slur "The Yid."

the German army from linking its Egyptian and Russian salients in the Middle East. When President Roosevelt asked to see the army's film coverage of the landings, Brigadier General William H. Harrison, head of the APS, could not bring himself to admit what had happened to that footage. Major Anatole Litvak had been detached from Capra's army unit to head the camera crew filming the American landings, but the ship carrying his exposed footage was sunk before it could even leave port. Field Photo, however, managed to obtain what it called "thorough coverage" of Allied troops under General Dwight D. Eisenhower landing at Algiers and Oran.

Ford and his thirty-two men from Field Photo, along with other cameramen from the army and navy, were temporarily assigned to duty under Zanuck shooting 16mm color film footage of the invasion for newsreels and a War Department documentary. Serving as motion picture adviser to the chief signal officer, Major General Dawson Olmstead, and assigned to the staff of Major General Mark W. Clark, Zanuck had a total of twelve camera crews in the field, commanded by Ford, Litvak, and Lieutenant Albert Klein of the APS. With a cigar clenched in his mouth and a .45 automatic pistol stuck in his belt, Zanuck exclaimed, "I wouldn't miss this show for all the cigars in Havana."

Noting Ford's arrival in his diary, Zanuck wrote, "Ford is anxious to get to the Tunis front and I shall assign him to one of the first American units to go into that area." Ford, Pennick, and two other OSS men were attached to Company D of the Thirteenth Armored Regiment of the U.S. Army. Boarding a British LCT (landing craft for tanks) and traveling mostly at night, the company arrived at the Algerian port of Bône in the midst of an air raid on the morning of November 18. On the road the next day, they managed to escape unscathed from a bombing by German planes. The company soon ran into more bombing at the Souk-el-Arba airport. "Not one of our entire tank group was injured," cameraman Robert Johannes later reported to the OSS. "We retaliated with fire from every form of gun we had, even pistols."

"I personally covered the landing at Bône, which was really tough," Ford wrote James Roosevelt after his return to the States. "From Bône we went to Tunisia. We were under dive [and] horizontal bombing, artillery and machine gun fire twenty-four hours a day for six weeks and subsisted on tea and English biscuits. Was I hungry! Lost 32 pounds, but got my outfit out with minor casualties. The Navy threw a Purple Heart at me so now I guess I have to buy a uniform, as all my personal gear was blown up."[14]

---

14. Ford's letter seems to imply that he received a Purple Heart for a minor injury he received in North Africa, but his only Purple Heart was the one for his wound in the Battle of Midway. He was notified of that award on February 2, 1943, and the medal was forwarded to him on July 7.

Ford and his men ran into their most sustained action after leaving Soul-el-Arba. Johannes recalled that German air raids "went on all night, every night, and during the daytime" as the company bivouaced on a farm outside Beja, hiding their tanks overnight among eucalyptus trees. "One JU-88 came over and bombed us, and a Spitfire night-fighter went up and got him. I was able to get some good shots of the JU-88 coming down in flames. The bombardier bailed out. I jumped into a jeep and with Commander Ford and C Sp Pennick, raced across ditches and gullies and picked him up. He had thrown away all identification, and when we arrived threw away his gun and surrendered to us. He said his best friends were in the plane and he wanted to see them. We drove to [the] crashed plane, but his pals were beyond recognition.

"We took pictures of the bombardier alongside his crashed plane. He objected, but he was told it was necessary. By that time, a [Free] French Army man came up and wanted to shoot our prisoner but we told him that he was our prisoner and was to be turned over to Intelligence for questioning. An American Intelligence officer arrived in a jeep a little later, evidently having seen the crash from his station, and we turned the prisoner over to him."

On November 29 Ford's group proceeded to Tebourba, "where heavy enemy resistance was encountered and our advance was stopped," Johannes said. The regiment was pinned down in a valley by a ferocious tank battle and German dive-bombing attacks. Finally, on December 6, Ford and his men left the continuing battle and returned to the rear with their footage. "Ford, regardless of danger, took his men where the best camerawork was to be done," OSS agent Tom Moon recalled. "Many area commanders, not anxious to have these men killed in their area, breathed a sigh of relief as they moved on." Ford departed from Gibraltar on December 19 aboard the *Samuel Chase* with Pennick, three cameramen, and a smuggled bottle of scotch for their Christmas celebration. The ship had to ward off three attacks by German submarines before arriving in Washington on New Year's Eve. The rest of the Field Photo unit wended its way back to London.

Only a small fraction of the many hours of color film shot by Field Photo cameramen wound up in Zanuck's 1943 documentary *At the Front in North Africa*. The most recognizably Fordian footage is a sequence of tanks being unloaded from landing craft at Bône. These beautifully photographed sunset shots show Ford's characteristic fondness for dramatizing otherwise uneventful action through the use of deep shadows and silhouettes. The documentary's most spectacular combat footage is the tank battle at Tebourba, shot from a hilltop closely overlooking German tanks under assault by American tanks and artillery. Ford himself makes a brief appearance in a comical sequence of soldiers relaxing and buying chickens from friendly Arabs at Souk-el-Khemis. Unshaven and wearing dark glasses, Ford is seen riding on a tiny burro. Although not identified on-screen, he was recognized by *Variety* reviewer *Wear.,* who wrote, "No explanation is made why Ford, producer-director of *How Green Was My Valley,* is there."

Upon his return to the States, Zanuck chronicled his experiences in a diary published by Random House in 1943 as *Tunis Expedition.* Reviewing the book in the *New York Times,* John K. Hutchens preferred it to *At the Front in North Africa,* a "feeble and even unprofessional job, the like of which would have meant—in Hollywood—an option not picked up." Released by Warner Bros. on February 25, 1943, the sluggishly paced documentary fails to offer much sense of the overall invasion; most of the running time is consumed with shots of convoys of troops and equipment moving through nondescript desert land-scapes. The army officially viewed Zanuck's material with a "lack of enthusi-asm." Capra considered it dismayingly weak by comparison with *Desert Victory,* the 1943 British Ministry of Information documentary on the African cam-paign against Rommel, which supplements its impressive battle footage with liberal use of night battle scenes staged in a studio. "I don't suppose our war scenes will look as savage and realistic as those we usually make on the back lot, but then you can't have everything," Zanuck admitted to General Olm-stead after filming was completed in December.

Zanuck commendably avoided such fakery, writing in a response to the *Times,* "I might have easily transposed *At the Front* from a straightforward piece of visual reporting to a bang-up documentary with propaganda over-tones. . . . Somehow, however, I am pleased that we resisted the temptation." But he ran into a public relations booby trap by including shots of himself wearing a helmet and a .45 automatic pistol, and a scene in which he fires a tommy gun at a German airplane. Zanuck was ridiculed in the press as a "Hol-lywood colonel," a strutting peacock who seemed to be trying to win the war single-handedly.[15]

The activities of Zanuck, Ford, Capra, and other Hollywood personalities in military service came under the cold eye of the U.S. Senate in February 1943, when Senator Harry S Truman's Special Committee Investigating the Na-

---

15. The loss of Litvak's footage, the derision that greeted Zanuck's documentary, and the acclaim the British received for *Desert Victory* so embarrassed the army that when it learned the British were compiling a new film called *Africa Freed,* it pulled strings to have some of the British footage incorporated into a Capra-produced documentary, *Tunisian Victory.* Containing even more faked footage than *Desert Victory* (parts of the North African campaign were restaged by Capra, John Huston, and George Stevens) and resorting to animation to cover many gaps in the action, *Tunisian Victory,* a joint venture of the War Department's Bu-reau of Public Relations and the British Ministry of Information, was released uneventfully by MGM in 1944.

tional Defense Program began looking into military filmmaking practices. The investigation focused on waste and inefficiency, alleged favoritism by Zanuck and the Academy Research Council in allocating production contracts to the studios, and allegations that studios were profiting from the "nonprofit" contracts. The committee also scrutinized the commissions granted to Hollywood filmmakers, as well as alleged conflicts of interest between their military and Hollywood activities, such as Ford and Capra receiving profit percentages from their old films while in uniform.

But the principal target was Zanuck. He was criticized for remaining on the Fox payroll at five thousand dollars a week for almost four months while on active army duty and for failing to place his ninety thousand shares of Fox stock in trust for the duration of his government service. Truman tartly suggested that the army should "send him to school and make a real Army officer out of him." Colonel Kirke B. Lawton, the newly appointed head of the Army Pictorial Service, conceded that Zanuck "was not putting full time on duty with the Signal Corps," and a secret investigation by the army inspector general in January 1943 found that Zanuck had violated the law by continuing to profit from his stock holdings, although no charges were filed against him.

"[W]ho cares about a few measly pennies or $50,000?" Zanuck angrily testified. "What does it matter if you can make a picture that will help someone kill a German, or save his own life?" Blasting the investigators for insinuating that he had personally profited from government films, Zanuck called it "a dirty, lousy outrage to do such a thing to a patriotic American, and I'm not going to stand for it. . . . I am to blame for being a sucker and trying to help my country. . . . They will never catch me, Major, ever doing anything again for anybody."

On April 5, 1943, Ford came under scrutiny by the committee when its chief counsel, Hugh Fulton, requested the names of civilians granted navy commissions. The navy forwarded a list that included Ford and twenty-five other members of "Field Photographic Intelligence." Fulton requested further information from the navy on Ford, Toland, Jack Bolton, and others "with respect to present and past financial connection with motion picture companies either by salary, fee, or stock ownership."

"Commander Ford has long been recognized as one of the most outstanding motion picture directors," Donovan responded in a May 3 letter to the chief of naval personnel detailing Ford's record of service in the Naval Reserve and his role in founding its prewar Photographic Unit. "At the present time he is still receiving dividends from several pictures which he directed on a percentage basis [*The Lost Patrol, The Informer,* and *Stagecoach*]. . . . These percentage dividends are now averaging approximately $2,000 yearly, on a di-

minishing basis.[16] John Ford holds 50 shares of stock in the Argosy Corporation, a corporation which was formed for the production of motion pictures.
This corporation produced one motion picture, *The Long Voyage Home,* which
Ford directed. The Argosy Corporation is not operating at present and has suspended production for the duration. Ford does not own any other motion picture stock."

Although the Senate investigation tended to spread overly broad innuendos,
blurring the facts of individual cases and displaying a biased attitude toward
the Hollywood men in uniform, it helped bring about a major reorganization
of army filmmaking, eventually resulting in the Academy Research Council
being dropped as the middleman for production contracts and Capra's unit
being transferred from the Special Services Division to the APS for reasons of
"economy." Zanuck was relieved of duty at his own request in May 1943, although he was mollified by the War Department's award of the Legion of
Merit in 1944 for "exceptional bravery under fire."

Ford escaped largely unscathed from the Senate investigation, thanks to his
undeniably vital role on the front lines with the OSS and his lack of any major
conflicts of interest, at least any that the committee could discover. Capra felt
that he and Ford had been rescued by Zanuck's willingness to sacrifice his own
military career. The fiascoes involving Zanuck and *December 7th* made Ford increasingly secretive about publicizing his military filmmaking activities, as well
as giving him an additional reason to ensure that his service record was carefully documented. Part of that effort was Field Photo's secret *ETO* (European
Theater of Operations) *War Diary* containing Johannes's account of serving
with him in North Africa.

Ford did devote some time during his service years to planning postwar
Hollywood projects. He had further discussions about *Salome, Where She
Danced,* considering Marlene Dietrich for the role of the Mata Hari–like spy,
before passing on the project. During his sojourn in North Africa, Ford often
distracted himself from the freezing cold by turning his mind to film ideas,
such as Graham Greene's novel *The Power and the Glory* and Nina Federova's
1940 novel about Russian émigrés in China, *The Family.* Ford wrote Dudley
Nichols in March 1943 that he was eager to discuss those projects, and in Sep-

---

16. That was somewhat misleading. According to his income tax returns, Ford earned $7,632 in profits from
his old movies in 1941; $2,757 in 1942; $3,096 in 1943; $25,485 in 1944; and $36,911 in 1945. His earnings included a $15,000 settlement Harry Wurtzel negotiated in the summer of 1943 from RKO for al-
lowing MGM to make *Bataan,* Tay Garnett's uncredited 1943 remake of Ford's 1934 film *The Lost Patrol,*
transposed to World War II.

tember he told Olive Carey he had been working on the remake of *The Last Outlaw,* which he was calling *Laramie.*

Ford also was monitoring the progress of MGM's plans for its film version of *They Were Expendable,* based on the 1942 best-seller by W. L. White about the exploits of U.S. Navy Lieutenant John Bulkeley and his PT boat crews in the early days of the war in the Philippines. Bulkeley was awarded the Medal of Honor in August 1942 for destroying Japanese planes and ships with his squadron of wooden boats as American forces made their desperate last stand. "The Wild Man of the Philippines" was even more famous for his daring rescue of General Douglas MacArthur. That March, Bulkeley commanded four PT boats transporting MacArthur, his family, and key staff members on the epic 620-mile journey through submarine-infested waters from Corregidor to Mindanao for their flight to Australia.

White's book, a first-person account by Bulkeley and three of his men, was part of a morale-boosting effort by Secretary of the Navy Frank Knox that included the planned film version and a May 1943 article in *Life* magazine by John Hersey, "PT Squadron in the South Pacific." Bulkeley recalled that Knox "wanted to promote the Navy and enhance the Americans, who were beaten up at that time [1942]. We were losing the war. Some admirals will say you always get hit, hit, *hit* in the first part of a war, then *you* start hitting. It was some time before we recovered. That's what Frank Knox wanted to counter by public relations."

What interested Ford, however, was the book's depiction of the gallantry of men willingly sacrificing themselves for a lost cause.

"Well, it's like this," one of Bulkeley's officers told White. "Suppose you're a sergeant machine-gunner, and your army is retreating and the enemy advancing. The captain takes you to a machine gun covering the road. 'You're to stay here and hold this position,' he tells you. 'For how long?' you ask. 'Never mind,' he answers, 'just hold it.' Then you know you're expendable. . . . You know the situation—that those few minutes gained are worth the life of a man to your army. So you don't mind it until you come back here where people waste hours and days and sometimes weeks, when you've seen your friends give their lives to save minutes."

"I was very bitter about the thing," Bulkeley admitted to me in 1987. "We went over there with 111 men and only 9 men came back alive. [The War Department] put eighty thousand soldiers over there, and that was a political decision on the part of the president and [Secretary of War Henry L.] Stimson that we were going to show the Asiatic race that we supported them, that we did not back off from the Japanese. But the war plan was totally, utterly hopeless. You could not send a battle fleet out there and defeat the Japs and bring aid and so forth to the Philippines. We were not only too far away, we weren't ready. To try to defend the Philippines was stupid, we couldn't do it. But we had to put up a fight."

After arriving in Washington from homecoming parades and rallies in New York, the newly promoted Lieutenant Commander Bulkeley spent several hours briefing the screenwriter assigned to *They Were Expendable,* Frank W. "Spig" Wead, the former navy flier who had turned to writing after his crippling injury and worked with Ford on the 1932 film *Air Mail.* "Knox picked him to do the writing, knowing full well Ford and Wead were close," Bulkeley said. Wead had returned to active duty as a navy lieutenant commander and helped plan the carrier war against the Japanese, serving as operations officer to Admiral C. T. Durgin, who described him as "a great man who did a remarkable job under very difficult circumstances." Another Ford crony, James Kevin McGuinness, was assigned by MGM as the executive in charge of *Expendable.*

Despite all this persuasion, Ford kept temporizing about directing the film. Reluctant to go off active duty to make a Hollywood war movie, he told McGuinness that if he did so, "[E]very congressman in America would be after my ass." McGuinness and Wead tried to allay that anxiety by suggesting that Ford donate his salary to Navy Relief. But Ford had a deeper concern stemming from his sense of responsibility toward the subject. At a time when Hollywood felt obliged to depict the war in a strictly gung ho, flag-waving fashion, he was not convinced that MGM would want a true, unvarnished depiction of that tragic chapter of the war, succinctly described by Bulkeley: "In the Philippines, we were living off the land with no pay and no chow for six months—all we cared about was gasoline and torpedoes. It was grim."

I'm back at the desk for a while," Ford wrote James Roosevelt from Washington on March 20, 1943. "Routine work for various Government agencies. Working 18 hours a day; very little of it military and naval nature. . . . Merian Cooper has been relieved as Chief of Staff for Chennault (politics) and is back in the country. We talked about Hollywood and after the war. We have some great propositions, if you would care to talk about it." That overture to the president's son, who had worked as a producer for Samuel Goldwyn before the war, seemed a shrewd political move on Ford's part, but Jimmy Roosevelt preferred a postwar career in politics, serving six terms in Congress. The discussions between Ford and Cooper, on the other hand, laid the groundwork for their postwar reactivation of Argosy Pictures.

Ford finally found an apartment in the overcrowded capital in the summer of 1943, renting furnished quarters on the third floor of 1636 Connecticut Avenue for $125 a month. An African-American man named James Jackson chauffeured him to work in a 1941 Buick. Ford described Jackson as a "good and trusted servant in my family for many years. . . . James is a World War [I] veteran, has been decorated twice, and [was] a close and trusted friend and servant of both the late Will Rogers and myself at the Fox Studios in Hollywood." Ford also had a maid whom he described to Spig Wead as "that aphrodisiacal Afro-American gal."

There is no evidence of Ford's carrying on actual extramarital liaisons in those hectic years. He told Mary he missed her so much they might even share a bed together when the war was over. But in the meantime, Ford amused himself by engaging in a prolonged flirtation with his secretary, Vangie Ostrander. He teasingly inserted bawdy remarks into his dictation, such as this complaint to one of his overseas officers in February 1944: "Vangie is still a virgin. . . . I might add that I also am virgo intacta although I became a grandfather last week." The same day Ford wrote Wead, "The only consolation in this town is our girl Vangie, who still says 'No,' emphatically no!" Vangie added her own postscript: "Uncle Spig, what should I do with that old goat[?]"

When he completed *The Battle of Midway,* Ford told Parrish to run the film for Gregg Toland and Sam Engel, who still were busy putting together their original version of *December 7th.* As Toland and Engel watched Ford's majestic color sequence of a burial at sea to the accompaniment of "My Country, 'Tis of Thee," Engel jumped out of his chair in the projection room and shouted, "The sonofabitch stole our scenes! That's exactly what we have in our picture, the stuff we told him about in Pearl Harbor!"[17] As they walked out, Engel was beside himself: "Don't you see what's happened? The bastard has sabotaged our picture! Everything we've been working on for six months!" After Parrish recounted Engel's outburst, Ford wryly admitted, "Maybe he's right."

Ford's devious way of showing up his insubordinate underlings was underscored by the implicit contrast between the stunning authenticity of his combat footage in *The Battle of Midway* and the glaring phoniness of *December 7th.* Although the faked footage of the Pearl Harbor bombing has turned up over the years in many subsequent documentaries, naively presented as the real thing, it was viewed as an embarrassment at the time by people within the

---

17. There is no burial at sea in either the long or short version of *December 7th,* but unedited footage for such a sequence exists at the National Archives.

government who knew the difference between genuine combat footage and a Hollywood facsimile. The prevailing attitude of disdain can be gauged by a comment made in 1943 by Office of War Information chief Elmer Davis when previewing a film made by Capra's army unit, *The Negro Soldier:* "Is not that the tank shot of Pearl Harbor? If so, it should not be used. That event should not be commemorated in a studio tank shot."[18]

While giving Donovan official authorization for the *December 7th* project, Stimson added a handwritten note stating the film would never be made public without the permission of the War Department. That caveat proved prophetic, for *December 7th* touched sensitive nerves in many quarters, most of all in Ford's own branch of service. The major roadblock to the film's release was that Admiral Harold R. Stark, commander of U.S. naval forces in Europe, had been chief of naval operations at the time of the Pearl Harbor debacle. Stark complained, "This picture leaves the distinct impression that the Navy was not on the job, and this is not true. . . . I am not concerned with minor inaccuracies, but great harm will be done and sleeping dogs awakened if the picture is released as it now stands, leaving the impression that the Navy was asleep."

This time Ford had stepped on the wrong toes. His passionate concern with inadequate preparedness was not calculated to enhance his popularity among the military brass, who already resented his contempt for authority and his casual approach to military discipline. *December 7th* gave them the opportunity to bring the maverick filmmaker in line. Sharing the concern of the Joint Chiefs of Staff that an uncontrolled film unit like Ford's could produce material detrimental to national morale, President Roosevelt issued a directive that all Field Photo material henceforth would be subjected to censorship. The navy reacted to the long version of *December 7th* "by confiscating the print and ordering Ford to lock up the negative," Parrish reported. "Toland went into a deep depression and requested duty as far away from Washington as possible. Ford sent him to Rio de Janeiro [in April 1943] to set up a Field Photo branch there."

Although the full-length *December 7th* was quietly available for screening at the National Archives for many years, that version remained largely unknown until 1991, when it was released on videocassette by Kit Parker Films as *December 7th: The Movie* ("BANNED FOR 50 YEARS BY THE U.S. GOVERNMENT"), with subtitles added for the Japanese-language sequences.

---

18. Far more elaborate re-creations of the attack appear in the 1970 U.S.–Japanese film *Tora! Tora! Tora!* and 2001's *Pearl Harbor.*

By today's standards, the critique of military unpreparedness offered in the long version seems far less controversial than its elaborate sections on Hawaii's Japanese-American population. Xenophobic in the extreme, the film argues that Hawaiians of Japanese descent owe their primary loyalty to Japan. In one sequence, such ordinary citizens as a gardener, female barbers, a taxi driver, and dance-hall girls are shown acting as undercover agents for the Empire of Japan, passing along vital intelligence about U.S. military forces at Pearl Harbor. Others are seen taking photographs of navy vessels and reporting to the Japanese consulate, which passes its intelligence along to a Nazi agent.

Paying lip service to the idea of tolerance—Harry Davenport's "Mr. C." claims, "I wouldn't, nor would anyone, undertake to separate the loyal from the disloyal"—*December 7th* includes scenes of Japanese-Americans engaging in patriotic rituals with "as American a spirit as exists in any New England community." But what the film gives with one hand it takes away with the other: Mr. C. bluntly declares that "when Tokyo speaks, they all listen." The closing of Japanese-American businesses, schools, and Shinto temples is depicted with approval, and Mr. C. goes so far as to describe Shintoism as "their so-called religion." Walter Huston's Uncle Sam uncomfortably reminds him that the First Amendment provides for freedom of religion, but the voice of "conscience" contemptuously replies, "Is it an infringement of those rights to prohibit American citizens from worshipping the head of a foreign government? . . . If that's Americanism, it's very hyphenated."

Belatedly realizing that allowing such an incendiary film to be completed on his watch was not to his credit, Ford followed his own advice and decided to be "inky" during the controversy over its suppression.

When the navy requested that Field Photo make a short film for showing to war workers as part of its Industrial Incentive Program, Ford saw a way of salvaging *December 7th*. He assigned Robert Parrish to recut the picture—saying, "Remember, if anyone asks you what you are working on, always say you're working on something else"—and asked Budd Schulberg and James Kevin McGuinness to write new narration. The abbreviated, thirty-four-minute version was approved by the navy and the War Department in 1943 and was screened for servicemen as well as industrial workers.

This version still focuses some attention on the intelligence failures preceding the bombing, including the mystifying lack of reconnaissance patrols around the island of Oahu. *December 7th* scathingly notes that the American planes at Hickam Field were lined up in rows, making them easy targets for destruction. But the film shifts from decrying disaster into a prolonged and somewhat forced mood of patriotic uplift. Americans are depicted fighting back against the second wave of attacks before rebuilding and resupplying Pearl Harbor in preparation for the job ahead.

Ford and Parrish removed the contentious debate between Uncle Sam and Mr. C., keeping just one brief shot of Uncle Sam symbolically asleep. While excising all the material about Japanese spies in Hawaii,[19] they kept the section on the suppression of Japanese culture and religion. Ironically, the shortened version omits the few positive things Toland and Engel had to say about Japanese-Americans and their acknowledgment of the existence of detention camps in Hawaii. Ford and Parrish briefly acknowledge the humanity of Japanese-Americans by including shots of a child and an elderly couple anxiously watching the skies during the bombing. But that minimal gesture of sympathy is overshadowed by the film's propagandistic rhetoric about the "diabolical" nature of the bombing and its gloating over "dead Japs."

Like *The Battle of Midway* a year earlier, *December 7th* won an Oscar for best documentary short subject. At the Academy Awards ceremony on March 2, 1944, at Grauman's Chinese Theater in Hollywood, the Oscar for *December 7th* was accepted by Jack MacKenzie Jr., who had done some of the filming at Pearl Harbor as well as at Midway. "It was a master stroke to have Jack MacKenzie accept the award," Jack Bolton wrote Ford. "He was cute as a button and got a tremendous hand." (MacKenzie was killed in a jeep accident near Hollywood on August 10, 1945, at the age of twenty-seven.)

Ford later admitted that he couldn't understand why *December 7th* won the award. But he was happy to take credit for it nonetheless. If you mentioned to Ford that he had won four Academy Awards, he would snap, "Six," ignoring the fact that the Oscars for *The Battle of Midway* and *December 7th* were not awarded to him personally.[20] The Oscar for *The Battle of Midway* was awarded to the navy and Twentieth Century–Fox, and the navy and Field Photo won the Oscar for *December 7th*.

Ford had become such a hot potato by the end of the summer of 1943 that Donovan literally decided to ship him on a slow boat to Asia. Temporarily posted to the China-Burma-India Theater of Operations (CBI) as a "technical observer," Ford left New York on September 19 aboard a freighter to Cal-

---

19. Some of that footage was incorporated into Frank Capra's even more xenophobic army propaganda film *Know Your Enemy—Japan*. So controversial that it was not released to the troops until August 9, 1945, three days after Hiroshima and the day the second atomic bomb was dropped on Nagasaki, *Know Your Enemy—Japan* was pulled from release on August 29 and did not receive its first public screening until 1977.

20. Although no one else has won four Oscars as best director, the filmmaker with the most Oscars remains Walt Disney, who won twenty-six.

cutta with Jack Pennick and a Field Photo cameraman, Jack Swain. The journey lasted fifty-five days and took them through stops at Cuba, Australia, and Ceylon.

Ray Kellogg was named deputy chief of Field Photo upon Ford's departure. Although Ford remained nominally in charge, it was Kellogg who "directed most of the activities of the Branch since that time," according to an October 1945 Field Photo document. Kellogg became acting chief when Ford went on inactive status in October 1944 to direct *They Were Expendable*. Serving as acting deputy branch chief was Warrant Photographer Guy V. Thayer.

If Ford in effect was demoted or shoved aside in September 1943, he didn't mind, because he was tired of all the paperwork and bureaucratic wrangling in Washington. He enjoyed the long, restful cruise and was pleased to be heading back into the field.

Ford's four-month CBI mission also served important political objectives for Donovan. The OSS unit in the Far East, established in May 1942, included bases in India, Burma, and Ceylon, but cooperation among the U.S., British, and Chinese allies was often tenuous. Donovan was eager to expand the OSS presence in India and China, but the British demanded to supervise all OSS operations on the subcontinent. Donovan planned his own visit to China in early December to implement the new arrangements with the British, resolve operational problems at the OSS base in Burma, and insist on greater cooperation from General Tai Li, the ruthless head of the Chinese secret service.

A Field Photo documentary called *Victory in Burma*, commissioned in April 1943, was designed to help flatter the British into greater cooperation with the OSS. Among Ford's principal duties in Burma was helping to complete the film, which was being made by Hollywood director Irving Asner under the supervision of the Field Photo chief in CBI, Lieutenant (jg) Charles Guy Bolte III, who was based in New Delhi. Donovan also wanted Ford to obtain filmed evidence of successful OSS operations in Burma in order to appease members of Congress who were increasingly skeptical about the value of the agency.

During his preliminary sojourn in New Delhi, Ford had a reunion with Gene Markey and became acquainted with U.S. Army Major General Albert C. Wedemeyer, who became a lifelong friend. A member of Mountbatten's staff in India before replacing General Joseph W. Stilwell as Generalissimo Chiang Kai-shek's chief of staff and commander of American forces in China in 1944, Wedemeyer did all he could to facilitate the work of the OSS, unlike General Douglas MacArthur, who barred the OSS from his command in the South Pacific, seeing them as rivals to his personal intelligence staff.

Before Pearl Harbor, Wedemeyer was sympathetic to the isolationist aims of the America First movement, but in his capacity with the army's War Plans Division, he ironically "became the Victory Program planner of a war I did not want." In his 1958 memoirs, Wedemeyer wrote, "The fact that Japan's attack had been deliberately provoked was obscured by the disaster at Pearl Harbor and by the subsequent loss of the Philippines, where the American garrison was regarded as expendable by an Administration bent on getting us into the European war by the back door. The noninterventionists, together with those who realized that Communist Russia constituted at least as great a menace as Nazi Germany, henceforth held their peace although well aware that President Roosevelt had maneuvered us into the war by his patently unneutral actions against Germany and the final ultimatum to Japan."

As a hard-line anti-Communist, Wedemeyer became a sharp postwar critic of Stilwell and George C. Marshall over their China policies and believed that World War II resulted in "the extension of totalitarian tyranny over vaster regions of the world than Hitler ever dreamed of conquering." Wedemeyer exerted a strong influence on the rightward turn of Ford's political beliefs during the cold war.

The immediate problem facing both Donovan and Ford in Burma was Colonel Carl Eifler, the hard-boiled commander of the OSS unit in Burma, Detachment 101. Also known as the Kachin Rangers, the guerrilla unit was largely composed of Kachin tribesmen from the hills north of Myitkyina. From its base on a tea plantation at Nazira, near the border of Burma in the Indian province of Assam, 101 supported a string of Burmese jungle outposts. The unit was known for its fierce fighting spirit, but the relationship between Donovan and Eifler had grown tense. Considering Eifler unreliable and insubordinate, Donovan planned to deal with him personally.

Ford got off on his own bad foot with Eifler. He was late reporting to Nazira because he was waiting for tailored uniforms to be made in Calcutta. He called Eifler to explain the situation. Thinking Ford was an army man, Eifler profanely threatened him with court-martial.

"Why, you old bastard," Ford shot back, "who the hell do you think you are talking to?"

Both men must have been impressed with each other's mettle, for when they finally met at Nazira in late November, they exchanged warm greetings. "Immediately the cameramen went to various camps, and the cameras went into action," OSS man Tom Moon recalled. "From Dibrugarh and Chabua the C-47 planes dropping supplies into Burma were accustomed to seeing the last-minute arrival of a jeep and watch as one of Ford's men ran toward the plane, his camera in one hand and a bottle of beer in the other." While visiting Nazira on December 7–9, Donovan relieved Colonel Eifler of his command. Eifler took some of the films made by Ford's unit back to Washington to boost the morale of OSS personnel with reports from the front and rally their support for 101 operations.

Field Photo cameramen such as Swain, Robert Rhea, Arthur "Butch" Meehan, and Wesley Berry documented the training of Kachin guerrillas by OSS personnel, as well as jungle reconnaissance, supply missions, and combat missions. Their film *Galahad Forces* shows the use of Kachins to screen the advance of Merrill's Marauders and the attack on Myitkyina by Brigadier General Frank D. Merrill's infantrymen. The camaraderie between the Kachins and OSS men is portrayed in Fordian terms in *Burmese Troops,* which includes the presentation of awards to native soldiers and a celebratory dance. Some of the Kachin guerrillas were led by Father James Stuart, a real-life John Ford character, a militant clergyman like those played by Harry Carey in *The Soul Herder,* Henry B. Walthall in *Judge Priest,* and Ward Bond in *The Searchers.* A bearded Dominican priest who claimed to have been a member of the Irish Republican Army, Father Stuart is described in *OSS Camera Report: China-Burma-India* as an "Irish priest—OSS—for twenty years a medical missionary in Burma. One day his congregation was tortured and killed by the Japs. They left him for dead—and now he's doing a swell job for us."

Ford personally participated in some of the filming behind enemy lines. During mid-December shooting on *OSS Camera Report: China-Burma-India,* he parachuted into the jungle from a C-47. This was the only time in his life that Ford had to make a parachute jump, and it was particularly terrifying for him because he and Jack Swain had just filmed a supply drop in which several chutes failed to open. Bob Rhea strapped a camera to his ankle to record his jump as the group dropped into the midst of dense vegetation, where they were met by a small group of Kachins led by Father Stuart. Ford remembered saying several Hail Marys while descending.

Ford's directorial touch is clearly visible throughout much of *Preview of Assam,* a nine-minute film made "to introduce a strange country to those whose war assignments it may concern." The framing and cutting style are characteristically Fordian, as are the film's dramatic use of shadows and backlighting and its eulogizing of a disrupted agrarian society forced to deal with the coming of war. But this film resembles other Ford wartime documentaries in its frequent lapses into brutality and even bloodthirstiness. As Tag Gallagher points out, the viewpoint on war in Ford's documentaries is "unequivocal compared to the story pictures, wherein military duty gone astray is a constant theme." Teaching Kachin guerrillas "how to kill," Americans in *Preview of Assam* demonstrate the making of Molotov cocktails and other instruments of "the gutter fighting which stimulates their imaginations." Referring to the

Kachins, the narrator says, "They are industrious pupils because they have long known what we have more recently learned, that the only good Jap is a dead Jap."[21]

On December 2, with Ford and Pennick, Donovan flew over "the Hump," the air route over the Himalayas between India and China, to inspect OSS bases at Kunming and force compliance by Tai Li with the Sino-American Cooperation Agreement. Concluding his trip in New Delhi, "Donovan examined and approved projects for the OSS's penetration of French Indochina, Thailand, and the Dutch East Indies—operations that marked the real start of thirty years of U.S. involvement in Southeast Asia," according to his biographer Anthony Cave Brown.

Ford stayed in CBI after Donovan's departure, helping to organize the OSS station in China under the cover of the Fourteenth U.S. Air Force, commanded by General Claire Chennault. Ford's acquaintance with Chennault through Merian Cooper was instrumental in smoothing the way for the station, which proved one of the most successful OSS enterprises in China. Field Photo made a film called *Chinese Commandos* for OSS instructors of commando units at the Kunming training compound. Ford spent much of his time in China teaching Chennault's men the "Ippy Dippy" technique. While personally photographing terrain from the air between Chunking and Kunming, he braved antiaircraft fire on those reconnaissance flights, some of which were protected by fighter-plane escorts. Ford and Pennick left New Delhi on January 14 for a grueling nine-day plane trip to Washington via the British colony of South Arabia, Egypt, British West Africa, and Brazil.

From *The Battle of Midway* onward, the films shot by Field Photo show a very Fordian preoccupation with mourning the human cost of war. The dead are frequently commemorated on-screen in funerals and other graveyard rituals. Sometimes Ford found that he had to mourn the deaths of his own men in Field Photo. Twelve of them died during the war, several in their early manhood.

OSS Camera Report: China-Burma-India contains a sequence eulogizing OSS personnel killed in Burma on January 18, 1944. One was the young Field Photo cameraman Butch Meehan, who volunteered to take the place of an ill navy comrade on what the film describes as a routine assignment. Twenty-one OSS men were killed when three planes were shot down by eighteen Japanese

---

21. This line alludes to the infamous slogan of the Indian wars, "The only good Indian is a dead Indian," reputedly derived from General Philip H. Sheridan's comment, "The only good Indians I ever saw were dead."

Zeroes. Crosses are shown in a jungle graveyard as the narrator says, "There they are—shipmates walked in to bury 'em. Took 'em three weeks—hell of a jungle. Some day we'll go back in force and build 'em a fitting resting place. But now the work must go on."

Ford was "heartbroken" to learn of Meehan's death upon his return to Washington. "Writing letters to the next of kin is not a pleasant duty," he admitted to Spig Wead. On February 2, 1944, the day after his fiftieth birthday and the day before the birth of his first grandson, Ford sat down and wrote one of those letters to Butch Meehan's mother, Louise, and his father, Hollywood cameraman George Meehan:

> It is with the deepest sorrow that I write to you and Mrs. Meehan about Arthur. By now I understand you have been informed officially of his heroic death. George, it is hard for me to put it into words—he was such a wonderful lad, one of the finest I've ever known. I am heartbroken to think he has gone. He had volunteered to take the place of one of his buddies who was down with fever. It was a dangerous mission and Butch went down with his machine gun blazing.
>
> We are stunned with grief back here, but of course our sorrow is nothing compared to yours. He was such a swell kid—brave, considerate, hard-working, always thinking of the other guy, never of himself—it is so ironic that Fate should cause him to go that way doing the other guy's job.
>
> I am trying to get several days' leave so I might come to the Coast and see you and your wife, if you wish. Perhaps I could tell you better in words what I'm trying to say on paper, but I know nothing I can ever say or write will ease the cold fact that our Country, our Navy, and our own hometown Hollywood have lost the bravest, cleanest, most lovable boy that ever made the Supreme Sacrifice for the things he loved and for which he fought.
>
> John Ford, Commander, USNR

Ford continued to reflect on Butch Meehan's death and what such a loss means to a commanding officer. Offering condolences nine days later to Meehan's immediate superior, Guy Bolte, Ford wrote, "The worst time possibly in a young officer's life is when he looks upon his own dead for the first time, but knowing you as I do, I know this perhaps will be the deciding factor in your life and you will be a tougher, wiser, and better guy for it. . . . I know now that you need no incentive to work harder and that your intellect has been sharpened by your sorrow."

Ford's sense of responsibility for young men entrusted to his care may have saved the life of Harry Carey Jr. At the urging of Dobe's parents, Ford pulled strings to get him reassigned from duty as a navy corpsman in the South Pacific to a safe job in Washington developing film for Field Photo. "Have been working like hell on Dobe's case," Ford wrote Olive Carey before the 1944 transfer. "Goldie, don't let Harry worry about the kid. It's a serious matter trying to play around with Fate. . . . Goldie, you know that I am Irish and fey and I know everything will be all right."

When Ollie tried to thank Ford for getting Dobe out of harm's way, Ford gruffly replied, "Oh, go fuck yourself."

"Ford punished people for eliciting his love," Garry Wills observed.

Ford's deepest feelings about a commander's responsibility for the young men serving under him were summed up most movingly in *The Searchers*. Midway in his wanderings, Ethan Edwards (John Wayne) returns to the frontier home of Brad Jorgensen (Harry Carey Jr.), who has been killed on the search. "You got my letter about your son Brad" is Ethan's wary greeting to the young man's father, Lars Jorgensen (John Qualen), who offers his hand in fellowship and understanding. But that gesture cannot purge Ethan's sense of guilt, for he later confesses disconsolately to Lars and his wife (Olive Carey), "I got your boy killed."

Upon his return to Washington from CBI in January 1944, Ford found that in his absence things at Field Photo headquarters had become "FUBAR," military slang for "Fucked Up Beyond All Recognition."

"We are working like hell, complete reorganization, everybody here is working 18 hours a day, everybody here is going completely nuts," he confided in a letter to Bolte. "I have lost my tan and all the weight I put on and gradually became a wreck. We now find we are understaffed by a ratio of 10 to 1. Everybody, including Grotsky, now writes commentary, speaks 'em, photographs 'em, and then criticizes 'em. Grotsky, I might add, as a writer of narration stinks."

Ford was elated when Donovan informed him of a new overseas assignment. The order came down from SHAEF, General Dwight D. Eisenhower's Supreme Headquarters Allied Expeditionary Force. "I understand there is to be a sporadic raid of sorts on the Continent in the near future and I am leaving the middle of next week to take part in same," Ford indiscreetly revealed in a letter to Spig Wead on March 28. "It will be a big job in charge of all blue-clad seagoers."

The "raid" was the Normandy invasion.

. . .

Before departing on April 18, Ford had a brief and bizarre meeting with the man who would serve as the prototype for one of his greatest films.

John Bulkeley, by now a commander and about to leave on his own secret European mission with the OSS, visited Ford at the Carlton Hotel with Mark Armistead. In William B. Breuer's 1989 *Sea Wolf: A Biography of John D. Bulkeley, USN,* Bulkeley's account of the meeting is erroneously placed in London: "We went up to Pappy Ford's room in Claridge's, and Mark Armistead beat on his door so damned long and hard that I thought he was going to knock it off the hinges. After a few minutes of ham-fisted pounding, a gruff voice inside bellowed, 'Well, come on in, goddam it!'

"Pappy was still in bed, and he propped open one eye. No doubt he had a king-sized hangover and was mad as hell over being so rudely disturbed. But when Mark introduced me, Ford leaped out of bed, stood at strict attention, saluted me, and said: 'I'm proud to salute the man who rescued General MacArthur!'

"I didn't know quite how to react. Pappy had just been promoted to captain and outranked me, and he was standing at attention—stark naked."

Bulkeley told me the incident took place in Ford's Washington hotel room shortly after Ford was promoted to captain by Donovan on April 3, 1944. Differing in other respects from the account in *Sea Wolf,* the version of Ford's behavior Bulkeley gave me was even more outrageous.

"I went to see him and he was bare-tail, absolutely naked in that damn bed. He loved to do that for shock effect. He had men in there and he had women in there, hangers-on trying to get a job or something. He had a big plate of food, eating with his fingers like a Roman emperor.

"The opening statement [from Ford] was, 'See that closet?' 'Yup.' 'Open it up.' I opened it up and there was a captain's uniform with four stripes. He said, 'You see that? I'm a captain.' I said [sarcastically], 'Yes. What are you captain of?' He picked up that big plate of food and threw it at me, and I ran out the door. He didn't even bother getting out of bed, he just reared up and *whammo!*

"Typical Ford—a show. That was a show for effect." Ford always loved "playacting," Bulkeley recalled.[22]

---

22. Ford's behavior may have been influenced by Major General Orde Wingate, the flamboyant organizer of British guerrilla operations in Burma. At their meeting in Burma, Wingate greeted Ford in the nude. OSS man Tom Moon's description of Wingate, who was killed in a March 1944 plane crash, sounds much like Ford: "Whatever was the traditional or accepted approach, he would take the opposite side. He returned politeness with rudeness. . . . He delighted in receiving visitors to his camp in the nude. The higher their rank or position, the more he delighted in their uneasiness as he would lie naked on his cot."

As late as March 1944, Ford told MGM's Jim McGuinness that he had decided against making *They Were Expendable*. But McGuinness countered with an eloquent argument that the film offered a rare opportunity to re-create a great moment of history while it was still fresh in living people's memories, and that the story was as important to "America's heroic tradition" as the Alamo, Ticonderoga, and Valley Forge. Perhaps Ford's meeting with Bulkeley, however riotous, helped bring home to Ford that sense of opportunity. Shortly before leaving Washington for the invasion, Ford wrote McGuinness, "Been thinking a lot about the story and if the Channel job goes well would like to come back and do it. Would like to get that dough to build a clubhouse for the kids when the war is over. . . . I frankly admit, my dear Seamus, that I am getting as enthusiastic as hell about *They Were Expendable.*"

Ford's intentionally vague and misleading orders from the navy on March 31, 1944, were to "proceed to the British Isles . . . and thence proceed to such other places as may be necessary in connection with accomplishing various reconnaissance flights in combat areas in preparation of strategic motion picture sequences from the air." It was on April 10, according to an OSS document, that "John Ford was placed in charge of all Allied Naval Photographic endeavor on the European invasion."

Ford arrived in London on the night of April 19 to begin assembling camera crews and equipment for "Operation Overlord," as the long-awaited Allied invasion of Europe was code-named. The June 6 landings on the coast of France would involve 175,000 fighting men, 50,000 vehicles, more than 5,000 ships, and almost 11,000 airplanes. British prime minister Winston Churchill called this "the most difficult and complicated operation ever to take place."

Recalling his "small, ant-like part in [Operation] Overlord," Ford said, "I was in charge of cinema photography, but in all honesty I was really more or less a logistic[s] officer. It was up to me to see that everybody who should have a camera had one. . . . My group was there to photograph everything we could for the record."

According to the OSS, "Commander Ford first undertook the gigantic task of analyzing the entire plan of the invasion, with the view in mind of deploying personnel to obtain maximum coverage. A serious shortage of both personnel and equipment existed for a task of this magnitude." Ford's job involved supervising "U.S. Navy, U.S. Coast Guard, British, Dutch, Polish, and French camera installations," he subsequently wrote in a report to the OSS. "Not having sufficient men to place on British ships [the mission of the British Second Army was to attack the beaches east of Omaha Beach], I enlisted the aid of a very dear friend, Lt. Col. George Stevens, famous Hollywood Motion Picture Director, who volunteered to cover their activities for me [heading a unit of ten U.S. Army photographers]. This he did subsequently and did a splendid job with his outfit and continued with us from D-Day until D plus 8 [June 14]. . . . [23]

"After the men were assigned, I held separate meetings with the Navy, Coast Guard, Army, Canadian, British, and the different national camera groups. We ran pictures, blackboard sketches, and I gave a talk on OSS camera methods, each talk averaging about an hour and a half. They were told primarily that they should show their own particular groups at War."

In the early days of their training for combat, Ford told his crewmen, "One thing I'll promise you, I'll never send any of you on a job I wouldn't tackle myself." And he vowed to go ashore with them on D-Day.

To augment the work of his combat photographers, who would be shooting mostly Kodachrome color film as well as black-and-white footage, Ford "had the idea of installing fixed cameras and camera mounts aboard landing craft that were to make the initial assault on D-Day," the OSS reported. "There were 152 of these cameras, so installed as to automatically begin operating as the third man or third vehicle left the craft." Five hundred 35mm Eyemo cameras, each loaded with four minutes of film, were mounted on the front of the landing craft; fixed cameras also were mounted on tanks.

This automated coverage "turned out to be most successful and was probably the best film shot during the invasion of the beaches," Ford told the OSS. ". . . The credit for this job is due to the efforts of Lt. Mark Armistead, USNR., OSS, who did a miraculous job with his men covering the entire embarkation coast by working 24 hours a day for six days."[24]

At Belfast on May 29, Ford boarded the destroyer USS *Plunket*, "which I knew would be in a position to get around and contact the other men." The *Plunket* set out to sea as the last ship in one of many giant Allied convoys, but

23. Another American filmmaker who took part in the D-Day landings was Samuel Fuller, then a twenty-one-year-old soldier with the U.S. Army's First Infantry Division, known as "The Big Red One." Fuller survived the assault on Omaha Beach and re-created it in his 1980 film, *The Big Red One*. He and Ford became good friends after the war, and Ford often paid visits to the locations of Fuller films. Every year on Fuller's birthday (August 12), his phone would ring and he would hear Ford barking, "Fuck the Big Red One!" Then Ford would hang up. Fuller's wife, Christa, was shocked when she picked up the phone shortly after they were married and heard Ford's greeting, not realizing it was an affectionate running gag between the two men.
24. Prior to that assignment, Armistead had been busy since January 1944 doing his "Ippy Dippy Intelligence" photographic reconnaissance of the French shoreline. He continued his reconnaissance in the final months of the war, even making flights over Russian-held Eastern Europe before other Allied governments protested the mapping of their terrain for the postwar benefit of American military intelligence. Ford had to save Armistead from being court-martialed.

wound up leading its convoy. The sea was rough and the destroyers pitched and rolled, making almost everyone aboard miserably seasick. Ford marveled that the men on the smaller landing craft "had enough guts left to get out and fight." They did so valiantly, even while many in the first assault wave were cut down by German machine guns and shells before they could make shore.

Giving Armistead orders for the landing of the camera unit, Ford said, "I'm in command. You're second. I'll take the toughest spot, you take the second toughest spot."

When asked by journalist Pete Martin to describe his D-Day experiences for a twentieth-anniversary article in the *American Legion Magazine,* Ford said that his memories came in "disconnected takes like unassembled shots to be spliced together afterward in a film. . . . I was too busy doing what I had to do for a cohesive picture of what I did to register in my mind. . . . I was reminded of that line in *The Red Badge of Courage* about how the soldiers were always busy, deeply absorbed in their individual combats."

At about 6:00 A.M. the *Plunket* dropped anchor near Omaha Beach. Mined booby traps laid by the Germans protruded at sharp angles from the shallow water. From his ship Ford could see and hear men on the small landing craft vomiting as they headed into combat. About midmorning, Ford and others on the *Plunket* were loaded aboard DUKWs (amphibious trucks, *ducks*). Then they headed off toward shore.

Ford remembered "watching one colored man in a DUKW loaded with supplies. He dropped them on the beach, unloaded, went back for more. I watched, fascinated. Shells landed around him. The Germans were really after him. He avoided every obstacle and just kept going back and forth, back and forth, completely calm. I thought, *By God, if anybody deserves a medal that man does.* I wanted to photograph him, but I was in a realtively safe place at the time so I figured, *The hell with it.* I was willing to admit he was braver than I was."

And yet, in the words of the OSS report on Ford's actions that day, "Knowing full well he would be subjected to unusual exposure to enemy fire without means to take cover, he personally took charge of the entire operation and was the first of his unit to land."

"The landing was rather soft, as I had figured," Ford told the OSS. "We suffered no casualties of a serious nature. Only one of our men, John Flynn, Sp2/c, USNR, was blown in the water, lost his camera and gear, but being a superb swimmer managed to swim to another destroyer."

When Ford hit the beach, he "ran forward and started placing some of my men behind things so they'd have a chance to expose their film. I know it doesn't make it blazingly dramatic, but all I could think was that for the most part everything was all so well coordinated, fitted perfectly, went beautifully. . . . In action, I didn't tell my boys where to aim their cameras. They took whatever they could." Ford ordered the cameramen not to stand while filming but "made them lie behind cover." Even so, the men had no weapons, only their cameras. Ford paid tribute to those cameramen by observing that "facing the enemy defenseless takes a special kind of bravery."

The OSS wrote of Ford himself, "After landing he visited all of his men at their various assignments, and served as a great inspiration by his total disregard of danger in order to get the job done."

While Ford remained in France, his film footage of D-Day was rushed back to London for processing and editing in accord with his prior instructions. Squads of cutters worked around the clock—four hours on, four hours off—under the supervision of producer Alan Brown.

The OSS stated that "an overall D-Day report, complete with sound, was completed on D plus 5 [June 11], and was shown to Mr. Winston Churchill. Copies were also flown to President Roosevelt and Mr. Stalin." That secret photographic report has never been seen publicly. Some of Ford's D-Day footage appeared in newsreels and government documentaries such as the nineteen-minute *United States Coast Guard Report Number 4: Normandy Invasion*. None of the footage was shown to the public in color, and only a small fraction of the black-and-white footage was exhibited; Ford thought the reason was that the U.S. government was "afraid to show so many American casualties on the screen."

In a 1998 article in the *New Yorker*, historian Douglas Brinkley, director of the Eisenhower Center at the University of New Orleans, reported that some of Ford's missing color footage had been located by Melvyn R. Paisley, a former assistant secretary of the navy, and amateur military historian and film collector Lars Anderson. The footage had been shunted around the country before being misfiled in a National Archives facility at College Park, Maryland. The Eisenhower Center, Brinkley wrote, "is now working with the director Steven Spielberg and others to preserve the color film." Spielberg won an Academy Award for directing the 1998 film *Saving Private Ryan,* which includes a stunning twenty-three-minute re-creation of the Omaha Beach landing Ford and his men risked their lives to commemorate on film.

After D-Day, Ford wrote in his official report, "We had many mishaps and adventures, but these naturally have no part in this record." The mishaps occurred when he went on a bender, badly needing to unwind from the supreme tension of the invasion. The adventures took place in the company of the naval officer described by General Douglas MacArthur as "that bold buckaroo with the cold green eyes," Johnny Bulkeley.

Once the initial landings were completed, Ford rounded up his cameramen and "summarily kicked them all back on their ships," he told the OSS. Then he "disobeyed orders . . . and went forward to the taking of Grandcamp [a nearby seaside resort]. This was excused because I was studying infilteration [sic] methods which might later be used by OSS."

One of Ford's most unnerving experiences was an encounter on June 11 on the Cherbourg Peninsula with an army friend, Colonel Russell "Red" Reeder, commander of the Twelfth Infantry Regiment of the Fourth Infantry Division. Reeder had been wounded by an 88mm round and was sitting with a leg so badly injured that it later had to be amputated. When Ford approached, Reeder asked if he had any orange juice. Ford offered him brandy instead, but the wounded man kept demanding orange juice. Ford recalled that he and Reeder "had a laugh about that long afterward at West Point.[25] In a moment of crisis, people get funny fixations."

Physically and emotionally spent, Ford eventually made his way to a French house serving as headquarters for a combat camera outfit of the Army Air Forces First Motion Picture Unit, headed by Major William H. Clothier.

Ford had tried to recruit Clothier into Field Photo at the beginning of the war, offering him a commission as a navy lieutenant (jg), but Clothier preferred the higher rank of a captain in the AAF, for which he shot Wyler's *Memphis Belle* in 1944. Six Field Photo cameramen were temporarily assigned to Clothier, including navy Photographer's Mate First Class Junius J. "Junior" Stout, son of Hollywood cameraman Archie Stout. Junior Stout and another Field Photo cameraman, Brick Marquard, had been chosen by Ford as the lead cameramen in the D-Day landings, hitting the beach with U.S. Army Rangers in the first wave of the invasion, to scout positions for the other photographers. Stout and Marquard subsequently filmed the post–D-Day construction of Mulberry artificial harbors, built with concrete caissons ("Phoenixes") towed across the English Channel and sunk in line off the French coast. The two cameramen received Silver Stars for their valor during the invasion, although Stout's had to be awarded posthumously.[26]

---

25. At a field hospital, Reeder was presented with the Distinguished Service Cross. In the postwar years, Reeder served as the United States Military Academy's assistant athletic director and wrote dozens of books about American military history. Ford became reacquainted with him in 1954 while at West Point filming *The Long Gray Line,* based on *Bringing Up the Brass,* based on the autobiography of the Academy's athletic trainer, Marty Maher, who wrote the book with Reeder's sister, Nardi Reeder Campion.

26. Stout died off the coast of the German-held island of Jersey, one of the Channel Islands, when the plane in which he was riding was shot down on October 30, 1944. His father later photographed Ford's *Fort Apache* and *The Sun Shines Bright* and was second-unit cameraman on *The Quiet Man.* Marquard was an assistant cameraman on postwar Ford features and director of photography on the director's last film, *Chesty: A Tribute to a Legend,* a documentary about U.S. Marine Lieutenant General Lewis B. "Chesty" Puller, filmed in 1968–70 and released in 1976.

Ford settled into a sleeping bag at Clothier's house and began drinking Calvados. He drank steadily for days on end. Once he even broke into an officer's locker to find more bottles of the apple brandy. At night Ford would roam around outside, getting into scrapes with French officers because he couldn't remember his password. Clothier had to stay up late each night talking with Ford and was disgusted when Ford urinated in his sleeping bag. Finally Clothier summoned Armistead to take Ford off his hands. Ford made it up to Clothier after the war by hiring him as camera operator on *Fort Apache* and eventually as director of photography on *The Horse Soldiers, The Man Who Shot Liberty Valance, Donovan's Reef,* and *Cheyenne Autumn.*

Ford's adventures with Bulkeley came about because of Bulkeley's assignment to the London branch of the OSS under Colonel David Bruce. Before the invasion, Bulkeley commanded three PT boats on highly dangerous clandestine missions across the English Channel. He worked with the British and the Free French "running spies into France and bringing 'em back out again. I really don't know who the hell I worked for. The least you know about what you're doing, the better off you are. You never looked at these people, their faces, so you wouldn't be able to recognize them again under torture. No matter what, if you get caught you're gonna die. Oh, you always have hope you might be able to fool 'em, but you don't fool 'em very long. If the SS can ever get ahold of you, it's the end of the matter." Bulkeley's PT boats also transported saboteurs, picked up downed aviators, and served as couriers for clandestine matériel and intelligence between Britain and the French underground.

As part of the invasion forces, Bulkeley was put in charge of a fleet of sixty-nine PT boats patrolling a quarter mile from the French coast "to repel [German] E-boats coming into the assault area." Those patrols continued until D+38—July 14. He later received the Croix de Guerre from Charles de Gaulle for "conspicuous gallantry and extraordinary bravery in action" while serving in the Normandy invasion. Admiral Bulkeley, who died in 1996, would have been astonished to read in Garry Wills's 1997 book *John Wayne's America* that "Bulkeley's boat had been put at Ford's disposal as a kind of water taxi during the landings at Normandy."

Bulkeley told me that it was on June 15 or 16 that Mark Armistead, a passenger on his PT boat, received a radio call from Ford on the USS *Augusta* (the heavy cruiser serving as flagship for the Western Naval Task Force) asking permission to come aboard Bulkeley's boat. Already wary of Ford from their previous encounter in the Washington hotel room, Bulkeley was taken aback by the great director's unkempt appearance as he was lowered over the side in a bosun's chair.

"I really didn't know much about the man, didn't pay much attention to him," Bulkeley recalled. "I had other things to worry about. Anyway, he came aboard my boat, and his first words were that he was going to be the director of the movie *They Were Expendable* and that he came to discuss who was going to play my part." Ford confided to Bulkeley that MGM wanted to cast Spencer Tracy in the lead role, "and he didn't like Spencer Tracy. He had not very many nice words to say about Spencer Tracy, for whatever reason."

"Who do you think ought to play your part?" Ford asked Bulkeley.

"How in the hell would I know?" Bulkeley replied. "You're supposed to be the movie genius!"

"And that was the end of the matter," recalled Bulkeley. "I had enough sense to know that guy was going to do exactly what he wants to do. The real thing he was over there for, he used me as a cat's-paw. He wanted to get over to Caen [ten miles inland], up where the fighting was at that time. Shortly thereafter he bailed out and went up there. Now, what'd he do? Typical of all directors and people like that who study human nature, he wanted to see men in actual combat and visualize and try to memorize the emotion of how men were acting while facing great danger in war. He'd translate that into his pictures, from his memory. He loved that kind of thing. He was up there for two or three days and then he came back and brought me a rifle; he must have been up against the Germans' front line."

While on Bulkeley's PT boat intermittently in the weeks following D-Day, Ford gradually impressed Bulkeley with his working knowledge of ships and navigation. Ford seized the opportunity to make an intimate study of Bulkeley's character and behavior under fire and to draw out his feelings about the events in the Philippines. Ford savored the irony of being on a PT boat in the midst of combat with the man whose story MGM had been begging him to direct for two years. Ford was deeply impressed with Bulkeley's disdain for the "monkey business" that went with being a "Hollywood hero," as well as with the commander's blunt-spoken professionalism.

"The whole thing happened at a time when the country was looking for heroes," Bulkeley told him, adding, "I hope they never make the goddam thing into a movie."

"This isn't going to be some goddamned two-bit propaganda flick," Ford promised. He explained that he had been resisting the idea of going on inactive status to make the film. "But I'm going to solve the situation by waiting until the war is over. Then I'll make *They Were Expendable.*"

Although the OSS, through Ford's unit, supplied the French underground, Ford's claim to have been with Bulkeley when the PT boat commander ran agents into and out of occupied France seems to be false. The director told Bogdanovich that he "worked with [Bulkeley] a lot" in an area around Bayeux that was "pretty well populated with the SS and Gestapo. So instead of drop-ping an agent in, we took a PT boat, which Johnny always skippered himself. . . . We'd go in there on one engine, drop an agent off or pick up in-formation, and disappear." However, when I asked Bulkeley if Ford went with him on those missions to France, Bulkeley replied, "No, no, never. No, that all happened before."

Bulkeley's boat did get into some running skirmishes with German E-boats while Ford was aboard. "I don't call that *much* action, or like the invasion of France," Bulkeley said. "Three times we had a German E-boat trying to come down into our line and break through. And three times we went after 'em. We sank one and we chased the others all the way back. Ford was just watching and dodging. Now, there's a number of books been written about him, like *Pappy*—I've read 'em all. One of the books [Dan Ford's] says that over in Nor-mandy we got tangled up with a German E-boat and got a whole bunch of machine-gun fire on the boat and he almost got clobbered. That's not quite true. We got laced up with a whole bunch of holes in the boat, along our wa-terline, but they didn't come near him."

Nevertheless, said Bulkeley, Ford reacted to being under fire by doing "ex-actly what any brave man would do—daring fate. He was no coward at all. He was like any typical Irishman there. He loved the excitement of it and he loved danger. He was just great." An amateur photographer, Bulkeley habitually wore a camera around his neck to take snapshots behind enemy lines. Accord-ing to Dan Ford's account of the supposedly near-fatal E-boat attack, Ford jokingly accused Bulkeley of waiting to take the first photograph of a cele-brated director's corpse. Asked about that story, Bulkeley scoffed, "I wasn't particularly worried [about Ford's safety]. Anyone's around me takes their chances, and he recognized that.

"John Ford made a lot of stuff up, you know. Too much for me. I know some of the stuff I heard him talk about was phony. He loved to portray him-self and see whether you'd bite. Sometimes he'd tell one of these tall tales which I know damn well wasn't true, but I never challenged him. I was always very careful about that. For that reason he tolerated me or I tolerated him. You don't argue with that man. And furthermore, you've got to recognize, as I did, that man is truly a genius. He's a great man."

After D-Day, Ford began to see the role of an observer and recorder of combat as increasingly insignificant next to the experience of being a part of the action. While on Bulkeley's boat, "John Ford ignored PR," the skipper re-called. "He wanted to be a rear admiral in combat. He liked the real stuff, people who had accomplished something or were doing something. He'd seen too many phonies and he didn't like that kind of business. He was fascinated by the Medal of Honor, for whatever reason. He sought me out all the time. And I'm privileged to have that. I don't think I'd normally do that, because there was too much difference in age, too much difference in outlook."

Ford returned to England on June 21. From Claridge's, he wrote his family that he had taken three hot baths in a single day and shaved off a beard that made him resemble his brother Frank. Ford eventually accompanied Bulkeley on a three-day mission into Yugoslavia, which Bulkeley said occurred while he was operating out of the Mediterranean in preparation for Operation Dragoon, the Allied invasion of southern France on August 15. Ford's military records show that he traveled from England to France on July 29, left the next day on a five-day round-trip to an undisclosed location, and returned to London on August 4. Andrew Sinclair writes in his Ford biography that the filmmaker accompanied Bulkeley on a PT boat mission to support the Yugoslav Partisans: "Ford was anti-Communist and supported Tito's rival, Mihailovic, but the émigré leaders were hopeless and British intelligence was antagonistic. The whole operation was 'too full of lousy Oxford dons and aristocracy,' Ford said later. 'Princes and dukes and God knows what kind of White Russians.'" According to Sinclair, Ford considered such leadership unworthy of the "proud, brave people of Yugoslavia." Frank Capra told me that when he visited Yugoslavia in 1971, President Tito handed him a medal to present secretly to the ailing Ford back in Hollywood for performing a World War II rescue mission.

However, when I asked Bulkeley about his mission to Yugoslavia with Ford, the admiral replied, "Well, that was only a minor one, a very minor one. It occurred mostly at night. Tito was a full-blown Commie. Mihailovic was the good guy, the non-Commie, but he was overwhelmed by this other gentleman [Tito]. It was the British job to supply Mihailovic's people. The OSS dropped a lot of stuff in to 'em. We just went in to the west coast of Yugoslavia and dropped a bunch of people off and a bunch of ammunition and so forth. John Ford just went for the ride. He could make a tall tale up out of nothing." As for Tito, some footage of the Partisan leader at his mountain headquarters is included in the Field Photo films *Farish Report* and *Unfinished Report,* but when asked about Tito, Bulkeley said, "I never even saw the guy." (Mihailovic was executed in 1946, after Marshal Tito became president of the Federal People's Republic of Yugoslavia.) Bulkeley was "skeptical" that Ford undertook "any 'actions' with the Partisans. . . . I believe this [is] one of those red-herring trails that Ford loved to put out."

Bulkeley not only refused Ford's offer to serve as technical adviser on *They Were Expendable* but also declined to watch the filming. "That brands you as a so-called Hollywood hero, and I want no part of that," Bulkeley explained.

"Maybe I'm foolish, but I felt very self-conscious about the whole thing. I just don't like all this monkey business. And I knew Ford was going to do it exactly as he wanted. One of my officers, Tony Akers, became the so-called technical director or assistant."[27] Bulkeley found the film "very authentic. So many other things happened that John Ford couldn't possibly deal with, but he picked the major things that had dramatic impact and followed as close as he could to the actual happenings."

Fourteen years after Ford's death, Bulkeley reflected on the enigmatic personality of his old friend and comrade: "I've been with him very often but I never really got to know the man. I don't understand him, really. He's a very eccentric man. He has too many facets. It's pretty hard to understand a man like that, to get down deep underneath him and understand. He must have known himself."

During Ford's long period of hesitation over making *They Were Expendable*, MGM ordered rewrites of Spig Wead's script from producer-director Sidney Franklin and screenwriter Budd Schulberg. After Franklin was assigned to the project, Ford wrote McGuinness in August 1943, "Spig tells me emphatically to forget about it. It involves too much sacrifice and humiliation for me to get into a routine where I couldn't protect myself."

MGM misguidedly thought that adding scenes with the family of the Bulkeley character would give the film broader appeal. Wead complained to McGuinness that "the guy is a very real guy to both of us, and I am sure that any attempt to work his wife and children into the picture (if that is what is meant by 'character development') will hurt the piece rather than help it. . . . One hears talk that the studios are all cold on war pictures, which is another worry; but there hasn't been a really good war picture yet."

As late as February 1944, Ford was still complaining to Wead that MGM "had some very quaint ideas about bringing it up to date. . . . Up to date? The thing will never be dated. Just what do they mean by up to date? Maybe a nice love story, or flashbacks to Kelly's home life [Lieutenant Robert B. Kelly, who narrated most of White's book, was the model for John Wayne's Lieutenant (jg) Rusty Ryan]. However, I told Jim it was out of the question for me. . . . The thing will probably be ske-rewed [*sic*] up." Eventually managing to do the picture his own way, and continually rewriting the script with Wead

---

27. Ensign Anthony B. Akers later became President John F. Kennedy's ambassador to New Zealand and assistant secretary of the U.S. Air Force. Kennedy himself was recruited into the PT boat service by Bulkeley at the personal request of Ambassador Joseph P. Kennedy, who, Bulkeley recalled, "wanted Jack to get into PT boats for the publicity and so forth, to get the veterans' vote after the war."

during production, Ford also vetoed MGM's suggestion of an epilogue show-
ing Bulkeley and his men returning to the Philippines with General
MacArthur's troops in late 1944. "We are sticking to fact," Ford told the *New
York Times* during the shooting. "Lieutenant Bulkeley did not go back to the
Philippines. We were together quite recently in Normandy."

Since Ford owed one more picture to Twentieth Century–Fox under his
ten-film prewar contract and was exclusively tied to Fox until that contract
was fulfilled, Darryl Zanuck was unhappy with his plan to work for MGM.
But Zanuck couldn't buck the navy brass, and he had to content himself with
Ford's written agreement on October 23, 1944, to direct a film within six
months after his discharge from the navy. A further Hollywood complication
arose when Ford asked Gregg Toland on September 16, 1944, to "co-direct
with me on *Expendable.*" Toland had been placed on inactive status with the
navy so he could work on the film, but his Hollywood employer, Samuel
Goldwyn, made it impossible for Toland to do so. Instead, Ford hired another
Field Photo member, Lieutenant Commander Joseph H. August, as cinematographer. Special effects expert James C. Havens, who had assisted Toland
in re-creating the bombing of Pearl Harbor, helped mount the battle scenes
for *Expendable.*

Four days after making his unsuccessful pitch to Toland, Ford formally requested that the navy place him on inactive status to direct *Expendable.* The request was granted on October 20. Contradicting his later claim that he was
forced to make the film against his will, he explained that Secretary of the
Navy James Forrestal and the chief of Navy Public Relations, Rear Admiral
A. S. Merrill, were "anxious to have this film produced as a matter of naval
policy. The Metro-Goldwyn-Mayer Company refuses to do the picture unless
I personally direct the film. Personally, I concur heartily in their request as the
picture will have a big Navy motif which at the present would be very
timely. . . . It is also understood by the aforementioned gentlemen that all re-
munerations I receive from the film will be turned over to a charitable fund
for servicemen and that I shall not retain any part of the resultant financial returns." Even while making the film, Donovan later wrote, Ford remained "in
constant communication with his headquarters in Washington, D.C., on the
progress of the numerous photographic projects of strategic and documentary
importance."

On October 30, the eve of his departure for Hollywood to begin preproduction, Ford wrote General Wedemeyer, "I am getting a big chunk of dough
for the picture, which I am turning over into a trust fund for Pennick and the
boys. That at least clears my conscience a bit. It will give Pennick a place to
store his loot." Ford's $300,000 salary became the seed money for the Field
Photo Memorial Home. More familiarly known as the Field Photo Farm or

simply the Farm, it was a gathering place in the San Fernando Valley for veterans of Ford's unit on Memorial Day and other ceremonial and social occasions, as well as a refuge for members of the unit who were down on their luck or out of favor with their wives.

Taking a skeptical view of Ford's decision to endow the facility, Garry Wills wrote, "Ford's generosity in this act has been exaggerated by authors who do not realize that Senator Truman's investigations of war waste had made it unwise to the point of impossibility for producers and directors to draw Hollywood money while in the service. . . . It no doubt galled Zanuck when Ford used the Navy to break his contract in making *Expendable*, and then finessed the double-dipping problem by using his salary from the movie to prolong his own happy military experience at the Field [Photo] Farm."

Aptly described by Andrew Sinclair as Ford's "last command," the Farm was established on an eight-acre estate in Reseda purchased for $225,000 from Hollywood executive Sam Briskin. Incorporated on November 30, 1944, the nonprofit Field Photo Homes Inc. had as its first directors Ford's business manager, Fred Totman, and the ubiquitous James Kevin McGuinness and Spig Wead. The legal details were handled by Donovan's Wall Street law firm, Donovan, Leisure, Newton & Lumbard.

For Ford, the Farm was his "living war memorial" to the men he lost in the war. Its melancholy centerpiece was the chapel, with a roster of their names:

Dean A. Cline
Thomas M. Evans
Robert Halprin
Daniel Hogan
Jack P. MacKenzie Jr.
D. C. MacFarlane
Arthur J. Meehan
Sergei A. Mihailoff
Nelson B. Paris
Edwin R. Roach
Junius J. Stout
Harold Wenstrom

After Joseph H. August died in 1947, his name was added to the honor roll.

In a striking example of casting against type, Ford gave the lead role in *They Were Expendable* to Robert Montgomery, the suave MGM actor known primarily for his roles in romantic comedies. The film's commander of Motor Torpedo Boat Squadron Three was named Lieutenant John Brickley rather than Bulkeley because of a navy regulation against a living member of that service being portrayed on-screen under his real name. Reviewing *Expendable* in the *Nation,* James Agee wrote that Montgomery, like Ford, "evidently learned a tremendous amount through the war. . . . [His] sober, light, sure performance is, so far as I can remember, the one perfection to turn up in movies during the year."

Montgomery's wartime service began in 1940 as a volunteer ambulance driver for the American Field Service in France. After duty as an assistant naval attaché at the U.S. Embassy in London, he served as Bulkeley's executive officer during PT boat combat in the Southwest Pacific in 1943. Montgomery later was operations officer of a destroyer squadron during the Normandy invasion. At one point he spotted Bulkeley on his PT boat and waved, not realizing that the man standing on the bridge next to Bulkeley was John Ford. For his wartime service, Lieutenant Commander Montgomery was awarded a Bronze Star and became a chevalier of the French Legion of Honor.

"I was assigned Robert Montgomery as my executive officer of Motor Torpedo Boat Squadron Seven," recalled Bulkeley, "and I wondered why in the world this man was assigned to me as lieutenant commander. He knew nothing about PT boats. And he was with me and did well. Now, all Montgomery was doing was watching me carefully and preparing himself to portray me. I don't think John Ford had anything to do with it, but he may have—you never could tell what the guy was up to. If you look at that movie carefully and me when I was much younger, Montgomery and I look alike. Furthermore, our habits and the way we work, the way we lead, we're very close together. Ford got someone who could copy my mannerisms and my speech. Good performance by Montgomery."

MGM star Robert Taylor was the first choice for the role of Brickley's executive officer, the character based on Lieutenant Robert Kelly. Taylor proved unavailable, so John Wayne was cast as the impetuous, short-tempered Rusty Ryan. Ford also found memorable parts for other members of his Stock Company, including Jack Pennick, Russell Simpson, Harry Tenbrook, and Ward Bond. Bond remained in the cast despite being hit by a car in Hollywood in July 1944. His right leg was so badly injured that it was almost amputated before Wayne and MGM intervened. Ford loyally arranged Bond's scenes so that he anchors them while remaining largely motionless or, by the end of the film, hobbling around on a crutch.

"I had everyone portrayed in the movie sign a release through MGM, including Bob Kelly," Bulkeley recalled. "Bob Kelly turned around . . . and sued 'em because they portrayed him as he actually is, a very rambunctious Irishman, very difficult to get along with. Now, I never had any problem with Kelly. I could read him, I could master him. I'm even tougher than he is. But he's a very brave man, he's got a Navy Cross. He's a *good* man, good sailor, but he's a stubborn bastard and he's one of these guys who shoots his mouth off when he should be listening, so that's where he gets in trouble." Bulkeley added with a chuckle, "Because of that, he's portrayed pretty accurately by John Wayne." Kelly's suit for $50,000, filed in a Boston federal court, brought him only $3,000.

U.S. Army Lieutenant Beulah Greenwalt Walcher—the nurse who served as the basis for the book's "Peggy" and the film's Second Lieutenant Sandy Davyss (Donna Reed)—also filed a lawsuit objecting to her characterization. According to Bulkeley, what most riled Kelly and Walcher is the way Ford "very subtly" suggests that Ryan and Sandy sleep together following her farewell dinner with the squadron. Walcher claimed in her lawsuit that she did not have a romance with Kelly, only a "friendship." After watching the movie, a federal court jury in St. Louis awarded Walcher $290,000 for what she considered "a humiliating invasion of privacy" that "cheapened her character." Attorneys for Loews, the parent company of MGM, unsuccessfully argued that Sandy was a composite character and that Donna Reed's portrayal was "highly restrained and completely inoffensive."

It's hard to imagine any woman objecting to being played on-screen by Donna Reed. During the war, her combination of wholesome Iowa beauty and understated sexual allure made her "popular with the GI's, who attached her autographed photo to foxholes, torpedo shacks, and bomber noses," wrote her biographer, Jay Fultz. "One homesick battalion in North Africa designated her as 'the girl we would most like to come home to.'" Reed also danced regularly with servicemen at the Hollywood Canteen.

Montgomery recalled that when the twenty-four-year-old MGM contract player first appeared on the set of *Expendable*, Ford studiously ignored her for half an hour. Told he needed to approve her costume, Ford "snarled" that he didn't have to bother with Reed or her costume. But Reed "was very intelligent," observed Montgomery. "She didn't let Ford upset her: she used his attitude—played off it. It gave her strength." Before long, Reed "won the respect of the crusty Ford," her biographer reported. "Her portrayal of the nurse reminded him of the dedicated servicewomen he had seen during combat duty. . . . She was authentic, he said, 'as typical as a Liberty-head dime.'"

"Donna Reed has more *gravitas* than most women in war films. In *They Were Expendable* she stands among the men, silently heroic, too involved with coping to have time for illusions or sentimentality or even wisecracks. As the bombs fall outside the underground hospital on Corregidor, she assists the surgeon, her face in the makeshift light reflecting pain and fatigue. Not a word is necessary, just the natural nobility of that face held in closeup." In the quietly moving dinner scene, Sandy appears luminous in her olive drab, thanks in part to a felicitous Fordian touch. Just before the scene was shot, the director "pulled from his pocket a string of pearls and presented it to Donna. The gesture demonstrated his mastery in establishing the right emotional pitch. In effect, the director was honoring the nurses taken prisoner at Corregidor. Deeply moved, Donna faced the camera thinking, as she would for years afterward, about their fate."

There is a personal resonance to the director's warily affectionate depiction of Sandy. Her relationship with Ryan, the navy man more at ease around boats than around women, recalls Ford's courtship of *his* army nurse, even down to the humorous byplay between Ryan and Sandy about which one outranks the other, a running joke between Jack and Mary throughout their marriage. And the injury for which Sandy treats Ryan, a shrapnel wound in the right hand, is similar to the wound Ford suffered at Midway.

With its direction credited to "Captain John Ford, USNR," *They Were Expendable* signified a new level of aspiration in Ford, a deepened conception of his role as the official cinematic chronicler of American history.

Location filming began early in February 1945 around Key Biscayne, Florida. The navy took six PT boats out of service to be used in the picture. James C. Havens, credited as second-unit director, was largely responsible for shooting the action scenes of PT boats under aerial attack; MGM planned to list Havens as the director of the battle scenes, but his credit was changed at the urging of the Screen Directors Guild. The destruction of the Cavite Navy Yard by Japanese bombers was simulated with dummy buildings constructed around permanent structures at the Miami Coast Guard Station. Ford also took advantage of a brush fire on an island in Key Biscayne, directly in camera range. "Perfect!" he said. "That's Manila burning!"

In addition to Ford, Montgomery, Wead, August, and Havens (a captain in the Marine Corps Reserve) had their military ranks listed in the credits. In such company, a mere Hollywood civilian was hopelessly out of place. Ford's resentment of John Wayne's avoidance of military service came out early in the filming, in an extraordinarily humiliating act of cruelty. It happened when they were shooting the scene of Charles Trowbridge's Admiral Blackwell inspecting Brickley's squadron after watching the PT boats going through their paces in Manila Bay. "Those boats of yours maneuver beautifully," the admiral tells Brickley. "But in wartime, I'm afraid I prefer something more substantial." As the admiral's car drives off, Montgomery and Wayne had to salute forlornly, with their backs to the camera. They did the scene twice, seemingly without flaw. When Ford called for a third take, Wayne murmured to Montgomery, "What's wrong with it?" Montgomery had no idea.

"Halfway through the third take," Montgomery recalled, "Ford called

'Cut!' Then—and there must have been at least a thousand people crowding round, watching the shooting—he yelled out at Wayne, for everyone to hear: 'Duke—can't you manage a salute that at least looks as though you've been in the service?'" Montgomery, who had served four terms as president of the Screen Actors Guild, commented, "It was outrageous, of course. I walked over to where Ford was sitting and I put my hands on the arms of his chair and leaned over and said: 'Don't you ever speak like that to anyone again.'"

Wayne walked off the set for the only time in his career, and shooting was halted for the day. "I told Ford he'd have to apologize," Montgomery recalled. "He blustered at first—'I'm not going to apologize to that son of a bitch . . .'; then he came out with a lot of phony excuses—'What did I say? I didn't mean to hurt his feelings.' He ended up crying."

Ford's edgy emotional state may have been a contributing factor in the serious accident he suffered near the end of the production schedule. On May 17, while on a camera platform at MGM directing inserts for battle sequences, Ford stepped backward and plunged to the floor, suffering a fracture of the upper end of the right shinbone, also affecting the knee joint. Ford insisted that only Montgomery and Wayne be allowed to lift him to a stretcher. As they escorted him for treatment at Cedars of Lebanon Hospital, a woman kept staring at Ford in the elevator. Finally he growled, "Alcoholic!" After all the hazards he had faced in actual combat, it was ironic that Ford's only incapacitating injury during the war came on a Hollywood soundstage.

The day following Ford's accident, Montgomery and Wayne were visiting him when MGM's Eddie Mannix called to find out when the director would come back to work. Ford surprised Montgomery by telling the executive that he would let Montgomery direct the rest of the picture. However, McGuinness wired the navy a few days later that Montgomery was "SHOOTING ONLY PROCESS BATTLE ACTION CUTS UNTIL [Ford's] RETURN. LAST SEQUENCE REMAINS FOR FORD TO DIRECT." Ford was supposed to spend three weeks in traction at the hospital but returned to MGM a week early, with his leg in a cast, to direct the final dramatic sequence of Brickley and Ryan departing by plane from the Philippines. Pleased with Montgomery's directorial contributions, Ford told him after seeing the first assembly, "I couldn't tell where I left off and you began."[28]

The making of *They Were Expendable* found Ford in a mood to memorialize. Shortly after the start of preproduction, he learned of the wartime deaths of

28. The experience encouraged Montgomery to direct five films of his own, from the 1947 film noir classic *Lady in the Lake* to the 1960 biopic of Admiral "Bull" Halsey, *The Gallant Hours,* starring James Cagney.

two young men he knew and loved. Within a ten-day period, he lost both Junior Stout and Francis Wai, the son of his Hawaiian friends Kin and Rosina Wai. The twenty-seven-year-old Wai, a former star athlete at UCLA, was killed on October 20, 1944, in the assault on the Japanese-held island of Leyte and was posthumously awarded the Distinguished Service Medal. After Stout died on October 30, he was posthumously awarded the Air Medal and the Purple Heart in addition to his Silver Star.

Ford's "grace notes" in *Expendable*—those moments of poetry he cherished because they were not necessary to the plot but enabled him to express his deepest feelings—include a brief sequence showing two crosses in a makeshift jungle graveyard. A pair of ensigns, running through the jungle with boyish exuberance, stop abruptly at the graves of their comrades and genuflect in a moment of silent prayer. This elegiac tone suffuses the entire film and makes it clear why Ford delayed so long before making it. Such an honest and downbeat meditation on war would not have been possible if the film had been made in 1942 or '43.

Released on December 20, 1945, *Expendable* was able to level with the postwar public about the painful choices and heroic sacrifices that had been necessary to the ultimate victory. And though Ford made the film in the final months of the war, when the American desire for revenge against the Japanese was at an apocalyptic pitch, he avoids demonizing the enemy, whose sailors and soldiers are never shown on-screen. Instead, Ford compassionately focuses the audience's attention at several key moments on the distraught faces of Asian civilians, stressing the universality of suffering in war: the announcement of the bombing of Pearl Harbor in a Manila nightclub is heard over a closeup of a distraught Japanese woman; a Filipina singer (Pacita Tod-Tod) tearfully delivers her moving rendition of "My Country, 'Tis of Thee" as military officers file out of the club (an incident that Ford said actually happened); and the sequence of the destruction of the Cavite Navy Yard concludes with the "Navy Hymn" (also known as "Eternal Father, Strong to Save") being played over an eloquent close-up of another Filipina watching from dockside as her man is evacuated onto a PT boat.

They Were Expendable's verisimilitude, richness of texture, and sense of spontaneity are the by-products of Ford's three and a half years witnessing and recording actual warfare. Ford said he approached the film as a "documentary," using no reflectors to supplement exterior lighting and maintaining a realistically low light level for interiors. "A documentary, yes," commented Admiral Bulkeley, "but with good actors."

The film's most passionate admirer, the young British critic and future director Lindsay Anderson, described it as "a heroic poem." *Expendable* offers a heightened image of reality, suffused with the director's personal feelings. In this transitional film between Ford's wartime service and his return to Hollywood mythmaking, we see the elements of his postwar style coalescing. Joseph H. August's magnificent black-and-white photography, the crowning achievement of his illustrious career, is as intricately composed as *The Informer* but far more subtle in its unobtrusively orchestrated patterns of light and shadow.[29] Ford's visual and dramatic style now expresses his feelings with a blend of emotional simplicity and the seemingly effortless artistry of a master craftsman.

Ford's military service made him fascinated with the intricacies of leadership and the fatherly nature of the leader's role. The central dramatic conflict of *Expendable* is between duty and personal ambition, maturity and immaturity. Before hearing the news of Pearl Harbor, Ryan fills out his application for transfer to a destroyer, explaining that he "can't build a navy reputation riding a plywood dream." Brickley tartly replies, "What are you aiming at—building a reputation or playing for the team?" Despite his initial scorn for Brickley's "fatherly advice," the impetuous Ryan gradually matures under his influence, submerging his ambition and sublimating the sadness of his doomed love affair as he learns to perform his duties as the squadron's executive officer.

These themes had personal significance for screenwriter Wead, the former navy flier whose recklessness left him crippled. Wead's screenplays for Ford's *Air Mail* and Hawks's *Ceiling Zero* (based on the writer's own play) also revolve around the clash between a headstrong, romantic subordinate and his tightly controlled, emotionally isolated commander. Brickley and Ryan can also be seen as the two halves of Ford's personality—the leader who has to suppress his personal desires for the sake of the team and the reckless, anarchic individualist he has to bring under control. Ford's sensitive direction of Montgomery, subtly stressing Brickley's balancing of personal emotion with the outward control necessary for leadership, demonstrates that a commander's cool, reserved exterior should not be confused with inhumanity.

Before the war, in such films as *The Grapes of Wrath* and *How Green Was My Valley,* Ford had begun focusing on the breakup of traditional families and communities under the pressures of the modern world. In *They Were Expendable,* Ford depicts an ad hoc "family" of military men and women that gradually breaks up in the service of a higher cause, national survival in the face of

---

29. After becoming the property of Ted Turner, *They Were Expendable* was colorized by American Film Technologies in the late 1980s for showings on TNT and elsewhere. An attempt to screen the colorized version on Danish television in 1990 was stopped by the Association of Danish Film Directors with the assistance of the Directors Guild of America and DGA member Dan Ford, standing up for his grandfather's moral and artistic rights.

enemy aggression. One of the film's most moving scenes is our last glimpse of "Dad," the elderly shipyard owner played by Russell Simpson, best known as Pa Joad in *The Grapes of Wrath*. Refusing to leave his shipyard despite an imminent Japanese invasion, Dad tells Ryan, "I worked forty years for this, son. If I leave it, they'll have to carry me out." Ford cuts to a heroic low angle of Dad sitting on his porch with his rifle across his knees, checking his jug to make sure he has an ample supply of liquid courage, as the sound track plays Danny Borzage's accordion rendition of "Red River Valley" from *Grapes*.

Against the wisdom and endurance of the veterans, Ford poignantly juxtaposes the fresh-faced innocence of the ensigns (Marshall Thompson, Arthur Walsh, and Cameron Mitchell) and, most memorably, the anonymous teenage sailor seen in close-up toasting the retiring Doc (Jack Pennick) by draining a glass of milk. This theme of the military as an extended family resonates in Brickley's farewell to the members of his squadron left behind with the army on Bataan: "You older men, with longer service records—take care of the kids. Maybe . . . that's all. God bless you."

What Bogdanovich calls Ford's theme of "the glory in defeat," the acceptance of devastating losses for a transcendent purpose, is encapsulated in the admiral's advice to the reluctant Brickley: "Listen, son, you and I are professionals. If the manager says, 'Sacrifice,' we lay down a bunt and let somebody else hit the home runs. . . . Our job is to lay down that sacrifice. That's what we were trained for, and that's what we'll do." Ironically, the ultimate sacrifice depicted in the film is Brickley's acceptance of the order to abandon the men who have served under him, echoing MacArthur's earlier evacuation of the Philippines.

By the time of *They Were Expendable*, Ford was "already out of synch with the prevailing *Zeitgeist*," Sarris observed. "What could have seemed more perverse than Ford's celebration of gallant defeat in the aftermath of glorious victory? It was as if the director had become nostalgic for certain values he felt slipping away irretrievably in the noisily opportunistic postwar world. Indeed, there was something anachronistic back in 1945 in Ford's invocations of unquestioning self-sacrifice, a dogged devotion to duty, an ingrained sense of responsibility, and a transcendental faith in a nation's worthiness to accept the fearsome sacrifices of its expendable individuals."

Ford's anachronism was more clearly apparent in retrospect than at the time of the film's release. *Expendable* has been described as a box-office flop, but it actually did good business, bringing in rentals of $3.25 million, enough to rank it among the year's top twenty films. *New York Times* reviewer Bosley Crowther underestimated the American public when he wrote, "It is in no wise depreciatory of . . . *They Were Expendable* to say that if this film had been released last year—or the year before—it would have been a ringing smash. Now, with the war concluded and the burning thirst for vengeance somewhat cooled, it comes as a cinematic postscript to the martial heat and passion of the last four years." From today's perspective, of course, that sobriety is one of its most admirable qualities, and many people also thought so in 1945.

Some reviewers damned *Expendable* with faint praise—the *New Yorker* superciliously remarked that it "has the freshness and simplicity of a well-told adventure story for juveniles"—but most appreciated the film's ambition and eloquence. Howard Barnes of the *New York Herald Tribune* called it "an abiding testament to the valor that made victory possible. . . . The greatest of film directors has lost none of his cunning or artistry during the years he has been in Navy uniform. . . . Ford, who should certainly know, has glossed over none of the agony which accompanied a rear-guard action. . . . It is only a pity that Ford did not cut his picture more drastically. It would have been more unified and even more dramatic."

The complaint about overlength was frequently heard at the time (the film runs two hours and sixteen minutes) and even in retrospect from Ford himself, who astonished Anderson in 1950 by saying that he intended the film to run only an hour and forty minutes. Anderson protested that such drastic cutting could not be done without ruining the film. "I think I know more about making pictures than you do," said Ford. This may have been a defensive reaction to criticism on Ford's part or simply an example of his perversity, needling an earnest admirer by affecting a pose of insensitivity.

Ford in fact exercised unusually close supervision of the editing, but he objected to studio recutting and to Herbert Stothart's symphonic score, claiming he wanted a sparser use of music. Nevertheless, the film's deliberate pacing, solemnly majestic musical accompaniment, and bitterly anticlimactic finale keep it faithful to the grim experience of the men who fought in the Philippines. Those who objected to its downbeat mood may have been expressing their own weariness with war.

"For what seems at least half of the dogged, devoted length of *They Were Expendable* all you have to watch is men getting on or off PT boats, and other men watching them do so," Agee observed in the *Nation*. "But this is made so beautiful and so real that I could not feel one foot of the film was wasted. . . . Visually, and in detail, and in nearly everything he does with people, I think it is John Ford's finest movie."

Ford's daughter sarcastically described him as a "ribbon freak." His military records and personal correspondence files offer ample evidence of his vigorous and largely unsuccessful campaigning for a variety of postwar military honors.

This disheartening postscript to Ford's otherwise exemplary World War II service lends further irony to the comical scene in *They Were Expendable* of Ensign Gardner vainly attempting to interest members of the squadron in the news that each has been awarded the Silver Star for rescuing MacArthur. The men are too busy repairing a damaged PT boat and performing other chores to pay attention to the news. While reflecting the serviceman's healthy cynicism about the value of medals in relation to deeds, the scene may also have been Ford's way of satirizing his own anxiety about military honors. He confided to a navy colleague in January 1946, "The only thing I would really be interested in would be a Silver Star, being [*sic*] a combat medal." But as a noncombatant, even one who had put himself in harm's way on numerous occasions, he was a dubious candidate for the award.

Ford's lobbying for a Silver Star began while he was filming *Expendable*. He thought he deserved the award for his actions and wounding during the Battle of Midway. On March 23, 1945, he wrote Captain John Roper in the office of Secretary of the Navy Forrestal: "Since my Naval combat career seems ended, I would like mightily to have the Commendation Ribbon at least to be buried in. As by the date you see the Commendation Ribbon was not then official—likewise the Silver & Bronze Stars. I was originally recommended for a medal but received the Citation instead." Asking Roper to bring his request for a Silver Star to Forrestal's attention, Ford added, "You will notice the wound was not mentioned in the citation due perhaps to [a] slipup. John, it's very brash of me to take up your time and I apologize most humbly. I can only say that I would like something for Mary & the Kids to be proud of."

The matter was referred to the Pacific Fleet Board of Awards, which noted with surprising asperity that while Ford had received a citation for his actions at Midway from the commandant of the Fourteenth Naval District, "evidently his performance of duty was not deemed sufficiently outstanding to merit the award of a Letter of Commendation by the CinC [commander in chief, Admiral Nimitz], U.S. Pacific Fleet." As a result, the Navy Board of Decorations and Medals wrote Forrestal on May 11, "Commander Ford has received the Purple Heart in recognition of his wounds received at Midway Island. The Board recommends that no further action in regard to a personal decoration be taken in his behalf." Nimitz and Forrestal concurred.

Undaunted, Ford enlisted Donovan and others in his quest for a Silver Star as well as a Distinguished Service Medal (for his services in the Normandy invasion). Donovan at the same time recommended him for the Legion of Merit, which was approved by Forrestal on December 9, 1945. The award was given on January 31, 1946, for Ford's "exceptionally meritorious conduct in the performance of outstanding services to the government of the United

States as Chief of the Field Photographic Branch, Office of Strategic Services. . . . Energetic and resourceful, he worked tirelessly toward the preparation and direction of secret motion-picture and still photographic reports and ably directed the initiation and execution of a program of secret intelligence photography." Describing Ford's extensive participation in combat photography, the citation recognized him for "rendering this vital service under extremely difficult and dangerous combat conditions. . . . By his brilliant service in a highly specialized field, Captain Ford contributed materially to the successful prosecution of the war."

But that great honor was followed by yet another disappointment. Four days after receiving the Legion of Merit, Ford was rejected for the Distinguished Service Medal, an award Frank Capra had received in June 1945 for his army filmmaking. The Board of Decorations and Medals told Forrestal that "the nature of the duties performed by Captain Ford were [sic] not such that they may be appropriately classified as a performance of duty in a position of great responsibility."

To fulfill his military ambitions, Ford would need another war.

Home is the sailor, home from sea . . ."

After completing *They Were Expendable* and spending two months in Washington wrapping up the affairs of Field Photo, Ford was released from navy service on September 29, 1945. Like most former servicemen, Ford took some time readjusting to civilian life. "Living in Hollywood, that is a bit difficult," he admitted to his Irish cousin Lord Killanin, "but now I am rested, my health is better, I have discarded my crutches and am walking now with only the aid of my father's old blackthorn from Spiddal."

Like Frank Capra, George Stevens, William Wyler, and other Hollywood colleagues who had served in the war, Ford was no longer content to be a studio contract director. He had been a military commander running what amounted to his own ministudio for the U.S. government, and he told Zanuck he did not want to return to a subordinate position in Hollywood. With Merian C. Cooper, Ford was busy making plans to go independent in their ambitiously revamped, freshly reincorporated Argosy Pictures.

But Ford first owed Zanuck another movie, and for all his bravado, he could not help feeling anxious about his future in Hollywood. He joked to a Fox colleague in September 1944, "If you should see [studio executive] Bill Goetz and Nunnally [Johnson], ask them if they will have room, when the War is over, for an old broken-down second-unit director. Salary no object."

CHAPTER ELEVEN

"I AM A DIRECTOR
OF WESTERNS"

Contrariety was perhaps his most consistent attribute.

A. J. A. SYMONS,
THE QUEST FOR CORVO

AT THE FAMOUS meeting in October 1950 when the Screen Directors Guild was torn apart over the issue of the Hollywood blacklist, the leading figure in the guild, who had been sitting in enigmatic silence throughout the evening, finally rose to address his colleagues. "My name is John Ford," he said. "I am a director of Westerns." What Ford went on to say about the matter at hand would have a powerful effect on the consciences of his fellow filmmakers. But one director present, Douglas Sirk, recalled that Ford's opening remark "set off a big discussion: people were so surprised that the great John Ford had chosen to categorize himself like that. They couldn't understand it. They would have rather expected him to step forward as the creator of *The Grapes of Wrath*."

After coming to America from Germany, Sirk had been surprised to find that Ford "was famous more for films like *The Grapes of Wrath* which to me aren't nearly so impressive as some of his Western work. But you know I love the Western. Now, there weren't too many Hollywood directors then who would have agreed, and even less critics. . . . [So Ford's remark] caused perplexity in Hollywood. It was the first time people there started to think about the Western as a medium worthy of great attention, except as a solid, ever-saleable piece of merchandise. There was no understanding of the place of the Western in the American cinema, or of the place of pictures in American culture."

Ford's act of self-definition at that pivotal moment in the history of Hollywood, and indeed in the history of the United States, reflected the profound transformation he had undergone in World War II. His identification with the military ethos and his growing sense of himself as a national poet made him turn his postwar filmmaking efforts largely to themes of American history. Wearing military fatigues and a navy baseball cap with a captain's eagle, Ford ran his sets like an extension of Field Photo. When he showed up at Hollywood events, it was often in full navy regalia. "Ford used to make quite a big scene about wearing his uniform to anything," recalled Vicky Wilson, Mark Armistead's daughter. "He would say to my dad, 'I don't want to wear my uniform. Don't put me in the position of having to wear it.' But if Dad wouldn't press him, he would be heartbroken."

Believing that the traditions he valued were under threat, Ford consciously set out to keep the values of pioneer America alive in the minds of his fellow countrymen. "Making Western pictures of that era has been a crusade with me since the war," he told a correspondent in 1949. Pointing to the commercial success of his films about the U.S. Cavalry, he added, "I am sure that means there are millions of people left [in the United States] still proud of their country, their flag, and their traditions."

Although as Darryl F. Zanuck reminded Ford in 1945, the cessation of hostilities meant that the filmgoing public was turning its attention away from what it considered the tiresome subject of World War II, Ford's obsession with war continued unabated. Of the ten films he directed between 1946 and 1951, three take place during the Indian wars (the Cavalry Trilogy comprises *Fort Apache, She Wore a Yellow Ribbon,* and *Rio Grande),* one during World War I *(What Price Glory),* one during World War II *(When Willie Comes Marching Home),* and one during the Korean War (the documentary *This Is Korea!). The Fugitive,* based on Graham Greene's novel *The Power and the Glory,* is set in a godless totalitarian state that in Ford's hands evokes the specter of Russian communism. Of the other three films he made in that period, all Westerns, only the religious allegory *3 Godfathers* entirely escapes the martial pattern. *My Darling Clementine* paints the Earp–Clanton feud in militaristic terms and *Wagon Master* deals with a group of peaceful Mormon pilgrims menaced by a band of murderous outlaws.

To be sure, Ford's increasing preoccupation with the West was partly dictated by box-office considerations. During the war, the Western genre had been eclipsed by combat films, but large-scale Westerns subsequently underwent a dramatic revival, remaining a Hollywood staple until the late 1950s, when the market became glutted with television Westerns. With its stylized treatment of frontier violence and nation building, the Western film displaced martial concerns into a context safely distanced from the sociopolitical uncertainties of the postwar era. The genre's popularity reflected a continued need among the American public for mythic parables of national identity in an age when America was grappling with the disturbing responsibilities of its new-found superpower status. "When in doubt, make a Western" was Ford's commercial as well as artistic mantra, and it proved almost infallible for him.

Even while seeking refuge in the mythos of the Old West, however, a film-maker could not avoid grappling, however obliquely, with the problems in the world outside the theater. Beneath the surface prosperity and complacency of postwar America, the country had to contend with widespread labor unrest, changing sexual mores and balances of power between men and women, in-creasingly urgent demands for greater racial equality, and the omnipresent anxieties over cold war issues and the threat of nuclear annihilation. As West-ern film historian Michael Coyne observes, rather than merely serving as "a relic of a simpler, more innocent past," the Western after World War II became "a vital medium for reflecting and articulating crucial issues of modern Amer-ican society. . . . While the Western was implicitly bound up with pride in the American experience, it could also be used with impunity to reproach twen-tieth-century political realities. The genre functioned as both a contained in-dictment and a reaffirmation of America, past and present." The deeper meanings we now find in the best Westerns from that period were not always as apparent to contemporary observers, who had a harder time seeing beyond genre conventions. This was just fine with Ford and other filmmakers who wanted to express themselves freely in the genre without attracting unwel-come attention from McCarthyites and others suspicious of Hollywood's pa-triotic bona fides.

However, Ford told his grandson that one reason he enjoyed making West-erns was that he could avoid dealing with political and sociological issues. Al-though true enough in a narrow sense, this claim is somewhat misleading. Ford displaced rather than ignored such issues. Beginning with the first film he made after being discharged from the navy, *My Darling Clementine* (1946), he retreated extensively into the American past to seek historical or mythic an-swers to the problems that troubled him in the present. In returning to the genre that had served seven years earlier as his vehicle for examining the social stresses of the depression era, he was searching for what he considered the core American values and testing them under fire. As deeply engaged politically as any director dealing with issues "ripped from today's headlines," Ford invited his audience to contemplate root causes and participate in an emotional and intellectual dialogue with his work, at times constructing scenes in a quasi-Brechtian fashion.

Ford created his own Western world, a fantasy domain in which he could be the undisputed king. "Jack lived in a dreamland, or rather he lived in Fordland," said actor-producer Charles FitzSimons, who appeared in his equally fantastic *Quiet Man*. Ford himself explained, "I like to make Western pictures because I like the people that I work with. I like to get out on location, I like to leave this place with the smog and fog and traffic and speedways and freeways. I like to get out and live in the open: you get up early, you work late, you eat dinner with an appetite, you sleep well. . . . When I come back from making a Western on location, I feel a better man for it." By living that life and translating it to the screen he was romanticizing and mourning a simpler, now-vanished way of life. But he continued to criticize what he saw as flaws in American society, past as well as present, and as his view of the present day grew darker, he became increasingly alienated from mainstream American culture.

The theme of the breakup of families, already an important element in his prewar films, became increasingly central in Ford's work after 1945, both as a reflection of his own disappointments about family life and as a metaphor for what he saw as the disintegration of social unity and purpose, reflecting a world increasingly out of control. One postwar project he was never able to film was *The Family*. Based on the novel by Nina Federova, the script by Laurence Stallings and Frank S. Nugent deals with an impoverished White Russian family living in the British Concession in Tianjin, China, in 1937. Their "Granny" tries to keep them together when they are trapped in a boardinghouse during a Japanese bombing raid with an alcoholic British woman, a Chinese high school teacher, and Japanese spies. "However, John assured me that it would have no political implication," Hedda Hopper gullibly reported in 1948, quoting Ford as saying, "It's simply the story of the disintegration of a family after it had been uprooted."

The Family seems quintessentially Fordian material, but Hollywood probably regarded it as too remote and downbeat to appeal to an American audience. Ford continued trying to film it as late as 1950, when he went to New York to offer the role of Granny to Greta Garbo. The director's bleak view of the changing world would also have been reflected, albeit humorously, in his remake of *The Last Outlaw*. That Rip Van Winkle story set in the modern West remained on his agenda even after the death of Harry Carey in 1947.

Ford's deeply ingrained feeling of rootlessness, as an Irish-American keenly aware of his family's displacement from their Connemara Eden, led him to romanticize the past with mounting intensity as he aged and America changed around him. His lovingly rendered depictions of some aspects of traditional communities in Ireland and the Old West stood in powerful contrast to what he saw as the soullessness of contemporary America. But he did not merely idealize archaic communities or indulge in uncomplicated optimism. His view of American society in these films steadily darkened, showing communities decimated by violence, riven from within, and surrounded by hostile forces threatening to tear them apart.

The result was a postwar body of work that became more nakedly individualistic, more deeply emotional, in many ways more pessimistic, fascinatingly and sometimes maddeningly self-contradictory, often defiantly quirky and self-indulgent to the point of perversity. Living in his imagined nineteenth-century Eden, extrapolated from the world just before he was born, the director created his own recognizably "Fordian" value system, a reflection of his own inner desires and conflicts. The unabashedly personal approach of his films, disguised as genre filmmaking, helped marginalize Ford with critics, academia, and, after the early 1950s, the Hollywood establishment. To them his work seemed merely crotchety in its stubborn anachronism rather than gloriously anachronistic, as he meant it to be. Defiantly opposed to prevailing postwar trends in movies, Ford largely disdained the voluptuous pessimism and probing psychoanalytical approach of film noir as well as avoiding, with some important exceptions, the overtly liberal aura of social consciousness typified by such critically acclaimed films as *The Best Years of Our Lives, Gentleman's Agreement, All the King's Men,* and *High Noon.*

While Ford's late 1940s Westerns have some reactionary elements, some also take antiracist and antiwar stands that seem subversive by the prevailing standards of Hollywood in that era. Those who simplistically equate Ford's politics with John Wayne's might be surprised to learn that when *She Wore a Yellow Ribbon* was filming in Monument Valley at the time of the 1948 presidential election, the only two people in the company who cast their absentee ballots for Harry S Truman rather than the Republican Thomas E. Dewey were Ford and Dobe Carey. Hearing some cast members claiming that the tax policies of Roosevelt and Truman were communistic, Ford disgustedly interjected, "I don't know what you guys are talking about. You all became millionaires off Roosevelt."

The mass audience of Ford's time tended to be reassured by the elements in his work that tastemakers deplored as old-fashioned. Less bothered by the director's outwardly conservative stance, the public probably responded with subconscious fascination to the more disturbing and provocative aspects of his films. No doubt Ford would not have remained commercially viable for so long if he had not been simultaneously reactionary and progressive. In any case, the public showed far more enduring loyalty to this great American artist than the critics did, but eventually—and inevitably—Ford fell out of step with the public as well. The price of being a national mythmaker is being discarded when the myth falls out of favor.

. . .

Ford still owed Darryl Zanuck a picture. But he turned down a new long-term contract at Fox that would have guaranteed $600,000 a year and, as before, the occasional freedom to make pet projects elsewhere. Ford was determined to run his own show. He did not want to have to keep cajoling studio executives who had rejected his cherished projects such as Maurice Walsh's Irish yarn "The Quiet Man" and Greene's novel *The Power and the Glory*. He wanted the ability to green-light those films himself.

Ford carved out his new independence in what initially seemed highly favorable conditions. Box-office receipts, robust during the war, reached a new peak of $1.69 billion in 1946, a record that stood for twenty-eight years even without adjustment for inflation. Favorable tax laws encouraged filmmakers to set up independent companies, and many took advantage of the opportunity. But the postwar euphoria in Hollywood was short-lived. Returning veterans were beginning to stay home from movies, more concerned with making a living and starting families. The social upheavals of a society readjusting from war to peace were depicted in the biggest box-office hit of 1946, Wyler's realistic and often downbeat masterpiece *The Best Years of Our Lives*. Early the following year began a sharp decline in moviegoing that would intensify with the spread of television in the late forties and provoke a major crisis in Hollywood by the early fifties. A contributing factor to this malaise was the 1948 Supreme Court decision in the Paramount case, compelling the studios to divest themselves of their theater chains. Marking the beginning of the end for the Hollywood studio system, this accelerated the downturn in production, resulting in the layoffs of thousands of industry workers.

The splintering of power in Hollywood eventually gave new strength to independent producers as well as to stars and their agents, who found themselves able to dictate terms to studio executives. But most filmmakers who tried to go independent immediately after the war found themselves too far ahead of the curve. The most prominent such venture was the Liberty Films partnership of Capra, Stevens, Wyler, and production executive Sam Briskin. Liberty made a deal to release its films through RKO but quickly folded because of the commercial failure of its first production, Capra's 1946 *It's a Wonderful Life*. Not only did independent filmmakers find it difficult to withstand a single flop, their independence was a somewhat illusory concept, for they could not function without releasing films through a studio's distribution apparatus.

With Merian C. Cooper, who had retired from the Army Air Forces and would be named a brigadier general in the Air Force Reserve in 1950, Ford incorporated the reorganized Argosy Pictures Corporation on January 2,

1946. Ford was chairman of the board of the privately held company and Cooper its president. The company name—derived from the Italian and variously meaning "a large merchant ship," "a fleet of ships," or "a rich supply"—symbolized Argosy's predominantly masculine orientation as well as Ford's identification with the U.S. Navy. Argosy's initial capitalization was approximately $500,000, half contributed by Ford and Cooper and the other half by twelve of their former OSS colleagues, including Wild Bill Donovan, David Bruce, William Vanderbilt, and Donovan's law partner and OSS right-hand man, Otto C. "Ole" Doering Jr. Doering arranged the financing with Cooper while Ford was in preproduction on his picture for Zanuck, *My Darling Clementine.* That April, Argosy's principal asset signed an exclusive contract with the company that obligated him to direct at least one picture a year for three years, with an annual salary of $150,000 (Ford's remaining obligation to Fox was excepted from the deal); Cooper's salary was set at $50,000 per year. Ford's stock ownership in Argosy was shared with Mary, and Cooper's with his wife, actress Dorothy Jordan, and their children.

Argosy's legal business was handled by Doering on behalf of Donovan's law firm, then known as Donovan Leisure Newton Lumbard & Irvine. Donovan's personal finances had suffered badly during the war, and he returned to the law firm after leaving government service in January 1946. He also became involved in a new business–private intelligence enterprise, the World Commerce Corporation. Because of his wartime friction with military intelligence, Donovan was passed over by President Truman when the Central Intelligence Agency was created in 1947 to replace the OSS, which had been liquidated in October 1945. Donovan and his fellow Argosy investors hoped to make use of their extensive international contacts for film production.

Shortly before America entered the war, Ford's agent, Harry Wurtzel, had talks with Fox, RKO, and Universal about the possibility of entering into a multiple-picture production deal with Argosy, with only some of the pictures to be directed by Ford. After Ford and Cooper returned from service, however, they initially considered bypassing the major studios and setting up Argosy as a large fish in a small pond. They had talks with Republic Pictures, the B-movie company in North Hollywood that made mostly Westerns and kept John Wayne unhappily under contract as its leading box-office attraction. Republic president Herbert J. Yates, a notorious philistine who came from the film-laboratory business and punctuated conversations by spitting streams of chewing tobacco, harbored an inchoate dream of elevating Republic to major-studio status. To that end he initiated a program of pictures with somewhat higher budgets and considerably higher artistic aspirations, signing Ben Hecht to make the ballet melodrama *Specter of the Rose* in 1946 and Orson

Welles to direct a low-budget version of Shakespeare's *Macbeth* in 1947. Yates saw even greater possibilities for prestige in having Ford as a staff producer. But talks collapsed because Argosy not only wanted a stock ownership position in Republic but also insisted on remaining an independent company selling its pictures to the studio for distribution.

On September 27, 1946, Argosy concluded a four-picture distribution deal with RKO, the studio that had allowed Ford to make some of his most self-consciously "artistic" films of the thirties, notably *The Informer.* RKO had since undergone management upheavals and was the weakest of the five major studios. Ford and Cooper later regarded the deal as unfavorable, but in fact it was as good as they could have expected. Their contract, later extended to include a fifth picture, called for Argosy and RKO to split the costs and profits and Argosy to retain creative control as well as ownership of the pictures (with the exception of the jointly owned *Mighty Joe Young,* Cooper's 1949 children's version of his RKO classic *King Kong).* If the first picture was successful, Ford would be allowed to make *The Quiet Man.* Argosy set up shop on the RKO-Pathé lot leased by David O. Selznick at 9336 W. Washington Boulevard in Culver City, where Cooper had made *King Kong,* Selznick had shot much of *Gone with the Wind,* and Orson Welles had made *Citizen Kane.*

The backing of Argosy's outside investors gave Ford and Cooper valuable leverage in controlling the content of their own films, but that power existed only within certain limits. Out of necessity, Ford soon found himself turning to Westerns, which he called "potboilers," to keep his company viable. Ford's use of such a self-denigrating label was belied by the artistry and emotion he lavished on those films, which include some of his finest work. But while concentrating on the Western genre ensured his bankability, it also meant that Ford was marginalizing himself with reviewers and the Hollywood establishment. His most fervent critical supporters increasingly were to be found outside the United States. With rare exceptions, American reviewers in that era still treated Westerns with knee-jerk condescension, no matter how ambitious or groundbreaking they were. Nor would Hollywood ever give Ford an Oscar for one of his Westerns. But such snobbery only encouraged his stubborn individualism.

In one of his letters to Mary toward the end of the war, Ford wrote that he was looking forward to spending his time in a rocking chair. A well-earned rest—like Ol' Mose Harper's in *The Searchers*—was Ford's first priority after his return from service. But, as always, Ford's restless nature could not be satisfied at home.

Katherine Cliffton, who became Argosy's story and research editor in 1947, observed:

I felt he lived his life on the set. He felt directly in charge of morale. He was there to see his people become a unit. A director is a kind of king. He loved the set. He loved being in charge. He was a man inclined to be home on the set or in Hawaii [on the *Araner*]. His films *are* his life—his films are his epitaph. Ford took to bed if he wasn't on the set. He would be sitting up in bed holding court. On rare occasions he would come downstairs for an hour or so. His bed was his office and his library and everything else.

Whenever I came to talk to him, he was sitting up in bed reading or watching television. I worked in the household for a long time cataloguing his library. He said, "I don't want cards, I want a big book." He had about six thousand volumes. They came in so fast, they almost defied cataloguing. I brought him a lot of stories; I was supposed to bring him an armload of books for personal reading. They lined his room and his study. It wasn't an orderly room he lived in.

To catalogue it, I had to study him. I found out his areas of interest and had a book full of authors, titles, categories—suspense, Civil War, Irish stories and lore, poetry, biographies, and historical novels. He read a lot and read very rapidly; he had to hold the page up to his face. He didn't mind reading a book over again if he liked it. *The White Company* and *Sir Nigel* [by Sir Arthur Conan Doyle], he said, were the two finest historical novels ever written. He loved suspense novels and had his favorites he liked to follow—[Agatha Christie's] Poirot, the Gideon books [by J. J. Marric, the pseudonym of John Creasey], he read them all.

On the set or on location, Ford similarly immersed himself in a seductive fantasy world, but one of his own creation. He had his own arbitrary code of conduct, rewards, and punishments, and when he was on a Western location, he had elaborate rituals to put everyone into a suitably Fordian mood after working hours. Around a campfire under the stars of Monument Valley, there were singsongs and "something different happening every night," Henry Fonda recalled. There were weekend dances, footraces, and barbecues with Ford's beloved "Navvies." The director's inner circle was invited to play games of pitch in his room at Goulding's lodge; Ford started each game with a pile of silver dollars, and it was understood that he was always allowed to win. Drinking was strictly forbidden for everyone from the director on down. On location for *My Darling Clementine,* Fonda was put in charge of the nightly entertainment: "I was the camp director of Camp Juneluska, we called it—'The Camp for Boys between the Ages of Fourteen,' I remember that was the phrase. There would be a program every night, and during the day when you're on the set between takes, you're talking about it and planning it and organizing it. Anyway, it was something that people got to look forward to." At the end of each evening, Ford would give a silent cue to the company bugler, Fonda remembered, "[A]nd he would disappear into the woods there. Suddenly when it had got to the last song, whatever it was, he would blow taps from way back in the woods. And I tell you that people would cry with nostalgia. It was like being a child again at camp."

Ford's next order of business after resting up in 1945 was to establish his homes away from home—the *Araner* and the Field Photo Farm. Reclaiming the *Araner* from navy patrol duty, Ford found it in relatively good shape thanks to the watchfulness of Frank McGrath, but Pat and Barbara were pressed into service to scrape off a layer of black paint used for camouflage. Ford had a priest bless the boat to remove the curse of war.

When the IRS questioned the Fords' continued tax write-offs for the use of the *Araner* as a business expense, Mary said in a 1952 affidavit, "Mr. Ford has a very limited social life, and practically without exception entertains only Navy or business associates in our home or aboard the yacht. . . . His cabin aboard the ship is equipped with library shelves filled with reference books, recording equipment, and other materials to work with during the time he is aboard. He spends most of his time in his cabin going over scripts and other material he uses in his work." Of course, she didn't mention the time he spent drinking and carousing on the boat. "We never spoke of his drinking within the household," Katherine Cliffton recalled.

Much as the *Araner* provided Ford with a refuge from his home on Odin Street, the Field Photo Farm in the San Fernando Valley offered a surrogate family life that helped compensate for his failure to achieve a satisfying relationship with his own family. Much of Ford's creative energy in late 1945 and early 1946 went into setting up the Reseda retreat for his war buddies and Stock Company members. Improvements were paid with the $75,000 remaining from his directing fee for *They Were Expendable*. He continued to subsidize the Farm by putting out thousands of dollars most years in gifts and loans.

Ole Doering became president of Field Photo Homes after the war and was added to its board of governors along with Ray Kellogg, Merian Cooper, and Rear Admiral I. C. Johnson. In a double-edged gesture, John Wayne, who never felt entirely comfortable at the Farm because of his noncombatant status, was named to its "honorary board of advisors." With its clubhouse, bar, and living quarters (six bedrooms, one permanently reserved for General

Donovan); the nondenominational chapel imported from Ford's home state of Maine, whose altar displayed a Catholic crucifix, a Protestant cross, and a Jewish Star of David; a parade ground, complete with cannon; and a baseball field, swimming pool, tennis court, and stables, the Field Photo Farm became Ford's earthly Valhalla for gatherings of his loyal men and the ghosts of their honored dead. In the words of its constitution, "The aim of the organization shall be to ever respect and hold before all men the shining example of our comrades who made the supreme sacrifice in order that we, as a nation, may continue to enjoy those freedoms that are the foundation of our country's greatness and are the birthright of all peoples." The egalitarianism of that lofty declaration was qualified by a sign at the entrance of the Farm reading "NO WOMEN EXCEPT ON VISITORS' DAY."

The members of the Farm all had one thing in common—Ford was their "Pappy." He expected to be treated with suitable deference. Not only a memorial to his war dead, whose medals were on display in the clubhouse in thirteen glass cases, the Farm was something of a living memorial to Ford himself, with a large oil painting of the director displayed over the fireplace. Based on a photograph taken while Ford was directing *The Long Voyage Home,* the George Schreiber painting depicts Ford standing in front of a camera, hands on hips, pipe jutting from his mouth, and wearing a yachting cap. The dedication ceremony for the Farm on April 14, 1946, included a presentation to Ford of "his" two Oscars for *The Battle of Midway* and *December 7th.* Those Oscars went on display under the painting, along with the ones Ford received for *The Informer, The Grapes of Wrath,* and *How Green Was My Valley.*

Mary Ford was deeply involved in the affairs of the Field Photo Farm. Like the Hollywood Canteen, it filled the void in her family life. She decorated the place and took charge of catering and other arrangements for most events at the Farm, including the annual St. Patrick's Day party and the Founder's Day party, a celebration of Ford's birthday. Ford personally took charge of the elaborately staged Memorial Day and Christmas ceremonies. Planning for each of those events went on for months, and each board member would be assigned particular tasks, as in a military operation. Everyone involved in the Memorial Day ceremony was expected to be in uniform. When Harry Carey Jr. finally protested that he had grown out of his navy uniform, Ford ordered, "Rent one!"

The 1948 Memorial Day ceremony was a typical Ford patriotic extravaganza. It began with the men of Field Photo and the OSS falling in during the presentation of the colors, marched from the chapel with a fife-and-drum escort. Then came paraplegics in wheelchairs from the nearby Birmingham Hospital, who had a permanent invitation to use the pool and other facilities. Reports were read on the condition of graves of members of the Field Photo and the Military Order of the Purple Heart. Ray Hyke, a navy veteran who usually played aging cavalry officers in Ford movies, read Lincoln's Gettysburg Address. Hyke was followed by the keynote speaker, General Donovan.

The main part of each year's ceremony was the reading of the roll call of departed comrades. In 1948, Ray Kellogg and George O'Brien had the duty. The chorus sang softly and muffled drumrolls punctuated O'Brien's reading of the thirteen names, with Kellogg repeating after each, "Lost in action." Taps was sounded, and the event concluded with bagpipers marching to the tune of "The Wearing of the Green." The roll call response was eventually modified to "Died for his country" as Ford expanded the list to include others in his personal pantheon, such as President John F. Kennedy.[1]

The main event at the Christmas party was the arrival of Santa Claus on a stagecoach escorted by six mounted stuntmen. Santa was played by actors such as Andy Devine, Charles Kemper, Alan Hale, Burl Ives, and Mike Mazurki. Riding atop the coach was Danny Borzage, playing "Jingle Bells" on his accordion, accompanied in later years by Jimmy Stewart. Santa would disembark at the clubhouse to distribute presents to the children. For the adults, the prevailing atmosphere of bonhomie and nostalgia at these events was lubricated with plenty of liquid refreshments.

On occasion Ford hosted parties for other groups. In September 1956 he threw a Western barbecue and lobster feed for several hundred American Legion members from Maine and others in town for the Legion's national convention. Dan Dailey was master of ceremonies for the entertainment program Ford directed, which included strolling singers, cowboys and Indians, square dancing, and a stunt show featuring John Wayne and fellow horsemen charging into a crowd of Mexican extras.

Free of the self-imposed tension of filmmaking, when he kept himself on the wagon and dominated the company by playing mind games and barking orders in military fashion, Ford presided over events at the Farm as a benevolent paterfamilias. Henry Fonda felt that Ford's tyrannical personality had mellowed somewhat as a result of his war experiences.

"There was a streak of cruelty about him; he had too sharp a tongue and he would go to elaborate lengths to show people up," Cliffton said, "and yet he would do nice little things for people that nobody saw. One time he called

---

1. Mark Haggard, a young filmmaker who became friendly with Ford in his later years, preserved on film one of the last of Ford's Memorial Day services. *John Ford: Memorial Day 1970,* released in 1974, was filmed at the Motion Picture and Television Country House and Hospital, where the chapel was moved after the Farm had to be sold in 1965.

a priest when I was there—maybe he called the priest *because* I was there. The priest had a boys' choir that sang at the Field Photo Farm. Ford said, 'I know some of the boys don't have blue suits. I want to give them blue suits because I didn't have a blue suit to graduate in from high school.' Nobody knew about this but me."

The symbolic role of the Field Photo Farm in Ford's postwar existence became clear when Harry Carey died of cancer at his Brentwood home on September 21, 1947, at the age of sixty-nine.

Ford was one of four people present at the deathbed of his first leading man. The others were a doctor, a nurse, and Harry Carey Jr. Ford's guilt over his long estrangement from Carey helps account for his extreme emotional reaction. Olive Carey, who was on her porch when Harry died, recalled that "Jack came out and he took hold of me and put his head on my breast and cried, and the whole front of my sweater was sopping wet. For at least fifteen or twenty minutes he cried, just solid sobbing, solid sobbing, and the more he cried, the stronger I'd get. It was very good for me, it was wonderful. Oh, God, he shook and cried."

The funeral, elaborately staged by Ford, was held at the Farm on September 24. Ollie always regarded it as "one of the best funerals ever done." Wearing a black suit, a string tie, and cowboy boots, Carey's body lay in state in the chapel overnight with an honor guard of four sailors. His last horse, Sunny, was tethered to the railing outside, wearing an empty saddle. Danny Borzage played "Red River Valley" on his accordion as a thousand mourners, many of them in uniform, took their places on the lawn near the chapel. As the navy pallbearers carried the casket from the chapel, the Jester Hairston Choir, an African-American singing group, offered spirituals. An Episcopalian minister conducted the services, Wayne read Tennyson's poem "Crossing the Bar," and Burl Ives sang Harry's favorite song, "Goodbye, Old Paint." Afterward, Ford provided the beer for an Irish wake. Frank Capra told Dobe Carey that the funeral had been "Ford's greatest production."

In contrast, Hollywood's July 1948 rites for D. W. Griffith were a potent symbol for Ford of the industry's shameful and hypocritical neglect of its greatest pioneer. Ford and Mae Marsh, the Griffith leading lady who became a regular in the Ford Stock Company—both of them cast members of *The Birth of a Nation*—were among only six people who paid respects to Griffith at the funeral home on July 26 (Cecil B. DeMille was another). The next day when the funeral was held at the Hollywood Masonic Temple, studio executives and producers who would not give Griffith a job in his later years vied to be seen in mourning. Ford made his own statement by staying away from the event. Whether consciously or not, he echoed his feelings about Griffith's death in *The Man Who Shot Liberty Valance,* when a forgotten pioneer (John Wayne's Tom Doniphon) has his humble coffin laid out in a livery stable and is mourned privately rather than publicly by three friends, the only people who understand his true importance.

From time to time, members of Ford's surrogate family would be expelled for failing to show him the required deference. Like most World War II veterans, Robert Parrish was preoccupied with making a living, starting a family, and saving money to buy a house. After a couple of visits to the Farm, he decided that he didn't want to perpetuate his service years in a largely male clubhouse.

Perhaps sensing that resistance, Ford invited Parrish and his wife to dinner at Odin Street. Describing the improvements under way at the Farm, Ford proudly said that in the chapel, "anyone and everyone will be welcome— Protestants, Jews, Catholics, Communists—everyone. What do you think of the idea?"

Parrish bluntly replied, "I think you should bulldoze the farmhouse, the chapel, the hitching post, the stained-glass windows, the swimming pool, the stables—the whole thing. Then I think you should subdivide the eight acres into fifty-foot lots and build low-cost duplex houses for returning veterans."

Ford slowly lit and relit his pipe four times before he finally spoke: "Like I said before, everyone will be welcome, regardless of race, creed, or color."

The next time Parrish saw Ford was at Carey's funeral. Parrish attended with another Field Photo veteran, screenwriter Daniel Fuchs. When they met up with Ford outside the chapel after the service, Ford turned to his warrant officer and said, "Guy, as soon as the morbidly curious civilians leave, we'll break out the beer and start the wake." Then he walked away. Parrish saw him only once in the next twenty-one years.

After they discussed such projects as the swashbuckler *Captain from Castile* (later filmed by Henry King with Tyrone Power as the Spanish conquistador) and a new version of Irvin S. Cobb's Judge Priest stories with the lynching scene intact, Zanuck suggested that Ford consider remaking the 1939 Fox Western *Frontier Marshal.* Directed by Allan Dwan and starring Randolph Scott as Wyatt Earp and Cesar Romero as the Doc Holliday character, it was adapted by Sam Hellman from Stuart N. Lake's biography *Wyatt Earp: Frontier Marshal,* which had already been filmed once before by Fox, with George O'Brien in 1934. Lake's influential book in turn has only a *very* loose connection with the facts about Earp's checkered career as a Western gambler, cattleman, church deacon, lawman, and occasional gunfighter.

Winston Miller, the principal screenwriter of what eventually became *My Darling Clementine,* played the George O'Brien character as a boy in *The Iron Horse.* Miller claimed that he and Ford "made up the story" of *Clementine* around the legendary Gunfight at the O. K. Corral without ever watching the Dwan film. But in fact Ford ran *Frontier Marshal* on October 31, 1945, and told Zanuck that it would provide an excellent story for a Technicolor Western starring Henry Fonda as Earp and Tyrone Power as Holliday. Describing Hellman's screenplay as about 40 percent accurate, Ford suggested it needed more historical detailing as well as exterior locations in Monument Valley or the Painted Desert to broaden its canvas.

To Fonda, Ford was less diplomatic. "Shit," he said, "I can do better than that."

Nevertheless, the two films have many similarities, and Hellman receives a story credit on *Clementine.* Miller, who shares the screenplay credit with producer Samuel G. Engel (a Field Photo veteran), found Ford "a touchy guy" to work with, but marveled at how Zanuck managed to exert his influence over the director: "Zanuck had an idea that he suggested and Ford thought it was terrible. Zanuck said in effect, 'Jack, if any other director was going to do the picture, I wouldn't even suggest it to him, but you can pull it off . . . ,' and Ford ate it up. Zanuck played him like a flute." One of Zanuck's most important suggestions was the ending. In the first draft of the screenplay, the story ended in a graveyard with Earp and Clementine Carter (Cathy Downs) each admitting plans to stay in Tombstone, Arizona. Zanuck suggested that Earp instead should say good-bye to Clementine at the edge of town and, before riding away, hint that he may return.

Ford's most important contribution to the script was his ruthless editing. He threw out a number of unnecessary scenes and heavily cut its garrulous and overly expository dialogue, turning *Clementine* into a terse morality play leavened with robust but underplayed humor and many purely visual interludes. The director added a few lines of his own during the filming, including two of the drollest dialogue exchanges in any Ford movie. Expressing admiration for Clementine after she has helped Doc Holliday (Victor Mature) operate on Chihuahua (Linda Darnell) in the saloon, Wyatt turns to the grandfatherly old Irish bartender, Ford regular J. Farrell MacDonald, and asks, "Mac, you ever been in love?" Mac replies, "No—I been a bartender all me life." Ford also inserted the gag with Clementine on the porch of the Mansion House inhaling deeply and murmuring, "The air is so clear and clean—scent of the desert flower," to which Wyatt embarrassedly replies, "That's me—barber." The film's most memorable bit of business, Fonda's whimsical balancing act on the porch as he sits in a chair with his legs doing bicycle motions on a fence post, was improvised on the spot by the director. "I guess more people have asked me about this balancing act than almost anything else I've done," Fonda said in 1971.

Ford claimed to have based *My Darling Clementine* on his memories of what Wyatt Earp, back in the silent days, told him about the Gunfight at the O.K. Corral. "So in *My Darling Clementine*," Ford told Bogdanovich, "we did it exactly the way it had been. They didn't just walk up the street and start banging away at each other; it was a clever military maneuver." Knowledgeable as he was about Western history, Ford undoubtedly knew that his brilliant and imaginative staging of the event—in which, among other fabrications, Doc Holliday and Old Man Clanton are killed—was not the way it actually happened. Most modern historians have described the gunfight, which took place in a cramped vacant lot a block from the corral, as a cold-blooded power play by the Earp faction against the Clanton gang. Wyatt Earp was not even the town marshal at the time; that position was held by his brother Virgil. The gunfight took place on October 26, 1881, not in 1882 as the film implies by inscribing that date on the tombstone of Wyatt's brother James, who in fact was the oldest, not youngest, of the Earps. "It's always simplicity that you should go after in any case," Ford believed. "In the scenario, the music, the acting, the style."

Ford and his writers went to considerable lengths to whitewash Earp, making him seem almost noble, despite his admitted love of poker and his resort to vigilante justice in what he calls "strictly a family affair." The actual Earp brothers considered themselves primarily "sporting men" rather than lawmen and were known to their enemies as "the fighting pimps." In Tombstone they served as the hired guns of the Republican business community in opposition to the ranchers, mostly Democrats, who protected outlaws such as the Clantons. The 1881 gunfight attracted widespread attention because duels of that kind were rare in the West, contrary to the impression conveyed by Hollywood. But few historians even today are able to agree on Wyatt's character or the significance of his convoluted political entanglements in Tombstone. Furthermore, Earp biographer Casey Tefertiller notes that the gunfight "erupted so quickly that not even the participants were quite certain exactly what had just happened."

That left fertile ground for mythmaking and tale spinning long before Ford took the shabby episode and "turned it into a wonderful tale of good and evil," as Tefertiller calls it. "*My Darling Clementine* captured the essence of the story without being burdened by either the facts or the furious social questions that swirled around Tombstone." Still, at one point during preproduction, Ford seemed to become uneasy about how far the script was veering from history and suggested that the names of the characters be fictionalized. Zanuck disagreed, feeling that an aura of authenticity would help distinguish *Clementine* from ordinary Westerns.

Katherine Cliffton felt that "*My Darling Clementine* was kind of phony. Earp [in real life] was a man of many parts—he had a piece in a whorehouse, et cetera. Doc Holliday was not such a lovable character as he was in that film. Ford later was more cynical, maybe. He couldn't make someone a hero *and* a heel [in *Clementine*]—he could later on. Movies were fairy stories in the thirties and forties because they had to be."

Each generation of filmmakers has twisted the Earp story for its own ideological purposes, from the law-and-order fables of the depression era to the cynically revisionist works of the 1960s and beyond (including Ford's own portrayal of a thoroughly corrupt Wyatt Earp in 1964's *Cheyenne Autumn*, played by James Stewart). In the idealistic worldview of *My Darling Clementine* there are no moral ambiguities intended in the epic battle between good (the Earps) and evil (the Clantons). Ford's 1946 version has been seen as an allegory of the winning of World War II or, alternately, the struggles of the cold war, with the Earps representing the American public, slow to anger but ruthless when wronged, and the Clantons representing the Axis powers or Red Menace (take your pick).

There is no doubt that Ford's military experiences deeply influenced the way he tells this archetypal story, which presents Wyatt as a shrewd, no-nonsense commander in the Johnny Bulkeley vein. But if Ford's romanticization of Earp indicates a buoyant postwar optimism about the American future, as some have argued, it is a guarded optimism deeply shaded by loss and qualified by the brutal way the victory is achieved. The name of the town, after all, is Tombstone.

Clementine emphasizes the devastation caused by frontier warfare, the cost of making the territory fit for "young kids . . . to grow up and live safe." Ford's especially poignant treatment early in the film of the death of James Earp (Don Garner) was influenced by the deaths of young men in his wartime command. The director's characteristic concern with family disintegration is depicted with even greater finality in *Clementine* than in his prewar films. Both families wind up decimated by their confrontation: the Clantons are wiped out, while two of the four Earp brothers are killed along with their ally Doc Holliday. Ford's idealization of family life is further qualified by his depiction of the murderous Clantons. Perhaps the director was exorcising some of his own worst tendencies as a father in having Ward Bond's Morgan Earp kill off Old Man Clanton (Walter Brennan), an abusive, whip-wielding psychopath who in the screenplay was allowed to ride off alone.

But the Manichaean opposition between the Earps and the Clantons is relatively unusual in Ford's West, where characters are usually painted in subtler shades of gray. *My Darling Clementine* is the kind of Western tale to which Jorge Luis Borges was referring when he wrote that "the ethical preoccupation of North Americans, based on Protestantism, has led them to present in the cowboy the triumph of good over evil." While the American Western, partly for that reason, has been regarded as a "subordinate genre," Borges adds, "One must admit, however, that it is a branch of the epic and that the brave and noble cowboy has become a worldwide symbol."

Fonda had a lock on the role of Wyatt from the beginning of Ford's involvement in the project, but casting Doc Holliday, traditionally a malleable character, proved more difficult. James Stewart was seriously considered. He had the gauntness usually associated with the consumptive dentist (who is a surgeon in the film). But after four years at war, Stewart decided to return to the screen in the lead role of *It's a Wonderful Life*. Ford enthusiastically accepted Zanuck's suggestion of Victor Mature, believing that his decadent sensuality suited Doc's self-destructive personality, even if this casting results in Doc "looking about as tubercular as a Kodiak bear," Allen Barra notes in *Inventing Wyatt Earp: His Life and Many Legends*. Barra speculates Ford didn't want Doc confused with John Carradine's Hatfield, "the gaunt gentleman gambler and defender of Southern womanhood in *Stagecoach,* who is clearly a variation of the Holliday legend," although Hatfield could hold his liquor and Doc couldn't. Less inclined to celebrate drunkenness after managing to remain sober throughout large stretches of the war years, Ford puritanically condemned the aspects of himself he saw in Doc, the self-loathing alcoholic. Ford was concerned about Mature's own tendency to drink and put on weight. After a fatherly chat from the director, Mature agreed to be a good boy, but Ford rode him mercilessly during the shooting just for insurance.

Fox ingenue Jeanne Crain was originally cast as Clementine, the kind and upstanding WASP heroine from back East who switches her allegiance from Doc to Wyatt. The character perhaps reminded Ford of his patrician friend from Portland High School, Alnah James. When Zanuck decided that Clementine was too small a role for an actress being groomed for stardom, Ford suggested Donna Reed or Anne Baxter before they agreed on the newcomer, Downs. Ford found parts in *Clementine* for many of his favorite character actors, including Bond, Jane Darwell, Russell Simpson, Mae Marsh, and his brother Frank as Dad, the town drunk in a Union army cap.

One actor Ford was not allowed to cast was Stepin Fetchit. In February 1945, the black comedian had written the director that he needed work. Ford came up with the role of Buttons, a factotum occupying an indispensable place in Earp's life much like Jeff Poindexter's with Judge Priest. Among other duties, Buttons was to have brought Earp his chair so the marshal could await the morning stagecoach. Telling Ford that he personally enjoyed Stepin Fetchit's performances, Zanuck wrote that casting the comedian in a 1946 movie would invite strong criticism from Negroes. Walter White of the increasingly militant National Association for the Advancement of Colored People had warned Zanuck and other Hollywood executives that Stepin Fetchit embodied what was considered an offensive and unacceptable racial stereotype. As Andrew Sarris so eloquently wrote of this instance of blacklisting, for postwar liberals it was "[b]etter that Fetchit be permanently unemployed than that he serve as a reminder of a shameful blind spot on both sides of the Mason-Dixon line. But for Ford, Mr. Fetchit was an old friend and a familiar face, and he had to make a living like everyone else."

Clementine has prompted criticism in recent years for its portrayal of Darnell's Chihuahua, the Mexican-Indian saloon girl (i.e., prostitute). The dark and sultry Fox actress first acted for Ford in *Drums Along the Mohawk* before Zanuck changed his mind and replaced her with Dorris Bowdon; Darnell is still visible in some long shots. Unlike Dallas in *Stagecoach,* Chihuahua is a prostitute *without* a heart of gold. Wyatt treats her with puritanical and racist contempt ("I'll run you back to the Apache reservation where you belong"). Ford uses her blatant sexuality and treachery as a symbol of the frontier wildness Wyatt is trying to "civilize." As Robin Wood observed in a 1971 essay on the director, Ford "can only tolerate Chihuahua when she is shot and dying, whereupon he promptly sentimentalizes her." The white supremacist attitude of the film is also made clear in the incident that wins Earp the job of marshal in Tombstone, his subduing of drunken, hell-raising Indian Charlie (Charles Stevens). When Earp's shave is disrupted by gunshots, he demands, "What kind of a town is this, anyway? Selling liquor to Indians." Before kicking Indian Charlie in the rump, he says harshly, "Indian, get outta town and stay out."

What is most memorable about *Clementine* is not its pulp-novel story line but Ford's relaxed, spacious filming style. After having second thoughts about color, he was pleased when Zanuck agreed to let him shoot in black and white. Joe MacDonald's beautifully atmospheric cinematography gives a palpable sense of the "clear and clean" desert air surrounding the nascent community of Tombstone. Art directors James Basevi and Lyle Wheeler created Tombstone against the spectacular vistas of Monument Valley, moving the action from the southern to the northern part of the state to lend it more mythic dimensions. The loving way the director details daily life in a rowdy frontier town, from the Bon Ton Tonsorial Parlor with its brand-new barber's chair ("Come all the way from Chicago") to the skeletal church rising at the border of town and wilderness, shows the imprint of Ford's four years as a documentary filmmaker and his growing fascination with conjuring up magical images of vanished Americana. Filmed from April through June of 1946, *Clementine* was relatively lavish for a Western of that time, costing more than $2 million. Zanuck was determined to make it both a critical and box-office hit, "*big time all the way.*"

The urge to settle down, so common among returning war veterans, is the key to Wyatt Earp's character in *Clementine*. Like Ford returning from the Normandy invasion, Earp celebrates his return to "civilization" by shaving off his nomad's beard. This canny, self-controlled man efficiently doing "a job of work" wants nothing more than to plant himself in his chair and watch the world go by from the porch of the local hotel, the Mansion House (which shares the name of a historic Dublin building). But Earp first has to finish the job of taming the wildness around him and inside him. Fonda's tightly wound, deliberate movements offer Ford plenty of "grace notes"—Ford loved to watch Fonda walk and constructed scenes for that reason—yet there are signs of dandyism and cold fanaticism in the characterization that Ford treats with some ambivalence. Perhaps he was already having some doubts about Fonda and keeping one eye on the wings where John Wayne was waiting to take over as a more relaxed, more adaptable Fordian hero.

The church dedication scene, one of the touchstones of the Western genre, represents the concept of civilization in its purest and most appealing form. Ford's favorite hymn, Robert Lowry's "Shall We Gather at the River," plays reverentially under the tracking shot of Earp escorting Clementine down a long, pillared walkway, the barber saluting his handiwork as they pass. They proceed up the dusty street toward the half-built church spire, outlined almost transparently against the sky and framed by two American flags flowing in the breeze. Announcing that he's "read the Good Book from cover to cover and back again, and I've nary found a word agin' dancin'," the deacon (Russell Simpson) breaks out his fiddle to start the festivities "by havin' a dad-blasted good dance!" Accompanying are Francis Ford on the violin and J. Farrell Mac-Donald on the piano. Ford gives us lyrical low-angle shots of the congregation square-dancing on the wooden planks against the bright midday sky. The group parts so Earp can waltz stiffly but gracefully with "his lady fair," to the same 1879 tune by James A. Bland that was used for Fonda's dance in *Young Mr. Lincoln,* "Oh, Dem Golden Slippers." The finest sequence in Ford's body of work to date, this poetic interlude remains one of the glories of his career.

However, after Ford turned in his cut of *Clementine,* Zanuck wrote him a memo on June 25 complaining that "the picture does not live up to my own personal anticipation" and that it needed a "major and radical cutting job." Concerned about what he considered continuity gaps and inconsistencies, Zanuck added, "Anything that appears even slightly obvious or formula will look ten times as bad in this type of film." He urged Ford to let him take over the editing as he had done on *The Grapes of Wrath* and *How Green Was My Valley*. Ford evidently was unwilling to make the changes Zanuck demanded. Reshoots were ordered in July from director Lloyd Bacon, including the graveyard scene of Wyatt speaking to his dead brother, James, an echo of Will Rogers's graveyard scene in *Judge Priest*. Distractingly filmed in front of a process screen, the scene may have been reshot to change James's age, given on the tombstone as eighteen although specified as twenty in the shooting script. Also filmed after Ford's departure was the night scene on the back porch of the saloon, also using a process screen, of Doc demanding that Clementine leave town; this replaced Clementine's calling him a coward as they walk through town. Another bit was added of Doc joining the Earps for the gunfight and reporting Chihuahua's death.

A nitrate print of the 1946 preview version, about ten minutes longer than the release version, has been preserved by the UCLA Film and Television Archive in cooperation with the Museum of Modern Art. Dan Ford wrote that Zanuck's cuts mostly involved broad comedy bits that Ford had added during shooting. But if so, those cuts were made before the film was previewed. What the reediting of the preview version demonstrates is Zanuck's characteristic impatience with Ford's leisurely style, his emphasis on mood and grace notes. Some nuances of characterization, including a bit more complexity for Chihuahua, were left on the cutting-room floor, and unfortunately the church dedication sequence was trimmed of opening shots of people arriving in wagons to the tune of "Oh! Susanna." At numerous points more obvious musical cues replaced the preview version's subtler use of underscoring. The most important change was to have the music of the title song begin playing when Clementine steps off the stagecoach, at a time when neither Earp nor the audience knows her name. In the preview version, the music begins much later in the sequence and is played more delicately.

Zanuck also had the film's ending partly reshot. The preview audience laughed at a bit of business Ford had added, a shot of Earp shaking Clementine's hand rather than giving her the conventional kiss at the fade-out. Though Ford's ending was "completely satisfactory to me," Zanuck told producer Samuel Engel in a September 4 memo, "I do feel that it will be honest, legitimate and reasonable if Henry looks at the girl, smiles, leans over and kisses her on the cheek. It is a goodbye kiss and nothing more. He *does* like her. The audience *knows* he likes her. Now is no time for us to get smart."

The critical reception failed to do the film justice. Most of its admirers were somewhat condescending to the genre and its detractors tended to overlook the qualities that set it apart from more routine Western fare. But *Clementine* performed impressively at the box office, with a worldwide gross of $4.5 million, reestablishing Ford as a reliable commercial director. Over the years *Clementine* has become a much-imitated classic and at times the object of affectionate parody, notably in Ford aficionado Burt Kennedy's slyly witty *Support Your Local Sheriff!* (1969) with James Garner as the marshal and Walter Brennan spoofing his Ford role. Screenwriter Kevin Jarre paid tribute to Ford in his Wyatt Earp movie, *Tombstone* (1993), by including a character named Father Feeney (played by Sandy Gibbons).

Ford always remained embittered over Zanuck's changes, and he may have regretted the film's historical oversimplifications. When asked by French critic Jean Mitry in 1954 whether *My Darling Clementine* was one of his favorite films, Ford replied, "My children liked it a lot. But I—you know."[2]

Noting that "some of the worst films have been done by great directors," Graham Greene, in his 1984 appearance at London's National Film Theatre, attacked "Henry" Ford's "intolerable" film version of *The Power and the Glory,* "where he gives the illegitimate child to the chief of police instead of to the priest, which was the whole subject of the novel." If not the worst film of Ford's career, *The Fugitive* is a leading candidate for that distinction.

Argosy purchased film rights to Greene's novel from Alexander Korda for $50,000 in November 1945. Seeing this as an opportunity to replicate the artistic success of *The Informer,* Ford hired Dudley Nichols to adapt the book. But Ford evidently had some doubts about his old collaborator, for in early 1946 he offered the job to *New York Herald Tribune* film critic Richard Watts Jr., who had offered advice and moral support on the earlier film but felt uncomfortable about becoming a screenwriter. After struggling with the censorship problems involved in depicting the alcoholism and lechery of Greene's "whiskey priest," Nichols suggested to Ford that they turn the story into "an allegory of the Passion Play." Ford worked so closely with Nichols on the final draft that Nichols thought the director deserved to share writing credit. Perhaps Nichols was also trying to share the blame, for it was the last time he received credit on a Ford film.

---

2. This disagreement may explain why Ford did not go ahead with plans to direct the 1947 Fox film *The Ghost and Mrs. Muir.* Philip Dunne's script of the romantic ghost story, based on the novel by R. A. Dick (Josephine A. C. Leslie), was directed by Joseph L. Mankiewicz. Ford enthusiastically agreed to Zanuck's suggestion of casting Katharine Hepburn opposite Rex Harrison, but Gene Tierney played Mrs. Muir for Mankiewicz.

Before starting shooting, Ford admitted to Darryl Zanuck that *The Fugitive* was "really not a sound commercial gamble but my heart and my faith compel me to do it." Ford's misguided piety helps explain why he so distorted the story; Henry Fonda, who played the cowardly priest, thought Ford's Catholicism made him uncomfortable with the theme of Greene's book, which the Vatican's Holy Office later condemned because it was "paradoxical" and "dealt with extraordinary circumstances." Ford utterly failed to grasp that paradox—that God works his will on earth through deeply fallible human beings. Instead, as Greene put it, Ford "gave all the integrity to the priest," which robbed the character of complexity and threw what little dramatic interest the film has to the fanatically antireligious lieutenant (Pedro Armendáriz). In his quest to kill the last remaining priest in his totalitarian country, the secretly superstitious and libidinous lieutenant is puritanically trying to stamp out the stubborn contradictions of his own nature.

Alas, the film is not about the lieutenant but revolves around the grotesquely miscast Fonda, with his hangdog expression, Midwestern whine, and brown shoe-polish makeup. Fonda knew he was all wrong for the part and tried to pass it off to the stage actor and director José Ferrer, a native of Puerto Rico, who was cast as the priest but subsequently proved unavailable.[3] To coax Zanuck into loaning Fonda and allowing him to use the *Fugitive* title, which Fox controlled, Ford decided to overlook their imbroglio over *Clementine* and promise to make another film for the studio, on one condition. Ford would do so only if Zanuck personally produced the picture, a gesture the executive found highly gratifying.

Mexico was Ford's preferred setting for drunken revelry between pictures, so it's ironic that he chose it as the setting for his grand religious statement (a prologue spoken by Bond diplomatically abstracts the locale of this "very old story that was first told in the Bible . . . and is still being played in many parts of the world"). Wine is outlawed in the puritanical, anticlerical country of the film, yet Ford offered Fonda the role of the priest when they were getting drunk on the *Araner* on a prewar cruise to Mazatlán. Even Ford's most hedonistic sprees were restrained by his essentially puritanical nature, as Fonda suggested when describing another trip they took to Mazatlán with Bond and John Wayne a few months after filming *The Fugitive:* "The first four or five days Ford came to

---

3. Ferrer's lack of availability was blamed on his commitment to play Cyrano de Bergerac on the stage. He was later accused of Communist sympathies but cleared himself by appearing as a friendly witness before the House Committee on Un-American Activities in May 1951. When Ferrer was nominated for an Academy Award earlier that year for his film version of *Cyrano,* Ward Bond vainly campaigned against the actor on political grounds, declaring, "This man is not good for the business."

town with us. After that he was too drunk to leave his boat. We'd start at the Hotel Central, and then we'd pick up a three-piece mariachi band and go from bar to bar, saloon to saloon, whorehouse to whorehouse. You went to the whorehouses just to sit and drink and listen to the mariachis play. You didn't fuck. You didn't think you should. Those whoores [*sic*] looked grungy."

The Fugitive was filmed entirely on Mexican locations and at Estudios Churubusco in Mexico City from November 4, 1946, through January 27, 1947. Ford wisely surrounded himself with some of Mexico's finest filmmaking talent, including the country's leading star, Armendáriz, and an actress internationally celebrated for her beauty, Dolores Del Rio. Emilio Fernández, who had directed the pair in their 1944 hit *María Candelaria,* was Ford's associate producer (in Mexico he was regarded as Ford's "codirector"). Known as "El Indio," Fernández had such a notoriously bad temper that he made Ford look like a pussycat. The part-Cuban actor Melchior "Mel" Ferrer, who had directed radio programs as well as a 1945 low-budget film, served as a "directorial assistant." Most importantly, Ford hired Mexico's finest cinematographer, Gabriel Figueroa, a master of chiaroscuro who had studied in Hollywood under Gregg Toland.

Fellow Motion Picture Alliance member Hedda Hopper, far more militant than Ford on the subject of Communism, asked him in February 1948 if it was true that "labor unions had forced him to hire known Communists to work on the film." Ford "snorted at the idea" but told her with careful ambivalence, "All you have to do is to remember the theme of the picture, and you'll know that a Communist wouldn't touch it with a ten-foot pole. We fully expect to be panned by every left-wing reviewer in the country. The picture is anti any political party that forbids the complete freedom of worship. You may hear much about Communists in Mexico, but if they are causing any serious trouble, I never noticed it. Of course, there is plenty of rumor. If a man merely asks for a raise in pay, he's likely to be tagged a Red."

Perhaps concerned that his last observation reflected too closely on the American political scene, Ford turned to Merian Cooper and added, "If there was anything pro-Communist about the picture, you can be sure that Cooper wouldn't have been co-producer. He spent ten months in a Russian jail [after being shot down while serving in the Polish air force after World War I], and completely lost all interest in anything Red."

Ford's motivations for making *The Fugitive* may have had as much to do with his own dimly perceived psychological conflicts as they did with his conscious religious and political allegiances. He told Hopper the film was about "the soul of a man that is being harried and chased," and he confided to Watts that the religious aspects of Greene's novel were not as important to him as the theme of a man searching for his mission in life. Greene's "whiskey priest" resembles Ford in being a bad Catholic, a guilt-ridden alcoholic and philanderer. The sanitized character on-screen is an ineffectual weakling and anxious teetotaler who seems both spiritually and physically impotent, as Ford may have seen himself in the depths of his alcoholic self-pity. But he seems to identify as strongly with the lieutenant, a priest manqué whose aggression is a cover for his spiritual anguish, and with the "good thief" played by Ward Bond. Known as "El Gringo," Bond's character physically resembles Ford, with his slouch hat, dark glasses, and dirty clothing.

Ford's conscious intentions in making *The Fugitive*—his ostentatious desire to bear witness to his faith and start off his new company with an "artistic classic" like *The Informer*—fatally undermined the film. The religious themes are all externalized, expressed through formalistic compositions, virtuosic lighting patterns, and ponderous pacing that turn the film into a lifeless series of holy-card tableaux. Departing from his usual practice of shooting under all weather conditions, Ford would "*wait* for the light" with Figueroa, depriving the film of all spontaneity. While creating an atmosphere of puritanical repression, Ford carried his worst artistic tendencies far beyond the extremes of *The Long Voyage Home,* indulging in an orgy of Irish and Latin religious sentimentalism over the motifs of self-sacrifice, martyrdom, and betrayal and over the iconography of the Virgin Mary and Mary Magdalene; Del Rio's Maria Dolores is an overly literal illustration of Ford's Madonna/whore complex. The final effect of this outward show of conventional piety is a feeling of distance and insincerity. Nichols blamed Ford for seeming "to throw away the script" while shooting the film in Mexico: "I disliked it intensely," he said.

When the film was released in November 1947, some reviewers predictably were snowed by what Bosley Crowther of the *New York Times* called the "monolithic beauty" of this "strange and haunting picture . . . Mr. Ford has accomplished in it a true companion piece to *The Informer.*" But James Agee in the *Nation* described *The Fugitive* as "a bad work of art, tacky, unreal, and pretentious" about "a creeping Jesus. . . . I doubt that Jesus ever crept, and I am sickened when I watch others creep in His name; I dislike allegory and symbolism which are imposed on and denature reality as deeply as I love both when they bloom from and exalt reality." Yet Agee paradoxically listed the film among the year's best offerings, praising Ford for "grandeur and sobriety of ambition . . . however distasteful or misguided."

Although *The Fugitive* has few defenders today, Ford defiantly told Bogdanovich, "It came out the way I wanted it to—that's why it's one of my favorite pictures—to me, it was perfect." Fonda considered that pure Fordian blarney: "[H]e knew, the perverted sonofabitch, he knew that it wasn't good in the end, but he damn well wouldn't admit it."

The Fugitive proved a quixotic, self-defeating gesture for someone trying to launch a new film company. As of 1951, RKO's books showed a modest return of $1,158,870 in worldwide rentals for the film, on a negative cost of $1,124,326. The negative cost did not include the additional expenses of marketing, and the film was carried as a substantial money-loser. All those years, Argosy remained hundreds of thousands of dollars in debt to RKO and the banks that financed the picture. The box-office failure of Argosy's first production caused the cancellation of *The Quiet Man,* which RKO feared would be another runaway art-house project, and obliged Ford to play it safe by concentrating on Westerns for the next few years.

Despite the box-office success of the Argosy Westerns *Fort Apache* and *She Wore a Yellow Ribbon,* the standard Hollywood accounting methods used by RKO ensured that Argosy never saw enough of the profits from those pictures to make much inroad into its accumulated indebtedness for *The Fugitive,* other bank loans and production advances from RKO, overhead, and interest. Donald Dewar, Argosy's vice president from 1947 through 1950, recalled that the company "never recovered" from *The Fugitive.* "They made some wonderful, moneymaking pictures there, but it was all going to cover the obligations. Plus, we began to see a defensive mechanism on the part of the bankers and RKO: 'How do we know that Ford isn't going to do this again?' You know, you could make any kind of picture at all in that period and make money. Except for *The Fugitive.*"

Ford's penchant for religious allegory found a far more congenial vehicle in *3 Godfathers.* This unabashedly sentimental 1948 Technicolor Western is perhaps the most ravishingly beautiful film he ever made, an allegory whose symbolism largely does "bloom from and exalt reality."

Produced by Argosy for MGM between the RKO films *The Fugitive* and *Fort Apache, 3 Godfathers* offered Ford a creative way of expiating his guilt feelings over his treatment of Harry Carey. Carey starred in their 1919 version of the Peter B. Kyne story about three bandits rescuing a baby in the desert, *Marked Men.* About a year before his father died, Dobe Carey asked him why he hadn't worked with Ford in more than a decade. "He won't ask me," the old man replied. "But you will—not till after I croak—but then you will. You can bet on it. His Irish pride kept us from making up, but he's also loyal. That's Irish, too." Sure enough, on the very day of Harry's death, Ford informed Olive Carey that he was planning to remake *Marked Men* with Dobe as the boyish and superstitious outlaw William Kearney, "the Abilene Kid." His fellow outlaws are played by John Wayne, as the tough and irreligious Robert Hightower, and Pedro Armendáriz, as the stalwart Mexican bandit Pedro Roca Fuerte, whose name alludes to Saint Peter, the "rock" upon whom Jesus built his church.

Dobe Carey was "introduced" in *3 Godfathers,* even though he had already appeared in three other films, including Howard Hawks's classic 1948 Western *Red River.* For Ford, the ceremonial gesture was important, marking the beginning of Dobe's long membership in the Ford Stock Company as its perpetually youthful, good-hearted "Kid." Ford's attitude toward his surrogate sons was always ambivalent, however, and he warned Dobe before they started filming *3 Godfathers,* "You're going to hate me when this picture is over, but you're going to give a great performance."

Ford was true to his word. During location filming at Furnace Creek Ranch in Death Valley in May 1948, with the heat reaching 130 degrees, Ford rode Dobe so mercilessly that the young actor thought he might actually die while shooting his death scene. Ford continually needled Dobe by saying, "My God, Audie Murphy begged me for this part!" Realizing that Ford's cruelty stemmed from his mixed-up feelings of obligation and resentment, Dobe would think, "Gee, if you were mad at my dad, don't take it out on me."

In Ford's best work, spiritual qualities are expressed through the physical world, not through abstract symbolism. The slow torture of the desert crossing in *3 Godfathers,* the harsh beauty of the scorched landscapes, the constant threat of death from thirst, and the howling wind (a traditional symbol of the presence of God) keep the film's spiritual undercurrents firmly rooted in the physical. The desert crossing gradually takes on the character of a religious pilgrimage as the three "wise men" encounter their haunting nativity scene. A dying woman (Mildred Natwick) entrusts them with her newborn son, whom she names Robert William Pedro Hightower. Transformed by responsibility, the outlaws reveal their innate nobility by sacrificing their chance of escape to save the child. Ford's religious imagery occasionally lapses into inorganic symbolism, such as when Wayne's character miraculously encounters a donkey that leads him and the baby to the town of New Jerusalem. *Marked Men* ended with Harry Carey dying while fulfilling his mission. But *3 Godfathers* celebrates Bob's redemption in warmly communal final sequences resembling a Sunday afternoon hoedown at the Field Photo Farm: a raucously comic trial followed with the townspeople gathering at the train station to serenade Bob with "Bringing in the Sheaves" and "Shall We Gather at the River" as he heads off for his year in prison.

Ford surprised Dobe at the end of shooting by having his father's horse, Sunny, brought to MGM for the dedication scene. Silhouetted against a sunset on a stylized studio hilltop, to the tune of "Goodbye, Old Paint," Ford's frequent stunt coordinator and second-unit director, Cliff Lyons, poses as Harry Carey, "Bright Star of the early western sky." This tableau, which dissolves directly into the introductory shot of Dobe, is a moving example of the continuity of generational tradition that runs throughout Ford's work. Although *3 Godfathers* has been brushed aside by most critics as minor Ford, and though it must be seen on the big screen to be fully appreciated, the heartfelt emotion Ford brought to the film has helped it become something of a popular classic in recent years, thanks to frequent airings on television.

The simplicity of the film's sentiment is balanced by the sophistication of its visual style. It is no coincidence that Ford's four most beautiful color films— *3 Godfathers, She Wore a Yellow Ribbon, The Quiet Man,* and *The Searchers*—are all the work of a modest, meticulous, largely unsung cinematographer named Winton C. Hoch. Hoch respected Ford's "consummate artistry," but his proud, rather aloof temperament made him averse to the ass-kissing submissiveness that "Pappy" encouraged among his coworkers.

Trained as a research physicist at the California Institute of Technology, Hoch was known as an expert in color cinematography, an area in which Ford felt somewhat ill at ease. Hoch did laboratory work on color processes for the Technicolor Corporation in the 1930s before becoming a cameraman. He came to Ford's attention when shooting Victor Fleming's 1948 *Joan of Arc.* After watching some of Hoch's rushes, Ford demanded bluntly, "Who determines the setup?" Hoch got his job on *3 Godfathers* by answering, "If you want to, *you* do. And if you don't want to, I'll be glad to do it." The first day of shooting in Death Valley, Ford decided to test him under field conditions. The director strode out into the desert and stopped atop a sand dune, musing aloud, "You know, this could make a hell of a shot." Hoch started to suggest a tracking shot instead, prompting a tirade from Ford that ended with, "I tell you where the camera goes." As Carey recalled, Hoch at that point "decided to be one of the team," replying simply, "Sorry, Jack."

Hoch was always a perfectionist, and he admitted that the care he took with setups sometimes clashed with Ford's more casual working methods. Ford would fret while Hoch moved prop cacti and sagebrush around the desert to balance his compositions, creating a harmonious effect that subtly enhances the visual beauty of the films. For his efforts, he was mocked by Ford as "a very, very pedantic cameraman." Ford's gift for composition was more instinctive. His visual directions were usually terse and sketchy, but once he said where to put the camera, he knew from experience how the shot would look.

When Hoch and I watched *The Searchers* together, the cameraman called attention to a group composition of the family moving onto the porch in the opening scene, taking their places with effortlessly fluid and beautiful movement. He exclaimed, "There's Ford's genius—right there."

Ford's two young grandsons, Timothy and Daniel, were among the few people "unafraid" of the Old Man, a journalist wrote in 1953. "His two adult children, Patrick and Barbara, say they have never outgrown their childhood terror of him."

Struggling to establish his own identity in Hollywood, Pat nevertheless "hated being independent," Katherine Cliffton observed. He failed in an MGM tryout arranged by his father through Jim McGuinness and could only find uncredited work rewriting scripts or doing research for Argosy. It was not until 1950 that Pat finally saw his name on the screen, as the cowriter of *Wagon Master* with Frank Nugent.

Barbara served an apprenticeship in her father's cutting room on *They Were Expendable* before being hired as an assistant editor to Jack Murray on *She Wore a Yellow Ribbon* and other Ford films. "Lots of people denigrated her," said Cliffton, "but I didn't hear her cutting denigrated in any way. She was a pretty good cutter, and when she was working she worked very hard." But in her personal life, Barbara was undisciplined, impulsive, and emotionally vulnerable. "Most men were afraid to date Barbara Ford because they were scared shitless of her father," said actor Bruce Cabot.

Ford sometimes made clumsy attempts to find a husband for Barbara. Once when the Ford and Carey families had a reunion, Jack and Harry "got pissy-ass drunk," Olive Carey remembered. "Harry passed out and I got him to bed. . . . I can't get Ford to go to bed. Mary's gone to bed, she's passed out, too. So I go into the kitchen and there's Jack, and he's got a crying jag on, drooling all down his chin, and crying his eyes out about Barbara and Dobe should get married—that's all there is to it, got to carry on the tradition, got to combine the Fords and the Carey family."

Bearing out the truth of Charles Dickens's observation that people coming from unhappy childhoods often escape into disastrous early marriages, Barbara defied her parents to marry the brilliant but self-destructive actor Robert Walker. The twenty-five-year-old Barbara met Walker, twenty-nine, in early June of 1948 at a party in Newport Beach aboard the *Araner*. Still distraught over his divorce from actress Jennifer Jones, who had left him for producer David O. Selznick, Walker had recently carried on a tempestuous affair with Ava Gardner. To his close friend Jim Henaghan, a writer for the *Hollywood Reporter,* Walker confided that he was through with actresses, "And I'll steer clear of beautiful women too. I'd like to meet a girl who's so unglamorous that no man would think of trying to take her away from me." So Henaghan, who knew John Ford, made the mistake of introducing Walker to Ford's daughter.

"I fell in love with him instantly, the very same day Jim introduced us—and I'm probably still in love with him," Barbara said near the end of her life, in an interview for Beverly Linet's 1986 book *Star-Crossed: The Story of Robert Walker and Jennifer Jones.* "The thing that first impressed me was his lack of ego. He wanted to talk about what interested *me*—which was film editing. He was curious about my background, about my growing up in a show-business atmosphere. . . . Bob had fabulous humor, great compassion. He was a gentleman and probably too sensitive for his own good. They tell me I have a good sense of humor too, so that is one of the things that attracted us to each other."

Barbara and Bob spent a good deal of time that month at Catalina on the *Araner*. Ford and his cronies "were all crazy about Bob," Barbara thought. Her unreflective attraction to Walker, a man whose charm could disappear quickly when he turned vicious and violent under the influence of alcohol, may have been a subconscious manifestation of her unhealthy devotion to her similarly troubled father. Toward the end of her life, she made a telling comparison: "Funny, the foolish little things you notice—and become so important in memory. I remember that Bob and Daddy could switch glasses. Both had bad eyes, and occasionally I'd hear Daddy say, 'Hey, Bobby, you've got my glasses on,' which he did. Daddy adored Bob, and vice versa."

When Barbara announced her intention to marry Walker, her parents objected because it was so abrupt and because he was divorced and not a Catholic. Nevertheless the Fords acquiesced and planned a wedding at Odin Street on their own anniversary, July 3. Then Walker decided to be married on the *Araner*. Henaghan, who "knew [Walker] wasn't in love with her," persuaded him to postpone the nuptials. But on July 8, Walker hastily arranged a small civil ceremony for that evening at the Beverly Hills Club. Columnist Louella O. Parsons later reported that Barbara's parents were "upset" by that perfunctory event, to which they were not invited.

Within a week, the marriage was foundering. Walker canceled their plans for a honeymoon in Carmel and told Barbara he wanted her to meet his family in Utah. So far, all his parents had seen of his new bride was the wire-service wedding picture in their local newspaper. His mother told Bob, "Well, she may be a nice girl, but she sure looks like a female Barry Fitzgerald." Barbara commented, "I didn't take that slur seriously, dismissing it as Bob's wicked sense of humor."

Another person upset by the wedding was Jennifer Jones, who made frequent telephone calls to the newlyweds' apartment. Walker seemed agitated by the attention of his highly neurotic ex-wife, but his problems went much deeper than that. "Nothing I did seemed to please him, and I desperately wanted to make him happy," Barbara recalled. "I was insanely in love with him." Walker was rumored to be bisexual, and he showed little sexual interest in Barbara, who later insisted, "I knew there was talk that our marriage had never been consummated. But it *was*."

On August 14, Walker attacked her physically and she phoned her parents for help. Henaghan recalled, "I got a frantic call from John Ford, who said, 'Jim, someone has to save her from Walker. He's been beating the hell out of her.' So I rushed to his apartment, where I found her sobbing on the sofa. Bob was in the bedroom. I confronted him and demanded, 'Have you been beating her?' He replied, 'Yeah, I can't stand her.'"

During Barbara's divorce proceedings in December, Mary Ford testified that when Barbara called her, "I rushed over to my daughter's apartment. Mr. Walker told me, 'Take her, I don't want her. Take her back where she came from.'" Four days after the breakup, Parsons told her readers, "John and Mary Ford have their little girl home with them again—but I know they are just as unhappy about the separation as they were when Barbara and Bob married without inviting them to the wedding."

A divorce on the grounds of "extreme and grievous mental cruelty" was granted on December 16, Barbara's twenty-sixth birthday. Walker's short, unhappy life came to an end in 1951 under circumstances that are still mysterious. Allegedly in a state of drunken despondency, he was injected with a sedative that caused respiratory failure. Barbara Ford's life seemed blighted by her unfortunate early marriage and her increasing emotional dependency on her father. Barbara and her father "looked alike, thought alike, and sometimes drank alike," Mary said.

The central paradox of Ford's existence was now dismayingly clear: This sensitive artist whose work valued the concept of family above all else was an abysmal failure in his own family life.

Who better than an Irishman could understand the Indians, while still being stirred by the tales of the U.S. Cavalry? We were on both sides of the epic." The ambivalence suggested by that remark Ford made late in life helps account for the lack of a critical consensus over his Cavalry Trilogy—*Fort Apache* (1948), *She Wore a Yellow Ribbon* (1949), and *Rio Grande* (1950)—films that to this day remain some of his most powerful and yet most problematical work.

Frank Nugent, the *New York Times* critic who had been lured to Hollywood by Darryl Zanuck in 1940, was still without a screenwriting credit six years later when he spent two weeks watching Ford shoot *The Fugitive* and chatting with him on location in Mexico. Nugent was there to gather material for a *New York Times Magazine* article, "Hollywood Invades Mexico."

After Ford returned to RKO in early 1947, Nugent dropped in to see him.[4] Ford began musing about a subject for another movie:

"The Cavalry. In all Westerns, the Cavalry rides in to the rescue of the beleaguered wagon train or whatever, and then it rides off again. I've been thinking about it—what it was like at a Cavalry post, remote, people with their own personal problems, over everything the threat of Indians, of death. . . ."

---

4. Nugent claimed this meeting occurred after he had finished writing "Hollywood's Favorite Rebel" for the *Saturday Evening Post*. However, that profile of Ford was not published until July 1949 and included anecdotes about his work as a Ford screenwriter.

Nugent agreed that sounded like a fine idea for a movie. Ford stunned him by asking him to write the screenplay, loosely based on "Massacre," James Warner Bellah's 1947 *Saturday Evening Post* story about a Custer-like martinet who needlessly provokes an Indian massacre of his entire command. Providing Nugent with dozens of books on the period, Ford sent him to explore the Indian country of the Southwest. When Nugent returned, Ford told him, "Now just forget everything you've read and we'll start writing a movie."

That remark has been taken as a sign of Ford's indifference to historical truth in the cavalry films. But with *Fort Apache,* he intended to avoid the failings of *My Darling Clementine.* The director's interest in American history had deepened during World War II, and he wanted to offer a rich and accurate depiction of life on a frontier military outpost in the post–Civil War era while using it as a microcosm of national values and conflicts.

"I did a lot of research on military and technical things for *Fort Apache,*" recalled Katherine Cliffton, who is credited as the film's research editor. "It wasn't usual in those days. He wanted to know what was right, even if he chose to overlook it. He was a quick study, and he had a lot of pride. If he opened his mouth to speak Chinese, he would be darn sure he was right. He wouldn't want to have someone say, 'You used a plural instead of a singular.' One of the things he would have his writers do was a biography of every character. Even a lesser character like George O'Brien [as Captain Samuel Collingwood in *Fort Apache*] was provided with a tragic history they could throw back at him [Nugent writes that Collingwood became a heavy drinker after conspicuously failing to lead a charge at the Civil War battle of Spotsylvania in 1864]. With Wayne [as Captain Kirby York], he'd lost his wife. Ford would have a biography so you knew how to include little remarks and little matters of precedence.

"One day Ford said to me, 'Here, do these up as soon as you can.' You hardly ever said to him, 'What?' There was a body of legend about him— you never ask the Old Man questions. So I staggered home under eight or ten books on the Civil War, Stonewall Jackson, and J. E. B. Stuart. In a day or two, I wrote quite exhaustive synopses. He said, 'That's good.' Before I finished I knew about Shiloh and Antietam and the fact that the Civil War began and ended on the same man's property.[5] I think he had me do this for good conversation—he wanted someone to talk to, and we did, at great length."

5. The first major battle of the Civil War, Bull Run, was fought in 1861 on the Manassas Junction, Virginia, farm of Wilmer McLean, at whose home in Appomattox Courthouse, Virginia, General Ulysses S. Grant accepted the surrender of General Robert E. Lee in 1865.

Cliffton and *Fort Apache*'s technical advisors, retired U.S. Army Major Philip Kieffer and Katharine Spaatz (daughter of General Carl Spaatz), thoroughly studied the customs, manners, and physical details of army life on the frontier. They pored over Matthew Brady photographs and such histories as H. H. McConnell's *Five Years a Cavalryman: Or, Sketches of Regular Army Life on the Texas Frontier, 1866–1871* and two memoirs by Elizabeth B. Custer, *Following the Guidon* and *"Boots and Saddles": Or, Life in Dakota with General Custer.* The latter volume provided, among other details, the ambience of a military ball; Ford wanted to use *Boots and Saddles* as the title for the film, which was shot as *War Party,* but RKO studio chief Ned Depinet personally prevailed on him to call it *Fort Apache.* Such period songs as "Garry Owen" (Custer's marching theme, née "The Daughters of Erin"), "The Girl I Left Behind Me," and "She Wore a Yellow Ribbon" were incorporated in the superb score by Richard Hageman.

The unusually thorough research helped Ford and art director James Basevi give a convincing atmosphere to the fort, constructed at the Corrigan Ranch (also known as Corriganville) in Simi Valley, California, and on RKO soundstages. The location work was filmed first in Monument Valley and nearby in Utah at Goosenecks State Park on the San Juan River, rather than in the less picturesque terrain in the eastern central part of Arizona where the actual Fort Apache was located. Determined to produce a moneymaker to turn around Argosy's fortunes, Ford agreed to a plea from Cooper in early August 1947 to trim the budget from $2,520,000 by cutting a few days off the shooting schedule. After reducing the budget to $2,299,914, Ford filmed *Fort Apache* with great efficiency, bringing it in at only $2,156,771.

Originally planned in Technicolor, *Fort Apache* was instead filmed by cinematographer Archie Stout in black and white, which was both more cost-efficient and more appropriate for the story's somber quality. Stout started off on a bad foot with Ford when he tried to change some of the director's camera setups, but he pleased Ford with his innovative use of infrared photography for sculptural lighting of men on horseback and striking cloud and dust effects. Unaccountably disparaging Stout's work, Lindsay Anderson claimed with particular unkindness that Ford only used the cameraman because his son was killed as a member of Field Photo during World War II.

Ford acknowledged that his principal visual influence for *Fort Apache* was Frederic Remington, whom he had first imitated in the 1918 Western *Hell Bent.* Remington's starkly beautiful paintings of cavalrymen, often tragic in tone, provided inspiration for the entire Cavalry Trilogy, along with the more romantic Western paintings of Charles M. Russell. Russell's colorful landscapes and Indian scenes were imitated by Ford in his magnificent imagery of

Indians on the march in *She Wore a Yellow Ribbon*. The Western painter
Charles Schreyvogel, a rival of Remington's, also left his imprint on the director. "My father kept a copy of a collection by Schreyvogel close by his bedside," Pat Ford recalled. "He pored over it to dream up action sequences for his
films." From this rich synthesis of styles and his own painterly eye for composition and movement, Ford developed a Western iconography distinctively his
own, instantly identifiable in distant long shots of lines of riders outlined
against the horizon, swift tracking shots of charging troopers arrayed in depth,
and low-angled vistas of brilliantly costumed Indians parading majestically past
the camera.

Each of the Cavalry Trilogy—which, it should be emphasized, evolved into
a trilogy without being planned that way—is based on one or more of Bellah's
stories from the *Post*. An unreconstructed Southern white supremacist who
claimed descendancy from Confederate heroes, Bellah was described by his
son James Jr. as "a fascist, a racist, and a world-class bigot. I think my father had
great contempt for Ford, not as an artist but from the social standpoint. He referred to Ford as a shanty Irishman and considered him a tyrant." Despite Bellah's ambivalence toward certain aspects of military life (he writes that "the
occupational disease of the Army is insanity"), his stories are rendered virtually unreadable today by their racist invective against Indians, not to mention
their lurid violence and pulpish persiflage. It's hard to believe that as late as
1947 a writer could use the phrase "the white man's burden" without irony,
yet Bellah did so in "Massacre," in which he also writes that "[t]he smell of an
Indian is resinous and salty and rancid" and refers to Indians as having "im-
passive Judaic [*sic*] faces." In his unfilmed story "The Devil at Crazy Man,"
Bellah mischaracterizes the Indian wars as "a race war against the white man"
while giving these words to a cavalry officer: "I hope it is cholera at this concentration of Cheyenne, Arapaho and Pawnee on Crazy Man Creek. God,
how I hope it's cholera! . . . Pray for it."

Ford and Frank Nugent, a political liberal who was half Irish and half Jewish, tossed out Bellah's demented rhetoric and turned the author's view of Indians on its head in *Fort Apache,* the first major Hollywood film of the postwar
era to portray Native Americans as noble, dignified, and unjustly treated. Nugent's novelistic screenplay provides the intricate social texture and varied
gallery of characters so sorely lacking in "Massacre." The screenwriter even
specified some shots that critics might assume are "director's touches," such as
the metaphorical image of the bugler being shot and his riderless horse leading the regiment into battle.

The central character is Lieutenant Colonel Owen Thursday (Henry
Fonda), a fictionalized version of General George Armstrong Custer, whose

reckless expedition into Sioux territory in 1876 led to the massacre of his entire battalion of Seventh Cavalry at the Little Bighorn. Ford, like his brother Francis, had long been fascinated by the figure of Custer. In 1912, Francis directed and starred in the Bison film *Custer's Last Raid*. Jack unsuccessfully tried to find backing for a Custer story called *Glory Hunter* in 1935, and worked in some brief but stirring images of the cavalry in *Stagecoach*. Before Ford managed to make his Custer film, Raoul Walsh offered a bizarrely sympathetic depiction of the general in *They Died with Their Boots On* (1941), starring Errol Flynn. Though a stirring piece of filmmaking, the Walsh film brazenly distorts history by making Custer sympathetic to the Indians who slaughter him: he makes his suicidal last stand to prove a point about political corruption in Washington. *Fort Apache* and Ford's other cavalry films were strongly influenced by Walsh's visual romanticism and composer Max Steiner's rousing use of "Garry Owen" and other music associated with the U.S. Cavalry.

It's ironic that while Ford uses the real names of historical characters in *My Darling Clementine* but falsifies their history, in *Fort Apache* he uses (mostly) fictional names and yet by taking such superficial liberties remains true to the essential facts of history. Ford harbored no illusions about Custer or the mythology surrounding his massacre. When I asked Ford about his cavalry films, he replied, "The cavalry weren't all-American boys, you know. They made a lot of mistakes. You just mentioned Custer, that was a pretty silly goddam expedition."

Despite his absorption in the military ethos, Ford always retained a fairly skeptical attitude toward the military brass. His sense that he never quite belonged on their social level, despite all his flattery and social climbing, caused him both jealousy and resentment. In *Fort Apache* and other films, he turns the phrase "West Point training" into a running joke connoting a narrow, by-the-book approach that fails to understand the complex situations soldiers face on the field of battle.

Ford's sharp critique of flawed military leadership in *Fort Apache* makes the film far more compelling dramatically than either *She Wore a Yellow Ribbon* or *Rio Grande*. They too explore questions of leadership, but with relatively conventional protagonists. A vainglorious martinet who bitterly resents his exile to "this godforsaken outpost," Colonel Thursday intends to use his command to transform himself into a figure of glory, "The Man Who Brought Cochise Back." Thursday's hubristic utterance of that phrase—prompting a shocked look from Captain Collingwood—anticipates Ford's exposure of the falsified image of Western heroism presented by Ransom Stoddard (James Stewart) in *The Man Who Shot Liberty Valance* (1962), whose screenplay was cowritten by Bellah.

Ford's contempt for the kind of officer Thursday represents is humorously conveyed when the new commanding officer lectures his men by saying, "The uniform, gentlemen, is not a subject for individual, whimsical expression." That is exactly how Ford regarded *his* uniform—and other issues of military discipline—while on active duty in World War II. Thursday's rebellious second-in-command, Captain York, represents the Fordian military tradition of intelligence, flexibility, and respect for the enemy; he shows the humanity Captain Ford manifested in his war documentaries.

The climactic confrontation between Thursday and York comes at the Noncommissioned Officers' Dance on the night before the regiment departs on its fatal mission. York has just returned from the Apache camp across the Mexican border, where he has persuaded Cochise (Miguel Inclan) to return with his people to talk peace, accompanied by only a small detail of cavalrymen. But upon receiving this news, Thursday callously informs York that the entire regiment will move out at dawn to face the Apaches. York's outraged protest, which defines Ford's own respectful attitude toward Native Americans in *Fort Apache,* should confound anyone who thinks that John Wayne always played Indian haters:

> York: Colonel Thursday, if you send out the regiment, Cochise'll think I've tricked him.
>
> Thursday: Exactly. We *have* tricked him. Tricked him into returning to American soil. And I intend to see that he stays here.
>
> York: Colonel Thursday, I gave my word to Cochise. No man is gonna make a liar out of me, sir.
>
> Thursday: *Your word* to a breech-clouted savage? An illiterate, uncivilized murderer and treaty-breaker? There's no question of honor, sir, between an American officer and Cochise.
>
> York: There is to me, sir.

Fonda would be absent from the screen for seven years after *Fort Apache,* appearing in the title role of *Mister Roberts,* the Joshua Logan–Thomas Heggen stage play about navy life in World War II. On Fonda's last night in California, Ford phoned him and growled, "I hear you're going back to New York to do some goddamn play." But when Fonda opened at New York's Alvin Theatre on February 18, 1948, Ford sent him a telegram expressing the love and support of his "Pappy" and the Ford Stock Company.

The transition from Fonda to Wayne as the essential Fordian hero already was complete by the time of *Fort Apache,* the first Ford film in which Wayne had top billing. Fonda's brilliant, largely unheralded performance as the tragically isolated Thursday taps into an aspect of the actor's personality not often displayed on-screen but which Ford fully understood after knowing him closely and working with him for several years. As Peter Fonda wrote in his 1998 memoir, *Don't Tell Dad:* "Dad played the part of Colonel Thursday, an unsmiling, bitter, strict hard-ass. When people ask me what it was like growing up as Henry Fonda's son, I ask them if they have seen *Fort Apache.*" Ford's switch in allegiance from Fonda to Wayne has been viewed as a reflection of the director's own change from prewar idealism to a growing postwar disillusionment, but that overly tidy formulation misrepresents the complexity of his work as well as of the characters both Fonda and Wayne played for Ford. It is Wayne who plays the humane, outspoken liberal and would-be peacemaker in *Fort Apache;* Fonda is the arrogant, self-centered bigot and warmonger. And yet York's character is not without troubling ambiguities, as the film's controversial ending sequence demonstrates.

In a 1971 essay on *Fort Apache,* Russell Campbell described the Arizona military outpost as Ford's "devoted attempt to realize an ideal: the organic community. It is an ideal at odds with the main current both of the American dream and of the American experience; its closest approximation in practice was probably in the early religious settlements—and among the Indians." The civilizing influence of women in the West is a major theme in *Fort Apache.* Colonel Thursday is humanized by his solicitude, however mistaken at times, for his teenage daughter, Philadelphia (Shirley Temple). Repeating visual motifs from *Wee Willie Winkie,* Ford again uses Temple's innocent, wide-eyed perspective as a means of acclimating the audience. The older women in the fort, such as Anna Lee's Emily Collingwood and Irene Rich's Mrs. O'Rourke, serve as the higher arbiters of order, overruling some of the more irrational demands of their menfolk, although Ford emphasizes the women's distress at being unable, any more than the men, to prevent the disaster brought on by Colonel Thursday.

The intricate social strands of the community come together in two formal balls, the Washington's Birthday Dance and the Noncommissioned Officers' Dance with its Grand March. Campbell describes these Fordian dance sequences as "occasions for carefree spontaneity and the affectionate celebration of fellowship within strict traditional conventions. Heavy drinking and horseplay co-exist with meticulously formal dress and conspicuous gallantry to the ladies . . . [giving] delightful visual expression to a conception of life infused with communal spirit and molded by inveterate patterns." Both dances are rudely and metaphorically disrupted by Colonel Thursday.

This is a community defined largely by its Irishness, by the traditional rituals and familial relationships of immigrants (including one named O'Feeney) striving to assimilate themselves into the larger American society through devoted military service. Recently arrived Irishmen, along with immigrants from Germany and elsewhere, composed a large segment of the cavalry during the Indian wars. Many of the Irishmen were veterans of the Civil War—on both sides, like Ford's uncle Mike—and still ostracized from mainstream American society. They saw the army, dirty job though it was, as a profession that would keep them out of poverty and demonstrate their allegiance to their new country. But as the gruesome combat with Indians dragged on and controversies raged over the government's Indian policy, the army suffered "a sharp decline in public favor because of the unwanted war in the West," military historian S. L. A. Marshall writes in *Crimsoned Prairie: The Indian Wars.* "The common soldier who had lately saved the nation had that quickly ceased to be a popular hero. In fact, he became nigh an object of scorn."

While reflecting that dissension, particularly in *Fort Apache,* Ford's cavalry films nevertheless find positive value in the army as a democratic institution. As the closing narration of *She Wore a Yellow Ribbon* puts it, "From Fort Reno to Fort Apache, from Sheridan to Starke, they were all the same—men in dirty-shirt blue and only a cold page in the history books to mark their passing. But wherever they rode, and whatever they fought for, that place became the United States."

The Irishness of Ford's cavalry is a sign of the egalitarianism it manages to maintain despite the rigidity of the military caste system, and the traditional Irish reverence for home, family, and clannish village life is replicated in the fort with a cohesiveness often lacking in American cities. Ford cleverly played up this aspect of the script in winning approval from Hollywood's censorship office, the Production Code Administration (PCA), for what he knew was a daringly revisionist treatment of American history. Submitting the script in July 1947 to the head of the PCA, fellow Irish Catholic Joseph I. Breen, Ford included a letter describing *Fort Apache* as a soundly patriotic story that would recognize the contribution of Irishmen to the history of the West.

For Ford and his Irish soldiers, military rank can be comforting and rewarding, but only if it does not interfere with the more basic human values of respect and civility. Thursday's destructive snobbery is exposed in his vain attempt to destroy the budding relationship of his daughter with Lieutenant Michael O'Rourke (John Agar) by reminding the young man's father, Sergeant-Major Michael O'Rourke (Ward Bond), of "the barrier between your class and mine." Destroying a potential family, and particularly one's own lineage, is a violation of all that Ford holds most sacred. Thursday openly displays an anti-Irish bias, remarking scornfully, "Place seems to be full of O'Rourkes," and addressing the lieutenant as "O'Brien" or "Murphy," as if to say, "They all look alike to me." Although Lieutenant O'Rourke is a West Point graduate, his father is a noncom with a strong Irish brogue, and even considering that the senior O'Rourke holds the Medal of Honor, earned through service with the Sixty-ninth Irish Brigade during the Civil War, fails to redeem this Irish-American family in Thursday's eyes.

Ford's view of the cavalry is not ethnocentric, however, but an acknowledgment of American cultural diversity. He pointedly includes members of other ethnic groups in his cavalry films, such as Sergeant Beaufort, the ex-Confederate played by Mexican actor Pedro Armendáriz in *Fort Apache;* German-American troopers Sergeant Hochbauer (Michael Dugan) and Corporal Krumrein (Fred Libby) in *Yellow Ribbon;* Franco-American Captain St. Jacques (Peter Ortiz) in *Rio Grande;* Woody Strode's Top Sergeant Braxton Rutledge and his fellow African-American Buffalo Soldiers of the Tenth Cavalry in *Sergeant Rutledge* (1960); and Polish-American Top Sergeant Stanislas Wichowsky (Mike Mazurki) in *Cheyenne Autumn* (1964). Even Indian scouts are respected members of the cavalry in *Rio Grande,* although many contemporary viewers would regard them as traitors to their own people.

Ford's stress on ethnic diversity within the ranks—further qualified by the segregated status of the Tenth Cavalry—demonstrates the director's conception of the military as a force for assimilation and a means of reconciling former enemies from the Civil War. Nowhere is the point made more movingly than in the death scene of the elderly Trooper Smith (Rudy Bowman) in *Yellow Ribbon.* A former Confederate general in the Civil War, Trooper Smith is given a military burial by Captain Tyree (Ben Johnson) and other Confederate veterans in the cavalry. With the permission of their commanding officer, Captain Nathan Brittles (John Wayne), a makeshift rebel flag is placed over the coffin.

The ethnic humor in Ford's cavalry films serves a function much like that of the "low comedy" supplied by Falstaff and other foils to the heroes in Shakespeare's history plays. Ford uses broad physical and verbal comedy to parody the dramatic plot and puncture the pomposities of the leading characters, giving equal importance to the common man and the king. The Irish sergeants in *Fort Apache,* particularly Victor McLaglen's Falstaffian Sergeant Mulcahy, mock the form of military rituals while giving Ford's military its true core of humanity, expressed with oblique wisdom and heartfelt emotion. As the malapropian Mulcahy puts it, they serve as "the morals of decorum." Low-comic interludes do not bother sophisticated modern audiences watching Shakespeare's history plays, perhaps because the archaic language makes everything in them seem equally stylized. But the same kind of humor is widely dismissed as an artistic flaw in Ford, even in the official biography by his own grandson, whose discomfort with such raucous ethnic humor may reflect the embarrassment of a more assimilated generation distanced from the popular culture of its roots.

Perhaps the deepest underlying cause of some people's distaste for Ford's comedy lies in its subversive nature. To Jean Mitry, who wrote a critical study of his work in 1954, Ford explained that he liked "to discover humor in the midst of tragedy, for tragedy is never wholly tragic. Sometimes tragedy is ridiculous."

The juxtaposition of two "retirement scenes" in *She Wore a Yellow Ribbon* perfectly illustrates this philosophy. The first scene, with Wayne's aging Captain Brittles inspecting his troops for the last time, is unabashedly sentimental, but the second, with McLaglen's Sergeant Quincannon sparking a drunken donnybrook in the Fort Starke saloon, is broad slapstick comedy. The ritualistic award giving and speech making of the first scene are parodied by the ritualistic drinking and brawling of the second. And while Ford introduces a few comic touches into Brittles's farewell, he gives a darker shading to Quincannon's by having Brittles admit setting up the brawl to put Quincannon in the guardhouse and out of harm's way until his time to retire. Looking at retirement as both tragic and ridiculous, Ford engages the subject with his Irish duality of perspective. This way of seeing the world was best summed up by Karl Marx, who wrote in 1852: "Hegel remarks somewhere that all great world-historic facts and personages appear, so to speak, twice. He forgot to add: the first time as tragedy, the second time as farce."

Not only is Ford's fondness for Irish humor often viewed as an artistic weakness, it has drawn some surprisingly harsh reactions from critics who evidently regard the Old West as an exclusive hunting preserve for WASPs. Reviewing *Fort Apache* in the *Nation,* James Agee wrote that "there is enough Irish comedy to make me wish Cromwell had done a more thorough job." Agee's reference is to the English political and military leader Oliver Cromwell, whose army rampaged through Ireland in 1649–50, dispossessing Catholics of their land and slaughtering thousands of men, women, and children. Agee's "joke" about Irish genocide could be understood, if not excused, as a distant relic of a less sensitive time were it not for the fact that it was published three years after the Nazi Holocaust.

What to make, then, of Ford's own attitude toward the subject of genocide? The frontier military community Ford idealizes in *Fort Apache* has its own tragic flaw: it is insular and archaic by definition as well as circumscribed and shadowed by the tragic consequences of war. This community is as artificial as the fort itself, erected in the midst of a desert, in territory still in the process of being taken by force from the Indians. Ford's cavalry films recognize, with varying degrees of explicitness, that the national unification the community represents is achieved only at the tragic cost of Indian genocide. The role of the Indians in his cavalry films is endlessly debated by film scholars, with some considering Ford relatively enlightened by the standards of his time and others accusing him of being severely limited by ethnocentrism and a tendency toward racial stereotyping. There is, in fact, no simple answer to this important question.

While people often tend to see what they want to see in Ford films, some of the confusion stems from the contradictory nature of the films themselves. It's hard to understand, for example, how the same man could make *Fort Apache* and then only two years later direct *Rio Grande,* which caricatures Indians as the worst kind of drunken, lustful, and bloodthirsty savages. And yet Ford insisted in 1968, "My sympathy is all with the Indians," reflecting his point of evolution after making *Cheyenne Autumn,* his ambitious but deeply flawed epic about a displaced Indian tribe trying to return to its ancestral homeland. Ford's conflicted attitudes toward the subject of Native Americans are apparent in his most memorable depiction of an individual Indian, the warmly affectionate yet still somewhat stereotypical portrait of Pony That Walks (Chief John Big Tree) in *Yellow Ribbon.* Though characterized as a wise man who vainly tries to bring peace, the elderly Kiowa chief, who has been shunted aside by younger leaders, has his dignity undercut by being made to shout drunkenly, "I am a Christian! Hallelujah!"

It should come as no surprise to learn that Ford was honored by those on both sides of the epic. The Navajos made him an honorary member of their tribe, and their opponents, the United Veterans of Indian Wars, gave Ford an award in 1950 for his "outstanding contributions toward preserving the true glory of America's colorful frontier history" in his films dealing with Indians. Ford's ability to empathize with both cavalry and Indian points of view accounts for much of the tension and strength of *Fort Apache.*

Nowhere is that more clearly demonstrated than in the film's controversial ending, in which York (now a colonel himself) covers up Thursday's misdeeds to some gullible newspapermen who regard Thursday as a mythic figure, "the hero of every schoolboy in America." Robin Wood claims that York's white-washing of Thursday's image "does violence to the previous development of the Wayne character and to the whole drift of the preceding narrative."

After listening to a reporter (Frank Ferguson) naively describing the glorious imagery of a painting titled *Thursday's Charge,* York responds with a cold stare and measured words: "No man died more gallantly. Nor won more honor for his regiment. . . . They're better men than they used to be. Thursday did that. He made it a command to be proud of." While arguably true on a superficial level, York's words conceal the truth that Thursday's men died for nothing. Campbell describes York as "a fervid opponent of the official line. Yet he does not once disobey a command. . . . York is the obedient rebel. . . . Despite all evidence to the contrary, the captain continues to place his trust in the ultimate virtue of the system to which he belongs. He questions, but he does not defy." Much, indeed, like Ford himself. When Bogdanovich asked if he agreed with York's decision, Ford replied, "Yes—because I think it's good for the country. We've had a lot of people who were supposed to be great heroes, and you know damn well they weren't. But it's good for the country to have heroes to look up to."

Ford's commentary on his own film, offered when the country was bitterly divided over the Vietnam War, was reductive and simplistic, clouded by the heightened conservatism of his later years. This clearly is a case in which we should trust the tale, not the teller. The remarkable achievement of *Fort Apache* is that it enables us to see through the historical lie while understanding and sympathizing with men who are suicidally following the example of a leader, Colonel Thursday, aptly described by Sergeant-Major O'Rourke as "the madman."

When York takes leave of the newspapermen to lead his troops on another campaign, he lifts into his arms the grandson of Colonel Thursday, calling the toddler "the best man in the regiment." Michael Thursday York O'Rourke is a living embodiment of memory, tradition, and the future, like the children named after the title characters of *3 Bad Men* and *3 Godfathers.* York then puts on the same kind of antiquated forage cap that Thursday affected. No longer is York wearing the slouch hat Thursday criticized as "individual, whimsical expression." This gesture implies York's tragic submission to Thursday's vainglory and, through this "obedient rebel," the submission of the cavalry itself. As the troop marches out of the fort, Ford fatalistically repeats the same camera setups he used when Thursday led the men to massacre, while on the sound track he reprises the anthem of doom, "The Girl I Left Behind Me."

Filmmaker Jean-Marie Straub cited York's gesture to illustrate his contention that Ford is "the most Brechtian of all filmmakers, because he shows things that make people think . . . by [making] the audience collaborate on the film." But the meaning of this gesture seems to have escaped Wood and others who have criticized the ending as a betrayal. And as Tag Gallagher notes, "Conservatives, meanwhile, were blind to Ford's ridicule and revisionism, and saw only celebrations of tradition; their interpretations reinforced progressive rejection of Ford. For example, *Fort Apache:* here is a picture glorifying the Indians and debunking myths of the 7th Cavalry; yet it is incessantly cited as a typical example of exactly the opposite and of everything wrong with John Ford."

She Wore a Yellow Ribbon begins with a shot of the flag of the Seventh Cavalry and the words "Custer is dead." This ravishingly beautiful Technicolor film is a lyric poem about mortality, the bittersweet story of an old cavalry officer coming to terms with the necessity of turning over his command to a younger generation. Wayne's extraordinarily moving performance as Captain Brittles reflected the fifty-four-year-old director's sense of his own marginality in a changing Hollywood. Perhaps it also drew from Ford's feelings about the way General Donovan had been put out to pasture by President Truman.

Brittles's very name suggests the fragility of his hold on existence, and he is not above indulging in self-pity, as when he exclaims, "God help this troop when I'm gone!" Turning toward this mythic figure of wisdom and dignity, who is superannuated even within the world of 1876, showed Ford's growing identification with the values of a vanished era in American history. Brittles's closest antecedent in Ford's work is Will Rogers's Judge Priest, another figure from the nineteenth century; these lonely and isolated men share the habit of communing with a dead wife in a graveyard. And like the judge, Brittles intervenes to bring peace to a world starting to spin dangerously out of control. In an emphatic close-up, Brittles nods his agreement with the words of his old friend Pony That Walks, "Old men should stop wars." Brittles even bends army regulations to do so, briefly reassuming command from his young replacement, Lieutenant Flint Cohill (John Agar), to prevent him from ordering a rash charge into an Indian stronghold as Colonel Thursday did in *Fort Apache*.

Written by Nugent and Laurence Stallings from two Bellah stories, "War Party" and "Big Hunt," and a first-draft screenplay by the author, *Yellow Ribbon* spends far too much time on the tiresome romantic triangle involving Cohill, blue-blooded Lieutenant Ross Pennell (Harry Carey Jr.), and saucy tease Olivia Dandridge (Joanne Dru). All three show signs of maturation by the end of the film, but Ford takes the old man's point of view so one-sidedly that he is unable to imagine either Cohill or Pennell ever achieving Brittles's stature. This is the first sign of an intolerance of the young generation that would become increasingly pronounced in Ford's later work. Brittles grudgingly reconciles himself to retirement only after Major Allshard (George O'Brien) convinces him that otherwise he would undermine Cohill's leadership: "Every time he'd give an order, men would turn around and look at you."

Brittles's difficulty in restraining his hotheaded subordinates is shared by

Pony That Walks, who disgustedly admits, "Young men do not listen to me. They listen to 'big medicine.'" The poignant fellowship between these two old-timers of different races is unusual for a Western from that time, but Ford's reliance on such easy sentimental gestures toward Indians even as he portrays them as considerably more savage than in *Fort Apache* shows the effect of his growing conservatism. It's probably no accident that the bellicose new leader of the Kiowas is played by a well-known African-American character actor, Noble Johnson, and is distinctively dressed in a red shirt, suggesting an analogy with cold war politics: the Indians as Communists or racial agitators and Brittles as Truman, the anti-Communist Democrat trying to keep the peace in an uncertain world by ensuring that minor skirmishes don't escalate into all-out war. Nugent later complained that he and Stallings were unhappy when Ford cut what they considered a key expository scene from the script, but the script is second-rate, with a far less compelling story line than *Fort Apache*. Ford concentrates his attention on the elements that genuinely engage him, the development of Brittles's character and romantic visual beauty.

Ford started to give John Wayne more complex roles only after seeing his performance as the aging, tyrannical cattle baron in Howard Hawks's epic Western *Red River*. "I never knew the big son of a bitch could act," Ford said to Hawks of Wayne's Tom Dunson. Most of *Red River* was filmed in 1946, and when Hawks ran into editing problems, Ford helped make some cuts. Ford also advised Hawks to have Walter Brennan narrate the film rather than using a written diary to tie together the episodic narrative. The earlier version, falsely advertised as the "Restored Director's Cut" when it was released on videotape, runs seven and a half minutes longer than the 1948 release version.[6]

Hawks told me that he consciously imitated Ford's visual style for some scenes in *Red River*: "I learned right in the beginning from Jack Ford. . . . I think he's got the greatest vision for a tableau, a long-shot, of any man. . . . Every time I run into a scene that I think Ford does very well, I stop things and think, 'What would he have done there?' And then I go ahead and do it, because he gets more use out of a bad sky—he goes right on shooting whether the weather's bad or good, and he gets fabulous effects." When Hawks was

---

6. Ford gave similar editing assistance to director Budd Boetticher on his 1951 Republic film *The Bullfighter and the Lady*, produced by John Wayne. Boetticher wrote Ford in November 1950 that he would "greatly appreciate" help with the editing. "I am in perfect accord with you in the belief that I have become too close to the picture." Boetticher later complained that Ford had cut much of the friendly relationship between two bullfighters played by Robert Stack and Gilbert Roland because he thought it made them seem like homosexuals. But in a January 1952 letter, Boetticher expressed appreciation to Ford for reducing the film from 124 to 87 minutes. The original cut has been restored by the UCLA Film and Television Archive.

about to shoot the funeral scene in *Red River,* cinematographer Russell Harlan said, "We better hurry, there's a cloud coming across that mountain right behind." Hawks recalled, "I waited until the cloud got near, thought of Ford, and started the scene. Then we started the burial service, and the cloud passed right over the whole scene. I told Jack, I said, 'Hey, I've made one almost as good as you can do—you better go and see it.'"

Ford and Hawks in later years often received praise for each other's films, and Ford was always happy to accept kudos as the director of *Red River.* Its far-reaching influence on Ford is clearly demonstrated by Wayne's brilliant performances in *Yellow Ribbon* and as the vengeful Ethan Edwards in *The Searchers.* Furthermore, Ford did not begin working with Harry Carey Jr. until his talent was demonstrated with his impressive bit part in *Red River,* and Ford cast Joanne Dru in *Yellow Ribbon* and *Wagon Master* after seeing her as the sultry Tess Millay in Hawks's Western; Dru became Barbara Ford's closest friend. On one of her visits to the Fords' home, Dru recalled, Ford was drinking in his bedroom and she and Barbara were outside: "Barbara was showing me a little doll's house she had had as a child, when suddenly we heard this noise. We looked up and Papa was peeing out the window. He said, 'Good afternoon, girls.'"

Winton C. Hoch won an Academy Award for his color cinematography of *Yellow Ribbon.* Hoch said Ford gave him only two specific instructions before shooting started: "I want Remington color" (Ford did not mention Russell to the cameraman) and "I want a red shirt on one of the Indian chiefs." In Bogdanovich's documentary *Directed by John Ford*, Ford claimed Hoch shot the celebrated thunderstorm sequence in *Yellow Ribbon* with "under protest" written on the clapperboard. "He did it under protest and won the Academy Award," Ford sneered.

"In other words, I didn't know what the hell I was doing," Hoch snapped when I reminded him of the story. The way Ford told it, Hoch didn't think there was enough light to shoot the sudden storm that arose on location in Monument Valley; yet the sequence is hair-raisingly effective precisely because of its unstable, naturalistic quality. "The fact is I have *never* shot under protest," Hoch claimed. "Jack Ford, the old buzzard, would never sacrifice a good story for want of a few facts. See, Ford would take turns working over various members of the crew. I've seen him really hang guys from the yardarm. No exceptions—Duke Wayne was *very* respectful to Pappy. But I was never really worked over properly, so I guess he figured it was about time I got my comeuppance."

The cameraman's version of that incident is confirmed by Harry Carey Jr., who wrote in *Company of Heroes* that the brewing storm made the sky devoid of light except for flashes of lightning. Ford called a wrap, then looked around and said to Hoch, "Winnie, what do you think?"

Hoch replied, "It's awfully dark, Jack. But I'll shoot it. I just can't promise anything."

Referring to the lens aperture, Ford told Hoch to "open her up and let's go for it. If it doesn't come out, I'll take the rap."

But even if Hoch did not shoot that scene "under protest," he reportedly did so on other occasions during the filming. Henry Brandon, who acted for Ford in *The Searchers* and *Two Rode Together,* heard about the filming of *Yellow Ribbon* from his brother Hugo, who was an assistant to Hoch on that picture. Henry related, "Ford would say, 'Use such-and-such a filter.' Hoch would say it would be too dark. Ford would say, 'Don't argue with me. Use it.' Hoch would come to Hugo and say, 'Put a notation: "Shot under protest." ' He did that [several] times on *She Wore a Yellow Ribbon* and he won the Academy Award. I told that to a cameraman later, and he said, 'Well, shit, [Ford] knew more than any of us.'"

Send the commie bastard to me, I'll hire him," Ford once declared. That remark has been quoted to demonstrate his bona fides on the question of blacklisting in Hollywood. The anti-Communist witch-hunt damaged the lives of many in the film industry and still has serious repercussions today. But Ford's defiant statement does not tell the whole story of his dealings with the blacklist, which were considerably more ambiguous.

The plain and obvious historical fact is that no director working in Hollywood during the blacklist era—roughly 1947 through 1960—could hire someone who was blacklisted, other than a screenwriter working under an assumed name or through a front. There is no record of Ford working with blacklisted people while the blacklist remained in force. Perhaps if he had made a public issue out of hiring someone on the blacklist, as Kirk Douglas and Otto Preminger did in 1960 on behalf of screenwriter Dalton Trumbo, history might have been different. But anyone who wanted to continue working in Hollywood during the fifties had to accept the blacklist as the status quo. The moral compromises involved, though different for each individual, were unavoidable, unless one was prepared to take the only completely uncompromising positions available, joining the ranks of the blacklisted or otherwise quitting the business.

Nevertheless, Ford was among the relatively few people in Hollywood who from time to time did take some principled stands against the blacklist. His dramatic act of leadership in preventing the Screen Directors Guild from issuing a blacklist of its own members in 1950 was his most celebrated moment as a participant in Hollywood politics. And yet, throughout what Trumbo called "the time of the toad," Ford was also a prominent member of the organization that spearheaded the Hollywood blacklist and zealously provided information to the House Committee on Un-American Activities (HUAC), California's Tenney Committee, and other witch-hunting organizations, the Motion Picture Alliance for the Preservation of American Ideals.

So which was the real John Ford—the one who opposed blacklisting as un-American, a violation of constitutional principles of freedom of speech and association, or the one who collaborated in blacklisting people whose political beliefs made them accused of being un-American? As so often happened in his life, the real John Ford was an uneasy blend of contradictions. During the greatest moral drama in the history of Hollywood, he was "on both sides of the epic."

At first, the rebel in Ford instinctively resisted the forces of reaction. "Ford was a very loyal American," said Katherine Cliffton, "but he also was very much irritated by the blacklist."

Having rejoined the board of the Screen Directors Guild in May 1946, Ford also served on its Veterans Committee, along with Frank Capra and William Wyler. George Stevens, an outspoken liberal, was guild president when HUAC launched its 1947 hearings into alleged Communist influence in Hollywood. Also known as the Thomas Committee, after chairman J. Parnell Thomas (R-N.J.), HUAC included among its members Richard M. Nixon, a Republican freshman from California. On September 18, the committee issued pink subpoenas to forty-three Hollywood people. Among them were so-called friendly witnesses, including Louis B. Mayer, Jack L. Warner, Ronald Reagan, and various members of the Motion Picture Alliance, such as McGuinness, Adolphe Menjou, and Robert Taylor. Nineteen Hollywood liberals and leftists subpoenaed became known as the "Hollywood Nineteen" or the "Unfriendly Nineteen," although not all were called to testify at HUAC's October hearings. The nineteen included five members of the SDG—Herbert Biberman, Edward Dmytryk, Lewis Milestone, Irving Pichel, and Robert Rossen—as well as actor Larry Parks and such prominent radical writers as Dalton Trumbo, John Howard Lawson, Ring Lardner Jr., and Bertolt Brecht.

The SDG fought back. On October 7, it established a Special Committee to Investigate Thomas Committee Subpoenas, also known as the Special Committee to Protect Members Called to Washington. Ford was named chairman. The other members included Stevens, guild vice president William Wyler, board members John Huston and George Sidney, and Ford's partner Merian C. Cooper. That September, Wyler, Huston, and Philip Dunne had formed the Committee for the First Amendment (CFA), a broad coalition of Hollywood liberals and others opposed to the HUAC investigation. Although the FBI regarded the CFA as a "Communist front," the CFA in fact tried to steer an uneasy middle course between defending the civil rights of the Hollywood Nineteen and declaring their own opposition to Communism, a strategy that proved disastrous.[7] By trying to place distance between themselves and the Hollywood Nineteen, they were playing into the hands of those who wanted a Hollywood blacklist. The liberal wing of the SDG made the same error.

Ford's committee was galvanized into action on the first day of the hearings, October 20, by the free-swinging testimony of director Sam Wood, the founding president of the Motion Picture Alliance. Wood described what he said were Communist efforts to infiltrate the SDG: "There is a constant effort to get control of the guild. In fact, there is an effort to get control of all unions and guilds in Hollywood. I think our most serious time was when George Stevens was president [for the first time, in 1941–43]; he went in the service and another gentleman [Mark Sandrich] took his place . . . and it was turned over to John Cromwell [in 1944]. Cromwell, with the assistance of three or four others, tried hard to steer us into the Red River, but we had a little too much weight for that." Asked by the committee's chief investigator, Robert E. Stripling, to name those other SDG members, Wood replied, "Irving Pichel, Edward Dmytryk, Frank Tuttle, and—I am sorry, there is another name there. I forget."

Tuttle testified before HUAC in 1951 that there were seven directors who had been Communist Party members: himself, John Berry, Herbert Biberman, Jules Dassin, Dmytryk, Michael Gordon, and Bernard Vorhaus. But Tuttle added, "The work of the directors in the Screen Directors Guild was very ineffectual as far as any real Communist angle was concerned. About all they were able to do was to propagandize for liberal candidates and the candidature of our own people during guild elections to the board of directors. I think only Mr. Biberman, Mr. Dmytryk, and I were ever elected to the board. As you can see, there were so few directors who were Communists that the Communists were content to have elected as many liberals as possible."

---

7. Ford was not a member of the CFA, whose members included Humphrey Bogart, Henry Fonda, John Garfield, James Gleason, Katharine Hepburn, Myrna Loy, Fredric March, Donna Reed, Edward G. Robinson, Spencer Tracy, Claire Trevor, Walter Wanger, and Charles Winninger (later the star of Ford's *The Sun Shines Bright*). The CFA sent a delegation to Washington that October to support the Nineteen, but their protest dissolved in recriminations within the group over whether they were there "supporting *rights,* not causes," as Dunne put it.

The Motion Picture Alliance, founded in 1944, was "organized in self-defense," Wood told HUAC. "We felt that there was a definite effort by the Communist Party members, or Party travelers, to take over the unions and the guilds of Hollywood, and if they had the unions and guilds controlled, they would have the plum in their lap and they would move on to use it for Communist propaganda." He estimated that in 1947 the MPA had "probably 1,100 members, but then we have the heads of labor and they control a great many votes. We have a lot of people, thousands more of people, who are indirectly interested with us through other associations."

As a result of such efforts, Wood declared, "at the present time Hollywood is pretty well aware" of attempts by Communists to influence the filmmaking process. "It has really caused everyone to be a watchdog. . . . I think it was [because of] inexperience that any material crept through. Now that they are aware of it they kept a pretty good eye on them. It isn't only what they get in the films, it is what they keep out. If a story has a good point, that sells the American way of living, that can be eliminated and you wouldn't miss it. If you picture some official, or the banker, as a dirty 'so and so,' we can see that, and out it goes."

Ford's work entered into the discussion when Stripling asked if Wood was familiar with Hollywood films that "portray what we might call the sordid side of American life." Expressing opposition to motion picture censorship, which he believed would be under the control of Communist "stooges," Wood volunteered a defense of a controversial film directed by his fellow MPA member: "Well, I think there are all sides of life and I think they should be photographed. . . . I think that if a story has a good point to it—I mean, *Grapes of Wrath*—things happen in America and I think we should show it."

Stripling persisted, "I believe Mr. [Eric] Johnston [president of the Motion Picture Association of America], when he appeared before the committee, made some mention of Russia's desire to obtain certain pictures which might portray the worst side of the United States. Do you know of any pictures that they have endeavored to obtain to show in Russia?"

"I don't know as they would be anxious to show that picture," Wood insisted, "because, after all, as poor as they were, they did have a piece of ground, and they did have an automobile, and they are at liberty to get the automobile and travel across the country."

Later in the questioning, Congressman Nixon returned to the subject of films like *The Grapes of Wrath*: "As a matter of fact, isn't it true that there are many pictures which point out the weak features of our own American system which have been made by people whose loyalty, insofar as communism is concerned, is absolutely unquestioned? In other words, people who are anti-

Communist have made, and will continue to make, pictures which point up weaknesses in our American system?"

Wood replied, "Yes, sir; if it is a good subject, they make it."

"You believe it is essential to maintain that privilege?"

"Yes, sir; I do. It is very important. I think we should have freedom to make the things that are important."

But when HUAC chairman Thomas, referring to alleged Hollywood Communists, promised, "We will take care of them when their turn comes," Wood said bluntly:

"I will help you, sir."

In response, Ford's committee sent a telegram later that day to Chairman Thomas and Speaker of the House Joseph W. Martin Jr. (R-Mass.):

EVERY SIGNATORY OF THIS TELEGRAM IS AN AMERICAN CITIZEN, OP-POSED TO COMMUNISM. MAKING MOTION PICTURES IS OUR BUSINESS. OUR HOMES AND OUR FAMILIES ARE IN HOLLYWOOD. WE ARE PROUD TO BELONG TO THIS INDUSTRY. NOW OUR INDUSTRY IS FACED WITH A CONGRESSIONAL INVESTIGATION. WE RECOGNIZE THE RIGHT OF CON-GRESS TO INVESTIGATE, BUT WE FIRMLY BELIEVE THAT AN AMERICAN CITIZEN SHOULD NOT HAVE HIS REPUTATION ATTACKED BY ANYONE WITHOUT THE RIGHTS WHICH WE BELIEVE WERE THE INTENT OF THE CONSTITUTION TO GIVE.

WE DO NOT BELIEVE THE CONSTITUTION INTENDED TO GIVE ANY EXECUTIVE, LEGISLATIVE OR JUDICIAL BODY OF OUR GOVERNMENT THE RIGHT TO SUBJECT THE GOOD NAME OF ANY CITIZEN TO ATTACK WITHOUT PERMITTING HIM FULLY AND FREELY TO DEFEND HIMSELF. WE BELIEVE THESE RIGHTS OF DEFENSE SHOULD INCLUDE THE RIGHT TO MAKE A STATEMENT IN HIS OWN BEHALF, TO BE REPRESENTED BY COUNSEL, AND TO HAVE THE PRIVILEGE OF CROSS-EXAMINATION OF WITNESSES AGAINST HIM. WE PETITION THAT THE PRESENT CONGRES-SIONAL INVESTIGATION OF THE MOTION PICTURE INDUSTRY BE SO CONDUCTED, AND WE MAKE THIS PETITION DIRECTLY TO CONGRESS.

IF THERE ARE TRAITORS IN HOLLYWOOD OR ANYWHERE ELSE, LET THE FEDERAL BUREAU OF INVESTIGATION POINT THEM OUT. LET THE ATTORNEY-GENERAL BRING THEM BEFORE THE COURTS. BUT AS CITI-ZENS, LET THEM HAVE A FAIR TRIAL, PROTECTED BY THE GUARANTEES OF THE CONSTITUTION. SUCH IS THE BILL OF RIGHTS.

Taking this stand involved some courage, but as Huston later acknowl-edged, the telegram was "just a little sheet lightning in the air." The fact that

the signers felt it necessary to declare their own hostility to Communism indicated that they were more concerned about their own careers than about the
fate of the "unfriendly" witnesses, whom they were willing to use as scape-
goats to demonstrate their own probity.

At the SDG board meeting on October 21, both Ford and Wyler expressed
outrage over Wood's allegation about Communist influence in the guild,
scorning it as patently false. Ford sarcastically remarked, "Of all the pictures
made in Hollywood, there is only one I have seen that smacked of Communism and followed the 'party line' from end to end. The little number called
For Whom the Bell Tolls. That followed the Marxist line right on down."

Ford evidently enjoyed the irony that both the director (Wood) and star
(Gary Cooper) of the film version of Hemingway's novel about the Spanish
civil war were leading members of the Motion Picture Alliance (Cooper testified before HUAC as a friendly witness on October 23). But Ford's jab also
implicated the screenwriter of *For Whom the Bell Tolls,* his longtime collaborator Dudley Nichols, an outspoken liberal and opponent of the MPA. Showing how far Ford had come politically from the days when he supported those
who fought for the Spanish Republic, his remark threw a spotlight on his attempts to steer a somewhat contradictory course over the issue of blacklisting.

"I don't know Sam Wood," Ford went on, "but I read these preposterous
statements in the papers. What can we do?"

Veteran B-movie director Edward L. Cahn suggested sending a telegram to
HUAC chairman Thomas expressing the guild's resentment of Wood's
charges.

Ford said, "I would suggest as chairman of the committee that you write
down a simple two-line statement just saying Mr. Wood's statement is untrue
and send a copy to Parnell Thomas and to Millie [Lewis Milestone]."

Lesley Selander, a director of B Westerns, objected.

"I've had doubts in my mind regarding three or four board members in the
past," he said. "They're left-handed in my mind."

"Left-handed," Ford repeated. "You mean Communists?"

"I don't say Communists. They don't just think the way I do, or the way
they really should think regarding our government and our laws."

"But, regarding the guild itself?" asked Ford. ". . . Listen, I'm a Roman
Catholic and a state of Maine Republican. . . . My objection to this whole
thing is that Wood's stand was in bad taste. As a guild member I think like
Willy [Wyler] and resent it very, very much. I object to calling names. Right
and left and center of the road. There is no such thing if we live up to the context of our Constitution. I mean we're all liberals, because it's a liberal Constitution. Thomas Jefferson was probably the greatest of all liberals and he was
considered a leftist at that time."

The SDG board finally authorized another telegram to Thomas and House Speaker Martin, signed by Stevens and the board, but it was much milder in tone than the one previously sent to Congress by the special committee and, as Ford had suggested, limited itself to contradicting Wood's allegations: "THE BOARD OF DIRECTORS OF THE SCREEN DIRECTORS GUILD FEELS CALLED UPON TO DENY THE TESTIMONY OF MR. SAM WOOD RE-GARDING COMMUNISTIC ACTIVITY IN THE SCREEN DIRECTORS GUILD AND IT IS OUR CONSIDERED BELIEF THAT MR. WOOD'S RE-MARKS ARE WITHOUT FOUNDATION."

Milestone, Dmytryk, Pichel, Biberman, and Rossen wired Stevens on October 21, bitterly reporting how HUAC responded to SDG's demand that they be treated fairly:

> TODAY ONE OF OUR ATTORNEYS BELIEVING WITH US AND YOU THAT ANY CITIZEN HAS THE PRIVILEGE OF CROSS-EXAMINATION AT-TEMPTED TO ASK MR. THOMAS FOR THAT RIGHT AND WAS FORCIBLY THROWN OUT OF THE COMMITTEE ROOM. ALL INDICATIONS THUS FAR POINT TO COMPLETE DOMINATION OF THE SCREEN EITHER BY THE THOMAS COMMITTEE IF THEY CAN ACHIEVE IT OR BY THEIR AC-KNOWLEDGED FIFTH COLUMN IN HOLLYWOOD, THE MOTION PICTURE ALLIANCE.

The only action that could stop such a subjugation of the guild and the industry, the five directors told Stevens, was the "IMMEDIATE ARRIVAL HERE OF OFFICIAL DELEGATION FROM SCREEN DIRECTORS GUILD TO DE-MAND OPPORTUNITY TO REFUTE WOOD'S PERJURED TESTIMONY."

Ford and Huston volunteered to go to Washington to offer support to the Hollywood Nineteen on behalf of the guild. Huston flew there with the CFA delegation, but Ford traveled separately and kept a much lower profile. Neither man testified before HUAC. That Ford may have been somewhat conflicted about the issues involved is evident from his meeting in Washington on November 4, five days after the hearings ended, with Senator Ralph Owen Brewster (R–Maine). Brewster claimed a "lifelong friendship with John Ford, whom I consider a very great American." That would have made them strange bedfellows indeed, for when Brewster was governor of Maine from 1925 through 1929, his "xenophobic stand against Catholic and immigrant influ-ences won him the support of the politically powerful Ku Klux Klan in Maine," according to a 1995 history of the state. Ford visited the senator's apartment to vouch for (as Brewster put it) the "character and achievements" of MGM chief Louis B. Mayer, who had come under scrutiny from HUAC for making the pro-Soviet film *Song of Russia* with Robert Taylor in 1943.

Brewster reported to Mayer that the director "worship[s] at your shrine." Ford offered his private testimonial shortly after the MGM chief appeared as a friendly witness before HUAC and gave the names of three screenwriters— Trumbo, Lester Cole, and Donald Ogden Stewart—whom he considered Communists. Perhaps it was no coincidence that the next film Ford directed, *3 Godfathers,* was for MGM.

Ten of the Hollywood Nineteen were cited for contempt of Congress on November 24, 1947, and later that month, the blacklist began officially when three of the Hollywood Ten lost their jobs. Hollywood was faced with a decision about the future of the Hollywood Ten and the principle involved in hiring or firing them. Instead, at a meeting on November 24 and 25 at the Waldorf-Astoria Hotel in New York City, the Association of Motion Picture Producers, the Motion Picture Association of America, and the Society of Independent Motion Picture Producers, reacting to mounting public hysteria in support of HUAC, formulated a policy of blacklisting that included the Hollywood Ten and anyone else accused of being a Communist. Few believed that the blacklist announced in the "Waldorf Statement" would stop with ten people.

"The decisive collapse," wrote Ceplair and Englund, "was the producers' unexpected recourse to the blacklist. . . . [But] evidence exists to indicate that an important minority of powerful studio bosses—Mayer, Goldwyn, [Dore] Schary [then with RKO], [Harry] Cohn [of Columbia]—were looking for a way to arrive at a different conclusion. If strong intra-industry support for the Ten had been forthcoming from some of the highly influential moderate and liberal screen artists who enjoyed social and professional access to high-level studio management, a number of key moguls might have hesitated."

Ford and other representatives of the Hollywood guilds held a critical but unpublicized emergency meeting at MGM from 11:00 A.M. to 4:00 P.M. on November 28, with representatives of the West Coast committee set up by the producers to implement the Waldorf Statement. As chairman of the committee, Mayer hosted the meeting, accompanied by RKO's N. Peter Rathvon, independent producer Walter Wanger, and Edward Cheyfitz, a representative of the Association of Motion Picture Producers and the Motion Picture Association of America. In addition to Ford, attending for the guilds were William Wyler for the SDG; Ronald Reagan, president of the Screen Actors Guild;[8] Sheridan Gibney, president of the Screen Writers Guild, and the SWG's vice president, George Seaton, and treasurer, Harry Tugend.

---

8. Reagan was playing a double game. While defending the civil rights of alleged Communists as a friendly witness before HUAC, he was secretly cooperating with the blacklist by acting as an FBI informer.

The producers sought support from the guilds for blacklisting and at the same time tried to offer reassurance that they were not intending a witch-hunt. That contradictory stand was a measure of the studios' confusion about how to proceed in the face of congressional pressure but without legal precedent for purging employees on political grounds. While expressing anger over the defiant behavior of the Hollywood Ten, Mayer and his fellow producers placed the principal blame on members of the Motion Picture Alliance and other friendly witnesses who had raised exaggerated national alarm about the extent of Communist influence in Hollywood. Fearing legal jeopardy, the producers would not officially acknowledge the existence of a blacklist, but they frankly admitted to the guild representatives that there already was a blacklist and some people had to be sacrificed to appease HUAC. Mayer's group stressed that they needed the help of the three principal talent guilds in formulating a blacklisting procedure that would hurt as few people as possible.

The guild representatives wanted to know why they had not been consulted before the Waldorf Statement was formulated. The producers blamed time pressure and the threat of the RKO board of directors to resign unless the studio announced a policy against employing Communists. Ford forcefully declared that the producers only came to the guilds when they were in a jam and needed help. Pointing out that their bylaws protected members from losing their jobs for such reasons, the guild representatives said that they would have to take up the issue with their boards. Reagan and Gibney also pointed out that blacklisting was prohibited by California state law, the Taft-Hartley Act, and the Wagner Act. Any action on the matter by the three guilds, Reagan urged, should be conducted on a unified basis.

In his report on the meeting to the SDG board on December 1, Wyler said that the producers' primary concern was the possible loss of box-office revenues due to the current political controversy. He reported that he had gone directly from the meeting at MGM to confer with the board of the Writers Guild, who believed the producers were trying to pass the buck to the guilds to work out an acceptable solution. At another meeting between producers and guild representatives on December 3, Mayer said he was most concerned about protests and other actions being taken by the American Legion and other anti-Communist groups.

The courage necessary to stop the blacklist was not forthcoming from either the studios or the guilds. Despite their representatives' venting of anger and distrust, the three guilds capitulated in short order, allowing the few to be sacrificed in a vain attempt to protect the many from the shame that ensued. A member of the Hollywood Ten, screenwriter Albert Maltz, later wrote, "One is destroyed in order that a thousand will be rendered silent and impotent by fear."

Ford was conspicuously absent, for unexplained reasons, from the open SDG membership meeting held to discuss the issue on December 2 and from the following day's meeting with the producers. *Daily Variety* noted that Ford would be leaving town over the weekend (December 5–7) for a cruise to Acapulco aboard the *Araner*. Frank Nugent and Laurence Stallings went with him for story conferences on *The Family.* They completed the script, but the film's mid-January start date in Mexico was postponed. Although he later tried to revive the project, its political overtones may have had something to do with Ford's hesitation in early 1948. Any movie dealing with Russians, even White Russians in this instance, could have become controversial in such a climate.

Ford did take one more public stand against HUAC. As commander of the Motion Picture Chapter of the Military Order of the Purple Heart, he had a statement of protest read to the membership. In a clever attempt by Ford to defuse possible objections, the statement was read by Audie Murphy, the baby-faced actor from Texas who was the most-decorated American soldier in World War II, a recipient of the Medal of Honor and three Purple Hearts, and a member of the Committee for the First Amendment:

> WHEREAS the overwhelming majority of employers and employees of the Motion Picture Industry, the fifth largest industry in the United States, are unquestionably loyal to the ideals and principles established in our Constitution;
> AND WHEREAS hundreds of the aforesaid employers and employees served honorably in the Armed Forces during the recent emergency;
> AND WHEREAS certain members of the United States Congress have, for their personal aggrandizement, engaged in repeated Communist witchhunts which have been defamatory and slanderous to the entire Motion Picture Industry;
> AND WHEREAS these witchhunts have been carried on without regard to facts;
> AND WHEREAS such unethical tactics, for the selfish interests of such members of Congress, have been harmful to an entire industry and have proven to be a waste of the taxpayers' money;
> NOW THEREFORE BE IT RESOLVED that the Motion Picture Chapter of the Military Order of the Purple Heart, composed of those members of the Motion Picture Industry who have won the Purple Heart decoration for wounds received while engaged in action against an enemy of the United States, does hereby condemn the Gestapo methods used by some members of Congress, and does pray that they employ their time and our money to build

much needed homes for the disabled veterans, to augment the hospital facilities available to our permanently wounded, and to educate a larger percentage of our American public to the real American way of life.

Murphy ate those brave words in 1948. Under the auspices of Hedda Hopper, he made a public recantation of his anti-HUAC activities by charging that Communists had attempted to infiltrate veterans' groups.

On February 22, 1948, the Motion Picture Chapter held its annual Purple Heart dinner in honor of the order's founder, whom Captain York calls "General George Washington" at the Washington's Birthday dance in *Fort Apache*. General Douglas MacArthur, then the supreme Allied commander in Tokyo, sent a telegram to Ford's group with the "warm and affectionate greetings of their comrade in arms." To spread the message about Hollywood's patriotism, Ford had a recording made of the dinner program and sent to all Purple Heart chapters in the congressional districts represented by members of HUAC. A condensed version was broadcast coast-to-coast on the ABC radio network on the day of the event.

In his speech, Ford recalled that Washington "placed more value on the durable man—the soldier who could take it day after day in the lines—than on any mere pyrotechnical display of grandstand bravery. . . . [A]nd tonight the people who make pictures are happy that they can be on the air to prove that not all Hollywood battles are cream-puff punches from the Sunset Strip. Most of the thousands who make up the Hollywood scene have thrown real punches on many stricken fields, and taken many a grievous blow."

By any rational standard, Ford's illustrious war record should have put his patriotism beyond question. But his liberal stands during the New Deal era were bound to seem somewhat suspect to hard-line anti-Communists during the postwar Red Scare, which was not only a symptom of the cold war but also a delayed reaction against the New Deal.

In the Orwellian language of the witch-hunt, Ford had been a "premature anti-fascist" in the 1930s, helping found the Motion Picture Artists Committee to Aid Republican Spain and speaking out against Hitler in 1938 as a member of the Hollywood Anti-Nazi League. He had been prominently pro-labor, helping found the SDG and serving on the committee conducting the guild's first contentious negotiations with the studios, as well as joining strikers on what HUAC considered the "Communist-inspired" picket line at the *Hollywood Citizen-News*. Through his work as vice president of the Motion Picture Democratic Committee, Ford supported the social programs and pro-interventionist stand of President Roosevelt. As a filmmaker, he had called attention to flaws in the American political and economic system by making *The Grapes of Wrath*. Ford's wartime work had criticized America's lack of military preparedness, and now, in 1947, he was making a film that examined the mistreatment of Indians and the dangers of fanatical military leadership, *Fort Apache*.

In short, John Ford had used his talent, lent his name, spoken out, and contributed money for causes that many people by 1947 had come to regard as "pinko."

His political activities had not escaped FBI notice over the years. The bureau opened a file on Ford in the late 1930s due to his tendency to support what J. Edgar Hoover's men considered "Communist Party front groups," including the Motion Picture Artists Committee and the John Steinbeck Committee for Agricultural Workers. Ford's role in organizing the SDG was viewed as suspicious by the FBI, which noted, "This effort was made by a small group of motion picture directors who professed the 'progressive' position . . . in reality the term 'progressive' meant sympathy for the Communist cause. This small group included John Ford." Despite charges in Ford's file that he was "long a fellow traveler" or even a Communist Party member, a 1943 FBI report conceded that his political activities "were of a mild nature, and in all probability he is an innocent."

First-generation Americans often feel an anxious need to prove and keep on proving their "Americanism," and Ford was no exception, as seen in his postwar lobbying for medals even beyond his Legion of Merit and Purple Heart. Ford's need to demonstrate his anti-Communist credentials through membership in the Motion Picture Alliance for the Preservation of American Ideals from its inception in 1944 meant that he was increasingly willing to endure the opprobrium of the liberals and leftists he formerly had been allied with in Hollywood. This is not to say that he was not sincere in his growing opposition to Communism as the cold war intensified. Spending four years hobnobbing with military brass and sharing common cause with Wild Bill Donovan and their fellow members of the OSS had caused a sea change in Ford's personal politics.

Ford's growing involvement with the MPA's anti-Communist crusade led him to become a member of its executive committee in 1949, implicating him more deeply in political tactics he would have found repugnant before the war and even as late as 1948. Influenced by the apocalyptic rhetoric of the cold war and the growing apparatus of the national security state instituted by President Truman in 1947, Ford, like many jittery Americans, seemed increasingly willing to compromise basic civil liberties as a way of holding the line against the Soviet Union and protecting the United States from what they saw as the serious threat of internal subversion.

As Garry Wills wrote in *John Wayne's America,* "People ask, 'What happened to Ford?' There is no mystery. He was a typical Democratic cold warrior. . . . [I]t was the Democratic President, Harry Truman, who gave [Wisconsin Republican senator Joseph] McCarthy the tools for his extreme tactics—the Attorney General's List of subversive organizations, the classification of secrets, and government security clearances. As Truman's adviser Clark Clifford admitted, the internal threat of Communism was deliberately exaggerated by Truman in order to win the 1948 election. Ford was an honorary member of the Cold War elite that forged such policies." Seen in that light, Ford's vote for Truman in 1948, although cast in defiance of Wayne and others in the MPA who were Thomas E. Dewey supporters, does not seem a particularly liberal stand.

In his 1947 HUAC testimony, Adolphe Menjou made the somewhat exaggerated boast that the "eternal vigilance" of the Alliance "has prevented an enormous amount of sly, subtle, un–American class-struggle propaganda from going into pictures." Between 1947 and 1951, pressure to expand the blacklist gained momentum in Hollywood, thanks largely to the efforts of the Alliance. Its 1947 recruitment campaign boasted, "FIRST . . . WE ORGANIZED. THEN . . . WE SURVIVED. THEN . . . WE GREW. NOW . . . WE ATTACK." The MPA's central role in the blacklist is made clear by Larry Ceplair and Steven Englund in *The Inquisition in Hollywood:* "During the [HUAC] hearings he held in Los Angeles in May 1947, Parnell Thomas told the press that 'hundreds of very prominent film capital people have been named as Communists to us.' The providers were the Motion Picture Alliance for the Preservation of American Ideals." Among those who testified behind closed doors at those hearings were MPA members Menjou, McGuinness, Robert Taylor, and Leo McCarey. Following HUAC's public sessions that October and the issuance of the Waldorf Statement, the MPA campaigned for the studios to implement their blacklisting policy more systematically. The MPA continued to provide dossiers to HUAC, encouraging the committee to conduct a more thorough round of hearings, as indeed happened in 1951.

"Unfortunately, we have received little support from top executives," the Alliance declared in May 1950. "Some, stupidly, have even opposed us, and a few have tried to destroy us. We know that, within the next year, motion pictures will again come under Congressional fire because of our Communists. . . . We know pretty well ourselves who they are. . . . America is insisting on a complete delousing. Let us, in Hollywood, not be afraid to use the [insecticide] D.D.T. on ourselves. We don't need much of it."

After the outbreak of the Korean War on June 25, 1950, the MPA called on the Los Angeles City Council to adopt "measures compelling Communists in this community to register, so that our enemies may be identified and our citizenry afforded full measure of protection against sabotage and treason." At an MPA meeting in March 1951, Hedda Hopper received a prolonged standing ovation when she declared that "the life of one soldier in Korea is worth all the careers in Hollywood," and another conservative newspaper columnist, Victor Reisel, was cheered when he urged an immediate "preventive war" against the Soviet Union with the dropping of atomic bombs on Soviet and Chinese strongholds.

Screenwriter John Lee Mahin, who worked with Ford on *Mogambo* (1953) and *The Horse Soldiers* (1959), served with him on the MPA's executive committee. "We didn't want the blacklist, but those things happened," Mahin claimed in an interview Todd McCarthy and I conducted with him in 1979. "It's not our fault that they joined the Communist Party, and I didn't give a damn if they worked or not. I could care less. I used to kid Dalton [Trumbo] and Jack [John Howard] Lawson, I'd say, 'You're gonna get in trouble because the American Legion and the Catholic Church are gonna have you black-listed. You're gonna scare these guys to death, and you're gonna get black-listed.' And, by God, they were. *We* didn't blacklist them. Some of them were very good writers." Despite his largely unrepentant attitude toward his own role in blacklisting, Mahin admitted, "There was a lot of damage done by stu-pid people." He conceded in retrospect that, contrary to the claims of the MPA, Hollywood radicals were "no threat to pictures" or to the American way of life: "If they were a threat to the American way of life, the American way of life isn't worth a shit, you know?"

Ford's decision to join the MPA's executive committee when Wayne suc-ceeded Robert Taylor as president in March 1949[9] may have been a form of protective coloration to shield himself from political danger from the right. But it is an inescapable fact that Ford remained prominent in the MPA for much of the blacklist era, lending his considerable prestige to the organization while it was helping to broaden the purge of Hollywood leftists from a rela-tively small number of people into the hundreds. Newspaper reports indicate that Ford continued to serve as a member of the MPA's executive committee through at least 1955, and among Ford's papers are his MPA "associate mem-ber" cards for 1957–58 and 1959–60. His federal tax returns indicate de-ductible contributions to the organization of $400 in 1947, $5 in 1954, and $1 in 1955.

---

9. Other members of the executive committee at the time included Bond, McGuinness, Mahin, Menjou, McCarey, Gary Cooper, Clark Gable, Pat O'Brien, and Cliff Lyons. Republic Pictures president Herbert J. Yates joined the committee by 1950. The right-wing Hollywood labor leader Roy M. Brewer, a leading force in blacklisting, was committee chairman.

Ford did not become an officer until after he saw the momentum begin to turn decisively against the left. Similarly, when Wayne became MPA president, "His role, finally, was to emerge after the battle and shoot the wounded," Wills notes. "[B]y [1949] the Alliance had won, Congress was calling the shots, the studios had capitulated, and actors were making overtures of preemptive co-operation. To step in then was joining a bully, not an underdog."

Philip Dunne was overly generous in his comment that Ford's reputation later suffered from people "finding him guilty by association with his rightist friends, John Wayne and Ward Bond." If Ford had associated with Wayne and Bond (another leading figure in the MPA) only while making movies, that would be a different matter. But though he tried to distance himself in various ways from their crude and fanatical brand of anti-Communism, Ford consciously and publicly participated with Wayne and Bond in the MPA, tarnishing his own reputation by associating himself with their political activities. Wayne told Ford's grandson that he considered the director a moderating influence within the MPA, but *pace* Ford's good friend Barry Goldwater, moderation in the pursuit of injustice is no virtue. Ford was playing a tricky and dangerous game with his divided loyalties during the blacklist era. Perhaps even he did not know in the end where the dividing line of his loyalties was drawn.

The fact that neither Wayne nor Bond fought in World War II may well have prompted them to overreact during the cold war by becoming superpatriots. Wayne increasingly seemed to identify himself with his own screen image, serving as a self-appointed spokesman for and embodiment of American patriotic values. The Duke's naïve and simpleminded views about Communism were in full cry when he played the title role of a HUAC investigator in the 1952 melodrama *Big Jim McLain*. Attacking such prestigious films as *All the King's Men* and *High Noon* as un-American and accusing Hollywood of being a hotbed of Communism hardly made Wayne popular with studio executives. Although he served four terms as president of the MPA, Wayne said in his 1971 *Playboy* interview, "Our organization was just a group of motion-picture people on the right side, not leftist and not Commies. . . . There was no blacklist at that time, as some people said. That was a lot of horseshit. Later on, when Congress passed some laws making it possible to take a stand against these people, we were asked about Communists in the industry. So we gave them the facts as we knew them. That's all. The only thing our side did that was anywhere near blacklisting was just running a lot of people out of the business."

Waving the flag so self-righteously did not harm Wayne's image with his loyal fans, who first made him the number one box-office star in 1950 and still continue to rank him high among their favorite actors. Many of his fellow countrymen came to regard Wayne as what writer-director John Milius dubbed him: "The Last American." But Wayne's conspicuous identification with right-wing causes resulted in greater damage to his reputation among liberals and intellectuals than Ford's reputation has suffered from his more conflicted and less widely publicized political views. Many American tastemakers still find it hard to take Wayne seriously as an actor even in the classic films he made with Ford and Hawks.

Ward Bond's film roles became less frequent as his life became increasingly consumed with Red hunting. Nine of the twenty-eight features he appeared in between 1947 and his death in 1960 were directed by Ford. Bond evidently did not understand the significance of his casting as the leader of a Western lynch mob in Nicholas Ray's *Johnny Guitar* (1954). Ford's liberal screenwriter on *The Grapes of Wrath,* Nunnally Johnson, probably spoke for many in Hollywood when he declared that Bond and his ilk made him "ashamed of the whole industry. . . . Think of John Huston, having to go out and debase himself to an oaf like Ward Bond and promise he'd never be a bad boy again, and Ward Bond would say, 'All right, then, we clear you, but we've got our eye on you.'"

Ford's conflicted attitude toward Bond was expressed in his 1969 comment that Bond was "a great, big, ugly, wonderful guy. But he was a terrific snob. This was the greatest snob I have ever known. Now, I don't understand snobbery. Ward's father was a coalminer—which is a very honorable profession. *My* father was a saloonkeeper—which is even more honorable. But Ward was striving for better things." Dobe Carey reported, "Ford said Ward would do anything that made him feel important, even at the expense of stomping on people, 'cause he was just too thickheaded to really analyze it and see what a phony thing it was."

When Bond invited Ford to a party honoring Joseph McCarthy, Ford reacted with unequivocal disgust: "You can take your party and shove it. I wouldn't meet that guy in a whorehouse. He's a disgrace and a danger to our country." Nevertheless, Ford gave Bond increasingly important film roles during the blacklist era. With characteristically perverse humor, Ford often cast the profligate Red-baiter as a militant man of God—the Bible-reading sergeant major in *Fort Apache,* the hymn-singing sheriff in *3 Godfathers,* the Irish priest who runs an IRA cell in *The Quiet Man,* and Captain Reverend Sam Clayton, the minister who commands a squad of Texas Rangers in *The Searchers,* barking the word "Bible!" as if calling for a gun. (These characters probably owed something to Ford's wartime colleague Father James Stuart, who epitomized the Catholic idea of the "Church militant." When welcomed by Ford to Los Angeles in 1947 on his first visit to the United States, Father

Stuart was described by the *Los Angeles Times* as "one of the fightingest Irish priests of them all . . . who had the Japs in Burma buffaloed.")

In his roles as a fighting clergyman, and even more so as the benevolent Mormon elder in Ford's 1950 Western *Wagon Master,* Bond often seems to represent the director's own moral authority and sense of tolerance. In *The Wings of Eagles,* Bond plays a thinly disguised caricature of Ford himself, the hard-boiled but sentimental director "John Dodge." But as long as they worked together, Ford behaved with sadistic cruelty toward Bond, making sarcastic remarks and playing elaborate practical jokes that invariably bounced off his rhinoceros-thick hide. "Duke and I were always spending most of our time thinking up tricks to play on Ward," Ford recalled. "If we spent half the time, just one quarter of the time, reading the script or trying to help the story, we'd have made better pictures."

Ford's bad-mouthing of Bond to other people became increasingly pointed over the years. "He and Ward had a strange friendship—it was on and off all the time," said Anna Lee. "Pappy was very fond of Ward in a lot of ways, and then Ward would do something that would be entirely against what he felt was right. I've got a picture of Pappy and John Wayne with three horses standing with their rears into the camera, and Ford's signature underneath saying, 'Guess who?' [Making fun of Bond's prominent posterior was a running joke with Ford.] I think he thought Ward was a little stupid. He didn't have much respect for him, though he was fond of him."

When Ford called himself "a state of Maine Republican" at the SDG board meeting on October 21, 1947—the second day of the HUAC hearings—it was the first recorded instance of Ford referring to himself as a Republican.

He repeated the phrase to the general guild membership when blacklisting was under debate in 1950 (both times Ford spoke behind closed doors, and his self-description was not reported in the press). Maine Republicans are traditionally more independent, if not more liberal, than many of their GOP colleagues. But for a man who had described himself during the New Deal era as "a definite socialistic democrat—*always* left" and whose immigrant father had been a Democratic Party ward boss, announcing a conversion to Republicanism was a stunning development. Even if Ford's change of party affiliation initially was partly for show—it did not affect his vote for President Truman in the 1948 presidential election—he supported the conservative Ohio senator Robert A. Taft for the Republican presidential nomination in 1952 as a member of the Citizens for Taft Committee headed by General Albert C. Wedemeyer. After Ford backed the moderate Republican Dwight D. Eisenhower over liberal Democrat Adlai Stevenson in the general election, Vice President

Richard Nixon wrote Ford in March 1953 to express his "personal appreciation for all that you did to make possible our overwhelming victory."

Ford's strategic retreat into the safer haven of conservative politics during
this period found echo in the increasingly nostalgic and pessimistic worldview
of his films. He never surrendered his stubborn sense of independence or his
highly idiosyncratic approach to the telling of American history, but after
1947 he increasingly identified himself with traditional values he saw as being
threatened by irrational, virtually uncontrollable world events.

By 1950, Ford's public comments on the issue of communism no longer
made reference to protecting civil liberties but were simply boilerplate cold
war rhetoric, devoid of subtlety or nuance. Speaking at an American Cancer
Society event that April when Wild Bill Donovan became the group's national
chairman, Ford said Donovan had been enlisted to do battle with both the
physical disease of cancer and the spiritual disease of Communism. Communism, Ford warned, was threatening to metastasize from behind the Iron Curtain throughout the United States, and it had to be attacked severely.

The question remains: What *did* happen to Ford? What changed him from
a liberal defender of civil liberties to a reactionary crusader against the Red
Menace? As was so often the case when people succumbed to that atmosphere
of fear, it appears that philosophical issues may have been less critical than the
personal experience of being under the accusation of disloyalty.

In the summer of 1950, around the time the Korean War started, Ford was
shocked to learn that his loyalty to the United States was being questioned.
The incident involved a former naval officer who had served during World
War II in an important position with Field Photo. After the war, the officer
had gone on to become an executive with a Hollywood independent film
company. In 1948, he contacted the U.S. Army Signal Corps about the possibility of making films for the government. That October, he was told that he
was considered a bad security risk. He dropped the matter until 1950, when
he made further inquiries and learned that his case was in the hands of the secretary of defense. The Field Photo veteran was told that both he and his former commanding officer, John Ford, were considered security risks by the
Signal Corps, and that Ford no longer had clearance to view Signal Corps
films.

As can readily be imagined, Ford went ballistic when he received this piece
of intelligence. Friends in both Hollywood and the navy were eager to intervene in his behalf. But Ford wanted to keep the matter from going public. He
delegated his brother-in-law and assistant director, Wingate Smith, to make a
quiet inquiry into the matter. Smith had served in the army in both world wars
and in 1950 held the rank of lieutenant colonel. On August 2, 1950, he made

a written request for information on Ford's status to Major General Kirke B. Lawton, the deputy chief signal officer, who had been head of the Army Pictorial Service during part of World War II. Smith disavowed any concern for the security problems of Ford's former subordinate and conceded that it was possible someone might have cause for complaint against him. The message was clear: Ford was not willing to go to bat for his ex-colleague and was only concerned about himself.

Lawton responded that the case was currently under investigation with the provost marshal of the army. "I have no information against Ford except that [the subject of the investigation] is in his employ," Lawton wrote Smith. (Either Lawton was mistaken on that point or was referring to the fact that in 1950 the man was associated with the Field Photo Farm.) "I will appreciate it if you will give me further information to run down the statement that the Signal Corps will not let Jack Ford view their films."

In his letter to Lawton, Smith declared that he and other (unnamed) veterans of World War II were eager to take part in filming the hostilities in Korea. Ford had already described himself to the Bureau of Naval Personnel in July 1949 as "more than anxious to return to active duty in case of an emergency. I am sure I would be of value to the effort with my knowledge of motion pictures." Ford wrote that he was qualified for combat photography as well as "preparation of pictures for propoganda [sic] or military effort." *Daily Variety* reported in August 1950 that a loyalty oath would be required from anyone involved in making government films on the "current global crisis," and that all prospective government filmmakers would be investigated by the FBI and the army's Counterintelligence Corps. Similar screening procedures had been followed in the last war, but the paper noted that "more caution is being exercised as regards total loyalty to this country than was evident during World War II."

The matter of Ford's loyalty apparently was soon resolved in his favor. By October, the navy was making arrangements for him to travel to Korea to make a combat documentary, filmed in early 1951 and released by Republic Pictures that August as *This Is Korea!* Ford's eagerness to volunteer his services during the unpopular "police action," as well as the sharp rightward turn of his Hollywood feature films and personal politics in 1949–50, may have been partly a reflection of his need to demonstrate his patriotism anew.

Ford was a central figure in one of the great symbolic events in Hollywood political history, the 1950 battle within the Screen Directors Guild over its imposition of a loyalty oath and blacklisting for its own membership.

As part of a drive by the Motion Picture Alliance to require a non-

Communist oath from everyone in the film industry, a group of right-wing directors headed by Cecil B. DeMille proposed such an oath for the SDG membership in the summer of 1950. In addition to his work with the MPA, DeMille helped run the Motion Picture Industry Council, set up in 1949 to attack alleged Communists and serve as a clearance board for people willing to profess repentance. DeMille even had his own intelligence service, the De-Mille Foundation for Americanism, which compiled dossiers on the "leftist" affiliations of his fellow directors and supplied them to HUAC and the Ten-ney Committee.

A non-Communist affidavit was already required of guild officers. The Taft-Hartley law required that if a labor organization wanted to be protected by the National Labor Relations Board, each of its officers had to sign such an affidavit. Ford's affidavit as an SDG board member was received by the guild on June 6, 1950, and he signed another the following year. But because SDG president Joseph L. Mankiewicz was not in favor of extending the oath to the full membership, DeMille took advantage of Mankiewicz's absence on a Eu-ropean vacation to push a resolution supporting the oath through the SDG board at an emergency meeting on August 18, 1950. Numbered ballots con-tributed to an atmosphere of fear in which only fourteen directors dared to check the "no" box under the text of the proposed oath. There were 547 "yes" votes and 57 ballots were not returned; no record exists today of how individual members voted, since the ballots were destroyed at the general membership meeting in October.

The loyalty oath bylaw and a provision requiring the guild to send produc-ers a list of directors who refused to sign the oath were approved at the SDG board meeting of October 9. But the blacklist provision caused a strenuous debate, sparked by Mankiewicz's opposition and his warning that any wide-spread revolt against the oath could lead to civil war within the guild. When he used the word "blacklist," Mankiewicz recalled, "I looked right at Jack Ford when I said it, and Ford jumped a foot. He didn't want any part of a blacklist, which I'd hoped would be the case."

According to Mankiewicz, Ford responded: "My closest friend is Merian Cooper and he happens to be a brigadier general in the United States Army, and last night, as we were having dinner, Coop said he wouldn't sign any god-dam loyalty oath and he said what we were making was a blacklist, and if a brigadier general in the Army tells me it's a blacklist, then it's a goddam black-list!" Ford said that not only Mankiewicz would be among those blacklisted by the guild for not signing the oath, but Cooper as well. Cooper told Ford that even if DeMille put a pistol to his head, he would not sign a loyalty oath that was not required by the government.

After winning Ford's moral support, Mankiewicz told the board he would not sign the member's oath, even though he had signed one as a guild officer. But the oath for members, including the blacklist provision, passed with only four dissenting votes, from Ford, Frank Capra, Mark Robson, and Clarence Brown (as guild president, Mankiewicz did not have a vote on the board). Unwilling to let the matter rest, Mankiewicz pressed for a general membership meeting to make clear to directors that they were in danger of being blacklisted if they refused to sign the oath. Ford expressed strong opposition to calling such a meeting because he feared it would set the membership against the board. Mankiewicz backed off the next day in a telephone conversation with Ford.

But after *Daily Variety* on October 11 made public the bitter divisions within the guild over the oath, the DeMille faction formed a committee to recall Mankiewicz from his presidency. Ford and Cooper were among eight board members who did not join the fifteen-member committee, which Capra had joined, fearful of questions about his own loyalty as a naturalized American citizen. Recall ballots, which did not contain a space for a no vote, were sent only to members not thought to be Mankiewicz supporters. Meanwhile, a group of Mankiewicz allies headed by John Huston succeeded in filing a petition for a membership meeting. The recall balloting and plans for a general membership meeting on October 22 went ahead even after Mankiewicz tried to defuse the recall movement by voluntarily signing the members' loyalty oath.

Edward L. Bernds, a B-movie director opposed to the loyalty oath, recalled the climate of fear surrounding the issue: "I consulted with my wife about it: Was I going to be a chicken and sign, or should I take the high moral ground and not sign? If you wouldn't sign, you were through. Until that time [when the SDG's general membership meeting took place], there was a very definite threat that we would lose our jobs if we wouldn't sign. The studios were just as scared as we were."

The tumultuous meeting in the Crystal Room of the Beverly Hills Hotel was attended by 298 people, most of them members of the SDG. Mankewicz denounced the actions of DeMille and the recall committee as "so foreign to everything I have ever known or learned or thought as an American." DeMille countered by reading a list of alleged Communist front groups with which he said some Mankiewicz supporters had been affiliated. "To accentuate the fact that we weren't born in this country," as Fred Zinnemann put it, DeMille mocked the accents of Billy Wilder, William Wyler, and Zinnemann when he read their names, referring to them as "Vilder," "Vyler," and "Tzinnemann." The audience "booed him until he sat down," Mankiewicz remembered. "When DeMille heard those boos, he knew the meeting had turned against him. He was beat."

Several directors, including Wyler, Stevens, and Rouben Mamoulian, gave impassioned speeches against DeMille. The Russian-born Mamoulian, recalling that he and other founders of the guild had been accused of being "red, left, revolutionaries" in the 1930s, expressed anguish over DeMille's nativism. "It was the first time anybody had ever mentioned my accent," Mamoulian told me in 1985. "That man sat there with his red face—it was a terrible moment, and it has haunted me all this time. DeMille said we should be governed by real Americans, that there were too many accents, and I said I was a better American than he was, because he was just born here and I *chose* the place. We saved the guild. They were going to start wearing marching shoes."

Throughout the meeting, Mankiewicz "was wondering, and I knew quite a few others were wondering, what John Ford thought. He was kind of the Grand Old Man of the Guild and people could be influenced by him. But he just sat there on the aisle wearing his baseball cap and sneakers, didn't say a word. Then after DeMille had made *his* big speech, there was silence for a moment and Ford raised his hand."

Edward Bernds remembered that when Ford joined the fray, it had the effect of "a battleship just blowing the canoes and rowboats away. He was the biggest director in the business. He stood up—dramatic pause—'My name is John Ford'—as if they didn't know. 'I am a director of Westerns'—as if they didn't know. It was the theatrical way he did it—this was not accidental."

After drawing laughter by identifying himself as "a director of Westerns," Ford said, "I am one of the founders of this guild. I must rise to protect the board of directors in some of the accusations made here tonight. Before I continue, I would like to state that I have been on Mr. Mankiewicz's side of the fight all through it. I have not read one item of print in the newspaper or trade papers. I have not read one telegram or one ballot or one recall notification. I have been sick and tired and ashamed of the whole goddamned thing. I don't care which side it is. If they intend to break up the guild, goddammit, they have pretty well done it tonight. . . .

"We organized this guild to protect ourselves against producers. By producers I don't mean men of the caliber of Zanuck or the late Irving Thalberg or some of the nine men we have as executive producers. I mean the little man that creeps in and says that Russians stink. We organized this guild to protect ourselves against those people."

But, said Ford, "Now somebody wants to throw ourselves into a news service and an intelligence service and give out to producers what looks to me like a blacklist. I don't think we should . . . put ourselves in a position of putting out derogatory information about a director, whether he is a Communist, beats his mother-in-law, or beats dogs. . . .

"I repeat again that I did not meet in Mr. DeMille's office, as a matter of fact, and I must admit I would be proud to meet there. I think he is a great guy. . . . I don't agree with C. B. DeMille. I admire him. I don't *like* him, but I admire him. Everything he said tonight he had a right to say . . . you know, when you get the two blackest Republicans I know, Joseph Mankiewicz and C. B. DeMille, and they start a fight over Communism, it is getting laughable to me. I know Joe is an ardent Republican. I happen to be a state of Maine Republican.

"I think Joe has been vilified, and I think he needs an apology. . . . I admire C. B.'s guts and courage even if I don't agree with him."

Ford warned that if Mankiewicz "is recalled, your guild is busted up." He added, "Everybody has apologized. Everybody has said their say, and Joe has been vindicated. What we need is a motion to adjourn." But Mankiewicz insisted on discussing the conduct of the recall committee. Ford, to a huge round of applause, picked up on a suggestion made earlier by others, saying, "I believe there is only one alternative, and that is for the board of directors to resign and elect a new board of directors. They are under enough fire tonight. It appears they haven't got the support of the men that elected them."

Ford's motion was carried. The twenty-five signers of the petition supporting Mankiewicz—the men who had been vilified by DeMille—were given a vote of confidence.

"A great night," Bernds recalled. "I was so euphoric that I bounced all the way home, because I was so upset about the rightwingers getting away with this loyalty oath. Ford unleashed the broadsides against DeMille. To see that man just shrivel and shrink as Ford spoke, it was a great triumph for moderation."

But Ford immediately began backtracking from his brave public stand, sending a letter to DeMille the following day commending him for displaying gentlemanly behavior at the event. DeMille responded with a warm letter of appreciation for this apologetic overture. Notes taken by a member of DeMille's staff indicate that on October 24, Ford amplified his views in a conversation with DeMille: "That meeting Sunday night was a disgusting thing to see—not a wolf pack, but [a] mice pack attacking you. That was your greatest performance. I just wish you could have seen yourself—a magnificent figure so far above that goddam pack of rats. I have recommended men for courage in battle, but I have never seen courage such as you displayed Sunday night. God bless you, you're a great man. I have talked to many men in Hollywood in the last two days, including Joseph Mankiewicz, and all agree you will emerge from this greater than ever."

Following the board's resignation, five remaining members of the guild's junior board elected new officers on October 25. Mankiewicz remained president and Ford was named vice president. But on the following day, in an act of capitulation that he never adequately explained, Mankiewicz wrote the guild membership asking them to sign the loyalty oath "as a voluntary act." Mankiewicz's contradictory actions left the final impression that he felt the real issue was not the oath but the undemocratic way the guild had enacted it. The oath was ratified by the SDG membership on May 27, 1951; the only other Hollywood guild to take such action was the Screen Producers Guild. At the end of his term that month, Mankiewicz left office voluntarily and moved to New York, with George Sidney replacing him as president. The loyalty oath remained part of the guild bylaws until 1966, when the U.S. Supreme Court upheld a lower court's ruling that the guild could not deny membership to directors who refused to sign it.

Ford's longtime friend and colleague Frank Capra, who had flipflopped in 1950 on the issue of the SDG's loyalty oath and blacklisting, faced questions about his own loyalty to his adopted country. Despite his lifelong Republicanism and his record as a maker of patriotic films both in Hollywood and for the army, Capra came under suspicion during the Red Scare for his associations with left-wing screenwriters and his occasional flirtations with liberal causes. Capra tried to demonstrate his patriotic bona fides by serving as an FBI informer and participating in the political clearing of screenwriters for State Department projects. But in December 1951, the Defense Department denied him a security clearance for work on Project VISTA, a think tank studying war plans at the California Institute of Technology.

Among the charges made against Capra by the Army–Navy–Air Force Personnel Security Board was that he had "for a number of years closely associated with motion picture writers and other individuals reported to be or to have been members of the Communist Party." Capra also was "reported to have been active in attempts to halt Congressional investigation of Communist influence in the motion picture industry." Another charge was that he was "a member of a Communist inspired picket line" in the 1938 strike at the *Hollywood Citizen-News.*[10]

On December 19, Capra wrote Ford asking for help. Capra's professional colleague of the longest duration, Ford was one of the few friends he had left in Hollywood whom he could trust on such a delicate matter. Ford's record of patriotism and military service made him a valuable character reference, and he was a man unafraid to speak his mind even in those perilous times.

10. Capra's political problems are discussed more fully in my 1992 biography *Frank Capra: The Catastrophe of Success,* and the revised 2000 paperback edition in which some of the material in this chapter also appears.

"AM SHOCKED AT LETTER," Ford replied in a telegram to Capra. "WHAT WERE WE FIGHTING FOR?" Writing the security board on December 24, Ford expressed a similar dismay about the government investigating the loyalty of his friend, whom he called a "truly great American."

Capra had sent Ford a copy of the letter from the security board containing the charges against him and outlined the responses he intended to make. In regard to the charge about the strike at the *Hollywood Citizen-News*, Capra claimed he merely had been observing the picketing, not participating in it. He insisted that photographs arranged deceitfully by director Herbert Biberman had made it appear otherwise for purposes of Communist propaganda. Capra did not have to mention to Ford that a photo published in the *Hollywood Citizen-News Striker* had shown both of them with Biberman supporting the strike on behalf of their guild, nor that Biberman had gone to jail in 1950 as one of the Hollywood Ten. But Capra claimed to have been unaware in 1938, like other guild members, that Biberman and another director, Frank Tuttle, were Communists.

Ford attempted to explain his and Capra's involvement in the strike to the security board by echoing Capra's story that they were only casual observers and not picketers. Ford even implied that they had happened upon the picket line by accident. He insisted that Capra would never join a picket line except to protest something "drastically opposed" to his "beloved" country. "Oh, what a lot of shit," screenwriter Philip Dunne commented in 1985 when I told him of Ford's explanation. Clearly recalling how Capra, Ford, Biberman, and Screen Actors Guild president Robert Montgomery walked the picket line along with him as representatives of their respective guilds, Dunne said, "Capra was there formally as president of the [directors'] guild. Ford has this completely wrong. Jack was not a rational man, he was an emotional man, and he liked to heighten the dramatic interest. This is an emotional letter. This is a silly letter, a crazy letter. Ford had very decent instincts, but he was being pushed around by Ward Bond and John Wayne. He could have been drunk when he wrote it."

Although Ford had been among the founders of the SDG in 1935 and Capra did not join until 1937, Ford told the security board with exaggeration that he and Capra had begun working together in the guild about sixteen years earlier when it was infiltrated by the " 'Commies,' 'Fellow Travelers,' 'Bleeding Hearts' or whatever you want to call them." Ford claimed that all but a tiny fraction of the guild had joined him and Capra in successfully fighting to keep the leftists out of the organization.

The security board's charge that Capra tried to "halt Congressional investigation of Communist influence in the motion picture industry" stemmed in part from his initial ambivalence toward HUAC, which had been noted in the files of the FBI and Army Intelligence. An FBI informant stated that Capra had been among "certain prominent persons in the motion picture industry in Hollywood [who] had been interested in plotting a line of attack" on HUAC in October 1947; Capra and the others "had considered going to Washington and appear[ing] as friendly innocent witnesses," but the plan "had been vetoed by [deleted]." Capra's vote against the SDG loyalty oath bylaw was noted in his HUAC file after being reported in October 1950 by the Communist Party newspaper the *Daily Worker* (which mentioned Ford's and Capra's opposition to the blacklist provision of the bylaws). Capra's changed attitude toward HUAC's investigation of Hollywood was reported in 1951 by a film producer serving as a confidential State Department informant. According to an FBI report on Capra, the informant said that when Capra was solicited for funds on behalf of the Hollywood Ten, who went to prison in 1950 after being convicted of contempt of Congress, he replied, "Let the bastards rot in jail."

Ford told the security board that he had never heard Capra speak out against the HUAC investigation. Calling it a "publicity stunt," Ford declared that he had opposed the investigation "loudly and vociferously." Ford's spirited defense helped Capra receive a conditional security clearance for Project VISTA in January 1952, for which Capra sent Ford an emotional letter of gratitude. But Ford's service to Capra came partly at the expense of one of Capra's screenwriters.

Capra conceded in his initial letter to Ford that there was some substance to the charge that he had associated with writers who were Communists, but he tried to minimize it by singling out Sidney Buchman as his only close writer associate whom he had had inklings was a Communist. Buchman testified before HUAC in September 1951 that he had been a member of the Communist Party at the time he wrote Capra's 1939 classic *Mr. Smith Goes to Washington*. In a lengthy document sent to the security board in his own defense on December 29, Capra named the names of several colleagues as Communists or suspected Communist sympathizers, including Buchman and Herbert Biberman.

Following Capra's lead, Ford also named Buchman's name to the government, and rather casually at that, as if the act of naming someone to a board investigating the loyalty of American citizens was a relatively incidental matter. Ford wrote the board that as far as he knew, Capra's "only friends with communistic leanings was [*sic*] one Sidney Buchman," and that their relationship had ended in an argument over Buchman's political views, particularly over the writer's disagreements with policies of President Franklin D. Roosevelt. Ford's inaccurate account of Capra's relationship with the blacklisted Buchman and their supposed differences over the Roosevelt Administration was based on misleading information provided by Capra. Ford's statement demonstrates a reckless willingness to pass on damaging gossip about a colleague's political views.

Ford's Red-baiting proclivities were demonstrated again in 1953, this time in reference to a fellow director who had been a member of his SDG committee combating HUAC six years earlier. Ford cabled his Irish relative Lord Killanin, "Your letter received with the discouraging news that the Reds—one John Huston—are seeking refuge in our lovely Ireland. This aint [sic] good, he is not of the right wing."

The reality—and absurdity—of the blacklist hit Ford closer to home when a member of the Ford Stock Company found herself unable to work because of suspicions about her political beliefs. Despite being English, Catholic, and a self-described "Winston Churchill conservative," Ford regular Anna Lee spent years on the blacklist after her name appeared in the anti-Communist organ *Red Channels.*

In June 1956, Lee wrote Ford about the situation. After a period of not knowing why she was on the blacklist, she discovered that she was being confused with someone else. Stressing to Ford that she was not against the blacklisting of actual Communists, Lee told him an injustice had been done in her case. Although insisting that she had managed to clear herself, she admitted that she was making her living by writing television scripts under an assumed name. She had not acted in a feature film since 1952.

"If it hadn't been for Ford, I probably wouldn't have been working now," Lee told me in 1987. "Of course, he was absolutely furious. He said, 'They can't do this to you.' And he immediately called somebody in Washington, got ahold of the head guys. He said, 'I've seen that it's out and you'll be all right from now on.' But even so, every time I signed a contract with a studio I had to sign a little rider which said, 'I'm not now and never have been a Communist, etc., etc.' I had to sign it and then I was allowed to work." In 1957, Lee made her first feature since being blacklisted, *Gideon's Day,* which Ford directed in England for Columbia Pictures, and the following year she returned to Hollywood filmmaking in Ford's *Last Hurrah,* also for Columbia.

Although this story demonstrates Ford's loyalty to a friend in trouble, the fact that he could get someone off the blacklist simply by picking up the phone raises disturbing questions: Why did Ford have such power? How often did he use it? Was it appropriate for *anyone* to be able to say if someone should or should not work? And by clearing Anna Lee, did Ford facilitate and tacitly approve the blacklisting of the woman with whom she had been confused?

The difficulty of trying to make a socially conscious film during the Red Scare was demonstrated when Ford was assigned by Darryl Zanuck to direct the film version of Cid Ricketts Sumner's novel *Quality.* Published in 1945, the book tells the story of a nurse named Patricia Johnson who is African-American but passes for white (hence her nickname "Pinky") until she undergoes a crisis of conscience and identity after returning to her southern home. When the Academy Award for the best picture of 1947 went to *Gentleman's Agreement,* the Twentieth Century–Fox film about a gentile posing as a Jew to expose anti-Semitism in America, Zanuck decided, "Let's do it again with a Negro."

Ford owed Fox a picture because of the favors Zanuck had done to facilitate the making of *The Fugitive.* The director seemed a good choice for *Quality* because of his sensitive handling of a controversial subject in *The Grapes of Wrath* and because he was one of the few Hollywood directors of his generation who often included African-American characters in his films and treated them sympathetically. Because of the HUAC investigation of Hollywood, however, the studios rapidly began losing interest in films exposing problems in American life. Even Zanuck was affected by the new wave of timidity that descended over Hollywood in 1948. *Variety* reported in August that "studios are continuing to drop plans for 'message' pictures like hot coals." *Quality* was among the casualties, but only temporarily. It was reactivated in a hurry when two other movies on racial themes were announced, *Home of the Brave* and *Lost Boundaries.*

Dudley Nichols had adapted *Quality* into a screenplay for Ford. Philip Dunne was called in as a script doctor on the film, ultimately titled *Pinky.* He wrote a memo suggesting, among other things, that instead of Pinky's white boyfriend leaving her upon learning her secret early in the story, he should decide to stay with her on the condition that she continue passing for white, but finally she herself ends the relationship to remain with her people.

"Zanuck called a meeting about a week later," Dunne recalled. "I went in and he was sitting there with a letter on his desk and Ford was sitting with him chewing on a handkerchief. Zanuck said, 'I want to read you something.' The letter was from Dudley Nichols, and I suppose he was feeling miffed because his script had been superseded. We share credit, by the way; he had written a fine script and I used a lot of it. The whole burden of this letter was that Dudley could not conceive of a white man being willing to marry her under these circumstances.

"So when I heard this, I thought, 'Well, now, here's Dudley Nichols, who was Ford's writer on all those pictures they did together—and here is Zanuck reading Dudley Nichols's letter to me—here goes, it's all getting unstuck, it's gone, what'll I do?' Zanuck looked at me with this little evil look."

Addressing himself directly to Dunne, Zanuck said, "That to me is a perfect example of the Hollywood liberal mentality."

The executive turned to see Ford's reaction.

"Well," said Ford, "Dudley always was a sort of a white nigger, anyway."

Laughing uproariously at the story, Dunne described Ford's remark as "perfectly awful. *Awful!* I knew what he meant, though. My brother once said, 'When the time has come to mediate, Dudley wants to fight. When the time has come to fight, his heart begins to bleed.' This is absolutely true of Dudley. And, of all things, to write a really disgusting letter."

With the support of Ford and Zanuck, Dunne rewrote the script as he had proposed. Jeanne Crain, who had originally been cast as the nurse in *My Darling Clementine,* was given the starring role of Pinky. The great black actress and blues singer Ethel Waters was cast as her stalwart grandmother, Dicey, a long-suffering woman whose habitual subservience makes it difficult for her to come to terms with Pinky's dilemma. Ethel Barrymore, to whom Ford had served Holy Communion as a boy in Portland when she was "the First Lady of the American Theater," was cast as Miss Em, the imperious white woman who becomes Pinky's benefactor.

Ford began shooting *Pinky* in March 1949. He went into the job unhappy because Zanuck refused to let him shoot on location in the South, which he considered essential. Then Ford ran into problems working with Ethel Waters, and Zanuck had discussions with Ford about reshooting some of her scenes to make them seem less theatrical. "It was a professional difference of opinion," Zanuck recalled. "Ford's Negroes were like Aunt Jemima. Caricatures. I thought we're going to get into trouble. Jack said, I think you better put someone else on it. I said, finish out the day, and I took Ford off the picture. Some directors are great in one field and totally helpless in another field."

Ford had been suffering from a relatively mild case of shingles, a viral infection causing skin blisters. After receiving a memo from Zanuck on March 15 about the reshoots that were needed, Ford stayed home in bed the following day. Soon after that, Dunne related, "I got a call from Zanuck. He said, 'I've got to take Ford off the picture.' I said, 'What's happened?' He said, 'Well, put it this way, let's say he's got a bad case of shingles.' So I knew something was up. Then he told me later. The cover story was he had shingles. And I used that [in his autobiography, *Take Two: A Life in Movies and Politics*] because I didn't want to hurt anybody. But the real story was that he drove Ethel Waters crazy. I never saw the stuff he shot, but this is what Zanuck felt: he said the stuff was 'unbelievable.' Ford had the old-fashioned race views; he had her moaning spirituals. He just didn't *understand*."

"I fought with John Ford on *Pinky,*" Zanuck admitted to Elia Kazan, the director of *Gentleman's Agreement,* who was asked to take over *Pinky* on short notice. Kazan insisted on reshooting all of Ford's footage, which he felt "showed a lack of interest and involvement." A great admirer of Ford, Kazan sought him out for advice after coming to Hollywood to direct the 1945 Fox film *A Tree Grows in Brooklyn*. When Kazan asked Ford how he got his ideas about staging a scene, Ford grumpily replied, "From the set. Get out on the location early in the morning before anyone else is there. Walk around and see what you've got."

"Oh, then look at the script and fit the scene into the location?" asked Kazan.

"No," Ford growled, "don't look at the fucking script. That will confuse you. You know the story. Tell it with pictures. Forget the words."

"What else?"

"The actors," said Ford. "Don't let them act. Direct it like you were making a silent."

Like Orson Welles, Kazan used Ford's films to learn directing technique, watching *Stagecoach* and *Young Mr. Lincoln* over and over. As *Pinky* shows, Kazan's psychologically complex style is far more focused on the characters' inner lives than Ford's, which tends to look at people through their behavior in changing social roles. Yet Kazan regarded Ford as "a great artist, because he likes the past. He is a modern man, but he can see that those frontier values were important. And that's why I say I'm closer to Ford than to anybody—not only because of the way I shoot, that's superficial, but because I have one foot in now and one foot in the past."

Like Ford, Kazan came to dislike *Pinky* in part because of its studio-bound nature. But he also found fault with the leading lady Ford left him. Jeanne Crain, said Kazan, was "the blandest person I ever worked with . . . not only was she white in her face but also white in her heart."

"That's exactly why she was cast," Dunne said with exasperation. "None of these people who criticize this can understand that she *had* to be cast that way. The whole point was that she had to look absolutely white. All they did was give her brown contact lenses. The message of the picture was very simple: People were wonderfully deferential to her until they found out and they turned completely, 180 degrees. I thought she did a beautiful job and I thought Kazan did a good job directing."

Kazan learned from Zanuck that Ford "hated Ethel Waters and Ethel Waters hated him. He did not like the way the picture was turning out. So he went to bed." Ford's crew explained to Kazan that Ford "didn't know what to do with her. He couldn't curse her, as he did with 'Duke' Wayne. When he indicated the least disfavor with what she was doing, her reaction was not fear but resentment and retreat." Kazan managed to develop a good working relationship with Waters, but after they both had a few drinks at the wrap party, he asked her, "You don't really like any white people, do you, Ethel?"

"No, I don't," she admitted. "I don't like any fucking white man. I don't trust any of you."

Ford always spoke warmly of *When Willie Comes Marching Home* (1950), one of the few outright comedies he made after the war. "I feel I'm essentially a comedy director, but they won't give me a comedy to do," he complained. But the problem with *Willie* is that it's not very funny.

The story of a soldier named Bill Kluggs (Dan Dailey) who is stuck in his hometown throughout World War II—except for a brief overseas mission he's not allowed to talk about—has the outlines of a Preston Sturges film but lacks the zany, anarchic sense of satire that Sturges brought to his wartime farces *The Miracle of Morgan's Creek* and *Hail the Conquering Hero* (from which Ford borrows William Demarest as the hero's blustering father). In the tradition of Fordian self-sacrifice, Kluggs's devotion to duty is more grim than amusing and the character's wartime adventures are played mostly for drama. "Well, that was my racket for a while, and there wasn't anything funny about it," Ford told Bogdanovich in 1966. "I wonder what s.o.b. will be the first to make a comedy about Vietnam?"

Willie is based on a short story by Sy Gomberg about an episode in his own military career when he was shipped out on a Friday afternoon, shot down a Japanese plane over the weekend, and returned to base on a Monday. Ford's fondness for this satirical take on the nature of heroism no doubt stemmed from its echoes of his own clandestine activities during the war, a subject he rarely discussed until late in life. Mistakenly parachuting into occupied France, Kluggs is picked up by members of the Maquis underground, who use him as a courier to smuggle film of a Nazi secret weapon (similar to the V-2 rocket) back to London and the United States. Ford had his own adventures with the French Resistance (albeit somewhat exaggerated), and few people beyond the top brass and military intelligence saw the secret films of combat and enemy weaponry he made during the war. Kluggs's escape under fire in a PT boat is reminiscent of Ford's adventures with Johnny Bulkeley, and the cast includes three actors who were OSS men during the war, Peter Ortiz, Alberto Morin, and Ford's own aide-de-camp, Jack Pennick.

If *Willie* suffers from an excess of realism, another war comedy Ford made for Fox, *What Price Glory* (1952), suffers because of its utter lack of realism. The problem was not that Ford was unfamiliar with the original stage version, *What Price Glory?*, the classic 1924 comedy-drama set in World War I by Maxwell Anderson and Laurence Stallings, lately a Ford screenwriter. Ford had directed some second-unit scenes for Raoul Walsh's 1926 silent film version as well as for its sequel, *Hot Pepper* (1932). And in 1949, Ford mounted a traveling production of the play as a benefit for the Military Order of the Purple Heart.[11]

A spinoff from vaudeville acts he helped the organization stage for wounded veterans, *What Price Glory* provided Ford his first entrée into the theater since his boyhood job as an usher. "It was always Ford's wish to do a stage play because he loved actors for the theater," said cast member Pat O'Brien. "It was all for charity. None of us got a quarter." Performed from February 22 through March 11 in Long Beach, San Jose, Oakland, San Francisco, Pasadena, San Gabriel, and at Grauman's Chinese Theater in Hollywood, *What Price Glory* starred Ward Bond (in his stage debut) and O'Brien as the pair of perpetually quarreling military lifers who can never seem to shake each other, Captain Flagg and Sergeant Quirt. John Wayne also played his first theatrical role, as Lieutenant Cunningham. They were supported by a cast of other familiar movie faces, including Maureen O'Hara (as Charmaine), Gregory Peck, George O'Brien, Wallace Ford, Robert Armstrong, Oliver Hardy, Harry Carey Jr., Forrest Tucker, William Lundigan, Ed Begley, and Charles Kemper. The program proclaimed, "Entire Production Supervised by John Ford," listing George O'Brien as Ford's assistant and Harry Joe Brown as the producer.

Although Ford later claimed to have directed the play, he was not willing to risk his reputation on the stage, so he gave that job to Ralph Murphy. "Ford never once interfered with Murphy," Carey recalled. During the nightly rehearsals at the Masquers Club in Hollywood, Ford sat "out in the audience and never said a word, but he was at every rehearsal. He loved the stage [and was] fascinated with it." One night when Murphy was absent, Ford took over the direction. His principal contribution was to indulge in his favorite amusement of belittling Bond's performance.

Ford may have been attracted to the play in 1949 because it provided a safe way of venting some of his rebellious attitudes in an increasingly repressive climate. The Anderson–Stallings *What Price Glory?* offers caustic commentary on the pointlessness of World War I, yet it does so in the traditional mode of soldiers letting off steam by griping. In the end, these marines have no option but to do their duty, however much they question it. Ford biographer Andrew Sinclair plausibly suggests that Ford's Korean experience, which came after his stage production, made him unhappy with the play's antiwar message.

Ford's listless staging of the badly misconceived 1952 film version and Joe MacDonald's gaudy Technicolor photography of phony-looking sets of a

---

11. Unlike the play, the Ford and Walsh films do not have a question mark in their titles. Nor did Ford's stage production use the question mark.

French village reflect the director's utter disdain for the project. Zanuck had originally planned to film *What Price Glory* as a musical comedy, but Ford was angry because Zanuck wouldn't let him cast John Wayne as Flagg, so he sabotaged the film by refusing to shoot most of the musical numbers. "There wasn't one catchy tune in the whole score," Ford beefed. "A quarter of the way through I got disgusted with it." The shrill and unfunny bickering between James Cagney's Flagg and Dan Dailey's Quirt leaves the impression that the director was not even paying attention. And as he had done during the making of *When Willie Comes Marching Home,* Ford was rude to leading lady Corinne Calvet because she wasn't Maureen O'Hara, who had been his first choice for both films.

Phoebe and Henry Ephron's adaptation of *What Price Glory?* removed most of the sting from the dialogue and added a treacly romance between a young soldier who barely appears in the play, Lewisohn (Robert Wagner), and a French girl from a convent school (Marisa Pavan). Ford took out most of his hostility on Wagner, constantly referring to him as "Boob." One day Ford became so angry at the young actor that he suddenly knocked him to the ground in front of a large group of extras. Cagney helped Wagner to his feet. Only twenty-one at the time, Wagner was aghast at being decked by Hollywood's leading director. "I thought my career was at an end," recalled Wagner, who didn't understand what had provoked Ford to attack him. "For me he was just a miserable son of a bitch." No wonder Cagney remembered Ford as "truly a nasty old man."

This production also led to an unfortunate contretemps with the Ephrons, who came in wary of Ford because it was "bruited about that he was prejudiced" against Jews. Henry Ephron recalled in his autobiography that Ford enjoyed irritating their screenwriter friend Daniel Fuchs, a former member of Field Photo, by calling him "Fucks." The producer of *What Price Glory,* Sol Siegel, was greeted by the director each morning with "Hello, Sam." Clearly the Ephrons were not willing to play along with Ford's habit of roughhousing badinage, sometimes along ethnic lines.

"Phoebe only spoke to him once and that was a mistake," Henry recalled. "He took us down to the set of the French village on the back lot of the studio. We walked around, deciding which setups we would use in the script. As we got back into the studio car, Phoebe remarked how many churches there were in that little village.

"Ford shot back, 'Don't you think there are a lot of synagogues in a Jewish village?'"

The Ephrons left the studio car and walked away from Ford, Phoebe saying, "I'd like to get some fresh air," and Henry telling the director, "Mr. Ford, you stink."

As for *What Price Glory,* Archer Winston wrote in the *New York Post,* "The total result is deplorable, which is shocking when you see the name of John Ford as director."

By 1949, Ford and Cooper had become unhappy enough with their RKO coproduction deal to want out. Ford privately complained that Argosy was lucky if it could scrape up enough money to do one modestly budgeted picture a year. They still had not succeeded in setting up their much-delayed production of *The Quiet Man* at RKO, despite sporadic announcements and Cooper's efforts to finance Argosy's share using frozen American funds in England. Plans to film in Ireland during the summer of 1947 with the help of Ford's relative Lord Killanin fell through when Argosy and Sir Alexander Korda could not agree on cofinancing terms.

"Each year we would hold the summer open and each year there was no money and we couldn't make the movie," recalled Maureen O'Hara, who made a handshake deal with Ford in 1944 to play the female lead. "The script was taken to Fox, RKO, and Warner Bros., and all the studios called it a silly, stupid little Irish story. 'It'll never make a penny, it'll never be any good,' they said. And the years slipped by. John Wayne and I used to go to the studio and say: 'Mr. Ford, if you don't hurry up I'll have to play the widow-woman and Duke will have to play Victor McLaglen's role because we will be too old!' "

In May 1948, RKO was taken over by the reclusive industrialist Howard Hughes, whose broad-brush approach to doing business in Hollywood was demonstrated by his order after inspecting the studio lot: "Paint it." The following year, Hughes's mismanagement of RKO caused a temporary production shutdown.

The Red Scare was felt strongly at RKO. Production chief Dore Schary testified against blacklisting before HUAC in 1947, but he soon capitulated along with the rest of the Hollywood hierarchy. Following the issuance of the Waldorf Statement, RKO fired its two members of the Hollywood Ten, director Edward Dmytryk and producer Adrian Scott. The political atmosphere at Ford's home studio became even less hospitable under Hughes, whose "anti-Communist fervor was of obsessive if not downright paranoid and hallucinatory proportions," writes film historian Thomas Schatz. "He made it clear that any left-wing sensibilities on the screen or any fellow travelers on the RKO payroll would not be tolerated, and that he expected Schary's support in his efforts to ferret out any subversive activity at the studio."

Schary departed in July 1948 to become vice president in charge of production at MGM, where Ford and Cooper were making *3 Godfathers.* The previous October, when Louis B. Mayer gave his friendly testimony before

HUAC, Ford had taken care to build his private bridge to the MGM studio chief despite his own opposition to the HUAC hearings. Ford was wary of the smoothly functioning factory approach to filmmaking at MGM, where most directors were allowed little creative freedom, but Argosy had managed to have its way with *3 Godfathers*. By July 1949, Ford and Cooper were eager to capitalize further on Mayer's goodwill. Cooper wrote Mayer, "Quite frankly, the most happy association that I have had since I returned from the war has been with you. I have a definite six-picture offer from another studio but would most surely like to talk to you, because Ford and I want to stick to high quality product . . . and would appreciate your talking to us if you care to, at your earliest convenience." Cooper's talk of a six-picture offer evidently was just talk, and nothing came of the overture to Mayer. For Ford and Cooper, thinking small now seemed the most attractive option for exercising as much independence as they could within the rapidly crumbling studio system.

Argosy entered a fresh round of talks with Herbert J. Yates of Republic Pictures. To Ford's initial annoyance, John Wayne vigorously intervened to lobby Yates about bringing Ford to the studio, arguing that Ford's presence would help attract other important directors. Since the coming of television, Yates had become concerned that the market for low-budget program pictures would dry up, so he was willing to make somewhat more expensive pictures. One was Allan Dwan's 1949 World War II movie with Wayne, *Sands of Iwo Jima*. Knowing that the veteran Dwan was inclined to slough off his pictures by that stage of his career, Ford took him aside for a pep talk before shooting began and urged him to make a suitable tribute to the heroism of the U.S. Marines in World War II. Dwan delivered a powerful and moving film that brought Wayne his first Oscar nomination.

Yates was leery of giving Ford free rein at Republic. But Wayne convinced Yates that Ford was an economical director, and he managed to persuade Yates to let Ford make *The Quiet Man* by promising to star in it with Maureen O'Hara after they first made a black-and-white Western together for box-office insurance. No doubt that carrot was the deciding factor in luring Argosy to Republic, but Ford was loath to admit that his destiny was now in the hands of an actor he had once employed as a propman. But as the studio system collapsed, stars like Wayne assumed growing control over production decisions that once had been the prerogative of studio moguls and powerful directors such as Ford.

Meanwhile, Argosy fulfilled its RKO contract with Cooper's pet project *Mighty Joe Young* (1949) and Ford's low-budget *Wagon Master* (1950). The lyrically filmed saga of a wagon train of persecuted Mormons heading for their promised land in 1849, *Wagon Master* is one of Ford's masterpieces, a highly personal work of art disguised as a bread-and-butter Western.

Ben Johnson is the leading man of both pictures. Probably the most graceful horseman ever to make a career on-screen, the handsome and amiable young Oklahoman had been a champion rodeo performer before his first experience with Ford as a stuntman and Henry Fonda's riding double on *Fort Apache*. During the shooting of *Fort Apache*, recalled Johnson, "There was a munition wagon with three actors in it. It came by the camera and turned over, and it was dragging toward a sheer rock wall. I happened to be settin' on a horse, and I ran in and stopped the runaway. After everything was cleared away, John Ford came over to me and he says, 'Ben, you'll be rewarded for this.' So I thought, Well, I'll get another doubling job." Instead, Ford signed him to a seven-year acting contract. Seeing in this rough-hewn but effortlessly natural performer "a cross between Gary Cooper and John Wayne," Ford began grooming Johnson for stardom with his supporting roles in *3 Godfathers* and *Yellow Ribbon*.

Mighty Joe Young, the story of a lovable gorilla who escapes after being brought to Hollywood as a nightclub attraction, began production in 1946 as *Mr. Joseph Young of Africa*. Released in July 1949, Cooper's reunion with some of his old collaborators from *Kong* was directed by Ernest B. Schoedsack and written by Schoedsack's wife, Ruth Rose; the Oscar-winning stop-motion creature effects were by Willis O'Brien and his youthful protégé Ray Harryhausen. Ford said he had nothing to do with this innocuous piece of escapism, except for encouraging Cooper to cast Johnson as the rodeo performer who goes to Africa to "bring 'em back alive" for promoter Max O'Hara (the stentorian Robert Armstrong from *King Kong)*.

After two years of breathing the poisonous atmosphere of Hollywood politics, Ford found the location shoot for *Wagon Master* in Moab, Utah, literally a breath of fresh air. This is the kind of low-pressure, unpretentious, purely enjoyable movie that Hollywood has forgotten how to make.

Filmed quickly, simply, and inexpensively, far from civilization and producers, *Wagon Master* was a relaxed, communal effort with some of Ford's favorite actors, crew people, stuntmen, and extras. The company shot for nineteen days on location, from November 14 through December 3, 1949, finishing up with twelve days' work at the studio and the RKO ranch in Encino; the negative cost was only $848,853. Even more than usual for Ford, the production was a family affair. Patrick Ford collaborated on the script with Frank Nugent, from an uncredited story by the director; Barbara Ford was an assistant cutter; and the assistant directors included Ford's brother Eddie O'Fearna, brother-in-law Wingate Smith, and nephew Francis Ford Jr.

Ford took along on location a glaring reminder of the Hollywood witch-hunt, Ward Bond. But the director slyly cast his favorite whipping boy as a Mormon elder subjected to irrational persecution because of his religious beliefs and the spreading of false stories about his sexuality. Although celibate like most Ford heroes, Elder Wiggs is reputed to have horns under his hat and "more wives than Solomon hisself!—at least that's what folks around here say." His band of Mormons are forced to head west by a sheriff's posse that resembles a lynch mob. In the process, they learn to appreciate their unexpected kinship with other social outcasts, the kind of people Ford loves most: a band of friendly Navajos and a trio of disreputable showfolk who "have what I used to call in my sinnin' days a hoochie-kootchie show," as the elder explains to the members of his flock. Perhaps Ford was trying to teach Bond a lesson in tolerance by making him walk for a few weeks in the elder's shoes.

Ford began mulling over the story of *Wagon Master* while working with Mormon extras on location for *She Wore a Yellow Ribbon*. He admired their hardworking spirit and dancing skills, along with their devotion to a marginalized religious faith. *Wagon Master* was his way of paying tribute not only to the Mormons' pioneering courage in the face of ostracism but to the American democratic spirit as it existed in a simpler time when most people (other than Indians) were immigrants in transit from some place or another, searching for a new land to put down roots.

The director seems to have undertaken this project as a cleansing ritual, much like the sacramental river crossing the Mormons undergo, like a baptism, at the start of their westward journey. Ford finds in *Wagon Master* the purity of a vanished era when faith in the American future was the stuff of everyday life, a time when, at least in his fervently romantic imagination, it was still possible for Americans to transcend the divisive forces of social prejudice. *Wagon Master* did not come with the usual trappings of a protest film, but that's what it was, Ford's indirect protest of the darkness, suspicion, and hatred that had enveloped America by the middle of the twentieth century. Rather than situating his morality play in the unfamiliar terrain of a present-day community of outcasts, as he clumsily attempted to do in *Pinky*, Ford wisely sets it in the time and place that feels most comfortable to him, what Charles FitzSimons called "Fordland."

When Ford returned from location, he mischievously told his son and Frank Nugent, "I liked your script, boys. In fact, I actually shot a few pages of it." Ford shrewdly tightened the action and dialogue throughout, reducing Alan Mowbray's medicine show proprietor Dr. A. Locksley Hall to a few choice comic lines and minimizing the Mormons' own expressions of prejudice. Ford discarded some of the nastier insults directed at the irreligious but good-natured cowboys hired to lead the wagon train, Travis Blue (Ben Johnson, given the surname of Mary Ford's ancestors) and Sandy Owens (Harry Carey Jr.).

But the irony is still present when bluenosed Brother Perkins (Russell Simpson) says of the showfolk, "Don't think we oughta take up with their kind of people, elder."

Wiggs replies, "I ain't so sure but what the Lord didn't put these folks in our path for a reason. As I see it, the Lord ain't one to waste His energy. Now He's gone to a lot of trouble gettin' these people into this fix. And if I was *Him*, I wouldn't want anybody messin' up *my* plans."

"Well, uh," mutters Perkins sheepishly, "putting it that way . . ."

The bigoted sheriff who runs the Mormons out of Crystal City, prompting the previously reluctant Travis to sign on for the job of wagon master, is played by Cliff Lyons, a fellow member with Ford of the Motion Picture Alliance's executive committee. The sheriff's litany of venom takes in virtually all of the film's fellow travelers: "Mormons! Cleggses! Show folk! Horse traders!" (he doesn't have to add that he hates Indians as well). The Cleggs are a family of criminals who eventually take control of the wagon train. The reptilian Uncle Shiloh Clegg (Charles Kemper) whips his boys to keep them in line like Pa Clanton in *My Darling Clementine*. It's tempting to see the Cleggs, like the sheriff, as surrogates for Ford's Neanderthal colleagues in the MPA or the venal Parnell Thomas and his fellow members of HUAC. While reaching the very summit of Ford's optimism, *Wagon Master* acknowledges the bitter, real-world irony that even a utopian community cannot survive without occasional recourse to violence in self-defense. Delegating the job of killing the Cleggs to the two "horse traders," the Mormons commit an act of moral compromise that enables their community to survive and reach their "promised land" while at the same time calling into question the viability of their own principles.

Describing *Wagon Master* as an "avant-garde Western . . . one of the most purely lyrical films Ford has yet made," Lindsay Anderson remarked, "Ford often abandons his narrative completely, to dwell on the wide and airy vistas, on riders and wagons overcoming the most formidable natural obstacles, on bowed and weary figures stumbling persistently through the dust." From the stylized opening shootout filmed in the style of a silent movie through the final "curtain call" reprise of characters, *Wagon Master* flows along with an easy rhythm, luxuriating in the seemingly effortless beauty of Bert Glennon's cinematography and the accompaniment of nostalgic songs composed by Stan Jones for the Sons of the Pioneers. Ford's group compositions resemble classical friezes in motion, while his long shots have a dreamlike quality, aesthetically distanced through the choral accompaniment ("A hundred years have come and gone since 1849, / But the ghostly wagons rollin' west are ever brought to mind"). In such scenes as the river crossing, with a glorious shot of a glistening colt trotting up a hill ahead of a wagon pulled by a team of horses (reprised as the film's final shot), Ford gives *Wagon Master* a semi-documentary feeling, keeping the action rough and unrehearsed within harmoniously composed frames. By this point in his career, Ford's style has been perfected: it is a documentary vision of an ideal world.

Wagon Master received its share of favorable reviews in the United States— the *Hollywood Reporter* called it "another of [Ford's] vivid and realistic dramas of the Old West that will delight everyone who enjoys outdoor adventure"— but it was not regarded as anything more than a solid genre piece. Some reviewers even found it deficient by that modest standard. "The screenplay, unfortunately, attempts to avoid the usual clichés of Western films," complained the *Hollywood Citizen-News*. "A good many 'peaks' of dramatic conflict were passed up, such as when the Indians accosted the wagon train. The scenarists chose to make the Indians friendly. . . . And not even the flogging of a bandit for assaulting an Indian girl compensates for the conflict that might have been." Philip K. Scheuer of the *Los Angeles Times* noted that the realistic abruptness of the final shootout "is likely to disappoint action fans who are anticipating something more lingeringly spectacular and sadistic." Although Scheuer praised Ford for having "mellowed with the years, away from the old shoot-'em-up horse opera and toward a rough but affectionate regard for these early Americans as people," it says a great deal about the cultural climate of America in 1950 that Ford's *avoidance* of racism and sadism was considered a serious commercial drawback.

Even some of Ford's coworkers found it hard to recognize the film's true artistic value. Katherine Cliffton recalled, "Somebody asked him what was his favorite picture. He said *Wagon Master.* That wasn't *anything.* For the man who made *How Green Was My Valley* and *The Grapes of Wrath*—those were *works of art.* I thought he was spoofing somebody. I wanted to say, 'You're kidding.'" Ford was not kidding. He told Bogdanovich in 1966, "Along with *The Fugitive* and *The Sun Shines Bright,* I think *Wagon Master* came closest to being what I had wanted to achieve."

Ford's plans to make Ben Johnson a star never panned out. *Wagon Master* proved only a modest box-office performer, with rentals of about a million dollars, and the amiable Johnson, at least in his youth, lacked the quality Ingmar Bergman identified as essential for a movie star: danger. But we'll never know what would have happened if Johnson had not violated the code of the

Ford Stock Company by talking back to the Old Man on location for *Rio Grande.*

One night at dinner, Johnson and Dobe Carey were discussing that day's filming of the climactic battle sequence.

"Well, there was a lot of shootin' goin' on today, but not too many Indians bit the dust," Johnson said.

The room fell quiet.

Ford demanded, "What did you say?"

"I was just talkin' to Dobe, Mr. Ford," Johnson replied.

"I know. What did you say?"

"I was just talkin' to Dobe."

"Hey, stupid!" snapped Ford. "I asked you a question. What did you say?"

Carey related that Johnson rose from the table, strode over to Ford, and "said something to Ford that none of us could hear. Ben says that when he stopped, he told Jack what he could do with his picture, in no uncertain terms. He sure left no doubt in anyone's mind that he was ready to kill! There was an embarrassed silence. . . . Then Jack said, 'Oh, Jesus Christ, Dobe, go get him, for God's sake, and bring him back.' He knew he'd been wrong."

Carey could not persuade Johnson to return to the dinner table. No more was said about the incident. Though Ford had Johnson under contract for four more years, he did not use him in another film until 1963. Ford did offer Johnson a role in *The Sun Shines Bright* (1953), but became irate when the actor's agent had the temerity to demand a higher fee. Carey thinks that was the real reason Johnson was ostracized for so long from the Ford Stock Company. Either way, it was a stalemate between two men's implacable pride.

Finding movie parts scarce away from Ford, Johnson returned to the rodeo circuit, winning a world's championship. When he reemerged as a leading character actor in the late 1960s, he was older and heavier and his face was deeply lined with bitterly acquired wisdom. He made memorable appearances in such films as *One-Eyed Jacks, The Wild Bunch,* and *The Sugarland Express,* and Ford buried the hatchet by casting him as a cavalryman in *Cheyenne Autumn.* Johnson finally won an Academy Award as best supporting actor for his majestic performance as Sam the Lion, the owner of the small-town Texas movie theater in *The Last Picture Show* (1971). Directed by Ford acolyte Peter Bogdanovich, the film displays a poster for *Wagon Master* as Sam's next attraction at his "picture show." But because the script contained profanity and nudity, Johnson refused the part until Ford bullied him into playing it. "Good God, do you want to play Duke's second all your life?" Ford demanded.

Accepting his Oscar, Johnson graciously thanked "Mr. John Ford, who had a lot to do with my doing the show." Then he added, "This couldn't have happened to a nicer fella."

On January 4, 1950, Argosy signed a nonexclusive production deal with Republic Pictures. "This was no sudden decision," Republic president Herbert J. Yates told the press. "We've been thinking about the merger for a long time." Ford later claimed Argosy left RKO because it was offered a better financial deal by Republic, yet at the time he and Cooper had serious reservations about joining Yates's studio and only went with Republic because they had little alternative.

Argosy agreed to deliver to Republic at least one and not more than three films directed by Ford and produced by Cooper over the next two years. Ford's weekly salary was set at $3,000, about the same as he had received at RKO. Republic would finance and own the Argosy films, costing between $700,000 and $1.25 million each, and Argosy was to receive 50 percent of the net profits. Yates retained approval of the story, shooting script, budget, cast, and start date of each picture. No Argosy film could run longer than 10,000 feet (111 minutes). Republic could make any changes it deemed necessary for foreign release, but no changes were allowed for domestic release after a film was "fully and finally cut and edited by Ford, except [for] minor changes which may be required" by government censorship bodies or to obtain a seal from the Production Code Administration.

Unlike in their previous negotiations with Republic, Argosy had to settle for a deal that did not provide Ford and Cooper with stock ownership in the studio and ownership of their pictures. On the plus side, Argosy did not share production costs as it had with RKO. Republic's agreement to fully finance the pictures was an important factor in a depressed business environment. But Ford would have to operate under tighter budget constraints at Republic, and though he still enjoyed a considerable degree of artistic freedom, Yates held veto power over some of the most important creative decisions. This was among the elements in the deal that would prove most galling to Ford, who told me he considered Yates a "stupid" man.

Shortly after delivering the negative of *Wagon Master* to RKO in late February 1950 for April release, Argosy moved its headquarters from Culver City to the Republic lot at 4024 Radford Avenue in North Hollywood (now the CBS Studio Center in Studio City).[12] Ford took a stroll around the lot one

12. In the spring of 1951, Argosy sold RKO all five films it had made for the studio—*The Fugitive, Fort Apache, She Wore a Yellow Ribbon, Mighty Joe Young,* and *Wagon Master*—in exchange for RKO's agreement to pay off the remaining bank debt and interest.

morning in January and found comfort in its compact dimensions and the old-fashioned ambience of its aging sets, which he would use to such advantage in re-creating turn-of-the-century Kentucky for *The Sun Shines Bright*. Ford was in such a benign mood that when he encountered Yates, he bowed and offered a cordial greeting to the crusty studio chief.

Either party to the Argosy-Republic agreement was allowed to cancel it after the first picture, which meant that Ford had to ensure the success of that project if he wanted to make *The Quiet Man*. This time, Ford would not repeat the mistake he made when he kicked off his RKO deal with an art-house picture. He played it safe with another John Wayne Western. *Rio Grande*'s box-office rentals of $2.25 million finally bought the green light for Ford's dream project.

When Ford described *The Quiet Man* to Lindsay Anderson as "the first love story I've ever tried. A mature love story," he was overlooking *Rio Grande*. Though the plot of this 1950 Western centers on an illegal raid by the U.S. Cavalry to root out Apaches taking refuge across the Mexican border, *Rio Grande* is also a mature love story between an estranged husband and wife, played by Wayne and Maureen O'Hara.

Because of Ford's "need to creep with some wariness up to this ticklish subject" of sexuality, as Anderson put it, the director seemed to have undertaken *Rio Grande* as sort of a dry run for the highly charged romantic relationship between Wayne and O'Hara in *The Quiet Man*. Ford frequently spoke Gaelic when directing O'Hara in *Rio Grande,* anticipating the scene in *The Quiet Man* of her character using "the Irish" to seek advice about her marital problems from the parish priest (Ward Bond). Although Ford enjoyed teasing and bantering with O'Hara, he treated her with remarkable deference. "I think he was in love with Maureen," Olive Carey observed. During the filming of a scene in *The Wings of Eagles,* Katherine Cliffton recalled, "Maureen O'Hara fluffed her lines fourteen times. She'd blow it and he'd patiently say, 'Let's do it again, Maureen.' Then they went inside a house and he talked to her. Dan Dailey said, 'Oh, God, wait till he gets ahold of us. He'll take it out on us.' I don't think *any* director would mistreat someone as gorgeous as Maureen O'Hara."

Wayne's Lieutenant Colonel Kirby York in *Rio Grande* is an older, harder, and more disillusioned version of the character he played in *Fort Apache*.[13] He

---

13. Contrary to most commentaries on the film, there is nothing in *Rio Grande* to indicate that the name of Wayne's character is spelled "Yorke" or that he is anyone other than the man who served under Colonel Thursday. The spelling error apparently originated in McGuinness's script of May 5, 1950, but in the final daily production report on July 21, the name is spelled "York."

has been separated from his Irish wife, Kathleen, for the fifteen years since he burned her plantation during the Civil War under orders from General Philip H. Sheridan (J. Carroll Naish). When the Yorks' son, Jeff (Claude Jarman Jr.), fails at West Point, he enlists in the regular army and is assigned to his father's cavalry outpost. In a point-of-view shot the first time Colonel York sees his grown son among the new troopers, Ford cuts to a close-up of Dobe Carey before panning to Jarman, as if to suggest that the colonel, like the director himself, regards Dobe as a more natural son figure than his own flesh and blood. Kathleen arrives with ambivalent feelings toward Kirby and tries to convince Jeff to quit the army, telling him that "what makes soldiers great is hateful to me." This emotionally complex family drama is treated by Ford and his cast with great delicacy, intermittently elevating *Rio Grande* above its crudely racist and stridently jingoistic military plot, derived from Bellah's story "Mission with No Record."

Rio Grande was filmed as *Rio Bravo* and retitled *Rio Grande Command* until shortly before its release in November 1950. The original title, the Mexican name for the river marking its border with the United States, was dropped because someone raised a legal claim and Yates didn't think *Rio Bravo* sounded commercial anyway. (Howard Hawks used the title for his 1959 Western classic with Wayne, a sizable hit for Warner Bros.) After "much wrangling, fist-fights and harsh words" over the budget with Yates that left Ford "a nervous wreck," the director had to economize by shooting *Rio Grande* in Moab, Utah, rather than Monument Valley. The film was completed in thirty-two shooting days during June–July 1950 for a thrifty $1,287,185, slightly above Argosy's contractual budget ceiling.

Rio Grande bears the stamp of Ford's most reactionary cold war political views. This is due largely to his decision to hire the archconservative James Kevin McGuinness rather than the liberal Frank Nugent as the film's screenwriter. Nugent's sympathy for Indians, a thread that runs through much of his work with and without Ford, was not wanted for *Rio Grande*. Ford remained loyal to McGuinness after he lost his job as an MGM executive in 1949. McGuinness's friends claimed he had been forced out because of his anti-Communist zealotry with the Motion Picture Alliance. When the writer died of heart problems at the age of fifty-five on December 4, 1950, shortly after the release of *Rio Grande,* Ford paid his final tribute by attending the funeral.

Bellah's story, loosely based on an actual raid across the Rio Grande in 1873, provided the principal political theme of *Rio Grande:* breaking the law in pursuit of a supposedly greater goal is justified by the demands of American empire building. Lieutenant Colonel York (named Massarene in the story) is frustrated by the limits placed on his ability to wage war against the Apaches.

When a band of marauding Apaches crosses into Mexico, counting on international law that forbids the cavalry to pursue them, General Sheridan gives York a strictly verbal order: "I want you to cross the Rio Grande. Hit the Apache and burn him out! I'm tired of hit and run, I'm sick of diplomatic hide and seek."

In his 1992 book *Gunfighter Nation: The Myth of the Frontier in Twentieth-Century America*, Richard Slotkin identifies *Rio Grande* as a key example of the "Cold War Western," a postwar development in the genre whose function was "to interpret modern forms of industrial and ethnic strife and to rationalize the development of the republican nation-state into an imperial Great Power. . . . The problem of reconciling democratic values and practices with the imperatives of power is both the central contradiction of American Cold War ideology and the classic problem of democratic politics. And it was precisely this issue that the 'Cold War Western' addressed." By the time of *Rio Grande*, Ford's cavalry "is not merely the 'representative' of American democracy—the agent of its policy, the metaphoric expression of its values. Democracy and nation are now entirely identified with the military."

Rio Grande can be read as Ford's early-warning allegory of the Korean War, which broke out ten days after it began filming. The military's impatience with civilian control in *Rio Grande* was echoed by General Douglas MacArthur and his right-wing supporters, who harshly criticized the Truman policy of containing Communism through "limited war" rather than risking an escalation that could have led to nuclear warfare. MacArthur's demand that Truman let him expand the war across the Chinese border by bombing Communist supply depots was that general's way of declaring his desire to "cross the Rio Grande . . . and burn him out!"

After Truman fired MacArthur in April 1951 for insubordination toward presidential authority, Ford was one of millions of Americans who felt outrage. Ford took his autographed picture of Truman from the wall of his home and replaced it with an inscribed portrait of MacArthur, declaring that he wouldn't restore the president to his former position of honor until he offered an apology to the general. The mythic view Ford presented of MacArthur in *They Were Expendable* was carried forward in documentary footage the director shot for *This Is Korea!* on January 8, 1951, of a silhouetted MacArthur striding imperiously from his staff car in Tokyo. MacArthur reciprocated Ford's admiration by telling him of his sentimental fondness for *She Wore a Yellow Ribbon*, which he watched once a month, indulging his nostalgia for the frontier army posts of his youth; the general's favorite movie stars were John Wayne and Ward Bond. MacArthur's famous comment to Congress in April 1951 that "Old soldiers never die—they just fade away" was reminiscent of what Wayne's Captain Brittles said about *his* retirement: "Old soldiers, Miss Dandridge—some day you'll learn how they hate to give up."

Ford's demonization of the enemy in *Rio Grande* was a throwback to his lurid depiction of Indians in *Drums Along the Mohawk*. The director's latest reversal on the subject probably meant that he regarded the "Red Indians" in *Rio Grande* more as "Reds" than as Indians. Even the Production Code Administration criticized McGuinness's script for its blatant racism. "It is our considered opinion that it behooves the industry to see to it that Indians in Motion Pictures are fairly presented," Joseph Breen wrote Republic. Breen recommended omitting a description of the Apaches as "a scourge to your country and to mine—thieves and murderers," as well as a line stating, "These Apaches are the only Indians who kill and torture for the sheer lust of it." Both lines were omitted from the film, but the Indians' drunken and bloodthirsty behavior remained intact, including their rape and murder of a trooper's wife and their clearly signaled intention to slaughter the white children they have abducted. (In the actual 1873 raid, the abducted women and children were *Indians,* kidnapped in Mexico by Colonel Ranald Mackenzie and his cavalrymen and taken back to the reservation as hostages.)

Though Ford let his anti-Communist feelings run away with his reason in making *Rio Grande,* the family story engaged him on a more personal level, metaphorically evoking the tensions within his own household. Ford seldom showed greater psychological insights into the dynamics of a dysfunctional family than he did in *Rio Grande.* The clash between Kathleen's southern heritage and York's Yankee sympathies is a darker reflection of the perpetual teasing between Mary and Jack Ford over their family histories of fighting on opposite sides of the Civil War. York's estrangement from his son cuts more painfully close to the bone for Ford. The unusual degree of intelligence and dignity he grants to Jarman's Jeff York may have been a measure of Ford's self-recrimination over his coldhearted treatment of Pat.

The Yorks' final reconciliation has strong elements of wish fulfillment, but Ford makes it emotionally compelling despite its (qualified) sexism. Both husband and wife are willing to compromise to restore their marriage, sacrificing some of their stubborn pride and ideological rigidity for a mutually empowering partnership. The initially haughty Kathleen has "become Irish" once again by scrubbing Kirby's clothes to the tune of "The Irish Washerwoman" and taking her dutiful place among the cavalry wives waiting to receive their men home from battle. There is no more talk from her about a soldier's job being "hateful."

Yet the essential feistiness of O'Hara's screen personality—Wayne once called her "the greatest guy I ever knew"—is acknowledged in the film's ending sequence when she is rewarded with the playing of "Dixie." Her husband is taken aback by this gesture of General Sheridan's but accepts it with a wry smile as Kathleen twirls her parasol triumphantly. Like Lincoln's request to hear "Dixie" after the South's surrender in *The Prisoner of Shark Island,* this tribute to a defeated faction symbolizes the hope of national reconciliation that still remained alive for Ford as late as 1950.

World War II was the last war to be endorsed by the intellectual establishment as a valid artistic subject," Andrew Sarris observes. "Ford proceeded into the fifties to photograph the Korean War, an act symptomatic of his downfall with the taste-makers."

Ford arrived in Korea at the beginning of January 1951 to make his navy documentary *This Is Korea!* Shortly before that, the tide of the war had turned against the United Nations forces north of the thirty-eighth parallel separating North and South Korea. Hundreds of thousands of Chinese Communist troops poured across the border, forcing the First Marine Division to make its fighting retreat through the snow from the Choisin Reservoir. As Gallagher puts it, "Characteristically, Ford had found the moment of defeat." Over a sequence of American troops torturously encamped in blizzard conditions, the film tells us, "You remember Valley Forge? Well, look at it again."

Accompanied by his naval aide and Hollywood colleague Mark Armistead and two Field Photo cameramen from World War II, Charles Bohuy and Robert Rhea, Captain Ford left for Korea on December 26, 1950. He spent four weeks following the Seventh Fleet and the First Marine Division as the officer in charge of Pacific Fleet Photographic Team ABLE, supervising the filming of battle footage. Some footage from other navy and marine cameramen was also used in the documentary. When Bogdanovich observed to Ford that his portrait of the war turned out to be far grimmer than *The Battle of Midway* or *They Were Expendable,* Ford replied, "Well, that's the way it was . . . there was nothing glorious about it. It was not the last of the chivalrous wars."

The narration written by James Warner Bellah (with contributions by Frank Nugent) is politically unsophisticated in the extreme and often appalling in its bloodthirstiness. Almost no attempt is made to explain the causes or the strategy of the war. The viewer merely is told that Korea was a "peaceful land . . . until the ruthless Red hand of Communism reached out to snatch it." The low point of Ford's filmmaking career is the horrific sequence showing American troops using phosphorus grenades and flamethrowers against dug-in enemy soldiers, accompanied by these words from the narrator (John Ireland): "Fry 'em out—burn 'em out—*cook* 'em!"

That hardline anti-Communist rhetoric clashes oddly with Ford's honesty in reporting the essential futility of the war. The hellishness of the battle scenes is conveyed with overwhelming visual intensity, and while Ford sentimentally indulges in repeated shots of Korean refugee children being cared for by American troops, the film leaves little doubt about the war's toll on the civilian population. The camerawork and editing convey an almost absurdist sense of aimlessness on the part of the UN forces, who are shown marching hither and yon with no sense of strategy or purpose. The firepower from the other side is treated as an abstract force; the only enemy soldiers we see are POWs.

Calling *This Is Korea!* "simply a narrative glorifying American fighting men on land, sea, and air," Ford wrote the navy's chief of information, Rear Admiral R. F. Hickey, on March 21, "As to the object of the picture, I am simply acting on Admiral [Arthur W.] Radford's directive, and I repeat again there is no policy, politics or controversy of any sort involved." But at the end of the film, the ostensible ideological purpose of simply presenting the war to the American public without political explanation is turned against itself. Ford's superficial jingoism enables him to get away with the daringly fatalistic closing narration delivered by Irving Pichel: "Well, what's it all about? You tell us. Ask any of these guys what they're fighting for, and they can't put it into words. Maybe it's just pure cussedness and pride in the Marine Corps. A job to do— and duty."

Ford forged a valued friendship in Korea with the most decorated marine in American history, Lewis B. "Chesty" Puller. While attached to the First Marine Division, Ford shared a tent with Puller, who was promoted from colonel to brigadier general that January and won his fifth Navy Cross for commanding the rear of the First Marine Division in the epic retreat from the Choisin Reservoir. Using the low-angle perspective he usually reserves for idealizing heroic figures, Ford filmed a close-up of the bulldog-faced general growling into a field telephone: "Put some more fire down on those people. Thank ya." It's likely that Ford's pessimism about the war was influenced by his camaraderie with the blunt-spoken general, about whom he later made a sentimental documentary, *Chesty: A Tribute to a Legend* (1968–70, released in 1976). When Puller heard the situation in Korea described as a stalemate with the forces of Communist China, he snapped, "Stalemate, hell! We've lost the first war in our history, and it's time someone told the American people the truth about it. The Reds whipped the devil out of us, pure and simple."

From Korea, Ford and Armistead flew to Tokyo for a four-day layover en route to California. As he had done after D-Day, Ford unwound from the stress of war with a bout of hard drinking. After returning home and being placed on inactive status on March 7, he required surgery for a double hernia, complaining to Michael Killanin, "I've never climbed so many damned mountains in my life." Ford supervised the editing of *This Is Korea!* while engaged in preproduction on *The Quiet Man*. Republic, which was not eager to release the documentary but bowed to the wishes of Ford and the navy, made 150 theatrical and nontheatrical prints in its Trucolor process. The film received favorable reviews when released that August. A. H. Weiler of the *New York Times* praised the film for capturing "the horrible visage of war" with a sense of "tired understatement. . . . It is sobering to see the bloody wounded and the silent dead." *Motion Picture Herald*'s Tom Canning called it "the best piece of war reporting since the end of World War II. It has captured on film some of the flavor and the feeling for which the late Ernie Pyle was justly famed."

Even after making patriotic appeals to exhibitors, Republic had trouble finding bookings for the fifty-minute film. Most of the American public preferred to avert its eyes from the horrific reality of this increasingly unpopular war. Exhibitors reported that women were walking out of the picture because it was too gruesome and that parents who had sons in Korea did not want to see what was happening there. The issue of the public's disengagement is addressed within the film itself. Over footage of casualties being treated at a field hospital, the narrator urgently demands: "Aren't you glad you gave that pint of blood last week? Or did you? But you will now, won't you?" One exhibitor, Herman Rosen, made a point of telling Republic he considered it his patriotic duty to show *This Is Korea!* at his theater in Pearl Harbor because it was supported by army and navy personnel. Ford wrote Rosen a heartfelt letter of thanks, expressing the wish that there were twenty more people like him in the country.

Ford was awarded an Air Medal by the navy on March 9, 1951, for "meritorious achievement in aerial flight as Officer-in-Charge of Pacific Fleet Photographic Team ABLE during operations against enemy aggressor forces in Korea from 4 January to 2 February, 1951. Completing ten missions during this period, Captain Ford carried out daring photographic flights over active combat areas. By his courage, skilled airmanship and unswerving devotion to duty in the face of grave hazards, he contributed materially to the success achieved by his unit and upheld the highest traditions of the United States Naval Service."

After interviewing Mark Armistead, Ford biographer Andrew Sinclair claimed that the flight missions for which Ford received the medal were actually performed by Armistead while the director was inland with Chesty Puller. This would not have been the first time Ford exaggerated his military exploits to win a medal, but there is nothing in Ford's navy records to indicate that his Air Medal might have been unwarranted. Ford did spend some time photographing operations conducted from an aircraft carrier, the USS *Philippine Sea*, and it is also possible that he flew missions with Puller. "We fought together and we were tentmates," Ford says in his documentary on Puller. During the period when they were together, Puller "flew with pilots in a tiny observation plane, buzzing over the hills around Andong, Pohang and Yongchon, spying out the Chinese," according to the general's biographer Burke Davis. "They were often fired on, but Puller's battle luck held, and there were no hits. His missions were so daring and talked of so breathlessly by returning pilots that he was awarded an Air Medal for the daily flights in the last half of [January]." (That May, showing his appreciation for James Warner Bellah's uncredited work on the documentary, Ford successfully lobbied General Albert Wedemeyer to obtain Bellah an Air Medal for a 1944 army combat operation.)

Ford's Air Medal finally enabled him to achieve his navy dream of becoming an admiral. To do so, he had to retire from active duty; if he had waited three more years, he would have qualified for the pension awarded for twenty years' service in the Naval Reserve, but he preferred the immediate upgrade in rank made possible by his combat decoration. On March 29, 1951, he requested retirement because of physical disability. President Truman promoted Ford to rear admiral, USNR, on May 1, the official date of his retirement from active service.

Fifteen years after taking an option on Maurice Walsh's story "The Quiet Man," Ford finally rolled his cameras on June 6, 1951. He started with a scene involving his brother Frank, wearing a long white beard, on the grounds of the Ashford Castle hotel next to Lough Corrib in the County Mayo village of Cong. The breathtakingly beautiful Technicolor fantasy John Ford made in Ireland at the age of fifty-five was not the fiercely political *Quiet Man* he would have made at forty. Not only the mellowing effect of advancing age but also long years of painful and disillusioning experience went into the making of this fervently romantic tale of an exile's return, a film whose dark undercurrent runs largely beneath its beguiling surface.

Ford had spent much of the intervening years filming warfare throughout the world and re-creating battle scenes in Hollywood and the deserts of the American Southwest. His personal and professional allegiances thrown into turmoil by the cold war, he had lived for the past four years under the guilty shadow of ideological fratricide. Like John Wayne's Sean Thornton, who leaves America in revulsion after killing a man in the ring, Ford was in flight from violence, material success, and the unexpected consequences of the American Dream. *The Quiet Man* would be his own exorcism of the demon of battle. In a fitting paradox, Ford was in Ireland preparing this film about a warrior turned pacifist when he received the news that he had achieved the pinnacle of military success by becoming an admiral. John Wayne celebrated the event by pushing Ford into Galway Bay.

The Quiet Man is the story of an Irish-American's attempt to recapture the imagined innocence and beauty of his Irish boyhood. The urgency of that need is a measure of how Sean has spent his "wasted years across the wintry sea," as Maureen O'Hara's Mary Kate (Mary Ford + Kate Hepburn) sings in "The Isle of Innisfree," the Richard Farrelly song Ford uses to encapsulate Sean's longing and loss. But Sean is returning to a land he remembers mostly from his mother's stories. *The Quiet Man* is often criticized for not offering a realistic portrait of Ireland, but that completely misses the point. Masterfully filmed by Ford and Winton C. Hoch with what Manny Farber called "the sunless, remembered look of a surrealist painting," the Ireland of *The Quiet Man* is presented as the romantic fantasy of a troubled man who is doubly an exile. After being taken from his native Ireland as a child, he willingly abandons his adopted homeland of the United States, which Barry Fitzgerald's Michaeleen og Flynn dismisses with his pithy phrase, "America . . . Pro-hibition!" The rich blend of comedy and drama that makes *The Quiet Man* Ford's most beloved film reflects the cultural clash embodied in Sean himself, whose search for a fairy-tale homeland of transcendent "peace and quiet" reflects the anguished, sometimes neurotic longings of the Irish diaspora.

Anthony Burgess wrote of the expatriate Irishman James Joyce, "Exile was the artist's stepping back to see more clearly and so draw more accurately; it was the only means of objectifying an obsessive subject-matter." Always something of a mental exile, looking back to the imagined Eden his parents had left behind in Connemara, Ford had to leave America to examine, understand, and re-create himself at this definitive turning point in his life's passage.

Surrounded by family members, old friends, and newfound Irish cronies, Ford filmed the location scenes for *The Quiet Man* in Mayo and the picturesque "Joyce Country" in Galway, not far from his own ancestral home, with his Irish cousin Michael Killanin unofficially serving as line producer and the legendary IRA man Ernie O'Malley helping with the direction of crowds. Ford's journey back to his roots in the summer of 1951 was charged with more symbolic resonance than any other visit to Ireland he had made since the War of Independence. The *Connacht Tribune* reported that Ford "was deeply moved when he visited the family home in Tourbeg, Spiddal, and saw the room and very bed in which his grandfather had been born." He gave the title character the Gaelic equivalent of his own first name and a last name borrowed from his Thornton cousins. The man who liked to pretend that he had started life as Sean Aloysius O'Fienne spent five intensely emotional and creative weeks projecting himself through his favorite surrogate, John Wayne, into the role of Sean Thornton, "a quiet, peace-loving man come home from America to forget his troubles."

The local newspaper reported, "Director Ford's association with the people of Spiddal is already well-known, still a *Connacht Tribune* representative was surprised to hear a Hollywood Oscar winner, in his American accent, tell him he was still 'cineal bodhar' (deafened) from the drone of the plane engines on his journey to Ireland, and that he was a 'col cuigear' (cousin) of Michael Droighnea, a teacher from Furbough. Those who would like to have a long chat with Mr. Ford would be well advised to forget all about Hollywood and film stars and be prepared to discuss the people of Connemara, the Cong struggle towards Irish independence, the Irish language, and his Irish relations."

Nothing is more fiercely resisted in Hollywood than a deeply personal project. Ford climaxed his siege of the reluctant Herb Yates by dragging him along on a location scouting trip to Ireland with Ward Bond. The director was insistent that he needed $1.75 million to make the film properly, but Yates was lowballing him at $1.238 million. Ford wanted to show Yates the natural beauty his money could buy.

As Ford told the yarn, doubtless with a bit of enhancement, he took Yates to see a small thatched cottage in Connemara. Summoning tears for the occasion, Ford told the studio chief, "There it is, the house where I was born." Ford claimed the hard-boiled Yates also was crying when he responded, "You can do *The Quiet Man*. For a million and a half."

On June 1, 1951, Yates authorized a budget of $1,464,152. Maureen O'Hara recalled, "John Ford asked John Wayne and me to take a cut and because we had all waited so long and so badly wanted to make the movie we agreed. John Wayne accepted $100,000 [also forgoing his usual profit percentage] and I got $65,000." According to Republic Pictures documents in Ford's files, the film's negative cost was not $1.75 million, as reported by Dan Ford and others, but $1,446,661. That was $17,491 under budget, even with the $955 that Ford charged the production to fly his parish priest, Father Daniel J. Stack, S. J., to the Irish location.

Nevertheless, Yates anxiously sent telegrams to Ireland threatening to shut down the picture if Ford didn't stop wasting Republic's money. Ford managed to keep shooting despite the nearly constant Irish drizzle that helped give *The Quiet Man* its unique look. Hoch recalled that the rain was so persistent that it began to turn Maureen O'Hara's red hair a dull brown, necessitated frequent changes of costume, and caused havoc in close shots when rain would drip from the actors' noses. But Ford didn't know how to respond when Yates complained about the scenery, "Everything's all green. Tell the cameraman to take the green filter off" (*The Quiet Man* brought Hoch his second Academy Award). The studio chief's long-distance badgering was the subject of nightly ridicule around the company dinner table at Ashford Castle. Yates even started to rival Bond as a Ford scapegoat. Bond loyally climbed to the top of a ruined tower on the hotel grounds and scraped with a piece of slate on the inside wall, "FUCK HERB YATES." He then contrived to lure Wayne up the tower to see his handiwork.

One of the reasons Yates fretted so much over what he considered a "phony art-house picture" was that Wayne had a far more introspective role than he was accustomed to playing, even with Ford. Yates summoned Wayne to his office before shooting began and disclaimed responsibility for *The Quiet Man,* warning Wayne that it would damage his career. The actor always felt that he was contending with "a goddam hard script. For nine reels I was just playing a straight man to those wonderful characters, and that's really hard." But Wayne rises to the challenge with sensitivity, grace, and good-natured humor.

Katherine Cliffton proposed an intriguing casting alternative, suggesting to Ford that he cast Robert Ryan as Sean Thornton. A former boxer himself, Ryan was an extremely intelligent actor especially skilled at playing neurotically self-destructive characters. Ford told Cliffton, "You do your research and catalogue my library, and I'll direct the pictures." Almost twenty years later, Frank Capra was visiting Ford's home to talk about the foreword for his autobiography, *The Name Above the Title,* which Cliffton was ghostwriting in Ford's name. They were all talking at once when Ford suddenly turned to Cliffton and said, "Ryan would have been good."

"He *would* have been a good 'quiet man,' a man with a tragedy in his past," Cliffton told me. "But I understood Ford's thinking. He needed a star, he needed to sell tickets. And he didn't like advice. He liked to put people down. That was one of the bad things about him. He would go to elaborate lengths to show people up." And just as elaborate lengths to apologize. Ford might have been uncomfortable working with Ryan at that time because of the actor's liberal political views. But in choosing an alter ego for this intensely autobiographical film, how could Ford have settled on anyone but John Wayne?

Frank Nugent's screenplay for *The Quiet Man* is so finely crafted that it's surprising to learn that it was written in a ten-week rush shortly before shooting began. Ford had earlier commissioned Richard Llewellyn, the author of *How Green Was My Valley,* to expand Walsh's story into a novella, and Laurence Stallings also did some work on the project. Llewellyn finished a screenplay adaptation in early 1951, but by then Ford had become concerned about the political aspects of the story, which was still set during the Troubles and had the protagonist taking up arms with the IRA. Reviving that issue might have been controversial in the current political climate, even (or perhaps especially) in a comedy. As late as the final stage of editing, Yates urged Ford to cut the word *national* from the wedding toast "May they live in peace and national freedom," explaining that the phrase "national freedom" could make it difficult to play the film in Great Britain and the British Commonwealth. Ford acquiesed, and so there is a brief break in the sound track during the toast offered by the IRA man Forbes, played by one of Maureen O'Hara's real-life brothers, Charles FitzSimons, who thought "John Ford panicked a bit thinking the word 'national' might offend."

Though it would have been a small but significant gesture to keep that line intact, Ford made a sound artistic decision in otherwise minimizing the film's overtly political dimensions. The War of Independence seems an overly weighty and ultimately irrelevant setting for Walsh's conventional fantasy of wish fulfillment. The character in the story is a small man who whips a bully because he happens to be, secretly, a professional fighter. Sean's guilty reason for trying to avoid the fight was added by Ford and Nugent. Furthermore, in the story, the character's return to Ireland is based on simple nostalgia, not on a rejection of his immigrant dream of America.

Ford had suggested to Llewellyn that the character return home to aid his family, as Ford himself did during the Troubles. Nugent's final screenplay has Sean motivated purely by personal concerns, although he finds that he cannot help being drawn into the complex interactions of the community. Some pointed political references still remain in the film, however unspecific they may be, such as the wonderful line improvised by Ford for Fitzgerald's Flynn, "Well, it's a nice soft night, so I think I'll go and join me comrades and talk a little treason." The parish priest, Father Lonergan (Ward Bond), is involved in an IRA cell with Flynn, Forbes, and Sean McClory's Owen Glynn. To Forbes's insistence, "We're at peace now, man," Michaeleen slyly replies, "True, but I haven't given up hope." The film even contains what could be seen as subtle references to blacklisting, such as in Bond's priest threatening Victor McLaglen's tyrannical Squire Red Will Danaher by warning, "I'll read your name in the Mass on Sunday," and the squire keeping a book with the names of people who offend him. In a revealing self-referential joke by the director, the book is kept by a lickspittle named Feeney, delightfully played by the great Irish actor Jack MacGowran.

The film's Inisfree[14] is a hybrid of the Irish past and present, impossible to

---

14. The name of the village is inspired by William Butler Yeats's poem "The Lake Isle of Innisfree," as is the Farrelly song heard in the film. But the film spells the name with only one *n*.

pin down to any one specific time period. The train and automobiles suggest the mid-to-late 1920s, as does the information that peace is a relatively recent development. But villages in rural Ireland retained a similarly old-fashioned ambience well into the 1950s; indeed, it was only during the shooting of *The Quiet Man* that Cong was finally wired for electricity. The film's aura of time-lessness is a key to the strategy behind Ford's creation of a dreamlike atmosphere.

Donald S. Connery writes in *The Irish,* his study of modern Ireland: "The popular image of the natives is a kind of gummy Irish stew of comedians, colleens, characters out of *The Quiet Man,* drunk poets, IRA gunmen, censorious priests, and cantankerous old farmers who sleep with their boots on. It is as if time had stood still in the Ould Sod while other nations had moved on." But it is the very essence of Sean's dream that time has stood still, that the fairy-tale illusion of his childhood innocence can be recaptured. We are kept aware throughout of a conscious re-creative effort of the will (both Sean's and Ford's), and both the comedy and drama stem from the constant intrusion of reality into what Sean views as a dreamworld.

Ford lures us into the dream by lavishing all his gifts of composition on the Irish countryside, making Sean's passion for Mary Kate seem at one with his passion for the land itself. But the director continually undercuts Sean's romantic illusions by humorously showing us the prosaic reality that lies underneath. When he plants roses outside their home, White o' Morning, Mary Kate scolds him for being a "silly" romantic and lectures him on the best kind of manure (horse). When Sean proudly shows off his little thatched cottage to a neighbor, he is given a left-handed compliment: "It looks the way all Irish cottages should, and so seldom *do.* And only an American would think of painting it emerald green!" Sean tells the widow Tillane (Mildred Natwick) that during his hellish life in America, "Inisfree became another word for heaven to me." But thinking of her own lonely life, she snaps, "Inisfree is far from being heaven, Mr. Thornton." Mary Kate herself—that ravishing vision of whom Sean says, "Hey, is that real? She couldn't be"—turns out to be a fiercely independent woman so concerned with her household belongings and dowry that she refuses to sleep with Sean after their marriage until he fights her brother, Red Will, for the "three hundred years of happy dreamin' in those things of mine." But Sean is a "quiet man" because of his secret guilt and the knowledge that "I can't fight unless I'm mad enough to kill."

The Quiet Man contains versions of most, if not all, of the stereotypical Irish figures listed by Connery. The Irish, of course, are right to object if people think such a catalogue of popular images accurately defines their national character. But such arguments tend to ignore Ford's reasons for using "type" characters and "stage Irish" conventions. Even Connery admits, "The trouble is that every time I am solemnly told in Ireland that the stage Irishman does not exist, I meet one the next day." Take Barry Fitzgerald's Flynn, the village matchmaker and wise fool, one of the most memorable characterizations in all of Ford's work. If his performance is "stage Irish," it belongs to a time-honored theatrical tradition, that of Synge, Yeats, O'Casey, and Lady Gregory, of the Abbey Theatre, whose players Ford uses in a number of the secondary roles. Like the other villagers, Flynn is highly conscious of his own role-playing, which he treats with the wit it deserves. Ford's traditional delight in ethnic humor is seldom malicious and almost always an expression of love and fellow feeling, a delight in social difference coupled with an embrace of our common humanity. Ford's fascination with ethnic characteristics is one of his principal ways of analyzing the structure of a given society; if he treats such traits with humor, it is largely because he finds social hierarchies, other than those based on goodness and achievement, to be ridiculous, offensive, and worthy of mocking. Although the people in *The Quiet Man* may appear at first glance to be stereotypes, they either turn out not to be what they seem or, as in the case of Red Will Danaher, shining and memorable examples of human folly and weakness personified.

"I've always said the film was a Western made in Ireland rather than an Irish film," Lord Killanin pointed out, "but it did more for Irish tourism and the country than anything else. It was not very popular here at first and there were strong objections to the line from May Craig: 'Here's a fine stick to beat the lovely lady,' a line I suspect Jack Ford wrote into the script."

That line—actually, she says, "Sir, here's a good stick to beat the lovely lady"—continues to cause negative reverberations in some viewers today, particularly women who find Ford's treatment of courtship and marriage distressingly retro by today's standards and don't know what to make of Mary Kate's fierce insistence on upholding the old custom of the dowry. While it's true that Ford finds great enjoyment in the spectacle of Sean dragging Mary Kate through the fields after she refuses to sleep with him, it's important to understand that this is all a charade concocted by Mary Kate. Like the fight scene that follows, it is not so much a genuine physical battle as a piece of theater performed to make a point before the community. She has finally succeeded in getting her husband to stand up to her brother, make a public demand for her dowry, and fight for his wife's love. Sean's profession of love by going through this charade is what matters to her, even if he has to follow the tradition of acting like a caveman. The ironic amusement with which Sean, Mary Kate, and Ford approach the marital donnybrook is lost on humorless viewers who consider *The Quiet Man* an appalling demonstration of the problem of spousal abuse in rural Ireland.

In her 1978 book *On the Verge of Revolt: Women in American Films of the Fifties,* Brandon French describes *The Quiet Man* as, like many other Ford films, "a marriage of conservative and progressive elements. . . . Mary Kate's battle for status in her marriage—not merely to have but to *be* something of her own—challenges the bases of conventional marriage, just as her behavior in general defies conventional femininity. . . . Her break with tradition is epitomized at the end of the film when Mary Kate tosses away the stick which an old woman gave Sean to keep his wife in line. In doing so, Mary Kate rejects the notion of her husband's mastery, to which the older woman obviously acquiesced. But at the same time she rejects the opportunity to master him. . . . In *The Quiet Man,* Ford anticipated the sixties by eschewing war in favor of love and by showing that liberation must be a goal of *both* sexes if they wish to live together in true harmony."

During the shooting of *The Quiet Man,* Ford fell into a temporary state of abject depression. Worn down by Yates's harassment and suffering from a cold that he claimed exacerbated his old World War II injury, Ford took to his bed at Ashford Castle. Ford had been feuding with Maureen O'Hara and with his son, Pat, whom he had brought to Ireland at Mary's suggestion after filming began. Pat's contentious relationship with his father had previously flared on location for *Wagon Master.* Still, with Barbara Ford working as an assistant editor on *The Quiet Man* back at Republic and Francis Ford, Wingate Smith, and Eddie O'Fearna all accompanying Jack in Ireland, Mary felt that Pat would feel hurt to be left out of a family project. But after so many years of emotional neglect and abuse, nothing could heal the rift between father and son.

Visiting Ford in his hotel room, Wayne found him more disconsolate and vulnerable than he had ever appeared before: "Pappy didn't know whether or not he had a picture, and everything seemed to hang heavy." Inexplicably, it seemed to Ford that his dream project had turned to ashes. No doubt something deeper was troubling him, perhaps having to do with the sense that he had achieved most of his goals as a filmmaker and yet that somehow it still wasn't enough. Wayne volunteered to direct some footage of the horse-race sequence to keep the production moving. Ford accepted the offer but hastened back to work for the following day's shooting.

Ford's exasperation with the philistinism of Herb Yates grew during postproduction. Yates told Ford that his distribution managers did not consider *The Quiet Man* a good box-office title. Something that suggested an action picture would be preferable, said Yates, who wanted to call the film *The Prizefighter and the Colleen.* Other suggestions he passed along to the director included *The Fabulous Yankee, Hearts Across the Sea, Homeward Voyage, Uncharted Voyage, The Man Untamed,* and *The Silent Man.*

The Yates complaint that required the most delicate handling involved the length of the picture. After Ford turned in his 129-minute cut, Yates wrote him on October 16, "My experience has taught me that audiences, no matter how good a picture is, do not want any picture to run over two hours. Exhibitor reaction is the same. In fact, Loews [a leading theater chain] will not play a picture running over two hours, and this is true of other important first-run theaters." This was the same letter in which Yates urged Ford to censor the line about "national freedom." Ford's reaction to the letter can perhaps be gauged by the fact that it contains a large stain from a spilled cup of coffee. Contractually, Argosy was in a bind over the length because Ford was obligated to turn in a film running no longer than 111 minutes. Ford lobbied Yates by sending him a list of successful films exceeding that arbitrary length, including *Gone with the Wind, For Whom the Bell Tolls, How Green Was My Valley,* and *Fort Apache.* But Yates was not persuaded.

Finally Yates held a screening of *The Quiet Man* for a small group of invited guests, with Ford in attendance. The audience was thoroughly enjoying the movie, but just as the big fight scene started, the screen went white and the lights came up in the screening room. Yates asked what was wrong. Ford explained that since he had to cut the film down to under 120 minutes, he figured the easiest way was simply to cut the fight scene. Yates relented, and the film went out to theaters as Ford wanted. It became one of the year's biggest hits and one of the top moneymakers in the history of Republic Pictures. Ford, who was honored with his fourth Academy Award as best director for *The Quiet Man,* became thoroughly disgusted when Yates hypocritically took bows for a picture he had once tried to disown.

Today *The Quiet Man* continues to draw many thousands of tourists each year to Cong and other filming sites in Ireland, which have remained largely unchanged since 1952. It also seems to have a quiet following within Ireland itself. Leonard Maltin, who made the 1992 Republic documentary *The Making of* The Quiet Man, reports that videotapes of Ford's movie are hot sellers in Ireland. But they are often sold under the counter in video stores, as if they were a form of pornography. An Irish enthusiast, Gerry McNee, wrote an entertaining and informative history of the location shooting, *In the Footsteps of* The Quiet Man (1990), and that same year Spanish filmmaker José Luis Guerin made *Innisfree* [sic], a fascinating half-documentary, half-fictional exploration of the relationship between the film and the local people whose heritage Ford idealizes on-screen. *The Quiet Man* has become a St. Patrick's Day staple on American television and is embraced by many Irish-Americans as their fantasy image of their spiritual homeland. That it was for Ford as well, but the current popular viewpoint tends to emphasize the film's humor and sentiment at the expense of the story's underlying darkness, as is also the case with Capra's *It's a Wonderful Life.*

The Quiet Man was one of the last Ford films to be widely praised by American mainstream critics, although the praise upon its opening in September 1952 tended to be superficial and uncomprehending (the *New York Times* called it "a carefree fable of Irish charm and perversity") and there were frequent notes of disapproval (the *New Yorker,* never a bastion of support for Ford in *any* period, lamented that "the master who made *The Informer* appears to have fallen into a vat of treacle"). From this point onward, Ford's reputation tended to be much higher outside his native land and largely in the hands of a younger generation of critics.

Ford's international critical following began developing after the war with Lindsay Anderson and Gavin Lambert of the British film magazine *Sequence.* Anderson's autumn 1950 *Sequence* article "The Director's Cinema?" addressed the question, "Can, in fact, a director like John Ford be considered an artist at all?" Answering himself with qualified affirmatives, Anderson laid out some of the early framework for what would eventually become the French *politique des auteurs,* later known in America as the controversial *auteur* theory. In 1947, the first small book on Ford's work appeared in England, *An Index to the Films of John Ford,* written by William Patrick Wooten and published by the British Film Institute. French critics, notably Jean Mitry, gradually began to celebrate Ford as American films, unseen during World War II, returned to their cinemas. But in some circles of French criticism, there was resistance to Ford's rowdy Americanism and machismo.

Anderson's writings about Ford during the forties and fifties in *Sequence, Sight and Sound,* and the American magazine *Films in Review,* as well as his 1981 book *About John Ford* (begun but not published in the fifties as a BFI monograph), have had a lasting influence on everyone who has written about the director and his work. Yet for Anderson, Ford seemed to have peaked in the mid-forties with *They Were Expendable* and *My Darling Clementine,* and after that it was a rocky and mostly downhill road. Anderson's passionate embrace of Ford's lyrical idealism in those films would be sorely tested by the director's steadily darkening body of work from the early fifties onward. The critic increasingly displayed both outright dismay and an undertone of condescension indicating that he saw Ford less as a conscious artist than as a naïve poet. With his keen radar, Ford seemed to pick up on that slight before almost anyone else. Anderson's famous account of their 1951 meeting in Ireland, titled "The Quiet Man," fittingly was published in the final issue of *Sequence.* Ford mercilessly pulls the leg of his young admirer while honing the "illiterate cowboy" persona he would carry to even greater extremes in later years.

"Christ, I hate pictures," Ford told Anderson.

Anderson asked why, in that case, Ford went on directing them.

"Well, I like *making* them, of course. . . . But it's no use asking me to talk about art."

When Anderson brought up his favorite Ford film, *They Were Expendable,* Ford needled him by saying, "You really think that's a good picture? I just can't believe that film's any good."

Anderson was not the first critic to find Ford "pretty well interview-proof" or to be baffled by Ford's demeanor and his splendidly defiant refusal to play the game of artist. Nor would he be the last, as my own youthful interview with Ford in 1970 would demonstrate.

In Ashford Castle towards the end of our location shooting," recalled Andrew McLaglen, Victor's son and a second assistant director on *The Quiet Man,* "we had a big dinner planned with Ford sitting at the end of the table, and we were all at this long, long table. . . . He got up and made a very soul-searching kind of a speech. He said he was so happy to be here making *this* film, which was his dream film to make, with all the closest friends he had in the business— Duke and Victor and Ward and Maureen. And he said, 'This would be the perfect way for me to end my career.'" Before leaving Ireland, Ford also told reporters that he was thinking of retiring from directing, perhaps to help Lord Killanin build an indigenous Irish film industry.

Ford's sense of psychological release after finishing his work on *The Quiet Man* in Ireland produced the same kind of mingled euphoria and despondency he felt after making battle documentaries. He had made a vow with Jack MacGowran that neither would drink until the picture had wrapped. True to their word, as soon as the last location shot was taken on July 14, Ford and MacGowran went on a monumental bender. When Ford's scheduled flight arrived in New York, a Republic representative was shocked to find that the director was not on it. After investigating the matter, he learned that after boarding the plane, Ford had been so drunk that the pilot had to turn around and take him back to Ireland. Eventually located in Dublin, Ford made it home intact, efficiently completing studio interiors and process shots by August 3.

That October, writing from Hollywood to thank Sheila Killanin for her hospitality, Ford told her that "Galway is in my blood and the only place I have found peace." He admitted, "I was all choked up at leaving our beloved Ireland and was afraid I would burst into tears, which I did on reaching my berth and thereupon fell fast asleep and woke up in New York. . . . It seemed like the finish of an epoch in my somewhat troubled life. Maybe it was a beginning."

CHAPTER TWELVE

"GO SEARCHIN' WAY OUT THERE"

Knowing [Hollywood] *for what it is, a town of success and failure, of aspiration and achievement, of doubt and despondency, I have come to feel that the other* [great meccas of world history] *have been in their times no more and no less than this town of mine, not high monuments of man's accomplishment, but turbulent plazas of man's unceasing search for the something he can never find.*

FORD, "VETERAN PRODUCER MUSES,"
NEW YORK TIMES, 1928

OR A MAN who admitted, "Directing's like dope addiction," voluntary retirement was tempting but hardly a realistic option. By the time *The Quiet Man* was released in September 1952, Ford was already shooting another film, *The Sun Shines Bright. The Quiet Man* would have made a fitting valedictory, but it is fortunate for his admirers that Ford did not stop at that high point of worldly success and classical harmony. The final period of his long career—adventurously varied, riven with self-contradictions—was a time for retrospection and reevaluation. Despite intermittent failures and false starts, it was a period that produced at least four great films. Even the flaws of some of Ford's later work stem from his willingness to confront fresh and difficult subject matter that calls into question his own core beliefs.

The price the aging filmmaker paid for the stubbornly personal nature of his artistic quest was an increasing marginalization, not only within the film industry but also from his audience and eventually from his own country. As early as 1953, Ford was saying, "I don't want to make the kind of junk the screen is offering today, because we made those pictures better thirty-five years ago." Instead, in the words of Andrew Sarris, Ford became the American cinema's "strategist of retreats and last stands." He wore that isolation as a badge of honor. Much, indeed, as Judge William Pitman Priest does in taking his last stand for tolerance, tradition, and the enlightened rule of law in *The Sun Shines Bright.*

. . .

After a hit of the magnitude of *The Quiet Man,* most directors would have capitalized on the opportunity by attempting something on an even grander scale, but Ford used his commercial leverage to push through the kind of small, offbeat film David O. Selznick once scorned as "some uncommercial pet of his that we would be making only because of Ford's enthusiasm." Having been proved so spectacularly wrong on *The Quiet Man,* Herb Yates was in no position to refuse Ford's desire to end his Republic contract with a morality play about an elderly judge (Charles Winninger) in a small Kentucky border town around 1896. Ford described *The Sun Shines Bright* in 1968 as "really my favorite, the only one I like to see over and over again."

An informal remake of his 1934 Will Rogers film *Judge Priest, The Sun Shines Bright* was adapted by Laurence Stallings from three Irvin S. Cobb short stories, "The Sun Shines Bright," "The Mob from Massac," and "The Lord Provides." The remake had been on Ford's agenda ever since Fox cut the anti-lynching scene from the original film. Stepin Fetchit, whose character had been saved from lynching by Rogers, returned to play the same role in *The Sun Shines Bright,* the judge's factotum Jeff Poindexter. Ford's loyalty to the actor was probably one of the reasons he couldn't convince Darryl Zanuck to let him remake *Judge Priest* in 1945, for Zanuck didn't even want Stepin Fetchit to appear in *My Darling Clementine.*

Another key sequence Ford was determined to include in *The Sun Shines Bright* is the prostitute's funeral drawn from Cobb's story "The Lord Provides." Judge Priest shames the town by walking behind the hearse of the woman "taken in sin" (played by Dorothy Jordan, the wife of Merian Cooper). Townsfolk gradually join the procession as the judge leads them to a black church, where he preaches the eulogy. Ford had wanted to borrow the idea for *Clementine.* He asked screenwriter Winston Miller to write a scene showing Tombstone's banker inspiring other men in town to march in the funeral procession of Linda Darnell's Chihuahua. Miller argued that "it just doesn't work because she wasn't a whore with a heart of gold." Ford stubbornly replied, "Well, I don't know what you're writing, but on the screen it's going to look a hell of a lot like a whore's funeral." The director waited until he could do justice to the idea with the magnificent, almost purely visual sequence of the procession in *The Sun Shines Bright.*

Ford was allotted just thirty days of shooting on the low-budget production, which began shooting at Republic on August 18, 1952. Even so, he finished the film two days ahead of schedule. "The main thing we're up against today is economy," he told a visiting reporter from the *New York Times.* "You see how we've got to concentrate and go like hell. Ten years ago, we'd never shoot this fast."

But Ford's style by this point was so finely honed that he managed to turn the project's economy and simplicity into major assets. "Mostly, a true director's work is done before the picture's started," he said. "You get all the elements beforehand. You study the sets for photographic value; you get the best cameraman you can; you get the best location. And I always work closely with the writer in preparing the screen story. We always sit and talk it over and write it together. . . . My own personal view is that a short story, like these, makes the best picture, better than a long novel which you have to cut in length. With the short story, you develop the storyline better."

Stars were among the luxuries *The Sun Shines Bright* could not afford, which was just the way the director preferred it. "My most beautiful pictures are not Westerns," he told Bertrand Tavernier in 1966, "they're little stories without big stars about communities of very simple people." In a triumphant example of casting against type, Ford gave the role of Judge Priest to a sixty-eight-year-old character actor. A lovable, roly-poly former vaudevillian best known as Cap'n Andy in the original 1927 Broadway production of *Show Boat* and the 1929 and 1936 film versions, Charles Winninger is moving and hilarious as the superannuated judge, displaying a sense of irony and intelligence matching Stepin Fetchit's.

Closer to Ford's age and position in life than Sean Thornton in *The Quiet Man,* Winninger's Billy Priest is even more of a Ford surrogate figure. Like both *She Wore a Yellow Ribbon* and *The Quiet Man, The Sun Shines Bright* deals with a man on the verge of retirement who finds that he must stand up to fight one more time. By doing so, he is able to bring at least temporary peace to a world fast spiraling out of anyone's control. Like Captain Brittles and to some extent Thornton, Judge Priest comes to accept his obsolescence in a changing world whose values he can barely recognize.

Priestlike though this judge may be, he is far from saintly. He lives comfortably enough within the town's racist structure, lobbies for votes with patronage and persiflage, and merely chuckles when a friend half-jokingly calls him "a common, unscrupulous politician." A secret morning drinker whose regular excuse is "Jeff, I gotta take my medicine—I gotta get my heart started," he carefully conceals the extent of his tippling from the members of the Ladies' Anti-Liquor League, who control two hundred votes (i.e., their husbands'). In a characteristically double-edged remark, Jeff promises his friend and employer, "With the election comin' on, they'd have to tear my tongue out by the roots 'fore I'd tell it to them." But the human flaws of this outwardly buffoonish jurist serve to make him a more effective moral leader by giving him that highest of Fordian qualities, "heart."

With his sense of justice, humor, and human sympathy, Judge Priest is Ford's 1950s version of Henry Fonda's young Mr. Lincoln, who also stands down a lynch mob (though the men Lincoln saves are not black). A slick modern politician played by Milburn Stone is the antagonist in both films. In *Young Mr. Lincoln,* Stone is Stephen A. Douglas, and in *The Sun Shines Bright,* he is Horace K. Maydew, scathingly described by the judge as "the son of a carpetbagger from Boston." (Several other actors from *Young Mr. Lincoln* also reappear, including Arleen Whelan, Russell Simpson, Robert Homans, Jack Pennick, and, in his last performance, Francis Ford, sublime as the coonskinhatted moonshiner Brother Feeney.) Maydew poses as the representative of progress, building his campaign against the judge on derogation of the old Confederate and Yankee veterans who, for Ford, represent the heart of the town. "No longer," promises Maydew, "can an empty sleeve or a gimpy knee serve as a blanket to smother the progress of the twentieth century." The particular note of venom in this portrait of a heartless politician can be traced to screenwriter Stallings, a Georgian who lost his right kneecap as a marine lieutenant leading his platoon against the Germans at Belleau Wood during World War I; the leg was amputated in 1922.

Judge Priest seemingly throws away any hope of reelection by leading the prostitute's funeral—while watching the procession, Jeff says to himself, "Me 'n' the judge sho' ain't gonna get elected *now*"—and by facing down the lynch mob, the "Tornado Boys." These backwoods tobacco farmers come to town to scapegoat a black youth, U. S. Grant Woodford (Elzie Emanuel), for a sexual assault that turns out to have been committed by a white man (Grant Withers). The sheriff throws away his badge and turns tail, leaving only Judge Priest and the teenager's uncle, Pleasant Woodford (Ernest Whitman), to guard the jail. The courageous moral stands of these old men bring the town to its senses, and the judge is reelected with the votes of the repentant Tornado Boys, who march to the polls en masse. In the film's coda, which Lindsay Anderson compared to the magically harmonious resolutions of Shakespeare's comedies, the whole town of Fairfield passes in review, group by group, as the judge acknowledges the tribute from his front porch. The Tornado Boys march behind a banner reading "He Saved Us from Ourselves." The town's black folk are given the place of honor after the parade has gone by, walking on from the opposite direction to serenade the judge with "My Old Kentucky Home." As the judge disappears into his home, Ford leaves us with the image of Stepin Fetchit on the porch steps finishing Stephen Foster's tune on his harmonica.

Released only a year before the landmark Supreme Court decision *Brown vs. Board of Education,* which began the process of dismantling Jim Crow, *The Sun Shines Bright* may seem hopelessly old-fashioned in its portrayal of a discredited way of life. Reviewing the film for the *New York Times,* Howard H. Thompson expressed outrage that "after parading a handful of Negroes to and fro in quaking servility, the picture foists an inexcusably synthetic sequence about a near-lynching. For this ambivalent piety someone—never mind who—should be deposited head first in a mud-bank."

The film's detractors seem baffled by Ford's ability to empathize with people on both sides of the racial divide and by his willingness to show Christian charity even to racists, to "hate the sin but love the sinner." Frank Nugent observed that Ford "loves the Confederacy with all an Irishman's affection for lost causes." Ford undoubtedly was on more congenial ground depicting the twilight of the Old South, around the time of his own childhood, than he was in attempting to deal with the unsettled New South in *Pinky.* The director's sentimental depiction of the camaraderie of Judge Priest and his old cronies makes *The Sun Shines Bright* resemble a Memorial Day service at the Field Photo Farm. But Ford's romanticizing of the rituals of the Gideon K. Irons Encampment, United Confederate Veterans, does not mean that he whitewashes racial injustice or sentimentalizes the venal and hypocritical community of Fairfield.

Period films are as much about the time in which they are made as about the period they ostensibly portray. In its racial attitudes, Eisenhower's America of 1953 was not radically different from the America of *The Sun Shines Bright.* With the civil rights movement looming just ahead, Ford and Stallings preached an urgent sermon about the injustices of lynching and Jim Crow, about the tragedy of a nation still fighting the Civil War and refusing to live in brotherhood.

The blacks of Fairfield cannot control their own destiny except by influencing a sympathetic white man like Judge Priest, as Jeff Poindexter and "Uncle Pleas" Woodford do with such great subtlety. Ford has been unfairly accused of racial stereotyping for accurately depicting the mores of this segregated society without always spelling out what he is doing verbally. In one particularly brilliant directorial touch, he offers a devastating visual satire of racist mores: when Judge Priest from his bench tells U. S., "Come here, boy," both the teenager *and* his elderly uncle enter the frame from right and left at precisely the same moment. Still, through the deeply moving relationship that develops between Judge Priest and the magisterial Uncle Pleas, Ford offers evidence of the close emotional bond that exists between blacks and whites even in a segregated society.

Seeing Uncle Pleas in the courtroom, the judge asks in wonderment, "Are *you* the boy that brought Bainbridge Corwin's body back from Chickamauga?"

"Why, yessir, judge, you remember," Uncle Pleasant replies. "I brought him all the way back, in these two arms." When the judge murmurs that, yes, he does remember, Uncle Pleas adds mournfully, "Oh, what a time that was."

Ford offers guarded hope for the future by showing how a forward-looking man of integrity like Judge Priest can transcend the narrow limitations of his background. But the film also makes it clear that even the best of the nineteenth-century paternalistic system, which Judge Priest represents, is inadequate to deal with the Darwinian factionalism of twentieth-century America, other than to perform a limited holding action against incipient social breakdown and perhaps to set an example for a better society. Ford saw himself in Judge Priest, a veteran increasingly shunted aside by younger men hoping to take power, but still a leader of his community, an elder statesman who could lead it to a higher moral plane. When Ford stood up against blacklisting at the 1950 meeting of the Screen Directors Guild, his action had the same electrifying theatricality as the judge's appearance on the steps of the county jail. Ford's Hollywood was much like Judge Priest's Fairfield: a town filled with prejudice and hatred, haunted by a past war, torn with factional divisions, hiding guilty secrets: a town in a lynching mood. Like Judge Priest, Ford was no radical, and his hands were not entirely clean, but his imperfection did not prevent him from rising to an important occasion.

Unfortunately, few Americans heard what the film had to say. Not that Republic gave them much chance. "The only trouble was that when I left the studio, old man Yates didn't know what to do with it," Ford recalled. "The picture had comedy, drama, pathos, but he didn't understand it. His kind of picture had to have plenty of sex or violence. This one had neither; it was just a good picture." In what appears to have been a violation of Argosy's contract with Republic—which guaranteed Ford final cut in the United States unless scenes had to be omitted for censorship reasons—Yates cut ten minutes from *The Sun Shines Bright* before its domestic release. "Oh yeah, they ruined that," Ford told me disgustedly. "Well, they didn't ruin it, they *couldn't* ruin it. But they cut a lot out of it. You're working with a stupid lot of people, the executive producers, so what the hell, you've got to expect it. In this case a fella named Herbert Yates. He cut out a lot of the black stuff, the Negro stuff. Not a lot of it, but there were climatic[1] scenes and he cut 'em out and it hurt the picture."

---

1. Ford carefully enunciated the word *climatic,* meaning "atmospheric." But when the interview was included in my previous book on Ford, my editor insisted on rendering the word as "climactic," giving an entirely different meaning.

The full hundred-minute version, which played theatrically overseas, was rediscovered when Republic inadvertently used it as a master for the 1990 videotape release. Contrary to Ford's implication, not all the cut scenes involved the African-American characters. One shows Judge Priest returning the "captured" Yankee flag to the GAR Hall and taking the opportunity to do some political healing with his old adversaries; in a coda to that scene, the judge wearily exits the shadowy hall through an array of Yankee cannons as a melancholy chorus sings the Civil War song "Tenting Tonight on the Old Camp Ground." A briefer scene cut by Republic establishes Jane Darwell's socially prominent matron Amora Ratchitt as a devoted political ally of Judge Priest and the daughter of a Confederate hero.

The missing "climatic" scenes especially mourned by Ford include the original opening with Stepin Fetchit hurrying back from early-morning fishing to awaken Judge Priest, a comical sequence demonstrating the judge's dependence on his black friend and servant; and a transitional moment with the dignified carriage driver Uncle Zach (Clarence Muse) coming to the aid of John Russell's wastrel Ashby Corwin. As Ford indicated, the film was not mortally damaged by these cuts, but the opening sequence was an especially serious loss, since Ford wanted to establish Jeff's importance in the judge's personal life before we enjoy Jeff's tongue-in-cheek playacting in the courtroom.

Hacking up the film may have been Yates's way of exacting revenge against Ford for getting his way on the editing of *The Quiet Man* and making it a success despite the studio chief's lack of faith. Republic dumped *The Sun Shines Bright* on the market in a way that signaled and guaranteed failure. Released in May 1953, when *Variety* judged it "a lightweight comedy-drama, poorly plotted and overlong at 90 minutes," the film did not play the all-important New York market until March 1954, and then only in neighborhood theaters. Thompson of the *Times* claimed he could hardly imagine "a more laborious, pedantic, and saccharine entertainment package."

Now truly a prophet without honor in his own country, Ford could take solace from his growing reputation in England, due in large part to the proselytizing efforts of Lindsay Anderson, whose *Sight and Sound* review savored "the kind of positive poetry, full of faith and love of life, which Ford continues to create, alone. How glad we should be that he decided not to make *The Quiet Man* his last picture."

Before that review appeared, Anderson sent Ford copies of the notices by London's two leading critics. C. A. Lejeune of the *Observer* described the funeral sequence as "a triumph in the deployment of cinema; something we might have praised this side idolatry, if only it had been French." And Dilys

Powell wrote in the *Sunday Times,* "Perhaps life is not like a film by John Ford. Perhaps old gentlemen do not single-handedly deflect a murderous mob, perhaps an election crowd is not so easily shamed by example into Christian charity. But it seems to me that this is acceptable as an artist's abstract of life: not what life is, but what it ought to be. At any rate it sends you away not, as so many films do, nauseated and angry but with the mortal desire for happiness and justice appeased."

The *Sun Shines Bright* was the last Argosy picture. But considering Ford's bitterness toward Yates, it's surprising to discover that the director spent almost two years trying to set up another picture with Republic. Negotiations continued even after he and Cooper initiated a legal claim against the studio charging it with underreporting profits.

The project they tried to sell to Yates was *Four Leaves of a Shamrock,* an anthology of four Irish stories planned by Ford and Michael Killanin as a way of encouraging indigenous feature film production in Ireland. Eventually whittled down to *Three Leaves of a Shamrock,* the picture finally reached the screen in 1957 as *The Rising of the Moon,* although not for Republic but for Warner Bros. The picture was produced by Four Provinces Films, established in 1952 by Killanin and Irish director Brian Desmond Hurst, with Ford serving as a board member. The name of the company implied support for the reunification of Ireland, referring to the four provinces (Connaught, Leinster, Munster, and Ulster) of which the country was composed before the 1921 treaty with the British. *The Rising of the Moon* was not, as Killanin claimed, "the first feature picture made by an Irish company in Ireland"—as early as the 1910s, Sidney Olcott and actor-director J. M. Kerrigan (who later worked with Ford) had each made a series of films in the country—but Four Provinces represented a significant attempt to demonstrate that Ireland's human and natural filmmaking resources could be used for local benefit as well as being exploited by outsiders.

Talking to a reporter from the *Irish Press* during a break from filming a sequence for *The Rising of the Moon* at the Kilkee railroad station, Ford declared, "Ever since I can remember, I've wanted the country my parents came from to have its own film industry. For many years, Lord Killanin and myself have been planning it. Why shouldn't Ireland have its own film industry? We send our priests and doctors all over the world. In the last few decades our actors and writers have also been leaving our shores. Why should they have to go? Why can't we keep them at home? . . . If this film is a success it will usher in an era in which our exiled artists will be glad to come home and work for an Irish film industry."

In addition to the trio of properties adapted by Frank Nugent for *The Rising of the Moon*—Frank O'Connor's story "The Majesty of the Law" and the one-act plays "A Minute's Wait" by Michael J. McHugh and "The Rising of the Moon" by Lady Gregory—James Joyce's melancholy short story about marriage, "The Dead," was also considered (John Huston magnificently filmed Joyce's story as a feature in 1987). Ford's files are full of correspondence with Killanin about their ideas for unmade projects, including film versions of Maurice Walsh's story "Bad Town Dublin," Liam O'Flaherty's *Famine*, Sir Arthur Conan Doyle's medieval adventure novel *The White Company*, and James Stephens's picaresque Irish novel *The Demi-Gods*.

Despite the strong box-office performance of *The Quiet Man*, foreign receipts reported by Republic had not been as substantial as Argosy expected. Ford and Cooper consulted the Donovan law firm, which arranged for Republic's books to be audited by Price, Waterhouse. The result was a legal claim by Argosy that foreign box-office receipts on their films had been improperly credited and accounted by Republic. Nevertheless, negotiations on the Irish project continued until Ford wired Killanin in July 1954: "Having acrimonious legal business complications with Monsieur de la Republic [Yates]. Suing in process. Just won't pay his obligations. . . . So stall, procrastinate and linger." Ford added that it was "[a]bsolutely impossible for me personally to do business" with Yates failing a resolution of the legal claim.

Ford blamed Cooper for what he considered inadequate vigilance toward Republic, and their relationship never recovered; even in his old age, Ford could hardly speak of Cooper without complaining about his financial stewardship of Argosy. The director's wrath even briefly affected his relationship with John Wayne, whom he blamed for helping lure him to Republic. Disgusted with Yates's treatment of Ford, Wayne left Republic after his contract expired with *The Quiet Man*. The final straw came when the studio chief started nickel-and-diming Wayne over his own dream project, *The Alamo*, for which Patrick Ford had written a screenplay in the late 1940s. With producing partner Robert Fellows, Wayne signed a nonexclusive, multipicture deal with Warner Bros.

In the midst of his battles with Republic, Ford considered bringing a new partner into Argosy, producer-director Leo McCarey. Ford greatly admired McCarey's work, particularly his 1944 comedy-drama about Catholic priests, *Going My Way*. McCarey's Rainbow Productions loaned Argosy $360,000 and put up a completion bond of $220,000 to help finance *Fort Apache*. But by the early fifties McCarey's career was in the doldrums; his postwar obsession with communism seemed to have muddled his sense of humor. Nothing came of his talks with Argosy.

By the fall of 1954, perhaps operating under the theory that "the devil you know is better than the devil you don't know," Ford seemed to have reached a rapprochement with Yates. A start date for *Three Leaves of a Shamrock* was set around Ford's birthday the following February. But the deal fell through, and on January 10, he and Cooper adopted a plan of complete liquidation for Argosy while they pursued their claim against Yates.

Though still nominally involved with Argosy, Cooper took a new job in May 1952 as general manager of Cinerama Productions Corporation. He was brought aboard to oversee completion of the company's initial project, *This Is Cinerama*. Begun under the auspices of producers Lowell Thomas and Mike Todd, it was a collection of spectacular scenes designed to show off the Cinerama process, a gargantuan form of triptych cinematography invented by Fred Waller. Although offering stunning vistas projected on a wide, curved screen, enhanced by multitrack stereophonic sound, Cinerama was hampered by optical distortions and visible lines separating its three screen panels. But the public was elated by *This Is Cinerama*. After premiering in New York on September 30, 1952, it went on to become the third-largest-grossing movie ever released, bringing in $20 million despite costing only $512,000 and playing in only seventeen specially equipped theaters. Cooper followed the opening with a premature announcement that the company's next feature would be a Civil War epic directed by Ford. Ford personally benefited from Argosy's stock investment in Cinerama (he held on to some of his own shares until 1961), but he was hesitant to work in the process, which he considered cumbersome and unnatural.

Ford is usually regarded as an aesthetic conservative, but that is somewhat misleading. True, he always preferred black-and-white photography over color and he never stopped grumbling about the difficulty of composing shots in wide screen, but he was not fazed by the coming of sound and he even tried his hand with the transitory gimmick of 3-D. While visiting John Wayne on location in Mexico for John Farrow's 1953 Western *Hondo,* Ford directed two shots of Wayne and a line of cavalrymen for the 3-D movie, produced by Wayne and Fellows for Warner Bros. When I asked what Ford contributed to *Hondo,* Wayne snapped, "Jesus Christ, don't you people ever give me credit for *anything?*"

The wide-screen revolution of the early fifties, initiated by Cinerama and followed by Fox's CinemaScope in 1953, was the most important of the technical solutions the film industry devised to deal with the crisis caused by its phenomenally successful new rival, television. In February 1954, Zanuck tried to sell Ford on the advantages of CinemaScope by arguing that it suited his fondness for staging scenes in long shots. Ford proved Zanuck correct when he first worked in the Scope format on Columbia's picture *The Long Gray Line* (1955), using the screen shape expressively in keeping with the film's metaphor of life as a parade. Ford's later work in wide screen—including *The Searchers* (VistaVision), *Cheyenne Autumn* (Panavision 70), and *7 Women* (Panavision)—uses those formats even more effectively. Eventually Ford did direct part of a Cinerama film, MGM's 1962 epic *How the West Was Won*. His segment, *The Civil War,* worked against the format by emphasizing character over spectacle and using vertical objects such as fences and door frames to disguise the lines between the panels.

One of the major investors in Cinerama was Cooper's friend Cornelius Vanderbilt "Sonny" Whitney. A wealthy horseman, socialite, patron of the arts, venture capitalist, and cousin of David O. Selznick's financial backer John Hay "Jock" Whitney, Sonny Whitney was heir to the Minnesota Mining and Manufacturing Company fortune. When he was unable to buy a controlling interest in Cinerama, he and Cooper left in 1954 to form C. V. Whitney Productions, also called C. V. Whitney Pictures. With grandiose plans of making an "American Series" of films telling the history of the United States, the company bought the rights to two novels for Ford to direct, James Warner Bellah's 1953 collection of Civil War stories *The Valiant Virginians* and Alan LeMay's 1954 Western adventure saga *The Searchers,* both of which originally ran as serials in the *Saturday Evening Post* (the latter under the title of *The Avenging Texans).* "I promise that no C. V. Whitney picture will ever misrepresent or paint a false picture of the U.S. or its people," the financier somewhat ambiguously proclaimed. Ford signed an agreement with Whitney on November 29, 1954, to direct *The Searchers* and two additional films for $175,000 each and 10 percent of the net profits.

Argosy was liquidated in January 1956, and its three-year dispute with Republic finally resulted in a settlement that December. Republic agreed to pay Argosy's stockholders a total of $540,000, of which John and Mary Ford, who owned 24.75 percent of the stock, received $133,650, and Merian and Dorothy Cooper, who owned 11.3 percent, received $61,020 (Dan Ford erroneously reported in *Pappy* that John Ford and Merian Cooper each received $546,000 in the settlement). The Coopers used their proceeds to purchase a home in a military retirement community in Coronado, near San Diego. "Coop," who received a special Academy Award in 1952 "for his many innovations and contributions to the art of motion pictures," remained largely inactive in the industry until his death in 1973 just a few months before his former partner John Ford.

Although Jack Warner had expressed interest in making a multiple-picture deal with Argosy before the company folded, and subsequently offered Ford attractive terms on a nonexclusive long-term deal ($100,000 per picture plus 50 percent of the net and ultimate ownership of the negative), Ford preferred to remain independent for the rest of his career. Working as a freelancer, he was represented at the MCA agency by his former naval colleague Jack Bolton; MCA president Lew Wasserman stepped in to handle some of the personal negotiating with studio chiefs on Ford's behalf.

On projects Ford initiated, his agents and his business manager, Bea Benjamin, made releasing deals with studios through his own privately held company, John Ford Productions, incorporated on August 9, 1956; Benjamin served as secretary-treasurer. Ford owned most of the stock, but some shares were sold to friends, including Michael Killanin, the director's indispensable secretary and script supervisor Meta Sterne, and John Wayne. Wayne was vice president of the company and even attended regular board meetings. From January 1956 onward, Ford rented office space at the Hollywood and Beverly Hills headquarters of Wayne's Batjac company.

Ford's first film after leaving Argosy, *Mogambo,* was an atypical picture for the director, but it helped keep him bankable after the commercial failure of *The Sun Shines Bright.* MGM's elaborately mounted remake of its 1932 Clark Gable romantic melodrama *Red Dust* transplanted the story from a studio facsimile of Indochina to exotic locations in the British East Africa colonies of Tanganyika, Kenya, and Uganda. Elegantly photographed in Technicolor by Robert Surtees and Frederick A. "Freddie" Young, *Mogambo* was one of Ford's biggest hits, grossing $5.2 million. It helped rejuvenate Gable's career and elevate Grace Kelly to stardom, and it showed Hollywood that Ava Gardner was capable of more than looking glamorous. Both Gardner and Kelly received Oscar nominations, Gardner for best actress in her delightfully earthy role as playgirl Eloise Y. Kelly and Grace Kelly in the supporting category as Linda Nordley, a proper Englishwoman who falls equally hard for Gable's white hunter, Vic Marswell.

Ford's Motion Picture Alliance crony John Lee Mahin, who had written *Red Dust* from a play by Wilson Collison, did a slick job of rewriting for producer Sam Zimbalist. Zimbalist remained in Hollywood supervising the film by telegram while Ford was off in Africa from October 1952 through the following January. Ford was feeling his age on the distant and physically trying location. He came down with amoebic dysentery and began experiencing blurriness of vision. Commanding a company of 525 people headquartered in a three-hundred-tent camp in Tanganyika, Ford carried a gun like everyone else because of the Mau Mau rebellion in Kenya, although they were also protected by members of the Lancashire Fusiliers and the Queen's African Rifles.

During the filming, three people were killed when a lorry overturned. One was a twenty-six-year-old British assistant director, John Hancock. Press reports of the accident failed to mention the names of the two Africans who were killed, but the *Los Angeles Times* added, "A dozen more were injured in similar upsets."

"As a rule, the danger was never from animals," Surtees recalled. "It was from automobiles. We ran over a couple of kids."

Anxious to hasten his departure from Africa, Ford worried Zimbalist by making heavy cuts in the screenplay, rewriting exterior scenes to shoot them inside tents in a British studio, and refusing to shoot most of the animal scenes. Second-unit directors James C. Havens and Yakima Canutt filmed grainy animal footage that was awkwardly matched with studio scenes. Ford found the idea of actually killing a gorilla on-camera repugnant, so he "wouldn't shoot the gorilla stuff," said Mahin. "And he wouldn't shoot the stuff in the canoe. I don't know why. The scene in the canoe was when Ava Gardner said that the elephant reminded her of somebody. I didn't mean it as a phallic symbol, but everybody took it as that, because that son-of-a-bitch bull elephant raised his trunk! The ears were flapping! Maybe the guy who shot it thought it was a good idea. It always got a laugh."

Because *Mogambo* has what Mahin called "a much classier atmosphere" than *Red Dust,* and also perhaps because Gable is so much older, the remake lacks some of the raciness of director Victor Fleming's original, best remembered for Jean Harlow's bath in a rain barrel. But *Mogambo* still carries a substantial erotic charge. The sexual tensions in the love triangle are handled with an aplomb that might have seemed surprising from Ford if he hadn't made *The Quiet Man* a year earlier.

Ford convinced MGM to put Grace Kelly on its contract roster. He had spotted her playing an Irish immigrant in a screen test she made for an unmade picture. He was convinced that this Philadelphia Irishwoman with a patrician manner had potential beyond her rather pallid role as Gary Cooper's Quaker wife in the 1952 Western *High Noon.* Kelly's icy facade concealed a passionate sexuality that Ford brought out on-screen; behind the scenes she and Gable carried on an affair that echoed their relationship in the picture, whose title means "passion" in Swahili.

Ford resented the studio's casting of Ava Gardner. He had wanted (who else?) Maureen O'Hara, "and he wasn't shy about letting that be known," Gardner recalled. "He adored Gracie, but he was very cold to me. He called me in to see him before shooting began and he didn't even look at me."

Gardner angered him on the first day of shooting by commenting after a take, "Oh, boy, that was a real fuckup. We goofed everything."

"Oh, you're a director now," Ford replied. "You know so fucking much about directing. You're a lousy actress, but now you're a director. Well, why don't you direct something? You go sit in my chair, and I'll go and play your scene."

Ford "went on ranting like a madman," she recalled, until Gable "put his arm around me, gave me a squeeze, and walked off the set." Furious, Ford suspended shooting. An hour later, he sent Gardner a message politely asking her to return to the set. His manner remained frosty until he admitted a few days later, "You're damn good. Just take it easy." After that, they developed a marvelous rapport as Ford became enamored of her feistiness and boozy, teasing sense of humor. "I never felt looser or more comfortable in a part before or since," she declared in her autobiography. Ford, she thought, could be "the meanest man on earth, thoroughly evil, but by the time the picture ended, I adored him."

Frank Sinatra, whose marriage to Gardner was in the process of unraveling, spent some time on the location. Ford set Sinatra to work cooking spaghetti dinners. Introducing Gardner to the British governor and his wife, Ford said maliciously, "Ava, why don't you tell the governor what you see in this one-hundred-twenty-pound runt you're married to."

"Well," replied Gardner, "there's only ten pounds of Frank but there's a hundred ten pounds of cock!"

Ford blanched and said, "I'll never talk to that girl again." But the British couple found Gardner's remark hilarious.

After Sinatra flew back to Hollywood at his own expense to test for the role of Maggio in *From Here to Eternity*, a crisis occurred when Gardner discovered she was pregnant. She decided to go to London to have an abortion. Ford "tried quite desperately to talk me out of it," she remembered.

"Ava, you are married to a Catholic," he said, "and this is going to hurt Frank tremendously when he finds out about it."

"He isn't going to find out about it, and if he does, it's my decision."

Ford promised to shoot around her to disguise her condition: "I'll arrange the shots. We'll wrap your part up as quickly as we can. Nothing will show. Please go ahead and have the child."

She remained adamant. MGM put out the story that she "was bitten by an inquisitive virus germ and had to be flown back to London to recuperate," as the *Los Angeles Times* reported.

Despite that disappointment, Ford thought Gardner was "a real trouper. She was unhappy over Sinatra, but she worked her ass off just the same. I loved her." Sinatra returned to Africa in time for the company's Christmas celebration. Not realizing what had happened, he "sang Christmas songs," recalled

Gardner, "and the natives, draped in blankets, sang carols in French, and John Ford read 'The Night Before Christmas.'"

Ford's frustrations with the production and his own state of health boiled over when the company relocated to England in February. Shooting interiors with an obvious lack of creative involvement, "Ford did a murderous thing to Clark," Mahin recalled.

After shooting a take, Ford said, "Cut. We'll move over here."

"Jack," said Gable, "Ava and I think we can do this better. Can we have another take?"

"Oh, you can, that's fine, yes, we'll have another take," said Ford. "All right, you ready? Camera. Action."

Gable began, "Look, honey, I think—"

"Cut!" said Ford. "That was great, just great, Clark! Now we'll move over here."

Ford did this to Gable "in front of the crew and everything," said Mahin. "That's a dirty trick. See, when he gets mad he can get vicious. Striking back is vicious."

In the months after his return to Hollywood, Ford's life could have been summed up in Shakespeare's words, "When sorrows come, they come not single spies, / But in battalions!"

The blurred vision he began experiencing in Africa was the result of cataracts. The London doctor who made the diagnosis urged an operation. Fearing that could end his career, Ford temporized about returning home. Mary joined him in England to travel through the Riviera and across Italy before sailing home from Naples on the *Andrea Doria* in early April. Ford's eyes became so sensitive that he had to remain in his cabin, in the dark. During this terrifying period, he wrote Michael Killanin, "I know you will keep it confidential. It is hard for me to say this, but the facts are briefly that I am afraid I am going blind."

Ford stalled the operation until early July. After coming home from Good Samaritan Hospital, he sat in his darkened bedroom well into that fall, unable to read, watch television, or work. He had little else to do but brood over his future, meditate over his past, and seek solace from his religious faith. Although the operation went as well as could have been expected, Ford was left with permanent impairment to his vision in his left eye. According to Olive Carey, "He was told not to take off the bandage and he got fed up with it and took it off too soon. That's why one eye went blind. But he could see more with that one eye than a lot of people could with four."

For the rest of his life, he wore a patch over his blurred left eye, usually under his thick dark glasses. He had to read by holding a book just a few inches from his face. Sometimes he would lift up the patch to read, as a way of avoiding the disorienting effect of looking through only one eye or sometimes because the "good" eye was not working properly. In a sense, however, Ford enjoyed wearing the eye patch, for it gave him a piratical look that enhanced his forbidding image. Once when posing for an advertising portrait, Ford was asked to stop scowling. He refused. "They all think I'm a so-and-so," he explained. "Let's don't disappoint them."

The Searchers, filmed a year after his eye operation, is one of Ford's most spectacularly beautiful pictures, ample proof that his work was not seriously affected by his worsening vision. A lifetime of making pictures honed his visual style to a matter of instinct. There have been other great visual artists who have suffered from cataracts, including Titian, J. M. W. Turner, and Claude Monet; in some ways, distorted vision can cause an artist to create more striking, daringly stylized effects that transcend the constraints of realism. Ford's tendency toward bolder visual brush strokes in his later films and his diminishing interest in minute detail work can be attributed in part to his poor eyesight. But those traits can also be seen as a form of stylistic purification, a function of his tendency in old age to cut through extraneous clutter and focus more intently on the essence of things. It could be argued that by losing ocular clarity and depth perception, Ford was driven more deeply inward, giving his work greater emotional clarity and a sense of perception that was more spiritual than material.

One of his soundmen observed, "The Old Man can't hear, he can't see. All he can do is make good pictures."

Hearing the donnybrook in the village of Iniafree, Francis Ford's Old Dan Tobin leaps from his deathbed in *The Quiet Man,* hobbling down the street as he waves his walking stick, joyously rejuvenated. Alas, life did not imitate art. When Jack came home in the spring of 1953, in the midst of his own health crisis, he found his older brother gravely ill from cancer. Jack helped arrange a throat operation for Frank that June, but his health continued to deteriorate until he died on September 5 at the age of seventy-one.

Frank stirred briefly on his deathbed, recognizing Jack and Wingate Smith. "Frank had an easy passing and all his thoughts were about Ireland," Jack reported to Killanin. "His last hours all he could speak was Irish. The services [on September 8 at St. Ambrose Catholic Church] were in the Irish tradition . . . and he was carried to his grave by his brothers, sons and nephews in uniform. It was quite a galaxy including navy, marines, infantrymen, an air force general and myself."

Taking refuge in form and tradition, Jack gave Frank a grand militaristic funeral when a few simple words over a plain wooden coffin might have been more appropriate. Usually Fordian funerals are poetically appropriate to the emotion inspired by the subject, but here the impersonal panoply seemed to mask Jack's inability to resolve his feelings toward his loved and hated older brother, the man who made him what he was. "We gave him a good sendoff, didn't we?" Ford asked actor Frank Baker after the funeral. An old friend and colleague of both brothers, Baker always felt Jack had behaved badly toward Francis, so he would not give him the solace of an answer. Neither that day nor for years after, when Jack kept asking the same guilty question.

Today, few of the films Francis Ford directed in the silent days still exist in film archives. It is a sad irony that only through his younger brother has "Brother Feeney" achieved a measure of cinematic immortality.

Perhaps the worst calamity that can occur in a John Ford movie, one seen over and over again in the director's work, is the loss of a home. Ford had to face that loss himself when the city of Los Angeles took away his home of thirty years by right of eminent domain. The Hollywood Bowl needed to expand its parking lot, so in 1954 the city gave the Fords sixty days' notice to leave before bulldozing their hillside neighborhood on Odin Street. There was nothing they could do about the march of "progress" but accept a payment of $46,000.

The Fords put down $95,000 for a new home at 125 Copa de Oro Road in Bel Air, a more prestigious location just north of Sunset Boulevard and a block from the UCLA campus. Formerly owned by directors Frank Lloyd and William Wyler, this was a larger and more lavish house, with separate bedroom suites for Jack and Mary and a game room to house his medals, awards, and Western memorabilia. Among his cherished items—he swore they were authentic—were a pair of Buffalo Bill's gloves, a war bonnet from the Battle of the Little Bighorn, and one of Wyatt Earp's rifles. But the house on Copa de Oro never felt as homey as "the Little Grey House on the Hill."

"He shouldn't have ever had to move from there," said Waverly Ramsey, the Fords' cook at Odin Street since 1945. "It was just a lovely place. It hurt him having to move, because he had everything there, the children had grown up there, and it was *home*."

To get over his loss, Ford went on a bender aboard the *Araner*. He almost had lost her, too. On February 6, 1953, while he was in England, the *Araner* was seriously damaged in a severe windstorm at Santa Barbara harbor. The boat came loose from its moorings and became stranded on a sandbar with its bottom and sides damaged. The insurance company paid the damage of $4,098, but an inspection showed dry-rot and a myriad of mechanical and electrical problems. Ford considered selling the *Araner* in 1956, but he stubbornly continued to pour money into the boat, hanging on to his home away from home well after it became financially unwise.

Waverly Ramsey and her husband, Bill, who had joined her in working for the Fords shortly after World War II, continued in their employ at Copa de Oro. "We were like family," said Waverly Ramsey. "Mrs. Ford was a lovely lady—the nicest person I've ever met. When she would buy something for you, it would be the same thing she would get for herself. Mr. Ford was a nice person—he had a heart. He did a lot of things for a lot of people, and you never hear about it, he was that type of a person. He didn't talk too much. Everybody else could do whatever they wanted to do and have the run of the house, but he just liked to be to himself, he was a loner. He liked to read a lot. He maybe read till two or three o'clock in the morning if he wasn't working, and he'd sleep late. We'd take him a thermos of coffee and wake him up."

Bill Ramsey, whose official title was that of Ford's chauffeur, usually traveled with him as well, acting as his manservant. They became "as much friends as a master and servant can be," said Ford's researcher Katherine Cliffton. Once when Ford went to Las Vegas, he asked his business manager, Bea Benjamin, to make hotel reservations for himself and Bill, who was African-American. Waverly Ramsey recalled, "Miss Benjamin was going to send Bill across the tracks. Mr. Ford said, 'Where's Bill?' Mr. Ford could stay in this big place in Las Vegas, but Bill couldn't. And, really, Bill looked as white as a lot of white people. Mr. Ford told them, 'If Bill can't stay here, I'm leaving too. You don't want him, you don't want me.' So that broke that down." Another time, Ford sent Bill to run an errand at the headquarters of the Academy of Motion Picture Arts and Sciences. Bill was made to go in the back entrance, and from that point on, Ford refused to have anything more to do with the Academy, even though he had been one of its founding members.

One of the few positive developments in Ford's personal life during the early fifties was his daughter's second marriage, to the actor and singer Ken Curtis, who had also been married previously. A Colorado native whose father had been a sheriff, Curtis was a big-band singer before becoming a singing cowboy in Hollywood. Barbara met him on a Republic dubbing stage in 1950, when he was doing the song accompaniments for *Wagon Master* as a member of the Sons of the Pioneers, a popular group of cowboy balladeers. They began dating and were married in Las Vegas two years later, on May 31, 1952. Just as she had done when she married Robert Walker, Barbara failed to notify her parents about the ceremony until it was safely over.

But Ken had a far more solid personality than Walker, and their marriage went smoothly for a few years. John Ford was fond of his mellifluous-voiced son-in-law, who was always available for impromptu serenading and other chores, almost like a valet. Sometimes he would even trim Ford's toenails. Ford rewarded Curtis with substantial supporting roles in such films as *Rio Grande, The Quiet Man, The Searchers, The Wings of Eagles, The Last Hurrah,* and *Cheyenne Autumn,* as well as with the lead in a 1956 short film for the navy, *The Growler Story.* Jack and Mary were delighted when Barbara became pregnant in 1958. Hedda Hopper reported that the Curtises were "on the verge of adopting a baby" when they received the news. But Barbara suffered a miscarriage and was never able to have children, much to her parents' chagrin.

Another mainstay of Ford's existence, the Field Photo Farm, fell into jeopardy by the mid-fifties. As the war receded into memory and Ford's men became more engrossed in their families and careers, attendance at the Farm began to wane. It was in danger of going the way of Judge Priest's clubhouse for Confederate veterans in *The Sun Shines Bright,* so empty that a knock on the door makes the judge muse aloud, "All that's left of us is here. Maybe it's a ha'nt . . . a ghost!" The Farm was running in the red, and Ford had to make up the losses out of his own pocket. The board of directors found it increasingly difficult to turn down frequent offers for the real estate. But Ford kept holding out against the inevitable, sentimentally unwilling to surrender the personal Valhalla he had created for his honored dead.

Subsist, subsist!"

The advice of old Martin Maher (Donald Crisp) to his son (Tyrone Power) in *The Long Gray Line* (1955) echoes Ford's directorial credo. Serving for more than fifty years as West Point's athletic trainer, Irish immigrant Martin Maher Jr. is not "a career man," but a functionary who doggedly does his job out of a sense of duty and pride, even though he questions its ultimate purpose. Marty is not even very good at his job, admitting, "It took me thirty or forty years just to get the hang of it, y'know." When he arrives from Ireland, he becomes a waiter but keeps breaking all the dishes; later he becomes swimming coach but doesn't know how to swim. And yet by his example and leadership, Marty inspires generations of young soldiers.

Adapted by screenwriter Edward Hope from *Bringing Up the Brass,* the autobiography of an actual West Point character, *The Long Gray Line* has all the trappings of an Eisenhower-era patriotic spectacle designed to glorify the American military system. President Eisenhower himself is a character in the film, humorously played by Harry Carey Jr. as a young cadet and by Elbert Steele in the framing sequences of Marty reminiscing to Ike at the White House. After approving Columbia's request to portray him, the president was given Hollywood's standard reverential treatment in the contemporary scenes: he is shown with his back to the camera as an almost disembodied presence, the way Jesus Christ was portrayed in Bible movies. But *The Long Gray Line* is one of Ford's most schizoid films, embodying the director's profoundly contradictory attitudes toward the military and the American Dream. "What *is* this place?" Marty asks on arriving at West Point. "Is it maybe a prison or—or is it a looney house? . . . Oh, what a fine ruin it'd make."

One by one the young men of the U.S. Military Academy file up to receive their diplomas, one by one they march off to a succession of wars, and one by one their death notices return to the Point—all seen through the eyes of a man who is there so long that the faces begin to blur, the sons take the places of the fathers, and the past seems to hang over the present like a shroud. The childless Marty Maher becomes paterfamilias to the West Point community, the academy's Mr. Chips. But that position carries its own crushing burden, for only Marty and his wife, Mary (Maureen O'Hara), have been around the Point long enough to feel the full extent of the waste. After learning of the death of one of his surrogate sons in World War I, Marty says, "The finest young men in the world—we bring 'em here, train 'em, teach 'em—duty, honor, and country— then send them out to be killed. I'll have no more to do with it."

But all he can do is stand by impotently and watch the endless parade of death. "Everything that I treasure in my heart, living or dead, is at West Point," he tells the president. "I wouldn't know where else to go." In old age, Marty is reduced to a grim reverie, letting his mind wander away from the Irish songs being played by the cadet marching band at his retirement ceremony to fantasize the return of Mary, his father, and others of his beloved dead. The director's Irish Catholic mysticism enables him to find a transcendent sense of meaning in the life of Marty Maher, who in most ways seems a failure. Marty is sustained by his faith in his adopted country and in the sacrificial value of the profession of arms, however absurd that faith may seem in the face of bitter reality.

The Long Gray Line suffers from the overly broad comedy of its first half, which offers too stark a contrast with the nightmarish darkness that follows. Tyrone Power, who was not only a partner in Ford's Irish filmmaking venture but also lived across the street from the director on Copa de Oro Road, gives a buffoonish and corny performance as the mustachioed and heavily brogued Marty Maher, so encrusted with stereotypical Irishness that it's hard to see the character through all the shtick. O'Hara's deftly stylized performance, on the other hand, offers a witty interplay between ethnic role-playing and genuine emotion, conveyed with great economy of gesture. Ford's view of the immigrant experience is extremely ambivalent: Marty transforms himself from "another mick waiter" into an American icon, but at the price of submerging his cherished Irish independence. Still, his temperamental inability to fit into a military mold and his lovable incompetence are stubborn signs of rebellion, and Ford may have exaggerated Marty's Irish mannerisms to make a point about his anarchic unwillingness to assimilate fully into American life.

The Long Gray Line was a box-office success when it opened in February 1955, grossing $5.6 million on a negative cost of $1.748 million, and its darker implications went largely unremarked at the time. Some reviewers poked fun at Ford's ethnic intransigence, seeing it as a sign of sentimental backwardness. The *New Yorker* observed that "there are many occasions when the institution on the Hudson seems to be a colonial outpost of the Irish Republic. . . . There is seldom even a hint that West Point training is supposed to provide something more than an emotional jag."

As a companion piece, Ford made a ten-minute film in CinemaScope for Columbia and the U.S. Treasury Department entitled *The Red, White and Blue Line.* Along with several minutes of scenes from *The Long Gray Line,* the short shows Power, O'Hara, Crisp, Betsy Palmer, and William Leslie gathering around the Maher dinner table to talk about U.S. savings bonds, and Columbia employees waiting to purchase bonds in what the narrator (Ward Bond) calls a "red, white and blue line." During the scene with his cast members, Ford tilts the camera above the set to let two lighting technicians join the discussion. Crisp, still in character as the lovably tyrannical Irish patriarch modeled on Ford's own father, makes a delayed entrance ambling in from the kitchen with a plate of Irish stew.

Among the brightest elements in *The Long Gray Line* is the performance of Betsy Palmer. The twenty-six-year-old stage and television actress made her film debut under Ford's direction. Palmer gives an uncommonly vivacious performance as Kitty Carter, a forthright modern woman who marries a West Point cadet (Leslie), gives birth to another (Robert Francis),[2] and becomes a warm and loving part of the Mahers' extended family. Palmer and Ford worked so well together in the spring of 1954 that he cast her later that year in his ill-fated film version of *Mister Roberts.* "From the moment we met I could tell that he liked me very much," she recalled.

> There was a nice warmth and ease. He has a good approach to women. He sort of treats you like a fella. Sometimes I'd be stand-

---

2. Francis died with two other people on July 31, 1955, in the crash of a small plane taking off from a parking lot in Burbank. The twenty-five-year-old actor, who also appeared in the 1954 film of *The Caine Mutiny,* was en route to a promotional appearance for *The Long Gray Line.*

ing watching a scene and he'd come stand next to me and drape his arm over my shoulder as if I were one of the gang.

I think he respected me tremendously for what I brought in, I did my homework, so he had stuff to work with. I know Mr. Ford, which is what I always called him, always had *his* homework done, and yet he worked very spontaneously. He was always deeply engrossed on the set, very introspective. He created as he went along, really in the moment. He put in my playing the piano in *The Long Gray Line.* He said, "I heard her messing around on the piano. I want her to play." I never was consciously aware of him giving me directions so much as just encouraging me to go in different directions and let me be the actress I was. I have always found that directors who have been actors, maybe not even for a long time, usually understand the actor's predicaments and problems. They've been through it, they know what it's about, so they're more open and understanding.

Mr. Ford would put a handkerchief in his mouth—it was always a nice clean handkerchief—and he would talk around it instead of taking it out of his mouth. It was his way of meditating. He would walk around pulling on it, *talking,* and you just hoped you grasped what it was he was saying, because it was quite muffled. But that was all right—what he wanted read through. You'd pick up from him with your sensory system.

I wasn't afraid of him. I think that's what he liked about me, that I was strong. See, he likes women sort of on the boyish side. When I did *Mister Roberts* [as the navy nurse Lieutenant Ann Girard], I remember him directing me to get more boyish all the time, and at one point I said, "Mr. Ford, I'm gonna come across like a lesbian." He said, "Palmer, will you just get your ass over there and do it the way I say." He just asks you to play it the way he would play it. That brings another color—you can do it as you think as a woman would, and then he'd bring in that little masculine side that makes it tomboyish. There are some of us women who are that way—we can climb ladders and do it comfortably. Hepburn is one, and Maureen is, in a wonderful Irish way.

He adored Maureen. They worked so well together. In *The Quiet Man,* running across the moors, hair blowing, she really was very strong. Maureen had a wonderful soft quality and was very soothing with that lovely Irish lilt, but she needed some fire set under her at times. They said when he was doing *The Quiet Man,* in order to get any fire going with Maureen he had to make her angry. He would refer to her "fat ass" and get her kinda steaming. Then they'd shoot and she'd have the energy. I saw him tease her that way. He would say, "Listen, Maureen, get your fat Irish ass over here." The fire is there, but it was banked down, and he knew how to unlock it.

Ford was especially cross with O'Hara during the making of *The Long Gray Line* because of a romantic involvement she was having with another man. O'Hara blew up over Ford's constant badgering and declared she would never work with him again. They did make another film together, *The Wings of Eagles,* and in later years O'Hara dutifully appeared at tributes to Ford, who honored her with a cameo appearance on the 1957 NBC-TV program *This Is Your Life: Maureen O'Hara.* But their relationship was never again as close or intense as it had been on *The Quiet Man.* When hoping to cast her in his 1957 film *The Rising of the Moon,* Ford told Michael Killanin, "She's a greedy bitch, and I wonder if she'd accept our terms. Of course her name on an Irish film has value." Further dropping his guard in a 1966 conversation in France with Bertrand Tavernier, Ford spoke of O'Hara with shocking vehemence, sounding like a spurned lover: "L'une des actrices que je déteste le plus est Maureen O'Hara. Tout le monde a cru que j'étais son amant. En fait, je la haïssais et elle me haïssait, mais elle convenait très bien aux rôles." ("Maureen O'Hara is one of the actresses I most detest. Everybody believed that I was her lover. In fact, I hated her and she hated me, but she suited her roles very well.")

When O'Hara was asked in a 1999 interview if she worked so well with Ford because they were temperamentally similar, she responded with a touch of asperity, "Frankly, I'm a bloody good actress and he let me use the talent I was born with. I was never happy with the things Hollywood made me do. I felt there were chains around me. But the first time I worked with Ford, the chains were gone. I could do any damn thing I wanted to and it was all right. He gave me freedom. Some of the directors used to direct every little movement of your hand! It's like being in a prison! Ford put you in a situation and let you fight your way out of it. . . . Yes, he was tough, very tough. You could get mad at him off the set, but in the time between 'Roll it' and 'Cut' he was a pleasure to work with."

On *The Long Gray Line,* Ford openly transferred his affections from O'Hara to the tall, statuesque blonde Betsy Palmer. Dobe Carey observed that Ford "developed a huge crush" on Palmer when they made their two films together. "He liked her. He *really* liked her."

When I asked Palmer about that, she replied, "I was pretty naïve at that time in my life, but I think the message might have been coming through. I just said, 'No, no, no, no.' I thought of him as sort of a father figure. He was a little scary. I was a little spooked sometimes because he looked as though he could be a very tough fella, and I just didn't want to get involved. I was in love with a doctor named Vincent Merendino. I met him just before the filming. And Mr. Ford respected that I was attached to the doctor. I said I was going to marry him. Mr. Ford said, 'We'll marry you up here at the Point. I'm going to give you away.' I wouldn't let that happen, but I was married when I was doing the movie.

"Mr. Ford was not a handsome man. In fact, if you saw him out on the street and didn't know who he was, you'd just walk by him and not pay too much attention. I think that in his heart and his soul he felt he was handsome, but he looked in the mirror, as we all do. I'm sure he had the *soul* of a lover. He always loved to have me come to his office and have lunch [during the making of *The Long Gray Line*]. We'd sit and chat, we talked about intelligent things, it wasn't just show business. And we'd work on the script a little bit, talk about scenes. But when he'd get into a political vein, I would shy away, because I felt very uneducated politically. Sometimes other people would come in too. Maureen would sometimes have lunch with us. Ty [Power] would too. So it wasn't always just me.

"Mr. Ford was a very romantic man in a strange way. Maybe the word 'sentimental' is better. Because he had a gruffness externally, but his sensitivity showed through with his work. He was not a gallant, and yet he was a very respectful man, always kind to me."

Mister Roberts (1955), a project that started so promisingly for Ford and his old friend Henry Fonda, turned into an outrageous debacle, the kind that could have ended the career of a lesser director.

The long-running play by Joshua Logan and Thomas Heggen was adapted from Heggen's seriocomic 1946 novel about a U.S. Navy cargo ship during the waning days of World War II in the Pacific. Fonda spent almost four years onstage playing the ship's beloved executive officer, Lieutenant (jg) Doug Roberts, who longs for a taste of actual combat while serving dutifully on the USS *Reluctant* as it makes its regular run "from Tedium to Apathy and back again—with an occasional side trip to Monotony." Directed by Logan and produced by Leland Hayward, the play became a huge popular favorite because of its lifelike portrayal of the frustrations and dreams of the average seaman. Fonda's performance was one of the great triumphs of his career.

In 1953, Warner Bros. announced that Logan would direct the film version. But Hayward asked him to step aside in favor of Ford, arguing, "Ford is money in the bank. He guarantees the success of the picture." Ford signed an agreement in March 1954 to direct *Mister Roberts* for $175,000, with no profit participation. Unhappy about being shunted aside, Logan later cast aspersions on Ford, including the false claim that Ford never bothered to see the play. Fonda told Lindsay Anderson that Ford came to see the play four or five times, although on repeat visits he spent most of his time backstage.

Logan further claimed that when Fonda asked Ford why he did not use his reserved seats, Ford replied, "Why should I look at that homosexual play?"

"That anecdote had traveled quickly through all the cast, and for a while John Ford was the most unpopular man at New York's Alvin Theatre," Logan wrote after Ford's death. "I still don't know what he meant by that remark, as the whole emotion of the play is of men yearning for women." Ford might have been reacting to a line Fonda spoke in the play about the resourcefulness of Ensign Pulver: "Eighteen months at sea without liberty, where'd he get the clap?" Fonda's autobiography notes that while that line was usually cut for censorship reasons, it was reinserted whenever Ford or another of the star's close friends came to see the play. But Logan's report that Ford called *Mister Roberts* "a homosexual play," like his claim that Ford never saw the play, may be apocryphal, an attempt by an embittered man to undermine Ford's reputation.

Perhaps the major reason Hayward hired Ford was that it "virtually ensured that the Navy would agree to cooperate, given the director's work during the war and his making of *They Were Expendable*," wrote navy film historian Lawrence Suid. The navy initially resisted official cooperation with *Mister Roberts,* largely because the captain (played on-screen by James Cagney) was such a petty and choleric tyrant. Donald Baruch, director of the Defense Department's Motion Picture Production Office, thought the captain was "far from being the type of man the Navy should want to admit to." Baruch's assistant, Major Clair Towne, told Columbia that the story had "other objectionable characteristics, of course, not the least of which is the basic character of Mister Roberts himself." That rather myopic comment presumably was a reference to Roberts's insubordinate attitude toward his captain.

Ford used his pull with the navy's Office of Information and with Admiral Robert B. Carney, chief of naval operations, promising to sanitize some of the raunchier aspects of the play. "Of course, we had to wash out the vulgar language, but that doesn't detract from the comedy, in my opinion," Ford told the *New York Times* before shooting began. Commander Merle MacBain, a navy information officer who served as one of the film's technical advisers, reported in July 1954, "We finally got the project cleared all the way up to the White House." Flattering Ike in *The Long Gray Line* was paying dividends.

No doubt it was partly to placate his branch of the service that Ford encouraged Cagney to turn the captain into more of a buffoon than a villain, resulting in one of the rare bad performances in the actor's great career. Logan wondered, "[W]hat has Ford made Cagney do, play the captain like an old New England bumbler, without any hatred, without darkness, without threat? He's all Down East accent, and comic at that. Without a villain there's no threat—without threat there's no story."

The navy supplied ships and personnel and allowed the company to use the Naval Air Station at Midway, where Ford had filmed *The Battle of Midway* twelve years earlier. Ford took members of his cast and crew on a tour of the islands that included the powerhouse from which he and Jack MacKenzie Jr. had filmed the 1942 battle. Jack Lemmon, Ford's Ensign Pulver, was amazed at how "you can see nothing but holes in that tower from the bullets, the machine guns firing at them."

Hard as it is to believe now, Warners and Hayward had doubts about Fonda playing Roberts on-screen. They worried that his long absence from Hollywood might have lessened his drawing power and that the forty-nine-year-old actor might seem too old to play the twenty-six-year-old Roberts. Logan, who had become estranged from Fonda, approached Marlon Brando, whose casting was announced by Warner Bros. in January 1954. But when Hayward asked Ford in February if he wanted Brando or William Holden, Ford said, "Bullshit! That's Fonda's part."

Fonda played Roberts's quiet decency to perfection. But the film's freshest element was Lemmon's casting as Frank Thurlowe Pulver, the conniving, lubricious goldbrick who serves as the ship's "laundry and morale" officer. The part brought Lemmon an Oscar, his first, for best supporting actor. He had come to Ford's attention in a most peculiar way.

Following Lemmon's film debut opposite Judy Holliday in George Cukor's 1954 Columbia film *It Should Happen to You,* Columbia's head of talent in Hollywood, Max Arnow, decided to give him a screen test for the role of Marty Maher in *The Long Gray Line.* For the elaborately produced reel of film, directed by Richard Quine, the boyish-looking actor was made up as an old man. "Christ, I was so Irish I couldn't understand myself!" Lemmon recalled.

> Ford would not look at the test. He told [Columbia president] Harry Cohn that he wanted Ty Power, he didn't want an unknown, and I was too damn young anyhow, makeup or not, to be playing a seventy-something-year-old man. Although Ford would not look at the test, Maurice Max, who was an assistant editor on the lot, ran the dailies for everybody. One day, just for the hell of it, at the end of Ford's dailies he put on my scene doing the part that Ford had just been seeing Power do.

The lights came on and Ford said, "Who the hell was that?" Max could hear him through the intercom. Jerry Wald was there, the second in command to Cohn. Jerry explained that I was a kid who had done a lead with Judy Holliday and so forth. Ford stood up and said, "Well, I'll tell you something, he's a lousy old man but he'd be a damn good Pulver." Max ran and told me that, and I said, "Well, Jesus, I hope something happens out of it."

Weeks later, I was on the lot one day and dropped in on Ford's set just to see what was going on. This guy with a cap, a patch over his eye, an old coat, pair of sneakers, baggy gray old pants, chewin' on a handkerchief, came up to me and said, "Are you that kid Lemmon who did the picture with Judy?" I said yeah. I thought he was a grip who had been on the film or something. He said, "I understand you want to play Pulver." I said, "Jesus, yes, I want to play Pulver, of course." He said, "Then spit in your hand." I said, "What?" He said, "It's an Irish custom. Spit in your hand." So he spit on his hand and he stuck it out and I pretended to spit in my hand. He shook my hand, said, "I'm Ford and you're Pulver," and walked away.

As soon as location filming began at Midway on September 1, Lemmon realized that Ford was

a tricky son of a bitch. Cagney warned me. When we got to Midway Island to start shooting, we sat around the first night and read through the script twice. Ford talked about the script and the film. I don't remember a damn thing he said, I was too excited. Jimmy and I were listed to do the first scene for the next morning, and that night before we all went to bed, Jimmy said to me, "Don't be surprised if you don't get called in the morning." I said, "Well, we *are* going to be called. They're gonna pick us up." Nobody picked us up, no nothin'. This went on every single night and morning for two weeks, we never worked.

We were having fun. Jimmy was teaching me a few tap dance steps and telling me marvelous stories of the old days. At the end of about the first week, Jimmy started thinking. He said, "I think we should start rehearsing everything except what's ever on the call sheet. Because the son of a bitch is never gonna have us do the scene that's on the call sheet. We ought to especially work on that long scene where we first meet." We started rehearsing it every day, breaking each other up. We really got it down cold.

Then suddenly our names were *not* on the call sheet, and Cagney said to me, "Watch out."

The next day at mid-morning, a guy came running up and said, "Mr. Cagney, Mr. Lemmon, Pappy wants you right away. They're shootin' you guys." We said, "What scene?" He said, "I don't know." We jump in the putt-putt, we go to the ship, it was just offshore. Ford's got the camera set up for the first scene where we meet, which was not on the call sheet, naturally. He wanted to shoot the whole scene in one [shot] and then maybe a little bit of coverage. We said, "Fine." He said, "Let's rehearse." We did. He looked kind of surprised. He said, "All right, let's try one. Just do what you're doing." We did one, he liked it, and we did it again and printed it. I think he just popped in a little bit of coverage, and *boom!* we were through early. I remember as we were leaving, Ford looked over at me and smiled. Then he gave Cagney a look like, "You son of a bitch, you *knew.* You knew I pulled something."

You'd think he'd just say, "Why don't you guys get to know each other and rehearse the scenes? Be ready, because I'm not sure when I'll be doing them." Of course, other directors have done this sort of thing. I personally don't like it. I resent it as an actor, because in a peculiar way it's saying, "You're better if I surprise you and you don't know what you're doing than if I leave you alone and let you act." I knew the whole goddam script anyhow by the end of the second week.

After his long stage run in the title role, Fonda had a fiercely protective attitude toward the play. He resented the tinkering Ford had done with screenwriter and playwright John Patrick, the Pulitzer Prize–winning author of *The Teahouse of the August Moon,* and with Frank Nugent, whose shooting script incorporated some material Logan had jettisoned from the novel. Concerned that Ford had lost much of the play's poignancy by overemphasizing its comedic aspects, Fonda resented the way he changed the timing of lines and added bits of comic business. The coarseness in the portrayals of most of the enlisted men and the cartoonishness of Cagney's captain badly clash with Fonda's eloquent underplaying of Roberts. Fonda was also upset about Ford's cavalier attitude toward casting secondary roles with members of his Stock Company who didn't match the stage characters.

"It has to do with the fact that Ford, for all his greatness, is an Irish egomaniac, as anyone who knows him will say," Fonda said later. "And when you got right down to it, he didn't know what to do with *Mister Roberts* that wasn't repeating what was successful in New York. He was trying to do things to the play that would be his in the film. Those of us who had been close to the play, Leland, Josh, and I, and others, felt Ford was tampering with something that was pretty good to begin with, and we weren't happy about it."

Ford in fact was doing what he always did with a script, transmuting the material into his own style of storytelling. In the view of Dobe Carey, who plays Stefanowski in the film, Fonda "should have known, having made his greatest films with Ford, that Ford does a lot of improvising. Hank should have gotten some—I wouldn't say hack—but a guy who would just shoot the script, not a creative man like Jack Ford." But it's also true that Ford's touch this time seemed clumsy, disrupting the play's careful balance of comedy and drama. And he was running up against an unpleasant fact of life about Holly-wood in the fifties. Decision-making power was shifting toward stars and pro-ducers. It was becoming hard for even a tyrannical director like Ford to push them around, as he had been accustomed to for decades.

Lemmon found himself in the middle of this awkward situation.

"Because Ford liked me and he liked what I was doing, he made up a whole bunch of junk for when I bring the nurses aboard—leaning on a hot gun, drinking dirty dishwater for soup and telling them to put more salt in it, all kinds of crap, and I hated it. But I did it. [The dishwater gag was repeated from *They Were Expendable,* with the same actor, Harry Tenbrook, playing 'Cookie.'] Ford was happy because I was doing things on the spur of the mo-ment, just making 'em up when he'd throw an idea. Hank was furious. He said, 'It wasn't in the play. It never would have been.' And if it wasn't in the play, it wasn't in the Bible as far as Hank was concerned."

Fonda told Lemmon, "Well, there's nothing much you can do about it, be-cause he's the director. But if you can screw it up, do it."

Political tensions also contributed to the schism between Fonda and Ford. "The whole [Ford] gang had gone way to the right," Peter Fonda recalled, "and my father kept his head on his shoulders. He thought the House Un-American Activities Committee was terribly un-American. He was incensed by it; he walked across the street to shake hands with someone who was black-listed. He and Ford and Wayne and Bond had open disagreements, and then Bond suggested he was a pinko, and that was that."

By the end of the first day's shooting on Midway, the issue of Ford's infi-delity to the play provoked a confrontation with Henry Fonda. It started as a peace parley called by Hayward. The star was summoned to Ford's room in the Midway BOQ (Bachelor Officers' Quarters). Fonda found Ford sitting in a wicker chair holding a drink. The director listened as Fonda began expressing his concerns in blunt language. The dialogue reportedly went something like this:

> *Ford:* Well, Hank, what do you think of the day's shooting?
> *Fonda:* I think it was shit.
> *Ford:* You traitorous bastard!

Recounting the incident in 1976, Fonda told me how shocked he was when Ford suddenly jumped up and slugged him in the face, knocking him sprawling and upending a water pitcher. But Fonda said he was more embarrassed than hurt. He left the room rather than getting into a serious brawl with the older man he called "Pappy."

The account Lemmon gave me in 1998 was somewhat different.

"I saw the whole thing. I woke up because I could hear 'em. I came down the hall and I looked in through the door, it was only partially closed, and they were screaming at each other. The argument basically was about the fact that they weren't sticking to the script. Ford took a swing at Fonda and missed. Fonda just held him with his hand on his chest, and Ford kept swinging like in a cartoon. He couldn't reach him, couldn't hit him. Then finally Hank just gave him a shove, pushed him back on the bed, and started for the door. I went paddlin' in my bare feet down the hall as fast as I could, not making any noise, and got back in bed."

Ford came to Fonda's room about a half hour later and apologized in tears. Their relationship was never the same again. Every time they finished a take, Ford would ask Fonda whether it met his approval, a ritual that made the actor even more uncomfortable. "Shoot it any way you like," Fonda would snap back. "I don't know what was in his mind," Fonda recalled, "but I do know he was stricken by what he had done, by hitting me."

Ford abandoned his longtime disciplinary habits and started boozing it up while working. He went on a serious binge after the company flew to Hawaii on September 24. He was staying on the *Araner* during a hiatus of a few days while waiting for the ship playing the *Reluctant* to arrive from Midway.

"Ford was mad at Hank and mad at Leland Hayward, and so he got drunk," Dobe Carey observed. One day, Ford caused an astonishing spectacle at the pool of the Niamalu Hotel, where the company was housed at Waikiki Beach. Betsy Palmer was sunbathing beside the pool with Dobe, Barbara Ford, and Barbara's husband, Ken Curtis. Dobe recalled:

> Betsy's lying in her swimming suit and she's got her straps pulled
> down so she won't have marks. And Kenny goes, "Oh, God."

Here comes the Old Man, and he's drunk. He's holding a great big beach towel wrapped around him. He goes, "Oh, *there* you are! There's old Dobe. Are you getting tan? Everybody getting tan? *Betsy's* getting tan?" She goes, "*Hi,* Pappy." And he goes, "Let's see." He pulls her top out, looks right at her tits, and says, "You're getting tan."

Everybody's watching now. He goes for the diving board. Kenny goes, "Oh, Christ!" Ford goes up, up, up, to the high board. He's got the cigar, he's got the patch, the glasses, and everything. And he drops the towel. He's bare-assed. In front of everybody, stark naked. And off he goes. Kenny and I jumped in and pulled him out. We were laughing; we almost drowned. Not too long after that, a doctor came and gave him a shot and they hauled him off.

"It was as bad as it could be," Fonda said, "and he finally had to be dried out in a hospital."

Ford went into the hospital on the evening of October 1. Shooting resumed six days later. Somehow Ford managed to complete the location work while openly guzzling one iced beer after another. "He had a case of beer," Lemmon remembered, "and then he started trying to direct the scene where all the canoes come out from the island and everything, and he was *pissed*. I went up onto the bridge to get a better look at what was going on. He was up there watching 'em all get ready for the shot, saying, 'Howdya like that? Issen that wonnerful?' He was definitely loaded and slurring his words. Apparently he went to Leland Hayward afterwards and said, 'I did something I can't do. I drank. And if you want me off the picture, I can understand it.' Hayward said, 'Nonsense.'"

But privately Hayward was becoming fed up with the situation. "Nobody knew who was in charge of what," he said. "Ford was pissed all day. Ward Bond, for Christ's sake, was directing the picture. At least he kept the cameras turning when Ford came to and until he passed out again."

The company returned to Hollywood on October 10, with about half of the picture completed. Ford resumed work at the studio two days later, rehearsing and shooting for four days before experiencing nausea and severe abdominal pains during a weekend at home. On Monday morning, October 18, Carey found Ford sprawled in his director's chair on a Warners soundstage, pants loosened and stomach grotesquely swollen.

"Will you look at this!" Ford exclaimed. "I can't even button my goddamned pants, for Chrissakes!"

Carey accompanied him to St. Vincent's Hospital for emergency surgery to remove his gallbladder. Ford's medical condition may have been exacerbated by his drinking binge. He seemed relieved to have found a way to get off the picture.

The following day, veteran director Mervyn LeRoy was borrowed from his Warners production *Strange Lady in Town* and assigned to complete *Mister Roberts.* LeRoy spent a few hours running the footage Ford had shot, then tried to direct the remaining scenes and retakes in what he considered an approximation of Ford's style. But LeRoy's work shows a deadly lack of imagination. Throwing out Nugent's script, he did little more than line up the actors in static groupings on cramped sets in front of phony backdrops and let them overact scenes from the play. In contrast, Ford's footage, even if it misses some of the inherent values of the material, is always visually alive. "Boy, did he have an eye!" said Lemmon. "And yet, I don't remember a single moment when I felt that any of his directions were for the camera, as opposed to a legitimate move for the actor—*ever.* But every frame was a beautiful picture. Probably as much or more than any director who ever lived, he combined the ability to stage beautifully with the eye of a painter."

One scene Lemmon was glad to reshoot, however, was Pulver's reading of the letter from Roberts to the crew before they realize that Roberts has been killed in action (some of Ford's wide shots were kept in the film). "I did not like the scene the first time I did it, with Ford," Lemmon said. "It was too indulgent, too big, too sentimental—you could see the acting much too much. I did it again with Mervyn and he let me be a lot simpler. That's the one we used. I went to see Pappy when he was back home, sick in bed after the operation. And his damn spies were everywhere. He said, 'I understand that you did the letter-reading scene again.' I said, 'Yeah, yeah, we had to do it again.' He said, 'And I understand you liked it better.' I said, 'Well, not me, no, who told you, wha wha . . .' He said, 'Well, that's good.' Ah, he was a character!"

Hayward eventually brought in a third director, Joshua Logan, to doctor the film. When Logan saw the rough cut, he "wanted to get a gun and shoot [Hayward] in the gut, and then drop the body on John Ford's front lawn. But that wouldn't take care of Ford himself, and what about Frank Nugent, who deserved to be skinned alive at least?" Working with LeRoy and with Ford's editor, Jack Murray, Logan filmed inserts and short connecting scenes, dubbed in new lines and reshuffled others, and reshot two important scenes—the ending with Pulver confronting the captain after throwing his palm tree overboard and the slapstick scene of Pulver filling a corridor of the ship with soapsuds.

Reshooting Ford's scene of the nurses' visit to the *Reluctant* was among Logan's top priorities, for there was only one nurse in the stage version and Ford "ruined [it] for me by having six girls come on and destroy the sexual intimacy of the scene." When Betsy Palmer returned from the location to her home in New York, she had "heard that Mervyn LeRoy was going to reshoot everything with the girls back in Hollywood. And I, with my big mouth, said, 'Well, *I'm* not going to go back there. Get another woman. Because I like what I did with Mr. Ford, and I don't want to be redirected.' I thought, 'How could it be any greater than it was when we were right there in Hawaii, on the water, on a real boat?'" LeRoy had not reshot that scene, and Jack Warner finally vetoed Logan's demand to do so. The nurses' visit to the boat was among the footage showing off the Midway location to best advantage, and Warner felt that redoing it on a Hollywood soundstage would make *Mister Roberts* "look like a smaller picture."

Ford and LeRoy shared directing credit, with Nugent and Logan receiving joint screenplay credit. Surprisingly, *Mister Roberts* received good reviews and became an enduring popular success after its release on July 30, 1955. Perhaps the underlying strength of the material was enough to carry the film despite its myriad deficiencies.

"I despised that film," Fonda said. "You can't tell an audience who saw only the movie, 'You should've caught the play.'"

Ford's scandalous behavior on *Mister Roberts* raised legitimate concerns about his physical and psychological fitness to continue directing. Despite his eminence in the industry, he needed to show that he could still be trusted to show up, stay sober, and work fast. But more than that, he needed to remind people what he could do when operating at the peak of his artistic powers.

Texas, 1836. A nine-year-old white girl named Cynthia Ann Parker was kidnapped by Comanches, Kiowas, and Caddoes at Parker's Fort on the Navasota River. She was renamed Naduah, and upon her maturation became the wife of Peta Nocona, war chief of the Noconi band. Recaptured in 1860, Naduah tried to return to her tribe but was held under guard and starved herself to death. Her son, Quanah Parker, became the last free war chief of the Comanches before surrendering his tribe in 1875.

This haunting and richly symbolic story from American frontier history inspired Alan LeMay, a novelist and sometime screenwriter, to write *The Searchers*. LeMay's novel about two Texans on an epic search for a kidnapped girl served as the basis for the 1956 Western that marked Ford's spectacular return to feature filmmaking. Frank Nugent's screenplay vastly improved on LeMay's gripping but often lurid and superficial novel, adding layers of psychological depth, humor, and social context.

"We are busy working on the script of *The Searchers*," Ford wrote Michael Killanin in March 1955. "It is a tough, arduous job as I want it to be good. I've been longing to do a Western for quite some time. It's good for my health, spirit, and morale."

The film centers on the most complex and fascinating character in Ford's entire body of work, Ethan Edwards (John Wayne). A former Confederate soldier, mercenary for Emperor Maximilian in Mexico, and freewheeling outlaw, Ethan enigmatically returns to his brother's family three years after the end of the Civil War. Ethan is secretly in love with his brother's wife, Martha (Dorothy Jordan), as we are told nonverbally by their gestures and by the couple's theme music, "Lorena," from a haunting Civil War ballad by Reverend H. D. L. Webster about an unconsummated adulterous romance ("We loved each other then, Lorena, / More than we ever dared to tell . . ."). Shortly after Ethan's return, Martha is raped and murdered, and her husband and son killed, by a band of Comanches led by Chief Scar (Henry Brandon). Scar carries off the two survivors of the massacre, nine-year-old Debbie Edwards (Lana Wood) and her womanly sister, Lucy (Pippa Scott), who herself is soon raped and killed. Ethan spends five years searching for Debbie with his young partner, Martin Pauley (Jeffrey Hunter), an adopted member of the Edwards family who (unlike the character in the novel) is part Indian.

Rather than launching C. V. Whitney Pictures with *The Valiant Virginians,* a Civil War spectacle that would have been more expensive and a less certain box-office draw, Sonny Whitney put Laurence Stallings's October 1954 screenplay on hold for the time being (the project was under development at Columbia). Whitney decided it would be wiser to start with a Western he could advertise as "The Biggest, Roughest, Toughest and Most Beautiful Picture Ever Made of America!" As Whitney's vice president in charge of production, Merian Cooper served as executive producer of *The Searchers.* Cooper and Ford entered into serious negotiations with Harry Cohn at Columbia on a coproduction and releasing deal, but despite Cohn's eagerness to make the film, they couldn't reach agreement on some key financing terms, so they went with Warner Bros. in April 1955.

The Searchers was stunningly photographed by Winton C. Hoch in Technicolor and VistaVision, a wide-screen process using a dual 35mm negative, resulting in an unusually sharp image and greater depth of field. Only two theaters in the country at the time were able to exhibit the double-frame image, so for other venues *The Searchers* was printed in conventional 35mm, still retaining much of its image quality.

In order to capture the story's epic sweep and changing landscape, *The Searchers* was filmed in two separate shoots during the winter and summer of 1955, ranging from Canada to Ford's favorite terrain, the desert southwest of Monument Valley. Pat Ford, who served as associate producer, organized the first stage of shooting, which began in March in the snows of Gunnison, Colorado. Although officially considered "second-unit" footage, these scenes involving Ethan, Martin, and actors playing cavalrymen and Comanches were directed by John Ford and photographed by Hoch. Stuntmen were used as doubles for the two stars: Terry Wilson doubled Wayne and Chuck Hayward filled in for Hunter. Without John Ford physically present but working from his instructions, the unit then filmed the buffalo-hunting scenes at Elk Island National Park in Edmonton, Alberta. Stunt coordinator Cliff Lyons, who also plays the cavalry officer Colonel Greenhill, served without credit as a second-unit director along with Pat Ford; close shots of the two stars were later filmed against process screens. Some buffalo were actually shot on camera, although the killing was performed by game wardens as part of the regular culling of the herd.

Principal photography, which took forty-nine shooting days and finished three days ahead of schedule, began in Monument Valley on June 16, 1955, with the opening sequence of Ethan arriving at the isolated Edwards home. Shooting continued on the Navajo reservation through July 13. A second unit directed by Pat and his uncle Ed O'Fearna picked up some shots, photographed by Field Photo veteran Alfred L. Gilks. Their footage included part of the battle at the river, one of the film's few sloppily directed and utterly implausible sequences. It was not only the challenge of shooting a complex outdoor story in a limited time period that made John Ford resort to others' help in rounding out *The Searchers*. He recognized that he had to conserve his diminishing physical strength, a working vulnerability that first surfaced on location for *The Quiet Man* and would manifest itself again, more seriously, during the filming of *Cheyenne Autumn*.

Perhaps the most memorable incident during the *Searchers* location shoot, at least the one most fondly recalled by members of the Ford Stock Company, involved the director's favorite whipping boy, Ward Bond, who plays the minister and Texas Ranger, Captain Reverend Samuel Johnson Clayton. During the day-for-night filming of Wayne's powerful speech recounting his discovery and burial of Lucy's violated body, Bond was fumbling around the set, half awake, in the process of morning ablutions.

"When Ford liked the take, he went, 'Right!'" recalled Dobe Carey. "We did the scene when Duke turns to me and says, 'What do you want me to do, draw you a picture?' and all that. So Ford went 'Right!'—and I heard, '*Mm-mm-mm.*' Ford turned around: 'What's the matter? What's wrong?' The camera operator said, 'The camera stopped.' '*The camera stopped?*' 'Yessir.' 'What's wrong with it?' 'Nothing.' Ford apologized to Duke and me and said, 'Let's do it just the same way—if you guys can do that the same way, you'll make me happy. I don't think you can, but'—a lot of crap. And I ran in, we did it again, and it was perfect. He went 'Right!' and that was it. Yeah, Ward had pulled the plug on the camera. Ward arrived on the set, and right where the camera was plugged in was where his electric razor fit. They didn't dare tell Ford. They figured Ford would kill him."

Luckily for all concerned, Wayne's performance was "even better the second time," Carey said. But Ford eventually *did* learn what happened. Winton Hoch told me that several years later, following Bond's death, he ran into Ford at a Hollywood event and told him about the electric razor. Ford's face turned white. He was uncharacteristically speechless, because he didn't have his favorite "horse's ass" to kick around anymore.

A happier occasion for the director was the Fourth of July party he threw on the reservation. The celebration included a barbecue, fireworks, songs, and competitions staged by the tribesmen, including horse races and footraces. The Navajos presented Ford with a deer hide inscribed to their old friend "Natani Nez" with words adapted from their ceremonial Yeibichai, or Night Chant:

IN YOUR TRAVELS MAY THERE BE
BEAUTY BEHIND YOU,
BEAUTY on BOTH SIDES of YOU,
and BEAUTY AHEAD of YOU.

The prevailing spirit of mutual generosity was somewhat marred by Ford's childish behavior in one of the competitions, "the Old Man's Race." Dobe Carey remembered, "Ford took his shoes off and got ready. He had a cigar in his mouth. They went, 'Get on your mark, get set,' and *boom!* There he goes. The others started on 'Go,' and of course, he won that race. But he didn't have to cheat. He could run like a son of a bitch. He was an amazing old bastard." Henry Brandon, the film's Indian chief, was also watching but had a different take on the race, insisting, "They *let* him win."

The previous day had seen the filming of the now-famous final shot of the door closing on Ethan as he returns to the wilderness. Echoing the opening shot of Martha opening a door to discover him riding in from the desert, this final visual bookend helps situate the story within Ford's characteristically ambivalent perspective toward the dichotomies of home and wandering. The framing device was not indicated in the script Ford took to location. It's fortunate for film history that Ford did not ask his cinematographer's opinion of the final shot. Winton Hoch told me that when Ford described the idea, all he could think was, "How corny can you get?"

Wayne had a bad hangover when the ending was filmed in the late afternoon of July 3. His condition may help account for Ethan's somewhat dazed and uncertain movements, so perfectly appropriate to the character's state of mind and body at the end of what Ford called the "tragedy of a loner." But Wayne was sharp enough to ad lib one of the most resonant gestures in the entire body of Ford's work, a gesture movingly encapsulating whole lifetimes of shared tradition. The actor recalled in Bogdanovich's *Directed by John Ford* that when he grabbed his right arm with his left as he stands in the doorway, he did so in spontaneous tribute to his idol, Harry Carey. One of the actors who has just passed Wayne to enter the house is Olive Carey. Wayne said he assumed the familiar Harry Carey stance—which can be seen in the ending sequence of Ford's debut feature with Carey, *Straight Shooting*—because "his widow was on the other side of that door, and he was the man Pappy said taught him his trade."

"It surprised me, yeah," Ollie Carey said with a smile more than thirty years later, "Harry always did it. It was an old gesture of his. Ford would let Harry do anything he wanted to do and then he'd maybe twist it a bit, but they worked like a team, they were wonderful together." She found the ending of *The Searchers* "a fabulous shot. It's a wonderful finish when he walks off."

The rest of the interiors for *The Searchers* were shot at the RKO–Pathé Studio in Culver City, Ford's base when he made *Fort Apache* and other films in the late forties. A few remaining *Searchers* exteriors were picked up in the Los Angeles area, including the climactic scene of Wayne lifting Natalie Wood into his arms and saying, "Let's go home, Debbie." That was shot in Bronson Canyon, part of Hollywood's Griffith Park, at midday on August 12, the penultimate day of shooting. After the company broke for lunch, they returned to the studio's stage 15 and started the afternoon's work with another of the film's classic scenes, one that required Wayne to undergo a complete emotional reversal from his morning's work.

Through a dreamlike haze of artificial snow falling against a blue-sky backdrop, Ethan and Martin are seen pausing on horseback as they temporarily turn back from their search. This is Ethan at his most implacable, declaring, "Injun'll chase a thing till he thinks he's chased it enough. Then he quits. Same way when he runs. Seems like he never learns there's such a thing as a critter'll just keep comin' on. So we'll find 'em in the end, I promise you. We'll find 'em—just as sure as the turnin' o' the earth."

The *Searchers* received high praise from some American reviewers. The *Hollywood Reporter* proclaimed it "undoubtedly one of the greatest Westerns ever made." *Look* magazine ran a lavish spread of photographs from *The Searchers,* including frame enlargements of some of the most memorable shots, and called the film "a Homeric Odyssey . . . a Western in the grand manner, the most roisterous since *Shane.*" But some reviewers seemed uneasy about the character of Ethan. *Variety's Holl.* complained that Ethan's motivations are "unclear. . . . Wayne is a bitter, taciturn individual throughout and the reasons for his attitude are left to the imagination of the viewer." None of the reviewers seemed to understand the film's central themes, since they hardly noticed Ethan's pathological racism. So deeply ingrained were such attitudes in the national culture of 1956 that few even realized something is terribly wrong with this most untraditional Hollywood Western "hero."

One 1956 observer who did recognize Ethan's racism was Lindsay Anderson, who reviewed *The Searchers* for the British film magazine *Sight and Sound.* For the last few years, this leading champion of John Ford had become increasingly troubled by the darkening of the director's vision. Revering the humane, optimistic qualities of such films as *They Were Expendable* and *My Darling Clementine,* Anderson did not know what to make of the fact that Ethan is "an unmistakable neurotic, devoured by an irrational hatred of Indians." Anderson pointed out that Ethan's search for his niece "seems, indeed, to be inspired less by love or honor than by the obsessive desire to do her to death, as a contaminated creature. Now what is Ford, of all directors, to do with a hero like this?"

Ford had portrayed racists before—notably Colonel Thursday in *Fort Apache,* who looks Cochise in the eyes while calling the legendary Indian chief a "recalcitrant swine"—but the virulent depths of Ethan's racism did represent something of a departure for the director. Wayne's performance is founded, as perhaps most great performances should be, on a deep emotional identification with the character. "I loved him and I loved playing him," the actor unequivocally declared in a 1975 interview. Wayne even named his youngest son, John Ethan, after the character.

When film historian Brian Huberman innocently praised Wayne's performance by telling him in 1974, "That was a great part you had as the villain," Wayne's face took on Ethan's fierceness. "He was no villain," Wayne said through clenched teeth. "He was a man living in his times. The Indians fucked his wife [*sic*]. What would you have done?" Wayne's remark about his "wife" is a revealing Freudian slip, although it's not clear whether he was thinking of Martha or Debbie, or both of them, as his "wife." This psychological twist offers an insight into what Wayne may have been feeling when he played Ethan, who struggles against his adulterous feelings for his brother's wife and is consumed with rage over the abduction and sexual possession of his niece by his Indian alter ego, Scar (if one entertains the idea that Debbie could be the *daughter* of Ethan and Martha, the incestuous overtones multiply). Wayne's identification with Ethan's horror of miscegenatory rape was so strong that it led him to distort the narrative, elevating forbidden feelings to what he regarded as defensible facts.

The making of *The Searchers* was unique in his experience with Ford, Carey wrote in his book about the director. Ford "was much more serious, and that was the tone that pervaded the cast and crew. The first scene I was in with Duke was the one where I discover that my family's prize bull has been slaughtered. When I looked up at him in rehearsal, it was into the meanest, coldest eyes I had ever seen. I don't know how he molded that character. . . . He didn't kid around on *The Searchers* like he had done on other shows. Ethan was always in his eyes."

"I've always thought [Wayne is] underrated as an actor," James Stewart told me in 1975. "I think *The Searchers* is one of the most marvelous performances of all time."

Ethan is a spiritual descendant of James Fenimore Cooper's Leatherstocking, the white frontiersman who carves a path through the wilderness for other pioneers but because of his violence is not fit to live among "civilized" people. D. H. Lawrence described Leatherstocking as "a man who turns his back on white society. A man who keeps his moral integrity hard and intact. An isolate, almost selfless, stoic, enduring man, who lives by death, by killing, but who is pure white. This is the very intrinsic-most American. He is at the core of all the other flux and fluff. And when *this* man breaks from his static isolation, and makes a new move, then look out, something will be happening."

Now what is Ford, of all directors, to do with a hero like Ethan?

The *Searchers* is often read in black-and-white terms by critics and scholars with a vested interest in proving or disproving the notion that Ethan's racism is shared by the director. But that either-or kind of argument is beside the point in dealing with such a complex work of art. A film of warring dualities, *The Searchers* gets to the heart of many of the unresolved contradictions that make the Western genre such a rich field for exploring American history and mythology.

The film's special quality owes something to Ford's powerful emotional imperative, in the wake of *Mister Roberts,* to restore his shaky hold on his artistic powers and shore up his standing in the industry. But Ford also seemed to be driven by psychological demons similar to those that motivate Ethan. The director's decision to tackle this difficult subject—dealing with racial and sexual issues most people in 1956 would have considered "unspeakable"—was a shrewd career move, showing a willingness to make a more "modern"-seeming Western for an audience that wanted greater psychological realism from the genre, such as in Anthony Mann's popular fifties Westerns with James Stewart as a neurotic, tormented frontiersman. But making *The Searchers* required real courage on Ford's part. Doing justice to the subject matter demanded an artistic commitment to imagine what could bring a man to the point of murdering his own flesh and blood in the name of racial purity.

Such an experience must have been unnerving. Indeed, Ford's behavior during the making of *The Searchers* showed signs of an inner disturbance unusually intense even by his own volatile standards. Ford had a major advantage over Wayne in being able to regard Ethan from a critical distance. He didn't have to be Ethan each night at the dinner table, and he could assign nobler aspects of himself to other characters, especially Martin Pauley. Nevertheless, even with all the help he had from Alan LeMay, Frank Nugent, and John Wayne in creating Ethan Edwards, Ford could not have conjured up the dark and crazy reality of the character if he had not recognized Ethan somewhere within himself. Before he started filming, Ford said *The Searchers* would be "a kind of psychological epic."

Using Ethan as his surrogate on "man's unceasing search for the something he can never find," Ford sends him "searchin' way out there" for the truth of the director's own divided personality. Like Ford, Ethan can be hard or tender, disciplined or wildly out of control, a vagabond or a family man, protective or destructive of his family, driven by love or hate. What Sam Clayton says of him is true of Ford as well: "You fit a lot of descriptions." With its complex portraits of Ethan, Martin, Debbie, and others torn between two cultures, *The Searchers* also allowed Ford to explore his ambivalent feelings about race and sexuality and about his own ethnic identity as a second-generation Irish-American. Taking him well beyond his usual formulas into uncharted personal and artistic territory, *The Searchers* examines the mass of tensions and contradictions that had been boiling up in Ford's life and work since the end of World War II. Ford's darkening vision of American history required such an unflinching look at some hard truths about what Leslie Fiedler called "[t]he heart of the Western . . . the encounter with the Indian, that utter stranger for whom our New World is an Old Home . . . leading either to a metamorphosis of the WASP into something neither White nor Red . . . or else to the annihilation of the Indian." The concentration on racial themes in Ford's postwar films leads him to an increasing preoccupation with miscegenation, extending beyond *The Searchers* into such films as *Sergeant Rutledge, Two Rode Together, Donovan's Reef,* and *7 Women.*

Although Indians continued to be crudely stereotyped in many fifties Westerns, a number of Hollywood films in that period dealt with racial issues in a complex and sensitive manner. A cycle of liberal pro-Indian films between 1950 and 1956 included *Broken Arrow, Devil's Doorway, Jim Thorpe—All American, Apache, White Feather,* and *The Last Hunt.* Prejudice against other ethnic groups was explored in such films as *Japanese War Bride, Bad Day at Black Rock, Love Is a Many Splendored Thing,* and *Giant,* but few films in that period dealt with the incendiary issue of prejudice against African-Americans. During the time *The Searchers* was written and produced, civil rights was in the process of replacing McCarthyism as the major domestic battleground. Encouraged by the Supreme Court's 1954 *Brown vs. Board of Education* decision outlawing segregation in public schools, the civil rights movement began in Montgomery, Alabama, on December 1, 1955, when Rosa Parks refused to yield her bus seat to a white man, triggering the citywide bus boycott led by Dr. Martin Luther King Jr. That history-changing event was still in progress when *The Searchers* was released.

"The emotional impact of *The Searchers* can hardly come from the issue of the kinship status and marriageability of an Indian in white society in 1956," claims film scholar Brian Henderson. "It becomes explicable only if we substitute black for red and read a film about red–white relations in 1868–1873 as a film about black–white relations in 1956." Henderson's argument denies the central importance of Native Americans in the history of the United States, implying that their near-genocide allows viewers of other races to ignore Indians' actual existence in the past and the present while seeing them only as signifiers for another race with more pressing demands. Ford did not confuse the struggles of African-Americans with those of Native Americans; both races have a long history in his films. But there is no doubt that by dealing so directly with the miscegenatory fears of white Americans in *The Searchers,* Ford was tapping into more generalized contemporary racial anxieties. It is a tribute to the film's richness that it can support a variety of broader allegorical meanings. Richard Slotkin points out in *Gunfighter Nation* that besides dealing with issues of American racial identity, *The Searchers* "is also a 'Cold War' Western which addresses issues of war and peace from the perspective of a microcosmic community forced literally to choose between being 'Red' and being dead. *The Searchers* brings these two concerns into the framework of a single, coherent, highly compressed fable and thus makes a crucial connection between the ideological basis of domestic racism and the ideological premises of the new, 'counterinsurgency' phase of the Cold War."

The Searchers subversively turns the concept of Western heroism inside out, showing the lone gunman who acts in the name of nascent civilization as a warped, destructive force. In fact, it is misleading even to consider Ethan the film's "hero." Ford told Jean Mitry before making *The Searchers,* "I should like to do a tragedy, the most serious in the world, that turned into the ridiculous." *The Searchers* mocks the very idea of solitary heroism by having the goals of the quest—the finding of Debbie and the killing of Scar—fulfilled by other people while Ethan's efforts are nihilistically concentrated on trying to kill his niece. It is the Shakespearean fool Ol' Mose Harper (Hank Worden) who repeatedly locates Debbie for Ethan, and it is the part-Indian Martin Pauley who kills Scar after spending five years preventing Ethan from killing Debbie. Ethan has to be content with scalping Scar's corpse, but the act proves cathartic, allowing him to redeem himself by sparing Debbie and returning her home. But his search would have ended much differently if it had not been for the influence of Martin and Mose.

In a further absurdist touch, the epic quest proves maddeningly circular, ending not far from where it began, thanks to Ethan's perpetual inability to catch up with Scar's nomadic band of "Nawyecka" Comanche (a name Ethan defines as "sorta like roundabout—man says he's goin' one place, means to go t'other"). Thanks to Hoch's magnificent VistaVision photography, Monument Valley is an almost surreally tactile physical presence in *The Searchers.* As Jean-Louis Leutrat and Suzanne Liandrat-Guigues observe in their essay "John Ford and Monument Valley," the architectural metaphor embodied by the vertical rock formations of Monument Valley "suggests depth and burial while at the same time commemorating disappearance and absence. . . . From *My Darling Clementine* onwards, Ford's perception of Monument Valley is as a place of funerals." Monument Valley never seemed so labyrinthine, so abstract a backdrop for moral drama, so nightmarishly difficult to escape as it appears in *The Searchers.* The pervasive sense of geographical unreality signaled by the opening title ("Texas 1868") is similar to the absurdist effect produced by cartoonists who have used Monument Valley as a surreal backdrop.

Ethan and Scar are locked in an insane vendetta like the Roadrunner and Wile E. Coyote, and everywhere they look is the same unchanging, primitive landscape, silently witnessing their futile cycle of revenge. As Michael Wilmington and I wrote in our 1971 essay on *The Searchers* in *Sight and Sound,* "As the search progresses, it becomes increasingly difficult to appreciate the difference between Ethan's heroism and the villainy of Scar, his Indian nemesis. Ethan hates Indians—is he envious of their freedom? Certainly Scar and Ethan are the only characters who fully understand each other, because their motives are so similar. . . . When the massacre occurs (the very day after Ethan's arrival), it has the disturbing feeling of an acting-out of his suppressed desires— destruction of the family and sexual violation of Martha. . . . Scar is not so much a character as a crazy mirror of Ethan's desires."

Initially Martin is mocked by Ethan as "Blankethead," but it is his divided racial identity ("I'm eighth Cherokee and the rest is Welsh and English—least that's what they tell me") that enables him to understand both white and Indian cultures and to transcend the hatred that drives them apart. Martin gains in stature as the search progresses, becoming a truly modern man, whereas Ethan is diminished, trapped in the destructive patterns of the past. The man with mixed blood, not the white supremacist, is the "intrinsic-most American." Martin is a classic outsider determined to prove he belongs in the dominant society, and as such he is akin to Ford's other noble outlaws. Perhaps he is so fully accepted at the end of *The Searchers* because he proved his worth by playing such a truly heroic role in the search, just as minority group members in America have long tried to win acceptance by serving in the military. Martin was Ford's middle name, and it is no coincidence that he cast an Irish-American actor as Martin Pauley; Jeffrey Hunter would go on to play key roles in two subsequent Ford films about ethnic assimilation, *The Last Hurrah* and *Sergeant Rutledge.*

In Nugent's script for *The Searchers,* when Captain Reverend Clayton swears in Martin as a member of the Texas Rangers, he does so without interruption. But Ford breaks up the scene with remarks from other characters and has Clayton momentarily forget the words of the oath. When Clayton asks "Where was I?" Ford has little Debbie remind him: "Faithfully fulfill." This is her subtle modification of the oath's more noncommittal requirement to "faithfully discharge your duties," a wording that means "to relieve of a burden." Rather than simply *discharging* his temporary duties as Clayton intends—a requirement that will not prevent Clayton from allowing Debbie to be sacrificed, which he admits is "a bitter thing to say"—Martin will, in the end, faithfully *fulfill* his oath by ensuring that Debbie is returned alive.

By preserving the last of his adopted family and reuniting with Laurie Jorgensen (Vera Miles),[3] his white fiancée, Martin symbolically ensures that America's future will be more ethnically blended; but even this hopeful note is qualified. No one in the film objects to the union of Martin and Laurie, but Martin naturally is disturbed by the virginal Laurie's shocking racist outburst (in her wedding dress) about Debbie: "Fetch *what* home? The leavin's of Co-

---

3. Third runner-up in the 1948 Miss America pageant as Miss Kansas, Miles made an uncredited appearance as a dancer in Ford's 1950 *When Willie Comes Marching Home.* The director rediscovered the beautiful and intense twenty-five-year-old actress while watching NBC TV's anthology series *Ford Theater* on June 2, 1955, two weeks before *The Searchers* began shooting. Miles was signed to a six-year contract by Alfred Hitchcock in October 1955 but worked for Ford that fall on his TV program *Rookie of the Year* and played the female lead in his 1962 feature *The Man Who Shot Liberty Valance.*

manche bucks, sold time and again to the highest bidder, with savage brats of her own. . . . Do you know what Ethan'll do if he has a chance? He'll put a bullet in her brain. I tell you, Martha would want him to." Given that mind-set in the Jorgensen family, it's hard to see how the lives of Martin or Debbie will be happy after their return to white society. Ethan's craziness is shared by the society he represents so well that in the end he must be expelled from it, like a bad dream.

Ford presents the Indian warrior in *The Searchers* strictly from the white point of view, as a terrifying and forbidding figure, yet not without recogniz-able human motivations of his own. *Look* magazine called Scar "the screen's most wicked, unregenerate Indian in a long time." Indeed, Ethan's doppel-gänger is the white man's nightmare of the Indian personified, a rampaging, out-of-control representation of the id. "Ford wanted me to be a ghost," re-called Henry Brandon. "He didn't want the still man to take pictures of me— he didn't want them in the lobby." Yet Scar's rationale for killing white settlers resembles Ethan's rationale for killing Indians: Scar tells him, "Two sons killed by white men. For each son I take many scalps." Even this degree of human-ization was too much for one reviewer, Courtland Phipps of *Films in Review*, who criticized the film for "a sentimental attitude toward the Indian which is the equivalent of an indictment of the white man."

By not actually showing Scar's gruesome depradations, Ford forces the viewer to imagine these horrors. This deeply troubling strategy, which forces the viewer to experience the same feelings of loss and anger that fuel Ethan's racial hatred, runs the risk of making the film itself seem racist, as in the scene of Ethan confronting the rescued white women who have been driven mad by their life with the Indians. "It's hard to believe they're white," says an army doctor. Ethan replies, "They ain't white—anymore. They're Comanch'." The powerful close-up showing Ethan's revulsion, emphasized by Ford with a rare tracking shot, could make it seem that we are regarding these women from Ethan's subjective point of view. But Ford offers an alternative by subsequently revealing Debbie as a strong, sane, and beautiful "woman grown" showing no apparent ill effects of her years with the Indians.

Another controversial sequence, Martin inadvertently buying an Indian wife he calls Look (Beulah Archuletta), begins with jovial humor and wistful Max Steiner music, but ends brutally with Martin literally kicking Look out of bed on their wedding night. Clearly intended as amusing, this sexist "gag" is soon followed by Look's death along with other Indians at the hands of Custer's Seventh Cavalry. This abrupt reversal of tone, a particularly wrench-ing sign of the film's schizoid emotional attitudes toward race and sexuality, recalls the inconsistent way Ford treats the part-Indian prostitute Chihuahua in

My Darling Clementine: mocking her sexuality before sentimentalizing her in death. Despite his honorary membership in the Navajo tribe, Ford's attitude toward Indians remained that of an intermittently sympathetic outside observer. He rarely even tried to "get inside" his Native American characters in the way he does with whites.

While part of Ford thought it appropriate to use Look's humiliation as comic relief, his better part was responsible for the horrific imagery of her burned-out village. This elegiac sequence evokes the 1869 massacre of the Cheyenne at the Washita River by the Seventh Cavalry, as well as photographic images of the 1890 Wounded Knee massacre. Ford uses Custer's marching tune, "Garry Owen," to accompany shots of the cavalry ignominiously herding along the captured survivors. The director's jaundiced attitude toward the cavalry in *The Searchers* goes beyond his critique in *Fort Apache* and anticipates his final Western, the pro-Indian *Cheyenne Autumn;* in fact, Ford first commissioned a screen treatment of that subject from his son, Pat, and Dudley Nichols in 1957, soon after making *The Searchers.*

The most glaring flaw in *The Searchers* is Debbie's improbable change of heart when Martin, after jumping from the rock formation the Navajos call John Ford Point, comes to rescue her in Scar's tepee. Almost instantly reversing her earlier determination to stay with "my people," as she calls the Comanches, she screams when awakened but then gives him a tight hug, exclaiming ecstatically, "Oh, yes, Marty! Oh, yes, Marty." Her behavior disturbingly resembles that of a rape victim who consents to the act out of a sense of self-preservation accompanied with a panicky loss of self-image. That this second violent abduction of Debbie's young life is carried out by a member of her own family makes it all the more troubling. Ford's cultural background made him unable to imagine any other solution than Debbie's unmotivated reversion to her original ethnic identity, even if he leaves some doubt about her future.

By contrast, Ethan's change of heart when he rescues Debbie feels entirely credible. The war between his savage and humane impulses is what makes Ethan such a fascinating character. His gesture of lifting Debbie and suddenly swinging her into his arms—while her fists are clenched to fight for her life— seems an almost involuntary gesture from Ethan, a spontaneous reaction to a long-buried memory. It echoes the first time we saw him with the child Debbie, lifting her into his arms within the illusory shelter of the Edwards home. The climactic scene's documentary-like roughness, with the camera operator momentarily losing the actors' faces as if he did not expect Wayne to lift Natalie Wood, helps make Ethan's transformation convincing and deeply satisfying.

The young French film critic and future nouvelle vague filmmaker Jean-Luc Godard was reduced to tears by his first screening of *The Searchers,* and later mused, "Mystery and fascination of this American cinema. . . . How can I hate John Wayne upholding Goldwater and yet love him tenderly when abruptly he takes Natalie Wood into his arms in the last reel of *The Searchers*?"

In light of Scar's function as Ethan's doppelgänger, it is poetically appropriate that Scar is played by a white man, and one with a subtly "alien" ethnic identity of his own by postwar American standards. With his fierce, muscular appearance, Henry Brandon was often cast in Indian roles, but he was actually a native of Germany, born Heinrich Kleinbach. He first appeared as an Indian in the 1948 Bob Hope comedy *The Paleface,* and he played a variety of other ethnic types before *The Searchers,* ranging from an Arab in *The Garden of Allah* to a Polynesian in John Wayne's *Wake of the Red Witch* and the lead role of the Chinese master criminal in the 1940 serial *Drums of Fu Manchu.* The Navajos working on *The Searchers* teasingly referred to Brandon as "the Kraut Comanche."

Ford's conflicted attitudes toward Indians and sexuality were reflected in his relationship with Brandon on *The Searchers,* which the actor described as "combative." When I interviewed him in 1987, Brandon proved an unusually acute observer of Ford's behavior and personality.

If Ford had taken the advice of his casting director, Jim Ryan, Brandon would not have been hired to play Chief Scar. During Brandon's interview for *The Searchers,* Ryan started shaking his head in Ford's direction when he learned that Brandon was German. But it was "too late," the actor recalled. "Ford said, 'We'll roach his hair up high.' That's when I knew I had the part. He didn't say I had the part. I waited till I was safely on film and said to Ford, 'Mr. Ford, I've lost lots of native parts—Indians, Arabs—because of my blue eyes. He come you cast me?' He said, 'Brandon, hasn't it occurred to you that the exception, dramatically speaking, is always more exciting than the rule?' I used that line many times when that objection came up, and I always got parts by quoting Mr. Ford.

"Ford was right. He loved to cast against type, and, of course, I as an actor love to do that. I remember one of the reviews picked it up, calling me 'the Indian chief with blazing blue eyes.' They weren't criticizing it, they thought it was interesting. When they got to know me the Indian extras would call me 'the Kraut Comanche.' Now of course I don't play them anymore because Indians have gotten to be good actors themselves."

Brandon did his best to bring some humanity and irony to the part of Scar. And he felt that Ford was "very fair-minded" on the subject of Indians. "On the train going to the location I couldn't sleep. Ford was in the dining car poring over the script. He said, 'Sit down. I want to talk to you. How do you feel about an Indian sleeping with a white woman?' I said, 'Wouldn't bother me a bit.' He said, 'Umm.' Like, 'That's good.' He didn't want me to feel I was playing a villain. I've always tried to find a *reason* for the villain's actions. I can't play just the hatred, I have to know why. He wanted to make sure I did not play the hatred.

"The Indian language in the script was written in an attempt to speak phonetic Comanche. I had a very literary technical advisor, a Navajo. I said, 'Mr. Ford, if I were allowed to change these lines into Navajo, I could feel some sort of truth.' Ford's attitude was, 'To hell with historical details. Give them what they expect.' My hairdo with the roaching up high was actually a Nez Perce hairdo. The Navajo hairdo is pulled back—there's no way you can avoiding making yourself look like a squaw. I know what his reasoning was, though I didn't hear him express it. It made me look ten times as good-looking as I am, and there are very few Nez Perce left, or Comanches, who would know the difference. The rest of the audience wouldn't know." (In a January 1955 production memo, Ford candidly admitted that he did not want the Comanche costumes to be entirely authentic, since the Comanches were Southern Plains Indians and the film was set in the desert. He instructed the costume designers to incorporate the styles of the Navajos, which he found more pictorially effective in any case.)

Ford's directions to Brandon about playing Scar were somewhat confusing, reflecting the director's own ambivalence about the character.

"When we were doing my first scene on location in *The Searchers,* Ford said, 'Brandon, get off the horse. I don't want you underplaying the part. I've just been over in England doing a picture [*Mogambo*] with those goddam Englishmen. They all go, "Nyah nyah nyah"—no emotions, no feeling at all. Play it broad, play it *big*.' A few weeks later when we were back at the studio doing interiors, we were watching rushes and he said, 'Too big—cut it in half.' Well, if it was anybody else I would have said, 'But you *told* me.' But with Ford you didn't object.

"Ford knew I did a lot of classical acting, Shakespeare and such. One day at lunch our eyes met at the table—his one eye and mine. He said, 'You know Shakespeare didn't write those plays at all, it was that guy Francis Bacon.' I immediately turned my back and started a conversation with a guy next to me. I didn't want to get into *that* subject at all; I knew there would be an argument. Later on, he said to me, 'Jesus Christ, you're hamming! What are you doing? I don't want any of that goddam Shakespearean acting.' I told myself, 'Don't say anything. Don't say anything.'"

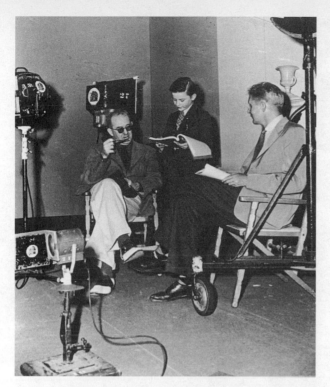

Screenwriter Philip Dunne (*right*) rehearses "the real auteur of the picture," as he wryly described child actor Roddy McDowall, with Ford on the set of *How Green Was My Valley* at Twentieth Century–Fox in 1941. TWENTIETH CENTURY–FOX/ACADEMY OF MOTION PICTURE ARTS AND SCIENCES

On the Malibu set of the Welsh mining village for *How Green Was My Valley* in 1941, Ford shares a lighthearted moment with two Irish brothers who were longtime members of his Ford Stock Company, Barry Fitzgerald and Arthur Shields. TWENTIETH CENTURY–FOX

"Well done, Massie Hughes": John Ford making his cameo appearance in *The Battle of Midway*, in the sequence of the rescued fliers U.S. NAVY/TWENTIETH CENTURY-FOX

"Yes—this really happened": three frame enlargements from the sequence of the raising of the American flag under fire on June 4, 1942, in Ford's World War II documentary *The Battle of Midway* U.S. NAVY/TWENTIETH CENTURY-FOX

Ford's most controversial World War II project was his 1943 U.S. Navy documentary *December 7th,* which he codirected with the great cinematographer Gregg Toland. In this frame enlargement from the 1943 *March of Time* documentary *Show Business at War,* Ford and Toland are screening footage from their documentary about America's lack of preparedness for the 1941 Japanese attack on Pearl Harbor. TIME, INC./TWENTIETH CENTURY-FOX

While on leave from the U.S. Navy during the closing days of World War II, Ford directed *They Were Expendable* (1945), his tribute to the men who made a gallant last stand in the Philippines during the early days of the war. Robert Montgomery (*left*) plays Lieutenant John Brickley, based on Lieutenant John D. Bulkeley, the navy hero who later became a close friend of Ford's; John Wayne is Brickley's rebellious second-in-command. MGM/WISCONSIN CENTER FOR FILM AND THEATRE RESEARCH

Henry Fonda as the megalomanical Colonel Owen Thursday and John Wayne as his principled second in command, Captain York: a frame enlargement from a scene just before the climactic battle in Monument Valley in Ford's 1948 cavalry Western *Fort Apache* RKO

"No man died more gallantly, nor won more honor for his regiment": a frame enlargement from one of the most controversial scenes in Ford's work, York's lying to newspapermen in order to cover up Colonel Thursday's misdeeds at the end of *Fort Apache* RKO

Much of the pleasure in watching a Ford movie is revisiting our favorite members of the John Ford Stock Company, such as Jane Darwell, Mae Marsh, John Wayne, and Hank Worden, seen here in the sentimental finale of *3 Godfathers* (1948), Ford's remake of his 1919 silent *Marked Men*. MGM

Former Civil War enemies reunited under a common flag: the death of Trooper Smith in *She Wore a Yellow Ribbon* (1949), with Ben Johnson, John Wayne, and Rudy Bowman (*on ground*) as the ex–Confederate general–turned–U.S. cavalryman RKO

"He's a lonely man—a very lonely man": John Wayne as Lieutenant Colonel Kirby York in the cavalry Western *Rio Grande* (1950) REPUBLIC PICTURES/ WISCONSIN CENTER FOR FILM AND THEATRE RESEARCH

In a loose moment, Ford once called his Irish romantic comedy *The Quiet Man* (1952) "the sexiest picture ever made." On a windblown night in Connemara, John Wayne's Irish-American exile Sean Thornton breaks local traditions to kiss a fiery Irishwoman he has only just met, Maureen O'Hara's Mary Kate Danaher. A slap in the face from Mary Kate will soon follow. REPUBLIC PICTURES

"Sir, here's a good stick to beat the lovely lady": John Wayne's Sean Thornton and Maureen O'Hara's Mary Kate Danaher settle their marital dispute with the entire community of Inisfree (including the provider of the stick, May Craig) as their witnesses in this much-debated satirical scene from *The Quiet Man*. REPUBLIC PICTURES/WISCONSIN CENTER FOR FILM AND THEATRE RESEARCH

These two legendary Irish-Americans, James Cagney and Ford, had a prickly relationship during the making of *What Price Glory* (1952), Ford's badly botched film of the classic play about World War I by Maxwell Anderson and Laurence Stallings. TWENTIETH CENTURY–FOX

The film Ford described as "really my favorite, the only one I like to see over and over again": *The Sun Shines Bright* (1953). In this melancholic remake of *Judge Priest*, Charles Winninger plays the aged Kentucky judge who provides a lesson in tolerance to his bigoted community. REPUBLIC PICTURES

The most complex character in Ford's work, John Wayne's Ethan Edwards in *The Searchers* (1956), returning home to the woman he secretly loves, his sister-in-law, Martha (Dorothy Jordan). Over the years, *The Searchers* has come to be regarded as one of the greatest American films, a profoundly moving study of the racism underlying much of the Western genre. WARNER BROS.

An original poster for Ford's three-part Irish film *The Rising of the Moon* (1957) WARNER BROS.

Ford's favorite "horse's ass," Ward Bond, spoofed the director as "John Dodge" in *The Wings of Eagles* (1957), adopting many of his mannerisms and props. John Wayne plays Ford's friend Frank W. "Spig" Wead, the former navy man who turned to screenwriting after a crippling injury. MGM/STATE HISTORICAL SOCIETY OF WISCONSIN

After more than three decades working for his "Coach," John Wayne still hangs on Ford's every word on location in Louisiana for their 1959 Civil War film *The Horse Soldiers*. UNITED ARTISTS

America's racial tensions became an urgent preoccupation of Ford's work during the turbulent decade of the 1960s. Woody Strode plays the title role in *Sergeant Rutledge* (1960), with Jeffrey Hunter as a fellow U.S. Cavalry officer who reluctantly arrests him on a trumped-up charge of rape and murder. Strode was one of the director's closest friends of his later years. WARNER BROS.

John Wayne as Tom Doniphon and James Stewart as Ransom Stoddard in Ford's last great Western, *The Man Who Shot Liberty Valance* (1962). The summation of the director's views on the interrelationship of legend and reality in American history, *Liberty Valance* mourns the inevitable passing of the rugged individualism represented by Doniphon, the man who actually performs the deed that makes the fraudulent Stoddard a celebrated political figure. PARAMOUNT PICTURES

Ford on location in Kentucky for "The Civil War," a segment of the 1962 Cinerama spectacle *How the West Was Won*, with cast members George Peppard (*left*) and Claude Johnson (*right*) CINERAMA/MGM

Ford's flawed but heartfelt tribute to Native Americans: Ricardo Montalban, Victor Jory, and Gilbert Roland as the defiant leaders of the uprooted Cheyenne nation in *Cheyenne Autumn* (1964) WARNER BROS.

Ford briefly dallied with the new sexual frankness of the 1960s when he directed Julie Christie as Irish prostitute Daisy Battles in *Young Cassidy* (1965). But Ford fell ill while directing this film about playwright Sean O'Casey and was replaced as director by Jack Cardiff. MGM

Anne Bancroft as the humanistic Dr. Cartwright, an atheist who sacrifices herself for a group of missionary women and a newborn child in Ford's last feature film, *7 Women* (1966) MGM

"The last place on earth": 7 *Women* was reviled by many reviewers but has since been hailed as a masterpiece by some critics. Ford considered it his finest achievement in direction. Assembled around the table in the Chinese mission are (*from left*) Sue Lyon, Mildred Dunnock, Anne Bancroft (*seated*), Margaret Leighton, Hans William Lee, unidentified actress, Eddie Albert, and Betty Field. MGM

Ford in a particularly crusty mood with his Boswell, Peter Bogdanovich, on location in Monument Valley for the young filmmaker's 1971 documentary *Directed by John Ford* CALIFORNIA ARTS COMMISSION/AMERICAN FILM INSTITUTE

A Portrait of the Artist as an Old Man: at his office in Beverly Hills on August 19, 1970, the seventy-six-year-old "ex-director" reluctantly poses for the author's camera. JOSEPH MCBRIDE

John Ford (*in profile, left*) prompts reminiscences from Lieutenant General Lewis B. "Chesty" Puller, USMC (Ret.), in a frame enlargement from the director's last film, the documentary *Chesty: A Tribute to a Legend* (completed in 1970). JAMES ELLSWORTH PRODUCTIONS/DYNA-PLEX, INC./ROBERT H. DAVIS

Chesty Puller at the tomb of Confederate general Robert E. Lee, another frame enlargement from *Chesty: A Tribute to a Legend* JAMES ELLSWORTH PRODUCTIONS/ DYNA-PLEX, INC./ROBERT H. DAVIS

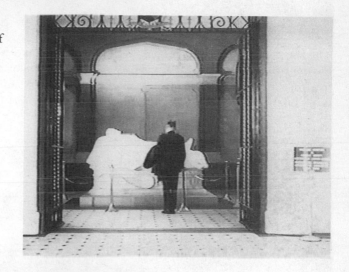

The poet and the president: the dying Ford being honored by President Richard Nixon with the Medal of Freedom on March 31, 1973. At the same nationally televised ceremony in Beverly Hills, Ford received the first Life Achievement Award from the American Film Institute. CARSON PRODUCTIONS/AMERICAN FILM INSTITUTE/CBS TELEVISION

The last gathering of the John Ford Stock Company: Memorial Day 1973 at the Motion Picture Country House and Hospital, Woodland Hills, California. Harry Carey Jr. and Anna Lee kneel before Donald Crisp and John Ford. JOHN STAFFORD/COURTESY OF ANNA LEE

The seventy-nine-year-old Ford, painfully shrunken with terminal cancer but happy to see old friends one last time, at the Woodland Hills reception three months before his death with (*from left*) Ford's brother-in-law and assistant director Wingate Smith; Crisp; and a Ford aficionado, cinematographer Alex Ameripoor JOHN STAFFORD/COURTESY OF ANNA LEE

At the studio when they filmed Scar's discovery of Debbie in a graveyard, Ford asked Brandon, "Did you look at yourself in the mirror after he put war paint on you?'

"Yes, Mr. Ford."

"Pretty scary, isn't it?"

"It sure is."

"I don't want you to do anything after you look down at her. I don't want any play of emotions, any facial expressions. I just want you to draw a blank."

Ford's attitude toward Brandon had turned sour at the start of the location shooting. Brandon spent a lot of time sunning himself on the rocks of Monument Valley in order to darken his body for the part. Ford seemed troubled by the actor's display of muscular sensuality. Thinking that Brandon was flaunting his physique, Ford reportedly made a homophobic remark about the actor.

"I didn't wear any body makeup," Brandon explained. "I have a low boiling point and perspire a lot. I knew if I got out on the desert location, Indian paint would be running because it's water-based. Before reading for the part I worked out, I shaved my chest, and I went outside for weeks and got a terrific tan. The first couple of days on *The Searchers,* I would put on just a bikini and lie in the sun so I wouldn't have to put on body makeup. The Indians thought I was crazy sitting out in the sun. We were on location three weeks and I don't think I went in front of the camera once. It was broiling hot. There was hardly any shade. I kept working on my tan. It was tough lying out there."

For most of Scar's scenes in Monument Valley, Ford used Brandon's double, Chuck Roberson, to play Scar in long shots. Brandon recalled that Ford "would call me into a scene and humiliate me by brushing me aside and saying, 'Call Chuck,' and bring my double in. I finally realized it was some kind of vendetta. I was getting madder and madder about it. I lost my temper one day.

"We were moving to another location and I was about to board the extras' bus and a Jeep roared up. Wayne was driving, Ford was in it. He said, 'You got two choices. You can go with me with the first unit, or you can go with my son, who's doing some drive-by pickups.' Well, that was a terrible thing to say, but I guess he was getting tired of this. I said, 'If I went with your son, I wouldn't have the benefit of your brilliant direction, Mr. Ford.' Wayne just stared with his mouth wide open; I had never seen him like that before. Ford's one eye just glared. He stuck his stogie in his mouth and drove away. He didn't speak to me for two weeks.

"God, he was an evil bastard."

Ford's combativeness throughout the shooting "seemed so inconsiderate and so unnecessary," Brandon felt. "He liked to push people to see how far they could go. Maybe that was how he would get effects out of actors. I think he respected me for getting mad at him. He didn't like people groveling. Bond would grovel. He would be running around clearing ashtrays, yessing Ford and laughing at his jokes. On that whole picture, Ford treated Bond terribly, and we could never figure out why. Bond would go out in the kitchen and eat with the black help because Ford would yell at him across three tables and put him down."

Brandon speculated that Ford's cruelty toward Bond, "which of course I secretly enjoyed," was motivated in part by the director's disgust over Bond's political extremism: "Bond was a horror. He and Hedda [Hopper] ran the blacklist. They put dozens of actors and directors out of work. Well, if you do that to a cowboy—if you take his horse—you'd get hung.

"Ford could excuse acting boners, like blowing a line, more than he could excuse action blunders, like an actor failing to do a running jump onto a horse. But on one scene, Bond was blowing lines. I could see Ford get madder and madder. Ford turned and said to me in German, 'Der kerl ist kein Schauspieler, er ist ein Hosenscheisser!'—'He isn't an actor, he's a pants-shitter!'

"An hour later they all came up to me and asked, 'What did he say?' And they all roared laughing. Every once in a while when Ford didn't want someone to know what he was saying, he'd talk to me in German, pretty well but not very gramatically correct. Ford liked to act as if he knew a lot of languages. I think he knew a bit in each one. He was talking Hawaiian once with a Hawaiian on the set. He liked to show off. When he did that I'm sure he prepared himself beforehand and stunned people with it.

"Bond was good in those parts, you can't take it away. Ward was a shit *and* he was a good actor. He was lucky he had Ford to teach him. People are always better in Ford's pictures. Ward was, so was Wayne, so was I. I never saw Ford praise an actor, ever, for something he'd done. He'd do it by indirection."

When Ford shot the intense scene of Martin challenging Ethan over his last will and testament, only the actors and a minimal crew were allowed to be present. "Ford didn't want anybody around—it would ruin the concentration," Brandon explained. "I went in on my belly through the brush, using my Army Signal Corps training. That night, Ford was studying the script, didn't look up. Suddenly he said, 'How'd you like the kid today?' He'd seen me crawling up the fucking hill. I said, 'He made me cry today.' See, he didn't like to praise an actor, so he made *me* do it. Hunter just loved me for it. The way Ford did it was so sly, so cruel, so mean.

"I roomed with Johnny Qualen on location. Of course, he was an old member of the Ford family. [Before playing Lars Jorgensen in *The Searchers*, Qualen had given memorable performances in such Ford films as *The Grapes of Wrath* and *The Long Voyage Home*.] One day Johnny came from shooting and he was crying. He said, 'I thought the Old Man loved me. He was so hateful to me today, screamed at me, called me names.' Several days later, back at the studio, I was in the john, standing at the urinal. Ford came in, stood at the next stall, and said, 'That roommate of yours'—by now he *wasn't* my roommate, we were all back in Hollywood, living at our own homes—'he's a mirror actor. He practices his part in front of the mirror.' I said, 'That's not true. All the time I roomed with him, he never practiced his part in front of a mirror.' Ford said, 'I told him to turn left and he turned right. That's a mirror actor.' What can you say? I guess there are things Ford can't abide.

"The still man on *The Searchers* was a little guy who adored John Ford, and Ford just treated him terribly. He never let him line up for a shot after the scene was taken. He made him take it during the action, which of course made for a much better shot. Ford didn't want to hear any noise from his still camera, so he'd watch the rehearsal carefully, and if someone or something made a noise he'd take a shot. I asked him, 'Why do you admire this man who treats you so terribly?' He said, 'I'll tell you why. When my wife died—she was somebody nobody in the company knew—Mr. Ford phoned everybody in the company and told them they had to come to the funeral. We had very few friends, and it was a small church. The church was so crowded you couldn't get in.'" (Ford's gesture was reminiscent of Judge Priest turning out the townsfolk for the prostitute's funeral in *The Sun Shines Bright*. Ford put a similar scene into *The Last Hurrah,* when Mayor Skeffington, to comfort the widow, turns out a crowd of political cronies to attend Knocko Minihan's wake.)

Brandon's most lasting impression of Ford's personality was his "vicious sense of humor. On *The Searchers* he had a bit actor cum extra wrangler type who had trouble following his direction and had to do it over and over. The guy was hard of hearing and didn't hear what Ford was saying, but he didn't have the guts to say, 'I didn't hear you.' Ford turned to the entire company and asked, 'Is there anybody here who speaks Texan and can translate for this asshole?' It was so funny, but the poor guy—if you had given him a loaded gun, he would have blown his brains out.

"At the end of the location, we all could have hung John Ford, but then you go to the premiere and you see he's made you look greater than you ever looked in your life, so you're eager to do it again. When you're working with a genius, you put up with a lot."

The *Searchers* opened on May 26, 1956, and became a substantial hit, grossing $4.45 million. Despite the fact that it also received some rave reviews, the

Academy of Motion Picture Arts and Sciences not only failed to nominate *The Searchers* for best picture, it did not nominate Ford's film for a single Oscar in a competition dominated by *Around the World in 80 Days, Giant,* and *The King and I,* none of which is as highly regarded today.

The Academy's inattention to a genuine American classic reflected the snobbism of that era's cultural elite toward Westerns, typified by *New Yorker* critic John McCarten, whose supercilious review occupied only three sentences. McCarten could see no difference between *The Searchers* and the most run-of-the-mill Hollywood oater: "The thing has to do with the search for a couple of maidens some nasty Comanches have abducted shortly after the Civil War, and it certainly contains plenty of action." Robert Ardrey offered an even more scathing dismissal in *The Reporter:* "And the same John Ford who once gave adults *The Informer* must now give children *The Searchers.*"

Even the avant-garde French film magazine *Cahiers du Cinéma* published a notorious two-sentence dismissal (unsigned) of *La Prisonnière du Désert* in October 1956: "Nostalgia from Ford for his old Westerns: nostalgia from Fordians for his old skills. Regrets at seeing a good scenario spoiled: annoyance at the everlasting sight of acting in the Irish style, above all by the females." But by 1962, the film's stature had so increased among the French that it placed at the top of a *Cahiers* critics' poll on the greatest American sound films.

Although an enduring favorite of John Wayne fans, *The Searchers* was largely ignored by American critics and film historians for many years. It was not until the early seventies that *The Searchers* became the "Super-Cult Movie of the New Hollywood," as Stuart Byron called it in a 1979 *New York* magazine article about its influence on leading young American directors. During the intervening period, the film's influence flowed obliquely into the culture through other artists it inspired. Ethan's cynical catchphrase "That'll be the day" made a big impression on Buddy Holly and Jerry Allison when they saw *The Searchers* at the State Theater in Lubbock, Texas. Their breakthrough song of that title, first recorded in July 1956 by Buddy Holly and the Crickets, became the number one hit in both the U.S. and Britain during the fall of 1957. And during the late fifties, a seventh grader making amateur films in Phoenix, Steven Spielberg, shot a two-reel Western in a friend's backyard imitating *The Searchers,* using a backdrop of Monument Valley painted on a bedsheet. In 1967, Jean-Luc Godard included a reference to *The Searchers* in *Weekend,* but this *hommage* failed to enlighten the American art house audience, since the subtitler thought *La Prisonnière du Désert* was the French title for something called *Prisoner of the Desert.*

Signs that a new generation of American film critics was beginning to rediscover Ford's unjustly neglected masterpiece began appearing in the sixties.

In his groundbreaking 1967 book on the director, Peter Bogdanovich declared that "the bold, vigorous strokes of *The Searchers* . . . require more artistry than the direction of *The Informer.*" Bogdanovich's 1971 Ford documentary begins and ends with the opening and closing scenes of *The Searchers.* In his influential 1968 survey *The American Cinema,* Andrew Sarris put Ford in his "Pantheon," using *The Searchers* to help make the case for Ford's artistry.

Unlike contemporary reviewers, Sarris was open and alert to the previously "unspeakable" themes of *The Searchers,* to the forbidden Ethan-Martha relationship and "the racist, revenge-seeking furies that have seared his soul," as Sarris wrote in a 1971 *Film Comment* essay on the film. However, the psychological interrelationship between Ethan and Scar, the absurdist aspects of the search, and Ford's transference of the heroic mantle from Ethan to Martin largely escaped attention until Michael Wilmington and I published our essay "Prisoner of the Desert" in the autumn 1971 *Sight and Sound,* which Byron described as the "seminal" study of *The Searchers.* Ford asked for a copy and sent a note with thanks for "the upbeat kindly way you treated me" in that and other articles.

In 1972, *The Searchers* made its first appearance on the *Sight and Sound* list of the greatest films ever made. Starting at number eighteen in the magazine's polling of international film critics (conducted every ten years), Ford's film climbed to fifth place in 1992. The seventies saw an explosion of *Searchers* influence on leading young American directors, including Martin Scorsese, Steven Spielberg, George Lucas, Michael Cimino, and John Milius, who borrowed from or imitated Ford's film in such otherwise diverse pictures as *Taxi Driver, Close Encounters of the Third Kind, Star Wars, Hardcore, The Deer Hunter, Dillinger,* and *The Wind and the Lion.* In addition, screenwriter Alan Sharp adapted a passage of dialogue from *The Searchers* for Robert Aldrich's 1972 Western *Ulzana's Raid.* Scorsese had Harvey Keitel and Zina Bethune discuss *The Searchers* at length in his 1967 feature *Who's That Knocking at My Door?,* and he used a clip from *The Searchers* in his 1973 *Mean Streets,* although he had to use a scene without John Wayne, who refused to appear in an R-rated movie.

"The dialogue is like poetry!" Scorsese said of *The Searchers.* "And the changes of expression are so subtle, so magnificent! I see it once or twice a year." Spielberg told Byron he had watched Ford's film a dozen times, including twice on location for *Close Encounters.*

Some of these filmmakers have challenged *The Searchers* and tried to go beyond Ford's limitations. Scorsese asked screenwriter Paul Schrader for what they came to call "the 'Scar' scene" in *Taxi Driver.* Schrader explained, "I feel, and other people feel, that the one thing *The Searchers* lacks—and it is a great film—is a scene between Scar, the Comanche chief, and Natalie Wood. . . . If

Ford had had the guts to show that their life together had some meaning, it would have made the ending—when John Wayne 'rescues' her—bitterly sweet."

After *The Searchers,* Ford fantasized about spending the remainder of his life sailing around the Hawaiian Islands on the *Araner.* Like John Wayne and Lee Marvin on their Polynesian island in *Donovan's Reef* (1963), Ford looked to Hawaii as his earthly paradise. But Ford knew that he would not be happy spending his remaining years in some distant outpost. Furthermore, the *Araner* was rotting at the beams, and Ford was not a wealthy man. He had always avoided investing in real estate, a seemingly irrational decision, particularly for an Irishman with an ancestral love of the land. Something in Ford, perhaps an atavistic sense of guilt over rising too far above his humble Irish roots, prevented him from pursuing riches for their own sake. He told himself that he needed to keep doing "a job of work" to earn a living, but the truth was that he lived to keep working.

While waiting for Sonny Whitney to make up his mind about doing *The Valiant Virginians,* Ford dashed off a couple of half-hour television programs in October and November 1955, *Rookie of the Year* and *The Bamboo Cross.* His willingness to cross over into the "enemy" camp might have seemed demeaning for a man of his stature, but this pragmatic move was a survival tactic, a bravura demonstration of his professional efficiency and his ability to work even at the accelerated pace demanded by series television.

Moreover, Ford's enthusiastic plunge into the new medium demonstrated again his largely unheralded adaptability to technical evolution. As early as July 1948, he and Merian Cooper announced that they were considering making television films for Argosy. The *New York Times* reported that they had been experimenting for sixteen months with a method of TV shooting that "utilizes the fastest elements of stage, screen, and radio to produce high entertainment tempo . . . [with] the possibility of combining live actors with motion pictures." (In 1949, Ford tried his hand at radio, directing two half-hour programs on NBC under the auspices of the Screen Directors Guild, condensed versions of *Stagecoach* and *Fort Apache,* both starring John Wayne.)

Michael Killanin asked Ford in 1958 what he thought filmmakers should do about television, since "There is one hand pulling us towards the making of good but cheap pictures for TV and the other trying to make feature pictures of quality." Ford replied that in choosing a project, the story was his foremost consideration. "As for TV," he said, "I think it has interesting possibilities for the future, and let's face it, *The Rising of the Moon* [their 1957 Irish trilogy] was shot in such a way that it could be used as three TV stories. In the long run, the length or time of a picture depends on the story. Let's find the right stories to make, then decide their scale and market potential!"

Rookie of the Year shares five cast members with *The Searchers:* John Wayne; his teenage son Patrick; Vera Miles; Ward Bond; and child actor Robert Lyden. Like Ford's radio version of *Fort Apache, Rookie of the Year* was made for an SDG series called *Screen Directors Playhouse.* Pat Wayne, Ford's godson, already had played small parts in several of his features. Ford offered Pat a glittering showcase for his title role of Lyn Goodhue, a baseball phenom whose father is hiding a shameful past. Larry Goodhue, aka Buck Garrison (Bond), a character clearly modeled on Shoeless Joe Jackson, was one of the "Black Sox" who threw the 1919 World Series. When small-town sportswriter Mike Cronin (John Wayne) uncovers the story, he realizes it could be his ticket back to New York but agonizes over what it could do to Lyn's career. Mike nobly decides to spike the story, but the crusty New York sports editor (James Gleason) tells him every sportswriter knows it and no one will print it.

Sharply written by Frank Nugent from a story by W. R. Burnett and directed by Ford with a masterful economy of style, *Rookie of the Year* has a relaxed lightness of touch perfectly suited to the intimacy of the new medium. Besides gratifying Ford's love of baseball—he once said that he liked animals, baseball, and people, in that order—the show reverberates with the artistic stimulation he always drew from a morally ambiguous dramatic situation. And with its theme of a conspiracy of silence to cover up a historical shame, *Rookie of the Year* echoes *Fort Apache* as well as adumbrating *The Man Who Shot Liberty Valance.* Seated in his director's chair on an empty soundstage, wearing his trademark slouch hat and dark glasses, Ford appeared at the end of the previous week's program to give a preview of *Rookie of the Year.* Its airing by NBC on December 7, 1955, came a day after the same network's airing of *The Bamboo Cross.*

The Bamboo Cross is so appallingly bad, such a grotesque self-parody, that it seems to have been directed by John Ford's evil twin. This ham-handed morality play about American nuns menaced by rabid Chinese Communists, filmed in November 1955 for *The Jane Wyman Fireside Theater,* is noteworthy only for its superficial resemblance to Ford's infinitely superior 1966 feature *7 Women.* Ford initiated the making of *The Bamboo Cross* as a tribute to the Maryknoll missionaries, to whom he was a benefactor. He received a token salary of one dollar. The Maryknoll order flattered him that April with an award and an invitation to speak at an ordination ceremony for priests at its Ossining, New York, headquarters.

Unfortunately, it was the audience that paid the penance. *The Bamboo Cross* shows the deleterious effect Ford's doctrinaire Catholicism and anti-

Communism had on his work when he attempted to use his emotionally held but intellectually underexamined beliefs as a film's sole raison d'être. The usually adroit dramatist and screenwriter Laurence Stallings must have been caught in a weak moment when Ford inveigled him into the task of adapting the play by Theophane Lee.

Wyman ably plays Sister Regina, a Maryknoll missionary accused by the local Communist leader, the grotesque King Fat (Kurt Katch), of murdering infants with "poison cakes," i.e., Communion wafers. As often happened in fifties Hollywood, the theme of informing crept into the story: King Fat wants Sister Regina to give false testimony blaming a priest for ordering the children's deaths, which were actually caused by disease. She and another nun, leeringly described by King Fat as "unmarried ladies," are saved by a young Communist, Mark Chu (Jim Hong), who sees the light and sacrifices his life to win them safe-conduct passes to the British garrison. The show ends with Sister Regina cradling the dead Mark as in a pietà.

The black-and-white morality of *The Bamboo Cross* is somewhat redeemed by the gray elegance and bleak spareness of Ford's visual style (the cinematographer was John MacBurnie). But Ford's "Chicoms" are absurd caricatures whose melodramatic villainy would seem overdrawn in a Saturday-matinee serial. Fortunately for the director's reputation, *The Bamboo Cross* remains one of his most obscure works.

One might wonder whether Ford made this "Red Menace" screed partially with tongue in cheek, were it not for the fact that in 1953 he was among 216 people signing a petition urging President Eisenhower to continue opposing the admission of Communist China to the United Nations. Other signers included George C. Marshall, Herbert Hoover, General A. C. Wedemeyer, Admiral Chester Nimitz, General James H. Doolittle, John Dos Passos, Merian Cooper, Robert Montgomery, and Adolphe Menjou.

The *Searchers* was nearing the end of postproduction in January 1956 when Whitney reactivated *The Valiant Virginians.* Under Ford's direction, Pat Wayne was to play the central role of a Southern teenager named Roan Catlett, who fights for the Confederacy and returns to the Shenandoah Valley to find that his home has been burned by Union soldiers under General Philip Sheridan (the same disaster that befalls Maureen O'Hara's character in *Rio Grande)*. John Wayne would have joined his son in the film, perhaps as the Confederate general Stonewall Jackson. Whitney envisioned the Civil War epic (which Ford wanted to retitle *The Young Virginians*) as part of his much-ballyhooed "American Series," a trilogy beginning with *The Searchers* and ending with a film he rather bizarrely described as being about Ethan Edwards's descendants invading Normandy Beach during World War II.

But after planning a fall 1956 production start for *The Valiant Virginians,* Whitney balked. Despite the financial success of *The Searchers,* his financial advisers persuaded him to ease out of moviemaking and buy a chain of television stations, a safer investment given the radical change in American viewing habits. On December 26, Whitney told Ford he was canceling their ambitious film project. Somewhat upset because he had spent a year in preparation, Ford nevertheless was relieved to be free of Whitney, whom he had come to regard as a dilettante.

Two weeks later, Ford complained in a letter to Wayne that the pleasure seemed to have gone out of moviemaking. Ford was beginning to experience the frustrations and humiliations many directors of his generation faced with the breakup of the studio system. Not only did they find themselves wasting much of their precious remaining time on projects that eventually fell through, but they were forced to assume the tedious money raising and logistical tasks the studios once had absorbed for them. Add to these complications the problems of advancing age, illnesses, and waning energy, and it's easy to see why Ford was becoming discouraged.

Like one of his characters, Ford always sought the cure for depression in wandering far from home. In the spring of 1956, he escaped for a while from the troubles of Hollywood by embarking with gusto on his long-delayed Irish project *Three Leaves of a Shamrock.* As he had written Michael Killanin in 1954, "[F]or the sake of my artistic soul I long to get back to Ireland and make our simple little story." Ford wanted to retitle it *Irish Coffee,* but Killanin discouraged that notion. Produced by Four Provinces on location from late March through early May 1956, mainly in counties Galway and Clare, the trilogy was released in 1957 as *The Rising of the Moon.*

Ford originally envisioned the film as a star-studded extravaganza in CinemaScope and color, with roles for such internationally known actors as Maureen O'Hara, Barry Fitzgerald, Donald Crisp, and a rising English actor, the protean Alec Guinness. Ford even made an overture to Katharine Hepburn for a segment to have been based on a traditional Irish ghost story. He apologized that he couldn't offer her much money, since he himself was working for the Screen Directors Guild minimum of $3,333 to help encourage film production in Ireland. But as he sentimentally admitted to Kate, he was not getting any younger and he wanted to direct her one more time. During their abortive romantic involvement in the thirties, they had talked about traveling to Ireland together. But now Hepburn proved less sentimental than Ford, passing up his offer to undertake a six-month tour of Australia with the Old Vic.

Out of financial necessity, Ford scaled back his elaborate early plans. The Four Provinces/Warner Bros. production budget "would just about have covered what he normally gets paid for directing," screenwriter Frank Nugent (who also worked for scale) noted with only slight exaggeration. The final production cost was $256,017, $104,771 under budget. Working with what cast member Maurice Good called "amazing speed and a concentration which baffles even seasoned veterans among actors and technicians," Ford completed the film in just thirty-five shooting days, ten days ahead of schedule.

Ford wound up with only one box-office name in the cast. His Bel Air neighbor Tyrone Power signed on as a Four Provinces board member and filmed brief introductions for the segments in a Dublin studio under Killanin's direction, an idea that Ford did not receive with enthusiasm. (The original plan was for Ford himself to do the introductions outside his ancestral home in Spiddal, reminiscing at one point about his trip to Ireland during the War of Independence in 1921.) Resisting suggestions to use Power as an actor in the "1921" segment, based on Lady Gregory's play *The Rising of the Moon,* Ford even threatened to turn over the direction of that segment to Brian Desmond Hurst if Power appeared in it.

By then Ford had come to believe strongly in the wisdom of using a cast of less stellar but uniformly superb Irish players, who provided authenticity as well as making the film a truly democratic ensemble piece. Most were recruited from the Dublin stage, including the brothers Jimmy and Joseph O'Dea, Donal Donnelly, and Maureen Potter. Some, like Cyril Cusack and Noel Purcell, were film veterans as well. Ford brought back some actors from his previous films about Ireland, including Denis O'Dea from *The Informer,* Eileen Crowe from *The Plough and the Stars* and *The Quiet Man,* and Jack Mac-Gowran, also from *The Quiet Man.* Ford did import a British cinematographer, Robert Krasker, best known for his work on Carol Reed's 1949 classic *The Third Man.* But as technical advisers, Ford enlisted his old friend Ernie O'Malley, the legendary IRA commandant, along with Lennox Robinson, the venerable playwright and former manager of the Abbey Theatre.

Ford softened his habitually gruff manner a bit for Irish consumption. When a reporter from the *Irish Times* was listening, Ford used "a gentle, conversational tone" with a nervous actor who spoke too softly. "I want to hear you all over the Claddagh," directed Ford, referring to an ancient fishing village that is part of Galway city.

When a group of chattering children crowded around the set at the Kilkee railroad station and could not be stilled, Ford rose from his chair and approached them, explaining politely, "All we want is a little peace and quiet while we're shooting." The children ignored him.

"QUIET!" bellowed Ford.

The sound of his voice "reverberated from hill to hill of Kilkee's blue mountains," another journalist reported. "The silence that descended on those children was little short of supernatural. Then, grinning quietly, John Ford got on with that take."

The Rising of the Moon begins with a story Power describes in his introduction as being "about nothing, yet perhaps it's about everything." Frank O'Connor's "The Majesty of the Law" tells of the reluctant visit of a Galway police inspector (Cyril Cusack) to serve an arrest warrant on an old man (Noel Purcell) who makes his home next to the ancient ruins of his family castle. One of those "Ferocious O'Flahertys" who were related to Ford's family of Galway Feeneys, Old Dan has had a violent disagreement with a bumptious neighbor named O'Feeney (John Cowley). But most of the friendly conversation between Dan and the policeman tactfully avoids that issue. Instead it is an eloquent lament for the loss of tradition in the modern world, showing that Ford, with all his preference for visual storytelling, loved the music of words and understood their potency:

> Liquor-making takes time. There was never a good job done in a hurry, for there are *secrets* in it. Every art has its secrets, and the secrets of distilling are being *lost*. Hear, when I was a boy, there wasn't a man in the barony but had a hundred songs in his heart. But with the people going here, there, and everywhere, and off to Canada, Australia, America, So' Boston . . . with the coming of the automobiles and . . . and . . . and the films, and the raddio [*sic*] and that other new thing along with it—all the songs are lost, and all the *secrets* are lost.

The film's directorial tour de force is its center section, "A Minute's Wait," from Michael J. McHugh's play about a train that can never seem to leave a country station because of all the riotous disruptions, unexpected arrivals, and musical celebrations. This farcical metaphor for Irish life, with its large cast of sharply drawn comic characters, is brilliantly orchestrated by Nugent and Ford. Their symbolic foils are a stuffy old English couple (Michael Trubshawe and Anita Sharp Bolster) who never seem to get the joke.

While "A Minute's Wait" can be appreciated as Ford's paean to the irrepressible anarchy of the Irish spirit, it also reinforces the insidious notion of Ireland as a backward island filled with lovable incompetents who haven't yet made it into the twentieth century. Ford's use of an old-fashioned train with an engine built in 1886 was deliberately anachronistic, provoking a complaint from the director of the West Cork Railway, who could not understand why Ford refused a modern train with a diesel engine. "He'll find out when the tourists come over next summer," Ford grumbled, in what Nugent took as an allusion to the tourist craze for jaunting carts provoked by *The Quiet Man*. Stubbornly oblivious to the Irish people's need to take pride in their growing modernism, the major political cause in Ireland during that period, Ford was indulging his own personal romantic vision of rural Ireland as a land of escape from the modern world, frozen dreamlike in the time of his childhood.

The "1921" segment is a throwback to the heavy-handedly expressionistic style of *The Informer,* with a vertiginously tilted camera (à la *The Third Man*) liberally used for "artistic" effect. This pretentious device distracts from the otherwise suspenseful drama of an IRA man, Sean Curran (Donal Donnelly), escaping from a British prison. In updating Lady Gregory's 1907 play to the War of Independence, Ford and Nugent added the characters of two Abbey Theatre actresses (Doreen Madden and Maureen Cusack) who masquerade as nuns to infiltrate the prison (one brazenly displays her American passport when caught, as Ford must have done during his own 1921 escapade). Drawing a Pirandellian connection between playacting and revolution makes explicit an underlying theme of the first two segments, that "stage Irish" behavior is one of the secret weapons the Irish people have evolved to manipulate and outwit their adversaries. "Act the dummy," the Irish warder (Joseph O'Dea) says sotto voce to a confederate as they lay plans for Curran's prison break, pretending to be bungling fools.

Among the greatest pleasures of Ford's work are the many interwoven correspondences among his films, including the use of actors in roles that echo and comment upon their previous work for the director. Such is the frisson of seeing the street singer from *The Informer,* Denis O'Dea, turn up here as Sergeant Michael O'Hara, the Irish policeman who becomes Curran's last obstacle to freedom. Anyone who remembers O'Dea singing "The Minstrel Boy" in *The Informer* ("The minstrel boy to the war has gone / In the ranks of death you'll find him") will hear its echoes throughout the scene at Galway's historic Spanish Arch, with O'Hara confronting the fugitive, who is disguised as a ballad singer peddling copies of the IRA ballad "The Rising of the Moon." To rekindle O'Hara's old revolutionary fervor, his wife (Eileen Crowe) sings him the song, proving what Old Dan said about songs containing "the *secrets.*" Finally realizing Curran's true identity, O'Hara decides to let him go free. Unlike Gypo Nolan, O'Hara is willing to forgo an informer's reward for the sake of his country. Explaining his action to a fellow policeman, he admits, "I suppose there's a bit of treason in us all, more or less."

Maurice Good, who plays O'Hara's timid young partner, was thrilled to be cast in a Ford film, since he was a devoted student of the director's work. But he was chagrined when Ford "set to work bawling me off and reducing me to a state of nervous despair" in front of hundreds of onlookers at the Spanish Arch. Recalling this "most awful onslaught," Donnelly told Lindsay Anderson how Ford bullied "his worshipper" to get the effect of "real fear" in his performance. "I'm sure that's absolutely fine, you know, in screen terms, but in terms of human behavior it's appalling. I know it works, but as an actor I can't stand it." Ford later seemed uncharacteristically apologetic, telling Good, "You know I was fooling you? You were all right, but I just had to make you so damned scared—you forgive me, don't you? The scene was grand, Maurice. . . . You know the way to play a scene when you're supposed to be frightened: don't forget it, and don't ever be scared of a movie director again."

The Rising of the Moon had its world premiere at the Metropole Cinema on May 16, 1957, as part of the Dublin International Film Festival. Opening theatrically in Ireland the following month, it began American play dates in July. Most American reviewers saw the film in stereotypical terms as an entertaining but quaintly old-fashioned piece of Irish blarney. But James Powers of the *Hollywood Reporter* clearly understood that Ford's theme in all three segments "is liberty, personal liberty, pugnacious and persistent, and it is told with wit, skill, and charm. Your appreciation of [the film] may be tempered by the degree to which you are Irish, by derivation or inclination, but even the most benighted Englishman could not deny the humor and the emotion that underlies it."

Ironically, it was the Irish (some of them) who expressed outrage over *The Rising of the Moon*. The city of Belfast in Northern Ireland banned it out of fear that "1921" might incite latent revolutionary sentiments. But even in the Irish Republic, the film provoked trouble. Describing it as "a vile production and a travesty of the Irish people," a member of the Limerick County Council, D. P. Quish, won approval for a resolution demanding that Warner Bros. withdraw it from showing throughout the world. As the Irish correspondent for *Variety* put it, another member, Gerard Hayes, declared that "if *The Rising of the Moon* was to be a criterion of what [the] Irish film industry was going to be like, then the least said about it the better." These huffings and puffings in Limerick took place only after the film had been in release for a full six months.

Due in part to the tepid critical response, but also to Warners' unenthusiastic and unimaginative marketing, the film never found the audience it deserved. As of 1965, rentals in the U.S. and Canada amounted to only $112,984; internationally it took in another $107,534. This disappointment essentially put an end to Ford's fond hopes of starting an Irish film industry. Truth be told, those hopes were mostly Killanin's anyway. As their long correspondence makes clear, Ford was willing to do his bit for the cause but lacked the emotional and ideological commitment required to devote a large part of his time and energy to establishing an Irish film industry. No matter how much he liked to moan about Hollywood, he had spent decades working within the studio system, and even as he saw it collapsing around him, he continued trying to find comfort within its familiar parameters. He and Killanin continued exchanging ideas about various projects and well into the 1960s kept trying to launch a production of *The White Company* with such names as Laurence Olivier, Alec Guinness, and John Wayne.

But the flowering of an indigenous Irish film industry was an idea whose time would not come until the 1990s, long after Ford's death.

Few directors would want to make a biographical film about one of their screenwriters. But Ford genuinely loved and admired Lieutenant Commander Frank W. "Spig" Wead. Asked about *The Wings of Eagles,* his 1957 film about Wead, Ford said, "I didn't want to do the picture, because Spig was a great pal of mine. But I didn't want anyone *else* to make it."

While it may have been virtually impossible to dramatize Wead's contributions to such films as *Air Mail* and *They Were Expendable,* Frank Capra's *Dirigible,* and Howard Hawks's *Ceiling Zero,* the story of Wead's personal life was powerful dramatic material. In Ford's hands, Wead's trajectory from daredevil navy flier to paraplegic to successful writer is more than the simplistic "triumph over handicap" fable others would have made of it. With its deglamorized, often magnificently understated performance by John Wayne, *The Wings of Eagles* pays tribute to Wead's courage in overcoming a catastrophe that would have destroyed a lesser man. Rather than giving up after breaking his neck in an accident at home, Wead learned to walk with crutches and used his navy experiences to forge his new career as a writer of short stories, books, plays, and movies. But *The Wings of Eagles* is essentially the tragedy of a man who failed to appreciate those who loved him most, his family.

Dan Ford suggests that the film is a disguised autobiography of his grandfather. Both Ford and Wead had restless, wandering natures that made them gravitate to lives of action, but because of physical infirmities they had to be content with largely vicarious adventures. Both turned to moviemaking as a substitute for military careers. Both found ways of serving in World War II, but as observers rather than combatants. And, most significantly, both men were unable to balance their careers with satisfying home lives. They neglected their families for the sake of their careers, and also perhaps because feelings of sexual inadequacy made them prefer masculine companionship.

Ford admitted, "I have never approached a subject with such fear and trepidation as I did the story of Spig Wead." The film's uncomfortably close-to-the-bone feeling for the director no doubt accounts for its emotional rawness and frequent incoherence, its bizarre changes of tone, and Ford's ruthlessly un-sentimental approach to his alter ego's character flaws.

For a film about a screenwriter, *The Wings of Eagles* has remarkably arch and witless dialogue, such as the toast that Min Wead (Maureen O'Hara) giddily offers to her husband, "Star-spangled Spig! Damn the martinis, full speed ahead, and don't give up the ship!" The screenplay by Frank Fenton and William Wister Haines had been in development at MGM since 1953. Ford accepted it, warts and all, but he hated the title, with its pretentious biblical overtones, and urged the studio to call the film simply *The Spig Wead Story*. The shooting from September 10 through October 4, 1956—with location work at the U.S. Naval Air Station in Pensacola, Florida, and aboard the USS *Philippine Sea*—was uncharacteristically dilatory for a Ford picture, going eight days over the thirty-nine-day shooting schedule and requiring almost three days of retakes.

Like Pat O'Brien's Duke Talbot in *Air Mail* and James Cagney's Dizzy Davis in *Ceiling Zero,* Wead is portrayed as a childish and irresponsible character who performs dangerous stunts as a naval aviator and constantly becomes involved in juvenile pranks. Wead abandons his family after his wife, beleaguered be-yond endurance, refuses to follow his wanderings from base to base. His two daughters know him only as a man who appears in aviation newsreels. But un-like in those earlier films directed by Ford and Hawks from writings by Wead, there does not seem to be much, if any, critical distance between the director and the character in the first part of *The Wings of Eagles*. Ford claimed to have been a participant in some of the actual hijinks he re-creates, and the humor is more disturbing than funny, particularly since Wayne is much older than the young man he is supposed to be playing. This is one case in which the direc-tor's tendency to balance tragedy with low comedy unquestionably works to a film's detriment. The scenes of Wead's injury, despondency, and determina-tion to walk are so emotionally involving that they seem to come from another movie.

It is only when Wead finally comes home, trying to patch up his domestic life, that he becomes incapacitated. In his anxious unfamiliarity with the re-sponsibilities of fatherhood, he overreacts when he hears one of his daughters crying in her sleep. Dashing out his bedroom door and tumbling down the stairs, he breaks his neck. What does this reflect but an overcompensation for the guilt he feels toward his family? As in *The Searchers,* Ford presents the home as the most dangerous place in the world, a fascinating paradox for a director with such emotional attachment to home as a symbol of community and con-tinuity.

Unexpectedly faced with the prospect of a lifetime of helpless dependency,

Wead stubbornly rejects Min's loyal offer to stay with him. To the demands and rewards of a mature loving relationship and a stable family life, Wead still prefers the superficial and sterile heartiness of male camaraderie and his vicarious participation in the escapist adventures of war and moviemaking. Ford portrays Wead's choices as destructive rather than noble; neither he nor his family ever recovers from his tragic flight from responsibility, disguised as martyrdom.

Ford reverts to comedy, this time with more success, during the prolonged sequence of Wead struggling to move his little toe. His former mechanic, "Jughead" Carson (Dan Dailey), assigned as Wead's nurse, masks his concern with a smoke screen of wisecracks and even a song-and-dance routine. Carson's seeming callousness (and Ford's) is actually a way of facing the unbearable. Making a joke out of Wead's infirmity gradually banishes his self-pitying despondency and restores his fighting spirit. Carson seems totally devoted to Wead, almost as if in an unspoken homosexual attachment, and becomes more of a "wife" to Wead than Min ever manages to be. Wead's sexual impotence turns him into the perpetual observer, fantasizer, and romanticizer of history, a personally dysfunctional but artistically creative role in life much like that played by Ford himself. Wead cannot reverse the fate he has made for himself: belatedly realizing that "[i]f it isn't a family, it's—it's nothing," he attempts a reconciliation with Min, only to have Pearl Harbor intervene and send him back into navy service. Maureen O'Hara, in her final Ford film, offers a shrewdly observed characterization of an acerbic modern woman forced to find her own identity while struggling with drink and loneliness, but this aspect of the film seems disappointingly spotty because some of her drinking scenes had to be cut as a result of objections from the Wead children.

Ford put himself into *The Wings of Eagles* in the self-parodying persona of "John Dodge," humorously played by Ward Bond, with all the familiar Fordian regalia (lifted from the director's home and office): pipe, dark glasses, handkerchief, secret cache of booze, Western memorabilia, pictures of Harry Carey and Tom Mix, and Oscars. Merian Cooper's wife, Dorothy Jordan, plays the demure Southern secretary Dodge calls "Stonewall." Gruff and jocular, Dodge treats Wead in the same sympathetic yet unpitying manner Ford employs for telling Wead's story. When Wead asks Dodge what he should write about, the director barks, "People! Navy people!"

In the final sequence, Wead, having suffered a heart attack, is given a sentimental apotheosis as he is retired from active duty. With his old navy buddies paying their respects, he is transported to another ship via breeches buoy, gliding over the gray ocean on mechanical wings. A shipboard band plays a mournful "Aloha." But if, as Ford said of Wead, "[l]ife disappointed him," he has no one to blame but himself.

Alohas occupy most of the running time of *The Growler Story,* a short film Ford directed for the chief of naval operations, Admiral Arleigh Burke, in November–December 1956. Shot at Pearl Harbor, with Mark Armistead producing, this little-known picture re-creates a celebrated incident in navy history, when the captain of the submarine *Growler* (SS-215), Commander Howard W. Gilmore (played by Ken Curtis), sacrificed his life for his men. While the sub was patrolling in the area of the Solomon Islands on February 7, 1943, Gilmore was badly wounded on the bridge during an attack by a Japanese gunboat. Realizing he could not get below in time to save his ship, Gilmore remained on deck, ordering, "Take her down." He was posthumously awarded the Medal of Honor.

An intermittently moving but extremely self-indulgent piece of Fordian sentiment, *The Growler Story* was made in 16mm color as a training exercise for the Pacific Fleet Combat Camera Group. Under the circumstances, the film can be forgiven its amateurish aspects, such as a shaky sense of period, clumsy zoom shots, and rudimentary staging of battle action. The use of nonactors in bit parts actually works to its benefit, giving the film the feeling of a poetic documentary. *The Growler Story* virtually disregards its narrative line to concentrate on Fordian grace notes, such as a navy band playing a dirgelike rendition of "Faraway Places" as the families of the crewmen say their good-byes and watch the ship slowly leave Pearl Harbor.

Ford spends less time on Gilmore than he does indulging weird riffs on Ward Bond's character, Quincannon, a flabby-chested navy lifer with an Irish brogue. Incongruously paired with an attractive young wife and eight children (Ford's way of teasing Bond about his illusion that he was God's gift to nubile women), Quincannon orders his children to stand at attention and salute when he leaves for sea. Firing a torpedo at a Japanese ship, he beats his breast and intones solemnly, "God rest their heathen souls!" But as soon as the Japanese are blown to perdition, Quincannon bursts into a devilish grin.

Ford officially reported to the navy that he found the production a "wonderful experience," but he was irritated by interference from an admiral assigned as technical adviser, who kept insisting that *The Growler Story* was supposed to be a training film, not a mood piece about heroism. Ford privately complained to John Wayne that Bond had been even more insufferable than usual on the Hawaiian location, so distracted by his social climbing with navy brass that he kept slipping in and out of character.

Well into his seventies, Ford continued to perform such services for the navy, which gave him the opportunity to go on temporary active duty and parade around in his admiral's uniform, topped off with his distinctive dark glasses and eye patch. In February 1957, Ford supervised navy photographic crews in a training exercise aboard an aircraft carrier, re-creating air and sea combat during the Battle of Midway.

One reason Ford kept up his navy contacts was that he was still trying to wangle a Navy Cross for the Battle of Midway fourteen years after the fact. Admiral John Dale Price, USN (Ret.), his technical adviser on *The Wings of Eagles* and an old friend of Spig Wead (Price was played on-screen by Ken Curtis), proposed Ford for the medal. Ford's Midway colleague F. M. "Massie" Hughes, by now a rear admiral himself, lobbied the Navy Board of Medals and Awards. But Hughes wrote Price in December 1956, "Jack did a very courageous deed in filming the events on that day of the attack and certainly carried out his task with utter disregard of his own hide. Yet, I don't know how we could reopen the case, after the Award Board that acted on the Midway recommendations threw out or reduced every recommendation that was submitted. . . . I was recommended along with the squadron commanders for a Navy Cross and only got a commendation ribbon." Ford was also unsuccessful in his 1956 attempt to obtain a Croix de Guerre from the French government for his World War II service.

Ford remained in close contact throughout the postwar years with his old friend Johnny Bulkeley, who visited him every few months in Hollywood. Ironically, it took Bulkeley twelve years longer than Ford to be promoted from captain to rear admiral, the rank he attained in 1963. Basking in the reflected glory of having his own personal naval hero in tow, Ford took Bulkeley on the sets of his films, as well as to social functions and even to meetings with producers.

"Every time I was out there, I always took a half day off to see him," Bulkeley recalled. "I'd ride with him and he would be thinking, and I'd be very careful to keep my big mouth shut, not to interrupt his thinking. You gotta be very careful with that guy. I always answered any questions, I never got into any arguments with him, and I never once mentioned that he had that damn patch over his eye. I happened to be present when some producer asked him what the patch was for in his eye. Old Ford looked at him and said, 'I don't ask what's wrong with your nose.'

"One time John Wayne was going to have a reception at his home in the [San Fernando] Valley, and I was invited. [Wayne's wife] Pilar had this reception, beautifully done, with a hell of a lot of people in black tie. They were going to show the movie *They Were Expendable.* Now, John Ford and John Wayne that afternoon had been out looking at Wayne's boat, an old converted minesweeper called the *Wild Goose,* and I happened to be with them. These two guys were dressed in dungarees—grossly informal, let's put it that way—and they both started getting pretty tight. Anyway, I left there to go up to Wayne's home. And these two guys came in—tight. Now, John Ford really *wasn't* tight. He just wanted to make a scene, a grand entrance, and Pilar got taken in. She was shocked, and ordered the servants not to give these two any more alcoholic drinks. Well, that infuriated John Ford and infuriated Wayne. But John Ford made one hell of an entrance. Everyone knew who the hell he was. Everyone was going to talk about that for ages. Then, when he settled down and showed the movie, he was right back in his element again. Producers who were prominent people, very able, would come running up, kneel down, and listen to what he had to say."

Bulkeley noted that Ford, as a ploy, often pretended to be drunker than he actually was: "When I saw him on sets, he was cold sober, all business, and professionally straight. But he drank when he wanted to drink, and he drank for the pleasure of it. You didn't throw any nasty glances at him or anything deprecating, because he'd pick it up and that would be a disloyalty. You do that, you're dead, you're finished, he won't have anything more to do with you. He was putting on a big act to see how you'd react to him. I knew that rascal."

One of Ford's most anomalous works is *Gideon's Day,* a British detective movie he filmed in the fall of 1957. Starring Jack Hawkins as the beleaguered Scotland Yard chief inspector George Gideon, it was something of a lark, enabling Ford to gratify his enjoyment of suspense novels and J. J. Marric's Gideon series in particular. He also wanted to help his longtime friend and Stock Company member Anna Lee get off the blacklist; in her first movie role since 1952, the British-born actress plays Gideon's devoted wife, Kate. Costing only $543,600—$12,994 under budget—*Gideon's Day* was filmed in London as a joint venture of John Ford Productions and Columbia (British) Productions Ltd., with Michael Killanin producing. Ford's salary was $150,000, and he was to receive half of the net profits, an attractive arrangement indeed.

Telling the story of what Gideon dryly calls "an average day in my life," this fast-paced, often tongue-in-cheek, engagingly modest film written by T. E. B. Clarke contains a large cast and a myriad of dramatic and comedic episodes. They range from the death of a disgraced colleague, the investigation of a sex murder, and the cracking of a robbery ring to the betrothal of the inspector's daughter with a young constable (the daughter is charmingly played by Anna Massey, Raymond's daughter, in her film debut). Since no Irish issues are involved, Ford is able to adopt a benign attitude toward British police methodology. The director's usual mockery of the British is transformed into poking good-natured fun at the code of politeness and reserve Gideon and his colleagues (such as Michael Trubshawe's serenely unflappable Sergeant Gully) are expected to follow in capturing even the most loathsome criminals.

Like the director himself, George Gideon is a highly professional but often irascible man, a pipe smoker and heavy drinker whose position of responsibility requires the fielding of a constant barrage of questions and emergencies. Once again, a Ford hero is flawed by his neglect of wife and family for the sake of duty. Lee's Kate is unbelievably tolerant of his endless broken promises, though we sense repressed loneliness in her unnatural state of cheer. "Never marry a policeman," Kate warns her daughter, but the girl seems fated to disregard her advice.

Befitting the overriding importance the film places on doing a good "job of work," Ford directed *Gideon's Day* with unpretentious dispatch and deft, seemingly effortless craftsmanship. But its modest virtues hardly deserve the extravagant accolade perversely bestowed by *Cahiers du Cinéma:* "The freest, most direct, least fabricated film ever to sprout from one of Her Majesty's studios."

After opening in England in March 1958, *Gideon's Day* was treated atrociously by Columbia. It was not released in the United States until the following February, and then only as a second feature in black-and-white prints, cut by a third to only fifty-four minutes and retitled *Gideon of Scotland Yard.* Not surprisingly, the film failed to earn back its costs. When the Los Angeles County Museum of Art obtained a first-generation 35mm Technicolor print from London to show in a 1994 Ford retrospective, Frederick A. Young's lovely pastel photography finally could be seen to full advantage.

America's political mood was starting to thaw by the late 1950s. The civil rights movement was gaining momentum, McCarthyism was fading, and the Democratic Party was undergoing a resurgence as the Eisenhower era came to an end. In Hollywood, the blacklist was showing signs of imminent collapse.

The employment of blacklisted screenwriters under other names became an open secret, and something of a farce, when Dalton Trumbo's story for *The Brave One* (1956) won an Academy Award for the nonexistent "Robert Rich." In January 1959, after it had become widely known that the blacklisted Carl Foreman and Michael Wilson had written the Oscar-winning screenplay for *The Bridge on the River Kwai* (credited to novelist Pierre Boulle) and that Ned Young had cowritten *The Defiant Ones* (1958) under an assumed name, a successful drive was mounted within the Academy of Motion Picture Arts and Sciences to rescind its rule prohibiting blacklisted writers from winning Oscars (the rule took effect too late to cover *The Defiant Ones,* which also received the Oscar for best screenplay). Shortly before the rule was changed, Ward Bond, who had been the president of the Motion Picture Alliance for the Preservation of American Ideals since 1955, publicly declared, "They're all working now, all these Fifth Amendment Communists. There's no point at issue. We've just lost the fight, and it's as simple as that." In 1960, Kirk Douglas and Otto Preminger finally broke the blacklist when they separately insisted on listing Trumbo as the screenwriter of their films *Spartacus* and *Exodus.*

Given these momentous changes in the political mood of his country and his industry, it was not coincidental that Ford's former liberal allegiances, which had lain dormant if not totally dead during Hollywood's age of darkness, began to manifest themselves once again in his work. There was a clear element of opportunism in Ford's latest political transformation. Returning to his political roots took far less courage in the late fifties than he would have needed to stick to them throughout the blacklist era. But it was also true that Ford's newfound sense of ideological freedom allowed some of his better instincts to resurface. His candid examination of racism in *The Searchers* indicated that Ford was becoming more open to challenging ideas, but few seemed to understand the film's sociopolitical implications, and it was not until he directed his 1958 film version of Edwin O'Connor's *The Last Hurrah* that Ford explicitly repositioned himself on the liberal side of the fence.

As soon as Ford read O'Connor's best-selling 1956 novel about the last campaign of an old Irish-American politician, Mayor Frank Skeffington, he sent a telegram to Columbia Pictures president Harry Cohn and told him he liked the book so much that he would do the film version for nothing. Not that Ford meant the offer to be taken literally: his salary was $125,000, plus 25 percent of the net. Although John Ford Productions took a bank loan for half of the film's production cost, Columbia had final cut. That caused Ford some problems. Shortly before the film's release, he publicly declared that he "had hoped to make a controversial picture," but that Columbia executives removed about a reel and a half of material they thought was "just too daring. 'It's liable to offend people,' they said. . . . Everybody had to get in on the act and save the picture. In the end we put back two reels, and it comes out the way I made it."

Ford didn't specify which scenes made Columbia anxious, but Frank Nugent's adaptation offers a scathing portrait gallery of Skeffington's enemies, an amalgamation of reactionaries, bigots, and buffoons. Ford paints them with the sharp brush he used for characterizing such figures in his Popular Front period. Spencer Tracy's Skeffington notes that one of his foes, newspaper publisher Amos Force (John Carradine), is a former member of the Ku Klux Klan: "I've never been certain why he quit exactly, although I've always suspected it was because he had to buy his own sheet. Little things like that, you know, drive a man to tolerance." And despite having been a supporter of the Eisenhower-Nixon Republican ticket in 1952, Ford includes a sly parody of Richard Nixon's infamous Checkers speech in *The Last Hurrah*. The opposition candidate Kevin McCluskey (Charles FitzSimons), a vapid tool of right-wing forces, bumbles his way through an embarrassingly gauche television appearance displaying his frozen-faced wife, his small children, and a dog rented for the occasion. The dog spoils the show by barking noisily through the candidate's remarks. Even its casting is an impish Fordian joke: a mongrel Irish terrier.

O'Connor's finely observed study of Irish-American life and the decline of old-fashioned machine politics in the age of television based its principal character on the legendary James Michael Curley, who not only served four terms as mayor of Boston, four terms as a congressman, and one term as governor of Massachusetts, but also two terms in prison. Historian Francis Russell pointed out in 1959 that O'Connor's Skeffington is "a retouched Curley, less violent, more urbane. After Curley's first resentment had worn off, he began to see the Skeffington portrait as an asset. The book had toned down his ruthlessness, emphasized his benevolence. . . . For a while Curley took jokingly to calling and signing himself Skeffington. From originally intending to sue O'Connor, he ended up by congratulating him."

Coyly set in "A New England City" (a laughably transparent legal disclaimer), the film goes even further than the book in presenting Skeffington as an urban Robin Hood. Curley's popularity was based on forcing the Yankees to subsidize extensive public works programs for the benefit of the working class. The film dramatizes this strategy while taking pains to exonerate the mayor from involvement in the system of kickbacks and patronage that Curley was also well known for practicing. Ford not only revels in attacking Skeffington's foes, he approaches Skeffington through his own pair of rose-colored glasses. Raymond Durgnat aptly described the film as "a nostalgically brawling farewell to the corrupt old Tammany-type boss . . . who, though as anachronistic, now, as the gunfighter, had a rough and ready moral grandeur to him."

The story struck a family chord in the director, bringing back memories of the political activities of his father and his uncle, Judge Connolly, on behalf of Portland's Irish-American community. Skeffington was the latest in the honorable line of Ford's benevolent, wisely humorous, but privately melancholy political figures, following in the tradition of Abraham Lincoln and Judge

Priest. The sociopolitical milieu of *The Last Hurrah* must also have reminded the director of his lost silent film *The Prince of Avenue A,* with Gentleman Jim Corbett as the son of an Irish-American ward boss. Ford's sentimental identification with Skeffington and everything he represents precludes any critical distance from the character.

Despite Curley's grudging fondness for the novel—his favorite part was the most lovingly protracted deathbed scene since Dickens—he professed outrage over the screen adaptation. After a private screening, Curley sued Columbia Pictures in August 1958, claiming that the film invaded his privacy. That was two months before its release and three months before Curley's own death at age eighty-three. Curley should have been delighted with Tracy's affectionate portrayal of a legendary figure even an adversary calls "an engaging rogue." When asked about the lawsuit, Ford responded, "If this is Curley—if Curley thinks he is Frank Skeffington—then instead of suing I would advise him to run for governor again." According to Curley's obituary in the *New York Times,* "Columbia contended it had paid Mr. Curley $25,000 for signing a release before the story was filmed. The Curley legal forces insisted the signature was a forgery. Before that aspect could be considered, a settlement was made out of court for a sum that was not disclosed." It was later reported that the final settlement was $15,000.

Ford took an unusually long time casting the lead role because he was stubbornly avoiding the obvious choice. Such names as James Cagney, John Wayne, and even Ward Bond were considered. Perhaps thinking of *Citizen Kane,* with its chilling portrait of another powerful American political figure, Ford made an offer to Orson Welles, whose Skeffington would have been less openhearted than Tracy's. "When the contracts were to be settled, I was away on location," Welles told Peter Bogdanovich, "and some lawyer—if you can conceive of such a thing—turned it down. He told Ford that the money wasn't right or the billing wasn't good enough, something idiotic like that, and when I came back to town the part had gone to Tracy."

It was Katharine Hepburn who finally intervened to help Ford and Tracy patch up their long-standing feud; by happy coincidence, O'Connor had provided Skeffington's late wife with the name of Kate. Her portrait is prominently displayed on the landing of the mayor's home in the movie; like Will Rogers's Judge Priest and other Ford heroes, Skeffington regularly communes with his loved one's memory image, although without words. Tracy turned fifty-eight while working on *The Last Hurrah* and was in poor health. He missed some days of shooting and often had to go home around midday. Without telling Tracy, Hepburn persuaded Ford to act as if quitting early was his idea. "God, I'm exhausted," Ford would tell Tracy when he saw the actor starting to fade. "You know, I think we've done a full day's work, and I don't know why the hell you don't go home." As a result of Ford's solicitude, the film finished eight days over its thirty-five-day schedule, but he still managed to bring it in for $255,654 under his budgetary allotment of $2,574,604.

The most delightful and touching aspect of *The Last Hurrah* is that it served as Ford's last grand reunion with many of Hollywood's most beloved old character actors, including Pat O'Brien, Donald Crisp, James Gleason, Basil Rathbone, Frank McHugh, Edmund Lowe, Frank Albertson, and Jane Darwell. Such nostalgic casting was not the director's original plan. He discussed importing several of the little-known Irish thespians from *The Rising of the Moon* to play Skeffington's cronies. But in the end, the only one of his "Irish players" to appear in the film was FitzSimons, from the cast of *The Quiet Man*. A brother of Maureen O'Hara, the former barrister had come to Hollywood to pursue a producing career. Casting a native Irishman as McCluskey was fitting because he is chosen by the Yankee establishment to oppose Skeffington in a cynical ploy to split the Irish-American vote. Crisp's cardinal, a longtime Skeffington foe as Boston's patrician William Cardinal O'Connell was to Curley, bemoans the fact that a young idiot like McCluskey represents "the hope of the future. . . . Is this the best we can do?"

That generational despair is one of the film's central themes. The mayor's son (Arthur Walsh) is a thoughtless playboy, and the leading Yankee banker (Rathbone) has a mentally deficient son (O. Z. Whitehead); Ford cast those parts with two of his Stock Company's perennial juveniles. Offering some balance are the mayor's sportswriter nephew Adam Caulfield (Jeffrey Hunter), who becomes his surrogate son, and the cardinal's thoughtful young aide, Monsignor Killian, played by Ford's own son-in-law, Ken Curtis. What gives these characters stature and potential in Ford's eyes is their respect for tradition, Adam through his uncle and the monsignor through his church. Adam gladly accepts the mayor's offer to observe his last reelection campaign for its "historical interest." Because of television and radio, "the old-fashioned political campaign in a few years will be extinct as the dodo," Skeffington says. "[T]his is your last chance to catch the act." But neither Adam nor Monsignor Killian offsets the alarming impression conveyed by the mayor's two unworthy successors, McCluskey and "Junior" Skeffington.

Such jaundiced portraits of the young, increasingly common in Ford's later films, clearly reflect his bitter disappointment over his own son. As FitzSimons put it, "Ford so wanted his son to deliver, and the son didn't." Ford carried a heavy burden of guilt over the history of emotional neglect that had blighted his son's life. By the time Patrick turned forty in 1961, it was obvious that he would never have a major career of his own in filmmaking. Lacking his father's drive and self-confidence, to say nothing of his prodigious talent, but sharing his alcoholism and prickly personality, Pat suffered from Hollywood's perception that he existed merely as a dim shadow of the man who allowed so many other people to call him "Pappy." Pat made further attempts to branch out on his own. As vice president in charge of production for C. V. Whitney Pictures, he produced the 1958 feature *The Missouri Traveler* (also known as *The Young Land*), a nostalgia piece directed by Jerry Hopper and starring Brandon de Wilde and Lee Marvin. Pat collaborated with Nugent and others in writing a 1959 British colonial adventure film, *Northwest Frontier* (also known as *Flame over India*), but both projects proved forgettable. Pat's only important credits came at the sufferance of his father, who just once granted his son a full producer's title, along with Willis Goldbeck, on *Sergeant Rutledge* in 1960. Pat's disenchantment with being the son of John Ford could only have been exacerbated by *The Last Hurrah,* with its clear message of emotional disinheritance.

While mourning the loss of the paternalism and traditional sense of community that Skeffington represents, Ford harbors no illusions about the survival of those values in the modern era. In Skeffington's imminent obsolescence, Ford can see his own growing irrelevance to modern American culture. Both the director and his protagonist emotionally live in the past. One of the most touching scenes in all of Ford's work is the mayor showing his nephew the old tenement where he and two of his political enemies were born and raised. As Skeffington points out the upper window where his family lived, Ford mixes in the sound of a baby crying with the gently wistful music of the Irish lullaby "The Castle of Dromore." Skeffington similarly blurs past and present in his traditional political practice of pitting the haves against the have-nots, uniting the Irish and other non-WASP groups against the Yankee establishment.

Candidly admitting to Adam that he is still motivated by an injustice done to his mother when she served as a maid to a prominent Yankee family, Skeffington delights in such stunts as invading the Yankee sanctum sanctorum, the Plymouth Club, whose members are "still breathing the same air they brought over on the *Mayflower*." To compound his calculated outrage to WASP sensibilities, the mayor pointedly takes along two of his closest and most ethnically identifiable aides, an Irishman (Edward Brophy) and a Jew (Ricardo Cortez). Skeffington's grandstanding personalizes a problem that would be more effectively addressed through the courts. But rather than criticizing Skeffington for his role in perpetuating these ancient ethnic feuds, Ford sentimentally revels in the mayor's inability to put the past behind him.

The positive value of the fading Irish-American communal traditions the mayor represents is conveyed most movingly in the film's extended centerpiece, Knocko Minihan's wake.[4] Knocko was a singularly unpopular man, but Skeffington loyally turns out a mob of supporters to pay their respects. Initially repulsed by the way a religious ritual becomes a political rally, Adam changes his mind after seeing the previously disconsolate widow (Anna Lee) enter the room on the arm of the mayor, who tells her, "Just a few of Knocko's friends." In the novel, Skeffington provides an eloquent defense of this kind of multilayered ritual, telling Adam, "Life wasn't exactly a picnic for our people in those days. They were a sociable people but they didn't get much chance for sociability. They were poor, they worked hard, and they didn't have much in the way of diversion. Actually, the only place people got together was at the wake. Everybody knew everybody else; when somebody died, the others went to pay their respects and also to see and talk to each other. It was all part of the pattern. They were sorry for the family of the deceased, to be sure, but while they were being sorry they took advantage of the opportunity to have a drink and chat with the others who were being sorry, too. . . . All in all, I've always thought the wake was a grand custom, and I still do." And if it is necessary to lie about the deceased to make the widow happy, Ford implies that such duplicity in the service of a greater good is "part of the pattern" that makes society function.

The townspeople's parade honoring the judge in *The Sun Shines Bright* is bitterly echoed when Skeffington walks home alone after his defeat, the new mayor's victory parade marching in the opposite direction behind him, with a band playing "Hail, Hail, the Gang's All Here." Skeffington repeats the words of the song with quiet irony when he is lying on his deathbed and his cronies arrive to say their farewells. As the consolations of memory became ever more central to his life and work, Ford enjoyed ending his films with a ceremonial assemblage of the cast, a curtain call. *The Last Hurrah* offers a melancholy variation on that motif, ending with the members of the Skeffington Stock Company filing up a staircase to see the mayor's body, casting outsized shadows on the wall as they slowly fade into history.

As Ford's cinematic wake for the immigrant society from which he emerged, *The Last Hurrah* has powerful emotional resonance. But as a portrait of the changes in modern American life, it is flawed by Ford's sentimental myopia. By identifying so closely with Skeffington, Ford misses the salient sociopolitical facts that rendered the Curley/Skeffington brand of politics extinct. It was not a Machiavellian resurgence of the old Yankee bloc that

---

4. As a private Fordian gag, the director cast the Latino actor Perry Lopez as Knocko's corpse. Lopez had played Rodrigues in *Mister Roberts* and would become best known as Detective Lou Escobar in *Chinatown*.

eventually turned Mayor Curley out of office but the economic rise of the Irish and other immigrant groups into the middle class, blurring the old class antagonisms and disrupting the old ethnic coalitions. Simply blaming Skeffington's defeat on the ignorance of a malleable new generation is a sign of Ford's own inability to understand or adapt to the changing American scene.

Ironically, just two years after the film's release, the nation would elect its first Irish Catholic president, a young man from Boston whose grandfather, John "Honey Fitz" Fitzgerald, was succeeded as mayor by James Curley in 1913. John F. Kennedy's ability to overcome an old ethnic barrier in American political life showed how thoroughly Irish-Americans had been absorbed into the social mainstream; Kennedy laid the foundation for that victory by cultivating an Anglophile persona that seemed more Yankee than traditionally Irish. His election demonstrated the fallacy of Ford's glib dismissal of the coming generation of politicians as a bunch of imbeciles. Still, Ford could not help being immensely pleased by the rise of a young Irish Catholic to the nation's highest office. He said that for the first time in his life, he felt like a full-fledged American citizen.

Ford's boss at Columbia, Harry Cohn, died on February 27, 1958, the morning of the fourth day of filming on *The Last Hurrah*. First hired by Cohn in 1935 to make *The Whole Town's Talking*, Ford was one of the few people in Hollywood who would admit to genuine personal fondness for the legendary tyrant: "He was the kind of a man whose nod and handshake were worth more than a contract drawn up by a score of Philadelphia lawyers."

When a Columbia executive came on the set to notify Ford that Cohn was dead, the director became distraught. The loss of his old friend was another sign that the age of the studio system was passing into memory, leaving Ford increasingly surrounded by people he neither knew nor respected.

"I'm dismissing the company," said Ford.

"But you can't do that," the executive protested, "it's never been done at Columbia!"

"It's being done now."

At Cohn's nondenominational funeral service on March 2, held on adjoining Columbia soundstages, Ford sat in the front row next to Abe Lastfogel, head of the William Morris Agency. After a soprano sang *Ave Maria*, Danny Kaye rose without introduction and went to a microphone to speak Cohn's eulogy (written by Clifford Odets): "Himself little educated, he admired, almost to a fanatic degree, talent. Talent itself was a quality which bred in him a deep respect, almost as though the gifted human being was set aside, as if God had put a special mark on his forehead. . . ."

When Kaye finished speaking, Ford turned to Lastfogel and asked, "Who is that intelligent young rabbi?"

In 1863, General Ulysses S. Grant sent a Union army brigade commanded by Colonel Benjamin H. Grierson on a six-hundred-mile raid through Mississippi into Louisiana to cut railroad lines and distract Confederate troops from Grant's drive toward Vicksburg. This incident, which historian James M. McPherson calls "the most spectacular cavalry adventure of the war," served as the basis for *The Horse Soldiers,* a 1956 novel by Harold Sinclair that attracted the interest of screenwriters John Lee Mahin and Martin Rackin, who were looking for a film to produce together. "We took out an option on this book," Mahin recalled, "and we said, 'The perfect guy [to direct it], a Civil War buff, is Ford.' He fell for it like a ton of bricks when we took it to him. We wanted Gable to play Duke's part first, and we almost had him. Ford was wonderful, but that was an unfortunate picture. Bad movie."

Many of the problems, as Ford realized, stemmed from the laboriously contrived screenplay. Although *The Horse Soldiers* features some of William H. Clothier's most beautifully atmospheric cinematography (including a sequence humorously re-creating the taking of a Matthew Brady photograph), much of the running time is wasted on a tediously manufactured conflict between Wayne's Colonel John Marlowe (the Grierson character) and William Holden's army doctor, Major Henry Kendall. Saddled with an overly convenient hatred of doctors, Marlowe treats Kendall with irrational viciousness, addressing him as "Croaker" but rarely with the joshing tone Ford habitually used in employing that insulting term for a physician. Emotionally identifying with the doctor, Ford gave him an Irish surname rather than the name in the script, Curtis.

After the picture opened in June 1959, Mahin "snuck into a performance, because it wasn't making much money, and I wondered why. I was sitting next to a woman. The scene came on where they had to haul in the wounded at the station. Holden was treating Wayne, and Wayne was mad at Holden, and she said, 'Oh, for God's sake! No man would feel that way about doctors!'"

Nor does the contentious romance between Marlowe and a captured Southern woman, Hannah Hunter (Constance Towers), seem credible, except during their final scenes of parting, when they develop a more mature human understanding (the music underneath is "Lorena," the Civil War ballad about unrequited love Ford previously used in *The Searchers*). Ford broke his rule against using blondes in Westerns after his eye wandered to the statuesque Towers at a Hollywood social event. "After a conversation regarding my Irish heritage and navy relatives, Mr. Ford decided to test me," she recalled. Towers had a good rapport with the director, who cast her again in *Sergeant Rutledge*

(1960) and became the godfather of her two children, one of whom, Michael Ford McGrath, was named after him. But her inexperience showed opposite Wayne and Holden in *The Horse Soldiers*. Her comic scenes tend to be too arch and her dramatic scenes too earnest. "Maybe it would have been better without that girl in it," Mahin conceded. Ford cast the African-American tennis star Althea Gibson as Hannah's maid, Lukey, whose presence enables him to remind the audience of the realities of slavery, but all too glancingly.

"I have never, in all my life, met any man who knew as much about the history of the Civil War as John Ford," Clothier said. "He can tell you the name of every general who was in the Union army and the Southern army. He is absolutely familiar with every piece of wardrobe that was worn by troops in the Civil War. When we would go on location for instance, on *The Horse Soldiers*, which was a Civil War film— Mr. Ford would have a box of books which was larger than his wardrobe."

Considering Ford's long-standing fascination with the subject—he told Gavin Lambert in the early 1960s that the Civil War was his major interest in life, with movies secondary—it is odd that *The Horse Soldiers* was Ford's first and only full-scale feature on the war. *The Prisoner of Shark Island* concerns the war's bitter aftermath, *Judge Priest* contains a magnificent Griffith-like flashback to Gettysburg, and *The Civil War,* Ford's segment of the 1962 Cinerama spectacle *How the West Was Won,* briefly but poetically depicts a farm boy's baptism of blood at the Battle of Shiloh. For the most part, the Yankees and Confederates who wander throughout Ford's films are living the war only in their memories. His longtime research assistant Katherine Cliffton admitted, "I was waiting for his big Civil War picture."

When I asked Ford why he hadn't made more films on the Civil War, he testily replied, "You have to find a story first, McBride," a ludicrously evasive answer considering that the Civil War is undoubtedly the richest and most dramatic period in American history. At the time I didn't know of Ford's attempt to make *The Valiant Virginians*. But with the major exception of *Gone with the Wind,* Hollywood traditionally has not had great success with Civil War movies; the conventional wisdom is that the subject remains too troubling and divisive for American audiences. Perhaps that marketing problem is what motivated United Artists to begin the trailer for *The Horse Soldiers* with a shot of marching Union soldiers incongruously accompanied by a choir singing the Confederate anthem "Bonnie Blue Flag."

Ford's personal embellishments on the screenplay of *The Horse Soldiers* included adding the opening sequence with Ulysses S. Grant giving Marlowe his orders aboard a boat on the Mississippi River. Grant is played by Stan Jones, the composer of songs for such Ford films as *Wagon Master, Rio Grande,* and *The Searchers,* as well as the theme song for *The Horse Soldiers*. In 1956, Laurence

Stallings suggested to Ford that he make a film about Grant, and Ford became intrigued by the idea of telling the story of a disgraced drunkard who went on to become the commanding general of the Union army and president of the United States. "He understood Grant, the drinking and all," Mahin observed. Ford never made a feature about Grant, but both *The Civil War* and *The Colter Craven Story,* the 1960 episode he directed for Ward Bond's *Wagon Train* television series, show Grant at Shiloh, the worst debacle of his military career. The haunting flashback about Grant in the TV program also includes scenes of his life before the war.

Ford's most important addition to the script of *The Horse Soldiers* was the sequence of the boy soldiers marching off to fight for the Confederacy, the one great passage in an otherwise mediocre film. A heartbreaking image of war's sacrifice of the young, it pirouettes from near tragedy to bittersweet comedy as Marlowe's men gallantly pretend to be routed by the cadets. Ford based the sequence on the 1864 Shenandoah Valley Battle of New Market, in which Union troops were run off by cadets from the Virginia Military Institute; Bellah had used the incident in *The Valiant Virginians.* Filming took place near the end of the location shoot, with 150 cadets between the ages of nine and sixteen from Jefferson Military College in Washington, Mississippi, the alma mater of Confederate president Jefferson Davis. The cadets' uniforms were copied from an actual 1850s-vintage college uniform preserved by a Natchez woman as a family heirloom. Jack Pennick spent a week drilling the boys in preparation for the filming and regaling them with his war stories. The cadets also became fond of veteran Ford stuntman and bit-part actor Fred Kennedy, who demonstrated his way of leaping into and out of his saddle.

But such bright moments were few during the making of *The Horse Soldiers.* This enervatingly complicated production provides an early illustration of what Joan Didion meant by her famous observation that the deal is the true art form of modern Hollywood. Six companies were involved in the contractual negotiations—United Artists, the Mirisch Company, and the personal companies of both producers, the director, and both male stars—a process that took several months. Not much energy seemed left over for the picture, which cost about $5 million, $175,000 going to Ford and $750,000 each to Wayne and Holden. Each star was granted 20 percent of the profits, and Ford was allotted 10 percent of the producers' share. Ford complained to Killanin that after subtracting $2.1 million in above-the-line costs (the salaries of the stars, writer-producers, and director), there was "no money to make the picture." It must have been galling to Ford that his former prop boy was now earning almost five times his own salary. In the final years of Ford's career, his bankability increasingly depended on Wayne's willingness to star in his films.

The director's grumpy mood throughout the production of *The Horse Soldiers* was aggravated by the hovering presence of Martin Rackin, who was precisely the kind of slick Hollywood wheeler-dealer Ford always tried to avoid. "Marty drove him crazy, because Marty was always cracking jokes," Mahin recalled. "He'd say, 'Get that son of a bitch off my neck, he's driving me crazy. See, you have humor, he has jokes.' I wondered if he was trying to split me and Marty to get his way. But he wasn't. It was just that Marty irritated him.

"We both walked on the set one day and they were doing the banquet scene, where [Hannah] served [the Yankees] food in her house. Ford was using a pretty well known bit actor, Walter Reed, he had him in a Union outfit. He had already played a Confederate officer. Well, he's a guy whose face you remembered, but here he was in two uniforms. We didn't know how to tell Ford. I said, 'I'll tell him,' and Marty said, 'Don't, Jesus, he'll go crazy.' So we went to Duke and said, 'We want some advice, how do you tell this guy?' Duke says, 'Well, you just go tell him. I agree with you. Jesus, we've already cranked two hours on this guy.' Finally we went down on the set and told him. Ford said, 'All right, all right, that's it! You take over, you take over!' Wouldn't accept the fact. We just cut around him." (Perhaps Ford was thinking of his uncle who, it was said, fought for both the Union and the Confederacy.)

The location work in Mississippi and Louisiana from October 28 through December 5 was logistically complicated and physically arduous for the sixty-four-year-old director. Ford took some pleasure in being reunited with his former silent cowboy star, Hoot Gibson, whose improbable casting as an elderly Union soldier attracted more attention from nostalgic locals than either Wayne or Holden. Ford also slipped into a remarkably benign mood with Hank Worden, the wizened character actor who was making his seventh Ford film in eleven years. Worden recalled, "Everybody used to call him Pappy. When we were shooting *Horse Soldiers*, we were out on location in front of one of the old mansions, out in the country. I said, 'Pappy, what am I supposed to do here?' He stopped and looked at me and said, 'Hank, you know I'm not that much older than you are. How would you like to call me Jack, and we'll keep it on an even keel.' I said, 'Thank you, sir, very much. Thank you, Jack.' And of course that was a privilege, because not everybody called Mr. Ford Jack."

But the director had to contend with some formidable egos on *The Horse Soldiers*, including his own. Wayne was preoccupied with long-distance pre-production planning for his pet project, *The Alamo*. According to his wife, Pilar, Wayne "made this movie the exception to his own self-imposed rule of not drinking while he was working. Holden, who also had a problem with alcohol, drank steadily while on location. Ford nagged and lectured Duke and

Holden, miserable because he wouldn't permit himself to join their parties." Pilar had become addicted to sleeping pills and was in the throes of withdrawal when she arrived on location. Two days later, she recalled, she "began hallucinating. I was told that I tried to slash my wrists." She was sent back to Hollywood to recuperate. Meanwhile, three people suffered broken legs, including Ford's son, Patrick, who served as his location scout.

On the morning of December 5 in Natchitoches, Louisiana, Ford was wrapping up location work, shooting parts of the climactic battle scene at Williams Bridge. Later that day he was planning to film the Union soldiers crossing the river. Before lunch, Ford asked Fred Kennedy to perform a routine horse fall.

The stuntman can be seen in *The Horse Soldiers* playing one of the troopers who is most solicitous of Hannah when she is forced to accompany their southward march. Previously, Kennedy's most memorable role for Ford was as Heinz, the grizzled veteran who befriends Trooper Jeff York after their fistfight in *Rio Grande*. When Kennedy worked on *The Horse Soldiers,* he was forty-eight years old. Ford did not know that the stuntman had broken his neck two years earlier, but he was reluctant to assign any stunts to Kennedy, who was clearly out of shape. Still, Christmas was nearing, and "the Old Man was trying to be nice, trying to give Fred a little extra dough," recalled actor Hank Worden, who was present that day.

Throughout the location shoot, Ford had been teasing Kennedy by trying to persuade Constance Towers to give him a kiss. So when they were ready to film Kennedy taking a fall from his horse, Bill Clothier suggested that once he hit the ground, it would be amusing for Towers to run in, throw her arms around Kennedy's neck, and kiss him. Ford agreed.

"Fred had done many stunts for Ford, but he had taken on some weight and wasn't as agile," Worden observed. "So when he did his fall, he didn't turn over as much as he should. He was on his back when he hit the ground. It broke his neck."

Not realizing what had happened, Ford pushed Towers forward into the shot. She walked in and bent down over the stuntman. He was lying almost motionless, gasping for breath, a Union army cap strapped to his head. Looking up in alarm, Towers exclaimed, "He's hurt."

Kennedy's face was turning blue when Ford rushed in with the company's first-aid man, John Leber. Towers and two stuntmen in Confederate uniforms held Kennedy's head slightly above the ground as she touched his shoulders gently. Leber and Ford administered oxygen. Leaning down to see if Kennedy was breathing, Leber said simply, "Dead."

"Ford was pretty shook up, and he walked away by himself," Worden remembered. The assistant director, Wingate Smith, "tried to comfort him a little. Wingate was crying and probably the Old Man was—that may be one reason why he walked away. Connie was crying, we were all feeling pretty bad. The Old Man sort of waved Wingate off, and Wingate left him alone for a minute to get control of himself."

Ford and Leber accompanied Kennedy to a local hospital, where he was pronounced dead on arrival. Ford called an abrupt halt to the location shooting and sent the company back to Hollywood. That night the director and Clothier paid their respects to Kennedy's body at a nearby church while his brother Roy, a wrangler on the picture, made arrangements to take him home. Ford returned to Los Angeles the following day.

Some work remained at the Goldwyn and MGM studios and in the San Fernando Valley before *The Horse Soldiers* finished shooting in January. But Ford never filmed the river crossing scheduled for the day of Kennedy's death or the script's ending sequence of the troopers marching wearily but triumphantly into Baton Rouge. "I guess he just got sick of it," Mahin said. Mahin claimed that in lieu of filming the battle at Williams Bridge as the script specified, Ford hastily threw together the ending of Colonel Marlowe galloping across an exploding bridge toward enemy lines after lighting the fuse with his cigar. (Wayne is doubled on horseback by Chuck Hayward.) But Mahin's memory faltered in that respect, for both the battle and the exploding bridge were filmed largely as written. Furthermore, in the screenplay the concluding march seems superfluous, a forced attempt at uplift, so Ford's decision to drop it arguably was aesthetically valid.

Nevertheless, Mahin disagreed with Ford's decision to end *The Horse Soldiers* in such an elliptical and downbeat manner: "I said, 'Marty, we've got to shoot [the original ending in the script].' I pleaded with the Mirisch brothers. They said, 'No, we've got Ford, Holden, and Wayne, we'll make a million.' I said, 'This picture goes right out the window. It's a little shaky up to there anyway, so let's at least have a finish.' They said, 'No, we won't spend the money.' "

Fred Kennedy's death was the first time someone had died in front of Ford's camera, other than in his combat documentaries; the three deaths during the filming of *Mogambo* occurred off the set in a vehicle accident. Ford was devastated to see a man die as a result of his direction. He had always loved stuntmen; he had been a stuntman himself, had even been seriously injured performing a stunt for his brother Frank in the silent days, and Fred Kennedy was a loyal member of his Stock Company.

"Duke told me," Pilar Wayne recalled, "that Ford couldn't seem to forget the accident and get on with his work, blaming himself for Kennedy's death. He began drinking heavily and lost interest in finishing the film." When Wayne returned home from location, he told her, "Ford just doesn't seem to care anymore. Hell, he looks and acts like a beaten man."

CHAPTER THIRTEEN

"THERE'S NO FUTURE IN AMERICA"

*I'm sorry the show didn't have a happier
ending. Maybe I can do better next time. . . .*

MAYOR SKEFFINGTON (SPENCER TRACY)
IN *THE LAST HURRAH* (1958)

IN THE EARLY summer of 1959, Ford was interviewed by Colin Young for a
Film Quarterly article on veteran Hollywood directors. Young asked Ford if
he had been making the kinds of films he wanted to make. "No!" barked
Ford. "I don't want to make great sprawling pictures. I want to make films in
a kitchen. . . . The old enthusiasm has gone, maybe. But don't quote that—oh,
hell, you can quote it." Nevertheless, Ford was not yet ready for retirement.
"Now is the time," he said, "to do the films I want to do. At sixty-four [actu-
ally sixty-five] I am too old for anything else."

After the disastrous experience of *The Horse Soldiers,* Ford spent all but two
weeks of the ten-week period from January 24 through April 15, 1959, cruising aimlessly around Hawaii with Mary on the *Araner.* He was mulling over his
future options in an industry and a society that were changing almost beyond
his comprehension. More and more, he was thinking of working outside the
United States. Michael Killanin was trying to negotiate a purchase of the film
rights to their pet project, Arthur Conan Doyle's novel *The White Company,*
which they hoped to film in Ireland, England, or on the Continent. They had
no luck obtaining financial backing for what would have been an expensive
period piece; even before *The Horse Soldiers* opened to so-so business that June,
their approach to the Mirisch Company was rebuffed. Killanin and Ford halfheartedly discussed a project to be filmed in Germany, a mystery story called
The Judge and the Hangman, starring John Wayne and Spencer Tracy. In March
1959, Dudley Nichols expressed interest in writing the script, but he soon fell
ill; the screenwriter whose artistic ambitions had helped Ford discover his own
strengths and limitations died of cancer in January 1960.

Ford's world, like Frank Skeffington's, was rapidly getting smaller in these autumnal years. Tyrone Power died of a heart attack in Spain while filming King Vidor's *Solomon and Sheba* in November 1958. Grant Withers, a member of the Ford Stock Company (*My Darling Clementine, Fort Apache, Rio Grande, The Sun Shines Bright*) and a poker-playing buddy of Ford and Wayne, despairing of his problems with booze and pills, committed suicide in March 1959. That November, the gargantuan Ford regular and sometime leading man Victor McLaglen was felled by a heart attack. December saw the death of Russell Simpson, the character actor whose nine roles for Ford included Pa Joad in *The Grapes of Wrath*. In November 1960, Ford would lose Ward Bond and Clark Gable only eleven days apart.

One of the deaths that hit Ford the hardest was that of Wild Bill Donovan, his wartime patron in the OSS. In declining health for more than two years with arteriosclerotic atrophy of the brain, General Donovan died at Washington's Walter Reed Army Hospital on February 8, 1959. "We have lost the last hero," President Dwight D. Eisenhower remarked.

Ford managed to revive his spirits that spring in the way he knew best, by taking a working vacation. He traveled to Taiwan and Korea on temporary active duty in the navy from April 15 through May 9 to make two short orientation films for the Department of Defense. Designed for showing to servicemen, civilians, and dependents posted to those countries, *Taiwan—Island of Freedom* and *Korea—Battleground for Liberty* were commissioned by the Office of Armed Forces Information and Education. These were part of a "People-to-People" series initiated by CINCPAC (the navy's commander in chief, Pacific) to foster better relations with the citizens of friendly Asian countries.

Ford held a four-hour meeting at his home on June 16, 1958, to organize a Hollywood advisory committee for the series. George O'Brien, a captain in the Naval Reserve, was chosen as project officer and was delegated to make a location scouting trip that fall. Ford also recruited Frank Capra, a retired army colonel; director George Sidney, a major in the Air Force Reserve; John Lee Mahin, a retired air force captain; and Ford's MCA agent and World War II colleague Jack Bolton, a retired captain in the Naval Reserve. Capra, then in the process of being politically rehabilitated to work in Hollywood, declined Ford's offer to direct one of the orientation films, but he and the other committee members served as advisers on Ford's Korea and Taiwan films as well as on scripts about such countries as the Philippines, Vietnam, and Cambodia.

Mark Armistead, a commander in the Naval Reserve, came aboard to help Ford and O'Brien produce *Taiwan,* which was narrated by Glenn Ford, a lieutenant commander in the navy who admired Ford but never had another chance to work for him. Both films were photographed in 16mm color by air force cameramen from the Lookout Mountain Air Force Laboratory in Los Angeles and were principally directed by Ford, although some scenes in *Korea* were directed by its screenwriter, U.S. Navy Lieutenant Commander Eric Strutt. Strutt wrote *Taiwan* in collaboration with Mahin and W. T. Blume.

The political agenda behind the People-to-People project, as the Defense Department privately explained to the committee members, was to counter-act Communist propaganda about American imperialism. The scripts for both of Ford's films contain some anti-Communist rhetoric, but they are mostly low-key and chatty, following the guideline to "Use the Cold War mission, without using the term."

Their primary message is that American personnel should behave abroad in a way that reflects well on the United States, showing respect for the people and customs of their host countries: "Remember, we are not part of an oc-cupation force." The *Taiwan* script calls for a Chinese airman to suggest, "I think if we just forget we are Chinese and American, and remember we are all people, we will get along fine." And about the Koreans, a character says, "Some people call them 'the Irish of the Orient.' They are a proud people . . . and want to be treated as equals." The *Korea* script diplomatically notes that "because democracy is new to the country, there are bound to be a lot of bugs to work out of the system . . . and it isn't right for us to be critical." But an American briefing officer speaks more propagandistically about Taiwan, then under the authoritarian rule of Generalissimo Chiang Kai-shek: "I think you'll be impressed by the personal freedom, the political freedom, the press freedom, and the religious freedom you will meet here. It is just the exact op-posite from conditions that exist on the Communist-held mainland."

Arriving in Taipei on April 20, Ford and O'Brien turned up at a press con-ference looking roguish in identical eye patches. They spent ten days in Tai-wan, shooting location scenes with both actors and nonactors. Korean location filming took place in the first week of May in Seoul, Pusan, and along the DMZ separating South and North Korea. Both documentaries in-clude framing footage filmed in Los Angeles at the Lookout Mountain studio with young Hollywood actors: a briefing for American airmen assigned to Taiwan and a discussion among four Americans in a Seoul apartment.

The most dramatic episode that took place on Ford's trip to Asia was his ro-mantic entanglement with a pretty Korean model and actress named Heran Moon, who recalled spending three days with him in Korea. In scenes Ford di-rected on May 7 at Seoul's Kyung Bok Palace, Heran plays a tour guide es-corting schoolgirls and talking with O'Brien, who filled in when another actor failed to appear. After Ford's departure the following day for Tokyo and Pearl Harbor, he sent gifts to the young woman, including movie makeup and photographs of them together in Korea. The most intimate photo, taken at the palace, shows Ford with a makeup pencil applying last-minute touches to her mouth; in another, the director holds her face while giving directions for her scene with O'Brien.

For the next eight months, Heran bombarded Ford with love letters. "All I want to tell is how much I miss you," she wrote. "I just close my eyes and think and remember everything we shared and calm down myself! . . . Darling, you brought me many things, happiness and others. I don't want to lose you, please don't go away from me. I want you to know that you are my life." Heran became worried because Ford seldom responded to her letters. Eventually, she began imploring him to help find her acting jobs in Hollywood, on his films or others. Their correspondence abruptly ended.

Hollywood today is a market for sex and horror," Ford complained to Colin Young in what would become a familiar and tiresome refrain of his later years. He added, "I don't want any part of that." While they were talking, Ford was interrupted by his secretary, Meta Sterne, who announced that "the girl" had arrived to discuss his new film.

"What girl?" demanded Ford.

"The girl in the picture," replied Sterne. "The girl who gets raped."

"Well, tell her to wait, she's not going to get raped yet."

Turning to Young, Ford deadpanned, "I'm really going to have to read that story."

Those jocular comments revealed Ford's conflicted state of mind about "sex and horror" as he approached the delicate and volatile subject matter of *Sergeant Rutledge* (1960). Not only did this Western take advantage of the new climate of sexual frankness but it did so through the prism of race relations, the most controversial political issue in the country at that time. Reviewers who failed to notice what Ford was saying about racism and miscegenation in *The Searchers* were permitted no such luxury with the bluntly provocative *Sergeant Rutledge*.

The original screenplay by James Warner Bellah and Willis Goldbeck deals with the court-martial of Sergeant Braxton Rutledge (Woody Strode), a black officer in the Ninth Cavalry Regiment, United States Colored Troops. Despite his exemplary service record, Rutledge is accused of the rape and murder of a white teenage girl (Toby Richards) as well as the murder of her father, his commanding officer. In the course of farcical legal proceedings reflecting the absence of genuine justice for blacks in that era, Rutledge, who admits only to killing the commanding officer in self-defense when discovered with the girl's body, is shown to be a scapegoat for white racism and sexual hysteria. Even his sympathetic defense counsel, Lieutenant Tom Cantrell (Jeffrey Hunter), is not entirely convinced of Rutledge's innocence until the actual murderer, the fort's white sutler (Fred Libby, who played one of the Cleggs in *Wagon Master*), breaks down and confesses to the sex murder.

Sergeant Rutledge was inspired by a Frederic Remington picture of black cavalrymen on the western frontier. Goldbeck brought the Remington image to Bellah with "the thought that no one yet had bothered in any way to present the story of the colored soldier and his contribution to the western march of American empire," as Bellah put it. This reactionary notion, coupled with Bellah's violent prejudices against blacks and Indians, did not augur well for the project. What *Sergeant Rutledge* might have been without Ford is abundantly clear in Bellah's novelization of the film. Though Bellah musters a certain admiration for Rutledge as a figure of courage, he can't express it without being patronizing. Rutledge seems less intelligent in the book than he does on-screen, and the author finds a familiar outlet for his prurient racist fantasizing: by the second page, a white girl has been gang-raped and murdered by nine marauding Indians.

In January 1959, Bellah and Goldbeck offered Ford their first version of the screenplay, then titled *Captain Buffalo*. Ford, as Bellah put it, "pointed out certain deformities that could be corrected by deft surgery." The writers spent ten days of "hard labor" with Ford in Hawaii aboard the *Araner* as the director performed that surgery. Bellah and Goldbeck completed the script while Ford was shooting his orientation films in Taiwan and Korea.

Returning to the studio for which he had directed *The Searchers,* Ford made a good deal with Warner Bros. for *Sergeant Rutledge,* earning him $250,000 for directing and presenting the film through John Ford Productions. (Goldbeck and Patrick Ford received the producer credits.) Working for the eighth and last time with the masterful cinematographer Bert Glennon—who had shot such Ford classics as *Stagecoach, Young Mr. Lincoln,* and *Wagon Master*—Ford filmed *Sergeant Rutledge* with great efficiency from July 16 through August 31, 1959. Starting with nine days of location work in Monument Valley, he finished eight days ahead of his forty-three-day shooting schedule.

By this late stage in his career, Ford had achieved an elegant simplicity and precision of style that some have mistaken for a perfunctory attitude toward his craft. If Ford now seemed less interested in visual beauty for its own sake, this was not simply a function of advancing age and fading eyesight but a result of his pruning away of inessentials to focus attention on the themes, ideas, and emotional situations that most urgently concerned him. More and more obsessively, these revolved around conflicts over race, the most seemingly intractable problem festering within the American psyche. Ford deliberately sought in his remaining years to rectify some oversights and imbalances in his work, finding stories about groups that he usually had relegated to supporting status—blacks, Indians, and women—and giving them the starring roles.

As a student of American history, Ford was pleased to be able to pay tribute to the black cavalrymen known as Buffalo Soldiers. In the film, Lieutenant Cantrell says the sobriquet was bestowed by Indians who saw the black troopers wearing buffalo coats and caps. However, in his 1967 book *The Buffalo Soldiers: A Narrative of the Negro Cavalry in the West,* William H. Leckie writes, "The origin of the term 'buffalo soldier' is uncertain, although the common explanation is that the Indian saw a similarity between the hair of the Negro soldier and that of the buffalo. The buffalo was a sacred animal to the Indian, and it is unlikely that he would so name an enemy if respect were lacking. . . . Men of the Tenth [Cavalry], and later of the Ninth, accepted the title and wore it proudly. Indeed, the most prominent feature of the regimental crest of the Tenth Calvary was a buffalo." The Ninth and Tenth Regiments of the U.S. Cavalry were formed in 1866 with freed slaves and black soldiers who had fought with distinction for the Union in the Civil War; the Tenth Cavalry's commanding officer was Colonel Benjamin Grierson, the man who led the raid commemorated by Ford in *The Horse Soldiers.*

Facing some of the roughest terrain and hardest fighting during the Indian wars, the Buffalo Soldiers were first sketched by Remington on an 1888 visit to Arizona. Considering them "charming men with whom to serve," he wrote, "As to their bravery, I am often asked, 'Will they fight?' This is easily answered. They have fought many, many times. The old sergeant sitting near me, as calm of feature as a bronze statue, once deliberately walked over to a Cheyenne rifle-pit and killed his man." Pointing out that the soldiers belied the stereotypical images of "black brutes" and buffoons, Remington noted, "The physique of the black soldiers must be admired—great chests, broad-shouldered, upstanding fellows."

Ford similarly idealizes the Buffalo Soldiers by contrasting them to Indians, whom he portrays as one-dimensional savages. From a modern perspective, using one racial stereotype to dispel another seems a glaring contradiction. Although Ford avoids Bellah's excesses in depicting Indian savagery, there is no doubt what Rutledge means in the film when, finding himself under siege with a white woman, Mary Beecher (Constance Towers), he gives her a pistol: "They'll have no mercy on you, lady, they'll have no mercy." To Ford, the overriding issue is that, like the Irish in his cavalry films, African-Americans are able to strive toward integration into the American mainstream through loyal military service, a consideration outweighing the tragic irony that they prove their fitness for citizenship by killing Indians. As William Loren Katz writes in *The Black West*, "If any of these men felt they were mercenaries hired by whites to crush red men there is no evidence of this in the historical literature. . . . The Buffalo Soldiers served their country during an age of mounting anti–Negro violence and hostility and, paradoxically, helped bring the white man's law and order to the frontier."

Ford's racial perspective in *Sergeant Rutledge* is that of an enlightened nineteenth-century liberal. He cannot appreciate how much harder it has been for African-Americans than for Irishmen to achieve total assimilation outside the safely sexless situation of military life. Nor can he comprehend why blacks might not find such assimilation desirable. And yet Ford offers one astonishing scene that calls into question everything that he, Rutledge, and America represent. Rutledge's temporary desertion is provoked by his heartrending exchange with Trooper Moffat (Naaman Brown), who dies in his sergeant's arms against the timeless backdrop of Monument Valley:

> *Moffat:* My three little girls . . . what's gonna happen to them, Brax?
>
> *Rutledge:* Some day, Moffat, they gonna be awful proud of you.
>
> *Moffat:* (laughs bitterly) Some day. You always talkin' about some day, like it gonna be Promised Land here on earth. Brax! We're fools to fight the white . . . white man's war.
>
> *Rutledge:* It ain't the white man's war. We're fighting to make us proud. Some day your little girls . . . Moffat, do you hear me? (he dies) Moffat!

Like *The Last Hurrah* before it, *Sergeant Rutledge* manifests an increased level of self-consciousness in Ford's treatment of American history. Knowing he was in the final stage of his long career, and perhaps also because he was tired of reviewers missing the point, Ford brought a new element of didactic urgency to his work. These late films give the sense that the director is passing along his accumulated wisdom and feelings—his testament—before it is too late. Ford's growing disillusionment with American society as it entered the turbulent 1960s hastened this development. Fittingly, Ford's late films deal with characters who, to a large extent, are able to stand outside of history at the same time as they are living it. Rutledge is one such character, a man who realizes that the ultimate meaning of his personal struggle can only be fully realized when he has become history. He is willing to sacrifice himself to that end: turning away help offered by his fellow Buffalo Soldiers, he says that "the Ninth's record's gonna speak for us all some day, and it's gonna speak clean."

. . .

In a 1966 interview with Samuel Lachize, a critic for the French Communist Party's official newspaper *L'Humanité,* Ford became incensed when Lachize pointed out that some people thought his work had racist aspects. Although Lachize stressed that he disagreed with that view, Ford responded with great agitation: "The people who say such things are crazy. I am a Northerner. I hate segregation, and I gave jobs to hundreds of Negroes at the same salary the whites were paid. . . . Me, a racist? My best friends are black: Woody Strode, and a caretaker [Bill Ramsey] who has worked for me for thirty years."

Ford reminded Lachize that he had made *Sergeant Rutledge,* whose title caracter was "nobler than anybody else in the picture." The director said that unnamed executives had told him a movie about a "nigger" would lose money because it could not be shown in the South. "I got angry and told them they could at least have the decency to say 'Negro' or 'colored man,' because most of those 'niggers' were worth better than they. When I landed at Omaha Beach there were scores of black bodies lying in the sand. Then I realized that it was impossible not to consider them full-fledged American citizens."

Woody Strode's majestic performance is the centerpiece of *Sergeant Rutledge.* Strode went on to make three more films for Ford, playing an Indian chief in *Two Rode Together,* John Wayne's African-American sidekick in *The Man Who Shot Liberty Valance,* and a Chinese warrior in *7 Women.* Such versatility was not as much of a stretch as it may have seemed, since Strode had a mixed racial heritage, part African-American and part Native American (Creek and Blackfoot).

After playing varsity football with Jackie Robinson at UCLA, Strode and another teammate, Kenny Washington, became the first black players in the National Football League when they joined the Los Angeles Rams in 1946. Strode played his first film role in 1941, but it was not until after he spent years in the Canadian Football League and as a professional wrestler that he began to make a major impression on-screen. His breakthrough roles were those of a rebellious GI in Lewis Milestone's 1959 Korean War film *Pork Chop Hill* and the gladiator who ignites the slave insurrection in Stanley Kubrick's *Spartacus* (1960). When Ford decided to cast him as Rutledge, Warner Bros. urged the director to use a better-known black actor such as Sidney Poitier or Harry Belafonte. "They aren't tough enough!" Ford replied, and that was that.

Strode's statuesque physique, large moonlike eyes, and bald head make him look almost superhuman. The film's theme song, "Captain Buffalo," describes a mythic figure "who is built like Lookout Mountain, taller than a redwood tree . . . John Henry was a weakling next to Captain Buffalo." This idealized quality is a double-edged sword, making Rutledge seem both more and less than a man. While his fellow troopers serenade Rutledge with the song, Ford shows him from a low angle posed heroically against a smoke-filled sky. When Mary Beecher asks Lieutenant Cantrell, "Who's Captain Buffalo?" he explains, "Captain Buffalo is a—well, he's the ideal soldier, you know. Giant-size, kind of a Paul Bunyon. I guess they're laying it on a little thick now for Rutledge, try to give him confidence and cheer him up." Mary replies, "What a wonderful way to do it." Here Ford is laying out his mythmaking strategy for all to see and hear, while simultaneously insisting on its validity.

Ford's working relationship with Woody Strode demonstrated both his need to prove his racial enlightment and his deep, unacknowledged ambivalence on the subject of race. Since Strode had never before played such a complex role, Ford resorted to some of his favorite tricks to goad him into a strongly emotional performance. The abuse Ford meted out to Strode was similar to that he meted out to white performers such as John Wayne and Victor McLaglen. But Ford's characteristic bullying tactics, especially his habit of cruelly jabbing into an actor's most sensitive areas, took on an uglier, sometimes inexcusable edge when directed at an African-American.

Strode recalled in his autobiography that Ford acted out each scene for him. But the director would become irate if he thought Strode wasn't paying close enough attention. "He'd stomp on my feet, slug me, throw rocks at me. One time he said, 'BEND OVER, YOU SON OF A BITCH!' and swatted me with the butt end of my rifle.

"I thought the old bastard hated me."

Strode had to suppress a desire to "hurt that old man."

One time, the actor reported, Ford "really upset me. I was supposed to be spying on the Indians. I was sneaking through the bushes, he hollered, 'WOODY, YOU SON OF A BITCH, QUIT NIGGERING UP MY GOD-DAMNED SCENE!'

"I had been tiptoeing, like I was scared. He wanted me to move with intelligence and cunning. Sergeant Rutledge wasn't a tiptoer; he was proud and dignified. . . . I almost had a nervous breakdown doing *Sergeant Rutledge,* but it helped me become an actor."

Indeed, Strode played the role with enormous conviction and passion. His most powerful scene comes when, responding to taunts from the bigoted white prosecutor (Carleton Young), Rutledge rises up in impassioned self-defense to explain that he returned from deserting "because the Ninth Cavalry was my home. My real freedom. And my self-respeck. And the way I was desertin' it, I wasn't nothing but a swamp-runnin' nigger. And I ain't that! Do you hear me? I'm a *man.*" To get Strode into a suitably agitated emotional state, Ford resorted to the old trick he had used with Victor McLaglen on *The Informer.*

The day before the scene was shot, Ford invited Strode to his son's house and offered him a large drink of hard liquor. Strode, who usually avoided drinking during production, accepted. He eventually became so drunk that Pat Ford found him raising a ruckus on Sunset Boulevard. Strode awoke the next morning in John Ford's sitting room with a terrible hangover. Reviewing the script in his bed, Ford pretended not to see Strode sneaking out the door. Pat hustled him off to the studio, where the director started the day by berating the actor for drinking. Strode remembered being "all pissed off, emotional, teetering right on the edge."

As Ford calculated, the combination of a hangover, merciless chastisement, and the wrenching content of the scene brought forth a lifetime of feelings: "John Ford wanted to know if we could get away with saying 'nigger' on the screen, and I said why not? It would be the first time a black man ever called *himself* a nigger on the screen. And I wanted to hit home."

When Strode finished his speech, becoming so emotional that he started crying and broke his chair in "the truest moment I ever had on the screen," Ford could not handle the real-life anguish he had summoned forth. He said brusquely, "Now, Woody, stop those tears. It's a sign of weakness."

In *Making Movies Black: The Hollywood Message Movie from World War II to the Civil Rights Era,* Thomas Cripps claims that Rutledge is "exonerated by a jury of good white people, but the evidence against him is so stacked and his innocence so trickily proved that, in this decade in which Eldridge Cleaver described rape as a political act, the stereotyped black brute reasserted itself in white memory." Cripps bases his reading on faulty premises. Far from being "a jury of good white people," the court-martial is portrayed by Ford as cynical, corrupt, and racist, and Rutledge is exonerated not by the jury or even the evidence but by the guilty man's sudden confession. Ford scathingly mocks the white courtroom spectators, who include a gang of would-be lynchers brandishing a rope and a gaggle of officers' wives taking prurient delight in being shocked by testimony about rape and innuendos about black sexuality (among them, not coincidentally, is Mae Marsh, who jumped to her death in Griffith's infamous *Birth of a Nation* while being pursued by a rapacious black man).

Cripps's claim that *Sergeant Rutledge* reinforces the stereotype of the black brute is also mistaken; if anything, the film can be faulted for playing into the Uncle Tom stereotype. In most ways the personification of manliness, Rutledge nevertheless is sexually neutered by the racist strictures of his society. Cantrell bases his defense partly on Rutledge's careful deference to Jim Crow in Mary Beecher's presence. Ford's emphasis on Rutledge's sexless, subservient nature qualifies the message of a film designed to show that blacks should be treated with full equality. In its brutal frankness about the sexual roots of white racism there is further ambivalence, for to make us understand and reject such prejudice, Ford daringly plays into those feelings with Gothic imagery straight from a horror film.

Rutledge's first appearance comes in a nocturnal close-up as his hand suddenly clasps the mouth of the blonde heroine. Mary tells the court that "it was as though he'd sprung up at me out of the earth. . . . It was like a nightmare!" Prompting similar feelings in the audience by conjuring up the imagery of the black brute mixed up in what Rutledge calls "white woman business," Ford powerfully implicates the spectator in his or her own racism before proceeding to attack and dispel it. If a residue of disturbing feelings lingers after the denouement, that is because *Sergeant Rutledge* is filled with raw, unresolved tensions that have not found an entirely satisfying artistic form. But Ford is honest enough to recognize and deal with his own complicity in racism, and he deserves credit for addressing such issues head-on.

If Woody Strode had any of his own reservations about *Sergeant Rutledge,* he did not express them. He preferred to focus on the unique opportunity Ford had given him to play a heroic role at a time when American Negroes were risking their lives for social equality and black males were still not allowed to express the full range of their manhood on-screen. *Sergeant Rutledge* was a box-office flop, but in a 1971 interview with Charlayne Hunter for the *New York Times,* Strode said proudly, "You never seen a Negro come off a mountain like John Wayne before. I had the greatest Glory Hallelujah ride across the Pecos River that any black man ever had on the screen. And I did it myself. I carried the whole black race across that river."

Ford suffered through an unaccustomed experience in the wake of *Sergeant Rutledge:* unemployment. The only project he really wanted to make at the time was *The White Company,* but no one was buying. Nor was anyone pursuing his services as a director. From September 1959 until June 1960, Ford had no feature film of his own before the cameras, the longest fallow period this workaholic had faced since his eye trouble in the early fifties. Restless and lacking companionship for trips on the *Araner* because so many of his old buddies were either busy or dead, Ford spent much of his time hanging around other people's sets, including those of Ward Bond's television series *Wagon Train* and John Wayne's epic feature *The Alamo.*

Ford regarded both ventures with ill-concealed jealousy and resentment. He saw them as rebellious acts by actors he had created out of the roughest clay but who now were disloyal enough to want success on their own terms, independent of their tyrannical father figure. This was particularly galling to

Ford because it came at a time when his own career was faltering. It was hard enough to deal with a new set of stars, producers, and studio executives who were not cowed by his four Academy Awards and whose implicit attitude was, "What have you done lately?" But when Ford's favorite whipping boy became a household name for playing Major Seth Adams in *Wagon Train*—an MCA series modeled (without credit) on Ford's own *Wagon Master*—that was too much for the Old Man to handle gracefully.

First broadcast on NBC in September 1957, *Wagon Train* became the number-two series the following season, trailing only CBS's *Gunsmoke*. Among the other *Wagon Train* regulars were two of Ford's favorite stuntmen, Terry Wilson and Frank McGrath. Bond stubbornly resisted the transition from movies to television until Ford told him, "Listen, you dumb Irishman. Don't you act for a living? Well, then you'd better act." This came during a time when Bond was having trouble getting work in movies, perhaps because he had alienated so many people with his blacklisting activities. Now that it was getting safer to have dissenting political opinions in Hollywood, Ford's estrangement from Bond may have been a delayed reaction to the actor's role as Hollywood's self-appointed political scourge as well as to Bond's influence on Ford's own continued entanglement with the Motion Picture Alliance. Despite Bond's public admission of defeat in his anti-Communist crusade, his success in *Wagon Train* did nothing to soften his political views and made him an even more shameless social climber. When Ford learned that Wayne had agreed to make a guest appearance on *Wagon Train,* Ford declared, "I taught him better than that. I've given up on Bond, the big, ugly, stupid gorilla, but I thought Duke had more intelligence."

The *Alamo* had been John Wayne's dream project for more than a decade. The heroic saga of the Texans besieged by Mexican troops in 1836 at the Alamo mission in San Antonio de Bexar has a strongly Fordian theme. These are men who sacrifice their lives for the benefit of future generations, who are (to quote *The Last Hurrah*) "victorious in defeat." Francis Ford played a villainous Mexican spy in the first film made about the Alamo, *The Immortal Alamo,* produced in and around San Antonio by the Méliès company in 1911, with William Haddock directing. When John Ford and Merian Cooper formed Argosy Pictures, Wayne approached them with the idea of doing a large-scale Alamo movie. Pat Ford wrote a first screenplay at Argosy in 1948, centering on the character of Davy Crockett. John Ford and Wayne announced the movie that year while visiting the actual Alamo during a location-scouting trip to Texas for *3 Godfathers.* Eventually, concerns about the cost and profitability of the Alamo project caused Ford and Cooper to pass on it.

Herbert Yates similarly resisted making *The Alamo* at Republic Pictures, believing that its commercial prospects would be limited by the story's ending. For years when Wayne shopped *The Alamo* around Hollywood, studio executives said they would make the picture if only he would work with Ford or another top director. Ford himself cautioned Wayne that producing and directing as well as acting would be far too daunting a task. But Wayne had come to regard the story of the Alamo defenders as his political credo ("This picture is America," he proclaimed), and he was determined that this film would be the realization of his long-standing ambition to become a director. He wanted to convince the world that, as he tells Linda Cristal in *The Alamo,* "I'm not as stupid as I look from the outside."

Eventually, Wayne was able to get his way by raising $10.4 million in production money, mostly from Texas millionaires. Wayne's Batjac production for United Artists began shooting September 9, 1959, in the 70mm Todd-AO format, on an elaborate set designed by Alfred Ybarra at the ranch of James T. "Happy" Shahan outside Brackettville, Texas. Wearing three hats as producer, director, and star (in the role of Davy Crockett), Wayne worked from a final shooting script by his crony James Edward Grant.

Over the years, John Ford had continued to offer advice to Wayne on the production and the casting, such as urging the unconventional choice of British actor Laurence Harvey to play Colonel William Travis, a martinet somewhat reminiscent of Henry Fonda's Colonel Thursday in *Fort Apache.* Many of the other *Alamo* cast and crew members were veterans of Ford pictures. (Harvey's wife, who accompanied him on location, was British actress Margaret Leighton, later cast in Ford's *7 Women.*)

When shooting finally began on *The Alamo,* Ford could not stay away. He confided to Michael Killanin that he was eager to go to Texas and "cast a paternal eye on Duke Wayne." Though Wayne did not invite him to do so, Ford showed up on September 19, claiming that he had come to Brackettville for a vacation.

Makeup man Monty Westmore saw Ford's car pull up in a cloud of dust and followed him to see what would happen. Wayne was directing a scene with Harvey and Richard Widmark (as Jim Bowie) inside the Alamo set. When Wayne called, "Cut—I think that's a print," Ford's voice was heard saying, "No, it's not." After a pause, Wayne ordered the actors to do the scene again. They did. This time when Wayne called "Cut," everyone looked at Ford. "Print it," ordered Ford, who proceeded to take a seat in Wayne's director's chair.

The same thing kept happening day after day. "Goddammit, Duke," Ford would say, "that's no way to play it. Here, try it this way." After one scene between Wayne and Widmark was completed to the actors' satisfaction,

Ford growled, "Do it again." Wayne asked, "*Why*, Coach?" and Ford replied, "'Cause it was no damn good."

Although Wayne was loath to admit it, he did need plenty of help on *The Alamo*. The daily pressure of his multiple duties was staggering. And as a first-time director, he had some serious limitations, not only in staging large-scale action scenes but also in handling actors. Hank Worden, who plays the Parson in *The Alamo*, told me that the difference between Ford and Wayne as directors was that Ford knew when to yell at actors and treat them roughly, but Wayne did so indiscriminately. Worden was the kind of actor who did not respond well to bullying, and Ford, a master psychologist, directed him accordingly. But with Wayne he felt intimidated and found it much harder to be relaxed on-screen.

Wayne naturally fumed at Ford's overt challenge to his authority on the set. If he had not managed to bring Ford under control, Wayne would have lost the respect of his company, ended any hope that *The Alamo* would be considered a John Wayne film, and destroyed his chances of ever directing again. So Wayne asked his cinematographer, Bill Clothier, "What the hell am I gonna do?" Pointing out that he had more crewmen than he needed, Clothier suggested, "Let's give the Old Man a second unit."

Aware of Ford's depressed condition, Wayne behaved with remarkable compassion, particularly since some of his own money was on the line. "I don't care what it costs," said Wayne, "but I am not going to let him feel rejected. I'd rather spend a million dollars than hurt his feelings." Telling Ford that second-unit director Cliff Lyons couldn't handle all the action, Wayne had Grant write extra scenes for Ford to shoot. Clothier estimated that it cost $250,000 to let Ford have his own unit. In four separate visits, Ford wound up spending forty-seven days on location, amounting to about half of the entire shoot.

Wayne's son Michael, whose official title was "assistant to producer," was delegated to serve as Ford's assistant. Placating Ford was a "rough position," he found, because his father ordered him not to let Ford use any of the principal cast members. Instead Ford's second unit occupied its time shooting battle footage of the Mexican army and other scenes involving extras. Michael Wayne's recollection of the *Alamo* filming was of continually butting heads with Ford, who kept trying to get him to disobey his father's edict.

Nevertheless, Ford did find ways of doing some work with the principal actors. Among his papers is a letter from Widmark on September 30, 1959, thanking Ford for the privilege of being directed by him. Ford loyally pretended that none of his footage was used in *The Alamo*, a fiction also maintained by John Wayne, who understandably was sensitive to the gossip that

Ford was largely responsible for whatever quality the film had. In fact, some of Ford's scenes do appear in the film, and not only some spectacular battle footage and other shots of Santa Anna's troops. Ford directed all or parts of such scenes as: the humorous initial meeting between Crockett and Flaca (Cristal) and their flirtatious exchange later in her room, ending with a very Fordian shadowy long shot in the hallway; the church basement scene with Crockett, Bowie, and others discovering an ammunition supply and killing a man over it; the poignant farewell between Jocko (John Dierkes) and his wife, Blind Nell (played by Veda Ann Borg, the wife of Andrew McLaglen); the scene of Smitty (Frankie Avalon), the young courier from the Alamo, seeking help from General Sam Houston (Richard Boone); and the serio-comic deaths of two of Crockett's Tennesseeans (Rudy Robbins and Chuck Roberson).

Ford was not exactly disinterested, then, when he lent his prestige to the promotion of *The Alamo*. In a quote used in the publicity and advertising campaigns, he proclaimed, "*The Alamo* is the greatest picture I've ever seen. It will last forever, run forever, for all peoples, all families everywhere."[1] Despite such overblown hype—and Ford's was far from the worst example—the film holds up surprisingly well today when seen in its fully restored 1992 version. Although overly long and garrulous, as well as highly uneven, it's filled with colorful characters and vignettes and sometimes achieves a genuine epic grandeur. Wayne lapses too often into corny speechifying, but no one can doubt the passion that went into this ambitious piece of personal filmmaking. Ironically, *The Alamo* did better at the box office *outside* the United States— most Americans already knew the ending—and while its reputation as a disaster is unwarranted, the film earned no money for Wayne and dampened his directing ambitions.

One day while visiting the set of *Wagon Train,* Ford told Bond about his dream of making a biographical film on Ulysses S. Grant. He had figured out a way to tell at least part of Grant's story within the format of the series. Bond reacted with enthusiasm, and Ford (who received a directing fee of only $3,500) put together a script with writer Tony Paulson. *The Colter Craven Story,* a one-hour program filmed in May 1960, centers on one of Ford's favorite character types, the drunken doctor. Ford regular Carleton Young plays a doctor so traumatized by his Civil War experiences treating wounded soldiers at the Battle of Shiloh that he later finds it impossible to perform surgery. To get Craven in shape for an emergency cesarean delivery, Major Adams tells him

---

1. When Ford listed his ten favorite movies for *Cinema* magazine in 1964, *The Alamo* slipped to tenth place, with *The Birth of a Nation* ranking first.

the story of an old friend from Illinois, "Sam" Grant (Paul Birch, the same actor who plays Grant in *The Horse Soldiers*).

The haunting eleven-minute flashback begins with Grant coming home to Galena in 1854 after being kicked out of the army for drunkenness. Throughout this elliptical passage, Ford conveys emotion with the utmost economy, and nowhere more beautifully than in a long shot of Grant's wife and children waiting on a shadowy street corner as he alights from a steamboat. Treated as a failure by his father (Ford's house windbag, Willis Bouchey), Grant is the butt of the town's malicious gossip. Ford gets in a jibe at Bond's McCarthy-era rumormongering. Tired of hearing what "folks say" about Grant, Adams disgustedly tells a pair of busybodies, "You can't always believe what 'folks say.'" After some humorous scenes of Grant helping Adams and his veteran drill sergeant (the indispensable Jack Pennick) organize the Second Illinois Volunteers, Grant returns to government service at the war's outbreak.

Eventually Grant is reunited with Adams—who at first does not recognize him—in the aftermath of Shiloh on April 7, 1862. The costly victory by the Union army resulted in the two sides suffering more than twenty thousand casualties; Adams describes this as "one of the worst days in American history." Using a battle that almost ended in Grant's worst military setback as the subject of an inspirational sermon is rather paradoxical, but in the eyes of both Adams and Ford, the lesson is Grant's heroic refusal to quit under adversity. The impressionistic Shiloh sequence includes a cameo by John Wayne as General William Tecumseh Sherman; Wayne is credited under the pseudonym "Michael Morris," the birth name of Lord Killanin as well as a reference to Wayne's boyhood name, Marion Michael Morrison. Ford and Bond argued over Ford's refusal to shoot a close-up of Wayne; Ford thought Bond wanted the world to see that he was the star and Wayne a mere guest star. The director prevailed, and Wayne was shown only in long shot.

In the midst of one of his own periodic attempts to kick the drinking habit, Ford makes the wretched Dr. Craven's alcoholic self-hatred uncomfortably believable, treating his problem with empathy rather than condescension, although the script reflects the then-prevalent belief that alcoholism is a psychological problem rather than a disease. The framing sequences involving the doctor suffer from being far too extended. Flatly filmed in nondescript locations, they are poorly matched with footage from some of the most beautifully photographed sequences from Ford's classic *Wagon Master*, incorporated to give the program greater visual scope. Ford became so carried away with this assignment that he delivered a seventy-two-minute program in the usual six days of shooting. Consideration was given to expanding *Colter Craven* into a two-part episode, but instead it was decided to cut the program by nineteen minutes to squeeze it into the normal one-hour time slot.

Ford came out of the experience with mixed feelings about directing for television. He complained that TV "is a fine thing if you don't like to eat and sleep. You can't build a scene the way you can in the movies. There's no time." And he had to deal with commercial interference. While he was shooting a scene with Grant, an agency representative for one of the show's sponsors objected to Grant being shown smoking a cigar.

"What's wrong with the cigar?" Ford asked.

"Our sponsor makes cigarettes and prefers no cigars or pipes be used."

"Give the sponsor my compliments," replied Ford, "and tell him to [expletive deleted in published interview]."

But Ford said he basically enjoyed his work on *Wagon Train* because "I have developed most of my pictures from short stories. That's what I like about TV; it has to be of necessity a short story. Tight and fast. . . . In fact, I want to do some more."

By the time Ford's episode aired on November 23, 1960, Ward Bond was dead.

Bond had been recklessly abusing his body. Indulging his eating, smoking, and drinking habits, he could not resist partying with newfound wealthy friends even while working long hours on the series. To keep his weight under control, he had been popping amphetamines without concern for their effect on his heart; Ford, however, was anxious about his old friend's health. On November 5, while visiting Dallas to attend a Cowboys football game and hobnob with friends, including broadcaster Gordon McLendon and right-wing oil tycoon Clint Murchison, Bond died of a heart attack in his hotel room at the age of fifty-seven.

Ford was also in Texas at the time. He was busy directing a Western for Columbia Pictures with James Stewart and Richard Widmark, *Two Rode Together,* at Happy Shahan's Brackettville ranch. Shahan had added another side of the San Antonio street to the sets left over from *The Alamo.* He called his combined film location and tourist attraction the Alamo Village.

"The news hit the set," recalled Henry Brandon, who was playing the Indian chief Quanah Parker. "I saw this whispering going on. I'm very nosy, so I went over to see what they were whispering about. Andy Devine, Wingate Smith, and somebody else [Ken Curtis] were saying, 'Who's gonna tell him?' Wingate said, 'I guess I will.' Andy said, 'I guess I will.' So they went over and I tagged along to see how Ford would take it. He just stood and stared. And then he turned to Andy Devine and said, 'Well, I think you're gonna have to be my horse's ass now.' Then he said, *'Wrap!'* We all went home at 10:00 A.M. It was a day of mourning. But he had to make a joke of it when you'd expect tears. Under all the abuse and everything, he loved the guy but he never showed it. Ford would never react the way you'd expect him to react. If you'd tell him a funny story he'd scowl. If you'd tell him a tragic story he'd laugh like hell." (Stuntman Chuck Roberson, who also was present when Ford heard the news, recalled seeing tears falling from beneath Ford's dark glasses.)

Ford chartered a small plane and traveled to Dallas with Curtis and Dobe Carey to join Bond's widow, Mary Lou. They accompanied the actor's body back to Hollywood, but on the day of the funeral at the Field Photo Farm, November 7, Ford was back in Texas to resume filming. Although he called for three minutes of silence on the set, his absence from the funeral (Mary attended in his place) may have been a further sign of Ford's ambivalence toward Bond and his political activities.

According to Ford's daughter, Barbara, while Bond was lying in state in the Farm's chapel, vandals stole his body; it was returned by the time of the funeral. Draped in flowers and an American flag, Bond's open casket was displayed beside a cannon on the lawn. The ceremony included typically Fordian sentimental touches, with singing by Curtis ("And He Was There"), Carey ("Come, Come Ye Saints"), and the Sons of the Pioneers ("The Song of the Wagon Master"). John Wayne offered the eulogy, calling Bond "a wonderful, generous, big-hearted man." Ford waited two more days before issuing a bland statement of his own: "Ward will always be with us wherever actors gather for talk or stuntmen get together for a card game. They'll remember. He was a great character—and a great guy."

Bond died just in time to miss the start of a new era of more liberal American politics with the election of President John F. Kennedy on November 8. At the time of his death, Bond was serving his fifth year as president of the widely despised Motion Picture Alliance (of which Ford remained an advisory committee member as late as July 1961). Bond's own political beliefs had never changed. In 1959, when Soviet premier Nikita Khrushchev received a friendly welcome in Hollywood, he protested by flying the American flag over his home at half-staff. In his final political statement, a posthumously published letter to the Hollywood Citizen-News, Bond charged that "self-described 'Civil Liberties' organizations" were taking action to "legally hamstring effective law enforcement control of dope, pornography, and subversive activities."

"Ward was a giant among Americans, a magnificent patriot who died fighting for his country," the MPA's executive director, Albert J. MacDonald, claimed in a letter to the membership. "The United States is the worse for his going. It was no coincidence that Ward Bond was the third President of MPA (Jim McGuinness and Sam Wood were the others) to die in office, of a heart attack. . . . The front rank of the anti-Communist struggle is no place for those unwilling to give everything to it."

Disheartened by Bond's passing, Ford quickly wrapped up location work on *Two Rode Together* and came home to complete the film at the Columbia ranch that November. He fell into a perilous state of despair, seeking oblivion with a drinking binge aboard the *Araner*. After drinking steadily for almost three weeks, he had to be hospitalized in Honolulu for alcoholic dehydration.

Although it has strong competition from *The Fugitive* and *What Price Glory*, Ford described *Two Rode Together* as "the worst piece of crap I've done in twenty years." The story, based on Will Cook's 1960 novel *Comanche Captives*, can be seen as a remake of *The Searchers* from a far more cynical perspective, but Ford's attitude toward the project seems so contemptuously indifferent that it is hard for the audience not to respond in kind. With its slapdash and blatantly ugly visual style, frequently cartoonish acting, crude caricaturing of Indians, and flippant treatment of serious themes, *Two Rode Together* represents one of the lowest points of the director's career. Ford clearly took on the project mostly to keep busy and for the money, $225,000 and 25 percent of the net profits; Ford's fee included his son's $25,000 salary for serving as his executive assistant. As Willis Goldbeck put it, Ford became "so anxious to make pictures, he'd go out and do anything."

Stewart and Widmark play the searchers in *Two Rode Together*, a marshal and a U.S. Cavalry officer uneasily paired on a mission to bring back white captives. Unlike Ethan and Martin in *The Searchers*, these two men are thoroughly jaded, lacking any belief in the point of their search. Stewart's Marshal Guthrie McCabe is unabashedly mercenary, hardly caring about the consequences, while Widmark's more compassionate Jim Gary vainly tries to spare the families of the captives from suffering tragic disillusionment. When a teenage Comanche named Running Wolf (David Kent) is reunited with his deluded white mother (Jeanette Nolan), he kills her and is lynched by the other white pilgrims. The stunningly beautiful leading lady of *The Alamo*, Linda Cristal, plays a Mexican captive woman living in a forced marriage with the Indian warrior Stone Calf (Woody Strode). She reluctantly allows herself to be brought back into white society—like Debbie at the end of *The Searchers*—only to become the uncomfortable object of prurient disapproval.

Two Rode Together could have served as a truly provocative reexamination by Ford of the repressed and otherwise unexplored areas of *The Searchers*, but Frank Nugent's screenplay and Ford's direction never rise to the level of seriousness such a treatment would demand. Ford's casual willingness to reduce the themes of his earlier masterpiece to crude, simplistic inversions shows how disillusioned he was becoming with the recycling process of Hollywood moviemaking. His nihilistic mockery of his own material stamps this as another of Ford's "evil twin" movies.

In his devastatingly funny review of *Two Rode Together* several years later, Manny Farber wrote that it "has the discombobulated effect of a Western dreamt by a kid snoozing in an Esso station in Linden, New Jersey. . . . The movie is a curious blend of modern blat and a senile impression of frontier culture that derives from the cheapest and oldest movies about prerailroad days in Indian territory. There is a wild, non sequitur quality . . . a free-for-all atmosphere in which not one detail or scene goes with another. In general, it is Widmark and Stewart, like two Pinter characters, separated out from a stiff (despite the yelling and flouncing), corny TV-styled production going on behind them." Farber expressed astonishment that such jarring elements "are the responsibility of John Ford, a director generally noted for making movies with a poetic and limitless knowledge of Indians, ranging farthest across the landscape of the American past, and being the moviemaker's Mr. Movie."

"I thought it was pretty bad," agreed Shirley Jones, *Two Rode Together*'s overripe ingenue. "I never figured out what it was all about, and I'm not at all sure Ford knew, either. Of course, Jimmy Stewart went at it like he was doing a masterpiece. Without him and Widmark, it might have been—*would* have been—an all-time turkey." Coming off her Oscar-winning supporting performance as a prostitute in *Elmer Gantry,* Jones seems grotesquely awkward as an unsophisticated young girl in blond pigtails. Dobe Carey reported that "Uncle Jack had a big crush on her," as he had once had on Betsy Palmer.

Ford's darkening sense of humor in his old age made him indulge this opportunity to parody his own work. As Quanah Parker, Henry Brandon found himself playing "in essence the same part as I played in *The Searchers,*" although it could be said more accurately that he was playing the *son* of Scar, since the mother of the actual Quanah was the captive Cynthia Ann Parker, the model for Scar's white wife, Debbie, in *The Searchers*. Brandon recalled that before his first appearance in *Two Rode Together,* "They had all this buildup to this formidable Indian chief Quanah Parker, this killer, this terrible son of a bitch. Jimmy Stewart and Richard Widmark ride up to my tent. Jimmy Stewart says something and I say, 'Lie.' I was very menacing. Ford gets me aside and says, 'No, I think he's amused by it.' That's better."

Describing *Two Rode Together* as a "hodgepodge of incidents and pieces of business from every Western Jack ever made," Dobe Carey observed that Ford acted as if he were "on a vacation, doing exactly what he damned well pleased." It wasn't as much fun for Carey, though. He had a drinking problem at the time, and after Ford spotted a bottle of whiskey in his room at the Fort Clark Guest Ranch, Dobe openly admitted that he planned to drink after work. Ford made no objection but moved him into a room across from his own. One day when they were filming Carey's comical brawl with Widmark and Ken Curtis, Carey knew that something was up: "Before Ford started getting ready to be nasty, he had physical tipoffs. He had a tendon in his neck that would start [pulsating], and he'd start chewing on his handkerchief. I'd say, 'Oh, shit.'" Ford made Carey, unlike the other actors, perform the entire brawl without the help of a stuntman. Between takes, Carey was lying on his stomach next to Widmark, catching his breath, when Ford came over to them. "Ford wanted to fix Widmark's neckerchief or something, because he was always fussing with your clothes. So Ford just put his knee on my back as hard as he could. And three ribs went 'Pop!' Broke three ribs. He was doing it because I told him I was gonna drink. That whole fight was my payback for drinking."

Ford had to fight to cast Woody Strode because Columbia executives, like some later critics, thought it odd for a black actor to play an Indian, not realizing that Strode was part Indian himself. "Ford got him out of black parts and into Indian parts, for which Woody was always very grateful," Brandon commented. Strode did not object to playing the kind of savage in *Two Rode Together* that his character was falsely accused of being in *Sergeant Rutledge*. And despite the fact that Ford was forging a friendly relationship with Strode—or perhaps *because* of it—the director continued his rough treatment of the actor during the making of *Two Rode Together*.

Ford became irate one night when Strode disobeyed orders and got drunk with an Indian chief and other Navajos from Monument Valley. After they set fire to an old wagon so they could circle the flames in their war dance, Ford came running out of his room in his nightgown, cursing and loudly demanding to know what was happening. At breakfast the next day, Strode took his tray and went to sit at Ford's table along with Stewart and Widmark. "Ford refused to let me eat at the table with them," Strode recalled.

The director said, "Woody, you can't eat with us. You're a nigger. You have to sit by yourself."

Strode sheepishly objected, "Papa, what could I do? When the Chief tells you to drink, you drink." It took Strode thirty-one years to register a stronger protest, but he did so by documenting the painful incident in his 1990 autobiography.

What keeps *Two Rode Together* watchable despite all its absurdities is Stewart's character. McCabe's outrageous cynicism is startling for a Ford protagonist but bracingly unsentimental and highly amusing. McCabe's bitterness toward the futility, corruption, and racism of the Western ethos reflects Ford's growing disenchantment with the frontier mythology he formerly celebrated. The marshal's mercenary attitude toward his job may also reflect Ford's sardonic comment on his own willingness to accept a project for which he had little regard. But one can sense the delight with which Ford seized upon the creative opportunity to work with Stewart. Ford had thought of casting him as Doc Holliday in *My Darling Clementine* and Major Kendall in *The Horse Soldiers*. "He was good in anything," Ford said of Stewart. "Played himself but he played the character. . . . People just liked him." Explaining Ford's interest in working with him, Stewart said modestly, "I think Hank [Fonda] put in a word for me."

On *Two Rode Together*, "All the things I'd heard about [Ford] were there," Stewart told me. "But they were a help instead of something that you—I can see that if somebody went in with fear or resentment—I was determined not to have that. It ended up a friendship. It was just a wonderful experience not only to know him but to be close enough in his work to realize what a master he was."

Stewart always claimed that "Ford just didn't like the spoken word very much" and that he was a primarily visual storyteller. But that cliché, which Ford also propagated, does not apply to the three films and one television program he did with Stewart. All of Stewart's roles for Ford are dialogue-heavy; Ford clearly enjoys hearing Stewart talk and his way of putting a humorous spin on his lines. Some Ford intimates felt that Stewart was playing the director in *Two Rode Together*, with the emphasis on his malicious sense of humor. "I never heard that," Stewart said with a chuckle.

The character of McCabe draws equally from Stewart's increasingly complex, worldly image in his postwar films, particularly his series of Westerns for director Anthony Mann. The more mature Stewart has a very dark sense of humor indeed. "The longer I got in the business," Stewart commented, "the more I realized how much humor had to do with presenting things, and how much a lack of humor just wasn't successful. It doesn't need to be a smile, just a feeling that you have in the way you react to things and the way your lines come out. It's true humor—you're not trying to be funny in the movie, you're not trying to make jokes, but it's a thing that's in you, yourself, that comes if you're talking to your wife or your friend. Something that's God-given. Ford had that humor, absolutely. And he was able to pick right up on humor—if it was just that half second that happened, he'd pick it right up."

"I was crazy about old Jack!" Richard Widmark said. "I caught him in his late days, when he was kind of bumbling around like Mr. Magoo—but he was great! . . . If he wanted to go fast, he could make the television people look like they were standing still. . . . One morning, Jimmy and I were eating breakfast, and a guy said that Jack wanted to see us. We went over. He came out in his pongee nightgown, which barely covered important areas—and with his patch and his 'ceegar.' It was a beautiful day, no clouds, sun shining. He looked up at the sky and said, 'Hell, we can't shoot in this weather. Why don't you fellows go back to bed?' About two that afternoon, we went out to the location, and did about a six-page scene in two hours. . . . Stewart and I are sitting near a riverbank and talking. It's a very good scene."

Perversely, in that long, uninterrupted shot, Ford does not show the river. Throwing away a chance to display some scenery behind the actors, he filmed their conversation from the *middle* of the river.

"Ford walked down the bank and walked right out into the river," Stewart recalled. "Well, everybody knew what that meant, so the cameraman and the crew followed him right out. He turned around and told Dick Widmark and I, 'Sit down over there.' Ford said to the cameraman, 'Get the two of 'em here, about like that.' It wasn't an easy thing to build something that would keep the camera from sinking, it was kind of a muddy bottom. And it was a long scene. We did the whole thing in the two-shot. Ford was out in the river when we were doing it. He said, 'Right,' and walked away. And that was it—Ford used to say 'Right' instead of 'Cut.' The sound man said, 'The sound—I hear a river.' Ford just said, 'Well, that's your problem.'

"Actually, it turned out to be a very interesting scene. The fact that there were no over-the-shoulder shots, just this two-shot, gives the impression that these two people just decide to sit down and figure out what's happened and what's going to happen. It helped establish timing and emphasis if you went straight through a scene without cutting. That's always been a help to me.

"Ford had an amazing method of directing. He didn't get everybody around a table and say, 'Now, here, this is this scene and you're so-and-so.' He left it pretty much up to you as an actor to have worked on the scene and to have pretty much worked out your idea of what it should be. Ford would sit there and say, 'All right, try it out.' He gave you a chance to do it. Then he would say, 'Maybe if you waited before you crossed, see how that works.' You have the script, you know the story, you know the scene, and he's set up the scene visually. Then he lets you move around in the scene, whether it's on a horse or in a bar, whatever it is. He'd say to the stuntmen, 'This is what I want, and I want it to be rough. I want you to get the scene so that it's quite a shock to everybody.' I think this is good."

But why *did* Ford shoot that scene in *Two Rode Together* from the middle of the river? One theory was that he wanted to punish the crew by making them stand up to their hips in the chilly water. But Stewart didn't think that was the case. Dobe Carey suggested another reason for Ford's perverse mood that day, one that Stewart perhaps was too embarrassed to recall or perhaps didn't even realize.

Ford and Stewart "had a flippant kind of relationship, lots of humor be-tween them," Carey said, "but I had a feeling that Jimmy made him edgy, had something that Jack knew he could never quite control the way, say, he ran roughshod over Wayne for so long. Maybe it was just Jimmy's talent and Jack's awareness that he had the real stuff in front of him. You could feel something building up with Jack for some time [on *Two Rode Together*]. All the deference he'd been showing Jimmy and Dick, that went completely against the grain. So he latched onto the two things that Jimmy and Dick had in common—they both wore toupees and had hearing problems.

"So he's out there in the middle of the river, with them sitting on the bank, and he starts talking lower and lower. You could hardly hear him if you were standing right next to him, but Jimmy and Dick, they're not ready to admit that they can't hear a damn word. They just keep nodding and nodding. Finally, Jack has established his point and he yells for everyone on the crew to gather around him in the water. When everybody's sloshed over to him, he throws up his arms in this great dramatic gesture and goes, 'Fifty years in this goddam business, and what do I end up doing? Directing two deaf hairpieces!'"

Virtually no American reviewers recognized in 1962 that *The Man Who Shot Liberty Valance* was John Ford's artistic summation. It was, after all, "just another John Wayne Western." And a blatantly old-fashioned one at that, a black-and-white movie with aging stars (Wayne and James Stewart) playing characters much younger than themselves, with a melodramatically oversize villain (Lee Marvin) and literally oversize comic relief (Andy Devine), and a visual starkness to its decor that hearkened back to the look of early silent Westerns.

But if Ford was behind his time in most superficial ways, he was ahead of the public consciousness in more important respects. With its profoundly skeptical reexamination of American history and mythology, a prophetic quality in anticipating the public's loss of faith in government, and an acknowledgment of the growing brutality in American life and the Western genre, *The Man Who Shot Liberty Valance* now clearly stands out as the most important American film of the 1960s.

Ford initiated the project, paying $7,500 for the film rights to the 1949 *Cosmopolitan* short story by Dorothy M. Johnson, which appealed to his twin fascinations with Westerns and mystery stories. James Warner Bellah and Willis Goldbeck (who also served as the film's producer) were assigned to write the screenplay in March 1961. Since Wayne had just signed a long-term deal with Paramount, Ford approached that studio after packaging the major elements. Ford raised half of the $3,207,000 budget through John Ford Productions. His own salary was $150,000 and 25 percent of the net profits, with Pat again receiving $25,000 as his executive assistant. Wayne received $750,000 and 7.5 percent of the gross receipts, while Stewart received $300,000 and the same percentage as well as half ownership of the picture after twelve years (Paramount and Ford's company each kept 25 percent ownership). Ford's deal with Paramount was announced in the trade press on April 10, but it took several more months before the studio gave the green light to begin shooting. While waiting, Ford directed his segment of *How the West Was Won*. *Liberty Valance* was filmed from September 5 through November 7, 1961,[2] finishing $84,850 under budget. It was released on April 18, 1962, to good box-office returns, including a domestic gross of $3.2 million.

What Stewart aptly called the film's "fascinating" story was provided by a woman who spent most of her life in the West. A journalism professor at the University of Montana at the time the film was produced, Johnson was a well-regarded author of sophisticated Western fiction containing powerful historical resonances and often a strongly allegorical bent. Her stories "The Hanging Tree" and "A Man Called Horse" were made into films as well, and she wrote an authoritative 1969 biography of Sitting Bull. However, Ford and his screenwriters added some important elements to Johnson's story about a transplanted easterner who builds his political career on the myth that he killed a western outlaw named Liberty Valance.

The characters of Pompey (Woody Strode), the friend and servant of Wayne's rancher Tom Doniphon, and Dutton Peabody (Edmond O'Brien), the comical but courageous editor of *The Shinbone Star,* are among Ford's most important additions. The film also brings in more political context for the gunfight, making Liberty Valance (Marvin) into a hired gun of the cattle barons opposed to statehood. Most crucially, perhaps, Ford differs from Johnson in having Senator Ransom Stoddard (Stewart) confess the truth about his duel with Valance rather than keeping it a shameful secret. Returning to Shinbone around 1910, the aged Stoddard reveals that the fatal shot was actually fired from an alleyway by Doniphon, who has died in obscurity; it was only some weeks or months after the duel that Stoddard himself learned the truth from Tom. Ford's Catholic beliefs may have suggested that Stoddard should attempt to cleanse his guilt over this far-reaching deception by publicly confessing. Stoddard's admission to the current editor of the *Star,* Maxwell Scott (Carleton Young), contributes another crucial layer of historical irony, for the editor refuses to print the story. Scott declares, "This is the West, sir. When the legend becomes fact, print the legend."

Reviewers of *Liberty Valance* found it "creaky" (A. H. Weiler of the *New York Times*), lacking in "sophistication" (*Tube.* of *Daily Variety*), or "a parody

---

2. On the day before the end of shooting, the Bel Air fire destroyed many homes near the Fords', which escaped undamaged. When Mary asked Jack if she should safeguard his Oscars and other trophies, he replied, "No, just get the pictures of my mother and father."

of Mr. Ford's best work" (Brendan Gill of the *New Yorker*). Ford took the unusual step of writing Bosley Crowther, the lead reviewer of the *Times,* to alert
him to the fact that the film was deliberately stylized like a silent Western, but
the point seemed to sail over Crowther's head. Offering an uncomprehending
assessment of the film that sounded like a premature obituary for the director's
career, Crowther described *Liberty Valance* as "a strangely synthetic sort of film,
an almost slapdash entertainment that is a bit of a baffling oddity." Crowther
thought that "the story's moral values are as disconcertingly confused as its two
or three styles of storytelling," and concluded that the veteran filmmaker's latest work "might be regarded as a baleful evidence of a creeping fatigue in
Hollywood."

The contemporary American observers who best appreciated the film's his-
torical significance were Andrew Sarris and Peter Bogdanovich, whose comments helped lay the foundation for Ford's eventual critical rediscovery by the
Sarris-inspired auteurist school of American critics. In his 1963 monograph
"The American Cinema"—published in the avant-garde New York magazine
Film Culture and subsequently used as the basis for his influential book of
the same title—Sarris called *Liberty Valance* one of Ford's "major works."
Bogdanovich, a young film enthusiast and aspiring director, programmed a
fourteen-film Ford series at Dan Talbot's New Yorker Theater in 1963. His
program notes described *Liberty Valance* as "perhaps [Ford's] most deeply felt
personal statement."

It was clear from these reactions that to fully understand the meaning of the
film, a viewer almost has to be well versed in Ford's previous work. But historical memory was spotty at best among most mainstream reviewers in the
early sixties, and even today some people who admire other Ford Westerns
downgrade *Liberty Valance* because it lacks the scenic values and the buoyant
energy of such classics as *Stagecoach, My Darling Clementine,* and *The Searchers.*

Ford's characteristic desire to confound people, particularly those people
who insisted on regarding him in a stereotypical light, only intensified as he
grew older. A wonderfully revealing example occurred during the shooting of
Liberty Valance when Ford received an offer from New York's Metropolitan
Opera Company to direct one of its upcoming productions. The opera they
asked him to direct was Puccini's *The Girl of the Golden West.* Doubtless the
Met's management thought it was flattering him, but Ford found the offer insulting, as if the Met were implying he was simply a "dirty old *cowboy*." He
sent back a message saying that he would be happy to direct an opera for the
Met, but that instead of *The Girl of the Golden West,* he wanted to direct Puccini's *La Bohème.*

If people wondered why he was making a "dirty old *cowboy*" movie like
Liberty Valance instead of some lavish epic in color and wide-screen, Ford de-

fiantly set out to show them that he did not give a damn. The film's lack of fancy "production values" was Ford's statement about going back to the basic values of moviemaking. Capturing the incomprehension of viewers expecting something more lavish, more visually ambitious, and perhaps also more celebratory from Ford at that stage in his career, Manny Farber (in his 1962 *Film Culture* article "White Elephant Art vs. Termite Art") complained about the "pale, neutral film life" of *Liberty Valance* and its setting in "an unreal stage town . . . where the cactus was planted last night."

It is often mistakenly assumed that Ford shot *Liberty Valance* in black and white because he couldn't afford to use color. There was even a rumor that *Liberty Valance,* like *Gideon's Day,* was actually filmed in color but was released in black and white. Cinematographer William H. Clothier denied those stories, explaining that Ford thought color would have made it impossible to achieve the crucially important interplay of light and shadow he needed for the climactic gunfight, which is seen twice from radically different perspectives. Ford's contract with Paramount in April 1961 specified that the film would be shot in black and white. He may have felt about *Liberty Valance* the way Howard Hawks felt about *Red River:* "Some things I think go well in black-and-white; they give you a feeling of being *older,*" Hawks explained. Another misapprehension about *Liberty Valance* is that Ford filmed it largely on the Paramount Western street and other interior sets simply because he was too cheap, tired, and/or lazy to bother with his usual visual splendor.

But *Liberty Valance* is not a film about landscapes or scenery, it is a film about ideas, an allegory of American history. One of Ford's most theatrical pictures, with a limited number of sets and an intimate concentration on the performers, it has more in common visually with the chamber dramas of Carl Theodor Dreyer than with *The Searchers* and other Ford Westerns in which the physical milieu is as important a presence as the characters. Ford virtually abstracts the physical backdrop of *Liberty Valance* to heighten the importance of dialogue, the emotional language of faces and bodies, and the symbolic use of gestures and objects. The almost total *absence* of landscape from *Liberty Valance* is itself a statement of Ford's loss of faith in the ideal of the American frontier; the civilization of Shinbone seems a dead end. The film's austerity, its masterful economy of style, and its concentration on memory marks it as very much an old man's movie. In the range, depth, and clarity of its play of ideas, and in Ford's self-conscious explication of his worldview after more than four decades of filmmaking, *Liberty Valance* is the director's cinematic testament. He would make one more great film before retirement, *7 Women,* but that valedictory work is something of an aberration in his career, not the grand summation represented by *The Man Who Shot Liberty Valance.*

. . .

Offering one of Ford's richest galleries of characters, *Liberty Valance* brings in a few newcomers who expand the Fordian universe in ways that point provocatively toward an uncertain future. But it also indulges in unabashedly nostalgic casting that, in the cases of Wayne and Stewart, places the actors' iconic status above any question of realism. Wayne, fifty-four when he appeared in the film, hardly ages from beginning to end, although he's still in the youthful courting stage with Vera Miles's Hallie at the start of the long flashback sequence, when Stewart pretends to be "a young man fresh out of law school" despite being fifty-three years old.

Ford seemed anxious about whether Wayne still wanted to work with him. When he called Wayne's house in April 1961, he became upset, thinking that the person answering the phone was Wayne pretending to be someone else. Wayne wrote Ford to assure him, "I certainly would not be too tired to talk to a man whom I consider my best friend—that I have a feeling of blood kinship with." This may have been an early indication of a pattern Dobe Carey observed in Ford's later years of Wayne and other stars trying to avoid the director: "It's terrible, because Duke loved him like he was his Dad, although they were not that far apart in age. And Dick Widmark just adored him. Widmark said, 'I treasure the days that I worked for John Ford. Even the days that I didn't agree with what he was doing, I still thought he's a genius.' But Duke and those guys, a lot of times I think they would actually stay away because they knew the Old Man was gonna say, 'Listen, I got a script. Let's talk about makin' a movie.' "

Sending Wayne the script of *Liberty Valance* in July 1961, Ford praised it highly, an unusual move on his part. He pointed out somewhat defensively that, for a change, they would not be going on location with this picture. Ford compared it to *Stagecoach,* which not only demonstrated his level of ambition on *Liberty Valance* but also served to remind Wayne that most of his scenes in *Stagecoach* were filmed on a studio lot. Nevertheless, Wayne was not happy with the character of Doniphon. He later complained that Ford "had Jimmy Stewart for the shit-kicker hero. He had Edmond O'Brien for the quick-witted humor. Add Lee Marvin for a flamboyant heavy, and, shit, I've got to walk through the goddam picture."

Those who have seen Woody Strode as the stalwart black hero of *Sergeant Rutledge* can best appreciate the contrast Ford intends to be drawn between that character and Strode's more subservient but still dignified Pompey in *Liberty Valance.* Pompey accurately represents the way most African-Americans had to live in the age of Jim Crow, being excluded from white establishments (such as Hank's Saloon, run by Jack Pennick) but quietly playing a vital role in the community. Pompey's close relationship with the man he calls "Mister Tom"—they live and work together, Pompey saves Tom from committing suicide, and Pompey is the only mourner at Tom's funeral until the Stoddards arrive from out of town—makes him virtually Tom's "wife." This is Ford's commentary on both men's outsider status and their mutual banishment from "civilization," which is always defined by Ford largely in terms of feminization. Their seemingly asexual but emotionally intertwined relationship embodies what Leslie Fiedler, in his 1960 book *Love and Death in the American Novel,* describes as "the archetypal image, found in our favorite books, in which a white and a colored American male flee from civilization into each other's arms."

In one of the richest female performances in Ford's work, Vera Miles as Hallie is a more mature and somber version of her spirited Laurie from *The Searchers.* Hallie works in the restaurant of a Swedish couple whom critics often describe as her parents, but it is unlikely that a young woman of that era would be on a first-name basis with her parents, as Hallie is with Peter and Nora Ericson, played by Miles's father from *The Searchers,* John Qualen, and *Two Rode Together*'s Jeanette Nolan. Miles also brings echoes of *Rookie of the Year,* in which she points a gun at Wayne to stop him from writing a story exposing the truth about an American icon; in both the TV show and the film, the story is burned rather than printed, but in *Liberty Valance,* Miles wants the truth to be revealed. Repeated viewings of *Liberty Valance* show that most of the important decisions in the story are Hallie's: she encourages Ranse to stay in town and open a school, she keeps him from leaving in the face of Valance's threat, she gets Tom to save Ranse's life by killing Valance, and she even plants the idea for Ranse's transformation of the territory with his congressional irrigation bill. When Scott asks Senator Stoddard to tell the story of Shinbone's past, it is only when Hallie nods her assent that Ranse does so. But if the film pays tribute to Hallie's fortitude and imagination, it also emphasizes that her choice of Ranse over Tom, setting this momentous chain of historical events in motion, was a tragic mistake.

The newcomers to Ford's world include Edmond O'Brien, whose casting as Peabody, the grandiloquent champion of the freedom of the press, draws on his background as a Shakespearean actor: he played Cassius and Marc Antony in Orson Welles's Mercury Theatre production of *Julius Caesar* in the late 1930s and Casca in MGM's 1953 film version of the play. In *Liberty Valance,* Peabody uses Shakespearean locutions and quotes from Henry V's St. Crispin's Day speech to bolster his own courage. When I acted with O'Brien in Welles's 1970s film *The Other Side of the Wind,* he told me what a joy it had been to work with Ford, who called his fellow Irishman "Éamon" and allowed as much rehearsal time as O'Brien needed to amplify his baroque performance.

On his most complex scene, the drunken soliloquy in the newspaper office ending with Peabody tipping his hat to his own shadow, he spent the entire morning rehearsing with Ford. Then they shot the scene in one long take and broke for lunch. After finishing his work on *Liberty Valance*, O'Brien wrote Ford, "In all the years, I have never enjoyed an acting experience so much."

The villains are memorably played by three actors who represented the growing trend toward psychopathic behavior in the Western genre, which would reach its epitome a few years later in the work of Ford's most important successor as a Western director, Sam Peckinpah. Peckinpah made his first major impact with *Ride the High Country*, released the same year as *Liberty Valance*. The Peckinpah Stock Company would come to prominently feature Strother Martin, who appears in Ford's film as Valance's wild-eyed sidekick, Floyd, the one who giggles with sadistic glee as his boss whips Dutton Peabody nearly to death. Valance's quietly sinister sidekick, Reese, is hawk-faced Lee Van Cleef, who later in the decade would go on to a starring career in Italian "spaghetti Westerns," including some directed by Sergio Leone.

Ford was not a total stranger to psychopathic characters—Valance's penchant for whipping his henchmen is borrowed from Pa Clanton's treatment of his sons in *My Darling Clementine*, and the names of Floyd and Reese are borrowed from two of the Clegg brothers in *Wagon Master*. But Ford was headed into a whole new dimension with Lee Marvin's Valance, one of the screen's most riveting incarnations of pure evil. Playing the role without a shade of ambiguity, Marvin has the starkness of a figure from a medieval morality play. While some would disparage Valance as a throwback to the simplistic morality of old B Westerns, there is a raw, disturbing believability to Marvin's performance that goes well beyond the norm in the genre up to that time. Perhaps the director's experiences in World War II, and Marvin's, had shown them a thing or two about fascism and its psychological roots in sadism.

The ineffectual forces of law and order in *Liberty Valance* are burlesqued through the character of Marshal Link Appleyard, an obese coward delightfully played as a Shakespearean fool by Ford regular Andy Devine. Sarris eloquently summed up his function in the film: "Devine, Ford's broad-beamed Falstaff, must stand extra guard duty for the late Ward Bond and Victor McLaglen. Ford, the strategist of retreats and last stands, has outlived the regulars of his grand army. . . . Through the entire flashback, Andy Devine fulfills his duties as town marshal by cowering behind doorways to avoid Liberty Valance. Yet Devine's mere participation in the fierce nobility of the past magnifies his character in retrospect. For Ford, there is some glory in just growing old and remembering through the thick haze of illusion." (Actually, in one scene late in the film, the marshal *does* take a brave stand against Valance, urging him to call off his vendetta against Ranse. But that is a striking exception to his usual behavior.)

During the shooting, Ford outdid himself with his vicious abuse of Wayne. One time when Wayne suggested something, Ford berated the actor before the entire company: "Jesus Christ, here I take you out of eight-day Westerns, I put you in big movies, and you give me a stupid suggestion like that!" Ford taunted Wayne about how Woody Strode had served in World War II and he hadn't, a jibe that infuriated Wayne. Ford also made malicious comparisons between Wayne's athletic career and Strode's. "Duke," Ford said, "there's the real football player." The tension that engendered almost led to a serious incident. When Wayne was having trouble controlling his horse-drawn buckboard during the scene at the burning ranch, Strode reached for the reins, but Wayne knocked him away. When the scene ended, Strode "was ready to kick his ass." Ford ran over, shouting to the younger man, "Woody, don't hit him! We need him!"

Ford's baiting of Wayne probably reflected his growing anger over Wayne's superior position in the industry. Perhaps Ford rationalized his behavior as a way of getting Wayne in the right mood to play the alienated and marginalized Tom Doniphon. As was usually the case, Wayne's instincts as an actor were superior to his conscious understanding of his screen persona. When Wayne's longtime assistant, Mary St. John, tried to tell him that Doniphon had an intriguing ambiguity, Wayne replied, "Screw ambiguity. Perversion and corruption masquerade as ambiguity. I don't like ambiguity. I don't trust ambiguity." But ambiguity is what Ford drew from Wayne in his eloquently underplayed performance. As Manny Farber observed, "Wayne's acting is infected by a kind of hoboish spirit, sitting back on its haunches doing a bitter-amused counterpoint to the pale, neutral film life around him." Farber appreciated Wayne's "engaging professionalism and a hipster sense of how to sit in a chair leaned against the wall . . . a craggy face filled with bitterness, jealousy, a big body that idles luxuriantly, having long grown tired with rough-house games played by old wrangler types like John Ford."

Wayne wondered why Ford was treating Stewart so kindly by comparison. About halfway through the shooting, the Duke asked, "How's it come that you've gone through this whole thing and you've never been at the bottom of the list? What is it, you've been red-appl'in' the Old Man?" Stewart admitted that he "got a little smug about it." Near the end of the production, they were getting ready to shoot the funeral scene with Strode in old-age makeup and powdery white hair, wearing blue overalls and a tattered vest. "Ford came over to me and asked what I thought of the costume," Stewart recalled. "I said it was a bit Uncle Remus–like and then immediately wished I'd bitten my tongue. I knew I'd make a mistake. 'Well, what's wrong with Uncle Remus?' he asks. And then he's yelling, 'Hey, Woody, Duke, everybody come over here. Look at Woody, look at his costume. One of the *players* seems to have some objection. One of the *players* here doesn't seem to like Uncle Remus. As a matter of fact, I'm not at all sure he even likes Negroes.' . . . I wanted to shoot myself. I wanted to crawl into a mouse hole. And I looked at Duke Wayne, and he was beaming like a cat that had just eaten the mouse." Wayne came over to him and said, "Well, welcome to the club. I'm glad you made it."

Stewart enjoyed regaling audiences with that anecdote as an example of Ford's eccentric sense of humor. But Stewart biographer Donald Dewey suggests that Ford had picked up on the conservative actor's real-life discomfort about associating with African-Americans. Stewart's attitude manifested itself in complaints during the sixties and seventies that movies had fallen under the influence of such special-interest groups as "teenagers and colored people." Lucille Gipson, a black woman who worked for Stewart's relatives in Pennsylvania, described him as a "gentleman," but said, "He *hated* the idea of having to say more than a hello directly to us. . . . He didn't know how to act with black people, like it was something special he was afraid of not being able to do right, so better stay away from us altogether."

Ford uses that attitude subtly in *Liberty Valance*, such as when Ranse presses a wad of bills into Pompey's hand and says in a condescending tone, "Po'k chop money." In the schoolroom scene, Ranse pompously preaches brotherhood but harshly corrects Pompey's grammar when the black man, earnestly reciting his history lesson, says of the Declaration of Independence, "It was writ by Mr. Thomas Jefferson of Virginia." In that scene, Ford frames Pompey with a portrait of Abraham Lincoln on the wall behind him; Stoddard, who fancies himself the territory's founding father, is juxtaposed with a portrait of George Washington, the slave-owning "Father of His Country."

When Bogdanovich commented that Ford's view of the West had become increasingly sad over the years, as reflected in the progression from *Wagon Master* to *The Man Who Shot Liberty Valance,* Ford replied, "Possibly—I don't know—I'm not a psychologist. Maybe I'm getting older."

Even more than most Ford pictures, *Liberty Valance* is filled with a complex network of cross-references to the director's other work. And in most instances, the mental process of cutting back and forth between them underscores the extent to which Ford's vision of America had darkened over the years. In particular, *Liberty Valance* can be seen as something of a remake of *My Darling Clementine,* Ford's classic portrait of the civilizing of a "wide-open town." Both films revolve around a mythic duel, and even the names of the towns share a macabre similarity: Tombstone and Shinbone. But comparing Henry Fonda's cool, methodically effective, honest, and idealistic (if also racist and violent) lawman in *Clementine* to James Stewart's shaky, often hysterical, ultimately fraudulent and cynical lawmaker in *Liberty Valance* vividly demonstrates Ford's loss of faith in what Peabody mockingly describes as "the spectacle of law and order." When Hallie goes to the ruins of Tom's home to pick a cactus rose for his coffin, we hear Alfred Newman's wistful "Ann Rutledge" theme from *Young Mr. Lincoln*. The theme is used at several other emphatic points in the sparsely scored *Liberty Valance,* suggesting that Tom is Hallie's lost love, as Ann was Lincoln's, and that Hallie plays a similarly inspirational role in Ranse's political career. But Ranse is no Lincoln, and Tom's despondent burning of his own home is an even darker twist on the Indians' burning of the Edwards home in *The Searchers.*

For Ford, born the year after Frederick Jackson Turner delivered his valedictory speech on "The Significance of the Frontier in American History," *Liberty Valance* represents the true closing of the frontier, both his own mythic frontier and that of the film genre he helped create. "The story of the Western from its heyday to the 'Bicentennial Westerns' of 1976 is basically one of loss of faith in America," Michael Coyne writes in his 1998 book *The Crowded Prairie: American National Identity in the Hollywood Western*. Ford was, as always, a leading figure in that development. Caught up in the tragic rush of history, his characters in *Liberty Valance* make choices that seem wrong in retrospect but at the time seem almost inevitable. Perfectly balancing the genre's irreconcilable contradictions, Ford makes a film with a populist thrust but an ultimate skepticism about the value of "progress." In terms of psychohistory, the killing of Valance, a rampant Western id-figure like Scar in *The Searchers,* means the purging of the unbridled force of the libido from the frontier town of Shinbone, leaving in its wake Tom's coffin, the feeble old Pompey, and the desiccated Stoddard couple. The wilderness may have become a garden, but it has become poisoned at its heart. Ford strikes this theme from the opening shot of the train bearing the Stoddards back to Shinbone: as the train leaves the frame, Ford lingers a moment on its black smoke hovering over the otherwise pristine landscape, visually showing that "progress" is a polluting force.

Ford's view of history in *Liberty Valance* could be summed up in Mao Zedong's famous adage, "Political power grows out of the barrel of a gun." But far from celebrating such a brutal process, Ford deplores its effect on the future of American civilization. The killing of Valance, while taming the forces of anarchy and making room for civilization to prosper, renders obsolete the pioneer values of self-reliance represented by Tom Doniphon and corrupts Ransom Stoddard's moral character. But Ford's view of Tom, the true Western hero, is not simply elegiac. As Peter Wollen observes, "By shooting Liberty Valance he has destroyed the only world in which he himself can exist, the world of the gun rather than the book; it is as though Ethan Edwards had perceived that by scalping Scar, he was in reality committing suicide." Ford's staging of the gunfight from a dual perspective, with the alleyway from which Tom fires becoming the film's equivalent of the "grassy knoll," prefigures the ambiguities surrounding the following year's assassination of President John F. Kennedy. The kind of public skepticism that watershed event unleashed is at the heart of *Liberty Valance,* whose hidden story of behind-the-scenes manipulation suggests that American history and the democratic process itself are something of a sham, a confidence trick played on the public by slick politicians and compliant reporters.

The editor's line "When the legend becomes fact, print the legend" has prompted a surprising amount of confusion in commentaries on the film. Despite its tragic personal implications for Stoddard, who realizes he is forever doomed to living under a false image, and despite what the line implies about the veracity of American history, some have made the mistakes of confusing the artist with his characters and overlooking the context in which the line appears, assuming that "Print the legend" is Ford's justification for his own role as a longtime fabricator of Western legends. The film clearly refutes that notion, for as Bogdanovich succinctly observes, "Ford prints the fact." In the script as well as in Bellah's novelization, editor Scott attributes this saying to his predecessor, prefacing the line with, "As the late and great Dutton Peabody used to say, 'It ain't news. . . .'" The studio's dialogue continuity indicates that Ford filmed the scene that way before the reference to Peabody was cut in the final editing stage. Peabody is portrayed as such a strong champion of journalistic truth-telling that Ford probably realized it would have been out of character for him to take such a cynical stance. Unlike Scott, who presumes that the public is better served by being fooled, Ford ruthlessly exposes the myth-making apparatus that underlies much of history and much of the director's own work in the Western genre. A similar revisionist impulse motivates Ford in *Fort Apache* and in such late films as *Sergeant Rutledge* and *Cheyenne Autumn.*

Hallie's placing of the cactus rose on Tom's coffin in the penultimate scene of *Liberty Valance* beautifully symbolizes Ford's mourning for the lost possibilities of American history. The rose itself represents the flowering of new life in the desert, which Stoddard's irrigation bill has helped make possible. But now the rose has been uprooted and is lifeless, like Tom, like Hallie's dreams. When Stoddard notices the rose and realizes that Hallie is still in love with Tom, the composition is as intricate as the ambiguities of his position in history: the rose is in the foreground as he moves forward in middle frame to shut the door of the coffin room, stopping when he sees the rose, with the door half-closed and Hallie's solitary figure visible in profile in the far background. Sarris again: "Everything that Ford has ever thought or felt is compressed into one shot . . . photographed, needless to say, from the only possible angle."

Ford's deep pessimism toward the American future is summed up in the film's coda on the train heading back East. Bringing a cuspidor to Senator Stoddard, the unctuous conductor (Willis Bouchey) tells him, "Nothing's too good for the man who shot Liberty Valance." Stoddard's face is bleak with resignation. Just before that final moment, Hallie glances out the train window and says of the Western landscape, "Look at it. Once it was a wilderness. Now it's a garden. Aren't you proud?" Ranse does not respond; we see only a troubled flicker in his eyes. Michael Wilmington and I wrote of this scene in our 1974 book on Ford: "Once the historical process has been given a catalyst, it can't be stopped: that is the tragedy. And the reason Ford 'prints the fact' is to ask the public, '*Are* you proud?' "

In 1976, I spent two days on the set of John Wayne's last film, *The Shootist,* watching the shooting of the scene in which Stewart diagnoses Wayne's gunfighter with terminal cancer. During a break in the filming, I gave Stewart a copy of our book on Ford. When I went to interview him at his home a few days later, Stewart said he had been thinking about what we wrote on the last scene of *Liberty Valance.* In his silent reaction to Hallie's question, he agreed, lies the meaning of the film, Ford's implied question to modern Americans about what has happened to their country since the closing of the frontier: "*Are* you proud?"

The Civil War, the antiwar parable Ford contributed to MGM's *How the West Was Won* (1962), again shows the discrepancy between the mythic version of history and the brutal reality. A darker recapitulation of his Shiloh sequence in *The Colter Craven Story,* Ford's masterfully directed episode of the Cinerama spectacle, just twenty-two minutes in length, has the simplicity and compression of a work of lyric poetry. Using fence posts, pillars, trees, and other objects to block out the lines separating the three panels of the cumbersome Cinerama process, Ford paradoxically deemphasizes spectacle to focus on history's intimate human dimensions. Coming at the midpoint of this highly uneven epic celebrating America's Manifest Destiny, *The Civil War* introduces a cautionary note amid all the bombastic jingoism. The latent ambiguities of James R. Webb's screenplay are fully realized in Ford's direction but otherwise tend to be submerged by the sheer scale of the production.

Ford directed *The Civil War* in May–June 1961. Joseph LaShelle, who had been Arthur C. Miller's camera operator on *How Green Was My Valley,* served as cinematographer. The opening and closing scenes of the Ohio farm from which Zeb Rawlings (George Peppard) goes off to war were shot first, on location near Paducah, Kentucky. The Shiloh sequence was filmed at MGM and at the Corrigan Ranch in the Simi Valley, where Ford had shot the scenes of the fort in *Fort Apache*. The four other parts of *How the West Was Won* were directed unimaginatively by two journeymen who, like Ford, had begun their careers as prop boys in the silent days at Universal, Henry Hathaway and George Marshall. Salaries on the project were reduced to allow part of the proceeds to benefit St. John's Hospital in Santa Monica, where Ford himself would be treated in later years. Ford received $50,000, and John Wayne a token $25,000 for his role as General Sherman (this time under his own name).

As an unblinking portrait of the horrors of war, *The Civil War* is surpassed in Ford's work only by his documentary *This Is Korea!* Giving only an impressionistic treatment of the actual battle—two nocturnal shots of a long line of cannons firing and snippets of footage from the 1957 MGM Civil War film *Raintree County*—Ford concentrates on the gory aftermath. Intensified by the scale of the huge Cinerama/Ultra Panavision imagery, his Shiloh is a landscape out of a nightmare, with piles of corpses being buried in a trench and a makeshift operating room that resembles a butcher shop. "It had been the bloodiest day of the war on the Western front," says the narrator (Spencer Tracy). "In the morning it had looked like a Confederate victory. But by nightfall no man cared to use the words 'win' or 'lose.'" Zeb, all naive excitement when he departed for war, wanders through the carnage dazed and bloody, saying, "It ain't quite what I *expected*—there ain't much glory in lookin' at a man with his guts hangin' out."

Picking up where *The Colter Craven Story* left off, Ford and Webb elaborate on Grant's despondency over his lack of preparedness for the Confederate attack. Grant (Harry Morgan) tells Sherman that he is prepared to resign because of "the general lack of confidence in me" and the false rumors that he had been drinking before the battle. Wild-eyed and disheveled, Sherman replies, "A month ago they were saying I was crazy, *insane*. Now they're calling me a hero. But hero or crazy, I'm the same man. Doesn't matter what the people think. It's what *you* think, Grant." Sharing the generals' sense of alienation from an uncomprehending and vindictive public, Ford takes the long view of history in presenting Shiloh as a temporary stumbling block in the Union's progress to ultimate victory. But it *does* matter what the people think. Zeb has been eavesdropping with a newfound friend, a Confederate deserter (Russ Tamblyn) who tempts him to run away. When the Reb realizes Grant's identity and lifts his gun to assassinate the general, Zeb bayonets his friend, then shakes his lifeless body, demanding, "Why did you make me *do* that?" As in *Liberty Valance,* the inexorable logic of history runs away with people's common humanity.

The framing sequences of Zeb's leavetaking from his mother (Carroll Baker) and his homecoming after her death are filmed with an artless simplicity that conveys a sense of primitive harmony with the land and an overwhelming sense of loss. At the end, striking a self-consciously heroic pose on the steps of his home, Zeb tells his brother of his plans to go West, join the cavalry, and fight Indians. This seemingly illogical development of Zeb's character after his disillusionment at Shiloh is presented by Ford as a tragic submission to the nation's warlike destiny. Ford's remarkably somber view of American history in *The Civil War* largely escaped critical notice. Although *How the West Was Won* was a box-office hit following its release in November 1962, its most tangible benefit for Ford was the beginning of his fruitful association with the film's producer, Bernard Smith. An urbane man who had been editor in chief of the publishing firm of Alfred A. Knopf before becoming a story editor for Samuel Goldwyn Pictures and other production companies, Smith formed a joint venture with Ford in 1962 that would result in the last two features of the director's career, *Cheyenne Autumn* and *7 Women.*

As Ford's physical world constricted and he was able to spend less and less time on the *Araner,* watching baseball games became one of his principal means of recreation. He and Mary held season tickets at Dodger Stadium, and although he could watch television only sparingly because of his worsening eyesight, he said, "I look at sports events, chiefly baseball, and like to see Perry Mason. That's about it." Ford's headgear on film sets, a major component of his gruff common-man persona, gradually changed from navy caps to baseball caps. For years he proudly wore a St. Louis Cardinals hat, a present from the team's legendary star Stan "The Man" Musial; in *Donovan's Reef,* child actor Tim Stafford (Anna Lee's son) similarly wears a hat given to him by Musial. Ford sometimes sported caps he received from Willie Mays of the San Francisco Giants and Joe Adcock of the Milwaukee Braves. Near the end of his career, Ford switched to a well-worn Dodgers hat, a gift from pitcher Don Drysdale, wearing it during much of the shooting on *7 Women.* Ford was touched when the Braves' home-run champion Henry Aaron, one of the men he most admired, paid a visit to the set of *Sergeant Rutledge.* The African-American ballplayer later told Ford he had seen the film six times.

As a diversion after *The Man Who Shot Liberty Valance,* Ford made his second television show about baseball, *Flashing Spikes.* The ABC program, starring James Stewart and hosted by Fred Astaire, was aired around the time of the

World Series in October 1962 and has cameo roles for Drysdale and the Dodgers' broadcaster, Vin Scully. Written by Jameson Brewer from a novel by Frank O'Rourke, this one-hour program, like 1955's *Rookie of the Year,* deals with a former player who was banned from major league baseball because of a bribery scandal.

Stewart's Slim Conway still loves the game so much that he hangs around training fields like a ghost and plays with a semiprofessional barnstorming team of old-timers called by the very Fordian name of the Wanderers. Ford clearly identifies with Slim's marginalization, his battered physical condition, and his dogged persistence in practicing his craft despite the jeers he receives from heartless spectators and vindictive journalists. When Conway takes a fatherly interest in a promising young Yankee player, Bill Riley (Patrick Wayne), and tries to pass along his skills and sense of tradition, the young man finds his own integrity called into question. Ultimately, both Riley and Conway are cleared of suspicion, and Conway manages to convince the sympathetic baseball commissioner (Jack Warden) that the old bribery charge was a frame-up.

Made by Astaire's Avista Productions for his *Alcoa Premiere* series, *Flashing Spikes* intersperses solid dramatic and comedic scenes (photographed in black and white by Bill Clothier) with shoddy visual corner cutting typical of television production in that era, including the clumsy use of baseball stock footage. But Ford literally has a field day with the semipro game, replete with delightful character-revealing vignettes and sharp satire of the mob mentality. Stewart's intensely concentrated, unglamorized performance endows Conway with genuine nobility and stature. "It was one of the first television things I'd done," Stewart recalled. "And Ford was a tremendous help to me, because this was sort of a new experience. Oh, God, it looked like we did the whole thing in ten minutes! Ford just called me up and said, 'I have something I'd like you to do.' And I don't think I even knew that it was *on* television. [*Laughs*] He just said, 'We're down at so-and-so, the studio [Revue],' and I went down. But it was a good experience, just like they all were with Ford." Ford also found room for another cameo by John Wayne, this time as a cigar-chomping marine sergeant umpiring a ballgame in Korea; he is billed as Michael Morrison.

Ford's reworking of the ostracization theme of *Rookie of the Year* makes it clear that while both these programs ostensibly are about baseball, their subtext is the Hollywood blacklist. *Rookie of the Year,* featuring blacklist ringleader Ward Bond as the banned player, cautiously argued that a son shouldn't be made to pay for his father's sins. *Flashing Spikes,* made in a far more liberal climate, centers on the flagrant injustice involved in one particular case of blacklisting. When asked by the commissioner why he didn't try to clear himself earlier, Conway replies with exasperation, "I got up, I defended myself, I denied it, but nobody believed me." Referring to that "nasty" time when he was the victim of a crooked witness "namin' names," Conway says, "People didn't take their baseball lightly in those days. . . . and there were quite a few innocent ballplayers on my ballclub. But rumors are rumors, so—well, I never want to see anything like that again. You know, that business almost closed out baseball. We might never have heard of Gehrig—DiMaggio—Musial."

Although the charge of taking a bribe is morally distinct from the constitutionally guaranteed expression of unpopular political beliefs, Ford is clearly trying to set the record straight on his distaste for blackballing of any kind. But by approaching the subject obliquely and being several years too late with his public display of moral indignation, Ford made little impact with *Flashing Spikes.*

Ford's loss of faith in America's future became increasingly plain to see as the social tensions of the 1960s deepened. The values he most revered—home, family, justice, tradition, the military—were being mocked, attacked, or simply disregarded. His ideal of communal harmony faded as the country splintered into warring ethnic factions. America was changing in ways he could not fully understand or accept.

In the final phase of his career, Ford directed three feature films (*Donovan's Reef, Cheyenne Autumn,* and *7 Women*), and started a fourth he was not able to finish (*Young Cassidy*). All but one of those films are set outside the United States, and as Robin Wood observes, "Ford's flight from his own country—I think in artistic terms it amounts to that—to the Pacific, to China, or back to Ireland, is interrupted only by his account of the desperate trek of the Cheyenne back to their native country." Reversing the pattern of Ford's prewar films, which often dealt with immigrants coming to America to seek a better life, these late works explicitly question the validity of the American Dream, a departure Ford anticipated with Sean Thornton's return to Ireland in *The Quiet Man.*

The South Seas island of Haleakaloa in *Donovan's Reef* (1963), Peter Wollen observes, is "a kind of Valhalla for the homeless heroes of *The Man Who Shot Liberty Valance.*" And for Ford himself, whose fantasies of a happy retirement transformed this raucous comedy into his personal vision of an earthly paradise. Shortly before the film opened, Ford called it a "spoof picture—a whammy, crazy sort of thing. We're not trying for any prizes." Representing Ford at his most uninhibited, *Donovan's Reef* requires similar indulgence from the spectator. This mulligan stew of knockabout comedy, pictorial beauty, boozy sentimentality, and earnest preachments about multiculturalism is a litmus test for one's preexisting attitudes toward Ford's idiosyncrasies.

Donovan's Reef centers around two old navy buddies (John Wayne as Michael Patrick "Guns" Donovan and Lee Marvin as Thomas Aloysius "Boats" Gilhooley) whooping it up on an island in French Polynesia. They felt no desire to return home to America after World War II, finding a happier and more peaceful existence among the islanders who helped them win the war. Another navy comrade, Dr. William Dedham (Jack Warden), stayed on to run a hospital for the natives, while Donovan (like Ford's father in Maine) opened the saloon that provides the film's title. The periodic visits of Gilhooley, whose fondness for mayhem is far more anarchic than that of his longtime sparring partner, are celebrated by drunken brawling in *Donovan's Reef.*

Loosely based on "The South Sea Story" by the uncredited James M. Michener, whose stories also served as the basis for the Rodgers and Hammerstein musical *South Pacific, Donovan's Reef* was languishing in Paramount's story files (under the working title *Climate of Love*) when Ford came to the studio to make *Liberty Valance*. Laboring on the property over the years were eight screenwriters, including Edmund Beloin, who wound up with the story credit after a Writers Guild of America arbitration. John Wayne's favorite screenwriter, James Edward Grant, was hired by John Ford Productions in February 1962 to write a shooting script. Grant's level of sophistication in the romantic comedy genre was summed up in his remark to Frank Capra, "All you gotta have in a John Wayne picture is a hoity-toity dame with big tits that Duke can throw over his knee and spank, and a collection of jerks he can smash in the face every five minutes." While this formula bears more than a passing resemblance to *Donovan's Reef,* Grant followed it all too crudely for Ford's taste in his screenplay completed on April 5, so the director brought in Frank Nugent for an extensive eleventh-hour rewrite, hoping Nugent would impart some of the flavor of his script for *The Quiet Man.*[3]

Acting as his own producer, taking a flat fee of $250,000 and no ownership share, Ford made the film with his usual efficiency in forty-seven days of shooting from July 23 through September 25, finishing $34,959 under his budget of $3.62 million. A commercial success, *Donovan's Reef* grossed $5,753,600 in the first five years of release. Nevertheless, the haphazard creative atmosphere resulted in a film that not only seems even more spontaneous

---

3. During November 17–19, 1962, Ford stepped in to direct scenes for another Grant screenplay, the John Wayne–Maureen O'Hara Western comedy *McLintock!*—a Batjac production for United Artists. The film's director, Andrew V. McLaglen, Victor's son and Ford's second assistant on *The Quiet Man,* had fallen ill. Actress Stefanie Powers recalled Ford's dramatic arrival on the Tucson location, stepping out of a car and pushing aside Wayne and O'Hara as he marched up to cinematographer William Clothier and announced, "Let's go to work, Bill." Powers marveled that everything Ford did was "so absurdly dramatic."

and relaxed than most Ford pictures but often looks as if the director made it up as he went along, a very mixed blessing creatively.

By the time location filming took place on the Hawaiian island of Kauai, Ford was rarely traveling to Hawaii anymore aboard the *Araner.* Because the yacht's continued upkeep and repair was such a drain on his dwindling financial resources, he wanted to rid himself of his former home away from home, but Mary was balking. "*Araner* to her is a status symbol," Ford wrote Pat in 1963. "She hates the boat—won't use it, but refuses to give it up. . . . It's crippling us." Since it was difficult to find a buyer for the thirty-seven-year-old boat, Ford considered giving it to the navy or operating it as a charter vessel. In the meantime, to recoup some expenses and as a nostalgic commemoration of his old way of life, Ford leased the *Araner* to Paramount for $5,000 and displayed it on-screen as one of Donovan's business enterprises.

As Graham Greene observed of Frank Capra's *Lost Horizon,* "Nothing reveals men's characters more than their Utopias." Lushly filmed in Technicolor by William Clothier, Ford's romantic daydream of a society divorced from time and trouble offers a superficially alluring means of escape from the contemporary American rat race to a more sensual and tolerant environment. But the Haleakaloa of *Donovan's Reef* is also a colonial Utopia where white men lord it over the natives in benevolent fashion and wallow in infantile regression, drinking and brawling and wenching without responsibility. Ford can't help taking vicarious pleasure in the excesses of Donovan and Gilhooley, but most viewers will agree with Dr. Dedham that they are "worse than a couple of kids." Still, the balletic saloon fights of these two aging Irish roughnecks, like the perpetual brawling of Quirt and Flagg in *What Price Glory,* have a strong element of Fordian self-parody. Before Donovan and Gilhooley begin their annual orgy of wreckage, they have this sublime exchange:

> *Donovan:* (cautioning) No fights.
> *Gilhooley:* Guns, uh—no fights? Twenty-two years—tradition—
> legion—
> *Donovan:* (corrects him) Legend.
> *Gilhooley:* —and the crowd.

The arrival of the doctor's long-lost daughter from Boston, Amelia (Elizabeth Allen), complicates the men's blissful existence. Initially the viewer is led to believe that Amelia, the heir to a Yankee shipping fortune, is a starchy, puritanical blue blood; the Dickensian opening scene at a Boston board meeting presents the family as stuck in the nineteenth century. In a panic, Donovan pretends that the doctor's half-caste children are his own, fearing Amelia will react to them with knee-jerk racism. But the threat Amelia represents is more in his mind than in reality. She turns out to be one of Ford's most spirited and attractive female characters, with an adaptable modernism that represents the director's qualified hope for the future. Amelia's lack of prejudice shames Donovan and the others for putting the children through an unnecessarily painful and humiliating experience. Like so many Ford characters, Amelia is an alienated outsider who longs for a home and hopes to reconstruct her shattered family life.

Robin Wood argues that Amelia's "capitulation" to the island's way of life is "so rapid (and so perfunctorily charted) that by halfway through the film there seems absolutely no reason why she should not simply be Told All, and the resulting plot-maneuvers to eke out the narrative before the final denouement become tedious and irritating in the extreme. . . . The tiresome and protracted buffoonery of *Donovan's Reef,* far from embodying any acceptable system of values, merely conceals an old man's disillusionment at the failure of his ideals to find fulfillment." While disagreeing with Wood about the development of Amelia's character, which I find charted with subtlety and humor (largely in visual terms), I think the film suffers instead from Ford's overidentification with Donovan's anxiety about miscegenation, even in the form that is least threatening to white society, a white man with a woman of another race. While clearly Ford is critical of Donovan's machinations to hide the truth from Amelia, a director more fully accepting of miscegenation would not have dragged them out for so long. Ford's ostentatious display of tolerance sometimes seems forced, as if he doth protest too much, and his fantasy of a harmonious multicultural society is flawed by racist mockery of the Chinese characters who make up the island's serving class. But the interactions of Amelia with her island family are genuinely moving, particularly her tentative relationship with Lelani, the young Polynesian princess (Jacqueline Malouf). As Wollen notes, *Donovan's Reef* is "part of a general movement which can be detected in Ford's work to equate the Irish, Indians, and Polynesians as traditional communities, set in the past, counterposed to the march forward to the American future, as it has turned out in reality, but assimilating the values of the American future as it was once dreamed."

The romantic relationship between Donovan and Amelia is problematical for modern viewers, since Ford revels defiantly in unregenerate sexism. "When I direct a scene I always want to make the leading lady fall down on her derrière," Ford said in 1964. Donovan literally manhandles Amelia and at the end makes the arrogant (and incorrect) boast, "I made a human being out of you." Amelia gives back as good as she gets, but the scene in which Donovan spanks her, accompanied by some traditionally Neanderthal John Wayne dialogue—"Amelia, you have a mean Irish temper, but I love it. From now on, I wear the pants in this family"—comes off as coarse and mean-spirited. Unlike the humorous scene of Sean's dragging Mary Kate through the fields in *The Quiet Man*—a charade she engineers herself—Amelia's humiliation is private, lacks a redeeming ironic social context, and becomes simply a celebration of male domination to which the female acquiesces.

Elizabeth Allen had a splendid working relationship with Ford: she called him "Sean" and he called her "Liz" or "Stinky." Given the evidence on-screen, it's hardly surprising to learn that Ford became infatuated with the lively young actress. When Allen visited Ford near the end of his life, they reminisced fondly about the night he came to her hotel room on Kauai and fell asleep listening to opera before she pointed him back to his own room. Wistfully regretting that he had never managed to seduce her, Ford joked that she was more interested in Cesar Romero, who was playing the island's rakish governor. Allen's gentle deflection of Ford's clumsy moves did not prevent him from casting her again in *Cheyenne Autumn,* as saloon girl Guinevere Plantagenet in the Dodge City sequence. Her undying affection and loyalty were demonstrated when she was one of the two Ford leading ladies who attended his burial service (the other was Anna Lee).

Westerns are understood and appreciated the world over, as much or more in other countries as here," Ford observed after directing his last Western, *Cheyenne Autumn* (1964). "When I go to Japan, I am more readily recognized and treated more as a celebrity than I am in my own country. When I go to England, I am often paid the respect of being asked to lecture, as I have at Oxford and Cambridge, and am often asked to discuss in particular a film such as *Wagon Master,* which is totally forgotten here. This is all to the good. As a moviemaker, my audience is the world, not just the U.S."

Ford's consciousness of his marginalized status within his native country during the final years of his career intensified his already strong emotional identification with members of minority groups opposed to the dominant culture. *Cheyenne Autumn,* an ambitious but problematic attempt to tell "how the West was won" from the Indian side of the story, was the logical outgrowth of this process of radical alienation. Ford was able to finance his revisionist epic only when he and producing partner Bernard Smith caught Jack Warner "in a weak moment." The most expensive film of Ford's career, *Cheyenne Autumn* was originally budgeted at $4,166,167 but grew in scale before filming began and was completed at a negative cost of $6,587,122, including Ford's own salary of $200,000. Ford-Smith Productions helped finance the Warner Bros. picture, which originally was to have been fully funded by the studio; Ford and Smith were to receive 40 percent of the net profits, but the film proved a box-office as well as critical disappointment.

Cheyenne Autumn is based on "what to most people must seem to be only a footnote in history," the heroic, 1,500-mile flight of 286 dispossessed Cheyenne Indians from their reservation in Oklahoma back to their Yellowstone homeland in 1878–79. Announcing the film to the *New York Times* in July 1963, when it had the working title of *The Long Flight,* Ford said, "I've killed more Indians than anyone since Custer. This is their side." He embellished on that remark to Bogdanovich three years later: "I've killed more Indians than Custer, Beecher, and Chivington put together, and people in Europe always want to know about the Indians. There are two sides to every story, but I wanted to show their point of view for a change. Let's face it, we've treated them very badly—it's a blot on our shield; we've cheated and robbed, killed, murdered, massacred and everything else, but they kill one white man and God, out come the troops."

Andrew Sarris called attention to "two striking incongruities in Ford's statement: first, his assumption of more genocidal guilt than his own films have actually earned in the way of a hard and fast body count, and, second, his disconcertingly sophisticated awareness that his reputation was more secure abroad than at home, and that, indeed, towards the end of his career he remained commercially and critically viable only because of the European market." Sarris felt that Ford may also have made the film as a last gesture toward the New York critical establishment, which had been largely dismissive of his work in the Western genre since *Stagecoach* twenty-five years earlier.

Such specific concerns probably did factor into Ford's thinking, but *Cheyenne Autumn* is a mournful, meditative, and poetic work of art, made from the vantage point of an artist's old age, taking a long view of both national and cinematic history. Ford's ambitious attempt to rectify what he perceived as an imbalance in his own work is a testimony to his concern with his artistic legacy and his deep-seated sense of justice. Made at the close of John F. Kennedy's "New Frontier," that brief period of guarded (and somewhat illusory) optimism for America's potential as a forward-looking, multicultural society, *Cheyenne Autumn* offers a somber lesson about a tragic period of American history along with a vision of racial reconciliation and healing. "Possibly you can only think of the past," the film's Quaker schoolteacher, Deborah Wright (Carroll Baker), tells the cavalry officer pursuing the Cheyenne, Captain Thomas Archer (Richard Widmark). "But I'm here to think about the future."

Unfortunately, the scope of Ford's ambition was circumscribed by commercial realities and compromises, even as the physical scale of the project inflated into gargantuan proportions. Ford had been considering making a film on the Cheyenne migration from at least the early 1950s, but the political climate of the blacklist era was not congenial to such a project. The final screenplay by James R. Webb, the writer of *How the West Was Won,* is an unwieldy amalgamation of material from two historical novels on the same subject, *The Last Frontier* (1941) by Howard Fast (uncredited) and Mari Sandoz's *Cheyenne Autumn* (1953).

Howard Fast openly proclaimed his Communist Party membership until breaking with the party in 1956 as a result of Nikita S. Khrushchev's denunciation of Joseph Stalin's crimes. Fast served three months in prison in 1950 for contempt of the House Committee on Un-American Activities and was attacked by the FBI as an author whose "main aim in writing is to use American history to denounce America." In fact, Fast's work defends civil liberties, self-determination, and minority rights over a wide historical canvas ranging from the ancient world (*Spartacus; Moses, Prince of Egypt*) through the American Revolutionary War (*Conceived in Liberty, Citizen Tom Paine, April Morning*), the Reconstruction era (*Freedom Road*), and modern America (*The Passion of Sacco and Vanzetti, Silas Timberman,* the *Immigrants* cycle).

Katherine Cliffton, who served as Ford's principal researcher on *Cheyenne Autumn,* recalled that the director "liked Howard Fast's *The Last Frontier,* but for some reason or another they didn't buy Fast's book." The film rights had been purchased by Columbia Pictures for producer-writer Sidney Buchman. A 1949 screenplay adaptation for Columbia by Ted Sherdeman, titled *The Cheyenne Massacre,* is among Ford's papers. Buchman himself, who was named to the security board by Frank Capra and Ford in 1951, was blacklisted after admitting his former Communist Party membership to HUAC in 1951 but refusing to name others; his defiance of a second HUAC subpoena in 1952 resulted in a suspended one-year jail sentence for contempt of Congress, and he did not work again in films under his own name until the 1960s.

In *Being Red: A Memoir* (1990), Fast gives his version of what happened to Columbia's plans to make the film: "The project had been shelved. Forever, as it turned out. You see, John Ford, the great director of that time, had been pleading with me to talk Buchman into allowing him, Ford, to direct *The Last Frontier.* He said, to quote him, 'I'll direct it right out of your book, your dialogue and nothing else. No fuckin' screenwriter—no, sir. Right from the book.' And he would have too, and it would have been a splendid film.

"But then Columbia Pictures . . . was told by [FBI director] J. Edgar Hoover that no film was to made from my book, whereupon Columbia shelved it. John Ford, furious, frustrated by a blacklist he had only contempt for, went to Warner Bros. [in the early 1960s], told them that the story was in the public domain, and then slipped my book to a screenwriter and told him to go ahead and do the screenplay. Neither honest nor decent, but Ford was not strong on those virtues, and the project went ahead. Meanwhile, Columbia Pictures obtained a copy of the screenplay, gave it to their lawyers with my book, and then slapped a hold on the completed film, with the prospect of a large and disgraceful plagiarism suit against Warner Bros. Warner settled out of court, paying Columbia a huge sum of money and giving them a large piece of the completed film, which was released under the title *Cheyenne Autumn*. As far as I was concerned, my share of the booty amounted to nothing. After all, Columbia owned the book."

A story outline Ford commissioned in 1957 from his son, Pat, and Dudley Nichols for a film about the Cheyenne migration has been lost. Richard Widmark has said that he commissioned his own research on the subject long before Ford cast him: "I brought the material to Ford, but he didn't want to make it. Some years went by; Old Jack still had all my research, and then he offered me *Cheyenne Autumn*." Webb's screenplay drew in part on memoranda and a ninety-page treatment written by Pat Ford after extensive story conferences with his father in late 1962 and early 1963.

Summarizing the director's conception of the film at that stage of preproduction before Warner Bros. began interfering, Pat wrote Bernard Smith, "The Cheyennes are not to be heavies, nor are they to be ignorant, misguided savages without plan or purpose to their war-making. Their motives must be clearly expressed in the beginning of the picture. If there is to be a heavy, it must be the distant United States government, a government blind to the plight of the Indians. The Army is to be portrayed as an underpaid, undermanned force, all but forgotten on a distant frontier, a group of dedicated men trying to maintain a virtually impossible peace despite Washington's mismanagement. The 'Penny Dreadful' press of the period is no help with its stories of 'savage red men' and of buckskin knights-errant to inflame the imaginations of a semi-literate public."

What John Ford originally had in mind was an unadorned, black-and-white film with the bleak look of *The Grapes of Wrath*. Pat Ford noted that the characters of both stories start out on their journeys from miserable surroundings in the Oklahoma dust bowl. His father, Pat specified, wanted the Indians not to speak English but to "serve, in his words, as a 'Greek Chorus.' Since lack of communication was one of their chief causes of trouble, it would be ridiculous to show them speaking the national language."

Of course, a sympathetic view of Indians was not unprecedented in John Ford's work, as demonstrated by such films as *Fort Apache* and *Wagon Master* and the Washita River massacre sequence in *The Searchers*. Nevertheless, *Cheyenne Autumn* dramatically reverses the terms of much of Ford's work in the Western genre. It is a far cry from his treatment of Indians in *The Iron Horse* and *Stagecoach* and even in such late works as *Sergeant Rutledge* and *Two Rode Together.* As Wollen points out in his 1969 book *Signs and Meaning in the Cinema,* "[P]art of the development of Ford's career has been the shift from an identity between civilized versus savage and European versus Indian to their separation and final reversal, so that in *Cheyenne Autumn* it is the Europeans who are savage, the natives who are heroes." The Cheyenne are seen in typically Fordian terms, as a civilized community striving for survival but threatened by crises from within, even as they fend off the external source of chaos and destruction, the U.S. Cavalry.

For a time Ford vacillated between *The Last Frontier* and *Cheyenne Autumn* as source material for his film. He asked Woody Strode his opinion of the two books, "because he knew I wouldn't look at the story like an intellectual," recalled Strode, who told Ford, "Papa, you'll have to use both books to tell the whole story." Fast's novel, while highly sympathetic to the Indians and scathingly critical of U.S. government policies, tells the story from the viewpoint of the white pursuers, principally Captain Murray, a hard-nosed cavalryman trying to do what he considers his duty but troubled by the irrationality of official policy. Sandoz, on the other hand, closely follows the Indian characters in her romantically idealized treatment of the subject.

Even though Fast does not receive screen credit on *Cheyenne Autumn,* the film's basic structure, the character of Captain Archer, and many of its important incidents (including the Dodge City sequence) bear strong similarities to *The Last Frontier.* In a September 1963 letter to an attorney vetting the research conducted for Ford's film, Bernard Smith claimed that Captain Archer is a composite of several historical figures, particularly Lieutenant William Philo "White Hat" Clark, who was renowned for his sympathy toward Indians; that the Dodge City sequence, although farcical, is largely based on fact; and that the film's somewhat fictionalized treatment of Secretary of the Interior Carl Schurz (Edward G. Robinson) also has a factual basis. Smith added that some changes were being made in the script to eliminate material for which historical sources could not be found.

Katherine Cliffton was assigned to verify the historical data from *The Last Frontier* in original sources, such as Dodge City and New York newspapers. She said that Ford bought the rights to the Sandoz book (for $10,000) as another way of "trying to protect himself. They paid something to Columbia anyway." According to legal correspondence in Ford's files, Ford-Smith Productions made the settlement in exchange for Columbia's agreement not to sue. After the film was released, Fast pursued a claim for credit, but the screen credits remained unchanged, stating only that the film was "suggested by" Sandoz's book. "Where *Cheyenne Autumn* went wrong," Cliffton felt, "was in trying to put into it what [Ford] admired in Fast's book. That film was a terrible disappointment. It was meant to be his grandest. To me it didn't come off; it was a poor imitation of his better films."

However, it could be argued that Ford should have used more, rather than less, of Fast's book, a far sharper piece of writing than Sandoz's novel. Unwilling or unable to adapt *The Last Frontier* openly despite the more liberal climate that had allowed Fast's *Spartacus* to be filmed successfully in 1960, Ford may have had residual concerns about possible political reaction to *The Last Frontier* and its author. But Ford's desire to incorporate two differing dramatic approaches to the story reflected an even deeper ambivalence. He would have been better advised to worry less about narrative evenhandedness and take a more unified point of view.

While marshalling his gifts of visual composition to eulogize the Cheyenne at every turn, Ford still tends to tell the story less from the Indians' point of view than from that of Captain Archer, who is dispatched to bring them back to the reservation. Like Captain York in *Fort Apache,* Archer, who also serves as the film's narrator, is the obedient rebel. Sympathetic to the Indians but conflicted by his need to follow unjust orders, however halfheartedly, Archer acquires stature from his principled opposition to the tragically inflexible attitude represented by the grossly caricatured Captain Oscar Wessels (Karl Malden). Like Ford, Wessels regards himself as an expert on Indians. But he follows a Prussian code of military discipline ("Orders are orders") whose (over)emphasis in the film is clearly meant to recall the argument used by the Nazi defendants at the Nuremberg Trials filmed by Ford's Field Photo unit. The only way *Cheyenne Autumn* can resolve this impasse and achieve a semblance of a happy ending is to drag in a Great White Father, Carl Schurz, as a deus ex machina. The transparency of this consolatory device, made even more dubious by poor process photography of Schurz's peace parley with the Cheyenne,[4] only serves to underscore the essential tragedy of American Indian history. Nevertheless, Ford movingly evokes his personal icon of healing when Schurz addresses a photograph of Abraham Lincoln borrowed from its place of honor in Ford's home, saying, "Old friend—old friend, what would *you* do?"

By cutting back and forth between cavalry and Indian perspectives on these events, Ford mostly succeeds in muddying the issues and reducing narrative

---

4. Spencer Tracy was originally cast as Schurz but was unable to travel to location because of illness. When he finally had to drop out of the film, process plates shot on location for the backdrop of the peace parley were awkwardly combined with studio shots of Robinson.

identification with *both* the white and the Indian characters. The root of this fatal conceptual flaw is Ford's inability to resolve the contradictions of his own dual allegiances, which he summarized with his comment, "Who better than an Irishman could understand the Indians, while still being stirred by the tales of the U.S. Cavalry? We were on both sides of the epic."

Besides Howard Fast's name, another conspicuous omission from the writing credits of *Cheyenne Autumn* is the name of Patrick Ford. The director's son was bitterly unhappy when he was passed over as screenwriter in favor of Webb after doing all his crucial preliminary work, which went unacknowledged on-screen. Relegated to the job of supervising the cavalry on the Monument Valley location, Pat was paid only $10,000 for his services, compared with the $100,000 Webb received for the screenplay (along with 10 percent of the net profits). This painful drama of filial humiliation was played out against the backdrop of recent conflicts between Pat and his father that strained their already tenuous relationship to the breaking point.

By 1963, Pat had left the movie business in disgust and was living in Hawaii with his second wife, the former Carroll Anderson, with whom he had a daughter, Mary Blue, in 1961. Discouraged over his prospects in the island economy, Pat wrote an eight-page letter on April 24, 1963, to his father's business manager, Bea Benjamin, asking for a loan of $20,000 to use as down payment on a ranch in California. Pat could hardly have made the request at a worse time. As Ford explained in a seven-page handwritten response to his son, that very day Barbara had moved back home after breaking up with Ken Curtis (they would be divorced in 1964), and Warner Bros. had backed out of its agreement to make *Cheyenne Autumn* (temporarily, as it turned out). The studio's view of the project, wrote Ford, was "Too much money—not enough 'stars.' We have no other offers or interest in the property. . . . so I'm not working, and no prospects in sight."

Ford spilled out his own money anxieties to Pat, laying most of the blame on Mary, whom he characterized as a hopeless spendthrift. When challenged about her spending, Mary accused him of hiding his assets and using his money to keep another woman. Although Ford's yearly income was still substantial, it had begun to decline, from $267,505 in 1961 to $189,988 in 1962 and $184,873 in 1963; his 1964 earnings would plunge to $136,915. Ford admitted to his son that he had thought of divorcing Mary but rejected the idea because he was "a strong believer in the marriage vow. . . . [But] perhaps I should turn everything over to her and go to Europe on a tax dodge stint—maybe I could leave a comfortable estate that way. (No! I'm not pessimistic—just Irish.) Of course, she'd piss everything away in a year." Lapsing into self-pity, Ford returned to the subject of Pat's loan request: "Ten years ago it would have been so simple! Now—take heart. After all, I've not much time left." But he added that he was grateful for being Irish, since "I always feel better and fight harder" when facing negative odds.

Pat's discontent boiled over into a serious confrontation on the *Cheyenne Autumn* location with producer Bernard Smith. John Ford sided with Smith and cut his remaining ties with his son. By the summer of 1964, Pat was working as a garage mechanic and his wife as a policewoman. That July, Pat made one last, futile gesture toward his father, offering him an old script he had written about Irish jumping horses. In a self-pitying cover letter, Pat took some of the blame for his failure in the movie business, but he could not resist some scapegoating of Jewish studio executives.

John Ford's relationship with his son never recovered from the *Cheyenne Autumn* incident. They saw each other occasionally over the years, but when Ford signed his last will and testament shortly before his death in 1973—superseding a 1970 will providing for his children to split what remained of the estate following Mary's death—he included the following provision: "I specifically request that no share of my estate be distributed to my son, PATRICK MICHAEL FORD." Pat never returned to the film business after 1964, making his living as a rancher, teacher, and parole officer for the county of Los Angeles. "Pat wanted to go his own way," Waverly Ramsey, the family cook, observed. "He just wanted to be Pat Ford. He didn't want to be 'John Ford's son.' He wanted to do it on his own."

"Pat and I were always good friends," said Dobe Carey. "We were the same age—Pat was born in April of 1921 and I was born in May. Pat didn't get along with a lot of people. He didn't even get along well with his Dad, and yet he always bragged about his father. But that was the saddest thing I've ever seen—Ford's relationship with his son. He didn't know how to have a relationship with his son. He didn't know how to communicate. He had a better relationship with me than he had with his own son."

But Dobe had his own experience of Ford's inability to cope with fatherly feelings: "He punched me once. He didn't hit very hard. He punched me because I got the giggles at something—he kissed me. He was *real* drunk this time. It was when Ken Curtis was married to Barbara; I was over visiting Kenny. Kenny said, 'Oh, Christ, you picked a bad time to come over, Dobe, because here comes the Old Man.' And here comes the chauffeur, Bill Ramsey, and he's got the Old Man with him. I see from the way that he's helping him out of the station wagon that Ford is drunk. Kenny had this beautiful singing voice, and I guess Ford wanted Kenny to sing or something, so he came over to see him and Barbara.

"Ford came in and said, 'Hello, Old Dobe.' We were sitting in an alcove, because that's where the record player was. He's got this Irish music playing and he's sitting on a little bench, getting very sentimental. He had a very wet mouth when he was drunk, and I was very clean-shaven in those days and very young, in my thirties. He leaned over and he kissed me on the cheek. He said, 'My son, my son'—very drunk. And he drooled on me. Well, Kenny runs into the bathroom and flushes the toilet. Then I know he's in there rolling around on the floor. So I'm smiling, and boom! Ford hits me right here [in the jaw]. He thought I was laughing at him, but I was laughing because Kenny was laughing. And then he started to cry, he started sobbing. He gave me a pretty good crack. But he was something else—a very complex man."

Like her parents and brother, Barbara Ford battled her own problem with alcoholism. She worked as an editor on the *Ben Casey* television series and for the TV production company MTM before leaving the business to remain with her mother until Mary died at age eighty-six in 1979. In her final years, Barbara went on "a big bender," Dobe said. "They put her in a sanitarium in Santa Barbara." When she came out, she lived with Dobe and his wife, Marilyn, for two months. "We were her family, see." Barbara rented an apartment and found a job through the CETA program, teaching minority children how to type. The job paid four dollars an hour "and she *loved* it," Dobe said. Then she was hired by Peter Bogdanovich to help edit his 1985 film *Mask,* her last job in the film industry. Although Barbara's relationship with her father was more loving than combative, she, like Pat, never seemed to be able to emerge fully from the shadow of John Ford's domineering but neglectful fatherhood. A heavy smoker, Barbara died of lung cancer at the age of sixty-two in 1985; according to Dan Ford, she "died sober." Pat died the following year of a heart attack at the age of sixty-five.

Commenting on John Ford's personal inability to achieve the kind of family life he idealized in his movies, and on the problems that helped cause the premature deaths of Ford's two children, Admiral John D. Bulkeley reflected in 1987, "Pat was a young man—he was far younger than I am. They're all dead now. There's no family left. Isn't that a terrible tragedy of a great man?"

Around the same time Ford's relationship with his son was worsening, the director's friendship with Woody Strode was becoming closer. Strode wrote in his memoir that they had a "father-son relationship." In 1963, the actor moved into Ford's house to take care of him, much as Pompey did for Tom Doniphon in *The Man Who Shot Liberty Valance.* The director had suffered a back injury and asked Strode if he "could stay here a few days and help massage this stuff out of my back."

"I sat up in a big armchair all night," Strode recalled, "and when the pain woke him up, I went to work.

"Finally he said, 'Woody, why don't you get comfortable and go lie down in my green room [the room adjacent to his bedroom].'"

Strode instead arranged a pillow and quilt and slept at the foot of Ford's bed. "Sometimes I'd get up at four in the morning and massage his back until he could go back to sleep," the actor recalled. "I had no idea a few days would turn into four months. . . . As the weeks turned into months, he got to feeling better. We'd sit together in his green room, read books and talk all day."

Ford was "lonely," Strode realized. The actor's hero worship bolstered Ford's ego at a time when Hollywood was starting to shut him out, his virility was waning, his old friends were rapidly dying off, and John Wayne, who had long served as his surrogate son, had grown too important and distant to fill that role any longer. Strode found that he had "replaced all those friends. Pat Ford told me, 'Woody, you know my father and I don't get along too well. What you're doing for him, I can't provide.'"

So Ford and Woody Strode talked about the director's favorite subject, American history, and Strode told Ford all his football and wrestling stories. They never talked about movies. Strode's wife, Luana, and their children visited almost daily to swim in the pool. Strode tried to help Ford cut back on his drinking, which sometimes led to acrimonious exchanges reminiscent of Pompey's stern but loving care of the despondent Doniphon after the gunfight in *Liberty Valance*. Once when Ford asked Strode to go downstairs and get him a glass of gin, Strode refused. Raising his eye patch for emphasis, Ford threatened never to cast the actor in another one of his movies. Strode simply dared the old man to fight if he wanted the glass of gin.

Strode's caretaking and tough love served as a tonic for Ford, but Pat seemed jealous and resentful of Strode's closeness to his father. He also seemed concerned that people might think that there was something sexual going on between his father and the statuesque former athlete. "Pat Ford had heard all the gossip that was floating around Hollywood about me living with his father," wrote Strode. "I guess people figured I was trying to take advantage of John Ford in his old age."

The matter came to a head when Jack and Mary took Strode to a funeral. Worried about what people would think, Pat asked his father to let Strode sit with him and his two sons, but Ford insisted on having the actor at his side. The stares they drew together made Strode understand the "awkward situation" his presence in Ford's house had caused. Pat said after the service, "Woody, all these people are worrying about what the old man is doing with you. Everyone's asking."

Feeling uncomfortable, Strode told Ford it was time for him to leave, since he had been staying at the house for four months. "Oh, my God, go home!" said Ford. Strode later admitted feeling "very emotional" about their leavetaking.

They remained good friends but saw each other only intermittently in the years that followed. There clearly was a homoerotic element in their relation-ship, at least on Ford's part. The soothing massages he received from the pow-erfully built former athletic hero gave Ford probably the only sustained and satisfying physical contact he had with another person in his old age.

It's no exaggeration to say that Woody Strode was the last great love of John Ford's life. The loss of that intimate relationship served to deepen Ford's sense of isolation.

The artistic compromises Warner Bros. forced on Ford in *Cheyenne Autumn* are most evident in the casting of the principal Indian roles. Pat Ford told Bernard Smith in January 1963 that the director wanted "honest to God Indi-ans—Navajos probably" to play Little Wolf and Dull Knife. Those are the two chiefs whose power struggle divides the tribe during its long march. Realizing that his father's notion of casting nonprofessional Indian actors would seem impractical to financiers, Pat suggested that the roles be played by two popu-lar actors with Indian blood, Richard Boone and Anthony Quinn. John Ford came around to the idea of casting Quinn as Dull Knife, but proposed to Warners that the part-Indian Strode be cast as Little Wolf.

After the studio exercised its leverage, however, Ford wound up with non-Indians in all the principal Indian roles, including the veteran Mexican-born actors Ricardo Montalban as Little Wolf and Gilbert Roland as Dull Knife. Sal Mineo, the Italian actor from the Bronx best known as Plato in *Rebel Without a Cause*, was cast as Little Wolf's troublemaking son, Red Shirt, and Mexican actress Dolores Del Rio, who previously had appeared in Ford's film *The Fugi-tive*, was given the part of the young brave's mother, Spanish Woman. The el-derly chief Tall Tree is played by an Anglo actor, Victor Jory. With his gaunt, leathery appearance, the Alaska native is the most convincing of these actors playing Indians in *Cheyenne Autumn*. But given its ostensible project of coun-teracting Hollywood clichés about Indian life, the film is seriously damaged by its lack of ethnic verisimilitude. Most of the Indians' scenes are played in En-glish. While Ford does manage to include a fair amount of untranslated Indian dialogue, it is in Navajo, not Cheyenne, because most of the extras were re-cruited from Monument Valley.

For the lead female role of the white Quaker missionary who willingly ac-companies the Cheyenne, Ford wanted a middle-aged actress who could con-vincingly play a spinster. Instead he was assigned the young and glamorous Carroll Baker. Although Baker was affecting as the Kentucky farm woman in Ford's episode of *How the West Was Won*, she brought to *Cheyenne Autumn* the distracting cinematic baggage of her sultry roles in such films as *Baby Doll* and *The Carpetbaggers*. She approached the challenge with a seriousness belying her image, acquitting herself honorably. But the recurrent emphasis on Deborah

Wright's romantic involvement with Captain Archer seems intrusive and distasteful in such a tragic context, even if the script makes Archer's adherence to military discipline the major obstacle between them.

Somewhat surprisingly, given Ford's habit in his old age of inveighing against the new climate of sexual permissiveness in Hollywood filmmaking—he said in 1969 that he would consider it a "mortal sin to direct the dirty pictures of today"—the director contemplated filming a scene for *Cheyenne Autumn* of Carroll Baker bathing nude in a river. Perhaps Ford had this titillating diversion inserted in the script merely as a ploy to help arouse interest from Warners, although he rationalized it as nonsexual. In any case, he wisely had second thoughts, much to the actress's disappointment. "I enjoy posing in the nude," Baker said at the time. "I even say, 'Let's take some more'—if the pictures are beautiful and not vulgar. You can't win them all. And I'm not about to argue with Mr. John Ford!"

Cheyenne Autumn began shooting on September 23, 1963. Several weeks of location work were scheduled for Monument Valley; Moab, Utah, the site of Arches National Monument; and Gunnison, Colorado. "For a guy pushing seventy it sounds like a tough physical task," Ford wrote Michael Killanin. "But Thank God I am THE Irish peasant of the peasants . . . and they never stop working until past ninety." Ford commanded a huge company totaling 865 people at its full complement. At times he seemed to relish what he knew could be his last opportunity to play the role of "Natani Nez." He had his repertoire of pet expressions, such as "I guess I'll have to pull a rabbit out of my hat." Once, when he was trying to stage a complicated scene involving Baker, Widmark, and Malden, he turned to cinematographer William Clothier and muttered how he would have to pull a rabbit out of his hat. Then he proceeded to do just that. The practical joke had literally been on his mind all morning as he waited for the perfect dramatic moment.

But Ford could work no miracles with his own physical health. He was seriously showing his age during the making of *Cheyenne Autumn*. Harry Carey Jr., who acted in the film, recalled, "What he used to do was he kept everything in his head and he didn't take notes. Barbara, his daughter, said he did his homework at night. Now, the script girl [Meta Sterne] would take all this down [during shooting], but she would never go up and say, 'Don't forget, you didn't get the shot of here and didn't get the reverse of that.' If she did, he would get mad. So he never had any place to look for help when he got old and needed reminding of things. He didn't ever ask anybody to help him out. And I think sometimes when he got older he'd lose some of the continuity. But his brain was still sharp. God, he was always sharp. He was sharp up until he went into a coma!"

For a man of Ford's advancing age and frail condition, worn down by too many years of heavy drinking and smoking, the production of *Cheyenne Autumn* proved too demanding both physically and creatively. He experienced circulation problems in his legs from hardening of the arteries, and he suffered from fatigue and depression that led him to delegate some of his directing duties.

According to Pat Ford, his father began taking steroids in the later part of his career as a way of artificially boosting his waning energy. Ford also developed an overreliance on sleeping pills and uppers that interfered with his productivity on *Cheyenne Autumn*. Clothier had the increasingly difficult task of waking Ford each morning at Goulding's. One time, Clothier continued into Ford's bathroom and threw all his pills in the toilet. Then the cameraman went outside to wait for Ford to get dressed. Fifteen minutes later, Ford came charging out of his room, complaining, "Some sonofabitch flushed my pills down the toilet."

"I did," admitted Clothier.

Ford shot back, "What would you do if I flushed all your *lenses* down the toilet?"

Wingate Smith eventually had to call in a doctor to take care of Ford when he became incapacitated; Smith found that Ford had been hiding part of his stash of pills inside hollowed-out books. George O'Brien, who was acting in another Ford Western forty years after *The Iron Horse,* tried to help his old friend out of his funk. O'Brien sat at Ford's bedside reminiscing about happier times, but Ford kept repeating, "It's just no fun anymore."

Second-unit director Ray Kellogg, a loyal veteran of Ford's Field Photo unit, picked up the slack during Ford's down periods on *Cheyenne Autumn*. When Ford was busy shooting, Kellogg often worked simultaneously in an effort to speed up the production. Progress was complicated further by inclement weather, and when the company left Utah, the film was five days behind its shooting schedule. Kellogg was a competent but undistinguished craftsman, and the inclusion of his footage helps account for the uneven quality of *Cheyenne Autumn*. But his work paid off in practical terms: when the film finished shooting on January 6, it was four days *ahead* of its seventy-five-day schedule.

Clothier's majestic Technicolor photography brought *Cheyenne Autumn* its only Academy Award nomination. Many of the Super Panavision 70 images have an almost three-dimensional depth, exquisitely molded with slanting light and shadow. Ford arrays his Indians with effortless mastery throughout the rock formations of Monument Valley in elegiac compositions stressing their natural relationship with the land in contrast to the violent and awkward eruptions of action emanating from the cavalry intruders. But unlike *The Searchers,* in which Ford's unrealistic use of Monument Valley geography helps emphasize the story's dreamlike quality as a "psychological epic," *Cheyenne Autumn* is hampered by the seeming circularity of the Indians' journey. Their trek through the valley's relatively small area, interrupted only occasionally by other kinds of terrain, works against the film's epic quality, highlighting the static feeling of the compositions and making Ford's deliberate, repetitive rhythm seem ponderous.

Nor does Ford entirely succeed in making the cavalry's halfhearted pursuit seem dramatically credible. Wingate Smith recalled that as a result of Fred Kennedy's death on *The Horse Soldiers,* Ford seemed skittish about stunts on his later pictures, worrying so much about safety that he seldom asked stuntmen to perform the spectacular horse falls and other feats of derring-do that contributed to the excitement of his earlier Westerns. Ford appeared unusually nervous and indecisive while preparing to film the scene of a prairie fire set by the Cheyenne to confuse their pursuers. When the scene was shot, however, Ford characteristically remained seated close to the action and, unlike the rest of the crew, did not move back from the flames until he ordered the cameraman to cut. "Well," Smith commented with an admiring smile, "he always likes to be the last."

The young journalist and aspiring filmmaker whose work did more than anyone else's to keep Ford's reputation alive in his final years spent three weeks in Monument Valley watching the filming. Peter Bogdanovich was then in the process of writing a series of articles on Hollywood filmmakers as a way of gaining entrée to the business and cultivating influential mentors such as Ford, Howard Hawks, and Orson Welles. With some difficulty, he managed to persuade the editor of *Esquire,* Harold Hayes, to let him write a Ford profile.

"Ford didn't like to talk about himself or about making movies," Dobe Carey noted. "The guy who was the most successful at getting him to talk was Peter Bogdanovich. But Peter was very lucky—he got off on the right foot. This couple came out across the desert—it was Peter and Polly [Platt, his first wife]. And this assistant started to run 'em off. He said, 'Go away, because Jack Ford doesn't like interviews.' And Ford saw it. He said, 'No, let 'em come in.' And he got 'em chairs, he sat 'em down, and he got 'em a room to stay. So Peter just lucked out. Then we were sitting up there around the table at Goulding's. He said, 'Mr. Ford, what's this and what's that?'—he started firing questions. I went, 'Oh, Jesus, he's gonna get eaten alive!' And he got away with it. A lot of times Ford would oversimplify things, but Peter did manage to score better than most people."

Bogdanovich was impressed that Ford, on their first meeting, pronounced his last name correctly and recognized it as Serbian, the first person he had ever known to do so. Ford's producing partner, Bernard Smith, interrupted the conversation with a comment on a business matter. Scowling, Ford turned back to Bogdanovich and pointed out:

"There's a word for what he just said."

"Yes?"

"*Govno,*" said Ford.

"I broke up," Bogdanovich recalled. "The word is the Serbian equivalent for 'shit.'"

Ford also charmed Polly, whom he dubbed "Teepee-That-Walks" after seeing her walking around the location wrapped in an Indian blanket. But Ford sometimes became exasperated at Bogdanovich's incessant questions and amused himself by pulling the leg of his earnest young admirer. One night when Bogdanovich asked Ford to name his favorite of all his films, the director solemnly replied, *"Arrowsmith."* On other occasions, Ford would say, "Jesus *Christ,* Bogdanovich! Can't you ever end a sentence with anything but a question mark? Haven't you *heard* of the declarative sentence?"

Producer Smith grew increasingly angry over the presence of Bogdanovich and Platt in Monument Valley. When Wingate Smith assigned them the small room used by the producer on his intermittent visits to the location, Bernard Smith became irate and threatened to fire Ford's brother-in-law if the couple was still there the next time he returned. "Listen, Bernie," said Ford, "you give Bogdanovich here my room and I'll double up with someone down below." The producer quickly backed down, and Ford told Bogdanovich, "Stay as long as you want."

Late in the morning of Friday, November 22, 1963, Ford was at White's Ranch in Moab, Utah, filming the violent climax of *Cheyenne Autumn,* the long shot of Little Wolf shooting Red Shirt. At that same moment in Dallas, Texas, "the New Frontier" of the 1960s was coming to an end with the assassination of President John F. Kennedy. The news reached Ford and company a short while later. Distraught, Ford called a wrap and spent the rest of the day in his motel room.

"I loved Kennedy," Ford reflected in 1966. "He was a fantastic man, humorous, intelligent, generous. His assassination was a terrible blow to America." Accepting the Warren Commission finding that Kennedy was killed by Lee Harvey Oswald, Ford commented, "Oswald was a wretched fool who caused the country immense harm, what with [Lyndon] Johnson being such a despicable man. He is a murderer."

Shortly after dawn on the morning after the assassination, Ford dressed in his World War II fatigue jacket, assembled the company, and held a brief memorial ceremony. Taps was sounded as the flag was lowered to half-staff.

Sounding drained and dispirited, Ford made a brief speech expressing faith in the continuity of the republic despite the loss of its young president. The company stood in silent prayer. Quickly finishing the Utah location work with four establishing shots, they prepared to return to Hollywood the following day.

Like most Americans, Ford was impressed with Jacqueline Kennedy's stoic grandeur in the aftermath of her husband's murder. Following the nationally televised funeral services in Washington on November 25, Ford made an emotional suggestion about Mrs. Kennedy's future to a Dallas acquaintance, Gordon McLendon. The producer of three low-budget pictures with Ford's son-in-law Ken Curtis in 1959–60, McLendon had broadcast a live radio report from the Dallas Trade Mart as the presidential limousine sped past en route to Parkland Hospital. Comparing Jacqueline to Joan of Arc, Ford asked McLendon to pass along to his friend, Lyndon Johnson, the notion that she should be appointed as United States ambassador to Italy to help perpetuate the mythic impact of her husband's death and funeral rites.

With his increasingly apocalyptic view of American history confirmed by real-life events, Ford resumed work on November 26, shooting interior scenes at the studio in Burbank. Not simply content with mocking the racist hysteria of the western frontier in the burlesque Dodge City sequence, Ford scathingly spoofs the terminal decadence of the Western genre.

James Stewart's cynical, "blind as a bat" Wyatt Earp, a semiretired fussbudget who can hardly be bothered to look up from his poker game to perform his functions as town marshal, is the reductio ad absurdum of Henry Fonda's calmly authoritative lawman in *My Darling Clementine*. After performing a comical operation on a rowdy cowboy he shoots in the saloon, Stewart's Earp confounds the townsfolk's lynch mob mentality by leading the local yokels in a circular chase during their farcical hunt for fugitive Indians in "the Battle of Dodge City." In the end, the rumored menace is revealed as one lone, forlorn Indian on the horizon.

Earp's contempt for the public's fickleness and gullibility is matched by that of the editor of the *New York Globe* (Charles Seel), who arbitrarily decides, upon hearing the news from Dodge City, "We're going to take a different tack. From now on we're going to grieve for the noble red man. We'll sell more papers that way." If much of *Cheyenne Autumn* suffers from Ford's reversion to the excessively rhetorical tradition of Dudley Nichols, the satirical Dodge City sequence stands as Ford's subversive autocritique.

On December 18, the company arrived in Colorado for three days of filming snow scenes in bone-chilling conditions. Ford found the location a trial. He sprained his ankle and gobbled down so many codeine tablets that he became badly incapacitated. Some of his directing duties had to be taken over by Richard Widmark. In a scene reminiscent of the lowest moments of the shooting of *Mister Roberts,* Dobe Carey described the sad spectacle of a disoriented Ford emerging from a station wagon, with his pants on backward, only to fall on his face in the snow.

So how is it possible to make a case for *Cheyenne Autumn*? Ford's last Western may be a failure, but it is an honorable failure. Although one can regret that commercial compromises and Ford's own artistic limitations prevented him from realizing his more rigorous original conception, it is important to look at *Cheyenne Autumn* not for what it might have been but for what it is. Although seriously flawed dramatically and diminished by its inability to make the Indians three-dimensional characters, the film is far more successful as a work of visual poetry, particularly when seen on the big screen as it was intended. The most genuinely moving scenes are almost entirely visual, such as the tribe's early-morning departure from the reservation, the old chief's funeral, the massacre at Fort Robinson, and the final transfer of the "sacred bundle" from Little Wolf to Dull Knife.

Given Ford's ethnocentric perspective, telling the story predominantly from the white officer's point of view may have been the most honest approach he could have taken toward the Indian community he is portraying, just as Jean Renoir made *The River* from the viewpoint of a British family living in India, realizing that as an outsider he could hardly pretend to speak for the native community. *Cheyenne Autumn* draws much of its fascination, and much of its confusion, from looking at American history from a point of view that is simultaneously traditional and subversive. The desire of the Cheyenne to reclaim their ancestral homeland is, like Sean Thornton's return to Ireland in *The Quiet Man,* a desperate flight from the reality of the present day. Their once-great nation has been reduced to a pitiful fragment; the most vital young man, Red Shirt, must be killed by the chief at the end because he threatens the truce that enables the tribe to live in peace. Ford ends with a nostalgic recapturing of primitive serenity, but the ending is bittersweet because we know that in Fordian terms any such return to the conditions of the past, however intensely desired, must prove a transitory illusion.

The American public in 1964 was not in the mood for the melancholy history lesson Ford offered them with *Cheyenne Autumn.*

After a lavish premiere for junketing members of the world press in Cheyenne, Wyoming, on October 3, 1964, and a foreign premiere in London on October 15 (neither of which the director attended), Ford's valedictory Western was given the kind of slow rollout that was standard for roadshows in that period but had the unfortunate side effect of allowing months for bad word of mouth to spread. Exclusive hard-ticket runs in five American cities began during the Christmas season; the national release took place the following spring. U.S. rentals amounted to a disappointing $3,135,989, but as Ford expected, *Cheyenne Autumn* was more popular overseas, bringing in $4,471,668. Including television revenues, the total rentals were $8,284,281, but because of the relatively high cost of making and distributing the picture, it failed to show a profit.

The critical reception in the United States was largely derisive, with few reviewers showing any sense of historical perspective about the film's significance in Ford's long and distinguished career. In a *Life* magazine review headlined "John Ford's Trojan Horse-Opry," Richard Oulahan called it a "turkey . . . just a great big, gorgeous kiddie show," claiming that "the poor Indian has been done in again." Stanley Kauffmann of the *New Republic* described the film as "a pallid and straitened version of the best Ford, with no new ideas and, what is perhaps worse, fumbling use of the old ones. . . . The cast is beyond disbelief." "Ford has apparently forgotten everything he ever knew, about actors, about cameras, about the Indians, and about the West," agreed *Newsweek* in a review entitled "End of the Trail?"

Newsweek's review prompted an eloquent defense from a young Ford admirer and future director, Mark Haggard. In a letter to the editor, he wrote that *Cheyenne Autumn* is "not one of John Ford's best films, but it is a good and competent one and shows that age has not hampered his abilities; rather, it reveals that at 70 he is still exploring and experimenting, moving in a new direction as an artist."

Another positive voice was that of Bosley Crowther of the *New York Times*. Crowther's favorite Ford film was *The Grapes of Wrath,* and he responded to the social significance of *Cheyenne Autumn,* a quality he had failed to discern in the more artistically successful film *The Man Who Shot Liberty Valance.* Crowther hailed *Cheyenne Autumn* as "a beautiful and powerful motion picture . . . a stark and eye-opening symbolization of a shameless tendency that has prevailed in our national life—the tendency to be unjust and heartless to weaker peoples who get in the way of manifest destiny. . . . [T]here is tragic and epic grandeur in the enactment of the whole exodus theme." Crowther subsequently proposed that the New York Film Critics Circle give Ford a special lifetime achievement award, but his motion was rejected.

The aspect of *Cheyenne Autumn* that most baffled reviewers was the Dodge City sequence, which, ironically enough, now seems the movie's finest sequence. *Daily Variety* reviewer Whitney Williams criticized the satirical interlude as "simply out of place" in offering "laughs [that] project no valid reason for their presence." Williams felt the whole film was "sorely in need of trimming; its good passages suffer from an over-leisurely style of narration." That advice from the trade paper was heeded by Warner Bros. In the opening road-show engagements, Warners broke the sequence into two parts to make room for an intermission. The second part, showing "the Battle of Dodge City," was cut before the wider American release. Ford and Smith were unhappy about this mutilation, as well as with prior cutting done by the studio in the Fort Robinson massacre sequence and other parts of the film, but they had no recourse, since their contract with Warners, like most of Ford's other contracts in the later years of his career, gave the studio final cut. Warners restored the missing Dodge City footage for the 1990 home-video release, although only in the pan-and-scan format. The entire sequence was finally seen in the letter-boxed format on the American Movie Classics cable television network, which aired the restoration without fanfare in its August 1999 Ford festival.

After Bogdanovich sent Ford a manuscript copy of his *Esquire* article on the making of *Cheyenne Autumn,* Ford angrily described it as "nauseating" and complained that it portrayed him as a foulmouthed, over-the-hill old drunk. "The Autumn of John Ford," as published in April 1964, was a highly sympathetic portrait of the artist as an old man, treating Ford with the seriousness and scholarship he so richly deserved. But Ford still took offense at the article's title, which implied that he was nearing the end of his career. If anything, Bogdanovich was being kind in his assessment of the director's continued viability in Hollywood. With the commercial failure of *Cheyenne Autumn,* and the growing perception that Ford's physical and creative powers were slipping, his remaining years in the industry would become decidedly wintry.

The former Bull Feeney felt a strong identification with the "worker playwright" Sean O'Casey, who emerged from lower-class Dublin and moved uneasily into the world of art. Relishing a second chance to do right by O'Casey after his botched filming of *The Plough and the Stars* almost thirty years earlier, which had left O'Casey reluctant to approve another film adaptation of his work, Ford showed immediate interest when approached by producers Robert D. Graff and Robert Emmett Ginna Jr. in 1963 to direct a movie about the writer's early life, *Young Cassidy.*

The screenplay by John Whiting is based on six autobiographical works by O'Casey collectively titled *Mirror in My House.* Although re-creating such events in O'Casey's life as the riotous 1926 stage premiere of *The Plough and the Stars, Young Cassidy* follows the source material in giving its protagonist one of the names the playwright (christened John Casey) adopted before settling on Sean O'Casey. The problems of this MGM film began with the overly episodic script, which lacks thematic focus, obfuscates the complex relationship between O'Casey's politics and his work, and spends far too much time on romantic entanglements that make Johnny Cassidy (Rod Taylor) seem like a Dublin version of Tom Jones.

Ford publicly praised the script in Bogdanovich's *Esquire* article but privately told Katharine Hepburn he doubted it would make a good film. Still, *Young Cassidy* offered the chance for one last working visit to Ireland. To accommodate the project's modest budget, he agreed to cut his usual salary to $50,000 and 5 percent of the producers' share of the profits. Owing to his touchy relationship with the relatively green producers, he brought Michael Killanin aboard as associate producer to serve as a buffer. Ford even had a clause inserted in his contract stating: "During the principal photography of the picture, Mr. Ford will not be interfered with in the pursuit of his directorial efforts."

However, he felt that Graff and Ginna usurped many of his prerogatives during preproduction. They disagreed with his desire to shoot in gritty black and white, they quarreled with him about casting and choice of locations (Ford preferred the more old-fashioned Limerick, the producers preferred to shoot around obstacles in Dublin), and they lectured the director about not indulging in stage-Irishness. Ford was convinced that they thought he was an alcoholic and an anti-Semite. These long-distance squabbles occurred while Ford was preoccupied with the difficult editing process on *Cheyenne Autumn*. Spreading himself far too thin after such a grueling shoot, Ford wore himself down by making two preproduction trips to Ireland in April and May 1964. But he seemed anxious to avoid another protracted period of unemployment, and *Young Cassidy* was set to begin shooting on July 14. Following location work in Ireland, studio scenes were to be filmed at MGM's Elstree Studios in London.

Sean Connery was originally cast in the title role, but the Scottish actor had to pull out before shooting started in order to fulfill a commitment for his third James Bond movie, *Goldfinger*. Connery's Australian replacement, Rod Taylor, also seemed too bluff and hearty for the role but managed an adequate Irish accent with the coaching of cast member Jack MacGowran. Oddly, Ford and his producers cast Irish actors mostly in minor roles, giving other important parts to British performers Maggie Smith, Flora Robson, Julie Christie, Michael Redgrave, and Edith Evans.

Graff and Ginna, who had visited with Ford the previous December in Los Angeles, were alarmed when he showed up for his May location scouting trip so intoxicated that he had to be helped off the Aer Lingus flight in a wheelchair. Ford's relationship with the producers never recovered from the shock. Drinking Black Velvet, Ford performed irascibly at a press conference with Graff, Ginna, Lord Killanin, and Taylor at Dublin's Shelbourne Hotel on the evening of July 9. When asked what the film would cost, he snapped, "It's none of your goddam business." Ford went off the record to tell a story about the reactions of some of his Spiddal relatives to *The Quiet Man,* but spied a young reporter taking notes anyway. "This is OFF the record," he barked. Lifting his black eye patch, he said, "This looks an *earnest* young man—maybe some day he's gonna write a *book.*"

Ford's mind often seemed elsewhere. "Tell me," he asked the assembly, "who was at Ernie O'Malley's funeral—did they do the right thing by him? Did he get military honors?" O'Malley, the IRA commandant general and memoirist, had been dead and buried since 1957, shortly after working with Ford on *The Rising of the Moon.*

Toward the end of the memorably raucous event, *Times* writer Seamus Kelly reported, "the great director was using an Americanised version of Connemara Gaelic with great freedom, fluency, and point. A woman journalist dared to address him as 'Mr. Ford,' and asked: 'Can you really speak Irish?' The maestro lifted the black eyeshade once again, looked out from under it like Balor, and said: 'Where d'ya get that Ford? O'Feeney to *you.*'"

Ford remained irascible throughout the first thirteen days of shooting. Killanin realized there would be serious trouble when he found two grocery bags full of Scotch bottles among Ford's personal effects. As he had done on *Mister Roberts,* Ford found illness a providential excuse to back out of a bad decision. The shooting was put on hold for four days so he could recover from a case of strep throat that had brought his weight down to only 139 pounds, 30 pounds below his normal figure. When his doctor, Maynard Brandsma, arrived from Los Angeles, Ford was found to be "badly debilitated," a production spokesman told the press. Resigning from the film on the doctor's advice, Ford rested at the Killanins' Dublin home before leaving for home via London on August 4. From there he went on to Hawaii for two months' recuperation. Graff and Ginna, who were just as relieved by Ford's departure as Ford was, quickly replaced him with Jack Cardiff, who had directed several films but was best known as the cinematogapher of such films as *Black Narcissus* and *The Red Shoes.* Cardiff directed most of *Young Cassidy,* although it is billed as "A John Ford Film."

Although somewhat redeemed by Smith's exquisite performance as Nora, Cassidy's lower-middle-class lover who lacks the courage to share his life as an artist, the film is generally a parade of clichés presented in an overly gaudy and modern color scheme. Some of Ford's work still shines through the overall mediocrity, including the love scene between Taylor and Christie, who plays the improbably gorgeous and tanned Dublin prostitute Daisy Battles. Again determined to show that he could direct an erotic scene as vividly as any young filmmaker, Ford directed Christie to act out Daisy's seduction of Cassidy with unashamed bluntness. As Cassidy kisses her against a wall, Daisy's chemise starts falling below her shoulders. Ford's original scene continued with Cassidy's head dropping beneath the frame line and one of Daisy's breasts slipping out of her clothing. Unfortunately, Cardiff partially reshot the sequence to eliminate the nudity, and in the release version Daisy's neckline does not match between shots.

When *Young Cassidy* opened in London in February 1965 and in the United States the following month, "many critics praised John Ford's direction for scenes I had done myself," Cardiff complained. "One critic commented, 'It is easy to see the difference between John Ford's direction and Cardiff's.' Another declared: 'The riot sequence is superb—obviously the work of the master, John Ford.' I suppose I should have been flattered that my work should be considered to be the work of the master, but in fact I was indignant."

I want to do a story about women," Ford announced one day to his producing partner Bernard Smith. Ford suggested filming "Chinese Finale," a 1935 short story by British author Norah Lofts about an atheistic doctor who sacrifices herself to save the lives of a group of missionary women and a newborn baby. The result was *7 Women* (1966), the last feature film in Ford's nearly fifty-year career as a director.[5] A true *film maudit*, it was reviled by most American reviewers but appreciated by overseas viewers better versed in Ford's body of work. Even some Ford scholars and biographers continue to treat *7 Women* as an embarrassing aberration, yet there also are those (such as myself) who regard this mordant drama of religious fanaticism, sexual repression, and social breakdown as one of Ford's masterpieces.

The most provocative of the late films in which Ford undertakes a searching reassessment of his own cinematic mythology, *7 Women* was made partly to confound the shortsighted critics who had failed to treat him with the understanding and deference he deserved. An unidentified friend of Ford's told the *New York Times,* "Jack resents the fact that some people think of him as a director of cowboy pictures. So he decided to remind them of his versatility." With typical perversity, however, Ford took pains to deny any such intentions when I asked him about *7 Women*. "No, it was just a job of work," he said. "I've directed women before." The truth, as always with Ford, lies somewhere in between.

---

5. In my earlier book on Ford, I gave the title as *Seven Women,* as have many other writers on Ford. But in examining Ford's correspondence, I realized that he preferred the title as it actually appears on the screen, *7 Women.* Using the numeral rather than the word—as he did with the titles of *3 Bad Men* and *3 Godfathers*— probably appealed to his pictorial sense, which manifests itself in his bold, graceful handwriting.

"Chinese Finale" probably put Ford in mind of the story that served as his unofficial model for the caustic attack on bourgeois hypocrisy in *Stagecoach,* Guy de Maupassant's "Boule de Suif." Anne Bancroft's whiskey-drinking, pants-wearing, humanistic, self-sacrificial Dr. D. R. Cartwright follows in the Fordian traditions exemplified by more than one character in *Stagecoach.* Not only does Dr. Cartwright share the traits of Claire Trevor's Dallas and Thomas Mitchell's Doc Boone but Bancroft recalled that during the filming of *7 Women,* Ford "used to call me 'Duke.' And I tried to be John Wayne too." With her earthy humor, sensuality, and poignant rootlessness, Dr. Cartwright also resembles Ava Gardner's Eloise Y. Kelly in *Mogambo.* Margaret Leighton's fanatical mission leader, Agatha Andrews, is a barely repressed lesbian who cannot admit her own desires and scorns Dr. Cartwright as a "scarlet woman." At first glance, Andrews may seem an anomaly in Ford's work, but she has clear precursors in Henrietta Crosman's rigid, vindictively puritanical mother in the first half of *Pilgrimage* and the members of the "Ladies' Law and Order League" in *Stagecoach,* who run Dallas and Doc out of town to the tune of "Shall We Gather at the River."

Yet among the most fascinating aspects of *7 Women* is the way it inverts and inflects patterns from the director's earlier films, revisiting familiar Fordian themes in a fresh and often startling manner. In her role as a deranged martinet who leads her isolated outpost into disaster at the hands of an alien people she views with racist contempt, Andrews is perhaps most similar to one of Ford's *male* characters, Henry Fonda's Colonel Thursday in *Fort Apache.* "Everyone who joined this mission enlisted in a war," she declares. "They are soldiers, Dr. Cartwright, soldiers in the Army of the Lord."

Set in what one character describes as "the last place on earth," the border of China and Mongolia, *7 Women* takes place in 1935, during what its prologue calls "a time of lawlessness and violence." This mission is not a British establishment, as in the original story, but is run by the "Unified Christian Missions Educational Society" of (where else?) Boston. It is a precarious outpost of American cultural imperialism at its most arrogantly pious and foolishly naive. Andrews proclaims, "This bandit, this . . . Tunga Khan as you call him, wouldn't dare to molest us. We are American citizens."

"I hate preaching . . . I hate sanctimoniousness," Ford said in 1966, and mockery is his choice of weapon. People who dislike *7 Women* usually think the story has *unintentional* comic overtones: they are oblivious to the dark strain of absurdist humor Ford brings to this story of innocents abroad, humor that offers counterpoint to the film's otherwise overwhelmingly grim vision of disorder and incipient mortality. In Anne Bancroft's words, what Dr. Cartwright "was fighting about with those women at that mission was that there was too much yin in their situation and not enough yang."

Such satirical humor was entirely lacking in the previous adaptation of "Chinese Finale" as a half-hour American television program in 1960, with Jan Sterling as Dr. Cartwright and Hilda Plowright as Andrews. Directed by Robert Ellis Miller, that bare-bones version (only four women) portrays the doctor as grimly idealistic and Andrews as rigidly moralistic but not entirely unreasonable. At the end, Andrews realizes the error of her ways and actually offers the doctor a blessing. In addition to restoring and augmenting the doctor's cynical, Rabelaisian humor, Ford's far bleaker interpretation portrays Andrews as a woman who gradually loses all grasp on reality when her fragile sense of authority is destroyed by a series of uncontrollable events—her own attraction toward the virginal young missionary Emma Clark (Sue Lyon), the menopausal pregnancy of Florrie Pether (Betty Field), the arrival of Dr. Cartwright, an outbreak of cholera, and the invasion of the mission by bandits.

The elegantly structured screenplay by British writers Janet Green and John McCormick, the married couple whose previous credits included the "social problem pictures" *Sapphire* and *Victim,* creates a finely nuanced gallery of characters while fleshing out the original story's somewhat schematic ironies. Smith worked directly with the writers at their home in Paris, and Ford communicated his suggestions by correspondence. Ford was disappointed when he could not persuade the writers to join him for story conferences in Hawaii aboard the *Araner,* and he was irritated when they would send revisions from Paris via telephone while he was shooting. In truth, Ford was delighted with their work, but he still exercised his habitual droit de seigneur over the screenplay, if largely for show.

As Anna Lee recalled, "He'd take the script and he'd read a scene and then he'd rip it up and he'd say, 'All right, now what would you like to do?' He'd give you your lines, but he would never write them down. Bernie Smith came on the set looking worried one morning and said, 'Mr. Ford, we're running over schedule. We are about two days over schedule.' Ford said, without even looking up, 'Oh, that's very easy to manage, Bernie.' He tore the pages out of the script and said, 'Now we're on schedule.'"

Ford tightened the dialogue throughout, particularly reducing the excessive rantings of Andrews and Lee's equally racist British missionary, Mrs. Russell, as well as omitting a sarcastic suggestion by Dr. Cartwright that Andrews should go to the island of Sappho. The director added such visual grace notes as Dr. Cartwright wryly studying herself in a mirror before her tryst with the simian Tunga Khan (Mike Mazurki), her contemptuous gesture in flinging away his robe when it lands in her lap during the wrestling match, and her poignant farewell embrace by Miss Argent (Mildred Dunnock). Ford also inserted occasional lines of dialogue, including Dr. Cartwright's memorable parting shot as she serves Tunga Khan poisoned tea: "So long, you bastard." (An intermediate version of the script has the doctor saying much less effectively, "So long, you grinning ape!")

The film's apocalyptic vision of destruction, set in an expressionistically stylized, vaguely Sternbergian nightmare of China, the most alien earthly landscape the American imagination could conceive, metaphorically reflects the turbulent period in which it was made. During the mid- to late sixties, Ford was becoming increasingly despondent over the collapse of traditional social order brought on by such events as the Vietnam War, the Cultural Revolution in China, and the riots in America's black ghettos. Ford's personal malaise was deepened by the harsh national reviews of *Cheyenne Autumn,* most of which appeared shortly before he began shooting *7 Women,* and by his own increasingly frail state of health.

French writer Romain Gary, a friend of Ford's since the 1940s, observed that Ford seemed to have aged a full decade in the two years between *Cheyenne Autumn* and *7 Women.* Wingate Smith, once again serving as Ford's assistant director, thought the cancer that ultimately killed him might have been present as early as the making of *7 Women.* But Ford kept delaying a checkup, fearing what he might discover. Anna Lee saw the depressing impact that Ford's physical condition had on the mood of the film: "I think towards the end of his life he changed, because he obviously knew he was a sick man. I'm sure he did on *7 Women,* because he used to say things once or twice that worried me."

In retrospect, *Chinese Finale* would have been a poetically apt title for Ford's Hollywood valediction, but the aging director was touchy about such autumnal language and did not consciously plan this film as his "finale." He wanted to call the picture *The Mandarin Coat*—after the brilliantly colored garb mockingly worn by the doctor in her final scene—but MGM disapproved. Ford and Smith chose the final title out of a list supplied by the studio that also included *The Yellow Robe, Wind from Mongolia,* and *The Last Place on Earth.*

The director's first choice to play Agatha Andrews was his old friend Katharine Hepburn. But much to Ford's dismay, Hepburn could not see herself playing the mission leader, a part she found totally unsympathetic. Rosalind Russell was also considered, but Smith felt that she, like Hepburn, would have brought overly familiar mannerisms to the role. The producer had the inspired idea of casting British actress Margaret Leighton, whose brilliant performance subtly captures the self-hatred, tormented isolation, and despair that underlie religious fanaticism.

Smith discussed the role of Dr. Cartwright with Ingrid Bergman, who proved unavailable, and Ford halfheartedly considered Jennifer Jones but demurred because of excessive pressure from her husband, producer David O. Selznick (who to Ford would always remain the Man Who Turned Down *Stagecoach*). Ford became excited over the idea of casting his *Young Cassidy* leading lady, Maggie Smith, as Dr. Cartwright. But the producer argued that it would be hard to accept the British actress as an American, even if Leighton could play one convincingly. Instead, he persuaded Ford to give the role of the doctor to Kentucky-born Patricia Neal, a warm, sultry, mature actress of Irish descent who won an Oscar for 1963's *Hud* and had recently starred with John Wayne in Otto Preminger's *In Harm's Way*.

For supporting parts, Bernard Smith suggested Mildred Dunnock, and Ford chose Anna Lee and Dame Flora Robson, who had played Johnny Cassidy's mother. Although Smith initially preferred Carol Lynley as Emma, MGM executive Red Silverstein pushed for Sue Lyon, the nymphet from Stanley Kubrick's *Lolita*. Lyon's acting skills were limited, but Ford and Smith went along with her because Silverstein promised to reciprocate by approving the rest of their casting choices and green-lighting the production. Lyon drew the highest salary of any cast member, $150,000, compared with $125,000 for Neal (who also had a $25,000 deferment to be paid out of the first profits). Although the young actress's line readings are often clumsy, despite the extra rehearsal time the director devoted to her, Ford effectively uses Lyon's combination of innocence and nubile sexuality as Emma becomes a locus of the power struggle between Andrews and Dr. Cartwright.

In early November 1964, his work on *Cheyenne Autumn* completed, Ford moved into an office at MGM to begin preproduction on *7 Women*. "There were a lot of people there who hadn't really heard of him, young people who would ask, 'Who?'" recalled cast member Eddie Albert. "And Ford was called upon to express his superior values to these people."[6]

MGM launched *7 Women* with a luncheon for the Hollywood press on February 1, 1965. The event was something of a sham, at least on Ford's part, because it was held in honor of his "seventieth" birthday when it was actually his seventy-first. Ford admitted to a reporter that he was not looking forward

---

6. One young person who knew Ford's work well and came to learn from him during the mid-1960s was Steven Spielberg. The teenager, an ambitious amateur filmmaker, talked his way into a brief interview with Ford. Showing the nervous Spielberg his collection of Western prints, Ford growled, "When you understand what makes a great Western painting, you'll be a great Western director." Ford gave Spielberg a piece of advice that offered an insight into his own visual style. He told the young filmmaker never to have the horizon in the exact center of a shot, but always to compose a shot with a high or low horizon. Ford ended their encounter by saying, "And never spend your own money to make a movie. Now get the hell out of here."

to the occasion: "At my age I have little room for cake and sentiment." But when it was over, he told Associated Press reporter Bob Thomas, "It has been a wonderful day. The lunch was charming, and I've had calls from just about everyone I know." He added, "I can still lick anyone around."

Principal photography began on February 8 and lasted through April 12, with pickup shots on April 20–21. The production cost of 7 *Women* was a relatively modest $2,298,181, but Ford's salary was a substantial $255,328. Ford-Smith Productions had a half ownership of the picture, but MGM retained final cut. Studio production reports show that Ford filmed most scenes quickly and efficiently, saving time for additional scenes and his silent grace notes. Nevertheless, in part because of retakes necessitated when Patricia Neal fell ill on her third day of shooting and had to be replaced by Bancroft, 7 *Women* finished $120,871 over budget and six days over its forty-day schedule.

Most of the film takes place inside the artificial world of the walled mission, a set on MGM's stage 15 designed by art director Eddie Imazu, whose work was the subject of a promotional featurette, *John Ford's Magic Stage.* Only three days were spent filming outside the studio in late March, at Glenmoor Ranch in Sutton Canyon near Chatsworth, for scenes around the mission gate, footage of the bandits on horseback, and other exteriors.

When *Los Angeles Times* reviewer Philip K. Scheuer visited the mission set, Ford told him that making the film was "a lot of fun but I have to keep on my toes the whole blank-blank [*sic*] time. Here are seven distinct personalities, all with definitive reactions and all crowded onto this cramped set. And, of course, when I was working with men like Duke Wayne, I could always say, 'Shut up, you guys!' But I tell them, 'I can't say it to you ladies.'"

"We all expected him to use his usual invective against the actresses," Anna Lee remembered. "The only time he did pick on a woman slightly was with Flora Robson. He wasn't happy when she told him that she wanted the 'Dame' put on her [dressing room] shingle. He muttered a lot about that. But he was expecting people to say, 'Well, he's going to be nasty,' and deliberately, I think, he set out to be as charming and as nice as he could. He couldn't have been nicer all the way through that picture."

Ford was so charming to Sue Lyon that one day she arrived on the set wearing a beanie reading "JOHN FORD IS A SWEETIE-PIE." Jane Chang, who plays the Mandarin princess Miss Ling, told me that Ford was infallibly gracious to her as well. When they filmed the scene of her character being humiliated by Tunga Khan, who throws dirty rags in her face, Ford stepped in afterward to wipe Chang's face with his handkerchief. Chang laughed as she remembered having to hold her breath because Ford's handkerchief was so disgusting. As he attended to her, she could see crew members snickering behind the director's back. But on another occasion, Chang was pleasantly astonished when Ford suddenly started ad-libbing dialogue for her in Mandarin Chinese. She was most grateful that he gave her ample opportunity to express strong emotion, unlike other Hollywood directors who eventually drove her out of the business by insisting that she remain stereotypically blank-faced and "inscrutable."

"I was very happy to be in a film directed by the great John Ford," Patricia Neal recalled, "and, in our very first meeting, felt I understood him perfectly. He was the boss and no one would cramp his act. I thought he was a darling." After finishing work on February 17, Neal returned to her rented home in Pacific Palisades. That night, while bathing one of her daughters, she suffered the first of a series of strokes. The thirty-nine-year-old actress, pregnant with her fourth child, was taken to the UCLA Medical Center in Westwood, where she had two additional brain hemorrhages. The third, while she lay unconscious in the X-ray room, was the most devastating. After a seven-hour brain operation, Neal was reported in "very critical" condition. For two weeks she was believed to be near death.

Ford-Smith Productions issued the incapacitated actress a check for $20,000 of her salary to help with medical bills, a payment they were not legally obligated to make; her husband, author Roald Dahl, wrote Ford a heartfelt letter of thanks. During her month's stay in the hospital, Neal received visits from Ford and Mildred Dunnock, among other friends and colleagues. She surprised everyone by emerging from her coma and being able to leave the hospital on St. Patrick's Day. Even though she had to use a wheelchair, was partly paralyzed, and suffered from speech impairment, she was well enough two months later to hold a press conference at the airport en route home to England. Eventually, Neal made an extraordinary recovery, chronicled in Barry Farrell's moving 1969 book, *Pat and Roald,* and the 1981 TV movie adaptation, *The Patricia Neal Story.* She triumphantly resumed her screen career in 1968 with *The Subject Was Roses.*

Neal's illness came as "an awful shock to everyone" working on *7 Women,* Anna Lee remembered. As a sudden reminder of the fragility of human life, the catastrophe shadowed the experience of making the film and probably helps account for its pervasive sense of melancholia. The morning after Neal's hospitalization, the show went on with the scene of Agatha Andrews covertly expressing her sexual attraction toward Emma. A $50,000 offer was quickly made to Bancroft to step into the starring role.

The two actresses were friendly professional rivals. They had appeared together onstage in *The Miracle Worker,* and the year before Neal won her Oscar for *Hud,* Bancroft won the award for starring in the film version of *The Mira-*

cle Worker. Without even reading the screenplay of *7 Women,* Bancroft left New York on February 19 and reported to MGM that weekend for wardrobe fittings. She began playing Dr. Cartwright on February 24 with a retake of the doctor's arrival at the mission on a donkey. Bancroft found Ford "infinitely patient in explaining his reasons for what he wants. At the same time, he is in complete command." Lee thought Bancroft's Italian Catholic background gave her a temperamental affinity with the Irish Catholic director. Her marvelous performance brings out all the richly varied humor, compassion, and spirit of Dr. Cartwright

To compensate for the effort involved in being so pleasant to the rest of the cast, Ford found a handy scapegoat in Eddie Albert, who appropriately plays the meek, henpecked mission teacher, Charles Pether. "He *crucified* Eddie on that picture," said Lee. "Because he was the only man [among the missionaries], you see, and Pappy always had somebody he liked to pick on. He put him down and made sarcastic remarks to him. Eddie stood it very well. I think Pappy was so afraid that somebody would get too uppity on a picture, he wanted to put them in their place right away."

"Before we shot," Albert recalled, "Ford was sick and he invited me to come over to his house. He was in bed. He said, 'Tell me how you see this character.' I hadn't done much study on that, but he asked me another question or two and I was really conversing, because I had nothing but respect for him. All of a sudden he said, 'Are you going to run the show?' He was putting me in my place. His problem was that he did that all his life, because he was far superior to most of the actors, and he was right. But he had to do it in a kind of a theatrical way—'Don't fuck around with me, kid. I'm gonna cut you up.' He'd suck you in. We'd be talking very pleasantly and he'd tell a few jokes. Then *I* told a joke and it was just what he wanted. He said, 'Look, you're not taking this too seriously?' He caught me off guard—'What'd I do?' All of a sudden he was a different man.

"I also got in trouble with him early in the shooting. About four o'clock he would stop for tea and we were all sitting there, him at the head of the table, while he would talk. Most of us were pretty terrified. He was talking about the Catholic cathedrals. He was explaining what a cathedral was and he named them all. I said, 'There's another one in Italy, you know.' Shit, I was so sorry I did this! He said, *'What?'* I said, 'I think there's another cathedral in Italy. . . .' He left me lying there. The next day he called again for tea and said, 'Mr. Albert, you are correct. There is another.' But it was a dubious victory, because from that time on, he would trick me all the time. He watched for times to put me back in my place. One time he asked me, 'Would you cut my toenails?' I said sure. And I got the feeling that he wanted to be *seen* with me cutting his toenails. I was onto him, but I admired him and almost loved him. That can be easily twisted around—I suppose somebody else would say I was kissing his ass.

"Whether you liked it or not, he had to win. Nine times out of ten he was right, but he was also childish in his wanting to win. He was in charge, but he also knew that it was his last picture and that he was very old, so he had his little doubts. He was not quite sure that he'd overcome this story yet. And I think he was very sensitive to the fact that that's about the end of him in Hollywood."

The school of liberal-humanist Ford criticism that grew out of the writings of Lindsay Anderson in *Sequence* and *Sight and Sound* found eloquent expression in Robin Wood's 1971 *Film Comment* essay on Ford's late work, which mourned the director's "acknowledgment of the disintegration of everything he had believed in." Unfortunately for Ford's shaky reputation at the time among intellectuals and academics, Wood found little to value in *7 Women:* "The essence of the film is a thinly concealed nihilism. The lack of real religious feeling in Ford prevents him from finding any transcendent spiritual values in the missionaries and their work; any positive belief in the mission as a community, or as an epitome of civilization, is made nonsense of by its futility, by its inner tensions and outer ineffectuality."

It's true that Ford finds no transcendent spiritual value in the "Christian Endeavor" movement represented by Agatha Andrews and her followers. Ford's personal ambivalence toward organized religion was encapsulated in a comment he made late in life when Bogdanovich asked, "Are you Catholic?" "I am a Catholic," Ford replied, "but not very Catholic." Nevertheless, Ford was prone to making ostentatious proclamations of faith in his old age, as if to reassure the world, and himself, that he was a true believer. He loved the outward pomp of Catholicism almost as much as he did that of the military. Two days after the start of filming on *7 Women,* Ford received the highest honor for a Catholic layman when he was invested with the cape and jewel of a Knight of Malta by Pope Paul VI. But religious leaders in Ford movies are usually either dangerous fanatics or well-meaning but ineffectual eccentrics. Since the missionaries in *7 Women* are Protestants, and Yankees to boot, not Catholics as in Ford's pietistic anti-Communist tract *The Bamboo Cross,* the director feels free to satirize their delusions.

But Ford never confuses satire with nihilism. Perhaps Katharine Hepburn's disdainful incomprehension of the screenplay's Agatha Andrews inspired Ford to approach the character with greater understanding. Leighton's performance evokes a powerfully moving sense of pity for a woman who, however destructive her actions, never loses her tragic stature. Ford well knows the hidden vulnerabilities of an authoritarian personality.

The slight hint of lesbianism in the original story is made more overt in the film when Andrews appears unannounced at the door of Emma's room and surreptitiously inspects the girl's half-clothed body. The mission leader's hands reach toward Emma, tentatively smoothing her hair, before Andrews retreats in anguished uncertainty. Wood quips that Ford's direction of this scene "looks as if someone had explained to him what a lesbian was five minutes before shooting and he hadn't had time to recover from the shock." Yet the scene in question, like the doorway scene in *The Searchers* of Captain Reverend Clayton discovering Martha's infidelity, is delicately played and directed. It stirs nothing but empathy for a woman tragically torn between her attenuated beliefs and her almost uncontrollable physical desires. The inability of this hypocritical puritan to deal with her repressed sexuality is the first sign of her imminent breakdown.

Ford allows all the women to be fully human rather than simply comic caricatures like the fire-breathing ministers in *Steamboat Round the Bend* and *Drums Along the Mohawk* or allegorical stick figures like the cast of *The Fugitive*. One of the most heartrending scenes in *7 Women* is Andrews's confession of her loss of faith, a realization that comes, significantly, when Emma lies gravely ill, beyond the power of prayer. The doctor listens with compassionate fascination as Andrews confides, "I've always searched for something that . . . isn't there. And God isn't enough. [*Whispers*] God help me. He—isn't enough."

Such a confession, however evocative of the existential searches in many earlier Ford films, does not constitute an expression of nihilism by the director. Ford's closest emotional and spiritual affinities are not with people who preach Christianity but with those who practice its principles in their daily lives, such as (paradoxically) the unbelieving Dr. Cartwright. The doctor takes her last name from her function in the story, metaphorically "building" the cart that carries the others to safety in the penultimate scene. When Bogdanovich asked Ford why the doctor sacrifices herself for the others, his answer was blunt and emotional: "I think that's a rather naive question, Peter. She was a doctor—her object in life was to save people. She was a woman who had no religion, but she got in with this bunch of kooks and started acting like a human being."

Superficially, the mission functions like a fort in one of Ford's Westerns, marking the arbitrary boundary between "civilization" and the wilderness. But the false and sterile values of the missionaries, whose rigidly artificial world is shattered by repeated incursions of uncontrollable outside life, serve as a negative model of Ford's idea of true civilization. They are foils for Dr. Cartwright's humanism. Comparisons with other Ford films leave out much that is fresh and provocative about 7 *Women,* but they also serve as reminders that the director's underlying value system did not change in any fundamental way. Dr. Cartwright resembles John Wayne's Captain York, Colonel Thursday's reasonable and principled antagonist in *Fort Apache;* and while the bandits are too broadly sketched to function as anything but allegorical figures, they could be equated with the Indians in *Stagecoach,* whose function is simply to provide a test of survival for the white characters. For such reasons, and because 7 *Women's* "last place on earth" clearly symbolizes the exhaustion of the American frontier ethos, Richard Combs argues that the film could be considered "Ford's last Western," a logical outgrowth of the dead-end feeling of *The Man Who Shot Liberty Valance* and the revisionism of *Cheyenne Autumn.*

Nevertheless, the sexual and racial aspects of 7 *Women* remain somewhat problematical even for an admirer of the film, especially since, for all its affinities with the Western genre, it falls outside that genre's stylized conventions. "Ford's barbarians," notes Wood, "are merely brutes: he can't conceive of them as possessing any natural fineness, and their vitality is presented as exclusively destructive." A more nuanced portrayal of the bandits would have added another level of complexity to the story, as in Frank Capra's film *The Bitter Tea of General Yen* (1933), a romance between a puritanical American woman and a Chinese warlord who is portrayed with a fascinating blend of brutality and sensitivity. Ford was after something far more basic with his bandits, as Sarris points out: "They are the worst kind of males the female psyche can envisage. These rampaging males wander around the countryside raping, killing, plundering, and worst of all, smashing all the windows, furniture, and bric-à-brac. They affront every canon of order imposed upon the male by the female since the beginning of time."

One would be inclined to let Ford indulge his obsessions were it not for the uncomfortable similarities between the portrayal of a war-torn China in 7 *Women* and the war in Vietnam. The American involvement in Vietnam dramatically escalated when the marines landed at Da Nang on March 8, 1965, while Ford was in the midst of filming 7 *Women.* His portrayal of blundering white do-gooders in Asia, of xenophobia masquerading as benevolence, seems right on target; seen today, Ford's harrowing images of a massacre of Chinese men, women, and children cannot help summoning up images of the 1968 My Lai massacre. Yet the analogy breaks down because the massacre in 7 *Women* is not committed by Americans against Asians, but by Asians against other Asians; the scene's horrific statement about the human potential for brutality is blurred by the racist implication that somehow Asians are more brutal than Caucasians. Like *Cheyenne Autumn, 7 Women* gives the sense of Ford venturing bravely into new territory, well beyond his usual belief structure, yet not quite searching far enough to satisfy the demands of complete honesty.

The same ambivalence surrounds the film's treatment of miscegenation, an insistent theme in Ford's later work. Dr. Cartwright allows herself to become Tunga Khan's concubine in exchange for food and medical supplies, and finally for the freedom of the people in her care. At the end, she appears in the shadowy corridor of the mission, silhouetted in her dazzling Mandarin coat. Ford has spent the entire film preparing us for this moment of poetry. As he explained, "I tried to keep the film down to a monotone, to start, and later on, when the girl put on the kimono, I went into rather vivid color for a sudden change." After her sardonic farewell toast to Tunga Khan, she downs her cup of poisoned tea, smashing it to the floor in anguish, as the screen darkens around her and the camera pulls rapidly back to the keening of a saxophone in Elmer Bernstein's magnificent score. This startling finale to Ford's feature directing career employs the kind of expressionistic lighting device he used to isolate his characters in *Mary of Scotland* and *Sergeant Rutledge*. Like Katharine Hepburn's martyred queen, Dr. Cartwright goes to her death with tragic grandeur, mingled with her human dread of oblivion.

Samuel Fuller, generally a great admirer of Ford's work, told me he was bothered by the ending of *7 Women* because he thought the doctor's decision to kill herself rather than submit to Tunga Khan was based on racist assumptions. As Fuller put it, "If he was *Cary Grant,* she wouldn't have killed herself." Of course, if Cary Grant had played Tunga Khan, *7 Women* would be *The Bitter Tea of General Yen.* Certainly such an egalitarian love relationship between people of different races would have been beyond the ethnocentric limits of Ford's imagination. But it's worth noting that the doctor kills herself after, not before, she first sleeps with Tunga Khan. This is not quite the avoidance of the "fate worse than death" in nineteenth-century melodrama. In fact, in the earlier scene of Dr. Cartwright's waiting to go to bed with the bandit leader, she appraises him coolly, appearing more amused than horrified by what she is about to do. To the crazed Andrews, the deal is an unspeakable humiliation: "He only wants her because she's white and he's yellow." But the doctor's apparent submission to Tunga Khan is a pragmatic decision, not only allowing her charges to escape but also avoiding, by suicide, what surely would be a brutal sexual bondage offering little hope of survival. Given the film's apocalyptic context, her suicide seems an existential statement rather than an expression of racist revulsion. The aging director says "so long" to his audience with one of the cinema's most haunting images of the terror and wastefulness of impending death.

Ford's visual mastery is evident in his graceful command of the wide Pana-vision frame, making subtly dramatic use of Joseph LaShelle's delicately shad-owed cinematography and choreographing movement with a virtuosity that never calls attention to itself. "In sequences with a large number of people he pays meticulous attention to every movement and gesture," observed 7 *Women* cast member Flora Robson. "It is almost as though he were directing a ballet. Very likely this goes back to his training in the silent film days when the cam-era alone had to tell the story. With Ford, the actor is continually conscious of the fact that he is making a motion picture and that it must move, move, move. His scenes are never static or dominated by the dialogue."

Before 7 *Women* was released, MGM exercised its prerogative of final cut and trimmed the film by six minutes, diminishing but not destroying the story's complexity. The most important missing scene is a powerful confronta-tion early in the film between Argent and Andrews. Like Captain Colling-wood in *Fort Apache,* Argent has been requesting a transfer. But when the letter from "headquarters" arrives, she is brutally informed by Miss Andrews that she is incapable of handling more than a subordinate position and that "the Lord has created some to command and some to serve." In one of Mil-dred Dunnock's finest moments on-screen, Argent tearfully responds, "Pride is a sin, too, Miss Andrews." This scene is necessary to understanding Argent's hostile expression when Andrews subsequently tells the doctor with bitter irony, "This is Miss Argent, my assistant. She's so loyal and devoted I don't know what I'd do without her." These complex dynamics also help motivate the climactic scenes when Argent finally summons up the courage to embrace Dr. Cartwright and tell off her former commander.

As a way of intentionally heightening the mission's feeling of enclosure—initially reassuring to its inhabitants, then illusory, and finally claustrophobic—the film eliminated the story's device of the bandits moving the women through the Chinese countryside to captivity at another location. Instead the bandits invade the mission and take over its living quarters while imprisoning the women in a shed. With unforced religious symbolism, they witness the ar-rival of new life as a baby is born under desperately inhospitable conditions. But reviewers who assumed that Ford simply wanted to avoid going outside with 7 *Women* were mistaken, for the uncut version of the film reveals that Ford had a radically different visual strategy. As counterpoint to the vise-tightening within the mission walls, he filmed two additional exterior seg-ments later cut by the studio: a strikingly expressionistic sequence of the bandits pillaging a nearby village and a comical courting scene with the bandit known as Lean Warrior (Woody Strode) picking flowers for Dr. Cartwright. The courtship scene sets up the wordless rivalry between the two bandits climaxing with Tunga Khan breaking Lean Warrior's neck as they wrestle to impress the doctor.

The missing footage quietly reappeared in pan-and-scan television prints during the 1970s. But the prints of 7 *Women* currently in television and home-video release are the eighty-seven-minute release version. Turner Entertainment, which now owns the film, does not even have a 35mm print available for screenings in the United States. When the Los Angeles County Museum of Art asked the company to make a new print for the museum's 1994 Ford retrospective, Turner said it could not justify the expense. Such indifference to Ford's legacy is not entirely the fault of the film's owners, since there has never been much demand for 7 *Women* from audiences of *any* kind.

Any hopes MGM might have had for 7 *Women* evaporated after its first public preview on July 16, 1965, at the Academy Theatre in Pasadena, California. The preview cards offer a revealing snapshot of the American public's attitude toward John Ford at the close of his Hollywood career.

Although 161 people in the Pasadena audience said they would recommend the film to their friends, compared with 110 who said they wouldn't, the negative comments seemed unusually vitriolic. Not surprisingly, women generally appreciated 7 *Women* more than men, but many women were more repulsed by the violence of the bandits. A large proportion of viewers of both sexes seemed offended by Ford's satirical view of organized religion and his exploration of racial and sexual taboos. Underlying even some of the most laudatory responses was a sense that Ford, despite his superficially old-fashioned narrative style, was offering a highly disturbing view of the chaotic world outside the theater at a time when the American public's preferred movie entertainment was the reassuring romantic escapism of *The Sound of Music.*

"Did John Ford 'flip his lid' or is he getting senile?" one viewer wrote on her preview card. "Egads, I haven't seen such an inane, corny, ridiculous, stupid, asinine, lousy movie in years! . . . Who was the weirdo atheist author?"

"I think that to laugh or make any religion ridiculous is poor taste to say the least!" another viewer complained. "I am surprised at John Ford."

Then there were such favorable responses as the following:

"Very good film. Makes one think about the true religions of his heart."

"This film completely depressed me but that's because it was so good. I wish it didn't make me feel so bad but I guess that's what makes a film exciting if you can really get so much out of it."

"Powerful actors. Great contrast. Bancroft swashbuckling like Fairbanks. Bring us more women of true heroic proportion."

"Script was terrific. Directing, acting terrific. One of the best movies. Humorous, dramatic, everything added to make a great motion picture."

But the most vociferous responses made the strongest impression:

"Too many scenes of perversion. I'm not a Puritan, but do perverts have to make so many pictures and why must they force their perversions on the public."

"Slept through most of it—didn't think it would ever get started."

"Stunk."

"Could be recut into a fair comedy."

"It's a shame John Ford has lost his talent."

That preview, followed by negative trade press reviews in December, explains why MGM dumped the film on the market on double features with such films as *24 Hours to Kill* and *The Money Trap,* beginning January 5, 1966. In the ultimate ignominy, the New York opening of *7 Women*—which *Variety* reported was delayed for four months "to avoid the slings and arrows of such [reviewers] as Bosley Crowther and Judith Crist"—was held in a grind house on Forty-second Street. To borrow a phrase from Samuel Goldwyn, the public stayed away in droves. Theatrical rentals amounted to only $433,075 in the domestic market and $504,357 in foreign countries.

That would have been ruinous enough, but what really ended Ford's Hollywood career was the condescending critical reception to the film, colored by the long-standing bias of the male-dominated critical establishment against "women's pictures" and the myopic vision of reviewers who couldn't see beyond the fact that Ford was reworking a genre identified with the 1930s. Veteran *Daily Variety* reviewer Whitney Williams typified that attitude: "It's the theme itself that militates against any more than passing interest; back in program days this was a more or less stock subject and appears old-fashioned now." *Time* chuckled over "the plight of some rather interesting actresses, trapped on MGM's chintzy Chinese soundstage with absurd situations, hoked-up direction, and dialogue like wet firecrackers." Barely bothering to mention the story line of this "Chinese-based Western in which Mongolian bandits replace the redskins," Arthur Knight of the *Saturday Review* described the characterizations as "hopelessly overemphatic and utterly implausible. . . . I suspect that [Ford's] admirers among the auteur critics will be hard put to explain away this work of The Master."

When the dean of American auteurists, Andrew Sarris of the *Village Voice,* ventured out into the wilds of Forty-second Street to review *7 Women,* even he "braced [him]self for the worst." But he felt Ford's "standing would not be jeopardized if he chose to direct the Three Stooges in a nudist movie, much less seven actresses in a Chinese adventure. I could have saved my defensive rationalizations. . . . The beauties of 7 *Women* are for the ages, or at least for a later time when the personal poetry of film directors is better understood between the lines of genre conventions. Ford's gravest crime is taking his material seriously at a time when the seriousness of an entire medium is being threatened by the tyranny of trivia." Two years later, Sarris wrote in *The American Cinema,* "The last champions of John Ford have now gathered around 7 *Women* as a beacon of personal cinema."

Another insightful contemporary appraisal was offered by Richard Thompson, a young critic for the University of Chicago magazine *Focus!*: "7 *Women* is Ford's most pessimistic film to date, culminating a progressive reappraisal of the myths he once celebrated and created," Thompson wrote in 1967. "The dark vein of *Two Rode Together, The Man Who Shot Liberty Valance,* and *Cheyenne Autumn* is now fully realized. Ford, of course, is The Old Order. Like Duke Ellington, Ford goes his own way, following his vision regardless of stylistic change around him. The sympathy Ford expresses for the old-way heroes in his films of progress is a personal sympathy. When Ford constructs a film with disorder in control at the end, what does it signify for Ford? For his art, and for films? For his view of America?"

I was a bit reluctant to raise the painful subject of 7 *Women* when I met Ford in 1970, but he responded with brio, "Sure, go ahead. It's one of my favorite pictures. See that plaque up there? The London Film Festival gave me that for 7 *Women*. It's the British equivalent of an Oscar."

"Were you surprised when it didn't do well with the American audience?"

"Unh-unh. It was over their heads."

"You made it knowing that the Americans wouldn't like it, then."

"No, I didn't give a God damn whether they liked it or not. I thought it was a swell story and a good script, so I did it."

In a letter to a woman who wrote him in praise of 7 *Women,* Ford was even more contemptuous toward those who had rejected his last feature. He labeled unfriendly American reviewers Communists. And he defiantly described 7 *Women* as his finest work as a director. He made a similar remark to French interviewer Claudine Tavernier, saying of the American critics who panned 7 *Women,* "They are all Communists, these critics, and they detest cinema." But it wasn't necessary to be a Communist to shun John Ford's Chinese finale. In 1976, I asked John Wayne what he thought of 7 *Women*. He admitted he had never seen it. Why not? I wondered, unable to conceal my surprise. Sounding sad and somewhat embarrassed, Wayne replied, "Well, I—*you know.*"

The prolonged fit of drunken despair that followed the making of 7 *Women* was disturbingly different from Ford's earlier benders.

Stumbling around the *Araner* as it sailed aimlessly along the coast of Hawaii, he railed to his grandson Dan about what a bad idea it had been to make *7 Women* and how it would end his career. The film was still months away from opening, but he knew. After weeks of heavy boozing, Ford had to be taken from the boat by ambulance one night in August and transported to a hospital for a couple of days of drying out. At his age, this was a frightening event, and his doctor in Hawaii warned him against a recurrence.

For the next seven years, until illness finally made him accept retirement, America's greatest filmmaker could not find a job in the industry he had helped create. He kept trying to get a picture off the ground even though project after project fell through. A lasting indictment of the Hollywood system, Ford's ostracism was not only a sign of his fading physical and commercial viability but also a reflection of the myopia of the times, when it seemed that any longhaired kid who had never made a movie was more bankable than an old master with decades of experience.

Living in the *Easy Rider* era turned Ford into a raging bull. When a writer from *Esquire* came to call and asked if he had seen the X-rated Oscar winner for best picture of 1969, *Midnight Cowboy,* Ford snapped, "No! Especially not that! I don't like porn—these easy, liberal movies. A lot of junk. I don't know where they're going. They don't either." An accompanying photograph showed Ford sitting in his den in near darkness, glowering down into the camera, an apt image of the elderly giant's wrathful isolation from the contemporary scene.

"This town is terrible," commented director Burt Kennedy, a friend of Ford's. "If you make a bad picture like *7 Women* at his age, the studios are off of you. I always said Ford was so rough when he was younger, because he was getting even for what was going to happen when they dumped him."

The combination of box-office failure, dismissive reviews, failing health, difficulty in obtaining insurance, his conservative political views, and his stubborn preference for such unfashionable genres as war movies and Westerns made Ford seem unemployable in the eyes of studio and bank executives. Ford told me in 1970 that he would "still enjoy doing a Western. If a story came along, I'd go out and do it now, but hell, they're not coming. I get two or three scripts a week, but they're remakes or rewrites of pictures I've already done. Or they're all filthy or sexy, and that would be against my nature, my religion, and my natural inclinations to do those things."

Ford was planning to follow *7 Women* with another film for MGM, *The Miracle of Merriford.* Adapted by Willis Goldbeck and James Warner Bellah from a 1955 novel by Reginald Arkell, it was a comedy about American ex-soldiers returning to a British town after World War II to rebuild a church they damaged during the war. Ford saw the project as a satire of the cultural clash between Americans and Britons, with humor similar to that of *The Quiet Man*. He wanted James Stewart and Dan Dailey in the leads, and was considering such other actors as Julie Christie, Jack Hawkins, and Cecil Kellaway. MGM announced in June 1965 that the film would begin shooting that October, but it was canceled after the studio read the script. Although Ford claimed the reason was that it didn't have enough sex, the bad preview of *7 Women* in July probably had something to do with the cancellation of another Ford project set in the past and dealing with religion. The following summer, Ford approached Walter Wanger, his producer on *Stagecoach* and *The Long Voyage Home,* in an unsuccessful attempt to set up *The Miracle of Merriford* as a TV movie.

Ford also wanted to make a biographical film about Wild Bill Donovan, claiming that he had promised the dying Donovan he would do so. Encouraged by Ole Doering, Donovan's right-hand man and later the legal counsel of Argosy Pictures, Ford began thinking about *O.S.S.* in earnest while working on *7 Women*. By then he and other former members of the wartime spy agency were becoming more open about talking about once-secret experiences, and books about the OSS and Donovan were proliferating. Donovan's life was full of colorful and controversial material, but that was one of Ford's problems: it made for a sprawling story that would have been difficult to structure as a movie. Furthermore, gung ho patriots like Donovan had fallen out of fashion during the Vietnam War era. Ford naturally thought of John Wayne to play Donovan and Anna Lee as his wife, Ruth. When I asked Ford how *O.S.S.* was coming, his response spoke volumes about his isolated position in contemporary Hollywood: "Not very well. It's hard to get a writer out here, you know. I mean, I don't know any of the writers."

One writer he did know was John Lee Mahin. According to Mahin, in the late 1960s, "Ford called me and said, 'I'm going to do my last picture, and by God I'm going to do what I want to do—*Midway*.' He was there. He was going to use some actual footage. He had some wonderful footage. An Italian company was going to put up the money, the money was there, and [producer] Al Ruddy, the guy who [later] did *The Godfather,* was in on it. I even wrote the opening. And suddenly the money wasn't available, and that was the last we heard of it."

The central characters were to have been two brothers: one breaks the Japanese code and the other dies piloting a fighter plane. Mahin described what he and Ford planned as the beginning of the picture, a scene involving Admiral Chester W. Nimitz, commander-in-chief of the U.S. Pacific Fleet, and Admiral Husband E. Kimmel: "Pearl Harbor on Christmas Day, 1941. We opened on Nimitz arriving. He replaced Admiral Kimmel, who was the goat. That morning they heard tapping on the *Arizona*. She was overturned, and the men had been living there for two and a half weeks. . . . [Nimitz and Kimmel] went over to the *Arizona* and Nimitz saw an old grizzled diver with a diving suit on who had just come up and was getting his breath. The young ensign said, 'Any sound?' He said, 'This morning we heard it here,' and he tapped the hull a couple of times and got no answer. And the old diver just burst into tears and said, 'Holy Jesus Christ.' Then they went away on the barge and on the sound track you heard 'God Rest Ye Merry, Gentlemen.' . . . Ford and I had a good feeling about it. He said, 'John, we'll do it the way it was.' . . . I was just going to take his dictation from what he wanted to say and write the scenes out."

A *Midway* feature was made by the Mirisch Company for Universal in 1976, directed in undistinguished fashion by Jack Smight. According to Admiral Bulkeley, Ford also wanted to direct *Tora! Tora! Tora!*, the 1970 American-Japanese coproduction about the bombing of Pearl Harbor, which was codirected by Richard Fleischer, Toshio Masuda, and Kinji Fukasaku for release by Twentieth Century–Fox. Ford had helped Gregg Toland restage the bombing for their 1943 documentary *December 7th*, but he could have done so on a far more ambitious scale for this $25 million production. Originally, the Japanese segments of *Tora! Tora! Tora!* were to have been directed by Akira Kurosawa, who was replaced after a few days of shooting. Kurosawa not only emulated Ford's work in such films as *The Seven Samurai* and *The Hidden Fortress* but also sported dark glasses in imitation of Ford. What a shame the world was deprived of a film about World War II jointly directed by Ford and Kurosawa.

Ford's international reputation was stronger than ever before, as demonstrated by his much-ballyhooed visit to Paris in 1966 for a reissue of *Fort Apache*, known in France as *Le Massacre de Fort Apache*. His trip was arranged by two young admirers, Pierre Rissient and Bertrand Tavernier, partners in a small company that promoted and sometimes also distributed American films; a noted film critic, Tavernier later became a major French director.

When Rissient went to meet Ford at the airport, he found the great filmmaker so drunk he was unable to walk. The two press attachés spent much of the next ten days trying to keep Ford sober enough for a few hours of interviews each day. Although he complained to his hosts that they never stopped talking about movies, Ford seemed to thrive on his spirited exchanges with several journalists and critics, including Samuel Lachize of *L'Humanité*. "I don't mind talking with a Communist," said Ford. "I'm a liberal." As a way of explaining his uninhibited mood and self-destructive behavior, Ford declared, "I can do whatever I want now, because I'll never make another picture. They won't let me make one. . . . I am a tough old retired director. Well, half-retired."

Determined to help Ford keep working, Rissient shrewdly suggested in late 1967 that he make a film of Maupassant's "Boule de Suif," but this time in France rather than Monument Valley. Ford flew to Paris on January 4, 1968, for a two-week trip to drum up interest. In the hope of impressing potential backers with his sobriety, he stayed on better behavior. Rissient suggested Leslie Caron for the lead role of the gallant prostitute. But according to Tavernier, Caron passed on the role because she felt that Ford, who did not like to move his camera, was less "modern" a director than one who did, such as Nanni Loy, an Italian best known for his 1962 film *The Four Days of Naples*.

In February 1967, Ford went to the Mediterranean on a three-week tour of temporary active naval service with Mark Armistead. The official purpose was to give a seminar on navy filmmaking, but Ford seemed to regard the trip as a nostalgic R&R cruise. At Marseilles, Ford and Armistead boarded the missile cruiser USS *Columbus*, the flagship of a cruiser-destroyer flotilla commanded by then Rear Admiral John Bulkeley. "Ford and Mark Armistead came all the way down there to 'consult' on something or other," Bulkeley recalled. "He used that excuse, but what the hell he was consulting about, I never knew. I gave him my cabin and I slept someplace else when he was on the ship. He just loved to stay in bed there all the time."

After that Ford only rarely traveled. Along with Jean Renoir and Fritz Lang, he attended the Montreal Film Festival in 1967, which was holding a revival of his first feature, *Straight Shooting*, recently rediscovered in the Czech Film Archive. Another expedition, in June 1970, took Ford to New York to see Katharine Hepburn in *Coco*, her musical about designer Coco Chanel. Ford went backstage, where the rest of the company stood around and gaped at the sight of the great director in their midst. Particularly since he had failed to come see her onstage as their romance was winding down in the late 1930s, the visit meant a great deal to both Hepburn and Ford.

Ford spent much of his time at home in bed during his later years. He even allowed a crew from a French television series to film a hilarious interview with him in bed. Wearing pajamas, barefoot, drinking, and smoking a cigar, Ford alternated fluidly between French and English with interviewer André S. Labarthe, mischievously parrying his questions and bantering with the crew. The half-hour interview was filmed August 31, 1965, and broadcast the following June 16 on the ORTF series *Cinéastes de notre temps* under the title "Entre chien et loup: John Ford" ("In the Twilight: John Ford").

Ford's use of his bed as a personal throne room also was memorialized in an evocative painting by R. B. Kitaj, *John Ford on His Deathbed*, showing him surrounded by characters from his movies. When Kitaj visited Ford's home for the sitting, he brought along his son, the future screenwriter and Ford admirer Lem Dobbs. For a June 1968 interview with the BBC TV, however, Ford got dressed to be filmed in his den but indulged his puckish sense of humor toward the British, unmercifully teasing interviewer Philip Jenkinson, who proved a remarkably good sport. Aired that August as *My Name Is John Ford: I Make Westerns*, Jenkinson's program is one of Ford's most entertaining and insightful interviews.

Ford still maintained an office until the early seventies, usually going in to work accompanied by his dachshunds, Sophie and Mariah, who rode along with him in the Chrysler station wagon chauffeured by Bill Ramsey. One of the reasons Ford persisted despite his failing health and his frustrations with the movie industry was that he was experiencing serious financial problems. Although his grandson estimated Ford's net worth in 1965 at $1.7 million, the Fords' living expenses remained relatively high while his income level was steadily falling.

Many of their assets were tied up in stock held by their bank for loans to pay income taxes. Although Ford earned $102,309 in 1966, more than half of that income came from stock dividends, largely on his holdings in AT&T and General Motors. John Ford Productions, of which Ford owned 88 percent, was showing sizable operating losses by the late sixties, as much as $110,935 in 1969. Furthermore, the Internal Revenue Service and the California Franchise Tax Board in 1967 filed levies against the Fords and John Ford Productions for underpayment of back taxes totaling $250,364. The levies stemmed from overestimated business expenses dating back to 1960, particularly those relating to the upkeep of the *Araner*, whose ownership had been transferred to the production company in 1960. The IRS levies, which amounted to all but $10,341 of the total, were paid off by July 1967. Ford finally unloaded the *Araner* in 1969 to E. E. Wright and Ronald M. Hunts for $25,000 cash and an interest in a resort; Ford's longtime home away from home was turned into a cruise ship, renamed the *Windjammer*.

Another drain on Ford's resources was the Field Photo Farm, which he had been subsidizing for many years with gifts and loans. Some of the land had to be sold in 1961 to keep the Farm solvent. After the clubhouse was destroyed by fire on January 8, 1969, the land, remaining buildings, and other property owned by Field Photo Homes were donated to the Motion Picture and Television Relief Fund, which sold the land for $276,825. The chapel was moved to the grounds of the Motion Picture Country House and Hospital in Woodland Hills. It was dedicated anew as the John Ford Chapel on October 19, 1969, an event celebrated with a screening of *The Quiet Man*.

Ford's annual Memorial Day ceremonies were moved to the site of the industry retirement home.

Ironically, Ford was employable in his final years only as an actor playing himself. He was the crusty star attraction of Bogdanovich's *Directed by John Ford* and Dan Ford's TV special *The American West of John Ford*, both of which appeared in 1971.

Bogdanovich began work on his lovingly crafted film in 1968, the year after the first publication (in England) of his seminal interview book *John Ford*, drawn from talks with Ford at his Bel Air home during the summer and fall of 1966. *Directed by John Ford*, made for the American Film Institute and the California Arts Commission, contains a lavish array of film clips illustrating Ford's role as a chronicler of American history, as well as interviews with John Wayne, James Stewart, Henry Fonda, and Ford himself. The documentary is eloquently narrated by Orson Welles, who recorded his commentary at a Howard Johnson's motel in Hollywood during a twenty-minute break from directing *The Other Side of the Wind* in the spring of 1971.

After agreeing to travel to Monument Valley, a journey he insisted on making by train, Ford stonewalled Bogdanovich during their filmed interview, answering Bogdanovich's questions with such comebacks as, "I wouldn't know," "Yeah, *uh-huh*," and "Cut!" Initially taken aback by such intransigence, Bogdanovich came to see that Ford's monosyllabic responses could be used effectively as "comic relief" to the artistry of the film clips, demonstrating Ford's principle of letting his work speak for itself. When asked how he shot the breathtaking land rush sequence from *3 Bad Men*, Ford replies, "With a camera."

"Jack used to call Peter Bogdanovich his 'favorite horse fly,' because he was always hanging around," Olive Carey reported. "I remember him saying, 'Get rid of that horse fly, will you?' Poor Bogdanovich—he gave him a *bad* time. Oh, Jesus! Nice guy, I like Peter, but he was one of those pestering guys, he just wouldn't stop [asking questions]."

Another example of Ford's malicious humor came when I asked him what he thought of Bogdanovich's book. "Pardon the expression, he's full of shit," Ford deadpanned. "I read the first three pages and threw it away. There wasn't a bit of truth in it. Instead of a character study, it was a caricature. What do you expect from a Yugoslav? Oh, he's a very good friend of mine, but as I repeat again [pointing to my tape recorder]—is this thing going? He's full of shit." Ford even affected ignorance of *Directed by John Ford*, saying of his trip to Monument Valley with Bogdanovich, "Well, if it was an interview, I didn't know it. I chatted with him up there. Was he filming it?"

Ford belied his own remarks by purchasing two hundred copies of the book to give to his friends and by twice making public appearances to take bows with *Directed by John Ford.* Following the world premiere at the Venice Film Festival on September 6, 1971, Ford was presented with the festival's highest award, the Golden Lion, in a ceremony at the Doge's Palace. That November, attending an invitational premiere held at the Directors Guild of America Theater in Hollywood, Ford accepted plaudits from various speakers, including California governor Ronald Reagan.

By then Bogdanovich had become Hollywood's hottest director with *The Last Picture Show.* The black-and-white period film, with its Fordian visual style and elegiac feeling, initiated a new wave of nostalgia that, in turn, helped make Ford's own films more accessible to a younger audience. Bogdanovich had invited Ford to visit him and Ben Johnson on the *Last Picture Show* location in Archer City, Texas. But those plans had to be dropped when Ford fell and fractured his pelvis.

"The most stupid accident," as he called it, occurred on October 15, 1970, when the seventy-six-year-old Ford tripped over a package of laundry on the steps of his own home. "And I'm a parachutist," he said ruefully. Ford was in traction at St. John's Hospital in Santa Monica until he went home on November 17. For several months after that he had to use a wheelchair and a walker. Although he was lucky to survive the pelvic fracture—such an injury often proves fatal to elderly people, particularly to alcoholics, with their depleted reserves of energy—this blow marked the beginning of the end for John Ford.

It probably was no coincidence that Ford suffered the incapacitating injury shortly after the death that September of Bill Ramsey. Distraught over the loss of the man he considered one of his closest friends, Ford wrote Katharine Hepburn that Bill "passed away in my arms." Waverly Ramsey subsequently retired from domestic service. She and Bill were replaced by another African-American couple, Oscar and Lizzie Tippins.

The American West of John Ford, broadcast on CBS TV on December 5, 1971, was thrown together in a matter of months by Dan Ford and three other producers under the influence of *Directed by John Ford* and Bogdanovich's interview book. The TV special is noteworthy for its filmed reunion between Ford and Henry Fonda, patching up their sixteen-year feud, and for some poignant glimpses of Ford reminiscing about happier times while visiting the site of the old Fox back lot (now Century City) and making his last trip to Monument Valley in June 1971. But the show contains some factual errors, such as John Wayne saying (twice) that the first time he ever worked with Ford was on *Stagecoach,* although their working relationship actually began in 1926 on *Mother Machree,* and Wayne's claim that no man or horse was ever injured on a Ford picture, even though Fred Kennedy, who was killed on *The Horse Soldiers,* is seen in a clip from his fight scene from *Rio Grande.*

During the preparation of his grandson's documentary, Ford had the opportunity to watch some of his old movies again. "When I saw some of those grand things I did when I was a young man, I was excited," he admitted. "Hadn't seen them since the day they were finished."

Ford's last piece of directing came that June during the making of the TV special in Monument Valley. Looking frail and shielded from the desert sun by an umbrella, Ford had fun staging a stunt with John Wayne being shot off a horse. Doubled in long shot by Chuck Roberson, Wayne landed hard on his rear end in the closer shot. Ford ordered crewmen to hurl dirt at the Duke and directed him to "rub your butt" after finding that he had landed on a rock. Ford could not help butting in on other scenes, saying to director Denis Sanders, "Denis! Denis! Would you mind a suggestion from a retired director?" and, "Denis, better get it quick. There's a half light on Duke. You're a lucky director to have it."

The two days of shooting in Monument Valley ended with a barbecue thrown by the Navajos in honor of Ford and Wayne. It was a nostalgic reunion for all of them, because it was the first time the director and his favorite actor had been back there together since *The Searchers.* Standing with Ford on the overhanging rock the Navajos call "John Ford Point," Wayne said, "I came back to reminisce, and I got the feeling that maybe Pappy came back to say good-bye." As it turned out, this was the last time either man went to Monument Valley.

Ford had one more Western he wanted to make there, *Appointment with Precedence.* Also called *The Josh Clayton Story,* it was to have starred Fred Williamson as the first black graduate of West Point to command a black cavalry unit. Because Ford still dreamed of filming Arthur Conan Doyle's novel *The White Company,* some of his associates referred to the Western as *The Black Company.* It was based on an original story by Robert Johnson, one of the black troopers in *Sergeant Rutledge.* There was a role for Woody Strode as a sergeant resentful of his new commander, and cameos for Stewart, Fonda, and Wayne.

Ford began working on the project toward the end of 1971, assigning James Warner Bellah to work on the treatment with Johnson. "I've been sitting around for a long time, and although my mind was working, my feet were beginning to itch," Ford told the *New York Times,* noting that the story not only had exciting action scenes but "exciting *ideas.*" There was some interest from Italian producers if the film could be made for under $2 million. Ford asked Wingate Smith to draw up a $1.5 million budget. Smith spent his final years in the business working on the *Green Acres* TV series and on commercials before falling ill with the leukemia that would kill him in 1974. He knew that Ford's budget was unrealistic but went through the motions to humor the ailing director.

Recognizing that he was a prophet without honor in his own country, Ford followed the lead of most rejected prophets: he thought of going into exile.

Ford's films were more popular in Italy than in the United States. Sergio Leone, whose films with Clint Eastwood had prompted the boom in "spaghetti Westerns," paid elaborate homage to Ford with his 1968 Western *Once Upon a Time in the West,* largely shot in Monument Valley with a cast including Fonda and Strode. Much in demand by Italian filmmakers, Strode lived in Rome much of the time between 1969 and 1973. He and Ford talked about working together in Italy or Spain. Ford found another screenplay, a low-budget Western with religious overtones. He wanted it rewritten to transform the white protagonist into Woody Strode, and he needed someone to put up the $20,000 purchase price. According to Ford, in the late summer of 1970, one of his representatives mentioned the director's interest in the script, and the asking price shot up to $50,000. Nothing more was heard of the project. In March 1972, *Variety* reported that Strode or Williamson would star in a Ford film called *The Grave Diggers,* an original by Bellah and his son James Jr. about Benjamin Davis, the first black West Point graduate to retire with the rank of major general. This was the last Ford project announced to the press.

"He wanted to work so bad," Dobe Carey remembered. "Working was like a vacation for him. He *loved* his work. When Hollywood wouldn't have him and he couldn't get a job, he actually called Walt Disney and asked him for a job. I think he was always interested in making *The Last Outlaw* again, even then. He wanted to make it with Duke. Oh, I wish it had happened. It would have been marvelous—Duke as an older guy, getting out of prison in the thirties. Duke always wanted to do it."

But after a while, Ford became resigned to his inactivity. One day at his home when he was told that a studio chief was calling, Ford said, "Tell him I can't come to the phone because I'm sitting here talking with my good friend Woody Strode."

The unmade Ford project that sounded the most promising was *April Morning,* the story of a teenage boy from New England who comes of age at the Battle of Lexington in 1775. John Wayne was to play the boy's father, a Massachusetts blacksmith. Perhaps a sense of guilt helped attract Ford to the 1961 novel by Howard Fast, who also wrote *The Last Frontier,* the uncredited source for *Cheyenne Autumn.* By 1966, when Ford started shopping the Revolutionary War project around Hollywood, Fast's political record was no longer an issue. Samuel Goldwyn Jr., whose father had produced Ford's *Arrowsmith* and *The Hurricane,* came aboard as producer of *April Morning.*

The script was by Michael Wilson, an ex-marine who was the principal screenwriter on *Friendly Persuasion,* William Wyler's film about a Quaker youth's baptism of fire during the Civil War. Wilson received no credit for that screenplay in 1956 because he was still on the Hollywood blacklist, but he was able to begin writing under his own name again in 1965. When I asked Ford about *April Morning* in 1970, he said, "Well, it's still coming. No company wants to do it. It's a great script. It's the best script I've ever read." Ford described the project as follows: "A boy and a man, a boy and his father. His mother. It's not really a battle story, it's a character sketch. The only historical character we use is Paul Revere."

Frank Capra, he added, had "a great story about Valley Forge, but nobody would go for it."

"Why?"

"These are an ignorant lot of bastards."

"Did they think the public wouldn't buy it?"

"No, they say, who the hell's interested in George Washington? I heard one producer say that to him. I says, 'I am, for one, and I know millions of other people are.' He says, 'Ah, that's dead fish, nobody's interested in the American Revolution.' I said, 'You ever read the *history* of the American Revolution?' He says, 'Hell no, I had better things to do.' I says, 'They didn't teach you in the sixth grade, when you graduated?' He says, 'What do you mean, I went through to the *eighth* grade.'"

In the late 1930s, Capra had wanted to film Maxwell Anderson's 1934 verse play *Valley Forge* with Gary Cooper as General George Washington. Columbia bought the film rights, but studio president Harry Cohn ultimately vetoed the project, partly because of the long-standing Hollywood belief that movie audiences aren't interested in the Revolutionary War but primarily because the looming war in Europe made it seem unwise to produce a film whose villains were the British. In March 1971, Ford and Capra decided to team up to film *Valley Forge* as a benefit for the Motion Picture Country House Relief Fund, as *How the West Was Won* had been for St. John's Hospital.[7] Capra was to direct the exteriors and Ford the interiors, with Ford receiving top billing. To keep the budget under $2 million, salaries were to be minimal, with numerous stars making appearances in small parts and Southern California locations

---

7. As so often happened in Ford's career, his brother Francis had been there first. In 1914, Francis directed the four-reeler *Washington at Valley Forge,* in which he played a spy trying to murder the general.

being used for battle scenes. Two major interior sets depicting Valley Forge were to be constructed at an ice-skating rink so that the actors' breath would be visible; the other major set, a Philadelphia ballroom, was to be built on a soundstage.

To help with the production, Ford and Capra initially enlisted Brigadier General Frank McCarthy, a World War II colleague of Capra's who had produced *Patton;* George C. Scott was asked to play Washington. By June 1971, however, Martin Rackin became involved as producer. Ford was so eager to make the film that he was willing to overlook the irritation he had felt toward Rackin during the making of *The Horse Soldiers* and his disgust over Rackin's 1966 remake of *Stagecoach.* Rackin wrote a five-page proposal for *Valley Forge* and submitted it to Cinema Center Films. Pitching the film as a major event for the upcoming 1976 U.S. bicentennial celebration, Rackin stressed that it would not be simply a flag-waving spectacle or an anti-British tract, but a human drama like *A Man for All Seasons* or *Patton* that would appeal to audiences of every political persuasion. Rackin tried to make the film seem relevant to the contemporary debate over war, peace, and patriotism by stressing the agonizing complexity of Washington's decisions and trials in the snows of Valley Forge.

Cinema Center Films showed interest, but Columbia balked at selling its film rights to *Valley Forge.* Ford tried to apply some pressure by giving an interview in November 1971 to Vernon Scott of United Press International: "We are having some troubles obtaining the rights to the property. But Frank and I would coproduce and codirect the picture [which was to have been billed as a John Ford–Frank Capra Production]. We've been friends for many years and there would be no conflict. Because the profits would go to the Country House, all the actors would work for scale. And so far we've had a great response from the stars. I'm looking forward to it."

Ford's other Revolutionary War project remained on his wish list until his retirement, but when I asked him, "What do you think the chances are of persuading them to let you make *April Morning?*" he replied, "Very slim." Fifteen years after Ford's death, Goldwyn and fellow executive producer Robert Halmi made *April Morning* as a TV movie with Delbert Mann producing and directing. Chad Lowe played the boy and Tommy Lee Jones his father.

Goldwyn, in a 1974 interview, blamed the widespread disillusionment toward American history in the Vietnam War era for his inability to find backing for Ford to direct *April Morning.* "It was a heartbreaking experience," Goldwyn told me. "Ford had wonderful ideas. He had so many ideas that were so bloody modern." They almost reached a deal at MGM, Goldwyn said, but it was scuttled by a studio executive with the following comment:

"There's no future in America."

That must have been the final straw for Ford. Even if he, in his own way, also despaired about America's future, hearing such a cynical dismissal of his nation's heritage must have made Ford feel that his contempt toward modern Hollywood was fully justified. "If that were John Wayne" hearing the remark, said Admiral Bulkeley, "you'd get a fist in your face."

The United States government always remained John Ford's most loyal employer.

In 1968, during the waning days of the Johnson administration, the United States Information Agency (USIA), the government's foreign propaganda arm, hired Rear Admiral Ford to serve as executive producer of a documentary justifying American involvement in the Vietnam War. *Vietnam! Vietnam!* is the most dismaying entry in the Ford filmography, a film that paints such a simplistic and often historically inaccurate view of America's most controversial war that even the USIA found it embarrassing. Although the location filming in Vietnam by director Sherman Beck was completed in December 1968, the jingoistic fifty-eight-minute documentary was not released until September 1971, and then only in a limited, halfhearted fashion.

Perhaps the most troubling aspect of this little-known episode of Ford's life is that privately he had a highly skeptical view of the Vietnam War. After making two trips to Vietnam in the winter of 1968 and the spring of 1969, Ford wrote his high school classmate Alnah Johnston, "What's the war all about? Damned if I know. I haven't the slightest idea what we're doing there." But when asked to lend his name and talents to the cause, Ford reflexively fell into the "My country, right or wrong" attitude of his service as a government filmmaker in World War II and Korea. Perhaps he was partly influenced by his characteristic attachment to lost causes, for by the time he joined up, seven months after the Tet Offensive, the Vietnam War was already widely regarded as a disaster for the United States and had split the nation into bitterly opposed camps of "hawks" and "doves." Once again, Ford had found the moment of defeat.

Vietnam! Vietnam! offers a graphic, often horrific view of the war's effect on the Vietnamese civilian population, but at the same time it promotes a simplistically prowar message, portraying the American involvement as an idealistic crusade to liberate a tyrannized agrarian people. There are striking visual and thematic similarities between *Vietnam! Vietnam!* and Ford's 1939 feature about the American Revolutionary War, *Drums Along the Mohawk*. But it seems to have escaped Ford entirely that America's intervention in a distant civil war against Communist guerrillas seeking to reunite their divided nation could hardly be compared with the American colonists' fight to free themselves from British rule. Ford's attempt to depict the Vietnam experience in such archaic terms was a sign of how seriously out of touch he had become with the changing contemporary world. In a provocative 1971 essay on Ford's politics in *The Velvet Light Trap,* Russell Campbell wrote, "Given time and detachment, Ford could conceivably create a tribute to the resistance of the Vietnamese people fully as powerful as his salute to the Cheyenne. Their dislocation is, if only Ford would see it, comparable."

But he would not see it, at least for public consumption. When Bogdanovich asked him in 1966 if the soldiers in *Fort Apache* were right to obey Colonel Thursday even though he foolishly led them to their deaths, Ford replied that the soldiers were right, because "he was the colonel, and what he says—goes; whether they agree with it or not—it still pertains. In Vietnam today, probably a lot of guys don't agree with their leader, but they still go ahead and do the job." Ford's comment characteristically oversimplifies his own far more complex film while showing how different his conscious attitudes often were from the subtler implications of his work.

If, as Andrew Sarris put it, Ford's willingness to make a film about the Korean War was "an act symptomatic of his downfall with the taste-makers," his willingness to make a film about the Vietnam War showed how utterly alienated he had become in only a few short years from the liberal audiences he had courted in such films as *Sergeant Rutledge* and *Cheyenne Autumn.* Ford's support for John F. Kennedy earlier in the decade gave way, in the years following the assassination, to public backing of former Kennedy rivals Barry Goldwater and Richard Nixon, and of California governor and future Republican president Ronald Reagan.

On his visit to France in 1966, Ford claimed he was a "liberal Democrat," and maybe somewhere in his heart he still was, but at home he talked and behaved like an archconservative. Ford said in France that he did not vote in the 1964 presidential election because "Goldwater didn't have a serious platform and I hated Johnson." But he admitted to Katharine Hepburn in 1973, much to her dismay, that he had voted for both Goldwater and Nixon in presidential elections. Asked in his 1968 BBC-TV interview what aspects of American society most dismayed him, Ford replied, "I'm worried about these [antiwar] riots, these students." He added, "I think our ancestors would be—can you say 'b-l-o-o-d-y'? I think they'd be bloody well ashamed of us if they saw us now."

Ford was capable of a more nuanced view of the trouble in the streets. Speaking to Bogdanovich in 1966, he drew a caustic comparison between the Los Angeles Police Department's suppression of the 1965 Watts riots and the U.S. Cavalry's attempt to stop the desperate flight of the Cheyenne in *Cheyenne*

Autumn. However, when it came to a contemporary foreign war involving the United States—even a new kind of "unconventional" war of counterinsurgency in which many Americans felt their country was on the wrong side—Ford reacted with knee-jerk patriotism, closing his mind to opposing views and acting as if the trumpet were summoning him back to serve in World War II.

John Wayne's anxiety to prove his patriotic bona fides in spite of his lack of World War II service led him to become a leading supporter of the Vietnam misadventure. In 1967, Wayne narrated a flag-waving Defense Department documentary about South Vietnam, *A Nation Builds Under Fire,* and starred in as well as codirected the cartoonishly hawkish feature *The Green Berets.* But unlike Wayne, Ford had nothing left to prove and nothing to gain from supporting the war so uncritically, except perhaps an emotional outlet. Ford's mindless bellicosity in that period may have been partly an angry response to his rejection by American audiences, critics, and studio executives. His alienation from liberal tastemakers and countercultural youth made him identify more strongly with the military than ever before.

Ford had done some consulting on a proposed film about Vietnam for the Defense Department's People-to-People series of orientation films in the late 1950s, before the United States assumed an active military role in that country. The USIA's Vietnam project, originally titled *Inside Vietnam,* was more propagandistic in intent than the People-to-People series, more like Frank Capra's aggressively rhetorical *Why We Fight* films from World War II. Sherman Beck, the director of *Vietnam! Vietnam!,* was a World War II veteran of the Army Signal Corps who had been directing USIA films since 1949. Beck told me in a 1972 interview that internal debate over the Vietnam project "got pretty hot. There were people in the USIA who did not want it made and there was tremendous friction—not friction, dissension—between people who wanted it made and people who didn't want it made." Beck said that unlike previous "soft-sell" films on Vietnam, *Vietnam! Vietnam!* was intended "to mount a more frontal attack on the entire subject."

Ford was brought into the project by Bruce Herschensohn, an outspoken hawk who at the time was director of the USIA's Motion Picture and Television Service. "In return for your advice and counsel on the film, we will pay you the rather dismal sum of $5,000," Herschensohn wrote Ford on September 3, 1968. "Your credit will read 'John Ford Presents (Title)' and also 'Executive Producer: John Ford.' These credits will be an immeasurable help to the success of our film and, more importantly, to the success of building respect for our policies. . . . P.S. If you want to go to Vietnam, you're invited."

Ford had not been eager to go to Vietnam. In May 1966, he wrote Michael Killanin, "The Navy wants me to do a temporary tour of duty [to give a seminar on filmmaking], and they gave me my choice between a place called Vietnam and the Mediterranean. They can request me back but they cannot order me back. Under the circumstances, I think I'd prefer the Mediterranean. I am tired of foxholes." The tour of duty to which he was referring was the 1967 cruise he spent largely with Bulkeley on the USS *Columbus.* By September 1968, Vietnam had become such a major battleground that Ford felt he could not refuse an offer to go there for his country. This time, however, he would not be going into the combat zone in uniform: the navy refused that request since it did not consider his duty with the USIA related to his status as a flag officer in the Naval Reserve, a decision he accepted with surprising equanimity. He went instead as a civilian working for the USIA.

Principal photography on the documentary began in Vietnam under Beck's direction on October 1, continuing for nine weeks; Ford's first visit to the country came near the end of that period. After Nixon's election on November 6, work on the film continued only "out of sheer bureaucratic momentum," a USIA official told Tad Szulc of the *New York Times.* In June 1971, the same month that postproduction was finally completed, Szulc reported that USIA director Frank Shakespeare had decided not to release the film because "the changing military and political situation in Vietnam, as well as domestic political considerations, now raised doubts on the film's value as convincing and productive propaganda."

The *Times* report may have embarrassed the USIA into releasing *Vietnam! Vietnam!* that September; otherwise it might have been left to a quiet oblivion. Although at the time the most expensive film the USIA had ever made ($252,751), it was shown by only twenty-nine of the agency's 176 posts during its first eight months of release. Retired by the USIA in 1975, the film has been cleared for domestic use since 1990, when a law was passed providing for USIA films to be made available to the American public twelve years after their overseas release.

The USIA's cautiously worded description of *Vietnam! Vietnam!* at the time of its release stated that it "deals exclusively with the decade of the 1960s and closes as of Dec. 31, 1969. It covers reasons why the United States and its Allies became involved in Vietnam and the problems arising from our involvement during the decade. It does not include current events in Vietnam nor the continuing de-escalation of our military participation subsequent to the 1960s. Its purpose therefore is historical."

Ford gave me a characteristically cryptic explanation of his creative involvement: "Just supervised it. Nothing to direct. What I did is generally went out there and said, 'That'd be a good thing to shoot, let's shoot that.'" Although there are some obviously non-Fordian visual elements in the film (zoom shots, telephoto lenses, rack focusing), many sequences seem very Fordian in emphasis, particularly those dealing with the war's disruption of families, farms, and villages, and the suffering of women, children, and old men. The concentration on civilians, rather than on military hardware and derring-do, in the film's first section, "Vietnam: The People and the War," is typical of Ford, and early sequences heavily romanticizing the pastoral life of the Vietnamese before the coming of war (the narrator refers to "the serenity of life and earth and family and prayer") are reminiscent of the introductory sections of such films as *Drums Along the Mohawk, December 7th,* and *The Civil War.* The second section, "Vietnam: The Debate"—a presentation of the debate between American hawks and doves, loaded to make the doves seem naive, glib, and even treasonous—is distressingly, but recognizably, in line with Ford's pronouncements about student protesters.

But while Ford exercised his influence on the project at every stage, particularly in postproduction, he did not direct any of it himself. "See, the problem was this—Vietnam was a tough go," Beck told me. "I covered the country like a blanket. Ford couldn't have done it physically. He and Herschensohn met before I was brought into the picture and it was decided that I would go over and come back with a story along the lines that were laid down by Herschensohn. I went with a three-man crew—a cameraman, an assistant cameraman, and a soundman. Ford came over to Vietnam to check the locations I had photographed and see if he wanted to add anything to it or request any additional coverage. . . . When Ford arrived in Vietnam, I met him at the airport and his comment was that he hates producers. He said, 'As far as I'm concerned, Sherm, you're the director. This is your film. I'm here to do whatever I can to help make it a good one.' I spent quite a bit of time with Ford at the Caravelle Hotel in Saigon when he arrived. We did a lot of talking up there in his room."

Both of Ford's grandsons served in Vietnam, Dan in the army and Tim in the merchant marine. "Of course, their grandmother is proud, but I shiver in my boots," Ford wrote Killanin. But he told me that while in Vietnam, "I had one very happy experience. I went up there and decorated my grandson, Daniel, my son's boy. He got the Silver Star and several Purple Hearts. He can do without the Purple Hearts, we've got enough of those in the family, but the Silver Star is a pretty high decoration for a kid up there, and they don't come up with the rations." Ford wrote in a letter shortly after his return that he had been flown to field headquarters by the army to decorate his grandson. However, Dan Ford reported that their rendezvous took place in the Caravelle Hotel and that he received no decoration from his grandfather.

Back in California, Ford engaged a journalist named Tom Duggan to help him outline the film. Duggan "actually spent more time than I did with Ford," said Beck. An ex-marine and former TV and radio talk show host, and a long-time editorial page columnist for Hearst's *Los Angeles Herald-Examiner,* Duggan was a flamboyant figure who relished political controversy. He hit it off well with Ford, who also had Duggan do some preliminary writing on his next film, his documentary about Chesty Puller (although the only writer credited on that film was Jay Simms, for writing the narration). Shortly after returning from his research trip to Vietnam, Duggan was injured in a car crash on the Pacific Coast Highway near Malibu on May 24, 1969, and died five days later at the age of fifty-three.

Ford "was completely responsible for the completion of the film," said Beck. "We turned in 60-odd thousand feet [eleven hours] of film which was edited and completed under his supervision. It was done by his editor, Leon Selditz, on the West Coast. I spent one week on the coast talking to Selditz, identifying footage." The newsreel footage, including the entire second half of the film, was selected and edited by Ford and Selditz. Charlton Heston, who served as head of "Democrats for Nixon" before switching sides officially, was recruited to narrate the film in his best orotund manner.

Vietnam! Vietnam! is not entirely an aberration in Ford's career—Raymond Durgnat, describing Ford's view of history as "the homeric American white-wash," referred to *Drums Along the Mohawk* as *Drums Along the Mekong*—but it tends to exaggerate certain tendencies in Ford that are usually restrained by aesthetic and historical distance. One reason Ford's war propaganda films are so much less complex than his war dramas is that his instincts are so much finer than his conscious attitudes. *The Battle of Midway* is Ford's finest documentary, and one of his greatest films, precisely because it minimizes rhetoric and propaganda and simply observes the realities of aerial attack, battle fatigue, and homesickness. By contrast, the scenes of civilian suffering in *Vietnam! Vietnam!* are used to stir audience outrage against the Vietcong, and follow the propagandistic tradition of placing great stress on the enemy's abuse of women and children. Nevertheless, the film's atrocity scenes are so appalling, and the combat scenes so unromantic, that even the most fervent hawk would be forced to reflect on the obscenity of war.

The South Vietnamese in this film could best be compared to Ford's "good" Indians in *Drums Along the Mohawk*: their folkways are presented with reverence, fascination, and dignity, yet there is an undertone of condescension and distrust that eventually is translated into political terms when the American "advisers" arrive. The implication is that the Vietnamese are basically a simple, pacific people whose northern family branch has been led astray by evil outside agents (i.e., the Soviets)—remarkably similar to the way the bad

Indians in *Drums* are manipulated by evil John Carradine into fighting for the British. Ford's explanation of black unrest in the United States was just as simplistic: he said in his 1968 BBC-TV interview, "They're being influenced from outside. Some other country . . . and the poor Negroes are getting the blame."

"Establishment" antiwar figures such as Senator J. William Fulbright, Senator Ernest Gruening, and Dr. Benjamin Spock are treated with relative respect in the second part of the film, but the student protesters and their anti-establishment candidate for president, Senator Eugene McCarthy, are treated with outright contempt. Footage of a U.S. antiwar march is counterbalanced with romantically staged shots of South Vietnamese soldiers marching and singing as the narrator says, "In South Vietnam, there were other parades where cries of 'Hell no, we won't go' were nonexistent; for without defense their families and country would live no more."

Although the antiwar side is allowed to speak out in what the narrator calls "[a] great free debate, perhaps the greatest of all time," their statements are directly answered by such figures as former presidents Dwight D. Eisenhower and Lyndon Johnson, Dean Rusk, Nelson Rockefeller, and Ronald Reagan. After Fulbright calls the Vietnam War "the kind of peripheral struggle" that should be engaged but "isn't of the kind of importance that would cause great nations to go to an all-out war," Ford cuts to Eisenhower saying bluntly, "If you're going to fight a war, I believe in winning—because you're losing lives. And this is one thing that ought to be the number-one priority. And whenever you get into a war, my own ideas are, get everything you can, as fast as you can, use everything you can and get it over with." Taken to its logical conclusion, this exchange would seem to imply that the U.S. should have used nuclear weapons in Vietnam.

The longest, and last, statement by a politician in the film is an excerpt from a speech by President Nixon at the United Nations, beginning, "Since I took office as president, no single question has occupied so much of my time and energy as the search for an end to the war in Vietnam. . . ." The film does not acknowledge Nixon's violation of his 1968 campaign pledge that he had "a secret plan" to end the war: his secret plan proved to be a prolongation of the war with intensified air power while bringing home the troops and ending the draft in order to neutralize the antiwar movement. The emphasis the film places on Nixon's speech and the dilemma of American prisoners' wives, a major propaganda theme of the Nixon administration, is a clear indication of the political metamorphosis the film underwent during the long editing process.

But by 1971, even the USIA realized how simplistic *Vietnam! Vietnam!* seemed as the United States went into the final stages of its so-called Vietnamization program, abandoning South Vietnam to the hopelessly inept, de-moralized, and corruption-riddled Saigon army and a desperate escalation of American air power. *Vietnam! Vietnam!* made "a lousy final chapter" for Ford's career, Sherman Beck regretfully told me in 1972.

"The guy is so old now that it's difficult to see in him the greatness that was there for his entire working life. I think the Old Man's rather lonely. We worked out there on the Goldwyn lot, and while we worked in the cutting room Joel McCrea would wander in and [director] Tay Garnett would wan-der in. All these older guys who are part of the history, they're still around and they're lonely, unhappy people because they feel they no longer are function-ing in the industry they love. This is one of the things that characterizes Ford."

The last film Ford directed was his sentimental documentary about his tent-mate in Korea, Lieutenant General Lewis Burwell "Chesty" Puller, USMC (Ret.), history's most decorated marine. Originally intended as a television special, *Chesty: A Tribute to a Legend* began filming at Puller's home in Saluda, Virginia, in August 1968, and finished shooting on April 8, 1970, when John Wayne's hosting segments were filmed on the Old Tucson set of Howard Hawks's Western *Rio Lobo* (also the last film in Hawks's career). After receiv-ing a single public showing in 1976, *Chesty* was finally released to the home video market several years later.

James Ellsworth, a Virginia businessman who became wealthy making plas-tic straws, produced *Chesty* in association with Dyna-Plex, Inc. of Newport Beach, California, and Robert H. Davis. Ellsworth earlier had tried to produce a feature film based on *Marine!*—the 1962 Puller biography by Burke Davis, to which Allan Dwan had been attached as director before his retirement. Ford and Wayne volunteered their services on the documentary, which Ford said he directed "out of friendship for Chesty." The $144,000 budget was guaranteed in part by Ellsworth's investment in another picture called *Door to Door Maniac*, starring country singer Johnny Cash; the final cost of *Chesty* was reported by Ellsworth as $225,000. Ellsworth talked in a staccato voice at a breakneck pace, and Ford, who had serious hearing problems under the best of circumstances, admitted that he never could understand what his producer was saying.

Wearing a cowboy outfit as he hosts this overly elliptical and impressionis-tic documentary, Wayne calls Puller "a sweet, tough, gentle, hard-boiled" ma-rine. If that paradox had been more fully explored, *Chesty* might have amounted to something more than reveristic montages of mostly impersonal war footage (some from Ford's *This Is Korea!*) interspersed with visual grace notes of Chesty sadly wandering around in retirement. Resembling a gruffer version of Charles Winninger's Judge Priest, the bulldog-faced general is sim-ilarly portrayed as a gallantly anachronistic old-timer who has been unfairly snubbed for being too outspoken. Puller's poor physical condition, the result of several strokes, makes this point in painfully graphic terms.

When the day came for Puller to be interviewed on camera, he was distraught because it was not long after his son, Lewis Jr., was severely wounded in Vietnam on October 11, 1968. Serving as a marine lieutenant commanding an infantry platoon, Lewis lost both legs and fingers on both hands in the explosion of a booby-trapped howitzer round. He later wrote a powerful memoir, *Fortunate Son: The Autobiography of Lewis B. Puller, Jr.* (1991), which won the Pulitzer Prize for biography.

"Trying to get Chesty to get some life into it," as cinematographer Brick Marquard put it, Ford inserted himself in the scene at Puller's home so he could ask his questions face-to-face. But Ford, seen only from the back, never asks Puller about his son, and Lewis Jr. is not even mentioned in the documentary, which was completed and copyrighted in 1970. Asked what impact his wounding had on his father, Lewis Puller said that "it almost killed him." As for himself, he said, "I tried to follow in his footsteps and it had disastrous consequences." The omission of this aspect of Chesty Puller's life is a sign of the film's failure to grapple with the troubling implications of its subject matter. Lewis B. Puller Jr. committed suicide in 1994.

Chesty gave Ford one last opportunity to sentimentalize over the lost cause of the Confederacy. Chesty's grandfather, Confederate Major John W. Puller, was killed with J. E. B. Stuart in a cavalry battle at Kellys Ford during the Civil War. As a result, Chesty "had an almost mystical respect for many of [the Confederacy's] generals and wished that he could have apprenticed with them," his son recalled. A few lovely shots stand out in *Chesty* to remind one of the poetry Ford could summon up from simple situations: long shots of cadets marching at Chesty's alma mater, the Virginia Military Institute in Lexington, Virginia, acquire a haunting resonance as the young men turn into silhouettes by marching into a deep foreground shadow, an image recalling the march of the boy soldiers in *The Horse Soldiers.*

Later in the film, some VMI cadets march past the elderly Puller standing beside a cannon. After Chesty returns their salute, his body sags and his face turns melancholy, just like Captain Brittles after he takes his final salute before retirement in *She Wore a Yellow Ribbon.* Other scenes of Chesty in Lexington—visiting the tomb of his boyhood hero Stonewall Jackson and Robert E. Lee's tomb in a chapel on the Washington and Lee University campus—also have great elegiac force. The musical score by Jack Marshall (father of future producer-director Frank Marshall) effectively uses such familiar Fordian tunes as "Red River Valley" and the Civil War–era "Bonnie Blue Flag" and "Lorena," as well as the marine marching song, "The Halls of Montezuma."

The extent to which Ford saw Chesty Puller as a sentimental projection of himself, cast aside by a country that no longer valued its heroes, is made clear in the parade sequence near the end of the film. This old man's dreamlike reverie—fulfilling the wish Puller made on his retirement, "to see once again the face of every marine I ever served with"—is similar to the quasi-mystical finale of the West Point cadets marching to honor Marty Maher in *The Long Gray Line*. Ford and Marquard used six cameras to film the lavish Marine Corps tribute to Puller on January 28, 1969, at the Marine Barracks in Washington, D.C.

As Puller watches the marines marching past in the cold winter light, Ford's voice is heard saying, "Standing behind the cameras, amidst all the panoply and glory . . . I looked at Chesty's face. In his eyes I could read his thoughts—the thousands of men he had commanded in peace and war—the battles he had won—trying to recall the faces of his boys—above all the great sadness of leaving his beloved Corps. There were tears in the eyes of many—especially in mine."

Chesty: A Tribute to a Legend ends with a shot of Wayne on the Western set bidding adieu to Puller—and Ford's filmmaking career—by saying, "They say old soldiers never die. Good luck, old soldier. We need men—*heroes*—like you in this country today." But the impression this film leaves with a thinking viewer can be summed up in the famous line from Bertolt Brecht's play *Galileo*, "Unhappy the land that needs heroes."

Ford directed Wayne's segments at Old Tucson the day after the actor received his Academy Award for Henry Hathaway's *True Grit*. As the fat, drunken marshal Rooster Cogburn, Wayne wore an eye patch like Ford's. When Wayne returned to work on *Rio Lobo*, all the people on the set had their backs turned to him. They turned around to reveal that they all were wearing eye patches—as was Wayne's horse. While sitting around the set watching Wayne working with Hawks, Ford would turn to the crew and say, "Look at that famous Academy Award winner now. He does it in one take. When he worked for me, it took fifty."

Two versions exist of Ford's *Chesty:* the original runs an hour and the release version runs twenty-eight minutes. When I asked Ford if he was pleased with the original version, he said, "Well, as a matter of fact, it's too long. We had to pad it too much. The first three-quarters are great, then we have to pad it a little bit. The finish is really good. I'm very pleased with it, yes." The long version allows the battle footage to run at excessive length, particularly in a montage near the end that supposedly reprises Chesty's career but has little relevance to the subject. After failing to attract a buyer despite being cut in half by Ford's editor and associate producer, Leon Selditz, *Chesty* languished on the shelf for several years. In the meantime, Chesty Puller died in October 1971 at age seventy-three, three years to the day after his son's mutilation in Vietnam.

In December 1974, I decided to try to raise some interest in *Chesty* by writing an article about the film in *Daily Variety*. Still no buyer emerged, so I arranged for *Chesty* to have its world premiere at the Los Angeles International Film Exposition (Filmex) in Century City on April 4, 1976. Unfortunately, the screening backfired. Filmex scheduled it at eleven on a Sunday morning on a double bill with *The Candidate,* a film that guaranteed a young, liberal audience. No introduction or explanation was offered to the audience of what they were about to see. From the first sight of John Wayne in his cowboy outfit, sporadic outbursts of uneasy laughter marred the event. At the end there were boos, mingled with applause from a few diehard Ford aficionados. The headline over my review in weekly *Variety* provided a stark epitaph for Ford's illustrious filmmaking career:

"Anti-Climax: John Ford Booed."

A notoriously difficult interview subject throughout his lifetime, but never more so than in his old age, Ford "was likely to want to talk about his socks more than about his work," Colin Young observed. I experienced that frustration firsthand when I spent an hour trying to interview Ford in August 1970.

At the time I was twenty-three years old and working as a reporter for the *Wisconsin State Journal* in Madison. Since the previous fall, I had been writing a critical study of Ford's films with Michael Wilmington. My July 2 letter to Ford requesting an interview had gone unanswered, so I called his office on August 4 from a pay phone in the *State Journal* lunchroom. When Ford came on the line, he sounded surprisingly cordial. I told him we were writing a book about him, and he growled, "My God! What for? You certainly picked a dull subject."

He picked up my letter and said he hadn't looked at his mail for a month. Playing the professional Irishman in approaching him, I had added "County Mayo" in parentheses after my name, and Ford read the words aloud, accenting the last syllable as the natives do. Warming up, he told me that his people had come from a neighboring county, Galway, and that his wife was a McBride. Then I really laid it on, mentioning that one of my ancestors had come to America after deserting from the British army.[8] Telling me about *his* ancestor who he claimed had deserted from the British army during the Rev-

8. Actually, as I later learned, the first of my ancestors to emigrate from Ireland to North America, James Gavin of County Armagh, deserted from the British *navy.* Conscripted in England, he jumped ship when it arrived in Newfoundland in 1820, assuming his mother's maiden name, Carey, to avoid recapture. Other ancestors of mine came from County Mayo, including my great-great-grandparents Patrick Flynn and Bridget Foy, sister of the vaudeville star Eddie Foy Sr., whose children performed with him as "The Seven Little Foys."

olutionary War, thirty years earlier than mine, Ford said, "Well, if your name's McBride and your ancestor deserted from the British army, you're all right." Then he said I could have the interview since I had "the proper ethnic background," adding, "Otherwise I'd tell you to go to hell."

On August 19, I arrived at Ford's office on a busy thoroughfare in Beverly Hills. The surprisingly spartan suite was located on the first floor of a nondescript office building at 321 S. Beverly Drive. I was welcomed by Ford's secretary, Rose Lew, a friendly but understandably skittish woman who bore a striking resemblance to Dorothy Jordan in her role as "Stonewall," John Dodge's secretary in *The Wings of Eagles.* Not realizing that Ford kept most of his trophies at home, I had expected to find his office, like Dodge's, crammed with memorabilia. A few items did stand out: paintings of Monument Valley and of Ford in his admiral's uniform; a photograph of the USS *Columbus,* inscribed by "your friend and shipmate" Johnny Bulkeley; and portraits of James Cagney and Will Rogers.

Dour and unruly, Ford was wearing deck shoes with rubber soles, baggy off-white trousers, and a blue shirt with his belly poking through the buttons. His remaining white hair was sticking out in every direction. His eye patch hung askew over his left eye, and his remaining eye fixed me with a basilisk stare—when he looked in my direction, mainly when he was irritated. There was a hum of activity inside the office. People were being ushered in and out, phones were ringing, letters were being thrust into his hands, but the bustle had a melancholy cast: this was a director who hadn't been able to make a feature for nearly five years.

During our hour together, Ford repeatedly asked his secretary if a phone call had come through from "the Italian gentleman, or the gentleman from Italy." As I discovered later while reading through his correspondence, the call he was hoping to receive involved the Italian Western he wanted to make with Woody Strode. Ford's impatience and gruffness with me was understandable. I did not realize that I had arrived in the midst of one of his final attempts to set up a deal for a movie. Surely one of the most irksome things that could have happened at this vexing moment in his career was for some kid to come into his office and pepper him with questions about his past and his future.

The session began on a cordial note, with Ford showing me snapshots of his wife and himself at their golden anniversary celebration on July 6 at the John Ford Chapel of the Motion Picture Country House and Hospital. Carroll Baker, who was living in Rome at the time, had arranged for a special blessing to be sent by Pope Paul VI. During the ceremony, the Fords exchanged their wedding vows for the third time. Afterward they greeted friends at a reception and cut pieces of a towering wedding cake.

When I handed back the pictures, Ford pulled open a drawer and proferred a cigar. Stupidly, I said I already had one, then tried to make up for my faux pas by saying, "Mine's only a nickel cigar." To which he replied, "Well, these are seven-and-a-half-cent cigars." He spat bits of his cigar into a wastebasket next to his desk, and when he took a pill ("My wife's gonna call and say, 'Be sure that Mr. Ford takes his pill' "), he stuck out his tongue and gargled in mock disgust.

Then Ford started quizzing me about my background. He asked me where I had gone to college, and when I said the University of Wisconsin, he startled me by asking, "Is that Madison or Ann Arbor?" I wondered if he was going senile or perhaps putting me through some kind of unnerving test. Then he asked what *village* I was from in County Mayo. Mortified, I confessed that I couldn't remember. Ford looked at me as if I were the reincarnation of Cromwell himself. But I didn't understand why his mood had turned so sour until I saw *The American West of John Ford* more than a year later.

In a segment of the TV special filmed the week after my visit to his office, Ford told Henry Fonda, "I had a kid, somebody come out the other day, came in fear and trembling to interview me. So I put him right at ease, I says, 'I don't like to be interviewed, I never liked interviewers.' . . . But he said he was from County Mayo, so we got along fine until I found out he *wasn't* from County Mayo, he was from *Iowa!*" Fonda commented, "The result, I gathered, satisfied him, but didn't give the writer much material to work with."

Ford cut in, "I didn't tell him *anything*."

Using his partial deafness as a ploy to avoid answering questions he didn't feel like answering, Ford perversely had me sit on his deaf—and blind—side, and made me shout questions several times ("I'm deef as hell in this ear, you know"), even spelling out words, to get them across. If you have to shout a question over and over, you begin to wish you had never asked it.

A prime example of Ford's stonewalling techniques came, probably not co-incidentally, when I brought up one of his most politically controversial films, saying, "You gave an unusual treatment of the cavalry in *Fort Apache*."

Ford replied, "I don't remember what the hell it's all about."

"It's kind of a Custer's Last Stand. With Henry Fonda."

"Oh, that's right, yeah. Yeah, it's all right."

"I understand that John Wayne felt uneasy about being in *Fort Apache* because he thinks Custer was a disgrace to the cavalry."

"Oh, that's a lot of crap. I don't think he's ever heard of Custer."

After some more chat along these lines, I asked a question that really seemed to rankle him:

"What did you think of Wayne finally getting the Oscar after so many years?"

"Isn't that rather a useless question?"

"Well, did you see *True Grit?*"

"Unh-unh. I was *delighted* when he won it. I went out and pioneered, campaigned for him and everything else. Come on, Mac, for Chrissake, those are stupid questions. For a man from Mayo, whose forebears are from Mayo, to ask . . ."

As the hour wound down, I could see that Ford was eager to get back to work. I told him, "I'm sorry I asked some silly questions."

"Well, it isn't that, but everybody asks the same questions, all you people, and I'm sick and tired of trying to answer them, because I don't know the answers. I'm just a hard-nosed, hard-working . . . ex-director, and I'm trying to retire gracefully."

"So you don't like people asking you about your old movies?"

"No, I've forgotten them, I don't know what they're about. I'm just trying to live out my life in peace and comfort and quiet. So I'm going to say *au revoir,* God bless you, County Mayo *go deo* [forever]. . . ."

"*Eirinn go bragh* [Ireland always]."

"County Mayo *go bragh.*"

When I turned off the tape recorder, Ford said he appreciated my visit but added, "This is positively the last interview I'm going to give." (In fact, he wound up doing a few more.) As a farewell present, I gave him a copy of a book I had edited two years earlier for the Wisconsin Film Society Press, *Persistence of Vision: A Collection of Film Criticism.* I opened it to the dedication page, which read "To John Ford." He lifted his eye patch and held the book close to his face to read those words. Dropping his veneer of brusqueness, he seemed genuinely touched, telling me, "Oh, that's sweet."

The dream of all Ford interviewers was that he would suddenly let down his guard to become voluble and eloquent, answering every question freely, thoughtfully, and expansively, sharing his inner thoughts, his philosophy of art and life. That almost never happened. But Austrian novelist Peter Handke made it come true by presenting an idealized "interview" with Ford in his 1972 novel *Der kurze Brief zum langen Abschied* (*Short Letter, Long Farewell*). For Handke's protagonist, a German visitor making a pilgrimage from Boston to Los Angeles, Ford is a modern-day shaman because he has a vision of the American Dream that is in danger of being forgotten: "I'm going to ask him to tell me what he used to be like and how America has changed since he stopped making pictures."

While painting Ford's home in Bel Air with somewhat fanciful detail in the book's closing scene, Handke captures the metaphorical truth of the aged director's surroundings, an incongruous oasis of old-fashioned Americana in the midst of an alien landscape. Ford is attended by a mute and crippled house-keeper, an Indian woman who acted in some of his pictures, and by his wife, described as being from "a family of Irish immigrants who had settled in Maine." Mary plays "Greensleeves" on the harmonium in his bedroom. The atmosphere outside is ominously heavy with approaching rain and flashes of lightning over the surrounding hills; dark shadows fall over the grass in Ford's garden as he smokes a cigar and muses about his country and its people. "We hardly dream at all any more," regrets Handke's Ford. "And when we do have a dream, we forget it. We talk about everything, so there's nothing left to dream about."

Ford reflects on the mysteries of personality and public image: "There are postures that make you feel like yourself. 'Yes,' you think, 'this is really me.' Unfortunately you're usually alone when that happens. Then you try it with people around and you're not yourself anymore, you fall into a pose. That's no good. It's ridiculous. It's your thoughts you want people to get a glimpse of, not your idiosyncrasies. One day you tell the truth, and you're startled. You're so happy you can't bear it; you try to tell the truth again, and then of course you lie. . . .

"Whenever I hear people talking about me, I have a feeling that it's too soon. My own experiences aren't far enough back. I'd rather talk about what other people have experienced before me. That's why I've always preferred to make pictures about things that happened before my time. I don't feel much nostalgia for my own past; what makes me nostalgic is things I never got around to doing and places where I've never been."

And yet, as alluring as this image of Ford might be, I still prefer the flinty, defiantly unyielding reality, the man who simply made great works of art while refusing to demystify the process. As the painter Pierre Auguste Renoir once observed, "The trouble is that if the artist knows he has genius, he's done for. The only salvation is to work like a laborer, and not have delusions of grandeur."

Shortly after returning home from the Venice screening of *Directed by John Ford,* Ford began his long farewell.

Suffering from abdominal pain so severe that he could no longer avoid see-ing his doctor, Ford underwent exploratory surgery that October of 1971 at St. John's Hospital in Santa Monica. The doctor found a massive inoperable malignancy, diagnosed as a form of colorectal cancer, specifically cancer of the rectum. After the operation, which Ford almost did not pull through, he was told that his illness was terminal. He was also suffering from atherosclerotic heart disease, blockages in the arteries of his heart.

Wingate Smith was hospitalized at the same time Ford underwent his surgery. Smith was suffering from the leukemia that would kill him in 1974. John Wayne "licked the Big C" after being diagnosed with lung cancer in 1964, but his wheezing on one lung was painful to witness on-screen, and he would succumb to metastatic stomach cancer in 1979. Ford was terribly shaken by Wayne's initial bout with the disease. Keeping vigil at the hospital with Wayne's wife, Pilar, Ford said in a broken voice, "He is like a son to me." Pilar recalled that Ford "tried to give me what little strength he had left. But he couldn't hide the fear in his eyes. . . . We both knew the glory days were gone. The Ford bunch had ceased to exist."

"All those guys weren't taking care of themselves physically," Admiral Bulkeley noted in 1987. "If John Ford had the same [colorectal cancer screening] examination every year that I have to have, whether I like it or not, to be fit for duty, if he caught it early enough, Ford probably would have been around today."

When Ollie Carey paid visits to the dying Ford at Copa de Oro, "He was in bed, still smoking that silly-ass cigar, chewin' on it. Last time I saw him, it was pretty rough." When she left the house, she broke down uncontrollably on the way to her car. In Ford's final months, she said, "He was unhappy, he was miserable, he was in pain all the time."

On May 18, 1972, Jack and Mary purchased a multiple grave plot at Holy Cross Cemetery in Culver City, in a rolling green valley near the graves of his brothers Francis and Edward. Late that year the Fords sold their home and, with Barbara going along to help care for them, moved to the desert near Palm Springs. They bought a six-bedroom, Spanish-style home in Palm Desert with the aptly named address of 74-605 Old Prospector Trail. Oscar and Lizzie Tippins went along to care for them. Ford underwent regular outpatient chemotherapy treatment at the Eisenhower Medical Center in nearby Rancho Mirage.

Asked why she and Jack moved to the desert, Mary said in 1977, "I developed Parkinson's disease, and Jack broke his hip. And we had a house with a beautiful winding stairway, a beautiful place. We loved every inch of it, but neither of us could go up or down stairs, so we had to get a place on one floor. And so many of our friends had retired and moved out here. . . . He always loved the desert. You can tell by his Monument Valley work. I'm just glad he didn't move us to Monument Valley! He said, 'Well, let's take a look at Palm Springs.' And our friend Frances Rich—[actress] Irene Rich's daughter—has a place down here, and she and Katie Hepburn were here, and they said they'd look around and see what they could find, and they phoned us that they'd found this house. So we just wandered down here, and Jack got real sick and couldn't be moved. Barbara hates and despises it—not much to do for a young person."

Ford spent his remaining days in a hospital bed in his air-conditioned bedroom, attended by nurses on three shifts around the clock. Usually he kept the curtains drawn against the heat and the outside world for which he now had little use, but when the curtains were open he could see the hills to the south, surrounding the Torrez Martinez Indian Reservation. In the room, which stank of cigars and illness despite air conditioning, Ford kept a few of his personal totems, such as a statue of the Virgin Mary with burning votive candles and a silver-mounted black saddle on a sawhorse. Much of his time was spent reminiscing with old friends who came to visit, including other retired filmmakers who lived in the area, such as Howard Hawks, Frank Capra, Henry Hathaway, and Clarence Brown. William Wyler, George Stevens, Robert Parrish, and Peter Bogdanovich also came to call. Even Henry Fonda paid a visit ("[N]ice man, Hank," Ford remarked). Next to his bed Ford kept a plastic bucket filled with half-smoked cigars. He would rummage around in the bucket for a suitable butt, then politely offer the bucket to his visitor.

In March 1973, Dan Ford began assembling material for the official family biography, *Pappy,* which did not appear until 1979, the same year Andrew Sinclair published the first Ford biography. Mary convinced Jack to cooperate with his grandson's project. In a series of audiotaped interviews with Dan, Barbara, actress Elizabeth Allen, and others, Ford offered some of his most relaxed and candid reminiscences.

Katharine Hepburn also helped prod his memories when she came to spend a week in Palm Desert. In their extraordinarily moving, wide-ranging conversations, Ford listened with fascination as Hepburn shrewdly drew him out on the complexities of character that made him such a multifaceted artist. Drawing comparisons with Spencer Tracy's equally perverse Irish temperament, she observed that for both men, their artistry was a refuge from the difficulties of everyday life. "The easiest thing Spence did was act," she said. "I'm sure the easiest thing John did was to direct."

Admitting that he had a personality in perpetual conflict with itself, Ford told Hepburn with equanimity, "I took life as it came along." With warmth and humor, he expressed admiration for her unconventional approach to life, as well as gratitude for their friendship that reached back four decades.

"Now you're so sweet to everyone," she teased. "This is not your true self."

Ford was chosen in February 1973 as the first recipient of the American Film Institute Life Achievement Award, given annually since then to a filmmaker "who has in a fundamental way advanced the art of filmmaking in America and whose work has stood the test of time." Calling Ford "the most important director since the late D. W. Griffith," the AFI honored itself by honoring Ford at a time when his reputation was at a low ebb with audiences and critics, although not with many of his fellow filmmakers.

Orson Welles, Ingmar Bergman, Akira Kurosawa, Frank Capra, Howard Hawks, Elia Kazan, Samuel Fuller, and others described Ford as the greatest living director; Sam Peckinpah and Arthur Penn emulated his work even while boldly challenging it with their revisionist Westerns; the American cinema's brightest newcomers, such as Martin Scorsese, Steven Spielberg, and George Lucas, regarded Ford as one of their masters; and Sidney Lumet declared, "There's one general premise: almost anything that any of us has done you can find in a John Ford film."

But the AFI tribute on March 31, 1973, was something of a fiasco, thrown together hastily when President Richard Nixon agreed to attend the event at the Beverly Hilton Hotel in Beverly Hills. Nixon's primary business in California was meeting with the president of South Vietnam, Nguyen Van Thieu, at San Clemente. Nixon's presence at the Ford tribute, although a heartfelt expression of his admiration for the director and his work, left an aura of political controversy around Ford's last hurrah. Several thousand people, including Jane Fonda and Tom Hayden, staged an antiwar protest outside. Ford himself made controversial statements in support of Nixon.

The program, televised by CBS two days later as *The American Film Institute's Salute to John Ford,* was slipshod. Standing in front of a salmon-pink curtain through which the United States Marine Band could be seen, master of ceremonies Danny Kaye told long, irrelevant stories and introduced other entertainment that seemed inappropriate to the recipient. When Leslie Uggams appeared, Ford could be heard saying loudly, though not on the air, "Who is *that?*" Uggams proceeded to serenade John and Mary Ford with the theme song from the trendy French film *A Man and a Woman.*

A more fittingly nostalgic serenade was a medley of Irish songs from *The Quiet Man* sung by Maureen O'Hara. John Wayne, James Stewart, and Jack Lemmon were among those who paid warm tributes to "Pappy." Others among the nine hundred dinner guests included an impressive array of Hollywood and political figures, ranging from Cary Grant, Fred Astaire, Clint Eastwood, and Steven Spielberg to Ronald Reagan, Barry Goldwater, and Henry Kissinger, whose date for the evening was Liv Ullmann.

The tribute was strangely short on clips from Ford movies. A montage produced by Peter Bogdanovich did not appear until more than halfway through the program, and Bogdanovich publicly complained that it had been severely edited for television. Although a montage of Ford's japery from *Directed by John*

Ford was also included, reaction shots of the honoree during the tribute were scarce on the broadcast, probably because he was so obviously dying, a breach of etiquette for a prime-time television entertainment program. It seemed that the AFI and CBS regarded both Ford and his work as something of an embarrassment.

The authentic life achievement award party was held before the AFI dinner in Ford's hotel room, for some members of his Stock Company who could not afford the $125 ticket price, including Olive Carey, Anna Lee, and Danny Borzage. Richard Widmark also dropped in before heading to the ballroom. Ollie recalled that Ford "was having a glass of wine and he was a little loaded, goofy, from pills. They'd filled him full of tranquilizers, evidently. Then he got up at [the dinner] and he really and truly didn't know where he was. Pitiful." She said that when she watched the event on television, "I cried like a baby because I hated to see him up there—just horrible."

Bogdanovich felt Ford was putting on something of an act for the cameras: "The funny thing is—and this is only a feeling of mine—I do not believe finally that *he* cared very much. Certainly he made damn sure to get through the evening all right—a great effort, for he was already very ill by then; he made the appropriate speech and the proper signs of emotion. . . . But I could swear the tear was not there and the rest of it just a gallant performance. . . . He knew he was dying and that none of this really mattered; he had created what he could, and all the rest was show."

About ten days after the show, when the Fords were back in Palm Desert, his Life Achievement Award was returned for repairs. Somehow the Silver Star from the AFI had become smashed out of shape.

J ohn Ford is one of my heroes in every sense of the word," former president Richard Nixon wrote me in 1988. When Ford and Nixon entered the Beverly Hilton ballroom for the AFI tribute, Nixon generously departed from protocol and let Ford precede him. As the Marine Band played "Hail to the Chief," Ford was pushed along in his wheelchair by his chauffeur, Oscar Tippins. It was as if this son of an immigrant Irish saloonkeeper had become president for a night.

Ford's relationship with Nixon was not always as warm as it was that night. Although Ford had supported the Eisenhower-Nixon ticket in the 1952 election and continued to vote Republican through the rest of the decade, he evidently voted for fellow Irish Catholic John F. Kennedy in the 1960 presidential election. But Ford's philosophical affinities with Nixon were rekindled during the Vietnam War era, when he became an emotional supporter of the embattled president. According to Admiral Bulkeley, Ford visited Nixon in

Washington on more than one occasion "in the very early part of the presidency, the first term, here in Washington. Nixon being from California, he had an interest in Hollywood."

In those meetings, Bulkeley said, Ford "used to taunt Nixon quite a bit." Taunting was characteristic Ford behavior, even with officials in high places. But it may also have reflected a certain lingering ambivalence toward Nixon as well as resentment over being excluded from Nixon's inner circle. In early 1969 while working on *Vietnam! Vietnam!* Ford actually lobbied to become an aide to the newly elected president. He enlisted George Murphy, the former Hollywood song-and-dance man who had become a Republican senator from California, to write navy secretary John H. Chafee on his behalf. Chafee responded to Murphy on March 6, 1969: "Your admiration of one of our most distinguished and loyal Americans, John Ford, is equally shared. His desire to achieve the designation of Naval Aide or Assistant to the President of the United States on an honorary basis is fully understandable.

"Unfortunately, appointments of this nature are not within the purview of my office. The President selects his aides and provides the names of these officers to the appropriate military service so that the administrative details may be completed. In the absence of a request from the President, I do not believe it would be appropriate for me to nominate Admiral Ford for a position on the White House staff.

"We are, however, deeply appreciative of Admiral Ford's contributions to the Navy, and of your interest in his behalf."

Nixon's decision to attend the dinner in Ford's honor came in the wake of the Paris peace agreement that finally began the process of ending the Vietnam War and during the mounting Watergate crisis that would end his presidency sixteen months later. If Nixon was, in one sense, wrapping himself in Ford's reputation like a flag to help ward off his enemies, it's also true that the embattled president was reaching out to Ford for emotional and spiritual sustenance, trying to gain strength from the great filmmaker who symbolized America's better aspirations. Not everyone, of course, had come around to that view, and it was a bitter irony that Ford's status was rising at a time when he could no longer work. While conservatives admired Ford all the more for being out of fashion with the intellectual establishment, and while some on the radical left admired him for his subversive streak and questioning of American mythology, for many in the middle it would take Ford's death to make him acceptable by removing his work from the clamorous context of contemporary political issues.

As part of the AFI ceremony, President Nixon awarded Ford the nation's highest civilian honor, the Medal of Freedom. The citation read as follows:

In the annals of American film, no name shines more brightly than that of John Ford. Director and filmmaker for more than half a century, he stands preeminent in his craft—not only as a creator of individual films of surpassing excellence, but as a master among those who transformed the early motion pictures into a compelling new art form that developed in America and swept the world. As an interpreter of the Nation's heritage, he left his personal stamp indelibly imprinted on the consciousness of whole generations both here and abroad. In his life and in his work, John Ford represents the best in American films and the best in America.

In his remarks at the dinner, Nixon called Ford "a great man, one of the geniuses of his profession," adding that "there are rare occasions—and this is one of them—when [the president] speaks for *all* the people." Although AFI director George Stevens Jr. had noted earlier in the evening that many of Ford's films no longer exist, Nixon declared, "I'm an unabashed movie fan. I think I've seen virtually all of the 140 [*sic*] movies."

And in a clumsy attempt at wit, Nixon said of Ford, "I have noted tonight that he has been characterized in several different ways. Some have called him 'Boss,' and others have called him 'Jack,' and most have called him 'Pappy.' But there was one term that I did not like. They called him a '*Rear* Admiral.' John Ford was never 'Rear.' And as commander in chief of the armed forces, [I declare that] for the balance of this evening, John Ford is a full admiral." Ford had tried unsuccessfully in 1969 to receive such a promotion, and he seemed mostly amused by the temporary promotion on the TV show, applauding but shaking his head. When Nixon told him sotto voce, "I don't have the admiral's cap with me," Ford facetiously replied, *"Aww."* But Ford was greatly appreciative when Nixon later had an admiral's hat sent to his home.[9]

Ford made two brief acceptance speeches, one for the AFI award and one for the Medal of Freedom. In neither speech did he speak of his art, remaining adamant to the end that his films should speak for themselves.

Holding a cigar, he admitted that he was "overcome with gratitude" to receive the award from the AFI. "I wish I had the words to express my feelings, but I don't. . . . Tonight is the most momentous occasion in the history, in the

9. That April 27, Ford was honored for his navy films with the U.S. Navy's Distinguished Public Service Award. Assistant Secretary of the Navy Robert D. Nesen presented the award at Ford's home in Palm Desert.

annals, of motion pictures. Tonight [for] the first time, the chief executive of our nation has honored a public motion picture event with his presence. This is a night long to be remembered—it certainly will be by me. Thank you, Mr. President. You have added dignity and stature to our image."

Accepting the Medal of Freedom, Ford referred to the recent return of the first American POWs from Vietnam since the signing of the peace agreement, and he quoted the first man who stepped off the hospital plane at Clark Air Force Base in the Philippines, Navy Captain Jeremiah A. Denton Jr.

When the gaunt men marching in pairs were handed over to the U.S. government in a televised ceremony on February 12, 1973, it was like a homecoming scene in a John Ford movie. Denton, after seven years as a POW, said, "We are happy to have had this opportunity to serve our country under difficult circumstances. We are profoundly grateful to our commander in chief and to our nation for this day." He added, in a shaky voice, "God bless America." Before his election to the U.S. Senate in 1980, the Alabamian chronicled his Vietnam experiences in the 1976 book *When Hell Was in Session,* which was made into a 1979 TV movie starring Hal Holbrook.

Addressing Nixon after the president fastened the Medal of Freedom around his neck, Ford said, "Thank you, sir. As Captain Jeremiah Denton said (hope I get through with this, I'm about ready to bust out in crying), as Captain Denton said as he set foot for the first time in many years on continental American soil [*sic*], 'I'm stunned and bewildered at this reception.' He ended with, 'God bless America.' I quote his words with feeling. . . .

"In a recent telephone conversation with the president, he said, 'What is your reaction to the prisoners coming home?' I said, 'Frankly, sir, I broke down, I blubbered and cried like a baby. Then I reached for my rosary and said a few decades of the beads, and I uttered a short little prayer—not an original prayer, but one that's spoken in millions of American homes today. It's a simple prayer—it's simply, "God bless Richard Nixon." ' Thank you."

As Tag Gallagher so eloquently put it, Ford's "God bless Richard Nixon" seemed incongruous with his satire of Nixon's Checkers speech in *The Last Hurrah,* "but Nixon was president, and needed blessing."

In his White House diaries, Nixon's chief of staff H. R. Haldeman evaluated Ford's speech in the brutal terms of realpolitik. After noting that "Ford did a magnificent job" of rising to the occasion physically, Haldeman wrote that the director's tribute to Nixon was "an extremely impressive moment, and one that nobody there, I don't think, will ever forget. It really stuck it to the anti-Nixon types in the film crowd."

On June 18, Bruce Herschensohn, who had sponsored Ford's *Vietnam! Vietnam!* at the USIA and was now serving as a Nixon staff member, wrote in a memo to the president: "As you know, Rt. [Retired] Rear Admiral John Ford has cancer. Two nights ago his health was failing so fast he was given the Last Rites, but he made a tremendous comeback yesterday and I spoke to him on the phone last night. He sounded his old self and kept repeating to me, 'President Nixon is the greatest President. No one can put a shadow over what he has accomplished. This visit with [Soviet President Leonid] Brezhnev [who had arrived in the U.S. on June 16] is more important that all those hypocritical [expletive deleted in memo] in the Senate [Watergate] Committee and the media who are out to get him. They're going to fail. He's a great, great man.'"

That July, when Nixon was lying ill with viral pneumonia at Bethesda Naval Hospital, he called Ford at his home in Palm Desert. This was the period when the existence of the White House taping system was being revealed. Nixon said, "I was lying here and I couldn't sleep, and I thought I'd call and chat with John." Following their conversation, Ford sent Nixon a get-well message. Nixon replied, "I have always felt that the best medicine of all—and I might add, the easiest to take—is the kind wishes from friends, and I am deeply grateful for your expression of goodwill." Adding his "appreciation and warmest personal regards," he signed himself "RN." This letter of August 16, 1973, is the last piece of correspondence in Ford's files before his death.

I asked former president Nixon to give me his thoughts on Ford for this book. Dated January 6, 1988, the manuscript he sent me is titled "Reflections on John Ford":

> Unfortunately I was not privileged to know John Ford personally as well as I would have liked. But I feel that I knew him intimately through the motion pictures he produced. If I had a choice today between a rerun of any John Ford motion picture and the current Academy Award winner, I would choose his.
>
> What made his pictures great? Some say the message. Others say the quality of the picture apart from any message. I would answer the question in a different way. All of John Ford's pictures had a message. But unlike many current pictures which emphasize a message, the message in his pictures never overwhelmed the movie. For example, it is impossible to see some of the currently popular anti-Vietnam movies without coming away with the conviction that the message was so powerful and so politically biased that it overwhelmed the movie.
>
> John Ford was to motion pictures what Tolstoy was to literature. *War and Peace* and *Anna Karenina* both had powerful messages but they would have been great novels without the message. All

of John Ford's movies had powerful messages. But all of them would have been great movies without the message.

What was the message which characterized John Ford movies? They all stood for what are now considered to be unfashionable, square values—honor, courage, character, decency, the good guys win, the bad guys lose. But the greatness of John Ford is that he eloquently demonstrated the fact that his movies could celebrate those unfashionable, square values without being smarmy or mushy. He also proved that a movie can be great without being dirty. Yet his sex scenes were far more powerful than those in today's movies, which proceed on the false assumption that the way to make sex appeal powerful in a movie is to make it more explicit.

I came to know John Ford during the Vietnam War years while I was in the White House. Polls have indicated that over 90 percent of Hollywood's best writers, producers, actors, and directors were passionately opposed to the war in Vietnam. The John Waynes, the Bob Hopes, and the John Fords were considered to be rather strange aberrations from this generally fashionable view.

I vividly recall a telephone conversation I had with John Ford when I informed him that I was coming to California to present the Medal of Freedom to him. We both knew that his illness was fatal but one would never know it from the strength of his voice and of his convictions. He was particularly moved by the scenes of the POW's coming home. He congratulated me for the strong policies which he felt had contributed to bringing them home. His last words were, "No amnesty for the draft evaders."

Some critics will say that this indicates that he was a hard-hearted, bloodthirsty warmonger. They totally miss the mark. He hated war, as I did. But he knew that in Vietnam, in spite of some mistakes that were made in conducting the war, America's goals were noble ones. He knew too that those who did their duty and went to Vietnam deserved praise, not condemnation. He was appalled that the Mayor of New York had said, "Our best young men went to Canada." What appalled him was not the fact that they fled to Canada in order to evade the draft. He understood why any young person would not want to go to Vietnam and get his butt shot off. What he objected to was their pretensions of higher morality—their looking down on those who did serve, the "dummies" who went to Vietnam and got their butts shot off. He believed as I did that our best young men went to Vietnam—even though they were not the best educated or the wealthiest or members of what would generally be described as the elite class, the brightest and the best in our society.

I don't see many Hollywood motion pictures these days and I am sure that there are some good ones. But what concerns me as I believe it would have concerned John Ford, is the tendency for many Hollywood pictures to reflect life in Hollywood rather than life in the United States. Many movies are sick because those who write, produce, direct, and act in them are sick. It just isn't considered fashionable to portray the old virtues that John Ford stood for. Even more important, it isn't considered to be commercial. This new negativism pervades the elite classes not just in Hollywood but in New York, Washington, and the other great financial and corporate centers of the United States.

A goody-two-shoes portrayal would not be a true picture of America. But I would suggest that Hollywood moviemakers would be well advised to travel through America and see what it really is—the good, the bad, and the ugly, with the good prevailing over the bad and the ugly by a factor of ten to one.

John Ford in his life and in his motion pictures celebrated courage, loyalty, honor, strength, sacrifice, patriotism. He did it so well that people by the millions flocked to see his movies. What America and the world needs today are more John Fords who share his values and reflect them in their work.

Like so many other observers before and since, Nixon saw what he wanted to see in Ford's work. Viewing Ford's films as an uncritical celebration of American history and traditional American values is, of course, a gross oversimplification. Ford needs to be rescued from the excesses of some of his admirers, including those who would prefer to "print the legend" rather than facing more complex truths about Ford and his country. But people who admire or dislike Ford's films must also take into account that Ford can be embraced—for more or less valid reasons—by those on all sides of the political spectrum, from Richard Nixon, Ronald Reagan, and Wild Bill Donovan to Sergei Eisenstein, Jean-Luc Godard, and Oliver Stone.

What made Ford a great popular artist is that he reflected so many facets of the people he addressed. He was able to do so because he had so many warring factions within himself. Like Whitman, he "contained multitudes." In the final analysis, Ford's artistic personality has to be seen as one of perpetual conflicts, contradictions, and paradoxes. If he never entirely resolved the issues that obsessed him, if he often seemed to dispute himself and sometimes acted against his own principles and ideals, that was part of the fuel that powered his creativity. What made him such a flawed human being was also what made him such a great artist. Those who expect artists to be ideal human beings fail to understand the nature of art. Often the greatest art comes out of torment, and some of the most important artists, such as Mozart and Tolstoy and Ford, lived in a riot of complication and frequent public absurdity. In Ford's case, his films are usually far more complex than his public stands were on the issues of his time.

William Butler Yeats could have been commenting on Ford when he wrote, "We make of the quarrel with others, rhetoric, but of the quarrel with ourselves, poetry."

The last gathering of the John Ford Stock Company took place on May 28, 1973.

Ford went to the Motion Picture Country House and Hospital in Woodland Hills for his final Memorial Day ceremony at the John Ford Chapel. He mustered up the strength to give the eulogy for the dead of his Field Photo unit. Among those paying their respects at the reception afterward were the ninety-four-year-old Donald Crisp, Anna Lee, Harry Carey Jr., Wingate Smith, Ray Kellogg, James Basevi, Carleton Young, and Mark Armistead. It was a warmly emotional reunion with a classic Fordian ending. While the reception was still in progress, Ford walked out the door on the arm of his chauffeur, Oscar Tippins, nobody noticing that he had gone, like Ethan Edwards walking away from his family at the end of *The Searchers.*

Alex Ameripoor, an Iranian-American cinematographer, went to the reception so he could meet his favorite filmmaker. "I said a few things to Ford," he recalled, "but of course he didn't hear me. I said, 'I'm sitting in the presence of history.' And he replied, '*What?* What do you mean?' After I repeated the statement twice, Ford finally got the point and looked at me as if saying to himself, 'Big deal.'" Ford had a more emotional farewell with his longtime character actor Frank Baker, a resident of the home. Ford had a drink of Scotch in Baker's bungalow before being wheeled back to his car and saying, "Well, I guess this is it. I'd like you to know that you're one of the very few people I ever respected. You never crawled on your belly to me."

Ford had signed his last will and testament at the Beverly Hilton Hotel on the day of his Life Achievement Award tribute. Under his legal name of John A. Feeney, Ford cut his son out of his inheritance, an act that raised eyebrows in the press and caused unhappiness among his family. Scott Eyman's Ford biography reports that Pat had written his father a letter "saying that Ford should not accept the Medal of Freedom from Nixon, that the President was sure to be impeached over Watergate, and that to associate with a criminal-to-be would negate any honor he might bestow." Until then, Ford and his son had a "quasi-relationship," Eyman writes. "Whenever Jack got mad at Pat, he would threaten to cut him out of the will, and Pat would respond by saying he had a county pension anyway. . . . The letter about Nixon changed everything." Shortly before the AFI ceremony, Dan Ford was in his grandfather's suite at the Beverly Hilton, helping him get dressed for the dinner. John Ford went into another room for a closed-door meeting of about fifteen minutes with his lawyer and business manager. "It was at that point, I believe, that Pat was cut out of the will," Dan Ford told Eyman. "It was never changed back." With the exception of a $10,000 bequest to Pat's daughter, Mary Blue, Ford left his estate in trust to his wife. Upon the widow's death, the remaining amount was to be divided equally between Barbara and his two grandsons; Dan and Tim were to inherit Barbara's share when she died. Shortly after Ford's death, Mary signed her own will, bequeathing part of her estate to Pat.

But there was not a great deal of money left. Even though Ford had earned an annual income of well over $200,000 for many years, his money had not been wisely invested, other than in his limited portfolio of blue-chip stocks. When the will was filed for probate, the estate was estimated at $500,000, excluding real estate. In 1976, Mary filed suit for $4.1 million against the executors of Ford's will, claiming that they had sold family assets at less than their true worth and had drawn up the will in such a way that taxes ate up most of the estate. Ford had never been much interested in money or very shrewd about its management and uses. He liked a comfortable home well stocked with books and liquor, he liked to wander on his boat, and he loved to work with as much freedom as he could muster within the Hollywood system. The rest, for him, was beside the point.

The last project to bear Ford's name was *Cowboy Kings of Western Fame: John Ford's Series of Famous Western Stars,* a portfolio of portraits of twenty-four Western movie stars by artist Will Williams, "presented" by Ford. Completed in the fall of 1973 and sold for $120 in a limited edition of five hundred copies, with Mary receiving a 10 percent royalty, the portfolio was of mediocre quality, but dabbling with it on his deathbed gave Ford some sentimental pleasure. He was able to pay tribute to such old friends as Harry Carey, Hoot Gibson, Tom Mix, Buck Jones, George O'Brien, Will Rogers, Ward Bond, James Stewart, and John Wayne.

In a posthumous message accompanying the portfolio, Ford wrote simply, "I consider myself very fortunate to have known all of these stars personally and I was privileged to direct most of them."

Ford was a past master at staging death scenes. His last months in Palm Desert, receiving a succession of friends at his bedside, provided him with a finale as grandly dramatic and even humorous, in its own way, as Frank Skeffington's epic deathbed scene in *The Last Hurrah*. In the words of one visitor, Katharine Hepburn, Ford faced death "like a gentleman. With great distinction."

But it took courage for him to behave with such grace and humor. The metastasizing cancer was eating him away. The side effects of terminal cancer and chemotherapy include nausea, loss of appetite, and inability to properly digest food; as a result, Ford suffered from malnutrition and anemia. He drank some Guinness stout every few hours to fortify himself and help ease the pain. But otherwise he refused painkilling medication until about two weeks from the end. His Catholic faith, casual though it may have been throughout most of his life, helped sustain him. A sense of justifiable pride in his accomplishments and his knowledge that he was surrounded by a small but loyal community of old friends buoyed his spirits and enabled him to face death with a certain serenity.

Admiral Bulkeley and Mark Armistead visited Ford about six months before his death. Asked how Ford handled his impending mortality, Bulkeley responded with military sangfroid: "We never mentioned it. You don't talk about those things. You *know* those things, you don't talk about them. He accepted it and recognized that it was terminal."

To Dobe Carey, who saw Ford about six weeks before he died, the Old Man was more emotionally open: "He was great. He would mention the fact that he was dying. He said, 'I'm dying, for Chrissake, at least you can . . .'— you know, he'd make a joke out of it. I asked him if he was in pain, and he said no. But you couldn't tell. He wouldn't say if he was."

When Ollie Carey called on the phone, Ford "sounded pretty good. He said he was gonna be all right. But he wasn't." Hepburn made cheery calls from England, where she was filming *A Delicate Balance*. Lindsay Anderson visited Ford in the desert, and Barbara told him, "It's only a matter of time. He's had the last rites: and last week we thought he'd gone. He had a giant hemorrhage and they rushed him to hospital in the middle of the night, but he fought his way out of it. He insisted on coming home."

Peter Bogdanovich, in Rome that summer directing *Daisy Miller*, called Ford several times. The last time they talked was on August 27. When Bogdanovich asked how he was doing, Ford said gamely but with painful effort, "Pretty well."

"I knew he didn't have long—he sounded so frail and helpless," Bogdanovich later wrote. "If you had seen or heard him on the set in control of eight hundred actors and technicians, it would have broken your heart."

"Much as I grieve for him," Anna Lee told me shortly after his death, "I was so thankful he went when he did, because there was practically nothing left of him. I had his arm and it was just like holding a bone in the sleeve of his coat."

When she saw Ford for the last time, two weeks before he died, she told him, "I love you, Sean Aloysius," and he said, "And I love you, Boniface." During the funeral mass, she remembered the difficulty she once had crying for a scene in one of his movies: "I told him, 'Sean, I'll cry at your funeral.' And, by God, I did."

"Jack was quite a guy," Howard Hawks recalled. "I saw more of him than anybody, almost, in his last few months because I'd just drop over to the house. He spent most of his time looking at old, old Westerns on television—you know, those cheap Westerns that were made in about a week. And he was still bright; he kept his senses. The last time I went out to see him [on August 28], he said good-bye to me. I walked out and stopped to speak to his daughter, and he yelled, 'Is Howard gone yet?' She said no. 'I want to see him!' He said, 'I want to say good-bye to you.' I said good-bye. He yelled again, 'Is he still there?' And he said, 'I want to say *good-bye* to you.' So I called Duke Wayne and said, 'Duke, you'd better get down here. I think he's going to die.' Duke got a helicopter and came down here, and the next day he died."

When Wayne visited on August 30, Ford greeted him by saying, "Do you miss Ward?"

"I sure do, Jack."

"Well, you're probably on the deathwatch, anyway," said Ford.

"No, you're the coach, you're the author, you'll bury us all."

"Well, I'll try to stick around a little while longer."

They drank brandies together while sharing jocular memories of Bond and their Young Men's Purity, Total Abstinence, and Yachting Association. Keeping up such bonhomie took heartbreaking effort, for as Wayne said later, "It's rough to put a fellow away that you spent forty-five years of your life with, in close communication."

Woody Strode arrived the next day from Italy, not long before Ford's death. Ford "was so tough I didn't believe he could die," Strode would write. But now the seventy-nine-year-old Ford "couldn't have weighed more than fifty pounds, his hair was all gone, his face looked like a skull. . . . He was propped up in bed having his last drink of whiskey. I said, 'Papa, I just got off the plane. Thanks for the telegram.' And I sat there on the side of his bed for six hours, holding his hand until he went into a coma."

John Martin Aloysius Feeney, known to the world as John Ford, died at 6:35 P.M. on August 31, 1973. Shortly thereafter the bulletin came over the Associated Press wire, hailing him as "the greatest American director of the sound film era, as D. W. Griffith was acknowledged the master of the silent movie." It was then that one could say of Ford, as Auden wrote of Yeats, "[H]e became his admirers."

"It was a beautiful death," Ford's sister Josephine Feeney told me at the West Hollywood mortuary where his body was lying in state, a tattered flag from the Battle of Midway draped over the closed coffin. "Jack knew we were all there, and there was no suffering. . . . He fell asleep about five o'clock and slept very quietly until the end." Also with him at the end were his wife and two children; his nephew, Father John Feeney, who had been a chaplain in Vietnam; and a nurse, Irene Maroni.

"He died in my arms," Woody Strode related to me. If not literally true, that was a very Fordian way of describing the death of the dauntingly powerful but emotionally vulnerable man to whom he was so loyally devoted. "His sister and I took an American flag and draped him in it. We got some brandy, toasted him, and broke the glasses in the fireplace."

Following a funeral mass celebrated by Timothy Cardinal Manning of Los Angeles at Blessed Sacrament Catholic Church in Hollywood on September 5, Ford was buried at Holy Cross Cemetery. Strode thought, "He should be buried in Monument Valley."

Although attended by many Ford Stock Company members and several of his fellow directors, the ceremonies were largely bereft of Fordian touches. But a soloist sang "The Battle Hymn of the Republic" as the coffin left the church, and as the mourners filed out behind it, the organist played "Bringing in the Sheaves," the tune Danny Borzage played on his accordion every morning when Ford arrived on the set. I searched Los Angeles flower shops for a cactus rose and finally found a small one to take to the church. Before the service, I placed it with the other flowers around the altar, but when the larger floral displays were taken to the cemetery, my cactus rose was left behind. At the graveside, a navy rifle squad fired a salute, a bugler blew taps, and Dan Ford, wearing his army uniform, presented the folded Midway flag to the widow.

As the coffin was being lowered into position over the open grave, hanging on chains from the jaws of a bulldozer, one of the grave diggers lost his grip and took a flying pratfall into a bouquet of flowers. "A bit of Fordian comedy," whispered Alex Ameripoor as we stood among a small group of people watching John Ford's body sinking into the grave. When Mary died in 1979, the grave was opened and Ford's coffin temporarily removed until it could be reburied with hers.

Fittingly for a man who loved to leave mystery and contradiction in his wake, there are three differing accounts of John Ford's last words.

One version is suitably solemn and Catholic, while the other two are earthy and irreverent. Just as Ford was the sum of his contradictions, it's possible that all three versions of his curtain line are true. Different people probably heard him say different things at different times as they came and went from the bedroom where Ford acted his final scene, trying out different endings to see which played best dramatically.

At the rosary vigil the night before Ford's funeral, Father Feeney told the congregation, "Stories of this man are legion, but I think the one which best sums up John Ford was what happened last Friday after he went into a coma. As we began saying the rosary, we heard his voice come out and say:

"'Holy Mary, mother of God . . .'

"This was a man who had dined with presidents and kings, and at the end it was his rosary beads clutched in his hands which gave him hope and consolation."

But others who were there that day insisted that the last words spoken by Ford came at the end of a mass celebrated at his bedside by Father Feeney. When the father put an "amen" to it, Ford asked:

"Now will somebody give me a cigar?"

Those were reported as Ford's last words in my *Sight and Sound* article on Ford's death, "Bringing in the Sheaves," and, in slightly different form, by Peter Bogdanovich in his *New York* magazine article "Taps for Mr. Ford."

But Dobe Carey, Ford's most intimate chronicler, offered a third version, related to him by Patrick Ford:

"Pat said that on the day Ford died, he had been in a coma for about six hours. He was still breathing. So they were just waiting for him to die. Evidently he had quite a peaceful passing. And the priest—now, Pat swore this is true—was standing at the head of the bed doing the last rites. He was going on and on and on. Pat said the Old Man's eyes opened and he went:

"'Cut!'"

SOURCES

Abbreviations used in these sections include: JF for John Ford (John Martin Feeney); AFI, American Film Institute; AMPAS, Academy of Motion Picture Arts and Sciences; Anderson, Lindsay Anderson, *About John Ford* (London: Plexus, 1981, and New York: McGraw Hill, 1983); Davis, Ronald L. Davis, *John Ford: Hollywood's Old Master* (Norman: University of Oklahoma Press, 1995); DF, Dan Ford, *Pappy: The Life of John Ford* (Englewood Cliffs, N.J.: Prentice-Hall, 1979); DFZ, Darryl F. Zanuck; DV, *Daily Variety;* FF, Francis Ford; Gallagher, Tag Gallagher, *John Ford: The Man and His Films* (Berkeley: University of California Press, 1986); HCJ, Harry Carey Jr.; HCN, *Hollywood Citizen-News;* HR, *Hollywood Reporter;* JFP, John Ford Productions; JM, Joseph McBride; JW, John Wayne; KH, Katharine Hepburn; *LAE, Los Angeles Examiner; LAHE, Los Angeles Herald-Examiner; LAT, Los Angeles Times;* Levy, Bill Levy, *John Ford: A Bio-Bibliography* (Westport, Conn.: Greenwood Press, 1998); Lilly, the John Ford papers at Indiana University's Lilly Library, Bloomington, Indiana; MF, Mary McBride (or McBryde) Smith Ford; *MPW,* the *Moving Picture Weekly;* n.a., no author listed; n.d., no date available; McNee, Gerry McNee, *In the Footsteps of* The Quiet Man (Edinburgh: Mainstream Publishing, 1990); M&W, Joseph McBride and Michael Wilmington, *John Ford* (London: Secker & Warburg, 1974; and New York: Da Capo Press, 1975); *NYT,* the *New York Times;* OH, oral history conducted by Dan Ford (Lilly); ONI, Office of Naval Intelligence; OSS, Office of Strategic Services; PB, Peter Bogdanovich, *John Ford* (London: Movie Magazine Ltd., 1967; Berkeley: University of California Press, 1968 and 1978 editions); R&O, Randy Roberts and James S. Olson, *John Wayne: American* (New York: Free Press, 1995); SDG, Screen Directors Guild (later the Directors Guild of America); Sinclair, Andrew Sinclair, *John Ford* (New York: The Dial Press/James Wade, 1979); SWG, Screen Writers Guild (later the Writers Guild of America); USN, United States Navy; USNR, United States Naval Reserve.

References to books and articles are listed fully the first time; subsequent references include only the author's last name (and, in the case of more than one book or article by a single author, the title).

EPIGRAPH

Ford's comment is from an interview by Walter Wagner in *You Must Remember This* (New York: G. P. Putnam's Sons, 1975).

INTRODUCTION: MY SEARCH FOR JOHN FORD (PP. 1–13)

During his high school days, John Feeney was referred to as "Bull" in various Portland (Maine) newspaper articles and articles in the Portland High School magazine, the *Racquet*. "They used to call me Bull Feeney," JF said in Patricia K. Gould, "John Ford Seeks 'Real Story' for Movie on Maine Visit," *Portland Press Herald,* June 7, 1947. The nickname was explained in Michael J. Lafavore, "John Ford: The Quiet Man from Portland," *Maine Life,* July 1976, and by his teammate Oscar Vanier in Toby Mussman, "Shades of Feeney: It's a Festival of Ford!" *Maine Sunday Telegram,* November 1, 1970. The phrase "the human battering ram" is quoted in DF from contemporary newspaper coverage of his grandfather's exploits.

Ford's comments to the author are from JF to JM, n.d. (November 1971), and an August 19, 1970, interview, parts of which were printed as JM, "County Mayo Gu [*sic*] Bragh . . . ," *Sight and Sound,* Winter 1970/71, and in M&W. JF's remark "I didn't tell him *anything*" was made to Henry Fonda on *The American West of John Ford* (CBS-TV, 1971).

JF's comments "The truth" and "I've led" are from Wagner. JF's niece Cecil McLean de Prida said in her OH that JF's father thought he would become a priest. JF's comparison of "The Irish and the colored people" is from George J. Mitchell, "Ford on Ford," *Films in Review,* June–July 1964. JF described William Jack as "the typical Yankee schoolteacher" in his OH, quoted in Levy. JF's "Look at the eyes" is from "John Ford" (interview), *Focus!,* October 1969, and "The secret" from JF/Barbara Ford OH, quoted by Gallagher; Barbara's comment on her father's eyes is in Sinclair. JF's confession that "I pose as an illiterate" is from an unpublished conversation with Hedda Hopper, April 13, 1962 (AMPAS), quoted in Gallagher; JF made the same remark publicly to Vernon Scott in a UPI dispatch, November 19, 1971. JF's explanation, "I simply direct pictures," is from his speech at a 1953 Republic Pictures ceremony; the untitled speech manuscript (Lilly) is quoted in DF.

Gallagher's comment on JF is from his book, as are the quotes from Frank Baker: "The real John Ford" was drawn from an unpublished 1977 interview by Anthony Slide and Robert Gitt, "Frank Baker"; "was always unhappy" is from Gallagher's own interview with Baker, as is FF's observation on JF. Sources of comments by other people on JF include Mary Astor, *A Life on Film* (New York: Dell, 1972); Philip Dunne, *Take Two: A Life in Movies and Politics* (New York: McGraw-Hill, 1980); Thomas Flanagan, "The Irish in John Ford's Films," Michael Coffey, ed., and Terry Golway, *The Irish in America* (New York: Hyperion, 1997); DF; PB; Alexander Jacobs, quoted in M&W; Lord Killanin in McNee; Robert Nathan, from an interview with the author; Darcy O'Brien, "Jack Ford and George O'Brien, A Long Voyage Home," *Recorder,* Fall 1996; Andrew Sarris, *The John Ford Movie Mystery* (Bloomington: Indiana University Press, 1975); and Milburn Stone, from Davis. The quotation from Walt Whitman is from his 1855 preface to the first edition of *Leaves of Grass.*

CHAPTER ONE: "'TISN'T THE CASTLE THAT MAKES THE KING" (PP. 15–36)

Jean Renoir's comment on Ford (epigraph) is from "About John Ford," *Action!,* November–December 1973.

Books on Irish and Irish-American history used for this chapter include *The Parliamentary Gazeteer of Ireland* (Dublin, London, and Edinburgh: A. Fullerton, 1844); Donal F. Begley, ed., *Irish Genealogy: A Record Finder* (Dublin: Heraldic Artists Ltd., 1981); Coffey and Golway, *The Irish in America;* David Fitzpatrick, *Irish Emigration 1801–1921* (Dublin: Dundalgan Press, 1984); Mr. and Mrs. Samuel Carter Hall, *Hall's Ireland,* first published 1841–43, condensed edition ed. by Michael Scott and published by Sphere Books Ltd. in London, 1984; Tom Hayden, compiler and ed., *Irish*

Hunger: Personal Reflections on the Legacy of the Famine (West Boulder, Colo.: Roberts Rinehart, 1997) (including Tim Pat Coogan's essay "The Lessons of the Famine for Today"); Robert Kee, *Ireland: A History* (London: Weidenfeld and Nicolson, 1980); Samuel Lewis, *A Topographical Dictionary of Ireland* (London: S. Lewis & Co., 1837); F.S.L. Lyons, *Ireland Since the Famine* (London: Weidenfeld and Nicolson, 1971); Kerby A. Miller, *Emigrants and Exiles: Ireland and the Irish Exodus to North America* (New York: Oxford University Press, 1985); Thomas H. O'Connor, Marie E. Daly, and Edward L. Galvin, *The Irish in New England* (Boston: New England Historic Genealogical Society, 1985); Cathal Póirtéir, ed., *The Great Irish Famine* (Dublin: Mercier Press, in association with Radio Telefís Éireann [RTE], 1995); and Cecil Woodham-Smith, *The Great Hunger: Ireland 1845–1849* (London: Hamish Hamilton, and New York: Harper & Row, 1962). Liam O'Flaherty's novel *Famine* (London: Victor Gollancz, 1937), dedicated to JF, was reprinted by David R. Godine in Boston, in a 1982 edition with an afterword by Thomas Flanagan.

Emigration figures are from Lyons and Miller. The saying "driven out of Erin" is quoted in Miller. The RTE documentary *When Ireland Starved* (1992) quotes the *London Times* on Irish emigration. "The most homesick" is from Thomas N. Brown, "Origins and Character of Irish-American Nationalism," *Review of Politics,* July 1956. President John F. Kennedy's "Remarks at Eyre Square in Galway," June 29, 1963, are in *Public Papers of the Presidents of the United States: John F. Kennedy, 1963* (Washington, D.C.: U.S. Government Printing Office, 1964). See also JM, "John Ford: The Quiet Man" (on JF's Irish heritage), *Irish America,* November 1999.

Genealogical and other information on the Feeney (Ford) family in Ireland was obtained by the author on his visit to Spiddal from sources including Ford relatives Paraic Feeney, Barbara Curran, and Tadhg O'Curraidhin; Father Tom Kyne was also helpful on local history. JF spoke to the author about County Mayo; his aunt Julia's information on the family's background was reported in JF to Michael Killanin, September 20, 1950, quoted in McNee. Other family history is from the author's interviews with Ford's sister Josephine Feeney and niece Cecil McLean de Prida; their OHs; JF's OH; JF's passport application, [April?] 1943, in which he identifies himself as "John Ford 'Sean O'Feeney'" and lists information about his parents' births, emigration, and naturalization (Lilly); DF; PB; and McNee. JF's comment on his parents in County Galway and his comparison of *Famine* to *The Grapes of Wrath* are from PB. JF spoke in his OH about the effect of the Famine on County Galway and Spiddal and about his father praying before leaving Spiddal.

Information on the O'Flahertys is from Flanagan's afterword to *Famine;* correspondence in Lilly between JF and Liam O'Flaherty; the Josephine Feeney and de Prida OHs; and DF. Mike Connelly's return to Spiddal is described in DF; JF spoke in PB and his OH about Mike's and other relatives' service in the U.S. Civil War. Charles FitzSimons discusses JF's Irish feelings in Davis. JF's remark to Eugene O'Neill is from DF. Information about the Morris family and the Feeneys' claim of blood ties is from McNee and Davis. Additional background on Lord Killanin is from 1999 obituaries: Richard Goldstein, "Lord Killanin, Olympic Leader, Dies at 84," *NYT,* April 26; "Former Olympic Committee President Dies at 84," *Irish Times,* April 26; and Peter Byrne, "Endearing Figure Who Bridged Many Divides," *Irish Times,* April 27. JF commented on the song "Down by the Glenside" in Bernardine Truden, "Hollywood's John Ford Directs New Irish Film," unidentified Irish newspaper (Lilly).

Thomas H. O'Connor provided a helpful overview of "The Irish in New England" in his essay in the anthology *The Irish in New England.* Books on Maine history consulted: William David Barry and Nan Cumming, *Rum, Riot, and Reform: Maine and the History of American Drinking* (Portland: Maine Historical Society, 1998); L. Whitney Elkins, *The Story of Maine: Coastal Maine* (Bangor, Me.: The Hillsborough Company, 1924); Richard W. Judd, Edwin A. Churchill, and Joel W. Eastman, eds., *Maine: The Pine Tree State from Prehistory to the Present* (Orono: University of Maine Press, 1995). For the history of Cape Elizabeth, Maine, see the notes for chapter 2.

Information on JF's birth is from John Martin Feeney, Record of Births, Town of Cape Elizabeth, Maine, February 1, 1894; Certified Abstract of a Certificate of Live Birth, State of Maine Department of Human Services, 1993. The dates on JF's coffin were observed by the author at JF's burial, Holy Cross Cemetery, Culver City, California, September 5, 1973; JF's correct year of birth was listed in M&W. Other family birthdates and vital statistics are from James Wilkinson, "An Introduction to the Career and Films of John Ford," M.A. thesis, UCLA, August 1960; Gallagher; Josephine Feeney, "Immediate Feeney Genealogy" (Lilly); and the OHs of Josephine Feeney and de Prida, which discuss JF's parents and his uncle Joe Connolly, as does JF's OH. JF's baptism is cited in Gallagher. Cannes Film Festival's JF retrospective is discussed in Joseph Reed, "John Ford Rides Again," *Vanity Fair,* April 1995; and Stephen Galloway, "Bard of the West," *HR,* May 12, 1995.

Information about the Feeney family name is from the author's interviews with Paraic Feeney and F. X. Feeney, and other sources, including Rev. Patrick Woulfe, *Irish Names and Surnames* (Baltimore: Genealogical Publishing Co., 1967, originally published in Dublin, 1923, by M. H. Gill & Son, as *Sloinnte Gaedheal is Gall/Irish Names and Surnames*); Edward MacLysagh, *The Surnames of Ireland* (Dublin: Irish Academic Press, 1985, sixth edition); and "Today: The Feeney Family," in the "Irish Kings and Their Heirs" column from an unidentified newspaper (c. 1920) (Lilly). Sources on FF's name change to Ford include de Prida's OH; JF's account to PB; and Wilkinson, which gives FF's account of naming himself after the automobile. Sarris discusses FF in *The John Ford Movie Mystery.* The *Portland Sunday Telegram* comments on FF's name choice in an article on JF, "Former Portland Boy Now in Forefront of Country's Greatest Movie Directors," May 10, 1925. The story about John T. Ford is from the author's interview with Olive Carey; information on John T. Ford is from the National Parks Service web site, "Ford's Theatre National Historical Site," *www.nps.gov/foth.* Lindsay Anderson's observation on JF's name is from *About John Ford.*

Books consulted on Portland history include Edward H. Elwell, *Portland and Vicinity* (Portland: Loring, Short & Harman and W. S. Jones, 1876 and 1881 editions, reprinted in 1975 by Greater Portland Landmarks, Inc.) (quoted); and Martin Dibner, *Portland* (Portland: Greater Portland Landmarks, Inc., 1972 and 1986 editions). JF's "I love Portland" remark is from the author's interview with Linda Noe Laine. Oscar Vanier's observation on JF is from Lafavore. Mary Ford's comment "Jack lies" is from the author's interview with Katherine Cliffton. Information on Feeney family residences in Portland: Tenth U.S. Census (1880), Cumberland County, Maine, Vol. 4 ED 52, Sheet 37, Line 40, references to the John Feeney family in Portland (obtained for the author by Daniel Cassidy); Portland city directories, 1870s–1920s; "John Ford in Portland," a document in the Portland Room of the Portland Public Library; Gerald Peary, "John Ford Slept Here," *American Film,* September 1990; Ray Routhier, "Celluloid Celebration: Ford Centennial," *Portland Press Herald,* May 7, 1995; and the author's visits to Feeney homes and other historical sites in Portland. JF's comment about African-Americans in Portland is quoted in Gallagher from JF's OH. Edwin O'Connor's novel *The Last Hurrah* was published by Little, Brown, Boston, 1956.

The author attended Portland's tribute to JF in July 1998. Program brochures included "John Ford: Hollywood & Monument Valley Gala," Merrill Auditorium, July 11, and "John Ford Memorial Tribute," Gorham's Corner, July 12. Articles on the tribute in the *Portland Press Herald*: Andrew D. Russell, "Sculpture to Honor City-Grown Filmmaker," May 2, 1996; Russell, "Portland Plans to Honor Native Son, John Ford," June 7, 1997; Russell, "John Ford Fans Gear Up to Honor a Hometown Boy," November 8, 1997; Russell, "Summer Film Festival to Honor Movie Legend," March 28, 1998; and editorial, "Portland's Public Art to Include John Ford," July 11, 1998. Other 1998 articles: Raymond Blair, "John Ford's Hometown Puts Him in the Spotlight," *LAT,* June 26; Mike Murphy, "Ford-Mania Coming Soon!" *Munjoy Hill Observer,* July; Ray Routhier, "Director John Ford Gets Hometown Tributes at Last," *Maine Sunday Telegram,* July 5; Routhier, "Portland Honors a Movie Legend: Native John Ford," *Maine Sunday Telegram,* July 12; and Michael Dwyer, "Thanks Ford Memories," *Irish Times,* July 25. FF's comment on Gorham's Corner is quoted in Sinclair from a film treatment by FF, "Cousin Joe." Ford's investiture as a Knight of Malta was reported in Levy and in Harold L. Cail, "John Ford, Maine Native, Is Honored by Pope Paul," *Portland Evening Express,* February 10, 1965. The *Press Herald* editorialized on JF's AFI Life Achievement Award in "He Made Good Films," April 4, 1973.

CHAPTER TWO: A FARAWAY FELLA (PP. 37–74)

The chapter title is borrowed from Pat O'Brien's description of James Cagney, quoted in John McCabe, *Cagney* (New York: Knopf, 1997). The epigraph by Fintan O'Toole, and his comments on the Irish and theatricality, are from his 1990 essay "Meanwhile: Back at the Ranch: Images of Ireland and America," in O'Toole, *The Lie of the Land: Irish Identities* (London and New York: Verso, 1997).

Information on Cape Elizabeth, Maine, is from Marcelin R. Berry, Miriam C. Chapman, Constance C. Murray, and Elizabeth B. Peterson for the Cape Elizabeth Historical Preservation Society, *Cape Elizabeth Past to Present* (Town of Cape Elizabeth, 1991); Chris Roerden, *Collections from Cape Elizabeth, Maine* (Town of Cape Elizabeth, 1965); the author's interview with the owner of JF's birthplace, Phineas Sprague Jr; the author's visit to the birthplace; and the OHs of JF, Josephine Feeney, and de Prida. For sources on JF's birth and his siblings, see notes for chapter 1. Josephine's calling JF her "baby brother" is from an interview with the author; in PB, JF recalled being "a fresh young kid." Sinclair quotes de Prida on the prejudice they experienced in Cape Elizabeth. Information on Peaks Island is from the author's tour of the island and interviews during that visit with Dan Ford, John Clement, and Catherine E. Plante; and from Ruth S. Sargent, *The Casco Bay Islands* (Dover, N.H.: Arcadia Publishing, 1995). JF's comment on boyhood boating is from Sinclair; his boating is also discussed in Levy.

Ford discusses various aspects of his childhood in his OH and his OH with Katharine Hepburn (audiotaped discussions cited as JF/KH OH). Josephine Feeney and de Prida in their OHs report that JF took after his mother and her artistic nature, and Josephine recalls that Barbara Feeney's sister was an artist; Barbara's remark "All the children" is from JF OH, quoted in Davis, as is de Prida's comment on JF being controlled by his mother. FF's description of his father, John Feeney, as "the greatest actor" is from Wilkinson; JF's story about his father and the flag is from Gallagher, and his comment on his father's storytelling is from Bernardine Truden, "An O'Feinne [sic] from Portland, Me., to Receive Eire Society Medal," *Boston Globe,* April 17, 1955. MF's comparison of JF's mother to Queen Victoria is from Sinclair; the Mother's Day 1929 Portland newspaper photo of JF and his mother (Lilly) is reproduced in Gallagher; Barbara Feeney's advice to MF, "Don't let anyone," was related to the author by Katherine Cliffton. Dudley Nichols comments on sexuality in JF's work in an April 24, 1953, letter to Anderson, published in *About John Ford.* Sinclair discusses JF's eyesight; Oscar Vanier's remark "He couldn't see" is from Mussman; JF comments on his eye for composition in PB; the story about JF watching Winslow Homer paint is from David Cook, *A History of Narrative Film* (New York: Norton, 1981); Manny Farber discusses JF's penchant for composition in depth in his review of *Two Rode Together, Artforum,* May 1969, reprinted in Farber, *Negative Space: Manny Farber on the Movies* (New York: Praeger, 1971). JF recalled his childhood visits to Ireland in JF OH and PB. Orson Welles comments on JF in Kenneth Tynan, "*Playboy* Interview with Orson Welles," *Playboy,* March 1967.

Portland's *Municipal Reports,* 1901–1914, contain an "Annual School Report" for each year, with information on each public school, teachers, curricula, textbooks, attendance, etc.; additional information on schools and teachers is contained in the Portland city directories. JF's Emerson Grammar School report card for 1905–06 is at Lilly. JF cited Marada F. Adams as influence: JF OH (in which he misremembers her first name as Miranda); further information on Adams is from *Municipal Reports* and Portland city directories. JF's diphtheria at twelve is cited in "Report of Physical Examination," October 10, 1941, in JF's USN personnel file (Lilly);

Portland diphtheria records: "Annual Report of the Board of Health," in the Portland *Munici-pal Report,* 1905; DF claims JF had the illness when he was eight years old. Sources on JF's sister Maime's nursing and JF's reading include DF and de Prida's OH.

JF discussed his ushering and acting experiences at Portland's Jefferson Theatre in his OH and JF/KH OH; DF reports his hazing by Sidney Toler. Other information on the Jefferson Theatre, and on actors and plays JF might have seen while working as an usher, is from James Moreland, "A History of the Theatre in Portland, 1794–1932," Volume II, Portland, 1938 (unpublished; available in the Portland Room of the Portland Public Library); Jefferson Theatre programs (Portland Room); Portland newspaper articles and advertisements. JF's memory of Ethel Barrymore: Hedda Hopper, "Ford Keeps Ahead of Young Producers," *LAT,* May 8, 1962. JF's recollection of acting on Peaks Island: author's interview with Olive Carey; "How long": Mrs. D. W. Griffith (Linda Arvidson), *When the Movies Were Young* (New York: E. P. Dutton, 1925, reprinted in 1968 by Benjamin Blom, New York). John Stewart, *Filmarama* (Metuchen, N.J.: Scarecrow Press, 1975), claims JF appeared in a 1901 play, *King's Carnival,* but Moreland lists no play with that title.

Information on early movie theaters in Portland: Moreland; Portland city directories, 1908–1914; and newspaper articles and advertisements. The Big Nickel ad appears in the June 1912 issue of the Portland High School magazine, the *Racquet.* The 101 Bison movies were regular attractions at the Big Nickel: "Gossip of Theaters," *Portland Evening Express & Advertiser,* September 8, 1913 (etc.). JF's comment "As a kid" is from Wagner; "In those days I read," from Sinclair. Frederick Jackson Turner's "The Significance of the Frontier in American History," *Proceedings of the State Historical Society of Wisconsin,* December 14, 1893, was reprinted in Turner's book *The Frontier in American History* (New York: Henry Holt, 1920). Henry Nash Smith's *Virgin Land: The American West as Symbol and Myth,* was published by Harvard University Press in 1950. Jorge Luis Borges's remark that "New England invented the West" is quoted from M&W; his observation on "the ethical preoccupation": *Introduccion a la literatura norteamericana* (in collaboration with Esther Zemborain de Torres) (Buenos Aires: Editorial Columba, 1967), translated as *An Introduction to American Literature* (Lexington: University Press of Kentucky, 1971).

JF discussed his high school years in his OH. Historical information on Portland High School during JF's years there (1911–15) is from Peter E. Gribbin, *A History of Portland High School, 1821 through 1981* (Portland: Portland High School, 1981); Gribbin, *The First Century of Portland High School Football, 1889–1989* (Portland: Dale Rand Printing, 1989); and the author's interview with Gribbin; as well as from the school magazine, the *Racquet.* Biographical information on William B. Jack is from "Jack Funeral Services to Be Held at 2 P.M. Saturday," *Portland Press Herald,* January 9, 1942; and Gribbin, *A History of Portland High School.* JF's story about William Jack and running away from home is from Gould; JF's claim "before I was twenty" is from his unpublished 1946 article "The Man's Story" (Lilly), quoted in Levy; his comments that William Jack was the greatest man he had ever met and the person who "set the pattern" of his life are from his OH, quoted in Davis.

Coverage of the Portland High School varsity football team, the Bulldogs, is from the *Racquet* and Portland newspapers, including "P.H.S. Outclasses Brunswick High, Winning 42 to 0," *Telegram,* October 5, 1913 ("fast and rugged backfield"); "P.H.S. Starts Season With Victory Over Deering High Team," *Telegram,* September 13, 1913 (JF ejected from game); and "Crimson Rivals Are Humbled by Blue and White," *Telegram,* October 26, 1913 ("the referee saw 'Bull' Feeney"). JF's comment "a young lawyer" and classmate's reply: "Movie Giant John Ford, Cape Native, Dies at 78," *Portland Evening Express,* September 1, 1973. JF described himself as "a pretty ugly fellow" in Bill Libby, "The Old Wrangler Rides Again," *Cosmopolitan,* March 1964. JF's recollection "In my first football game" is from JF, "The Man's Story," quoted in Levy; the *Racquet,* March 1914, commented on "Feeney's form" in "Athletics: Track."

JF spoke of his friendship with Alnah James Johnston in JF/KH OH; the friendship was discussed by JF's longtime research assistant Katherine Cliffton in her interview with the author.

Information on Miriam Ruth Burke is from de Prida's OH and the Portland High School Graduating Exercises program, June 18, 1914 (Portland High School and Lilly). Information on Edith Koon (Mrs. Kenneth Sills) is from de Prida's OH; Gribbin, *A History of Portland High School;* she is quoted in Lafavore (which also includes quotes from Vanier) and Mussman (which also includes quotes from Robert Albion, William Mahoney, and Vanier). The school building was described as "a poor specimen" in "Editorials," *Racquet,* March 1914. JF's membership on the executive board of his class is reported in "Class Notes," *Racquet,* Christmas 1912. Willis Goldbeck's comment on JF's "tremendous insecurity" is from Anderson. Lucien Libby's joke is from "Sayings of the Class Wits," *Racquet,* November 1913; Sinclair reports on JF working some of Libby's personality into Henry Fonda's title character in *Young Mr. Lincoln.* Libby's January 18, 1950, letter to JF is quoted in Scott Eyman, *Print the Legend: The Life and Times of John Ford* (New York: Simon and Schuster, 1999). Gallagher reports that JF wrote a parody of the school fight song. JF's jobs during those years included delivering fish (JF OH; de Prida OH), unloading trucks (Davis), and working for a shoe company (Gallagher). JF in his OH recalled dancing with one of the Fitzgerald girls; "At the school proms" is from "The Man's Story," quoted in Levy. JF's high school graduation: Portland High School Graduating Exercises program, June 18, 1914; "Portland High Graduates Its Largest Class" and "Graduating Class at Portland High," *Portland Evening Express,* June 18, 1914. JF toastmaster at senior class banquet: "Class Parts For P.H.S. Senior Class Banquet," unidentified Portland newspaper, n.d. (1914); "Class Notes," *Racquet,* May 1914.

Information on the history of Universal Pictures is from Bernard F. Dick, *City of Dreams: The Making and Remaking of Universal Pictures* (Lexington: University Press of Kentucky, 1997); I. G. Edmonds, *Big U: Universal in the Silent Days* (New York: A. S. Barnes, 1977); Richard Koszarski, *An Evening's Entertainment: The Age of the Silent Feature Picture, 1915–1928* (Berkeley: University of California Press, 1990); and a *DV* special issue on history of Universal (including an article by JM, "Business 101"), February 5, 1990. Ogden Nash's quip is quoted in Anthony Slide, *The American Film Industry: A Historical Dictionary* (Westport, Conn.: Greenwood Press, 1986).

A primary source on FF, his relationship with his family, his film career, and his work with JF, is FF's unpublished autobiographical manuscript, "Up and Down the Ladder," c. 1934, a typescript (312 pp.) in the Grover Jones papers at AMPAS. Gallagher has extensive information on FF in his book on JF and his article on FF, "Brother Feeney," *Film Comment,* November–December 1976 (which quotes FF on Abraham Lincoln). Other biographical information on FF is from "Portland Native Francis Ford Dies at 71 in Hollywood," *Portland Press Herald,* September 6, 1953; the OH of his son Philip Ford (John Phillips Ford); and Philip Ford's obituary, *Variety,* January 28, 1976. FF also comments on his background in "Francis Ford," *Universal Weekly,* November 1, 1913; and on his shift from stage to film in Mlle. Chic, "Talking to Francis Ford," *MPW,* May 13, 1916. Further information on FF's early film career and the Méliès company is from Frank Thompson, *The Star Film Ranch: Texas' First Picture Show* (Plano, Tex.: Republic of Texas Press, 1996).

The story about Barbara Feeney, FF, and the highwayman is from FF, "Up and Down the Ladder" (including her remark "I wish he had"); Truden; and Frank S. Nugent, "Hollywood's Favorite Rebel," *Saturday Evening Post,* July 23, 1949. JF spotting FF on-screen is from Phyllis Schuyler Thaxter, "Through the Stage Door," unidentified source, n.d. (1920s) (Lilly); de Prida's OH recalled that Judge Connolly located FF for the Feeneys; the story about Barbara watching FF in a serial is from "Up and Down the Ladder." JF recalled writing stories in his OH and in a letter to Donald Monteith, July 21, 1948. JF discussed his early interest in movies in his OH, quoted in Davis. JF's comment that FF "was a great cameraman" is from PB; his advice to Fred Zinnemann about regarding the camera as "an information booth" is quoted in M&W.

JF's OH recalled that Principal Jack urged him not to go to college, although DF says the opposite. Information on JF's application for Annapolis is from the author's interview with Vice

Admiral John D. Bulkeley, USN; JF OH; DF. JF discussed his unhappiness at the University of Maine in the JF/KH OH, in which he recalled the taunt "Hey, shanty!" (quoted in Davis). JF's comment "Hell, they kicked me out" and his recollection of taking night classes in American history at the University of Southern California are from Mark Haggard, "Ford in Person," *Focus on Film,* Spring 1971; JF spoke of going to California in his OH. "John Feeney is closely connected" is from *The Racquet 1863–1914 Alumni Number,* Portland High School, November 1914. JF's line "I want to be a tugboat captain" and Lindsay Anderson's comment are from Anderson's interview "The Quiet Man," *Sequence,* January 1952, reprinted in his book.

CHAPTER THREE: "A DOLLAR FOR A BLOODY NOSE" (PP. 75–100)

The chapter title is a Francis Ford quote from Richard Willis, "Francis Ford, of the Gold Seal Company," *Motion Picture Magazine,* June 1915. The epigraph is from the *MPW* review of JF's *The Scrapper,* June 2, 1917.

JF spoke to Wagner of traveling to California by train; his story about "the boss's daughter" is from Haggard. Sources on Joseph A. McDonough traveling with JF include Mussman (with Oscar Vanier quote); and a note in Lilly, n.a., attached to a letter from Jack Haley to McDonough, August 9, 1919. Information on McDonough's career in Hollywood is from James Curtis, *James Whale: A New World of Gods and Monsters* (London: Faber and Faber, 1998); and McDonough's obituary, *Variety,* May 17, 1944. JF's arrival in Los Angeles is described in DF. Allan Dwan told the author about FF building his home with lumber from Universal; Lefty Hough, then a Universal property man, also told the story in his OH. JF discussed his name change in his OH; FF playing a character named John Ford is mentioned in Marjorie Gilmore, "The She-Wolf (101 Bison)" (serialization of film), *Motion Picture Story Magazine,* 1913.

Information on Grace Cunard's background is from Hugh C. Weir, "She Has Written Four Hundred Scenarios: A Chat with Grace Cunard," *Universal Weekly,* September 4, 1915; "The Campbells Are Coming," *Universal Weekly,* October 16, 1915; Richard Henshaw, "Women Directors: 150 Filmographies," *Film Comment,* November–December, 1972; Kalton C. Lahue, *Ladies in Distress* (South Brunswick, N.J.: A. S. Barnes, 1973); Gallagher's book and his article "Brother Feeney." FF spoke of his confidence in Grace in the articles *"The Campbells Are Coming"* and Mlle. Chic, "Talking to Francis Ford." Grace's comment that she "promised both your mothers" is from her letter to JF and McDonough [February 1917?], quoted by Gallagher.

Lillian Gish remembered Hollywood in the early silent era in Jeanne Moreau's 1983 documentary *Lillian Gish* ("I thought I was"), and in conversations with the author. Additional information on early Hollywood is from FF, "Up and Down the Ladder"; Benjamin B. Hampton, *History of the American Film Industry from Its Beginnings to 1931* (New York: Dover Publications, 1970 edition), originally published as *A History of the Movies* (New York: Covici, Friede, 1931); and Bruce Torrance, *Hollywood: The First Hundred Years* (New York: New York Zoetrope, 1982). Information on Carl Laemmle Sr. and Universal Pictures is from Dick, *City of Dreams: The Making and Remaking of Universal Pictures;* Edmonds, *Big U: Universal in the Silent Days;* Koszarski, *An Evening's Entertainment: The Age of the Silent Feature Picture, 1915–1928;* Robert Mannering, "Perils of the Movies," *Theatre,* April 1914; and various articles in the *Universal Weekly,* including: "Universal City Making Wonderful Strides," September 13, 1913; "All Aboard for Universal City," January 31, 1914; "Universal Stage Largest in the World," April 25, 1914; "The New Universal City," September 5, 1914; and "Universal's Chameleon City," September 26, 1914. Diana Serra Cary wrote about actual cowboys appearing in early Westerns in her book *The Hollywood Posse: The Story of a Gallant Band of Horsemen Who Made Movie History* (Boston: Houghton Mifflin, 1975).

JF's possible involvement in *Lucile, the Waitress* is noted in PB. In its advertisement for *Lucille Love, The Girl of Mystery, Universal Weekly,* March 28, 1914, Universal boasts of "spending thousands"; Edmonds reports JF doubling in that serial. FF's observation on making serials ("You need a good memory") is from the Mlle. Chic interview. JF's comment on FF's influence

("Well, my brother Frank") is from PB. JF recalled digging ditches in his OH and the JF/KH OH. FF discussed JF as "a full-fledged assistant" and told how he "got his break" in "Up and Down the Ladder"; FF's "As a prop man" comment is from Wilkinson. JF's description of his work as "assistant, handyman" is quoted in Gallagher. Allan Dwan remembered JF as a property man and assistant in Peter Bogdanovich, *Allan Dwan: The Last Pioneer* (New York: Praeger, 1971), reprinted in Bogdanovich, *Who the Devil Made It* (New York: Knopf, 1997) ("His brother Francis"); Davis, from Dwan's OH ("The reason"); DF; and the author's interview with Dwan. MF's OH told the story of JF having a hammer in his pocket during a dance scene. Background on Lefty Hough is from Hough's OH and Kevin Brownlow, *The War, the West, and the Wilderness* (New York: Knopf, 1979). JF recalls his work as an assistant cameraman in the JF/KH OH.

Information on directors at Universal is from various articles in the *Universal Weekly*, including "The Universal's Remarkable Staff of Picture Producers," April 11, 1914. The *Universal Weekly* comments on FF's humor in *"The Campbells Are Coming."* Edmonds quotes an unnamed reviewer of *Three Bad Men and a Girl*. Richard Willis's observation in *Motion Picture Magazine* about FF's "quiet, almost sarcastic manner" is quoted in Gallagher, "Brother Feeney"; FF's line "Now, boys" is also from Willis; his comment "The joint is full" is from "Ford of the Films," *Irish Digest*, May 1952. The stories about the grenade, the powder bomb, the tent fire, and how JF "made the leap" are from Nugent, "Hollywood's Favorite Rebel." The date of JF's firing by Universal is established by his Universal Film Mfg. Co. pay slip, March 29, 1916; FF gives an account of the tent fire in "Up and Down the Ladder." JF's declaration about FF, "I want to see him *lashed*," is quoted in Gallagher from his interview with Frank Baker; Gallagher wrote that JF had a "pathological" attitude toward FF. Baker's comments on the relationship between JF and FF are from an interview with Anthony Slide and Robert Gitt, "Frank Baker," quoted in Gallagher.

Information on D. W. Griffith and *The Birth of a Nation* is from Karl Brown, ed. by Kevin Brownlow, *Adventures with D. W. Griffith* (New York: Farrar, Straus and Giroux, 1973); and Richard Schickel, *D. W. Griffith: An American Life* (New York: Simon and Schuster, 1984). JF is quoted on Griffith from PB and from Schickel, "Good Days, Good Years," *Harper's,* October 1970; in his OH, he remembered Griffith pouring a drink for himself. JF's comment on his early acting roles is from PB; Vanier's comment on JF's acting is from Lafavore.

Edmonds reports on theater managers in Portland replacing the name Ford with Feeney. The shooting of *The Strong Arm Squad* was reported in "Local Police Force Feature in a 'Movie,'" *Portland Evening Express,* November 20, 1915; and "Ten Fords in Francis' Vacation Film," *MPW,* January 1, 1916 (primarily about the shooting of *Chicken-Hearted Jim*); MPW reviewed *The Strong Arm Squad* in its issue of February 12, 1916. When interviewed by the author, JF claimed not to remember *Chicken-Hearted Jim*. Olive Carey related Al Stern's line about L-Ko comedies in an interview with the author; other information on the L-Ko Komedy Kompany is from various articles in the *Universal Weekly*. JF's work for L-Ko is established by his termination notices from the company, February 3 and 17, 1917.

The JF and Hoot Gibson quotes on living together are Cecilia Ager, "Then and Now," *NYT Magazine,* September 20, 1959; Gibson's background is from Brownlow, *The War, the West, and the Wilderness*. Mary Ford's OH recalled JF living with Mark Fenton. JF's address on Hollywood Boulevard appears in various JF correspondence, 1917–20 (Lilly). Information on JF's parents' visit to Hollywood in 1917 is from a note in JF's 1917 correspondence files (Lilly); and Maime Feeney McLean to JF, March 28, 1917. John A. Feeney's line about the Murphy bed is quoted in Davis; in a 1917 letter, the elder Feeney reminded JF to write home. JF's purchase of a horse, Woodrow, is reported in Stephen Drumman to JF, June 1, 1916.

JF's story of how he became a director at the opening of Universal City is from Peter Bogdanovich's documentary film *Directed by John Ford* (1971). Further information on those events is from the author's interview with Olive Carey (including JF taking a pay cut to become a di-

rector); Dwan's OH (on Laemmle being influenced by favorable reports about JF); PB; Ed-
monds; Koszarski; Dick; and "The New Universal City." Cecil McLean de Prida's OH recalled
JF codirecting a film with Eddie Laemmle. JF was listed as an assistant director in *Motion Picture
News,* October 21, 1916, and April 12, 1917. *The Tornado* was reviewed in *Moving Picture World,*
March 3, 1917; JF's comments on the film are from Wagner ("scared to death") and PB ("just a
bunch of stunts"); FF discussed it in Wilkinson; the fan letter from Mary Parks to JF is dated
August 12, 1917 (Lilly). *The Trail of Hate* was reviewed in *Exhibitors' Trade Review,* April 28,
1917; PB raises the question of directing credit. FF commented on *The Soul Herder* in Wilkinson. *Hell Bent* was reviewed in *Motion Picture News,* June 29, 1918.

Information on Harry Carey's background is from the author's interviews with Olive Carey
and HCJ; Olive Carey's OH; HCJ, *Company of Heroes;* Gallagher; and various articles in the *Uni-
versal Weekly.* The 1919 Universal advertisement of JF and Harry Carey is reproduced in
Brownlow, *The War, the West, and the Wilderness.* Harry Carey's reference to JF as "Young
Lochinvar" was reported to the author by HCJ. Olive's "bewitching smile" is mentioned in
"Harry Carey in *A Knight of the Range,*" *MPW,* February 5, 1916.

JF's 1915 insurance application: John A. Feeney, accident insurance application, Royal In-
demnity Co., October 8, 1915; see also John A. Feeney, insurance policy application, Pruden-
tial Insurance Co., April 6, 1909. Information on the draft in World War I is from Clyde E.
Jacobs and John F. Gallagher, *The Selective Service Act: A Case Study of the Governmental Process*
(New York: Dodd, Mead & Company, 1967); *This Fabulous Century, Vol. II: 1910–1920* (New
York: Time-Life Books, 1985 edition); and *The Draft?: A Report Prepared for the Peace Education
Division of the American Friends Service Committee* (New York: Hill and Wang, 1968). Hollywood's
outburst of patriotism was reported in "Movies Mobilized for War," *MPW,* March 31, 1917.

JF's draft card: John Augustin [sic] Ford, No. 14, Los Angeles Board, Class 1A, order no.
1291, serial no. 1296, registration certificate No. 122, registered June 5, 1917 (Lilly). JF's claim
to have served in U.S. Navy in World War I: JF OH; in other OHs, de Prida and James Warner
Bellah said JF did not serve in the war; Bellah said JF invented a role as a bluejacket, and de Prida
said he tried to become an aerial combat photographer and sought the benefit of his father's political influence. R. W. Abbott, War Department Office of the Chief, Motor Transport Corps,
Washington, D.C., wrote JF, October 31, 1918, about his request for a commission in the Army
Signal Corps. JF's subscription to Liberty Loan bonds at Universal: June 19, 1917, document
(Lilly). JF's sisters wrote him about the war: Maime to JF, March 28, 1917; Josephine to JF, 1917
(a note at Lilly attached to Josephine's letter, evidently from de Prida, provides information on
JF's attempts to enlist and his parents' attitudes toward military service).

Ed O'Fearna is discussed in the OHs of Josephine Feeney; de Prida; JF; Philip Ford;
Wingate Smith; and Lefty Hough. The Feeney brothers' feuds are described in Paul Harrison,
"The Film Director Who Never Goes to the Movies," unidentified publication, August 14,
1937 (Lilly). Hough's comment that the feud between JF and Ed "goes back to the days in
Maine" is from Brownlow, *The War, the West, and the Wilderness.* FF's decline is chronicled in
"Up and Down the Ladder"; Gallagher's book and his article "Brother Feeney"; Philip Ford's
OH; and Lahue.

CHAPTER FOUR: "A JOB OF WORK" (PP. 101–134)

The chapter title and epigraph are from PB. Olive Carey told the author about JF picking
up the phrase "a job of work" from her husband, Harry Carey.

JF wrote about Harry Carey's influence ("I learned a great deal") in "The Man's Story," quoted
in Gallagher; he spoke about Carey in PB ("Harry Carey tutored me"). John Wayne's comments
on Carey are from Ronald L. Davis, *Duke: The Life and Image of John Wayne* (Norman: University
of Oklahoma Press, 1998); and R&O. JF's insistence that his Carey Westerns "weren't shoot-'em-
ups" is from PB. Joseph Sistrom's description of Carey having "a good American face" is from the

author's interview with Frank Capra, quoted in JM, *Frank Capra: The Catastrophe of Success* (New York: Simon and Schuster, 1992). Olive Carey told the author that "Goodbye, Old Paint" was her husband's favorite song. Jean Renoir made his observation on Westerns to the author.

Carl Laemmle's comment on the length of *Straight Shooting* is from PB. Andrew Sarris's observations on JF's films are from his books *The American Cinema: Directors and Directions, 1929–1968* (New York: E. P. Dutton, 1968) ("evolved") and *The John Ford Movie Mystery* (on *Straight Shooting* and "would be ill-advised"); Philippe Haudiquet analyzed JF's "expressionist temptation" in *John Ford*, Cinéma d'Aujourd'hui series (Paris: Editions Seghers, 1968). Reviews of JF's silent Westerns are from *Moving Picture World* (1917): *The Secret Man*, October 13; *The Soul Herder*, August 11; and *Bucking Broadway*, December 22; *Exhibitors' Trade Review* (1918): *Three Mounted Men*, November 21, and *Hell Bent* (quoted in Gallagher); and *Photoplay: The Outcasts of Poker Flat*, 1919 (quoted in PB). JF discussed Peter B. Kyne's novella *The Three Godfathers* and the sharpshooting and "realism" in *Marked Men* with Billy Leyser, "It's the 'Little Things' That Count: Details Essential, Says Jack Ford," *Cleveland News*, January 27, 1920; JF comments on the *Marked Men* title in PB; JF's remark to William Wyler about *3 Godfathers* is from Davis. Sources on Frank Capra as an extra in *Outcasts* and another JF film include the author's interview with Olive Carey; JM, *Frank Capra*; Capra, "My Crazy Hollywood!" *Sunday Pictorial*, London, June 15, 1938; and Jim Tully, "Star Boss," *This Week*, November 14, 1937. Capra's observation on JF is from his autobiography, *The Name Above the Title* (New York: Macmillan, 1971).

Information on Wyatt Earp is from Bob Boze Bell, *The Illustrated Life & Times of Wyatt Earp* (Phoenix: TriStar-Boze Publications, 1993; third edition, 1995); Bogdanovich, *Allan Dwan: The Last Pioneer;* Brownlow, *The War, the West, and the Wilderness;* Davis; Josephine Sarah Marcus Earp, collected and ed. by Glenn G. Boyer, *I Married Wyatt Earp: The Recollections of Josephine Sarah Marcus Earp* (Tucson: University of Arizona Press, 1976); Wayne Michael Sarf, *God Bless You, Buffalo Bill: A Layman's Guide to History and the Western Film* (New York: Fairleigh Dickinson University Press, 1983); and Casey Tefertiller, *Wyatt Earp: The Life Behind the Legend* (New York: John Wiley and Sons, 1997). Davis quotes Wyatt and Josephine Earp on Hollywood. JF talked to PB about knowing Earp. The final screenplay of *My Darling Clementine* by Samuel G. Engel and Winston Miller is dated March 11, 1946; a version of the script was published in Robert Lyons, ed., *My Darling Clementine* (New Brunswick, N.J.: Rutgers University Press, 1984).

The unsigned contract offered to JF by the Universal Film Mfg. Co. is dated September 1917 (Lilly); the contract JF signed that month is in Lilly, which also has unsigned contracts sent by Universal to JF for the serial *The Strange Case of Cavendish*, July 31 and August 16, 1919. Universal reprimanded JF for morning tardiness in W. Sistrom to JF, March 22, 1919. Olive Carey's memories of living with JF at Newhall are from an interview with the author; her OH; and Gallagher. JF on Pardner Jones: PB. JF's Lexington Avenue address is from an envelope postmarked from Portland to JF, February 20, 1917. FF described JF as "durable" in Wilkinson. Olive Carey and Harry Carey Jr. told the author about the trouble between JF and Harry Carey that was started by J. Farrell MacDonald and Joe Harris. Other Olive Carey quotes are from HCJ, *Company of Heroes.* The Battling Nelson story; "According to legend"; and the post-1921 relationship of Harry Carey and JF were discussed in the author's interview with HCJ. Davis reports on Olive and Harry riding around Hollywood in a Lincoln. Reviews of *The Prince of Avenue A:* Marion Russell, unidentified source [1920] (Lilly); *Exhibitors' Trade Review*, January 17, 1920. JF said in his OH that he thought James J. Corbett had no acting talent. Information on JF's Fox salary and 1921 contract is from Gallagher. Information on the death of Buck Jones is from Edward Buscombe, ed., *The BFI Companion to the Western* (London: BFI/Deutsch, 1988; New York: Atheneum, 1990).

Sources on Janet Eastman Crothers include the author's interview with Olive Carey and her OH; Davis; Gallagher; and Eddie Laemmle to JF, September 5, 1919. Janet's leading role in *The Raid* is discussed in *MPW*, March 10, 1917, and a photograph of her in the role appears in the

March 17 issue. Janet's letters to JF include March 25, 1920; [March?] 1920; June 17, 1920 (asking why he's not writing); and her [1920?] letter with French writing.

Sources on Mary McBride [aka McBryde] Smith Ford include MF's OH; the author's interviews with Olive Carey and Dan Ford; de Prida's OH; JF's OH; DF; Gallagher; and an interview with Mary Ford (1977) by Anthony Slide and June Banker. Information on Mary's nursing background is from army surgeon general Rupert Blue to Mary McBryde Smith, April 25, 1917; Annie W. Goodrich, dean of Army School of Nursing, to Mary, October 19, 1918; Mary's nursing oath, October 28, 1918, Toledo, Ohio; and Col. C. P. Darnell, office of surgeon general of army, to Mary, January 6, 1919. MF's relative John Blue: "UDC Honors John Blue in Memorial Day Service Here," *Sandhill Citizen,* 1958 (Lilly).

Kevin Brownlow and John Kobal discuss Mira Hershey's dances at the Hollywood Hotel, quoting Viola Dana, in *Hollywood: The Pioneers* (New York: Knopf, 1979); additional information on the hotel is from Torrance. The Fords' marriage certificate: Mary McBride Smith and John Feeney, Los Angeles County, July 3, 1920 (includes information on her parents) (Lilly); an item on their wedding appeared in *Variety,* July 23, 1920. Davis quotes MF on the reaction of JF's friends to their wedding. Mary's comments on JF and her marriage are from Slide and Banker, except for "We had more fun" (from Sinclair). Dan Ford's observation that "Ford really married above himself" is from an interview with the author; de Prida's OH contains her observation on MF's first meeting with the Feeneys. Dan Ford's comments on JF's "identity crisis" and Mary's attitude toward his movie career as "flashy and 'low Irish'" are from *Pappy.*

The date of the Fords' rental of the Beechwood Drive house is from their lease with Henry Hotchner, June 30, 1920. Information on Hershey selling the Odin Street house (Majestic Heights Tract) to the Fords is from Hershey's deed to MF, October 5, 1920; see also MF and JF mortgage on a lot in Majestic Heights, same date. The Fords' Christmas card, 1926 (Lilly), is quoted in Davis. Information on JF's 1928 purchase of Rolls-Royce is from Sinclair ("This ought"); and W. S. Malin, IRS audit of JF's 1934 tax return, July 2, 1936 (Lilly). JF's income in 1920s and payments for advertising and publicity are listed in his tax returns (Lilly); his purchase of a secondhand 1919 Stutz Speedster is listed in his auto insurance policy, December 31, 1919.

The dates of birth of Patrick and Barbara Ford are listed in PB and Gallagher. MF's comment on their children is from Slide and Banker; JF's is from an interview, "To Spank or Not to Spank? That's Sure the Question!" *LAE,* May 16, 1925; de Prida's OH recalled JF beating Patrick with a razor strop, but not disciplining Barbara; Katherine Cliffton discussed the Fords' treatment of their children in her interview with the author. Gallagher reports that MF announced she was leaving JF. Information on MF's visit to *The Iron Horse* location is from Slide and Banker; MF's OH; and *Fox Folks Junior* (location newsletter), January 31, 1924; Priscilla Bonner, in her interview with the author, recalled MF's visit to the *3 Bad Men* location. MF commented on JF and actresses in her OH and Sinclair (reference to Madeleine Carroll). *Photoplay's* observations on JF's home life are from an article by Everly Watson, "There Is a Santa Claus" [1920s] (Lilly); Wingate Smith's remark on MF's fondness for reading is from Harrison. JF's abstinence pledge is at Lilly; MF's morning ritual and their "torpedo juice" are reported in Sinclair; Uncle Bunny's homemade wine is mentioned in MF's OH. Information on MF's friend Victoria Forde Mix is from MF's OH; Slide and Banker; and FF, "Up and Down the Ladder."

CHAPTER FIVE: DIRECTED BY JOHN FORD (PP. 135–164)

Sources on Irish history cited in the notes for the introduction were used again for this chapter. Tom Clarke's prophecy "between this moment and freedom" is quoted in Kee. The dates of JF's trip to Ireland in 1921 are established by his U.S. passport, November 15; List of First-Class Passengers, SS *Baltic,* New York–Liverpool, November 19; and List of First-Class Passengers, RMS *Olympic,* Southampton to New York, December 21. JF's account of the trip is from his letter to MF, n.d. [c. December 1921–January 1922], quoted in DF; JF discusses the Thorntons in his March 9, 1936, letter to Sean O'Casey. JF's comment "That's where *we* killed them" is from Sinclair's interview with Robert Emmett Ginna Jr. MF's OH discusses JF's offer to take her to Ireland and how she dealt with his trip. Her comment "I never asked him" is from Sinclair, as are that biographer's comments on the trip and on JF's support of the IRA. Martin Feeney's request for an IRA pension is discussed in his letter to JF, October 27, 1953, and in Ernie O'Malley to JF, December 9, 1953. O'Malley's *On Another Man's Wound* (London: Rich and Cowan, 1936) was reprinted in 1961 by Four Square Books, London, and its sequel, *The Singing Flame,* was published in 1978 by Anvil Books, Dublin. See notes for chapter 6 for information on JF's 1934 USNR commission. JF's tax write-offs for his trip and his stay in New York are in his 1921 IRS return. Martin Feeney's recollection of JF's visit is from DF, which also comments on the trip helping to resolve JF's "identity crisis."

Sources on Michael Collins traveling to Ireland with treaty proposals, December 2–3, 1921, include JF's letter to MF on his trip; Frank O'Connor, *The Big Fellow: Michael Collins & The Irish Revolution,* reprinted by Corgi, 1969; Jim Rees and Liam Charlton, *Arklow—Last Stronghold of Sail: Arklow Ships from 1850–1985* (Arklow, Ireland: second edition, 1986) (on boat accident); and Tim Pat Coogan, *The Man Who Made Ireland: The Life and Death of Michael Collins* (Niwot, Colo.: Roberts Rinehart, 1992); originally published as *Michael Collins,* Hutchinson (London), 1992. Anderson's book describes JF's account of the boat accident as "typical Ford." Philip Dunne's account of discussing Collins with JF is from Dunne's interview with the author. Lilly has the Republic of Ireland bond certificate made out to "Saul" [Sol] M. Wurtzel, November 15, 1921. The discussion about Indians and the Black and Tans is from "John Ford talks to Philip Jenkinson about not being interested in movies," *Listener,* February 12, 1970.

The making of *The Iron Horse* is chronicled in the Fox location newsletter *Fox Folks Junior* (1924); Sol Wurtzel's telegram appears in the January 12 issue, and Francis Powers's birthday tribute to JF, "Passing of the 29th [*sic*] Year," on February 14. Local coverage includes "Historic Film To Be Made Near Reno," *Nevada State Journal,* November 21, 1923; "Film People Ready to 'Shoot' Picture," *Nevada State Journal,* January 1, 1924; "Film Company To Operate Near Wadsworth," *Sparks* (Nevada) *Tribune,* January 2, 1924; Fox advertisement soliciting local extras, *Nevada State Journal,* January 3, 1924; "Old-Time Engine to Be Screened," *Sparks Tribune,* January 4, 1924; "Nevada Film at American" and advertisement for *The Iron Horse, Humboldt* (Nevada) *Star,* July 3, 1926.

JF recalls the filming in Mitchell and PB; he discusses "outdoor dramas" in "'Film Capital izes Stage Shortcomings,' Says Ford," *LAE,* May 3, 1925. George O'Brien discusses the filming of *The Iron Horse* in Leonard Maltin, "FFM Interviews George O'Brien," *Film Fan Monthly,* May 1971; Arthur Lund's account appears in "Risks Life to Film Stampede," unidentified Minnesota paper [1925?] (AMPAS); Lefty Hough reminisces in DF about bootleg booze and hookers; JF's fight with his brother Eddie is recalled in the Hough and Philip Ford OHs; Harold Schuster's reminiscences are from Brownlow, *The War, the West, and the Wilderness,* which also includes Hough's comment "The Ford outfit" and other information on the location filming, such as JF drawing inspiration from his uncle Mike's stories and songs. Darcy O'Brien's account of JF having "disappeared on location" is from his article "Jack Ford and George O'Brien, A Long Voyage Home." HCJ's *Company of Heroes* reports that Charles Russell was a guest at Harry Carey's Rancho. JF names Wurtzel the guardian of his children and executor of his estate in John Martin Augustine Feeney, Last Will and Testament (handwritten), February 9, 1927 (Lilly).

The cost of *The Iron Horse* is listed in Mitchell; film rentals are from Gallagher. The unsigned *NYT* review is dated August 29, 1924. Sources on the dinner party at Fox Hall include Gallagher and MF's OH (which also includes Barbara Feeney's remark to MF on why she preferred to stay at a hotel); JF's quip "I'd have to wear clothes" is from his letter to (unidentified) friends, quoted in a *Photoplay* item [1924]. Coverage of the Los Angeles premiere (1925) includes "*The*

Iron Horse Arrives," *HCN,* February 21; and Florence Lawrence, "*Iron Horse* Approved by Film Celebrities," *LAE,* February 22; details of the Grauman's Egyptian prologue, *The Days of 1863–1869,* are from a program (in May) for *The Iron Horse* (AMPAS).

One instance of JF's frequent protestation that he was "not a career man" appears in an interview by André S. Labarthe filmed on August 31, 1965, for the French broadcaster ORTF's series *Cinéastes de notre temps,* and first shown on June 16 of the following year under the title "Entre chien et loup: John Ford" ("In the Twilight: John Ford"). The unsigned *NYT* review of *Nero* is dated May 26, 1922; J. Gordon Edwards's stage acting is recalled by Francis Ford in "Up and Down the Ladder." Priscilla Bonner's reminiscences of the making of *3 Bad Men* are from her interview with the author. JF describes the land rush sequence in PB ("[S]everal of the company") and Maurice Zolotow, *Shooting Star: A Biography of John Wayne* (New York: Simon and Schuster, 1974). The stunt involving the baby is recalled in JF's OH and Hough's OH.

Coverage of JF's 1927 trip to Europe includes "Director on Long Jaunt," *San Francisco Call-Post,* February 26; "German Actors to Return with Ford," *Hollywood Citizen,* March 9; "Ford Praises Murnau's Touch," *Moving Picture World,* March 12 (quoting JF on *Sunrise*); "Director Abroad Hunting Locations," *Baltimore Sun,* March 20; "Philip Klein Signed to Write for Fox," *New York Review,* March 26; "Ford Back from Europe: Leaves for Hollywood," *New York Telegraph,* April 14; and "John Ford Back from Europe," *Film Daily,* May 7, 1927. Everson discusses *Sunrise* in *American Silent Film.* JF's comment to Fred Zinnemann is quoted in M&W. Sources on *Frozen Justice* include F. W. Murnau to Winfield Sheehan, November 16, 1925; Sheehan to JF, December 11, 1925; [Sheehan?] telegram to JF, December 12, 1926; Sheehan to JF, January 29, 1927. JF's description of *Four Sons* as his "first really good story" is from Mitchell; Gallagher reports that it was named film of the year by *Photoplay;* Fox's description of *Four Sons* as its "Biggest Success in Last Ten Years" is from *Moving Picture World,* April 21, 1928. The *Variety* review of *Hangman's House* is by *Rush.* [Alfred Rushford Grearson], May 16, 1928. JF's observations on the state of his art form are quoted from his article "Veteran Producer Muses," *NYT,* June 10, 1928, reprinted in Richard Koszarski, ed., *Hollywood Directors 1914–1940* (New York: Oxford University Press, 1976). Jean Renoir's comment on learning from JF "how not to move my camera" is from Davis.

Accounts of the 1926 encounter between Marion "Duke" Morrison (later known as John Wayne) include Miriam Hughes, "Oh, For a Hair Cut!" *Photoplay,* December 1930 ("You one"); JW in *Directed by John Ford* ("So, not being interested"); and DF ("That's enough"). JW's comments on his relationship with JF are from Davis ("wanted to be a director") and Zolotow ("He kept his distance"). JF's early impression of JW is from the *Time* cover story on JW, "The Wages of Virtue," March 3, 1952.

CHAPTER SIX: "WITHOUT A HARBOR, MAN IS LOST" (PP. 165–213)

The chapter title is from a line spoken by Will Rogers in JF's 1933 film *Doctor Bull.* The epigraph is from *Directed by John Ford,* also the source of JF's comment on talking pictures being "much easier to make than silent pictures."

Background on the coming of sound is from Douglas Gomery, "Problems in Film History: How Fox Innovated Sound," *Quarterly Review of Film Studies,* August 1976; Gomery, "The Coming of Sound: Technological Change in the American Film Industry" in Tino Balio, ed., *The American Film Industry* (Madison: University of Wisconsin Press, 1985 revised edition); and William K. Everson, *American Silent Film* (New York: Oxford University Press, 1978). In "Veteran Producer Muses," JF recalls that period as "a time of near panic." JF's comment on the use of music with *Mother Machree* is from his article "Thematic Presentations, A Wish for the Future," *Film Daily,* June 12, 1927. Orson Welles's observations on JF are from his interview with Tynan. JF's self-description as "a man of the silent cinema" is quoted in Sinclair; Lee Lourdeaux writes of JF's "fine Irish ear" in *Italian and Irish Filmmakers in America: Ford, Capra, Coppola, and*

Scorsese (Philadelphia: Temple University Press, 1990). The *NYT* review of *Napoleon's Barber* appeared on November 26, 1928. JF's description of Lumsden Hare's scenes in *The Black Watch* is from PB.

JF's comments on Ward Bond are from DF ("Who's that"); Davis ("very unsophisticated"); and HCJ, *Company of Heroes* ("Let's face it, Bond is a shit"). JF's romantic rivalry with Bond on location for *Salute* is recalled in R&O. Stepin Fetchit's reminiscences of working with JF and Duke Morrison (JW) on *Salute* are from his interview with the author, printed as JM (with uncredited foreword by Albert Johnson), "Stepin Fetchit Talks Back," *Film Quarterly,* Summer 1971, and reprinted in Brian Henderson and Ann Martin, eds., *Film Quarterly: Forty Years—A Selection* (Berkeley: University of California Press, 1999). Information on Kenneth Hawks and *Big Time* is from the author's interview with Kenneth's brother Howard Hawks, quoted in JM, *Hawks on Hawks* (Berkeley: University of California Press, 1982); and from Todd McCarthy, *Howard Hawks: The Grey Fox of Hollywood* (New York: Grove Press, 1997). JF's "Air Relief Fund" contribution is mentioned in E. A. Caldwell, IRS examining officer, to JF, November 4, 1932 (reporting on an audit of JF and MF for the 1930 tax year); JF's tax returns document his 1929–33 income; his stock ownership is listed in his tax returns, 1924–33.

The *Film Spectator* reviewed *Men Without Women* in "John Ford Gives Us Another Great Example of Screen Art," February 15, 1930 (quoted in Davis); Sarris discusses the film in *The John Ford Movie Mystery.* E. L. Doctorow's introduction to Sinclair Lewis's 1925 novel *Arrowsmith* is from the 1998 Signet Classics edition. Sources on JF filming *Arrowsmith* (1931) include Harrison ("If you're going to direct"); Jon Tuska's interview with H. Bruce Humberstone in his book *Close Up: The Contact Director* (Metuchen, N.J.: Scarecrow Press, 1976); and Davis (quoting Helen Hayes). The circumstances of JF's firing from *Arrowsmith* are reported in Gary Wills, *John Wayne: The Politics of Celebrity* (New York: Simon and Schuster, 1997), and Eyman, *Print the Legend.* JF's explanation of why he worked a baseball sequence into *Born Reckless* is from PB. The rarity of screenings of *Up the River* is discussed in Mark de la Vina, "1930 'B' Film Earns an A for Z Channel," *LAT,* September 30, 1986.

Sources on JF's contracts with Fox include the studio's agreement with JF, April 27, 1931, extending his contract to October 2, 1932 (with reference to his letter of December 23, 1930, about a three-month leave of absence); Twentieth Century–Fox Film Corp. to JF, October 23, 1944, referring to his contract dated September 1, 1934, amended September 28, 1937; and Eyman, *Print the Legend.* Harry L. Wurtzel (JF's agent) discusses freelancing in a letter to JF, December 10, 1931. The Fox reorganization is discussed in Benjamin B. Hampton, *History of the American Film Industry,* and Gomery, "The Coming of Sound: Technological Change in the American Film Industry." JF's comments on his status in Hollywood during that period are from JF to Harry Wurtzel ("a journeyman director"), quoted in Anderson; PB ("I did the best"; "In those days"); and Jean Mitry, "Recontre avec John Ford," *Cahiers du Cinéma,* March 1955, translated by Andrew Sarris and included in Sarris, ed., *Interviews with Film Directors* (Indianapolis: Bobbs-Merrill, 1967) ("to turn out films"). Jean Arthur and George Stevens commented on JF to the author; Howard Hawks spoke of Frank W. "Spig" Wead in an interview with the author, published in JM, *Hawks on Hawks.*

JF's recollection that there was "something special" about Duke Morrison in his youth is from Pilar Wayne, with Alex Thorleifson, *John Wayne: My Life with the Duke* (New York: McGraw-Hill, 1987). JW's comment on JF shunning him is from his OH, quoted in R&O, which also includes comments on the split between JF and JW. Bogdanovich's account of Raoul Walsh choosing JW for the starring role in *The Big Trail* is from his book *Who the Devil Made It,* which contains an interview with Walsh. JF's list of his favorite films for *Cinema,* 1964, is cited in Gallagher. How John Wayne was named is discussed in DF; Zolotow; and R&O. Barbara Ford's 1934 message to JW from her father is recalled by JW in Bogdanovich, "The Duke's Gone West," *New York,* June 25, 1979.

DF's account of JF's trip to the Far East with George O'Brien includes JF's account of leaving MF behind and O'Brien's description of JF as "the most private man I ever met." Other sources on the trip include an item in *LAE,* January 8, 1931; Gallagher (on O'Brien's lack of knowledge of a JF spying mission); Levy; and Darcy O'Brien, "Jack Ford and George O'Brien, A Long Voyage Home." JF's comment about his physical condition and O'Brien looking at him admiringly is from a January 1931 letter to MF, quoted in DF. Sources on JF's trip to Hawaii and the Philippines with MF include a Ford family radiogram to JF in Honolulu, December 12, 1931; JF's letter from the SS *Tzibaclak* to MF in Manila, January 28, 1932; SS *President Grant* entertainment program (with JF as entertainment chairman), March 2–8, 1932, Honolulu to San Francisco; and Passenger List (including JF and MF), SS *Wilhelmina,* Los Angeles to Hawaii with return to San Francisco, sailing October 31, 1932. JF's *Shanghai Interlude* project is reported in Elizabeth Yeaman, "Pomeroy's Film Firm to Make 12 Features," *HCN,* March 21, 1932; see also JF's 1932 tax return.

MF's automobile accident (1933) is reported in "Mrs. John Ford, Director's Wife, Hurt in Odd Accident," unidentified Los Angeles newspaper, September 29; an item in *LAE,* September 30; and "Mrs. Ford, Auto Fall Victim, Goes Home," *LAE,* October 1. Coverage of the suicide of John Willis Smith includes "John Ford's Kin's Suicide Revealed by Garage Blast," *LAE,* January 3, 1932; and "John Willis Smith Final Rites Today," *LAE,* January 6, 1932. MF's comment "The first thing Bobby [Barbara] says" is from a 1926 letter to JF, quoted in Levy. Wingate Smith's OH reports on Pat Ford's punishment for imitating his father; Pat's comment on their relationship is from his interview with James D'Arc, 1979, quoted in Wills. Biographical information on Wingate Smith is from his OH and his obituary, *DV,* July 30, 1974. A report on JF's examination by Dr. Harley J. Gunderson, September 27, 1934, is at Lilly.

Philip Dunne discussed JF's politics with the author. JF's comment about "a constant battle" is from Emanuel Eisenberg, "John Ford, Fighting Irish," *New Theater,* April 1936; he describes his working methods in Howard Sharpe, "The Star Creators of Hollywood: John Ford," *Photoplay,* October 1936. JF describes himself as "a definite socialistic democrat—*always* left" in a letter to his nephew Bob Ford, 1937, quoted in DF (see the notes for chapter 9). Information on the founding of the Motion Picture Directors Association and JF's presidency is from Slide, *The American Film Industry,* Gallagher; and list of MPDA members, *Film Daily,* June 12, 1927. The founding of the Screen Directors Guild is discussed in JM, *Frank Capra.* The text of JF's speech to the SDG (1933) is in Lilly. Rouben Mamoulian is quoted on the SDG from an interview with the author for JM, *Frank Capra,* which also quotes Mitch Tuchman's 1977 interview with King Vidor. Capra recalls his March 10, 1933, encounter with JF in *The Name Above the Title.* JF's comment on the purpose of the SDG ("to talk about") is quoted in Jerry Roberts, Ted Elrick, and Tomm Carroll, "Sixty Years of Action," *DGA Magazine,* November–December 1996/January–February 1997. Additional information on the 1933 Hollywood pay-cut crisis is from Larry Ceplair and Steven Englund, *The Inquisition in Hollywood: Politics in the Film Community, 1930–1960* (Berkeley: University of California Press, 1979). Frank Baker's story about JF's response to an old actor begging for money is from Gallagher's interview with Baker.

Gloria Stuart is quoted from the author's interview, published as JM, "Great Gloria: Gloria Stuart Tells How She Made a Titanic Comeback," *Cinemania Online,* December 19, 1997. Information on the background of Dudley Nichols is from Nichols's letter to Anderson, April 22, 1953; "Dudley Nichols, Award Winning Producer, Dies," *HCN,* January 5, 1960; and "Dudley Nichols Rites Today After Long Career, Top Pix," *DV,* January 6, 1960. Nichols discusses his relationship with JF, how he wrote his first script, and his penchant for "stylized symbolism" in his letter to Anderson. JF's response to an interviewer's question about "the theme of the family" is from Bertrand Tavernier, "Notes of a Press Attaché: John Ford in Paris, 1966," *Film Comment,* July/August 1994. Barbara Feeney's death (1933) is reported in "Mrs. John A. Feeney, 77, Mother of 3 Hollywood Directors, Dies," *Portland Press Herald,* March 27; and her obituary in the *Portland Evening Express,* March 27. I. A. R. Wylie's short story "Pilgrimage" appears in the *American Magazine,* November 1932; Fox's announcement of the film version is from an item in *LAE,* November 17, 1932. Henrietta Crosman's comment on *Pilgrimage* is quoted in a note on the film by Clive Denton, Toronto Film Society, July 26, 1982 (AMPAS). Norman Foster's re marks on JF are from his interview with the author.

Information on JF's purchase of the *Araner* is from "Preliminary Statement," April 27, 1961 (summary of tax information, Lilly); and W. S. Malin, tax audit, July 2, 1936 (referring to JF deducting expenses for taking Harry Cohn on the boat). JF's tax deductions for use of *Araner* are from his tax returns, 1934 ff.; MF recalls the boat as "terribly expensive" in Sinclair, which also contains the story about JF tossing a Nichols script overboard. JF recalls studying film projects on the boat in Sharpe. Darcy O'Brien's observation on the *Araner* is quoted in Davis. JW's comment on JF's drinking is from DF; sources on JF's trips to Mexico on the *Araner* include DF; R&O; and Davis (including the entries from the ship's log). Dunne's comments on socializing with JF on the *Araner* and JF's attitude toward the USN are from Dunne's interview with the author. For information on the wartime charter of the *Araner,* see the notes for chapter 10.

Sources on the Emerald Bay Yacht Club include the author's interviews with club members Philip Dunne and Vice Admiral John D. Bulkeley, USN; Sinclair; Gallagher; and DF. Differing accounts of the club's slogan are in Sinclair ("No Jews and no dues") and DF ("Jews but no dues"); Dunne's confirmation of the latter as the actual slogan is from his interview with the author, in which he also discussed his relationship with JF. Information on the Phoenix Park Murders is from Kee and Lyons. Wurtzel is described as the club's "Rabbi" in Nichols to C. E. Wingate Smith, n.d. (Lilly). Mark Armistead's OH recalls the club's initiation ceremony. Sources on the Young Men's Purity, Total Abstinence, and Yachting Association (aka the Young Men's Purity, Total Abstinence, and Snooker Pool Association) include Gallagher and DF.

JF's U.S. Navy career is summarized in "Rear Admiral John Ford, U.S. Naval Reserve, Retired," USN, October 2, 1952. JF's claim of "a few years spent before the mast" is from his application for a commission in the U.S. Naval Reserve, July 10, 1934. Sinclair claims that JF's "boyish" double life includes spying in 1921, 1929, and 1931–32; in "Jack Ford and George O'Brien, A Long Voyage Home," Darcy O'Brien comments on the "prepostcrousness" of the notion that JF was spying on his 1931 trip to Asia with George O'Brien. JF's USNR training report [c. 1941] mentions his 1934 activities and the course in "Naval and Combat Photography." Documents on JF's USNR commissioning in 1934 include his April 22, 1949, service record; medical exam, chief of the Bureau of Navigation, September 21, 1934; JF to chief of Bureau of Navigation, application for USNR commission, July 10, 1934; FF's notarized certification of JF's birth, August 30, 1934; letters of recommendation from Rear Admiral Frank H. Schofield, USN (Ret.)., September 7, 1934 (quoted), and Sol M. Wurtzel, 1934; report from the chief, Bureau of Medicine and Surgery, that JF was not qualified medically, September 14, 1934; endorsement by H. A. Jones, director, Naval Reserves, Eleventh Naval District, September 1, 1934 (quoted); JF medical exam, n.d.; JF biographical sheet [1941]; and JF's Brief of Record, USN, July 11, 1942.

The announcement that JF was to direct Will Rogers in *A Connecticut Yankee in King Arthur's Court* is from *LAE,* August 3, 1929. Rogers's comment on his Cherokee blood is from Jerry Belcher, "Will Rogers—a Mirror of America," *LAT,* August 15, 1985. Rogers discusses JF in his syndicated newspaper column, June 24, 1934 ("This old boy"), and July 1, 1934 ("used to direct"; "one of the likable things"), quoted in Bryan B. Sterling and Frances N. Sterling, *Will Rogers in Hollywood* (New York: Crown, 1984); JF's account of working with Rogers is also from that book. HCJ's account of his conversation with JF about Rogers is from his interview with the author. Stepin Fetchit told the author about the lynching scene that JF filmed for *Judge Priest* but was cut by the studio; Gallagher quotes JF on Rogers's speech against lynching. Stepin Fetchit's comment "Paht of the time" is quoted in Ben Yagoda, *Will Rogers: A Biography* (New York: Knopf, 1993); V. S. Naipaul praises the controversial African-American comedian in *A*

Turn in the South (New York: Knopf, 1989). G. K. Chesterton's observation on judges is from his story "The Man in the Passage" (1913), *The Penguin Complete Father Brown* (Harmondsworth, England: Penguin Books, 1981).

Irvin S. Cobb recalls the filming of *Steamboat Round the Bend* in "Unselfish Rogers Pictured by Cobb," *NYT,* August 22, 1935. Rogers's death and funeral are described in Yagoda. JF's invitation to Rogers to travel with him aboard the *Araner* to Hawaii is recalled by MF in Ray Coll Jr., "Shoreside Shorts," Honolulu paper [1935]; Rogers's response to JF, "You keep your duck," is from Sinclair, as is MF's recollection of JF going "all to pieces" after Rogers's death; JF's OH recalls his memorial service for Rogers. JF's comment on the studio's recutting of the film is from PB; Sterling and Sterling discuss the shot cut from the film of Rogers waving good-bye. Information on Darryl F. Zanuck and the formation of Twentieth Century–Fox is from Mel Gussow, *Don't Say Yes Until I Finish Talking: A Biography of Darryl F. Zanuck* (New York: Doubleday, 1971); and George F. Custen, *Twentieth Century's Fox: Darryl F. Zanuck and the Culture of Hollywood* (New York: BasicBooks, 1997).

CHAPTER SEVEN: SEAN AND KATE (PP. 214–244)

The epigraph is from Eisenberg. Sources on the relationship between JF and Liam O'Flaherty include DF and the JF-O'Flaherty correspondence in Lilly. JF recalls his friendship with Joseph Kennedy in Mitchell; information on Kennedy is from Richard J. Whelan, *The Founding Father* (New York: New American Library, 1964); David E. Koskoff, *Joseph P. Kennedy: A Life and Times* (Englewood Cliffs, N.J.: Prentice-Hall, 1974); and Lawrence J. Quirk, *The Kennedys in Hollywood* (Dallas: Taylor Publishing Co., 1996). Maurice Walsh's story "The Quiet Man" was published in the *Saturday Evening Post,* February 11, 1933; a revised version appeared in Walsh's collection *Green Rushes* (New York: Frederick A. Stokes Co., 1935). Sources on JF's interest in filming the story in 1935–6 include his 1935 IRS return; Walsh and JF agreements for sale of film rights, February 25, 1936 (signed by JF on April 9), and March 5, 1936; and McNee.

Douglas Gomery's comment on RKO is from his book *Movie History: A Survey* (Belmont, Ca.: Wadsworth Publishing Co., 1991). Sources on Merian C. Cooper include the author's interviews with Katherine Cliffton (Cooper's secretary and later story editor for the JF-Cooper production company Argosy Pictures) and Ronald Haver; Cliffton's OH; *Memo from: David O. Selznick,* selected and edited by Rudy Behlmer (New York: Viking Press, 1972); Brownlow, *The War, the West, and the Wilderness;* and Behlmer, "Merian C. Cooper Is the Kind of Creative Showman Today's Movies Badly Need," *Films in Review,* January 1966. The story about Cliff Reid and *The Lost Patrol* is from Michel Mok, "The Rebels, If They Stay Up This Time, Won't Be Sorry for Hollywood's Trouble," *New York Post,* January 24, 1939. Nunnally Johnson's description of Reid as "terrified" of JF is from DF; Robert Parrish, *Growing Up in Hollywood* (New York: Harcourt Brace, 1988), tells about Reid coming on the set of *The Informer* and JF hiring him for *They Were Expendable;* other comments on Reid are from Katharine Hepburn, *Me: Stories of My Life* (New York: Knopf, 1991); and Dudley Nichols to Anderson, April 22, 1953, published in Anderson, *About John Ford.*

O'Flaherty describes *The Informer* (London: Jonathan Cape, 1925) as "a sort of high-brow detective story" in his book *Shame the Devil* (London: Grayson and Grayson, 1934), quoted in Denis Donoghue's preface to *The Informer,* 1980 edition (New York: Harcourt Brace Jovanovich). Nichols's screenplay of *The Informer* was published in Harlan Hatcher, ed., *Modern British Dramas* (New York: Harcourt, Brace, 1941), and Hatcher, ed., *Modern Dramas* (New York: Harcourt, Brace, 1944); see also the unpublished shooting script by Nichols [1935]. Nichols comments on the script in his article "The Writer and the Film," in John Gassner and Nichols, *Twenty Best Film Plays* (New York: Crown, 1943); and Nichols to Anderson; see also "Nichols and Ford to Do Script on Cruise," *HR,* December 17, 1934. JF comments on non-verbal storytelling in his 1937 press release "Exclusive for William Boehnel: *N.Y. World Telegram*" (United Artists publicity files, State Historical Society of Wisconsin). JW's analysis of *The Informer* is from *Directed by John Ford;* JF's remark that the film "lacks humor" is from PB.

The production costs of *The Lost Patrol* and *The Informer,* and JF's earnings from those films, are from Nichols to Anderson; JF's 1933 and 1935 IRS returns; and Norman Hayward, IRS audits of JF for the tax years 1935 and 1936, July 29, 1937. Information on the story about Victor McLaglen getting drunk is from the author's interview with Vice Admiral John D. Bulkeley, USN; DF; Bob Condon, "John Ford, The Director? Sure, I Know Him," *New York,* n.d. (AMPAS); Parrish, *Growing Up in Hollywood;* and David Niven, *The Moon's a Balloon* (New York: G. P. Putnam's Sons, 1972); JF denies the story in Wagner and is also quoted from Condon. Other JF comments on the film are from Eisenberg; Sharpe; and Mitchell.

Darryl F. Zanuck's remark on *The Informer* is from Gussow. Reviews of the film (1935) include Andre Sennwald, *NYT,* May 10; *Land.* (Tom Landry), *Variety,* May 15; Otis Ferguson, *New Republic,* May 29; and *Picturegoer,* n.d. (AMPAS). JF's recollections of the Hollywood preview are from his OH and Mitchell ("like a leper"); Nichols relates to Anderson that RKO executives said they regretted making the film. The *NYT* and National Board of Review awards are listed in Levy; information on the 1936 Oscar ceremony and controversy is from JM, *Frank Capra;* and Mason Wiley and Damien Bona, *Inside Oscar: The Unofficial History of the Academy Awards* (New York: Ballantine Books, 1993). Nichols's letter rejecting his Oscar and JF's statement accepting his award is from "Dudley Nichols Turns Down Academy Award," *HR,* March 9, 1936; the SDG statement that "No one can respect" the Academy is from an SDG newsletter quoted in Wiley and Bona. DF says that because JF accepted his Oscar in 1936, the SDG voted him out of office and he remained inactive in the guild for the rest of his life. However, the SDG files indicate that JF was elected treasurer on January 17, 1936, and held that post until Rowland V. Lee was elected on May 15, 1938; JF was reelected to the SDG's board of directors at that meeting (see also "Capra Elected Prez of Directors' Guild," *Variety,* May 18, 1938) and remained on the board until May 19, 1940; after returning from World War II, he rejoined the board on May 19, 1946, and subsequently served in other guild posts. The history of the SDG contract talks is in JM, *Frank Capra,* including material from the author's interviews with Capra ("because they had") and Dunne ("a company of gentleman"); Capra's "stooging" comment is from *The Name Above the Title.* JF's 1937 statement on the SDG is from his "Exclusive for William Boehnel: *N.Y. World Telegram.*"

Sources on Katharine Hepburn's life, career, and family background include Hepburn, *Me;* Michael Freedland, *Katharine Hepburn* (London: W. H. Allen, 1984); Anne Edwards, *A Remarkable Woman: A Biography of Katharine Hepburn* (New York: William Morrow, 1985); and Barbara Leaming, *Katharine Hepburn* (New York: Crown, 1995). KH's remark that she "sort of came over on the *Mayflower*" is from an interview with the author, quoted in JM, *Frank Capra.* Dr. Thomas Hepburn's statement on eugenics is from proceedings of the Connecticut Society of Social Hygiene, quoted in Leaming; KH's expression of shock over the size of the Feeney family is from the JF/KH OH, 1973 (audiotapes at Lilly).

JF's comment on KH ("When they gave me") is from Sharpe, "The Star Creators of Hollywood"; his comments to KH are from DF ("You're a hell of a fine girl"); "Men Behind the Stars: John Ford," *Motion Picture,* October 1936 ("You'll give"), and Leaming ("Listen, Katharine" and "This is a goddam lousy scene"); Leaming describes the incident with the pipes and JF directing KH's screen test in 1932. Sarris's criticism of Maxwell Anderson's play *Mary of Scotland* is from *The American Cinema.* KH's comments on Mary Stuart and finding JF "fascinating but impossible" as well as "an extremely interesting man" are from *Me.* The story about KH putting a mark on JF's shirt is from Freedland. Pandro S. Berman's comment on JF is from Davis; John Carradine's story is from Jordan R. Young, *Reel Characters: Great Movie Character Actors* (Beverly Hills, Ca.: Moonstone Press, 1987).

Sources on the JF-KH romance and its effect on JF and his marriage include DF; Leaming; Edwards; Davis; and Bogdanovich, "The Cowboy Hero and the American West . . . as Directed by John Ford," *Esquire,* December 1983. Cecil McLean de Prida's observations on the romance in her OH, and her report of MF saying "Jack is very religious," are quoted in Davis. Letters by Dan Ford and Selden West on Leaming's book, and a reply by Leaming, are from the *NYT Book Review,* May 14, 1995. Tom Hepburn's statement to his sister and George Cukor's entry in the *Araner* log are from Leaming; the intimate photograph of KH and JF aboard the *Araner* is printed in DF. The JK/KH OH tapes are quoted from Davis ("I'm not sure"; "half pagan"; "a remarkable woman") and Gallagher ("being able"; "enormously rough"); the comments on split personalities by KH and JF are cited by Leaming. Claire Trevor commented on JF, MF, and KH in an interview with the author. The Fords' quotes on their golden anniversary are from an item in *Time,* July 20, 1970; and the author's interview with Linda Noe Laine (MF's "I've been married fifty years"). Other comments by MF on JF, their marriage, and his films are from Slide and Banker. DF reports that MF regarded her husband's movie career as "flashy and 'low Irish'"; Leaming describes MF as "monstrous" and claims she habitually called JF "shanty Irish."

Letters from KH to JF quoted in this chapter include: March 1, 1937 ("I can only say"), from Davis; and April 10, 1937 ("Oh Sean"; "must say yes and no"), from Gallagher and Davis. The letter to JF from "Mimi" is dated [December 5?], 1938 (Lilly). Information on JF's visit to his father in 1936, his father's death, and the aftermath include KH to JF, June 27, 1936; and Leaming. JF's jocular expression of affection is from his January 16, 1937, letter to KH; the incident at the St. Louis hotel is from Leaming and a letter by Emily Perkins to JF [January 1937]; JF's letter to Perkins is dated January 25, 1937. The end of JF's romantic relationship with KH is clear from her letter of April 10, 1937.

JF's offer to Sean O'Casey to write the screen adaptation of *The Informer* is reported in Garry O'Connor, *Sean O'Casey: A Life* (New York: Atheneum, 1988). The riot over the 1926 Abbey Theatre production of O'Casey's play *The Plough and the Stars* is discussed in Sean McCann, ed., *The Story of the Abbey Theatre* (London: Four Square Books, 1967). Spencer Tracy's rejection of a role in *Plough* and JF's reaction are recalled by KH in the JF/KH OH. JF's comment "For these pictures" is from Sharpe. Sam Briskin's arguments with JF over *Plough* are reported in JF's OH and in PB. Sources on RKO's reshooting and JF's bender include JF's OH; Leaming; KH, *Me;* and PB (in which JF also remarks on the cutting of *Mary of Scotland*). JF's attempt to have his name removed from *Plough* is reported in Leaming; his claim that his version was released in Ireland and England is from PB.

CHAPTER EIGHT: "NO PLACE FOR AN AUTEUR" (PP. 245–268)

The chapter title is a description of Darryl F. Zanuck's Twentieth Century–Fox from Philip Dunne, *Take Two: A Life in Movies and Politics* (New York: McGraw-Hill, 1980). Additional quotes from Dunne are from the author's interview; Dunne, *Take Two;* and Dunne, "No Fence Around Time," introduction to *How Green Was My Valley: The Screenplay for the Darryl F. Zanuck Film Production Directed by John Ford* (Santa Barbara, Ca.: Santa Teresa Press, 1990). The chapter epigraph is from Sarris, *The American Cinema.*

JF's comments on DFZ are from Gussow ("Darryl's a genius") and DF ("Napoleon complex"); DFZ's praise of JF's work is from Gussow. The argument between JF and DFZ over Warner Baxter's accent is reported in Tom Stempel, *Screenwriter: The Life and Times of Nunnally Johnson* (San Diego: A.S. Barnes, 1980); and Davis. DFZ/Fox's rural nostalgia policy is discussed in Custen. JF's proposal to remake *La Grande Illusion* is from his March 1, 1938, letter to DFZ (Lilly); DFZ's March 2 reply is in *Memo from Darryl F. Zanuck: The Golden Years at Twentieth Century–Fox,* selected, ed., and annotated by Rudy Behlmer (New York: Grove Press, 1993). Jean Renoir's recollection of JF is from *My Life and My Films,* trans. by Norman Denny (New York: Atheneum, 1974). JF's criticisms of DFZ for lacking "artistic integrity" and making "safe commercial pictures" are from DF.

Anecdotes about JF dealing with extras and Fox executives are from William Clothier's OH (about an unidentified 1930s film) and from the author's interview with Bulkeley (about *How*

Green Was My Valley). JF's working methods are discussed by Arthur C. Miller in Fred C. Bal-shofer and Miller, *One Reel a Week* (Berkeley: University of California Press, 1967). JF's OH comments on violating the rule of screen direction in the *Stagecoach* chase; Winton C. Hoch's observations on JF's violations of the rule and on the scene in *She Wore a Yellow Ribbon* are from the author's interview with Hoch, parts published as JM, "Winton Hoch: 'A Damn Good Job,'" *Film Comment,* November–December 1979. Selznick remarks on JF's secretive personality in a memo to J. H. Whitney, August 11, 1937, from *Memo from: David O. Selznick.*

JF's claim not to be proud of his work is from Gussow. Parrish discusses JF's postproduction practices in *Growing Up in Hollywood* and Max Wilk, *The Wit and Wisdom of Hollywood* (New York: Atheneum, 1971). DF describes JF looking at rushes with a magnifying glass on the set of *The Prisoner of Shark Island;* JF told Gussow about his "tacit agreement" that DFZ would cut his films. DFZ's filmmaking credo ("They don't call them") is from Gussow; DFZ comments on the rushes of *Young Mr. Lincoln* in a memo to JF, March 22, 1939, in *Memo from Darryl F. Zanuck;* DFZ's jocular comment on JF's style in a memo to John Steinbeck and Elia Kazan, May 3, 1950, is also from that collection. JF's letter to DFZ on *Drums Along the Mohawk* is quoted in Davis; JF's phrase "grace notes" appears in his "Notes for Jim McGuinness on [*They Were*] *Expendable,*" [1944] (Lilly); JF recalls the scene cut from *Lincoln* in PB; his remark to DFZ about cutting *The Grapes of Wrath* is from Wilk. Sources on DFZ's changes in *My Darling Clementine* and JF's reaction include John A. Gallagher, "Winston Miller" (interview), *Films in Review,* December 1990; *Memo from Darryl F. Zanuck;* and the preview version of the film, restored by UCLA Film and Television Archive. DF praises DFZ's recutting JF's work to reduce "broad sight gags"; but in *The John Ford Movie Mystery,* Sarris criticizes the idea that DFZ made JF a greater artist.

The *Shark Island* production schedule is from a Fox cast list [January 1936?] (Lilly); and from Levy, who also reports on Fox's purchase of story rights. Information on Dr. Mudd is from Edward Steers Jr., *His Name Is Still Mudd. The Case Against Dr. Samuel Alexander Mudd* (Gettysburg, Pa.: Thomas Publications, 1997); and James E. T. Lange and Katherine DeWitt, "Life of Assassination Figure Muddier Than Known," the *Washington Times,* August 30, 1997 (quoting Frederick Stone). Haudiquet observes in his book that JF had "an obsession with justice." Information on Frank McGlynn Sr. is from FF, "Up and Down the Ladder." Sources on the JF–Carey plans to remake *The Last Outlaw* include the author's interviews with Olive Carey and HCJ; distribution agreement between JF and United Artists Corp., January 5, 1945 (State Historical Society of Wisconsin, United Artists legal files); and amendment, United Artists Corp. and Argosy Pictures Corp., April 22, 1946.

Sources of production information on *Wee Willie Winkie* include "The Making of a Great Picture" in the Fox souvenir book for the film, 1937 (AMPAS); Balshofer and Miller; and Shirley Temple Black, *Child Star: An Autobiography* (New York: McGraw-Hill, 1988); Temple describes it as her favorite film in Jeanine Basinger, *Shirley Temple* (New York: Pyramid Communications, 1975). JF recalls his teaming with Temple in Gussow; Davis reports he was far from happy about it; his initial "indifference" is reported in Black. JF's greeting to Temple, their nicknames for each other, and his chant "Shirley Temple is unfair" are reported in "—And Shirley Met Ford," Fox souvenir book. JF's OH recalls his delight that Temple whispered cues to a British actor. Temple's comment on the contrast between JF's exterior and interior personalities is from Basinger. DFZ's remarks at the July 25, 1936, story conference on *Winkie* are from *Memo from Darryl F. Zanuck.* Black describes Victor McLaglen's death scene; sources on the funeral scene include Balshofer and Miller; PB ("We've got everybody"); and Gussow ("D. Z. said").

Graham Greene's review of *Wee Willie Winkie* from *Night and Day,* October 28, 1937, is reprinted in David Parkinson, ed., *The Graham Greene Film Reader: Reviews, Essays, Interviews & Film Stories* (Manchester, England: Carcanet Press, 1993, and New York: Applause Books, 1995), which also contains Greene's *Captain January* review from the *Spectator,* August 7, 1936. The Fox libel suit over *Winkie* is quoted from Parkinson, which also contains a report on the suit reprinted from the Law Reports of the London *Times,* May 23, 1938; Greene comments on the suit in "Memories of a Film Critic," *International Film Annual,* 1958, reprinted in his autobiography *Ways of Escape* (New York: Simon and Schuster, 1980), and in Parkinson. Norman Sherry's comment on the suit is from *The Life of Graham Greene, Volume I: 1904–1939* (New York: Viking Penguin, 1989), which also includes Greene's phrase "that bitch Shirley Temple" (quoted from a letter to Elizabeth Bowen); Basinger's analysis of Temple's screen personality is from *Shirley Temple.* Greene's comment on *The Fugitive* is from Quentin Falk, *Travels in Greeneland: The Cinema of Graham Greene* (London: Quartet Books, 1984).

JF's joke about making films for money is from Labarthe's interview, "Entre chien et loup: John Ford" ("In the Twilight: John Ford"), *Cinéastes de notre temps,* 1966; JF's comment on the profitability of films is from his interview with the author. Ben Hecht's work on *The Hurricane* is reported in William MacAdams, *Ben Hecht: A Biography* (New York: Scribners, 1990); other production information on the film is from JF's OH; Davis; and UA publicity material, 1937 (State Historical Society of Wisconsin). PB reports JF's uncredited direction of scenes in *The Adventures of Marco Polo.* Information on William Faulkner's work on *Submarine Patrol* and *Drums* is from Joseph Blotner, *Faulkner: A Biography* (New York: Random House, 1974). DFZ's demand about "keeping the war out of" *Submarine Patrol* is quoted from Davis; JF comments on the Nancy Kelly incident and "adverse criticism from my own studio" in his letter to William Dover of Fox, October 29, 1938, quoted in Davis; JF's claim of engine trouble is reported by DF. JF tells PB of his dislike for the story of *Four Men and a Prayer;* JF's comment that a director "must hypnotize himself" is from Wagner. David Niven's story about *Four Men* is from *The Moon's a Balloon.* Josephine Feeney's OH points out that C. Aubrey Smith resembled her father, John A. Feeney.

Chapter Nine: Natani Nez (pp. 296–334)

JF's nickname "Natani Nez" was explained to the author by Billy Yellow; references to the name appear in JF's OH and PB.

Ceplair and Englund report that JF was a founder of Motion Picture Artists Committee to Aid Republican Spain and attended the party for Ernest Hemingway; JF's OH discusses Hemingway. Information on JF's involvement with the Motion Picture Democratic Committee is from the author's interview with Philip Dunne and Dunne, *Take Two.* Sources on JF and the Hollywood Anti-Nazi League include the author's interview with Gloria Stuart; Ceplair and Englund; Nancy Lynn Schwartz, completed by Sheila Schwartz, *The Hollywood Writers' Wars* (New York: Knopf, 1982); and "Anti-Nazis Hear Warning," *LAT,* January 31, 1938. Bob Ford's letter to JF, September 30, 1937, and JF's [September?] 1937 reply (quoted from DF) are in Lilly; an undated note following JF's letter, citing Cecil McLean de Prida, claims the letter was never sent. Sources on the 1938 strike of the *Hollywood Citizen-News* include the author's interview with Dunne; JM, *Frank Capra;* SDG minutes, May 23 and June 6, 1938; Schwartz; "Film Directors Give Aid," *Hollywood Citizen-News Striker,* June 1, 1938; and "Summary of Information" (on a House Committee on Un-American Activities [HUAC] citation about Frank Capra's involvement in the strike), G-2, October 10, 1951, in Capra's Army Intelligence file.

DF's largely skeptical and dismissive account of his grandfather's spying for the Office of Naval Intelligence (ONI) was written before JF's U.S. Navy file was released, showing the full extent of his spying missions before World War II while a member of the U.S. Naval Reserve (USNR) (see references in following paragraphs); the author examined the file at Lilly in 1998. MF's OH discusses JF's spying and her involvement, which is also detailed in Davis. Henry Fonda's OH gives a misleading description of JF's behavior in Mexico.

Among the sources of information in JF's USN files are his service record, April 22, 1949; and his official USN biography, "Rear Admiral John Ford, U.S. Naval Reserve, Retired," October 2, 1952. William J. Donovan, director of the Office of Strategic Services (OSS) in World War II, which included Ford's Field Photographic Branch, reports to Rear Admiral Harold Train, director of ONI, April 27, 1943, that JF "devoted himself to the study of intelligence matters" in the USNR before World War II. JF is described as "fully qualified as an intelligence officer" by Commander W. H. Vanderbilt, USNR, head of strategic services for ONI, April 8, 1943, in JF's Annual Fitness Report. JF outlines his "research covering camera photography and camouflage problems" in Mexico and Hawaii in his October 1, 1935, Annual Fitness Report, with October 5, 1935, comments from H. A. [Captain Herbert A.] Jones, commanding officer, director, and instructor, Naval Reserves, Eleventh Naval District. JF mentions "several Naval Intelligence assignments" in his Annual Fitness Report, September 15, 1941, and comments in his USN Biographical Sheet [1941] that he had made "numerous voyages [on the *Araner*] to Hawaii, Panama, the Mexican Coast, and various places on the Pacific."

Documents on JF's spying missions in Mexico include C. Young, commandant's office, Eleventh Naval District, to JF, May 6, 1936 (authorization for visit to Mexico); JF's 1936 report to ONI on Scammon Lagoon in Baja California, quoted in DF ("close enough"); John Staples, ONI, to commandant, Eleventh Naval District, July 25, 1936 (noting that JF had contributed "valuable and most interesting data" on Scammon Lagoon); Lieutenant Commander A. A. Hopkins to JF, 1936 (commending him for the "considerable *importance*" of his reports); JF to Capt. Ellis Zacharias, USN, "Subject: Baja California and the Gulf of California," [December?] 1939; J. R. DeFrees, commandant, Eleventh Naval District, to JF, January 16, 1940 (commending JF on his "initiative in securing the valuable information" during his 1939 Baja California and Gulf of California mission); and C. A. Blakely and W. W. Waddell, commandant's office, Eleventh Naval District, to JF, February 6, 1941 (granting permission for his 1941 mission to Mazatlán and La Paz). Japanese attacks on the U.S. mainland during World War II are discussed in Bert Webber's books *Retaliation: Japanese Attacks and Allied Countermeasures on the Pacific Coast in World War II* (Corvallis: Oregon State University Press, 1975), and *Silent Siege: Japanese Attacks against North America in World War II* (Fairfield, Wa.: Ye Galleon Press, 1984).

Darryl F. Zanuck rejects JF's Custer project *Glory Hunter* in his letter to JF, April 13, 1935. JF's comment on the Western genre in the 1930s is from his interview with the author; Western production figures are from Buscombe, *The BFI Companion to the Western*; Buscombe, *Stagecoach* (London: BFI Film Classics, 1992); and R&O. JW's comment that playing a singing cowboy made him feel like "a goddam pansy" is from Ronald L. Davis, *Duke: The Life and Image of John Wayne* (Norman: University of Oklahoma Press, 1998). "Stage to Lordsburg" by Ernest Haycox appeared in *Collier's*, April 10, 1937; Wingate Smith's OH reports that Pat Ford discovered the story; JF says in PB that the story reminded him of Guy de Maupassant's "Boule de Suif"; information on JF's purchase of the story is from Buscombe, *Stagecoach*. Nichols's screenplay of *Stagecoach* was published in Gassner and Nichols, *Twenty Best Film Plays;* Nicola Hayden, ed., *Stagecoach: A Film of John Ford and Dudley Nichols* (New York: Simon and Schuster, 1971); and Richard Anobile, ed., *Stagecoach* (New York: Avon Books, 1975); the date the script was written is from DF. JF reports Ben Hecht's contributions to *Stagecoach* in MacAdams.

JF's two-picture deal with Cooper and Pioneer Pictures is discussed in Ronald Haver, *David O. Selznick's Hollywood* (New York: Knopf, 1980), which includes Cooper's comments on the deal arousing the ire of studio heads and JF being "the very best director alive." DFZ's refusal to read the *Stagecoach* script, and the rejection of the project by MGM, Paramount, and Warner Bros. are reported in DF; Harry Cohn's agreement to let JF make the film if he would also make *Golden Boy* is from "Shiker" to "Pops" [1938?] (Lilly). Trevor's comments on JF and *Stagecoach* are from her interview with the author. JF's interest in filming *Salome, Where She Danced* is discussed in his letter to an unidentified recipient, July 2, 1943; JF to Spig Wead, February 11, 1944; and MF to JF, January [24?], 1944; other information on the film is from Matthew Bernstein, *Walter Wanger, Hollywood Independent* (Berkeley: University of California Press, 1994).

Cooper's comments on JF and Selznick and on pitching *Stagecoach* are from Haver. Selznick's 1937 comments about JF in *Memo from: David O. Selznick* include his telegram to John Hay Whitney and John Wharton, June 29 ("We must select the story"; "outstanding failures"); memo to Dan O'Shea, July 16 ("annoyed"); and memo to Whitney, August 11 ("somewhat wounded"). Sources on Selznick projects offered to JF include Selznick's 1937 telegram to Whitney and Wharton, cited above *(Lafayette Escadrille);* O'Shea to JF, December 1, 1937 *(The Little Shepherd of Kingdom Come);* and David Thomson, *Showman: The Life of David O. Selznick* (New York: Knopf, 1992) (Benedict Arnold). KH's comment that JF "loved his hits—adored his failures" is from *Me;* JF tells PB how he financed his pet projects. JF's salary figures on *The Hurricane* and his Fox pictures are from Gallagher; his salary on *Stagecoach* is from Buscombe, *Stagecoach;* Capra's salary is from JM, *Frank Capra.* JF's comment that "Duke wasn't ready" until *Stagecoach* is from Wayne and Thorleifson; sources on Wayne's casting include DF; R&O; Davis, *Duke;* and Bogdanovich, "The Duke's Gone West."

The budget, production cost, and 1939 box-office gross of *Stagecoach* are from "*Stagecoach*: Tentative Budget," Walter Wanger Prods. (1938); and Buscombe, *Stagecoach.* Locations and shooting dates are from those sources and "John Ford Takes His *Stage Coach* [*sic*] Out—," *DV,* November 8, 1938. Other production information is from an unsigned memo, "Indians," to Dan Keefe of Wanger Prods., October 28, 1938 (Lilly). JF and Nichols discuss *Stagecoach* in Michel Mok, "The Rebels, If They Stay Up This Time, Won't Be Sorry for Hollywood's Trouble," *New York Post,* January 24, 1939.

Information on Monument Valley is from the author's 1973 visit; "The *Stagecoach* Country" in "That Amazing *Stagecoach* and Some Interesting Facts About Its History and the Strange People Who Depended Upon It . . . ," production notes, Walter Wanger Prods., 1939 (AMPAS); Robert de Roos, *Monument Valley* (Flagstaff, Ariz.: Northland Press, 1965); Carlo Gaberscek, *Il West di John Ford* (Udine, Italy: Arti Grafiche Friulane, 1994); Bette L. Stanton, *"Where God Put the West": Movie Making in the Desert, A Moab–Monument Valley Movie History* (Moab, Ut.: Four Corners Publications, 1994); Davis; Wills; Neil M. Clark, "Desert Trader," *Saturday Evening Post,* March 29, 1947 (on Harry Goulding); Todd McCarthy, "John Ford and Monument Valley," *American Film,* May 1978; Edward Buscombe, "Inventing Monument Valley: Nineteenth Century Landscape Photography and the Western Film," 1995, from *Fugitive Images: From Photography to Video,* ed. by Patrice Petro (Bloomington: Indiana University Press, 1995), article reprinted in *The Western Reader,* ed. by Jim Kitses and Gregg Rickman (New York: Limelight Editions, 1998); and articles in *Arizona Highways:* April 1956, "Trip to Monument Valley," "The Valley That Nobody Knows," "Monument Valley," R.C., "Guest Book in the Valley," and Allen C. Reed, "John Ford Makes Another Movie Classic in Monument Valley" *(The Searchers);* September 1981, William R. Florence, "John Ford . . . the Duke and Monument Valley," and Virginia Greene, "Some of the Photos That Sold Monument Valley"; July 1999, Jeb J. Rosebrook and Jeb Stuart Rosebrook, "John Ford's Monument Valley"; and December 1999, "Monument Valley Filtered." JF comments on Monument Valley in his interview with Bill Libby. JF tells PB he drove through the valley before making *Stagecoach;* the stories about the Careys and George O'Brien introducing JW to Monument Valley are from Zolotow; the story about JW introducing JF to the site is in R&O. Wingate Smith's OH recalls the snow on the *Stagecoach* location. George Herriman's use of Monument Valley is discussed in Patrick McDonnell, Karen O'Connell, and Georgia Riley de Havenon, *Krazy Kat: The Comic Art of George Herriman* (New York: Harry N. Abrams, 1986).

Background on the Navajo people *(Diné)* is from Clyde Kluckhohn and Dorothea Leighton, *The Navaho* [*sic*], revised edition (Cambridge, Mass.: Harvard University Press, 1974, first published in 1946), which includes population and per-capita income figures for 1940; 1990 U.S. census data are from "Navajo Nation Profile" (1999) on the Web site *www.navajoland.com.* Varied reports on the money spent by the *Stagecoach* company in Monument Valley include Burt Kennedy, "A Talk with John Ford," *Action!* September–October 1968 ("[W]e left $200,000"); McCarthy ("about $60,000"); and Clark, "Desert Trader" ($45,000). The Navajos' unhappiness about Apaches being cast in *Stagecoach* is reported in "The *Stagecoach* Country." Navajos interviewed by the author include Billy Yellow, Lillian Bradley Smith (daughter of Lee Bradley), Barbara White (granddaughter of Lee Bradley), and Ella Begay (Portland, Maine, 1998); and George Holliday et al. (Monument Valley, 1973). Information on Hosteen Tso is from the author's interview with HCJ; PB; Davis; McCarthy; Clark; and Stanton. Chief John Big Tree is recalled in JF's OH and Buscombe, *The BFI Companion to the Western*. Tony Hillerman's novel *Sacred Clowns* was published by HarperCollins in 1993. JF defends his treatment of Indians in Eric Leguèbe, "John Ford," in *Le Cinéma Americain par ses auteurs* (Paris: Guy Authier, 1977) (the quotation is translated in Gallagher). In his OH, JF remembers kissing Navajo babies; the Navajos singing "Happy Days Are Here Again"; and the actor who plays Geronimo in *Stagecoach*. JW offers his views of Indians in Richard Warren Lewis, "*Playboy* Interview with John Wayne," *Playboy*, May 1971, reprinted in G. Barry Golson, ed., *The Playboy Interview* (New York: Playboy Press, 1981); the author's interview with a Navajo U.S. Army veteran who threatened to shoot JW was conducted in Monument Valley, 1973.

The actors' salaries for *Stagecoach* are listed in Buscombe, *Stagecoach*. Claire Trevor's comments on JF and *Stagecoach* are from her interview with the author; Louise Platt discusses Trevor in Dennis McLellan, "Memories of a Trailblazer," *LAT*, March 28, 1999. Olive Carey's comments on JF's walk and personality, and HCJ's observation that JF was a "tender, loving man . . . intrigued with machoism," are from their interviews with the author. JF's rough treatment of JW during the making of *Stagecoach* is reported by DF; Davis, *Duke;* and R&O. JW's account of how JF's bullying had the whole cast on his side, and his comment to JF that "I'm playing you," are from *Directed by John Ford*. JF's praise of JW's performance is from R&O. Allan Dwan's observation that JF acted as a "hypnotist" with JW and other actors is from Davis, *Duke*. The help JW received from Yakima Canutt and Paul Fix is reported in Canutt, *Stunt Man: The Autobiography of Yakima Canutt,* with Oliver Drake (New York: Walker and Co., 1979); and Davis, *Duke*. Canutt recalls his *Stagecoach* stunts in *Stunt Man;* additional information is from the author's interview with Canutt; in PB, JF recalls discussing the chase with Frank S. Nugent. Thomas Mitchell is quoted from Bob Thomas, ed., "John Ford and *Stagecoach,*" *Action!* September October 1971 ("That's all right"), and Nick Clooney, "Monument Memories," *American Movie Classics Magazine*, September 1995 ("the meanest").

Information on the press preview of *Stagecoach* is from Trevor and the preview program, Fox Westwood Theatre, Westwood Village (Los Angeles), February 2, 1939 (AMPAS). JF's monitoring of the preview from Maine is reported in Alta Durant, "Gab," *DV,* February 3, 1939. *Stagecoach* reviews (1939) include V. K., *Motion Picture Herald*, February 17; n.a., *DV,* February 3; n.a., *HR*, February 3; and Nugent, *NYT,* March 3. The film's preservation is reported in "Wayne Gifts *Stagecoach* to Institute," *Variety*, February 25, 1970.

The ending lines of Mark Twain's *Adventures of Huckleberry Finn*, 1884, are quoted in this section. D. H. Lawrence's description of the American landscape is from *Studies in Classic American Literature* (New York: Thomas Seltzer, 1923). Leslie A. Fiedler's observation about the loss of "the distinction between high literature and popular culture" is quoted from *The Return of the Vanishing American* (New York: Stein and Day, 1968). Also quoted are Smith, *Virgin Land;* André Bazin, "The Evolution of the Western" from Bazin, *What Is Cinema?,* translated and ed. by Hugh Gray (Berkeley: University of California Press, 1967); J. A. Place, *The Western Films of John Ford* (Secaucus, N.J.: Citadel Press, 1973); and Wills, *John Wayne's America*.

Robin Wood's essay *"Drums along the Mohawk"* appears in Ian Alexander Cameron and Douglas Pye, eds., *The Movie Book of the Western* (West Sussex, England: Ward Lock, 1996), also published as *The Book of Westerns* (New York: Continuum, 1996). JF discusses color films in PB. Claudette Colbert's comment on the filming and Katherine Cliffton's on JF's attitude toward Indians are from their interviews with the author. The production difficulties on *Drums* are discussed in JF to DFZ, July 17, 1939; DF; and Davis.

Orson Welles describes JF as an old master in the Tynan interview; he calls JF his "teacher" in Dilys Powell, "The Life and Opinions of Orson Welles," the *Sunday Times,* London, February 3, 1963. Welles's comment to the author on watching *Stagecoach* "Every night for more than a month" is quoted from JM, *The Book of Movie Lists: An Offbeat, Provocative Collection of the Best and Worst of Everything in Movies* (Chicago: Contemporary Books, 1998). Welles also discusses *Stagecoach,* as well as the making of *Citizen Kane* and the citation he received from JF, in Welles and Peter Bogdanovich, *This Is Orson Welles* (New York: HarperCollins, 1992), and the revised edition (New York: Da Capo Press, 1998). Sarris comments on *Kane* and *How Green Was My Valley* as "the beginnings of a cinema of memory" in *The American Cinema,* which also describes the "double vision" of JF's style.

JF talks about *Young Mr. Lincoln* in PB, which also describes the director's "extraordinary sense of intimacy" with Abraham Lincoln. DFZ's comment on screenwriter Lamar Trotti is from his memo to JF, December 3, 1938, in *Memo from Darryl F. Zanuck.* Henry Fonda recalls the making of *Young Mr. Lincoln* in Mike Steen, *Hollywood Speaks: An Oral History* (New York: Putnam, 1974); Fonda's 1970 discussion about the film with JF is from *The American West of John Ford.* Pauline Moore Watkins remembered the filming in an interview with the author and in Watkins to JM, April 9, 1998; she provided the author with the script scene for her screen test as Ann Rutledge; see also Gregory William Mank, "The Hollywood Adventures of Pauline Moore," *Films in Review,* July/August 1994. Arthur C. Miller's filming of the Ann Rutledge scene is mentioned in Balshofer and Miller. Fritz Lang is quoted on *Fury* in Bogdanovich, *Who the Devil Made It.* Sergei M. Eisenstein, *"Mr. Lincoln by Mr. Ford,"* written in 1945 and published in *Iskusstvo Kino,* 1960, was partially reprinted in Eisenstein, ed., and translated by Jay Leyda, *Film Essays* (New York: Praeger, 1970).

John Steinbeck's novel *The Grapes of Wrath* was published by Viking, New York, in 1939. Steinbeck's comment on the book's title is from his letter to Elizabeth Otis, September 10, 1938, quoted in Jackson J. Benson, "The Background to the Composition of *The Grapes of Wrath,"* in Peter Lisca, ed., with Kevin Hearle, *The Grapes of Wrath: Text and Criticism,* 1972 (updated edition, New York: Penguin USA, 1997). Steinbeck's series of articles on migrant farmworkers in the *San Francisco News,* October 5–12, 1936, is collected as *The Harvest Gypsies: On the Road to the Grapes of Wrath,* introduced by Charles Wollenberg (Berkeley, Ca.: Heyday Books, 1988). Wollenberg reports that Steinbeck asked DFZ if he believed the book. Okie migration figures are from Alan Brinkley, *"The Grapes of Wrath,"* in Mark C. Carnes, Ted Mico, John Miller-Monzon, and David Rubel, eds., *Past Imperfect: History According to the Movies* (New York: Henry Holt, 1995). Zanuck's comments on purchasing the film rights to *Grapes* are from DFZ, "Zanuck Finds Odds Longer Than Roulette's," *LAT,* November 21, 1954. Steinbeck discusses the film in letters to Elizabeth Otis, December 15, 1939, and Fonda, November 20, 1958, in Elaine Steinbeck and Robert Wallsten, eds., *Steinbeck: A Life in Letters* (New York: Viking, 1975).

Nunnally Johnson's screenplay *The Grapes of Wrath* was published in Gassner and Nichols, *Twenty Best Film Plays;* see also Johnson's revised temporary script, August 5, 1939, with an added final scene, November 1, 1939. Thomas Flanagan's comment on the film is from his essay "The Irish in John Ford's Films" in Coffey and Golway; JF draws connections with "my Irish tradition" in PB. JF's claim that he never read the novel appears in George Bluestone, *Novels into Film* (Baltimore: Johns Hopkins University Press, 1957). His comments on why he made the film are from Mitchell. Information on the film's production is from Bluestone; Gussow; Warren French, *Filmguide to* The Grapes of Wrath (Bloomington: Indiana University Press, 1973); DF; Joseph R. Millichap, *Steinbeck and Film* (New York: Frederick Ungar, 1983); and Wollenberg's introduction to *The Harvest Gypsies;* Jay Parini, *John Steinbeck: A Biography* (New York: Henry Holt, 1995); and Custen. Philip Dunne discussed Jane Darwell and Louise Dresser with the author; Beulah Bondi comments on her testing for the role of Ma Joad in Young, *Reel Characters.* JF remarks on Gregg Toland's photography in PB; JF's comments on his original ending are from PB ("logical end") and Gussow ("on a down note"). JF recalls in his OH and in the Wagner interview that he told DFZ to direct the ending.

The New York premiere of *Grapes* is described in Michel Mok, "Slumming with Zanuck," *Nation,* February 3, 1940. Information on the film's box-office returns is from Gallagher and Custen. Woody Guthrie's review, "Woody Sez: A Review of *The Grapes of Wrath,"* *Daily*

Worker, 1940, is reprinted in Henrietta Yurchenco, assisted by Marjorie Guthrie, *A Mighty Hard Road: The Woody Guthrie Story* (New York: McGraw-Hill, 1970); Joe Klein discusses Guthrie's writing of the song "Tom Joad" in *Woody Guthrie: A Life* (New York: Knopf, 1980); Guthrie's credo is quoted in Hal Ashby's 1976 biographical film *Bound for Glory.* Frank S. Nugent's review of *Grapes* is from the January 25, 1940, *NYT;* Nugent's hiring by Fox is discussed in Ezra Goodman, *The Fifty-Year Decline and Fall of Hollywood* (New York: Simon and Schuster, 1961); Gussow; and Nugent's obituaries (December 31, 1965) in *NYT,* "Frank S. Nugent, Screen Writer and Former Film Critic, Dead," *NYT,* and by Thomas M. Pryor in *DV,* "Services Today for Frank Nugent, Caustic Critic as Well as Author of Pix." Welles comments on *Grapes* in *This Is Orson Welles.*

Eugene O'Neill's one-act plays *The Long Voyage Home, The Moon of the Caribees, Bound East for Cardiff,* and *In the Zone* were published as *The Moon of the Caribees* and *Six Other Plays of the Sea* (New York: Boni & Liveright, 1919). O'Neill's telegram to JF, June 1940, is from Travis Bogard and Jackson R. Bryer, eds., *Selected Letters of Eugene O'Neill* (New Haven, Ct.: Yale University Press, 1988). JF's account of the genesis of his film version of *The Long Voyage Home* is from "John Ford" (interview), *Focus!* October 1969. Sources on JW's performance and his lessons from Osa Massen include Davis, *Duke;* and R&O; JF's advice to Parrish about directing JW is quoted in Davis. Production information on *The Long Voyage Home* is from Bernstein. Information on the artists visiting the set is from JF, "How We Made *The Long Voyage Home*," *Friday,* August 9, 1940 (including a photo of JF with the artists); "Movie of the Week: *The Long Voyage Home*," *Life,* November 11, 1940; and R&O. Information on Cooper's activities in this period is from Behlmer, "Merian C. Cooper Is the Kind of Creative Showman Today's Movies Badly Need." Sarris comments on *Tobacco Road* in *The American Cinema;* Nunnally Johnson's criticism of the film is from his letter to Lindsay Anderson, January 24, 1955, published in Anderson, *About John Ford.*

The organization and training of JF's unofficial Navy Volunteer Photographic Unit (formed in 1939) is discussed in William Stull, "'Hollywood's Own' Film Unit Volunteers to Film the Navy," *American Cinematographer,* October 1941, including the making of the unit's film about the California State Guard. JF's comment about "carrying out the original plan" for which he had been commissioned is from his USN Biographical Sheet [1941]. Sources on his prewar studies of training films and aerial and sea photography include JF, Annual Fitness Report, October 10, 1936; Annual Fitness Report, September 23, 1937; and JF, n.d., report on training duties (c. 1940–41), which includes his description of his duties as recruiting officer of the Naval Reserve Photographic Section, officially organized in 1940 ("tactics, ballistics, and training"). W. W. Waddell, commandant of the Eleventh Naval District, in his comments on JF's January 10, 1941, Annual Fitness Report, states to the chief of the Bureau of Navigation, February 21, 1941, that JF "visualized the great importance of photography" in combat. JF's claim to have "pioneered combat and sea photography" for the USN is from his Annual Fitness Report, September 15, 1941.

The plan for the organization that became the Field Photographic Branch of the Office of Strategic Services, commanded by JF, is described in "Comment and Summary on Proposed Naval Photographic Organization" [c. 1940], signed by JF; Lieutenant Commander Edmund H. Hansen, USNR; Lieutenant Commander Frank W. Wead, USN (Ret.); Lieutenant Commander Alfred J. Bolton, USN (Ret.); and Captain Merian C. Cooper, Air Corps Reserve, USA. JF's orders to active duty in the USN from the chief of the Bureau of Navigation are dated September 11, 1941; see also JF, n.d., report on training duties. JF comments on his New York Critics award and Small Arms Expert's medal in his USN Biographical Sheet [1941].

Background to the production of *Sex Hygiene* and other U. S. Army training films is from a volume in the series *United States Army in World War II* (Washington, D.C.: Office of the Chief of Military History, Department of the Army): Dulany Terrett, *The Technical Services: The Signal Corps: The Emergency,* 1956; see also Gussow; Custen; and William K. Everson, "John Ford Goes to War—Against VD," *Film Fan Monthly,* May 1971 (including DFZ's comment "He don't scare me"). JF is quoted on *Sex Hygiene* from PB, and Gene Fowler Jr. from Davis.

Sources on the filming of *How Green Was My Valley* include the author's interviews with Dunne, Anna Lee, and Roddy McDowall (including his remark about Jackie Coogan); Dunne, *Take Two;* "No Fence Around Time" in Dunne, *How Green Was My Valley;* Balshofer and Miller; Gussow; and Custen. The actors' chant "We haven't changed a line" was recalled by Dunne in his interview with the author. DFZ's remarks at the "*How Green Was My Valley* Conference on First Draft Continuity of May 18, 1940," May 22, 1940, are from *Memo from Darryl F. Zanuck.* Sources on William Wyler working on *How Green* include the author's interview with Dunne; and Jan Herman, *A Talent for Trouble: The Life of Hollywood's Most Acclaimed Director, William Wyler* (New York: G. P. Putnam's Sons, 1995). *Time*'s review, November 24, 1941, mistakenly credits JF with the decision to use narration.

Information on McDowall's background is from his *NYT* obituary by Mel Gussow, "Roddy McDowall, 70, Child Star and Versatile Actor," October 4, 1998. McDowall's observations on JF's direction are in DF and in McDowall's interview with Maureen O'Hara, "Sitting Pretty," *Premiere,* July 1991 ("He was so terrific"). O'Hara discusses *How Green* in that interview and recalls the filming of the wedding scene in Anderson's documentary "John Ford" (*Omnibus 25* series for the BBC TV, 1992). François Truffaut's observation on JF and O'Hara is from his 1973 essay "God Bless John Ford" in *Les Films de ma vie* (Paris: Flammarion, 1975), trans. by Leonard Mayhew as *The Films in My Life* (New York: Simon and Schuster, 1978). Sources on JF's arguments with Sara Allgood include the author's interview with Dunne; McDowall, "Sitting Pretty"; and Davis. Information on the 1942 Academy Awards ceremony is from Wiley and Bona.

CHAPTER TEN: "YES—THIS REALLY HAPPENED" (PP. 335–415)

The chapter title is from the narration of JF's 1942 documentary *The Battle of Midway.* The epigraph is from Sinclair.

The principal sources of information on the Battle of Midway are Vice Admiral Chester W. Nimitz, commander-in-chief, U.S. Pacific Fleet, to commander-in-chief, U.S. Fleet, "Battle of Midway" online action report, June 28, 1942 (National Archives and Records Administration); and Gordon W. Prange, with Donald M. Goldstein and Katherine V. Dillon, *Miracle at Midway* (New York: McGraw-Hill, 1982). Additional sources include Samuel Eliot Morison, *History of United States Naval Operations in World War II, Vol. IV: Coral Sea, Midway and Submarine Actions, May 1942–August 1942* (Boston: Little, Brown, 1949); James L. Mooney, ed., *Dictionary of American Naval Fighting Ships* (Washington, D.C.: Naval Historical Center, Department of the Navy, 1969); A. J. Barker, *Midway: The Turning Point* (New York: Ballantine Books, 1971); Mark Healy, *Midway 1942: Turning-Point in the Pacific,* Osprey Military Campaign Series No. 30 (Oxford: Osprey Publishing, 1993); and Thomas B. Allen, "Ghosts and Survivors Return to the Battle of Midway," *National Geographic,* April 1999. Forrest C. Pogue's comments on the Japanese expansion in the Pacific after Pearl Harbor are from his book *George C. Marshall: Ordeal and Hope* (New York: Viking, 1966).

JF is quoted on his experiences at Midway from the following sources: JF interview, unidentified newspaper [1942] (Lilly) ("Those Marines"); "Narrative by Cmdr. John Ford, USNR, Photographic Experiences from Pearl Harbor, December 7, 1941–August 17, 1943," Office of Naval Records, Washington, D.C., quoted in Prange, *Miracle at Midway* ("goofy for a bit"; "one big chunk"; "a good place"; "a very lucky hit"; also the source of Captain Cyril T. Simard's comment "Well, forget the pictures"); Axel Madsen's interview with JF, *Cahiers du Cinéma,* October 1966 ("I shot film"); PB ("time for the colors to go up"; "I did all"); and Philip Jenkinson's interview with JF, *My Name Is John Ford: I Make Westerns* (BBC TV), 1968 ("I just kept"; "I am really a coward"; "wounded pretty badly"). Jack MacKenzie Jr.'s recollections of filming *The Battle of Midway* with JF are from Alvin Wyckoff, "as related by" MacKenzie, "Fighting

Cameramen," *American Cinematographer,* February 1944; MacKenzie's obituary appears in *Variety,* August 22, 1945. Other sources on JF's experiences at Midway include his OH; DF; Nugent, "Hollywood's Favorite Rebel"; WJD to adjutant general, War Department, recommending JF for Silver Star, September 27, 1945; and Secretary of the Navy James Forrestal, JF Legion of Merit citation, January 31, 1946. JF's 1942 travel to Pearl Harbor and Midway is documented in COI to chief, Naval Operations, January 20, 1942; Simard, U.S. Naval Air Station, Midway, to JF, May 28, 1942 (on JF's verbal orders from Nimitz); and WJD to adjutant general, War Department. JF's travel orders from Midway to Los Angeles are dated June 13, 1942. JF's OH discusses the order from Nimitz and learning from Commander F. M. "Massie" Hughes, USN, commander, Patrol Squadron 23, that the Japanese code had been broken and an attack on Midway was expected. Sources on JF's reconnaissance flight with Hughes are JF's OH and Hughes to JF, June 3, 1942.

Documentation of JF's navy honors includes "Citation for Distinguished Service—Midway, Cmdr. JF, USNR," n.d., signed by Rear Admiral D. W. Bagley, USN; JF navy personnel record, October 6, 1944 (also includes record of Purple Heart); and JF's Legion of Merit citation from Forrestal. JF's Midway wound is described in his "Medical History" slip, June 4, 1942, signed by Lieutenant Commander Frederick S. Foote, MC, USNR; see also JF to Chief Pharmacist's Mate Mayfield at U.S. Naval Air Station, Midway, July 3, 1942; and Captain C. F. Behrens, MC, USN, "Special Examination and Treatment Request," U.S. Naval Hospital, Bethesda, Md., July 22, 1943. Additional documentation on JF's Purple Heart is from the notification by the chief, Naval Personnel, to JF, February 7, 1943; the medal was forwarded to JF on July 7, 1943, by the Navy Department Bureau of Navigation. JF's telegram to MF, June 8, 1942 ("OK"), is quoted in Davis, MF recalls their reunion in Slide and Banker. Nugent's description of JF as "the official eye of the American high command" is quoted in Anderson.

Press coverage of JF at Midway (1942) includes Robert Trumbull, "Japs, Too Groggy to Answer Bell, Missed Chance to Score," *LAT,* June 12; "FORD FILMED BATTLE OF MIDWAY," *HR,* June 18; Louella O. Parsons column, "John Ford Hollywood No. 1 Hero," June 18; "Director Wounded as He Makes His Greatest Pic Aided by Hollywood Boy," *HR,* June 18; "Director Ford Wounded," *LAE,* June 19 (war extra); Parsons, "John Ford Hit by Shrapnel in Midway Raid," *LAE,* June 19; "Filming Midway Epic May Win Ford Award," *Portland Press Herald,* June 20; and "Lieut. Comdr. Ford to Attend Maine Legion Convention," *Press Herald,* June 23. Mark Twain on courage is from his novel *The Tragedy of Pudd'nhead Wilson* (Hartford: American Publishing Co., 1894).

Henry Fonda comments on *The Battle of Midway* in *Directed by John Ford.* Other sources include *"The Battle of Midway:* Dialogue Continuity"; notes by James Kevin McGuinness, "FIRST RUNNING . . . BLACK & WHITE"; Parrish, *Growing Up in Hollywood;* Parrish, *Hollywood Doesn't Live Here Anymore* (Boston: Little, Brown, 1988) (including the discussion between JF and Walter Wanger, Sam Engel's comments on the film, and JF's response to Engel's outburst); and Lieutenant Arthur E. Arling, USNR, "Cameramen in Uniform," *American Cinematographer,* October 1943. JF's "comment to Parrish about the editor's mother and Parrish's description of the audience reaction to *The Battle of Midway* at the Radio City Music Hall are from DF. Theatrical bookings are reported in *The Film Daily Yearbook,* 1943. Sarris comments on the film in *The American Cinema,* and William T. Murphy in "John Ford and the Wartime Documentary," *Film & History,* February 1976. Information on *Midway* (1976) is from Lawrence Suid, *Sailing on the Silver Screen: Hollywood and the U.S. Navy* (Annapolis, Md.: Naval Institute Press, 1996).

Information on JF's documentary *Torpedo Squadron 8* is from PB and the author's viewing of the film at the UCLA Film and Television Archives' JF retrospective, 1994. Sources on the Twentieth Century–Fox project *Torpedo Squadron 8* include Suid; *The Film Daily Yearbook,* 1943; A. J. "Jack" Bolton, Eleventh Naval District Public Relations office, to JF, November 2, 1942; and a *NYT* item, February 6, 1944. T. M. P. [Thomas M. Pryor] reviews *Wing and a Prayer* in the August 31, 1944, issue of *NYT.* Philip Dunne's recollection of his talk with JF about *The Battle of Midway* and VT-8 is from the author's interview with Dunne.

Ford's U.S. Navy service records at Lilly (containing dates and other information) include: JF, Navy Biographical Sheet [1941]; Brief of Record, July 11, 1942; partial transcript, March 14, 1946; Rear Admiral JF, USNR Ret., 73847, "Ships and Stations during 7 December 1941 to 31 December 1946," n.d.; service record, April 22, 1949; and his 1952 USN biography, "Rear Admiral John Ford, U.S. Naval Reserve, Retired." JF's orders to report to active USN duty and additional duty with COI were issued by C.W. Nimitz, chief, Bureau of Navigation, to Lieutenant Commander JF, USNR, September 11, 1941; JF's report of compliance with orders was signed the same date. JF's promotion to commander, USNR, on October 7, 1941, is from Brief of Record; Cooper's recommendation to WJD of JF's promotion is dated September 9, 1941; James R. Murphy, COI, discusses the modification of JF's duties in a letter to Commander Edward V. Hayes, Department of the Navy, May 18, 1942.

JF's living habits in Washington, D.C., are reported by Frank Farrell, "John Ford Dons Naval Uniform Because 'It's the Thing to Do,'" *New York World-Telegram,* November 1, 1941; his attire is described by Jerry Klutz, "The Federal Diary," unidentified Washington newspaper, January 26, 1942 (Lilly). JF's April 5, 1942, letter to MF reports he is feeling healthy; his OH recalls his promise to her that he wouldn't drink for the duration. DF describes Mary's loneliness during the war years. Sinclair reports JF told MF he was leaving home for a couple of days and that she saw him for only twenty-four hours during those years. JF's letter of October 2, 1941, chiding MF for calling long-distance is quoted by Davis, who also reports JF's dinner with the Roosevelts on October 29, 1941. The Fords' remarriage in Washington, D.C., December 1941, is cited in Levy. Parsons's interview with MF is from her June 20, 1942, *LAE* column. Bolton to JF, November 2, 1942, describes MF as "pretty miserable" about JF's absence from home. Her OH reports that she learned of the impending Doolittle Raid. JF's tender letter from sea to MF is dated June [26?], 1943, and is quoted from Eyman, *Print the Legend.* JF tells MF in his letter of July 26, 1943, that they might share a bed; her wry comment about JF "falling in love with me" is quoted in E. R. "Ray" Kellogg to JF, July 29, 1944. Information on the Hollywood Canteen is from MF's OH; Ray Hoopes, *When the Stars Went to War: Hollywood and World War II* (New York: Random House, 1994); Slide and Banker; and Bolton to JF, November 2, 1942. MF's gratitude for the Canteen is reported in Sinclair.

Lists of personnel in JF's Naval Reserve unit include: chief, Bureau of Navigation, to commandant, Eleventh Naval Reserve, September 7, 1940; director, Naval Reserve, Eleventh Naval District, to chief, Bureau of Navigation, January 23, 1941; "Commissioned Men," n.d. (Lilly); and Stull, "'Hollywood's Own' Film Unit Volunteers to Film the Navy." The unit's strength when JF joined COI is reported in his Officer Qualifications Questionnaire, [c. 1943]. Cooper's wartime service is described in Behlmer, "Merian C. Cooper Is the Kind of Creative Showman Today's Movies Badly Need." JF's strengths and weaknesses as a naval officer are evaluated in his Annual Fitness Report by Captain I. C. Johnson, USN (Ret.), director of Naval Reserve, Eleventh Naval District, September 15, 1941. JF's joke about "navy wives" is from the author's interview with Dunne.

The principal source of information on William J. Donovan (WJD) and the Office of Strategic Services (OSS) is Anthony Cave Brown, *The Last Hero: Wild Bill Donovan* (New York: Times Books, 1982). Additional sources include Edward Hymoff, *The OSS in World War II* (New York: Ballantine Books, 1972); R. Harris Smith, *OSS: The Secret History of America's First Central Intelligence Agency* (Berkeley: University of California Press, 1972); Ceplair and Englund; Bradley F. Smith, *The Shadow Warriors: O.S.S. and the Origins of the C.I.A.* (New York: Basic Books, 1983); John Ranelagh, *The Agency: The Rise and Decline of the CIA* (New York: Simon and Schuster, Touchstone edition, 1987); Tom Moon, *This Grim and Savage Game: OSS and the Beginning of U.S. Covert Operations in World War II* (New Haven, Conn.: Burning Gate Press, 1991); Maochun Yu, *OSS in China: Prelude to Cold War* (New Haven, Conn.: Yale University Press, 1996); and David K. E. Bruce, "The National Intelligence Authority," *Virginia Quarterly Review,* Summer 1946. WJD's remark about putting Stalin on the OSS payroll is from Robert

Hayden Alcorn, *No Bugles for Spies: Tales of the OSS* (New York: David McKay, 1962). Abraham Polonsky's recollection of the anti-Communist bias of the OSS and Army Intelligence in the final year of the war is from Ceplair and Englund. The presidential authorization of the Office of the Coordinator of Information (COI), "Executive Order 8826: Designating a Coordinator of Information," July 11, 1941, is reprinted in Hymoff.

JF's Field Photo budget for 1942 is from Brown; the incorrect figure is reported in Davis; JF's estimate of $5 million as the first-year cost of unit operations is from JF to Merian C. Cooper, January 24, 1941. The War Department and *Why We Fight* film budgets are reported in JM, *Frank Capra*. JF discusses his OSS activities ("Our job") in Ted Thackrey Jr., "Secret Exploits of Daring OSS Group Revealed," *LAHE*, July 15, 1962. Primary information on films made by the OSS/Field Photographic Branch includes films on deposit at National Archives, as well as printed descriptions of the films on file at the Archives and on its Web site, *merrimack.nara.gov:80* (see Filmography for list of titles). Information on the *Iceland* film is from Mark Armistead's OH and from WJD to adjutant general, War Department, recommending JF for the Legion of Merit, September 27, 1945. Sources on *Canal Report* include: COI to chief, Bureau of Navigation, December 18, 1941; chief, Bureau of Navigation, to JF, December 20, 1941; [JF], "Notes for Commentation [*sic*]," December 1941 (Lilly); and Parrish's recollection in Davis. Parrish discusses the shelved film about the State Department Building in *Growing Up in Hollywood;* sources on the shelved film about the National Gallery of Art include Parrish, *Hollywood Doesn't Live Here Anymore* (Boston: Little, Brown, 1988), and Frederick A. "Freddie" Spencer to JF, August 20, 1943. Information on *War Department Report* is from a *Washington Daily News* article [1943] (Lilly). The films on Nazi war crimes and the Nuremberg trials are discussed in Armistead's OH; Parrish, *Growing Up in Hollywood;* Joseph E. Persico, *Nuremberg: Infamy on Trial* (New York: Viking Penguin, 1994); Kellogg to JF, November 20, 1945; and Kellogg's telegram to JF, November 23, 1945.

Armistead's OH states that Field Photo filmed more than fifty combat missions; his aerial reconnaissance and mapping work are also discussed in his OH, as well as in the author's interviews with Admiral John D. Bulkeley and Vicky Wilson (Armistead's daughter); Sinclair; and Joe Farruggia and R. Cort Kirkwood, "Our Top-Secret Weapon," *American Movie Classics Magazine,* September 1995. Armistead comments in his OH and in Sinclair about life on his yacht and JF's personal habits. Information on the Cunningham Combat Camera is from Armistead's OH; Parrish, *Growing Up in Hollywood;* Benjamin Perlman, director, Naval Reserve, Eleventh Naval District, "Photographic Personnel for the Naval Reserve," to chief, Bureau of Navigation, January 23, 1941; and Forrestal's citation of JF for the Legion of Merit.

The bombing of Pearl Harbor, including the issue of whether President Franklin D. Roosevelt deliberately provoked the attack, is discussed from varying viewpoints in such books as Pogue; Prange, in collaboration with Goldstein and Dillon, *At Dawn We Slept: The Untold Story of Pearl Harbor* (New York: McGraw-Hill, 1981); John Toland, *Infamy: Pearl Harbor and Its Aftermath* (New York: Doubleday, 1982); and Robert B. Stinnett, *Day of Deceit: The Truth About FDR and Pearl Harbor* (New York: Free Press, 2000). Bruce's comment on the failure of the intelligence agencies at Pearl Harbor is from his article "The National Intelligence Authority." The Fords' experiences at the home of Rear Admiral Andrew C. Pickens on December 7, 1941, are reported in Slide and Banker; Sinclair; and MF's OH.

Orders issued in 1942 for the production of *December 7th* include Secretary of the Navy Frank Knox to COI (WJD) [January]; WJD to Knox, January 13; COI to chief, Naval Operations, January 20; and WJD's directive to JF, May 12. Secretary of War Henry L. Stimson's caveat about the film is from his letter to WJD, December 3, 1942. An unattributed one-page outline titled *The Story of Pearl Harbor: An Epic in American History* was sent by Atherton of COI to JF at Pearl Harbor, February 5, 1942. JF's unedited 1942 footage of *Pearl Harbor* (*Damage*) (including rebuilding of damaged ships) is at the National Archives. JF wrote MF on April 7, 1942, about staging scenes for *December 7th* in Hawaii; his activities there and his other work on the film are discussed in Parrish, *Hollywood Doesn't Live Here Anymore;* Parrish also writes about *December 7th* in "Directors at War: John Ford," *American Film,* July–August 1985. The documentary footage of the Pearl Harbor attack filmed by C. P. Daugherty, Plc, and Lieutenant Commander Edward Young is discussed in L. J. Wiltse, assistant chief of staff to the commander in chief, U.S. Pacific Fleet, to Knox, June 27, 1942. Elmer Davis's comment on the tank shot is quoted in JM, *Frank Capra.*

Gregg Toland's assignment to Brazil in April 1943 is reported in U.S. naval attaché, Rio de Janeiro, to Naval Command, OSS, June 17, 1944. Admiral Harold R. Stark's opposition to *December 7th* is discussed in Spencer to JF, August 20, 1943; Stark is quoted from Murphy, "John Ford and the Wartime Documentary." FDR's directive about censorship of Field Photo films is reported in Sinclair. The screenings of *December 7th* for servicemen and industrial workers are reported in WJD to adjutant general, War Department, September 27, 1945. The Oscar for *December 7th* is discussed in JF's OH and Bolton to JF, March 3, 1944; JF's inaccurate claim to have won six Oscars was reported by Bogdanovich to JM and is quoted in M&W.

Sources on the Doolittle Raid include the author's interview with General James H. Doolittle, USA; Lieutenant Colonel Carroll V. Glines, USAF, *Doolittle's Tokyo Raiders* (New York: Van Nostrand Reinhold, 1964); Glines, *The Doolittle Raid* (New York: Orion Books, 1988); Mooney; Prange, *Miracle at Midway;* Suid; "Doolittle's Tokyo Raid," U.S. Air Force Museum Web site, *wpafb.af.mil.* (quoting a 1980 Doolittle interview); JF to Captain Ellis M. Zacharias, USN, March [?], 1943; and Zacharias to chief, Naval Personnel, August 13, 1943. FDR's comment about Shangri-La is from his press conference of April 21, 1942, in *Complete Presidential Press Conferences of Franklin D. Roosevelt,* Vol. 19 (New York: Da Capo Press, 1972). Unedited Army Air Forces Doolittle Raid footage is filed in National Archives under the titles *Lt. Col. James H. Doolittle and Flight Take Off from the Carrier "Hornet" on Tokyo Raid* and *Tokyo Raid.*

Information on Hollywood personnel in uniform is from "To the Colors!" *The Film Daily Yearbook,* 1943. Dunne told the author about his attempt to join Field Photo; see also Dunne, *Take Two.* Sources on the activities of John Wayne and Ward Bond as noncombatants during World War II include R&O; Davis, *Duke;* Wayne and Thorleifson; and Wills. R&O quotes the February 1942 letter from Gen. Lewis B. Hershey, director of Selective Service, granting JW a draft deferment. JW's letter to JF, May [?] 1942, requesting to join Field Photo, is quoted in Davis, *Duke,* and R&O, which questions JW's claim to have received a letter from WJD stating that he could join the unit. JW's later application to Field Photo is mentioned in Spencer to JW, May 27, 1943, and JW to JF, August 1, 1943, cited in R&O, including JW's comment that he needs a last "fling" before entering the service. Dunne told the author that JW was offered a job by JF and turned him down. JW's comment that he should go on a USO tour is quoted in Wills. JW's certificate from WJD, OSS, October 1, 1945, stating that he "Honorably Served the United States of America as a Member of the Office of Strategic Services," is among JF's papers at Lilly. MF's June 1, 1943, letter to JF, quoted in Gallagher, asks him to write JW about Esperanza "Chata" Baur; JF obliquely chides JW about Chata in his letter of July 9, 1943, quoted in Wills. MF's letter to JF on November 18, 1943, about the Bond and Wayne marital breakups is cited in R&O; Pat Ford's letter to JF on December 18, 1943, mentions MF's decision not to intervene with the Bonds. The vodka incident is reported in DF and R&O. MF's complaint to JF that Bond and JW are "bound for destruction" is also from her June 1, 1943, letter quoted by Gallagher. JF's question about how "Uncle Ward" looks in a tin hat and binoculars is from a letter to JW, January 1942, quoted in Davis; JF's acerbic comment about the "heroism" of Bond and JW is from his [March?] 1942 letter to MF, quoted in R&O. MF's comment that she "could never help John Wayne" is from Slide and Banker.

Information on JF's income for 1941–44 is from his tax returns for those years and from JF to Arthur D. Welch, August 12, 1942. Documentation on the USN charter of the *Araner* includes Commander W. J. Morcott, USN (Ret.), port director, NTS: San Pedro, Eleventh Naval

District, to MF, January 15, 1942; T. L. Gatch, assistant judge advocate general of USN, to JF, February 9, 1942; charter between JF and United States of America, August 29, 1942; N.W. Gokey, Navy Bureau of Ships, to JF, June 12, 1944, terminating charter; MF and JF acknowledgment of return of the *Araner,* July 12, 1944; and "Film Director Turns Yacht Over to Navy," *LAT,* February 3, 1942. Frank McGrath's assignment to the *Araner* as JF's personal watchdog is reported in MF's OH and Sinclair.

In a letter to his agent Harry Wurtzel [January 1942] (Lilly), JF comments on Jews and Catholics and their special stake in the war; the same letter suggests that Wurtzel hire a Jewish lawyer to threaten a journalist planning an article JF thought would be unsympathetic. The journalist was Tom Wood, who became an Argosy publicist on *Fort Apache,* according to "*Fort Apache* Cost Breakdown as of March 6, 1948"; other correspondence about Wood's planned article includes JF to JW, January 12, 1942, and Wurtzel to JF, January 1942. JF's instruction to Wurtzel to hire a "hebe lawyer" to handle a difficult negotiation (with RKO regarding the MGM film *Bataan*) is in his letter of July 6, 1943, the phrase is quoted in Gallagher. JF's ethnic badinage with Wurtzel in his correspondence includes addressing him as "Herschell" [*sic*] in his letter of July 10, 1943; Wurtzel signs himself "Herschel" to JF, July 15, 1943; JF's use of the name is quoted in Gallagher. JF refers to a Jewish doctor as "The Yid" in his letter to MF, October [4?], 1943. JF's comment "I'm a bit ashamed that a great warrior like me should be in mockie-land while the good people are fighting" is from his October 30, 1944, letter to Major General Albert C. Wedemeyer, USA ("mockie-land" is quoted in DF as "'movie land'"). Eyman quotes "mockie-land" correctly in *Print the Legend* while still absolving JF of being anti-Semitic. The meaning and derivation of "mockie" are explained in the *Oxford English Dictionary,* second edition (Oxford: Clarendon Press, 1989); and *Dictionary of American Regional English,* Vol. III (Cambridge, Mass.: Belknap Press of Harvard University Press, 1996).Wedemeyer's anti-Semitic views are discussed in Joseph W. Bendersky, *The "Jewish Threat": Anti-Semitic Politics of the U.S. Army* (New York: Basic Books, 2000). JF's OH tells of his work helping repatriate Jewish refugees from Budapest; see also Gallagher. JF's donations to Jewish charities are listed in his IRS returns, 1929, 1955, 1961, and 1966; information on his gift of a silver menorah to Temple Israel of Hollywood is from his 1962 correspondence with Captain Alan Brown, USNR; Jack Fier of Columbia Studios; and the rabbi of Temple Israel, Dr. Max Nussbaum. Samuel Fuller comments on JF's religious pluralism in *Il Etait une Fois . . . Samuel Fuller: Histoires d'Amérique racontées par Samuel Fuller à Jean Narboni et Noël Simsolo* (Paris: *Cahiers du Cinéma,* 1986) (quotation translated by JM). Bea Benjamin's OH discusses JF's attitude toward Jews.

MF's complaint about the Hollywood Canteen being dominated by Jews is from her letter to JF, December 8, 1943; her complaint about John Garfield and SAG is from her January [24?], 1944, letter to JF. Pat Ford refers to MF's struggle against alleged Communist influence at the Canteen and compares her to a Prussian aristocrat in his December 18, 1943, letter to JF. MF's OH claims Dalton Trumbo and other leftists tried to take over the board of directors. MF's Christmas 1943 letter to JF reports her happiness over Eddie Cantor's presents. Pat's complaint about working with Jews in Navy Public Relations is from his January 27, 1944, letter to JF; Pat's August 24, 1943, letter to JF comments on Wingate Smith's resentment of having to answer to Jewish officers in the U.S. Army.

Information on Pat's wedding to Jane Mulvany is from Levy. Sources on Pat's college graduation and USN service include (1942): Pat to MF, July 21; JF to Commander William J. Marcott, USN (Ret.), Eleventh Naval District, July 29; Bolton to JF, November 2; and (1943): Pat to JF, July 20. Pat's 1944 request for transfer to Gene Markey's unit is discussed in Markey to JF, February 25; JF to Pat, March 6; and Lieutenant Commander Off (ONI) to Markey, March [7?]. The birthdates of the Ford grandsons, Timothy and Daniel, are from "Family Data" in the "(Jack Aloysius Feeney)" file at Lilly. JF describes Timothy to Wead as "absolutely beautiful," March 28, 1944; Vangie Ostrander's comment on "Grandpappy" JF is from her letter to Wead,

February 26, 1944. JF mentions Barbara Ford's directing ambitions in his August [17?], 1943, letter to her, and discusses her plans to work for him after the war in his [July 1943] letter to Sidney V. Smith, Y2C, USNR. Barbara's interview for *The Song of Bernadette* is reported in Harry Wurtzel to JF, December 2, 1942. Sources on Francis Ford's enlistment and discharge include DF; MF to JF, April [21?], 1943; and JF to Corporal FF, April 22, 1943. Information on the internment of Cecil and Larry de Prida is from JF's correspondence files, June 1943–February 1945; State Department press release, February 2, 1944; and Harrison Carroll's column, "John Ford's Niece Saved at Manila," 1945.

Information on Frank W. "Spig" Wead is from R&O; Zolotow; "Lieutenant Commander Frank Wead: Biography," Columbia Studios, August 1941 (AMPAS); Commander Frank Wead, "Biographical Information," MGM, June 2, 1944 (AMPAS); Vice Admiral C. T. Durgin, USN (Ret.) to JF, May 3, 1955; and obituaries (1947): "Frank Wead, Novelist and Playwright, Dies," *LAT*, November 17; "Frank Wead Dies; Movie Writer, 52," *NYT*, November 18; "Commander Frank W. Wead," *Variety*, November 18; and Bob Considine's column, "On the Line," *LAE*, November 21. Wead's assignment to *They Were Expendable* is reported in Bolton to JF, November 2, 1942, and was discussed by Bulkeley in his interview with the author.

Sources on JF in North Africa include his orders from the vice chief, Naval Operations, August 14, 1942; orders from WJD to JF, August 21, 1942; Major James S. Simmerman, commander of Thirteenth Armored Regiment, July 8, 1943, entry in JF's service record; DFZ to JF, July 27, 1945; the "African Invasion" section of Field Photo's "ETO War Diary," July [?], 1945, including a statement by CSp (P) Robert Johannes, November 1944; DFZ, *Tunis Expedition* (New York: Random House, 1943); and JM, *Frank Capra*. JF reports his activities at Bône and in Tunisia to James Roosevelt in a letter of March 20, 1943 ("I personally covered"). Moon describes Ford filming regardless of danger. JF's return from Gibraltar to Washington is reported in Jack Pennick to Simmerman, June 10, 1943. JF's thinking about postwar film projects while in North Africa is related in his letter to Dudley Nichols, March 22, 1943. See notes for chapter 9 on *Salome, Where She Danced*; other information on Hollywood films and projects is from Harry Wurtzel to JF, January 14, 1942 (*The African Queen* option); JF's correspondence with Wurtzel, June–July 1943 (*Bataan* settlement); and JF to Olive Carey, September 18, 1943 (*Laramie [The Last Outlaw]*). *At the Front in North Africa* is reviewed by *Wear.* in *Variety*, March 3, 1943. The review of *Tunis Expedition* by John K. Hutchens, "War Front Diary," appears in *NYT Book Review*, April 11, 1943; DFZ's letter to the editor is in the April 25 issue. DFZ's citation for "exceptional bravery" is reported in Gussow. Information on *Tunisian Victory* is from JM, *Frank Capra*, drawing from sources including the author's interviews with John Huston and George Stevens.

Sources on the Truman committee investigation of army filmmaking include *Hearings Before a Special Committee Investigating the National Defense Program* (Part 17, U.S. Senate, February 16 and April 3, 1943) and committee records at the National Archives declassified at the request of the author, including 1943 correspondence: Commander L. N. Miller, liaison officer, Bureau of Naval Personnel, to undersecretary of the navy (Clearing Office), "Information as to civilians granted commissions by Navy Department," April 13; Commander H. A. Houser, USN, to Hugh Fulton, chief counsel of the committee, April 14; Fulton to Houser, April 22; Mr. Haller to Mr. Ansberry, "SUBJECT: Navy Movie Commissions," April 22; Fulton to Houser, April 26; and WJD to chief, Naval Personnel, May 3 (quoted). DFZ's testimony at the army inspector general's secret hearing is from Custen.

Additional information on U.S. Army filmmaking in World War II is from the army's series *The United States Army in World War II*: Terrett, *The Signal Corps: The Emergency*: George Raynor Thompson, Dixie R. Harris, Pauline M. Oakes, and Terrett, *The Signal Corps: The Test*, 1957; and Thompson and Harris, *The Signal Corps: The Outcome*, 1966; as well as from Thomas William Bohn, *An Historical and Descriptive Analysis of the "Why We Fight" Series* (New York: Arno Press, 1977); and JM, *Frank Capra*. Frank Capra's belief that he and JF had been rescued by DFZ is expressed in a letter to his wife, Lucille, July 4, 1943 (Frank Capra Archive, Wesleyan University), cited in JM, *Frank Capra*. JF's recommendation of Capra to Chief of Staff General George C. Marshall was reported to the author by Capra: see JM, *Frank Capra*, with additional information from the author's interview with Brigadier General Frank McCarthy, secretary to Marshall in World War II. *Know Your Enemy—Japan* is discussed in JM, *Frank Capra*, and William J. Blakefield, "A War Within: The Making of *Know Your Enemy—Japan*," *Sight and Sound*, Spring 1983.

Books containing information on the Motion Picture Alliance for the Preservation of American Ideals (MPA) include Ceplair and Englund; Schwartz; Zolotow; and Otto Friedrich, *City of Nets: A Portrait of Hollywood in the 1940s* (New York: Harper and Row, 1986). Press coverage of the MPA's formative period includes (1944): "Leaders of Film Industry Form Anti-Red Group," *LAT*, February 5; "M.P. Alliance Formed to Fight Subversive Forces," *HR*, February 7; MPA, "Statement of Principles" (advertisement), *DV* and *HR*, February 7 ("We believe"); "Pic Leaders Open War on Film Isms," *DV*, February 7; A. U., "Heading Right Way," *DV*, February 7; "Alliance To Work in Co-Operation With Legion," *DV*, February 8; "Film Anti-Red Drive Backed," *LAE*, February 15; John T. McManus, "Speaking of Movies: Reaction's Rump," *PM*, February 15; "Red Influence in Films Hit," *HCN*, February 23; "Labor Joins in Drive Against Reds in Films," *LAE*, March 2; McManus, "Speaking of Movies: Know-Nothing Nostradamus," *PM*, March 13; *Sid.*, "Time To Name Names," *DV*, March 15 (reprinted from *Variety* of same date); Fred Stanley, "Tempest in Hollywood," *NYT*, April 23; "Film Alliance Approves Fight on Communism," *LAT*, April 29; Hedda Hopper column, "Looking at Hollywood," *LAT*, May 6; "Film Industry Is Defended by Unions, Guilds," *DV*, June 29; and "Guilds Attack Hearst-Backed Film Alliance," *PM*, July 2; see also: "Sam Wood Taken by Heart Attack," *LAT*, September 23, 1949.

Zolotow reports that JF was a founding member of MPA, and JF's 1944 U.S. income tax return includes the deduction of a forty-dollar contribution to MPA. The names of other founding members are from Zolotow; MPA, "Statement of Principles"; and articles listed above; Zolotow reports that formative meetings were held in McGuinness's home. Articles on JW as MPA president include "Wayne Heads Film Alliance," *LAE*, March 24, 1949, and "N.Y. Trial To Bare Red Spy Facts, Stripling Says," *HCN*, [March] 1949 ("We don't want"). The charge of anti-Semitism against the MPA is reported in "Film Alliance Approves Fight on Communism." Sam Wood's will is discussed in Ceplair and Englund.

Bulkeley quotes are from the author's interview, except where otherwise indicated. Additional sources of information on Bulkeley include William B. Breuer, *Sea Wolf: A Biography of John D. Bulkeley, USN* (Novato, Ca.; Presidio Press, 1989), and Rachel L. Swarns, "Vice Adm. John D. Bulkeley, 84, Hero of D-Day and Philippines" (obituary), *NYT*, April 8, 1996. Bulkeley's comment on his recruitment of John F. Kennedy into the PT boat service is from Breuer; see also Chandler Whipple, *Lt. John F. Kennedy—Expendable!* (New York: Envoy, 1962), and Joan and Clay Blair Jr., *The Search for JFK* (New York: Berkley, 1976). The accounts of JF's first meeting with Bulkeley are from the author's interview with Bulkeley and from Breuer.

Information on JF's visit to the China–Burma–India Theater is from the author's interview with Major General Albert C. Wedemeyer, USA; JF's OH; Sinclair; DF; Moon; WJD to chief, Naval Personnel, August 11, 1943; chief, Naval Personnel to JF, August 27, 1943; JF to U.S. naval liaison officer, Calcutta, November 21, 1943 (reporting that date); JF to U.S. naval observer, Chunking, China, December 2, 1943 (reporting that date); and JF flight and travel records, December 1943–January 1944 and January 24, 1944. Ray Kellogg's direction of most Field Photo Branch activities as acting chief after JF's departure for CBI is reported in Stephen M. Newmark, acting chief, Field Photo Branch, to CO, Navy Command, October 29, 1945. Guy V. Thayer's service as acting deputy branch chief under Kellogg is reported in Kellogg to Lieutenant Commander A. C. Liggett, USNR, November 1, 1944. Sources on the OSS in China include Field Photo/OSS films at National Archives; Moon; and Yu. Information on Father James Stuart is from Moon and various Field Photo/OSS films made in Burma. "The only good Indian" and General Philip H. Sheridan's statement about "The only good Indians" are from Buscombe, *The BFI Companion to the Western*. General Wedemeyer is quoted from his book *Wedemeyer Reports!* (New York: Henry Holt, 1958); other information on Wedemeyer is from the author's interview; Wedemeyer's OH; "Albert C(oady) Wedemeyer," *Current Biography,* 1945; Pogue; and Barbara W. Tuchman, *Stilwell and the American Experience in China, 1911– 1945* (New York: Macmillan, 1971).

The deaths of Field Photo cameramen Junius J. "Junior" Stout and Arthur "Butch" Meehan are recorded in "Field Photo Personnel," n.d. (Lilly); and "Allied War Cemetery," *Evening Post* (Island of Jersey), November 7, 1944. Information on Stout and Brick Marquard photographing Mulberry harbors is from Pete Martin's interview with JF, "We Shot D-Day on Omaha Beach," *American Legion Magazine,* June 1964, and Forrestal's posthumous presentation of the Silver Star to Stout [1945?] (Lilly); see also Guy Hartcup, *Code Name Mulberry: The Planning, Building and Operation of the Normandy Harbours* (London: David & Charles, Newton Abbot, 1977, and New York: Hippocrene Books, 1977). Information on Stout's other decorations is from Award of the Air Medal, Ninth Air Force [1945?], and Commander R. J. Hardy, USN, Bureau of Naval Personnel, to Archibald J. Stout, awarding the Purple Heart [1945?] (Lilly). JF's correspondence on Meehan (1944) includes his letter to George (and Louise) Meehan, February 2; Louise Meehan to JF, February 5; JF to Lieutenant (jg) Guy Bolte III, USNR, February 11 ("heartbroken"; "The worst time"); and JF to Wead, February 11 ("Writing letters to the next of kin"). The death of Francis Wai (1944) is reported in Bill Gee, "Francis B. Wai Was a Fine Athlete; Services Tuesday," *Honolulu Star-Bulletin,* September 7, 1949 [*sic*]. Harry Carey Jr.'s service in Field Photo is discussed in HCJ, *Company of Heroes,* and in JF to Olive Carey, September 18, 1943; JF's response when Ollie thanked him for recruiting her son, and Garry Wills's comment, are from Wills, *John Wayne's America.*

Information on D-Day is from Stephen E. Ambrose, *D-Day, June 6, 1944: The Climactic Battle of World War II* (New York: Simon and Schuster, 1994); and Cornelius Ryan, *The Longest Day: June 6, 1944* (New York: Simon and Schuster, 1959). JF's USN orders to "proceed to the British Isles" are dated March 31, 1944; JF's letter to Wead about the "sporadic raid" is dated March 28. The official OSS comments on JF's role in filming the invasion are from Lieutenant Colonel Lewis M. Gable, GSC, for Colonel James R. Forgan, GSC, CO, OSS Detachment, ETOUSA, to commander, U.S. Naval Forces in Europe, June 27, 1945, recommending JF for the Distinguished Service Medal. JF's reminiscences of D-Day, the preparations, and the aftermath are from his three-page report to Secretariat, "Report of Officer Returning from the Field," September 9, 1944; and Martin, "We Shot D-Day on Omaha Beach." JF's promise to his crewmen is from Nugent, "Hollywood's Favorite Rebel"; his comment to Armistead ("I'm in command") is quoted in Sinclair.

The discovery of JF's D-Day footage is reported in Douglas Brinkley, "The Color of War," *New Yorker,* July 20, 1998. Information on JF's return to England is from his orders of June 20, 1944, and JF to his family, June 27. Information on Colonel Russell "Red" Reeder is from Richard Goldstein, "Russell Reeder, 95, Leader In Invasion on D-Day, Dies," *NYT,* March 1, 1998; JF's account to Martin misremembers the date of his 1944 encounter with Reeder as June 6. JF's birthday greeting to Samuel Fuller was recalled for the author by Christa (Mrs. Samuel) Fuller.

Sources on Bulkeley's activities during the Normandy invasion include the author's interview with Bulkeley; Breuer; JF, "Report of Officer Returning from the Field"; and press coverage (1944): E. D. Ball, "Famous Pacific PT Boat Hero, John Bulkeley, Headed Patrol of Vicious Craft in Invasion," *Tyler* (Texas) *Telegraph,* June 9; "Bulkeley Dishes It Out," *Newsweek,* June 19; and "Bulkeley Is Busy," *Newark Evening News,* June 22. JF gives accounts of his adventures with Bulkeley in PB and Mitchell; other accounts are in DF and Wills. Bulkeley's comment "The whole thing happened" is from his interview with the author; JF's response to Bulkeley ("This isn't") is from Breuer. JF's discussions with Bulkeley about casting *They Were*

Expendable are from the author's interview with Bulkeley and from Breuer ("Who do you" exchange). Information on the OSS supplying the French Resistance through JF's unit is from PB and from Newmark to CO, Naval Command. Accounts of the Yugoslavian mission in which JF participated include the author's interviews with Bulkeley and Capra; Bulkeley's letter to JM, March 15, 1988 ("skeptical"); and Sinclair. Information on William Clothier's World War II activities is from Clothier's OH; Scott Eyman, "On and Off Poverty Row" (interview), *Take One*, November–December 1973; and Lieutenant M. E. Armistead, USNR, to Junius J. Stout et al., July 28, 1944; JF's bender at Clothier's is reported in the Clothier and Armistead OH's.

JF's comment on Washington desk work is from his March 20, 1943, letter to James Roosevelt. JF's lease with Abra M. Warren for his Connecticut Avenue apartment is dated June 6, 1943; his 1941 Buick is mentioned in his "Application for Supplemental and Occupational Mileage Ration," OPA, October 12, 1943. JF's chauffeur James Jackson and JF's maid are discussed in Ostrander to Fred Totman [April 1943?]; JF to Wead, April 11, 1944 (quoted); JF To Whom It May Concern, April 13, 1944 (quoted); and JF to Amon Carter, April 13, 1944 JF's description of Jack Pennick is from his letter to Howard Barnes of the *New York Herald Tribune*, July 22, 1943; WJD's comment on Pennick was quoted by Kellogg in his eulogy at Pennick's memorial services at the Field Photo Memorial Home, August 20, 1964, from the script of the services (Lilly). JF's humorous comments on Ostrander are from his February 11, 1944, letters to Bolte ("Vangie is") and Wead ("The only consolation," with Ostrander's postscript, "Uncle Spig").

W. L. White's book *They Were Expendable* was published in 1942 by Harcourt, Brace & World, New York. John Hersey's article "PT Squadron in the South Pacific" is the May 10, 1943, cover story in *Life*. Anderson calls JF's film of *They Were Expendable* "a heroic poem"; PB discusses JF's theme of "the glory in defeat." JF's OH comments on the incident involving the Filipina singer. Comments by Wead and JF on MGM's script changes include Wead to McGuinness, July 19, 1943; JF to McGuinness, August 5, 1943 ("Spig tells me"), and JF to Wead, February 1944 ("had some very quaint"). JF's expression of concern that Congress "would be after my ass" if he went off active duty to make a Hollywood war movie (quoted from a letter to McGuinness, n.d.), and the proposal by McGuinness and Wead that he donate the money to Navy Relief, are from DF. JF's statements of enthusiasm for the film project and about building a "clubhouse" are from his "Notes for Jim McGuinness on [*They Were*] *Expendable*" [1944] (Lilly); JF's earlier decision not to make the film is challenged by McGuinness in his [March?] 1944 letter to JF arguing the story's importance to "America's heroic tradition." JF's characterization of Forrestal and Rear Admiral A. S. Merrill, chief of Navy Public Relations, as "anxious to have this film produced," and JF's statement that he will turn over his fee to a fund for servicemen are from his letter to the chief, Naval Personnel, September 20, 1944; JF's comment about plans for his "big chunk of dough" is from his October 30, 1944, letter to Wedemeyer.

Information on JF being placed on inactive status to direct *Expendable* is from USN and OSS correspondence, September–October 1944, and JF, "Ships and Stations During 7 December 1941 to 31 December 1946," which states that he left his OSS duty on October 27. JF's July–September 1944 itinerary is from his request for per diem payments, 1944. Information on JF's Fox contract is from George Wasson to JF, October 4, 1944, and Twentieth Century–Fox Film Corp. to JF, October 23, 1944 (signed agreement). Information on JF's contract with Loews for *Expendable* is from James B. Donovan, OSS, to F. L. Hendrickson of Loews, April 27, 1945, referring to a December 20, 1944, agreement superseded by a March 5, 1945, agreement. JF asks Toland to codirect *Expendable* in a letter of September 16, 1944; second-unit director James C. Havens's credit is discussed in J. P. McGowan of SDG to JF, July 20, 1945. Information on Bond's auto accident is from Kellogg to JF, July 29, 1944, and R&O. Sources on Robert Montgomery's wartime service and return to Hollywood include the author's interview with Bulkeley; R&O; Anderson; "Robert Montgomery Enlists as War Ambulance Driver," *LAT,* May 27, 1940; "Montgomery Joins Embassy," *LAT,* August 2, 1941; "Robert Montgomery to Be Put on Inactive Duty by Navy," *LAT,* October 9, 1944; Pryor, "Home Is the Sailor," *NYT,* February 4, 1945; Bob White, "Lt. Comdr. Montgomery Doffs Brass Hat to Daub on Grease Paint Again," *LAT,* April 29, 1945; "The Story's Dynamite in *They Were Expendable,*" *Cue,* December 8, 1945; and Hopper, "Bob Montgomery Sees Need of War Pictures," *LAT,* January 13, 1946.

JF's declaration "We are sticking to fact" in *Expendable* is from Stanley, "The Hollywood Agenda," *NYT,* February 4, 1945. JF's remark on the brush fire is from an MGM press release, "Movie Magic Recreates Jap Manila Attack," 1945 (AMPAS). Montgomery's remark to Donna Reed about JF is recalled in Montgomery's interview with Anderson in *About John Ford;* also quoted is Jay Fultz, *In Search of Donna Reed* (Iowa City: University of Iowa Press, 1998). Information on JF's hospital stay and Montgomery filling in as the film's director is from McGuinness's wire to Markey's office, quoted in Naval Command to Charles Cheston, OSS, May 22, 1945; JF's fracture is described in Dr. John C. Wilson To Whom It May Concern, July 9, 1945. Montgomery's comments on JF and *Expendable* are also from his interview in Anderson, as are JF's comments to Montgomery, Eddie Mannix, and the woman in the hospital ("Alcoholic!"), and JW's question to Montgomery ("What's wrong"). JF's comments to Anderson about *Expendable,* including his statement that he approached the film as a "documentary," are from their *Sequence* interview published as "The Quiet Man" and reprinted in *About John Ford.* JF indicates his unusual degree of involvement with the editing in a May 29, 1945, letter to Markey.

Reviews of *Expendable* include (1945): *Film Daily,* November 23; Howard Barnes, *New York Herald Tribune,* December 21; *New Yorker,* December 22; Bosley Crowther, *NYT,* December 26; and (1946): James Agee, *Nation,* January 5; see also Anderson, "*They Were Expendable* and John Ford," *Sequence,* Summer 1950. Sarris comments on the film in *The John Ford Movie Mystery.* The box-office performance is reported in Gallagher and R&O. Sources on Lieutenant Robert Kelly's lawsuit over *Expendable* include Zolotow and the author's interview with Bulkeley; those sources also provided information on Lieutenant Beulah Greenwalt Walcher's lawsuit, as does 1948 press coverage of her suit: "Corregidor Nurse Wins $290,000 in Film Suit," *LAT,* December 4, and "Metro Loses 290G Privacy Suit," *Variety,* December 6. The colorization of *Expendable* is discussed in "AFT, Turner Pact to Colorize Classics," *HR,* November 25, 1987; and JM, "Colorized Pic Is Dane Bane," *DV,* April 12, 1990.

Documents at Lilly on the Field Photo Farm include Donovan, Leisure, Newton & Lumbard to Totman, October 31, 1944; Articles of Incorporation of Field Photo Homes, Inc., filed November 30, 1944, State of California; *The Field Photo Homes Inc.,* booklet, n.d. (includes names of wartime dead); Constitution, August 18, 1946; and "Method of Operation," February 21, 1964. Other information on the Farm is from DF; Davis; Sinclair; HCJ, *Company of Heroes;* Wills; and Philip K. Scheuer, "John Ford Hasn't Forgotten His Wartime OSS Buddies," *LAT,* April 22, 1956.

Barbara Ford's description of her father as a "ribbon freak" is from Sinclair. Information on JF's pursuit of medals and decorations includes his letters seeking the Silver Star: JF to Captain John Roper, USN, March 23, 1945 ("Since my Naval combat career"), with a memo from Lieutenant (jg) C. J. Barry, USN, to Captain H. G. Patrick, Navy Department Board of Decorations and Medals [BDM], n.d.; and JF to Commander H. A. MacDonald, USN (Ret.), Navy Photographic Services, January 22, 1946 ("The only thing"). Other information (1945) on JF's request for the Silver Star is from BDM to Nimitz, April 5; president, Pacific Fleet Board of Awards, to Nimitz, April 20 ("[E]vidently his performance"); Selden B. Kennedy, BDM, to Forrestal, May 11; n.a., "Rough Draft, Subject: Captain John Ford, USNR/Recommendation for award of Silver Star," September 12 (Lilly); WJD to adjutant general, War Department, September 27 (recommending Silver Star and Legion of Merit); and (1946): Otto C. Doering Jr., to JF, March 22. Information on the denial of the Silver Star (1945) is from W. L. Ainsworth, Board of Awards, April 20; Nimitz to Forrestal, May 6; and Forrestal's endorsement of the denial, May 19. Sources on the recommendation for the Distinguished Service Medal include Gable of OSS to commander, U.S. Naval Forces in Europe, June 27, 1945; MacDonald to JF,

January 14, 1946; and Doering to JF. Information on the denial of the DSM is from R. W. Hayler, BDM, to Forrestal, February 4, 1946 ("the nature of the duties"). Sources on JF's Legion of Merit include R. W. Hayler, BDM, to Forrestal, September 27, 1945, approved by A. L. Gates for Forrestal, December 9, 1945; and the citation issued by Forrestal, January 31, 1946.

Information on JF concluding his wartime service is from JF, "Ships and Stations During 7 December 1941 to 31 December 1946"; Doering to chief, Naval Personnel, July 23, 1945; order of release from active duty, chief of Naval Personnel to JF, September 27, 1945; and Notice of Separation from Naval Service, signed by JF, September 29, 1945. JF's comments about returning to Hollywood are from his letter to Killanin, c. fall 1945 ("Living in Hollywood"), quoted in Sinclair; DF (his remark to DFZ); and JF to James Basevi, September 12, 1944 ("If you should see").

CHAPTER ELEVEN: "I AM A DIRECTOR OF WESTERNS" (PP. 416–519)

The chapter title is a comment by JF at the October 22, 1950, SDG special membership meeting, quoted from Kenneth L. Geist, *Pictures Will Talk: The Life and Films of Joseph L. Mankiewicz* (New York: Scribners, 1978), which includes a partial transcript of the meeting; Geist and Eyman, *Print the Legend,* are the sources of JF's other comments on that occasion. Douglas Sirk's recollections of the meeting are from Jon Halliday, *Sirk on Sirk* (New York: Viking, 1972). Additional sources on the SDG controversy over the Mankiewicz recall are listed later in this section. The chapter epigraph is from A. J. A. Symons, *The Quest for Corvo: An Experiment in Biography* (London: Cassell, 1934).

General information on postwar Hollywood is from Balio, *The American Film Industry;* Thomas Schatz, *The Genius of the System: Hollywood Filmmaking in the Studio Era* (New York: Pantheon, 1989); Schatz, *Boom and Bust: Hollywood in the 1940s,* History of the American Cinema Series No. 6 (New York: Scribners, 1997); Gomery, *Movie History: A Survey;* and JM, *Frank Capra.* Political events of this period in Hollywood are documented in Ceplair and Englund; Schwartz; and Victor S. Navasky, *Naming Names* (New York: Viking, 1980), although those books say relatively little about the SDG. For a general history of the postwar Red Scare, see David Caute, *The Great Fear: The Anti-Communist Purge Under Truman and Eisenhower* (New York: Simon and Schuster, 1978).

JF's attitude toward wearing his uniform was discussed by Vicky Armistead Wilson in her interview with the author. JF's comment on "Making Western pictures" is quoted in Davis from JF to Thomas B. Dawson, November [?], 1949; JF's OH says that he made Westerns to avoid dealing with contemporary issues. His other explanations for why he enjoyed directing Westerns are from his interviews with BBC TV's Jenkinson ("I like to make") and Bill Libby of *Cosmopolitan* ("When I come back"). Charles FitzSimons's observation about JF living in "Fordland" is from Davis. Michael Coyne discusses the Western genre as a vehicle for critiquing modern American social issues in *The Crowded Prairie: American National Identity in the Hollywood Western* (New York: I. B. Tauris & Co., 1997). HCJ told the author that he and JF were the only members of the *She Wore a Yellow Ribbon* company who voted for President Truman in the 1948 election; JF's comment about FDR to conservative members of the cast is from Sinclair.

Sources on JF's project *The Family* include the first-draft screenplay by Laurence Stallings and Frank S. Nugent, n.d. (Lilly); Merian C. Cooper to C. R. Everitt of Little, Brown, November 29, 1945; Cooper's telegram to an unidentified recipient, December 13, 1945; "Scribes Set Sail to Script *The Family,*" *DV,* December 4, 1947; Hedda Hopper, "John Ford Pictures May Tumble More Traditions," *LAT,* February 22, 1948; and an *LAE* item, February 13, 1950. JF's rejection of a long-term Fox contract is reported in Gallagher. Information on *The Last Outlaw* project is from the author's interview with HCJ; JF's legal files (Lilly); and contracts between JF and United Artists Corp., January 5, 1945, and between Argosy Pictures Corp. and UA, April 22, 1946 (UA collection, State Historical Society of Wisconsin).

Argosy's prewar talks with Fox, RKO, and Universal are mentioned in Harry Wurtzel to JF

(1941), September 19, November 5, 10, and 22. Other sources on the history of Argosy include DF; Otto C. Doering Jr. to JF, March 22, 1946; contract between Argosy and JF, April 18, 1946, and "Contract Digest," April 16, 1946; "Argosy Pictures Corp. Personnel List" (1947); Grady Johnson, "A Paean to Economy," *NYT,* June 27, 1948; list of Argosy stockholders of record, H. Lee Van Hoozer (Argosy secretary), January 6, 1956; Doering to Cooper, May 3, 1965; and Eyman, *Print the Legend* (including Donald Dewar's comment that the company "never recovered" from the box-office failure of *The Fugitive*). Information on Argosy's 1946 discussions with Republic Pictures Corp. is from Dewar to Cooper, January 17, 1946; and Cooper to Herbert J. Yates of Republic, January 18, 1946. Information on the RKO-Argosy deal is from "Summary of Film Earnings" *(The Fugitive),* RKO, January 25, 1951; DF; and Edwin Schallert, "Ford Closes Four-Film Deal; *Fugitive* First," *LAT,* October 2, 1946. JF describes his Argosy Westerns as "potboilers" in Kennedy, "A Talk with John Ford." Cooper's retirement as a brigadier general in the AF Reserve is reported in Behlmer, "Merian C. Cooper Is the Kind of Creative Showman Today's Movies Badly Need"; WJD's postwar activities and the creation of the Central Intelligence Agency are discussed in Brown and Ranelagh.

Henry Fonda's comment about JF's personality being mellowed by his war experiences is from DF. JF tells MF in his letter of March [28?], 1945, that he is ready for a rocking chair. Katherine Cliffton's recollections of JF's personality, reading habits, drinking, and purchase of suits for the members of a boys' choir are from her interview with the author. JF's fondness for games of pitch is reported in HCJ, *Company of Heroes,* and Nugent, "Hollywood's Favorite Rebel." Fonda's memory of "something different happening every night" on location in Monument Valley is from *Directed by John Ford.* Information on the purchase of Reseda property for the Field Photo Farm is from "Memorial Home," *Motion Picture Herald,* April 20, 1946; and Price, Waterhouse & Co. to Board of Directors, Field Photo Homes, Inc., April 23, 1948. The Farm's postwar officers are listed in "Field Photo Memorial Home," [October?] 1945; its constitution (quoted) is from August 1946. The warning "NO WOMEN" is quoted in Parrish, *Growing Up in Hollywood.* Other information on the Farm is from DF; HCJ, *Company of Heroes;* Parrish, *Growing Up in Hollywood;* Davis; Field Photo Memorial Day program, 1948 (Lilly); Scheuer, "John Ford Hasn't Forgotten His Wartime OSS Buddies"; "John Ford Puts on Maine Party," the *Maine Legionnaire,* September 1956; and Mark Haggard's 1974 short film *John Ford: Memorial Day 1970.* The reconstituted Emerald Bay Yacht Club is discussed in DF and in Ward Bond to JF, November 13, 1945. Sinclair reports on a priest blessing the *Araner;* MF's affidavit to the IRS about their use of the boat is dated March 12, 1952 (Lilly).

Sources on Harry Carey's death and funeral include the author's interview with Olive Carey; HCJ, *Company of Heroes;* Gallagher; and newspaper articles (1947): "Harry Carey, 37 Yrs. In Pix, Dies," *DV,* September 22; "Harry Carey, Stage, Screen Veteran, Dies," *LAE,* September 22; "Film Notables at Rites for Actor Harry Carey," *LAT,* September 25; and "Tribute Paid Harry Carey," *L.A. Daily News,* September 25. Capra's description of the funeral as "Ford's greatest production" was reported by Olive Carey. Sources on D. W. Griffith's funeral and visitors to the funeral home include Ezra Goodman, *The Fifty-Year Decline and Fall of Hollywood* (New York: Simon and Schuster, 1961); Lillian Gish, with Ann Pinchot, *The Movies, Mr. Griffith, and Me* (Englewood Cliffs, N.J.: Prentice-Hall, 1969) (on JF, Mae Marsh, and Cecil B. DeMille at funeral home); Robert M. Henderson, *D. W. Griffith: His Life and Work* (New York: Oxford University Press, 1972); and Schickel, *D. W. Griffith: An American Life.*

JF discusses *Captain from Castile* in a letter to DFZ, September 25, 1945; JF's proposal to remake *Judge Priest* is mentioned in DFZ to JF, August 2, 1945. JF reports to DFZ on November 1, 1945, about viewing *Frontier Marshal;* JF's remark about the film to Fonda is from Anderson. Winston Miller's comments on *My Darling Clementine* are quoted from John A. Gallagher, "Winston Miller" (interview), *Films in Review,* December 1990; see also Robert Lyons, "Interview with Winston Miller" in Lyons, ed., *My Darling Clementine* (New Brunswick, N.J.: Rutgers University Press, 1984). Stuart N. Lake's *Wyatt Earp: Frontier Marshal* was published in 1931 by Houghton Mifflin in Boston. Allen Barra discusses Victor Mature's Doc Holliday in *Inventing Wyatt Earp: His Life and Many Legends* (New York: Carroll and Graf, 1998). JF's observation about "simplicity" is quoted by Lyons from Axel Madsen, "Cavalier Seul," *Cahiers du Cinéma*, October 1966. Information on the Gunfight at the O.K. Corral is from Tefertiller, *Wyatt Earp: The Life Behind the Legend;* and John Mack Faragher, "The Tale of Wyatt Earp," in Carnes, *Past Imperfect: History According to the Movies.* JF's claim to have filmed the gunfight accurately is from PB. Jorge Luis Borges discusses the Western genre in *An Introduction to American Literature.*

JF's agreement with Twentieth Century–Fox Film Corp. for *My Darling Clementine* was signed on December 4, 1945. Sources on *Clementine* script changes include "Added Scenes & Retakes" in the shooting script, July 8 and 10, 1946; Lyons, including a transcript of the film, discarded scenes from the script, and notes on the changes; DFZ to JF, June 25, 1946; DFZ to Lloyd Bacon, July 13, 1946, and DFZ to Samuel Engel, September 4, 1946, in Behlmer, ed., *Memo from Darryl F. Zanuck.* DFZ's suggestion of the film's original ending is from "Conference with Mr. Zanuck (on First Draft Continuity of February 22, 1946)," March 5, 1946 (Lilly); DFZ's memo to Engel discusses reshooting the ending. JF's suggestion of using fictional names for characters in *Clementine* is discussed in his letter to DFZ, January 25, 1946, and DFZ's January 29 reply. Information on the song "Oh, Dem Golden Slippers" is from Fulton Brylawski to Cliffton, November 2, 1949. Fonda reports in his interview for Anderson's *About John Ford* that JF added the "Scent of the desert flower" exchange; JF's improvisation of Fonda's fence balancing act is recalled by the actor in *The American West of John Ford;* Fonda also discusses the scene in *Directed by John Ford.*

Correspondence between JF and DFZ on casting proposals for *Clementine,* including Mature, James Stewart, Donna Reed, Anne Baxter, and Stepin Fetchit, is from November 1945–March 1946. Stepin Fetchit asks JF for work in his letter of February 16, 1945; Sarris's comment on JF's employment of the actor is from *The John Ford Movie Mystery.* JF tells DFZ in a letter of January [11?], 1946, that he would be pleased to make the film in black and white. Levy says *Clementine* was filmed in May–June 1946, but a letter from DFZ to JF, April 16, 1946, records that shooting has started, and DFZ to JF, June 25, that it has finished. The cost of *Clementine* and DFZ's assertion that the film needs a "major and radical cutting job" to be "*big time* all the way" are from his June 25 memo to JF in *Memo from Darryl F. Zanuck.* Gallagher reports the film's box-office gross. DFZ's decree that a kiss be added to the ending is from his memo to Engel. JF's disparaging remark about *Clementine* ("My children liked it") and his comment about seeking "to discover humor in the midst of tragedy" are from his interview with Jean Mitry, *Cahiers du Cinéma,* translated by Andrew Sarris, in Sarris, ed., *Interviews with Film Directors.* Robin Wood's observations on *Clementine* are from his essay "Shall We Gather at the River?: The Late Films of John Ford," *Film Comment,* Fall 1971. JF's interest in *The Ghost and Mrs. Muir* is discussed in 1946 correspondence: DFZ to JF, March 28; JF to DFZ, March 29; and DFZ to Fred Kohlmar and Philip Dunne, June 24, in *Memo from Darryl F. Zanuck;* see also Dunne, *Take Two.*

Graham Greene's comments on *The Fugitive* are from his Guardian Film Lecture in 1984 at the National Film Theatre, London, in Parkinson, *The Graham Greene Film Reader.* Information on Argosy's purchase of film rights to Greene's novel *The Power and the Glory* from Alexander Korda is from Cooper's telegram to Korda, November 27, 1945; Korda's telegram to Cooper, November 28, 1945; and "Sold to Argosy," *NYT,* June 30, 1946. Dudley Nichols to JF, March 9, 1943, indicates they had discussed the project; but before hiring Nichols to adapt the novel, JF offered the job to Richard Watts Jr., as discussed in Watts to Cooper, January 14, 1946, and JF to Watts, January 24, 1946. Nichols discusses the problems of adapting the novel and his dislike for JF's direction of his script in his April 22, 1953, letter to Anderson; Nichols's comment that JF deserves cowriting credit is from his October 31, 1946, letter to JF. JF's statement that he wants to make *The Fugitive* because of his religious convictions is from his October 17, 1946, letter to DFZ, quoted in R&O; Fonda tells Anderson that JF knew the film was not good. JF's remark that the film is about "the soul of a man" is from Hopper, "John Ford Pictures May Tumble More Traditions"; JF's comments on filming *The Fugitive* in Mexico, labor, and communism are from Hopper, "His Hobby Is Collecting Oscars," *Chicago Tribune,* February 22, 1948.

JF's arrangements with Fox for Fonda and the *Fugitive* title are from JF to DFZ, October 17 and 24, 1946, and DFZ to JF, October 23 and 24, 1946. Fonda discusses his casting, his suggestion of José Ferrer, and Ferrer's unavailability in Anderson; Ferrer's HUAC testimony on May 23 and 25, 1951, is from the committee's hearings on *Communist Infiltration of Hollywood Motion-Picture Industry;* Ward Bond's comment that Ferrer "is not good for the business" is from "Bond's Campaign Costs Ferrer Teachers' Award; Invokes Pegler, Sokolsky," *DV,* March 14, 1951. Fonda's recollection of his trip to Mazatlán with JF et al. after *The Fugitive* is from Fonda, as told to Howard Teichmann, *Fonda: My Life* (New York: New American Library, 1981). The cost and gross of *The Fugitive* are reported in Price, Waterhouse & Co. to Argosy board of directors, October 7, 1947; and "Summary of Film Earnings"; shooting dates and locales are from Levy. Information on Emilio Fernández's involvement with *The Fugitive* is from Paulo Antonio Paranagua, trans. by Ana M. Lopéz, *Mexican Cinema* (London: British Film Institute and IMCINE, 1995); Cooper to Charles Woram, Estudios Churubusco, August 31, 1946; and Woram to Cooper, September 23, 1946. Reviews include Bosley Crowther, *NYT,* December 26, 1947; and James Agee, *Nation,* January 10, 1948, reprinted in *Agee on Film.* JF's comment on the film being "perfect" and his recollection that he would "*wait* for the light" are from PB.

JF's meeting with Stallings in London during World War II was reported to the author by Cliffton. Harry Carey's explanations to his son of why he hadn't worked with JF in more than a decade are from HCJ, *Company of Heroes* ("He won't ask me") and Gene Vier, "Harry Carey Jr. Recalls His Dad," *LAT,* November 24, 1979 ("His Irish pride"). HCJ's recollections of JF's cruelty on *3 Godfathers* are from *Company of Heroes* and Gallagher ("Gee, if you were mad"). Additional information on the Death Valley shoot is from Lowell Farrell, production manager, "Facts About Death Valley Location," April 3, 1948. Winton C. Hoch's comments on JF and their exchange at rushes for *Joan of Arc* are from the author's interview with Hoch, parts published as JM, "Winton Hoch: 'A Damn Good Job.'" The JF–Hoch exchange on the first day of shooting *3 Godfathers* is from HCJ, *Company of Heroes.* JF calls Hoch "a very, very pedantic cameraman" in *Directed by John Ford.* Hoch's comment about "Ford's genius" was made to the author during a screening of *The Searchers* at the Los Angeles County Museum of Art. See also JM, *"3 Godfathers," Film Comment,* July 1973.

In his 1951 interview with Anderson for *Sequence,* "The Quiet Man," JF comments on playing it safe by concentrating on Westerns after the box-office failure of *The Fugitive.* Information on the cancellation of *The Quiet Man* in the late 1940s is from DF; R&O; McNee; Cooper's telegram to Korda, October 26, 1946; Cooper to JF, August 6, 1947; "To Use Blocked Sterling in Filming of *Quiet Man,*" the *Film Daily,* July 15, 1948; and JF to Donald Monteith, July 21, 1948.

Cliffton spoke with the author about Pat and Barbara Ford. Grady Johnson's observation that JF's grown children were afraid of him although his grandsons were not is from "John Ford: Maker of Hollywood Stars," *Coronet,* December 1953. Information on Pat's writing jobs in this period is from Sinclair. JF's OH recalls taking Barbara to cutting sessions on *They Were Expendable.* Sources on the Barbara–Robert Walker marriage and divorce include Beverly Linet, *Star-Crossed: The Story of Robert Walker and Jennifer Jones* (New York: G. P. Putnam's Sons, 1986); the 1948 *LAT* articles "Hollywood Pair to Be Married Aboard Yacht," June 30; "Robert Walker Weds Daughter of John Ford," July 9; "John Ford's Daughter Sues Robert Walker," September 24; and "Mrs. Walker Granted Divorce on Birthday," December 17; and Louella O. Parsons column, "Robt. Walker, Wife Separate," *LAE,* August 17, 1948. Bruce Cabot's observation about most men being afraid to date Barbara is from Edward Z. Epstein, *Portrait of Jennifer: A Biography of Jennifer Jones* (New York: Simon and Schuster, 1995). MF's comment about the similarity between Barbara and JF is from Sinclair. Olive Carey's story about JF's "crying jag" is from Wills.

JF's ambivalent statement about the U.S. Cavalry and the Indians ("Who better than") is from Leguèbe, "John Ford," in *Le Cinéma Americain par ses auteurs* (quotation translated by Gallagher). The initial JF-Nugent meeting about *Fort Apache* (working title: *War Party*) and Nugent's claim to have finished his *Saturday Evening Post* profile of JF by that time are from Nugent's letter to Anderson, May 3, 1953; the profile, "Hollywood's Favorite Rebel," appears in the July 23, 1949, issue of the *Post*. Nugent's article "Hollywood Invades Mexico" (partly about the making of *The Fugitive*) is in the *NYT Magazine,* March 23, 1947. James Warner Bellah's story "Massacre," originally published in the *Post,* February 22, 1947, is reprinted in his collections *Massacre* (New York: Lion Books, 1950), and *Reveille* (New York: Fawcett Gold Medal Books, 1962), as is "The Devil at Crazy Man" (1947). James Warner Bellah Jr.'s description of his father is quoted in Davis; the senior Bellah is also described in Wills. Title suggestions for *Fort Apache* are documented in an unsigned January 19, 1948, memo in JF's production files; JF to Joe Breen, July 17, 1947 (in which JF describes the story as patriotic and pro-Irish); and an Argosy memo, January 19, 1948. Nugent's biographies of characters in *Fort Apache* are in his story outline for *War Party* [1947], which also includes Nugent's suggestion of the riderless horse.

Cliffton discussed Nugent's biographies with the author, as well as the research she and Katharine "Tatty" Spaatz conducted for the film. Other information on their research is from notes on books and music in JF's files, and 1947 correspondence: Thomas Geoly of Eaves Costume Manufacturing Corp. to Spaatz, May 8; Spaatz to Cliffton, June 21 (on Matthew Brady photos); JF to Breen; and Spaatz to Cliffton, July 24. S. L. A. Marshall discusses the U.S. Cavalry and its combat with Indians in *Crimsoned Prairie: The Indian Wars* (New York: Scribners, 1972). The influences of Frederic Remington and Charles M. Russell on JF are discussed in JF's OH; PB; Brian W. Dippie, *Remington & Russell: The Sid Richardson Collection* (Austin: University of Texas Press, 1994); and Scheuer, "Mormon Trek Pictured in John Ford *Wagonmaster* [*sic*]," *LAT,* April 8, 1950. Pat Ford is quoted from Eyman, *Print the Legend,* on Charles Schreyvogel's influence on his father. Locations for *Fort Apache* are listed in JF production files and in Gaberscek, *Il West di John Ford.*

Fort Apache budget and cost figures are from "*War Party* Budget Breakdown," July 25, 1947; Cooper to JF, August 6, 1947; and "*Fort Apache* Cost Breakdown as of March 6, 1948." Information on Archie Stout's use of infrared photography on *Fort Apache* is from *American Cinematographer* articles by Stout, "Dramatic Pictorialism with Infrared Film," August 1948, and George Turner, "Dust and Danger at *Fort Apache,*" June 1996. Agee's review of *Fort Apache* in the *Nation,* July 24, 1948, is reprinted in *Agee on Film.* Comments on the film's ending include those by JF in PB; Jean-Marie Straub, quoted in M&W; and Wood, "Shall We Gather at the River?: The Late Films of John Ford." JF's statement "My sympathy is all with the Indians" is from his interview with Jenkinson; his comment that the cavalry "weren't all-American boys" is from his interview with the author. JF's award from the United Veterans of Indian Wars is reported in "Indian Wars' Vets Salute John Ford," *DV,* October 16, 1950. Russell Campbell's comments on *Fort Apache* are from his essay "*Fort Apache,*" the *Velvet Light Trap,* August 1971; Karl Marx is quoted from "The Eighteenth Brumaire of Louis Napoleon," 1852.

Peter Fonda comments on his father's performance in *Fort Apache* in *Don't Tell Dad: A Memoir* (New York: Hyperion, 1998). JF's sarcastic remark to Henry Fonda about *Mister Roberts* (the play) is from Fonda and Teichmann; JF's telegram of best wishes to Fonda is dated February 18, 1948. Howard Hawks's comments on JF are from the author's interviews with Hawks, in JM, *Hawks on Hawks,* as is JF's remark about JW in *Red River* ("I never knew"). Sinclair and Gallagher report that JF and Hawks were praised for each other's work. Joanne Dru's anecdote about JF urinating is quoted in Sinclair from Dru's OH. Budd Boetticher's complaints about JF's cutting of *The Bullfighter and the Lady* are reported in Davis; see also PB; Gallagher; and Boetticher to JF, October 30 and November 7 and 11, 1950, and January 16, 1952 (the November 11 letter is quoted from Eyman, *Print the Legend*).

Documentation at Lilly on two Bellah stories, "War Party" and "Big Hunt," serving as the basis for *She Wore a Yellow Ribbon* includes n.a., First Detailed Treatment, n.d.; a screenplay by Bellah, n.d.; and a 1949 note on the stories in JF's files. "War Party," originally published in the *Saturday Evening Post* (1946), is reprinted in Bellah's collection *Massacre;* "Big Hunt," first published in the *Post* in 1947, is reprinted in both *Massacre* and *Reveille;* another of Bellah's *Post* stories reprinted in both collections, "Command" (1946), also was used for *Yellow Ribbon.*

JF's story about Hoch shooting the thunderstorm in *Yellow Ribbon* "under protest" is from *Directed by John Ford.* Hoch's comments on JF and *Yellow Ribbon,* and JF's instructions to Hoch about color, are from the author's interview with Hoch, parts published as JM, "Winton Hoch: 'A Damn Good Job.'" HCJ's recollection of Hoch and the thunderstorm is from *Company of Heroes.* Hoch's other objections during the filming were reported to the author by Henry Brandon, whose brother Hugo Brandon was an assistant to Hoch on *Yellow Ribbon.*

JF's comment "Send the commie bastard to me" is quoted in Gallagher, as reported by Maurice Rapf in 1976. Cliffton told the author that JF was "very much irritated by the blacklist." Testimony before the House Committee on Un-American Activities (HUAC) by Sam Wood, Louis B. Mayer, and Adolphe Menjou is from *Hearings Regarding the Communist Infiltration of the Motion Picture Industry,* HUAC, U.S. Government Printing Office, October 20–30, 1947. Frank Tuttle's HUAC testimony is from the committee's hearings on *Communist Infiltration of Hollywood Motion-Picture Industry,* 1951. Dalton Trumbo discusses the blacklist era in *The Time of the Toad: A Study of Inquisition in America and Two Related Pamphlets* (New York: Harper & Row, 1972). Albert Maltz's observation on blacklisting is from his book *The Citizen Writer* (New York: International Publishers, 1950), quoted in Ceplair and Englund. Ronald Reagan's FBI informing was revealed in 1985 by the *San Jose Mercury News* (California), based on documents obtained through the Freedom of Information Act: see "Unmasking Informant T-10," *Time,* September 9, 1985; see also Dan E. Moldea, *Dark Victory: Ronald Reagan, MCA, and the Mob* (New York: Viking, 1986), and Anne Edwards, *Early Reagan* (New York: William Morrow, 1987).

Information on JF's membership on the SDG board of directors is from SDG minutes, May 19, 1946; May 20, 1947; and May 28, 1950; his election to the interim board as first vice president is from the minutes of October 25, 1950. The SDG "Guild Committees" list indicates he was appointed to the Veterans Committee on June 4, 1946, and to the SDG Special Committee to Investigate Thomas Committee Subpoenas on October 7, 1947; JF became the chairman of that special committee, as indicated in the minutes of SDG's October 21, 1947, board meeting. Information on the non-Communist affidavit required of labor organization officers is from *A Guide for Labor Organizations,* National Labor Relations Board, 1948, and "Affidavit of Noncommunist Union Officer," NLRB. Sources on non-Communist affidavits signed by JF include an SDG document addressed to the guild's general counsel, Mabel Walker Willebrandt, on June 5, 1950 (with a written notation that JF's affidavit was filed on June 6, 1950); William S. Holman, executive secretary of SDG, to Claud[e] B. Calkin, affidavit compliance officer, NLRB, June 2, 1951 (mentioning a JF affidavit forwarded to NLRB on April 18, 1951); Willebrandt to Calkin, June 28, 1951, indicating that another JF affidavit, signed after his reelection to the SDG board in 1951, was forwarded to NLRB; and Calkin to Willebrandt, July 11, 1951.

The October 20, 1947, telegram from JF's SDG committee to Speaker of the House Joseph W. Martin Jr. and HUAC chairman J. Parnell Thomas is signed by SDG president George Stevens, JF, Cooper, John Huston, George Sidney, and William Wyler (copies in Lilly and SDG files); Huston comments on the telegram in his autobiography, *An Open Book* (New York: Knopf, 1980). "Louis" [Lewis] Milestone, Edward Dmytryk, Irving Pichel, Herbert Biberman, and Robert Rossen sent a telegram to Stevens, October 21; Stevens and the SDG board sent a telegram contradicting Wood's allegation to Martin and Thomas, October 22; the SDG telegram is quoted in October 23 coverage by *LAT,* "Directors Deny Red Activities," and *DV,* "Wood's Red Probe Charges Denied by Directors Guild" (with "SDG Board Raps Wood Testimony"). The discussion at the October 21, 1947, meeting of the SDG board of directors is quoted in Eyman, *Print the Legend,* from the minutes of the meeting. JF's self-description as "a state of Maine Republican" is also quoted by Geist from the minutes of the October 22, 1950, SDG special membership meeting; JF gives a similar self-description in his OH (1973). Sources on JF's support for Senator Robert A. Taft's 1952 presidential candidacy include JF to Taft, July 22, 1952, and Taft to JF, August 7, 1952; Wedemeyer's service as national chairman of the Citizens for Taft Committee is discussed in *Wedemeyer Reports!* Vice President Richard Nixon thanks JF in a letter of March 28, 1953, for supporting the Eisenhower-Nixon ticket in the 1952 presidential election.

Information on the Committee for the First Amendment is from the author's interview with Dunne; Dunne, *Take Two;* Ceplair and Englund; JM, *Frank Capra,* and from *DV* (1947): "The Committee for the First Amendment" (advertisement), October 21; "Committee for the First Amendment" (advertisement), October 24; "30 Filmites Leave on Protest Dash to Washington," October 27; "H'd [*sic*] Group Holds Press Sessions in Washington" and "HOLLYWOOD FIGHTS BACK!" (CFA advertisement), October 28; and "Thomas Committee Flayed by Stars on Broadcast," November 3. The FBI's description of the CFA as a "Communist front" is from a section of the January 16, 1952, FBI report on "FRANK RUSSELL CAPRA, aka Francesco Capra" (File No. 123-12626) released to the author through the Freedom of Information Act in 1992 and quoted in JM, *Frank Capra* (New York: St. Martin's Press paperback edition, 2000). The minutes of the October 21, 1947, SDG board meeting indicate that JF and Huston volunteered to go to Washington; JF's planned visit is mentioned in a telegram from Stevens and the SDG board to Milestone, October 22; Senator (Ralph) Owen Brewster mentions JF's presence in Washington and their "lifelong friendship" in a letter to Louis B. Mayer, November 5, 1947 (Lilly); Huston writes of his trip in *An Open Book.* Brewster's "xenophobic stand" is discussed in Richard W. Judd, "Hydroelectric Power Development" in Judd, Edwin A. Churchill, and Joel W. Eastman, eds., *Maine: The Pine Tree State from Prehistory to the Present* (Orono: University of Maine Press, 1995).

The Waldorf Statement appears as "Johnston Gives Industry Policy on Commie Jobs" in *DV,* November 26, 1947, along with "Drum Cited 10 Out of Pix." Sources (1947) on the emergency meeting at MGM that November 28 include a telegram from Mayer, Walter Wanger, Joe Schenck, Henry Ginsberg, and Dore Schary to Stevens, November 26; n.a., SDG document, December 1; Wyler's account of the meeting in "Proceedings," SDG board meeting, December 1; and "Guild Execs, Film Toppers Meet Today On Ousted 10," *DV,* November 28. Information on the December 2, 1947, SDG general membership meeting is from the "Proceedings" of the meeting and from Stevens to Capra, December 9, 1947 (including the text of the resolution adopted at the meeting requiring a non-Communist oath from SDG officers); the oath is quoted in *DV,* December 4, 1947, along with "Directors Fite [*sic*] Commies; Bar Them as Officers"; the members' oath is printed in an SDG advertisement in *DV,* October 13, 1950. JF's departure to work on *The Family* is reported in "Scribes Set Sail to Script *The Family*"; his attempt to revive the project is mentioned in an *LAHE* item, February 13, 1950. Mayer's concern about protests and other actions being taken by the American Legion and other anti-Communist groups is reported in the SDG document "Notes on Meeting Held at M.G.M. Wednesday, December 3, 1947, Attended by Producers' Committee and the Three Guilds."

The resolution presented by Audie Murphy to a meeting of the Motion Picture Chapter #1898, Military Order of the Purple Heart, is at Lilly (a note on the document lists the date as 1947); information on Murphy's war record and his recanting of his anti-HUAC stand is from

Don Graham, *No Name on the Bullet: A Biography of Audie Murphy* (New York: Viking, 1989). Sources on the February 22, 1948, Purple Heart dinner, and the ABC Radio network's nationwide broadcast on that date of a condensed recording of the event include: JF, Untitled Purple Heart Speech (Lilly); and 1948 correspondence: Lee Van Atta to JF, February 5; Capra to JF, February 23; JF to Capra, n.d.; and General Douglas MacArthur to JF, February [22?]. JF's FBI file, released through the Freedom of Information Act, is quoted in Eyman, *Print the Legend*. Wills characterizes JF in *John Wayne's America* as "a typical Democratic cold warrior." JF's description of Communism as a spiritual cancer is from the text of his speech to the American Cancer Society tribute to WJD, April 12, 1950 (Lilly).

Additional information on the October 22, 1950, SDG special membership meeting and the issues involved is from Geist (including quotes from the meeting transcript) and 1950 SDG documents: minutes, special board meeting, August 18; condensed minutes, board meeting, September 5; minutes, board meeting, October 9; recall petition, October 11; Mankiewicz to SDG members, October 26, published in *DV* as "Mankiewicz Asks Unity on SDG Oath," October 27; and Mankiewicz to SDG members, October 27. JF's flattering October 23, 1950, letter to Cecil B. DeMille is in DeMille's papers at Brigham Young University, Provo, Utah, as is the transcript of "Remarks by John Ford" to DeMille, October 24; DeMille's October 23 response to JF's letter is at Lilly. Information on DeMille, the Motion Picture Industry Council, and the DeMille Foundation for Americanism is from JM, *Frank Capra;* Geist; and Ceplair and Englund. Other sources include the author's interviews with Rouben Mamoulian and Edward L. Bernds; JM, *Frank Capra;* Parrish, *Growing Up in Hollywood;* PB; Huston, *An Open Book;* George Stevens Jr.'s 1984 documentary film *George Stevens: A Filmmaker's Journey;* Elia Kazan, *A Life* (New York: Knopf, 1988); and Fred Zinnemann, *An Autobiography: A Life in the Movies* (New York: Scribners, 1992) (including reproductions of the October 13, 1950, recall committee telegram to SDG members and the recall ballot). Information on the MPA-inspired mandatory industry-wide loyalty oath is from Ceplair and Englund; and *DV* articles (1950): "Spark All-Ind. Loyalty Oath," October 3; "MPIC Details Its Proposed 3-Part Loyalty Oath," October 11; "Proposed MPIC Loyalty Oath Is Referred to 10-Member Committee," October 19; and "MPA Walks Out of MPIC Talks; Renewing Drive on 'H'wood Reds,'" December 4.

Coverage of the Mankiewicz recall attempt in *DV* also includes (1950): "SDG Non-Red Oath Disclaimed," August 25; "SDG Schism on 'Blacklist,'" October 11; SDG announcement of balloting on non-Communist oath bylaw (advertisement), October 13; "Mankiewicz Recall to Fail" and "Text of Recall Telegram," October 16; Mankiewicz open letter (advertisement), October 16; "Important Notice to All Members of the Screen Directors Guild" (petition for open meeting; advertisement), October 16; "SDG Members to Meet Sunday on Mankiewicz Issue; Ct. Halts Recall," October 17; "'Recall the Recall' Move Reported in SDG Board Rapprochement," October 20; "May Ask SDG Board to Resign," October 23; "Mankiewicz Wins; SDG Bd. Out," October 24; and "Choose Temporary SDG Board and Officers," October 30; see also "Screen Directors Guild Split on 'Loyalty Oath,'" *Daily Worker,* October 18, 1950; David Robb, "Directors Guild Born out of Fear 50 Years Ago," *DV,* October 29, 1985; and Michael Cieply, "The Night They Dumped DeMille," *LAT,* June 4, 1987. The ratification by the SDG membership of the non-Communist oath is from "1951 Revised By Laws [*sic*] of SDG of A (Inc.)," May 27, 1951. The rejection by other industry guilds of a mandatory loyalty oath is reported in "MPA Walks Out of MPIC Talks; Renewing Drive on 'H'wood Reds,'" *DV,* December 4, 1950. JF's reelection to the SDG board is reported in "Geo. Sidney New Prez of Screen Directors Guild," *DV,* May 29, 1951. The voiding of the DGA loyalty oath is reported by *DV* in 1966 articles including "Court Orders DGA Admit 5 Who Nixed the Loyalty Oath," July 15; "Court Upholds Its Nix on DGA Loyalty Oath," August 24; and "U.S. Supreme Bench Upholds Upheaval of DGA Loyalty Oath," December 6.

Information on JF, Capra, and the Army–Navy–Air Force Personnel Security Board (ANAFPSB) is from JM, *Frank Capra;* the author's interviews with Chester Sticht (Capra's secretary) and Dunne; and Capra, Security Board File, submitted to ANAFPSB, December 29, 1951. Capra wrote JF requesting help on December 19, 1951, enclosing a copy of Victor W. Phelps, ANAFPSB, to Capra, December 14, 1951, on the denial of Capra's security clearance (quoted). JF's telegram in response to Capra [December 1951] is from Lilly and is quoted in JM, *Frank Capra*. JF's December 24, 1951, letter defending Capra to the ANAFPSB was released to the author in 1992 by the Department of Defense through the Freedom of Information Act; an earlier draft of the letter from Lilly is quoted in JM, *Frank Capra*. Capra thanked JF in a letter of January 14, 1952. The 1951 HUAC testimony of Sidney Buchman is from the committee's hearings on *Communist Infiltration of Hollywood Motion-Picture Industry*. Buchman was named by Capra to the ANAFPSB in his Security Board File. The report of an FBI informant that Capra had been among "certain prominent persons in the motion picture industry in Hollywood [who] had been interested in plotting a line of attack" on HUAC in October 1947 is from Capra's FBI file, first quoted in the 1993 Touchstone paperback edition of JM, *Frank Capra*. Capra's comment about the Hollywood Ten ("Let the bastards rot in jail"), reported in July 1951 by a confidential State Department informant, is from a section of the January 16, 1952, FBI report on "FRANK RUSSELL CAPRA, aka Francesco Capra" released to the author through the Freedom of Information Act in 1994 and quoted in JM, *Frank Capra*, St. Martin's Press paperback edition, 2000. Information on the strike at the *Hollywood Citizen-News* is from the author's interview with Dunne, parts quoted in JM, *Frank Capra*; Schwartz; SDG minutes, May 23 and June 6, 1938; "Film Directors Give Aid," *Hollywood Citizen-News Striker*, June 1, 1938; and "Summary of Information" (on a HUAC citation about Capra's involvement in the strike), G-2, October 10, 1951, in Capra's Army Intelligence file. JF's 1953 telegram to Michael Killanin describing Huston as a "Red" is quoted in McNee. Sources on Anna Lee's blacklisting include the author's interview with Lee; Lee to JF, June 11, 1956; her OH; and Gallagher.

For information on JF's founding membership in the MPA, see the notes for chapter 10. JF's MPA membership cards in his collection at Lilly are those for 1957–June 1958 (associate membership card A1242) and June 1959–May 1960 (associate membership card A1013). JF's payment of dues to the MPA is recorded in his IRS returns for 1944, 1947, 1954, and 1955. JF is listed as a member of the MPA's advisory committee in a July 24, 1961, letter to the MPA membership from its executive director, A. J. MacDonald (Lilly). Information on JF's membership on the MPA's executive committee is from "Motion Picture Alliance Sets Election Meet," March 7, 1949 (on his nomination); MPA stationery in JF's files (also including Herbert J. Yates as a committee member: see a 1950 mimeographed letter at Lilly from Roy M. Brewer, chairman of MPA executive committee, "IMPORTANT NOTICE! TO ALL MEMBERS OF THE M.P.A. EXECUTIVE COMMITTEE"); "Motion Picture Alliance Names Brewer President," *HCN*, June 1, 1953; "Elect Brewer, Leo McCarey Motion Picture Alliance Heads," *HR*, 1953 (AMPAS); and "M.P. Alliance Reelects Brewer," *HR*, May 7, 1954. JW's OH describes JF as a moderating influence within the MPA.

John Lee Mahin's comments on blacklisting are from an interview by the author and Todd McCarthy, parts printed as "Bombshell Days in the Golden Age: John Lee Mahin Interviewed," *Film Comment*, March–April 1980, and reprinted as "John Lee Mahin: Team Player" in Pat McGilligan, ed., *Backstory: Interviews with Screenwriters of Hollywood's Golden Age* (Berkeley: University of California Press, 1986). The MPA's 1947 statement "FIRST . . . WE ORGANIZED" is quoted in R&O. Schwartz reports the MPA's support for Thomas E. Dewey's 1948 presidential campaign. Ceplair and Englund discuss the MPA's campaign for blacklisting and its providing of information about alleged Communists to HUAC; see also "McGuinness Challenges Hollywood Witnesses Protesting Film Probe," *LAE*, October 17, 1947. The MPA's proposed resolution (1950) for the Los Angeles City Council to adopt measures compelling Communists to register is from Brewer, "IMPORTANT NOTICE! TO ALL MEMBERS OF THE M.P.A. EXECUTIVE COMMITTEE"; see also "M.P. Alliance Demands City Register All Communists," *DV*, July 20, 1950. The comments by Hopper and Victor Reisel at the March 1951 MPA meeting are from

"UCLA Student Honored as Film Group Rips Reds," *LAT,* March 23, 1951; see also the reference to Reisel's speech in R&O. The MPA's advocacy of using "D.D.T." on Hollywood is from "Demands Films Be 'Deloused' of Reds," *Los Angeles Evening Herald and Express,* May 15, 1950; and MPA, "Yes: Communism Again" (advertisement), May [15?], 1950, Hollywood trade press (AMPAS).

Dunne's comment that JF was found "guilty by association" with JW and Bond is from *Take Two.* Wills's observation about JW's role as MPA president being to "shoot the wounded" is from *John Wayne's America.* JW's denial that there was a Hollywood blacklist even though he conceded that people were run out of the industry for political reasons is from Lewis, *"Playboy Interview with John Wayne."* JW attacking *All the King's Men* and *High Noon* is from Davis, *Duke.* Coverage of JW's election as MPA president in 1949 includes: "Motion Picture Alliance Sets Election Meet," *HCN,* March 7; "Film Group to Install Wayne as President," *LAT,* March 24; and "N.Y. Trial to Bare Red Spy Facts, Stripling Says," *HCN,* March 30; JW's reelection is reported in "Anti-Red Film Group Elects Wayne to 2nd Term as Chief," *LAE,* March 20, 1950. John Milius's characterization of JW is from his interview with the author, published as "Milius Says *Apocalypse Now* Is a 'Descent into Hell,'" *DV,* September 2, 1975. Sources on JW's career thriving despite his blacklisting activities include Davis, *Duke;* R&O; and Wills.

Nunnally Johnson's comment that Bond and his ilk made him "ashamed of the whole industry" is from Stempel, *Screenwriter: The Life and Times of Nunnally Johnson.* JF's statement to Bond that Senator Joseph McCarthy was a "disgrace" is quoted in R&O from Elizabeth Allen's OH (Lilly). JF's description of Bond as "a great, big, ugly, wonderful guy" is from Haggard, "Ford in Person." HCJ discusses JF's view of Bond in Gallagher. JF's recollection of playing tricks on Bond with JF is from Haggard, "Ford in Person." Anna Lee discussed the "strange friendship" of JF and Bond in her interview with the author. The description of Father Stuart as "one of the fightingest Irish priests" is from "Fighting Priest of War in Burma Here for Visit," *LAT,* May 29, 1947.

Information on the Army Signal Corps viewing as security risks JF and a former naval officer who served in his OSS Field Photo Branch is from Lieutenant Colonel Wingate Smith to Major General Kirke B. Lawton, August 2, 1950; and Lawton to Smith [1950]; the former naval officer's association with the Field Photo Farm in 1950 is indicated in the Lilly files on the Farm. The report that a loyalty oath would be required from anyone involved in making government films on the "current global crisis" appears in *DV,* August 28, 1950, as "Reds Ruled Off Gov't Films." In his Annual Qualifications Questionnaire, Bureau of Naval Personnel, July 18, 1949, JF describes himself as "more than anxious to return to active duty in case of an emergency."

Sources on *Pinky* include the author's interview with Dunne; Michel Ciment, trans. by Susan Frazer, "An Introduction," in Jeanine Basinger, John Frazer, and Joseph W. Reed Jr., eds., *Working with Kazan* (Middletown, Ct.: Wesleyan Film program, 1973); Ciment, *Kazan on Kazan,* British Film Institute Cinema One series (New York: Viking, 1974); Gussow; Kazan, *A Life;* Dunne, *Take Two;* Jeff Young, *Kazan: The Master Director Discusses His Films: Interviews with Elia Kazan* (New York: Newmarket Press, 1999); DFZ letters to JF (1949): February 1, March 15, and March 16; and DFZ to Kazan, July 1, 1952, in Behlmer, ed., *Memo from Darryl F. Zanuck.* The report of the studios dropping plans for "message" pictures is from *Variety,* August 11, 1948, quoted in Ceplair and Englund. The screenplay of *Pinky* by Dunne and Nichols is dated March 5, 1949; DFZ to JF, February 1, 1949; Katherine Cliffton's synopsis for JF of the source novel by Cid Ricketts Sumner, *Quality,* is dated April 15, 1948. JF's contract for the film with Twentieth Century–Fox, dated January 24, 1949, was signed by JF on February 17, 1949. JF's (re)assignment to *Pinky* is reported in Parsons column, *LAE,* January 20, 1949. DFZ recalls to Gussow his "professional difference of opinion" with JF on *Pinky.* Kazan's discussion with JF about directing is from Kazan, *A Life.* JF's OH recalls Kazan watching *Stagecoach;* Ciment reports Kazan watching *Young Mr. Lincoln.*

The play *What Price Glory?* (1924) by Maxwell Anderson and Laurence Stallings appears in their book *Three American Plays* (New York: Harcourt Brace, 1926). Documents at Lilly on JF's 1949 stage production *What Price Glory* (whose title, like that of his 1952 film version, omitted the question mark) include a telegram from Stallings to Howard Reinheimer, January 3; play script with cast list; "Itinerary"; George O'Brien To Whom It May Concern, March 3; and programs (Masquers Club, Hollywood, n.d.; Grauman's Chinese Theater, Hollywood, March 11). JF's unwillingness to risk his reputation as a stage director was expressed to James Warner Bellah in a telephone conversation discussed in Bellah's letter to JF, December 8, 1948; JF's claim in his OH to have directed the stage production is cited in Davis. Press coverage includes (1949): Edwin Schallert, "Ford Sets Gala Cast for *What Price Glory* . . . ," *LAT*, January 13; "Stage Show to Aid Wounded," *LAE*, January 13; item in *LAE*, February 23; Schallert, "Filmland $1,000,000 Stars Do GI Benefit," *LAT*, February 27; and "War Play Ends Tour," *LAT*, March 2; see also Karyn Kay and Gerald Peary, "Talking to Pat O'Brien," *The Velvet Light Trap*, Fall 1975; and Michael F. Blake, "He Was Their Stage Coach," *LAT*, May 28, 1999. Sources on JF's film *What Price Glory* include Thomas M. Pryor, "Hollywood Scenes," *NYT*, September 1, 1951; production report, 1952 (Lilly); Sinclair; and Doug Warren, with James Cagney, *James Cagney: The Authorized Biography* (New York: St. Martin's Press, 1983).

The shooting dates, crew names, and negative cost of *Wagon Master* are from the Daily Production Reports, November–December 1949. Sinclair reports that JF began mulling the story while making *Yellow Ribbon*. JF's remark "I liked your script, boys" is quoted in Nugent, "In Remembrance of Hot-Foots Past," *NYT*, May 4, 1950. Anderson's description of *Wagon Master* as an "avant-garde Western" is quoted in M&W; his other comments are from his review in *Sequence*, New Year 1951. Other *Wagon Master* reviews (1950) include Scheuer; *HR*, April 5; and *HCN*, May 10; box-office results are from Gallagher. JF's high regard for *Wagon Master* is expressed in PB and was discussed in the author's interview with Cliffton.

Schatz comments on Howard Hughes's "anti-Communist fervor" in *The Genius of the System*. Cooper's July 1949 letter to Louis B. Mayer suggesting a production arrangement between Argosy and MGM is quoted in Eyman, *Print the Legend*. Information on the Argosy Pictures Corp.–Republic Productions Inc. agreement includes: "Digest of Republic Agreement," December 16, 1949; contract between Argosy and Republic, signed January 4, 1950, by JF and Yates (quoted); agreement between Argosy and JF, signed January 4, 1950; and 1950 press coverage: "Republic Gets Ford, Cooper," *LAE*, January 6; "Ford, Cooper Move over to Republic," *HR*, January 6; Hopper, "Argosy Film Unit Moves to Republic," *LAT*, January 6 (with Yates quote); and "Argosy Closing Out Its Offices," *DV*, March 3. JF's OH claims Argosy left RKO because Republic offered a better deal, but Van Hoozer to Cooper, December 17, 1954, indicates JF and Cooper had serious reservations about entering into the deal; the discussions between Yates and JW about JF coming to Republic are reported in JW's OH; R&O; and Zolotow; JF told the author he considered Yates "stupid." JF describes his stroll around the Republic lot in a letter to Richard Brooks, January 1950; JF's pep talk to Allan Dwan is from Dwan's OH, quoted in Gallagher.

JF comments on *Mighty Joe Young* in his OH and PB. The working title *Mr. Joseph Young of Africa* is from the production Staff List, October 29, 1947. Ben Johnson recalls the *Fort Apache* incident in an interview with Lucy Gray, n.d., unidentified source (AMPAS); other sources on the incident include the author's interview with Cliffton and a *DV* item on Johnson's contract, December 2, 1947; JF's praise of Johnson is from an Argosy press release on the actor, 1949 (AMPAS). The Johnson-JF argument is reported by HCJ in *Company of Heroes*, which also says JF offered Johnson a role in *The Sun Shines Bright*. JF's comment to Johnson urging him to appear in *The Last Picture Show* is quoted by Bogdanovich in Bill Krohn, "Le Renoir américain: Entretien avec Peter Bogdanovich," in Patrice Rollet and Nicolas Saada, eds., *John Ford* (Paris: Editions de l'Etoile/*Cahiers du Cinéma*, 1990). In a letter to JF on October 5, 1970, Bogdanovich thanks him for persuading Johnson. Johnson's Oscar acceptance speech is from Wiley and Bona.

The signed agreement between Argosy and Republic for *Rio Grande* (working title: *Rio Bravo*) is dated March 20, 1950. JF's comment about "much wrangling" on the film's budget is from his telegram to JW, June 1, 1950, quoted in McNee and R&O (both books mistakenly state that the telegram concerns the budget of *The Quiet Man*). Bellah's "Mission with No Record," originally published in the *Saturday Evening Post* (1947), is reprinted in *Reveille*. The 1873 Mackenzie raid into Mexico is discussed in Wills. In the *Rio Bravo* screenplay by James Kevin McGuinness, May 5, 1950, with revisions to June 6, JW's character is named "Yorke," but the name is spelled "York" in the Daily Production Report (final), July 21, 1950, which also lists the shooting schedule and number of production days. Breen comments on the script in a letter to Republic's Allen Wilson, May 12, 1950. Information on McGuinness being forced out of his job at MGM and on his death include JW's OH and the *DV* obituary of McGuinness, December 5, 1950; JF's attendance at McGuinness's funeral is mentioned in Stallings to JF, December 11, 1950.

Republic's financial statement on *Rio Grande,* September 25, 1953, provides information on the shooting (including the negative cost), and additional information is contained in *The Making of* Rio Grande, a documentary written and hosted by Leonard Maltin, Republic Pictures, 1993 (included on the Republic videotape of *Rio Grande*). The title changes are discussed in JF's OH; Yates to JF, May 3, 1950; Yates's telegram to JF [October 1950]; and an August 25, 1950, *DV* item on the semifinal title change to *Rio Grande Command*. JF's description of *The Quiet Man* as his "first love story" is from Anderson, "The Quiet Man"; Anderson's comment about JF warily approaching "this ticklish subject" in *Rio Grande* is quoted in M&W. JW's description of O'Hara as "the greatest guy" is from Davis, *Duke*. Richard Slotkin discusses *Rio Grande* and the "Cold War Western" in *Gunfighter Nation: The Myth of the Frontier in Twentieth-Century America* (New York: Atheneum, 1992).

At a Los Angeles County Museum of Art screening of *When Willie Comes Marching Home,* Sy Gomberg, author of the original story ("When Leo Comes Marching Home"), said it was based on his own wartime adventures. JF calls himself "essentially a comedy director" in Mitchell; his statement that there "wasn't anything funny" about World War II is from PB. The wartime experiences of Peter Ortiz and Alberto Morin are mentioned in a press release for *Willie,* then titled *Front and Center,* Twentieth Century–Fox, 1949. Corinne Calvet discusses JF's rudeness on *Willie* and on his film *What Price Glory* in *Has Corinne Been a Good Girl?* (New York: St. Martin's Press, 1983). Henry Ephron's charge that JF was biased against Jews, and the stories about Daniel Fuchs and Sol Siegel, are from Ephron's autobiography, *We Thought We Could Do Anything: The Life of Screenwriters Phoebe and Henry Ephron* (New York: Norton, 1977). Archer Winsten's *New York Post* review of *What Price Glory* is quoted in McGilligan, *Cagney: The Actor as Auteur* (New York: Da Capo, 1979). Robert Wagner discusses his mistreatment by JF in Davis, which also quotes JF's complaint about the songs written for the film. Cagney's description of JF as "truly a nasty old man" is from Warren and Cagney.

Information on the Korean War is from John Toland, *In Mortal Combat: Korea, 1950–1953* (New York: William Morrow, 1991); and Burke Davis, *Marine!: The Life of Lt. Gen. Lewis B. (Chesty) Puller, USMC (Ret.)* (Boston: Little, Brown, 1962); JF comments on the war in PB. Sarris's observations on JF's filming of war are from *The American Cinema*. Other information on Puller is from the author's interview with JF; JF's documentary *Chesty: A Tribute to a Legend* (1968–70, released in 1976; long and short versions); *Chesty Puller: The Marine's Marine* (*A&E Biography* series, 1998); and "Gen. Chesty Puller Dies; Most Decorated Marine," *NYT,* October 13, 1971.

Production dates of *This Is Korea!* are from DF and Vice Admiral C. T. Joy, USNR, commander, Naval Forces, Far East, citation awarding the Air Medal to JF [1951]; see also JF's orders for active duty, December 22, 1950; orders to depart for Pearl Harbor, December 26, 1950; and separation procedure, Long Beach, March 7, 1951; JF's Air Medal citation from Secretary of the Navy Francis P. Matthews, March 9, 1951; and J. P. McGowan, "Directors and Assistants in the Reserve Force," SDG press release, 1951. JF's time on the USS *Philippine Sea* is reported in Sinclair and DF; his letter to Killanin about climbing mountains in Korea is quoted in Davis. JF's accompaniment to Korea by Mark Armistead, Charley Bohuy, and Bob Rhea is reported in MF to Benjamin, January 15, 1951; Armistead's OH; Sinclair; and DF. Sinclair claims the missions for which JF received his Air Medal actually were performed by Armistead; JF's statement that he and Puller "fought together" is from *Chesty: A Tribute to a Legend;* Davis, *Marine!* states that Puller "flew with pilots in a tiny observation plane" during the period when JF was with him in Korea. Bellah's Air Medal is discussed in JF to Lieutenant General A. C. Wedemeyer, May 25, 1951; and Wedemeyer to JF, May 29 and July 23, 1951. JF's visit to Tokyo on January 8, 1951, to film MacArthur and JF's drinking on his Tokyo layover are reported in DF. Joanne Dru's OH reports that JF replaced his autographed picture of President Truman with one of MacArthur after the general was fired. MacArthur's fondness for *She Wore a Yellow Ribbon* is reported by JF in his OH and his interview with Bill Libby. Other information on MacArthur is from William Manchester, *American Caesar: Douglas MacArthur, 1880–1964* (Boston: Little, Brown, 1978); and David McCullough, *Truman* (New York: Simon and Schuster, 1992).

JF describes *This Is Korea!* as "simply a narrative" in his March 21, 1951, telegram to Rear Admiral R. F. Hickey, chief of information, USN. Lilly has separate narration scripts for the film by Bellah and Nugent. *This Is Korea!* reviews (1951) include A. H. Weiler, "Combat in the East," *NYT,* August 19; and Tom Canning, *Motion Picture Herald,* September 1. Republic's reluctance to distribute the documentary and the reactions of exhibitors and the public are reported in (1951): Yates to JF, May 12; JF's telegram to Yates, n.d.; J. R. Grainger (of Republic's New York office) to Yates, November 14; JF to Herman Rosen, November 26 (thanking him for playing the film); and Republic's list of exhibition contracts sold through September 22 (Lilly).

Documentation on JF's promotion to rear admiral and his retirement from active USN service (1951) includes: the chief of Naval Personnel to JF, February 15; JF to chief of Naval Personnel, asking for transfer to retired status, March 29; chief of Naval Personnel to secretary of the Navy, approving transfer to retired list, April 27; Secretary of the Navy Matthews to JF, May 5, citing action by President Truman on May 1 promoting JF to rear admiral on the date of his official retirement; Lieutenant DuBose, office of chief of Naval Personnel, to JF, May 5, notifying him of his transfer to the Honorary Retired List of USNR and advancement to rear admiral; and L. J., office of chief of Naval Personnel, to JF, May 5.

For sources on JF's 1936 purchase of film rights to Maurice Walsh's story "The Quiet Man," see the notes for chapter 7; JF and Republic made agreements selling and assigning story rights on May 25, 1951. Maureen O'Hara's comments on her handshake deal with JF in 1944 to make *The Quiet Man* and their frustrations in obtaining backing are quoted in McNee from an appearance she made in Ireland on RTE's *The Late, Late Show.* The comments on O'Hara's relationship with JF by Olive Carey and Cliffton are from their interviews with the author. The involvement of Richard Llewellyn, Nugent, and Stallings in the writing of *The Quiet Man* is reported in JW's OH; Llewellyn to JF, January 21, 1951; Parsons column, *LAE,* November 18, 1950; and Nugent, "Pubs, Pictures and 'Nice Soft Days' in Eire," *NYT,* August 5, 1951. The setting of earlier versions of the *Quiet Man* script during the War of Independence is indicated in documents at Lilly: "Undated Early Script Notes *The Quiet Man* (1949)"; notes on "Troubles" and "Terror" (n.d.); notes, n.d.; and notes (1951).

Sources on JF's trip to Ireland with Yates and Ward Bond include JF's account in Anderson (quoted); JF's OH; and the November 18, 1950, Parsons column. JF's position that he needed $1.75 million to make *The Quiet Man* is discussed in Grainger to JF, October 1950; the final budget is specified in Republic's agreement with Argosy, June 1, 1951; see also Van Hoozer to Doering, July 23, 1952. O'Hara's comment about JF asking her and JW to cut their salaries is from McNee. The negative cost is reported in Republic's statement on the film's income and costs, August 22, 1953. Yates's denigration of *The Quiet Man* as a "phony art-house movie" and warning to JW against making it are reported in DF; JW calls *The Quiet Man* "a goddam hard script" in Joe McInerney, "John Wayne Talks Tough," *Film Comment,* September 1972. Cliffton's suggestion of Robert Ryan for Sean Thornton, JF's responses, and her ghostwriting of JF's foreword to Capra's *The Name Above the Title* are from the author's interview with Cliffton. Anthony Burgess's observation on art and exile is from his book *Re Joyce* (New York: Norton, 1968, originally published as *Here Comes Everybody: An Introduction to James Joyce for the Ordinary Reader,* London: Faber and Faber, 1965).

Information on the location shooting of *The Quiet Man* in Ireland is from the author's visit to Cong, Ireland, and vicinity; the author's interview with Hoch; JM, "Winton Hoch: 'A Damn Good Job'"; McNee; Brian Barrett, "Innisfree [sic], Hollywood, Co. Mayo," the *Irish Independent,* July 14, 1951; and Nugent, "Pubs, Pictures and 'Nice Soft Days' in Eire." McNee quotes the June 23, 1951, report in the *Connacht Tribune* that JF "was deeply moved" when visiting his family's home in Spiddal and the paper's comment on "Director Ford's association with the people of Spiddal" in "Hollywood Takes Over Village of Cong," 1951. Additional production information is from *The Making of* The Quiet Man, a documentary written and hosted by Leonard Maltin, Republic Pictures, 1992 (included on Republic's fortieth anniversary videotape release of *The Quiet Man*).

Yates's complaint "Everything's all green" is from Davis; Bond's graffito about Yates is reported in McNee and Davis, *Duke.* Barbara Ford's work as assistant editor is mentioned in her letter to JF, June 20, 1951; MF's suggestion that Pat Ford be sent to Ireland is from her letter to JF, June 12, 1951; JF's illness on location and his problems with Pat and O'Hara are reported in Wayne's OH and DF; JF also comments on his illness in Anderson, "The Quiet Man." Information on JF's parish priest visiting the location is from Daniel J. Stack, S.J., to JF, June 29, 1951, and the invoice for Stack's trip, Republic to JF, August 13, 1951. Barrett reports that Ernie O'Malley helped direct crowd scenes. JW pushing JF into Galway Bay is from M&W. Killanin's description of *The Quiet Man* as "a Western made in Ireland" is from McNee.

Republic's concerns about the length of *The Quiet Man* are discussed in Yates to JF, October 16, 1951, quoted in McNee, and J. R. Grainger to JF, October 24, 1951; see also an October 1951 list in JF's files of lengths of various pictures (Lilly). The story about JF cutting the film for the private screening is from JF's OH and DF. Republic's title suggestions are discussed in Yates to JF, September 25, 1951; and JF to Grainger, November 21, 1951. FitzSimons reports JF's cutting of the word *national* in McNee; Yates urges the change in his October 16, 1951, letter to JF. Reviews of *The Quiet Man* (1952) include "Carry *Me* Back to Old Virginny," *New Yorker,* August 23; *NYT,* September 7; and Manny Farber's review in the *Nation,* 1952, reprinted in Farber, *Negative Space.* Donald S. Connery comments on *The Quiet Man* and Irish stereotypes in *The Irish* (New York: Simon and Schuster, 1968); Brandon French discusses the film in *On the Verge of Revolt: Women in American Films of the Fifties* (New York: Frederick Ungar, 1978). Information on the film's popularity and its impact on Irish tourism is from McNee; "*Quiet Man* Boosts Irish Tourist Biz," *Variety,* September 2, 1953; Luke Gibbons and Kevin Rockett, "The Green on the Screen," *Irish Times Weekend,* October 10, 1987; David McDonough, "*The Quiet Man* Has Tiptoed into the Parade," *NYT,* March 12, 1995; Alf McCreary, "*The Quiet Man*'s Ireland," *British Heritage,* August–September 1997; and Georgina Wroe, "Going Crazy Over Wayne's World," *Times Weekend* (London), June 13, 1998.

JF's comment "Christ, I hate pictures" and his needling about *They Were Expendable* are from Anderson, "The Quiet Man." Other Anderson articles on JF include "*They Were Expendable* and John Ford," *Sequence,* Summer 1950; "The Director's Cinema?" *Sequence,* Autumn 1950; and "John Ford," *Films in Review,* February 1951, reprinted in *Cinema,* Spring 1971, with introduction by Gavin Lambert. The first book on JF, William Patrick Wooten's *An Index to the Films of John Ford,* was published by the British Film Institute (London) in 1947. Andrew McLaglen's recollection of JF's speech at Ashford Castle is from *The Making of* The Quiet Man. JF discusses retirement and the Irish film industry in "Irish Film Company to Make Picture Next Year," *Connacht Tribune,* September 6, 1952. JF's bittersweet comments on leaving Ireland are from his letter to Lady Killanin, October 2, 1951, quoted in McNee.

Chapter Twelve: "Go searchin' way out there" (pp. 520–599)

The chapter title is from Stan Jones's theme song for *The Searchers*. The epigraph is from JF, "Veteran Producer Muses." JF's comment that "Directing's like dope addiction" is from Hedda Hopper, "Ford Keeps Ahead of Young Producers," *LAT*, May 8, 1962.

JF's disapproval of the "junk" being made in the film industry is from Grady Johnson's December 1953 *Coronet* profile "John Ford: Maker of Hollywood Stars." Sarris describes JF as a "strategist" in *The John Ford Movie Mystery*. JF's assertion that his "most beautiful pictures are not Westerns" is from Gallagher's translation of Bertrand Tavernier, "John Ford à Paris: Notes d'un Attaché de Press," *Positif*, March 1967. JF's fondness for the scene of a prostitute's funeral is from Lyons, "Interview with Winston Miller," in Lyons, ed., *My Darling Clementine*. Nugent's "In Remembrance of Hot-Foots Past" notes JF's love of the Confederacy. JF's comments on economy, preparation, and short stories as film sources are from Gertrude Samuels, "The Director—Hollywood's Leading Man," *NYT Magazine*, October 26, 1952.

The period of *The Sun Shines Bright* is specified in the introduction to the screenplay by Laurence Stallings, July 18, 1952. The writer's service in World War I is reported in John Driscoll, "Laurence Stallings," in Randall Clark, ed., *American Screenwriters: Second Series*, Dictionary of Literary Biography, Vol. 44 (Detroit: Gale Research Co., 1986). The filming dates for *The Sun Shines Bright* are from the shooting schedule (Lilly). JF's description of the film as "really my favorite" and his complaint about Republic's Herbert J. Yates not understanding it are from Kennedy, "A Talk with John Ford"; JF's comment on the studio's recutting is from his interview with the author. Reviews include *Variety*, May 6, 1953; H. H. T. [Howard H. Thompson], *NYT*, March 17, 1954; Lindsay Anderson, *Sight and Sound*, April–June 1954; and C. A. Lejeune, "Labour of Love," *Observer* (U.K.), and Dilys Powell, "Old and True," *Sunday Times* (U.K.), quoted in Anderson to JF, November 9, 1953.

The deferment of Argosy Pictures Corp. profits by JF and Cooper is reported in Cooper to JF [1953?]. Sources on Argosy's audit of Republic include (1953): Otto C. Doering Jr. to Cooper, April 28; Argosy (Cooper) to Republic (Yates), May 19; Argosy secretary H. Lee Van Hoozer to Cooper, September 1; Argosy to Yates, September 15; and JF's telegram to Michael Killanin [c. July 5, 1954], quoted from McNee. Information on Leo McCarey's talks with Argosy is from Barbara Ford's OH; Cooper to JF [1953?]; McCarey to JF [1953?]; Cooper's telegram to JF, February 23, 1953; and Mabel Walker Willebrandt to Cooper, JF, and Van Hoozer, December 2, 1953. A possible Argosy deal with Warner Bros. is discussed in Cooper to JF [1953]; Cooper to JF, January 5, 1955, discusses the possibility of dissolving Argosy and obtaining money from Republic.

Cinerama and CinemaScope are discussed in John Belton, *Widescreen Cinema* (Cambridge, Mass.: Harvard University Press, 1992); Gomery, *Movie History: A Survey*; and Behlmer, "Merian C. Cooper is the Kind of Creative Showman Today's Movies Badly Need." DFZ attempts to sell JF on CinemaScope in his letter of February 16, 1954. Cooper's involvement with Cinerama Prods. Corp. is reported in Belton; "Merian Cooper to Helm Production for Cinerama," *DV*, August 14, 1952; and Cholly Knickerbocker column, "Whitney Quits Cinerama After Row with Mayer," *LAE*, May 8, 1953. Sources on Argosy's investment in Cinerama include Cooper's February 23, 1953, telegram to JF; Argosy statement, December 18, 1954; and T. Edelschain, chief of IRS corporation tax branch to Doering, January 6, 1956, which also includes other financial and incorporation data on Argosy. Cooper's interest in JF directing a Cinerama film is from Belton; Cooper to JF [1953]; and Cooper to JF [1953?]. JF's retention of shares in Cinerama until 1961 is indicated in his California income tax return for that year. The citation for Cooper's special 1952 Oscar is from Wiley and Bona. Gallagher reports that JF directed two shots in *Hondo*; John Wayne's outburst about JF's contribution is from his interview with the author.

The amount and date of Republic's settlement with Argosy and the amounts paid to JF and Cooper are from *Otto C. Doering, Jr. and Lucy F. Doering vs. Commissioner of Internal Revenue, Tax Court of the United States*, filed January 4, 1963; and a breakdown of percentages of Argosy stock held by the Fords and the Coopers in Van Hoozer, list of stockholders of record, January 6, 1956; the erroneous figures for the amounts paid to JF and Cooper are reported in DF. Information on Argosy's dissolution is from Bea Benjamin to JF, January 3 and January 4, 1956; and Van Hoozer, list of stockholders of record. A. J. "Jack" Bolton's service as JF's agent is indicated in correspondence at Lilly. The incorporation of John Ford Productions (JFP) on August 9, 1956, and other details about the company are from minutes of the first meeting of JFP's board of directors, October 12, 1956; JFP's application to Division of Corporations, Department of Investment, State of California [1956]; and JF's U.S. corporate tax return, 1956. Information on JFP's rental of offices at Batjac is from Killanin's telegram to JF at Batjac, January 3, 1956; and Benjamin to JF on that date. Warner Bros.' offer of a long-term deal with JFP is discussed in 1956 correspondence: Benjamin to JF, June 14, and P. D. Knecht of Warners to Benjamin, October 3.

JF's travel to Africa to film *Mogambo* is detailed in "Itinerary for John Ford, Mrs. John Ford, and Mrs. Jane Ford," October 1952 (Lilly). Information on the African location shooting is from the author's interview with Mahin; DF; Ava Gardner, *Ava: My Story* (New York: Bantam Books, 1990); June Ellen Wayne, *Grace Kelly's Men* (New York: St. Martin's Press, 1991); Robert Lacey, *Grace* (New York: G. P. Putnam's Sons, 1994); Barbara Berch Jamison, "You Can't See the Jungle for the Stars," *NYT,* October 19, 1952; Morgan Hudgins, "Bivouac on the Trail of *Mogambo* in Africa," *NYT,* January 4, 1953; and Vic Heutschy and Ron Ross, "Filming a Motion Picture in Africa," *International Photographer,* July 1953. An MGM press release, November 17, 1952, mentions the cast and crew carrying guns. Producer Sam Zimbalist's concern over JF cutting the script is documented in telegrams to JF, December 24 and 31, 1952, and January 6, 13, and 14, 1953. The fatal accident and other injuries during production are reported in "Clark Gable's Film Aide Dies in Africa Crash," *LAT,* January 19, 1953; John Hancock's obituary, *Variety,* January 21, 1953; Philip K. Scheuer, "Witch Doctors' Help Costs MGM $14.25," *LAT,* March 1, 1953 ("A dozen more"); and Charles Higham, *Ava: A Life Story* (New York: Delacorte, 1974) (quoting Robert Surtees).

JF's reaction to Kelly's screen test is reported in Dore Schary, *Heyday: An Autobiography* (Boston: Little, Brown, 1979); and Lacey. Gardner's comments on her relationship with JF and their discussion about her decision to abort Frank Sinatra's child are from *Ava: My Story*; the remarks she and JF made to the British couple and Gardner's comments about the company's Christmas celebration are from Higham, as is JF's description of Gardner as "a real trouper." The story about JF's "dirty trick" on Clark Gable is from the author's interview with Mahin.

The quotation "When sorrows come" is from William Shakespeare's *Hamlet.* Information on JF's return to the United States is from the *Andrea Doria*'s list of passengers departing from Naples (1953); and MF to Benjamin, March 16, 1953. Sources on JF's eye problems include the author's interviews with Olive Carey and Admiral John D. Bulkeley; DF; and 1953 correspondence: JF to Killanin, n.d., quoted in Davis (confiding his fear of blindness); Brian Desmond Hurst to Killanin, April 21; Killanin to JF, September 20; and Meta C. Sterne to John O'Brien, October 21. The soundman's comment on JF's hearing and seeing was reported to the author by Cliffton. JF's remark "They all think I'm a so-and-so" is from Johnson's profile. Sources on Francis Ford's throat operation include Sterne's telegram to Dr. Ian Macdonald, May 4, 1953; and FF to JF, June 15, 1953; sources on FF's death and funeral (1953) include DF; Gallagher ("We gave him"); Wingate Smith's OH; cards from floral offerings, Field Photo Memorial Farm, September; "Francis Ford Rosary Slated," *LAE,* September 7; Sterne to Killanin, September 15, and JF to Killanin, September ("Frank had an easy passing"), both quoted in McNee.

The sale price of the Fords' Odin Street home and the purchase price of their Copa de Oro home are from JF's IRS return, 1954; MF talks about leaving Odin Street in Slide and Banker; JF's bender on the *Araner* after selling that house is reported in Sinclair; and the Copa de Oro home was described to the author by Waverly Ramsey and Cliffton. Davis reports on the gloves and war bonnet owned by JF; JF talks about Wyatt Earp's rifle in *The American West of John Ford*. Waverly Ramsey's comments on the Fords are from her interview with the author; Cliffton spoke to the author about JF's friendship with Bill Ramsey, whose errand to AMPAS was reported to the author by Bulkeley. JW's practical joke is described in Wayne and Thorleifson. The damage to the *Araner* is assessed in E. R. Cull, "Report of Accident" (1953), for Fireman's Fund Insurance Co. (Lilly). JF's consideration of selling the *Araner* is discussed in MF to Benjamin [June 16?, 1955], and Benjamin to MF, June 20, 1955. Liquidating the Field Photo Farm is discussed in Benjamin to Doering, March 20, 1956.

Ken Curtis's meeting with Barbara Ford is described in Curtis's OH. Biographical information on Curtis is from his publicity biographies, 1940s–70s (AMPAS); "This Man Kissed a Girl! On *Gunsmoke* That's News," *TV Guide*, June 27, 1964; and obituaries (1991): *DV*, April 30; "Ken Curtis, Festus on *Gunsmoke*, Dies," *HR*, April 30; Burt A. Folkart, "Ken Curtis; Played 'Festus' on *Gunsmoke*," *LAT*, April 30; and "Ken Curtis, Actor, 74, Festus on *Gunsmoke*," *NYT*, May 1. *LAE* reports Barbara's marriage to Curtis in "Barbara Ford Weds Curtis," June 1, 1952, and "Wedding Bells," June 2. Hedda Hopper reports Barbara's pregnancy and previous adoption plans in "John Ford Will Be Grandfather," *LAT*, January 21, 1958. Sources on Curtis's relationship with JF include the Curtis and HCJ OHs. Barbara's breakup with Curtis is reported in JF to Pat Ford [April? 1963], and Army Archerd's column, *DV*, July 23, 1964.

President Dwight D. Eisenhower's approval of his portrayal in *The Long Gray Line* by actors (Harry Carey Jr. and Elbert Steele) was reported in "Ike Okays Portrayal of Self as West Point Cadet in Col's *Line*," *DV*, October 16, 1953, and "Film Impersonating Ike (Boy and Man)," *Variety*, October 21, 1953; Steele's casting as the president is from a cast list issued by the Call Bureau Casting Service, August 1, 1954. Betsy Palmer's comments on JF and Maureen O'Hara are from the author's interview with Palmer, who also recalled her work in JF's short film *The Red, White, and Blue Line*. Information on the death of Robert Francis is from his *Variety* obituary, August 3, 1955, and from Palmer. JF's crossness with O'Hara while making *The Long Gray Line* is reported in Davis; JF's unhappiness over an affair O'Hara was having is revealed in JW's OH. JF's description of O'Hara as "a greedy bitch" is from a letter to Killanin, n.d., quoted in Davis; JF also discusses her in Tavernier, "John Ford à Paris: Notes d'un Attaché de Press" (English translation by JM). O'Hara's comments about working with JF are from Angela Fox Dunn, "Maureen O'Hara: John Ford's Favorite 'Rosebud,'" *amctv.com*, August 6, 1999. The cost and box-office gross of *The Long Gray Line* are from Gallagher. The *New Yorker* review, "When Shamrocks Last by the Hudson Grew," appeared on February 19, 1955.

The play *Mister Roberts* by Thomas Heggen and Joshua Logan (New York: Random House, 1948) is based on Heggen's 1946 novel, published by Houghton Mifflin, Boston. JF's agreement to direct the film version of *Mister Roberts* was made with Orange Prods., March 15, 1954. Joshua Logan's comments on JF and *Mister Roberts* are from Logan's book *Movie Stars, Real People and Me* (New York: Delacorte Press, 1978), which also includes JF's reported remark "Why should I look at that homosexual play?"; Jack Warner's edict not to reshoot the nurses' scene; and Leland Hayward's comments "Ford is money in the bank" and "Nobody knew who was in charge." The original plan for Logan to direct the film is discussed in his book and is reported in "Steam Up *Roberts* for Film Voyage," *DV*, September 2, 1953. The "Eighteen months at sea" line is discussed in Fonda and Teichmann, *My Life*. JF comments on sanitizing the play's language in "Mr. Ford's *Mister Roberts*," NYT, August 22, 1954. John Patrick's "First Treatment" for the film is dated April 12, 1954.

The film's casting is discussed in "Steam Up *Roberts* for Film Voyage"; "Anchors Aweigh," *NYT*, January 24, 1954 (on Marlon Brando); and "Fonda Will Re-Create Roberts' Role in Pic," *DV*, February 24, 1954. The criticisms of the play by Donald Baruch and Clair Towne are reported by Suid, quoting Baruch's memorandum for the record, September 23, 1953, and

Towne to George Dorsey (Columbia's Washington representative), September 30, 1953; Suid and Barbara Ford's OH mention JF's USN connections as a key element in his hiring; JF's use of his connections to get the project approved is reported in Captain A. McB. Jackson, USN, naval aide to Secretary of the Navy Charles S. Thomas, to Admiral Robert B. Carney, USN, chief of Naval Operations, July 21, 1954. The project's clearance is reported by Merle MacBain, Department of Navy Office of Information, to Admiral John Dale Price, USNR, July 23, 1954 (McBain and Price were the technical advisers on *Mister Roberts*). Production dates on *Mister Roberts,* as well as information on JF's hospitalization, are from "Daily Production and Progress Reports," September 14–October 12, 1954. Jack Lemmon discussed his screen test for *The Long Gray Line* and the filming of *Mister Roberts* in his interview with the author; Betsy Palmer also recalled the filming in her interview with the author; HCJ commented on Palmer to the author and in *Company of Heroes,* in which he reports JF's "huge crush" on the actress.

Fonda's criticism of JF as "an Irish egomaniac" is from Steen. Fonda and Teichmann quote JF's insistence on casting Fonda. Fonda's account of his fight with JF is from the author's interview with Fonda; Fonda's OH; and Fonda and Teichmann. Other accounts of the fight include the author's interview with Lemmon; HCJ, *Company of Heroes;* and PB. The dialogue between JF and HF during their confrontation was reported by HCJ to the author ("You traitorous") and by Logan, who heard it from Leland Hayward ("Well, Hank" and "I think it was"). McCabe, *Cagney,* reports Fonda telling JF, "Shoot it any way you like"; Fonda's comment "I don't know what was in his mind" is from Fonda and Teichmann. Fonda's advice to Lemmon to "screw it up" is quoted by Lemmon in his commentary on the 1998 Warner Bros. laserdisc version of *Mister Roberts.* Barbara Ford's OH reports that JF considered Fonda an ingrate. Peter Fonda's observation about the political friction between his father and JF is from Eyman, *Print the Legend.* Henry Fonda discussed his negative view of the film with the author and is quoted from Sinclair, citing the *Sunday Express* (London), September 13, 1959 ("I despised"), and from Fonda and Teichmann ("You can't tell an audience").

Sources on the incident with JF at the pool include the author's interview with HCJ and *Company of Heroes.* Fonda's recollection of JF being taken to the hospital to dry out is from Davis; Ken Curtis's OH also reports on JF's drinking during the filming. JF's gallbladder attack and replacement by Mervyn LeRoy are reported in Barbara Ford's OH; *Company of Heroes* (including JF's comment, "Will you look at this!"); and 1954 press coverage: "Film Director Ford Stricken," *LAE,* October 18; "LeRoy Pinch-Hits for John Ford, Ill," *DV,* October 19; "Ford Undergoes Knife, LeRoy Helming *Roberts,*" *HR,* October 19; and "John Ford Shows Gain," *LAE,* October 19.

The formation of C. V. Whitney Prods. is reported in "C. V. Whitney Bankrolls Film Co.," *DV,* November 12, 1954; "Whitney and Cooper Form Movie Firm," *HCN,* November 12, 1954; *"The Searchers," Look,* June 12, 1956; and Courtland Phipps, *"The Searchers," Films in Review,* June–July 1956 (which includes Whitney's promise about his company's plans). The agreement between JF and Whitney Pictures for *The Searchers* and two other films is dated November 29, 1954. Press announcements of *The Searchers* include "C. V. Whitney Bankrolls Film Co." and "John Ford to Meg 3 for Whitney Co.," *HR,* December 2, 1954. *The Searchers* advertisement quoted [1956] is at AMPAS. Information on distribution dealings for the film is from correspondence (1954): Lew Wasserman to Bolton, December 14; Cooper to Whitney, December 17; Van Hoozer to Cooper, December 17; and Cooper's December telegram to JF; and (1955): Harry Cohn's telegram to JF, January 1; Cooper to JF, January 5; and Jack Warner to JF, April 20.

Alan LeMay's novel *The Searchers* (New York: Harper and Brothers, 1954) was serialized in the *Saturday Evening Post* as *The Avenging Texans,* November 6, 13, 20, 27, and December 4, 1954. Information on Cynthia Ann Parker and Quanah Parker is from historical research by Jessica McBride and from T. R. Fehrenbach, *Lone Star: A History of Texas and the Texans* (New York: American Legacy Press, 1968). D. H. Lawrence's description of Leatherstocking is from

"Fenimore Cooper's Leatherstocking Novels" in Lawrence's *Studies in Classic American Literature*. JF's comment "We are busy working on the script of *The Searchers*" is from a March 1955 letter to Killanin, quoted in Davis; see Nugent's Revised Final Screenplay of *The Searchers* [1955]. Information on the song "Lorena" is from Arthur M. Eckstein, "Darkening Ethan: John Ford's *The Searchers* (1956) from Novel to Screenplay to Screen," *Cinema Journal*, Fall 1998.

Sources on the principal photography of *The Searchers* include the author's interviews with Henry Brandon, Harry Carey Jr., Olive Carey, Chuck Hayward, Winton C. Hoch, George Holliday, John Wayne, Natalie Wood, Hank Worden, and Billy Yellow; "Daily Production Reports"; the script breakdown; correspondence from location by Lowell Farrell; travel list, June 13, 1955; Reed, "John Ford Makes Another Movie Classic in Monument Valley"; Gaberscek, *Il West di John Ford*; and *A Turning of the Earth: John Ford, John Wayne and* The Searchers (1998), a documentary by Nick Redman included on the 1998 Warner Home Video videotape of *The Searchers*. Information on the VistaVision format is from Belton. The Bond incident with the electric razor was reported to the author by Hoch and HCJ; HCJ's comment on JW's performance in the scene is from R&O. JF discusses the film's Comanches in his "Notes on *The Searchers*," to Pat Ford, Nugent, Wingate Smith, and Frank Beetson, January 26, 1955. HCJ comments in *Company of Heroes* on the unusual seriousness of JF and JW during the making of the film. The inscription on the deer hide is reported in Reed, "John Ford Makes Another Movie Classic in Monument Valley"; a photo of the presentation appears in Rosebrook and Rosebrook, "John Ford's Monument Valley." Sources on the footrace on *The Searchers* include the author's interviews with HCJ and Brandon. McDonnell, O'Connell, and de Havenon, *Krazy Kat*, quotes the Navajo Yeibichai, or Night Chant. The *Look* article *"The Searchers"* describes Scar as a "wicked, unregenerate Indian"; Phipps criticizes JF for "a sentimental attitude toward the Indian." The Dudley Nichols–Pat Ford 1957 treatment of the Cheyenne story is discussed in Pat's January 21, 1963, letter to Bernard Smith.

Information on the second-unit snow scenes is from the author's interviews with Hoch and Hayward; Pat Ford to JF, Cooper, Lowell Farrell, Hoch, Lefty Hough, Wingate Smith, Cliff Lyons, Beetson, Art Cole, and Carl Gibson, February 15, 1955; *"The Searchers*: Tentative Schedule of Movements to Gunnison, Colorado," February 19, 1955, listing JF as part of the unit; "Daily Production Reports," February 28–March 4, 1955 (listing JF as second-unit director at Gunnison); Pat Ford to JF, Cooper, Farrell, and Van Hoozer, March 22, 1955; and *A Turning of the Earth*, which shows slates on many of the snow scenes and outtakes with JF's name listed as director. Information on second-unit scenes in Monument Valley is from the author's interview with Brandon and "Daily Production Reports," June–July 1955.

JW's comment that he "loved" Ethan is from F. Anthony Macklin, "I Come Ready: An Interview with John Wayne," *Film Heritage*, Summer 1975. JF's comments "I should like to do a tragedy" and "a kind of psychological epic" are from Mitry, "Recontre avec John Ford." JW talks in *Directed by John Ford* about imitating Harry Carey's gesture in the final shot of *The Searchers*; Hoch told the author he thought the shot was "corny"; Olive Carey's remarks also were made to the author. JF's description of *The Searchers* as "the tragedy of a loner" is from PB. Brian Huberman's talk with Wayne about *The Searchers* is quoted in R&O. James Stewart commented on JW and *The Searchers* in an interview with the author, quoted in JM, "James Stewart Delighted by Upward Swing in Westerns," *DV*, December 22, 1975.

Information on Vera Miles is from "Biographical Notes on VERA MILES," Twentieth Century–Fox [c. 1949] (AMPAS); Miles's publicity biography, September 6, 1956 (AMPAS); "Vera Miles Will Do 15 Pix for Hitchcock," *DV*, October 12, 1955; J. D. Spiro, "Vera Miles: Country Girl in Hollywood," *Milwaukee Journal*, May 13, 1956; and Mark Hemeter, "'Fighting Trim': Vera Miles Still a Doer," *New Orleans Times-Picayune/States-Item*, February 20, 1981. Miles's TV credits are listed in *Films in Review*, October 1971; information on her June 2, 1955, *Ford Theater* program is from James Robert Parish and Vincent Terrace, *The Complete Actors' Television Credits, 1948–1988*, Vol. 2: *Actresses* (Metuchen, N.J.: Scarecrow Press, 1990).

Gallagher reports box-office figures for *The Searchers.* Information on Buddy Holly, Jerry Allison, and "That'll Be the Day" is from Ellis Amburn, *Buddy Holly: A Biography* (New York: St. Martin's Press, 1995). Contemporary reviews of *The Searchers* (1956) include *Holl., DV,* March 13; Jack Moffitt, *HR,* March 13; John McCarten, *New Yorker,* June 9; the anonymous review in "Films Sortis a Paris du 8 Aout au 11 Septembre," *Cahiers du Cinéma,* October (trans. by JM); Lindsay Anderson, *Sight and Sound,* autumn; and Robert Ardrey, *The Reporter,* quoted in Stuart Byron, *"The Searchers:* Cult Movie of the New Hollywood," *New York,* March 5, 1979. "Prisoner of the Desert" by JM and Michael Wilmington, which Byron describes as the "seminal" essay on the film, first appeared in *Sight and Sound,* Autumn 1971, and was reprinted in *AFI Report,* July 1973, as well as being reprinted (with revisions) in M&W; JF requests a copy of the essay in a letter from his secretary Rose Lew to JM, October 13, 1971. JF's thanks for "the upbeat kindly way you treated me" in that and other articles is from JF to JM [c. November 1971, handwritten by JF on November 24, 1971, letter from JM to Rose Lew]. Information on the 1962 *Cahiers* critics' poll and the quotation from Jean-Luc Godard are from "Prisoner of the Desert"; *Sight and Sound* polls listing *The Searchers* are reported in Byron and in Roger Ebert, *Roger Ebert's Video Companion* (Kansas City, Mo.: Andrews and McMeel, 1996 edition).

Other critical commentary quoted on *The Searchers* includes PB; Slotkin, *Gunfighter Nation;* Jean-Louis Leutrat and Suzanne Liandrat-Guigues, "John Ford and Monument Valley," in Edward Buscombe and Roberta E. Pearson, eds., *Back in the Saddle Again: New Essays on the Western* (London: British Film Institute, 1998); Sarris, *"The Searchers," Film Comment,* Spring 1971; and Brian Henderson, *"The Searchers:* An American Dilemma," *Film Quarterly,* Winter, 1980–81. Fiedler's observation on the "heart of the Western" is from *The Return of the Vanishing American.* Martin Scorsese, Steven Spielberg, and Paul Schrader are quoted in Byron on *The Searchers.* Information on Spielberg's juvenile imitation of *The Searchers* is from the author's interview with Terry Mechling for JM, *Steven Spielberg: A Biography* (New York: Simon and Schuster, 1997).

James Warner Bellah's novel *The Valiant Virginians* was published by Ballantine Books, New York, 1953. Bellah's outline for JF's planned film version is dated May 3, 1954; Bellah's Full Story Continuity is undated; Stallings wrote a continuity outline, August 19, 1954, and a First Estimating Draft, October 12, 1954 (for Columbia); see also a letter from Columbia's Jerry Wald to JF, June 14, 1956. Whitney's go-ahead for *The Valiant Virginians* and his discussion of a World War II film as part of his "American Series" are from his January 19, 1956, letter to JF; the "American Series" concept is mentioned in the *Look* magazine article *"The Searchers"* and in "C. V. Whitney, Company Outline 5-Yr. Sked; *Chang* to be Refilmed," *DV,* March 29, 1956. Nugent to JF, April 24, 1956, mentions that Pat Wayne was to play the central role in *The Valiant Virginians;* JW's possible casting as Stonewall Jackson is discussed by Rev. Frederick G. Weber to Whitney, May 11, 1956. Whitney's plans for fall 1956 production of the film are indicated in a January 16, 1956, letter to JF; JF reports the film's cancellation to JW, December 26, 1956. JF's complaint that the pleasure has gone from filmmaking is from his January 17, 1957, letter to JW.

Levy provides information on 1949 radio programs hosted by JF: adaptations of *Stagecoach* (*NBC Theater,* January 9) and *Fort Apache* (*Screen Directors Playhouse,* NBC, August 5). Argosy's interest in making television films is discussed in "Joining the Parade," *NYT,* July 4, 1948. Information on *Rookie of the Year* is from the Production Budget, Hal Roach Studios, October 11, 1955. A copy of Theophane Lee's play *The Bamboo Cross,* n.d., is at Lilly, as is the television adaptation by Stallings, October 21, 1955; see also an item in *LAE,* September 27, 1955, on JF directing the program; JF's salary is reported in his 1955 IRS return, which lists a contribution to the Maryknoll Fathers (as do other IRS and California tax returns of JF's). JF's Maryknoll award and speech (1955) are reported in an *LAE* item, April 20; and in JF to Killanin, May 13. Television is discussed in Killanin's interview with JF, "Poet in an Iron Mask," *Films and Filming,* February 1958. The information that JF signed a petition to President Eisenhower is from Charles Edison, Joseph C. Grew, Walter Judd, John W. McCormack, H. Alexander Smith, and

John Sparkman of The Committee for One Million (Against the Admission of Communist China to the United Nations) to JF, November 5, 1953. JF's comment on liking animals, baseball, and people is quoted in Davis.

Background on Irish cinema history is from Arthur Flynn, *Irish Film 100 Years* (Ireland: Kestrel Books, 1996). The inaccurate claim that *The Rising of the Moon* was "the first feature picture made by an Irish company in Ireland" was made by Lord Killanin in the film's world premiere program, Metropole Cinema, Dublin, May 16, 1957. JF discusses his hopes for an Irish film industry in Tom Hennigan, "For Ford," *Irish Press,* April 29, 1956. Information on stories considered for *The Rising of the Moon* (working titles: *Four Leaves of a Shamrock, Three Leaves of a Shamrock*) is in Killanin to JF, March 15 and 25 and April 6, 1953, and July 16 and 26, 1954; Killanin to Manuel Baird, July 26, 1954; and Hurst to JF, September 7, 1954. JF's original intention to make the film in CinemaScope and color, and Nugent's working on the script for scale, are reported in "Memorandum on Mr. John Ford's Visit to Ireland 20th to 29th August, 1955," Four Provinces Prods.; JF's salary for the film is listed in his 1957 IRS return. Sources on the plans to make the film for Republic include 1954 correspondence: Killanin to JF, July 7; Killanin to Tyrone Power, October 11; and Killanin to Hurst, November 5; and Yates's Dublin announcement of the Irish venture, reported in "Pictures May Be Made Here," *Irish Press* [December?] 24, 1953. JF's overture to KH is from a [September?] 1954 letter. The project's postponement to 1956 is reported in Killanin's telegram to Cooper, January 12, 1955.

JF's statement about making the film "[F]or the sake of my artistic soul" is from his March 1954 letter to Killanin, quoted in Davis. JF's "gentle" tone with an actor is described in "Work Progresses on First Film by Irish Company," *Irish Times,* April 14, 1956; JF's handling of noisy children is reported in Hennigan, "Immortal Railway," unidentified Irish newspaper [1956] (Lilly). Maurice Good recalls the filming in "On Location with John Ford," *Irish Digest,* September 1956; JF's bullying of Good is also discussed in Anderson's interview with Donal Donnelly (in which Good is identified under the pseudonym of "Pat Ryan"). Nugent's comment on the film's low budget and JF's remark about why he refused to use a modern train are from Nugent, "Eire Happily Revisited," *NYT,* July 14, 1957.

The production cost and gross theatrical rentals of *The Rising of the Moon* are reported in a Warner Bros. distribution statement for the period ended January 30, 1965. Budget figures and the shooting schedule are from the Production Cost Ledger and the Shooting Schedule, March–May 1956. The original plan for JF to appear in the introductory segments is mentioned in Nugent, Suggested Treatment of Continuity, *Three Leaves of a Shamrock*, n d; JF's February 6, 1956, letter to Killanin indicates his resistance to using Power in the "1921" segment; Killanin's direction of the Power introductions is discussed in Killanin to JF, June 4 and 15, 1956, and January 18, 1957, and JF's telegram to Killanin, June 19, 1956. JF's idea of calling the film *Irish Coffee* is discussed in Killanin to JF, May 14, 1956, and JF's telegram to Killanin, June 18, 1956. The review by James Powers appears in the July 9, 1957, issue of *HR*. Information on the Dublin and New York openings is from "Record Dublin Gross for John Ford's Irish Film," *HR,* June 12, 1957; additional information is from the world premiere program. The denunciations of *The Rising of the Moon* by D. P. Quish and Gerard Hayes are reported in "Limerick Co. Council Protests Ford's *Moon*," *Variety,* February 19, 1958. Davis notes the film's banning in Belfast.

DF reports that JF talked about retirement after *The Searchers.* Sources on JF's plans with Killanin for a film of Arthur Conan Doyle's novel *The White Company* include the author's interview with Cliffton; DF; Killanin to JF, October 28 and December 19, 1958, and March 2 and 23, 1959; and other 1959 correspondence: Killanin to Bolton, January 26; Killanin to Conan Doyle, February 16; and Bolton to JF, March 19 (reporting the project's rejection by the Mirisch Company).

Information on the filming of *The Wings of Eagles* is from "Assistant Director's Reports," MGM, September 10–October 4, 1956; and JF to Admiral Arleigh Burke, chief of Naval Operations, October 8, 1956. For biographical information on the film's subject, Frank W. "Spig" Wead, see the notes for chapter 10. JF's comments "I didn't want to do the picture" and "[l]ife disappointed him" are from PB; his admission that he approached the subject in "fear and trepidation" is from his notes on the film, n.d. (Lilly), quoted in R&O. JF's claim to have participated in Wead's hijinks is in PB, which also discusses the film's use of JF memorabilia. DF discusses MGM's development of *The Wings of Eagles* and describes it as a disguised autobiography of JF. JF mentions his dislike of the title in PB; JF to JW, December 26, 1956 (which reports that MGM thought the film too comedic); and JF to JW, January 25, 1957. Davis, *Duke,* mentions the cutting of some scenes involving Maureen O'Hara.

Documents (1956) on *The Growler Story* include K. Craig, acting chief of Naval Personnel, to JF, October 30, orders for temporary active service; commander-in-chief, Pacific Fleet, telegram to JF, November 6, ordering him to report to Pearl Harbor; JF radiogram to Captain John McCain, office of the chief of Naval Operations, December 5 (calling the production a "wonderful experience"); and JF to JW, December 26 (including his complaint about Bond's behavior). Information on the USN submarine *Growler* (SS-215) is from *Dictionary of American Fighting Ships, Vol. III,* 1968, Navy Department, office of the chief of Naval Operations, Naval History Division. JF's irritation with the admiral who was technical adviser on *The Growler Story* is reported in Sinclair and in Mark Armistead's OH. The National Archives has *John Ford Footage Simulating Battle of Midway,* February 26, 1957 (unedited footage) and *Battle of Midway MN-1433* (unedited footage). JF's attempt to obtain the Navy Cross is discussed in Rear Admiral F. M. "Massie" Hughes, USN, to Admiral Price, December 17, 1956. JF's attempt to obtain the Croix de Guerre is discussed in Commander M. E. Armistead, USNR, to Contre-Amiral Jubelin, Attaché Naval, Ambassade de France, Washington, D.C., October 22, 1956; Lilly also has a draft of the letter in English. Admiral Bulkeley's observations on JF are from his interview with the author; Breuer reports on Bulkeley's promotion to rear admiral.

The July 1958 *Cahiers du Cinéma* review of *Gideon's Day* (aka *Gideon of Scotland Yard*) is quoted in Gallagher's translation. Information (1957) on JF's deal for the film is from the agreement between Columbia Pictures Corp. and JFP, January 10; employment agreement between JFP and JF, June 6; and agreement between Columbia (British) Prods. Ltd. and JF, October 1. The budget is from an agreement between Columbia and Columbia (British) Prods. Ltd., October 1, 1957.

Sources on the changing political mood in Hollywood in the late 1950s include Navasky; Ceplair and Englund; and "Some on Acad Bd. Would K.O. Rule Barring Oscar to Reds," *DV,* January 12, 1959 (with Ward Bond's comment "They're all working now"). Sources on Boston's James Michael Curley (the model for Mayor Frank Skeffington in *The Last Hurrah*) include William V. Shannon, *The American Irish* (New York: Macmillan, 1963); "James M. Curley Dies in Boston; Colorful Democratic Boss Was 83," *NYT,* November 13, 1958; "The Last Rites," *Time,* November 24, 1958; and Francis Russell, "The Last of the Bosses," *American Heritage,* June 1959. Curley's relationship to Skeffington, Curley's lawsuit against Columbia, and the settlement of the suit are discussed in "Curley Opposes Movie," *NYT,* August 20, 1958; "James M. Curley Dies in Boston; Colorful Democratic Boss Was 83"; and Russell; JF's comments "If this is Curley" and "had hoped" are from "Down with Rebecca," *Newsweek,* September 22, 1958. JF's telegram to Harry Cohn after reading Edwin O'Connor's 1956 source novel *The Last Hurrah* is reported in Thomas Wood, *"Last Hurrah* in Real Locale," *New York Herald Tribune,* May 25, 1958. Raymond Durgnat comments on the film in *The Crazy Mirror: Hollywood Comedy and the American Image* (London: Faber and Faber, 1969). Information on JF's deal and Columbia's right of final cut is from the minutes of the first meeting of the board of directors of JFP, October 12, 1956; Columbia and JF agreement, March 4, 1957; production-distribution agreement between Columbia and JFP, June 6, 1957; and agreement between Columbia and Guaranty Trust Co. of New York, 1958. Information on the budget, cost, schedule, and shooting dates is from the film's budget, February 18, 1958; and Hervey S. Shaw, Columbia's assistant treasurer, to JFP, June 8, 1959.

JF's consideration of James Cagney and JW for Skeffington is mentioned in Benjamin to JF, July 11, 1956; JF's thought of casting Bond is from JF to JW, January 17, 1957. Other preproduction information is from 1956 correspondence: Columbia's Jerry Wald to JF, May 21; Nugent to JF, November 23; and Bolton to JF, December 6; Cohn's notes on the [Nugent] second-draft screenplay, March 11, 1957; and the final-draft screenplay by Nugent, January 16, 1958. Orson Welles's explanation of why he lost the role of Skeffington is from Welles and Bogdanovich. KH's intervention to patch up the JF–Spencer Tracy feud is discussed in the JF/KH OH and in Leaming. Information on Tracy going home early is from "Assistant Director's Daily Reports," February 24–April 14, 1958; and Leaming. JF's comment "God, I'm exhausted" is quoted in Leaming and was recalled by KH in the JF/KH OH. JF's casting Perry Lopez as Knocko's corpse is reported by Wood, "*Last Hurrah* in Real Locale." Sources on Cohn's death and funeral and JF's tribute include Bob Thomas, *King Cohn: The Life and Times of Harry Cohn* (New York: G. P. Putnam's Sons, 1967); and Clifford Odets, "Eulogy for Harry Cohn" (delivered by Danny Kaye) in Bernard F. Dick, *The Merchant Prince of Poverty Row: Harry Cohn of Columbia Pictures* (Lexington: University Press of Kentucky, 1993). Charles FitzSimons's comment on JF's relationship with his son is from Davis, who also reports on Pat's alcoholism and JF's guilt over neglecting him emotionally. Information on *The Missouri Traveler* is from Bolton to JF, May 11, 1956, and the *Variety* review, January 15, 1958.

Harold Sinclair's novel *The Horse Soldiers* was published by Harper and Brothers in 1956. James M. McPherson's description of Grierson's Raid is from *Battle Cry of Freedom: The Civil War Era* (New York: Oxford University Press, 1988). The Final Estimating Script for *The Horse Soldiers* by Mahin and Martin Rackin is dated August 22, 1958 (JF collection, State Historical Society of Wisconsin). Mahin's comments on the film are from the author's interview with Mahin, parts quoted in JM and McCarthy, "Bombshell Days in the Golden Age: John Lee Mahin Interviewed." JF's interest in the Civil War was reported in the author's interviews with Cliffton and Gavin Lambert, and is mentioned in Tim Hunter, "An Interview with William Clothier," *On Film*, No. 2, 1970, and Lambert's introduction to Lindsay Anderson, "John Ford," *Cinema*, Spring 1971; JF also discussed the Civil War with the author. Stallings suggests U. S. Grant as a possible film subject in his December 3, 1956, letter to JF. Pat Ford reports on his *Horse Soldiers* location scouting in a letter to JF [September? 1958].

Anna Lee told the author about JF's rule against blondes in Westerns. Sources on Constance Towers's working relationship and friendship with JF include "Connie Towers: 'The Best Role since Scarlett O'Hara,'" *Look*, June 9, 1959; "Biography of Constance Towers," Warner Bros. publicity material for *Sergeant Rutledge* (1960); Dorothy Manners, "About Constance 'Connie' Towers: Modern Method," *LAE*, July 16, 1961; and Gregg Hunter, "Constance Towers, *The King*'s Anna, Says, 'You Have To Be Up All the Time To Perform a Major Musical Role,'" *Hollywood Drama-logue*, April 13, 1979.

Financial information on *The Horse Soldiers* is from the Budget, Mirisch Company, October 14, 1958; JF's contract with the Mirisch Co., October 17, 1958; and Production Notes, United Artists. JF's complaint about working with "no money" is from a letter to Killanin, n.d., quoted in Davis. Information on the filming of the military academy sequence is from the author's interview with Mahin and n.a., "Six Days with Horse Soldiers" (Lilly). Hoot Gibson's work on the film is reported in Ager, "Then and Now," and "Six Days with Horse Soldiers." Other *Horse Soldiers* filming information is from the author's interviews with Hank Worden and Chuck Hayward; the Shooting Schedule; the Final Estimating Script; Film Production Chart, *DV*, December 12, 1958; and Archerd's column, *DV*, January 7, 1959. Hayward told the author he doubled JW in the ending.

Sources on the death of Frederick O. "Fred" Kennedy (December 5, 1958) include the author's interviews with Worden, Hayward, and Mahin; the William Clothier and Curtis OHs; and 1958 press coverage: "Fall in Film Fatal to Actor Fred Kennedy," *LAT,* December 6, with AP photograph; "Veteran Hollywood Stunt Man Killed," *HCN,* December 6; obituary, *DV,* December 8; and "Second Broken Neck Fatal to Kennedy," *Variety,* December 10; the first-aid man is identified in the Shooting Schedule. Information on three people suffering broken legs on location is from "Second Broken Neck Fatal to Kennedy"; and John Gilbert, "Working with Ford" (Martin Rackin interview), *Sight and Sound,* Winter 1959/60 (mentioning Pat Ford's fracture). Pilar Wayne's recollections of the filming are from Wayne and Thorleifson. Information on JF's return from the location is from "Guests 1958" (Lilly).

CHAPTER THIRTEEN: "THERE'S NO FUTURE IN AMERICA" (PP. 600–720)

The chapter title is from the author's interview with Samuel Goldwyn Jr. (quoting an MGM executive), published in JM, "Last John Ford Pic, Tribute to Gen. Puller, Looks for Buyer," *DV,* December 26, 1974; Bulkeley's reaction is from his interview with the author. JF's admission that he had lost his "old enthusiasm" and his other remarks to Colin Young are from Young's article "The Old Dependables," *Film Quarterly,* Fall 1959. Information on JF sailing around Hawaii, 1958–59, is from DF; Bea Benjamin to Rip Yeager, December 12, 1958; MF to Benjamin, February 8, 1959; and "Honolulu—Travel John Ford 1958" (Lilly).

For sources on JF's project *The White Company,* see the notes for chapter 12. Information on JF's project *The Judge and the Hangman* is from his letter to JW, December 26, 1956; Killanin to JF, March 2, 1959; Bolton to JF, March 9, 10, and 19, 1959; Bolton's telegram to Killanin, May 11, 1959; and Louella O. Parsons column, "John Ford Plans to Direct First Mystery Thriller" [c. 1959]. Sources on Dudley Nichols's illness and death include Bolton to JF, March 19, 1959; "Dudley Nichols, Award Winning Producer, Dies," *HCN,* January 5, 1960; and "Dudley Nichols Rites Today After Long Career, Top Pix," *DV,* January 6, 1960. The death of Grant Withers is discussed in Zolotow. Information on the death of William J. Donovan is from Brown (including the comment by President Eisenhower) and "In Memoriam GENERAL WILLIAM J. DONOVAN 1883–1959" (a booklet of tributes in the New York press) (Lilly).

Information on JF's recruitment to supervise orientation films in the People-to-People series for the Office of Armed Forces Information and Education, Department of Defense, 1958–59, and his organization of a Hollywood production committee is from 1958 correspondence: John C. Broger, deputy director, Office of Armed Forces Information and Education, to JF, July 29; Broger to Admiral Felix B. Stump, USN, CINCPAC [July]; Charles C. Finucane, assistant secretary of Defense, to JF, August 7; Broger to JF, August 14; C. R. "Buck" Wilhide, Department of Navy, Office of Information, to JF, August 15; Captain George O'Brien, USNR, orientation film project officer, to JF, November 13; and Benjamin to Yeager, December 12; see also Eric Strutt to Broger, February 8, 1959. The "PLAN FOR DEPARTMENT OF DEFENSE PEOPLE-TO-PEOPLE FILM PROJECT" (including Taiwan and Korea films), February 26, 1959, is at Lilly, with a letter from O'Brien to JF and other committee members, November 13, 1961; see also "Orientation for People to People Films" (1959) ("Use the Cold War"). An undated letter from Brigadier General S. F. Giffin, USAF, director, Office of Armed Forces Information and Education, to Vice Admiral W. R. Smedberg III, chief of Naval Personnel, commends JF and other committee members for making two films, *Taiwan—Island of Freedom* and *Korea—Battleground for Liberty,* and developing other film projects on the Philippines and Southeast Asia. The involvement of JF and Frank Capra in these projects is discussed in JM, *Frank Capra.*

Strutt's script for *Taiwan—The Island Fortress* (working title) [1959] is at Lilly, as are a script breakdown [1959] ("Remember"); Strutt's script for *Korea—Land of the Morning Calm* (working title) [1959]; and Strutt, n.d. "Action Outline for Story of Korea (CINCPAC–Asian Project)." "John Ford Visits Korea" reports that Strutt directed parts of *Korea—Battleground for Liberty.* Additional correspondence and scripts for the series of orientation films are in the Frank Capra Archives at Wesleyan University, as is the August 22, 1961, "Outstanding Contribution Award" to Capra. JF's orders for temporary duty on his trip to make the *Taiwan* and *Korea* films are from the commander in chief, Pacific, April 14, 1959, and the commander, Naval Forces, Korea, May 8, 1959; JF's travel voucher, paid July 2, 1959, lists his itinerary and dates; the completion of his duty is recorded in commander in chief, Pacific, to JF, May 9, 1959; see also caption information in a press release accompanying a photograph of JF and O'Brien in Taiwan, 1959. Sources on JF working with Heran Moon at Kyung Bok Palace, Seoul, on May 7, 1959, include "John Ford Visits Korea" (press release), May 12, headquarters, United Nations Command, U.S. Forces Korea, Eighth U.S. Army; and photos by M/Sgt. Al Chang (Lilly), with caption information in a press release from the Office of the Chief of Information and Education, Department of the Army. Moon's letters to JF are at Lilly; her expressions of love are from her letter of June 21, 1959, quoted from Davis; other letters are dated June 14 and 29 and November 7 and 16, 1959, and February 6, 1960 (asking JF to help her find work in Hollywood).

Production information (1959) on *Sergeant Rutledge* (working title: *Captain Buffalo*) is from Willis Goldbeck to JF, January 15; Goldbeck's telegram to JF, March 25; contracts between JFP and WB, June 3 and 8; the Revised Estimating Script by James Warner Bellah and Goldbeck, June 11; and "Daily Production Reports," July 16–August 31. Bellah comments on the film in "The Birth of a Story," the introduction to his novelization of *Sergeant Rutledge* (New York: Bantam, 1960). William H. Leckie comments on the derivation of the sobriquet "Buffalo Soldiers" in *The Buffalo Soldiers: A Narrative of the Negro Cavalry in the West* (Norman: University of Oklahoma Press, 1967). Frederic Remington is quoted in William Loren Katz, *The Black West,* revised edition (New York: Anchor Books, 1973). Woody Strode discusses the film in Charlayne Hunter, "Woody Strode? 'He Wasn't the Star But He Stole the Movie,'" *NYT,* September 19, 1971; and Strode and Sam Young, *Goal Dust: An Autobiography* (Lanham, Md.: Madison Books, 1990). Thomas Cripps gives his critical viewpoint in *Making Movies Black: The Hollywood Message Movie from World War II to the Civil Rights Era* (New York: Oxford University Press, 1993). Information on Naaman Brown's uncredited role as Moffat is from "Daily Production Reports"; cast listing for *Sergeant Rutledge,* Call Bureau Cast Service, 1960; and the *Academy Players Directory* listing for Brown, Issue 83, 1959.

JF's comment on his racial attitudes is from an interview with Samuel Lachize in *L'Humanité,* quoted in Tavernier's 1967 *Positif* article "John Ford à Paris: Notes d'un Attaché de Press"; this and subsequent quotations from the Tavernier article are from the English translation by J. P. Coursodon in *Film Comment,* July–August 1994, "Notes of a Press Attaché: John Ford in Paris, 1966." Davis reports that John F. Kennedy's election to the presidency in 1960 made JF feel that he was a full-fledged American citizen.

JF calling Ward Bond a "dumb Irishman" and JF's conflicted views on working in television are from Dwight Whitney, "'Why That Old Blankety Blank!'" *TV Guide,* November 19, 1960. JF's remark about JW appearing on *Wagon Train* is quoted in Davis; JF's OH says that he refused to follow Bond's wishes to shoot a close-up of JW for their episode, *The Colter Craven Story* (1960). JF's fee and the month of filming are from the contract between Revue Studios and JFP for *The Coulter [sic] Craven Story,* April 29, 1960. The script at Lilly for *The Coulter [sic] Craven Story* by Tony Paulson, dated April 26, 1960, has JF's annotations. JF's handling of the objection to the cigar is reported in Hal Humphrey, "Director John Ford Leaves Crew of *Wagon Train* All Shook Up," *Los Angeles Mirror,* May 28, 1960. JF's seventy-two-minute cut of the program is mentioned in Whitney. Ratings for *Wagon Train* and *Gunsmoke* are from Alex McNeil, *Total Television: The Comprehensive Guide to Programming from 1948 to the Present,* fourth edition (New York: Penguin Books, 1996). Information on the Battle of Shiloh is from U. S. Grant, *Personal Memoirs of U.S. Grant,* 1885, and McPherson, *Battle Cry of Freedom.*

Sources on Bond's death and funeral include the author's interview with Henry Brandon; Barbara Ford in her OH with JF (including the information about Bond's body being stolen); photographs of the funeral (Lilly); DF; Zolotow; HCJ, *Company of Heroes;* Davis; and press coverage (1960); "TV Star Ward Bond Dies of Heart Attack," *LAT,* November 6; "Ward Bond

Dead; TV and Film Actor," *NYT,* November 6; "Heart Attack Kills Actor Ward Bond," *LAE,* November 6; Bond obituary, *DV,* November 7; Jeff Davis, "500 Attend Funeral Rites for Ward Bond," *Los Angeles Mirror,* November 7 (with JW quote); "Ward Bond Rites Held at Reseda," *HCN,* November 7; Bond obituary, *HR,* November 7; "Last Rites for Ward Bond of TV Conducted," *LAT,* November 8; "Film World Pays Tribute to Ward Bond," *LAE,* November 8; and "In Memoriam Ward Bond," the *Starboard Club,* 1960 (Field Photo Homes Inc. newsletter). Zolotow reports that Bond flew his flag at half staff when Nikita Khrushchev visited Hollywood in 1959. Bond's final political statement was his letter printed in *HCN* on November 7, 1960. JF's accompaniment of Bond's body from Texas is reported in "Ward Bond Body Flown Back to Los Angeles," *LAT,* and "Ward Bond Flown to L.A.," *LAE,* November 7, 1960. The silent tribute on the set of *Two Rode Together* is reported in Army Archerd's column, *DV,* November 8, 1960. JF's statement on Bond ("Ward will always be with us") is from "A Farewell to Ward Bond," *TV Guide,* November 19, 1960. The claim that Bond "died fighting for his country" is from the July 24, 1961, letter to MPA members by the organization's executive director, A. J. MacDonald (Lilly). DF reports JF's drinking binge after completing *Two Rode Together.*

Sources on JF, JW, and *The Alamo* include the author's interviews with Hank Worden, Chuck Hayward, and Louis S. Race; JF's OH; the documentary film *John Wayne's The Alamo,* MGM (1992) (included on the MGM laserdisc with the restored edition of *The Alamo*); Donald Clark and Christopher Andersen, *John Wayne's The Alamo: The Making of the Epic Film* (New York: Citadel Press, 1995); PB; Zolotow; Wayne and Thorleifson; R&O; Wills; Davis, *Duke;* and Rodney Farnsworth, "John Wayne's Epic of Contradictions: The Aesthetic and Rhetoric of War and Diversity in *The Alamo,*" *Film Quarterly,* Winter 1998–99. Wills reports on JF's earlier plans to make an Alamo movie with JW for Argosy Pictures. FF's involvement in the 1911 film *The Immortal Alamo* is discussed in Thompson, *The Star Film Ranch: Texas' First Picture Show.*

The dates of JF's visits to the Texas location of *The Alamo* are in his itinerary "Guests 1959" (Lilly). Information on JF's arrival on location is from Clark and Andersen; Zolotow; William Clothier's OH; and the author's interview with Race, an assistant director who heard the story from makeup man Monty Westmore. JF's comment that he wanted to "cast a paternal eye" on JW is from his letter to Killanin, September 1959, quoted in Davis. JF's comments on JW's direction are from R&O ("Goddammit, Duke") and Wills ("Do it again"). JW's discussion with Clothier about JF is from Eyman, "On and Off Poverty Row"; JW's comment about letting JF direct a second unit regardless of the cost is from Zolotow. Michael Wayne's recollections of being JF's assistant on the film are from Davis. Richard Widmark's letter of September 30, 1959, thanks JF for directing him. Information on the scenes JF directed is from the author's interviews with Hayward and Worden; JF's OH; Clark and Andersen; Eyman, *Print the Legend;* and *John Wayne's The Alamo.* JF's declaration that "*The Alamo* is the greatest" is quoted in Zolotow; JW's claim that "This picture is America" is from Davis, *Duke.* JF's list of favorite movies is from *Cinema,* 1964, and is reprinted in JM, *The Book of Movie Lists.*

Sources on *Two Rode Together* include the author's interviews with James Stewart, Henry Brandon, and HCJ; HCJ, *Company of Heroes;* Strode and Young; and Donald Dewey, *James Stewart: A Biography* (Atlanta: Turner Publishing, 1996). For sources on Quanah Parker and Cynthia Ann Parker, see the notes for chapter 12. JF disparaged the film as "crap" in DF. Willis Goldbeck's contention that JF was willing to direct anything in his later years is from an interview in Anderson by Kevin Brownlow (1970). JF's comment that Stewart "was good in anything" is from Bogdanovich, "Th' Respawnsibility of Bein' J . . . Jimmy Stewart" in *Pieces of Time: Peter Bogdanovich on the Movies* (New York: Arbor House/Esquire, 1973); Stewart playing JF is from JM, "Aren't You . . . Jimmy Stewart?" *American Film,* June 1976. Widmark comments on JF in Michael Buckley, "Richard Widmark (Part Three)," *Films in Review,* June/July 1986. Information on JF's deal for the film is from memorandum of agreement, JFP and Shpetner Prods., July 26, 1960; Benjamin memo on contract, July 26, 1960; and production-distribution agreement,

JFP, Shpetner Prods., and Columbia Pictures [1960]. Manny Farber's May 1969 review of *Two Rode Together* in *Artforum* is reprinted in his collection *Negative Space.*

Reviews of *The Man Who Shot Liberty Valance* (1962) include *Tube., DV,* April 11; A. H. Weiler, *NYT,* May 24; Bosley Crowther, "Film Odds and Endings," *NYT,* June 3 (see also JF to Crowther, March 5); and Brendan Gill, *New Yorker,* June 16. Farber comments on the film in "White Elephant Art vs. Termite Art," *Film Culture,* 1962, reprinted in *Negative Space;* Sarris in "The American Cinema," *Film Culture,* Spring 1963, and *The John Ford Movie Mystery;* and Bogdanovich in his program notes for "A Tribute to John Ford," New Yorker Theater, New York, 1963 (AMPAS).

Dorothy M. Johnson's short story "The Man Who Shot Liberty Valance" is available in William Kittredge, ed., *The Portable Western Reader* (New York: Penguin Books, 1997) (with background information on Johnson); the story was published in the July 1949 issue of *Cosmopolitan* and in Johnson's collection *Indian Country* (New York: Ballantine Books, 1953). Information on JF's purchase of film rights is from a contract between JFP and Paramount Pictures, March 31, 1961, referring to a March 1, 1961, contract between Johnson and JFP. The novelization by Bellah, based on his and Goldbeck's screenplay and Johnson's story, was published by Pocket Books in New York in 1962; the screenplay by Bellah and Goldbeck is dated August 31, 1961; see also the film's Dialogue Continuity, n.d. Information on JF's assignment of Goldbeck and Bellah to write the screenplay is from the writers' contract with JFP, March 20, 1961; and Curtis Kenyon (Paramount story editor) to Eugene H. Frank, March 22, 1961.

Sources on JF's deal with Paramount and JFP on *Liberty Valance* and the film's budget and production cost include (1961): JFP, Paramount, and Stewart, memorandum of agreement, April 5; rider to memorandum of agreement, April 5; contract between Paramount and JFP, April 5; supplement to memorandum of agreement, April 6; DF; Gallagher; "Poise Stewart, Wayne for Ford Pic at Par," *DV,* April 10; "Goldbeck Produces *Liberty Valance*," *HR,* September 1; Production Budget, September 8; Estimated Finishing Cost as of October 14; and (1963): Distribution and Production Advances as of March 30, 1963 (Paramount). The filming schedule and release date are from the *DV* Film Production Chart, November 3, 1961; Kenyon, "Data for Bulletin of Screen Achievement Awards," AMPAS, December 11, 1961; and Academy Awards eligibility records, AMPAS.

Sources on the Metropolitan Opera Company's offer to JF to direct *The Girl of the Golden West* include the author's interview with Katherine Cliffton; Archerd's column, *DV,* October 31, 1961; and JF in Bogdanovich, "The Autumn of John Ford," *Esquire,* April 1964, reprinted in condensed form in his collection *Pieces of Time.* The Bel Air fire is reported in "Fire Burns 250 Homes," *LAT,* November 7, 1961; JF's comment to MF is from Archerd's November 7 *DV* column. Sources on JF persuading JW to appear in *Liberty Valance* include the author's interview with HCJ; JW to JF, April 20, 1961, quoted in Davis; JF to JW, July 7, 1961; and R&O, from JW's OH. JW's "Screw ambiguity" comment is from R&O. Stewart's comments on the film are from his interviews with the author. Edmond O'Brien described his working relationship with JF in an interview with the author and in a February 22, 1962, letter to JF, quoted in Davis. Clothier explains the film's use of black and white in Tim Hunter, "An Interview with William Clothier"; and Eyman, "On and Off Poverty Row"; Howard Hawks's comment on black and white is from an interview with the author in JM, *Hawks on Hawks.* Stewart's anecdote about Strode's costume is from *Directed by John Ford* and Dewey; Stewart's racial attitudes are discussed in Dewey. JF's goading of JW is reported in Davis ("Jesus Christ") and Strode and Young. Bogdanovich's comment on JF's increasingly sad view of the West and JF's response are from PB. Also quoted in this section are Leslie A. Fiedler, *Love and Death in the American Novel* (New York: Stein and Day, 1960); Mao Zedong, *Quotations from Chairman Mao Zedong* (Beijing: Foreign Language Press, 1966); Peter Wollen, *Signs and Meaning in the Cinema,* British Film Institute Cinema One Series (London: Secker and Warburg, 1969); and Coyne, *The Crowded Prairie.*

Information on the locations and shooting dates for *The Civil War* is from "Schedule Sequence #3," *How the West Was Won,* MGM, May 17, 1961. Information on the salaries of JF and JW is from Gallagher, Zolotow, and Davis. Information on Bernard Smith's background is from "Production Notes on *Cheyenne Autumn,*" Warner Bros., 1964, and Robin Pogrebin, "Bernard Smith, 92, Who Edited Literary Giants," *NYT,* December 31, 1999; DF gives the date Ford-Smith Productions was formed. Stewart's comment on *Flashing Spikes* is from an interview with the author. JF discusses Henry Aaron and baseball hats in his OH and his TV watching in Hedda Hopper's syndicated column, May 8, 1962.

JF's description of *Donovan's Reef* as a "spoof picture" is from an interview with Eugene Archer, *NYT,* July 14, 1963. Wollen comments on the film in *Signs and Meaning in the Cinema;* Wood discusses JF's 1960s work in "Shall We Gather at the River?: The Late Films of John Ford"; Graham Greene's observation on utopias is from his review of *Lost Horizon, Spectator* (London), April 30, 1937, reprinted in Parkinson. Capra quotes James Edward Grant in *The Name Above the Title.* JF and Elizabeth Allen reminiscence about his sexual advances in the Allen–JF OH; their nicknames for each other are from a letter she wrote JF in 1963; JF comments on his treatment of leading ladies in Mitchell. Allen's and Anna Lee's attendance at JF's burial service is reported in JM, "Bringing in the Sheaves."

JFP's production agreement with Paramount for *Donovan's Reef* (then untitled) is dated February 23, 1962. The source material by James Michener, the ten screenwriters who worked on the project over the years, and the WGA arbitration are discussed by Paramount's Kenyon in his 1962 letters to Frank, February 21; JF, September 26; and Bernard Donnenfeld, Frank, JF, and Herb Steinberg, November 21. The film's shooting schedule is dated June 1962. Financial information is from Paramount documents at Lilly: "Detailed Production Cost to September 28, 1963"; "Account at Close of Period Ending January 1, 1966"; and "Account as of December 28, 1966." Information on the use of the *Araner* is from the licensing agreement between JFP and Paramount, July 10, 1962; and Benjamin to Yeager, July 16, 1962; JF comments on MF's conflicted feelings toward the *Araner* in his letter to Pat Ford, [April ?] 1963 (Lilly), quoted in Davis. JF's involvement in *McLintock!* is reported in his 1962 itinerary (Lilly); R&O; and Davis (quoting Stefanie Powers).

Information on the Ford-Smith Prods. deal for *Cheyenne Autumn* (working title: *The Long Flight*) is from the contract between Ford-Smith Prods. and Warner Bros., July 26, 1963 (unsigned copy and signed copy with deletion); the Warner Bros. and Ford-Smith Prods. agreement, November 6, 1963; and Warner Bros.' "Distribution Statement as of June 30, 1971" (also including the film's negative cost and rentals); see also "John Ford and Bernard Smith To Make *Long Flight* at WB; First Four Stars Are Set," *HR,* July 3, 1963, and "Title Change" (to *Cheyenne Autumn*), *HR,* September 27, 1963. Sources of JF's comments on the project include Bill Libby, "The Old Wrangler Rides Again" ("Westerns are"); Mitchell ("in a weak moment"); Archer ("I've killed more Indians than anyone since Custer"); and PB ("I've killed more Indians than Custer"); Sarris in *The John Ford Movie Mystery* notes "two striking incongruities" in JF's statement to PB. JF's conception of *Cheyenne Autumn* is summarized by Pat Ford in his January 21, 1963, letter to Smith, quoted in Sinclair. Wollen's observation about *Cheyenne Autumn* reversing JF's earlier perspective on Europeans and Indians is from *Signs and Meaning in the Cinema.*

The novels that served as sources of *Cheyenne Autumn* are Howard Fast, *The Last Frontier* (New York: Duell, Sloan & Pearce, 1941), and Mari Sandoz, *Cheyenne Autumn* (New York: McGraw-Hill, 1953). Sources on the screen adaptation include the author's interview with Cliffton; Sandoz, "*Cheyenne Autumn*: A Story That Had To Be Told," Warner Bros. press release, 1964; Ford-Smith Prods. to Sandoz, October 9, 1963; Sandoz, assignment of film rights to Ford-Smith Prods., October 9, 1963; and Fast, *Being Red* (Boston: Houghton Mifflin, 1990) (quoted). The First Estimating Draft of Ted Sherdeman's unproduced screenplay based on Fast's novel, *The Cheyenne Massacre* (aka *The Last Frontier*), Columbia, December 13, 1949, is at Lilly, as are the treatment, February 3, 1949, and Sherdeman to [S.] Sylvan Simon (the producer of the Columbia project), February 9, 1951. Widmark's recollection of bringing the story of the Cheyenne migration to JF's attention is from Buckley.

Smith's letter about the research conducted for *Cheyenne Autumn* is to attorney Martin Gang, September 16, 1963 (James R Webb Papers, State Historical Society of Wisconsin). Sources on the Ford-Smith Prods. settlement with Columbia regarding *The Last Frontier* include the author's interview with Cliffton and 1965 correspondence at Lilly: Nahum A. Bernstein (Fast's attorney) to J. L. Warner, January 27; P. D. Knecht (Warner Bros. attorney) to Bernstein, February 1; Bernstein to Knecht, February 5; and Knecht to Bernstein, February 19. Strode and Young comments on JF's request for the actor to read the novels and to play a role in the film. Information on Fast's history as a Communist Party member and his reason for leaving the party is from Fast, *Being Red;* and Natalie Robins, *Alien Ink: The FBI's War on Freedom of Expression* (New York: William Morrow, 1992). J. Edgar Hoover's description of Fast is from *Masters of Deceit* (New York: Henry Holt, 1958). The earlier FBI claim about Fast's "main aim in writing" is quoted in Robins. Information on Sidney Buchman is from JM, *Frank Capra,* and Navasky, *Naming Names.*

Shooting information on *Cheyenne Autumn* is from Warner Bros.' "Daily Production and Progress Reports," September 23, 1963–January 6, 1964; and "Production Notes on *Cheyenne Autumn,*" Warner Bros., 1964. Carroll Baker's comments on nudity are from "Carroll Baker Dresses Up for *Cheyenne Autumn,*" Warner Bros. press release, 1964. JF's statement that he wanted a middle-aged actress to play Deborah Wright is from PB; JF's definition of a "mortal sin" for a director is from "John Ford Raps Today's Pix & Stars," *Variety,* June 25, 1969. The shooting of the fire scene and Wingate Smith's comment are from Bogdanovich, "The Autumn of John Ford," reprinted in *Pieces of Time;* JF's skittishness about stunts is noted in Smith's OH. Spencer Tracy's replacement by Edward G. Robinson is reported in "Robinson Replaces Tracy," *Film Daily,* December 30, 1963. Barbara Ford's OH reports that the photograph of Lincoln used in the film is from JF's home.

JF's assurance about his stamina is from a letter to Killanin quoted in Sinclair. Pat Ford's report of JF's steroid use in the later part of his career is cited by Dan Ford in Davis. In his interview with the author, HCJ discussed JF's mental state in his old age; JF's disorientation during the Colorado filming of *Cheyenne Autumn* is described by HCJ in *Company of Heroes.* Other sources on JF's illness, fatigue, and depression during production include DF and Wingate Smith's OH. JF's problems with pills are discussed in Smith's OH; *Company of Heroes;* and Burt Kennedy, *Hollywood Trail Boss: Behind the Scenes of the Wild, Wild Western* (New York: Boulevard Books, 1997), which reports Clothier's confrontation with JF. Ray Kellogg's second-unit footage is listed in "Daily Production and Progress Reports," October–December 1963. George O'Brien's reminiscing with JF and JF's comment "It's just no fun anymore" are reported in DF.

Bogdanovich's accounts of Ford in Monument Valley include "The Autumn of John Ford" and Bogdanovich's introduction to the article in *Pieces of Time;* the article (in its condensed form) and the introduction are reprinted together in the 1978 edition of PB as "Introduction: A Meeting at Monument Valley." HCJ's interview with the author discussed JF's aversion to talking about himself or his work, and the arrival of Bogdanovich and Polly Platt on location. JF's crack about *Arrowsmith* is from HCJ, *Company of Heroes.* JF's exasperated remark to Bogdanovich about his questions ("Jesus *Christ*") is from Bogdanovich's article "The Cowboy Hero and the American West . . . as Directed by John Ford." JF complains about "The Autumn of John Ford" in a letter to Bogdanovich, December 6, 1963; JF's comment in the letter that the article is "nauseating" is quoted in Davis. JF's nickname for Platt and his comments to and about Bernard Smith are from PB. JF's line as part of his hat gag is quoted by Clothier in Eyman, "On and Off Poverty Row."

JF's comments on President Kennedy ("I loved Kennedy") and Lee Harvey Oswald are from Tavernier. Sources on Kennedy's assassination and its impact on JF and the *Cheyenne Autumn* company in Moab, Utah, include "Daily Production and Progress Reports," November 22–23,

1963; the JF–Barbara Ford OH; DF; and HCJ, *Company of Heroes.* JF's suggestion about Jacqueline Kennedy is from his letter to Gordon McLendon, November [26?], 1963.

The openings of *Cheyenne Autumn* are reported in "*Cheyenne Autumn* Toasted by World Press in Wyoming," *HCN,* October 5, 1964; and "Warner Bros. Scores Publicity Smash with *Cheyenne Autumn,*" *Boxoffice,* 1964. Bernard Smith expresses his and JF's unhappiness over the studio's recutting in a telegram to JF, October 5, 1964, and a letter to JF, October 12, 1964. Reviews include (1964): *Whit.* [Whitney Williams], *DV,* October 7; Richard Oulahan, "John Ford's Trojan Horse-Opry," *Life,* November 27; and Crowther, "Screen: John Ford Mounts Huge Frontier Western," *NYT,* December 24; and (1965): "End of the Trail?" *Newsweek,* January 11, and a letter in reply from Mark Haggard, "A New Direction," February 1; and Stanley Kauffmann, *New Republic,* January 23. Crowther's proposal of an award for JF is reported in Sarris, *The John Ford Movie Mystery.*

Sources on Pat Ford's work on *Cheyenne Autumn* include DF; Bogdanovich, "The Autumn of John Ford"; and Pat to Bernard Smith, January 21, 1963; Pat's unhappiness over credit and pay is from DF; his loan request and information on his living situation are from his letter to Benjamin, April 24, 1963, JF's response is his letter to Pat, [April?] 1963, quoted in Davis. JF's 1961–64 income figures are from his and MF's U.S. and California income tax returns. Pat's confrontation with Bernard Smith is reported in DF; Pat mentions his work as a mechanic and submits a script to his father in his letter of July 20, 1964. The "Last Will and Testament of John A. Feeney [aka John Ford]," signed March 31, 1973, is at Lilly; see also 1973 press coverage: "Notes on People," *NYT,* November 30; "John Ford's Will Disowns Only Son from 500G Estate," *DV,* November 30; "John Ford's Will: Son Pat Is Out, Various Trusts Set," *Variety,* December 5. Eyman, *Print the Legend,* reports that JF cut Pat out of the will because of their dispute over JF's acceptance of the Medal of Freedom from President Richard M. Nixon. Information on JF's 1970 will is from "Notes on People"; "John Ford's Will Disowns Only Son from 500G Estate"; and "John Ford's Will: Son Pat Is Out, Various Trusts Set." Woody Strode's comments on his relationship with JF in 1963 are from Strode and Young. HCJ's comments on JF kissing and punching him, and on Pat and Barbara Ford, are from his interview with the author. Sources on Barbara's later years include the author's interviews with HCJ, Admiral Bulkeley, and Dan Ford (she "died sober"); and her obituary, *Variety,* July 3, 1985. Information on Pat's alcoholism is from Gallagher and Davis. Sources on Pat's death include the author's interviews with Olive Carey and HCJ. The comments on Pat by Waverly Ramsey and Bulkeley are from their interviews with the author. Mary Ford's death on July 29, 1979, is reported in "Mary Ford Dies at 86; Film Director's Widow," *LAT,* July 30; obituary, *DV,* July 30; and "Mrs. John Ford, 86," *NYT,* July 31.

The description of Sean O'Casey as the "worker playwright" is reported in Declan Kiberd, *Inventing Ireland: The Literature of the Modern Nation* (London: Jonathan Cape/Random House, 1995), and (Cambridge, Mass.: Harvard University Press, 1996); O'Casey's memoirs and their film adaptation, *Young Cassidy,* are discussed in Stephen Watts, "O'Casey in a Movie 'Mirror,'" *NYT,* September 27, 1964. O'Casey's name changes are explained in O'Connor, *Sean O'Casey: A Life.* O'Casey's reluctance to allow another film of his work following *The Plough and the Stars* is reported in Seamus Kelly, "The Ford of the O'Feeneys?" *Irish Times,* July 10, 1964. The news that JF would direct *Young Cassidy* was reported on September 3, 1963, in "Ford Will Film Life of O'Casey," *NYT,* and "MGM to Biopic Sean O'Casey; Ford Directs," *DV.* The filming dates are from the Shooting Schedule, June 9, 1964; Robert Emmett Ginna Jr. to JF, June 19, 1964; "*Young Cassidy* Rolling," *HR,* July 15, 1964; and DF. JF's public praise of John Whiting's screenplay is from Bogdanovich, "The Autumn of John Ford," and JF's doubt that the script would make a good film is expressed in the JF/KH OH. The contract between Sextant and JFP for *Young Cassidy,* January 27, 1964 ("During the principal"), and JF's July 29, 1964, agreement with Sextant are at Lilly.

Sean Connery's casting in the title role is reported in Robert D. Graff to JF, December 30, 1963; a telegram from Ginna and Graff to JF, January 21, 1964; and the Sextant-JFP contract. JF's location scouting trip to Ireland is reported in DF and in Graff and Ginna to JF, May 27, 1964. DF discusses JF's disputes with Ginna and Graff; JF's disagreements with those producers are discussed in 1964 correspondence: Killanin to JF, February 28 and May 26; Graff and Ginna to JF, May 27; and JF to Ginna and Graff, June 5 and 11; and in Ginna, "No Blarney in Filming O'Casey's Work," *LAT* [1964]. The account of JF's July 9, 1964, press conference at Dublin's Shelbourne Hotel is from Kelly, "The Ford of the O'Feeneys?" Coverage of JF's departure from the film (1964) includes an item in the *Irish Times*, August 4; "John Ford Ill, Coming Home from Ireland," *HCN*, August 4; "Ailing Ford Quits Film," *LAT*, August 6; and "Cardiff at *Cassidy* Helm Replaces John Ford," *Film Daily*, August 10. JF's weight loss is noted in his May 2, 1965, letter to Killanin, quoted in Davis, which also reports Killanin's discovery of JF's Scotch bottles. JF's direction of an erotic scene with Christie and Rod Taylor is discussed in Sinclair, citing an unpublished manuscript by Ginna, "Intimations of John Ford." The JF footage remaining in the film is discussed in "Critics' Guessing Game," *Variety*, March 24, 1965, and Jack Cardiff, *Magic Hour* (London: Faber and Faber, 1996).

The story "Chinese Finale" appears in Norah Lofts, *I Met a Gypsy* (London: 1935, and New York: Knopf, 1936); the half-hour TV adaptation *Chinese Finale* was shown on NBC's *Alcoa Theatre*, March 7, 1960. JF's conflicting statements on directing women are from Philip K. Scheuer, "*Women* Keeps Ford Wary," *LAT*, March 24, 1965 ("I want to do a story about women"); and his interview with the author ("I've directed women before"). Information on the Ford-Smith deal on *7 Women* is from Saul N. Rittenberg of MGM, Bernard Smith Prods., and JFP, deal memorandum for *Chinese Finale* (working title), July 15, 1964; the negative cost and gross rentals are from the producer's participation statement from MGM for the period ended August 31, 1970. JF's arrival at the studio is reported in "Ford to MGM Offices," *HR*, November 2, 1964. Title suggestions are discussed in Bernard Smith, "New Titles for *Chinese Finale*," to JF, January 21, 1965. *Chinese Finale* scripts by Janet Green and John McCormick are dated October 7 and November 30, 1964 (the latter including the line "So long, you grinning ape!"); see also "Changes," April 5, 1965. Steven Spielberg recalls his encounter with JF in Randall Lane, "'I Want Gross,'" *Forbes*, September 26, 1994; Spielberg's account of JF's advice about how to frame the horizon is from an interview conducted by executive producer Richard Schickel for the 1998 American Film Institute/TNT series *100 Years . . . 100 Movies*.

Casting and script issues for *7 Women* are discussed in Bernard Smith's letters to JF, August 26 October 12, 1964; David O. Selznick campaigns for Jennifer Jones to play Dr. Cartwright in letters to JF, March–October 1964. KH's reasons for turning down a role and JF's dismay are discussed in the JF/KH OH, in which JF mistakenly remembers offering her the role of Dr. Cartwright and seems to confuse Anne Bancroft with Margaret Leighton; that KH was offered the role of Agatha Andrews is clear from KH's comments in the JF/KH OH and from Bernard Smith's September 29, 1964, letter to JF. Coverage of JF's "70th" birthday celebration (1965) includes Scheuer, "At 70, John Ford Still Makes History," *LAT*, February 1; "John Ford's 70th Feted," *HR*, February 1; and Bob Thomas, AP interview, February. An unidentified friend's report that JF "decided to remind them of his versatility" and JF's comment about having "little room for cake and sentiment" are from Peter Bart, "Ford's Ladies' Vehicle," *NYT*, January 31, 1965. Romain Gary's comment on JF aging is from Tavernier.

Production information is from the author's interviews with JF, Eddie Albert, Jane Chang, and Anna Lee; *John Ford's Magic Stage* (1965), an MGM featurette on the making of *7 Women* (included on the 1992 MGM/UA Home Video laserdisc edition of the film); Wingate Smith's OH (recalling JF showing early signs of cancer during the filming); MGM's press kit, including Production Notes (AMPAS); "Schedule: Budget"; "Final Production Budget," January 20, 1965; "Shooting Schedule"; "Daily Progress Reports," February 8–April 7, 1965; "Weekly

Production Cost," July 31, 1965; press coverage (1964): "Ford and Smith Set MGM Deal on *Chinese Finale,*" *HR,* March 16; "Bernard Smith Checks In," *HR,* May 18; "Traveling Man," *NYT,* July 12; "Smith Meeting with Waltman on *Chinese,*" *HR,* August 11; "Smith Preps *Finale,*" *DV,* October 21; "Smith Has 2 for MGM," *Film Daily,* November 2; and (1965): "*7 Women* To Shoot in Sutton Canyon," *DV,* March 26.

Patricia Neal recalls her working relationship with JF and being taken ill during the production of *7 Women* in her autobiography, *As I Am,* with Richard DeNeut (New York: Simon and Schuster, 1988). Other sources on Neal's illness and her replacement by Bancroft include Barry Farrell, *Pat and Roald* (New York: Random House, 1969); "*7 Women* Star Anne Bancroft Stage and Screen's Most Honored Actress" and "7 Women Who Were Glad to Be Ordered Around by John Ford," MGM publicity material, 1966; and 1965 press coverage: "Patricia Neal 'Very Critical,'" *DV,* February 19; "Bancroft Subs Neal in *Seven,*" *DV,* February 22; and "Just 2 Days to Refilm on *Seven*—Ford," *DV,* February 24. Neal's deal for the film is reported in Bernard Smith to Saul Rittenberg, MGM, November 9, 1964. Information on her payment is from the *7 Women* payroll ledger, December 31, 1965; the Final Production Budget; and Roald Dahl to JF, March 18, 1965; Bancroft's salary is also listed in the payroll ledger. Bancroft's recollection of JF calling her "Duke" and her comment on Dr. Cartwright are from David Ehrenstein, "Embracing Complexity," *LAT,* May 5, 2000. Bancroft's observation about JF being "infinitely patient" and the comments on JF by Sue Lyon and Flora Robson are from "7 Women Who Were Glad to Be Ordered Around by John Ford." Information on the Pasadena preview, July 16, 1965, is from "1st Preview—1st Report," MGM preview cards (total of 351) (Lilly).

Sources of JF comments on *7 Women* include his interview with the author; PB ("I think that's a rather naive question"); Scheuer, "*Women* Keeps Ford Wary" ("a lot of fun making the film"); Claudine Tavernier, "La 4ème Dimension de la Vieillesse," *Cinema 69,* June 1969 ("They are all Communists"); "John Ford" (interview), *Focus!* October 1969 ("I tried to keep the film"); and JF's letter to Mrs. Prescott, n.d. (AMPAS). Bogdanovich's question "Are you Catholic?" and JF's response are recalled in Krohn, "Le Renoir américain: Entretien avec Peter Bogdanovich," in Rollet and Saada, *John Ford.* JF's investiture as a Knight of Malta is reported in Levy and in Cail, "John Ford, Maine Native, Is Honored by Pope Paul." JF's comment "I hate preaching" is from Tavernier.

MGM's release of *7 Women* on double features is reported in (1966): Clyde Leech, "*Women* Dramatic," *LAHE,* January 6; "Two Metro Pix in Gumshoe Playoff," *Variety,* May 11; and Sarris's review in the *Village Voice,* May 26, reprinted in *The John Ford Movie Mystery;* Sarris's comment about "The last champions" is from *The American Cinema.* Richard Thompson's essay "John Ford's 7 Women," is from *Focus!* May 1967, and is reprinted as "*7 Women*" in JM, ed., *Persistence of Vision: A Collection of Film Criticism* (Madison: Wisconsin Film Society Press, 1968). Wood comments on the film in "Shall We Gather at the River?: The Late Films of John Ford." Other reviews include *Whit.* [Whitney Williams], *DV,* December 6, 1965; James Powers, *HR,* December 6, 1965; Arthur Knight, "Swinging on Some Stars," *Saturday Review,* January 8, 1966; and "Wild Eastern," *Time,* May 13, 1966; Richard Combs discusses the film in "At Play in the Fields of John Ford," *Sight and Sound,* Spring 1982. The comments on *7 Women* by Samuel Fuller and JW are from interviews with the author.

JF's illness in the summer of 1965 is discussed in DF and in Yeager to Bea Benjamin, August 15, 1965. JF's disdain for "these easy, liberal movies" is from Noel Berggren, "Arsenic and Old Directors," *Esquire,* April 1972. Burt Kennedy's comment on how Hollywood "dumped" JF is from Davis. JF's 1970 explanation of why he was not working is from his interview with the author. Sources on JF's project *The Miracle of Merriford* include PB; Al Truscony to JF, May 18, 1965; Russell Birdwell to JF, August 3, 1965; Edith Tolkin to Mr. Morton, August 27, 1965; JF to Walter Wanger, June 1966; JF to Hugo [only name listed], [June 15, 1966]; "John Ford to

Film *Miracle* at MGM," *HR,* June 17, 1965; and "John Ford's Future," *Variety,* June 23, 1965. Sources on JF's project about Donovan and OSS include the author's interviews with JF and Anna Lee; PB; Doering to JF, February 15 and May 27, 1965, and January 20, 1970; JF to Doering, May 5, 1970; and Kennedy, "A Talk with John Ford" (in which JF claims he promised the dying Donovan he would make the film). Mahin spoke to the author about JF's Midway project. Bulkeley told the author about JF's interest in making *Tora! Tora! Tora!;* the film's production is described in Suid, and Vincent Canby's *NYT* review is dated September 24, 1970.

JF's 1966 visit to Paris is covered in Tavernier, including quotes from interviews given by JF to various members of the press. Tavernier also reports on the proposed film of "Boule de Suif," which is discussed in Pierre Rissient to JF, October 20, 1967; JF's 1968 visit to Paris to help sell the project is noted in Benjamin to Yeager, January 18, 1968. JF's orders for 1967 temporary active naval service are from the commandant, Eleventh Naval District, January 30, 1967; Bulkeley told the author about JF's 1967 visit to his ship, which was noted in Bulkeley to JF, February 24; Archerd's column, *DV,* February 8; and an item in *Time,* February 17. JF's attendance at *Coco* is discussed in KH to JF, June 1970, and JF to KH [c. June 1970]. André S. Labarthe's JF interview, "Entre chien et loup: John Ford" ("In the Twilight: John Ford"), was filmed at JF's home in Bel Air, August 31, 1965, and was aired June 16, 1966, on *Cinéastes de notre temps,* ORTF. Philip Jenkinson's interview for BBC TV's *My Name Is John Ford: I Make Westerns,* broadcast in August 1968, was filmed at JF's home that June. Information on the painting of JF by R. B. Kitaj, *John Ford on His Deathbed* (completed 1983) is from the author's interview with Lem Dobbs. Waverly Ramsey told the author about JF's dachshunds.

JF's net worth in 1965 is listed in DF. Documentation (1967) on tax levies against JF, MF, and JFP includes IRS notice of levy on JFP to United California Bank, Hollywood, assessed April 21 (paid July 31); IRS notice of levy on JF and MF to United California Bank, April 21 (paid July 31); California Franchise Tax Board to JFP, June 8; Benjamin, JFP, to Franchise Tax Board, July 10; IRS to JFP, December 7; and IRS to JF and MF, December 7. JFP's operating losses in the late 1960s are reported in the company's IRS return, 1970 (containing information from 1964–70). JF's 1966 income is listed in the JF–MF IRS return, 1966. JF told Pat Ford in his [April ?] 1963 letter that much of his assets were tied up in stock held by the bank for loans to pay income taxes. The sale of the *Araner* to JFP is documented in U.S. Treasury Department, Bureau of Customs, "Bill of Sale of Enrolled or Licensed Yacht" by JF to JFP, December 20, 1960; the 1969–70 sale of the *Araner* is documented in "Ketch *Araner*" (advertisement), *Variety,* May 20, 1970; Richard S. Harris to Mr. Babcock, trust officer, California Canadian Bank, San Francisco [1970]; DF; and Sinclair. Sources on the disposition of the Field Photo Farm (1969) include DF; tax return of organization exempt from income tax, Field Photo Homes; corporation grant deed, Field Photo Homes Inc., to Motion Picture and Television Relief Fund, March 17; and "Dedicate John Ford Chapel at Country House," *DV,* October 20.

Sources on *Directed by John Ford* include the author's interviews with Peter Bogdanovich and Eric Sherman; "John Ford To Be Film Topic," *LAT,* July 15, 1968; Syd Cassyd, "AFI, Art Groups To Do Ford Documentary," *Boxoffice,* July 22, 1968; and Richard Patterson, "Making a Compilation Documentary," *American Cinematographer,* June 1972. The author was present when the commentary was recorded by Orson Welles at a Howard Johnson's motel in Hollywood in 1971. The comments on Bogdanovich by JF and Olive Carey are from their interviews with the author. JF's purchase of two hundred copies of PB was reported to the author in 1970 by Bogdanovich and Milton Luboviski of Larry Edmunds Bookstore, Hollywood. JF's award from the Venice Film Festival is reported in Thomas Quinn Curtiss, "John Ford Honored as Venice Film Fete Closes," *NYT,* September 7, 1971. Camilla Snyder reports on the Los Angeles premiere of *Directed by John Ford* in "Tribute to Director John Ford," *LAHE,* November 26, 1971. Sources on the making of *The American West of John Ford* include (1971): "John Ford at Wayne Camp," *Variety,* May 12; Wayne Warga, "Documentary About Master Film-Maker,"

It Was Made," *Action!* September–October; and Zolotow, "*The American West of John Ford Comes to Television with the Help of an Old Friend,*" *TV Guide,* December 4.

JF's plan to visit the Texas location of *The Last Picture Show* is mentioned in Bogdanovich to JF, October 23, 1970. Sources on Bill Ramsey's death (1970) include the author's interview with Waverly Ramsey; JF to KH, October 2, quoted in Davis; and KH to JF, October 8. JF's description of his fractured pelvis as the "most stupid accident" is from "Hollywood Sound Track," *Variety,* October 21, 1970; medical information on the injury is from Cameron B. Hall, M.D., To Whom It May Concern, November 18, 1970; Rose Lew (JF's secretary) to Juris Ubans, October 30, 1970; and Medicare hospital insurance benefits record, January 26, 1971, St. John's Hospital, Santa Monica, California.

Information on JF's project *Appointment with Precedence* is from A. H. Weiler, "John Ford Rides Again," *NYT,* April 23, 1972; and "John Ford's Return," *Variety,* April 29, 1972; Wingate Smith's admission that he humored JF by preparing a budget for the film is from Smith's OH; Smith's activities in his final years and his fatal illness are described in his *DV* obituary, July 22, 1974. Sources on JF's Italian Western project with Woody Strode include 1970 correspondence: JF's telegram to Strode, June 12; JF to Strode, June 17; JF to Roger Beaumont, August 19; and JF to Carroll Baker, September 11; the author was in JF's office on August 19 while JF was waiting for a phone call from Italy about the project. JF's project *The Grave Diggers* is described in "Black West Pointer as John Ford Pic; Deal Pends with Lee Winkler," *Variety,* March 29, 1972. HCJ told the author JF "wanted to work so bad." JF's explanation of why he couldn't come to the phone when a studio chief called is from the author's interview with Mark Haggard.

Sources on JF's project *April Morning* include the author's interviews with JF, Samuel Goldwyn Jr., and Zelma (Mrs. Michael) Wilson; JF to Goldwyn, April 26, 1966; JF to Hugo [1966]; JF to Killanin, June 15, 1970; and JM, "Last John Ford Pic, Tribute to Gen. Puller, Looks for Buyer." Maxwell Anderson's *Valley Forge* (1934) was published in his collection *Eleven Verse Plays, 1929–1939* (New York: Harcourt, Brace and World, 1939). Sources on the plans by JF and Capra to film *Valley Forge* include the author's interview with Capra; JM, *Frank Capra*; 1971 correspondence: Frank McCarthy to JF, March 30; Martin Rackin to JF, June 29, enclosing Rackin's "Proposal for the John Ford–Frank Capra Production of *VALLEY FORGE* by Pulitzer Prize–winning playwright Maxwell Anderson"; and Rackin to JF, October 12; and Vernon Scott, UPI dispatch, November 19, 1971. Francis Ford's film on George Washington/Valley Forge was *Washington at Valley Forge* (1914), with FF as "The Spy"; see the *Universal Weekly,* March 28, 1914. JF's disgust over Rackin's *Stagecoach* remake is reported in Tavernier.

JF's support for Governor Ronald Reagan is expressed in his [January?] 1967 telegram to Reagan; information on JF's service as vice chairman of the "Dinner with Governor Reagan" (April 9, 1970) include Lieutenant Governor Ed Reinecke to JF [April? 1970], and Reagan to JF, May 29, 1970. In the JF/KH OH, JF admits voting for Barry Goldwater and Richard Nixon for president. JF's self-description as a "liberal Democrat" and his claim that he did not vote in the 1964 presidential election are from Tavernier. JF's comment about antiwar protests and his explanation for black unrest are from Jenkinson; JF's observation on the Watts riots was reported to the author by Bogdanovich.

Sources on the United States Information Agency documentary *Vietnam! Vietnam!* include the author's interviews with JF and Sherman Beck, parts quoted in an article on the film by JM, "Drums Along the Mekong," *Sight and Sound,* Autumn 1972; Beck, "*Inside South Vietnam: Treatment of a Thirty-Minute Motion Picture for the United States Information Agency,*" April 29, 1968 (Lilly); Tad Szulc, "$250,000 U.S.I.A. Movie on Vietnam, 3 Years in the Making, Being Shelved," *NYT,* June 10, 1971; "John Ford Vietnam Footage Looks Dead," *Variety,* June 16, 1971; and the USIA transcript of *Vietnam! Vietnam!* (1971). JF expresses bewilderment over the Vietnam War in his letter to Alna[h] Johnston, May 21, 1969, quoted in Eyman, *Print the Legend.* Campbell discusses JF's attitudes toward the Cheyenne and the Vietnamese in his *the Legend*. Campbell discusses JF's attitudes toward the Cheyenne and the Vietnamese in his 1971 essay "*Fort Apache*." JF's comment on the soldiers following Colonel Thursday in *Fort Apache* is from PB.

JF's consultation on a Vietnam project for the People-to-People series (1958) is noted in Broger to Stump. JF's comment that the navy wanted him for a tour of duty is from his letter to Killanin, May 2, 1966, quoted in Sinclair. Bruce Herschensohn, director, USIA Motion Picture and Television Service, offers JF the job of executive producer on the USIA's Vietnam War documentary (later titled *Vietnam! Vietnam!*) in a letter of September 3, 1968. Information on the USN's refusal of JF's request for uniformed service in Vietnam (1968) is from Vice Admiral Charles K. Duncan, chief of Naval Personnel, to JF, December 4; and JF to Duncan, December 11. Sources on JF's trips to Vietnam include the author's interview with Beck; 1968 correspondence: Duncan to JF, December 4; Herschensohn to MF, December 6; and JF to Duncan, December 11; and JF's 1969 letter to Johnston. JF's comment on his grandsons, Dan and Tim, serving in Vietnam is from a letter to Killanin, n.d., quoted in Sinclair. JF recalled decorating his grandson Dan Ford in his interview with the author and his letter to Mr. Altshuler, Custom House, Terminal Island, California, January 22, 1969 (in which JF states he decorated Dan at field headquarters); Dan Ford's contradictory report is from Eyman, *Print the Legend*. Information on Tom Duggan and his work on *Vietnam! Vietnam!* and *Chesty* are from the author's interview with Beck; JF to George Putnam, June 3, 1969; and "Tom Duggan, 53, Dies of Injuries from Auto Crash," *LAT*, May 30, 1969. The clearance of *Vietnam! Vietnam!* for U.S. screenings is noted in the National Archives Internet database.

Contracts for *Chesty: A Tribute to a Legend* include an agreement between Dyna-Plex and James Ellsworth (with information on *Door to Door Maniac*); and an agreement between [Lieutenant General] Lewis B. Puller [USMC (Ret.)] and Ellsworth, December 16, 1969. Ellsworth's statement of the cost of *Chesty* is reported in JM, "Last John Ford Pic, Tribute to Gen. Puller, Looks for Buyer." Biographical information on Chesty Puller; his grandfather, Major John W. Puller; and Chesty's son, Lewis B. Puller Jr., is from Burke Davis, *Marine!*; Lewis B. Puller Jr., *Fortunate Son: The Autobiography of Lewis B. Puller, Jr.* (New York: Grove Weidenfeld, 1991), and his May 24, 1992, interview with Brian Lamb on C-SPAN's *Booknotes;* the documentary *Chesty Puller: The Marine's Marine;* "Gen. Chesty Puller Dies; Most Decorated Marine," *NYT,* October 13, 1971 (obituary); and "Area's 'Fortunate Son' Dies," the *Rappahannock* (Virginia) *Record,* May 19, 1994 (obituary of Lewis B. Puller Jr.). Information on Allan Dwan and the *Marine!* film project is from Bogdanovich, *Allan Dwan: The Last Pioneer.*

Sources on the filming and postproduction of *Chesty* include the author's interviews with JF, Ellsworth, Townsend, Richard S. Harris, and Marquard; "John Ford Winds Marine Corps Spec," *HR,* January 27, 1969; "John Ford to Direct Chesty Puller Vidshow," *DV,* April 22, 1970; Haggard, "Ford in Person"; and JM, "Last John Ford Pic, Tribute to Gen. Puller, Looks for Buyer." Chesty Puller's wish "to see once again the face of every Marine I ever served with" is quoted by JW in *Chesty: A Tribute to a Legend*. Sources on the eye-patch gag on the set of *Rio Lobo* include the author's interview with Hawks; McCarthy, *Howard Hawks: The Grey Fox of Hollywood*; and James Bacon, "When Ford Directs, He's the Star," *LAHE,* November 25, 1971 (with JF's comment on JW). The Bertolt Brecht quotation is from his play *Leben des Galilei* (*Galileo*) (1939). The 1976 review of *Chesty* by the author (whose *Variety* moniker then was Mack.) appears in two versions: "Sentimental Romanticism the Dominant Tone of John Ford's *Chesty,* Preemed at Filmex," *DV,* April 6; and "Anti-Climax: John Ford Booed," *Variety,* April 7 (condensed version).

The author wrote JF on July 2, 1970, requesting an interview; their first conversation was on August 4, 1970 (author's telephone notes). Parts of the author's tape-recorded interview with JF (August 19, 1970, Beverly Hills, California) appear in JM, "County Mayo Gu [*sic*] Bragh . . . ," *Sight and Sound,* Winter 1970/71, and in M&W. The author discusses his family history in JM, "In Pursuit of My Ancestral Heritage: From *The Seven Little Foys* to *Patriot Games*," *Irish America*, October–November 2000. The book dedicated by the author to JF is *Persistence of Vision: A Collection of Film Criticism*. Information on the Fords' golden anniversary celebration (1970) is from the author's interview with JF; Archerd's column, *DV*, June 25; an item and photograph in *Time*, July 20; and Carroll Baker to JF, July 22 (on the message from Pope Paul VI). JF and Henry Fonda discuss the author in *The American West of John Ford*. JF's letter to the author describing himself as "too old and tired" for a biography was written in November 1971 on JM to Rose Lew, November 24, 1971. Peter Handke's novel with JF as a character is *Der kurze Brief zum langen Abschied* (Frankfurt-am-Main: Suhrkamp Verlag, 1972), trans. by Ralph Manheim as *Short Letter, Long Farewell* (New York: Farrar, Straus and Giroux, 1974). Pierre Auguste Renoir's comment on "genius" is from Jean Renoir, trans. by Randolph and Dorothy Weaver, *Renoir, My Father* (Boston: Little, Brown, 1962).

Press coverage of the American Film Institute tribute to JF (Beverly Hills, California, March 31, 1973) includes: A. D. Murphy, "John Ford First AFI Lifetime Achievement Award Recipient," *DV*, February 28; "Medal of Freedom for John Ford," *DV*, March 2; "Nixon at Ford Fete," *DV*, March 5; Thomas M. Pryor, "John Ford Coming to Dinner," *DV*, March 26; Bacon, "Nixon Joins Stars at John Ford Fete," *LAHE*, April 2; Murphy, "Nixon Honors Films as 'Great Profession' in Awarding Ford, Vet Director, Freedom Medal," *DV*, April 2; Ron Pennington, "President Nixon, Industry Pay Homage to Director John Ford," *HR*, April 2; "Ailing Director Gets Nixon Kudos," AP, April 2; Bacon, "Great Night for John Ford and the Irish," *LAHE*, April 3; Snyder, "Ford: The Man and the Party," *LAHE*, April 3; "AFI Film Too Long for TV; Bogdanovich Protests Deletions," *DV*, April 3; "Bogdanovich Rips AFI Cuts on Telecast of Ford Fete," *HR*, April 3; and Archerd's column, *DV*, April 3. Information on the Stock Company gathering at the Beverly Hilton Hotel is from the author's interview with Olive Carey. Bogdanovich comments on the tribute in his article "Taps for Mr. Ford," *New York*, October 29, 1973, reprinted as "Taps" in the 1978 edition of PB. Sidney Lumet's comment on JF is from an unpublished article by JM and Michael Wilmington, "The Return of John Ford," July 1971.

The description of JF as "the most important director since the late D. W. Griffith" is from AFI director George Stevens Jr.'s award presentation on the televised version of the dinner, The *American Film Institute's Salute to John Ford* (CBS-TV, April 2, 1973). President Richard M. Nixon's remarks and JF's speeches at the dinner are from *The American Film Institute's Salute to John Ford*; JF's reading copy of the speech thanking Nixon [March 1973] is at Lilly. JF's citation for the Medal of Freedom is quoted in Sinclair; it was read by Nixon (with variations) on *The American Film Institute's Salute to John Ford*. Biographical information on Captain Jeremiah Andrew Denton Jr., USN, is from "Biographical Directory of the United States Congress,1774– Present," *bioguide.congress.gov*. Footage of Denton's homecoming and speech appears in the 1998 documentary film *Return with Honor* by Freida Lee Mock and Terry Sanders; see also February 13, 1973, press coverage: James P. Sterba, "First Prisoner Release Completed," *NYT*, and "POWs Sampling the Sweet Taste of New Freedom," *LAT*. H. R. Haldeman's comment on the AFI dinner is from his entry for March 31, 1973, in *The Haldeman Diaries: Inside the Nixon White House* (New York: G. P. Putnam's Sons, 1994).

Nixon's comment that "John Ford is one of my heroes" is from a letter to JM, January 5, 1988; Nixon's manuscript on JF, "Reflections on John Ford," is dated January 6, 1988. Nixon also recalls the AFI tribute in *RN: The Memoirs of Richard Nixon* (New York: Grosset and Dunlap, 1978). Bulkeley's comments on JF's relationship with Nixon are from his interview with the author. JF's desire to become a Nixon aide is discussed by navy secretary John H. Chafee in a letter to U.S. senator George Murphy, March 6, 1969; information on JF's pursuit of promotion to full admiral is from Admiral B. A. Clancy, vice chairman of Naval Operations, to Admiral John M. Will, USN (Ret.), September 5, 1969. The USN's presentation of its Distinguished Public Service Award to JF (1973) is reported by *DV* in "John Ford Navy Award

Recipient," April 26, and Army Archerd's column, May 1. JF thanks Nixon for his admiral's hat in a letter of May 4, 1973. Herschensohn's June 18, 1973, memo to Nixon about his conversation with JF is from the Nixon White House Central Files (staff member and office files) at the National Archives II in College Park, Maryland, quoted in Nicholas J. Cull, "Richard Nixon and the Political Appropriation of *Friendly Persuasion* (1956)," *Historical Journal of Film, Radio and Television,* June 1999. Nixon's July 1973 call to JF was reported to the author by Josephine Feeney and Cecil McLean de Prida, and is quoted in JM, "Bringing in the Sheaves," *Sight and Sound,* Winter 1973–74, reprinted in M&W; information on Nixon's hospitalization is from Stephen E. Ambrose, *Nixon: Ruin and Recovery, 1973–1990* (New York: Simon and Schuster, 1991); and Jonathan Aitken, *Nixon: A Life* (London: Weidenfeld and Nicolson, and Washington, D.C.: Regnery, 1993). Nixon's comment "I have always felt" is from his letter to Rear Admiral John Ford, USN (Ret.), August 16, 1973 (referring to a JF letter not in Lilly). The reference to Walt Whitman is a paraphrase of his poem "Song of Myself"; the observation about rhetoric and poetry is from William Butler Yeats, *Mythologies,* quoted in Kiberd.

JF's final days and death are reported in JM, "Bringing in the Sheaves." Information on JF's exploratory surgery in October 1971 is from Davis and from Wingate Smith's OH. Information on colorectal cancer is from Dr. Patrick E. McBride to JM, September 1999; and David E. Larson, M.D., editor in chief, *Mayo Clinic Family Health Book* (New York: William Morrow, second edition, 1996). The Certificate of Death for John Aloysius Ford aka Feeney, August 31, 1973, was filed September 5, 1973, in the Department of Health, Bureau of Vital Statistics Registrar, County of Riverside, California. JW's cancer is discussed in Wayne and Thorleifson; and R&O. JF's failure to have a timely colorectal cancer screening examination was noted in the author's interview with Bulkeley. Information on the Fords' purchase of a grave plot is in a bill from Cunningham & O'Connor Mortuary to Patrick Ford [1974].

Olive Carey's recollections of JF's "miserable" final months are from her interview with the author. MF's explanation of why she and JF moved to Palm Desert is from Slide and Banker. Sources on JF's visitors at Palm Desert include the author's interviews with Anna Lee, HCJ, and Hawks; Sinclair; DF; Davis; Parrish, *Growing Up in Hollywood* (with a description of JF's cigar bucket and personal totems); Davis; and Archerd's column, *DV,* February 8, 1973. Information on Dan Ford's research for *Pappy* is from DF and the JF/KH OH. JF's statement about taking life "as it came along" is from the JF/KH OH, quoted in Davis, as are KH's remark to JF about "your true self" and her comment about work being the "easiest thing" in the lives of JF and Spencer Tracy. Sources on JF's Memorial Day 1973 visit to the Motion Picture Country House and Hospital in Woodland Hills, California, include the author's interviews with Alex Ameripoor, Lee, and HCJ; Archerd's column, *DV,* May 31, 1973; JM, "Bringing in the Sheaves"; and Gallagher (quoting JF's comment to Frank Baker).

KH's comment that JF faced death "like a gentleman" is quoted in Sinclair from Ginna, "Intimations of John Ford." JF's drinking of Guinness stout on his deathbed is reported in R&O. Bulkeley told the author about JF's increasing devoutness and the fact that they did not discuss his fatal illness. JF's refusal of painkillers until less than two weeks before his death is reported in Bogdanovich, "Taps for Mr. Ford." Sources of comments by people who talked to JF as he was dying include the author's interviews with Olive Carey, HCJ, Lee, and Hawks in JM, *Hawks on Hawks*; and Bogdanovich, "Taps for Mr. Ford." JF's description of Henry Fonda as a "[N]ice man" is from Anderson, as is Barbara Ford's statement "It's only a matter of time." KH's cheery telephone calls are mentioned in her letters to JF, June 24, 1973, and [August 13?, 1973]. JF's exchange with JW during their last visit ("Do you miss Ward?") is from Stewart Slavin, "John Ford: 'A Warm, Kind Human,'" *LAHE,* September 3, 1973; their drinking of brandy and discussion about the Young Men's Purity, Total Abstinence, and Yachting Association are reported in R&O.

Sources on people present at JF's death on August 31, 1973, at Palm Desert, California, include the author's interviews with Josephine Feeney and Woody Strode ("He died in my arms"); JM, "Bringing in the Sheaves"; Strode and Young; and Irene Maroni to Miss [Lucille J.] Boston, January 31, 1974. Variant versions of JF's last words are given in JM, "Bringing in the Sheaves" ("Holy Mary, mother of God . . ." and "Now will somebody give me a cigar"); Bogdanovich's version of the cigar line ("Would someone please get me a cigar") is from "Taps for Mr. Ford." Pat Ford's report of JF's last word as "Cut!" is from the author's interview with HCJ.

The W. H. Auden quotation is from his poem "In Memory of W. B. Yeats," 1940, from *The Collected Poetry of W. H. Auden* (New York: Random House, 1945). Obituaries of JF (1973) include AP dispatch, August 31, 1973, quoted in M&W; Robert Rawitch, "Director John Ford, Winner of Six [*sic*] Academy Awards, Dies," *LAT,* September 1; "John Ford, Winner of 5 [*sic*] Oscars for Film Direction, Is Dead at 78 [*sic*]," *NYT,* September 2; Roger Greenspun, "John Ford: 1895–1973 [*sic*]," *NYT,* September 9; Stuart Byron, "John Ford 1895–1973 [*sic*]," *The Real Paper* (Boston), September 12; and "Old Master," *Time,* September 17. In fact, JF's true year of birth was 1894, his age when he died was 79, and he won four Oscars as best director.

Information on JF's funeral on September 5, 1973, at Blessed Sacrament Church, Hollywood, and his burial service that day at Holy Cross Cemetery, Culver City, is from JM, "Bringing in the Sheaves," including the comments by JW ("It's rough to put a fellow away"), Strode ("He should be buried in Monument Valley"), and Ameripoor ("A bit of Fordian comedy"). Other reports on the funeral (1973) include Archerd's column, *DV,* September 5; "Director John Ford Eulogized as an 'Incomparable Master,'" *LAT,* September 6; and "Ford Rites Draw Famous and Obscure," *LAHE,* September 6. JF is buried in Section M (Precious Blood), Lot 304, Grave 5, Holy Cross Cemetery and Mausoleum. The author saw the Midway flag on JF's coffin in 1973 and discussed it with his sister Josephine Feeney at the Cunningham & O'Connor Mortuary, West Hollywood; see also M&W. The author also saw JF's grave after it was emptied pending MF's burial in 1979.

JF's posthumous message "I consider myself very fortunate" is from *Cowboy Kings of Western Fame: John Ford's Series of Famous Western Stars,* portraits by Will Williams (Hollywood: Western Series, Inc., 1973). Information on that project includes a proposed agreement between Williams and JF, August 10, 1973; the contract between MF and Williams, February 10, 1974; press release, "The Great Director's Final Project" (1973); and Whitney Williams, *DV* review, November 26, 1973. Information on MF's will is from "Last Will and Testament," Mary McBryde Feeney, September 30, 1973, and another copy on the same date with handwritten revisions (both in Lilly). MF's lawsuit against the executors of JF's estate is reported in "Ford Widow Sues Executors of Estate," *HR,* September 30, 1976; and in Davis.

FILMOGRAPHY

Films and television programs involving John Ford are listed in order of release; films are feature length and in black and white unless otherwise indicated (some Ford films photographed in black and white were released with tinted sequences). Length is listed for short silent films (in reels) and World War II documentaries (in minutes, where available). For films made by Argosy Pictures, Ford and his partner Merian C. Cooper were the producers; Ford also served as a producer on some of his later films through his production company John Ford Productions, and some of his earlier films carried the credit "A John Ford Production." Films made by Ford-Smith Productions were produced by Ford's partner Bernard Smith.

Code for abbreviations: AFI (American Film Institute); b&w (black and white); D (Director); FF (Francis Ford); JF (Jack Ford, 1914–23; John Ford, 1923ff.); Fox (William Fox Studios, until 1935); JFP (John Ford Productions); 20th (Twentieth Century–Fox, 1935ff.); U (Universal); UA (United Artists); USIA (United States Information Agency); WB (Warner Bros.).

More complete filmographies are available in Peter Bogdanovich, *John Ford* (1967); Tag Gallagher, *John Ford: The Man and His Films* (1986); and Bill Levy, *John Ford: A Bio-Bibliography* (1999). Ford may have worked as a crewman on some silent films besides those listed here; see the text of this book for further details. This filmography includes some newly collected information.

Silent Films as Crew Member and/or Actor and Stuntman

1914
Lucille Love—The Girl of Mystery (U, 15-part serial); D: FF
The Mysterious Rose (U, two reels); D: FF

1915
Smuggler's Island (U, two reels); D: FF

The Birth of a Nation (Epoch) D: D. W. Griffith; JF was actor only
Three Bad Men and a Girl (U, two reels); D: FF
The Hidden City (U, two reels); D: FF
The Doorway of Destruction (U, two reels); D: FF
The Broken Coin (U, 22-part serial); D: FF
The Campbells Are Coming (U, four reels); D: FF

1916

The Strong Arm Squad (U, one reel); D: FF
Chicken-Hearted Jim (U, one reel); D: FF
Peg o' the Ring (U, 15-part serial); D: FF
The Bandit's Wager (U, one reel); D: FF
The Purple Mask (U, 16-part serial); D: FF

Short Silent Films as Director

1917

The Tornado (U, two reels); also writer and actor
The Trail of Hate (U, two reels); also writer and actor
The Scrapper (U, two reels); also writer and actor
The Soul Herder (U, three reels)
Cheyenne's Pal (U, two reels); also story

Silent Features as Director (unless otherwise indicated)

1917

Straight Shooting (U)
The Secret Man (U)
A Marked Man (U); also story
Bucking Broadway (U)

1918

The Phantom Riders (U)
Wild Women (U)
Thieves' Gold (U)
The Scarlet Drop (U); also story
Hell Bent (U)
A Woman's Fool (U)
Three Mounted Men (U)

1919

Roped (U)
Harry Carey Tour Promotional Film (U, one-half reel)
The Fighting Brothers (U, two reels)
A Fight for Love (U)
By Indian Post (U, two reels)
The Rustlers (U, two reels)
Bare Fists (U)
Gun Law (U, two reels)
The Gun Packer (U, two reels)
Riders of Vengeance (U)
The Last Outlaw (U, two reels)
The Outcasts of Poker Flat (U)

The Ace of the Saddle (U)
The Rider of the Law (U)
A Gun Fightin' Gentleman (U)
Marked Men (U)

1920

The Prince of Avenue A (U)
The Girl in No. 29 (U)
Under Sentence (U, two reels); D: Edward Feeney [later O'Fearna]; story by JF
Hitchin' Posts (U)
Just Pals (Fox)

1921

The Big Punch (Fox)
The Freeze Out (U)
The Wallop (U)
Desperate Trails (U)
Action (U)
Sure Fire (U)
Jackie (Fox)

1922

Little Miss Smiles (Fox)
Silver Wings (Fox); D: JF (prologue only), Edwin Carewe
Nero (Fox); D: J. Gordon Edwards; JF directed some scenes
The Village Blacksmith (Fox)

1923

The Face on the Barroom Floor (Fox)
Three Jumps Ahead (Fox); also writer
Cameo Kirby (Fox); first film in which JF is credited as "John Ford"
North of Hudson Bay (Fox)
Hoodman Blind (Fox)

1924

The Iron Horse (Fox)
Hearts of Oak (Fox)

1925

Lightnin' (Fox)
Kentucky Pride (Fox)
The Fighting Heart (Fox)
Thank You (Fox)

1926

The Shamrock Handicap (Fox)
3 Bad Men (Fox)

The Blue Eagle (Fox)
What Price Glory (Fox); D: Raoul Walsh; JF
　directed some scenes

1927
Upstream (Fox)
Seventh Heaven (Fox); D: Frank Borzage; JF
　directed some scenes

Part-Sound Features as Director

1928
Mother Machree (Fox)
Four Sons (Fox)

Silent Feature as Director

1928
Hangman's House (Fox)

Short Sound Film as Director

1928
Napoleon's Barber (Fox)

Part-Sound Features as Director

1928
Riley the Cop (Fox)

1929
Strong Boy (Fox)

Sound Features as Director (unless otherwise indicated)

1929
The Black Watch (Fox); D: JF, "Staged by"
　Lumsden Hare
Salute (Fox)
Big Time (Fox); D: Kenneth Hawks; JF as
　actor only

1930
Men Without Women (Fox); D: JF, "Staged
　by" Andrew Bennison; silent and sound
　versions
Born Reckless (Fox); D: JF, "Staged by"
　Andrew Bennison
Up the River (Fox); D: JF, "Staged by"
　William Collier Sr.

1931
Seas Beneath (Fox)
The Brat (Fox)
Arrowsmith (Goldwyn/UA)

1932
Hot Pepper (Fox); D: John G. Blystone; JF was
　second-unit director
Air Mail (U)
Flesh (MGM)

1933
Pilgrimage (Fox)
Doctor Bull (Fox)

1934
The Lost Patrol (RKO)
The World Moves On (Fox)
Judge Priest (Fox)

1935
The Whole Town's Talking (Columbia)
The Informer (RKO)
Steamboat Round the Bend (20th)

1936
The Prisoner of Shark Island (20th)
The Last Outlaw (RKO); D: Christy
　Cabanne; JF has co-story credit
Mary of Scotland (RKO)
The Plough and the Stars (RKO); additional
　scenes directed by George Nicholls Jr.

1937
Wee Willie Winkie (20th)
The Hurricane (Goldwyn/UA)

1938
The Adventures of Marco Polo (Goldwyn/UA);
　D: Archie Mayo; JF directed some scenes
Four Men and a Prayer (20th)
Submarine Patrol (20th)

1939
Stagecoach (Wanger/UA)
Young Mr. Lincoln (20th)
Drums Along the Mohawk (20th) (color)

1940
The Grapes of Wrath (20th)
The Long Voyage Home (Wanger/UA)

1941

Tobacco Road (20th)
How Green Was My Valley (20th)

Films Produced (1940–45) by John Ford's Field Photographic Branch, Office of Strategic Services (OSS)

1940

California State Guard Mobilization and Induction Ceremonies

1941

Sex Hygiene (U.S. Army Signal Corps, 30 min.)
Iceland (11 min.)
Canal Report

1942

Doolittle Raid: Ships in Task Force (unedited)
Task Force at Sea: On Way to Doolittle's Tokyo Raid (unedited)
Doolittle Raid: Fliers Take Off from USS Enterprise & USS Hornet (unedited)
The Battle of Midway (Navy/Field Photo, 18 min., color; JF also appears; also an air force version and a version for war workers)
The Battle of Midway (outtakes, color)
USS Yorktown (CV-5), in Battle of Midway (color)
Torpedo Squadron 8 (8 min., color)
Pearl Harbor (Damage)
U.S.S. Kearny (aka *Damage Repair of the WWII Destroyer*) (4 min.)
North African Invasion (unedited, 302 min., color)

1943

December 7th (two versions: 82 min. and 20 min.)
At the Front in North Africa (Signal Corps/OSS, 41 min., color); JF also appears
War Department Report (46 min.)
German Manpower (22 min.)
German Air Power (20 min.)
OSS Camera Report: China, Burma, India (17 min.)
Inside Tibet (39 min., color)
Preview of Assam (9 min.)

Homenaje a Mexico (Mexico National Celebration) (10 min.)
Maneuver Report No. 1 (24 min.)
Victory in Burma

1944

Burial of Air Crash Victims (4 min.)
We Sail at Midnight (Maritime Commission, 10 min.)
Personnel Inspection of Field Photographic Branch (6 min.)
Marshal Tito's Wartime Headquarters (4 min., color)
King George Inspects USS Augusta, LST, LCI, and LCTs at Portland, England
Normandy Invasion (Navy/Coast Guard/Field Photo/Allied governments)
Manuel Quezon: In Memoriam (18 min., color); JF also appears
German Reprisals; Destruction in Greece (53 min., color)
Japanese Surrender [Burma] (9 min.)
A Report on OSS Morale Operations in Italy (10 min.)
Campbell Missile (28 min.)
Cayuga Mission (outtakes, 11 min.)

1945

Mission to Giessen (7 min.)
Evacuation of Prisoner of War (3 min.)
A Report on Airborne Rockets Prepared by the Joint Committee on New Weapons and Equipment of the Joint Chiefs of Staff (color)
That Justice Be Done (on the Nuremberg Nazi War Crimes Trials, 10 min.)
Nazi Supreme Court Trial of the Anti-Hitler Plot, Sept. 1944–Jan. 1945 (44 min.)
Nazi Concentration Camps (59-min. compilation shown at the Nuremberg Trials, largely photographed by U.S. Army Lieutenant George Stevens)
The Nazi Plan (compilation shown at the Nuremberg Trials, assembled by Stevens and Budd Schulberg)
Nuremberg (76-min. record of the Nuremberg Trials, filmed and assembled by Ray Kellogg, Pare Lorentz, and Stuart Schulberg)

Also: 1942–45 (undated films, listed in alphabetical order)

Blind Bombing (14 min.)

Body Search (19 min.)

Brazilian Material OSS Unit No. 17 (color)

Burma Butterflies (9 min.)

Burma, Kachin Guerrilla Camp (9 min., color)

Burmese Troops (9 min., color)

Chinese Commandos (10 min.)

Crete (30 min.)

The E 2-Man Fol-Boat (8 min.)

The 8-Man Fol-Boat (6 min.)

Farish Report (11 min.)

Fate Conoscenza Colnemico: Uniformi Tedesche e Distintivi (Italian sound track, 14 min., color)

Galahad Forces (20 min.)

Ground to Air Transfer (11 min.)

House Search (27 min.)

Iconography (30 min.)

Japanese Background Study Program: Natural Resources of Japan: Part 2 (22 min.)

Japanese Behavior (50 min.)

Joan and Eleanor (18 min.)

Kachin State, Burma (11 min., color)

Kachin State, Burma, During World War II, Office of Strategic Services (7 min., color)

Kachin State, Burma, Office of Strategic Services Operations (10 min., color)

Meet the Enemy (Germany) (40 min.)

Morale Operations Field Report No. 1 (46 min.)

Nassau Training Report (10 min., produced by Field Photo for the Maritime Unit)

Nylon Rubber Boat (16 min.)

Office of Strategic Services Operations, Burma (8 min., color)

OSS Activities in Burma During World War II (8 min., color)

OSS Activities in Burma During World War II (note: this is a different film from the title listed above)

OSS Basic Military Training (25 min.)

OSS Training in Middle East (10 min.)

Pridi Phanomyong Meets Office of Strategic Services Officers (2 min.)

Project Eagle (16 min.)

Project Gunn (21 min.)

P.W.E. and M.O.—Cairo (16 min.)

Rescued Flyers (4 min.)

Seabees (44 min.)

S.I. in Action (14 min.)

Suspended Runway (22 min.)

This Is Japan (12 min.)

Undercover (80 min.)

Unfinished Report (17 min.)

Using the Lambertson Unit (8 min.)

Hollywood Features and Television Programs as Director (unless otherwise indicated)

1945

They Were Expendable (MGM)

1946

My Darling Clementine (20th)

1947

The Fugitive (Argosy/RKO)

1948

Fort Apache (Argosy/RKO)

3 Godfathers (Argosy/MGM) (color)

1949

Mighty Joe Young (Argosy/RKO); D: Ernest Schoedsack; JF was one of the producers

She Wore a Yellow Ribbon (Argosy/RKO) (color)

Pinky (20th); D: Elia Kazan; JF prepared this film but was replaced as director

1950

When Willie Comes Marching Home (20th)

Wagon Master (Argosy/RKO)

Rio Grande (Argosy/RKO)

1951

The Bullfighter and the Lady (Republic); D: Budd Boetticher; JF assisted with the editing

This Is Korea! (U.S. Navy/Republic documentary) (color)

1952

What Price Glory (20th) (color)

The Quiet Man (Argosy/Republic) (color)

1953

The Sun Shines Bright (Argosy/Republic)

Mogambo (MGM) (color)

1954

Hondo (WB) (color); D: John Farrow; JF directed two shots

1955

The Long Gray Line (Columbia) (color)

The Red, White and Blue Line (U.S. Treasury Department/Columbia documentary short) (color)

Mister Roberts (WB); D: JF and Mervyn LeRoy (color)

The Bamboo Cross (Lewman Ltd./Revue; *The Jane Wyman Fireside Theatre* series for NBC–TV)

Rookie of the Year (Hal Roach Studios; *Screen Directors Playhouse* series for NBC–TV)

1956

The Searchers (C.V. Whitney Pictures/WB) (color)

1957

The Wings of Eagles (MGM) (color)

John Ford Footage Simulating Battle of Midway/Battle of Midway MN–1433 (U.S. Navy, unedited); JF also appears

The Rising of the Moon (Four Provinces Films/WB)

The Growler Story (U.S. Navy, short) (color)

1958

Gideon's Day (Gideon of Scotland Yard in U.S., 1959) (JFP/Columbia [British] Prods.) (color, but released in U.S. in b&w)

The Last Hurrah (JFP/Columbia)

1959

The Horse Soldiers (Mirisch Co./UA) (color)

Taiwan—Island of Freedom (U.S. Department of Defense; short documentary) (color)

Korea—Battleground for Liberty (U.S. Department of Defense; short documentary) (color); some scenes directed by Lieutenant Commander Eric Strutt, USN

1960

Sergeant Rutledge (JFP/WB) (color)

The Alamo (Batjac/UA) (color); D: John Wayne; JF directed some scenes

The Colter Craven Story (MCA/Revue; *Wagon Train* series for NBC–TV)

1961

Two Rode Together (Ford–Shpetner Prods./Columbia) (color)

1962

The Man Who Shot Liberty Valance (JFP/Paramount)

Flashing Spikes (Avista Prods./Revue; *Alcoa Premiere* series for ABC–TV)

The Civil War (a 22-minute segment in *How the West Was Won*) (Cinerama/MGM) (color)

1963

Donovan's Reef (JFP/Paramount) (color)

McLintock! (Batjac/UA) (color); D: Andrew V. McLaglen; JF directed some scenes

1964

Cheyenne Autumn (Ford–Smith Prods./WB) (color)

1965

Young Cassidy (MGM) (color); D: Jack Cardiff; JF directed some scenes

1966

7 Women (Ford–Smith Prods./MGM) (color)

1971

Vietnam! Vietnam! (USIA documentary) (color); D: Sherman Beck; JF was executive producer

1976 (filmed 1968–70)

Chesty: A Tribute to a Legend (James Ellsworth Prods./Dyna-Plex, Inc./Robert H. Davis; short documentary) (color and b&w); JF also appears and co-narrates

Documentaries on Ford's Life and Work

1951

The Screen Director (Association of Motion Picture Producers/AMPAS/WB); D: Richard Bare; JF appears briefly in this short documentary directing JW in *The Quite Man*

1958

"The Western" (documentary; *Wide Wide World* series for NBC-TV); JF and John Wayne are among the guests on this show about Western movies

1965

Sean O'Casey: The Spirit of Ireland (Professional Film Services) (short documentary on making of *Young Cassidy*) (color)

John Ford's Magic Stage (MGM) (short documentary on making of *7 Women*) (color and b&w)

1966

"Entre chien et loup: John Ford" ("In the Twilight: John Ford") (*Cinéastes de notre temps* series for ORTF, Paris); D: Hubert Knapp; JF interviewed

1968

My Name Is John Ford: I Make Westerns (BBC TV) (color); D: Jonathan Philips; JF interviewed

1971

Directed by John Ford (California Arts Commission/AFI documentary) (color and b&w); D: Peter Bogdanovich; JF interviewed

The American West of John Ford (Group One/Timex/CBS-TV documentary) (color and b&w); D: Denis Sanders; JF appears and directs one scene

1973

The American Film Institute's Salute to John Ford (Carson Prods./AFI for CBS-TV) (color and b&w); D: Robert Scheerer

1974

John Ford: Memorial Day 1970 (short documentary of JF's Memorial Day service at the Motion Picture Country House and Hospital) (color); D: Mark Haggard

1989

John Ford's America (American Movie Classics documentary, including Ford home movies of the filming of *My Darling Clementine,* life aboard the *Araner,* and the Field Photo Farm) (color and b&w); D: Marino Amoruso

1990

Innisfree [sic] (PacoPoch A.V.S./Virginia Films/Televisión Española (TVE)/La Sept Cinéma/P. C. Guerin/Samson Films; feature-length documentary on the making of *The Quiet Man* and the village of Cong, Ireland) (color); written and directed by Jose Luis Guerin; consultant, Lord Killanin

1992

The Making of The Quiet Man (Republic Pictures; short documentary) (color and b&w); written and hosted by Leonard Maltin

"John Ford" (two parts; *Omnibus 25* series for BBC TV, U.K.) (color and b&w); D: Andrew Eaton; written and presented by Lindsay Anderson (condensed for A&E *Biography* series, U.S., 1993)

"John Ford" (*Creative People* series, NHK Family Productions, Japan) (color and b&w)

1993

The Making of Rio Grande (Republic Pictures; short documentary) (color and b&w); written and hosted by Leonard Maltin

1998

A Turning of the Earth: John Ford, John Wayne and The Searchers (Warner Home Video documentary) (color and b&w); D: Nick Redman

2002

John Ford Goes to War (Starz/Encore documentary on JF's World War II documentaries) (color and b&w); D: Tom Thurman; co-producer, Joseph McBride

ACKNOWLEDGMENTS

I've been working on this book, intermittently, for more than half my lifetime. The people who have helped me along the way—all those loyal family members, friends, and fellow Fordians—have become my personal Stock Company, without whom this dream project could not have been realized. Foremost is Ruth O'Hara, who encouraged me to pull together my three decades of research and finally get down to writing the book.

When I began researching John Ford at the University of Wisconsin, Madison, in the late 1960s, opportunities to see his films other than on television were rare. The Wisconsin Memorial Union held a brief Ford series in the fall of 1967, but not under ideal conditions. The screenings were held in the campus Stiftskeller to the sounds of rock music and clinking beer mugs, and it was disorienting to go to a screening of *They Were Expendable* directly from being teargassed in a protest against the Dow Chemical Company for manufacturing napalm used in the Vietnam War. *She Wore a Yellow Ribbon* was shown in Professor Russell Merritt's film class, but only a black-and-white print could be obtained, and the screening was disrupted by boorish catcalls.

My friend Michael Wilmington and I took a Greyhound bus to see *The Searchers* for the first time at the Clark Theater in Chicago's Loop. We handful of Fordians on the Union Film Committee finally managed to bring a spectacular original 35mm print of the film to the campus Play Circle in May 1970, but President Nixon's invasion of Cambodia and the killings at Kent State provoked a riot in Madison that brought the National Guard to occupy the campus. Hardly anyone made it through the lines of troops to see *The Searchers*. So we brought the film back exactly a year later, and the students rioted to commemorate the earlier event, with the National Guard again taking over the campus. We began to wonder if what became known as "The Annual *Searchers* Riot" somehow was being provoked by our inflammatory act of showing the film.

A more congenial setting for showing Ford films was the Wisconsin Film Society. Because I was president, I was able to indulge my subversive tastes for *Wagon Master* and *The Sun Shines Bright* before small but appreciative audiences as long as I showed enough Fellini and Bergman films to keep us solvent. (Years later I met Ingmar Bergman when he made a brief visit to Hollywood, and he was delighted to find a fellow Ford aficionado at his press conference, telling me as he left the room, "We will talk about John Ford"; alas, we didn't get the chance.) At the Film Society I was aided and abetted by Wilmington, Wayne Merry, Mark Bergman, Ken Mate, and Gerald Peary; future filmmakers Errol Morris, Andrew Bergman, and Mark Goldblatt were among our loyal members. Sudipta Chatterjee of the Green Lantern Cooperative in Madison allowed me to screen Ford films in the wee hours of the morning. I also watched Ford films in the RKO collection at the State Historical Society of Wisconsin's Wisconsin Center for Film and Theatre Research, whose wonderful film archive was ably curated by Elizabeth Dalton and later by Maxine Fleckner Ducey.

By 1969, I was working as a reporter for the *Wisconsin State Journal* but still spending much of my free time watching and writing about movies. I asked Wilmington to join me in writing a critical study of Ford. Our *John Ford* took two years to write, but because American publishers had no interest in the subject, the book did not see publication until 1974, the year after Ford's death. First published in London by Secker & Warburg, *John Ford* was edited by David Wilson for the British Film Institute's Cinema Two series; Da Capo Press published the American edition in 1975 and has kept it in print ever since. With his many brilliant insights into Ford, Mike, now the film critic of the *Chicago Tribune,* helped me understand my favorite filmmaker in ways I could not have done alone.

But there were many Ford films about which we had not written, and no biography had yet been published on this most enigmatic of filmmakers. I started seeking out and interviewing Ford collaborators, as well as continuing to track down films I hadn't seen. Shortly after I moved to California in the summer of 1973—with a memorable three-day pilgrimage to Monument Valley along the way—Ford died. I kept getting distracted from the biography by other projects. More books on Ford were published in the seventies and eighties, but none, I felt, managed to capture the essence of the man.

When I met Ruth O'Hara, a brilliant and passionate Irishwoman newly arrived in America, I thought that I was living the story of *The Quiet Man* in real life, albeit in the reverse geographical direction. To my amusement, I discovered that Ruth considered *The Quiet Man* too filled with stereotypically quaint images of Ireland for her liking. My influence, and her years of living in America, have since helped her appreciate the film as an Irish-American's seductive fantasy of his ancestral homeland, even if she still finds some aspects of it deplorable. Our spirited and fruitful disagreement over *The Quiet Man* proved to be a sign of our stimulating intellectual colloquy on many subjects, which continues undiminished to this day. Meanwhile, Ruth's appreciation for (most of) Ford's work and for my earlier Ford book rekindled my enthusiasm for this biographical project. She and her mother, Esther "Hetty" O'Hara, expertly guided me on a research trip to Ireland. Over the years Ruth has watched many Ford films with me, sharing her insights into his work, psychology, and ethnic heritage. While pursuing her own career as a research psychologist at Stanford University, Ruth also provided much-needed advice and encouragement during the writing and editing stages.

My children, Jessica and John McBride, were a great help to their "Pappy" on this project, as they are in every aspect of my life. The first movie Jessie watched, when she was ten days old, was Ford's *3 Godfathers,* projected for her on a classroom screen in Madison. One of the most memorable times she and I have spent together was our trip to New Salem and Springfield, Illinois, to research the historical background of *Young Mr. Lincoln.* She is now an award-winning journalist on the *Milwaukee Journal Sentinel* and a budding novelist; it is a delight to share writing ideas with my richly talented daughter. John, now an urbane and multitalented teenager, enjoys teasing me about the ordeal I put him through in 1994 by taking him to see forty Ford movies in a two-month period. But he admits to having enjoyed some of them, especially *The Man Who Shot Liberty Valance, The Grapes of Wrath,* and *3 Godfathers,* as well as anything else with Harry Carey Jr. John generously joined me in watching and critiquing many more Ford movies in the years that followed, and his comments are always fresh and illuminating. Like Jessie before him, he has already outpaced me in many areas of knowledge and gladly fills me in when I need a quick rundown on something like DNA or nuclear physics.

Ruth O'Hara's parents, Noel and Hetty, were immensely helpful on this book, sharing their knowledge of Irish history and culture and patiently answering my many questions on those subjects. The late Noel O'Hara, a fine writer and scholar with a particular interest in Irish-American literature, supplied me with thought-provoking research material. With the help of Henry Cairns, proprietor of Town Hall Bookshop in Bray, Ireland, and the staff of the Bray Public Library, Noel tracked down the information that helped me to confirm that Michael Collins was a fellow passenger of Ford's on their December 1921 boat trip across the Irish Sea. Hetty, a marvelous teacher, helped me understand Ford's roots when we visited County Galway, and passed on to me her family recollections of the War of Independence and the Irish civil war, as did Noel's mother, the late Mary O'Hara, who lived through those events.

The companionship of the rest of the O'Hara clan in California has helped sustain me over the years: Susan and Stuart Bennett; Una Harris and her children, Siúan and David McGahan; Fiona O'Kirwan; and Gwenn and Karl Van Dessel and their children, K. J. and Natasha. As always, I am fortified by the encouragement and support of my siblings and their spouses: Dennis McBride and Karen Barry; Genevieve McBride and Steve Byers; Mark McBride and Kim Stanton-McBride; Michael and Kerin McBride; Dr. Patrick and Kim McBride; and Timothy McBride and Shirley Porterfield. I am fortunate to have as my nieces and nephews John and Catherine Caspari and Barbara, Donovan, Gabrielle, Gillian, Lauren, Lindsay, Meredith, Philip, Pierce, Raymond Erin, Ryan, and Sean McBride. My aunts Bobby Dunne, Mickey Lorch, and Sister M. Jean Raymond McBride are an abiding source of joy.

As I celebrate my fortieth year as a professional writer, I thank my late mother, Marian Dunne McBride, a journalist and politician who launched my career by helping me write and sell an article about my Little League teammate Greg Spahn, son of the legendary Milwaukee Braves pitcher Warren Spahn, to *Young Catholic Messenger* in 1960. And I thank my late father, Raymond McBride, whose long career with the *Milwaukee Journal* included a stint as movie reviewer. My recounting of my dad's love for one of his favorite films, *Stagecoach,* brought a smile to the saturnine face of John Ford, the only time Ford smiled during the hour we spent together.

After moving to Los Angeles, I augmented my Ford education by attending retrospectives at the University of Southern California; the UCLA Film and Television Archive (where I also viewed a rare 35mm print of *At the Front in North Africa*); and the Los Angeles County Museum of Art. I thank LACMA film curator Darlene Ramirez for asking me to moderate a 1994 panel on Ford that also included Peter Bogdanovich, Tag Gallagher, and Leonard Maltin. Shelley Ruston and Gage Rickard invited me to conduct a 1981 series of Ford screenings and lectures at the Santa Barbara Museum of Art. I have spoken frequently on Ford and Irish cinema at the kind behest of Daniel Cassidy, who heads the Irish Studies Program of New College of California in San Francisco, for which I am now an adjunct professor of film and literature. Eric Sherman, one of the cinematographers of Bogdanovich's documentary *Directed by John Ford,* invited me to speak on Ford to his class at the Malibu College of Directing, and Jonathan Kuntz brought me as a guest speaker to his UCLA class on Ford.

Other people and institutions who have enabled me to see Ford films over the years include American Movie Classics; Audio Films, Chicago; ARP Videos; DOC Films at the University of Chicago; Eddie Brandt's Saturday Matinee, North Hollywood; Harrison Engle; Tag Gallagher; William F. Gavin and Robert H. Leeper of the United States Information Agency, who arranged my 1972 screenings of *Vietnam! Vietnam!;* Mark Haggard; Kino International; Bill Krohn; the Library of Congress; the National Archives; Non-Fiction Video; Frank Pedi and James Dier of Films Incorporated, Skokie, Illinois; the Starlight Roof, South Pasadena, California; Vintage Video; and the Z Channel, Los Angeles. For allowing me to see *Chesty: A Tribute to a Legend* before its release, I thank James Ellsworth and Charles C. Townsend; for giving Ford's last film its world premiere in 1976, I am grateful to Gary Essert and Gary Abrahams of the Los Angeles International Film Exposition (Filmex).

The seminal works of scholarship for anyone writing about Ford are those by Bogdanovich, Andrew Sarris, and Lindsay Anderson. I have endlessly consulted Bogdanovich's interview book *John Ford* (London: Movie Magazine Ltd., 1967, and Berkeley: University of California Press, 1968 and 1978 editions) and his 1971 film *Directed by John Ford* (California Arts Commission/American Film Institute). Sarris's *The American Cinema: Directors and Directions, 1929–1968* (New York: E. P. Dutton, 1968) was the bible for film buffs of my generation, and Sarris provided further inspiration with *The John Ford Movie Mystery* (Bloomington: Indiana University Press, 1975). Bogdanovich and Sarris also have been generous in their personal guidance of this fellow Fordian. Although Anderson vehemently disagreed with some of my views on Ford, particularly with my admiration for *The Searchers,* he pioneered the study of Ford with his pieces in the British film magazines *Sequence* and *Sight and Sound.* His eloquence is preserved in his book *About John Ford* (London: Plexus, 1981; New York: McGraw-Hill, 1983) and his 1992 BBC TV special *John Ford,* directed by Andrew Eaton. I am grateful to my friend and colleague Gavin Lambert for standing up to his old friend Anderson in defense of my first book on Ford. Tag Gallagher turned up fresh information and insights with his *John Ford: The Man and His Films* (Berkeley: University of California Press, 1986) and his article on Francis Ford, "Brother Feeney," in *Film Comment,* November 1976. Other useful groundwork was done by Ford biographers Andrew Sinclair in *John Ford* (New York: The Dial Press/James Wade, 1979) and Ronald L. Davis in *John Ford: Hollywood's Old Master* (Norman: University of Oklahoma Press, 1995).

That prodigious film scholar Anthony Slide published my article on *Straight Shooting* in his British magazine *The Silent Picture* and many years later provided me with his and June Banker's illuminating 1977 interview with Mary Ford for use in this book. Tony also helped me with other research leads, such as introducing me to Priscilla Bonner and pointing me to Francis Ford's autobiography "Up and Down the Ladder" in the Grover Jones collection at the Academy of Motion Picture Arts and Sciences.

Personally as well as professionally, I miss Alex Ameripoor, an Iranian-born cinematographer whom I met at Ford's funeral. Alex not only could recite the entire sound tracks of Ford movies but understood Ford's personality and sense of humor to a rare degree. His premature death in 1986 deprived his friends of a great inspiration and companion. I have also been stimulated by the camaraderie and conversation of other fellow scholars, journalists, and Ford aficionados, including John Belton, Edward L. Bernds, Robert S. Birchard, John Boorman, Kevin Brownlow, Stuart Byron, Claude Chabrol, Charles Champlin, Sherrie Connolly, Arthur M. Eckstein, Harrison Engle, Samuel Fuller, Linda Gross, Mark Haggard, Ronald Haver, Avie Hern, Albert Johnson, Bill Krohn, Maria Elena de las Carreras Kuntz, Jonathan Lethem, Blake Lucas, Todd McCarthy, Patrick McGilligan, Dennis McLellan, Leonard Maltin, Jawad Mir, Thomas M. Pryor, Jean and Dido Renoir, Lee Sanders, Slobodan Sijan, Bob Thomas, Richard Thompson, François Truffaut, and Wendell Wethington. I also thank my good friends Felipe and Martha Caseres and their son Felipe, Lynn Garrison, Gary and Jillian Graver, Charles Horton, Lou and Judy Race, Marjorie Robbins, John Sanford, Michael Schlesinger, Henry Sheehan, Don Shull, and Rowena Silver.

The most enjoyable part of writing a book is getting to know so many fascinating people in the course of the research. I am deeply grateful to the 121 people who gave me interviews for this book: Eddie Albert; Alex Ameripoor; Marino Amoruso; Jean Arthur; Gertrude Astor; Sherman Beck; Jane Beckwith; Ella Begay; Edward L. Bernds; Robert S. Birchard; Peter Bogdanovich; Priscilla Bonner; John Boorman; Dan Borzage; Henry Brandon; Katherine Cliffton Bryant; Vice Admiral John D. Bulkeley, USN; Yakima Canutt; Frank Capra; Harry "Dobe" Carey Jr.; Marilyn Carey; Olive Carey; Claude Chabrol; Charles Champlin; Jane Chang; John Clement; Iron Eyes Cody; Claudette Colbert; Ruth Clifford Cornelius; Barbara Curran; Philip J. "Jack" Dawson; Cecil McLean de Prida; Síle de Valera; Lem Dobbs; General James H. Doolittle, USA; Amanda Dunne; Philip Dunne; Allan Dwan; Florence Eldridge; James Ellsworth; Elizabeth Evitts;

Also, Martin Joseph Feehan; F. X. Feeney; Josephine Feeney; Paraic Feeney; Stepin Fetchit; Henry Fonda; Dan Ford; John Ford; Norman Foster; Christa Fuller; Samuel Fuller; Lillian Gish; Samuel Goldwyn Jr.; Peter E. Gribbin; Mark Haggard; Ronald Haver; Howard Hawks; Chuck Hayward; Winton C. Hoch; George Holliday; John Huston; George M. Kelly; Father Tom Kyne; Linda Noe Laine; Gavin Lambert; Anna Lee; Jack Lemmon; Roxana Johnson Lonergan; John Lee Mahin; Rouben Mamoulian; Brick Marquard; Margot McCain; Brigadier General Frank McCarthy, USA (Ret.); Roddy McDowall; Jane McPhllips; Rita McPhillips; Terry Mechling; John Milius; Cameron Mitchell; John Mitchum; Robert Nathan;

And, Edmond O'Brien; Pat O'Brien; Tadhg "Tim" O'Curraidhin; Esther O'Hara; Mary O'Hara; Noel O'Hara; Dr. Ruth O'Hara; Betsy Palmer; Catherine E. Plante; Abraham Polonsky; Thomas M. Pryor; Louis S. Race; Waverly Ramsey; Jean Renoir; Benny Rubin; Eric Sherman; Lillian Bradley Smith; Phineas Sprague Jr.; John Stafford; George Stevens; James Stewart; Chester Sticht; Woody Strode; Gloria Stuart; Bob Thomas; Charles C. Townsend; Claire Trevor; Helen Leech Walsh; Pauline Moore Watkins; John Wayne; Major General Albert C. Wedemeyer, USA (Ret.); Orson Welles; Barbara White; Vicky Armistead Wilson; Zelma (Mrs. Michael) Wilson; Hank Worden; Billy Yellow; Randy Yellow; and Fred Zinnemann.

Several of these people were especially generous with their time and encouragement. The wonderful Carey family—Olive Carey, her son Harry "Dobe" Carey Jr., and his wife Marilyn—provided a living link to both Ford as a young man and Ford as the "Pappy" of the Stock Company to which Ollie, Dobe, and the elder Harry Carey belonged. Dobe's splendid memoir *Company of Heroes: My Life as an Actor in the John Ford Stock Company* (Metuchen, N.J.: Scarecrow Press, 1994) is the best account of what it was like to work with Ford.

Other people who provided extraordinary help and support on this project include Anna Lee and her husband, novelist Robert Nathan; Philip Dunne and his wife, Amanda; and Admiral Bulkeley. I am indebted to former president Richard M. Nixon for graciously providing me with his written reflections on Ford for this book.

To understand Ford, it was essential for me to learn firsthand how he is regarded by members of the Diné—the Navajo people—who worked with him in Monument Valley. The hospitality I received on my visit there in 1973 was remarkably generous. George Holliday, a Navajo who appeared in several Ford films, served as my knowledgeable tour guide, taking me to the places where Tombstone once rose in *My Darling Clementine* and the pioneer home was burned in *The Searchers*. During my 1998 visit to Portland, Maine, for the dedication of the Ford statue and other festivities honoring the native son, I had the privilege of interviewing Billy Yellow, whose grandson Randy Yellow kindly served as translator for the venerable Navajo shaman and Ford Stock Company member. I also had delightful interviews with three women who came from the reservation to honor Ford and shared with me their memories and observations of Natani Nez: Ella Begay, Lillian Bradley Smith, and Barbara White. Jefferson L. Begay, chief of staff to the president of the Navajo Nation, also was generous with his assistance in 1998. Patricia Scott Rodney, who went from teaching Steven Spielberg in elementary school to teaching on Indian reservations in Arizona, enthusiastically tutored me about that beautiful state and its Native American heritage.

Gene Ward Smith, another friend I made during the writing of my Spielberg biography, alerted me to the events honoring Ford in Portland. My research trip to Portland was aided by Jessica Turner of the Convention and Visitors Bureau of Greater Portland. Linda Noe Laine invited me to her Peaks Island picnic during the Ford festivities and gave me an interview about her experiences with Ford. I had convivial and informative talks with Michael Dwyer, the visiting film correspondent of the *Irish Times,* and Portland history maven Ruth Riddick, a writer for the local newspaper *Mainebiz.*

Catherine E. Plante organized my tour of Peaks Island, with the knowledgeable assistance of Officer John Clement of the Portland Police Department and the hospitality of Joyce Neal, occupant of the former Feeney home on the island. Former Portland mayor Philip J. "Jack" Dawson was helpful during my visit. Phineas Sprague Jr., the owner of Ford's birthplace in Cape Elizabeth, generously allowed me a tour of the farmhouse, conducted by Zachary Hunter. I also received kind assistance from Elizabeth Evitts, who showed me around her apartment at 23–25 Sheridan Street in Portland, formerly occupied by the Feeneys, and Tina Campbell and Frank Mello III, who showed me the Feeneys' home at 65 Monument Street. Peter E. Gribbin, the historian of Portland High School, was extraordinarily helpful with my research, answering my questions about the history of the school, loaning me copies of his booklets *A History of Portland High School, 1821 through 1981* (Portland: Portland High School, 1981) and *The First Century of Portland High School Football, 1889–1989* (Portland: Dale Rand Printing, 1989), and allowing me to read copies of the school magazine, the *Racquet.*

This is an unauthorized biography of John Ford. On principle, I would never consider writing an authorized biography because I believe that doing so inevitably compromises a biographer's independence, to the reader's detriment and that of the historical record.

Although Ford boasted about not telling me anything when I interviewed him in 1970, I found our meeting not only informative and moving but also invaluable in enabling me to get a firsthand sense of his personality. So despite his crotchetiness, I thank "Himself" for his encouragement of my research and am pleased to know that he appreciated reading what Mike Wilmington and I wrote about him.

Ford's secretary Rose Lew offered gracious assistance. Ford's sister Josephine Feeney and niece Cecil McLean de Prida received me warmly in 1973. Ford's nephew Paraic Feeney could not have been more welcoming to the inquisitive American scholar who came on short notice to his home in Spiddal, Ireland. Ford relatives Barbara Curran and her husband Tadhg "Tim" O'Curraidhin showed me the ruins of the filmmaker's ancestral home and helped educate me on the history of Spiddal and County Galway. My friend and fellow film critic F. X. Feeney, a distant Ford relative, was a faithful ally throughout this project, watching Ford films with me and sharing his insights.

Dan Ford, the director's grandson and biographer, helped lay the groundwork for biographical study of Ford with *Pappy: The Life of John Ford* (Englewood Cliffs, N.J.: Prentice-Hall, 1979). The collection of Ford papers that Indiana University's Lilly Library obtained from Dan Ford—an unexpectedly rich though somewhat incomplete treasure trove—has been a great help to this study. I spent six weeks in the summer of 1998 reading through the papers at the library, where Saundra Taylor and her staff treated me with impeccable professionalism and integrity. Staff members who helped me included Rebecca Cape, Cinda May, Dana M. Ohren, and especially Helena Leech Walsh. A native of Ireland who ran errands for the production staff of *Young Cassidy* while Ford was directing the film in Dublin, Helena gave me the benefit of her sharp observations of Ford and Irish history. Her kindness and generosity made my stay in Bloomington pleasant as well as productive.

I spent many months doing research in the invaluable collections of the Margaret Herrick Library of the Academy of Motion Picture Arts and Sciences in Beverly Hills, California. Linda Harris Mehr and her fine staff were always knowledgeable and helpful. I made several important discoveries among the various collections of papers at the Wisconsin Center for Film and Theatre Research of the State Historical Society of Wisconsin, where I could count on the loyal support of Barbara Kaiser. Among the other libraries and archives I utilized were the University of Wisconsin Memorial Library, Madison; the genealogy libraries of the Church of Jesus Christ of Latter-Day Saints, Salt Lake City and Los Angeles; the University Research Library of the University of California, Los Angeles; the University of Southern California libraries, including the USC Cinema-Television Library, Los Angeles; the Maine Historical Society, Portland; and the public libraries of Madison and Milwaukee, Wisconsin; and Los Angeles, Pasadena, Beverly Hills, and Glendale, California.

In Ireland, I was given enthusiastic research assistance by Father Tom Kyne of St. Ende Parish, Spiddal, and the staffs of the *Irish Times* and the *Irish Press,* who allowed me access to their clipping files on Ford. Ruth O'Hara and I spent a memorable afternoon in Ireland discussing the country's history with Martin Joseph Feehan, who also gave me copies of Ernie O'Malley's books *On Another Man's Wound* and *The Singing Flame;* I thank Paul Feehan for introducing me to his father and for his other help over the years. I found important information on Ford's Maine background at the Thomas Memorial Library, Cape Elizabeth, with the help of reference librarian Jane Beckwith; and at the Portland Public Library and its Portland Room, with expert guidance by assistant librarian Margot McCain. Ford's birth records were obtained from the Town of Cape Elizabeth and the State of Maine Department of Human Services. Daniel Cassidy provided me with information from the 10th U.S. census (1880) and his research into Irish-American life at the time of Ford's youth. In Maine, I had a pleasant talk about Ford with Éamon de Valera's granddaughter Síle de Valera, Ireland's minister for Arts, Heritage, Gaeltacht, and the Islands.

Through the kind intervention of Admiral Bulkeley, I was able to obtain records and other information on Ford's U.S. Navy service from the Naval Office of Information in Washington, D.C. I thank Rear Admiral Jimmie B. Finkelstein, the navy's chief of information, and his staff members Commander Kendell Pease, Anna C. Urband, and Sheila A. Graham. For assistance at the Naval Historical Center, I thank Charles R. Haberlein Jr., H. A. Vadnais Jr., and Dean C. Allard. Other research information and materials were provided by Book City, Hollywood; Ned Comstock of the USC Cinema-Television Library; Blake Edwards; Nadine Goff; David Shepard; the Museum of Modern Art, New York; Darlene Ramirez; Howard Prouty; Ellen Mastroianni; Pauline Moore Watkins and her son Thomas Machamer.

For providing stills, I thank the Academy of Motion Picture Arts and Sciences; American Movie Classics; Alex Ameripoor; Russell Campbell; Collectors Bookstore, Hollywood; Walter Donohue, *Projections 4*/Faber and Faber; Eddie Brandt's Saturday Matinee; Peter E. Gribbin and Portland High School; the Larry Edmunds Bookshop, Hollywood; Anna Lee; the Museum of Modern Art/Film Stills Archive; the Office of Strategic Services; Photofest, New York; Producers & Quantity Photo, Inc., Hollywood; Don Schneider; John Stafford; the UCLA Theater Arts Library/William Wyler Collection; the U.S. Navy; Rob Daly, Videostill, Hollywood; the Wisconsin Center for Film and Theatre Research; and the companies that produced and released John Ford's films.

Publications that have printed my writings on Ford include *Sight and Sound, Film Comment, Film Quarterly, AFI Report,* the *Velvet Light Trap,* the *Silent Picture,* the *Real Paper* (Boston), and *Irish America.* I particularly thank the following magazines for material incorporated in this book: *Sight and Sound* for "County Mayo Gu [*sic*] Bragh . . . ," Winter 1970/71; "Drums Along the Mekong," Autumn 1972; and "Bringing in the Sheaves," Winter 1973–74; *Film Quarterly* for "Stepin Fetchit Talks Back," Summer 1971, reprinted in Brian Henderson and Ann Martin, *Film Quarterly: Forty Years—A Selection* (Berkeley: University of California Press, 1999); and *Film Comment* for "Bombshell Days in the Golden Age: John Lee Mahin Interviewed," March–April 1980 (with Todd McCarthy), reprinted as "John Lee Mahin: Team Player" in Pat McGilligan, ed., *Backstory: Interviews with Screenwriters of Hollywood's Golden Age* (Berkeley: University of California Press, 1986).

I thank the editors of publications that helped keep me going during the writing of this book by giving me assignments to write columns, articles, and reviews. They include Barbara Epstein of the *New York Review of Books;* Patricia Harty of *Irish America* magazine; Michael Anderson of the *New York Times Book Review;* Alan Andres and Katharine Whittemore of *American Movie Classics Magazine;* Ray Greene, Kim Williamson, and Christine James of *Boxoffice;* Jeff Schwager and Jim Emerson of *Reel* magazine and *Cinemania Online* (with Rudy Brueggemann at the latter); and Richard Stayton, Tara McCarthy, and Lisa Chambers of *Written By.*

Once again, Maurice L. Muehle provided invaluable legal advice and enthusiastic support for my writing endeavors. Maury's integrity and skill have been a bulwark of my career for more than ten years now, and I greatly benefit from his keen knowledge of literature and film. Maury's helpful staff includes Lanla Gist, a writer herself who takes a special interest in my work.

A good agent is such a precious discovery that I count myself extremely fortunate to be in the wise and diplomatic hands of Richard Parks. He has gone the extra mile for me many times now on our two books together and has helped make my writer's life much smoother than it otherwise would be. In London, I am ably represented by Richard's associate, Barbara Levy of the Barbara Levy Literary Agency.

At St. Martin's Press, Calvert Morgan Jr. acquired this project and skillfully guided the manuscript through its early stages. Tim Bent took over the book after Cal left and completed the editing process expertly and with sympathetic understanding. The book has benefited from the wise legal reading of Henry R. Kaufman; the enthusiastic efficiency of Tim's assistant Julia Pastore; the copyediting of Adam Goldberger, Juli Barbato, and Josette Haddad; and the elegant design by Michelle McMillian. I also thank my editor at Faber and Faber, Walter Donohue, for acquiring this book in the U.K. I received invaluable assistance in the final stages of editing from Ann Weiser Cornell, my beloved partner in life and esteemed fellow author, whose fondness for John Ford films helped draw us together.

Joseph McBride
Richmond, California
April 2001

INDEX

Note: Films directed and/or produced by Ford are listed under his name; other films are listed under their titles. Principal references to Ford's films are in **boldface**.